HANDBOOK OF APPROACH AND AVOIDANCE MOTIVATION

HANDBOOK OF APPROACH AND AVOIDANCE MOTIVATION

Andrew J. Elliot

Editor

Psychology Press
Taylor & Francis Group
New York   Hove

Psychology Press
Taylor & Francis Group
270 Madison Avenue
New York, NY 10016

Psychology Press
Taylor & Francis Group
27 Church Road
Hove, East Sussex BN3 2FA

© 2008 by Taylor & Francis Group, LLC

Printed in the United States of America on acid-free paper
10 9 8 7 6 5 4 3 2 1

International Standard Book Number-13: 978-0-8058-6019-1 (Hardcover)

Library of Congress Cataloging-in-Publication Data

Elliot, Andrew J.
    Handbook of approach and avoidance motivation / Andrew J. Elliot.
        p. cm.
    Includes bibliographical references and index.
    ISBN 978-0-8058-6019-1 (alk. paper)
    1. Avoidance (Psychology) I. Title.

BF337.A92E45 2008
155.9--dc22   2008011859

Visit the Taylor & Francis Web site at
http://www.taylorandfrancis.com

and the Psychology Press Web site at
http://www.psypress.com

Contents

PART I   Introduction

Introduction and Overview

PART II   Neurophysiology and Neurobiology

Brain Systems and Mechanisms

Cortical Asymmetry

Cortex-Reflex Connections

Subcortical Processes

Neurotransmitters

PART III   Basic Dispositions, Goals, and States

PART IV   Evaluative Processes

PART V   Emotion and Well-Being

PART VI Cognition

PART VII The Self

PART VIII Social Context

Preface

Of the many conceptual distinctions present in psychology today, the approach–avoidance distinction stands out as one of, if not, the most fundamental and basic. The distinction between approach and avoidance motivation has a venerable history, not only within but beyond scientific psychology, and the deep utility of this distinction is clearly evident across theoretical traditions, disciplines, and content areas. The *Handbook of Approach and Avoidance Motivation* is designed to illustrate and highlight the central importance of this distinction, to serve as a one-stop resource for scholars working in this area, and to facilitate integration among researchers and theorists with an explicit or implicit interest in approach and avoidance motivation.

In an introductory chapter, I lay the groundwork for the volume by overviewing the history of the approach–avoidance distinction, explicating its fundamental role in motivational analyses of behavior, and providing definitional and terminological guidance. The main body of the *Handbook* is organized according to seven broad parts that represent core areas of interest in the study of approach and avoidance motivation (e.g., neurophysiology and neurobiology, evaluative processes). Each part contains a minimum of four chapters, each of which covers a specific aspect of approach and avoidance motivation. The coverage of the *Handbook* is not comprehensive (such coverage is an impossibility, given the widespread implicit, as well as explicit, use of the approach–avoidance distinction), but clearly encompasses the most central areas in the contemporary study of approach and avoidance motivation.

I could not be happier with the lineup of scholars that have made contributions to this volume. Those working in this area will recognize the names in the Table of Contents as an all star team of researchers and theorists in the area of motivation. Furthermore, these top-of-the-line scholars have uniformly provided chapters worthy of their reputation. In short, in this volume I am pleased to present outstanding chapters by the best minds in the field.

The *Handbook of Approach and Avoidance Motivation* is targeted toward those in academia, including advanced undergraduates, graduate students, postdoctoral students, and professors. The broad applicability of the approach–avoidance distinction will likely make the book a helpful resource for a diverse population. The volume may not only be used as a personal resource for researchers and theorists, but may also be used as a textbook for teachers of advanced undergraduate and graduate seminars; indeed I intend to use it in this capacity myself.

I hope you enjoy reading these chapters as much as I enjoyed editing them. The study of approach and avoidance motivation is clearly as vibrant and generative now as it has ever been!

Andrew J. Elliot

Editor

Andrew J. Elliot is a professor of psychology at the University of Rochester. He received his PhD from the University of Wisconsin–Madison in 1994. His research areas include approach and avoidance motivation, achievement and social motivation, the self, personal goals, subjective well-being, color, and parental, teacher, and cultural influences on motivation and self-regulation. He is currently an associate editor of *Personality and Social Psychology Bulletin*, is currently the motivation and emotion section editor of *Social and Personality Psychology Compass*, and has coedited the *Handbook of Competence and Motivation*. He has over 100 scholarly publications, has received research grants from public and private agencies, and has been awarded four different early and mid career awards for his research contributions.

Contributors

Adam A. Augustine
Department of Psychology
Washington University in St. Louis
Saint Louis, Missouri

Nicole M. Avena
Department of Psychology
Princeton University
Princeton, New Jersey

Yael E. Avivi
Department of Psychology
University of Miami
Coral Gables, Florida

Lindsay L. Barber
Department of Psychology
University of Missouri–Columbia
Columbia, Missouri

John A. Bargh
Department of Psychology
Yale University
New Haven, Connecticut

Roger D. Bartels
Department of Psychology
University of Minnesota
Minneapolis, Minnesota

Roy F. Baumeister
Department of Psychology
Florida State University
Tallahassee, Florida

Elliot T. Berkman
Department of Psychology
University of California–Los Angeles
Los Angeles, California

Gary G. Berntson
Department of Psychology
The Ohio State University
Columbus, Ohio

Jim Blascovich
Department of Psychology
University of California–
    Santa Barbara
Santa Barbara, California

Kristy L. Boyce
Department of Psychology
University of Oklahoma
Norman, Oklahoma

Margaret M. Bradley
Department of Psychology
University of Florida
Gainesville, Florida

John T. Cacioppo
Department of Psychology
University of Chicago
Chicago, Illinois

Christopher K. Cain
Center for Neural Science
New York University
New York, New York

Charles S. Carver
Department of Psychology
University of Miami
Coral Gables, Florida

M. Lynne Cooper
Department of Psychology
University of Missouri–Columbia
Columbia, Missouri

Leda Cosmides
Department of Psychology
University of California–
    Santa Barbara
Santa Barbara, California

Douglas Derryberry
Department of Psychology
Oregon State University
Corvallis, Oregon

Patricia G. Devine
Department of Psychology
University of Wisconsin–Madison
Madison, Wisconsin

Ed Diener
Department of Psychology
University of Illinois
Champaign–Urbana, Illinois

J. Richard Eiser
Department of Psychology
University of Sheffield
Sheffield, South Yorkshire
United Kingdom

Andrew J. Elliot
Department of Psychology
University of Rochester
Rochester, New York

Russell H. Fazio
Department of Psychology
The Ohio State University
Columbus, Ohio

Melissa J. Ferguson
Department of Psychology
Cornell University
Ithaca, New York

Jens Förster
Department of Psychology
University of Amsterdam
Amsterdam, the Netherlands

Nathan A. Fox
Department of Human Development
University of Maryland
College Park, Maryland

Ronald S. Friedman
Department of Psychology
University of Albany,
State University of New York
Albany, New York

Cheryl A. Frye
Department of Psychology
State University of New York–Albany
Albany, New York

Philip A. Gable
Department of Psychology
Texas A&M University
College Station, Texas

Shelly L. Gable
Department of Psychology
University of California–
Santa Barbara
Santa Barbara, California

Seth Gitter
Department of Psychology
Florida State University
Tallahassee, Florida

H. Hill Goldsmith
Department of Psychology
University of
Wisconsin–Madison
Madison, Wisconsin

Samuel D. Gosling
Department of Psychology
University of Texas–Austin
Austin, Texas

Takeshi Hamamura
Department of Psychology
University of British Columbia
British Columbia, Canada

Cindy Harmon-Jones
Department of Psychology
Texas A & M University
College Station, Texas

Eddie Harmon-Jones
Department of Psychology
Texas A & M University
College Station, Texas

Steven J. Heine
Department of Psychology
University of British Columbia
British Columbia, Canada

E. Tory Higgins
Department of Psychology
Columbia University
New York, New York

Bartley G. Hoebel
Department of Psychology
Princeton University
Princeton, New Jersey

Anne L. Hurst
Department of Psychology
College of William and Mary
Williamsburg, Virginia

Carroll E. Izard
Department of Psychology
University of Delaware
Newark, Delaware

Amanda C. Jones
Department of Psychology
University of Texas–Austin
Austin, Texas

Douglas T. Kenrick
Department of Psychology
Arizona State University
Tempe, Arizona

Sander L. Koole
Department of Psychology
and Education
Vrije Universiteit
Amsterdam, the Netherlands

Julius Kuhl
Department of Psychology
University of Osnabrück
Lower Saxony, Germany

Peter J. Lang
Department of Clinical and Health
Psychology
University of Florida
Gainesville, Florida

Randy J. Larsen
Department of Psychology
Washington University in St. Louis
Saint Louis, Missouri

Amy Latimer
School of Kinesiology and
Health Studies
Queens University
Ontario, Canada

Jean-Philippe Laurenceau
Department of Psychology
University of Delaware
Newark, Delaware

Joseph E. LeDoux
Center for Neural Science
New York University
New York, New York

Kathryn Lemery-Chalfant
Department of Psychology
Arizona State University
Tempe, Arizona

Ash Levitt
Department of Psychology
University of Missouri–Columbia
Columbia, Missouri

Debra Lieberman
Department of Psychology
University of Hawaii
Manoa, Hawaii

E. J. Masicampo
Department of Psychology
Florida State University
Tallahassee, Florida

Joseph Moskal
Department of Biomedical
Engineering
Northwestern University
Evanston, Illinois

Sadia Najmi
Department of Psychology
Harvard University
Cambridge, Massachusetts

Jaak Panksepp
Department of Veterinary
and Comparative Anatomy,
Pharmacology, and Physiology
Washington State University
Pullman, Washington

Carly Peterson
Department of Psychology
Texas A&M University
College Station, Texas

E. Ashby Plant
Department of Psychology
Florida State University
Tallahassee, Florida

Pedro Rada
Laboratory of Behavioral
    Physiology
University of Los Andes
Merida, Venezuela

Bethany C. Reeb
Department of Human
    Development
University of Maryland
College Park, Maryland

Marjorie Reed
Department of Psychology
Oregon State University
Corvallis, Oregon

Madeline E. Rhodes
Department of Psychology
State University of New York–Albany
Albany, New York

Ira J. Roseman
Department of Psychology
Rutgers University
Camden, New Jersey

Alexander J. Rothman
Department of Psychology
University of Minnesota
Minneapolis, Minnesota

Peter Salovey
Department of Psychology
Yale University
New Haven, Connecticut

Abigail A. Scholer
Department of Psychology
Columbia University
New York, New York

Aaron Sell
Department of Psychology
University of California–
    Santa Barbara
Santa Barbara, California

Meli S. Sheldon
Department of Psychology
University of
    Missouri–Columbia
Columbia, Missouri

Michelle N. Shiota
Department of Psychology
Arizona State University
Tempe, Arizona

Carolin J. Showers
Department of Psychology
University of Oklahoma
Norman, Oklahoma

Regina M. Sullivan
Department of Zoology
University of Oklahoma
Norman, Oklahoma

Jerry Suls
Department of Psychology
University of Iowa
Iowa City, Iowa

Daniel Sznycer
Department of Psychology
University of California
Santa Barbara, California

Amelia E. Talley
Department of Psychology
University of Missouri–Columbia
Columbia, Missouri

Maya Tamir
Department of Psychology
Boston College
Chestnut Hill, Massachusetts

Todd M. Thrash
Department of Psychology
College of William and Mary
Williamsburg, Virginia

Dianne M. Tice
Department of Psychology
Florida State University
Tallahassee, Florida

John Tooby
Department of Anthropology
University of California–Santa
    Barbara
Santa Barbara, California

Donna J. Toufexis
Department of Psychiatry and
    Behavioral Sciences
Emory University
Atlanta, Georgia

Daniel M. Wegner
Department of Psychology
Harvard University
Cambridge, Massachusetts

Ladd Wheeler
Department of Psychology
Macquarie University
Sydney, New South Wales,
    Australia

Donald A. Wilson
Department of Zoology
University of Oklahoma
Norman, Oklahoma

Jhon T. Wlaschin
Department of Psychology
University of Minnesota
Minneapolis, Minnesota

Eric Youngstrom
Department of Psychology
University of North Carolina–
    Chapel Hill
Chapel Hill, North Carolina

Part I

Introduction

Introduction and Overview

1 Approach and Avoidance Motivation

Andrew J. Elliot

CONTENTS

The distinction between approach and avoidance motivation has a long and rich history in intellectual thought in general, and scientific psychology in particular. In accord with Lewin (1935), approach motivation may be defined as the energization of behavior by, or the direction of behavior toward, positive stimuli (objects, events, possibilities), whereas avoidance motivation may be defined as the energization of behavior by, or the direction of behavior away from, negative stimuli (objects, events, possibilities). Approach and avoidance concepts and constructs have been utilized across a diversity of scholarly disciplines, theoretical traditions, and empirical content areas.

Attention to the approach–avoidance motivational distinction has not been constant over the years, but may be seen as waxing and waning at different periods. At present, there appears to be substantial interest in approach and avoidance motivation, but it is also the case that motivationally relevant theories, models, variables, and hypotheses continue to be espoused with little or no consideration of this fundamental distinction. In addition, when the approach–avoidance distinction is utilized in the contemporary literature it is rarely explicitly defined, and approach and avoidance motivation are often described and discussed using diverse terminology that tends to obfuscate links between findings and frameworks.

Accordingly, the broad aims of the *Handbook of Approach and Avoidance Motivation* are threefold. First, the handbook is designed to illustrate the importance and broad utility of the approach–avoidance motivational distinction. Second, it is designed to provide a ready resource for scholars interested in theoretical and empirical work in this area. Third, it is designed to reveal conceptual and empirical links and convergences across disciplines, research traditions, and levels of analysis that will, it is hoped, facilitate cross talk and cross-fertilization among researchers and theorists.

In this introductory chapter, I begin by overviewing the history of the approach–avoidance distinction. I then proceed to explicate the fundamental role of approach and avoidance motivation in the functioning of organisms across the phylogenetic spectrum. Next, I return to the definition of approach and avoidance motivation offered above, and elaborate on several conceptual considerations inherent within this definition. I continue by discussing terminological issues pertaining to the approach–avoidance distinction, and then I close with a brief overview of the various sections that comprise the contents of the handbook.

HISTORY

Distinguishing approach motivation from avoidance motivation may be considered one of the oldest ideas in the history of thought about the behavior of organisms. Scholars have made use of the approach–avoidance distinction for well over 2000 years. It first appeared in the writing of the ancient Greek philosopher Democritus of Abdera (460–370 B.C.E.). Democritus articulated an ethical hedonism in which the immediate pursuit of pleasure and avoidance of pain were prescribed as the guide for human action: "The best thing for man is to pass his life so to have as much joy and as little trouble as may be" (fragment 189, see Copleston, 1946, p. 125; see also Aristippus [435–356 B.C.E.] and Epicurus [342–270 B.C.E.]). Plato (427–327 B.C.E.) had Socrates (470–399 B.C.E.) espouse various hedonic notions in *Protagoras* and *Phaedo*, although it is unclear whether such positions should be attributed to Socrates or Plato himself.

The eighteenth century British philosopher Jeremy Bentham was the first to clearly postulate a psychological hedonism, in addition to an ethical hedonism; this form of hedonism moved beyond a prescription of how we ought to behave to a proto-scientific description of how we actually do behave. This principle is directly stated at the beginning of Bentham's *Introduction to the Principles and Morals of Legislation*: "Nature has placed mankind under the governance of two sovereign masters, pain and pleasure. It is for them alone to point out what we ought to do, as well as to determine what we shall do" (Bentham, 1779/1879, p. 1).

Within the field of scientific psychology per se, the approach–avoidance distinction was attended to from the beginning. Wundt (1887), for example, in his monumental *Principles of Physiological Psychology* (Vol. 3), conceptualized pleasure and pain as unique psychic elements brought into consciousness by sensation, emotion, and cognition (Marshall, 1889). In his classic *Principles of Psychology* (Vol. 2), James (1890) portrayed pleasure and pain as "springs of action," noting that pleasure is a "tremendous reinforcer" of behavior and pain a "tremendous inhibitor" of behavior (pp. 549–559). James even provided speculation on the neural mechanisms underlying "impulsive" and "inhibitory tendencies" (p. 550). Freud (1915) construed the procurement of pleasure and the avoidance of pain (i.e., unpleasure) as the basic motivational impetus underlying psychodynamic activity, and divided the superego into two parts—the ego ideal,

representing what the person should do, and the conscience, representing what the person should not do (Freud, 1923). Thus, James and Freud moved beyond a general focus on pleasure and pain per se to a focus on the specific ways that approach and avoidance behavior are produced and regulated.

In addition to these early pioneers, many prominent psychological theorists over the years have made use of the approach–avoidance distinction in their work. Thorndike (1911), in his "law of effect," described how responses followed by satisfaction are more likely to recur and responses followed by discomfort are less likely to recur. Jung (1921) posited that a fundamental difference between extroverts and introverts is that extroverts exhibit an interest in moving toward social objects, whereas introverts exhibit an interest in moving away from social objects. Tolman (1925) contended that a complete description of behavior must include reference to the end (i.e., goal) toward which or away from which the organism is moving. Pavlov (1927) identified two types of reflexive responses to stimuli, an orienting response toward the stimulus and a defensive response away from the stimulus. Lewin (1935) posited that goal objects in the life space have positive valences that attract and negative valences that repel. Horney (1937) discussed different strategies that individuals use to cope with their basic anxiety, including "moving toward" and "moving away." Skinner (1938, 1953) distinguished between reinforcers that strengthen responses and punishing stimuli that weaken responses, and differentiated positive reinforcement (the provision of a positive) from negative reinforcement (the removal of a negative).

Murray (1938) distinguished between two types of psychological needs, "adient" (positive) needs that impel the organism toward other objects, and "abient" (negative) needs that impel the organism away from other objects. Hull (1943) proposed two classes of acquired drives, conditioned appetitive drives (e.g., involving food) and conditioned aversive drives (e.g., involving pain avoidance), and his mathematical theory of instrumental behavior included parameters representing the tendency to respond (reaction potential) and inhibit responding (inhibitory potential). Miller (1944) detailed various dynamic conflicts that can result from incompatible valences (e.g., being attracted to and repelled by the same goal object). Hebb (1949) posited that stimulation below a certain threshold leads to pleasure and approach behavior, whereas stimulation above the threshold leads to pain and avoidance behavior. Sullivan (1953) introduced the notion of self-personifications, including the good me and the bad me. Rotter (1954) proposed that individuals' expectancies and values are largely a function of their experiences with prior rewards and punishments.

Maslow (1955) asserted that human beings have two basic sets of needs, deficit needs (e.g., safety) that involve striving to eliminate a negative-life situation and growth needs (i.e., self-actualization) that involve striving to attain a more positive-life situation. Cattell (1957) distinguished between the innate motives (ergs) of exploration (an appetitive motive) and escape to security (an aversive motive). Heider (1958) summarized the difference between "can" and "may" by stating that the former implies that if a person tries, he or she will succeed, whereas the latter implies that if a person tries he or she will not be punished. Mowrer (1960) differentiated between hoped for and feared states, and linked the presence and absence of these states to distinct emotions. Rogers (1961) stated that personal goals may either represent moving toward something positive or moving away from something negative. Erickson (1963) distinguished between basic trust and mistrust in articulating the crisis of the first psychosocial stage of development. Eysenck (1967) posited that introverts are "stimulus shy" due to high baseline levels of cortical arousal, whereas extraverts are "stimulus hungry" due to low baselines levels of cortical arousal. Bowlby (1969) proposed two distinct types of attachments, secure attachment that promotes challenge seeking and exploration, and insecure attachment that leads to caution and a preoccupation with safety and protection.

The aforementioned is but a sampling of the prominent psychological theorists who have implemented approach–avoidance concepts or constructs in their work. This listing emphatically documents the historical significance of the approach–avoidance distinction; it not only shows that the distinction has a long history, but also that it has a broad history. Indeed, the approach–avoidance distinction has been utilized in all of the major theoretical approaches that have been employed to scientifically explain behavior, regardless of how these approaches might be characterized: psychodynamic (e.g., Freud), behaviorist (e.g., Skinner), and humanistic (e.g., Maslow); dispositional (e.g., Murray) and situational (e.g., Thorndike); biological (e.g., Eysenck), affective (e.g., Mowrer), cognitive (e.g., Heider), and social cognitive (e.g., Rotter).

During the 1970s through the 1980s, many cognitive and social-cognitive theorists pitted cognitive against affective and motivational accounts of behavior. In this context, the approach–avoidance distinction was still utilized in theorizing to some degree, but in a much more limited way than in years past. It was with the acknowledgment in the 1990s that cognition, affect, and motivation are deeply intertwined, and need not be viewed as conceptual competitors, that motivational considerations in general, and the approach–avoidance distinction specifically, returned to prominence.

This return to prominence is noteworthy, because use of the approach–avoidance distinction in the contemporary scene would appear to differ from prior use in two important ways. First, until recently, the approach–avoidance distinction had been widely utilized and applied without taking a step back to explicitly define and articulate the nature of approach and avoidance motivation. Thus, philosophers, theorists, and researchers over the years have incorporated the approach–avoidance distinction in many different ways in their work, but they have not clearly explicated the conceptual space represented by approach and avoidance motivation per se. Recent work has directly attended to this issue (Elliot, 1999, 2006; Elliot & Covington, 2001). Second, until recently, the approach–avoidance distinction has been used to address specific issues regarding motivation, without considering its broader potential as an explanatory tool. Prior work has focused on a diversity of specific issues—on hedonism as the ultimate energizer of activity; on the various appetitive and aversive mechanisms, needs, and motives that underlie observable action; on the different valence-based variables that serve to guide and direct behavior, etc. However, there has been little consideration of how the approach–avoidance distinction might be used to integrate various types and levels of analysis to construct a more detailed and sophisticated account of motivation. Recent work has moved in this direction (Cacioppo & Berntson, 1994; Carver & Scheier, 1998; Elliot & Church, 1997; Higgins, 1997; Lang, 1995).

FUNDAMENTAL ROLE OF APPROACH AND AVOIDANCE MOTIVATION

The widespread use of the approach–avoidance distinction over the years undoubtedly reflects the fundamental role of approach and avoidance motivation in human functioning. Both approach and avoidance motivation are integral to successful adaptation; avoidance motivation facilitates surviving, while approach motivation facilitates thriving. This is the case with respect to physical and psychological adaptation alike (Elliot, 2006).

Approach and avoidance motivation not only plays a central role in the functioning of humans, but also in the functioning of organisms across the phylogenetic spectrum. Tooby and Cosmides (1990) have argued that the decision to approach or withdraw has been the fundamental adaptive decision that organisms have had to make throughout their evolutionary past. To paraphrase Schneirla (1959), the high road of evolution has been littered with the remains of species that have failed to acquire one or more mechanisms for accurately determining the beneficial or harmful potential of environmental stimuli. As such, all animate life, from the single-cell amoeba upward, is equipped with at least some basic form of approach–avoidance mechanism that produces or regulates movement toward potentially beneficial stimuli and away from potentially harmful stimuli.

In the amoeba, approach and avoidance motivation is obviously extremely rudimentary, representing approach and withdrawal tendencies "energized directly by protoplasmic processes set off by the stimulus" (Schneirla, 1959, p. 2). For example, a weak light will stimulate a local flow of protoplasm toward the light, often followed by a general movement in that direction, whereas an intense light will stimulate a local contraction of protoplasm, often followed by a general movement away from the light source. Schneirla (1959) argued that organisms at all levels of complexity possess approach-based mechanisms that evoke appetitive reactions and facilitate food-getting, shelter-getting, and mating, and avoidance-based mechanisms that evoke withdrawal reactions and facilitate defense, huddling, flight, and protection, in general. He proposed that the sophistication of these mechanisms varies considerably across species, with those of protozoa and other invertebrates being rudimentary and rigid, and those of higher organisms being more advanced and flexible.

Researchers have not only documented the existence of approach and avoidance mechanisms across phyla, but have also shown individual differences in approach and avoidance motivation within a variety of different species. Intraspecific differences in the tendency to approach or avoid novel stimuli have been documented in monkeys (Suomi, 1983), cats (Adamec, 1991), dogs (Goddard & Beilharz, 1985), wolves (MacDonald, 1983), cows (Fordyce, Goddard, & Seifert, 1982), goats (Lyons, Price, & Moberg, 1988), rats (Garcia-Sevilla, 1984), mice (Kagan, 1998), birds (Verbeek, Drent, & Wiepkema, 1994), snakes (Herzog & Burghardt, 1988), fish (Wilson, Coleman, Clark, & Biederman, 1993), and even some crustaceans (Wilson, Clark, Coleman, & Dearstyne, 1994). Perhaps most provocatively, some researchers have conducted factor-analytic studies seeking to demonstrate the presence of basic dimensions of "personality" in nonhumans. For instance, Budaev (1997) used factor analysis to examine the patterns underlying exploratory, predatory inspection, and schooling behavior in male guppies. Results

revealed two primary orthogonal factors that the investigator interpreted in terms of approach and avoidance motivation: an approach system "governing exploration and social attraction" and a fear avoidance system "governing responses to aversive stimulation" (p. 399). Comparable results suggesting independent, approach- and avoidance-based dimensions of "personality" have been obtained in factor-analytic studies of behavior with octopuses (Mather & Anderson, 1993), yellow-bellied marmots (Armitage, 1986), small-eared bushbabys (Watson & Ward, 1996), rhesus monkeys (Stevenson-Hinde, Stillwell-Barnes, & Zunz, 1980), and hooded rats (Maier, Vandenhoff, & Crowne, 1988).

It is not only just the organism's ability to determine the adaptive significance of stimuli that is central to survival, but also the speed at which these determinations are made (Berntson, Boysen, & Cacioppo, 1993; Orians & Heerwagen, 1992). As such, all (surviving) organisms are hard-wired or "pre-programmed" to make immediate approach–avoidance responses to particular classes of stimuli (Zajonc, 1984, p. 122). Zajonc (1998) contends that "approach–avoidance discriminations" (p. 592) are the primary and most elemental reaction of organisms to environmental stimuli, the initial response on which all subsequent responses are based. This is nicely illustrated in the amoeba's instantaneous, constitutionally ingrained approach or withdrawal response to light intensity, which is essentially a reflexive reaction to the light stimulus.

Humans, like protozoa, exhibit immediate, constitutionally ingrained approach and avoidance responses to certain classes of stimuli. For example, humans possess many different unconditioned exteroceptive reflexes that are commonly classified as orienting (e.g., the salivary reflex) or defensive (e.g., pain withdrawal and startle; Graham, 1973; Pavlov, 1927; Sokolov, 1963) and that may be considered manifestations of approach and avoidance motivation, respectively (Dickinson & Dearing, 1979; Konorski, 1967). One such reflex that has attracted significant research attention is the blink component of the startle reflex. This blink reflex is an involuntary response to an intense stimulus such as a loud noise, a bright light, or an electric shock, and occurs within 30–50 ms of stimulus onset (Bradley & Vrana, 1993). It serves the defensive function of protecting the eye from injury, and acts as a behavioral interrupt that clears processors to deal with potential threats in the environment (Lang, 1995; Öhman, 1997). The magnitude and latency of this primitive reflex has been shown to vary as a function of the motivationally relevant state of the individual prior to stimulus onset. That is, the blink reflex is stronger and its latency is shorter when the startle stimulus is presented to persons in a negative state (e.g., viewing unpleasant materials) relative to a positive or neutral state (e.g., viewing pleasant or neutral materials; Lang, Bradley, & Cuthbert, 1990).

An accumulating body of research indicates that people evaluate most if not all encountered stimuli on a good or bad dimension (Osgood, Suci, & Tannenbaum, 1957), and that they do so immediately, and without intention or awareness (Bargh, 1997; Zajonc, 1998). For example, in a set of studies on the "automatic evaluation effect," Bargh, Chaiken, Raymond, and Hymes (1996) used a subliminal presentation technique to prime participants with positively or negatively valenced words prior to a task in which they pronounced other positively or negatively valenced words as rapidly as possible. The subliminal presentation of any positively valenced word facilitated the speed of pronunciation of any other positively valenced word presented (and likewise for pairs of negatively valenced words), thereby demonstrating that participants processed the valence of the subliminally presented words even though there was no instrumental reason for doing so (Fazio, Sanbonmatsu, Powell, & Kardes, 1986). Although it is possible that immediate good or bad evaluations represent a form of automatic cognitive processing (Fiske, 1982), several theorists have suggested that such evaluations actually take place independent of the transformation processes typically implicated in cognition (Kuhl, 1986; LeDoux, 1987; Zajonc, 1980). Recent research has yielded supportive evidence, suggesting that the neural circuitry involved in the evaluative (good or bad) processing of stimuli is at least partially divergent from that involved in the perceptual (identification and discrimination) processing of stimuli (Crites & Cacioppo, 1996; LeDoux, Sakaguchi, & Reis, 1984; Murphy & Zajonc, 1993; Shizgal, 1999). Thus, automatic good or bad evaluations may be a direct response to stimuli, unmediated by any higher order cognitive processes.

Automatic evaluation is presumed to instantaneously evoke approach and withdrawal behavioral predispositions. Over the years, a number of theorists from the emotion (Arnold, 1960; Frijda, 1986; Lang, 1984; Lazarus, 1991), motivation (Corwin, 1921; Lewin, 1935; Mowrer, 1960; Young, 1959), and attitude (Bogardus, 1931; Doob, 1947; Osgood, 1953; Thurstone, 1931) literatures have posited that the positive or negative evaluation of a stimulus is inherently linked to a tendency to move toward or away from the stimulus, respectively. Empirical data support this proposition. In a set of reaction time experiments, Chen and Bargh (1999) had

participants either pull a lever toward them (an approach-based flexor reaction) or push a lever away from them (an avoidance-based extensor reaction) as quickly as possible when a positively or negatively valenced stimulus word appeared. Results indicated that participants reacted more quickly for positive than negative words when they were instructed to pull the lever toward them (the approach response), and more quickly for negative than positive words when they were instructed to push the lever away from them (the avoidance response; Cacioppo, Priester, & Berntson, 1993; Förster, Higgins, & Idson, 1998; Solorz, 1960). These results were obtained even when no mention was made of the evaluative content of the stimuli and when participants were not instructed to evaluate the stimuli in any way, prompting Bargh and Chartrand (1999) to conclude that automatic evaluation results in a behavioral predisposition toward or away from the stimulus "in a matter of milliseconds" (p. 475).

It is important to highlight that the action disposition associated with automatic evaluation is a predisposition, not an overt behavioral response per se. Positively and negatively evaluated stimuli produce a physiological and somatic preparedness for approaching and withdrawing (Arnold, 1960), but observable behavior may or may not correspond to this initial behavioral readiness (Lang, Bradley, & Cuthbert, 1997). Actually, in lower organisms, and in constitutionally ingrained responses in humans, evaluation does lead directly and invariably to observable approach or withdrawal behaviors. In much human behavior, however, behavioral predispositions represent an initial input that may be overridden by other inputs generated by other approach- and avoidance-based mechanisms or processes prior to an actual behavioral response being enacted. For example, the sight of a tasty dessert stimulus may automatically evoke an approach tendency at the physiological and somatic levels, but a more deliberate consideration of one's ever expanding waistline may lead to the overt act of pushing one's chair away from the dinner table.

Thus, in predicting observable behavior, particularly for complex organisms such as humans, with their flexible and creative self-regulatory repertoire (e.g., delay of gratification, impulse control, goal setting), one must consider the operation of multiple levels of approach and avoidance motivation (Cacioppo & Berntson, 1994), both at the same level of representation (Miller, 1944) and in hierarchical fashion (Elliot & Church, 1997). Indeed, in human behavior, approach and avoidance mechanisms and processes are multifarious, operating across the neuraxis from rudimentary reflexes to vaunted cortical processes (Berntson et al., 1993; Elliot & Thrash, 2002).

This prevalence of approach and avoidance mechanisms and processes bespeaks the central role of approach and avoidance motivation in survival and adaptation.

In sum, approach and avoidance motivation is manifest in and fundamental to all organisms, from protozoa to human beings. The greater the complexity of the organism, the greater the number and complexity of the approach–avoidance mechanisms and processes involved in the production and regulation of behavior. Given the fundamental nature of approach and avoidance motivation, and its ubiquitous presence in biological and psychological functioning, it seems reasonable to consider the approach–avoidance distinction an organizing principle in the study motivation (Berntson et al., 1993). That is, the approach–avoidance distinction may be seen as a unifying thread that can be applied to most, if not all, motivational concepts and constructs. As such, this distinction holds tremendous integrative, interpretive, and generative potential. The approach–avoidance distinction is certainly not sufficient to account for motivation, but it is necessary, and its broad and deep application is likely to yield much theoretical fruit.

DEFINITION AND CONCEPTUALIZATION

At the beginning of this chapter, I offered the following definition of approach and avoidance motivation: Approach motivation may be defined as the energization of behavior by, or the direction of behavior toward, positive stimuli (objects, events, possibilities), whereas avoidance motivation may be defined as the energization of behavior by, or the direction of behavior away from, negative stimuli (objects, events, possibilities). It may be helpful to elaborate on several aspects of this definition, given the fact that approach–avoidance motivation is rarely defined in explicit fashion.

First, being a motivational distinction, approach–avoidance encompasses both the *energization* and *direction* of behavior. Energization refers to the initial activation, instigation, or "spring to action" (James, 1890, p. 555) that orients the organism in a general way (Elliot, 1997). This energization may be very rudimentary, as in the amoeba's evolutionarily engrained orienting away from bright light, or may be more complex, as in the human being's dispositional tendency to orient toward an achievement task as a function of past socialization in competence-relevant settings. Importantly, this use of energization does not presume that the organism is passive until instigated to action; on the contrary, the organism is viewed as perpetually active, with instigation functionally representing a shift from one form of orienting to another (Atkinson & Birch,

1970). Direction herein refers to the guiding or channeling of behavior in a precise way. This guiding and channeling is typically in the service of an activated desire or concern (Elliot & Thrash, 2001).

Second, inherent in the approach–avoidance distinction is the concept of physical or psychological movement. Positively evaluated stimuli are associated with an approach orientation to bring or keep the stimulus close to the organism (literally or figuratively), whereas negatively evaluated stimuli are associated with an avoidance orientation to push or keep the stimulus away from the organism (literally or figuratively). As noted earlier, although positively and negatively evaluated stimuli produce (at minimum) a physiological and somatic preparedness for physical movement toward or away from the stimuli, respectively (Arnold, 1960; Corwin, 1921), this preparedness may or may not be translated directly into overt behavior. In advanced organisms, initial approach or avoidance inclinations may even be overridden or channeled in the opposite direction of the initial inclination (Elliot & Church, 1997).

Third, implicit in the aforementioned point is the notion that movement toward a positive stimulus and movement away from a negative stimulus each has two distinguishable forms. "Movement toward" can represent getting something positive that is currently absent or it can represent keeping something positive that is currently present (functionally, continuing toward). Likewise, "movement away" can represent keeping away from something negative that is currently absent (functionally, continuing away from) or it can represent getting away from something negative that is currently present (for a conceptual parallel, Herzberg, 1966). Thus, approach motivation not only encompasses promoting new positive situations, but also maintaining and sustaining existing positive situations, and avoidance motivation not only encompasses preventing new negative situations, but also escaping from and rectifying existing negative situations.

Fourth, positive or negative valence is construed as the conceptual core of the approach–avoidance distinction. A stimulus is positively or negatively evaluated by the organism, and this produces inclinations and efforts to approach or avoid the stimulus. "Positive" and "negative" are presumed to take on somewhat different meanings in different contexts, including beneficial/harmful, liked/disliked, and desirable/undesirable. Research indicates that these dimensions are conceptually and empirically comparable to a high degree, although some empirical work suggests that they may be separable in certain instances (Berridge, 1999). At present, given their substantial comparability, it seems best to construe beneficial/harmful, liked/disliked, and desirable/undesirable as functionally equivalent dimensions that may be subsumed under the positive/negative rubric (i.e., in essence, the three dimensions are conceptualized as indicators of a positive or negative latent variable). Nevertheless, it is possible that subsequent research will establish a need to distinguish among these dimensions in defining the approach–avoidance distinction.

Fifth, "stimuli" as used herein may represent concrete, observable objects/events/possibilities, or they may represent abstract, internally generated representations of objects/events/possibilities. Furthermore, stimuli are meant to connote an essentially limitless, idiographic array of focal objects/events/possibilities.

TERMINOLOGICAL CONSIDERATIONS

Many different terms and labels have been used over the years to cover the basic conceptual space that is covered by the definition of approach and avoidance motivation offered herein. Each of the different designations tends to be associated with a somewhat different emphasis. Three of the most common of these designations are considered in the following, in addition to approach–avoidance.

Hedonism (i.e., pleasure–pain). Hedonism has been conceptualized in many different ways in the philosophical and psychological literatures. In philosophy, the ancient Greeks, such as the Epicureans, used the term quite broadly to refer to seeking the pleasures and avoiding the pains of both the mind and the body, whereas the British empiricists used the term more narrowly to refer to the pleasures and pains of bodily sensation (Boring, 1950; Cofer & Appley, 1964). In psychology, hedonism has typically been defined in a narrow sense in terms of bodily sensation and experienced affect (Franken, 1994; Young, 1961). Rozin (1999) has recently proposed a more inclusive view of hedonism, defining pleasure as "a positive experienced state that we seek and that we try to maintain or enhance" and pain as "a negative experienced state that we avoid and that we try to reduce or eliminate" (p. 112). This more inclusive view of hedonism is more akin to the conceptualization of approach–avoidance motivation herein than is the normative view of hedonism in the psychological literature. Rozin's definition remains narrower than that presented herein, however, in that he uses the term "experienced" to refer to conscious experience, whereas nonconscious and even reflexive processes are included under the approach–avoidance rubric in the present definition.

Approach–withdrawal. The approach–withdrawal distinction was introduced to the psychological literature by Schneirla (1959), a comparative psychologist. Schneirla argued that motivational analyses should be grounded in overt behavioral actions, so that they are applicable to lower as well as higher organisms. Thus, he conceptualized approach and withdrawal motivation in terms of observable behavior toward stimuli and away from stimuli, respectively (i.e., approach–withdrawal motivation and observable physical movement were considered isomorphic). Davidson and colleagues (Davidson, 1992; Sutton & Davidson, 1997; Tomarken, Davidson, Wheeler, & Doss, 1992) currently utilize the approach–withdrawal distinction in broader fashion to refer to action tendencies as well as overt action per se. Approach and withdrawal tendencies are presumed to be grounded in differential cortical activation. Approach tendencies are linked to activation of the left prefrontal cortex, whereas withdrawal tendencies are linked to activation of the right prefrontal cortex. These approach–withdrawal tendencies are posited to be the foundational dimensions of emotional experience. The conceptualization of approach–avoidance proffered herein is similar to Davidson and colleagues' conceptualization of approach–withdrawal, in that approach–avoidance refers to action tendencies as well as overt action per se. However, their approach–withdrawal distinction is narrower than the approach–avoidance distinction espoused herein, in that approach–withdrawal focuses on the issue of energization at the biological level, whereas approach–avoidance herein covers both energization and direction, and is applicable to biologically based and psychologically based processes across the neuraxis.

Appetite–aversion. The "appetite–aversion" distinction was coined by Craig (1918), who conceptualized appetites and aversions in terms of internal states of agitation (i.e., energization) accompanied by a readiness to "consume" the "appeted" stimulus or "get rid of" the "disturbing" stimulus (pp. 93–94). Craig focused primarily on physiological instincts in his theorizing, and considered basic reflexive mechanisms to be outside the purview of his appetite–aversion analysis (as did Tolman (1932) who explicitly embraced Craig's distinction). In the contemporary literature, Lang and colleagues (Lang, 1995; Lang, Bradley, & Cuthbert, 1997) utilize the appetite–aversion distinction in their analysis of emotion and reflexive behavior. Emotion is characterized as a motivationally tuned state of action readiness, and two basic brain systems are posited to underlie emotion: appetitive (consummatory) and aversive (defensive). Reflexive behaviors are also characterized in terms of the appetitive–aversive distinction. In both instances, appetitive is meant to connote consummatory and approach oriented, whereas aversive is meant to connote defensive and avoidance oriented. More complex, "tactical" behavior is also thought to be organized in terms of this appetitive–aversive distinction, but little detail is offered in this regard (interestingly, approach–avoidance terminology per se is utilized when "tactical" behavior is [briefly] discussed; Lang, 1995, p. 373). The conceptualization of approach–avoidance offered herein is similar to Lang and colleagues' conceptualization of appetitive–aversive in that the approach–avoidance distinction is viewed as applicable to reflexive behavior. Indeed, given Lang and colleagues' incorporation of "tactical" behavior under the appetitive–aversive rubric, the two distinctions under consideration primarily differ in terms of emphasis. Reflexive behavior has been the central focus of the appetitive–aversive distinction, whereas it is simply one of many levels under consideration in the approach–avoidance distinction).

Approach–avoidance. The approach–avoidance distinction emerged from Kurt Lewin's work on Field Theory, specifically his conceptualization of the forces that accompany positive and negative valences. Lewin (1935) posited that stimuli have positive or attracting properties, or negative or repelling properties (i.e., valences) that are linked directly to tendencies to approach or avoid the stimuli. These positive and negative valences usually emerge from the organism's needs, meaning that approach and avoidance tendencies are typically activated in the service of need satisfaction. Working within a Lewinian framework, Miller (1944) helped popularize the approach–avoidance distinction with his systematic experimental research on approach–avoidance conflicts. In fact, it is not Lewin, but Miller (1937), as well as Hovland (1937) and Sears (1937), who first used the term approach–avoidance in print (in the published proceedings of an American Psychological Association symposium on conflict chaired by Clark Hull). Although, in most of Miller's experiments, approach and avoidance were operationalized in terms of movement toward or away from an object in physical space, Miller (1944), in accord with Lewin, explicitly stated that approach and avoidance are to be understood dynamically and functionally, not spatially (Dollard & Miller, 1950). That is, the experimental work on "spatial approach or avoidance" behavior (Miller, 1944, p. 432) was designed to be a simple, concrete analog of more complex, abstract motivational processes. McClelland and colleagues (McClelland, 1951; McClelland, Atkinson, Clark, & Lowell, 1953) were also instrumental in establishing the approach–avoidance distinction. These theorists focused primarily on approach and avoidance motives, characterized as

dispositional preferences for acquiring positive, hoped for experiences or states (e.g., the motive for success) or for avoiding negative, feared experiences or states (e.g., the motive to avoid failure). However, they also noted that the distinction between approach and avoidance motivation was applicable at the level of unlearned, reflexive mechanisms as well as motives (McClelland et al., 1953). Like Lewin (and Miller), McClelland and colleagues clearly conceptualized the approach–avoidance distinction in terms of underlying valence-based processes, rather than observable behavior per se.

In sum, it seems that the best way to cover the conceptual space under consideration is in broad fashion, and in terms of underlying motivational mechanisms and processes rather than observable behavior per se. The term "hedonism" has tended to represent a rather narrow set of psychological phenomena (i.e., sensory or affective), and the approach–withdrawal designation has typically been linked to an emphasis on physical movement as a direct indicator of motivation. Both of these terminological options seem unnecessarily restrictive. The designations "appetitive–aversive" and "approach–avoidance" have been proffered and used in highly similar fashion in the literature. Both of these designations are broadly applicable to all levels and degrees of complexity of valence-based mechanisms and processes, from the simple, constitutionally engrained instigation of fixed behavior in the single-celled amoeba to the highly complex, multiply determined, flexible regulation of the human being. Thus, from a conceptual standpoint, either of these options would suffice. Approach–avoidance has been selected herein because it is the more widely recognized of the two designations in the motivational literature, and because it is the easier of the two options to intuitively understand (particularly for the newcomer to the literature).

OVERVIEW OF THE HANDBOOK OF APPROACH AND AVOIDANCE MOTIVATION

The present volume is designed as a broad overview of research and theory on approach and avoidance motivation. Given the breadth of applicability of the approach–avoidance distinction, the breadth of the coverage in the handbook is substantial, encompassing a multitude of different constructs, levels of analysis, and disciplines. This breadth of coverage bears testimony to the foundational and pervasive importance of the approach–avoidance distinction in motivational accounts of behavior.

The scholars who have provided chapters to the handbook are widely recognized as outstanding contributors in their area of expertise. This is truly a stellar lineup, and they have, without exception, written excellent, cutting edge, insightful chapters that individually and corporately do justice to the topic of approach–avoidance motivation.

The first part of the *Handbook* is comprised of a single introductory chapter that provides an overview of the approach–avoidance motivational distinction. The second part grounds approach–avoidance in neurophysiology and neurobiology, covering a broad range of topics that include brain systems and mechanisms, cortical asymmetry, cortex-reflex connections, subcortical processes, neurotransmitters, hormones, and olfaction. Part three shifts to a variety of topics relevant to different types and levels of analysis, including basic personality dispositions (including traits and temperaments) in both human and nonhuman animals, the genetic basis of basic dispositions, domain-specific (i.e., achievement and social) motives and goals, and situation-specific motivational states. Part four focuses on the evaluative processes that make approach and avoidance such an integral aspect of motivated behavior; topics include the evolutionary basis of evaluation, the immediacy and automaticity of evaluation, the structure of evaluation, and asymmetries in evaluative processes.

The fifth part of the *Handbook* covers emotion and well-being, including the structure of emotions, the function of emotions, distinct emotional experience, the specific emotion of anger, and the general concept of psychological well-being. The sixth part focuses on cognition, specifically the topics of challenge and threat appraisal, mental control, orienting and attentional processes, and the framing of information. Part seven encompasses various topics relevant to the self, specifically, self-regulation, self-esteem and the self-concept, self-knowledge, and access to the self. The eighth and final part of the handbook covers the area of social context, including culture, stereotyping, social comparison, social exclusion, and last but certainly not least, sexual behavior.

Clearly much ground is covered in the handbook; this breadth of coverage nicely illustrates the widespread influence of the simple but powerful approach–avoidance distinction. Those new to this area will undoubtedly be astounded by how a seemingly simple distinction can be so enduring and generative. I believe that those who are seasoned veterans working in this area will also find much to learn in the pages herein.

ACKNOWLEDGMENTS

Preparation of this chapter was facilitated by a grant from the William T. Grant Foundation (Grant #2565).

REFERENCES

Adamec, R. (1991). Anxious personality in the cat. In B. Carroll, & J. Barrett (Eds.), *Psychopathology and the brain* (pp. 153–168). New York: Raven Press.

Armitage, K. (1986). Individuality, social behavior, and reproductive success in yellow-bellied marmots. *Ecology, 67,* 1186–1193.

Arnold, M. (1960). *Emotion and personality.* New York: Columbia University Press.

Atkinson, J. W., & Birch, D. (1970). *The dynamics of action.* New York: Wiley.

Bargh, J. A. (1997). The automaticity of everyday life. *Advances in Social Cognition, 10,* 1–61.

Bargh, J., & Chartrand, T. (1999). The unbearable automaticity of being. *American Psychologist, 54,* 462–479.

Bargh, J., Chaiken, S., Raymond, P., & Hymes, C. (1996). The automatic evaluation effect: Unconditional automatic attitude activation with a pronunciation task. *Journal of Experimental Social Psychology, 32,* 104–128.

Bentham, J. (1779/1879). *Introduction to the principles of morals and legislation.* Oxford: Clarendon Press.

Berntson, G., Boysen, S., & Cacioppo, J. (1993). Neurobehavioral organization and the cardinal principle of evaluative bivalence. *Annals New York Academy of Science, 702,* 75–102.

Berridge, K. (1999). Pleasure, pain, desire, and dread: Hidden core processes of emotion. In D. Kahneman, E. Diener, & N. Schwarz (Eds.), *Wellbeing: The foundations of hedonic psychology* (pp. 525–557). New York: Russell Sage Foundation.

Bogardus, E. (1931). *Fundamentals of social psychology* (2nd ed.). New York: Appleton-Century-Crofts.

Boring, E. G. (1950). *A historical of experimental psychology.* New York: Appleton-Century-Crofts.

Bowlby, J. (1969). *Attachment.* New York: Basic Books.

Bradley, M., & Vrana, S. (1993). The startle probe in the study of emotion and emotional disorders. In N. Birbaumer, & A. Ohman (Eds.), *The structure of emotion* (pp. 270–287). Seattle: Hogrefe & Huber.

Budaev, S. (1997). "Personality" in the guppy (*Poecilia reticulata*). *Journal of Comparative Psychology, 111,* 399–411.

Cacioppo, J., & Berntson, G. (1994). Relationship between attitudes and evaluative space: A critical review, with emphasis on the separability of positive and negative substrates. *Psychological Bulletin, 115,* 401–422.

Cacioppo, J., Priester, J., & Berntson, G. (1993). Rudimentary determinants of attitudes, II: Arm flexion and extension have differential effects on attitudes. *Journal of Personality and Social Psychology, 65,* 5–16.

Carver, C., & Scheier, M. (1998). *On the self-regulation of behavior.* New York: Cambridge University Press.

Cattell, R. (1957). *Personality and motivation: Structure and measurement.* Yonkers, New York: World Book.

Chen, M., & Bargh, J. (1999). Consequences of automatic evaluation: Immediate behavioral predispositions to approach or avoid the stimulus. *Personality and Social Psychology Bulletin, 25,* 215–223.

Cofer, C. N., & Appley, M. H. (1964). *Motivation: Theory and research*. New York: Wiley.

Copleston, F. (1946). *A history of philosophy,* Vol. 1. London: Burns, Oats, & Washbourne, Ltd.

Corwin, G. (1921). Minor studies from the psychological laboratory of Cornell University. *American Journal of Psychology, 32*, 563–570.

Craig, W. (1918). Appetites and aversions as constituents of instincts. *Biological Bulletin, 34*, 91–107.

Crites, S., & Cacioppo, J. (1996). Electrocortical differentiation of evaluative and nonevaluative categorizations. *Psychological Science, 7*, 318–321.

Davidson, R. (1992). Prolegomenon to the structure of emotion: Gleanings from neuropsychology. *Cognition and Emotion, 6*, 245–268.

Dickinson, A., & Dearing, M. (1979). Appetitive–aversive interactions and inhibitory processes. In A. Dickinson, & R. Boakes (Eds.), *Mechanisms of learning and motivation* (pp. 203–231). Hillsdale, NJ: Lawrence Erlbaum Associates.

Dollard, J., & Miller, N. (1950). *Personality and psychotherapy*. New York: McGraw-Hill.

Doob, L. (1947). The behavior of attitudes. *Psychological Review, 54*, 135–156.

Elliot, A. J. (1997). Integrating "classic" and "contemporary" approaches to achievement motivation: A hierarchical model of approach and avoidance achievement motivation. In P. Pintrich, & M. Maehr (Eds.), *Advances in motivation and achievement* (Vol. 10, pp. 143–179). Greenwich, CT: JAI Press.

Elliot, A. J. (1999). Approach and avoidance motivation and achievement goals. *Educational Psychologist, 34*, 149–169.

Elliot, A. J. (2006). Approach and avoidance motivation. *Motivation and Emotion, 30*, 111–116.

Elliot, A. J., & Church, M. A. (1997). A hierarchical model of approach and avoidance achievement motivation. *Journal of Personality and Social Psychology, 72*, 218–232.

Elliot, A. J., & Covington, M. V. (2001). Approach and avoidance motivation. *Educational Psychology Review, 13*, 73–92.

Elliot, A. J., & Thrash, T. M. (2001). Achievement goals and the hierarchical model of achievement motivation. *Educational Psychology Review, 12*, 139–156.

Elliot, A. J., & Thrash, T. M. (2002). Approach–avoidance motivation in personality: Approach and avoidance temperaments and goals. *Journal of Personality and Social Psychology, 82*, 804–818.

Erickson, E. (1963). *Childhood and society* (2nd ed.). New York: Norton.

Eysenck, H. (1967). *The biological basis of personality*. Springfield, IL: Charles Thomas.

Fazio, R., Sanbonmatsu, D., Powell, M., & Kardes, F. (1986). On the automatic activation of attitudes. *Journal of Personality and Social Psychology, 50*, 229–238.

Fiske, S. (1982). Schema-triggered affect. In M. Clark, & S. Fiske (Eds.), *Affect and cognition* (pp. 55–78). Hillsdale, NJ: Lawrence Erlbaum Associates.

Fordyce, G., Goddard, M. E., & Seifert, G. W. (1982). The measurement of temperament in cattle and effect of experience and genotype. *Proceedings of Australian Animal Production, 14*, 329–332.

Förster, J., Higgins, E., & Idson, L. (1998). Approach and avoidance strength during goal attainment: Regulatory focus and the "goal looms larger" effect (1998). *Journal of Personality and Social Psychology, 75*, 1115–1131.

Franken, R. (1994). *Human motivation*. Belmont, CA: Brooks/Cole Publishing Company.

Freud, S. (1915). Repression. In the standard edition of *Complete psychological works of Sigmund Freud,* Vol. XIV. London: Hogarth, 1957.

Freud, S. (1923). The ego and the id. In the standard edition of *Complete psychological works of Sigmund Freud*, Vol. XIX. London: Hogarth, 1947.

Frijda, N. (1986). *The emotions.* Cambridge: Cambridge University Press.

Garcia-Sevilla, L. (1984). Extraversion and neuroticism in rats. *Personality and Individual Differences, 5*, 511–532.

Goddard, M., & Beilharz, R. (1985). A multivariate analysis of the fearfulness potential in potential guide dogs. *Behavioral Genetics, 15*, 69–89.

Graham, F. (1973). Habituation and dishabituation of responses innervated by the autonomic nervous system. In H. Peeke, & M. Herz (Eds.), *Habituation: Vol. 1. Behavioral studies* (pp. 163–218). New York: Academic Press.

Hebb, D. O. (1949). *The organization of behavior*. New York: Wiley.

Heider, F. (1958). *The psychology of interpersonal relations.* New York: John Wiley & Sons.

Herzberg, F. (1966). *Work and the nature of man.* Cleveland, OH: Ward.

Herzog, H. A. Jr., & Burghardt, G. M. (1988). Development of antipredator responses in snakes. *Ethology, 77*, 250–258.

Higgins, E. T. (1997). Beyond pleasure and pain. *American Psychologist, 52*, 1280–1300.

Horney, K. (1937). *The neurotic personality of our time.* New York: Norton.

Hovland, C. I. (1937). Differences in resolution of approach-approach and avoidance–avoidance conflicts. *Psychological Bulletin, 34*, 719.

Hull, C. (1943). *Principles of behavior*. New York: Appleton-Century-Crofts.

James, W. (1890). *The principles of psychology* (Vol. 2). New York: Henry Holt & Co.

Jung, C. (1921). Psychological types. In Vol. 6 of *The collected works of C. G. Jung.* Princeton, NJ: Princeton University Press.

Kagan, J. (1998). Biology and the child. In N. Eisenberg (Ed.), *Handbook of child psychology* (Vol. 3, pp. 177–235). New York: John Wiley & Sons.

Kahneman, D., Diener, E., & Schwarz, N. (1999). Preface. In D. Kahneman, E. Diener, & N. Schwarz (Eds.), *Wellbeing: The foundations of hedonic psychology* (pp. 9–12). New York: Russell Sage Foundation.

Konorski, J. (1967). *Integrative activity of the brain: An interdisciplinary approach.* Chicago: The University of Chicago Press.

Kuhl, J. (1986). Motivation and information processing. In R. Sorrentino & E. Higgins (Eds.), *Handbook of motivation and cognition, vol. 1* (pp. 404–434). New York: Guilford.

Lang, P. (1984). Cognition in emotion: Concept and action. In C. Izard, J. Kagan, & R. Zajonc (Eds.), *Emotion, cognition, and behavior* (pp. 196–226). New York: Cambridge University Press.

Lang, P. (1995). Studies of motivation and attention. *American Psychologist, 50*, 372–385.

Lang, P., Bradley, M., & Cuthbert, B. (1990). Emotion, attention, and the startle reflex. *Psychological Review, 97*, 377–395.

Lang, P., Bradley, M., & Cuthbert, B. (1997). Motivated attention: Affect, activation, and action. In P. Lang, R. Simmons, & M. Balaban (Eds.), *Attention and orienting: sensory and motivational processes* (pp. 87–135). Florida: Lawrence Erlbaum Associates.

Lazarus, R. (1991). *Emotion and adaption.* New York: Oxford University Press.

LeDoux, J. (1987). Emotion. In F. Plum (Ed.), *Handbook of physiology* (Vol. 5, pp. 419–454). Bethesda, MD: American Physiological Society.

LeDoux, J., Sakaguchi, A., & Reis, H. (1984). Subcortical efferent projections of the medial geniculate nucleus mediate emotional responses conditioned by acoustic stimuli. *Journal of Neuroscience, 4*, 683–698.

Lewin, K. (1935). *A dynamic theory of personality.* New York: McGraw-Hill.

Lyons, D., Price, E., & Moberg, G. (1988). Individual differences in temperament of domestic dairy goats: Constancy and change. *Animal Behavior, 36*, 1323–1333.

MacDonald, K. (1983). Stability and individual differences in behavior in a litter of wolf cubs (*Canis lupus*). *Journal of Comparative Psychology, 97*, 107–119.

Maier, S., Vandenhoff, P., & Crowne, D. (1988). Multivariate analysis of putative measures of activity, exploration, emotionality, and spatial behavior in the hooded rat (*rattus norvegicus*). *Journal of Comparative Psychology, 102*, 378–387.

Marshall, H. R. (1889). The classification of pleasure and pain. *Mind, 14*, 511–536.

Maslow, A. (1955). Deficiency motivation and growth motivation. In M. Jones (Ed.), *Nebraska symposium on motivation* (pp. 1–30). Lincoln: University of Nebraska Press.

Mather, J., & Anderson, R. (1993). Personalities of octopuses (*Octopus robescens*). *Journal of Comparative Psychology, 107*, 336–340.

McClelland, D. (1951). *Personality.* New York: The Dryden Press.

McClelland, D., Atkinson, J., Clark, R., & Lowell, E. (1953). *The achievement motive.* New York: Irvington Publishers.

Miller, N. E. (1937). Analysis of the form of conflict reactions. *Psychological Bulletin, 34*, 720.

Miller, N. (1944). Experimental studies of conflict. In J. McV. Hunt (Ed.), *Personality and the behavioral disorders* (Vol. 1, pp. 431–465). New York: Ronald Press.

Mowrer, O. (1960). *Learning theory and behavior.* New York: Wiley.

Murphy, S., & Zajonc, R. (1993). Affect, cognition, and awareness: Affective priming with optimal and suboptimal stimulus exposures. *Journal of Personality and Social Psychology, 64*, 723–739.

Murray, H. (1938). *Explorations in personality.* New York: Oxford University Press.

Öhman, A. (1997). As fast as the blink of an eye: Evolutionary preparedness for preattentive processing of threat. In P. Lang, R. Simmons, & M. Balaban (Eds.), *Attention and orienting: sensory and motivational processes* (pp. 87–135). Hillsdale, NJ: Lawrence Erlbaum Associates.

Orians, G., & Heerwagen, J. (1992). Evolved responses to landscapes. In J. Barkow, L. Cosmides, & J. Tooby (Eds.), *The adapted mind* (pp. 555–579). New York: Oxford University Press.

Osgood, C. E. (1953). *Method and theory in experimental psychology.* New York: Oxford University Press.

Osgood, C. E., Suci, G., & Tannenbaum, P. (1957). *The measurement of meaning.* Urbana, IL: University of Illinois Press.

Pavlov, I. (1927). *Conditioned reflexes: An investigation into the physiological activity of the cortex* (Translated by G. Anrep), New York: Dover.

Rogers, C. (1961). *On becoming a person: A therapist's view of psychotherapy.* Boston: Houghton Mifflin.

Rotter, J. (1954). *Social learning and clinical psychology.* Englewood Cliffs, NJ: Prentice-Hall.

Rozin, P. (1999). Preadaptations and the puzzles and properties of pleasure. In D. Kahnaman, E. Diener, & N. Schwartz (Eds.) *Well-being: The foundations of hedonic psychology* (pp. 109–133). New York: Russell Sage Foundation.

Schneirla, T. (1959). An evolutionary and developmental theory of biphasic processes underlying approach and withdrawal. In M. Jones (Ed.), *Nebraska Symposium on Motivation* (pp. 1–42). Lincoln: University of Nebraska Press.

Sears, R. R. (1937). Resolution of conflicts between approach avoidance responses. *Psychological Bulletin, 34*, 719–720.

Shizgal, P. (1999). On the neural computation of utility: Implications from studies of brain stimulation and reward. In D. Kahneman, E. Diener, & N. Schwarz (Eds.), *Well-being: The foundations of hedonic psychology* (pp. 500–524). New York: Russell Sage Foundation.

Skinner, B. F. (1938). *The behavior of organisms: An experimental analysis.* Englewood Cliffs, NJ: Prentice-Hall.

Skinner, B. F. (1953). *Science and human behavior.* New York: Macmillan.

Sokolov, E. (1963). *Perception and the conditioned reflex.* Oxford: Pergamon.

Solorz, A. (1960). Latency of instrumental responses as a function of compatibility with the meaning of eliciting verbal signs. *Journal of Experimental Psychology, 59*, 239–245.

Stevenson-Hinde, J., Stillwell-Barnes, R., & Zunz, M. (1980). Individual differences in young rhesus monkeys: Continuity and change. *Primates, 21*, 498–509.

Suomi, S. (1983). Social development in rhesus monkeys: Consideration of individual differences. In A. Oliverio, & M. Zappella (Eds.), *The behavior of human infants* (pp. 71–92). New York: Plenum Press.

Sullivan, H. S. (1953). *The interpersonal theory of psychiatry.* New York: W. W. Norton.

Sutton, S. K., & Davidson, R. J. (1997). Prefrontal brain asymmetry: A biological substrate of the behavioral approach and inhibition systems. *Psychological Science*, 8, 204–210.

Thorndike, E. (1911). *Animal Intelligence*. New York: Macmillan.

Thurstone, L. L. (1931). Measurement of social attitudes. *Journal of Abnormal and Social Psychology*, 26, 249–269.

Tomarken, A. J., Davidson, R. J., Wheeler, R. E., & Doss, R. C. (1992). Individual differences in anterior brain asymmetry and fundamental dimensions of emotion. *Journal of Personality and Social Psychology*, 62, 676–687.

Tooby, J., & Cosmides, L. (1990). The past explains the present: Emotional adaptions and the structure of ancestral environments. *Ethology and sociobiology*, 11, 375–424.

Tolman, E. (1925). Behaviorism and purpose. *Journal of Philosophy*, 22, 35–41.

Tolman, E. (1932). *Purposive behavior in animals and men.* New York: The Century.

Verbeek, M., Drent, P., & Wiepkema, P. (1994). Consistent individual differences in early exploratory behavior of male great tits. *Animal Behavior*, 48, 1113–1121.

Watson, S., & Ward, J. (1996). Temperament and problem solving in the small-eared bushbaby (*Otolemur garnettii*). *Journal of Comparative Psychology*, 110, 377–385.

Wilson, D., Clark, A., Coleman, K., & Dearstyne, T. (1994). Shyness and boldness in humans and other animals. *Trends in Ecology and Evolution*, 9, 442–446.

Wilson, D., Coleman, K., Clark, A., & Biederman, L. (1993). Shy-bold continuum in pumpkinseed sunfish (*Lepomis gibbosus*): An ecological study of a psychological trait. *Journal of Comparative Psychology*, 107, 250–260.

Wundt, W. (1887). *Grundzüge der physiologishen psychologie*, (3rd ed.), Leipzig: Engelmann.

Young, P. (1959). The role of affective processes in learning and motivation. *Psychological Review*, 66, 104–125.

Young, R. K. (1961). *Motivation and emotion: A survey of the determinants of human and animal activity.* New York: Wiley.

Zajonc, R. B. (1980). Feeling and thinking: Preferences need no inferences. *American Psychologist*, 35, 151–175.

Zajonc, R. B. (1984). On the primacy of affect. *American Psychologist*, 39, 117–123.

Zajonc, R. B. (1998). Emotion. In D. Gilbert, S. Fiske, & G. Lindzey (Eds.), *The handbook of social psychology*, (4th ed., pp. 591–632). New York: McGraw-Hill.

Part II

Neurophysiology and Neurobiology

Brain Systems and Mechanisms

2 Emotional Processing and Motivation: In Search of Brain Mechanisms

Christopher K. Cain and Joseph E. LeDoux

CONTENTS

Emotion and motivation are deeply intertwined (LeDoux, 2002b). The stimuli that trigger us to react emotionally also motivate us to act. In this chapter we discuss brain interactions between emotion and motivation in escape behavior, a form of avoidance conditioning, using the vast base of knowledge that has been obtained about emotional processing through studies of fear conditioning. We next discuss appetitive conditioning and approach motivation in a similar fashion. We conclude with an integrated view of the brain mechanisms of avoidance and approach motivation. The final picture is far from complete, since much remains unknown. However, we hope to show that research on the brain mechanisms of avoidance and approach has solved different parts of similar puzzles. Considering the two together reveals a coherent view of the underlying circuitry and suggests a strategy for advancing our understanding of motivational processing by the brain.

DEVELOPING A FRAMEWORK

How does a neuroscientist interested in the details of brain function approach the study of emotion and motivation? Consider the following scenario. A child at the playground encounters a dog. At first he freezes in his tracks, but after a few seconds he runs behind his mother for protection. If we want to understand this behavior we could ask him what he was feeling during the experience and why he behaved as he did. He may respond that he is afraid of dogs and ran away to avoid being bitten. Assuming that we could trust his verbal report, which we should not (Larsen & Fredrickson, 1999), it is still very difficult to study the brain mechanisms of human subjective experiences like feelings (emotion) and wants and needs (motivation). Imaging techniques like fMRI are rapidly advancing, but even this technique reveals little about the precise workings of neurons and molecules in the brain. The techniques required to study detailed mechanisms of brain function, discussed below, usually cannot be used with humans for ethical and practical reasons. Animal research allows for use of these techniques, but it is unlikely that human subjective experiences are the same in lower species (LeDoux, 2002c). Even if they were, procuring a verbal report from a rat is not possible.

The strategy employed in our laboratory builds upon a distinction between emotions and feelings (Damasio, 1994; LeDoux, 1984). Emotions are states automatically elicited by significant stimuli. Stimuli associated with food, sexual reproduction, predatory defense, thermoregulation, and pain are some examples. Feelings, on the other hand, are cognitive representations of emotions. All animals have the capacity to detect and respond to significant stimuli independent of their higher cognitive capacities. For this reason, we focus on emotional responses and make no assumptions about conscious feelings that may accompany these responses, even though feelings may have an important impact on human behavior.

The predatory defense, or fear, system has been a particularly useful model for exploring questions about emotional processing. Stimuli associated with predators elicit defensive responses adaptive for the organism. By examining how the brain processes information about innate and learned fear stimuli, and how it generates specific defensive responses on the basis of this processing, the defense circuitry is being mapped. In this sense, emotion can be thought of as the process by which the brain computes the value of a stimulus for the purpose of responding adaptively. However, the same responses that are adaptive in some situations can become maladaptive when they are activated by stimuli that are not dangerous, or when activated in a recurring and prolonged way that exceeds the requirements of the situation.

Returning to our example above, note that when the child encountered the fear-eliciting stimulus (the dog) he first froze in his tracks and then fled. This is a common theme with emotional behaviors. Emotional stimuli have the capacity to both elicit emotional reactions (such as freezing) and to enable emotional actions (such as flight), often in that order. Thus, the emotional processing of sensory information in the fear system elicits defensive reactions, and this processing also motivates active responses that minimize exposure to the threat. The former is usually referred to as fear, and the latter as escape or avoidance.

In the introductory chapter of this book, Elliot (2006) defined avoidance motivation as "the energization of behavior by, or the direction of behavior away from, negative stimuli." This is indeed a useful starting point. We would like to extend this view. We propose that "energization" occurs when the brain's fear system is activated by a threatening stimulus. This energization is both general (nonspecific arousal systems, such as monoamine containing networks, are activated) and specific (fear responses, such as freezing behavior and associated visceral responses, are elicited). The "direction of behavior away from" the threatening stimulus also reflects the activation of the fear system. In this case, the fear system leads to the activation of motivational circuits that initiate goal-directed behavior.

Using this framework we have investigated brain mechanisms mediating fear and avoidance motivation with two specific behavioral protocols: classical fear conditioning and instrumental escape from fear (EFF) learning. Classical fear conditioning studies have demonstrated how the brain mediates the learning of an emotional association between a neutral conditioned stimulus (CS) and an aversive unconditioned stimulus (US), and how the CS subsequently arouses the brain and elicits "passive" conditioned responses (CRs). EFF studies, on the other hand, are beginning to shed light on how the CS can then serve as a motivating factor to initiate active responses that reduce exposure to the fear arousing stimulus.

TOOLS FOR STUDYING BRAIN MECHANISMS OF BEHAVIOR

The field of neuroscience has a wide arsenal of tools available for studying the neural basis of behavior. Some of these are traditional techniques, such as the lesion method, whereas others have only emerged in recent years, such as the creation of genetically engineered animals that allow studies of the molecular basis of behavior. In order to facilitate the discussion of brain mechanisms later in the chapter, we give a brief summary of common techniques.

LESIONS

Brain lesions have been widely used to investigate the functions of specific brain regions. In a typical learning experiment, a region of interest is damaged and behavior is assessed. Damage is usually induced by passing positive current through an electrode (electrolytic lesion) or by infusing a small volume of chemical into the region (excitotoxic lesion). The timing of the lesion relative to learning can further distinguish the brain region's role in the learning and memory process. For instance, lesions before training can implicate a region in learning, while postlearning lesions can implicate a region in memory storage or recall mechanism (Rodrigues, Schafe, & LeDoux, 2004). Electrolytic lesions are perhaps the simplest technique and offer the greatest control over the spatial extent of damage; however, electrolytic lesions also destroy fibers of passage and cannot be used to firmly attribute function to cell bodies in the lesioned region (Koo, Han, & Kim, 2004). Excitotoxic lesions destroy cell bodies in the infused region and spare fibers of passage; however, controlling the extent of damage is difficult given the unpredictable diffusion patterns of infused liquids.

"Disconnection" experiments are emerging as a clever and useful technique for studying the functional role of connections between two regions (LeDoux, Sakaguchi, Iwata, & Reis, 1986; Parkinson, Willoughby, Robbins, & Everitt, 2000b). In a classic disconnection experiment, asymmetrical unilateral lesions are produced leaving one intact nucleus type in each hemisphere of the brain. As long as unilateral lesions of either nucleus alone do not affect the behavior of interest, this technique implicates the interactivity of two nuclei in a brain process (Everitt & Robbins, 1992).

LOCAL PHARMACOLOGY

A related but less severe technique involves temporarily inactivating cells within a region prior to a particular phase of testing. This is achieved by infusing a chemical agent, via stereotaxically implanted cannulae, directly into a brain region. Muscimol, a $GABA_A$-receptor agonist, is perhaps the most commonly used inactivating agent (Blair, Sotres-Bayon, Moita, & LeDoux, 2005). In addition to sparing transmission in fibers of passage, temporary inactivation preserves the integrity of the brain region for subsequent phases of testing and allows for greater temporal resolution. However, inactivation also has some drawbacks. For instance, it is difficult to control the diffusion of the chemical agent and to restrict inactivation to the region of interest. If nearby structures are necessary for some aspect of the task, then inactivation may prove difficult.

Using a technique identical to inactivation, very small volumes of pharmacological agents can be infused into a specific brain region to implicate molecules in a particular behavior. The timing of the infusion relative to the stage of behavioral training can provide insight into whether a molecule in that region participates in learning, short-term memory (STM), long-term memory (LTM), or other nonspecific processes (Rodrigues et al., 2004). Of course, local pharmacology is also imperfect in that infused drugs can affect adjacent regions.

GENETIC MANIPULATIONS

The use of genetic manipulations to investigate the role of brain site-specific molecules is rapidly advancing, but is still imperfect. Knockout and transgenic mice are very useful for implicating a specific molecule in brain processing, although the majority of these manipulations are global (whole brain), or at least affect large portions of the brain (e.g., forebrain specific knockouts), and present at birth (often resulting in unwanted compensation by other molecules). More recently, researchers have taken to directly infusing constructs to manipulate gene expression in a site- and time-specific manner. The early results are promising and such techniques are likely to be used more often in the future (Rumpel, LeDoux, Zador, & Malinow, 2005).

NEURAL ACTIVITY

Rather than impairing a brain region to deduce its role in a particular behavioral process, it is also useful to record normal neural activity during the task. Multichannel single unit recordings have been widely and successfully used for this purpose (Schoenbaum, Setlow, & Ramus, 2003). Electrodes are chronically implanted allowing for the online recording of both field potentials and action potential activity in isolated neural units. By comparing spike frequency changes with different task phases or different behaviors one can begin to decipher whether neurons in a region participate in task-related sensory processes, motor processes, timing processes, or even plastic learning processes. Such techniques have been successfully used in the study of amygdala-dependent (Goosens & Maren, 2004) and striatum-dependent learning (Nicola, Yun, Wakabayashi, & Fields, 2004). One particularly useful aspect of single unit recording is that temporal components of recorded spike trains can encode an experience with a high degree of precision (Quirk, Armony, & LeDoux, 1997). Thus, spike timing information recorded from different structures during the same task can be used to track information flow through a particular circuit.

Immediate early gene (IEG) expression is another method for mapping the neural circuitry related to specific behavioral tasks. Some common examples of IEGs used for mapping include *cFOS*, *Arc*, and *Homer 1a*. These genes are transcribed in response to heightened neural activity and have distinguishable patterns of mRNA expression. For instance, *Arc* expression can be seen in the nucleus 2–10 min after neural activity and dissipates by 20 min. *Homer 1a*, on the other hand, takes 25–30 min to be expressed in the nucleus after activation. Thus, one can distinguish between brain regions involved in specific behaviors by eliciting the behaviors with a 25 min separation and then examining differential IEG expression (Petrovich, Holland, & Gallagher, 2005). IEG expression studies can be a powerful tool for implicating brain regions in specific behaviors and may complement electrophysiological studies.

AVOIDANCE MOTIVATION

The concept of avoidance motivation arose to explain why animals and people move away from, either physically or psychologically, certain environmental stimuli. Our natural inclination as introspective beings is to invoke some subjective state to explain why we, or other animals, avoid certain stimuli and situations. However, just as we defined emotions independent of conscious feelings, we also define motivations independent of conscious states. Motivations, in this view, reflect the activation, via emotional processing, of brain systems involved in goal-directed behavior. Avoidance motivation, specifically, can be defined in terms of brain processes that prevent

exposure or facilitate the removal of the organism from fear arousing stimuli. This is not to say that conscious factors never enter into motivation. But when we study motivation in rodents or other animals, it seems unnecessary, and in fact, counterproductive, to introduce conscious states as explanatory factors since the existence of consciousness in such creatures cannot be proven.

BEHAVIORAL PARADIGMS FOR STUDYING AVOIDANCE MOTIVATION

The following paragraphs focus on two research areas that are commonly studied in relation to avoidance motivation: classical conditioning and instrumental escape conditioning. However, it is important to note that there are a wide range of behavioral paradigms that fall under the umbrella of "avoidance motivation." For instance, animals will avoid situations that lead to the omission of reward (Papini, 2003) or the presentation of punishment (Bolles, 1967a). Interested readers are referred to the following works for further information regarding these, and other, avoidance behavioral paradigms (Brush, 1971; Denny, 1991; Reilly & Bornovalova, 2005).

Classical Fear Conditioning

Classical fear conditioning is a simple learning paradigm based on Pavlov's seminal work with dogs (Pavlov, 1927). Fear conditioning has been intensely studied by psychologists and neuroscientists because of its simplicity and its relevance to human learning and anxiety (Blanchard & Blanchard, 1969b; Bolles & Fanselow, 1980; Davis, Walker, & Myers, 2003; Fanselow & Gale, 2003; LeDoux, 2000; Rescorla, 1988; Seligman, 1971). This focus has been fruitful, and we now have a good understanding of how the brain mediates this emotional behavior.

In a typical fear conditioning experiment, rodents are presented with an emotionally neutral CS, often a tone, that is paired in time with an aversive footshock US. Prior to the pairing, subjects exhibit no defensive responses to the tone. After pairing, tone presentations elicit a cassette of defensive responses including freezing (Blanchard and Blanchard, 1969a), autonomic reactions (Schneiderman, Francis, Sampson, & Schwaber, 1974), neuroendocrine responses (Mason, Mangan, Brady, Conrad, & Rioch, 1961), and potentiation of somatic reflexes such as startle (Davis, 1986). Collectively these CS-elicited learned responses are referred to as conditioned fear responses. Fear responses elicited by the CS after pairing with the US indicate that associative learning took place during conditioning, provided that similar responses fail to occur when the CS and US are unpaired during training (Rescorla, 1967). Conditioned fear responses can last for the lifetime of the animal (Gale et al., 2004). Fear conditioning also establishes the CS as secondary incentive that can motivate avoidance behaviors (discussed below).

Instrumental Conditioning and EFF Learning

For many decades following Pavlov's work, conditioned fear (Mowrer & Lamoreaux, 1946; Solomon & Wynne, 1954; Bolles, 1969) and its neural basis (Sarter & Markowitsch, 1985) were commonly studied with avoidance protocols. We focus here on signaled active avoidance, although there are many procedural variations on this theme, such as passive avoidance (Blanchard & Blanchard, 1970) and Sidman avoidance (Sidman, 1953). In a typical active avoidance experiment, rats are presented with tone-shock pairings on one side of a two-compartment chamber. Movement to the opposite side terminates the tone and prevents the shock presentation. These avoidance responses (R_as) serve as the dependent measure of fear learning and animals exhibit R_as more frequently and with shorter latencies as training progresses. However, avoidance proved to be a difficult paradigm for the analysis and explanation of learning mechanisms. First, learning occurs on trials where the animal successfully avoids shock, and it was difficult to explain how absence of a US could reinforce a response. Second, researchers realized that avoidance was actually a complex learning process where animals first learned that the tone predicted shock, and then learned to escape the tone and prevent shock delivery. Two-factor theory arose hypothesizing that avoidance conditioning involves both classical fear conditioning and instrumental response conditioning (Miller, 1948; Mowrer, 1947). In the almost 80 years since the emergence of two-factor theory, researchers have heatedly debated the contents (i.e., S-S, S-R, or R-S), conditions (Pavlovian operations, instrumental operations, or both) and mechanisms (drives, perceptions, etc.) of avoidance conditioning. However, one idea was proposed early and remains a viable possibility today, escape from fear (EFF) (for review see Levis, 1989).

EFF learning was proposed to explain how classical conditioning and instrumental conditioning could interact to mediate active avoidance. The basic idea is that classical conditioning first establishes fear of the CS. Then on later trials, active responding is reinforced by fear reduction associated with CS-termination. Another way to say this is that the response is instrumental in leading to the reinforcement: fear reduction. Formally, this sort of learning is called conditioned negative reinforcement of a stimulus–response association. Importantly, expression of EFF learning is also believed to be motivated by fear. As training progresses, escape responding is motivated by fear of the CS and reinforced by CS-termination. Thus, EFF learning may be an ideal paradigm for studying how

fear processing can lead to the reinforcement and motivation of active instrumental responses. A major benefit of adopting this strategy is that the neural mechanisms of classical fear conditioning have largely been worked out giving us a firm foundation to examine aversive motivation and instrumental learning.

Despite the promise and simplicity of EFF, it has itself been the subject of considerable controversy over the years (Bolles, 1970; Levis, 1989; McAllister & McAllister, 1991). The main reason is that some researchers have had trouble reliably reproducing EFF learning (independent of avoidance conditioning) in the laboratory. Many have reported successful EFF learning, but failures to obtain EFF learning are also common (see Cain & LeDoux, 2007 for a complete list of references) and may be underreported. We recently conducted an extensive behavioral examination of EFF, using rearing as the escape response, in order to address reasons for the controversy and to suggest procedural improvements (Cain & LeDoux, 2007). We found that EFF training led to a twofold increase in CS-evoked rearing relative to yoked control animals (Figure 2.1A and B). This learning was long lasting (24 h) and response specific (no increase in other nonreinforced behaviors). Interestingly, successful EFF learning also resulted in a transition from passive freezing reactions to active escaping; rats that learned the EFF response showed no spontaneous recovery of freezing following the extinguishing CS presentations used for EFF training (Figure 2.1D). Importantly, expression of EFF learning was also motivated by fear of the CS; animals that went through EFF training did not rear differently than yoked controls until the CS was presented. Thus, our data lead us to conclude that instrumental escape responses can be reinforced by CS termination and be motivated by fear.

Any discussion of emotional motivation would be incomplete without mention of drives and incentives. Hull's drive theory (Hull, 1943) was devised to explain how new habits are learned and repeated. According to Hull, stimulus–response associations are formed because the stimulus evokes a drive, like hunger or pain, and the response results in reduction of that drive. Since not all motivating stimuli are innately motivating, studies on EFF learning expanded the notion of drive theory to include "acquired drives" (Miller, 1948). However, drive theory in its initial form was eventually replaced by incentive theory because of a number of problems. One such problem is that rats will work to obtain sweet-tasting saccharin even though it has no nutritive value and therefore cannot result in reduction of the hunger drive. Incentive theories discard hypothetical drive states and instead assume that external stimuli motivate behavior because they arouse emotion. Bolles (1967b) explained the difference by suggesting that

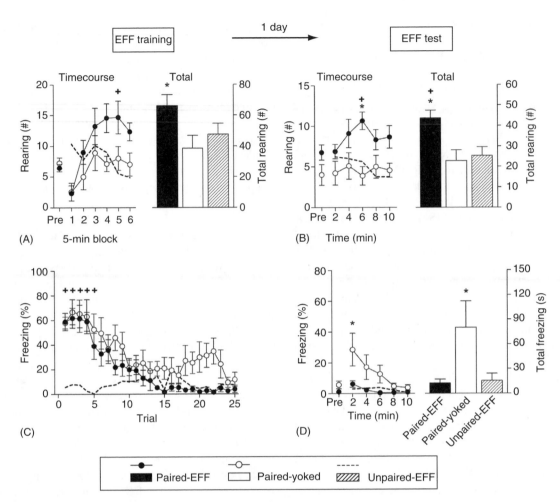

FIGURE 2.1 Escape from fear (EFF) learning represents instrumental learning that is motivated by fear and reinforced by fear reduction. One day after Pavlovian tone-shock pairings, rats were presented with 25 tone-alone presentations in a novel context (EFF training, left). For paired-EFF rats, rearing during a tone presentation led to its immediate termination (response–reinforcement pairing). Paired-yoked rats received identical tone presentations independent of their behavior. One day after EFF training, rats were presented with a single, continuous 10 min tone presentation to assess long-term EFF memory (EFF test, right). Rearing and freezing were assessed during both phases. Paired-EFF rats showed a twofold increase in the EFF escape response (rearing) during the training and testing session compared to paired-yoked rats (A and B). Unpaired-EFF rats had no fear of the conditioned stimulus (CS) and did not acquire the EFF response (enhanced rearing). Successful acquisition of this active escape response was also associated with less passive freezing to the tone (C and D). Further analysis demonstrated that EFF learning was response-specific and performance was motivated by fear (no difference in rearing in the absence of the CS; data not shown). From "Escape from fear: A detailed behavioral analysis of two atypical responses reinforced by CS-termination," by C. K. Cain and J. E. LeDoux, 2007, *Journal of Experimental Psychology: Animal Behavior Processes* 33, p. 455. Adapted with permission.

"drives push while incentives pull." For the purpose of studying brain mechanisms of emotion and motivation, we will assume that incentives do their work not by arousing subjective emotions, but rather by activating neuronal processing in specific brain regions. This activation reflects a brain state where performance of an instrumental response is a highly probable outcome.

BRAIN MECHANISMS RELATED TO AVOIDANCE MOTIVATION

Using the tools outlined in "Tools for Studying Brain Mechanisms of Behavior" of this chapter, a great deal of progress has been made in understanding the brain mechanisms of avoidance motivation. Research on classical fear conditioning has been especially successful at delin-eating the anatomical, cellular, and molecular mecha-nisms of avoidance reactions (e.g., freezing). Although research regarding the brain mechanisms of instrumental escape or avoidance (fear-related actions) has lagged behind, we outline a strategy with the potential for rapid progress using our knowledge of fear conditioning mechanisms as a foundation. However, as we will discuss in "Approach Motivation," findings from approach motiva-tion research may provide an excellent guide for dissecting avoidance motivation at the systems level.

Classical Fear Conditioning

Neural circuits. Considerable evidence suggests that the amygdala is critical for learning, storage, and expression of fear conditioning (LeDoux, 2000; Pare, Quirk, & LeDoux, 2004). The amygdala is composed of a dozen or so nuclei (Pitkänen, Savander, & LeDoux, 1997). Fear conditioning research has focused primarily on three of these: the lateral nucleus (LA), central nucleus (CE), and basal nucleus (B).

Neurons in the LA receive auditory (CS) and somato-sensory (US) inputs from thalamic and cortical process-ing regions (LeDoux, 1990; Mascagni, McDonald, & Coleman, 1993; McDonald, 1998; Romanski, LeDoux, Clugnet, & Bordi, 1993). Tone signals arrive in the LA as early as 12 ms following stimulus onset and the same neu-rons receive shock inputs (Bordi & LeDoux, 1994a,b; Clugnet, LeDoux, & Morrison, 1990; Romanski et al., 1993). LA neurons in turn connect with CE both directly and indirectly via projections to B (Pare & Smith, 1998; Pitkänen et al., 1997).

The LA appears to be critical for the acquisition and storage of fear conditioning. Both electrolytic and exci-totoxic lesions of the LA prevent acquisition and expres-sion of fear conditioning (Amorapanth, LeDoux, & Nader, 2000; Campeau & Davis, 1995; Gale et al., 2004; LeDoux, 1990). Further, temporary inactivation of the LA with muscimol prevents CS-elicited freezing when given before training or testing, but not if given immedi-ately after training (Muller, Corodimas, Fridel, & LeDoux, 1997; Wilensky, Schafe, & LeDoux, 1999). CE, via its projections to the hypothalamus and brainstem (Bellgowan & Helmstetter, 1996; Davis, 1998; De Oca, DeCola, Maren, & Fanselow, 1998; LeDoux, Iwata, Cicchetti, & Reis, 1988), appears to mediate the expres-sion of conditioned fear (Amorapanth et al., 2000; Goosens & Maren, 2001; Hitchcock, & Davis, 1986; Kapp, Whalen, Supple, & Pascoe, 1992; but see Koo et al., 2004). The role of B in fear conditioning is some-what controversial at present. Pretraining lesions of B have no effect on learning or expression (Amorapanth

et al.; Goosens & Maren, 2001; Nader, Majidishad, Amorapanth, & LeDoux, 2001; Sotres-Bayon, Bush, & LeDoux, 2004), but a recent study indicates that post-training lesions impair expression of learning (Anglada-Figueroa & Quirk, 2005). This suggests that B is not required for learning or expression of fear conditioning, but may participate in one or both of these processes under normal circumstances.

Taken together, anatomic, lesion, and inactivation studies strongly suggest that LA participates in the learn-ing and storage of fear conditioning while the B and CE participate at least in fear expression. Notably, LA manip-ulations that impair fear conditioning do not alter tone or shock sensitivity, the ability to freeze, or even nonasso-ciative learning processes such as shock-induced sensiti-zation (Fanselow & LeDoux, 1999). Thus, the LA appears to be selectively involved in associative learning about emotionally significant stimuli.

Synaptic plasticity. Short latency (<15 ms) auditory-evoked unit responses of LA neurons are enhanced fol-lowing behavioral fear conditioning (Collins & Pare, 2000; Quirk, Repa, & LeDoux, 1995; Repa et al., 2001). These changes are believed to reflect synaptic plasticity induced by the associative pairing of the tone and shock. To examine this, Rogan, Staubli, & LeDoux (1997) assessed auditory CS-evoked field responses in the LA, and CS-evoked fear behavior in freely behaving rats before, during and after fear conditioning. They found an increase in slope and amplitude of this response during fear conditioning that paralleled fear behavior and per-sisted (Rogan et al., 1997). Importantly, unpaired CS and US presentations produced no enhancement of this response or fear of the CS. These and other studies also highlight the thalamus→LA synapse as an important mediator of fear conditioning. The earliest CS-evoked LA responses occur <15 ms after tone-onset, are modi-fied by fear conditioning and are likely driven by direct connections from the thalamus (Quirk et al., 1995; Quirk et al., 1997; Rogan & LeDoux, 1995; Rogan et al.). Consistent with this notion, LA excitatory postsynaptic potentials evoked by stimulation of thalamic afferents are selectively enhanced in brain slices taken from fear-conditioned rats (McKernan & Shinnick-Gallagher, 1997).

Fear conditioning also results in synaptic plasticity in structures afferent to the LA (e.g., thalamus, cortex) (Quirk et al., 1997; Weinberger, 1995). However, this is unlikely to be essential for behavioral fear learning for two reasons: (1) inactivation of the LA prevents fear learning and memory indicating that these structures alone cannot support learning (Muller et al., 1997; Wilensky et al., 1999), and (2) plasticity in these afferent structures appears to depend on LA function (Armony, Quirk, & LeDoux, 1998; Maren, 2001). These findings suggest that fear conditioning changes the way a CS is processed in an emotional circuit involving LA, and this plasticity allows the CS to control expression of defensive responses after an aversive experience.

The demonstrated importance of the LA to learning and memory for fear conditioning, coupled with discoveries of synaptic plasticity in LA, led to a cellular hypothesis of fear conditioning (Blair, Schafe, Bauer, Rodrigues, & LeDoux, 2001). Briefly, prior to auditory fear conditioning, tone presentations result in weak depolarization of LA neurons and little to no activation of downstream brain areas mediating expression of defensive responses. However, when tone and shock stimuli are paired in time, neurons are strongly depolarized resulting in initiation of an LTP-like process that strengthens the synapses between auditory afferents and LA neurons. Following fear conditioning, tone presentations result in strong depolarization of LA neurons and activation of downstream brain areas mediating expression of defensive responses (Figure 2.2).

Molecular mechanisms of fear conditioning in LA. With mounting anatomical, physiological, and behavioral evidence implicating the LA in fear conditioning, more and more researchers have focused their efforts on unraveling the molecular signaling cascades important for learning and memory in this region. The majority of studies employ genetic and pharmacological manipulations coupled with fear conditioning to determine the function of specific molecules. Manipulations carefully timed with respect to training and testing allow researchers to distinguish between involvement in learning, STM and LTM processes (Rodrigues et al., 2004). Related studies have also probed the molecular mechanisms of LTP, usually using in vitro brain slice preparations while stimulating sensory afferents and recording in LA. In vitro LTP has been covered in detail elsewhere and the results are generally in agreement with in vivo manipulations (Sigurdsson, Doyere, Cain, & LeDoux, 2007). A detailed review of the large body of molecular work related to fear conditioning is beyond the scope of this chapter (for reviews see: Maren, 2001; Rodrigues et al.); however, we will highlight the contributions of a few key molecular players to illustrate how long-lasting changes in plasticity between sensory afferent and principal neurons in the LA are achieved.

There appear to be several important molecular stages to fear conditioning-related plasticity in the LA. First, receptors and ion channels at the synapse translate presynaptic activity into postsynaptic activation of intracellular signaling cascades. NMDA receptors, L-type voltage gated calcium channels, and metabotropic glutamate receptors are crucial for this process. When activated they couple neural activity to kinase cascades by elevating

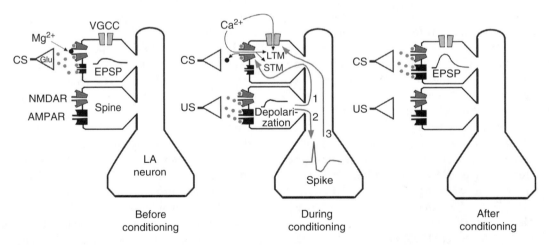

FIGURE 2.2 Schematic representation of the cellular hypothesis of fear conditioning in the lateral nucleus (LA). Before conditioning (left), conditioned stimulus (CS)-evoked release of glutamate from sensory afferents results in a weak AMPAR-mediated depolarization of LA neurons. During conditioning (middle), the addition of strong depolarization from unconditioned stimulus (US)-afferents opens NMDA receptors and L-type channels allowing calcium to enter the cell. Calcium triggers kinase cascades that lead to short- and long-term changes in AMPAR function. Thus, after conditioning (right), CS-afferents now evoke strong depolarization in LA neurons causing them to fire and drive downstream regions important for conditioned fear responses. From "Synaptic plasticity in the lateral amygdala: A cellular hypothesis of fear conditioning," by H. T. Blair, G. E. Schafe, E. P. Bauer, S. M. Rodrigues, and J. E. LeDoux, 2001, *Learning and Memory (Cold Spring Harbor, N. Y.)*, *8*, p. 229. Adapted with permission.

intracellular calcium. αCaMKII is particularly important for short-term memory/plasticity and may covalently modify existing synaptic proteins, like the AMPA receptor, to facilitate glutamatergic transmission. PKA and MAPK are important for long-term memory/plasticity. When activated they translocate to the nucleus to simulate CREB-mediated transcription. Long-term changes in synaptic transmission are ultimately achieved by transcription of the appropriate genes, translation of new proteins, and incorporation of these new proteins at the synapse. For instance, a very recent study demonstrates that the production and synaptic insertion of new AMPA receptors are critical for long-term fear conditioning memory (Rumpel et al., 2005). In addition to facilitating the function of existing synapses, transcription and translation may also be necessary to form new synapses between sensory afferents and LA neurons. Together, molecular work in the fear conditioning pathway demonstrates that synaptic receptors or channels, intracellular kinases, and nuclear machinery respond to CS–US pairings in a coordinated fashion to change CS processing in the LA.

Escape From Fear

As discussed above, brain studies of classical fear conditioning have advanced to the stage of providing detailed accounts of the circuitry, physiology, and molecular events important for the various phases of emotional incentive learning. Studies of aversive instrumental conditioning have not yet reached this point. One reason is likely related to the ongoing debate in psychological circles regarding just about every aspect of active avoidance conditioning (contents, conditions, mechanisms). Indeed, brain research on behavior is critically dependent on having at least a reasonable understanding of the important psychological processes involved (Maren, 2003). Another reason is that brain studies of avoidance more often than not investigate passive avoidance, and even within this realm, the results of brain manipulations have been mixed (Liang et al., 1982; Maren, 2003; Sarter & Markowitsch, 1985). Thus, we will save the discussion of brain mechanisms of avoidance for another day and here focus on EFF. Readers interested in the brain mechanisms of active avoidance are referred to the work of Michael Gabriel (Gabriel et al., 2003).

EFF research has been sporadic over the last half century and only one study to date has investigated brain mechanisms of EFF learning. Amorapanth et al. (2000) created selective electrolytic lesions of amygdaloid subnuclei to investigate their potential involvement in EFF learning. Lesions of the LA, CE, or B were made prior to fear conditioning and EFF training and both conditioned freezing and escape responding were measured. In this case, chamber crossing served as the escape response. The results were clear (Figure 2.3). LA lesions disrupted

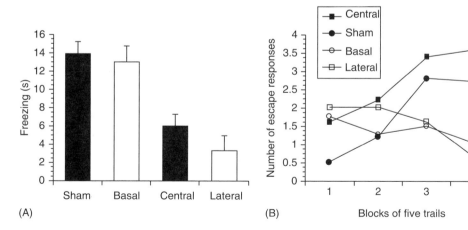

(A)   (B)

FIGURE 2.3 Escape from fear (EFF) learning depends on the lateral and basal, but not central, amygdala. Prior to behavioral training rats received bilateral electrolytic lesions of the lateral nucleus (LA), central nucleus (CE), or basal nucleus (B). Rats were first subjected to Pavlovian fear conditioning and then EFF training using chamber crossing as the escape response. LA and CE lesions disrupted performance of a passive fear reaction to the conditioned stimulus (CS) (A, freezing). LA and B lesions disrupted performance of an active EFF response (B, chamber crossing). These data suggest that LA is necessary for establishing the CS as a conditioned incentive. This information is then relayed to CE to initiate passive Pavlovian reactions and to B for active escape responding. From "Different lateral amygdala outputs mediate reactions and actions elicited by a fear-arousing stimulus," by P. Amorapanth, J .E. LeDoux, and K. Nader, 2000, *Nature Neuroscience, 3*, p. 74. Adapted with permission.

both conditioned freezing and EFF learning. CE lesions disrupted freezing but not escape responding. And B lesions disrupted escape responding but not conditioned freezing. Thus, consistent with the model proposed above, LA damage prevented the acquisition of CS-elicited fear, which is necessary for both fear reactions (freezing) and fear actions (escaping). The double dissociation between CE and B on freezing and EFF suggest that CE mediates fear reactions and B participates in the motivation and reinforcement of fear actions like instrumental escape learning.

Ongoing experiments in our laboratory are investigating the downstream brain regions potentially responsible for receiving information from B and translating it into instrumental escape responding. One possibility is the nucleus accumbens (NAcc) which contributes to appetitive-motivated action learning (Cardinal & Everitt, 2004; Ikemoto & Panksepp, 1999), including action learning about conditioned reinforcers (Kelley & Delfs, 1991; Robbins, Giardini, Jones, Reading, & Sahakian 1990). Anatomically, NAcc shares direct connections with B (Everitt & Robbins, 1992; Robbins, Cador, Taylor, & Everitt, 1989) and is situated at the "neural crossroads of emotion and movement" (Graybiel, 1976; Mogenson, Jones, & Yim, 1980) making it a particularly attractive candidate region. We will return to this possibility when we consider a "motive circuit" at the end of this chapter, integrating findings from both aversive and appetitive studies.

APPROACH MOTIVATION

Approach motivation research attempts to explain how environmental stimuli elicit behaviors that function to shorten the distance, either physical or psychological, between the animal and a desired outcome. Neuroscientists have been especially successful in explaining approach motivation at the systems level. We discuss below how this research may inform the study of avoidance motivation hopefully leading to a more comprehensive understanding of brain mechanisms of motivation.

BEHAVIORAL PARADIGMS RELATED TO APPROACH MOTIVATION

Appetitive conditioning has been intensely studied and many diverse behavioral paradigms have been employed to examine the brain mechanisms of appetitive motivation and learning. That CSs may acquire value as a result of temporal pairings with appetitive USs, like food, is widely accepted. Two basic observations support this notion.

First, rats will learn a new instrumental response that is paired with a Pavlovian CS (secondary reinforcement) (Fantino, 1977); they will work to receive a CS that was previously paired with food even though no food is delivered, as if the CS has acquired its own "motivational significance" (Holland & Petrovich, 2005). Second-order Pavlovian conditioning provides another example. For instance, rats will acquire an approach response to a tone if it is paired with a light that previously predicted food, even though no food is delivered in this session (Holland & Rescorla, 1975). Reviewing all of the various paradigms is beyond the scope of the present chapter, but we will focus on three that parallel our discussion of avoidance motivation above: Pavlovian conditioned approach, conditioned potentiation of feeding, and Pavlovian to instrumental transfer. The behavioral outcomes in these paradigms have been widely viewed as representing "conditioned appetitive motivational states," similar to our framework for discussing avoidance motivation in the previous section (Holland & Petrovich, 2005).

Conditioned Approach

Pavlovian conditioned approach, sometimes called autoshaping, is the appetitive equivalent of classical fear conditioning. Temporal pairings of an initially neutral CS (e.g., light) with an appetitive US (e.g., food) result in acquisition of an approach response to the CS on subsequent test trials. Conditioned approach is an example of a learned preparatory response, which likely evolved to bring an animal into contact with food using environmental cues as a guide. This is in contrast to consummatory responses, like licking and chewing, that are necessary for eating. Conditioned approach can be a powerful form of learning and even maladaptive (Hearst, 1975) where an animal will learn to approach the cue rather than the food itself. Pavlovian appetitive conditioning also establishes the CS as a secondary incentive, with the capacity to energize and direct other active behaviors.

Conditioned Potentiation of Feeding

The conditioned potentiation of feeding (CPF) model is a paradigm where a secondary incentive, established through Pavlovian conditioning, can motivate active responding. Rats are first subjected to standard Pavlovian conditioning (CS–US pairings) where the rat's behavior has no bearing on delivery of the stimuli. Following this training rats are sated and then given access to food pellets ad libitum. Under these conditions rats eat very little. However, following presentation of the appetitive CS, they will begin to consume pellets. Interestingly, a positive effect is achieved (more eating after CS presentations) even if the food source is moved to a new location. Thus, the effect of the CS presentation is not a result of conditioned approach, but rather a motivational consequence of appetitive conditioning (Holland & Petrovich, 2005).

Pavlovian to Instrumental Transfer

Our final example is a phenomenon known as Pavlovian to instrumental transfer (PIT) (Estes, 1948; Lovibond, 1983). Rats are trained in independent sessions with Pavlovian discriminative conditioning (CS+ or CS– trials, + representing US delivery) and instrumental conditioning (response-US pairings; e.g., lever pressing). Once these responses are well-learned, rats are placed in the instrumental chamber and responding is compared between CS+ periods and CS– periods. CS+ presentations lead to an increase in instrumental responding demonstrating that the CS+ may have acquired motivational properties during Pavlovian conditioning (Cardinal, Parkinson, Hall, & Everitt, 2002a; Holland & Gallagher, 2003). PIT can facilitate responding for a food reward that is different from that used as the US in Pavlovian conditioning (Balleine, 1994), a phenomenon dubbed "conditioned motivation" (Rescorla & Solomon, 1967). However, there are also outcome-specific forms of PIT where responding is facilitated only when the US in Pavlovian conditioning matches the reinforcement used for instrumental conditioning (Colwill & Rescorla, 1988). Thus, the PIT phenomenon provides further evidence that a motivational state can be conditioned and functioned to influence ongoing active behaviors. Note that PIT-like effects have been reported for aversive learning, although brain mechanisms of aversive PIT are not known (e.g. Brackbill and Overmier, 1979).

BRAIN MECHANISMS RELATED TO APPROACH MOTIVATION

Before summarizing what is known about the brain mechanisms related to the above tasks, it is important to point out that researchers in the appetitive field have employed a different strategy than those in the aversive field (generally speaking). To some degree, aversive emotion and motivation research has sacrificed comprehensive systems-level knowledge of aversive behavior in favor of detailed cellular mechanisms of the stages of simple Pavlovian conditioning. In the appetitive field, much more progress has been made in understanding the behavior at the systems level at the expense of detailed cellular mechanisms. Thus, the following sections will primarily focus on specific brain regions important for various aspects of appetitive conditioning and motivation.

Conditioned Approach

Interestingly, the amygdala appears to be critically important for establishing a CS as a conditioned incentive with appetitive Pavlovian conditioning. Studies of the amygdala in appetitive conditioning typically focus on distinctions between CE and the BLA (which includes the lateral, basal, and accessory basal nuclei). Lesions of CE, but not BLA, interfere with conditioned approach learning to a light CS paired with food (Parkinson, Robbins, & Everitt, 2000a). The BLA does, however, appear to have some role in Pavlovian appetitive conditioning. Hatfield, Han, Conley, Gallagher, and Holland (1996) found that lesions of the BLA, but not CE, impaired devaluation of an appetitive CR. They quantified "food-cup" behavior in rats that received light-food pairings, a complex of CRs related to approach. In order to "devalue" the US representation half of the rats received LiCl after consuming the food to make them sick. In normal rats, and CE lesioned rats, this approach CR was diminished on subsequent trials. BLA lesioned rats showed no evidence of the food devaluation and the approach CR to the light was unaltered. Interestingly, all rats, regardless of lesion, ate substantially less of the food after it was "poisoned" indicating that neither CE nor BLA mediates the food–sickness association. Together, these data suggest that both the BLA and CE are involved in appetitive incentive learning. The BLA may participate in associative learning between the CS and "sensory properties" of the US important for accessing current US value postconditioning (Balleine & Killcross, 2006). This profile is also taken as support for the BLA in generating consummatory responses to the CS with Pavlovian conditioning. In contrast, CE may function to associate the CS with general "affective" properties of the US important for preparatory responses like approach.

The ventral striatum, specifically the NAcc, forms strong reciprocal connections with the amygdala (especially B) and may be a key region for translating Pavlovian incentive learning into motivated action. Indeed, because of its connections with structures important for emotion processing and behavioral expression, the NAcc may represent a "limbic–motor" interface (Mogenson et al., 1980). Excitotoxic and dopamine-depleting lesions of the NAcc core region impair both the acquisition and performance of conditioned approach (Cardinal et al., 2002b; Parkinson, Olmstead, Burns, Robbins, & Everitt, 1999; Parkinson et al., 2000b; Parkinson et al., 2002). Disconnection lesions between the NAcc core and the anterior cingulate cortex (ACC) also impair discriminative conditioned approach (CS+ vs. CS–), but not conditioned approach using a single CS, leading to the suggestion that the ACC "disambiguates" CSs and prevents generalization (Cardinal et al., 2003).

Conditioned Potentiation of Feeding

CPF, where a Pavlovian CS can increase food consumption in sated rats, also appears to depend on the amygdala. BLA lesions specifically impair CPF without affecting conditioned approach responses (Gallagher & Holland, 1992). CPF was intact in CE lesioned rats. This basic pattern was repeated in a more elaborate second study (Holland, Petrovich, & Gallagher, 2002). Here the researcher's note that presentation of the CS to sated rats potentiated feeding independent of any approach CR. The food was placed in the opposite side of the chamber (relative to Pavlovian conditioning) so that any approach CR would actually impair feeding. Additionally, the researchers point out that CS presentations in CPF do not elicit immediate eating but rather a slowly developing increase in the amount of food eaten after the CS terminates. Thus, the authors argue, CPF reflects BLA-dependent learned motivation rather than any overt CR acquired during initial training. These data are also consistent with the notion that BLA participates in generating consummatory responses to a Pavlovian CS. Further disconnection lesion studies demonstrated that connections between the BLA and lateral hypothalamus, which is involved in feeding initiation, are important for CPF, as well as connections between the BLA and medial prefrontal cortex (Holland & Petrovich, 2005). However, disconnection lesions between the BLA and NAcc had no effect on CPF (Holland & Petrovich, 2005). Thus, at present, CPF appears to depend on an amygdalo-prefrontal-hypothalamic network that is critical for the control of feeding by learned motivational cues.

Pavlovian to Instrumental Transfer

In addition to potentiating eating, Pavlovian CSs can also facilitate food-seeking in PIT paradigms (Balleine & Killcross, 2006). Outcome-specific PIT, where instrumental responding for a US is increased by a CS that was previously paired with the same US, is disrupted by BLA lesions but not CE lesions (Blundell, Hall, & Killcross, 2001; Corbit & Balleine, 2005). In contrast, CE lesions disrupt conditioned motivation (US nonspecific or general PIT) whereas BLA lesions do not (Hall, Parkinson, Connor, Dickinson, & Everitt, 2001; Corbit & Balleine, 2005). These data were taken to suggest that both BLA and CE are involved in conditioned incentive learning, with the BLA mediating consummatory responses via associations with sensory properties of the US and the CE mediating preparatory responses via associations with general affective properties of the US.

PIT also appears to depend on the NAcc. Simple presentation of an appetitive CS increases dopamine levels in the NAcc core (Bassareo & Di Chiara, 1999; Ito, Dalley, Howes, Robbins, & Everitt, 2000) and dopamine antagonists abolish PIT (Dickinson, Smith, & Mirenowicz, 2000; Smith & Dickinson, 1998). In support of this, lesions of the NAcc core disrupt PIT (Hall et al., 2001). Given that general PIT also requires an intact CE, and that CE has no direct connections to the NAcc core (Everitt et al., 1999), dopamine release in the NAcc core from mesolimbic regions may be under control of CE projections that mediate conditioned incentive learning (Cardinal et al., 2002a).

A MOTIVE CIRCUIT?

A brain processing account of motivation must include an explanation of how emotional stimuli lead to the invigoration and direction of behavior toward positive goals and away from aversive ones. The brain state evoked by emotional stimuli has been called a "motive state" (Morgan, 1943; Gallistel, 1980) and studies in the aversive and appetitive fields suggest that the amygdala and NAcc are important mediators of this state (Kalivas & Nakamura, 1999). In the following paragraphs, we will outline a hypothetical motive circuit responsible for EFF learning. The model relies heavily on appetitive research demonstrating that the amygdala is important for incentive learning and that the NAcc is important for using incentive information to invigorate and guide active behaviors. In the appetitive context, invigoration is evidenced by the ability of a Pavlovian CS to facilitate active behaviors like eating (CPF) and food-seeking (PIT). The direction of behavior is represented by approach conditioning where a CS paired with food, for instance, results in movement toward the CS. It has been suggested that avoidance/escape behavior may be a form of approach, approach to safety (Ikemoto & Panksepp, 1999), and thus may rely on similar brain regions and mechanisms. The goal object in EFF learning is fear. Invigoration is evidenced by the demonstration that EFF responses are only expressed in the presence of the fear-eliciting CS. The EFF response is directed away from fear (toward safety) since it is instrumental in terminating the fear-eliciting CS.

Before describing the motive circuit as it relates to EFF, a brief discussion of dopamine transmission is warranted. Dopamine, especially NAcc dopamine, has been intensely studied for decades as it relates to reward-related processes (Salamone, Correa, Mingote, & Weber, 2005). Although NAcc dopamine was initially believed to mediate the primary motivational value of rewards like food and sex, this notion has been called into question. Mounting evidence suggests that NAcc dopamine is important for generating anticipatory/preparatory responses in the presence of a secondary incentive (e.g., CS paired with food), but not for consummatory responses. Thus, manipulations of NAcc dopamine affect how hard a rat will work for food (Aberman, Ward, & Salamone, 1998), but they do not generally affect how much food the rat will eat once it is obtained (Berridge & Robinson, 1998; Everitt et al., 1999; Ikemoto & Panksepp, 1999). Simple NAcc infusion of dopamine, or drugs that mimic dopamine, results in the invigoration of active exploratory behaviors such that the animals appear to be searching for something (Ikemoto & Panksepp, 1999). This may apply to aversive motivation as well, and in this context, it is important to note that fear-eliciting CS presentations cause dopamine (from ventral tegmental neurons) to be released in the NAcc core (Levita, Dalley, & Robbins, 2002; Pezze & Feldon, 2004). The amygdaloid CE, important for expression of fear conditioning and approach conditioning, projects to the ventral tegmental area (VTA) and may stimulate dopamine release in the NAcc (Cardinal et al., 2002a).

Figure 2.4 shows a hypothetical motive circuit as it relates to EFF. Recall that, in EFF, rats first learn to fear the tone through Pavlovian pairings with an aversive footshock. Then, in a separate session, tone presentations are terminated when the rat makes the appropriate escape response (e.g., rearing or chamber crossing). Early in the session, rats primarily freeze to the tone. But eventually they exhibit the escape response and the tone terminates (Figure 2.1). Fear-reduction associated with tone-termination is believed to reinforce the instrumental response, and tone-evoked fear is believed to motivate escape responding on subsequent trials.

In EFF, tone processing begins in the auditory system (thalamus, cortex) and is relayed to the LA. As a consequence of LTP generated by Pavlovian conditioning, activity in sensory afferents can now drive firing in LA neurons. This activity is then relayed to both the CE and B. CE outputs trigger expression of species-typical defensive responses (e.g., freezing) subserved by brainstem and hypothalamic regions. CE outputs also activate brainstem "arousal" centers like dopaminergic neurons in the VTA. Conditioned incentive information is relayed from B to the NAcc core region where this signal may be "gain amplified" (Everitt et al., 1999; Parkinson et al., 1999) by dopamine arriving from the VTA. This NAcc signal may access motor control regions in the cortex and brainstem via projections to the ventral pallidum. Thus, dopamine in the NAcc, triggered by the tone presentation, may invigorate behavior. The manner in which behavior is reinforced and subsequently directed is

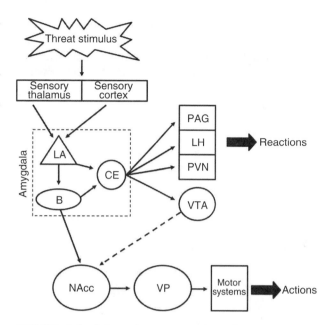

FIGURE 2.4 Schematic representation of a hypothetical brain motive circuit mediating escape from fear (EFF) learning. After fear conditioning, threatening stimuli, processed in the sensory thalamus and cortex, drive activity in the LA and CE leading to passive fear reactions (like freezing) and also activate arousal centers like the ventral tegmental area (VTA). Incentive information flows also from LA to B which projects to the nucleus accumbens (NAcc). The NAcc processing of incentive information invigorates and guides active behavior via projections to the ventral pallidum (VP) and downstream motor systems, with the aid of dopamine arriving from VTA. Note that early portions of this model are derived from work on amygdala-dependent fear conditioning and EFF learning (Amorapanth et al., 2000; LeDoux, 2000) while downstream portions of the model are borrowed from work in appetitive conditioning (Ikemoto & Panksepp, 1999; Kalivas et al., 1999; Cardinal et al., 2002a). Additional abbreviations: PAG, periaqueductal gray; LH, lateral hypothalamus; PVN, paraventricular nucleus; LA lateral amygdala; B, basal amygdala; CE, central amygdala.

presently unclear, although the incentive signal arriving from B seems critical. Some studies suggest that striatal processing of incentive stimuli facilitates the acquisition of instrumental stimulus–response (i.e., tone-escape) associations in the cortex, perhaps the motor cortex or the ACC. If true, this model can explain how fear-eliciting tone presentations can first elicit passive freezing and later lead to the acquisition of an active escape response. Note, however, that well-learned instrumental habits may no longer rely on incentive processing by the amygdala and NAcc (Ikemoto & Panksepp, 1999).

Although clearly very speculative, the present model draws on systems-level appetitive findings to build on the solid foundation of aversive incentive learning (fear conditioning) providing strong hypotheses about a motive circuit for EFF learning. These hypotheses are directly testable using currently available techniques. The model will surely be refined in the coming years as more experimental evidence comes to light. Other brain regions that may be included in the motive circuit include the prefrontal cortex (for motivated decision making and working memory), the hippocampus (for working memory and contextualizing motivated behavior), and the mediodorsal thalamus (for the coordination of information between limbic and motor circuits) (Cardinal et al., 2002a; LeDoux, 2002a; Kalivas, Churchill, & Romanides, 1999).

SUMMARY AND CONCLUSION

Emotion and motivation are deeply intertwined psychological processes related to human subjective states (feelings and wants/needs). As noted earlier, this presents a problem for neuroscientists interested in the brain mechanisms of behavior. In this chapter we outline a strategy for examining brain mechanisms of emotion and motivation focusing on fear-related behaviors. We argue that emotion and motivation result from information processing in brain systems that evolved to solve basic problems confronting the organism, like finding food and mates, and eluding predators. As such, we can begin to study emotion and motivation by examining how the brain detects and relays input stimuli and generates output behaviors. These are relatively easy tasks. More difficult, however, is understanding the plastic processes between inputs and outputs that determine the stimulus value and produce situation-appropriate responses.

The fields of approach and avoidance motivation have largely progressed independently and have had success at different levels of brain analysis. The aversive field, for instance, has made great strides in understanding the cellular and molecular events important for generating emotional reactions and establishing incentive stimuli. The appetitive field has advanced much further in understanding how incentives are used to generate behavior at the systems level. We, and others (Everitt et al., 1999), have argued that these different traditions may have much to learn from each other. For instance, considering the findings of the two fields together suggests that amygdala–striatum interactions may be particularly important for motivational learning. The result is the generation of a hypothetical "motive circuit" that may guide future research with the promise of

enriching our understanding of brain mechanisms of emotional and motivational behaviors.

REFERENCES

Aberman, J. E., Ward, S. J., & Salamone, J. D. (1998). Effects of dopamine antagonists and accumbens dopamine depletions on time-constrained progressive-ratio performance. *Pharmacology, Biochemistry and Behavior, 61,* 341–348.

Amorapanth, P., LeDoux, J. E., & Nader, K. (2000). Different lateral amygdala outputs mediate reactions and actions elicited by a fear-arousing stimulus. *Nature Neuroscience, 3,* 74–79.

Anglada-Figueroa, D., & Quirk, G. J. (2005). Lesions of the basal amygdala block expression of conditioned fear but not extinction. *The Journal of Neuroscience: The Official Journal of the Society for Neuroscience, 25,* 9680–9685.

Armony, J. L., Quirk, G. J., & LeDoux, J. E. (1998). Differential effects of amygdala lesions on early and late plastic components of auditory cortex spike trains during fear conditioning. *The Journal of Neuroscience: The Official Journal of the Society for Neuroscience, 18,* 2592–2601.

Balleine, B. (1994). Asymmetrical interactions between thirst and hunger in Pavlovian-instrumental transfer. *The Quarterly Journal of Experimental Psychology. B, Comparative and Physiological Psychology, 47,* 211–231.

Balleine, B. W., & Killcross, S. (2006). Parallel incentive processing: An integrated view of amygdala function. *Trends in Neurosciences, 29,* 272–279.

Bassareo, V., & Di Chiara, G. (1999). Differential responsiveness of dopamine transmission to food-stimuli in nucleus accumbens shell/core compartments. *Neuroscience, 89,* 637–641.

Bellgowan, P. S. F., & Helmstetter, F. J. (1996). Neural systems for the expression of hypoalgesia during nonassociative fear. *Behavioral Neuroscience, 110,* 727–736.

Berridge, K. C., & Robinson, T. E. (1998). What is the role of dopamine in reward: Hedonic impact, reward learning, or incentive salience? *Brain Research. Brain Research Reviews, 28,* 309–369.

Blair, H. T., Schafe, G. E., Bauer, E. P., Rodrigues, S. M., & LeDoux, J. E. (2001). Synaptic plasticity in the lateral amygdala: A cellular hypothesis of fear conditioning. *Learning and Memory (Cold Spring Harbor, N. Y.), 8,* 229–242.

Blair, H. T., Sotres-Bayon, F., Moita, M. A., & LeDoux, J. E. (2005). The lateral amygdala processes the value of conditioned and unconditioned aversive stimuli. *Neuroscience, 133,* 561–569.

Blanchard, R. J., & Blanchard, D. C. (1969a). Passive and active reactions to fear-eliciting stimuli. *Journal of Experimental Psychology, 68,* 129–135.

Blanchard, R. J., & Blanchard, D. C. (1969b). Crouching as an index of fear. *Journal of Comparative Physiological Psychology, 67,* 370–375.

Blanchard, R. J., & Blanchard, D. C. (1970). Dual mechanisms in passive avoidance: I. *Psychonomic Science, 19*(1), 1–2.

Blundell, P., Hall, G., & Killcross, S. (2001). Lesions of the basolateral amygdala disrupt selective aspects of reinforcer representation in rats. *The Journal of Neuroscience: The Official Journal of the Society for Neuroscience, 21,* 9018–9026.

Bolles, R. C. (1967a). Punishment. In: *Theory of motivation* (pp. 417–433). New York: Harper and Row.

Bolles, R. C. (1967b). *Theory of motivation.* New York: Harper and Row.

Bolles, R. C. (1969). Avoidance and escape learning: Simultaneous acquisition of different responses. *Journal of Experimental Psychology, 68,* 355–358.

Bolles, R. C. (1970). Species-specific defense reactions and avoidance learning. *Psychological Review, 77,* 32–48.

Bolles, R. C., & Fanselow, M. S. (1980). A perceptual-defensive-recuperative model of fear and pain. *Behavioral and Brain Sciences, 3,* 291–323.

Bordi, F., & LeDoux, J. E. (1994a). Properties of single units in areas of rat auditory thalamus that project to the amygdala. II. Cells receiving convergent auditory and somatosensory inputs and cells antidromically activated by amygdala stimulation. *Experimental Brain Research. Experimentelle Hirnforschung. Experimentation Cerebrale, 98,* 275–286.

Bordi, F., & LeDoux, J. E. (1994b). Response properties of single units in areas of rat auditory thalamus that project to the amygdala. I. Acoustic discharge patterns and frequency receptive fields. *Experimental Brain Research. Experimentelle Hirnforschung. Experimentation Cerebrale, 98,* 261–274.

Brackbill, R., & Overmier, J. B. (1979). Aversive CS control of instrumental avoidance as a function of selected parameters and method of pavlovian conditioning. *Learning and Motivation, 10*(3), 229–244.

Brush, F. R. (1971). *Aversive condtioning and learning.* New York: Academic Press.

Cain, C. K., & LeDoux, J. E. (2007). Escape from fear: A detailed behavioral analysis of two atypical responses reinforced by CS-termination. *Journal of Experimental Psychology: Animal Behavior Processes, 33*(4), 451–463.

Campeau, S., & Davis, M. (1995). Involvement of the central nucleus and basolateral complex of the amygdala in fear conditioning measured with fear-potentiated startle in rats trained concurrently with auditory and visual conditioned stimuli. *The Journal of Neuroscience: The Official Journal of the Society for Neuroscience, 15,* 2301–2311.

Cardinal, R. N., & Everitt, B. J. (2004). Neural and psychological mechanisms underlying appetitive learning: links to drug addiction. *Current Opinion in Neurobiology, 14,* 156–162.

Cardinal, R. N., Parkinson, J. N., Hall, J., & Everitt, B. J. (2002a). Emotion and motivation: The role of the amygdala, ventral striatum, and prefrontal cortex. *Neuroscience and Biobehavioral Reviews, 26,* 321–352.

Cardinal, R. N., Parkinson, J. A., Lachenal, G., Halkerston, K. M., Rudarakanchana, N., Hall, J., et al. (2002b). Effects of selective excitotoxic lesions of the nucleus accumbens core, anterior cingulate cortex, and central nucleus of the amygdala on autoshaping performance in rats. *Behavioral Neuroscience, 116,* 553–567.

Cardinal, R. N., Parkinson, J. A., Marbini, H. D., Toner, A. J., Bussey, T. J., & Robbins, T. W., et al. (2003). Role of the anterior cingulate cortex in the control over behavior by Pavlovian conditioned stimuli in rats. *Behavioral Neuroscience, 117,* 566–587.

Clugnet, M. C., LeDoux, J. E., & Morrison, S. F. (1990). Unit responses evoked in the amygdala and striatum by electrical stimulation of the medial geniculate body. *The Journal of Neuroscience: The Official Journal of the Society for Neuroscience, 10,* 1055–1061.

Collins, D. R., & Pare, D. (2000). Differential fear conditioning induces reciprocal changes in the sensory responses of lateral amygdala neurons to the CS(+) and CS(−). *Learning and Memory (Cold Spring Harbor, N. Y.), 7,* 97–103.

Colwill, R. M., & Rescorla, R. A. (1988). Associations between the discriminative stimulus and the reinforcer in instrumental learning. *Journal of Experimental Psychology. Animal Behavior Processes, 14,* 155–164.

Corbit, L. H., & Balleine, B. W. (2005). Double dissociation of basolateral and central amygdala lesions on the general and outcome-specific forms of pavlovian-instrumental transfer. *The Journal of Neuroscience: The Official Journal of the Society for Neuroscience, 25,* 962–970.

Damasio, A. (1994). *Descarte's error: Emotion, reason, and the human brain.* New York: Gosset/Putnam.

Davis, M. (1986). Pharmacological and anatomical analysis of fear conditioning using the fear-potentiated startle paradigm. *Behavioral Neuroscience, 100,* 814–824.

Davis, M. (1998). Anatomic and physiologic substrates of emotion in an animal model. *Journal of Clinical Neurophysiology: Official Publication of the American Electroencephalographic Society, 15,* 378–387.

Davis, M., Walker, D. L., Myers, & K. M. (2003). Role of the amygdala in fear extinction measured with potentiated startle. *Annals of the New York Academy of Sciences, 985,* 218–232.

De Oca, B. M., DeCola, J. P., Maren, S., & Fanselow, M. S. (1998). Distinct regions of the periaqueductal gray are involved in the acqcuisition and expression of defensive responses. *The Journal of Neuroscience: The Official Journal of the Society for Neuroscience, 18,* 3426–3432.

Denny, M. R. (1991). *Fear, avoidance, and phobias: A fundamental analysis.* Hillsdale, NJ: Lawrence Erlbaum Associates, Publishers.

Dickinson, A., Smith, J., & Mirenowicz, J. (2000). Dissociation of Pavlovian and instrumental incentive learning under dopamine antagonists. *Behavioral Neuroscience, 114,* 468–483.

Elliot, A. J. (2006). The hierarchical model of approach–avoidance motivation. *Motivation and Emotion, 30,* 111–116.

Estes, W. K. (1948). Discriminative conditioning II: Effects of a Pavlovain conditioned stimulus upon a subsequently established operant response. *Journal of Experimental Psychology, 38,* 173–177.

Everitt, B. J., Parkinson, J. A., Olmstead, M. C., Arroyo, M., Robledo, P., & Robbins, T. W. (1999). Associative processes in addiction and reward. The role of amygdala–ventral striatal subsystems. In: J. McGintry (Ed.), *Advancing from the ventral striatum to the extended amygdala* (pp. 412–438). New York: New York Academy of Sciences.

Everitt, B. J., & Robbins, T. W. (1992). Amygdala–ventral striatal interactions and reward-related processes. In: J. P. Aggleton (Ed.), *The amygdala: Neurobiological aspects of emotion, memory, and mental Dysfunction* (pp. 401–429). New York: Wiley-Liss, Inc.

Fanselow, M. S., & Gale, G. D. (2003). The amygdala, fear, and memory. *Annals of the New York Academy of Sciences, 985*, 125–134.

Fanselow, M. S., & LeDoux, J. E. (1999). Why we think plasticity underlying Pavlovian fear conditioning occurs in the basolateral amygdala. *Neuron, 23*, 229–232.

Fantino, E. (1977). Conditioned reinforcement: Choice and information. In: J. E. R. Honig & J. E. R. Staddon (Eds.), *Handbook of operant behavior* (pp. 313–339). Englewood Cliffs, NJ: Prentice-Hall.

Gabriel, M., Burhans, L., & Kashef, A. (2003). Consideration of a unified model of amygdalar associative functions. *Annals of the New York Academy of Sciences, 985*, 206–217.

Gale, G. D., Anagnostaras, S. G., Godsil, B. P., Mitchell, S., Nozawa, T., Sage, J. R., et al. (2004). Role of the basolateral amygdala in the storage of fear memories across the adult lifetime of rats. *The Journal of Neuroscience: The Official Journal of the Society for Neuroscience, 24*, 3810–3815.

Gallagher, M., & Holland, P. C. (1992). Understanding the function of the central nucleus: Is simple conditioning enough? In: J. Aggleton (Ed.), *The amygdala: Neurobiological aspects of emotion, memory and mental dysfunction* (pp. 307–321). New York: Wiley-Liss.

Gallistel, R. (1980). *The organization of action: A new synthesis*. Hillsdale, NJ: Erlbaum.

Goosens, K. A., & Maren, S. (2001). Contextual and auditory fear conditioning are mediated by the lateral, basal, and central amygdaloid nuclei in rats. *Learning and Memory (Cold Spring Harbor, N. Y.), 8*, 148–155.

Goosens, K. A., & Maren, S. (2004). NMDA receptors are essential for the acquisition, but not expression, of conditional fear and associative spike firing in the lateral amygdala. *The European Journal of Neuroscience, 20*, 537–548.

Graybiel, A. (1976). *Input–output anatomy of the basal ganglia*. Lecture at the Society for Neuroscience, Toronto, Canada

Hall, J., Parkinson, J. A., Connor, T. M., Dickinson, A., & Everitt, B. J. (2001). Involvement of the central nucleus of the amygdala and nucleus accumbens core in mediating Pavlovian influences on instrumental behaviour. *European Journal of Neuroscience, 13*, 1984–1992.

Hatfield, T., Han, J. S., Conley, M., Gallagher, M., & Holland, P. (1996). Neurotoxic lesions of basolateral, but not central, amygdala interfere with Pavlovian second-order conditioning and reinforcer devaluation effects. *Journal of Neuroscience, 16*, 5256–5265.

Hearst, E. (1975). Pavlovian conditioning and directed movements. In: G. T. Bower (Ed.), *Psychology of learning and motivation* (pp. 215–272). New York: Academic Press.

Hitchcock, J., & Davis, M. (1986). Lesions of the amygdala but not of the cerebellum or red nucleus block conditioned fear as measured with the potentiated startle paradigm. *Behavioral Neuroscience, 100*, 11–22.

Holland, P. C., & Gallagher, M. (2003). Double dissociation of the effects of lesions of basolateral and central amygdala on conditioned stimulus-potentiated feeding and Pavlovian-instrumental transfer. *The European Journal of Neuroscience, 17*, 1680–1694.

Holland, P. C., & Petrovich, G. D. (2005). A neural systems analysis of the potentiation of feeding by conditioned stimuli. *Physiology & Behavior, 86*, 747–761.

Holland, P. C., Petrovich, G. D., & Gallagher, M. (2002). The effects of amygdala lesions on conditioned stimulus-potentiated eating in rats. *Physiology & Behavior, 76*, 117–129.

Holland, P. C., & Rescorla, R. A. (1975). The effect of two ways of devaluing the unconditioned stimulus after first- and second-order appetitive conditioning. *Journal of Experimental Psychology. Animal Behavior Processes, 1*, 355–363.

Hull, C. L. (1943). *Principles of behavior*. New York: Appleton-Century-Crofts.

Ikemoto, S., & Panksepp, J. (1999). The role of nucleus accumbens dopamine in motivated behavior: A unifying interpretation with special reference to reward-seeking. *Brain Research. Brain Research Reviews, 31*, 6–41.

Ito, R., Dalley, J. W., Howes, S. R., Robbins, T. W., & Everitt, B. J. (2000). Dissociation in conditioned dopamine release in the nucleus accumbens core and shell in response to cocaine cues and during cocaine-seeking behavior in rats. *Journal of Neuroscience, 20*, 7489–7495.

Kalivas, P. W., Churchill, L., & Romanides, A. (1999). Involvement of the pallidal-thalamocortical circuit in adaptive behavior. *Annals of the New York Academy of Sciences, 877*, 64–70.

Kalivas, P. W., & Nakamura, M. (1999). Neural systems for behavioral activation and reward. *Current Opinion in Neurobiology, 9*, 223–227.

Kapp, B. S., Whalen, P. J., Supple, W. F., & Pascoe, J. P. (1992). Amygdaloid contributions to conditioned arousal and sensory information processing. In: J. P. Aggleton (Ed.), *The amygdala: Neurobiological aspects of emotion, memory, and mental dysfunction* (pp. 229–254). New York: Wiley-Liss.

Kelley, A. E., & Delfs, J. M. (1991). Dopamine and conditioned reinforcement. I. Differential Effects of Amphetamine Microinjections into Striatal Subregions. *Psychopharmacology (Berl), 103*, 187–196.

Koo, J. W., Han, J. S., & Kim, J. J. (2004). Selective neurotoxic lesions of basolateral and central nuclei of the amygdala produce differential effects on fear conditioning. *The Journal of Neuroscience: The Official Journal of the Society for Neuroscience, 24*, 7654–7662.

Larsen, R. J., & Fredrickson, B. L. (1999). Measurement issues in emotion research. In: D. Kahneman, E. Diener, & N. Schwarz (Eds.), *Well-Being*. New York: Russell Sage Foundation.

LeDoux, J. E. (1984). Cognition and emotion: Processing functions and brain systems. In: M. S. Gazzaniga (Ed.), *Handbook of cognitive neuroscience* (pp. 357–368). New York: Plenum Publishing Corp.

LeDoux, J. E. (1990). Fear pathways in the brain: Implications for theories of the emotional brain. In: P. Brain, S. Parmigiani, D. Maindardi, & R. J. Blanchard (Eds.), *Fear and defense* London: Gordon and Breach.

LeDoux, J. E. (2000). Emotion circuits in the brain. *Annual Review of Neuroscience, 23*, 155–184.

LeDoux, J. E. (2002a). The lost world. In: *Synaptic self* (pp. 235–259). New York: Viking.

LeDoux, J. E. (2002b). The mental trilogy. In: *Synaptic self* (pp. 174–199). New York: Viking.

LeDoux, J. E. (2002c). The emotional brain revisited. In: *Synaptic self* (pp. 200–234). New York: Viking.

LeDoux, J. E., Iwata, J., Cicchetti, P., & Reis, D. J. (1988). Different projections of the central amygdaloid nucleus mediate autonomic and behavioral correlates of conditioned fear. *The Journal of Neuroscience: The Official Journal of the Society for Neuroscience, 8*, 2517–2529.

LeDoux, J. E., Sakaguchi, A., Iwata, J., & Reis, D. J. (1986). Interruption of projections from the medial geniculate body to an archi-neostriatal field disrupts the classical conditioning of emotional responses to acoustic stimuli. *Neuroscience, 17*, 615–627.

Levis, D. J. (1989). The case for a return to a two-factor theory of avoidance: The failure of non-fear interpretations. In: S. B. Klein & R. R. Mowrer (Eds.), *Contemporary learning theories: Pavlovian conditioning and the status of traditional learning theory* (pp. 227–277). Hillsdale, NJ: Lawrence Erlbaum Ass.

Levita, L., Dalley, J. W., & Robbins, T. W. (2002). Nucleus accumbens dopamine and learned fear revisited: A review and some new findings. *Behavioural Brain Research, 137*, 115–127.

Liang, K. C., McGaugh, J. L., Martinez, J. L., Jensen, R. A., Vasquez, B. J., & Messing, R. B. (1982). Post-training amygdaloid lesions impair retention of an inhibitory avoidance response. *Behavioural Brain Research, 4*, 237–249.

Lovibond, P. F. (1983). Facilitation of instrumental behavior by a Pavlovian appetitive conditioned stimulus. *Journal of Experimental Psychology: Animal Behavior Processes, 9*, 225–247.

Maren, S. (2001). Neurobiology of Pavlovian fear conditioning. *Annual Review of Neuroscience, 24*, 897–931.

Maren, S. (2003). What the amygdala does and doesn't do in aversive learning. *Learning and Memory (Cold Spring Harbor, N. Y.), 10*, 306–308.

Mascagni, F., McDonald, A. J., & Coleman, J. R. (1993). Corticoamygdaloid and corticocortical projections of the rat temporal cortex: A Phaseolus vulgaris leucoagglutinin study. *Neuroscience, 57*, 697–715.

Mason, J. W., Mangan, G., Brady, J. V., Conrad, D., & Rioch, D. M. (1961). Concurrent plasma epinephrine, norepinephrine and 17-hydroxycorticosteroid levels during conditioned emotional disturbances in monkeys. *Psychosomatic Medicine, 23*, 344–353.

McAllister, D. E., & McAllister, W. R. (1991). Fear theory and aversively motivated behavior: Some controversial issues. In: M. R. Denny (Ed.), *Fear, avoidance, and phobias: A fundamental analysis* (pp. 135–163). Hillsdale, NJ: Erlbaum.

McDonald, A. (1998). Cortical pathways to the mammalian amygdala. *Progress in Neurobiology, 55*, 257–332.

McKernan, M. G., & Shinnick-Gallagher, P. (1997). Fear conditioning induces a lasting potentiation of synaptic currents in vitro. *Nature, 390*, 607–611.

Miller, N. E. (1948). Studies of fear as an acquirable drive: I. Fear as motivation and fear-reduction as reinforcement in the learning of new responses. *Journal of Experimental Psychology, 38*, 89–101.

Mogenson, G. J., Jones, D. L., & Yim, C. Y. (1980). From motivation to action: Functional interface between the limbic system and the motor system. *Progress in Neurobiology, 14*, 69–97.

Morgan, C. T. (1943). *Physiological Psychology*. New York: McGraw Hill.

Mowrer, O. H. (1947). On the dual nature of learning: A reinterpretation of "conditioning" and "problem solving". *Harvard Educational Review, 17*, 102–148.

Mowrer, O. H., & Lamoreaux, R. R. (1946). Fear as an intervening variable in avoidance conditioning. *Journal of Comparative Psychology, 39*.

Muller, J., Corodimas, K. P., Fridel, Z., & LeDoux, J. E. (1997). Functional inactivation of the lateral and basal nuclei of the amygdala by muscimol infusion prevents fear conditioning to an explicit conditioned stimulus and to contextual stimuli. *Behavioral Neuroscience, 111*, 683–691.

Nader, K., Majidishad, P., Amorapanth, P., & LeDoux, J. E. (2001). Damage to the lateral and central, but not other, amygdaloid nuclei prevents the acquisition of auditory fear conditioning. *Learning and Memory (Cold Spring Harbor, N. Y.), 8*, 156–163.

Nicola, S. M., Yun, I. A., Wakabayashi, K. T., & Fields, H. L. (2004). Cue-evoked firing of nucleus accumbens neurons encodes motivational significance during a discriminative stimulus task. *Journal of Neurophysiology, 91*, 1840–1865.

Papini, M. R. (2003). Comparative psychology of surprising nonreward. *Brain, Behavior and Evolution, 62*, 83–95.

Pare, D., Quirk, G. J., & LeDoux, J. E. (2004). New vistas on amygdala networks in conditioned fear. *Journal of Neurophysiology, 92*, 1–9.

Pare, D., & Smith, Y. (1998). Intrinsic circuitry of the amygdaloid complex: Common principles of organization in rats and cats. *Trends in Neurosciences, 21*, 240–241.

Parkinson, J. A., Dalley, J. W., Cardinal, R. N., Bamford, A., Fehnert, B., & Lachenal, G., et al. (2002). Nucleus accumbens dopamine depletion impairs both acquisition and performance of appetitive Pavlovian approach behaviour: Implications for mesoaccumbens dopamine function. *Behavioural Brain Research, 137*, 149–163.

Parkinson, J. A., Olmstead, M. C., Burns, L. H., Robbins, T. W., & Everitt, B. J. (1999). Dissociation in effects of lesions of the nucleus accumbens core and shell on appetitive Pavlovian approach behavior and the potentiation of conditioned reinforcement and locomotor activity by D-amphetamine. *Journal of Neuroscience*, *19*, 2401–2411.

Parkinson, J. A., Robbins, T. W., & Everitt, B. J. (2000a). Dissociable roles of the central and basolateral amygdala in appetitive emotional learning. *The European Journal of Neuroscience*, *12*, 405–413.

Parkinson, J. A., Willoughby, P. J., Robbins, T. W., & Everitt, B. J. (2000b). Disconnection of the anterior cingulate cortex and nucleus accumbens core impairs Pavlovian approach behavior: Further evidence for limbic cortical-ventral striatopallidal systems. *Behavioral Neuroscience*, *114*, 42–63.

Pavlov, I. P. (1927). *Conditioned reflexes*. New York: Dover.

Petrovich, G. D., Holland, P. C., & Gallagher, M. (2005). Amygdala and prefrontal pathways to the lateral hypothalamus are activated by a learned cue that stimulates eating. *The Journal of Neuroscience: The Official Journal of the Society for Neuroscience*, *25*, 8295–8302.

Pezze, M. A., & Feldon, J. (2004). Mesolimbic dopaminergic pathways in fear conditioning. *Progress in Neurobiology*, *74*, 301–320.

Pitkänen, A., Savander, V., & LeDoux, J. E. (1997). Organization of intra-amygdaloid circuitries in the rat: An emerging framework for understanding functions of the amygdala. *Trends in Neurosciences*, *20*, 517–523.

Quirk, G. J., Armony, J. L., & LeDoux, J. E. (1997). Fear conditioning enhances different temporal components of tone-evoked spike trains in auditory cortex and lateral amygdala. *Neuron*, *19*, 613–624.

Quirk, G. J., Repa, C., & LeDoux, J. E. (1995). Fear conditioning enhances short-latency auditory responses of lateral amygdala neurons: Parallel recordings in the freely behaving rat. *Neuron*, *15*, 1029–1039.

Reilly, S., & Bornovalova, M. A. (2005). Conditioned taste aversion and amygdala lesions in the rat: A critical review. *Neuroscience and Biobehavioral Reviews*, *29*, 1067–1088.

Repa, J. C., Muller, J., Apergis, J., Desrochers, T. M., Zhou, Y., & LeDoux, J. E. (2001). Two different lateral amygdala cell populations contribute to the initiation and storage of memory. *Nature Neuroscience*, *4*, 724–731.

Rescorla, R. A. (1967). Pavlovian conditioning and its proper control procedures. *Psychological Review*, *74*, 71–80.

Rescorla, R. A. (1988). Behavioral studies of Pavlovian conditioning. *Annual Review of Neuroscience*, *11*, 329–352.

Rescorla, R. A., & Solomon, R. L. (1967). Two-process learning theory: Relationships between Pavlovian conditioning and instrumental learning. *Psychological Review*, *74*, 151–182.

Robbins, T. W., Cador, M., Taylor, J. R., & Everitt, B. J. (1989). Limbic–striatal interactions in reward-related processes. *Neuroscience and Biobehavioral Reviews*, *13*, 155–162.

Robbins, T. W., Giardini, V., Jones, G. H., Reading, P., & Sahakian, B. J. (1990). Effects of dopamine depletion from the Caudate-Putamen and nucleus accumbens septi on the acquisition and performance of a conditional discrimination task. *Behavioural Brain Research*, *38*, 243–261.

Rodrigues, S. M., Schafe, G. E., & LeDoux, J. E. (2004). Molecular mechanisms underlying emotional learning and memory in the lateral amygdala. *Neuron*, *44*, 75–91.

Rogan, M. T., & LeDoux, J. E. (1995). LTP is accompanied by commensurate enhancement of auditory-evoked responses in a fear conditioning circuit. *Neuron*, *15*, 127–136.

Rogan, M. T., Staubli, U. V., & LeDoux, J. E. (1997). Fear conditioning induces associative long-term potentiation in the amygdala. *Nature*, *390*, 604–607.

Romanski, L. M., LeDoux, J. E., Clugnet, M. C., & Bordi, F. (1993). Somatosensory and auditory convergence in the lateral nucleus of the amygdala. *Behavioral Neuroscience*, *107*, 444–450.

Rumpel, S., LeDoux, J., Zador, A., & Malinow, R. (2005). Postsynaptic receptor trafficking underlying a form of associative learning. *Science*, *308*, 83–88.

Salamone, J. D., Correa, M., Mingote, S. M., & Weber, S. M. (2005). Beyond the reward hypothesis: Alternative functions of nucleus accumbens dopamine. *Current Opinion in Pharmacology*, *5*, 34–41.

Sarter, M. F., & Markowitsch, H. J. (1985). Involvement of the amygdala in learning and memory: A critical review, with emphasis on anatomical relations. *Behavioral Neuroscience*, *99*, 342–380.

Schneiderman, N., Francis, J., Sampson, L. D., & Schwaber, J. S. (1974). CNS integration of learned cardiovascular behavior. In: L. V. DiCara (Ed.), *Limbic and autonomic nervous system research* (pp. 277–309). New York: Plenum.

Schoenbaum, G., Setlow, B., & Ramus, S. J. (2003). A systems approach to orbitofrontal cortex function: Recordings in rat orbitofrontal cortex reveal interactions with different learning systems. *Behavioural Brain Research*, *146*, 19–29.

Seligman, M. E. P. (1971). Phobias and preparedness. *Behavior Therapy*, *2*, 307–320.

Sidman, M. (1953). Avoidance condtioning with brief shock and no exteroceptive warning signal. *Science*, *118*, 157–158.

Sigurdsson, T., Doyere, V., Cain, C. K., & LeDoux, J. E. (2007). Long-term potentiation in the amygdala: A cellular mechanism of fear learning and memory. *Neuropharmacology*, *52*(1), 215–227.

Smith, J. W., & Dickinson, A. (1998). The dopamine antagonist, pimozide, abolishes Pavlovian-instrumental transfer. *Journal of Psychopharmacology*, *12*, A6.

Solomon, R. L., & Wynne, L. C. (1954). Traumatic avoidance learning: The principles of anxiety conservation and partial irreversibility. *Psychological Review*, *61*, 353.

Sotres-Bayon, F., Bush, D. E., & LeDoux, J. E. (2004). Emotional perseveration: An update on prefrontal–amygdala interactions in fear extinction. *Learning and Memory (Cold Spring Harbor, N. Y.)*, *11*, 525–535.

Weinberger, N. M. (1995). Retuning the brain by fear conditioning. In: M. S. Gazzaniga (Ed.), *The cognitive neurosciences* (pp. 1071–1090). Cambridge, MA: The MIT Press.

Wilensky, A. E., Schafe, G. E., & LeDoux, J. E. (1999). Functional inactivation of the amygdala before but not after auditory fear conditioning prevents memory formation. *The Journal of Neuroscience: The Official Journal of the Society for Neuroscience*, *19*, RC48.

3 Effects of Early Experience on the Development of Cerebral Asymmetry and Approach–Withdrawal

Nathan A. Fox and Bethany C. Reeb

CONTENTS

Over 25 years ago, a study conducted by Davidson and colleagues demonstrated that frontal electroencephalographic (EEG) asymmetry was related to different expressions of emotion (Davidson, Taylor, & Saron, 1979). Numerous studies followed in the examination of the role of frontal EEG asymmetry in relation to emotional valence (Coan & Allen, 2004; Harmon-Jones, 2003), motivation (Davidson, 1995, 2004; Davidson, Jackson, & Kalin, 2000a; Harmon-Jones, 2004) and affect disorders, such as depression and anxiety (Gotlib, Ranganath, & Rosenfeld, 1998; Heller & Nitschke, 1998; Thibodeau, Jorgensen, & Kim, 2006; Tomarken & Keener, 1998).

Frontal EEG asymmetry has been viewed alternatively as a state-dependent measure of negative or positive emotion (Ahern & Schwartz, 1985; Coan, Allen, & Harmon-Jones, 2001; Davidson, Ekman, Saron, Senulis, & Friesen, 1990; Gotlib et al., 1998; Heller, 1990), as an index of approach or withdrawal motivation (Davidson, 1995; Davidson et al., 2000a; Fox, 1991, 1994), and as a trait measure reflecting the disposition to either express certain types of emotion or respond in a motivationally biased manner (Fox, Henderson, Rubin, Calkins, & Schmidt, 2001; Schmidt & Fox, 1994; Tomarken, Davidson, Wheeler, & Doss, 1992a; Wheeler, Davidson, & Tomarken, 1993).

Compared to other theories of emotional valence, the approach–withdrawal theory of EEG frontal asymmetry as proposed by Davidson has been suggested to best explain results observed in both studies of state and trait emotional valence as well as studies of affective disorders (Coan & Allen, 2004; Davidson, 1998a, 2004; Harmon-Jones, 2003, 2004). According to the approach–withdrawal model, increased activation of the left frontal cortex is associated with increases in appetitive, approach-related behavior that are typically displayed in the context of moving toward a desired goal. The approach system includes such emotions as joy, interest, and even anger. In contrast, increased right frontal activation is related to increases in defensive, withdrawal-related behavior that is displayed in the context of moving away from or avoiding threatening or novel stimuli. The withdrawal system includes such emotions as fear and disgust. This chapter serves two purposes: (1) to review studies that support the approach–withdrawal theory of frontal asymmetric activation and (2) to discuss the role of early experience in the development of motivationally related asymmetry by reviewing both the human and animal literatures.

MEASURES OF FRONTAL CEREBRAL ACTIVATION

Evidence for cerebral lateralization of affective information in the frontal cortex was initially observed in patients with lesion to the right or left frontal cortex (Gainotti, 1972, 1989; Morris, Robinson, Raphael, & Hopwood, 1996; Robinson & Downhill, 1995; Robinson, Kubos, Starr, Rao, & Price, 1984; Sackeim et al., 1982). In these studies, it was demonstrated that left frontal lobe lesions resulted in depressive symptomatology, while in contrast, patients with right frontal damage were more likely to develop manic symptomatology. Additionally, the more frontal (Robinson et al., 1984) and the more focal the lesions (Morris et al., 1996), the greater the symptomatology. These results suggest that the left and right frontal regions are specialized for differential emotional processing, and therefore should lead to asymmetric activation in a normal population when different emotional states are evoked. EEG is an ideal tool to investigate such activation, because it is noninvasive and allows for excellent temporal resolution. Studies investigating asymmetric activation have primarily focused on differences in the alpha frequency band (8–13 Hz) between the left and right frontal sites. Alpha power is used because it has been shown to be inversely related to activation (Shagrass, 1972). Therefore, lower alpha power reflects greater activation while greater alpha power reflects less activation.

FRONTAL ASYMMETRY AS A STATE OR TRAIT MEASURE OF APPROACH–WITHDRAWAL

Asymmetric frontal activation has been shown to change as a function of exposure to various stimuli believed to evoke the approach or withdrawal systems. In one study by Davidson and colleagues (1990), EEG was recorded while subjects viewed film clips that evoked either joy or disgust. Greater right frontal activation was found only during the periods in which subjects expressed the clear emotional expression of disgust rather than during the entire disgust-evoking film clip. In addition, greater left frontal activation was observed during segments in which subjects displayed a Duchenne's smile (Ekman, Davidson, & Friesen, 1990), a smile typically associated with genuine happiness (Ekman & Friesen, 1982). Such asymmetries were not observed when alpha power was averaged over the entire film clip suggesting that actual "feeling" or presence of the subject's affective state, as expressed by his or her facial expressions, is important in uncovering differences in frontal asymmetric activation. Similar frontal asymmetries were obtained in a study where subjects were asked to produce various facial expressions that reflect either approach or withdrawal emotional states (Coan & Allen, 2003b; Coan et al., 2001).

In another study, differences in frontal asymmetric activation were observed in the absence of facial expression during a task that manipulated reward and punishment (Sobotka, Davidson, & Senulis, 1992). During reward trials, subjects had to respond quickly to a particular target stimulus to receive a reward (monetary increase); the subject would not receive a reward if his or her response was not fast enough. During punishment trials, subjects would lose money if they were not able to respond quickly to the target stimulus or would not lose money if the response was fast enough. As predicted, greater right frontal activation was observed during punishment trials when compared to reward trials. Therefore, it was concluded that right-sided frontal activation is reflective of withdrawal-related emotions associated with aversion to punishment.

In the studies described above, increased left frontal activation associated with approach-related stimuli appears to be associated with positive emotional valence. However, this is not always the case, because studies conducted by Harmon-Jones have shown that anger, an emotion associated with approach but with a negative valence, is related to increased levels of left frontal asymmetry (for reviews see Harmon-Jones, 2003, 2004). To demonstrate that state measures of anger are related to left frontal activation, subjects were randomly assigned to one of two groups, one in which the subjects were insulted by another person and another in which subjects were treated in a neutral manner (Harmon-Jones & Sigelman, 2001). The goal of the study was to evoke an anger state in the subjects who received insults. Immediately after the treatment, resting EEG was collected. Results revealed that those who were insulted showed greater relative left frontal activation compared to subjects who were not insulted. In addition, the insult treatment was effective in inducing states of anger, because the subjects who had been insulted reported heightened levels of aggression and anger compared to those who were treated neutrally. These findings, investigating frontal activation and anger, give the approach–withdrawal theory of frontal EEG asymmetry further support because an emotion that is both approach-related and negative in valence is related to greater left frontal rather than right frontal activation.

INDIVIDUAL DIFFERENCES IN FRONTAL ACTIVATION

The research reviewed above compares approach and withdrawal-oriented emotional states by evoking various emotional states within the subjects. However, when the individual comes into the laboratory to have his or her EEG measured, he or she already varies in his or her own dispositional mood which, subsequently, should also influence baseline resting EEG measures. Therefore, frontal EEG asymmetry additionally has been investigated as a trait measure or tendency for individuals to respond in a motivationally biased manner (Hagemann, Naumann, Thayer, & Bartussek, 2002; Jackson et al., 2003; Sutton & Davidson, 1997; Tomarken, Davidson, & Henriques, 1990; Tomarken et al., 1992a; Tomarken, Davidson, Wheeler, & Kinney, 1992b; Wheeler et al., 1993). The approach–withdrawal theory of frontal EEG asymmetry suggests that individuals with greater right activation will be more vulnerable to experiencing negative emotional states and stronger withdrawal/inhibitory tendencies, such as those experienced in anxiety disorders. In contrast, individuals with decreased left frontal activation will be more vulnerable to experiencing decreased positive emotional states and weaker approach tendencies (Davidson, 1995; Davidson, 1998a).

In an initial study investigating the relation between resting EEG asymmetry and reported global negative and positive affect during emotion-eliciting film clips, Tomarken and colleagues (1990) found that resting alpha power asymmetry observed in female subjects predicted their reported feelings of negative affect during the clips. The greater the negative affect reported, the greater the

relative right frontal activation found during rest. These effects were observed independent of the subjects' mood state reported during the recording of the baseline measures.

In another study conducted by the same group, it was found that only among subjects with high test–retest reliability in resting frontal EEG measured over a 3-week time period did frontal asymmetric activation predict subjective emotional responses while watching emotionally valenced film clips (Wheeler et al., 1993). Subjects who showed greater left frontal activation stability during rest reported greater positive affect after watching the positive film clip, whereas those who showed greater stability in right frontal activation reported greater negative affect after watching the negative film clip. This pattern of findings remained even when baseline mood was statistically controlled. Other studies have also reported measures of resting EEG asymmetry to be highly stable over time periods ranging from several weeks (Tomarken et al., 1992b; Wheeler et al.) to months (Hagemann et al., 2002). Together, these results suggest that stability in frontal EEG asymmetry reflects possible trait patterns of approach–withdrawal and that this asymmetry measure may be used as an index of an individual's predispositional response to emotion-evoking stimuli. However, it should be noted that some studies find only moderate stability in EEG asymmetry (Vuga et al., 2006), but these results may be explained by the dual nature of resting asymmetry in that it has the potential to reflect both trait and state measures of the individual (Hagemann et al., 2002).

Additional studies have examined the relations between resting frontal EEG asymmetries and dispositional depressive moods, positive and negative affect, and anger. Using the Beck Depression Inventory (BDI) (Beck, Ward, Mendelson, Mock, & Erbaugh, 1961) to measure subjects' depressive mood, Davidson's group found that subjects with consistently high BDI scores had significantly less left frontal activation during baseline EEG collection compared to subjects who consistently scored low on the BDI (Schaffer, Davidson, & Saron, 1983). Using the Positive and Negative Affect Scale (PANAS) (Watson, Clark, & Tellegen, 1988) as a measure of dispositional mood, it was found that subjects who displayed greater stability as well as high levels of left frontal activation reported significantly greater dispositional positive affect and less negative affect when compared to those who displayed greater stability in right frontal activation (Tomarken et al., 1992a). In a study assessing trait anger, Harmon-Jones and Allen (1998) measured adolescent trait anger using the Buss and Perry Aggression questionnaire (1992). This trait anger measure was found to be associated with greater left activation and decreased right activation.

In a number of studies, individual differences in the strength of the behavioral activation system (BAS) and behavioral inhibition system (BIS) and its relations to frontal EEG asymmetry have been investigated. Gray (1975, 1994) hypothesized that the BAS is responsible for guiding and executing behaviors that are involved in obtaining a desirable stimulus while the BIS is responsible for guiding and executing behaviors involved in the removal of or moving away from an undesirable stimulus. Therefore, the BAS may be reflective of a dispositional tendency for motivational approach while the BIS may be reflective of a dispositional tendency for motivational withdrawal. In a study conducted by Sutton and Davidson (1997), frontal EEG asymmetry measured during rest was assessed in its relation to measures of BAS and BIS strength using Carver and White's (1994) BIS and BAS scales. Results revealed that subjects with greater left frontal activation had higher BAS scores while subjects with greater right frontal activation had higher BIS scores. In addition, subjects that displayed greater left frontal activation also displayed greater differences between BAS and BIS scores. Frontal asymmetry measures in this unselected population were not predictive of positive and negative affect using the PANAS (Sutton & Davidson, 1997) suggesting that measures of frontal asymmetry are more predictive of motivational tendencies as reflected by measures from the BAS/BIS scale rather than measures of positive and negative affect. Replications of these results have been reported for the relation between left frontal activation and the BAS scale (Coan & Allen, 2003a; Harmon-Jones & Allen, 1997; Hewig, Hagemann, Seifert, Naumann, & Bartussek, 2006), but the relation between the BIS scale and right frontal activation has been found to be inconsistent.

PSYCHOPATHOLOGY AND FRONTAL EEG ASYMMETRY

The literature reviewed thus far has primarily focused on frontal EEG asymmetry and how it relates to either state or trait measures of approach and withdrawal emotion-related affect. There are some studies that suggest that frontal asymmetric activation may also be a useful predictive assessment tool for dispositional biases for affective disorders. In a study conducted by Henriques and Davidson (1991), it was found that, similar to subjects who scored high on the BDI, clinically depressed subjects showed significantly less left frontal activation, referred to as left frontal hypoactivation, compared to control subjects with no history of depression. This direction of activation is predicted by the approach–withdrawal theory because states of depression should be associated with deficits in the approach motivation system, and thus decreased activation in the left frontal cortex should be observed (Davidson, 1998b). In addition, left frontal hypoactivation has been suggested to serve as a state-independent marker for individuals who are at greater risk for developing depressive symptomatology (Henriques & Davidson, 1990). For example, subjects who had a history of depression but were in remission at the time resting EEG was recorded and additionally did not differ in their emotional state from never-depressed controls still displayed left frontal hypoactivation compared to controls (Henriques & Davidson, 1990). Similar decreases in left frontal activity were also observed in subjects who suffered from seasonal affect disorder even after subjects were in remission following light therapy treatment (Allen, Iacono, Depue, & Arbisi, 1993).

If the approach–withdrawal theory predicts that decreased left frontal activation reflects a faulty motivational approach system, then what would be predicted when one has a hyperactive or faulty motivational withdrawal system? It is adaptive to show withdrawal behaviors when faced with a valid threat, but it is not adaptive to display heightened withdrawal when the target stimulus is considered harmless. However, in individuals who suffer from anxiety-related disorders, seemingly harmless situations are subjectively interpreted as threatening. Therefore, it is hypothesized that these anxious individuals would display heightened levels of right frontal activation compared to nonanxious individuals (Davidson, Marshall, Tomarken, & Henriques, 2000b). Resting EEG was recorded from controls and phobics who suffered from a fear of public speaking. Prior to recording EEG, subjects were told that they would have to give a public speech in front of a group of raters. EEG was then recorded while the subjects prepared and anticipated giving their speech. Increased right frontal activation was observed in the phobics compared to controls during the anticipation of giving a speech. Phobics also reported higher levels of anxiety and negative affect prior to giving their speech, suggesting that right frontal activation is increased in anxious individuals during tasks that evoke anxiety (Davidson et al., 2000b). These results and the results from depressed subjects suggest that tendencies to display certain patterns of frontal asymmetric activation may be a marker for affective disorders. However, it should be noted that some studies have found inconsistencies in the results (for review see Gotlib et al., 1998; Heller & Nitschke, 1998; Heller, Nitschke, Etienne, & Miller, 1997; Nitschke, Heller, Palmieri, & Miller, 1999; but see Davidson's (1998b) comments on some of these issues.

DEVELOPMENTAL ORIGINS OF FRONTAL EEG ASYMMETRY

The research reviewed above was conducted using adult populations. However, there has also been some research examining similar relations between motivational tendencies and frontal EEG asymmetry among infant and child samples. This research has covered ground similar to the adult work examining relations between frontal EEG asymmetry and the expression of different emotions (Fox & Davidson, 1986, 1987, 1988), indexing approach or withdrawal motivation (Davidson & Fox, 1992; Fox, 1991, 1994) or a trait measure reflecting temperamental bias or disposition (Calkins, Fox, & Marshall, 1996; Fox et al., 2001; Henderson, Fox, & Rubin, 2001; McManis, Kagan, Snidman, & Woodward, 2002).

Unlike studies with adults where short- and long-term stability of frontal EEG asymmetry has been examined (Allen, Urry, Hitt, & Coan, 2004; Debener et al., 2000; Tomarken et al., 1992b; Vuga et al., 2006), there are few studies of the stability of this metric in infants or young children. The exceptions are a study by Bell and Fox (1994) that examined stability in young infants over a 6-month interval and found modest stability (between age correlations ranging from 0.07 to 0.83) and a study by Jones, Field, Davalos, and Pickens (1997) that found moderate stability from infancy to early childhood (between age correlations ranging from 0.42 to 0.66). Underlying the lack of repeated measurement of frontal EEG asymmetry in infancy and early childhood is the issue of understanding the etiology of this pattern and the possible changes in asymmetry that may be a result of early experience.

We know little about the developmental origins of frontal EEG asymmetry. For example, is it present at birth or does it emerge over the first years of life? What, if any, are the effects of early experiences on the development of this metric? Recent findings in behavioral genetics have shown that heritability of frontal EEG asymmetry is relatively modest (<30% of the variance) between identical twins, suggesting that environment must play a substantial role in the development of frontal asymmetry (Anokhin, Heath, & Myers, 2006). Here, we review studies that will help elucidate possible experiential contributions in the development of frontal EEG asymmetry.

State Measures of EEG Asymmetry in Infant and Child Populations

An initial formulation of a developmental model for frontal EEG asymmetry was articulated by Fox and Davidson over 20 years ago (Fox & Davidson, 1984). This model was centered on research and theory articulated by the ethologist T. C. Schneirla, who proposed that a fundamental organization of the nervous system across phylogeny involved circuits specialized for approach and withdrawal behaviors (Schneirla, 1959). The tendencies to approach or withdraw could be elicited by stimuli based upon their hedonic value and intensity. Fox and Davidson (1984) proposed that at birth, areas of the cortex were lateralized to support the motor programs and cognitive processes underlying either approach or withdrawal. These areas were thought to be connected to more sub-cortical regions that were activated during the experience of either positive or negative emotions, such that certain emotions would be associated with approach behaviors while other emotions were associated with withdrawal. As infants developed a more complex repertoire of motor and cognitive behaviors in response to contexts eliciting approach or withdrawal, regions of the prefrontal cortex would come to be specialized for these complex behavioral responses.

As evidence of these developmental changes, Fox and Davidson reported on two studies with human infants. In the first, newborn infants were presented with different liquid tastes (sugar water, citric acid, and quinine solutions). Previous work by Steiner (1979) had demonstrated that newborns displayed discrete facial movements suggesting either approach (eye widening and lip pursing) or avoidance (disgust expressions) in response to these tastes. Fox and Davidson (1986) recorded EEG from frontal and parietal scalp locations while presenting these liquids to the newborns and later coded infant facial expressions. They reported finding right EEG asymmetry during facial expressions associated with disgust or avoidance and left EEG asymmetry during facial expressions associated with approach. Of note, there were no differences in the pattern of asymmetry between frontal or parietal sites, suggesting that at birth there is hemispheric specialization but not regional specialization for approach–withdrawal behaviors.

In a second study, Fox and Davidson (1987) observed 10-month-old infants' facial expression responses to approach of an unfamiliar adult and separation from their mother while recording EEG. The EEG recordings were synchronized to the video, and segments of EEG coinciding with the facial expressions were extracted for analysis. Examination of these data found significant asymmetric effects specific to the frontal leads. Emotions (interest, joy) linked with approach behaviors were associated with left frontal EEG asymmetry while emotions (fear, distress) linked with withdrawal were associated with right frontal EEG asymmetry. The data suggest that, at least by 10 months of age, there are clear regional differences in EEG asymmetry related to approach and withdrawal behaviors, with specificity for the frontal region.

EEG Asymmetry as a Trait Measure in Infants and Children

Although Fox and Davidson (1984) proposed a developmental model linking the emergence of emotions and approach–withdrawal behaviors to the development of frontal EEG asymmetry, they did not directly address the issue of the effects of early experience on its emergence. Rather, Davidson and Fox (1989) proposed that frontal EEG asymmetry may serve as a marker for temperamental disposition. In a study examining relations between baseline frontal EEG asymmetry and 10-month infant response to maternal separation, they reported that infants displaying right frontal EEG asymmetry were more likely to display distress at separation than those displaying left frontal EEG asymmetry (Davidson & Fox, 1989).

Fox and colleagues have since examined the role of frontal EEG asymmetry in infant temperament (Fox et al., 1995; Fox et al., 2001; Fox, Schmidt, Calkins, Rubin, & Coplan, 1996). In a series of studies, relations between infant temperament, social competence and behavior, and frontal EEG asymmetry have been examined. These studies have found that young children exhibiting right frontal EEG asymmetry are more likely to exhibit social withdrawal and behave in a socially maladaptive manner when interacting with unfamiliar peers (Fox et al., 1995; Fox et al., 1996; Fox et al., 2001). This pattern of frontal EEG asymmetry can be identified as early as nine months of age, and it, in combination with measures of infant negative or fearful temperament, predicts social reticence or withdrawal in the preschool and school age period. In addition, children who display stable patterns of behavioral inhibition over time also exhibit stable right frontal asymmetry. Interestingly, children who originally displayed a right frontal bias but changed over development from a more to a less inhibited behavioral profile displayed a change in their pattern from right to left frontal asymmetry (Fox et al., 2001). These results suggest that there are experiential factors that influence the stability of frontal EEG asymmetry across development. For example, in a longitudinal study of behavioral inhibition and frontal EEG asymmetry, inhibited children who were placed in daycare during the first year of life were more likely to change and became

less inhibited, suggesting early daycare experience as a possible modulator of EEG asymmetry (Fox et al., 2001). Thus, it would appear that frontal EEG asymmetry may be affected by early experiences involved in patterns of caregiving.

Early Experience and the Development of EEG Asymmetry

One interesting model for examining the effects of early caregiving experience on the development of frontal EEG asymmetry is maternal depression. Maternal depression has been shown to be related to an increased likelihood of the development of negative affect (Durbin, Klein, Hayden, Buckley, & Moerk, 2005; Field, Pickens, Fox, Gonzalez, & Nawrocki, 1998; Zahn-Waxler, Cummings, Iannotti, & Radke-Yarrow, 1984) as well as inhibition or withdrawal (Kochanska, 1991; Pauli-Pott, Mertesacker, & Beckmann, 2004) in infants and children. A variety of data suggest that women who are depressed, presenting either postpartum depression or a clinical history of major depressive disorder, display nonoptimal patterns of caregiving to their infants (Cohn, Matias, Tronick, Connell, & Lyons-Ruth, 1986; Cooper & Murray, 1997; Field, 1984; Field et al., 1988; Field et al., 1985). Specifically, studies have shown that mothers suffering from postpartum depression were more negative toward their 2-month-old infants and their infants were, in turn, less positive in face-to-face social interactions (Cohn et al., 1986; Cohn, Campbell, Matias, & Hopkins, 1990). Other research has found that the type of interaction patterns that infants have with their depressed mothers generalizes to those with nondepressed adults (Field, 1992). Field claims that infants appear to mirror the behavior of their depressed mothers (Malphurs et al., 1996), displaying less activity (Field et al., 1988), less contingent responsivity (Cohn et al., 1990), and more negative facial expressions (Cohn et al., 1990) compared to infants of nondepressed mothers.

Field and colleagues (Field, Diego, Hernandez-Reif, Schanberg, & Kuhn, 2003) have identified a number of individual differences in interactive styles among depressed women with their infants. Among them were those mothers who were "intrusive," "withdrawn," and those with typical "good" interaction skills. These different patterns were identified by careful observation and coding of the dyadic mother–infant interaction. "Intrusive" mothers were those who displayed rough physical contact, using what the authors describe as rapid staccato actions and tense or fake facial or vocal expressions (p. 239). In contrast, "withdrawn" mothers displayed flat affect, rare instances of vocalization or touching their infant and showed little face-to-face interaction. "Good" mothering was characterized as involving smiling, sensitive touching and contingent, responsive appropriate behaviors. Although infants of "good" mothering still displayed right frontal EEG asymmetry, this group showed the least lateralization compared to either withdrawn or intrusive mothering (Field et al., 2003). These results parallel findings reported by Hane and Fox (2006) in which quality of maternal care within a nondepressed sample influenced development of frontal EEG asymmetry where infants of mothers displaying high quality care were more likely to show a left EEG asymmetry bias. In contrast, infants who received low quality maternal care showed right EEG asymmetry suggesting that quality of maternal care in general may influence the development of EEG asymmetry.

Field and colleagues reported that the two aberrant styles of mothering (withdrawn and intrusive) resulted in different patterns of frontal EEG asymmetry in their infants. Infants of withdrawn mothers were more likely to display right frontal EEG asymmetry while infants of intrusive mothers were more likely to display left frontal EEG asymmetry (Diego et al., 2002; Diego, Field, Jones, & Hernandez-Reif, 2006a). As well, infants of mothers with these differing styles display different EEG patterns to face stimuli. Diego et al. (2002) found that infants of intrusive depressed mothers displayed a shift from left to right frontal EEG asymmetry when presented with facial expressions of surprise and sadness, while infants of withdrawn depressed mothers showed no such change in EEG asymmetry. The authors argue that these differences in infant baseline and reactive EEG reflect the different underlying physiologies of infants of depressed mothers, based upon their experience with one or another style of caregiving.

In another example of the effects of early experience on frontal EEG activity, Jones, McFall, and Diego (2004) reported that depressed mothers who breastfed their infants until the third month of life were less likely to show right frontal EEG asymmetry while infants of depressed mothers who were bottle fed exhibited a bilateral decrease in frontal EEG power. Although the precise mechanisms underlying the differences in frontal EEG activity are left unspecified, the effects of differential early experiences, whether they are behavioral or nutritional, on frontal EEG asymmetry are clear.

One obvious question that remains about the influence of maternal depression on the development of infants' frontal EEG asymmetry is whether the asymmetry is a result of the prenatal or the postnatal environment. Recent work by a number of labs has begun to examine the influences of depression in pregnant women on the developing fetus and subsequently on the newborn and infant child. This work stems from data from two sources. The first is research on the effects of depression in women during pregnancy on physical parameters and birth outcomes. For example, women suffering from depression have infants with more perinatal complications and these infants are more likely to have low birth weight (Diego et al., 2006b; Field, Diego, & Hernandez-Reif, 2006; Hoffman & Hatch, 2000). A second source is data on the effects of depression on the fetus, itself. For example, Field and colleagues (2001) found that fetuses of depressed women are less active and less responsive to stimulation (see also work by DiPietro, Hawkins, Hilton, Costigan, & Pressman, 2002; DiPietro, Irizarry, Costigan, & Gurewitsch, 2004). The data from Field and colleagues clearly demonstrate physiological effects on the fetus among women with depression. If that is the case, it calls into question the findings on changes in frontal EEG asymmetry of infants with depressed mothers. The effects on fetal development and the effects on neonatal development appear to be tangled and hard to parse apart.

EARLY EXPERIENCE AND DEVELOPMENT OF CEREBRAL ASYMMETRY IN ANIMALS

Because there is little control over the environment in human development studies, it is difficult to determine which environmental factors lead to observed frontal asymmetries. Therefore, examining environmental influences on brain asymmetry using nonhuman animal models may give some insight into how such asymmetry develops in humans. Occurrence of brain lateralization in nonhuman species has been known for several decades (for a review see Rogers & Andrew, 2002). Both nonhuman primates (Kalin, Larson, Shelton, & Davidson, 1998) and rats (Sullivan & Gratton, 1998, 2002) display similar patterns of asymmetry to emotional stimuli within the frontal cortex as that observed in behaviorally inhibited children (Calkins et al., 1996; Fox et al., 2001; McManis et al., 2002). Kalin and colleagues (1998), for example, showed that individual differences in frontal EEG asymmetry in monkeys were related to trait-like fear behaviors and cortisol response, where monkeys with greater right frontal activation had greater fear and higher levels of cortisol. In rats, lesions to the right medial prefrontal cortex (mPFC) led to increased entry into the open arms of an elevated plus maze and decreased avoidance of a quinine solution (Sullivan & Gratton, 2002) as well as decreased corticosterone and stress-induced ulcer development (Sullivan & Gratton, 1999). The relations between emotion-related behavior and brain asymmetry has been shown to be dependent on early life experiences (Denenberg, 1981; Lyons, Afarian, Schatzberg, Sawyer-Glover, & Moseley, 2002; Sullivan & Dufresne, 2006; Tang, 2003). Examining this literature within the framework of emotional development may help explain how EEG asymmetry develops in the human infant.

The first study examining early experience-induced asymmetry was conducted 30 years ago by Denenberg (1978). From postnatal days 1–20, litters of rat pups were exposed to a novel cage for 3 min per day while control litters remained undisturbed. This neonatal handling procedure has been shown to have a lifelong impact on the emotional development of the rat by decreasing emotionality in an open field test (Denenberg, 1962; Denenberg, 1964) as well as inducing a better adaptive stress response (Levine, 1957, 1960). This decrease in emotionality observed among the handled animals was shown to be influenced by a stimulation-induced right-shift in brain asymmetry. Handled rats with ablations to the right neocortex showed decreased emotionality while no differences were observed between handled animals with left ablations and those with intact brains (Denenberg, 1978, 1981). In contrast, nonhandled animals showed no cerebral asymmetry.

The observed asymmetry among handled animals parallels the right cerebral lateralization for emotional stimuli that is commonly observed in the human literature (for reviews see Davidson, 2003; Davidson et al., 2000a; Fox, 1991, 1994). Of interest is the finding that nonhandled rats do not display such lateralization, suggesting that some facet of stimulation early in life induces normal development of brain lateralization for emotional regulation (Denenberg, 1981). As well, neonatal stimulation may induce cerebral lateralization by enhancing the growth and development of callosal connections which then gives rise to more specialized brain function (Denenberg, 1981). In a more recent study, it was found that individual rats display differential levels of dopamine content where some rats were more left lateralized and some were more right lateralized (Thiel & Schwarting, 2001). Of these animals, the ones who were more right lateralized also displayed less emotionality. These results suggest that observation of brain asymmetry in relation to emotional stimuli in rats is not uncommon and further supports Denenberg's original hypothesis (Denenberg, 1981)—early experience actually induces a rightward shift in asymmetric activation at the population level. However, because this study did not control the localization of the lesions made within the neocortex, it is hard to

determine if the early stimulation effects are localized to a particular region or from where in the brain the frontal lateralization propagates.

EARLY POSTNATAL STIMULATION AND UNDERLYING NEUROBIOLOGY OF CEREBRAL ASYMMETRY: RAT MODELS

One region of the brain suggested to give rise to cerebral lateralization via early stimulation is the hippocampus (Sullivan & Gratton, 2003; Tang, 2003; Verstynen, Tierney, Urbanksi, & Tang, 2001; Tang, Zou, Reeb, & Connor, 2008). Enhanced negative feedback to a stressor observed among animals that received early life stimulation has been shown to be mediated by the increased number of glucocorticoid receptors (GRs) within the hippocampus (Meaney et al., 1985). Given the connections between the hippocampus and the frontal cortex (Thierry, Gioanni, Degenetais, & Glowinski, 2000), it is logical to explore the hippocampus as a possible brain region linked to differences in cortical asymmetry in animals exposed to early stimulation (Tang, 2003).

In studies examining the effects of early stimulation on hippocampal function, Verstynen et al. (2001) found that brief exposures to novelty during the first three postnatal weeks induced a right-shift in volumetric asymmetry in the hippocampus. As well, Tang and colleagues reported similar lateralization in hippocampal long-term potentiation (LTP) (Tang et al., 2008) and sensitivity of hippocampal LTP to exogenous corticosterone (Tang, 2003). In another study by Sullivan and Gratton (2003), the effects of neonatal handling on benzodiazepine receptor binding within the hippocampus and dentate gyrus were investigated. Handling was found to induce a rightward shift in benzodiazepine receptor binding (Sullivan & Gratton, 2003).

Increased sensitivity to corticosterone is an indirect measure of the number of active glucocorticoid receptors (GRs) within the hippocampus, suggesting that stimulated animals have a greater number of GRs on the right side of the hippocampus. Right-lateralized hippocampal GRs may lead to a right-shift in negative feedback to emotional stimuli and thus down-regulate activation within the neonatally stimulated animals' right frontal cortex. Similarly, benzodiazepines induce GABAergic inhibition perhaps leading to greater inhibition of right-sided stress-induced activation among handled animals. These studies offer direct evidence that neonatal stimulation induces a rightward shift in the hippocampus and indirect evidence that early stimulation-induced frontal asymmetry may originate from the hippocampus.

In addition to the study of early stimulation effects on hippocampal lateralization development, there are studies examining lateralization of dopamine, a catecholamine that acts as a modulator of prefrontal activation (for review, see Seamans & Yang, 2004; Thierry et al., 2000). Individual differences in the lateralization of postmortem dopamine content in the frontal cortices were related to levels of emotionality where greater elevations in right compared to left dopamine content predicted less emotionality in the rat (Thiel & Schwarting, 2001). Given these results, it was hypothesized that early life stimulation may influence the development of brain lateralization via the dopaminergic system within the prefrontal cortex (PFC). In separate experiments examining the effects of early handling on the development of mesocortical dopaminergic output, Sullivan and Dufresne (2006) found that early stimulation enhanced dopaminergic turnover in the right prefrontal cortex. Parallel to this lateralization in dopamine turnover, early stimulation decreased corticosterone to both repeated and acute stress. These results suggest that increased dopaminergic activation in the right frontal cortex may counteract levels of corticosterone by facilitating the return to basal levels of glucocorticoids as well as help inhibit activation of central amygdalar output and other cortical regions typically involved in stress regulation (Day et al., 2002). In addition, dopamine appears to modulate the excitability of hippocampal activity as it propagates to the prefrontal cortex (for a review, see Thierry et al., 2000). Thus, early experience leads to not only an increased downregulation of right frontal activity via increased right lateralized negative feedback to a stressor but also has additional control over hypothalamic–pituitary–adrenal (HPA) axis activation through increases in dopaminergic metabolism within the right prefrontal cortex.

EARLY EXPERIENCE AND CEREBRAL LATERALIZATION: NONHUMAN PRIMATE MODELS

Research in early stimulation and asymmetry has primarily focused on the rat. However, there has been one report of the effects of early life stimulation on the development of asymmetry in nonhuman primates' prefrontal cortex. Lyons et al. (2002) randomly assigned infant monkeys to one of three groups: low maternal foraging demand, high maternal foraging demand, or intermittent social separations. In the low foraging demand group, the mothers had easy access to an abundance of food, whereas in the high foraging demand group, mothers had to search longer and had to exert greater effort to acquire a similar amount of food. The intermittent separation group was fed regularly. However, the infants were exposed to brief 1-hr separations from their mother on a biweekly basis from postnatal weeks 13–21. Both high

foraging demand and intermittent separations have been shown to decrease emotionality as well as enhance cortisol stress response (Lyons, Martel, Levine, Risch, & Schatzberg, 1999; Rosenblum & Andrews, 1994). Four years following this early life stimulation procedure, structural magnetic resonance imaging was performed and white and gray matter volumes of the prefrontal cortex were measured.

Compared to monkeys raised in the low foraging demand group, monkeys who were raised in either the high foraging demand or intermittent separation groups displayed a right-shift in gray matter volume in the dorsolateral prefrontal cortex as well as an overall right-shift in prefrontal white matter volume (Lyons et al., 2002). In addition, only the monkeys who were exposed to intermittent separations early in life displayed greater right gray matter volume in the ventral medial frontal cortex. The authors suggest that this rightward shift in prefrontal volume may reflect a rightward increase in prefrontal GRs which more quickly activates negative feedback of the stress response system, thus down-regulating activation of the right prefrontal cortex. Similar to early stimulation effects and development of asymmetry in rats, early stimulation in nonhuman primates induces a rightward shift in lateralization.

The animal studies reviewed above have shown that early stimulation induces asymmetry in prefrontal cortex volume and dopaminergic turnover, as well as hippocampal response to corticosterone and benzodiazepines. However, it is likely that early stimulation induces asymmetry in several other regions of the brain, especially those which are known to be involved in the processing of emotional information. For example, the amygdala has been suggested to modulate right prefrontal cortex (for reviews see Davidson & Irwin, 1999; Davidson et al., 2000a; Fox, Henderson, Marshall, Nichols, & Ghera, 2005). The amygdala has connections to both the hippocampus and the prefrontal cortex (Sotres-Bayon, Bush, & LeDoux, 2005), suggesting that the neural connections between the amygdala and these brains regions or perhaps the neural activation of the amygdala itself may also be affected by early stimulation in an asymmetric fashion. However, studies have yet to be conducted to examine whether such lateralization occurs.

INTEGRATING HUMAN AND ANIMAL FINDINGS

What elements of early stimulation lead to these lateralized effects and how can animal studies inform us about the developmental origins of asymmetry in EEG in humans? It has been suggested that increased maternal care in the form of licking-grooming and arched-back nursing in rats mediates the observed effects of neonatal stimulation (Francis, Diorio, Liu, & Meaney, 1999; Liu et al., 1997). Therefore, it may be that the development of asymmetry in neonatally stimulated rats is also mediated by increases in maternal care. This may explain the results found by Hane and Fox (2006) where infants who received high quality maternal care display decreased right frontal activation compared to those who received low quality maternal care.

However, more recent studies in both primates (Parker, Buckmaster, Sundlass, Schatzberg, & Lyons, 2006) and rodents (Tang, Akers, Reeb, Romeo, & McEwen, 2006) show that increased maternal care does not necessarily produce early stimulation effects. One suggested alternative mechanism is stress inoculation, which directly results from early repeated exposures to novelty/stress (Parker et al., 2006). This mechanism may help explain the change in behaviorally inhibited children who were put into day-care at an early age (Fox et al., 2001). It is probable that exposure to the daycare environment provided infants and children exposure to an ever-changing, unpredictable environment, thus increasing the chances that the child will be exposed to new and stressful situations. Subsequently, this exposure would lead to the increased chance to learn how to self-regulate during these stressors, thus ultimately leading to better emotional regulation and stress "inoculation" for stress observed in later childhood. In contrast, those children who were more likely to remain stable in their behavioral inhibition profile were those who remained in the exclusive care of the parent during the first year of life, having little opportunity to interact with new and stressful situations to help "inoculate" them against stress during later life.

Another hypothesis proposed to explain early stimulation effects suggests that these effects are modulated by maternal care in which the early stimulation has a direct effect on the infant's stress response system and the mother acts to regulate the infant's stress response immediately after the infant has been exposed to novelty (Reeb, Romeo, McEwen, & Tang, 2006; Tang et al., 2006). If the mother is reliable in her caretaking toward the infant after the infant is exposed to novel stimuli, then this will act to alleviate the infant's stress response. After repeated encounters with stressors and reliable responses from the mother, this helps to shape a more adaptive stress response over time. However, if the mother is not reliable in her care toward her infant, a less adaptive stress response will develop. This may be related to what is occurring in infants with depressed mothers. Although reliability in caretaking behaviors has not been examined among

depressed and nondepressed mothers, it could be that mothers who are depressed may also be less reliable in maternal care compared to nondepressed mothers. If this were the case, then it would be expected that infant interactions with depressed mothers would lead to the development of right frontal activation while those with nondepressed mothers would lead to more left frontal activation. Differences in the development of EEG asymmetry observed between the infants of depressed mothers who are either intrusive or withdrawn in their caregiving style may also be explained by the reliability of maternal behavior. However, these patterns of reliability within depressed mothers remain to be tested.

SUMMARY AND CONCLUSIONS

In this chapter, we briefly reviewed the relations between approach–withdrawal motivation and frontal EEG asymmetry. There is a corpus of evidence that suggests that left frontal activation is approach related and right frontal activation is withdrawal related. This phenomenon has been described as a reflection of the evoked emotional state as well as a trait of motivational biases. Individual differences in EEG asymmetry are apparent at very early ages and early experience plays a role in influencing the development of such asymmetry. It is not yet clear which components of early experience, such as having a depressed mother, affect the development of EEG asymmetry or whether certain components of the environment increase the likelihood of stability in EEG asymmetry over a long period of time. Because isolation of such components is difficult in a human population, the use of animals in translational research may help illuminate specific environmental components that influence the development of EEG asymmetry. Although some animal research investigates the impact of early experience on development of cerebral asymmetry, further research as well as greater communication between animal and human researchers is needed.

REFERENCES

Ahern, G. L., & Schwartz, G. E. (1985). Differential lateralization for positive and negative emotion in the human brain: EEG spectral analysis. *Neuropsychologia, 23*, 745–755.

Allen, J. J., Iacono, W. G., Depue, R. A., & Arbisi, P. (1993). Regional electroencephalographic asymmetries in bipolar seasonal affective disorder before and after exposure to bright light. *Biological Psychiatry, 33*, 642–646.

Allen, J. J., Urry, H. L., Hitt, S. K., & Coan, J. A. (2004). The stability of resting frontal electroencephalographic asymmetry in depression. *Psychophysiology, 41*, 269–280.

Anokhin, A. P., Heath, A. C., & Myers, E. (2006). Genetic and environmental influences on frontal EEG asymmetry: A twin study. *Biological Psychology*, *71*, 289–295.

Beck, A. T., Ward, C. H., Mendelson, M., Mock, T., & Erbaugh, T. (1961). An inventory for measuring depression. *Archives of General Psychiatry*, *4*, 561–571.

Bell, M. A., & Fox, N. A. (1994). Brain development over the first year of life: Relations between EEG frequency and coherence and cognitive and affective behaviors. In G. Dawson & K. Fischer (Eds.) *Human behavior and the developing brain* (pp. 314–345), New York: Guilford Press.

Buss, A. H., & Perry, M. (1992). The aggression questionnaire. *Journal of Personality and Social Psychology*, *63*, 452–459.

Calkins, S. D., Fox, N. A., & Marshall, T. R. (1996). Behavioral and physiological antecedents of inhibited and uninhibited behavior. *Child Development*, *67*, 523–540.

Carver, C. L., & White, T. L. (1994). Behavioral inhibition, behavioral activation, and affective responses to impending reward and punishment. The BIS/BAS scales. *Journal of Personality and Social Psychology*, *67*, 319–333.

Coan, J. A., & Allen, J. J. (2003a). Frontal EEG asymmetry and the behavioral activation and inhibition systems. *Psychophysiology*, *40*, 106–114.

Coan, J. A., & Allen, J. J. (2003b). Varieties of emotional experience during voluntary emotional facial expressions. *Annals of the New York Academy of Sciences*, *1000*, 375–379.

Coan, J. A., Allen, J. J., & Harmon-Jones, E. (2001). Voluntary facial expression and hemispheric asymmetry over the frontal cortex. *Psychophysiology*, *38*, 912–925.

Coan, J. A., & Allen, J. J. B. (2004). Frontal EEG asymmetry as a moderator and mediator of emotion. *Biological Psychology*, *67*, 7–49.

Cohn, F., Matias, R., Tronick, E. Z., Connell, D., & Lyons-Ruth, D. (1986). Face-to-face interactions of depressed mothers and their infants. In E. Z. Tronick & T. Field (Eds.), *Maternal depression and infant disturbance* (pp. 31–45). San Francisco, CA: Jossey-Bass.

Cohn, J. F., Campbell, S. B., Matias, R., & Hopkins, J. (1990). Face-to-face interactions of postpartum depressed and nondepressed mother-infant pairs at 2 months. *Developmental Psychology*, *26*(1), 15–23.

Cooper, P. J., & Murray, L. (1997). The impact of psychological treatments of postpartum depression on maternal mood and development. In L. Murray & P. J. Cooper (Eds.), *Postpartum depression and child development* (pp. 201–220). London, UK: The Guilford Press.

Davidson, R. J. (1995). Cerebral asymmetry, emotion, and affective style. In R. J. Davidson & K. Hugdahl (Eds.), *Brain asymmetry* (pp. 361–387). Cambridge, MA: MIT Press.

Davidson, R. J. (1998a). Affective style and affective disorders: Perspectives from affective neuroscience. *Cognition and Emotion*, *12*, 307–330.

Davidson, R. J. (1998b). Anterior electrophysiological asymmetries, emotion, and depression: Conceptual and methodological conundrums. *Psychophysiology*, *35*, 607–614.

Davidson, R. J. (2003). Affective neuroscience and psychophysiology: Toward a synthesis. *Psychophysiology*, *40*, 655–665.

Davidson, R. J. (2004). What does the prefrontal cortex "do" in affect: Perspectives on frontal EEG asymmetry research. *Biological Psychology*, *67*, 219–233.

Davidson, R. J., Ekman, P., Saron, C. D., Senulis, J. A., & Friesen, W. V. (1990). Approach–withdrawal and cerebral asymmetry: Emotional expression and brain physiology, I. *Journal of Personality and Social Psychology*, *58*, 330–341.

Davidson, R. J., & Fox, N. A. (1982). Asymmetrical brain activity discriminates between positive and negative affective stimuli in human infants. *Science*, *218*, 1235–1237.

Davidson, R. J., & Fox, N. A. (1989). Frontal brain asymmetry predicts infants' response to maternal separation. *Journal of Abnormal Psychology*, *98*, 127–131.

Davidson, R. J., & Irwin, W. (1999). The functional neuroanatomy of emotion and affective style. *Trends in Cognitive Sciences*, *3*, 11–21.

Davidson, R. J., Jackson, D. C., & Kalin, N. H. (2000a). Emotion, plasticity, context, and regulation: Perspectives from affective neuroscience. *Psychological Bulletin*, *126*, 890–909.

Davidson, R. J., Marshall, J. R., Tomarken, A. J., & Henriques, J. B. (2000b). While a phobic waits: Regional brain electrical and autonomic activity in social phobics during anticipation of public speaking. *Biological Psychiatry*, *47*, 85–95.

Davidson, R. J., Taylor, N., & Saron, C. (1979). Hemisphericity and styles of information processing: Individual differences in EEG asymmetry and their relationship to cognitive performance. *Psychophysiology*, *16*, 197.

Day, H. E., Vittoz, N. M., Oates, M. M., Badiani, A., Watson, S. J., Jr., Robinson, T. E., et al. (2002). A 6-hydroxydopamine lesion of the mesostriatal dopamine system decreases the expression of corticotropin releasing hormone and neurotensin mRNAs in the amygdala and bed nucleus of the stria terminalis. *Brain Research*, *945*(2), 151–159.

Debener, S., Baeudecel, A., Nessler, D., Brocke, B., Heilemann, H., & Kayser, J. (2000). Is resting anterior EEG alpha asymmetry a trait marker for depression? *Neuropsychobiology*, *41*, 31–37.

Denenberg, V. H. (1962). The effects of early experience. In E. S. E. Hafex (Ed.), *The behaviour of domestic animals* (pp. 109–138). London: Bailliere, Tindall & Cox.

Denenberg, V. H. (1964). Critical periods, stimulus input, and emotional reactivity: A theory of infantile stimulation. *Psychological Review*, *71*, 335–351.

Denenberg, V. H. (1978). Infantile stimulation induces brain lateralization in rats. *Science*, *201*, 1150–1152.

Denenberg, V. H. (1981). Hemispheric laterality in animals and the effects of early experience. *The Behavioral and Brain Sciences*, *4*, 1–49.

Diego, M. A., Field, T., Hart, S., Hernandez-Reif, M., Jones, N., Cullen, C., et al. (2002). Facial expressions and EEG in infants of intrusive and withdrawn mothers with depressive symptoms. *Depression and Anxiety*, *15*, 10–17.

Diego, M. A., Field, T., Jones, N. A., & Hernandez-Reif, M. (2006a). Withdrawn and intrusive maternal interaction style and infant frontal EEG asymmetry shifts in infants of depressed and non-depressed mothers. *Infant Behavior & Development*, *29*, 220–229.

Diego, M. A., Jones, N. A., Field, T., Hernandez-Reif, M., Schanberg, S., Kuhn, C., et al. (2006b). Maternal psychological distress, prenatal cortisol, and fetal weight. *Psychosomatic Medicine*, *68*, 747–753.

DiPietro, J. A., Hawkins, M., Hilton, S. C., Costigan, K. A., & Pressman, E. K. (2002). Maternal stress and affect influence fetal neurobehavioral development. *Developmental Psychology*, *38*, 659–668.

DiPietro, J. A., Irizarry, R. A., Costigan, K. A., & Gurewitsch, E. D. (2004). The psychophysiology of the maternal–fetal relationship. *Psychophysiology*, *41*, 510–520.

Durbin, C. E., Klein, D. N., Hayden, E. P., Buckley, M. E., & Moerk, K. C. (2005). Temperamental emotionality in preschoolers and parental mood disorders. *Journal of Abnormal Psychology*, *114*, 28–37.

Ekman, P., Davidson, R. J., & Friesen, W. V. (1990). Duchenne's smile: Emotional expression and brain physiology, II. *Journal of Personality and Social Psychology*, *58*, 342–353.

Ekman, P., & Friesen, W. V. (1982). Felt, false, and miserable smiles. *Journal of Nonverbal Behavior*, *6*, 238–252.

Field, T. (1984). Early interactions between infants and their postpartum depressed mothers. *Infant Behavior & Development*, *7*, 527–532.

Field, T. (1992). Infants of depressed mothers. *Development and Pscyopathology*, *4*, 49–66.

Field, T., Diego, M., & Hernandez-Reif, M. (2006). Prenatal depression effects on the fetus and newborn: A review. *Infant Behavior & Development*, *29*, 445–455.

Field, T., Diego, M., Hernandez-Reif, M., Schanberg, S., & Kuhn, C. (2003). Depressed mothers who are "good interaction" partners versus those who are withdrawn or intrusive. *Infant Behavior & Development*, *26*, 238–252.

Field, T., Diego, M. A., Dieter, J., Hernandez-Reif, M., Schanberg, S., Kuhn, C., et al. (2001). Depressed withdrawn and intrusive mothers' effects on their fetuses and neonates. *Infant Behavior & Development*, *24*, 27–39.

Field, T., Healy, B., Goldstein, S., Perry, S., Bendell, D., Schanberg, S., et al. (1988). Infants of depressed mothers show "depressed" behavior even with nondepressed adults. *Child Development*, *59*, 1569–1579.

Field, T., Pickens, J., Fox, N. A., Gonzalez, J., & Nawrocki, T. (1998). Facial expression and EEG responses to happy and sad faces/voices by 3-month-old infants of depressed mothers. *British Journal of Developmental Psychology*, *16*, 485–494.

Field, T., Sandberg, D., Garcia, R., Vega-Lahr, N., Goldstein, S., & Guy, L. (1985). Prenatal problems, postpartum depression, and early mother-infant interactions. *Developmental Psychology*, *12*, 1152–1156.

Fox, N. A. (1991). If it's not left, it's right. Electroencephalograph asymmetry and the development of emotion. *American Psychologist*, *46*, 863–872.

Fox, N. A. (1994). Dynamic cerebral processes underlying emotion regulation. *Monographs of the Society of Research in Child Development*, *59*, 152–166.

Fox, N. A., & Davidson, R. J. (1984). Hemispheric substrates of affect: A developmental model. In N. A. Fox & R. J. Davidson (Eds.), *The psychobiology of affective development* (pp. 353–381). Hillsdale, NJ: Erlbaum Press.

Fox, N. A., & Davidson, R. J. (1986). Taste-elicited changes in facial signs of emotion and the asymmetry of brain electrical activity in human newborns. *Neuropsychologia*, *24*, 417–422.

Fox, N. A., & Davidson, R. J. (1987). Electroencephalogram asymmetry in response to the approach of a stranger and maternal separation in 10-month-old infants. *Developmental Psychology*, *23*, 233–240.

Fox, N. A., & Davidson, R. J. (1988). Patterns of brain electrical activity during facial signs of emotion in 10-month-old infants. *Developmental Psychology*, *24*, 230–246.

Fox, N. A., Henderson, H. A., Marshall, P. J., Nichols, K. E., & Ghera, M. M. (2005). Behavioral inhibition: Linking biology and behavior within a developmental framework. *Annual Review of Psychology*, *56*, 235–262.

Fox, N. A., Henderson, H. A., Rubin, K. H., Calkins, S. D., & Schmidt, L. A. (2001). Continuity and discontinuity of behavioral inhibition and exuberance: Psychophysiological and behavioral influences across the first four years of life. *Child Development*, *72*, 1–21.

Fox, N. A., Rubin, K. H., Calkins, S. D., Marshall, T. R., Coplan, R. J., Porges, S. W., et al. (1995). Frontal activation asymmetry and social competence at four years of age. *Child Development*, *66*, 1770–1784.

Fox, N. A., Schmidt, L. A., Calkins, S. D., Rubin, K. H., & Coplan, R. J. (1996). The role of frontal activation in the regulation and dysregulation of social behavior during the preschool years. *Development and Pscyopathology*, *8*, 89–102.

Francis, D., Diorio, J., Liu, D., & Meaney, M. J. (1999). Non-genomic transmission across generations of maternal behavior and stress responses in the rat. *Science*, *286*, 1155–1158.

Gainotti, G. (1972). Emotional behavior and hemispheric side of lesion. *Cortex*, *8*, 230–236.

Gainotti, G. (1989). Disorders of emotions and affect in patients with unilateral brain damage. In F. Boller & J. Grafman (Eds.), *Handbook of neuropsychology* (Vol. 3, pp. 345–361). Amsterdam: Elsevier.

Gotlib, I. H., Ranganath, C., & Rosenfeld, J. P. (1998). Frontal EEG alpha asymmetry, depression, and cognitive functioning. *Cognition and Emotion*, *12*, 449–478.

Gray, J. A. (1975). *Elements of a two-process theory of learning*. London: Academic Press Inc.

Gray, J. A. (1994). Three fundamental emotion systems. In P. Ekman & R. J. Davidson (Eds.), *The nature of emotion: Fundamental questions* (pp. 243–247). New York: Oxford University Press.

Hagemann, D., Naumann, E., Thayer, J. F., & Bartussek, D. (2002). Does resting electroencephalograph asymmetry reflect a trait? An application of latent state-trait theory. *Journal of Personality and Social Psychology*, *82*, 619–641.

Hane, A. A., & Fox, N. A. (2006). Ordinary variations in maternal caregiving influence human infants' stress reactivity. *Psychological Science, 17*(6), 550–556.

Harmon-Jones, E. (2003). Clarifying the emotive functions of asymmetrical frontal cortical activity. *Psychophysiology, 40*, 838–848.

Harmon-Jones, E. (2004). Contributions from research on anger and cognitive dissonance to understanding the motivational functions of asymmetrical frontal brain activity. *Biological Psychology, 67*, 51–67.

Harmon-Jones, E., & Allen, J. J. (1997). Behavioral activation sensitivity and resting frontal EEG asymmetry: Covariation of putative indicators related to risk for mood disorders. *Journal of Abnormal Psychology, 106*, 159–163.

Harmon-Jones, E., & Allen, J. J. (1998). Anger and prefrontal brain activity: EEG asymmetry consistent with approach motivation despite negative affective valence. *Journal of Personality and Social Psychology, 74*, 1310–1316.

Harmon-Jones, E., & Sigelman, J. (2001). State anger and prefrontal brain activity: Evidence that insult-related relative left prefrontal activation is associated with experienced anger and aggression. *Journal of Personality and Social Psychology, 80*, 797–803.

Heller, W. (1990). The neuropsychology of emotion: Developmental patterns and implications for psychopathology. In N. L. Stein, B. Leventhal & T. Trabasso (Eds.), *Psychological and biological approaches to emotion* (pp. 167–211). Hillsdale, NJ: Lawrence Erlbaum Associates.

Heller, W., & Nitschke, J. B. (1998). The puzzle of regional brain activity in depression and anxiety: The importance of subtypes and comorbidity. *Cognition and Emotion, 12*, 421–447.

Heller, W., Nitschke, J. B., Etienne, M. A., & Miller, G. A. (1997). Patterns of regional brain activity differentiate types of anxiety. *Journal of Abnormal Psychology, 106*, 376–385.

Henderson, H. A., Fox, N. A., & Rubin, K. H. (2001). Temperamental contributions to social behavior: The moderating roles of frontal EEG asymmetry and gender. *Journal of the American Academy of Child and Adolescent Psychiatry, 40*, 68–74.

Henriques, J. B., & Davidson, R. J. (1990). Regional brain electrical asymmetries discriminate between previously depressed and healthy control subjects. *Journal of Abnormal Psychology, 99*, 22–31.

Henriques, J. B., & Davidson, R. J. (1991). Left frontal hypoactivation in depression. *Journal of Abnormal Psychology, 100*, 535–545.

Hewig, J., Hagemann, D., Seifert, J., Naumann, E., & Bartussek, D. (2006). The relation of cortical activity and bis/bas on the trait level. *Biological Psychology, 71*, 42–53.

Hoffman, S., & Hatch, M. C. (2000). Depressive symptomatology during pregnancy: Evidence for an association with decreased fetal growth in pregnancies of lower social class women. *Health Psychology, 19*, 535–543.

Jackson, D. C., Mueller, C. J., Dolski, I., Dalton, K. M., Nitschke, J. B., Urry, H. L., et al. (2003). Now you feel it, now you don't: Frontal brain electrical asymmetry and individual differences in emotion regulation. *Psychological Science, 14*, 612–617.

Jones, N. A., Field, T., Davalos, M., & Pickens, J. (1997). EEG stability in infants/children of depressed mothers. *Child Psychiatry and Human Development, 28*, 59–70.

Jones, N. A., McFall, B. A., & Diego, M. A. (2004). Patterns of brain electrical activity in infants of depressed mothers who breastfeed and bottle feed: The mediating role of infant temperament. *Biological Psychology, 67*, 103–124.

Kalin, N. H., Larson, C., Shelton, S. E., & Davidson, R. J. (1998). Asymmetric frontal brain activity, cortisol, and behavior associated with fearful temperament in rhesus monkeys. *Behavioral Neuroscience, 112*(2), 286–292.

Kochanska, G. (1991). Patterns of inhibition to the unfamiliar in children of normal and affectively ill mothers. *Child Development, 62*, 250–263.

Levine, S. (1957). Infantile experience and resistance to physiological stress. *Science, 126*, 405.

Levine, S. (1960). Stimulation in infancy. *Scientific American, 202*, 80–86.

Liu, D., Tannenbaum, B., Caldji, C., Francis, D., Freedman, A., Sharma, S., et al. (1997). Maternal care, hippocampal glucocorticoid receptor gene expression and hypothalamic–pituitary–adrenal responses to stress. *Science, 277*, 1659–1662.

Lyons, D. M., Afarian, H., Schatzberg, A. F., Sawyer-Glover, A., & Moseley, M. E. (2002). Experience-dependent asymmetric variation in primate prefrontal morphology. *Behavioural Brain Research, 136*(1), 51–59.

Lyons, D. M., Martel, F. L., Levine, S., Risch, N. J., & Schatzberg, A. F. (1999). Postnatal experiences and genetic effects of squirrel monkey social affinities and emotional distress. *Hormones and Behavior, 36*, 266–275.

Malphurs, J. E., Field, T. M., Larraine, C., Pickens, J., Pelaez-Nogueras, M., Yando, R., et al. (1996). Altering withdrawn and intrusive interaction behaviors of depressed mothers. *Infant Mental Health Journal, 17*(2), 152–160.

McManis, M. H., Kagan, J., Snidman, N. C., & Woodward, S. A. (2002). EEG asymmetry, power, and temperament in children. *Developmental Psychobiology, 41*, 169–177.

Meaney, M. J., Aiken, D., Bodnoff, S. R., Iny, L. J., Tatarewicz, J. E., & Sapolsky, R. M. (1985). Early postnatal handling alters glucocorticoid receptor concentration in selected brain regions. *Behavioral Neuroscience, 99*, 765–770.

Morris, P. L., Robinson, R. G., Raphael, B., & Hopwood, M. J. (1996). Lesion location and poststroke depression. *Journal of Neuropsychiatry and Clinical Neurosciences, 8*, 399–403.

Nitschke, J. B., Heller, W., Palmieri, P. A., & Miller, G. A. (1999). Contrasting patterns of brain activity in anxious apprehension and anxious arousal. *Psychophysiology, 36*, 628–637.

Parker, K. J., Buckmaster, C. L., Sundlass, K., Schatzberg, A. F., & Lyons, D. M. (2006). Maternal mediation, stress inoculation, and the development of neuroendocrine stress resistance in primates. *Proceedings of the National Academy of Sciences of the United States of America*, *103*, 3000–3005.

Pauli-Pott, U., Mertesacker, B., & Beckmann, D. (2004). Predicting the development of infant emotionality from maternal characteristics. *Development and Psycopathology*, *16*, 19–42.

Reeb, B. C., Romeo, R. D., McEwen, B. S., & Tang, A. C. (2006). Explaining early stimulation effect: Maternal mediation or maternal modulation? *Developmental Psychobiology*, *48*, 623.

Robinson, R. G., & Downhill, J. E. (1995). Lateralization of psychopathology in response to focal brain injury. In R. J. Davidson & K. Hugdahl (Eds.), *Brain asymmetry* (pp. 693–711). Cambridge, MA: MIT Press.

Robinson, R. G., Kubos, K. L., Starr, L. B., Rao, K., & Price, T. R. (1984). Mood disorders in stroke patients: Importance of location of lesion. *Brain*, *107*, 81–93.

Rogers, L. J., & Andrew, R. (2002). *Comparative vertebrate lateralization*. Cambridge, UK: Cambridge University Press.

Rosenblum, L. A., & Andrews, M. W. (1994). Influences of environmental demand on maternal behavior and infant development. *Acta Paediatrica Supplement*, *397*, 57–63.

Sackeim, H., Greenberg, M. S., Weiman, A. L., Gur, R., Hungerbuhler, J. P., & Geschwind, N. (1982). Hemispheric asymmetry in the expression of positive and negative emotions. *Archives of Neurology*, *39*, 210–218.

Schaffer, C. E., Davidson, R. J., & Saron, C. (1983). Frontal and parietal EEG asymmetries in depressed and non-depressed subjects. *Biological Psychiatry*, *18*, 753–762.

Schmidt, L. A., & Fox, N. A. (1994). Patterns of cortical electrophysiology and autonomic activity in adults' shyness and sociability. *Biological Psychology*, *38*, 183–198.

Schneirla, T. C. (1959). An evolutionary and developmental theory of biphasic processes underlying approach and withdrawal. In M. R. Jones (Ed.), *Nebraska symposium on motivation* (pp. 1–42). Lincoln, NE: University of Nebraska Press.

Seamans, J. K., & Yang, C. R. (2004). The principle features and mechanisms of dopamine modulation in the prefrontal cortex. *Progress in Neurobiology*, *74*, 1–57.

Shagrass, C. (1972). Electrical activity in the brain. In N. S. Greenfield & R. A. Sternbach (Eds.), *Handbook of psychophysiology* (pp. 263–328). New York: Holt, Rinehart, & Winston.

Sobotka, S., Davidson, R. J., & Senulis, J. (1992). Anterior brain electrical asymmetries in response to reward and punishment. *Electroencephalography and Clinical Neurophysiology*, *83*, 236–247.

Sotres-Bayon, F., Bush, D. E. A., & LeDoux, J. E. (2005). Emotional perseveration: An update on prefrontal-amygdala interactions in fear extinction. *Learning & Memory*.

Steiner, J. E. (1979). Human facial expressions in response to taste and smell stimulation. *Advances in Child Development and Behavior*, *13*, 257–295.

Sullivan, R. M., & Dufresne, M. M. (2006). Mesocortical dopamine and hpa axis regulation: Role of laterality and early environment. *Brain Research*, *1076*, 45–59.

Sullivan, R. M., & Gratton, A. (1998). Relationships between stress-induced increases in medial prefrontal cortical dopamine and plasma corticosterone levels in rats: Role of cerebral laterality. *Neuroscience*, *83*(1), 81–91.

Sullivan, R. M., & Gratton, A. (1999). Lateralized effects of medial prefrontal cortex lesions on neuroendocrine and autonomic stress responses in rats. *The Journal of Neuroscience*, *19*(7), 2834–2840.

Sullivan, R. M., & Gratton, A. (2002). Behavioral effects of excitotoxic lesions of ventral medial prefrontal cortex in the rat are hemisphere-dependent. *Brain Research*, *927*, 69–79.

Sullivan, R. M., & Gratton, A. (2003). Behavioural and neuroendocrine correlates of hemispheric asymmetries in benzodiazepine receptor binding induced by postnatal handling in the rat. *Brain and Cognition*, *51*, 160–248.

Sutton, S. K., & Davidson, R. J. (1997). Prefrontal brain asymmetry: A biological substrate of the behavioral approach and inhibition systems. *Psychological Science*, *8*, 204–210.

Tang, A. C. (2003). A hippocampal theory of cerebral lateralization. In K. Hugdahl & R. J. Davidson (Eds.), *The asymmetrical brain* (pp. 37–68). Cambridge, MA: MIT Press.

Tang, A. C., Akers, K. G., Reeb, B. C., Romeo, R. D., & McEwen, B. S. (2006). Programming social, cognitive, and neuroendocrine development by early exposure to novelty. *PNAS*, *103*, 15716–15721.

Tang, A. C., Zou, B., Reeb, B. C., & Connor, J. A. (2008). An epigenetic induction of a right-shift in hippocampal asymmetry: Selectivity for short- and long-term potentiation but not post-tetanic potentiation. *Hippocampus*, *18*, 5–10.

Thibodeau, R., Jorgensen, R. S., & Kim, S. (2006). Depression, anxiety, and resting frontal EEG asymmetry: A meta-analytic review. *Journal of Abnormal Psychology*, *115*, 615–729.

Thiel, C. M., & Schwarting, R. K. (2001). Dopaminergic lateralisation in the forebrain: Relations to behavioural asymmetries and anxiety in male Wistar rats. *Neuropsychobiology*, *43*(3), 192–199.

Thierry, A., Gioanni, Y., Degenetais, E., & Glowinski, J. (2000). Hippocampo-prefrontal cortex pathway: Anatomical and electrophysiological characteristics. *Hippocampus*, *10*, 411–419.

Tomarken, A. J., Davidson, R. J., & Henriques, J. B. (1990). Resting frontal brain asymmetry predicts affective responses to films. *Journal of Personality and Social Psychology*, *59*, 791–801.

Tomarken, A. J., Davidson, R. J., Wheeler, R. E., & Doss, R. C. (1992a). Individual differences in anterior brain asymmetry and fundamental dimensions of emotion. *Journal of Personality and Social Psychology*, *62*, 676–687.

Tomarken, A. J., Davidson, R. J., Wheeler, R. E., & Kinney, L. (1992b). Psychometric properties of resting anterior EEG asymmetry: Temporal stability and internal consistency. *Psychophysiology, 29,* 576–592.

Tomarken, A. J., & Keener, A. D. (1998). Frontal brain asymmetry and depression: A self-regulatory perspective. *Cognition and Emotion, 12,* 387–420.

Verstynen, T., Tierney, R., Urbanksi, T., & Tang, A. (2001). Neonatal novelty exposure modulates hippocampal volumetric asymmetry in the rat. *Developmental Neuroscience, 12*(14), 3019–3022.

Vuga, M., Fox, N. A., Cohn, J. F., George, C. J., Levenstein, R. M., & Kovacs, M. (2006). Long-term stability of frontal electroencephalographic asymmetry in adults with a history of depression and controls. *International Journal of Psychophysiology, 59,* 107–115.

Watson, D., Clark, L. A., & Tellegen, A. (1988). Development and validation of brief measures of positive and negative affect: The PANAS scales. *Journal of Personality and Social Psychology, 54,* 1063–1070.

Wheeler, R. W., Davidson, R. J., & Tomarken, A. J. (1993). Frontal brain asymmetry and emotional reactivity: A biological substrate of affective style. *Psychophysiology, 30,* 82–89.

Zahn-Waxler, C., Cummings, E. M., Iannotti, R. J., & Radke-Yarrow, M. (1984). Young children of depressed parents: A population at risk for affective problems. In D. Cicchetti & K. Schneider-Rosen (Eds.), *Childhood depression: New directions for child development* (pp. 81–105). San Francisco: Jossey-Bass.

4 Appetitive and Defensive Motivation Is the Substrate of Emotion

Peter J. Lang and Margaret M. Bradley

CONTENTS

Survival is the primary motivation for living organisms—to preserve the life of the individual and to ensure the propagation of their genetic inheritance. Two broad classes of stimulus events are critical in this struggle: cues relevant to the *promotion* of genetic survival (e.g., food, drink, potential sexual partners) and those that indicate *threat* to survival (e.g., predators, natural disasters, accidents). It is proposed here that two overlapping neural circuits have evolved in the brains of complex animals to cope with these events: an *appetitive* motivational circuit that organizes responses to stimuli, promoting survival; and a second, *defense* motivational circuit that mediates reactions to threat. In this view, emotion accompanies activation of appetitive or defense systems, prompting pleasant or aversive affects, respectively. In humans, of course, overt responses to threat or appetite vary and are often inhibited or delayed. Nevertheless, preparatory, autonomic, and somatic reflexes that occur automatically mobilize the organism. In this sense, emotions can be usefully construed as survival-based *dispositions to action*.

In this chapter, we summarize key issues in the motivational study of emotion, beginning with a brief outline of its evolutionary foundations in reflexive physiology and behavior. We then provide an overview of emotion processing from affective cue to motivational activation, and conclude by assessing emotional reactions in a picture-viewing context, in which pleasant and unpleasant pictures prompt autonomic, somatic, and neural activity consistent with the idea that emotion stems from activation in fundamental appetitive and defensive motivational circuits that have evolved to sustain and protect life.

REFLEX FOUNDATIONS

The idea that motivation and emotion share a reflex foundation has had many adherents over the years. Konorski (1967), for example, proposed a motivational typology of unconditioned reflexes, keyed to the reflex's survival role. Exteroceptive reflexes were proposed to be either preservative (e.g., ingestion, copulation, nurture of progeny) or protective (e.g., rejection of noxious agents). He further suggested that emotional states reflect this two-system organization: Preservative emotions included such affects as sexual passion, joy, and nurturance; fear and anger were considered protective affects. Dickinson and Dearing (1979) developed Konorski's dichotomy into a theory of two opponent motivational systems, aversive and attractive, each activated by a different, but equally wide range of unconditioned stimuli. Masterson and Crawford (1982) further elaborated the concept in the context of defense, suggesting that a variety of different actions in response to threatening stimuli—such as fleeing, freezing, fighting, and defensive burying—are organized by a general "defense motivation system," and proposed that unpleasant emotional reactions in humans could be construed as a phylogenetic mammalian development that involved outputs from the same defense system.

In a motivational view, the *hedonic valence* of a stimulus is determined by the dominant motive system: stimuli that activate the appetitive system are pleasant (preservative/attractive) and mediate positive affects; stimuli that activate the defense system (protective/aversive) are unpleasant and mediate negative affects. Thus, evaluative reports of *pleasure/displeasure* roughly index which motivational system is activated by a stimulus event (i.e., appetitive or defensive).

APPROACH AND AVOIDANCE

In a simple organism such as a flatworm, motivated behavior can be almost entirely characterized by two survival-based reflexive movements: Direct approach to appetitive stimuli and withdrawal from aversive stimuli. On the basis of the overt behavior of such simple organisms, Schneirla (1959) defined approach and withdrawal as the basic reactions "applicable to *all* motivated behavior in *all* organisms." Schneirla surely intended this description to be metaphorical, considering that more complex animals react to threat or appetite with a great variety of specific behaviors, not all directionally oriented. For instance, a male rat's response to an aversive shock is various: If administered to the rat's feet in a closed, empty chamber, the animal freezes; if delivered by a prod from outside the cage, the rat flees; if suitable material is present, the rat will attempt to bury the shock apparatus; if another male is in the vicinity, approach, in the form of a fight, ensues (see Mackintosh, 1983, for a discussion of the data). These behaviors are all expressions of an evolved defense system. All are potentially useful in the appropriate context (although none may be of much help in the laboratory environment) and include the full range of directional reactions—withdrawal, approach, and immobility.

A similar mix of actions (and inaction) is apparent in the appetitive behavior of animals, e.g., in the stalking of predators and the mating dances of many species. Humans possess an even greater armamentarium of coping skills—a greater ability to delay or inhibit overt action, and to plan ahead: Although the insult of a boss may inflame, the wise employee does not throw the punch. Nevertheless, in a context of threat the physiology continues to mobilize for action, and in the hiatus between stimulus and withheld response, emotions are strongly experienced. Indeed, emotions are less about Schneirla's behavioral constructs of approach and withdrawal (or avoidance) than about different contexts in which a range of defensive and appetitive responses can potentially be deployed.

MOTIVATIONAL STRATEGY AND BEHAVIORAL TACTICS

In his famous treatise *On War* (1832/1976), Karl Von Clausewitz proposed the terms *strategy* and *tactics* to describe concepts guiding armies in the struggle to survive and achieve victory. In his view, a strategy is an underlying goal-directed principle governing the selection and implementation of specific actions that serve the end goal. Tactics are diverse, context-bound patterns of action that facilitate the current strategy, but do not mirror it. Thus, even though the strategic goal may be to attack and destroy an opponent's army, at times the best tactical action on a specific battlefield is to withdraw.

Applying this conception to the range of motivated behaviors (Lang, 1995), emotion's underlying action dispositions are organized around two strategic dispositions, appetitive/preservative and defensive/protective, that define broad motivational end goals that facilitate survival. Specific emotions, on the other hand, reflect tactical, context-determined actions, with anger, for instance, reflecting a disposition to defensive aggression. The same emotional label is often applied to a variety of different tactical behaviors. For example, hypervigilance, freezing, spontaneous defecation, disruption of motor control, and headlong flight are all seen to reflect "fear," despite the fact that they are very different in both physiology and function. Furthermore, even appetitive appearing behaviors, such as sexual approach, can occur in primates under threat (van Lawick-Goodall, 1971). Thus, beyond the broad strategic level of description—that emotions are pleasant or unpleasant and vary in their arousal/intensity—affects are elusive entities.

EMOTION PROCESSING: AFFECTIVE CUES AND MOTIVATIONAL ACTIVATION

In human beings, it is generally held that "affects" are reflected in three measurable response systems (Lang, 1968, 1994a): (1) expressive and evaluative language, (2) physiologic changes mediated by the somatic and autonomic systems, and (3) behavioral acts. This is the database of emotion, and a theory of emotion must cope with its breadth and diversity. The task is complicated by the fact that the correlations among and within systems are often quite modest when research subjects confront a situation designed to evoke a particular affect (Lang, 1968; Mandler, Mandler, Kremen, & Sholiton, 1961). That is to say, there has been little support for hypothesis (inspired by William James) that verbal report of a particular emotional feeling (e.g., anger, fear, anxiety) is reliably associated with specific physiological changes or patterns of action.

Considering the myriad of words in all languages that describe various emotions and shades of feeling, many researchers have proposed an alternative approach to the understanding of emotional states. They suggest that individual word descriptors might not define a catalogue of specific affects; rather, they hypothesize instead that organizing dimensions of affect underlie the emotional lexicon. Thus, work on natural language categories (Ortony, Clore, & Collins, 1988; Shaver, Schwartz,

Kirson, & O'Connor, 1987) suggests that people's knowledge about emotions is hierarchically organized, and that the superordinate division is between positivity (pleasant states: love, joy) and negativity (unpleasant states: anger, sadness, fear). Osgood and his associates (Osgood, Suci, & Tannenbaum, 1957), using the semantic differential, earlier showed that emotional descriptors could, in the main, be distributed along a bipolar dimension of affective valence—from attraction and pleasure to aversion and displeasure. A dimension of activation, from calm to aroused, also accounted for very significant variance. Similar conclusions have been drawn by other, independent investigators of verbal report (Mehrabian & Russell, 1974; Tellegen, 1985), and in early studies of facial expression (Schlosberg, 1952).

In effect, the organization of emotional language complements the view that there are motivational circuits in the brain, appetitive and defensive, that vary in activation or metabolic arousal. It is further proposed that the varying affects of humans reflect this motivational base. That is, while emotions may come in many shapes, determined by cultural factors and the tactical demands of context, they are fundamentally organized by their motivational determinants, and can thus be construed as primarily reflecting varying activation in underlying appetitive or defensive neural circuits that have evolved to mediate appropriate survival actions.

EMOTIONAL PERCEPTION

As already suggested, much of the "noise" in emotion analysis comes from the varying behavioral demands of the context in which affect is evoked. These tactical differences confuse comparisons, and encourage laboratory explorations of emotion that carefully control the context of its induction (Bradley, 2000). Thus, the research reviewed here investigates appetitive and defensive activation in the laboratory in a single, controlled experimental context—viewing emotional pictures.

Looking at pictures is a ubiquitous and ecologically natural human activity. Through exposure to magazines, films, and television, image processing may occupy as much as 10–50% of the waking life of children and adults (Reeves & Hawkins, 1986). It is generally accepted that pictures can evoke strong emotions, with many politicians, the media, and polls of the general public all maintaining that media depictions of sex and violence are not only affectively compelling, but may significantly influence societal morals, levels of aggression, and the incidence of criminal behavior.

From the perspective of laboratory research on brain and body reactions in emotion, picture-viewing tasks have many virtues. The individual is normally immobile when observing an object or event and artifacts due to motor activity do not disrupt sensitive measurements. Furthermore, a specific visual cue is both the implicit and explicit focus of current activity, and all research participants have the familiar (and quite elementary) processing task of simply looking at the picture. Thus, the reactions that are observed are those mediated reflexively by an emotional cue, appetitive or aversive, indexed as changes in brain activity, and as somatic and autonomic indices of attention and action mobilization—all of which can be evaluated relative to subsequent verbal report.

What Is Motivational Activation?

When an emotionally evocative picture is presented, it is assumed to activate appetitive and defensive motivational circuits that coordinate the body's response to stimulation. In general, neuroanatomical models of emotion propose that inputs from the visual sensory cortex and thalamus converge on subcortical structures, particularly the amygdala, which in turn projects to other sites in the limbic brain (e.g., the central gray and the hypothalamus). These projections mediate the somatic and autonomic nervous system innervation of muscles and glands, thereby facilitating vigilance and survival reflex action.

What is currently known about the connections between sensory cues and subcortical motivational structures comes from animal research, particularly from studies of aversive learning in the rat. In this species, as in humans, massive defensive reactions (autonomic and behavioral) are readily evoked by painful stimuli (e.g., electric shock). If aversive stimulation occurs reliably in the context of a previously innocuous stimulus (e.g., a light), features of the defensive behavior come to be evoked when the cue is presented alone. That is, the cue itself activates the defensive system, prompting compensatory actions and fear.

Considerable information is now available about this network's specific neurophysiology (see Davis & Lang, 2003, for an overview). Using anatomical and electrophysiological tools, the chain of probable neural activation can be traced, starting from the input end in the sensory system—proceeding through the necessary connecting structures, defining the links least prodigal in synaptic connections—to the autonomic and motor effectors (Figure 4.1). Input normally passes from the

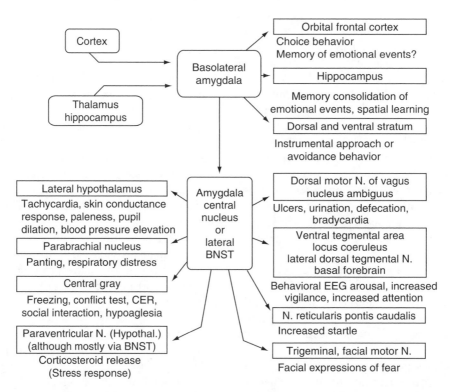

FIGURE 4.1   Inputs and outputs to the extended amygdala that may mediate psychophysiological responses in affective contexts.

sense organs to the sensory cortex, although the most simple sensory information (e.g., lights or tones) may require only thalamic processing (e.g., see the cortical lesioning studies of DiCara, Braun, & Pappas, 1970).

Information from the sensory system proceeds to the amygdala—first to its basolateral and then to its central nucleus. Outputs from the basolateral to the central nucleus and the extended amygdala appear to be critical in the increased processing of emotionally significant stimuli, whether they are pleasant or aversive. Outputs from the extended amygdala in turn project to many of the structures mediating the autonomic and somatic components of overt action. Direct output to the dorsal striatum and indirect output via the orbital frontal cortex appear to be involved in actual avoidance responses. Furthermore, output from *the basolateral nucleus* to the ventral striatum, as well as the orbitofrontal cortex, is likely a contributor to the execution of approach and choice behavior.

This circuitry constitutes motivational systems that are finely tuned to the probability that events will require survival action, e.g., that a remote threat will become an imminent danger, or that a sexual provocation will likely lead to pleasant consummation. In animals, increasing imminence prompts a more general mobilization of the organism, mediated by various neurotransmitters such as acetylcholine, dopamine, norepinephrine, as well as many peptides such as corticotropin releasing hormone (see Davis & Lang, 2003 for an overview). These substances act either within the amygdala or at various central target areas to facilitate neural transmission, and they are associated with increasing intensity of appetitive or defensive motivation (and are roughly correlated with reports of emotional arousal in humans).

TACTICAL RESPONSE

The subcortical circuit involving the amygdala appears to be a general mediator in responding to motivationally relevant cues. Consistent with this role, activation of the amygdala does not define a specific emotional response pattern. Rather, there are independent routes from the central nucleus to different response systems that produce highly varied outputs. For instance, when autonomic (blood pressure) and somatic (freezing) measures of aversive learning were measured in animals, lesion studies have indicated that these conditioned emotional responses are mediated by different structures, with the autonomic response dependent on an intact lateral hypothalamus, and the somatic component requiring an intact midbrain central gray area (Iwata & Ledoux, 1988). Furthermore,

amygdala projections have been implicated in a variety of other aversively motivated responses, i.e., in escape and avoidance learning (Ursin, 1965); in defensive/aggressive behavior (Blanchard & Blanchard, 1977; Roldan, Alvarez-Pelaez, & Fernandez de Molina, 1974), and, as we will examine in more detail later, in augmenting startle reactions (Davis, 1989).

This same defensive system also prompts varied hormonal and autonomic responses. For example, heart rate and blood pressure decrease in response to a conditioned tone (previously accompanied by shock) when animals are physically restrained; on the other hand, these same autonomic responses increase when the conditioned signal is presented to freely behaving animals (Iwata & LeDoux, 1988). The specific response selected—the tactical response in the defensive context—depends on specific contextual elements and previous learning. These findings do not support a hypothesis of immutable autonomic patterns associated with distinct aversive emotional states—fear, anxiety, anger, helplessness (depression?), and the like. They are consistent, however, with the hypothesis that specific aversive response patterns are tactical phenomena, determined by individual and contextual factors, all driven by the same defensive motivational strategy.

EMOTION AND COGNITION

Although emotions prompt reflex reactions mediated by evolutionarily older brain structures, primary reinforcers (e.g., pain) or simple stimulus associates such as tones or lights are often not the cues that engage human affects. Emotion is the companion of cognition—in reflecting on memories, dreaming, or imagining the future—and its processing involves broad cortical activation.

From the cognitive perspective, affective memory images can be thought of as associative networks of information that include encoded units representing a variety of features of an emotional event (e.g., bio-informational theory, Lang, 1979, 1984, 1994a). For instance, a possible cognitive network for a snake fearful individual would include information regarding the visual appearance of the snake, its meaning, and appropriate actions to take upon encountering a snake. That is, some of the linked representations are perceptual (i.e., *stimulus* units that code sensory features of the context, as the color, size, and location of the snake) and others are conceptual (i.e., *meaning* units, such as the proposition that all snakes are dangerous). A novel feature of bio-informational theory is its inclusion of *response* units (procedural knowledge) in the network. Many cognitive models tend to focus on the representation of sensory and semantic information in memory, without considering the necessary representations of associated behavioral outputs. In bio-informational theory, on the other hand, the retrieval of an emotional memory activates response units, which code associated overt actions (e.g., running) and reflex reactions (e.g., heart rate acceleration) that are part of the associative structure of emotional event memories. Response information is linked to input cues on the basis of both unconditioned and conditioned associations. Consistent with the use of these terms in the learning literature, unconditioned responses are innate, hard-wired links between stimulus features (e.g., sudden movement) and a particular action (e.g., startle response), whereas conditioned associations reflect links forged through experience.

WHAT MAKES AN INFORMATION NETWORK EMOTIONAL?

From an information processing perspective, all memories can be considered to be organized as associative networks. In what way then are affective memories different? Emotion networks are unique in that they include direct connections to the same subcortical motivational circuits activated by unconditioned appetitive and aversive stimuli. That is, they activate the same neural systems that mediate the formation of conditioned associations based on primary appetitive or aversive reinforcers. As noted previously, these motivational systems have evolved primarily to direct action, supporting the organisms' drive to survive. Their outputs are therefore those that facilitate information intake, motor recruitment, and action readiness, leading to the centrality of physiological (autonomic and somatic) expression in affective engagement. These reactions, coded as "response units" in the informational network and initiated via subcortical connections to a variety of structures implicated in arousal and action, are the foundation of emotional experience.

PROCESSING THE NETWORK

Network processing can be viewed as an iterative process in which input cues that match some network representations can, depending on the network's collective associative strength, result in activation of the entire network, including the response units. Although the probability of an emotional reaction increases as more network units match the input cues (Lang, 1985), impoverished sensory and conceptual matches, as in narrative descriptions or an evocative picture, can often prompt palpable affect if the association between network units is strong.

Furthermore, networks with high associative strength are more likely to be temporally sustained, with the activated information fed back into the system as a new cue, reactivating response units that mediate somatic and autonomic reflexes. Thus, whereas physiological responses are often considered outputs of emotional processing, their afferents can also serve as input cues. That is, while these cues are not particular to specific affects, they are in this sense "perceived" as James suggested (James, 1894, Lang, 1994b).

Emotional representations can therefore be cued (activated) in numerous ways. They are primitively cued by the external events and actions they represent. In human, these representations are also readily activated by language descriptions, moving and still pictures, and other symbolic stimuli that only resemble, or symbolize, the natural context. When symbolic emotional cues such as pictures are presented in the laboratory context, it is assumed that they engage the same cognitive network and neural circuit as would comparable sensory information in a reality context.

Of course, the observer "knows" that the picture is a symbolic representation, as this context information is associatively present when the network is activated (i.e., "it's only a picture"). Therefore, unlike our gross motor reactions to actual events (e.g., vigorous flight from an attacking animal), autonomic and neuromuscular responses to pictorial representations are muted—an "efferent leakage" that can be measured only by the bioelectric amplifier. In responding to media, the observer generally experiences only a "feeling," a disposition to behave of which there is limited overt evidence (Frijda, 1986). In this view, the media activate the same effector systems that would be engaged by an actual threatening or appetitive event. However, the final path to overt behavior is blocked, "gated out" by context driven inhibitory information.

LOOKING AT PICTURES: EMOTIONAL ENGAGEMENT

Numerous studies in our laboratory and that of others over the past decade have uncovered highly reliable patterns of physiological and behavioral reactions elicited when people view affective pictures (Bradley, Codispoti, Cuthbert, & Lang, 2000; Greenwald, Cook, & Lang, 1989; Lang, Greenwald, Bradley, & Hamm, 1993; Lang, Bradley, & Cuthbert, 2005). Whereas some reactions reflect whether a cue activates the appetitive or defensive system, others are primarily sensitive to the intensity of motivational activation, as illustrated in Figure 4.2.

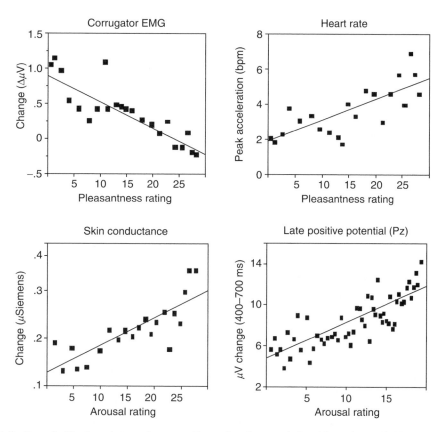

FIGURE 4.2 Distribution of affective pictures in a two-dimensional space defined by ratings of affective valence and arousal, and psychophysiological responses that vary with affective valence (corrugator EMG, heart rate) or affective arousal (skin conductance and cortical event-related potentials).

For instance, facial muscle activity during picture viewing is a marker of whether a cue activates the appetitive or defensive system. Corrugator (frown) muscle activity is reliably heightened for unpleasant pictures, as illustrated, whereas zygomatic (smile) muscle activity is greatest for pictures judged high in pleasantness. Heart rate is also responsive to the specific neural system activated. Unpleasant pictures generally prompt marked deceleration during viewing (recalling the "fear bradycardia" seen in animals), compared to pleasant pictures, as illustrated in Figure 4.2.

Other physiological responses, however, vary primarily with the degree of motivational activation, which is indexed by rated emotional arousal. Thus, skin conductance—an index of activity in the sympathetic nervous system—increases monotonically with increases in rated arousal, regardless of whether a picture is rated as highly pleasant or unpleasant (Figure 4.2). Similarly, event-related potentials (ERPs) measured at the scalp show a distinct, voltage-positive cortical response over the centro-parietal cortex, evoked directly by the picture stimuli that are also positively correlated with stimulus arousal (i.e., it is similarly enhanced for both pleasant and unpleasant arousing pictures) (Cacioppo, Crites, Gardner, & Berntson, 1994; Keil et al., 2002; Cuthbert, Schupp, Bradley, Birbaumer, & Lang, 1998). These measures index the intensity or activation level of the current motivational state, but are silent about which motivational system is dominant (i.e., appetitive or defensive). In the picture-viewing context, these responses presumably reflect heightened attention and preparation for action that is pertinent for both highly appetitive and highly aversive cues.

The results of factor analyses of self-report, physiological, and behavioral measures clearly support a two-factor solution. Pleasantness ratings, heart rate, and facial muscles load on a first *hedonic valence* factor, whereas arousal and interest ratings, viewing time, skin conductance, and cortical ERPs load on a second, *emotional arousal factor*. The cross-loadings for all measures are very low. The data are consistent with the view that reported affective experience is determined in significant part by the individual's motivational state. That is, negative affective valence (unpleasant experience) is associated with activation of the defense system; positive valence (pleasant feelings) is associated with activation of the appetitive system; facial EMG and heart rate index differences in which motivational system is engaged. Reports of emotional arousal are associated with activation of either motivational system, reflecting an increase in incentive strength and organismic mobilization and are reliably indexed by the magnitude of skin conductance reactions and the late positive potential. Taken together, the motivational states elicited by these affective cues (and the somatic, cortical, and autonomic substrates of their perception) appear to be fundamentally similar to those occurring when other complex animals "stop, look, and listen," sifting through the environmental buzz for cues of danger, social meaning, or incentives to appetite.

THE STARTLE REFLEX AND EMOTIONAL PRIMING

The autonomic and somatic outputs reviewed above are evoked directly by the presentation of a picture cue, prompting motivational activation via stored memory representations and their links to subcortical circuits mediating appetite and defense. Another measure of emotional activation can be obtained, however, by presenting a secondary stimulus (i.e., a "startle probe") at some point during the picture cue. This additional stimulus prompts a secondary reflex that is modulated in latency and magnitude by the motivational state evoked by the primary cue.

An abrupt sensory event in almost any modality will prompt a startle response, which consists of a chained series of rapid extensor–flexor movements that cascade throughout the body (Landis & Hunt, 1939). This reaction is a defensive reflex, facilitating escape in many species, and it may still serve a protective function in mammals, (i.e., in avoiding organ injury as in the eyeblink, or in retraction of the head and torso in the full body startle reflex to avoid attack from above) (Li & Yeomans, 1999). In human subjects, sudden closure of the eyelids is one of the first, fastest, and most stable elements in the reflex sequence; in rats, whole-body startle is measured in specially designed cages. Studies involving either animals or humans have found elevated startle amplitude in the presence of cues associated with shock (Bradley, Moulder, & Lang, 2005; Grillon & Davis, 1997; Hamm, Greenwald, Bradley, & Lang, 1993; Lipp, Sheridan, & Siddle, 1994).

Davis (1989, 2000) and Davis et al. (1987) have systematically investigated the neural circuitry underlying potentiation of the startle response during aversive learning in animals. When stimulated by an abrupt noise, the afferent path of the reflex proceeds from the cochlear nucleus to the pontine reticular formation; from there efferent connections pass through spinal neurons to the reflex effectors. This is the basic obligatory circuit, driven by the parameters of the input stimulus (e.g., stimulus intensity, frequency, steepness of the onset ramp). A second circuit, intersecting the primary reflex pathway, determines startle potentiation after fear conditioning. There is now overwhelming evidence that the amygdala is the critical structure mediating this effect. First, there are direct projections from the central nucleus of the amygdala to the reticular site which mediates potentiation (i.e., nucleus reticularis pontis caudalis); second, electrical stimulation of the amygdala's central nucleus enhances startle reflex amplitude; finally, and most important, lesions of the amygdala abolish fear conditioned startle potentiation (Davis, 1989).

The potentiation of the startle reflex in an aversive context reflects activation in some of the same subcortical structures implicated as central in the defensive motivational system. Reflex potentiation in the context of ongoing defensive activation can therefore be considered a case of motivational priming: That is, the induced defensive state of the organism primes (augments) an independently instigated reflex that is connected to the defense system, i.e., the startle response. According to this motivational priming hypothesis (Lang, Bradley, & Cuthbert, 1990, 1997) the magnitude of the defensive startle reflex reflects, in part, the ongoing motivational state of the organism.

When startle probes are administered while subjects view pictures, results have consistently conformed to the motivational priming hypothesis. The startle reflex is potentiated when participants view unpleasant stimuli; moreover, the reflex is reliably inhibited when viewing pictures judged as pleasant (Bradley et al., 2000; Bradley, Cuthbert, & Lang, 1999; Cook, Davis, Hawk, & Spence, 1992; Dichter, Tomarken, Shelton, & Sutton, 2004; Hamm, Cuthbert, Globisch, & Vaitl, 1997; Vanman, Boehmelt, Dawson, & Schell, 1996; Vrana, Spence, & Lang, 1988). These modulatory effects increase with greater activation in these motivational systems, as illustrated in Figure 4.3. However, the direction of effect is opposite for appetitive and defensive activation. When highly arousing unpleasant pictures are probed, the startle reflex is strongly potentiated. Conversely, the most arousing pleasant pictures (e.g., romantic and erotic couples) prompt the greatest startle inhibition (Bradley

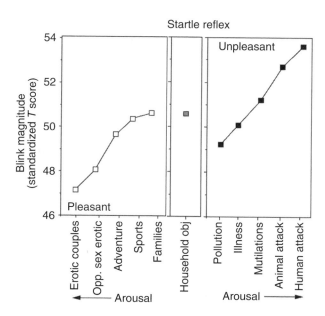

FIGURE 4.3   The magnitude of the reflexive blink response to a startling probe increases as unpleasant pictures become more arousing, but decreases as pleasant pictures become more arousing.

et al.). Thus, in addition to facial EMG and heart rate, modulation of the startle reflex is another, indirect index of whether a picture cue activates the defensive or appetitive motivational system.

ATTENTION AND ACTION

For humans and other animals, the first reaction to a novel cue is a reflexive, directional orientation to the stimulus (Pavlov, 1927). If the input is motivationally irrelevant, this "orienting reflex" rapidly habituates (Sokolov, 1963). Aversive cues, however, initially prompt systemic adjustments that facilitate sustained perceptual processing. For example, an animal orienting to the appearance of a distant predator shows a profound deceleration in heart rate, "fear bradycardia," not found in response to other events (Campbell, Wood, & McBride, 1997). "Freezing"—a statue-like inhibition of movement—accompanies the change in heart rate, along with increased overall sensory acuity. If the predator approaches (shows stalking behavior), somatic and autonomic activation increases progressively, culminating in defensive action.

Interestingly, a similar cascade of initial orienting occurs for the predator. Upon observing potential prey, the predator is likely to freeze, orient, and determine the precise spatial location and obstacles to capture. Humans show similar attention and action readiness when confronted with motivational cues (in life, and in the laboratory) responding reflexively with heightened attention to appetitive and aversive events even if the cues are not actual, but media representations.

Graham (1992) initially proposed that startle reflex inhibition is an index of attentional engagement, and recent research supports the view that attention and emotional arousal are interacting factors in startle reflex modulation (Bradley, Codispoti & Lang, 2006). Thus, startle probes presented in the context of unpleasant pictures that are rated relatively lower in arousal, such as pictures of sad events, pollution, people who are ill, actually prompt relative reflex inhibition compared to less interesting, neutral stimuli (Bradley et al., 2000; Cuthbert, Bradley, & Lang, 1996), suggesting reflex inhibition due to heightened attention. Evidence also suggests that startle reflexes are reduced for all picture contents when attention is initially engaged, and that this attentional inhibition may be greater in both appetitive and defensive activation (Bradley et al., 1993).

We interpret startle inhibition as indicating attention capture that is preferential for all motivationally relevant input. The data suggest that relative reflex inhibition is the modal reaction when attention is engaged, and that this reduced response increases with more interesting and more pleasantly exciting foregrounds. In this view, potentiated startle is the exceptional response, occurring only when attention is focused on very upsetting or threatening stimulus contents. As an aversive cue is more fully processed, defensive activation increases, prompting reflex potentiation, rather than inhibition, for the most arousing unpleasant pictures. The fact that inhibition of motor action (i.e., freezing) is an early initial reaction to a novel stimulus, and that defensive potentiation occurs later (and only to the most arousing unpleasant stimuli) is consistent with a sequence of defensive reactions from attention to action. That is, the initial reaction to threat is inevitably to stop, look, and listen (as prey do when first perceiving a predator in the distance), and only after information is gathered are the tactical responses of fight or flight deployed.

DEFENSIVE ACTIVATION

When a wild rat sees a human at some distance away, the rat freezes in a highly alert, attentive posture. As the human (or other potential predator) gradually approaches, the rat suddenly darts away, if escape is possible. If escape is not possible and the human gets very close, the rat will attack (Blanchard, Flannelly, & Blanchard, 1986). Defensive behaviors become increasingly apparent with a reduction in distance from predators and other dangerous or potentially painful stimuli (Blanchard & Blanchard, 1987). Given an available escape route, proximity is associated with an increased probability of active flight. In the absence of an escape option, the best defense may be attack. When the threat stimulus is distant, however, the rat "freezes and orients toward the predator".

Using concepts introduced by Timberlake (Timberlake, 1993), Fanselow (1991, 1994) has analyzed defensive behavior, describing three stages of increasing prey–predator proximity: (1) preencounter defense, which includes preemptive behavior that occurs in a foraging area where predators were previously encountered, (2) postencounter defense, which includes responses prompted by the detection of a distant predator, and (3) circa-strike defense, which includes behaviors that occur in the region of physical contact or its close imminence. Behavior shifts from preemptive threat vigilance at preencounter, to postencounter freezing and orienting to a specific predator cue, to the circa-strike stage when the organism engages in vigorous defensive action.

Electrical stimulation studies support this conceptualization (Davis & Lang, 2003, p. 414). Mild amygdala stimulation (electrical) first stops ongoing behavior (freezing), prompting bradycardia (Kapp et al., 1990) and EEG activation (Dringenberg & Vanderwolf, 1996). As stimulation increases, the animal becomes more active;

at high levels of stimulation, it vigorously attempts escape from the source of stimulation. Thus, a predator at some distance prompts mild activation of the amygdala, functionally increasing attention. As the predator comes closer, amygdala activation increases, now mediating overt defensive behavior, including escape.

As Fanselow (1991, 1994) proposed the switch from an attentional mode to active defense may involve a switch in activation from ventral to dorsal periaqueductal gray. Bandler and others (cf. Bandler & Shipley, 1994) have shown that the ventral periaqueductal gray projects to cardiovascular centers mediating bradycardia as well as those involving inhibition of the motor system. In contrast, the dorsal periaqueductal gray projects to centers mediating tachycardia and active escape behavior. Assuming a low threshold for projected amygdala activation in ventral periaqueductal gray, we might expect this structure to mediate attentional responses, subsequent to the amygdala's activation by a novel event. If the dorsal periaqueductal gray has a higher threshold for amygdala activation, however, its function would depend on greater activation in the amygdala (e.g., as with predator approach), prompting an abrupt switch from passive vigilance to full-scale action.

Lang et al. (1997) proposed an adaptation of the predator imminence model for explicating human brain and psychophysiological reactions to unpleasant and threatening cues, such as pictures. In the defense cascade model (Figure 4.4), we suggested that humans, when first seated in the psychophysiological laboratory, are functionally similar to an animal at the *preencounter stage*, i.e., moderately alert in an unfamiliar environment. For humans and other animals, presentation of an aversive picture (*postencounter*) prompts focused attention, "freezing," apprehension, and sympathetic arousal. During postencounter, physiological indices of attention at first increase with imminence and severity of the threatened consequence—greater skin conductance, increased heart rate deceleration, and some inhibition of the probe startle reflex. During this period, however, brain and body are also mobilizing for possible action.

One could conjecture that amygdala transmissions to the central gray are increasing with greater arousal (imminence of threat), ultimately switching the impact site from the ventral (freezing) to the dorsal (action) gray. The first motor consequence of this switch may be the change in direction of startle modulation, i.e., from an initial moderate reflex inhibition to reflex potentiation. Startle potentiation then progressively increases in magnitude with the aversiveness of stimuli (as probes occur more proximal to the circa-strike stage in the

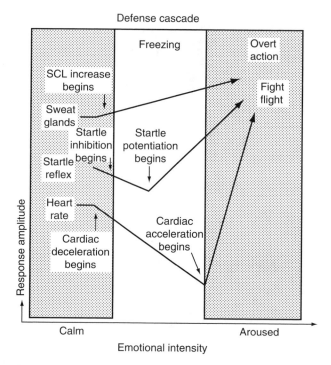

FIGURE 4.4 The defense cascade model describes a cascade of physiological reactions that occur as a threatening context, becomes increasingly more arousing, with changes in skin conductance, startle reflexes, and heart rate occurring at different rates.

animal model). With a further increment in threat the heart rate response also reverses the direction of change from orienting to defense (Graham, 1979, Sokolov, 1963)—from a parasympathetically mediated, fear bradycardia to action mobilization and sympathetically mediated cardiac acceleration.

The biological model of emotion presented here suggests that depending on level of stimulus aversion (threat, apprehension), the set of measured responses to a threat cue will vary with the level of defense system activation. Furthermore, the overt behaviors that may result with increasing imminence (closer to the circa-strike region) could look fearful (i.e., avoid), angry (approach), or, given overwhelming stress and no available coping behavior, hopelessness, and depression.

The model's predator is, of course, engaged in a parallel dance mediated by the appetitive system—first freezing and observing quietly the distant prey (food source), followed by stalking forward slowly, increasingly mobilized for what becomes, at the circa-strike stage, a final approach and attack. Overall, it is a parallel progression from attention to action, with a coincident increment in

appetitive arousal. While there are currently little data on the predator's anticipatory pleasures—joy of the hunt, satisfaction in its consummation—the neurophysiology of the process is likely to be similar to what is observed in defense.

The primitive similarities in appetitive and defensive behaviors suggest that the mediating neural circuits are overlapping and involve many of the same neural structures. Brain imaging studies have supported this view. Thus, although we might expect to find specific reward or fear centers in the brain, more often similar structures are found to be active in both pleasant and unpleasant emotion, and furthermore, variations in activation magnitude are more related to response vigor than to the direction of action. In effect, motive systems may be better conceptualized as circuit patterns of connectivity among brain structures rather than as specific anatomical sites that uniquely determine appetite and defense.

PICTURE PROCESSING AND THE BRAIN

As already noted, appetitive and threatening cues initially capture attention, presumably supporting increased information intake and evaluation of the environment. Research with primates has shown that the amygdala receives projections from all levels of the visual system. Furthermore, the occipital and ventral temporal processing areas of the visual system receive reciprocal projections from the amygdala (Amaral, Price, Pitkanen, & Carmichael, 1992), providing a feedback loop through which motivational activation can modulate processing in both primary and secondary visual centers.

Consistent with this model, viewing affectively engaging pictures results in reliable increases in visual neural activity. Lane et al. (1997), using PET, and Lang et al. (1998), using fMRI, presented evocative picture stimuli to normal participants and recorded blood flow changes in the caudal cortex. Compared to affectively neutral pictures, participants showed dramatically larger areas of activation (in the lateral occipital, posterior parietal, and inferior temporal cortex) for pictures with emotionally evocative content, and stronger changes in the BOLD signal. Subsequent fMRI research (Bradley et al., 2003) found that activation in these areas of the visual system progressively increases, covarying monotonically with the judged emotional arousal of picture cues—regardless of whether they were pleasant or unpleasant. Moreover, PET research with phobic participants has also found enhanced occipital activation when viewing pictures of specific fear objects (Fredrikson,

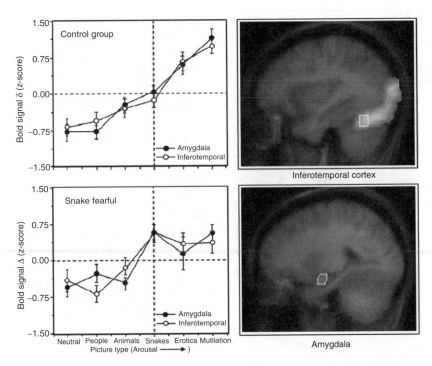

FIGURE 4.5 Neural activity in the bilateral amygdala and fusiform cortex (as measured by fMRI) is increased when viewing affectively arousing pictures, with clear covariation in activity between these neural structures.

Wik, Annas, Ericson, & Stone-Elander, 1995; Fredrikson et al., 1993).

If enhanced activity in the visual cortex is mediated by differences in amygdala activation, one expects a close covariation in neural activity in these structures. Recent data corroborate that activation of the amygdala covaries closely with the activation in the inferotemporal, visual processing area (Sabatinelli, Bradley, Fitzsimmons, & Lang, 2005) (Figure 4.5) with both highly pleasant and highly unpleasant pictures eliciting significantly greater activity in both structures. Furthermore, both sites increase in activation as rated emotional arousal increases. Finally, both structures showed heightened activity when snake phobics view pictures of feared stimuli, relative to the response of nonfearful participants (Figure 4.5). Replicating other studies, pleasant, as well as unpleasant, cues significantly affected amygdala activity, indicating that this subcortical structure is involved in the neural circuitry underlying both appetitive and defensive motivation.

At this stage of imaging research, very few motivationally relevant brain structures appear to be activated only in pleasant or unpleasant emotion. Possible exceptions are the nucleus accumbens and medial prefrontal cortex (Sabatinelli, Costa, Versace, Bradley, & Lang, 2007) that have been implicated in studies of a proposed

"reward" system and shown to be active in response to positive emotional pictures, e.g., of loved ones (Aron, Fisher, Mashek, Strong, & Brown, 2005), or pictures showing use of addictive substances (David et al., 2005). In a recent study, we examined these structures, specifically comparing the response to highly pleasant and highly unpleasant pictures (Sabatinelli et al., 2007). For unpleasant pictures (snakes, mutilated bodies), there was no significant activation in either structure. In contrast, for pleasant pictures (romantic or erotic couples), strong activation of both the nucleus accumbens and the medial prefrontal structures were reliably observed. Because pleasant and unpleasant pictures were equivalent in emotional arousal, the specific activation for pleasant and appetitive content is intriguing.

SUMMARY AND CONCLUSION

We have proposed that emotions are founded on appetitive and defensive motivational circuits in the brain that evolved because they promoted the survivability of individuals and enhanced the probability of their gene propagation. Originally, these circuits were activated in the context of cues that, on the one hand, signaled imminent danger or pain, and on the other, the availability of food or opportunities for sexual congress or nurturance of progeny. In this sense, emotions are based on reflexive action dispositions that increment vigilance and perceptual processing, and mobilize the organism for either the active acquisition of reward or, alternatively, for defense of the body's integrity. In complex animals, who are adaptable to context and capable of inhibition, delay, and future planning, however, gross behavioral reactions (such as vigorous approach or withdrawal) are not automatic or inevitably consequent (Elliot & Thrash, 2002).

Nevertheless, less evident preparatory reflexes, both somatic and autonomic, are automatically engaged in the context of motivational cues. Thus, in studies of emotional perception, the reflex reactions of human participants' parallel responses found when animal subjects are confronted with rewarding or threatening stimuli. Furthermore, these brain and body responses are reliably correlated with the hedonic valence and intensity of reported emotions. Finally, neural imaging studies indicate that the brain structures and circuits known to mediate survival reflexes in animal subjects are also engaged when human participants confront emotionally arousing stimuli, supporting the hypothesis that emotion is built on basic motivational circuits in the brain that have evolved to sustain life.

ACKNOWLEDGMENTS

This research was supported in part by grants from the National Institute of Mental Health (P50 MH 72850) and National Institute of Dental Research (DE 13956).

REFERENCES

Amaral, D. G., Price, J. L., Pitkanen, A., & Carmichael, S. T. (1992). Anatomical organization of the primate amygdaloid complex. In J. P. Aggleton (Ed.), *The amygdala: Neurobiological aspects of emotion, memory and mental dysfunction* (pp. 1–66). New York: John Wiley & Sons, Inc.

Aron, A., Fisher, H., Mashek, D. J., Strong, G., Li. H., & Brown, L. L. (2005). Reward, motivation, and emotion systems associated with early-stage intense romantic love. *Journal of Neurophysiology, 94,* 327–337.

Bandler, R., & Shipley, M. T. (1994). Columnar organization in the midbrain periaqueductal gray: Modules for emotional expression? *Trends Neuroscience, 17,* 379–389.

Blanchard, R. J., & Blanchard, D. C. (1977). Aggression behavior in the rat. *Behavioral Biology, 21,* 197–224.

Blanchard, R. J., & Blanchard, D. C. (1987). An ethoexperimental approach to the study of fear. *Psychological Records, 37,* 305–316.

Blanchard, R. J., Flannelly, K. J., & Blanchard, D. C. (1986). Defensive behavior of laboratory and wild *Rattus norvegicus. Journal of Comparative Psychology, 100,* 101–107.

Bradley, M. M. (2000). Emotion and motivation. In J. T. Cacioppo, L. G. Tassinary, & G. Bernston (Eds.), *Handbook of psychophysiology* (pp. 602–642). New York: Cambridge University Press.

Bradley, M. M., Codispoti, M., Cuthbert, B. N., & Lang, P. J. (2000). Emotion and picture perception: Emotion and motivation I: Defensive and appetitive reactions in picture processing. *Emotion, 1,* 276–298.

Bradley, M. M., Codispoti, M., & Lang, P. J. (2006). A multiprocess model of startle modulation during affective perception. *Psychophysiology, 43,* 486–497.

Bradley, M. M., Cuthbert, B. N., & Lang, P. J. (1993). Pictures as prepulse: attention and emotion in startle modification. *Psychophysiology, 30,* 541–545.

Bradley, M. M., Cuthbert, B. N., & Lang, P. J. (1999). Affect and the startle reflex. In M. E. Dawson, A. Schell, and A. Boehmelt (Eds.), *Startle modification: Implications for neuroscience, cognitive science and clinical science* (pp. 157–186). Stanford, CA: Cambridge University Press.

Bradley, M. M., Moulder, B., & Lang, P. J. (2005). When good things go bad: The reflex physiology of defense. *Psychological Science, 16,* 468–473.

Bradley, M. M., Sabatinelli, D., Lang, P. J., Fitzsimmons, J. R., King, W., & Desai, P. (2003). Activation of the visual cortex in motivated attention. *Behavioral Neuroscience, 117,* 369–380.

Cacioppo, J. T., Crites, S. L. Jr., Gardner, W. L., & Berntson, G. G. (1994). Bioelectrical echoes from evaluative categorizations: I. A late positive brain potential that varies as a function of trait negativity and extremity. *Journal of Personality and Social Psychology, 67,* 115–125.

Campbell, B. A., Wood, G., & McBride, T. (1997). Origins of orienting and defense responses: An evolutionary perspective. In P. J. Lang, R. F. Simmons, & M. T. Balaban (Eds.), *Attention and orienting: Sensory and motivational processes* (pp. 41–67). Hillsdale, NJ: Lawrence Erlbaum Associates.

Cook, E. W., Davis, T. L., Hawk, L. W., & Spence, E. L. (1992). Fearfulness and startle potentiation during aversive visual stimuli. *Psychophysiology, 29*(6), 633–645.

Cuthbert, B. N., Bradley, M. M., & Lang, P. J. (1996). Probing picture perception: Activation and emotion. *Psychophysiology, 33,* 103–111.

Cuthbert, B. N., Schupp, H. T., Bradley, M. M., Birbaumer, N., & Lang, P. J. (2000). Brain potentials in affective picture processing: Covariation with autonomic arousal and affective report. *Biological Psychology, 52,* 95–111.

David, S. P., Munafo, M. R., Johansen-Berg, H., Smith, S. M., Rogers, R. D., Matthews, P. M., et al. (2005). Ventral striatum/nucleus accumbens activation to smoking-related pictorial cues in smokers and nonsmokers: A functional magnetic resonance imaging study. *Biological Psychiatry, 58,* 488–494.

Davis, M. (1989). Neural systems involved in fear-potentiated startle. *Annals of the New York Academy of Sciences, 563,* 165–183.

Davis, M. (2000). The role of the amygdala in conditioned and unconditioned fear and anxiety. In J. P. Aggleton (Ed.), *The amygdala* (Vol. 2, pp. 213–287). Oxford, UK: Oxford University Press.

Davis, M., Hitchcock, J., & Rosen, J. (1987). Anxiety and the amygdala: Pharmacological and anatomical analysis of the fear potentiated startle paradigm. *Psychology of learning and motivation* (Vol. 21). New York: Academic Press.

Davis, M., & Lang, P. J. (2003). Emotion. In M. Gallagher & R. J. Nelson (Eds.), *Handbook of psychology* (pp. 405–439). Hoboken, NJ: Wiley.

DiCara, L., Braun, J. J., & Pappas, B. (1970). Classical conditioning and instrumental learning of cardiac and gastrointestinal responses following removal of neocortex in the rat. *Journal of Comparative and Physiological Psychology*, *73*, 208–216.

Dichter, G. S., Tomarken, A. J., Shelton, R. C., & Sutton, S. K. (2004). Early- and late-onset startle modulation in unipolar depression. *Psychophysiology*, *41*, 433–440.

Dickinson, A., & Dearing, M. F. (1979). Appetitive–aversive interactions and inhibitory processes. In A. B. Dickinson, R. A. Boakes (Ed.), *Mechanisms of learning and motivation* (pp. 203–231). Hillsdale, NJ: Erlbaum.

Dringenberg, H. C., & Vanderwolf, C. H. (1996). Cholinergic activation of the electrocorticogram: An amygdaloid activating system. *Exp. Brain Res.*, *108*, 285–296.

Elliot, A. J., & Thrash, T. M. (2002). Approach–avoidance motivation in personality: Approach and avoidance temperaments and goals. *Journal of Personality and Social Psychology*, *82*, 804–818.

Fanselow, M. S. (1991). The midbrain periaqueductal gray as a coordinator of action in response to fear and anxiety. In A. Depaulis & R. Bandler (Eds.), *The midbrain periaqueductal gray matter: Functional, anatomical and neurochemical organization* (pp. 151–173). New York: Plenum Publishing Co.

Fanselow, M. S. (1994). Neural organization of the defensive behavior system responsible for fear. *Psychonomic Bulletin Review*, *1*, 429–438.

Fredrikson, M., Wik, G., Annas, P., Ericson, K. A. J., & Stone-Elander, S. (1995). Functional neuroanatomy of visually elicited simple phobic fear: Additional data and theoretical analysis. *Psychophysiology*, *32*, 43–48.

Fredrikson, M., Wik, G., Greitz, T., Stone-Elander, S., Ericson, K. A. J., & Sedvall, G. (1993). Regional cerebral blood flow during experimental phobic fear. *Psychophysiology*, *30*, 126–130.

Frijda, N. H. (1986). *The emotions*. New York: Cambridge.

Graham, F. K. (1979). Distinguishing among orienting, defense, and startle reflexes. In H. D. Kimmel, H. van Olst, & F. Orelebeke, (Eds.), *The orienting reflex in humans. An international conference sponsored by the scientific affairs division of the North Atlantic Treaty Organization* (pp. 137–167). Hillsdale, NJ: Lawrence Erlbaum Associates.

Graham, F. K. (1992). Attention: The heartbeat, the blink, and the brain. In B. A. Campbell, H. Hayne, & R. Richardson (Eds.), *Attention and information processing in infants and adults* (pp. 3–29). Hillsdale, NJ: Lawrence Erlbaum Associates.

Greenwald, M. K., Cook, E. W. III, & Lang, P. J. (1989). Affective judgment and psychophysiological response: Dimensional covariation in the evaluation of pictorial stimuli. *Journal of Psychophysiology*, *3*, 51–64.

Grillon, C., & Davis, M. (1997). Fear-potentiated startle conditioning in humans: Effects of explicit and contextual cue conditioning following paired vs. unpaired training. *Psychophysiology*, *34*, 451–458.

Hamm, A. O., Cuthbert, B. N., Globisch, J., & Vaitl, D. (1997). Fear and startle reflex: Blink modulation and autonomic response patterns in animal mutilation fearful subjects. *Psychophysiology*, *34*, 97–107.

Hamm, A. O., Greenwald, M. K., Bradley, M. M., & Lang, P. J. (1993). Emotional learning, hedonic changes, and the startle probe. *Journal of Abnormal Psychology*, *102*, 453–465.

Iwata, J., & LeDoux, J. E. (1988). Dissociation of associative and nonassociative concomitants of classical fear conditioning in the freely behaving rat. *Behavioral Neuroscience*, *102*, 66–76.

James, W. J. (1894). The physical basis of emotion. *Psychological Review*, *1*, 516–529.

Kapp, B. S., Wilson, A., Pascoe, J. P., Supple, W. F., & Whalen, P. J. (1990). A neuroanatomical systems analysis of conditioned bradycardia in the rabbit. In M. Gabriel & J. Moore (Eds.), *Neurocomputation and Learning: Foundations of Adaptive Networks* (pp. 55–90). New York: Bradford Books.

Keil, A., Bradley, M. M., Hauk, O., Rochstroh, B., Elbert, T., & Lang, P. J. (2002). Large-scale neural correlates of affective picture-processing. *Psychophysiology*, *39*, 641–649.

Konorski, J. (1967). *Integrative activity of the brain: An interdisciplinary approach*. Chicago: The University of Chicago Press.

Landis, C., & Hunt, W. (1939). *The startle paradigm*. New York: Farrar and Rinehart.

Lane, R. D., Reiman, E. M., Bradley, M. M., Lang, P. J., Ahern, G. L., Davidson, R. J., et al. (1997). Neuroanatomical correlates of pleasant and unpleasant emotion. *Neuropsychologia*, *35*, 1437–1444.

Lang, P. J. (1968). Fear reduction and fear behavior: Problems in treating a construct. In J. M. Schlien (Ed.), *Research in psychotherapy* (Vol. 3, pp. 90–103). Washington, DC: American Psychological Association.

Lang, P. J. (1979). Presidential address, 1978: A bio-informational theory of emotional imagery. *Psychophysiology*, *16*, 495–512.

Lang, P. J. (1984). Cognition in emotion: Concept and action. In C. E. Izard, J. Kagan, & R. B. Zajonc (Eds.), *Emotions, cognitions, and behavior* (pp. 192–228). New York: Cambridge.

Lang, P. J. (1985). The cognitive psychophysiology of emotion: Fear and anxiety. In A. H. Tuma & J. D. Maser (Eds.), *Anxiety and the anxiety disorders* (Vol. 3, No. 2, 3–62, pp. 131–170). Hillsdale, NJ: Erlbaum.

Lang, P. J. (1994a). The motivational organization of emotion: Affect–reflex connections. In S. VanGoozen, N. E. Van De

Poll, & J. A. Sargeant (Eds.), *Emotions: Essays on emotion theory* (pp. 61–93). Hillsdale, NJ: Erlbaum.

Lang, P. J. (1994b). The varieties of emotional experience: A meditation on James-Lange theory. *Psychological Review, 101*, 211–221.

Lang, P. J. (1995). The emotion probe. *American Psychologist, 50*, 372–385.

Lang, P. J., Bradley, M. M., & Cuthbert, B. N. (1990). Emotion, attention, and the startle reflex. *Psychological Review, 97*, 377–395.

Lang, P. J., Bradley, M. M., & Cuthbert, B. N. (1997). Motivated attention: Affect, activation and action. In P. J. Lang, R. F. Simons, & M. F. Balaban (Eds.), *Attention and orienting: Sensory and motivational processes* (pp. 97–135). Inc, NJ: Lawrence Erlbaum Associates.

Lang, P. J., Bradley, M. M., & Cuthbert, B. N. (2005). International affective picture system (IAPS): Affective ratings of picture and technical manual. Technical Report A-6, University of Florida, Gainesville, Florida.

Lang, P. J., Bradley, M. M., Fitzsimmons, J. R., Cuthbert, B. N., Scott, J. D., Moulder, B., et al. (1998). Emotional arousal and activation of the visual cortex: An fMRI analysis. *Psychophysiology, 35*, 1–13.

Lang, P. J., Greenwald, M. K., Bradley, M. M., & Hamm, A. O. (1993). Looking at pictures: Affective, facial, visceral and behavioral reactions. *Psychophysiology, 30*, 261–273.

Li, L., & Yeomans, J. S. (1999). Summation between acoustic and trigeminal stimuli evoking startle. *Neuroscience, 90*, 139–152.

Lipp, O. V., Sheridan, J., & Siddle, D. A. (1994). Human blink startle during aversive and nonaversive Pavlovian conditioning. *Journal of Experimental Psychology, Animal Behavior Processes, 20*, 380–389.

Mackintosh, N. J. (1983). *Conditioning and associative learning.* New York: Oxford.

Mandler, G., Mandler, J. M., Kremen, I., & Sholiton, R. (1961). The response to threat: Relations among verbal and physiological indices. *Psychological Monographs, 75*, Whole No. 513.

Masterson, F. A., & Crawford, M. (1982). The defense motivation system: A theory of avoidance behavior. *The Behavioral and Brain Sciences, 5*, 661–696.

Mehrabian, A., & Russell, J. A. (1974). *An approach to environmental psychology.* Cambridge, MA: MIT Press.

Ortony, A., Clore, G. L., & Collins, A. (1988). *The cognitive structure of emotions.* Cambridge: Cambridge Press.

Osgood, C., Suci, G., & Tannenbaum, P. (1957). *The measurement of meaning.* Urbana, IL: University of Illinois.

Pavlov, I. P. (1927). *Conditioned Reflexes.* Oxford, UK: Oxford University Press.

Reeves, B., & Hawkins, R. (1986). *Masscom: Modules of masscommunication.* Chicago, IL: Science Research Associates.

Roldan, E., Alvarez-Pelaez, R., & Fernandez de Molina, A. (1974). Electrographic study of the amygdaloid defense response. *Physiology & Behavior, 13*, 779–787.

Sabatinelli, D., Bradley, M. M., Fitzsimmons, J. R., & Lang, P. J. (2005). Parallel amygdala and inferotemporal activation reflect emotional intensity and fear relevance. *NeuroImage, 24*, 1265–1270.

Sabatinelli, D., Costa, V. D., Versace, F., Bradley, M. M., & Lang, P. J. (2007). Pleasure rather than salience activates human nucleus accumbens and medial prefrontal cortex. *Journal of Neurophysiology, 98*, 1374–1379.

Schlosberg, J. (1952). The description of facial expression in terms of two dimensions. *Journal of Experimental Psychology, 44*, 229–237.

Schneirla, T. (1959). An evolutionary and developmental theory of biphasic processes underlying approach and withdrawal. In M. Jones (Ed.), *Nebraska symposium on motivation* (pp. 1–42). Lincoln: University of Nebraska Press.

Shaver, P., Schwartz, J., Kirson, D., & O'Connor, C. (1987). Emotion knowledge: Further exploration of a prototype approach. *Journal of Personality and Social Psychology, 52*, 1061–1086.

Sokolov, E. N. (1963). *Perception and the conditioned reflex.* Oxford, UK: Pergamon Press.

Tellegen, A. (1985). Structures of mood and personality and their relevance to assessing anxiety, with an emphasis on self-report. In A. H. Tuma & J. D. Maser (Eds.), *Anxiety and the anxiety disorders* (pp. 681–706). Hillsdale, NJ: Lawrence Erlbaum.

Timberlake, W. (1993). Behavior systems and reinforcement: An integrative approach. *Journal of Experimental Analysis of Behavior, 60*, 105–128.

Ursin, H. (1965). Effect of amygdaloid lesions on avoidance behavior and visual discrimination in cats. *Experimental Neurology, 11*, 298–317.

van Lawick-Goodall, J. (1971). *In the shadow of man* (pp. 172). Boston: Houghton Mifflin.

Vanman, E. J., Boehmelt, A. H., Dawson, M. E., Schell, A. M. (1996). The varying time courses of attentional and affective modulation of the startle blink reflex. *Psychophysiology, 33*, 691–697.

Vrana, S. R., Spence, E. L., & Lang, P. J. (1988). The startle probe response: A new measure of emotion? *Journal of Abnormal Psychology, 97*, 487–491.

Subcortical Processes

5 Dopamine and SEEKING: Subcortical "Reward" Systems and Appetitive Urges

Jaak Panksepp and Joseph Moskal

CONTENTS

INTRODUCTION

During the past three decades it has become increasingly clear that dopamine (DA) contributes heavily to brain mechanisms that allow animals to pursue a great variety of positive rewards and contributes to "reinforcing" effects that mediate appetitive learning. This incentive-motivational system mediates a general form of appetitive eagerness as well as a variety of addictions, from drugs to sex, from shopping to social bonding, and even the delights of music. How are all these varieties of motivational effects to be explained? This has become much easier now that a remarkable general-purpose emotional–motivational SEEKING system has been revealed during the past half century. It is one that appears to have been evolutionarily derived to mediate the appetitive desire to search for, to find, and to harvest the diverse fruits of the world needed for survival.

Animals and humans readily self-activate (i.e., self-stimulate) this brain system in addictive ways. Although most investigators, steeped in behavioristic traditions, have sought to explain the function of this system with traditional hand-me-down concepts such as *reward* and *reinforcement*, ethological observations are more consistent with the view that this is a positively motivated emotional action system—a SEEKING system—that helps animals pursue diverse aspects of their livelihood with eagerness. It mediates a certain kind of emotional–behavioral presence that includes vigorous investigatory sniffing, exploration, foraging and in hunting species, predatory urges (Figure 5.1). This primary-process substrate for desire, constructed of many neurochemistries, interacts with higher secondary and tertiary cognitive mechanisms that gradually generate positive expectancies and hopes about the world (Figure 5.2). The SEEKING system does not mediate the pleasure of sensation but the anticipatory exhilaration and euphoria of pursuing sensory pleasures. This system, like all emotional systems, has abundant attributes (Figure 5.3), and each could be used as an anchor for a more limited partial view of the system than the integrated whole.

Brain dopamine circuitry currently figures most prominently in understanding this experience-expectant

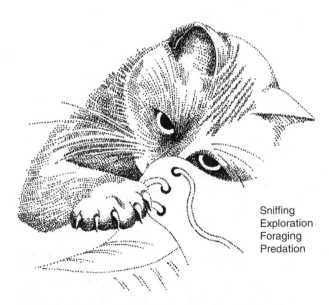

Sniffing
Exploration
Foraging
Predation

FIGURE 5.1 The SEEKING system in action, with some major behavioral manifestations highlighted. Reprinted from Figure 8.6 of *Affective neuroscience, the foundation of human and animal emotions* by Panksepp, 1998a. With permission of Oxford University Press.

SEEKING system and its many addictive urges. But there are many brain dopamine systems and much more than dopamine in the constitution of the SEEKING system (Figure 5.3). With respect to dopaminergic contributions, most of the above effects are more dependent on the subset of brain DA pathways that project upward from the ventral tegmental area (VTA) to the ventral striatal regions than the more lateral nigrostriatal ones arising from the adjacent substantia nigra *pars compacta* that innervate the dorsal striatal regions. The VTA DA projections (i.e., the mesocortical and mesolimbic DA pathways) terminate in frontal cortical and ventral striatal areas, especially the nucleus accumbens. Modern discussions of the specific natural (i.e., evolved) functions of mesolimbic and meso-cortical DA systems remain a controversial topic, which is commonly disconnected from relevant historical issues, such as the nature of self-stimulation reward and the various instinctual behaviors that can be evoked by electrically stimulating this circuitry. Also, there is currently little substantive discussion of the affective psychological states that accompany such brain stimulation, with people persistently using old behavioristic terms such as reward and reinforcement without adequately considering the types of natural psychobehavioral patterns this system mediates. Subjective experience remains a taboo topic among neurobehaviorists who typically conduct the animal brain and behavioral work needed to understand such neural systems (Panksepp, 1998a, 2005). From an affective neuroscience view, there exist many distinct rewards and punishments in the brain, and the process of reinforcement is mediated, in part, by affective changes within the nervous system (Panksepp, 2008).

Thus, there is a vast conceptual chasm between investigators pursuing behavioral neuroscience in animal models and those who would like to reap basic psychological and clinical insights from this work. The aim of this chapter is to provide an overview of the emerging ideas and ongoing controversies in this area and to articulate a unifying idea that puts the mass of available data into an evolutionary framework. This framework envisions that a complex dopamine energized SEEKING/foraging/expectancy emotional system can explain most of the motivational effects that have been described in the literature. This view, one of the oldest in the field, may have the strength to reconcile the many existing theoretical positions and advance linkages to clinical and other kinds of psychological thinking. This framework may help (a) to unify the many suggested functions of this so-called brain reward system, (b) to clarify the psychological role of brain DA in the emergence of positive affect and addictive urges, and (c) to promote a better understanding of learning—the topic that is of

The dopamine part of it

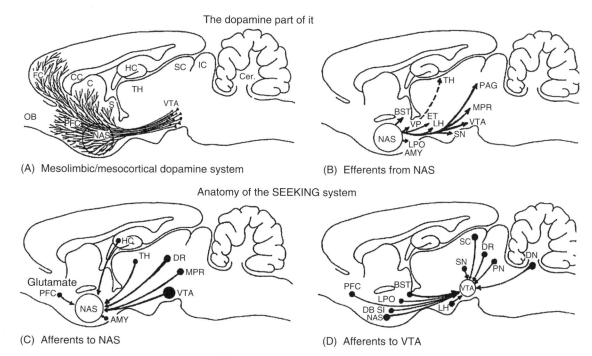

(A) Mesolimbic/mesocortical dopamine system

(B) Efferents from NAS

Anatomy of the SEEKING system

(C) Afferents to NAS

(D) Afferents to VTA

FIGURE 5.2　Schematic diagrams of the dopamine based SEEKING system on a sagittal depiction of the rat brain. (A) Ascending projections of A10 dopamine (DA) neurons localized in the ventral tegmental area (VTA) innervating to limbic regions including the nucleus accumbens septi (NAS), the mesolimbic DA system as well as cortical regions the mesocortical DA system. (B) Major efferent projections of the NAS. (C) Afferent projections to the NAS. (D) Afferent projections to the VTA. Abbreviations—AMY, amygdala; BST, bed nucleus of stria terminalis; C, caudate–putamen; CC, corpus callosum; DB, diagonal band of Broca; DN, dentate nucleus; DR, dorsal raphe; ET, entopeduncular nucleus; FC, frontal cortex; HC, hippocampus; IC, inferior colliculus; LH, lateral hypothalamus; LPO, lateral preoptic area; MPR, mesopontine reticular nuclei; OB, olfactory bulb; PAG, periaqueductal gray; PFC, prefrontal cortex; PN, parabrachial nucleus; SC, superior colliculus; SI, substantia innominata; SN, substantia nigra; TH, thalamus; VP, ventral pallidum. From "The role of nucleus accumbens DA in motivated behavior: A unifying interpretation with special reference to reward-seeking," by S. Ikemoto and J. Panksepp, 1999, *Brain Research Reviews*, *31*, p. 6.

greatest interest to neurobehaviorists. At the same time, readers should recognize the abundant debate that continues in the field (for overview, see Berridge, 2007).

BRAIN PLEASURE AND SEEKING URGES

Let us first focus on the nature of such brain emotional/motivational systems from a historical perspective. In 1953, Robert G. Heath discovered that he could evoke feelings of pleasure in humans by electrically stimulating specific parts of the brain (for an overview, see Heath, 1996). The epicenter for this effect was the septal area at the very front of the neural tube where the cerebral hemispheres mushroom laterally. Independently, in 1954 Olds and Milner discovered that animals would voluntarily apply electrical stimulation to specific parts of the brain, and the first brain area from which this type of *self-stimulation* was observed was also the septal area. Self-stimulation

from those sites is, behaviorally, comparatively relaxed and methodical; animals typically make one response to obtain one electrical stimulation of the brain (ESB). However, it was rapidly discovered that an even more vigorous, behaviorally "energized" self-stimulation could be obtained from the lateral hypothalamus (LH). Animals pressed the lever many more times than they needed to get all available ESBs when the stimulation activated the massive longitudinally coursing trajectory of the *medial forebrain bundle* (MFB) that connected the mesencephalon with ventral and medial frontal regions of the brain. This LH-MFB system was eventually found to be confluent with and strongly modulated by brain DA, especially fibers emerging from the VTA and terminating in the nucleus accumbens and frontal cortical regions. The underlying motivational-affective states underlying septal and LH-MFB forms of self-stimulation were probably quite different at an affective level. In order to understand

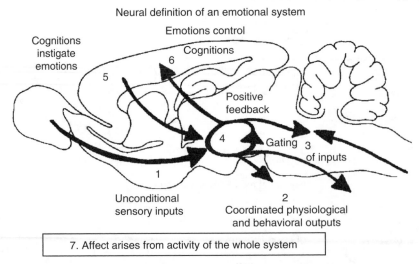

FIGURE 5.3   Proposed neural definition of an emotional system. These seven neural interactions are postulated to be character-istics of all major primary-process emotional systems of the brain. (1) A few sensory stimuli can unconditionally access emotional systems, but most inputs are developmentally learned; (2) emotional systems can promote coherent instinctual action outputs, as well as (3) modulate sensory inputs. (4) Emotional systems have positive-feedback components that can sustain emotional arousal after precipitating events have passed. Also, (5) these systems can be modulated by cognitive inputs and (6) can modify and channel cognitive activities. (7) The important criterion that emotional systems create affective states is not included, but it is assumed that arousal of the whole executive circuitry for each emotion is essential for elaborating emotional feelings within the brain, perhaps by interacting with other subneocortical brain circuits for organismic-visceral self-representation. Adapted from Figure 3.3 of *Affective neuroscience the foundation of human and animal emotions* by Panksepp, 1998a. With permission from Oxford University Press.

what DA contributes to these systems, we must conceptu-alize the larger functional networks in which DA oper-ates. For instance, a host of other neural components must be considered in the SEEKING network (Figure 5.2). One of the most recently identified neuropeptides would be orexin, concentrated in dorsolateral areas where ESB induced appetitive behavior is best evoked, which con-trols brain arousal in global ways, partly by facilitating all other major arousal systems of the brain including norepinephrine, histamine, acetylcholine, and dopamine itself (Sakurai, 2007).

It is now generally accepted that there are several types of self-stimulation in the brain. For instance, on the basis of discrimination experiments using stimulation of several distinct brain reward sites as conditional stimuli, the internal states evoked by stimulation of the medial septal area appear substantially different from that aroused during the frantic self-stimulation of MFB sites (Stutz, Rossi, Hastings, & Brunner, 1974). Specifically, ESB administered at different electrode sites along a psy-chologically homogeneous functional system, such as the rewarding aspects of the MFB, cannot be discriminated well, but stimulation applied to the MFB is comparatively easily discriminated from septal stimulation. On the basis

of our limited understanding of the corresponding sub-jective experiences in humans, it is septal stimulation, rather than MFB stimulation, that is more likely to be provoking pleasurable responses such as specific sexual feelings (Heath, 1996). MFB stimulation seems to gener-ate some other type of hedonically positive excitement (Panksepp, 1985; Fiorino & Phillips, 1999).

The psychological properties of these systems are of considerable interest to clinicians, but neurobehaviorists working on animals are understandably hesitant to par-ticipate in such discussions, preferring to maintain their focus on cellular and behavior-only levels of analyses. After all, emergent subjective experiences, such as affec-tive states, which probably arise from complex and wide-scale network dynamics, must be inferred since they cannot be monitored directly by any of the measurement tools of science. We will argue that it is essential to *theo-retically* entertain such possibilities, since many of the evolved network functions of the brain, such as emergent affective states, are essential for making sense of how the brain really works. Indeed, we may find that affective con-ceptions of certain globally acting state-control systems will shed more new light on how the brain mediates psychiatrically relevant mental disturbances than the currently popular information-processing models that envision the underlying substrates to be affectively vacuous learning systems.

Although there is abundant evidence that dopamine can facilitate learning (Kelley, 2004; Rosenkranz & Grace, 2002; Wise, 2004), the most abundant support for such views has typically come from *correlative* neurophysiological investigations of DA neurons in behaving animals (Schultz, 2006). However, dopamine *mediation* of learning may be secondary to the affective-behavioral properties of the kind of appetitive emotional arousal that the dopamine energized seeking system mediates, which we would suggest is the primary evolutionary function of this multifaceted system. Much of the evidence for reward learning signals comes from electrophysiological experiments which tell us much about what dopamine neurons are listening to (Figure 5.2C and D), but essentially nothing clear about what dopamine systems actually do upstream (Figure 5.2A) and downstream (Figure 5.2B) in the regulation of mind and behavior (Berridge, 2007; Panksepp, 2005). Essentially this same criticism could be made for the increasingly popular "incentive-salience" view of this appetitive system (Berridge, 2007). Dopamine arousal may be permissive in promoting the gating of reward related inputs (e.g., attributes 3 and 6 in Figure 5.3). This reflects a common mistake in neuroscience, where important parts of systemic functions are envisioned as the whole (Bennett & Hacker, 2003). The SEEKING system is here envisioned as an image of the integrated whole while most other approaches are dealing with important parts.

The unconditional (i.e., evolutionary-instinctual) function of the mesolimbic and mesocortical DA circuitry is to promote a special kind of psychobehavioral coherence—an exploratory/seeking urge (Figure 5.1) that allows various learning systems, probably situated in other parts of the brain (Figure 5.2), to operate more efficiently. Rather than being the governor of learning, the brain SEEKING system helps interface certain instinctual action urges, which promote specific types of affects, with environmentally linked learning processes that are represented mostly in other parts of the brain (e.g., Figure 5.3, attribute 6). In other words, dopamine activity may promote learning without directly mediating associative processes. This chapter will frame the functions of the mesolimbic/mesocortical DA system in terms of this psychobiological theory that has now been advanced for more than a quarter century (Panksepp, 1981 to present), with comparatively little impact on neuroscience because it asserts that unconditional emotional, affectively experienced, action urges are critically important aspects of understanding this system. In any event, a large number

of variants of this viewpoint, usually of more limited scope (with no psychological-experiential features), are penetrating into the mainstream of behavioristic thought. All these lines of thinking go back to preneuroscientific conceptions of incentive motivation (Bindra, 1974; Bolles, 1972; Toates, 1986). For a discussion of the more fine-grained neuroscientific details of this view, see Alcaro, Huber, & Panksepp (2007), and for closely related complementary views, see Berridge (2007).

Here we provide a more general overview, as we continue to advance the idea that it is as important for us to conceptualize the global psychobehavioral functions of this emotional network in the regulation of organismic actions as to focus on careful behavioral analyses and fine details such as the firing of individual dopamine cells during various behavioral tasks (Schultz, 2006). This dopamine based reward system has an intrinsic capacity to promote instinctual behaviors characterized by eager, forward-directed, investigatory activities (i.e., the characteristics of the appetitive, rather than consummatory, phases of goal-directed behaviors) that help construct well-blended affective-cognitive expectancies accompanied by positively valenced appetitive urges. Obviously such an experience-expectant system must participate in learning, but the more fundamental function is to promote a certain type of unconditional psychobehavioral attitude toward appetitive survival issues. Thus, this emotional system also participates in many stress-related and negative incentive behavioral processes, as in organismic seeking of safety. In a sense the SEEKING system may be the primordial emotional system of the brain for it participates to some degree in all the other emotional responses of the organism. We think the evidence is strong that this system operates in a global, energetic state-control manner, rather than one that is simply designed for "information processing" (Ciompi & Panksepp, 2004; Panksepp, 2003). The global functions of such evolved brain systems can frame, and provide interdisciplinary meaning, for the more molecular animal-brain studies.

In sum, we explore how DA participates in the global psychobiological processes that have been designed to unconditionally generate appetitive eagerness and to conditionally help construct the psychobehavioral competence to effectively anticipate future rewards. From the cognitive-emotional perspective, it was previously envisioned as a general-purpose expectancy system: Panksepp (1981). This type of functional conceptualization seems not to be congenial for many in modern behavioral neuroscience because it emphasizes instinctual, affective, and broad network properties of brain systems rather than the more discrete "information-processing," learning aspects. It is also premised on the not yet widely acknowledged assumption that a "network-doctrine" is as important for understanding the intrinsic psychobiological functions of the brain/mind as the "neuron-doctrine." Various brain emotional systems operate in global mass-action ways, where neuronal activities are contributing to "pressures" for action, rather than simply "processing" incoming information. A telling empirical point, too often ignored, is that single-cell recordings of DA neurons show that most are firing in similar ways, as if their collective "force" is more important than what any single cell is doing. This, of course, does not mean that such action systems do not promote information processing. They surely do, but much of that transpires in systems far upstream (e.g., hippocampus and neocortex) from the motivational urges that drive the core psychobehavioral motivational capacities of organisms, which are better studied ethologically than in the context of complex learning tasks.

We believe that such global brain/mind viewpoints may be more meaningfully related to human affective processes relevant for understanding primary-process motivational urges and psychiatric imbalances than traditional learning-system views (Kapur, 2003; Panksepp, 2005). Such globally operating state-control systems construct those "energetic" experiential-organic processes that provide a grounding for the cognitive details of mental life. Although all emotional systems promote learning, it is in the analysis of their evolved capacity to regulate actions and psychobehavioral coherence that the most psychiatrically useful principles may emerge (Panksepp, 2004, 2006). For instance, many neuropeptides (and the biochemical machinery for their biosynthesis and regulation) control and regulate ethologically distinct psychobehavioral attitudes that are disturbed in major psychiatric disorders (Panksepp & Harro, 2004). In this context, Freud's assertion in *Beyond the Pleasure Principles* (1920/1959, p. 61) was prescient: "No knowledge would have been more valuable as a foundation for true psychological science than an approximate grasp of the common characteristics and possible distinctive features of the instincts." Because the ethological concept of emotional instincts was never integrated into learning theory, we still have difficulty conceptualizing how many brain systems help establish motivational coherence.

CRITIQUE OF THE CONCEPTUAL CONUNDRUMS IN THE FIELD

On the basis of classical behavioristic assumptions, which (mis)guided and constrained psychological thinking through the middle of the 20th century (Panksepp, 2005,

2008), the most common interpretation of the MFB self-stimulation phenomenon was that the essential neural substrates of reward and reinforcement had been discovered. In fact, those concepts, so easy to define in operational terms, are devilishly difficult to define in terms of evolved brain functions. Although such behaviorist views remain prominent and influential to the present day (Robbins & Everitt, 1999; Wise, 2004), there is no assurance yet that a distinct unitary reinforcement process exists in the brain at least as it was classically envisioned as a glue-like promotor of stimulus–response and stimulus–stimulus associations. As a result of the persistence and sustained hegemony of those instinct-free traditions in *behavioral neuroscience*, impressively detailed but conceptually limited behavioristic theories continue to be constructed from electrophysiological studies of single-unit activity changes in dopaminergic neurons in motorically restrained animals during various learning tasks (Schultz, 2000, 2002, 2006). Such viewpoints are based more on the study of discrete operant responses rather than the study of the ethologically coherent behavior patterns promoted by these neuronal networks. Obviously, it is of foremost importance to understand the unconditional-instinctual aspects of brain systems, than in how they participate in learning. Results from such neurophysiological studies are finally converging with ideas, alluded to above, that have existed in the neuroethological literature for some time (Panksepp, 1971–2008).

Still, there remains abundant disagreement about the types of terminologies we should use to discuss such issues. Thus, exactly how does this reward or reinforcement system (again, both terms being delightfully ambiguous conceptually, if not operationally) achieve the remarkable feat of orchestrating appetitive urges and associated cognitive processes? Such questions lie at the heart of the many theoretical positions that remain prominent in this field.

At present, there are several rather distinct ways to envision how organisms manage their affairs through the various neural tools with which they have been endowed by evolution. Perhaps the most controversial view is that internally experienced *affect* is an important component of behavioral control (Panksepp, 2005, 2008). Most of the other theories rely on more neuro-mechanistically ruthless approaches that do not attribute any experienced psychological functions to complex neural network activities.

The *psychoethological* view advanced here asserts that organisms are intrinsically "active" because they have an extensive evolutionary repertoire of raw instinctual-emotional abilities, which include various primary-process affective experiences as part of these genetically provided tools for coping with various archetypal survival needs. It aspires to consider how internally experienced affective states help regulate behavior through learning. In other words, world events (e.g., conditional stimuli) achieve much of their power in behavioral control by recruiting instinctual neuro-affective emotional-action processes in an anticipatory fashion. In contrast, the more classical neuro-behaviorist view still does not acknowledge any such experiential brain emotional functions. Most behavioral neuroscientists do not acknowledge "active-affective organism" concepts, and only partly because they are harder to envision in an ultra-mechanistic way. However, if such brain functions do exist, as seems evident from abundant lines of evidence (Panksepp, 1998a, 2003, 2005), then one dismisses such evolutionary possibilities at the peril of never really understanding how the brain operates. A better appreciation of this dilemma may eventually promote an open-mindedness that currently continues to be in short supply in behavioral brain research.

Although there is abundant room for scientifically rigorous consilience between such views, the continuing disagreements and debates (Berridge, 2007) have deep roots in the ontological biases of the past (Panksepp, 2008). Those whose thinking is guided by the study of the natural psychobehavioral tendencies of animals tend to view various emotive systems in terms of the general-purpose evolutionary tools that nature provided to facilitate the pursuit of resources essential for survival. Investigators, whose thinking is guided more by general-purpose associative learning theories of the Anglo-American behavioristic tradition, tend to envision most brain systems in terms of the informational operations and the salience of incentives that allow animals to navigate the many vagaries of their external worlds. Both viewpoints have much to offer, but there have been few attempts to blend these perspectives into a harmonious whole, such as a general-purpose SEEKING system. The historical reasons for this are not hard to find.

CONFRONTATION BETWEEN BEHAVIORISM AND ETHOLOGY

Let us briefly consider some of the past intellectual forces that continue to haunt theorizing in this academic arena. In the 1950s, there was a major confrontation between the behaviorist and ethological visions of how to understand the systematic behavior patterns of organisms (Burkhardt, 2005). The former was based on traditional reinforcement-based learning theories (that have led to many current computational information-processing views of associative processes). The latter

was based on the view that evolution had provided organisms with a variety of basic tools for existence, best reflected in the natural behavior patterns exhibited in the wild. The latter approach eventually led to the working hypothesis that a variety of distinct mind–brain operating *systems* exist that control global psychobehavioral states of organisms (Panksepp, 1998a). The debate came to a head in a confrontation between Daniel S. Lehrman and Konrad Lorenz (Lehrman, 1953). No conciliatory resolution of that debate ever emerged (see Burkhardt, 2005, for an excellent historical perspective). Partly because of such conceptual polarities, we are left to this day, with many narrow views of the types of living skills the ascending DA circuits, that "energize" the extensive MFB self-stimulation SEEKING system, provide for animals. The continuing force of a learning-centered behaviorism can also be highlighted by the fact that an early ethological antecedent to the present views, that rewarding brain-stimulation unconditionally facilitates approach behaviors (Glickman & Schiff, 1967), has largely been ignored in recent neuro-behavioristic theory development.

Another consequence of this controversy is disagreement about how we should talk about and conceptualize the roots of animal behavior. Current learning-system views mandate traditional third-person observational language, where the focus is more on the relatively easily conceptualized attributes of the environment (e.g., incentive salience) that guide behavior than the internally evolved processes (e.g., seeking urges) that energize the coherent expressions of instinctual psychobiological tendencies. That such internal urges exist seems certain, but neurobehaviorists are typically not intellectually prepared to think or talk about them. This is partly because a behavior-only approach requires that science must forever conceptualize knowledge in third-person, externalized terms, while an ethological, especially a psychoethological, approach has the option (admittedly rarely taken) to conceptualize brain functions from more internal, psychodynamic, and affective perspectives, which can be related straightforwardly to human motivational and psychiatric concerns (Panksepp, 1998a, 2004, 2005, 2006). Because of advances in neuroscience, ethological and behavioristic reinforcement views can finally be synthesized in ways that may benefit both, and also open up stronger linkages to human concerns.

Much may be gained if we develop the mental flexibility to view the intrinsic psychobehavioral systems conjointly from both the external information-processing vantages and internal psychodynamic perspectives. A reasonable assumption is that the evolution of many higher brain mechanisms was based upon the preexisting capacity of neural tissue to represent affectively the internally coded, organically-based survival needs of organisms. At some point in evolutionary "deep time" such internal needs were surely unconscious (Berridge & Robinson, 2003). However, at some point in brain evolution, such neural functions led to the emergence of a proto-consciousness—instinctually driven affective states that represented the primal needs and urges of organisms (Panksepp, 2005). Affect is a very useful heuristic for providing simplified information about survival concerns to the higher cognitive apparatus for effective decision making (Panksepp, 2008).

Affective experience presumably solidified as a routine brain capacity when organisms needed added flexibility in their behavioral choices. In this evolutionary transition, the various instinctual-affective urges of organisms became comingled with the emerging higher cognitive systems that were evolutionarily emerging to help parse the seemingly infinite *differences* in the world. It is in the recognition of the evolutionary layering of brain–mind processes and blending of these phases of brain–mind evolution that a new synthesis—a reconciliation of seemingly polar viewpoints—may be achieved. In any event, that is the synthesis to which we aspire here.

BRIEF SYNOPSIS OF SELF-STIMULATION REWARD

Before proceeding further with these difficult issues, let us first briefly share a historical synopsis of the three major phases of inquiry into the nature of self-stimulation reward during the past 50 years.

FIRST PHASE OF SELF-STIMULATION RESEARCH (1954–EARLY 1970s)

The first two decades of work clarified the general neuroanatomy and behavioral characteristics of self-stimulation reward. Although stimulation along the MFB corridor could reinforce various behaviors, there were many behavioral anomalies, including rapid extinction and weak secondary reinforcement characteristics, that challenged investigators to generate new theoretical perspectives that ranged from multiprocess views (Deutsch, 1963) to unified incentive views (Trowill, Panksepp, & Gandelman, 1969).

As it became increasingly clear that self-stimulation reward had unusual properties that did not strictly simulate the effects of conventional rewards, investigators started to look more closely at the specific motivated behaviors

exhibited by animals. It was soon noted that animals would exhibit an enormous number of consummatory behaviors during free administration of such stimulation, and for a short time there was some hubris about the possibility that multiple motivational systems could be discovered that led animals to eat, drink, gnaw, hoard, retrieve babies, attack other animals, and so forth (Wise, 1968). However, this hope was eventually demolished by a series of influential experiments performed by Valenstein, Cox, and Kakolewski (1970) which indicated that all of these outwardly distinct motivated behaviors could be transformed from one to another simply by the appropriate arrangement of experiential factors. For example, if food was taken away from "stimulus-bound feeders," all animals started to exhibit alternative behaviors (e.g., drinking or gnawing) that effectively competed with the original behaviors, even if the originally removed goal-object was returned.

Valenstein et al. asserted that the brain reward substrate that was being studied was entirely "plastic" and its functions were guided by learning principles. Research on the diverse motivational properties of MFB stimulation ceased. Only a few insisted that this brain substrate could be conceptualized in terms of a unified emotional/appetitive model that could explain the diversity of observable behavioral manifestations (Panksepp, 1971, 1982a, 1986, 1992). Essentially, the claim was that this was the fundamental substrate that all the specific motivations, like hunger and thirst, use to recruit the investigatory and appetitive phases of behavior. When this intrinsic (i.e., evolved) function of the brain interacted with "world events," it helped establish behaviorally eager *expectations* about when rewards are available (Panksepp, 1981, 1982a). In philosophical parlance, the system unconditionally mediated "intentions in action" and only conditionally, "intentions to act."

This view readily explains why activities of so many neurons in the MFB trajectory correlate with the foraging activities of animals (Hamburg, 1971) and exhibit the capacity to anticipate forthcoming rewards (Olds, 1977). Very similar anticipatory changes in rat DA neurons have now been found in animals self-administering heroin (Kiyatkin & Rebec, 2001). All these findings are congruent with our original hypothesis that this system was more important for appetitive eagerness than consummatory rewards (Panksepp, 1981). However, our original foraging/expectancy interpretation was so far from the reward/reinforcement mainstream that it was largely ignored. It did not fit prevailing learning-theory biases. Moreover, the interests of most investigators shifted at that time, a quarter of a century ago, to the newly discovered *neurochemical* substrate for such behaviors—ascending brain DA systems. In other words, while the MFB is a very complex network of multiple neural components, the possibility emerged that DA circuitry, which coursed along the MFB trajectory, was the most important reward learning component. As a dopamine view of brain reward gained ascendancy, the intellectual controversy of motivational specificity and nonspecificity of the self-stimulation substrate, which engaged the previous generation, seemed ever less relevant. We think that was a mistake, for the older views pointed rather clearly to a new interpretation of the evolved functions of this neural circuitry (Panksepp, 1971, 1981), and variants of those conclusions are only now emerging into the limelight (Berridge & Robinson, 1998; Schultz, 2002).

Second Phase: The DA Pharmacology Years (Early 1970s–Early 1990s)

There had been some early hope that the discovery of well-organized sets of neurons using norepinephrine (NE) as their neurotransmitter might explain self-stimulation reward. As it turned out, NE is a general arousal system with little affective or motivational specificity. The discovery of brain DA and the subsequent clarification of ascending DA pathways (Ungerstedt, 1974) led to an explosion of research demonstrating the importance of DA in self-stimulation reward, with considerable initial controversy over whether these systems participated more in the sensory or motor aspects of reward sustaining behaviors.

Wise (1982) galvanized interest in new theoretical model building, by vigorously advancing the view that DA-secreting neurons constituted a fundamental substrate for pleasurable affective hedonics. He along with many students and other colleagues also solidified the idea that this was a core circuit for the mediation of a variety of drug addictions (Wise & Bozarth, 1987). In response to his seminal 1982 article on the topic, only a few argued for alternative views. Panksepp (1971, 1981, 1982a) suggested that the intrinsic function of this circuitry was well reflected in the characteristic behavior patterns evoked by stimulating the system, that is, forward, investigatory behaviors with abundant sniffing and the apparent seeking of reward objects. The claim was that an evolutionarily ingrained, affectively positive foraging urge was sustaining self-stimulation along the MFB of the brain (Panksepp, 1982b).

Since then, it has become increasingly evident that even though the stimulation of the DA system was hedonically positive, it was not the same type of affect as generated by the consumption of food and water. Rather, it resembles the effects produced by psychostimulants such as amphetamine and cocaine, which are also exquisitely effective in increasing exploratory behaviors at mild doses and obsessive stereotypies and compulsive grooming at high doses. In any case, it came to be generally agreed that the brain substrates of psychostimulant addiction, and other addictions as well, were closely aligned with those that mediated MFB reward, where the operational concept of reward often helped mask, rather than clarify, our conceptual ignorance (see Salamone & Correa, 2002, for a useful discussion).

Investigators who continued to be entranced by the possibility that self-stimulation reward might actually be simulating a pleasure-reward type process were eventually convinced by their own experiments that this type of ESB did not promote gustatory pleasure responses (Berridge & Valenstein, 1991). This epiphany led to their repackaging of the classical *appetitive-consummatory* behavior distinction into the synonymous but psychologically more provocative *wanting–liking* categories (Robinson & Berridge, 1993). This has now had widespread impact on conceptualizing psychobiological processes that may underlie addictive processes in the brain (Robinson & Berridge, 2003) even though these authors take pains to note that their psychological terms have no conscious psychological implications (Berridge & Robinson, 2003). The wanting concept was gradually amplified into the "incentive salience" view of DA function (Berridge & Robinson, 1998). From our perspective this is only a single attribute (albeit an important and now theoretically well-developed one) of a larger set of attributes (*vide infra*) that define and characterize all basic emotional systems (Figure 5.3, Panksepp, 1981, 1982a, 1986, 1998a, 2005).

Third Phase: DA Cell Neurophysiology (Late 1990–Present)

The discovery of ascending DA systems in the mammalian brain, along with the discovery that this system promotes most addictive behaviors, galvanized an impressive research tradition that has progressed independently of the earlier controversies. Advances in neuroscience have permitted investigators to study the single-cell activities of neurochemically specified neurons, such as the firing of DA cells, and develop techniques for monitoring the release of DA in the terminal fields with various in vivo techniques (e.g., voltammetry and dialysis). The characterization of exactly when DA cells are firing and releasing their contents in the context of learning and other behaviors has yielded many findings that are hard to embed in a simple reward–pleasure scheme.

At the single-cell level, DA neurons generally tend to fire more (i.e., to burst, which is accompanied by DA release: Cooper, 2002; Hyland, Reynolds, Hay, Perk, & Miller, 2002) when animals are anticipating reward rather than when they are consuming rewards. Unexpected rewards are especially effective in provoking DA neuron firing. This has led to a "reward prediction error" theory of DA function (Schultz, 2002, 2006), based largely on correlational rather than causal data, which states that DA systems fire when reward contingencies or the patterns of reward change. Let us try to envision this process from the internal psychobehavioral "point-of-view" of an active organism. Seeking urges should be aroused whenever there are unexpected goodies in the environment. The seeking of rewards should be tightly linked to, and integrated with, brain systems that encode environmental events in ways to maximize the probability of obtaining future rewards. This requires several psychobiological processes to be promoted concurrently—invigoration of investigatory-foraging tendencies, amplification of relevant perceptual processes (i.e., heightened incentive salience), and the facilitation and perhaps solidification of knowledge structures related to these sensory-motor activities (Figures 5.2 and 5.3). In short, the "reward prediction error-signal" hypothesis and the "foraging/seeking" views are compatible, more piecemeal, descriptions of what may be happening—one focusing on organisms from the outside (i.e., how the system responds to the patterning of external rewards), the other more from the inside (i.e., how evolution designed brain processes to optimally obtain the fruits of the environment). However, our ethological emotional view links up more readily and effectively with human psychological and psychiatric issues.

AFFECTIVE NEUROSCIENCE STRATEGY

Of course, it is understandable that neurobehaviorists who subscribe to the dictum that brain functions can only be legitimately described in subjectively neutral (i.e., objective), third-person terms are bound to resist terminologies that grant animals intrinsic psychobiological abilities. We believe this is rapidly becoming a counterproductive stance, especially when it comes to a discussion of the intrinsic emotional operating systems of the brain that have powerful affective consequences for the experiences of both humans and other animals (Panksepp, 2005). Of course, the traditional behavioral reply to such assertions has been that *there is no way we can ever see into the minds of other animals*. Such limits of objective observational methods are, of course, formally true in the study of many of the hidden aspects of nature (from subatomic particles to global force fields such as gravity), and certainly an excellent warning when it comes to making any assertions about individually acquired cognitive experiences (i.e., we have very inadequate mindscopes to probe the thoughts of individual animals). However, we would submit that it is currently shortsighted when it comes to class-general emotional operating systems that may mediate emotional feelings shared by many species of organism, including humans who can give us propositional self-reports. The only "mind-reading" we need to do at that level is to interpret the categorical primary-process emotional-affective status of the animals, which can be monitored using traditional behavioral approach–avoidance measures, rather than making any claims about secondary or tertiary processes (i.e., their thoughts about their emotional states).

With dramatic advances in our understanding of the neurochemistries of emotional systems and development of relevant psychopharmacologies (Panksepp & Harro, 2004), these working hypotheses can now be empirically evaluated in humans who can provide verbally compelling affective self-reports. Also, as we study the natural emotional behaviors of other animals, we may eventually develop empirical tools that will allow us to harvest comparable, albeit nonintentional, affective state feedback from other animals by studying their emotional behavior patterns, especially their vocalizations (Panksepp, 1998; Knutson, Burgdorf, & Panksepp, 2002), some of which are proving to be highly linked to the anatomies and neurochemistries of the seeking system (Burgdorf, Knutson, & Panksepp, 2000; Burgdorf, Knutson, Panksepp, & Ikemoto, 2001a; Burgdorf, Knutson, Panksepp, & Shippenberg, 2001b; Burgdorf & Panksepp, 2006; Burgdorf, Wood, Kroes, Moskal, & Panksepp, 2007). Thus, we would suggest that in the future, published behavioral neuroscience studies be encouraged to discuss their brain findings not only from the traditional external (i.e., objective) point of view, but also from more inferential internal (subjective) perspectives (Panksepp, 2005).

A relaxation of our positivistic scientific guard (that we can never know about the emotional feelings of other animals) has the potential to naturalize and humanize neuroscience research in ways that may reap scientific, psychiatric, and cultural benefits (Panksepp, 2007). The recognition that there are extensive functional systems in the brain that represent the internally experienced needs and urges of animals can realistically simplify our conceptual understanding of animal behaviors, although clarification of the underlying neural details of such complex networks as the SEEKING system remains an enormous undertaking (Alcaro et al., 2007; Di Chiara, 2002; Ikemoto & Panksepp, 1999). In any event, other animals, just like humans, probably seek to maximize positive affective states and minimize negative ones—they, in their cognitively simple anticipatory ways, and we humans, with all the cognitive complexity, the profound hindsight and foresight that we can muster. With their own more limited cognitive powers, other organisms can also seek desirable (affectively positive) and avoid undesirable (affectively aversive) events in advance of their appearance. The complexity of each species' higher cortical association areas (e.g., working memory regions of the dorsolateral prefrontal cortex) determines how far ahead in time members of each species can envision events. Humans can obviously plan far ahead in their desire to obtain favorable outcomes and minimize unfavorable ones, but these cognitive capacities do not appear to create basic affects. Raw affective experience appears to be an ancient subcortical function of the primary-process emotional systems of the brain (Panksepp, 2005, 2007).

Internal affective experiences probably facilitate the guidance of long-term behavioral choices. The seeking/wanting system that helps mediate exploration, appetitive eagerness, and intense interest in the resources of the world (Figure 5.1) is such a system. From a behaviorist view, it may help animals adapt to "reward prediction errors" (Schultz, 2000, 2006), even though that is a rather abstruse way to say something that can be expressed more plainly. But such conceptual simplification can only be achieved if we are willing to take a more internally-centered, intentional stance—one that recognizes that there is some type of very primitive self-centeredness (i.e., intentions-in-action) to emotional and motivational operating systems of the brain (Panksepp, 1998a, 2003).

Such views may require behavioral neuroscientists to confront the nature of the core self, perhaps an implicit, neurosymbolic type of SELF (e.g., Simple Ego Type Life form, postulated by some: Panksepp, 1998b, 2000, 2002, 2003). Such an intrinsic neurosymbolic representation of the organism, laid out in visceral and motor-action coordinates, could be a "ground" process for brain representations of organismic needs and desires. The possibility that the feeling component, which helps guide behavior, was achieved by affectively valenced emotional operating systems is evolutionarily plausible. Although clearly an intellectual challenge for most behaviorists, it is certainly possible that such a self-centric view may be ontologically correct for all mammals. Although often difficult to address empirically, the goal of scientific epistemologies is to reveal ontologically correct views of reality. In behavioral neuroscience, as well as in human evolutionary psychology (Panksepp & Panksepp, 2000), this requires a clear vision of the types of psychobehavioral operating systems—evolutionarily provided functional tools—that are foundational for organismic existence within the brain (Panksepp, Knuston, & Burgdorf, 2002).

With no consideration of coherent psycho-neuro-evolutionary positions, the tsunami of positivistic "facts" may continue to delay the emergence of functionally well-integrated forms of knowledge in psychologically relevant functional neuroscience. This, in our estimation, has been happening in the study of brain reward and brain DA systems. However, as flaws in classical behavioristic ideas have been revealed—for instance the possibility that reinforcement is fundamentally affective (Panksepp, 2005, 2007)—recently there has been a growing willingness to entertain new theoretical ideas, largely based on a flood of new evidence from modern technologies. Since there is presently such a growing mass of relevant data concerning DA functions that cannot be covered in this short chapter (Alcaro et al., 2007; Ikemoto & Panksepp, 1999; Kelley & Berridge, 2002; Nestler, 2005; Robbins & Everitt, 1999; Robinson & Berridge, 2003), we selectively focus on several major theoretical views about the motivational consequences of brain dopamine that have recently emerged: (a) the reward error-prediction signal hypothesis, (b) the wanting/liking distinction, (c) the response facilitation perspective, and (d) the response switching and novelty detection viewpoints. In our estimation, all of these views are congruent with the unifying hypothesis that the extended DA-illuminated lateral-hypothalamic/MFB continuum constitutes a coherently operating seeking system of the brain—it provides a coherent image of the "whole" which easily incorporates the more limited "parts." As we summarize the above views, we also argue that the seeking-euphoria approach to understanding brain-stimulation reward effectively sets the stage for a better understanding of the major addictive processes of the brain.

CURRENT PANDEMIC OF DOPAMINE THEORIES

Before summarizing this integrative seeking hypothesis, we emphasize that the available models need not be in competition with each other. To move the field forward, we need to be as clear about issues on which there may be agreement as on those where disagreement prevails. To help put issues into context, older historical perspectives will be highlighted as needed.

PREDICTIVE REWARD SIGNAL AND REWARD PREDICTION ERROR-SIGNAL HYPOTHESIS

This learning-theory behaviorist perspective, advanced by Schultz (2000, 2002, 2006), is based on (a) the consistent tendenc,y of DA neurons to briefly burst in response to unexpectedly rewarding events and novel, attention-grabbing events, followed by a rapid diminution of responding with repeated stimulus presentations; (b) as these cells stop responding to the unexpected presentation of rewards, they gradually become responsive to stimuli that predict rewarding events; and (c) these cells are then inhibited by the omission of rewards. Although the evidence for this view comes almost exclusively from dopamine neuron firing, which reflects inputs into the system, the theory is premised on the assumption that those changes also reflect what the dopamine system is doing downstream. Namely, as already noted, it is promoting a view about what dopamine does in the brain based on empirical observations of what this system is listening too, and hence it could easily be confusing neurophysiological correlates with neurochemical causes (Berridge, 2007; Panksepp, 2005).

Many similar neurophysiological observations, rarely acknowledged, were made three decades ago by a discover of self-stimulation reward (Olds, 1977). Olds spent the last phase of his career asking which areas of a rat's brain exhibited the first signs of appetitive conditioning using a simple classical-conditioning paradigm (tones paired with delivery of food). As summarized elsewhere (Panksepp, 1981, 1998a, Figures 15 and 8.3, respectively), the lateral hypothalamic continuum—where the most vigorous forms of self-stimulation are evoked—yielded the first signs of appetitive conditioning. This work was initiated before DA neurons had been anatomically and electrophysiologically characterized. Even though it did not tell us about the properties of dopamine cells, it indicated that there are an enormous number of neurons in the brain that have such learning abilities.

Olds's work is still informative about how appetitive learning is represented in the brain. His work should diminish eagerness to impute too much functional specificity to the dopaminergic aspects of this extended system. The lesson to be drawn from Olds's work is that an enormous number of neurons, in widespread brain areas, exhibit appetitive conditioning. Thus, it is premature to imply that correlated electrophysiological responses should be taken as indices of *causal* processes. Although all scientists appreciate such injunctions, we are perplexed that so many cognitive neuroscientists have been captivated by Schulz's dazzling correlational work.

However, such correlations are much more widely represented in the nervous system than is presently widely recognized, and there is little reason to believe that most are the causes rather than the consequences of learning. In any event, such neuronal changes would be expected from a system whose main function is to unconditionally facilitate resource acquisition. In fact, Olds's work suggested that we could readily conceptualize much of the extended lateral hypothalamic self-stimulation continuum as an appetitive motivation system (as opposed to an epicenter for consummatory reward or reinforcement). The "expectancy/SEEKING" view was among the first to emphasize that distinction (Panksepp, 1981, 1986).

The reward prediction error-signal hypothesis has arisen from the behaviorist learning and information-processing views of how brain functions should be analyzed. Nevertheless the ethologically based, emotional-systems perspective also provides a robust and complementary viewpoint on the integrated evolutionary function of this circuitry. Such global ethological views can be easily linked to information-processing views (Panksepp, 1986). For instance, MFB arousal with ESB facilitates theta activity in the hippocampus. This is essential for translating short-term information input into long-term memories and for establishing spatial maps and habit structures which guide foraging activities (see forthcoming discussion about hippocampal theta rhythm, elaborating this issue). This perspective leaves open the possibility that the actual reinforcement signal that solidifies learning (assuming such a signal truly exists in the brain) may be more closely linked with the offset of foraging urges (e.g., when glutamate systems are activated at the termination of DA burst firing), rather than directly to the DA release. This counter-intuitive possibility (at least from a direct DA learning-signal perspective) is congruent with the mass of data implicating facilitated glutamatergic transmission in learning. It also immediately raises the possibility that the now widely assumed DA "learning signal" is more of a correlated feature of neural change in relevant networks that shape resource seeking, rather than instructive signals that directly govern learning. Although dopamine may promote the efficiency of working memory processes (Goldman-Rakic, 1999), it may only serve a permissive role in the creation of learning.

In short, although proponents of the reward prediction error-signal hypothesis have provided a computationally tractable learning theory-type explanation for DA cell firing (Schultz, 2006), proponents of learning and "teaching signal" views typically overlook ethological evidence indicating that DA promotes sensory-motor arousability of foraging urges. From this latter viewpoint, DA largely recruits psychobehavioral resources that permit distant learning networks to operate more efficiently. When cognitive expectancies have been established in the higher cortical networks, downward influences (presumably glutamatergic) then provide feedback onto the subcortical seeking urges to sustain optimally focused foraging. Although DA can help promote learning by promoting foraging, it may have comparatively little direct effect on mediating the details of learning. In other words, since self-initiated actions bring animals in contact with relevant features of the environment, it is to be expected that this system promotes many opportunities to optimize the animal's knowledge base.

If we consider an automobile analogy, VTA DA neurons appear to be that part of the overall system that correspond to fuel flow in the system, allowing organisms to efficiently speed up search strategies, as they seek resources. Just as drivers familiarize themselves in new neighborhoods by utilizing the accelerator, brain DA may serve a similar role in allowing new learning to propel the forward-directed, investigatory seeking "energies" of the animal. Behavioral efficiency and steering functions are presumably provided by dynamically flexible patterns of DA release that are initially influenced unconditionally by sensory events but which rapidly come to be controlled by emerging cognitive structures. As animals shift from flexible foraging patterns to more habitual responses, there may be a shift of behavioral control from VTA-based DA circuits to the more lateral and dorsal nigrostriatal "habit" systems (Ikemoto & Panksepp, 1999). Schultz's work has made little distinction between these flexible and more habitual response patterns. In sum, even though learning will eventually be represented in the neuronal activities of the broader network (just as the flow of gas through the carburetor will change systematically as the driver navigates familiar terrain), many of the resulting DA changes may be the consequences rather than the causes of learning.

Instead of seeking major reinforcement or learning signals within the dynamics of DA networks, it may be more productive to consider how such an evolved foraging process links up with the causal learning mechanisms, as in the hippocampus and neocortex (Figures 5.2 and 5.3). In fact, there is one such neurophysiological mechanism, widely ignored by dopamine-intrigued learning theorists, that could be a major contributor to the dopamine associated information integration. This is the hippocampal theta rhythm that is regulated by ascending pathways that course through the MFB on their way to the septal area (Vertes & Kocsis, 1997). The relationship of theta to hippocampal information processing has been extensively documented (Pavlides, Greenstein, Grudman, & Winson, 1988), and this rhythm is tightly synchronized to the investigatory sniffing of animals instigated by the lateral hypothalamic reward or "expectancy/seeking" arousal (Rossi & Panksepp, 1992). Although brain DA is not essential for the manifestation of theta in the hippocampus, animals without dopamine exhibit very few theta bursts, presumably because of their exploratory inactivity (Whishaw et al., 1978). Since brain DA can facilitate the intensity of the theta rhythm (Miura, Ito, & Kadokawa, 1987), the learning/reinforcement that has been attributed to DA neurons may largely reflect feedback consequences of the learning process as opposed to the causes, as is assumed in the Schultz model.

In sum, most of the impressive correlational data harvested by Schultz and colleagues may be explicable from the view that the globally operating DA system that invigorates search-investigatory-seeking patterns simply establishes the essential neurobehavioral preconditions for other learning and memory systems to operate: for instance, those in the hippocampus as well as frontal cortical networks that elaborate reward-expectancy and foresight capacities of the brain (Rolls, 2005).

INCENTIVE SALIENCE AND THE WANTING–LIKING DISTINCTION

Because of anomalies with the simple consummatory-pleasure views of self-stimulation reward, Robinson and Berridge (1993) postulated that brain DA systems mediate "wanting"-type processes in the brain. To a substantial extent, this is a more delimited semantic variant of the expectancy/seeking concept. However, they proceeded to emphasize that the psychoneurological process that characterized their view was the postulated capacity of DA systems to promote "incentive salience." This concept essentially suggests that external stimuli associated with reward become more capable of attracting appetitive behaviors (Berridge & Robinson, 1998). This elaboration, important as it is theoretically (e.g., it could be linked to the gating of higher cognitive processes through glutamatergic linkages: Horvitz, 2002), in our view, is only one of the many defining attributes of all blue-ribbon, grade-A, emotional systems (Panksepp, 1982a, 1986, 1998). One of the proposed functions of each basic emotional network, such as the DA-facilitated SEEKING system, is to help gate incoming information and related cognitive perceptual processes relevant for the emotional arousal (Panksepp, 1982a, 1998a).

All emotional systems are special purpose learning systems with a variety of properties (Figure 5.3). From the affective neuroscience perspective, the defining criteria of emotional systems are that (1) the underlying circuits are genetically predisposed and designed to respond unconditionally to stimuli arising from major life-challenging circumstances, (2) the circuits organize diverse behaviors by activating and inhibiting action tendencies and concurrent autonomic-hormonal changes that have proved adaptive in the face of such life-challenging circumstances during the evolutionary history of the species, (3) emotive circuits change the sensitivities of sensory and perceptual processes that are relevant for the action tendencies that have been aroused, (4) neural activity of emotional circuits outlast the precipitating circumstances, (5) emotional circuits can come under the conditional control of emotionally neutral environmental events, (6) emotional circuits have reciprocal interactions with brain mechanisms that elaborate higher decision-making processes and consciousness, and (7) emotional circuits are critical in instigating affective feelings. The incentive salience view, correct as it may be in its restricted domain, focuses primarily on the third and perhaps sixth attributes to the exclusion of the others. Perhaps it is unwise to simply focus on one dimension of a multifaceted process?

RESPONSE FACILITATION PERSPECTIVE

Since the demonstration that the motor impairments of Parkinson's disease emerged from the deterioration of brain DA neurons, it has been recognized how important DA is for recruiting action tendencies. In a fine critique of the behaviorist concept of reinforcement, Salamone and Correa (2002) have emphasized how important DA is in recruiting brain/mind resources for sustaining work-related response requirements. When DA transmission is compromised, animals stop behaving sooner in progressive fixed-ratio and other long-interval schedules of reinforcement (Correa, Carlson, Wisniecki, & Salamone 2002). In simple terms, it may be that organisms without DA tire more easily—they simply do not have the normal psychic "energy" to sustain goal-directed behaviors. This, of course, is perfectly consonant with the historical use of coca-leaves among indigenous South Americans to sustain energy during tiring tasks such as long-distance running.

Neill, Fenton, and Justice (2002) have also pointed out that measures of brain DA metabolism indicate that DA release is related more to work output requirements than the reward input parameters of behavioral tasks. This is consistent with a growing body of data indicating that self-stimulation reward can be sustained independently of "DAergic" mechanisms (Garris et al., 1999). All of the above findings are consistent with the view that mesolimbic and mesocortical DA arousal evolved largely in the service of appetitive behavior sequences that can be ethologically characterized as foraging/investigatory/seeking urges.

RESPONSE SWITCHING AND NOVELTY RESPONSE VIEWPOINT

Ascending DA circuits interact with higher brain networks that elaborate perceptual and related cognitive processes. Thus, it has been suggested that one of the main functions of DA may be to facilitate switching between alternative behavior patterns (Oades, 1985; Redgrave, Prescott, & Gurney, 1999). This hypothesis is quite attractive, especially if one limits the behavioral switching to the manifestation of forward-directed foraging strategies. As new opportunities for resource acquisition emerge, animals that can shift their seeking activities accordingly will surely increase their survival chances.

Consistent with this view was the demonstration of the synaptic release of DA just as animals begin to explore new environments (Rebec, Grabner, Johnson, Pierce, & Bardo, 1997) and to interact with new social partners (Robinson, Heien, & Wightman, 2002). These findings are entirely concordant with the demonstration, at a single-unit level, that DA cells fire in response to novel attention-grabbing stimuli (Schultz, 2002), as well as with the global foraging/seeking/expectancy view of lateral hypothalamic reward processes.

Some of these theories can also deal cogently with the increasing evidence that DA systems can be activated by aversive events (Di Chiara, Loddo, & Tanda, 1999; Everitt et al., 1999). Not only do aversive events require efficiency in switching behavioral priorities, but also they should promote motivation to *seek* locations of safety. Clearly, a brain system that promotes searching–foraging urges might help animals efficiently escape threatening events (for a more extensive discussion see Ikemoto & Panksepp, 1999).

DISCRIMINATING AMONG THEORIES

If these theories were really orthogonal, causal experiments would be needed to discriminate all of the above hypotheses. We do not think such tests can be devised if all proposals merely reflect different facets of more global network properties. Of course, the diversity of DA receptors, and the enormous number of inputs to the relevant brain areas (Figure 5.2) (Ikemoto & Panksepp, 1999), highlights the complexity that needs to be faced (see Alcaro et al., 2007, for an attempt to do that).

However, as investigators try to dissect the overall network (McBride, Murphy, & Ikemoto, 1999), we should not forget that the parts contribute to a psychobehaviorally coherent whole, and it is essential to properly conceptualize the whole in order for the pieces to make much sense (Panksepp, 1998a, 2003). The seeking view can readily accommodate all of the above findings, as well as many others including the role of dopamine in novelty responses (Bardo & Dworkin, 2004) and the exquisite responsivity of dopamine networks to salient nonreward events (Horvitz, 2002), as well as behavioral and broad-scale incentive sensitization (Nocjar & Panksepp, 2002; Vanderschuren & Kalivas, 2000; Wywell & Berridge, 2001) and the human experience of euphoria (Drevets et al., 2001; Volkow, Fowler, & Wang, 2002) that characterizes this system. The more global seeking view can also productively impact clinical thinking (Kapur, 2003), especially in our understanding of the global underpinnings of cravings and addictive urges.

AFFECTIVE AND GENETIC SUBSTRATES OF ADDICTIONS AND CRAVINGS

A generalized brain function that encourages animals to become urgently engaged with resource-seeking clearly constitutes a core process in all addictions. Self-stimulation of the LH-MFB part of the circuitry has an obsessive-compulsive character to it. The discovery that many addictive drugs rely on this system to sustain the affect that contributes to the urgency with which animals seek certain drugs and natural rewards has provided a powerful theme now recognized by many investigators. The well-documented anatomy of this system, with its multitude of interactions with higher brain regions from frontal cortex to hippocampus, provides abundant linkages to learning mechanisms, and other neural adaptations, that can sustain addictive behaviors (for overviews see Berridge & Robinson, 1998; Di Chiara, 2002; Hyman, Malenka, & Nestler, 2006; Ikemoto & Panksepp, 1999; Kalivas & Nakamura, 1999; Koob & LeMoal, 2005; Nestler, 2005; Panksepp, Nocjar, Burgdorf, Panksepp, & Huber, 2004; Wise, 2004). Here we focus on three relevant themes that may be of clinical importance: (a) the nature of the neuropsychic affective-motivational changes that sustain addictions, (b) the types of behavioral measures that may give us some access to the hedonic experiences of other animals, and (c) the deep

nature of the neuro-adaptations that need to be studied to understand addictive motivational substrates of the brain.

AFFECTIVE SUBSTRATES OF PSYCHOSTIMULANT ADDICTION

There are probably several distinct neural pathways to addiction. For instance, brain systems that mediate psychostimulant addictions are substantially different from those that mediate opiate reward (Olmstead & Franklin, 1997), as well as other neurochemically distinct types of reward (Ikemoto & Wise, 2004; Tzschentke & Schmidt, 1998). It is incorrect to assume that addictions ride upon a single pleasure, reward, or reinforcement principle, even though all addictions do share seeking components, as mediated by the lateral hypothalamic foraging-reward continuum discussed above. The shared function of this system is an appetitive drive that probably feels hedonically positive when modestly aroused, but which, when amplified by the neuro-adaptations that accompany chronic drug use, can fade into craving and an aversive psychic urgency. This would be more akin to a disturbingly insistent psychological pressure (obsessive craving) than to an affectively positive feeling (Koob & Le Moal, 1997). Presumably a very different depressive negative feeling emerges during the reward dysregulation that accompanies drug withdrawal (Koob & Le Moal, 2001).

In any event, the emotional feelings and motivational urges that contribute to addictions are probably multifaceted. For instance, there are good reasons to believe that there are many positive affects in the brain (Ostow, 2003; Panksepp, 1998a, 2005), and we have postulated that to a substantial extent the positive affect engendered by opiates resembles social reward while that of psychostimulant reflects a positively valenced foraging urge. Indeed, just as various positive affects may contribute to the onset of drug addictions, various negative feelings during drug withdrawal help sustain addictive patterns. Both have been modeled in animals (Koob & Le Moal, 1997, 2001), but it would be desirable to have a measure of positive and negative affective status of animals that can be deciphered as readily as human self-reports of good or bad feeling.

CAN ANIMALS REPORT THEIR DESIRES?

We have recently argued that rat vocalizations can be used to model the positive and negative affective processes that mediate addictions in humans (Knutson et al., 2002; Panksepp et al., 2002). This radical assertion is based on our finding that the two major ultrasonic vocalizations

(USVs) of rats—the 22 kHz alarm calls and the 50 kHz positive social engagement calls—may be sufficiently robust emotional indicators of many negative and positive affective feelings so as to serve as a reliable index of affective likes and dislikes, in rats. Hopefully these will relate directly to the positive and negative hedonic changes that control addictive processes in humans (Panksepp et al., 2004). If USVs of rats can reflect direct read-outs of their affective states (Knutson et al., 2002; Panksepp & Burgdorf, 2000), the harvesting of vocalizations should nicely supplement important evidence derived from the more arduous conditioned place preference and aversion paradigms (Bardo & Bevins, 2000).

In brief, the 22 kHz calls are conditionally exhibited in environments that have been associated with the administration of affectively aversive drugs such as opiate receptor antagonists and lithium chloride. 50-kHz chirps, on the other hand, are emitted to affectively positive drugs such as opiates and psychostimulants (Burgdorf et al., 2001a; Knutson et al., 2002). In fact, 50-kHz calls are exhibited when CSs occur that predict a wide range of positive rewards such as food, play, sexual behavior, and rewarding electrical stimulation of the brain (Burgdorf et al., 2000, 2001a,b). Indeed, the neuro-circuitry of the 50-kHz USV is closely related to the ascending mesolimbic/mesocortical dopamine system (Burgdorf & Panksepp, 2006; Burgdorf et al., 2007). Thus, we would challenge the other views to explain the confluence between these positive-affect indicative vocalizations and the various dopamine theories that abound in the literature (*vide supra*).

Emerging knowledge of the 50-kHz USV circuitry highlights the importance of dopamine and glutamate within the basal forebrain, especially the nucleus accumbens and preoptic areas (Burgdorf et al., 2001, 2007; Wintink & Brudzynski, 2001). Indeed, it is well known that all addictive drugs increase DA levels in the nucleus accumbens (Di Chiara, 2002; Wise, 2004). The neurochemical generators of 22-kHz calls are also poorly understood, but there is a robust cholinergic component (Brudzynski, 2007). In the context of addiction, it is noteworthy that those calls are quite prominent during both opiate and psychostimulant withdrawal (Mutschler & Miczek, 1998; Vivian & Miczek, 1991, 1993), both of which evoke brain cholinergic overflow and aversive feelings in humans and animals (Brudzynski, 2007).

These potential measures of drug desire and drug withdrawal may be closely coupled to the spontaneous brain generators of various positive and negative affects. Indeed, with such ethological measures, of considerable face-validity, one may no longer have to infer affect *indirectly* from learned behavioral measures such as lever presses and spatial choices (Bardo & Bevins, 2000). The *directness* of this vocalization measure may facilitate mapping the underlying neuronal pathways of positive and negative affects that regulate drug craving, and thereby illuminate brain changes that constitute addictive urges (Burgdorf & Panksepp, 2006; Knutson et al., 2002; Panksepp et al., 2002, 2004).

NEURAL AND PSYCHOLOGICAL ADAPTATIONS LEADING TO ADDICTIONS

The phenomenon of sensitization, where organisms become increasingly responsive to drugs of abuse, especially psychostimulants, as a function of exposure, may highlight the neurochemical adjustments that promote addictive urges (Robinson & Berridge, 2003; Vanderschuren & Kalivas, 2000). Sensitized animals seek drug rewards more persistently than nonsensitized ones. This strengthening of reward seeking is also evident for conventional rewards such as sex and food (Nocjar & Panksepp, 2002). The final common pathway for sensitization and drug addiction is widely held to reflect increases in DA transmission in the nucleus accumbens (for a review see Wise, 2004). It appears that DA both "pushes" animals into environments to seek rewards and "pulls" them toward specific stimuli associated with positive feelings (rewards) in the past. Stress, a common pathway to relapse in recovering drug addicts, also increases DA release (Shaham, Erb, & Stewart, 2000), again highlighting why "rewarding" DA release in the brain should not be conceptualized as a simple sensory pleasure signal.

From a "brain pleasure/reward" perspective, sensitized DA circuitry might be expected to foster elevated levels of positive affect in a linear fashion. However, from an expectancy/seeking perspective, the function may be more an inverted-U, and a sensitized brain may simply experience more urgency to indulge in appetitive reward seeking behaviors. Under such conditions, the brain may actually become more susceptible to frustration if rewards are not forthcoming. Psychologically, sensitization may shift one from a modest and well-controlled feeling of "I want…" to an intense and more impulsive "I WANT IT NOW!" In short, it is presently widely accepted that in addition to a proper conceptualization of dopamine energized reward systems, one of the keys to unraveling the transition to addiction is a better understanding of the neurobiological and neuropsychological changes that accompany sensitization.

Although some of the neurochemical details of sensitization have been deciphered (Cornish & Kalivas, 2002;

McFarland & Kalivas, 2001; Stewart 2000; Vanderschuren & Kalivas, 2000), critical elements yet to be elucidated may reside in a more detailed characterization of the concomitant changes in the long-term gene transcription patterns that result from the use of drugs of abuse and the sensitization that results (Laakso, Mohn, Gainetdinov, & Caron, 2002). Several long-term changes in gene expression patterns such as ΔFosB have emerged as candidates for sustaining addictive urges (Nestler, Barrot, & Self, 2001). However, few psychobiologically relevant studies are available, and strategies need to be implemented that can allow us to decode how affective processes are amplified in the relevant circuits.

According to the view advanced here, it is not just brain dopaminergic cells, but changes in the extended lateral hypothalamic/MFB seeking continuum which sustain vigorous self-stimulation behavior, that will provide essential knowledge about the neuropsychological cascade that leads to addiction. This continuum contains many relevant neuropeptides including opioid, cholecystokinin, orexin, and neurotensin. Since metabolic mapping (Gallistel, Gomita, Yadin, & Campbell, 1985; Roberts, 1980) and cFos mapping of such neuronal activities (Arvanitogiannis, Flores, & Shizgal, 1997; Nakahara et al., 1999) have clarified the extended anatomy of a number of relevant brain circuits, molecular biology tools can now be used to determine exactly how the underlying brain substrates respond to repeated activations (Nestler, 2004). Recent technical advances, such as gene-chips or microarrays, now allow us to screen for psychologically-relevant changes in the expression of thousands of genes simultaneously in small tissue samples along the SEEKING and other emotional systems. Indirectly related brain areas that may facilitate associated learning effects (such as the hippocampus and orbital frontal cortex) are also ideal targets for analysis.

Promising targets for helping modulate desired affective changes may eventually be validated in human studies that carefully focus on psychological changes using new psychoethological measures (Panksepp, 1998a). For instance, the convergence of arousal promoting neuropeptides such as orexin and neurotensin onto the VTA provides vectors for medicinal development that may be useful in the treatment of addictive urges; many of these agents may work best in specific psychosocial contexts (Panksepp & Harro, 2004).

FUTURE PROSPECTS

There is a growing interest in linking the basic psychobiological data culled from animal models to the human condition (Depue & Collins, 1999). This important trend will be fostered if we develop more coherent psychobiological theories and animal models that can interface effectively with psychological and psychiatric issues. In general, behavioral neuroscientists continue to avoid the utilization of mental constructs (especially affective feeling dynamics) that may forge effective links to human emotional issues. In part, this is a hang-over of behavioristic/positivistic thought that insisted we put only externally observable factual peppercorns into the scientific grinder of knowledge, while ignoring overarching psychological ideas that describe the shared primitive emotional dynamics of human and animal minds.

Before we knew much about the brain, such cautionary strategies were more coherent than they are now. This caution is still reasonable if we are concerned with the cognitive contents (the channel-functions) of other minds (Panksepp, 2004). But it is retarding progress if extended to emotional processes that we probably share homologously with other animals: namely the basic affective state-control functions that generate fundamental emotional and motivational feelings (Panksepp, 2005, 2008). However, fears of anthropomorphism and zoomorphism remain so vast, that few useful neuro-mental integrative constructs can be found among the rapidly increasing mountain of unintegrated neurobehavioral facts. When these facts are integrated into a coherent, overarching theoretical framework, better intellectual commerce between our rapidly emerging knowledge of the animal brain and human psychiatric ailments should emerge (Panksepp, 2003; Panksepp & Harro, 2004).

In sum, our theoretical bias is that clearer images of the types of attentional, emotional, and motivational operating systems that exist in the subcortical reaches of the mammalian brain will give us excellent platforms to develop integrative working hypotheses that can effectively promote psychological understanding of motivational processes. The expectancy/SEEKING concept, which does not simply limit itself to dopaminergic neurons, is such a construct. It also recognizes that the DA system, which helps "light up," to energize, the potentials of many brain networks, operates as a coherent whole. It does not convey information in discrete, single-cell, information-processing terms. DA promoted SEEKING urges help mediate coherent psychobehavioral evolutionary functions that become more refined with specific life experiences, as cascades of interactions with higher cortico-cognitive processes are solidified. Thus, the clear and stable motivational response patterns seen in well-trained animals may no longer reflect the dynamics of

VTA dopaminergic SEEKING functions that allowed those habitual behavior patterns to emerge (Ikemoto & Panksepp, 1999; Kalivas & Volkow, 2005).

If such core emotional operating systems are capable of generating a primitive form of affective consciousness (i.e., raw feels), then it may be impossible to understand what the brain is really doing without investigators entertaining the reality of affective brain functions (Panksepp, 2005, 2007). Theoretical views that entertain the reality of psychoaffective concepts appear to have a better chance of linking up productively with human psychological issues than perspectives that remain strictly at third-person, behaviorally descriptive levels that are rigidly linked to learning-theory traditions. It seems likely that evolution provided animals with various attentional, emotional, and motivational operating systems that are self-referential. All mammals may possess affectively experienced "centers of gravity" for their decision-making processes.

As we begin to entertain such possibilities, we may begin to generate neuroscientific viewpoints that link up productively with a large number of human concerns. By taking psychoevolutionary perspectives to certain brain functions, we may also more easily reconcile the apparently conflicting claims of more narrow viewpoints. Indeed, we may find that the evolutionarily ingrained (initially "object-less") emotional operating systems of the brain "grasp" the world (i.e., they are designed to seek learning) in ways that hardly resemble the mindless associative-reinforcement learning models handed down from preneuroscientific eras. Were we to accept that other animals do have emotional lives, we may come to better understand how various simple maneuvers such as the provisioning of socially and object enriched environments reduce addictive urges in animals. Moreover, we may be able to construct more effective multimodal treatments for the many addictions that so profoundly impact the lives of human beings.

REFERENCES

Alcaro, A., Huber, R., & Panksepp, J. (2007). Behavioral functions of the mesolimbic dopaminergic system: An affective neuroethological perspective. *Brain Research Reviews*, 56, 283–321.

Arvanitogiannis, A., Flores, C., & Shizgal, P. (1997). Fos-like immunoreactivity in the caudal diencephalon and brainstem following lateral hypothalamic self-stimulation. *Behavioural Brain Research*, 88, 275–279.

Bardo, M. T., & Bevins, R. A. (2000). Conditioned place preference: What does it add to our preclinical understanding of drug reward? *Psychopharmacology*, 153, 31–43.

Bardo, M. T., & Dworkin, L. P. (2004). Biological connection between novelty- and drug-seeking motivational systems. *Nebraska Symposium on Motivation*, 50, 127–158.

Bennett, M. R., & Hacker, P. M. S. (2003). *Philosophical foundations of neuroscience*. Malden, MA: Blackwell.

Berridge, K. C. (2007). The debate over dopamine's role in reward: The case for incentive salience. *Psychopharmacology*, 191, 391–431.

Berridge, K. C., & Robinson, T. E. (1998). What is the role of dopamine in reward: Hedonic impact, reward learning, or incentive salience? *Brain Research Reviews*, 28, 309–369.

Berridge, K. C., & Robinson, T. E. (2003). Parsing reward. *Trends in Neuroscience*, 9, 507–513.

Berridge, K. C., & Valenstein, E. S. (1991). What psychological process mediates feeding evoked by electrical stimulation of the lateral hypothalamus. *Behavioral Neuroscience*, 105, 3–14.

Bindra, D. (1974). A motivational view of learning, performance, and behavior modification. *Psychological Review*, 81, 199–213.

Bolles, R. C. (1972). Reinforcement, expectancy, and learning. *Psychological Review*, 79, 394–409.

Brudzynski, S. M. (2007). Ultrasonic calls of rats as indicator variables of negative or positive states. Acetylcholine–dopamine interaction and acoustic coding. *Behavioural Brain Research*, 182, 261–273.

Burgdorf, J., Knutson, B., & Panksepp, J. (2000). Anticipation of rewarding electrical brain stimulation evokes ultrasonic vocalizations in rats. *Behavioral Neuroscience*, 114, 320–327.

Burgdorf, J., Knutson, B., Panksepp, J., & Ikemoto, S. (2001a). Nucleus accumbens amphetamine microinjections unconditionally elicit 50 kHz ultrasonic vocalizations in rats. *Behavioral Neuroscience*, 115, 940–944.

Burgdorf, J., Knutson, B., Panksepp, J., & Shippenberg, T. (2001b). Evaluation of rat ultrasonic vocalizations as predictors of the conditioned aversive effects of drugs. *Psychopharmacology*, 155, 35–42.

Burgdorf, J., & Panksepp, J. (2006). The neurobiology of positive emotions. *Neuroscience Biobehavioral Reviews*, 30, 173–187.

Burgdorf, J., Wood, P. L., Kroes, R. A., Moskal, J. R., & Panksepp, J. (2007). Neurobiology of 50-kHz ultrasonic vocalizations in rats: Electrode mapping, lesion, and pharmacology studies. *Behavioural Brain Research*, 182, 274–283.

Burkhardt, R. W. (2005). *Patterns of behavior*. Chicago: University of Chicago Press.

Ciompi, L., & Panksepp, J. (2004). Energetic effects of emotions on cognitions-complementary psychobiological and psychosocial finding. In R. Ellis & N. Newton (Eds.), *Consciousness and emotions* (Vol. 1, pp. 23–55). Amsterdam, PA: John Benjamins.

Cooper, D. C. (2002). The significance of action potential bursting in the brain reward circuit. *Neurochemistry International*, 41, 333–340.

Cornish, J. L., & Kalivos, P. W. (2001). Cocaine sensitization and craving. *Journal of Addiction Research*, 20, 43–54.

Correa, M., Carlson, B. B., Wisniecki, A., & Salamone, J. D. (2002). Nucleus accumbens DA and work requirements on interval schedules. *Behavioural Brain Research, 137*, 179–187.

Depue, R. A., & Collins, P. F. (1999). Neurobiology of the structure of personality: Dopamine, facilitation of incentive motivation, and extraversion. *Behavioral and Brain Sciences, 22*, 2511–2513.

Deutsch, J. A. (1963). Learning and electrical self-stimulation of the brain. *Journal of Theoretical Biology, 4*, 193–214.

Di Chiara, G. (2002). Nucleus accumbens shell and core DA: Differential role in behavior and addiction. *Behavioural Brain Research, 137*, 75–114.

Di Chiara, G., Loddo, P., & Tanda, G. (1999). Reciprocal changes in prefrontal and limbic DA responsiveness to aversive and rewarding stimuli after chronic mild stress: Implications for the psychobiology of depression. *Biological Psychiatry, 46*, 1624–1633.

Drevets, W. C., Gautier, C., Price, J. C., Kupfer, D. J., Kinahan, P. E., Grace, A. A., et al. (2001). Amphetamine-induced dopamine release in human ventral striatum correlates with euphoria. *Biological Psychiatry, 49*, 81–96.

Everitt, B. J., Parkinson, J. A., Olmstead, M. C., Arroyo, M., Robledo, P., & Robbins, T. W. (1999). Associative processes in addiction and reward. The role of amygdala-ventral striatal subsystems. *Annals of the New York Academy of Sciences, 877*, 412–428.

Fiorino, D. F., & Phillips, A. G. (1999). Facilitation of sexual behavior and enhanced DA efflux in the nucleus accumbens of male rats after D-amphetamine-induced behavioral sensitization. *Journal of Neuroscience, 19*, 456–463.

Gallistel, C. R., Gomita, Y., Yadin, E., & Campbell, K. A. (1985). Forebrain origins and terminations of the medial forebrain bundle metabolically activated by rewarding stimulation or by reward blocking doses of pimozide. *Journal of Neuroscience, 5*, 1246–1261.

Heath, R. G. (1996). *Exploring the mind–brain relationship.* Baton Rouge, LA: Moran Printing Inc.

Garris, P. A., Kilpatrick, M., Bunin, M. A., Michael, D., Walker, Q. D., & Wightman, R. M. (1999). Dissociation of dopamine release in the nucleus accumbens from intracranial self-stimulation. *Nature, 398*, 67–69.

Glickman, S. E., & Schiff, B. B. (1967). A biological theory of reinforcement. *Psychological Review, 74*, 81–109.

Goldman-Rakic, P. S. (1999). The "psychic" neuron of the cerebral cortex. *Annals of the New York Academy of Sciences, 868*, 13–26.

Hamburg, M. D. (1971). Hypothalamic unit activity and eating behavior. *American Journal of Physiology, 220*, 980–985.

Horvitz, J. C. (2002). DA gating of glutamatergic sensorimotor and incentive motivational input signals to the striatum. *Behavioural Brain Research, 137*, 65–74.

Hyland, B. I., Reynolds, J. N. J., Hay, J., Perk, C. G., & Miller, R. (2002). Firing modes of midbrain dopamine cells in the freely moving rat. *Neuroscience, 114*, 479–492.

Hyman, S. E., Malenka, R. C., & Nestler, E. J. (2006). Neural mechanisms of addiction: The role of reward-related learning and memory. *Annual Review of Neuroscience, 29*, 565–598.

Ikemoto, S., & Panksepp, J. (1999). The role of nucleus accumbens DA in motivated behavior: A unifying interpretation with special reference to reward-seeking. *Brain Research Reviews, 31*, 6–41.

Ikemoto, S., & Wise, R. (2004). Mapping of chemical trigger zones for reward. *Neuropharmacology, 47*(Suppl. 1), 190–201.

Kalivas, P. W., & Nakamura, M. (1999). Neural systems for behavioral activation and reward. *Current Opinion in Neurobiology, 9*, 223–227.

Kalivas, P. W., & Volkow, N. D. (2005). The neural basis of addiction: A pathology of motivation and choice. *American Journal of Psychiatry, 162*, 1403–1413.

Kapur, S. (2003). Psychosis as a state of aberrant salience: A framework linking biology, phenomenology and pharmacology in schizophrenia. *American Journal of Psychiatry, 160*, 13–23.

Kelley, A. E. (2004). Ventral striatal control of appetitive motivation: Role in ingestive behavior and reward-related learning. *Neuroscience Biobehavioral Reviews, 27*, 765–776.

Kelley, A. E., & Berridge, K. C. (2002). The neuroscience of natural rewards: Relevance to addictive drugs. *Journal of Neuroscience, 22*, 3306–3311.

Kiyatkin, E. A., & Rebec, G. V. (2001). Impulse activity of ventral tegmental area neurons during heroin self-administration in rats. *Neuroscience, 102*, 565–580.

Koob, G. F., & Le Moal, M. (1997). Drug abuse: Hedonic homeostasis dysregulation. *Science, 278*, 52–58.

Koob, G. F., & Le Moal, M. (2001). Drug addiction, dysregulation of reward, and allostasis. *Neuropsychopharmacology, 24*, 97–129.

Koob, G. F., & Le Moal, M. (2005). *The neurobiology of addiction.* New York: Academic Press.

Knutson, B., Burgdorf, J. & Panksepp, J. (2002). Ultrasonic vocalizations as indices of affective states in rat. *Psychological Bulletin, 128*, 961–977.

Laakso, A., Mohn, A. R., Gainetdinov, R. R., Caron, M. G. (2002). Experimental genetic approaches to addiction. *Neuron, 36*, 213–228.

Lehrman, D. S. (1953). A critique of Konrad Lorenz's theory of instinctive behavior. *Quarterly Review of Biology, 28*, 337–365.

McBride, W. J., Murphy, J. M., & Ikemoto, S. (1999). Localization of brain reinforcement mechanisms: Intracranial self-administration and intracranial place-conditioning studies. *Behavioural Brain Research, 101*, 129–152.

Miura, Y., Ito, T., & Kadokawa, T. (1987). Effects of intraseptally injected DA and noradrenaline on hippocampal synchronized theta wave activity in rats. *Japanese Journal of Pharmacology, 44*, 471–479.

Mutschler, N. H., & Miczek, K. A. (1998). Withdrawal from i.v. Cocaine "binges" in rats: Ultrasonic distress calls and startle. *Psychopharmacology, 135*, 161–168.

Nakahara, D., Ishida, Y., Nakamura, M., Kuwahara, I., Todaka, K., & Nishimori, T. (1999). Regional differences in desensitization of c-Fos expression following repeated self-stimulation of the medial forebrain bundle in the rat. *Neuroscience, 90*, 1013–1020.

Neill, D. B., Fenton, H., & Justice, J. B. Jr. (2002). Increase in accumbal dargic transmission correlates with response cost not reward of hypothalamic stimulation. *Behavioural Brain Research*, *137*, 129–138.

Nestler, E. J. (2005). Is there a common molecular pathway for addiction? *Nature Neuroscience*, *8*, 1445–1449.

Nestler, E. J., Barrot, M., & Self, D. W. (2001). Δfosb: A sustained molecular switch for addiction. *Proceedings of the National Academy of Sciences*, *98*, 11042–11046.

Nocjar, C., & Panksepp, J. (2002). Chronic intermittent amphetamine pretreatment enhances future appetitive behavior for drug- and natural-reward: Interaction with environmental variables. *Behavioural Brain Research*, *128*, 189–203.

Oades, R. D. (1985). The role of noradrenaline in tuning and dopamine in switching between signals in the CNS. *Neuroscience and Biobehavioral Reviews*, *9*, 261–282.

Olds, J. (1977). *Drives and reinforcements: Behavioral studies of hypothalamic functions.* New York: Raven Press.

Olmstead, M. C., & Franklin, K. B. (1997). The development of a conditioned place preference to morphine: Effects of microinjections into various CNS sites. *Behavioral Neuroscience*, *111*, 1324–1334.

Ostow, M. (2003). Mood regulation, spontaneous, and pharmacologically assisted. *Neuro-Psychoanalysis*, *6*, 77–86.

Panksepp, J. (1971). Aggression elicited by electrical stimulation of the hypothalamus in albino rats. *Physiology & Behavior*, *6*, 311–316.

Panksepp, J. (1981). Hypothalamic integration of behavior: Rewards, punishments, and related psychobiological process. In P. J. Morgane & J. Panksepp (Eds.), *Handbook of the hypothalamus, Vol. 3, Part A. Behavioral studies of the hypothalamus* (pp. 289–487). New York: Marcel Dekker.

Panksepp, J. (1982a). Toward a general psychobiological theory of emotions. *The Behavioral and Brain Sciences*, *5*, 407–467.

Panksepp, J. (1982b). Foraging–expectancy command circuitry of the brain: A functional theory of lateral hypothalamic self-stimulation. *Brain and Behavioral Sciences*, *5*, 67.

Panksepp, J. (1985). Mood changes. In P. J. Vinken, G. W. Bruyn, & H. L. Klawans (Eds.), *Handbook of clinical neurology. Vol. 1. Clinical neuropsychology* (pp. 271–285), Amsterdam, PA: Elsevier Science Publishers.

Panksepp, J. (1986). The anatomy of emotions. In R. Plutchik (Ed.), *Emotion: Theory, research and experience Vol. 3. Biological foundations of emotions* (pp. 91–124). Orlando: Academic Press.

Panksepp, J. (1992). A critical role for "affective neuroscience" in resolving what is basic about basic emotions. *Psychological Review*, *99*, 554–560.

Panksepp, J. (1998a). *Affective neuroscience, the foundations of human and animal emotions.* New York: Oxford University Press.

Panksepp, J. (1998b). The periconscious substrates of consciousness: Affective states and the evolutionary origins of the SELF. *Journal of Consciousness Studies*, *5*, 566–582.

Panksepp, J. (2000). Affective consciousness and the instinctual motor system, the neural sources of sadness and joy. In R. Ellis & N. Newton (Eds.), *The caldron of consciousness, motivation, affect and self-organization (vol. 16), advances in consciousness research* (pp. 27–54). Amsterdam, PA: John Benjamins.

Panksepp, J. (2002). *Foreword* to G. A. Cory Jr. & R. Gardner Jr. (Eds.), *The evolutionary neuroethology of Paul Maclean* (pp. ix–xxvii). London: Praeger.

Panksepp, J. (2003). At the interface of affective, behavioral and cognitive neurosciences. Decoding the emotional feelings of the brain. *Brain and Cognition*, *52*, 4–14.

Panksepp, J. (2004). *Textbook of biological psychiatry.* Hoboken, NJ: Wiley.

Panksepp, J. (2005). Affective consciousness: Core emotional feelings in animals and humans. *Consciousness and Cognition*, *14*, 30–80.

Panksepp, J. (2006). Emotional endophenotypes in evolutionary psychiatry. *Progress in Neuro-Psychopharmacology and Biological Psychiatry*, *30*, 774–784.

Panksepp, J. (2008). The affective brain and core-consciousness: How does neural activity generate emotional feelings? In: M. Lewis & J. Haviland (Eds.), *The handbook of emotions* (3rd ed., pp. in press,). New York: Guilford.

Panksepp, J., & Burgdorf, J. (2000). 50 kHz chirping (laughter?) In response to conditioned and unconditioned tickle-induced reward in rats: Effects of social housing and genetic variables. *Behavioral Brain Research*, *115*, 25–38.

Panksepp, J., & Harro, J. (2004). The future of neuropeptides in biological psychiatry and emotional psychopharmacology: Goals and strategies. In J. Panksepp (Ed.), *Textbook of biological psychiatry* (pp. 627–659). New York: Wiley.

Panksepp, J., Knuston, B., & Burgdorf, J. (2002). The role of emotional brain systems in addictions: A neuro-evolutionary perspective. *Addiction*, *97*, 459–469.

Panksepp, J., Nocjar, C., Burgdorf, J., Panksepp, J. B., & Huber, R. (2004). The role of emotional systems in addiction: A neuroethological perspective. *Nebraska Symposium on Motivation*, *50*, 85–126.

Panksepp, J., & Panksepp, J. B. (2000). The seven sins of evolutionary psychology. *Evolution & Cognition*, *6*, 108–131.

Pavlides, C., Greenstein, Y. J., Grudman, M., Winson, J. (1988). Long-term potentiation in the dentate gyrus is induced preferentially on the positive phase of theta-rhythm. *Brain Research*, *439*, 383–387.

Rebec, G. V., Grabner, C. P., Johnson, M., Pierce, R. C., & Bardo, M. T. (1997). Transient increases in catecholaminergic activity in medial prefrontal cortex and nucleus accumbens shell during novelty. *Neuroscience*, *76*, 707–714.

Redgrave, P., Prescott, T. J., & Gurney, K. (1999). Is the short-latency DA response too short to signal reward error. *Trends in Neurosciences*, *22*, 146–151.

Roberts, W. W. (1980). [^{14}C]: Deoxyglucose mapping of first-order projections activated by stimulation of lateral hypothalamic sites eliciting gnawing, eating, and drinking in rats. *The Journal of Comparative Neurology*, *194*, 617–638.

Robinson, D. L., Heien, M. L. A. V., & Wightman, R. M. (2002). Frequency of DA concentration transients increases in dorsal and ventral striatum of male rats during introduction of conspecifics. *Journal of Neuroscience, 22,* 10477–10486.

Robinson, T. E., & Berridge, K. C. (1993). The neural basis of drug craving: An incentive-sensitization theory of addiction. *Brain Research Reviews, 18*(3), 247–291.

Robinson, T. E., & Berridge, K. C. (2003). Addiction. *Annual Review of Psychology, 54,* 25–53.

Rolls, E. (2005). *Emotions explained.* New York: Oxford University Press.

Rosenkranz, J. A., & Grace, A. A. (2002). Dopamine-mediated modulation of odour-evoked amygdala potentials during Pavlovian conditioning. *Nature, 417,* 282–287.

Rossi, J. III, & Panksepp, J. (1992). Analysis of the relationships between self-stimulation sniffing and brain-stimulation sniffing. *Physiology & Behavior, 51,* 805–813.

Sakurai, T. (2007). The neural circuit of orexin (hypocretin): Maintaining sleep and wakefulness. *Nature Review Neuroscience, 8,* 171–181.

Salamone, J. D., & Correa, M. (2002). Motivational views of reinforcement: implications for understanding the behavioral functions of nucleus accumbens DA. *Behavioural Brain Research, 137,* 3–25.

Schultz, W. (2000). Multiple reward signals in the brain. *Nature Reviews Neuroscience, 1,* 199–207.

Schultz, W. (2002). Getting formal with DA reward. *Neuron, 36,* 241–263.

Schultz, W. (2006). Behavioral theories and the neurophysiology of reward. *Annual Review Psychology, 57,* 87–115.

Shaham, Y., Erb, S., & Stewart, J. (2000). Stress-induced relapse to heroin and cocaine seeking in rats: A review. *Brain Research Brain Research Reviews, 33,* 13–33.

Stutz, R. M., Rossi, R. R., Hastings, L., & Brunner, R. L. (1974). Discriminability of intracranial stimuli: The role of anatomical connectedness. *Physiology & Behavior, 12,* 69–73.

Toates, F. (1986). *Motivational systems.* Cambridge, UK: Cambridge University Press.

Trowill, J. A., Panksepp, J., & Gandelman, R. (1969). An incentive model of rewarding brain stimulation. *Psychological Review, 76,* 264–281.

Tzschentke, T. M., & Schmidt, W. J. (1998). Discrete quinolinic acid lesions of the rat prelimbic medial prefrontal cortex affect cocaine- and MK-801-, but not morphine- and amphetamine-induced reward and psychomotor activation as measured with the place preference conditioning paradigm. *Behavioural Brain Research, 97,* 115–127.

Ungerstedt, U. (1974). Brain dopamine neurons and behavior. In F. O. Schmitt & F. G. Worden (Eds.), *The neurosciences, third study program* (pp. 695–703). Cambridge, Mass: MIT Press.

Valenstein, E. S., Cox, V. C., & Kakolewski, J. W. (1970). Reexamination of the role of the hypothalamus in motivation. *Psychological Review, 77,* 16–31.

Vanderschuren, L. J., & Kalivas, P. W. (2000). Alterations in dopaminergic and glutamatergic transmission in the induction and expression of behavioral sensitization: A critical review of preclinical studies. *Psychopharmacology, 151,* 99–120.

Vivian, J. A., & Miczek, K. A. (1991). Ultrasounds during morphine withdrawal in rats. *Psychopharmacology, 104,* 187–193.

Vivian, J. A., & Miczek, K. A. (1993). Diazepam and gepirone selectively attenuate either 20–32 or 32–64 kHz ultrasonic vocalizations during aggressive encounters. *Psychopharmacology, 112,* 66–73.

Vertes, R. P., & Kocsis, B. (1997). Brainstem-diencephalo-septohippocampal systems controlling the theta rhythm of the hippocampus. *Neuroscience, 81,* 893–926.

Volkow, N. D., Fowler, J. S., & Wang, G. J. (2002). Role of dopamine in drug reinforcement and addiction in humans: Results from imaging studies. *Behavioral Pharmacology, 13,* 355–366.

Whishaw, I. Q., Robinson, T. E., Schallert, T., De Ryck, M., & Ramirez, V. D. (1978). Electrical activity of the hippocampus and neocortex in rats depleted of brain dopamine and norepinephrine: relations to behavior and effects of atropine. *Experimental Neurology, 62,* 748–767.

Wintink, A. J., & Brudzynski, S. M. (2001). The related roles of dopamine and glutamate in the initiation of 50-kHz ultrasonic calls in adult rats. *Pharmacology Biochemistry and Behavior, 70,* 317–323.

Wise, R. A. (1968). Hypothalamic motivational systems: Fixed or plastic neural circuits? *Science, 162,* 377–379.

Wise, R. A. (1982). Neuroleptics and operant behavior: The anhedonia hypothesis. *Brain and Behavioral Sciences, 5,* 39–87.

Wise, R. A. (2004). Dopamine, learning and motivation. *Nature Reviews Neuroscience, 5,* 483–494.

Wise, R. A., & Bozarth, M. A. (1987). A psychomotor stimulant theory of addiction. *Psychological Review, 94,* 469–492.

Wywell, C. L., & Berridge, K. C. (2001). Incentive-sensitization by previous amphetamine exposure: Increased cue-triggered 'wanting' for sucrose reward. *Journal of Neuroscience, 21,* 7831–7840.

Neurotransmitters

6 An Accumbens Dopamine– Acetylcholine System for Approach and Avoidance

Bartley G. Hoebel, Nicole M. Avena, and Pedro Rada

CONTENTS

Throughout a given day, we constantly make decisions as to whether we should, or should not, engage in various activities. This chapter addresses the neural mechanisms for enacting these approach or avoidance decisions and transforming information into action. We used microdial-ysis to measure dopamine (DA) and acetylcholine (ACh) in the nucleus accumbens (NAc) while rats were tested in a variety of animal models of approach and avoidance behaviors. As described below, each of the opposing behavior patterns suggests that approach involves the release of DA in the accumbens, whereas ACh is correlated with, or causes, avoidance. ACh creates a state that is at least inhibitory and sometimes aversive.

THE NUCLEUS ACCUMBENS: A SENSORY–MOTOR INTERFACE FOR MOTIVATION

ORGANIZATION OF THE ACCUMBENS: ANATOMY AND NEUROTRANSMITTERS

"Sensory" Input From the Limbic System

At the bottom level of the neuroaxis are the monosynaptic reflexes in the spinal cord, such as the knee-jerk reflex. Proceeding up the neuroaxis, one can find increasingly complex sensory–motor processing sites. This is most remarkable in animals that have maximized the evolutionary process of encephalization (Teitelbaum, 1971). Near the "top" is the somatosensory cortex with its input to the adjacent motor cortex. Using feeding behavior as an example, the taste-sensory cortex has the ability to respond to sensory stimuli, such as sugar in the mouth, and then relay this information to a nearby cortical area that gives a taste-related response modified by satiation signals (Rolls, 2006). This cortical sensory region must receive satiety signals from the gut as relayed by subcortical mechanisms for food approach and avoidance. On the motor side, the cortex can activate action-pattern ensembles for directing movements towards a place where food is available, or towards a place in body-coordinate space, such as the mouth (Graziano, 2006). This spatial dichotomy is manifest in two components of behavioral approach: appetitive behavior and consummatory behavior. Conversely, memories of unsafe food stimuli may direct action away from the mouth. This is avoidance and escape behavior.

The striatum contains the memory systems for sensory–motor associations (Izquierdo et al., 2006). It stores both approach and avoidance information. In this chapter, we will focus on the role of the ventral striatum, which includes the NAc. In this region the brain interprets input from the other limbic modules. The amygdala communicates issues of emotion, including aversion and fear (Yamamoto, 2007). The nearby ventral hippocampus conveys information regarding emotional context (Phillips, Drevets, Rauch, & Lane, 2003). The dorsal hippocampus provides spatial information and related memories (Bannerman et al., 2004; Redish & Touretzky, 1997). The taste associational cortex, mentioned above, provides taste signals that are already modified by sensory-specific satiety signals (Rolls, 2007). The thalamus relays information from the energy control systems in the hypothalamus (Kelley, Baldo, & Pratt, 2005), and the hypothalamus has some projections straight to the NAc (Yoshida, McCormack, Espana, Crocker, & Scammell, 2006). These limbic areas send information to the striatum to make go–no go decisions for action (Hoebel, 1988, 1997; Mogenson, Jones, & Yim, 1980; Mogenson & Yang, 1991; Robbins & Everitt, 1996; Rolls, 1995) as originally postulated by Mogenson and colleagues (Mogenson et al., 1980). For diagrams of these connections, see other reviews (Berthoud, 1999; De Olmos & Heimer, 1999; Kelley et al., 2005; Leibowitz & Hoebel, 2004; Robbins & Everitt, 2007).

The striatal networks for approach and avoidance are not only for selecting among inputs and opening or closing gates to the motor systems, but must also be viewed on a temporal or sequential dimension. As the animal learns which stimuli predict a reinforcer, the interface that deals with those stimuli gradually changes in sequential order from the accumbens shell to the accumbens core, and on up into the dorsal striatum (Haber, Fudge, & McFarland, 2000). A stimulus may elicit the response with less and less information needed about the original reinforcer (Robbins & Everitt, 1996). This reward "devaluation" (Balleine & Dickinson, 1998) may be a key feature of automatized responses in everyday life and also can become the basis for impulsive reactions in addiction and perhaps obsessive behavior.

"Motor" Output for Complex Behavior

The striatal output is sometimes called the extrapyramidal system to distinguish it from direct cortical–spinal projections of the pyramidal motor system. To get to the hindbrain motor output systems, the accumbens projects to the hypothalamus and midbrain, hence to the vagal motor system for gut actions and to the facial motor systems for action patterns such as chewing (Berthoud, 1999). To get into to the pyramidal system "fast track" to the spinal cord, the striatum projects via the globus pallidus and motor thalamus to the motor cortex.

All the striatal output cells have an intriguing shape that appears to have evolved to collect the myriad inputs on many dendrites, each with thousands of spines, each spine with synapses on its head and neck. Thousands of inputs from the brain regions cited above can synapse with a single output neuron, which must "decide" via electrochemical depolarization whether or not to fire an action potential.

Neuromodulation

The striatum, like most of the rest of the brain, receives inputs that use serotonin to arouse it (Jacobs & Fornal,

1999), norepinephrine to generate focused or scanning attention (Aston-Jones & Cohen, 2005), and DA to signal salient events and promote action in ways discussed below. These neuromodulators do not necessarily generate action potentials by themselves, but instead adjust the resting potential of postsynaptic neurons. For example, DA may slightly hyperpolarize the output neurons so that spontaneous firing is suppressed and strong excitatory inputs generate a burst of firing on a relatively silent background (Nicola, Woodward Hopf, & Hjelmstad, 2004; Peoples, Lynch, Lesnock, & Gangadhar, 2004). Thus, DA can modulate the effects of other neurotransmitters, such as glutamate, arriving from the input pathways listed above.

DA has different effects depending on which DA receptors are present and which postsynaptic neurons are involved. These receptors can change their binding characteristics as a means of local homeostatic modulation to compensate for excessive DA release, as in substance abuse (Di Chiara & Imperato, 1988), or diminished DA release seen in aging (Gerhardt & Maloney, 1999). Whereas the glutamate inputs enter the NAc and synapse on the heads of spines of the output neurons, DA synapses tend to be on the necks of the spines to better modulate the spread of excitatory current generated by glutamate (Li, Kolb, & Robinson, 2003).

Interneurons

Programming complex input–output relations for approach and avoidance requires interneurons. The striatum has many interneurons, but one other type stands out. They are relatively large neurons with vast branching dendrites. They appear to connect, in part, to the output cells. This connection is near the base of the dendrites and on the cell bodies, perfect for canceling out the glutamate and DA inputs and creating a "no go" signal by inhibiting the NAc output. These are the ACh interneurons that are the main focus of this chapter. We will argue that they play an essential role in avoidance behavior.

OVERVIEW OF THE HYPOTHESES

With this organizational overview in mind, we come to the main question for this chapter. What mechanism determines whether or not the animal engages in approach or avoidance behavior? In seeking a partial answer, we used microdialysis to measure DA and ACh in the NAc while rats were tested in a variety of animal models of approach and avoidance behaviors.

With an apology for the overemphasis on DA and ACh, a fascinating picture has nonetheless emerged. As described below, each of the opposing behavior patterns suggests that approach involves the release of DA in the accumbens, whereas ACh is correlated with, or causes, avoidance. ACh creates a state that is at least inhibitory and sometimes aversive. Put simply, accumbens DA signals "ok to go." It apparently potentiates actions designed for working hard to get, or get rid of, a stimulus. ACh signals "stop, it is unsafe." Gradually such responses get automatized in the striatum (Haber et al., 2000). The modernized version of the DA hypothesis of reinforcement is combined with our cholinergic hypothesis of satiety and aversion. Hypothetically, satiation occurs under the influence of ACh when DA is normal or high. ACh can cause aversion, including anxiety and behavioral depression, when DA is low. These individual hypotheses are refined and qualified in the following sections and gathered into a theory that is discussed in the last section of this chapter.

THE METHOD: IN VIVO MICRODIALYSIS

The technique of microdialysis is used in the experiments we will describe below. Rats are equipped with an implanted guide shaft aimed at the NAc. To sample extracellular levels of neurotransmitters, a probe is inserted through the guide shaft to the site of interest. The probe is made of a double-lumen hypodermic needle with a cellulose tip (Hernandez, Stanley, & Hoebel, 1986). During forward dialysis, neurotransmitters diffuse into the probe and then are collected for quantitative analysis by analytical chemistry. Conversely, using reverse dialysis neurotransmitters or drugs can be infused into the brain site of interest, diffusing into the surrounding brain tissue. Originally, one worried that the recovered DA was so far removed from the synapse that it might not be functional, but the "volume transmission" theory of neuromodulator function suggests that neurotransmitters like DA can act at a distance by diffusion (Guidolin, Fuxe, Neri, Nussdorfer, & Agnati, 2007). Besides, if reverse dialysis of DA agonists such as amphetamine (Hernandez, Lee, & Hoebel, 1987) could be behaviorally effective, then the DA that is released must be able to diffuse to receptors meant for the purpose of influencing behavior. Microdialysis samples are typically collected in 5- to 20-min periods before, during and after an event such as a meal or drug administration. More rapid sampling (e.g., 1 min) is also possible (Wise et al., 1995). By oxidizing DA on the tip of an electrode, measurements can be made in fractions of a second (Millar, O'Connor, Trout, & Kruk, 1992).

With the use of the microdialysis technique, as well as consideration of the results from other techniques, we will now examine situations involving approach and avoidance behaviors and can predict when and why a rat's brain will release DA and ACh in the NAc during the course of various behavioral tests.

DOPAMINE AND ACETYLCHOLINE IN APPROACH AND AVOIDANCE BEHAVIOR PATTERNS

It is well known from the literature on Parkinson's disease that DA in the nigrostriatal system is necessary to initiate movement. It is also clear that the balance of DA/ACh in the dorsal striatum determines the patient's ability to move (McGeer & McGeer, 1980). Therefore, effective treatments would increase DA levels and concurrently reduce the relative overabundance of ACh. Thus, pharmacotherapy sometimes consists of a DA precursor, L-DOPA, and a cholinergic blocker. It is as if DA facilitates going and ACh facilitates stopping.

Alongside the nigrostriatal DA pathway, as it ascends from the midbrain, is the mesolimbic DA pathway. It projects forward from the ventral tegmental area (VTA) of the midbrain, through the lateral hypothalamus to the limbic areas of the forebrain, including the NAc, amygdala, hippocampus, and frontal cortex. We hypothesized that the mesolimbic DA system in the NAc would be organized like its neighbor, the dorsal striatum, and would be equipped with a cholinergic "stop" system that opposed the DA function. If so, in our first example, DA would increase when a rat begins to eat, and ACh should be released when a rat slows its eating during the satiation process.

FEEDING AND SATIETY

Dopamine: Microdialysis studies have shown that feeding releases DA in the NAc (Hernandez & Hoebel, 1988; Hoebel, Hernandez, Schwartz, Mark, & Hunter, 1989; Radhakishun, van Ree, & Westerink, 1988). Further measures of subsecond release suggest that DA release is relatively high during food seeking (Roitman, Stuber, Phillips, Wightman, & Carelli, 2004). DA depletion with 6-hydroxy-dopamine suggests that DA is needed for instrumental work output (Salamone, Correa, Farrar, & Mingote, 2007). DA antagonists briefly increase operant responding for food, which then gradually declines, suggesting a loss of reward and not simply loss of motivation or motor impairment (Wise, 2006; Wise, Spindler, & Legault, 1978). In addition to reward and motivation, DA has roles in error signaling (Schultz, Tremblay, & Hollerman, 2000), salience or novelty (Bassareo, De Luca, & Di Chiara, 2002; Hooks & Kalivas, 1995),

incentive motivation (Robinson & Berridge, 1993) and learning (Di Chiara & Bassareo, 2007).

Di Chiara and colleagues find that a novel, unconditioned, palatable food stimulus releases DA primarily during the first experience, and this effect habituates with additional exposures, suggesting that DA in the NAc is involved in acquisition rather than maintenance of incentive motivation (Bassareo & Di Chiara, 1997). The first experience with a novel food raises DA selectively in the shell and not the core of the NAc (Bassareo & Di Chiara, 1999), and this increase is dependent on stimulation of mu-opioid receptors located in the VTA (Tanda & Di Chiara, 1998). We find similar results using sucrose. Ingestion of a sucrose solution releases DA in the NAc shell during the first exposure, but less on a second exposure, again suggesting that DA release in the NAc shell depends on the novelty of the stimulus (Rada, Avena, & Hoebel, 2005). DA released in response to the taste of sucrose is proportional to concentration, not the volume consumed (Hajnal, Smith, & Norgren, 2004). However, under certain feeding conditions DA in the NAc can be released with a palatable food, time after time, like a substance of abuse, as discussed in the section of this chapter on sugar bingeing.

Acetylcholine: ACh in the NAc appears to induce satiety. Feeding to satiety causes an increase in extracellular ACh in the NAc (Avena, Rada, Moise, & Hoebel, 2006b; Mark, Rada, Pothos, & Hoebel, 1992). Its overall muscarinic effect is to inhibit feeding at M1 receptors since local injection of the mixed muscarinic agonist arecoline will inhibit feeding, and this effect can be blocked by the relatively specific M1 antagonist pirenzepine (Rada and Hoebel, unpublished). The mixed, muscarinic agonist oxotremorine fails to inhibit lever pressing for food, but does inhibit self-administration of cocaine (Mark et al., 2006). Rats with accumbal ACh toxin-induced lesions eat more food than nonlesioned rats (Hajnal, Szekely, Galosi, & Lenard, 2000).

ACh release in the accumbens may be a manifestation of effective appetite suppressant therapies, and these therapies are, in theory, applicable to drug abuse as well. D-fenfluramine combined with phentermine (i.p.) increases extracellular ACh in the NAc at a dose that inhibits both eating and cocaine self-administration (Glatz et al., 2001; Glowa, Rice, Matecka, & Rothman, 1997; Rada & Hoebel, 2000).

To summarize, ACh release can oppose high DA levels and in this way contribute to satiation. The next section explores a condition in which accumbens DA is low and ACh is high. This may go beyond normal satiety, into the realm of an aversive state.

CONDITIONED TASTE PREFERENCE AND AVERSION

Some approach and avoidance responses are programmed in hindbrain sensory–motor interfaces. For example, in the decerebrate rat, hindbrain connections from the first taste-relay nucleus to the motor outputs are sufficient for neural responses that encode taste and produce facial expressions for food acceptance and rejection (Grill & Kaplan, 2002). In the intact rat, the taste code can be classically conditioned (Chang & Scott, 1984; Mark, Scott, Chang, & Grill, 1988). For conditioned taste preference and conditioned taste aversion, the amygdala and lateral hypothalamus are important in engaging approach and avoidance mechanisms for the rat to walk over to a food source, taste the options, and express a preference (Caulliez, Meile, & Nicolaidis, 1996; Kolakowska, Larue-Achagiotis, & Le Magnen, 1984; Touzani & Sclafani, 2001).

Conditioned taste preference and conditioned taste aversion are the simplest forms of learning that could inform us about the neural mechanisms of both food approach and avoidance. To eat, or not to eat, is often a life or death question faced by animals. The decision is clearly based on prior experience with tastes that signals nutrition or poison.

Dopamine: Using the technique of Sclafani and colleagues (Elizalde & Sclafani, 1990), animals were prepared with a microdialysis probe in the NAc, an indwelling catheter in the cheek for injecting the tastant, and a gastric fistula for injecting food in the stomach. They were allowed to drink a mildly bitter-tasting sucrose octaacetate solution that automatically triggered the injection of polycose into the stomach (Mark, Smith, Rada, & Hoebel, 1994). In this way, the mildly-bitter taste was repeatedly paired with nutrition. On other days, when they drank a citric-acid flavored solution, water was injected into the stomach. In accord with prior results, the animals soon developed a preference the bitter flavor when given a two-bottle choice. Why? One reason is that the bitter flavor had become a conditioned stimulus that resulted in the release of DA in the NAc (Figure 6.1). This neurotransmitter release was presumably instrumental in eliciting the approach behavior.

Conditioned taste aversion has an effect on DA release that is opposite to what is seen with conditioned taste preference. Initially, saccharin delivered through a catheter into the mouth is a preferred taste for rats, as suggested by copious drinking and a neural firing pattern in the nucleus tractus solitarius (NTS) like that seen with the taste of sucrose. However, when saccharin is made aversive by paring its taste with lithium chloride-induced nausea in Garcia's classic taste aversion paradigm (Rusiniak, Palmerino, Rice, Forthman, & Garcia, 1982), animals avoid drinking saccharin, and the taste signal in the NTS changes to resemble that of quinine (Chang & Scott, 1984). When the taste signal and the behavioral response to saccharin are "switched" in this way, microdialysis reveals a shift from saccharin-induced DA release to a decrease in DA (Mark, Blander, & Hoebel, 1991). There is clearly a conditioned decrease in neurotransmitter release underlying the conditioned avoidance behavior.

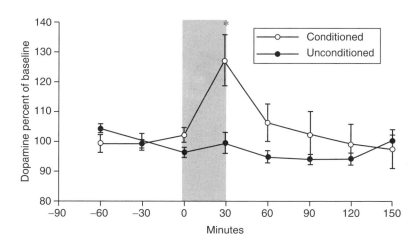

FIGURE 6.1   An example of learned dopamine (DA) release as measured by microdialysis. Extracellular DA in the NAc increases in response to a conditioned taste preference ($^*p <.01$). Details are provided in the text. From "An appetitively conditioned taste elicits a preferential increase in mesolimbic dopamine release," by G. P. Mark, S. E. Smith, P. V. Rada and B. G. Hoebel, 1994, *Pharmacology, Biochemistry, and Behavior*, 48, p. 651.

Acetylcholine: In the first major confirmation of the ACh–aversion hypothesis, conditioned aversion to saccharin significantly increased ACh release in the NAc (Mark, Weinberg, Rada, & Hoebel, 1995). This shows that accumbens ACh release is correlated with avoidance of an unsafe substance. Apparently DA/ACh balance in the accumbens reflects, in part, not just a taste dimension, but what Scott and Mark (1987) call a safety–toxicity dimension. Safe, nutritious substances normally release DA, and poisonous ones release ACh. The same taste can do either one, depending on learned physiological consequences.

The accumbens ACh–avoidance link is more than a correlation; it is causal. When neostigmine is microinjected locally into the NAc to block the degradation of ACh and thereby elevate extracellular levels in association with the taste of saccharin, a conditioned taste aversion is generated (Taylor, Davidson, Mark, Rada, & Hoebel, 1992). In other words, the high levels of ACh produced an internal stimulus (the unconditioned stimulus) like that of lithium chloride-induced nausea.

In summary, the increase in extracellular ACh in the NAc, in combination with a decrease in extracellular DA, can create an aversive state that is sufficient to cause a conditioned taste aversion, as shown by saccharin avoidance. In the next section we ask, if relatively high ACh is, in fact, aversive, will an animal work to escape it and in the process, lower ACh?

HYPOTHALAMIC SELF-STIMULATION AND STIMULATION-ESCAPE

The search for a behavior reinforcement system can be traced back to the 1950s when physiological psychologists focused on the reticular formation, with its role in promoting and inhibiting arousal, and the hypothalamus, with its dual roles in appetite and satiety. In an effort to electrically facilitate approach behavior, Olds and Milner (1954) serendipitously discovered intracranial self-stimulation. Miller and colleagues (Delgado, Roberts, & Miller, 1954) explored electrically induced eating, and Stellar, Teitelbaum, and Epstein (Stellar, 1994; Teitelbaum & Epstein, 1962) focused on medial and lateral hypothalamic lesions, which caused hyperphagia and aphagia/adipsia, respectively. The lateral hypothalamus was described as a feeding center, a view which was challenged repeatedly as the roles and respective functions of nerve fibers that pass through this brain region, as well as other feeding centers, were gradually discovered. We now know that there are many feeding systems in the hypothalamus including, as it turns out, the hypothesized lateral hypothalamic feeding

system (Morton, Cummings, Baskin, Barsh, & Schwartz, 2006) with outputs such as orexin cell groups. In the more medial aspects of the hypothalamus there are fibers from satiety systems, including some arising in the paraventricular nucleus (PVN) (Leibowitz & Hoebel, 2004).

Lateral hypothalamic electrode sites that elicit feeding, drinking, or mating are also sites where rats will electrically self-stimulate (Hoebel, 1976). The brain self-stimulation procedure typically consists of lever pressing for 0.5 s trains of 100 Hz stimulation. A stimulus-bound feeding site can, depending on stimuli available in the environment, be shifted to, for example, a drinking site, while producing both appetitive behavior and oral signs of aversion (Berridge & Valenstein, 1991). At sites that will elicit stimulation-bound feeding, satiety causes a relative shift from brain self-stimulation to stimulation-escape (Hoebel, 1976). Food deprivation potentiates self-stimulation at these sites (Carr & Wolinsky, 1993).

Some hypothalamic electrodes, when placed medial to the fornix, elicit an aversive state, as demonstrated operationally by stimulation-escape behavior, which is measured by lever pressing to turn off recurrent brain stimulation for 5 s. Some electrodes support both approach and escape, with the animal's choice of the two levers shifting from self-stimulation to stimulation-escape as a function of increased satiety or increasing body weight (Carr & Wolinsky, 1993; Hoebel, 1979).

The same principle is true of a hypothalamic site that can elicit mating. Brain self-stimulation in the posterior hypothalamus shifts to stimulation-escape after ejaculation (Hoebel, 1979). Self-stimulation at this site looses it reinforcing value after castration, and androgen-replacement therapy restores it (Caggiula & Hoebel, 1966). Thus, we have here an approach–avoidance system for male mating behavior.

Dopamine: According to our DA–ACh approach–avoidance theory, stimulation-induced approach behavior should involve the release of DA in the NAc, and stimulation-induced escape should reduce an aversive, ACh-mediated state. That is precisely what we find, but there is an interesting twist. DA is released during both brain self-stimulation and stimulation-escape, which suggests that DA is involved in both positive and negative reinforcement. The release of DA is involved in approach that gets, or gets rid of, the reinforcing stimulus (Rada, Mark, & Hoebel, 1998b). This may help explain why noxious stimuli, such as a tail shock, can release DA (Abercrombie, Keefe, DiFrischia, & Zigmond, 1989); it could be the result, in part, of escaping the aversive situation as well as a response to a novel stimulus.

Acetylcholine: There are at least three separate ACh systems in the brain. One is in the forebrain with major projections to the hippocampus and cortex. Another is in the midbrain and projects to the VTA. Some of the lateral hypothalamic outputs descend directly to the VTA and some to the parabrachial nucleus in the hindbrain, where mu-opioid receptors are critical for brain stimulation-induced feeding (Carr, Aleman, Bak, & Simon, 1991). This circuit apparently reaches the cholinergic nerves in the midbrain, because self-stimulation releases ACh from their terminals in the VTA. Blocking ACh in the VTA prevents brain self-stimulation and also will bring an ongoing meal to a halt (Rada, Mark, Yeomans, & Hoebel, 2000). Note this VTA cholinergic system normally facilitates the DA system. This is just the opposite function of the third ACh system, in the NAc, which is the subject of this chapter. It has interneurons scattered throughout the striatum, as described in the introduction.

The next interesting test of the accumbens ACh–aversion hypothesis was whether or not the animal that escapes brain stimulation is escaping accumbal ACh. Figure 6.2 shows ACh levels in the NAc for several groups

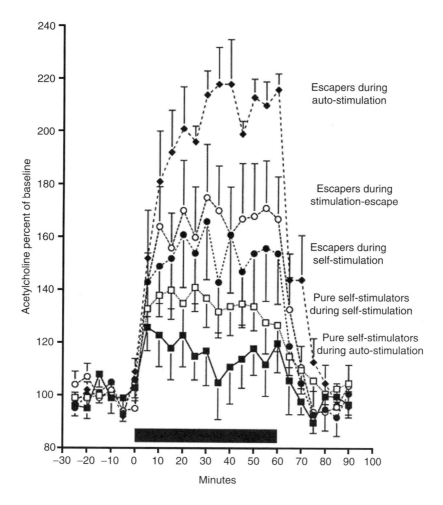

FIGURE 6.2 Extracellular acetylcholine (ACh) in the nucleus accumbens (NAc) is shown before, during and after 60 min of lateral hypothalamic stimulation in five situations. In the top curve (filled diamonds), extracellular ACh more than doubles in 'escapers' when they received inescapable stimulation. In the next curve (open circles) the same animals reduced their ACh release significantly by stimulation-escape responding. In the middle curve (filled circles) the escapers pressed a different lever for self-stimulation on a different day. Self-stimulation increased ACh half as much as inescapable stimulation. The bottom two curves are for different rats that were pure self-stimulators that failed to learn stimulation-escape (open squares and filled squares). They showed the smallest rise in ACh. From "Aversive hypothalamic stimulation releases acetylcholine in the nucleus accumbens, and stimulation-escape decreases it," by P. V. Rada and B. G. Hoebel, 2001, *Brain Research*, 888, p. 60.

of rats. These groups were trained to self-stimulate in 5-min periods. This alternated with 5-min periods of automatic, recurrent stimulation. They could sit there and be stimulated, or, if they found it aversive they could escape by lever pressing for a 5 s cessation of stimulation. Rats were then grouped according to whether they were (a) "pure self-stimulators" that did not press the escape lever, (b) those that would self-stimulate when they had the opportunity and also escape the automatic stimulation, and (c) those that did not self-stimulate and assertively pressed the escape lever, i.e., "escapers." In the top curve of Figure 6.2, note that the automatic stimulation increases ACh in the NAc to 200% of baseline in the rats that would have escaped it if they had been allowed to do so. The next, curve (second from the top) shows what happens when the "escapers" are allowed to avoid stimulation by pressing the lever to turn off stimulation; their ACh levels decrease (Rada & Hoebel, 2001). Thus, a neural consequence of stimulation-escape behavior is to reduce the level of accumbens ACh. DA is probably involved in the motivation to approach and press either lever, whether it is for stimulation (approach) or escape (avoidance). When ACh is relative high, this apparently stops brain self-stimulation and turns the animal's attention toward the problem of escaping the ACh-mediated state.

MOTIVATION AND DEPRESSION

If depression is in some ways the opposite of motivation and elation, then one might expect a depressed animal to display decreased extracellular DA and increased ACh.

Dopamine: A role for DA in mania has been suggested (Schwartz, Ksir, Koob, & Bloom, 1982). DA is needed for work output (Neill, Fenton, & Justice, 2002; Salamone et al., 2007), and we have already mentioned its role in incentive motivation (Berridge & Robinson, 1998) and reward. According to any of these views, one might expect an animal with low DA to either work in a manner that restores it or to give up and display response extinction. Persistent lack of responding is a characteristic of behavioral depression.

This field of behavioral neuroscience has an interesting history of animal models of "learned helplessness", "anhedonia", "behavioral despair", chronic "mild stress", and "social isolation" (Blanchard & Blanchard, 1990; Porsolt, Anton, Blavet, & Jalfre, 1978; Seligman, 1972; Willner, 2005; Wise, Spindler, deWit, & Gerberg, 1978). In the forced-swim test for behavioral depression, a rat is tested for escape efforts in a water tank, 2 days in a row (Porsolt

et al., 1978). Rats tend to give up trying to escape on the second day, as shown by less active swimming and more passive, immobile floating. Extracellular DA in the NAc does, indeed, decrease during the swim test when animals become behaviorally depressed (Rossetti, Lai, Hmaidan, & Gessa, 1993).

Acetylcholine: We hypothesized, based on the ACh–aversion hypothesis, that a rat undergoing the forced-swim test would have high levels of accumbal ACh when its escape behavior decreases. On the other hand, maybe ACh would be low due to successfully escaping the aversive situation by floating. Neither idea was quite right, but we were on the right track. ACh does not rise or fall during immobility. Instead, it decreases briefly after the animal is removed from the water the first day and then increases, with the interesting discovery that basal ACh is still high before going back in the water the second day when behavior will be depressed (Rada, Colasante, Skirzewski, Hernandez, & Hoebel, 2006). Thus, ACh levels seemed to reflect a long-lasting state correlated with behavioral depression the next day.

We tested the cholinergic receptor types, nicotinic and muscarinic, that might be responsible for this depression-related effect. Nicotinic receptors were unlikely to be involved, since we had shown that local nicotine releases DA via nicotinic receptors (Rada, Jensen, & Hoebel, 2001). Turning to the muscarinic receptors, Figure 6.3 shows that local bilateral injection of a muscarinic agonist arecoline depresses swimming behavior, and the relatively specific M-1 antagonist pirenzepine increases swimming (Chau, Rada, Kosloff, Taylor, & Hoebel, 2001). This is not a locomotor effect because there was no sign of hyperactivity in an open field. Thus, the M-1 type receptor is a candidate for accumbens-induced depression.

Classic antidepressants such as desipramine are well known to increase swimming behaviors in the forced-swim test (Detke, Rickels, & Lucki, 1995). Even a specific serotonin reuptake inhibitor such as fluoxetine (Prozac) will have this effect (Detke et al., 1995). Thus, the forced-swim test can identify antidepressant drugs that motivate escape behavior without causing general increases in locomotor activity. We find that fluoxetine delivered directly into the NAc by reverse dialysis causes an immediate increase in escape efforts (Chau, Rada, Kosloff, & Hoebel, 1999). The increase in synaptic serotonin caused by fluoxetine, in that one brain site, is sufficient to produce the antidepressant effect typically seen with 2 weeks of peripheral administration.

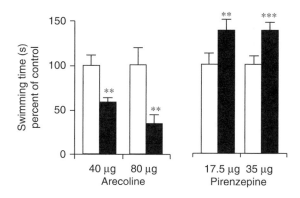

FIGURE 6.3 Swimming time following injections of cholinergic drugs in the nucleus accumbens (NAc) (black bars), compared with vehicle (white bars). Local injection of arecoline, a muscarinic agonist, decreased swim time (left graph); the animals gave up more quickly. Conversely, pirenzepine, an M1 receptor antagonist, increased swimming escape attempts in the manner of an antidepressant (right graph), but note this is a local injection; so this is a locally induced antidepressant effect. Swimming time following vehicle is normalized to 100% representing the control value. Swimming time following a drug injection on a different day is expressed as a percentage of control. Significant changes in the within-subject response to drug injections are indicated with asterisks ($^{**}p$ <.01, $^{***}p$ <.001). From "Nucleus accumbens muscarinic receptors in the control of behavioral depression: antidepressant-like effects of local M1 antagonist in the Porsolt swim test," by D. T. Chau, P. Rada, R. A. Kosloff, J. L. Taylor and B. G. Hoebel, 2001, *Neuroscience, 104*, p. 791.

If the accumbens ACh depression hypothesis is correct, then an antidepressant drug should lower ACh. When local fluoxetine is delivered by microdialysis into the NAc, it lowers extracellular ACh (Chau et al., 1999).

The mechanism of action is clear. Fluoxetine infused into the NAc inhibits ACh release, and judging by the similar action of a serotonin-1A receptor agonist, 8-OH-DPAT (Rada, Mark, & Hoebel, 1993), serotonin acts in part at serotonin-1A receptors to produce this effect. When the high basal ACh, due to the prior day's experience, is reduced, the animal spends more time trying to escape.

There are two anomalous results to explain. First, if ACh stops behavior or causes an aversive state, why would rats self-inject the cholinergic agonist carbachol into the NAc (Ikemoto, Glazier, Murphy, & McBride, 1998). This effect appears contrary to the theory that ACh can cause aversion or inhibit behavior. However, we find that when injected in the NAc, carbachol decreases ACh release via M2-muscarinic receptors and also releases DA, which explains self-injection (Rada, Paez, Hernandez, Avena, &

Hoebel, 2007). Second, why would the muscarinic antagonist scopolamine inhibit eating (Will, Pratt, & Kelley, 2006)? Scopolamine is a cholinergic antagonist that blocks most types of muscarinic receptors, including the M-2 receptor that is both postsynaptic and presynaptic. As a presynaptic autoreceptor on the cholinergic neurons, the M-2 type normally provides local negative feedback by inhibiting further release of ACh. Blocking the M-2 receptors releases ACh (Chau et al., 2001). This elevated level of ACh could act at postsynaptic receptors such as the M-1 type to suppress eating. Thus, rats may stop eating with scopolamine due to the release of ACh.

In summary, the results are consistent with the theory that DA can cause behavior activation as seen in the open-field locomotor test, and ACh can cause behavior depression as seen by the chronically elevated basal level on the second day of the swim test. The behavioral depression is mediated in part by a postsynaptic M-1 effect. Local fluoxetine raises extracellular serotonin, which then acts in part at serotonin-1A receptors to lower ACh. This reduces the ACh available at M-1 receptors and thereby alleviates behavioral depression.

DRUG SELF-ADMINISTRATION AND DRUG WITHDRAWAL

In this section, we describe animal models of drug dependence that amplify approach–avoidance responses. Most addictive drugs increase extracellular DA, and drug withdrawal releases ACh in the NAc.

Dopamine: In a classic paper, Di Chiara and Imperato (1988) reported that drugs of abuse delivered systemically increased extracellular DA in the accumbens as measured by microdialysis. At about the same time, we also adopted the Ungerstedt (Hurd, Kehr, & Ungerstedt, 1988) microdialysis technique and found that morphine, phencyclidine, amphetamine, and nicotine released DA from terminals in the NAc, even when infused locally (Hernandez et al., 1987; Mifsud, Hernandez, & Hoebel, 1989; Pothos, Rada, Mark, & Hoebel, 1991; Rada, Mark, Taylor, & Hoebel, 1996). The only exception we could find to the dopaminergic addictive-drug rule was the anxiolytic drug diazepam (Valium) given systemically, which has the potential for abuse without a large effect on DA release (Rada & Hoebel, 2005). One reason for diazepam dependence may be related to ACh release during withdrawal, as described below.

Acetylcholine: Withdrawal signs can be elicited in rats by giving them an addictive drug for a prolonged period and then administering the appropriate receptor antagonist. This can be done for morphine using naloxone, for local morphine using local methyl naloxonium, for nicotine using mecamylamine, and for diazepam using the benzodiazepine antagonist flumazenil (Koob, Maldonado, & Stinus, 1992; Rada & Hoebel, 2005; Rada et al., 2001; Way, Loh, & Shen, 1969). Rats received injections of morphine daily for a week, causing DA release each time as deduced from the microdialysis measurement on Day 7 (Pothos et al., 1991). Then on Day 8, they received naloxone, which causes DA to decrease and ACh to be released instead. These animals displayed wet-dog shakes and teeth-chattering, which are classic signs of opiate withdrawal. By injecting methyl naloxonium in a variety of brain sites, Koob et al. (1992) found that the locus coeruleus and the periaqueductal gray were highly sensitive in eliciting the activating physiological components of morphine withdrawal, and the NAc mediated aversion. Koob and colleagues have argued that withdrawal is also an aversive state that rats will work to escape. As evidence of anhedonia during withdrawal, they show that brain self-stimulation reward threshold rises during withdrawal from addictive drugs (Epping-Jordan, Watkins, Koob, & Markou, 1998; Markou & Koob, 1991; Schulteis, Markou, Cole, & Koob, 1995). If this state is due in part to accumbens ACh, then the DA–ACh theory predicts that naloxone give systemically, or methyl naloxonium infused locally in the accumbens, would cause the release of ACh in morphine-dependent rats. This is in fact the case. As shown in Figure 6.4, systemic administration of the opioid antagonist, or "local opioid withdrawal" in the NAc, not only lowers extracellular DA, but also releases ACh (Rada, Mark, Pothos, & Hoebel, 1991; Rada et al., 1996). The observation that local naloxone causes a withdrawal-like shift in DA/ACh balance shows in another way that the NAc has opioid receptors involved in drug withdrawal.

In summary, most addictive drugs activate dopaminergic functions. Some, such as the psychostimulants that release DA or block DA reuptake, will have effects in every DA terminal region. Others, such as the opiates, may act in part by way of DA cells in the VTA (Tanda & Di Chiara, 1998). In cases of pharmacologically induced withdrawal, ACh was released in the NAc. Having argued that high levels of ACh can be aversive, on the basis of conditioned taste aversion, antidepressant therapy and brain stimulation-escape behavior, we conclude that high ACh during drug withdrawal once again has an aversive component. If rats will press a lever that lowers ACh in the stimulation-escape paradigm, it is logical to suggest that they will also respond for drugs that lower ACh in

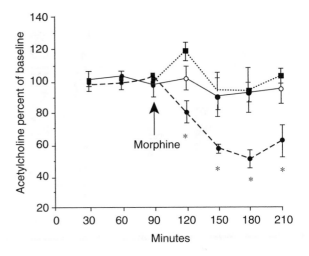

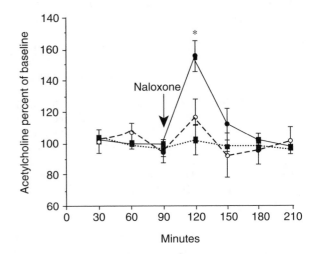

FIGURE 6.4 Top graph: Morphine injection (20 mg/kg i.p.) causes a significant decrease in extracellular ACh (closed circles), which was not apparent after repeated exposure to the opiate for 7 days (open circles). Control rats received saline (filled squares). Bottom graph: On Day 8, after morphine dependence was established, naloxone injection (20 mg/kg i.p.) causes a 55% increase in ACh levels (closed circles) that was accompanied by withdrawal signs such as wet-dog shakes and teeth-chattering. This did not occur in nondependent rats (open circles) nor rats pretreated with clonidine (filled squares). Control rats injected with saline (not shown) showed a similar lack of effect ($^*p < .05$). From "Systemic morphine simultaneously decreases extracellular acetylcholine and increases dopamine in the nucleus accumbens of freely moving rats," by P. Rada, E. Pothos, G. P. Mark, and B. G. Hoebel, 1991, *Brain Research*, 561, p. 355.

order to alleviate withdrawal. This would be a form of "self-medication." The case for ACh in withdrawal from psychostimulants has not yet been made. Interpretation of diazepam withdrawal was complicated by a rise in DA along with the ACh. Theoretically, the relative predominance of ACh might cause sufficient "aversion" such that the animal would self-medicate by taking more of the tranquilizer, to lower ACh.

Self-medication during withdrawal by taking the drug again may be one of the primary causes of relapse (Koob & Le Moal, 2005a,b). The aversive cholinergic component is possibly one factor underlying this type of drug relapse. To escape the mood and motivational effects of high ACh when withdrawing from morphine, alcohol or nicotine, the animal needs only to take more of the drug, which will raise DA and lower ACh.

One way to test these theories is to go beyond drugs that act wherever the receptors exist, and turn to natural means of activating the DA and opioid systems. Natural forms of sensory input, which act via normal routes to reinforcement, may shed new light on the motivational mechanisms for approach and avoidance.

SUGAR INTAKE AND SUGAR WITHDRAWAL

This section shows, in essence, that bingeing on sugar can be like taking a low dose of a drug of abuse.

Dopamine: Feeding behavior and cocaine both increased extracellular DA in the NAc at the same probe site and in the same animals (Hernandez & Hoebel, 1988). Based on this and similar evidence, many researchers have suggested that drugs of abuse act, in part, via the feeding reward and motivation system (Hoebel, Rada, Mark, & Pothos, 1999; Kelley & Berridge, 2002; Rada et al., 2007; Wise, 1988, 1989). Cocaine has more potent effects on extracellular DA than does food. Cocaine not only acts everywhere there are DA reuptake sites, but it does so every time the drug is administered. Cocaine, as well as opiates, causes local homeostatic compensations in terms of receptor trafficking and synthesis of neurotransmitters and receptors. Food could hardly be expected to have addictive effects with the magnitude of those drugs. Perhaps this is one reason the DA system that projects to the NAc evolved so that it stops firing when the food taste is no longer novel. DA cells primarily become active in response to novel conditioned stimuli, as described in the section on conditioned taste preference. Recordings from DA cells in the VTA of monkeys suggest that even the conditioned response to DA wanes, and a response reappears only when the conditioned stimuli fail to deliver the expected taste (Berns, McClure, Pagnoni, & Montague, 2001; Schultz, Dayan, & Montague, 1997). Thus, one might think we are well protected from the

addictive properties of DA under most nondrug circumstances. However, alternating feasting with famine is another story.

When we look at all the behavioral and environmental variables that potentiate drug abuse and apply them to feeding, an interesting effect emerges. A surge of DA can be released in the NAc every time the animal eats when trained to binge on sugar by alternating food deprivation and access to chow and a sugar solution to drink (Rada & Hoebel, 2005). Figure 6.5 is an example of repeated DA release caused by daily sugar bingeing. The control group with ad libitum access to 10% sucrose solution does not show the effect, nor does a group that only had sugar to drink twice, on Day 1 and again on Day 21. But the group with daily 12-h food deprivation followed by access to chow and the sucrose solution shows a sharp rise in DA, even on Day 21. Thus, in these rats with intermittent access to sugar, the DA effect was analogous to receiving a low dose of an addictive drug every day for 21 days. Concomitant signs of dependency appear.

The indications of "sugar addiction" parallel signs of drug addiction. These are fully described elsewhere (Avena, Rada, & Hoebel, 2008). In brief, they fall into three behavioral categories: (a) "binge eating," which refers to an unusually large meal, larger than an animal would take when feeding ad libitum (Avena, Rada, & Hoebel, 2006a), (b) "withdrawal," which occurs in response to fasting, or when naloxone is administered (Colantuoni et al., 2002), (Avena, Bocarsly, Rada, Kim, & Hoebel, 2008), (c) "craving," which, for lack of a better word, is defined as long-lasting signs of enhanced motivation seen during abstinence. These protracted effects include (a) "cross-sensitization", in which the animals are hyperactive in their exploration of an open-field when given a low dose of amphetamine (Avena & Hoebel, 2003) or cocaine (Gosnell, 2005), (b) the "deprivation effect", in which the animals engage in more lever pressing for sugar after 2 weeks of abstinence than ever before (Avena, Long, & Hoebel, 2005), (c) the "gateway effect", shown as taking more alcohol when sugar is denied (Avena, Carrillo, Needham, Leibowitz, & Hoebel, 2004), and (d) the "incubation effect" which refers to the growing motivation to lever press for sugar-associated cues. This phenomenon grows for as long as a month during sugar abstinence (Grimm, Fyall, & Osincup, 2005). We will discuss bingeing and withdrawal, since they both have results related to DA/ACh balance in approach and avoidance.

In addition to the repeated release of DA described above, we have found other neurochemical changes in the brains of sugar-bingeing rats during bingeing. First, with

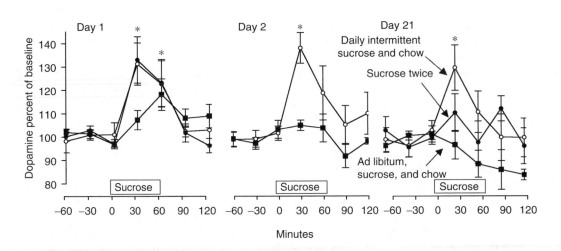

FIGURE 6.5   Only the animals on the intermittent sucrose and chow regimen maintained high dopamine (DA) release during the first hour for 21 days (open circles). Microdialysis samples were collected on Days 1, 2, and 21 of access. On Day 1, DA levels increased significantly for the control groups: sucrose-twice group (filled circles), ad libitum sucrose and chow (filled squares), but there was a blunting of this effect by Day 21. The ordinate indicates the hour (0–60 min) of sucrose availability for this test ($^{*}p <.05$). From "Daily bingeing on sugar repeatedly releases dopamine in the accumbens shell," by P. Rada, N. M. Avena, and B. G. Hoebel, 2005, *Neuroscience*, 134, p. 737.

regard to DA systems, receptor autoradiography performed after a month of intermittent sugar bingeing shows increased D-1 receptor binding and decreased D-2 receptor binding in the striatum relative to chow-fed controls (Colantuoni et al., 2001). These receptor alterations are like those reported for drugs of abuse (Alburges, Narang, & Wamsley, 1993; Unterwald, 2001). This decrement in D-2 receptor binding may be due, in part, to a decrease in expression of mRNA for the D-2 receptor (Georges, Stinus, Bloch, & Le Moine, 1999; Turchan, Lason, Budziszewska, & Przewlocka, 1997). Even in human drug addicts, and people who are obese, brain imaging reveals this telltale decrease in D-2 receptor binding, which is interpreted as an adaptation to excessive DA release (Volkow & Wise, 2005).

Enkephalin mRNA is also decreased in rats with intermittent sugar access (Spangler et al., 2004). Our finding is consistent with observations of Kelley's group (Kelley, Will, Steininger, Zhang, & Haber, 2003) using limited daily access to Ensure, a sweet-fat drink. It is likely that this decrease in production of enkephalin is related to the increase in mu-opioid receptors that we see in sugar-bingeing rats (Colantuoni et al., 2001). Intermittent bingeing releases DA, and presumably opioids, and alters DA and opioid receptor functions and gene expression, suggesting these neural systems compensate for the effects of intermittent deprivation and bingeing (Colantuoni et al., 2001; Rada et al., 2005; Spangler et al., 2004).

Acetylcholine: As described above, naloxone can cause withdrawal in rats pretreated with drugs of abuse, suggesting that these drugs act via endogenous opioid systems somewhere in the nervous system. The same is true of sugar after the animals are trained to binge. We obtain signs of anxiety during withdrawal in the sugar-bingeing rats, using both naloxone (3 mg/kg s.c.) and with 24-h food deprivation. Multiple signs of withdrawal have been detected during withdrawal in sugar-bingeing animals, including teeth-chattering and anxiety as measured by avoidance of the open arms of an elevated plus-maze (Colantuoni et al., 2002) (Avena, Bocarsly, Rada, Kim, and Hoebel, 2008). After naloxone treatment the animals are also prone to behavioral depression in the swim test (Kim, Avena and Hoebel, unpublished). In terms of neurochemistry, rats in withdrawal from a diet of intermittent sugar and chow show the predicted decrease in DA and increase in extracellular ACh in the NAc (Colantuoni et al., 2002), much like withdrawal from morphine, alcohol, or nicotine.

In summary, according to behavioral measures in three phases of addiction, rats with several weeks of experience bingeing on a sugar solution show many of the same behavior patterns as seen in animal models of drug dependency. This is due, in part, to the fact that they get daily "surges" of DA in the NAc. Apparently this involves changes in both DA and opioid systems, as described above. These changes contribute to withdrawal signs, which include behavioral manifestations of increased ACh release combined with relatively low extracellular DA.

We call these rats "sugar addicted," although others might prefer the term "sugar dependent." Even drug addiction is not called an addiction in the DSM-IV, although that may soon change. It is clearly established that animal models can capture many of the features of drug addiction (Koob & Le Moal, 2005a). As reviewed above, we have used a number of these models with the intermittent sugar diet and have found many of the same features. Given the careful step-by-step comparison between rats that self-administer cocaine, morphine, nicotine, and alcohol in binges and those that self-administer sugar in binges, it is clear that the drugs and sugar can have similar effects on behaviors that model addiction.

It is an interesting question whether social and scientific norms will be accepted such that the term addiction is applied to natural behaviors. The popular press already has articles about "addiction" to many different, highly-motivated behavior patterns, including many self-help books and Web sites that address food addiction. The differences between strong motivation and true addiction will have to be sorted out. The evidence outlined above certainly suggests that under certain circumstances, bingeing on a sugar solution can institute approach and avoidance effects like addictive drugs.

THE DA–ACh THEORY OF APPROACH AND AVOIDANCE

Five examples of approach and avoidance are reviewed above. On the approach side we discussed (a) eating, (b) a positive conditioned stimulus, (c) brain self-stimulation, (d) drug intake, and (e) sugar bingeing. These are contrasted with opposing behaviors, which are in the avoidance category: (a) satiation, (b) negative conditioned stimuli, (c) behavioral depression, (d) drug withdrawal, and (e) sugar withdrawal. All the approach situations have DA release in common. All the avoidance situations feature a rise accumbens ACh. It was noted that DA is an important factor in seeking both positive and negative reinforcers. In this sense, it is involved in the motoric aspects of both approach and avoidance behavior. The closely related problem is to identify the neural systems that provide each of the components of reinforcement processes. As summarized by Kelley et al. (2005), DA is important for the approach phase, opioids for the hedonic aspect of the feeding consummatory act, with glutamate and GABA in the NAc controlling the actual consummatory acts. ACh, on the other hand, promotes stopping. ACh seems to have dual roles by also contributing to an

aversive state, and may do so in conjunction with dynorphin acting at kappa opioid receptors, which are known to mediate aversion in the NAc while inhibiting the DA system (Nestler & Carlezon, 2006; Spanagel, Herz, & Shippenberg, 1990).

The evidence presented above in the feeding–satiety section suggests that postingestional stimuli release accumbens ACh, which stops appetitive behavior. The section on conditioned taste preference and avoidance strongly suggests that the taste of nausea-associated (i.e., unsafe) food, even if it is a sweet food, will both decrease DA and release ACh while stopping appetitive behavior. Elevated ACh in the NAc is sufficient to create a long-lasting aversion. The brain self-stimulation and stimulation-escape section suggest that if there is enough DA to support behavior output, the animal will work to avoid stimulation that releases ACh and thereby succeed in reducing its own ACh levels. It may be that ACh releases DA via nicotinic receptors for the approach behavior that is necessary for this negative reinforcement. In the section on behavioral exploration and depression it becomes clear that ACh acts via the M-1 muscarinic-type receptor to make a rat decrease escape efforts when DA is low. Basal ACh can remain elevated for hours, if not days. Elevated ACh is a cause of the depressed state as indicated by the action of local fluoxetine, which lowers ACh and augments efforts to escape the aversive situation.

Then we turned to addiction as a form of exaggerated approach and avoidance, first to drugs and then to sugar. Drug addiction is very powerful compared to natural addiction, but qualitatively the two are very similar. Once the components of sugar dependency were given operational definitions for comparison with drugs of abuse, the results mimicked drug addiction in terms of both behavioral abnormalities and neurochemical changes in the brain. In both cases, withdrawal lowered DA and released ACh instead. We conclude that the withdrawal state is an aversive condition that creates negative conditioned cues, and that animals would work to rectify this situation by performing acts that lower ACh, if they can trigger enough DA to do it. The most direct way to release DA and lower ACh might be to take the substance of abuse such as morphine, alcohol, nicotine, or sugar over again.

MORE EVIDENCE: HYPOTHALAMIC CONTROL OF DA/ACh BALANCE

If the accumbens DA/ACh theory is correct, then manipulations of other brain sites that start or stop ingestive behavior should, in at least some cases, release DA or ACh accordingly. A series of studies from our laboratory has shown that specific hypothalamic systems for feeding and satiety exert a predictable influence over DA/ACh balance in the NAc. Specifically, norepinephrine or galanin, which induces eating when injected in the PVN, increases DA release and lower accumbens ACh (Hajnal, Mark, Rada, Lenard, & Hoebel, 1997; Rada, Mark, & Hoebel, 1998a). Neuropeptide-Y did not have these effects even though it is orexigenic (Rada et al., 1998a). Satiety-producing doses of serotonin or cholecystokinin (CCK) in the PVN lowered accumbens DA, and the combination of serotonin plus CCK both decreased DA and increased ACh (Helm, Rada, & Hoebel, 2003). In summary, whenever DA or ACh release was increased by hypothalamic injections, the change was in the direction of feeding or satiety, respectively.

BULIMIA: ANOTHER TEST OF THE THEORY

Bulimic patients have a difficult approach–avoidance conflict. They want to eat, but do not want to gain weight. Some purge the calories, some exercise excessively, and others fast periodically or use artificial sweeteners (Klein, Boudreau, Devlin, & Walsh, 2006). As a test of the DA–ACh theory in an animal model of bulimia, rats were trained to binge on 10% sugar while the contents of their stomachs were purged using an open gastric fistula (Avena et al., 2006b). Bingeing released DA every day, just from the taste of sugar. The bouts of sugar intake were even larger than seen with normal sugar bingeing. Purging prevented the typical ACh increase that would normally accompany satiety. This is further evidence that ACh is part of the final common path for factors that inhibit ingestive behavior. In terms of approach and avoidance, one can surmise that the abnormal approach behavior in bulimia involves receiving repetitive DA release without ACh. Purging behavior may involve avoiding accumbens ACh.

SUMMARY

In all of the opposing behavior patterns described above, approach behavior involves the release of DA, whereas ACh is correlated with, or causes, avoidance. The data support the described hypotheses and generate an overall theory. As others have said, DA in the NAc is important for approach and behavior reinforcement, i.e., approaching again and again. We emphasize that this is true for both positive and negative reinforcement. ACh creates a state that is at least inhibitory and sometimes aversive. ACh apparently counteracts DA in some regards, such as during the satiation process, but also works with DA to

generate approach behavior that escapes the effect of ACh. Clearly, ACh is a major factor in stopping unsafe behavior. When DA is low, ACh apparently creates an aversive state that would be essential for learning avoidance. From our current vantage point, with a view limited largely to these two neurotransmitters in the NAc and their interaction with opioid systems, ACh can inhibit behavior when DA is high, and creates an aversive state when DA is low.

ACKNOWLEDGMENTS

This research was supported at various stages by USPHS grant DA-10608, MH-65024 and the M. and B. Lane and E. H. Lane Foundations.

REFERENCES

Abercrombie, E. D., Keefe, K. A., DiFrischia, D. S., & Zigmond, M. J. (1989). Differential effect of stress on in vivo dopamine release in striatum, nucleus accumbens, and medial frontal cortex. *Journal of Neurochemistry*, *52*(5), 1655–1658.

Alburges, M. E., Narang, N., & Wamsley, J. K. (1993). Alterations in the dopaminergic receptor system after chronic administration of cocaine. *Synapse (New York)*, *14*(4), 314–323.

Aston-Jones, G., & Cohen, J. D. (2005). An integrative theory of locus coeruleus–norepinephrine function: Adaptive gain and optimal performance. *Annual Review of Neuroscience*, *28*, 403–450.

Avena, N., Rada, P., & Hoebel, B. (2006a). Unit 9.23C Sugar bingeing in rats. In J. Crawley, C. Gerfen, M. Rogawski, D. Sibley, P. Skolnick, & S. Wray (Eds.), *Current protocols in neuroscience* (pp. 9.23C.1–9.23C.6). Indianapolis: John Wiley & Sons, Inc.

Avena, N. M., Carrillo, C. A., Needham, L., Leibowitz, S. F., & Hoebel, B. G. (2004). Sugar-dependent rats show enhanced intake of unsweetened ethanol. *Alcohol (Fayetteville, N. Y.)*, *34*(2–3), 203–209.

Avena, N. M., & Hoebel, B. G. (2003). A diet promoting sugar dependency causes behavioral cross-sensitization to a low dose of amphetamine. *Neuroscience*, *122*(1), 17–20.

Avena, N. M., Long, K. A., & Hoebel, B. G. (2005). Sugar-dependent rats show enhanced responding for sugar after abstinence: Evidence of a sugar deprivation effect. *Physiology & Behavior*, *84*(3), 359–362.

Avena, N. M., Rada, P., & Hoebel, B. G. (2008). Evidence of sugar addiction: Behavioral and neurochemical effects of intermittent, excessive sugar intake. *Neuroscience and Biobehavioral Reviews*, *32*(1), 20–39.

Avena, N. M., Rada, P., Moise, N., & Hoebel, B. G. (2006b). Sucrose sham feeding on a binge schedule releases accumbens dopamine repeatedly and eliminates the acetylcholine satiety response. *Neuroscience*, *139*(3), 813–820.

Avena, N. M., Bocarsly, M. E., Rada, P., Kim, A., & Hoebel, B. G. (2008). After daily bingeing on a sucrose solution, food deprivation induces anxiety and accumbens dopamine/acetylcholine imbalance. *Physiol Behav*. [Epub ahead of print].

Balleine, B. W., & Dickinson, A. (1998). Goal-directed instrumental action: Contingency and incentive learning and their cortical substrates. *Neuropharmacology*, *37*(4–5), 407–419.

Bannerman, D. M., Rawlins, J. N., McHugh, S. B., Deacon, R. M., Yee, B. K., Bast, T., et al. (2004). Regional dissocitations within the hippocampus–memory and anxiety. *Neuroscience and Biobehavioral Reviews*, *28*(3), 273–283.

Bassareo, V., De Luca, M. A., & Di Chiara, G. (2002). Differential expression of motivational stimulus properties by dopamine in nucleus accumbens shell versus core and prefrontal cortex. *The Journal of Neuroscience: The Official Journal of the Society for Neuroscience*, *22*(11), 4709–4719.

Bassareo, V., & Di Chiara, G. (1997). Differential influence of associative and nonassociative learning mechanisms on the responsiveness of prefrontal and accumbal dopamine transmission to food stimuli in rats fed ad libitum. *The Journal of Neuroscience: The Official Journal of the Society for Neuroscience*, *17*(2), 851–861.

Bassareo, V., & Di Chiara, G. (1999). Differential responsiveness of dopamine transmission to food-stimuli in nucleus accumbens shell/core compartments. *Neuroscience*, *89*(3), 637–641.

Berns, G. S., McClure, S. M., Pagnoni, G., & Montague, P. R. (2001). Predictability modulates human brain response to reward. *The Journal of Neuroscience: The Official Journal of the Society for Neuroscience*, *21*(8), 2793–2798.

Berridge, K. C., & Robinson, T. E. (1998). What is the role of dopamine in reward: Hedonic impact, reward learning, or incentive salience? *Brain Research. Brain Research Reviews*, *28*(3), 309–369.

Berridge, K. C., & Valenstein, E. S. (1991). What psychological process mediates feeding evoked by electrical stimulation of the lateral hypothalamus? *Behavioral Neuroscience*, *105*(1), 3–14.

Berthoud, H. R. (1999). An overview of neural pathways and networks involved in the control of food intake and selection. In H. R. Berthoud & R. J. Seeley (Eds.), *Neural and metabolic control of macronutrient intake* (pp. 361–388). New York: CRC Press.

Blanchard, D. C., & Blanchard, R. J. (1990). Behavioral correlates of chronic dominance–subordination relationships of male rats in a seminatural situation. *Neuroscience and Biobehavioral Reviews*, *14*(4), 455–462.

Caggiula, A. R., & Hoebel, B. G. (1966). "Copulation-reward site" in the posterior hypothalamus. *Science*, *153*(741), 1284–1285.

Carr, K. D., Aleman, D. O., Bak, T. H., & Simon, E. J. (1991). Effects of parabrachial opioid antagonism on stimulation-induced feeding. *Brain Research*, *545*(1–2), 283–286.

Carr, K. D., & Wolinsky, T. D. (1993). Chronic food restriction and weight loss produce opioid facilitation of perifornical hypothalamic self-stimulation. *Brain Research*, *607*(1–2), 141–148.

Caulliez, R., Meile, M. J., & Nicolaidis, S. (1996). A lateral hypothalamic D1 dopaminergic mechanism in conditioned taste aversion. *Brain Research*, *729*(2), 234–245.

Chang, F. C., & Scott, T. R. (1984). Conditioned taste aversions modify neural responses in the rat nucleus tractus solitarius. *The Journal of Neuroscience: The Official Journal of the Society for Neuroscience*, *4*(7), 1850–1862.

Chau, D., Rada, P. V., Kosloff, R. A., & Hoebel, B. G. (1999). Cholinergic, M1 receptors in the nucleus accumbens mediate behavioral depression. A possible downstream target for fluoxetine. *Annals of the New York Academy of Sciences*, *877*, 769–774.

Chau, D. T., Rada, P., Kosloff, R. A., Taylor, J. L., & Hoebel, B. G. (2001). Nucleus accumbens muscarinic receptors in the control of behavioral depression: Antidepressant-like effects of local M1 antagonist in the Porsolt swim test. *Neuroscience*, *104*(3), 791–798.

Colantuoni, C., Rada, P., McCarthy, J., Patten, C., Avena, N. M., Chadeayne, A., et al. (2002). Evidence that intermittent, excessive sugar intake causes endogenous opioid dependence. *Obesity Research*, *10*(6), 478–488.

Colantuoni, C., Schwenker, J., McCarthy, J., Rada, P., Ladenheim, B., Cadet, J. L., et al. (2001). Excessive sugar intake alters binding to dopamine and mu-opioid receptors in the brain. *Neuroreport*, *12*(16), 3549–3552.

De Olmos, J. S., & Heimer, L. (1999). The concepts of the ventral striatopallidal system and extended amygdala. In J. F. McGinty (Ed.), *Advancing from the ventral striatum to the extended amygdala: Implications for neuropsychiatry and drug abuse* (Vol. 877). New York: Annals of the New York Academy of Sciences.

Delgado, J. M., Roberts, W. W., & Miller, N. E. (1954). Learning motivated by electrical stimulation of the brain. *American Journal of Physiology*, *179*(3), 587–593.

Detke, M. J., Rickels, M., & Lucki, I. (1995). Active behaviors in the rat forced swimming test differentially produced by serotonergic and noradrenergic antidepressants. *Psychopharmacology (Berl)*, *121*(1), 66–72.

Di Chiara, G., & Bassareo, V. (2007). Reward system and addiction: What dopamine does and doesn't do. *Current Opinion in Pharmacology*, *7*(1), 69–76.

Di Chiara, G., & Imperato, A. (1988). Drugs abused by humans preferentially increase synaptic dopamine concentrations in the mesolimbic system of freely moving rats. *Proceedings of the National Academy of Sciences of the United States of America*, *85*(14), 5274–5278.

Elizalde, G., & Sclafani, A. (1990). Flavor preferences conditioned by intragastric polycose infusions: A detailed analysis using an electronic esophagus preparation. *Physiology & Behavior*, *47*(1), 63–77.

Epping-Jordan, M. P., Watkins, S. S., Koob, G. F., & Markou, A. (1998). Dramatic decreases in brain reward function during nicotine withdrawal. *Nature*, *393*(6680), 76–79.

Georges, F., Stinus, L., Bloch, B., & Le Moine, C. (1999). Chronic morphine exposure and spontaneous withdrawal are associated with modifications of dopamine receptor and neuropeptide gene expression in the rat striatum. *The European Journal of Neuroscience, 11*(2), 481–490.

Gerhardt, G. A., & Maloney, R. E., Jr. (1999). Microdialysis studies of basal levels and stimulus-evoked overflow of dopamine and metabolites in the striatum of young and aged Fischer 344 rats. *Brain Research, 816*(1), 68–77.

Glatz, A. C., Ehrlich, M., Bae, R. S., Clarke, M. J., Quinlan, P. A., Brown, E. C., Rada, P., & Hoebel, B. G. (2001). Inhibition of cocaine self-administration by fluoxetine or D-fenfluramine combined with phentermine. *Pharmacology, Biochemistry and Behavior, 71*, 197–204.

Glowa, J. R., Rice, K. C., Matecka, D., & Rothman, R. B. (1997). Phentermine/fenfluramine decreases cocaine self-administration in rhesus monkeys. *Neuroreport, 8*(6), 1347–1351.

Gosnell, B. A. (2005). Sucrose intake enhances behavioral sensitization produced by cocaine. *Brain Research, 1031*(2), 194–201.

Graziano, M. (2006). The organization of behavioral repertoire in motor cortex. *Annual Review of Neuroscience, 29*, 105–134.

Grill, H. J., & Kaplan, J. M. (2002). The neuroanatomical axis for control of energy balance. *Frontiers in Neuroendocrinology, 23*(1), 2–40.

Grimm, J. W., Fyall, A. M., & Osincup, D. P. (2005). Incubation of sucrose craving: Effects of reduced training and sucrose pre-loading. *Physiology & Behavior, 84*(1), 73–79.

Guidolin, D., Fuxe, K., Neri, G., Nussdorfer, G. G., & Agnati, L. F. (2007). On the role of receptor–receptor interactions and volume transmission in learning and memory. *Brain Research Reviews, 55*(1), 17–54.

Haber, S. N., Fudge, J. L., & McFarland, N. R. (2000). Striatonigrostriatal pathways in primates form an ascending spiral from the shell to the dorsolateral striatum. *The Journal of Neuroscience: The Official Journal of the Society for Neuroscience, 20*(6), 2369–2382.

Hajnal, A., Mark, G. P., Rada, P. V., Lenard, L., & Hoebel, B. G. (1997). Norepinephrine microinjections in the hypothalamic paraventricular nucleus increase extracellular dopamine and decrease acetylcholine in the nucleus accumbens: Relevance to feeding reinforcement. *Journal of Neurochemistry, 68*(2), 667–674.

Hajnal, A., Smith, G. P., & Norgren, R. (2004). Oral sucrose stimulation increases accumbens dopamine in the rat. *American Journal of Physiology. Regulatory, Integrative and Comparative Physiology, 286*(1), R31–R37.

Hajnal, A., Szekely, M., Galosi, R., & Lenard, L. (2000). Accumbens cholinergic interneurons play a role in the regulation of body weight and metabolism. *Physiology & Behavior, 70*(1–2), 95–103.

Helm, K. A., Rada, P., & Hoebel, B. G. (2003). Cholecystokinin combined with serotonin in the hypothalamus limits accumbens dopamine release while increasing acetylcholine: A possible satiation mechanism. *Brain Research, 963*(1–2), 290–297.

Hernandez, L., & Hoebel, B. G. (1988). Food reward and cocaine increase extracellular dopamine in the nucleus accumbens as measured by microdialysis. *Life Sciences, 42*(18), 1705–1712.

Hernandez, L., Lee, F., & Hoebel, B. G. (1987). Simultaneous microdialysis and amphetamine infusion in the nucleus accumbens and striatum of freely moving rats: Increase in extracellular dopamine and serotonin. *Brain Research Bulletin, 19*(6), 623–628.

Hernandez, L., Stanley, B. G., & Hoebel, B. G. (1986). A small, removable microdialysis probe. *Life Sciences, 39*(26), 2629–2637.

Hoebel, B. G. (1976). Brain-stimulation reward and aversion in relation to behavior. In A. Wauquier & E. T. Rolls (Eds.), *Brain-stimulation reward* (pp. 335–372). Amsterdam: North Holland Publishers.

Hoebel, B. G. (1979). Hypothalamic self-stimulation and stimulation escape in relation to feeding and mating. *Federation Proceedings, 38*(11), 2454–2461.

Hoebel, B. G. (1988). Neuroscience and motivations: Pathways and peptides that define motivation. In R. C. Atkinson, R. J. Herrnstein, G. Lindzey, & R. D. Luce (Eds.), *Stevens' handbook of experimental psychology* (pp. 547–625). New York: Wiley.

Hoebel, B. G. (1997). Neuroscience and appetitive behavior research: Twenty-five years. *Appetite, 29*, 119–133.

Hoebel, B. G., Hernandez, L., Schwartz, D. H., Mark, G. P., & Hunter, G. A. (1989). Microdialysis studies of brain norepinephrine, serotonin, and dopamine release during ingestive behavior: Theoretical and clinical implications. In L. H. Schneider, S. J. Cooper, & K. A. Halmi (Eds.), *The Psychobiology of Human Eating Disorders: Preclinical and Clinical Perspectives* (Vol. 575). New York: Annals of the New York Academy of Sciences.

Hoebel, B. G., Rada, P., Mark, G. P., & Pothos, E. (1999). Neural systems for reinforcement and inhibition of behavior: Relevance to eating, addiction, and depression. In D. Kahneman, E. Diener, & N. Schwartz (Eds.), *Well-being: The Foundations of Hedonic Psychology* (pp. 558–572). New York: Russell Sage Foundation.

Hooks, M. S., & Kalivas, P. W. (1995). The role of mesoaccumbens–pallidal circuitry in novelty-induced behavioral activation. *Neuroscience, 64*(3), 587–597.

Hurd, Y. L., Kehr, J., & Ungerstedt, U. (1988). In vivo microdialysis as a technique to monitor drug transport: Correlation of extracellular cocaine levels and dopamine overflow in the rat brain. *Journal of Neurochemistry, 51*(4), 1314–1316.

Ikemoto, S., Glazier, B. S., Murphy, J. M., & McBride, W. J. (1998). Rats self-administer carbachol directly into the nucleus accumbens. *Physiology & Behavior, 63*(5), 811–814.

Izquierdo, I., Bevilaqua, L. R., Rossato, J. I., Bonini, J. S., Da Silva, W. C., Medina, J. H., et al. (2006). The connection between the hippocampal and the striatal memory systems of the brain: A review of recent findings. *Neurotoxicity Research, 10*(2), 113–121.

Jacobs, B. L., & Fornal, C. A. (1999). Activity of serotonergic neurons in behaving animals. *Neuropsychopharmacology: Official Publication of the American College of Neuropsychopharmacology, 21*(2 Suppl.), 9S–15S.

Kelley, A. E., Baldo, B. A., & Pratt, W. E. (2005). A proposed hypothalamic–thalamic–striatal axis for the integration of energy balance, arousal, and food reward. *The Journal of Comparative Neurology, 493*(1), 72–85.

Kelley, A. E., & Berridge, K. C. (2002). The neuroscience of natural rewards: Relevance to addictive drugs. *The Journal of Neuroscience: The Official Journal of the Society for Neuroscience, 22*(9), 3306–3311.

Kelley, A. E., Will, M. J., Steininger, T. L., Zhang, M., & Haber, S. N. (2003). Restricted daily consumption of a highly palatable food (chocolate Ensure(R)) alters striatal enkephalin gene expression. *The European Journal of Neuroscience, 18*(9), 2592–2598.

Klein, D. A., Boudreau, G. S., Devlin, M. J., & Walsh, B. T. (2006). Artificial sweetener use among individuals with eating disorders. *The International Journal of Eating Disorders, 39*(4), 341–345.

Kolakowska, L., Larue-Achagiotis, C., & Le Magnen, J. (1984). Comparative effects of lesion of the basolateral nucleus and lateral nucleus of the amygdaloid body on neophobia and conditioned taste aversion in the rat. *Physiology & Behavior, 32*(4), 647–651.

Koob, G. F., & Le Moal, M. (2005a). *Neurobiology of Addiction.* San Diego: Academic Press.

Koob, G. F., & Le Moal, M. (2005b). Plasticity of reward neurocircuitry and the 'dark side' of drug addiction. *Nature Neuroscience, 8*(11), 1442–1444.

Koob, G. F., Maldonado, R., & Stinus, L. (1992). Neural substrates of opiate withdrawal. *Trends in Neurosciences, 15*(5), 186–191.

Leibowitz, S. F., & Hoebel, B. G. (2004). Behavioral neuroscience and obesity. In G. Bray, C. Bouchard, & P. James (Eds.), *The handbook of obesity* (pp. 301–371). New York: Marcel Dekker.

Li, Y., Kolb, B., & Robinson, T. E. (2003). The location of persistent amphetamine-induced changes in the density of dendritic spines on medium spiny neurons in the nucleus accumbens and caudate-putamen. *Neuropsychopharmacology: Official Publication of the American College of Neuropsychopharmacology, 28*(6), 1082–1085.

Mark, G. P., Blander, D. S., & Hoebel, B. G. (1991). A conditioned stimulus decreases extracellular dopamine in the nucleus accumbens after the development of a learned taste aversion. *Brain Research, 551*(1–2), 308–310.

Mark, G. P., Kinney, A. E., Grubb, M. C., Zhu, X., Finn, D. A., Mader, S. L., et al. (2006). Injection of oxotremorine in nucleus accumbens shell reduces cocaine but not food self-administration in rats. *Brain Research, 1123*(1), 51–59.

Mark, G. P., Rada, P., Pothos, E., & Hoebel, B. G. (1992). Effects of feeding and drinking on acetylcholine release in the nucleus accumbens, striatum, and hippocampus of freely behaving rats. *Journal of Neurochemistry, 58*(6), 2269–2274.

Mark, G. P., Scott, T. R., Chang, F. C., & Grill, H. J. (1988). Taste responses in the nucleus tractus solitarius of the chronic decerebrate rat. *Brain Research, 443*(1–2), 137–148.

Mark, G. P., Smith, S. E., Rada, P. V., & Hoebel, B. G. (1994). An appetitively conditioned taste elicits a preferential increase in mesolimbic dopamine release. *Pharmacology, Biochemistry, and Behavior, 48*(3), 651–660.

Mark, G. P., Weinberg, J. B., Rada, P. V., & Hoebel, B. G. (1995). Extracellular acetylcholine is increased in the nucleus accumbens following the presentation of an aversively conditioned taste stimulus. *Brain Research, 688*(1–2), 184–188.

Markou, A., & Koob, G. F. (1991). Postcocaine anhedonia. An animal model of cocaine withdrawal. *Neuropsychopharmacology: Official Publication of the American College of Neuropsychopharmacology, 4*(1), 17–26.

McGeer, P. L., & McGeer, E. G. (1980). Chemistry of mood and emotion. *Annual Review of Psychology, 31*, 273–307.

Mifsud, J. C., Hernandez, L., & Hoebel, B. G. (1989). Nicotine infused into the nucleus accumbens increases synaptic dopamine as measured by in vivo microdialysis. *Brain Research, 478*(2), 365–367.

Millar, J., O'Connor, J. J., Trout, S. J., & Kruk, Z. L. (1992). Continuous scan cyclic voltammetry (CSCV): A new high-speed electrochemical method for monitoring neuronal dopamine release. *Journal of Neuroscience Methods, 43*(2–3), 109–118.

Mogenson, G. J., & Yang, C. R. (1991). The contribution of basal forebrain to limbic-motor integration and the mediation of motivation to action. *Advances in Experimental Medicine and Biology, 295*, 267–290.

Mogenson, G. J., Jones, D. L., & Yim, C. Y. (1980). From motivation to action: Fundamental interface between the limbic system and the motor system. *Progress in Neurobiology, 14*, 69–97.

Morton, G. J., Cummings, D. E., Baskin, D. G., Barsh, G. S., & Schwartz, M. W. (2006). Central nervous system control of food intake and body weight. *Nature, 443*(7109), 289–295.

Neill, D. B., Fenton, H., & Justice, J. B., Jr. (2002). Increase in accumbal dopaminergic transmission correlates with response cost not reward of hypothalamic stimulation. *Behavioural Brain Research, 137*(1–2), 129–138.

Nestler, E. J., & Carlezon, W. A., Jr. (2006). The mesolimbic dopamine reward circuit in depression. *Biological Psychiatry, 59*(12), 1151–1159.

Nicola, S. M., Woodward Hopf, F., & Hjelmstad, G. O. (2004). Contrast enhancement: A physiological effect of striatal dopamine? *Cell and Tissue Research, 318*(1), 93–106.

Olds, J., & Milner, P. (1954). Positive reinforcement produced by electrical stimulation of septal area and other regions of rat brain. *Journal of Comparative Physiological Psychology, 47*(6), 419–427.

Peoples, L. L., Lynch, K. G., Lesnock, J., & Gangadhar, N. (2004). Accumbal neural responses during the initiation and maintenance of intravenous cocaine self-administration. *Journal of Neurophysiology, 91*(1), 314–323.

Phillips, M. L., Drevets, W. C., Rauch, S. L., & Lane, R. (2003). Neurobiology of emotion perception I: The neural basis of normal emotion perception. *Biological Psychiatry, 54*(5), 504–514.

Porsolt, R. D., Anton, G., Blavet, N., & Jalfre, M. (1978). Behavioural despair in rats: A new model sensitive to antidepressant treatments. *European Journal of Pharmacology, 47*(4), 379–391.

Pothos, E., Rada, P., Mark, G. P., & Hoebel, B. G. (1991). Dopamine microdialysis in the nucleus accumbens during acute and chronic morphine, naloxone-precipitated withdrawal and clonidine treatment. *Brain Research, 566*(1–2), 348–350.

Rada, P., Avena, N. M., & Hoebel, B. G. (2005). Daily bingeing on sugar repeatedly releases dopamine in the accumbens shell. *Neuroscience, 134*(3), 737–744.

Rada, P., Colasante, C., Skirzewski, M., Hernandez, L., & Hoebel, B. (2006). Behavioral depression in the swim test causes a biphasic, long-lasting change in accumbens acetylcholine release, with partial compensation by acetylcholinesterase and muscarinic-1 receptors. *Neuroscience, 141*(1), 67–76.

Rada, P., & Hoebel, B. G. (2005). Acetylcholine in the accumbens is decreased by diazepam and increased by benzodiazepine withdrawal: A possible mechanism for dependency. *European Journal of Pharmacology, 508* (1–3), 131–138.

Rada, P., Jensen, K., & Hoebel, B. G. (2001). Effects of nicotine and mecamylamine-induced withdrawal on extracellular dopamine and acetylcholine in the rat nucleus accumbens. *Psychopharmacology (Berl), 157*(1), 105–110.

Rada, P., Mark, G. P., & Hoebel, B. G. (1998a). Galanin in the hypothalamus raises dopamine and lowers acetylcholine release in the nucleus accumbens: A possible mechanism for hypothalamic initiation of feeding behavior. *Brain Research, 798*(1–2), 1–6.

Rada, P., Mark, G. P., Pothos, E., & Hoebel, B. G. (1991). Systemic morphine simultaneously decreases extracellular acetylcholine and increases dopamine in the nucleus accumbens of freely moving rats. *Neuropharmacology, 30*(10), 1133–1136.

Rada, P., Paez, X., Hernandez, L., Avena, N. M., & Hoebel, B. G. (2007). Microdialysis in the study of behavior reinforcement and inhibition. In B. H. Westerink & T. Creamers (Eds.), *Handbook of microdialysis: methods, application and perspectives* (pp. 351–375). New York: Academic Press.

Rada, P. V., & Hoebel, B. G. (2000). Supraadditive effect of D-fenfluramine plus phentermine on extracellular acetylcholine in the nucleus accumbens: Possible mechanism for inhibition of excessive feeding and drug abuse. *Pharmacology, Biochemistry, and Behavior, 65*(3), 369–373.

Rada, P. V., & Hoebel, B. G. (2001). Aversive hypothalamic stimulation releases acetylcholine in the nucleus accumbens, and stimulation-escape decreases it. *Brain Research, 888*(1), 60–65.

Rada, P. V., Mark, G. P., & Hoebel, B. G. (1993). In vivo modulation of acetylcholine in the nucleus accumbens of freely moving rats: I. Inhibition by serotonin. *Brain Research, 619*(1–2), 98–104.

Rada, P. V., Mark, G. P., & Hoebel, B. G. (1998b). Dopamine release in the nucleus accumbens by hypothalamic stimulation-escape behavior. *Brain Research, 782*(1–2), 228–234.

Rada, P. V., Mark, G. P., Taylor, K. M., & Hoebel, B. G. (1996). Morphine and naloxone, i.p. or locally, affect extracellular acetylcholine in the accumbens and prefrontal cortex. *Pharmacology, Biochemistry, and Behavior, 53*(4), 809–816.

Rada, P. V., Mark, G. P., Yeomans, J. J., & Hoebel, B. G. (2000). Acetylcholine release in ventral tegmental area by hypothalamic self-stimulation, eating, and drinking. *Pharmacology, Biochemistry, and Behavior, 65*(3), 375–379.

Rada, P., Pothos, E., Mark, G. P., & Hoebel, B. G. (1991). Microdialysis evidence that acetylcholine in the nucleus accumbens is involved in morphine withdrawal and its treatment with clonidine, *Brain Research, 561*, 354–356.

Radhakishun, F. S., van Ree, J. M., & Westerink, B. H. (1988). Scheduled eating increases dopamine release in the nucleus accumbens of food-deprived rats as assessed with on-line brain dialysis. *Neuroscience Letters, 85*(3), 351–356.

Redish, A. D., & Touretzky, D. S. (1997). Cognitive maps beyond the hippocampus. *Hippocampus, 7*(1), 15–35.

Robbins, T. W., & Everitt, B. J. (1996). Neurobehavioural mechanisms of reward and motivation. *Current Opinion in Neurobiology, 6*(2), 228–236.

Robbins, T. W., & Everitt, B. J. (2007). A role for mesencephalic dopamine in activation: Commentary on Berridge (2006). *Psychopharmacology (Berl), 191*(3), 433–437.

Robinson, T. E., & Berridge, K. C. (1993). The neural basis of drug craving: An incentive-sensitization theory of addiction. *Brain Research. Brain Research Reviews, 18*(3), 247–291.

Roitman, M. F., Stuber, G. D., Phillips, P. E., Wightman, R. M., & Carelli, R. M. (2004). Dopamine operates as a subsecond modulator of food seeking. *The Journal of Neuroscience: The Official Journal of the Society for Neuroscience, 24*(6), 1265–1271.

Rolls, E. T. (1995). Central taste anatomy and neurophysiology. In R. L. Doty (Ed.), *Handbook of olfaction and gustation* (pp. 549–573). New York: Marcel Dekker.

Rolls, E. T. (2006). Brain mechanisms underlying flavour and appetite. *Philosophical Transactions of the Royal Society of London. Series B, Biological Sciences, 361*(1471), 1123–1136.

Rolls, E. T. (2007). Sensory processing in the brain related to the control of food intake. *The Proceedings of the Nutrition Society, 66*(1), 96–112.

Rossetti, Z. L., Lai, M., Hmaidan, Y., & Gessa, G. L. (1993). Depletion of mesolimbic dopamine during behavioral despair: Partial reversal by chronic imipramine. *European Journal of Pharmacology, 242*(3), 313–315.

Rusiniak, K. W., Palmerino, C. C., Rice, A. G., Forthman, D. L., & Garcia, J. (1982). Flavor-illness aversions: Potentiation of odor by taste with toxin but not shock in rats. *Journal of Comparative Physiological Psychology*, *96*(4), 527–539.

Salamone, J. D., Correa, M., Farrar, A., & Mingote, S. M. (2007). Effort-related functions of nucleus accumbens dopamine and associated forebrain circuits. *Psychopharmacology (Berl)*, *191*(3), 461–482.

Schulteis, G., Markou, A., Cole, M., & Koob, G. F. (1995). Decreased brain reward produced by ethanol withdrawal. *Proceedings of the National Academy of Sciences of the United States of America*, *92*(13), 5880–5884.

Schultz, W., Dayan, P., & Montague, P. R. (1997). A neural substrate of prediction and reward. *Science*, *275*(5306), 1593–1599.

Schultz, W., Tremblay, L., & Hollerman, J. R. (2000). Reward processing in primate orbitofrontal cortex and basal ganglia. *Cerebral Cortex (New York: 1991)*, *10*(3), 272–284.

Schwartz, J. M., Ksir, C., Koob, G. F., & Bloom, F. E. (1982). Changes in locomotor response to beta-endorphin microinfusion during and after opiate abstinence syndrome—a proposal for a model of the onset of mania. *Psychiatry Research*, *7*(2), 153–161.

Scott, T. R., & Mark, G. P. (1987). The taste system encodes stimulus toxicity. *Brain Research*, *414*(1), 197–203.

Seligman, M. E. (1972). Learned helplessness. *Annual Review of Medicine*, *23*, 407–412.

Spanagel, R., Herz, A., & Shippenberg, T. S. (1990). The effects of opioid peptides on dopamine release in the nucleus accumbens: An in vivo microdialysis study. *Journal of Neurochemistry*, *55*(5), 1734–1740.

Spangler, R., Wittkowski, K. M., Goddard, N. L., Avena, N. M., Hoebel, B. G., & Leibowitz, S. F. (2004). Opiate-like effects of sugar on gene expression in reward areas of the rat brain. *Brain Research. Molecular Brain Research*, *124*(2), 134–142.

Stellar, E. (1994). The physiology of motivation. 1954. *Psychological Review*, *101*(2), 301–311.

Tanda, G., & Di Chiara, G. (1998). A dopamine-mu1 opioid link in the rat ventral tegmentum shared by palatable food (Fonzies) and non-psychostimulant drugs of abuse. *The European Journal of Neuroscience*, *10*(3), 1179–1187.

Taylor, K. M., Davidson, K., Mark, G. P., Rada, P., & Hoebel, B. G. (1992). Conditioned taste aversion induced by increased acetylcholine in the nucleus accumbens. *Society for Neuroscience Abstracts*, *18*, 1066.

Teitelbaum, P. (1971). The encephalization of hunger. *Progress in Physiological Psychology*, *4*, 319–350.

Teitelbaum, P., & Epstein, A. N. (1962). The lateral hypothalamic syndrome: Recovery of feeding and drinking after lateral hypothalamic lesions. *Psychological Review*, *69*, 74–90.

Touzani, K., & Sclafani, A. (2001). Conditioned flavor preference and aversion: Role of the lateral hypothalamus. *Behavioral Neuroscience*, *115*(1), 84–93.

Turchan, J., Lason, W., Budziszewska, B., & Przewlocka, B. (1997). Effects of single and repeated morphine administration on the prodynorphin, proenkephalin and dopamine D2 receptor gene expression in the mouse brain. *Neuropeptides*, *31*(1), 24–28.

Unterwald, E. M. (2001). Regulation of opioid receptors by cocaine. *Annals of the New York Academy of Sciences*, *937*, 74–92.

Volkow, N. D., & Wise, R. A. (2005). How can drug addiction help us understand obesity? *Nature Neuroscience*, *8*(5), 555–560.

Way, E. L., Loh, H. H., & Shen, F. H. (1969). Simultaneous quantitative assessment of morphine tolerance and physical dependence. *The Journal of Pharmacology and Experimental Therapeutics*, *167*(1), 1–8.

Will, M. J., Pratt, W. E., & Kelley, A. E. (2006). Pharmacological characterization of high-fat feeding induced by opioid stimulation of the ventral striatum. *Physiology & Behavior*, *89*(2), 226–234.

Willner, P. (2005). Chronic mild stress (CMS) revisited: Consistency and behavioural–neurobiological concordance in the effects of CMS. *Neuropsychobiology*, *52*(2), 90–110.

Wise, R. A. (1988). The neurobiology of craving: Implications for the understanding and treatment of addiction. *Journal of Abnormal Psychology*, *97*(2), 118–132.

Wise, R. A. (1989). Opiate reward: Sites and substrates. *Neuroscience and Biobehavioral Reviews*, *13*(2–3), 129–133.

Wise, R. A. (2006). Role of brain dopamine in food reward and reinforcement. *Philosophical Transactions of the Royal Society of London. Series B, Biological Sciences*, *361*(1471), 1149–1158.

Wise, R. A., Newton, P., Leeb, K., Burnette, B., Pocock, D., & Justice, J. B., Jr. (1995). Fluctuations in nucleus accumbens dopamine concentration during intravenous cocaine self-administration in rats. *Psychopharmacology (Berl)*, *120*(1), 10–20.

Wise, R. A., Spindler, J., deWit, H., & Gerberg, G. J. (1978). Neuroleptic-induced "anhedonia" in rats: Pimozide blocks reward quality of food. *Science*, *201*(4352), 262–264.

Wise, R. A., Spindler, J., & Legault, L. (1978). Major attenuation of food reward with performance-sparing doses of pimozide in the rat. *Canadian Journal of Psychology*, *32*(2), 77–85.

Yamamoto, T. (2007). Brain regions responsible for the expression of conditioned taste aversion in rats. *Chemical Senses*, *32*(1), 105–109.

Yoshida, K., McCormack, S., Espana, R. A., Crocker, A., & Scammell, T. E. (2006). Afferents to the orexin neurons of the rat brain. *The Journal of Comparative Neurology*, *494*(5), 845–861.

Hormones

7 The Role and Mechanisms of Steroid Hormones in Approach–Avoidance Behavior

Cheryl A. Frye and Madeline E. Rhodes

CONTENTS

Steroid hormones are important trophic factors that profoundly influence the brain and behavior. This chapter summarizes what is known about the role of steroid hormones in mediating approach–avoidance behavior, with an emphasis on the research findings from the author's laboratory. This chapter covers the following topics. First, an overview about steroid hormones (estrogen, progestins, and androgens), their fluctuations and sources, is provided. Second, information about the mechanisms of these steroids is presented. Third, the models or research paradigms that have been used to examine steroids' role in approach–avoidance motivation is discussed. Fourth, findings are presented about how (effects and mechanisms) estrogen mediates approach–avoidance behavior. Fifth, effects and mechanisms of progestins underlying approach–avoidance motivation are discussed. Sixth, the role of androgens in mediating approach–avoidance is covered. Finally, these findings are summarized, their

potential implications are reviewed, and areas for future research are raised.

BACKGROUND ABOUT STEROID HORMONES, FLUCTUATIONS, AND SOURCES

Hormones are chemical messengers produced and released by glands. Endocrine effects of hormones refer to when they are released from peripheral endocrine glands into the bloodstream, where they then can act at distant target tissues. In general, hormones do not cause behavioral effects, rather hormones influence central, peripheral, and sensory nervous system processes so that specific stimuli are more likely to elicit responses (given the appropriate behavioral or social context). The relationship between hormones and behavior is bidirectional: hormones can affect behavior and behavior can also influence hormone secretion.

All steroid hormones are derived from cholesterol, which is produced from acetate in the liver. Steroid hormones in vertebrates are produced primarily by the gonads and adrenals and have a characteristic 3-, 6-carbon ring and one conjugated 5-carbon ring structure. Steroid hormones are fat-soluble and can passively diffuse through all cell membranes. As such, they are typically not stored, but are released almost immediately upon production. Because steroid hormones are not particularly soluble in water, carrier proteins transport them to target tissues, which are tissues that have receptors that enable accumulation or responsiveness to steroids. Behaviorally effective concentrations of hormones are very low, typically in the nanogram or picogram range, even when expressed as concentrations in centiliters of plasma. As such, steroid hormones have potent effects on physiology and behavior (Nelson, 2005).

There are a number of sex differences in fluctuations of steroid hormones. Although both females and males secrete, and can respond to, estrogens, progestins, and androgens, females typically have higher estrogen and progestin concentrations than do males, and males have higher androgen levels than do females. Prior to sexual maturation, the sexual dimorphisms in levels of these steroid hormones are modest. After puberty, there are more pronounced fluctuations in concentrations of these steroid hormones. Among sexually mature females, levels of steroid hormones vary cyclically over reproductive cycles, whereas, among males circadian variations are most prominent. Across reproductive cycles, during the follicular phase, estrogen, progestin, and androgen levels of females are generally low and similar to basal (low) concentrations typically observed among males, later in the day. However, during the luteal phase and pregnancy, estrogen, progestin, and androgen levels of females are much higher than are those of females in the follicular phase, or among males. Among sexually mature males, androgen secretion varies in a circadian pattern, with androgen levels typically peaking earlier in the day and waning through the remainder of the day. Another sex difference in steroid hormone secretion occurs later in life. At menopause, the ovarian cessation in production of estrogen, progestins, and androgens, is relatively abrupt and occurs in a few years. In contrast, men experience a decade-by-decade decline in androgen levels which peak during young adulthood and typically reaches nadir (a low point) between the sixth to ninth decade of life.

Changes in hormonal milieu that occur with puberty, the menstrual cycle, pregnancy, or menopause may influence arousal, mood, or cognition directly or indirectly by altering the context-dependent effect of environmental and behavioral events (Kimura, 2002; Pfaff, Berrettini, & Joh, 2000; Steiner, Dunn, & Born, 2003). In support, during the luteal phase of the menstrual cycle, when steroid concentrations are high, a number of functions are enhanced including hypothalamic pituitary adrenal (HPA) axis responses (Kirschbaum & Hellhammer, 1999; Roca et al., 2003), social cognition (Macrae, Alnwick, & Milne, 2002; Penton-Voak et al., 1999), cognitive functions (Kimura, 2002), and mood (Protopopescu et al., 2005; Sanders, Warner, Backstrom, & Bancroft, 1983). Negative mood and physical symptoms are more pronounced after menstruation onset, when levels of steroid hormones are lowest (Bäckström et al., 1983; Schmidt, Nieman, Danaceau, Adams, & Rubinow, 1998). As well, explicit memory and mood are poorer late in the 3rd trimester of pregnancy, when steroid hormone levels have already peaked and are beginning to decline (Keenan, Veldhuis, & Yang, 1998). Indeed, decline in steroid hormones that occur with menstruation, late in pregnancy and after delivery, and with the menopausal transition may modulate the activity of the HPA axis. These variations in HPA processes could contribute to a number of dimorphisms in basic functions, such as approach and avoidance processes, as well as the prevalence of various stress-related disorders, including depression and schizophrenia (Kajantie & Phillips, 2006; Kudielka & Kirschbaum, 2005; Steiner et al., 2003).

We have investigated sex differences in HPA responsiveness and how this alters approach–avoidance interactions between conspecifics. Exposure of rats to restraint stress during gestation produces HPA hyper-responsiveness in adult offspring that results in more deleterious effects among females than males. Using an animal model of prenatal stress exposure (45 min of restraint on gestational day 17), we observed that among adult offspring there were robust alterations in steroid hormone secretion, a number of steroid-dependent behaviors and in morphology of the hippocampus, a steroid-sensitive brain region (Frye & Orecki, 2002a,b; Frye & Walf, 2004; Frye & Wawrzycki, 2003; Schmitz et al., 2002). One behavioral difference observed that is particularly relevant for this chapter was social interaction. Female rodents typically demonstrate more social interaction (i.e., time spent grooming, sniffing, following with contact) with a same-sex conspecific than do their male counterparts (Figure 7.1, left). Social interaction of females, but not males, was reduced in this paradigm among rats exposed to prenatal stress (Figure 7.1, right). These findings illustrate that females may be particularly vulnerable to effects of stress to disrupt social/approach behaviors.

Although traditional endocrine glands are a source of estrogens, progestins, and androgens, these steroid

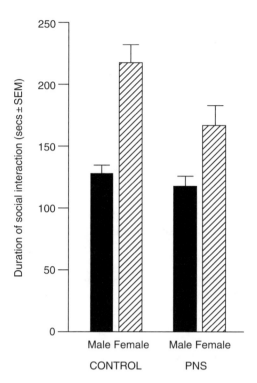

FIGURE 7.1 Time spent engaging in social interaction with a conspecific of male (solid bars) and female (striped bars) rats either exposed (PNS) or not (CONTROL) to gestational stress.

hormones are secreted from a number of tissues. The steroid hormones, 17β-estradiol (E_2), progesterone (P_4), and testosterone (T) are primarily secreted from gonadal sources, females' ovaries and males' testes. E_2, P_4, and T are also secreted by the adrenals of females and males. When an individual is not exposed to extreme stressors, the concentrations of these steroid hormones typically secreted by the adrenals are usually much lower than is produced by the ovaries and testes. However, the adrenals do have a capacity to produce substantial concentrations of these steroid hormones most prominently during stress-related activation of the HPA axis. During pregnancy, the placenta is a significant source of these steroid hormones. Steroid hormones secreted by these peripheral glands readily enter the bloodstream and permeate all biological tissues, including the brain, due to their lipophilicity which is related to their formation from the precursor cholesterol. In addition to classic secretion of steroid hormones from peripheral sources having central effects which are referred to as endocrine effects, there is also evidence that the brain is an endocrine gland and that production of steroids within the brain can act at nearby targets, which are known as paracrine effects.

Glial cells in the central and peripheral nervous system have been demonstrated to produce estrogens, progestins, and androgens independent of the peripheral tissues. Central biosynthesis (neurosteroidogenesis) involves transport of cholesterol, the precursor for all steroid hormones, by mitochondrial benzodiazepine receptors (MBRs) from the outer to the inner mitochondrial membrane (Papadopoulos, 2004). The P450 side chain cleavage enzyme (P450scc) then converts cholesterol to pregnenolone, from which various estrogens, progestins, and androgens can be formed through its conversion by metabolic enzymes, which are localized in different concentrations across brain regions. Biosynthesis of neurosteroids can occur rapidly in response to meaningful environmental or behavioral events (Barbaccia, Serra, Purdy, & Biggio, 2001), which can then have acute, neuromodulatory, paracrine (or "neurotransmitter-like") effects on adjacent neural tissues (Baulieu, Robel, & Schumacher, 2001).

Although *de novo* production of estrogen (Balthazart et al., 2006; Bernardi, Pluchino, Stomati, Pieri, & Genazzani, 2003; Forlano, Schlinger, & Bass, 2006) and progestins (Baulieu, Schumacher, Koenig, Jung-Testas, & Akwa, 1996) and androgens (Melcangi, Magnaghi, Galbiati, & Martini, 2001) has been demonstrated by glial cells independent of peripheral tissues, the most widely studied neurosteroid is a progestin that is often referred to as allopregnanolone. The chemical, or "trivial," name for allopregnanolone is 5α-pregnan-3α-ol-20-one: it is abbreviated in the literature a number of ways, most commonly as 3α,5α-THP. Allopregnanolone is formed in two ways, via central metabolism from P_4 secreted by peripheral glands and by *de novo* biosynthesis in glial cells. Peripheral P_4 is metabolized by activity of 5α-reductase and 3α-hydroxysteroid oxidoreductase enzymes. As such, allopregnanolone may have effects as a result of traditional endocrine actions. That is, in neurons, allopregnanolone may be formed as a metabolic product of peripherally secreted P_4. Paracrine effects of allopregnanolone formed through local biosynthesis in glial cells may exert neuromodulatory effects on proximal cells (Baulieu et al., 1996). These redundant, multiple sources of allopregnanolone (from metabolism of P_4 from peripheral endocrine glands and *de novo* synthesis in glial cells) and other neurosteroids have led to the notion that neurosteroids may be essential neuromodulatory agents involved in maintaining homeostasis of physiological and behavioral functions.

Evidence that allopregnanolone, and other neurosteroids, can have actions through nontraditional endocrine substrates (Rupprecht, 2003), including targets that typically underlie stress and anxiety responses that play a role in neuropsychiatric disorders (Rupprecht &

Holsboer, 2001) have bolstered this premise. Although P_4 can alter HPA axis responses to stressors, actions of allopregnanolone likely account for these effects on arousal (Roca et al., 2003). Allopregnanolone's neural effects are independent of intracellular progestin receptors (PRs) (Bitran, Shiekh, & McLeod, 1995; Reddy, O'Malley, & Rogawski 2005), and involve biphasic effects to potentiate the inhibitory actions of γ-aminobutyric acid (GABA) by modulation of $GABA_A$ receptors, similar to benzodiazepines (Majewska, Harrison, Schwartz, Barker, & Paul, 1986; N-Wihlbäck, Sundstrom-Poromaa, & Backstrom, 2006). Consistent with this GABAergic mechanism, P_4 and allopregnanolone administration decreases anxiety, aggression, and negative mood, in moderate concentrations (Andréen et al., 2006; Bitran et al., 1995; Fish, Faccidomo, DeBold, & Miczek, 2001; N-Wihlbäck et al., 2006; Reddy et al., 2005). Given these effects and implications, the various mechanisms through which steroid hormones and neurosteroids can have their effects need to be considered further and are discussed below.

MECHANISMS OF STEROID HORMONES

There are many possible mechanisms by which steroid hormones can influence behavior. Due to the multiplicity of mechanisms, a comprehensive discussion, or investigation, of all of these is beyond the scope of this review. However, one manageable approach to begin to understand divergent mechanisms of steroid hormones is to consider the two different broad categories of steroid actions. First, steroids can have traditional actions at cognate intracellular steroid receptors. Second, steroids may have actions that are independent of these classic actions at intracellular steroid receptors, which may involve targeting specific membrane receptors, neurotransmitter substrates ($GABA_A$, NMDA receptors), second messengers (mitogen activated protein [MAP] Kinase, AKT, CREB), and growth factors (EGF, TGF, and IGF). An overview of these different types of mechanisms is discussed further below.

Functional effects of steroid hormones have traditionally been considered to involve "genomic" actions at intracellular steroid receptors. Intracellular steroid receptors have been identified for each steroid hormone (estrogen, progestin, and androgen) and have the following characteristics. Intracellular steroid receptors have a high affinity for a specific class of steroids, which ensures that steroids will enter and be retained in specific steroid containing target cells. Intracellular steroid receptors also have specificity for a class of steroids. For example, estrogen receptors (ERs) exhibit a high degree of specificity for E_2, and other classes of hormones, such as progestins and andro-

gens, do not activate ERs when present in physiological concentrations. Third, there are a finite number of intracellular steroid receptors and the biological response is graded and saturable. That is, steroid receptors can be induced, but steroids do not cause new receptors to be formed. When there is sufficient steroid present or a threshold concentration of steroid is reached, all receptors become saturated and bound; hence, a biological response mediated by steroid receptors may be all-or-none like occupancy of ERs.

Classic or "genomic" actions of steroid hormones are when steroids bind to steroid receptors to form steroid-receptor complexes, which produce biochemical changes within target cells that are responsible for the biological response to the hormone. Traditionally, it was thought that after steroids diffuse into neural cells and bind with their specific intracellular receptors, the steroid-receptor complex moves into the cell nucleus for which it has acquired an affinity (Fannon, Vidaver, & Marts, 2001). Now it is known that steroid receptors are nuclear factors that initiate interaction with steroid in the nucleus (MacGregor & Jordan, 1998). The complex then binds to specific acceptor sites on the chromatin within the cell nucleus and this attachment enables specific portions of the DNA to be accessible to enzymes. Transcription of mRNA from a segment of the DNA is followed by the mRNA leaving the cell nucleus and interacting with ribosomes in the cytoplasm to direct the formation of new proteins (Etgen, 1984; Falkenstein, Tillmann, Christ, Feuring, & Wehling, 2000; O'Malley & Means, 1974). The cell's functional response to the steroid is then carried out by these newly formed proteins. These traditional actions at intracellular steroid receptors that result in transcription and translation of new proteins can occur minimally in 15 min and often require hours to days (Pfaff & McEwen, 1983).

An abundance of data suggests that steroids' functional effects can occur independent of traditional actions at intracellular steroid receptors. The mechanism(s) of steroids that do not involve actions at intracellular steroid receptors (and direct actions on DNA) are often labeled "non-genomic." One of the first indicators that steroid hormones might have different mechanisms of action was the discovery that there are variable time frames for functional effects (Selye, 1942). The time frame for genomic and nongenomic actions of E_2 is the most divergent compared to that of the other steroid hormones (progestins and androgens) that have been investigated. Because the most is known about genomic and nongenomic actions of E_2, a few of the nongenomic mechanisms of E_2 are mentioned here.

Estrogen can alter neurons, their membrane, their energy functions, the production and function of neurotransmitters, and neuromodulators; as well, E_2 alters the structure and function of glial cells, even in cells that do not have ERs. Some of the actions of E_2 that contribute to these effects are described below. Estrogen can alter caveolae, or membrane invaginations, and thereby the availability of specific (receptor) membrane proteins (Toran-Allerand, 2000). Estrogen can alter the expression of genes involved in mitochondrial functions (Bettini & Maggi, 1992). The synthesis and secretion of neurotransmitters that modulate neuronal excitability are influenced by E_2 (Gibbs, Hashash, & Johnson, 1997; McCarthy, Felzenberg, Robbins, Pfaff, & Schwartz-Giblin, 1995; McMillan, Singer, & Dorsa, 1996). Astrocyte functions are altered by E_2 (Day et al., 1993; Stone et al., 1998). Growth factors (Duenas et al., 1994; Gibbs, 1998, 1999; Gibbs, Wu, Hersh, & Pfaff, 1994; Singh, Meyer, & Simpkins, 1995) that influence dendritic branching (Shughrue & Dorsa, 1993) and synaptogenesis (Ferreira & Caceres, 1991) are also altered by E_2. Estrogen's potential targets for nongenomic actions may include second messengers, such as cAMP, MAP kinase cascade and phosphatidylinositol 3-kinase pathways (Honda et al., 2000; Linford, Wade, & Dorsa, 2000; Migliaccio et al., 1996; Murphy & Segal, 2000; Watters, Campbell, Cunningham, Krebs, & Dorsa, 1997; Wise et al., 2000; Zhou, Watters, & Dorsa, 1996). These mechanisms may account for some of the rapid effects of E_2 through phosphorylation, as well as provide for mechanisms by which E_2 may have actions with longer latencies (Wise et al., 2000). Of course, it is most likely that functional effects of E_2 may involve integrated mechanisms of nongenomic and genomic actions (Vasudevan, Kow, & Pfaff, 2005).

The diversity of genomic and nongenomic actions of progestins has been less well-characterized compared to that of E_2. In general, it is accepted that P_4 and its 5α-reduced metabolite, dihydroprogesterone (DHP), bind with high affinity for intracellular PRs. However, the product of DHP's conversion by 3α-hydroxysteroid dehydrogenase, allopregnanolone, does not bind with high affinity to intracellular PRs in physiological concentrations (Iswari, Colas, & Karavolas, 1986; Rupprecht, 2003; Smith et al., 1974). Rather, allopregnanolone has actions via $GABA_A$, NMDA, dopamine, and sigma receptors, and the downstream signal transduction factors that mediate these receptors' actions (Frye, Walf, & Petralia 2006a).

The mechanisms by which androgens exert their effects are similar to, albeit less well characterized, than that of progestins. In general, it is accepted that T and its 5α-reduced metabolite, dihydrotestosterone (DHT), bind with high affinity for intracellular androgen receptors (ARs). However, the product of DHT's conversion by 3α-hydroxysteroid dehydrogenase, 3α-diol, does not bind with high affinity to intracellular ARs in physiological concentrations (Cunningham, Tindall, & Means, 1979; Verhoeven, Heyns, & De Moor, 1975). Rather, 3α-diol has actions via $GABA_A$ and NMDA receptors (Frye, McCormick, Coopersmith, & Erskine, 1996; Gee, 1988; Pouliot, Handa, & Beck, 1996).

The diversity of the sources of steroid hormones and the multiple substrates through which they can potentially exert their effects, underscore the need to have circumspect experimental paradigms with which to elucidate their role, mechanism, and central sites of action involved in approach and avoidance. As such, the various approaches that have been used to understand the role of steroid hormones in approach–avoidance processes are summarized below.

MODELS OF APPROACH–AVOIDANCE MOTIVATION

One of the most long-standing methods of experimentally examining approach and avoidance has been to use sexual behavior as a model. Generally, two components of sexual behavior have been considered. The first is the appetitive component, which is typically considered sexual drive or sexual motivation. Sex drive, the motivation to engage in sexual behavior, is one of the most powerful forces among humans and other mammals. Cross-culturally, in both Western and non-Western societies, young people participate in premarital sexual activities despite severe consequences, which can include death sentences for unmarried couples that engage in sexual intercourse (Ford & Beach, 1951). Threat of contracting the life-threatening sexually transmitted disease, syphilis, did not curtail the sexual liberation observed during the 1920s in North America (Quetel, 1990). Today, many men and women have reported that during sexual arousal they were so motivated to engage in sexual activity that the possible consequences of pregnancy or contracting AIDS, or other sexually transmitted diseases, were not considered (Quetel, 1990). One would think that understanding sexual motivation may be considered a priority to curtail the aforementioned negative outcomes. However, it is often viewed that sexual motivation may be somewhat unique compared to other motivated behaviors insofar as sexual arousal or hormones may contribute to the "clouding of logic" and impair decision-making processes. Perhaps because of the difficulties associated with carrying out this research, there has been very little funding to address this aspect of human sexual behavior (Nelson, 2005). As such, what is known about sexual motivation has primarily come from animal studies, which typically examine the work that animals will do (or impediments they will overcome) to gain access to a mate.

The second component of sexual behavior, the consummatory component, which focuses on sexual performance or potency, has been more readily examined experimentally. What and how we know about the role of estrogen, progestins, and androgens in mediating these various components of sexual behaviors is discussed below.

ESTROGEN, PROGESTINS, ANDROGENS, AND SEXUAL BEHAVIOR OF FEMALES

Estrogen, progestins, and androgens mediate the various components of female sexual behavior including: attractivity (stimulus value of a female to a male), proceptivity (solicitation behaviors of females toward males), and receptivity (state of responsiveness of females toward males; Beach, 1976). At puberty, when the ovaries begin to secrete estrogen, progestins, and androgens in a cyclic fashion, sexual behavior of rodents coincides with increases in these steroid hormones (which are coordinated with ovulation) if there is appropriate, sexually relevant stimuli. In contrast to primates, which have peak estrogen and androgen levels that coincide with ovulation, rodents also have high levels of progestins at ovulation.

Among rodents, and some other species, sexual motivation and behavior are mediated by hormones. Estrogen and progestins mediate both the appetitive and consummatory aspects of female sexual behavior in rodents, with slightly different roles. Estrogen is absolutely essential for initiation of attractivity and receptivity (consummatory components), whereas, progestins play a greater role in mediating appetitive behaviors including proceptivity, and the onset and duration of attractivity and receptivity (consummatory components) of sexual behavior. Among primates, sexual performance is independent of hormonal control, however, sexual motivation of primates and rodents may be influenced by androgen levels (Hull, Muschamp, & Sato, 2004).

ANDROGENS AND SEXUAL BEHAVIOR

Androgens mediate the appetitive phase of male sexual behavior, the courtship phase, and the consummatory phase, which involves copulatory behaviors. At puberty when the testes begin to secrete androgens, the motivation to seek sexual contacts, sexual performance, and copulatory ability increases. In general, castration reduces these behaviors and androgen replacement reinstates

them, but there is considerable individual variability, cross-species differences, and effects of sexual experience prior to castration that mediate the nature of these effects. For example, the high baseline preoccupation with sexual material exhibited by persons convicted of sex crimes may contribute to the lack of effect produced by chemical or other types of castration that have been used to try to aid in the rehabilitation of such persons. Because the sexual experience of animals can be controlled in an experimental setting, the following discussion focuses on results from animal models.

As described above, endocrine factors may influence the expression or motivation for sexual behavior by changing the threshold at which specific behaviors are elicited in response to relevant stimuli. However, many social and environmental factors may also influence these parameters. For example, among males, the availability of females, as well as whether they are attractive or novel, influences the level of sexual motivation and performance that is expressed. In support, during mating, the presence of female rodents (particularly novel ones), or the sensory cues associated with females, can influence androgen levels of male rodents (Bronson & Desjardins, 1982; Purvis & Haynes, 1974). Notably, this secretion of androgens can be classically conditioned to environmental stimuli, such that androgen-dependent behaviors can then be observed with exposure of castrated rats to conditioned stimuli (Graham & Desjardins, 1980). It is not surprising that steroid hormones alter reproductive behaviors; however, it is notable that stimuli associated with mating can also influence steroid hormone secretion.

One approach that has been utilized to account for the possibility that extraneous stimuli can become a conditioned stimuli and influence steroid hormone secretion is to utilize a very sparse mating environment. In a laboratory setting, assessment of sexual behavior is typically conducted with a single male and female in a very small space, such as an empty aquarium, so that as many variables as possible can be controlled. Mating in this setting also occurs very rapidly and appears to primarily involve the male approaching the female and the female avoiding the male, to the extent possible in this environment. The benefit of this standard mating approach is that the results can more be clearly interpreted. However, this paradigm is limited because approach and avoidance behaviors are almost exclusively exhibited by males and females, respectively, which precludes the expression of the normative range of this behavioral repertoire.

Naturalistic mating differs from standard mating in a number of ways. In natural habitats, there is more environmental and social complexity. For example, rats typically do not mate in pairs, as occurs in the standard mating task. In the wild, several male and female rodents mate in groups. Moreover, naturalistic mating occurs in larger spaces, which enables females to solicit sexual contacts and also to escape sexual contacts. Thus, in the natural environment, there are additional cues, space, and stimuli that may serve as unconditioned stimuli that may enable more successful mating.

We, and other laboratory investigators, have utilized a semi-natural, paced mating paradigm to mitigate the limited validity of the standard mating paradigm. Paced mating uses a test arena that selectively enables females to demonstrate both approach and avoidance behaviors. Paced mating uses an arena that is approximately four times larger than aquaria, which are typically used in standard mating. Moreover, the pacing chamber is divided by a barrier that has a small hole at the bottom that allows a female, but not a male, to traverse the two sides of the chamber and solicit sexual contacts. This paradigm is more ethologically relevant and allows both approach and avoidance behaviors to be more readily examined.

Although reproductive behavior clearly involves approach and avoidance and is the most relevant complex behavior in terms of evolution and adaptation, a clear limitation of using reproductive behavior as the sole model for understanding approach–avoidance processes is the complexity of the behavioral repertoire involved in mating. Because of this limitation, we have utilized other behavioral tasks to compliment our investigation of hormonal control of approach–avoidance behaviors. The behaviors exhibited in these other tasks may represent approach and avoidance responses that would precede or contribute to mating behavior in another context. By examining effects of hormones in mating paradigms and comparing these effects to those observed in standard behavioral assays of exploration, anxiety, and social behavior, we are able to dissociate more clearly the endocrine-behavior relationship without confounds of social interactions altering endocrine parameters.

A few of the models that we have used in our laboratory are reviewed below. Typically, rodents are tested sequentially in a battery of tasks. Initially, performance in the open field is assessed. This is immediately followed by performance in the elevated plus maze. Following examination in these two tasks, approach–avoidance and reproductive and endocrine responses are evaluated in the standard or paced mating tasks. Over a longer period of time, the hormones found to mediate approach and avoidance in the above tasks are evaluated for effects in the conditioned place preference paradigm. As such, this procedure enables us to elucidate the role and mechanisms

of hormones on approach and avoidance in both reproductive and nonreproductive contexts.

The open field is a classic conflict task that has been used to assess approach–avoidance behavior. The open field capitalizes on the nocturnal nature of rodents and their role as prey animals. Rodents typically remain in, or seek out, dark, enclosed places. The open field assesses the extent to which an animal will venture to the center of the open field, away from the protected perimeter of the apparatus. In our laboratory, the open field paradigm is as follows. Rats or mice are placed in the corner of a brightly lit open field with 48-square or 16-square grid floor, respectively. The path that the rat travels in the open field is traced for five minutes. The number of central squares entered in the open field is considered approach behavior to a novel or aversive stimuli (a brightly lit open space). Conversely, entries in the peripheral squares are considered an avoidance response, as the animal is avoiding the negative stimuli.

The elevated plus maze is another conflict task often used to assess approach–avoidance behavior. In the elevated plus maze, as in the open field, the tendency for rodents to prefer dark, enclosed places and to avoid open places and heights, is used to assess approach–avoidance behavior. In our laboratory, rats or mice are placed at the center of the elevated plus maze, which has two open and two closed arms. The amount of time an animal spends on both the open or closed arms and the number of entries into the open and closed arms is recorded in a five-minute test. Approach behavior is considered time spent on the open arms, as animals are approaching a negative stimulus (open elevated space), and time in the closed arms is considered avoidance of the negative stimulus. Notably, prior experience or habituation in this task can significantly alter performance, such that the approach–avoidance aspect of the task may be compromised, as such in this and all tasks, performance of naïve animals is examined.

We have also used conditioned place preference in our laboratory to assess approach–avoidance behavior. Conditioned place preference has traditionally been used to determine the rewarding effects of compounds by establishing the contingent associations between an agent administered and environmental stimuli paired with the agent (White & Carr, 1985). In our laboratory, we have used conditioned place preference to assess the ability of steroid hormones to alter an animal's preference for a particular area of the conditioning chamber. Following two days of habituation to the apparatus, baseline preference for one side of the conditioning chamber is assessed. Rats are then subjected to two cycles of four conditioning days. On two of the conditioning days, rats are administered a steroid hormone immediately before placement on the originally nonpreferred side of the chamber. The other two days of conditioning consist of administration of vehicle followed immediately by placement in the originally preferred side of the chamber. Following completion of conditioning trials, rats are given a test trial to determine whether side preference has changed as a function of steroid treatment. If an animal has switched its preferred side following pairing with steroid administration, we consider this approach to a previously nonpreferred environment. Although this paradigm can also be used to assess avoidance of previously conditioned appetitive stimuli, we have not utilized this approach because the steroids of interest to our laboratory are clearly eliciting dramatic approach responses in this and other paradigms.

Because steroid hormones have profound, pervasive effects, one of the clearest ways to demonstrate effects of hormones in particular processes is to examine effects following extirpation of the primary source of endogenous steroid secretion (ovaries or testes) and after steroid hormone replacement with physiological levels. The removal of the primary source of a hormone to determine its behavioral effects is a classic technique in endocrinology. In brief, first the gland that is the source of a hormone influencing a behavior of interest is surgically removed. Second, the behavioral effects of removing the gland are observed. Third, the hormone of interest is replaced by exogenous administration with injections. Fourth, whether reinstatement of the hormone reverses the effects of the removal of the gland is assessed behaviorally. The following pages describe findings from our laboratory that primarily have used this extirpation and replacement paradigm with estrogens, progestins, and androgens to evaluate the effects of these steroids in the models of approach–avoidance discussed above.

ESTROGENS AND APPROACH–AVOIDANCE

Estrogen plays a necessary role in initiating reproductive behaviors and may be important for mediating some of the approach–avoidance responses involved in the mating process. Ovariectomized rats, with circulating E_2 levels at nadir, show little to no sexual responsiveness in either standard or paced mating paradigms (Frye & Rhodes, 2006; Petralia & Frye, 2004). E_2 administration to ovariectomized rats increases approach to, and solicitation of, a novel stimulus male in both standard and paced mating paradigms (Frye & Rhodes, 2006; Petralia & Frye, 2004). Moreover, rats that are reproductively senescent demonstrate lower

levels of receptivity and show less pacing behavior than do rats that are the same age (1 year old) but are reproductively competent. Reproductively senescent rats (2 years old) demonstrate the typical mating posture of rodents (lordosis) 60% (±25) of the time after being mounted by a sexually experienced male rat in a pacing arena, whereas 1-year-old reproductively competent rats demonstrate this response 85% (±10) of the time (Figure 7.2, first bar). Reproductively senescent rats also show reduced pacing behavior (% exits after intromissions from a male rat; 12%±8) compared to reproductively competent rats (30%±14; Figure 7.2, second bar). As well, mice that are aged and reproductively senescent (2 years old) administered E_2 also demonstrate lower levels of receptivity (1±1% occurrences of lordosis in response to male mounting) than do their 1-year-old counterparts administered E_2 (12±6%).

The mechanisms through which E_2 may mediate approach–avoidance responses in sexual behavior paradigms may involve actions of E_2 at the ERα, rather than the ERβ, isoform of the ER. In support, systemic administration of selective ER modulators (SERMs) with selective

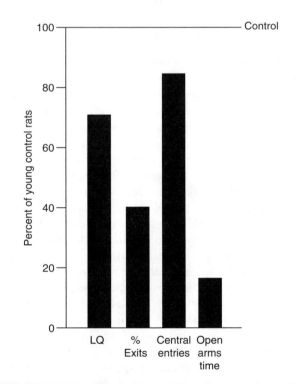

FIGURE 7.2 Lordosis quotients (LQ), percentage of exits following mating contacts (% exits), central entries in the open field (central entries), and time spent on the open arms of the elevated plus maze (open arms time) of reproductively senescent rats presented as percent of young control rats.

actions at ERα-(PPT, 17α-E$_2$), facilitate sexual receptivity in the standard mating paradigm, compared to vehicle or ERβ-selective SERMs (DPN, coumestrol; Rhodes & Frye, 2006; Walf & Frye, 2005). Moreover, ERαantisense oligonucleotide administration to the lateral ventricle, which reduces ERαexpression in the hypothalamus, inhibited sexual receptivity in the standard mating paradigm (Walf, Rhodes, Meade, Harney, & Frye, 2006). Together, these data suggest that E$_2$ can facilitate sexual behavior and that these effects may be due in part to actions at ERα in the hypothalamus.

We have examined the role of E$_2$ in mediating approach–avoidance responses in the open field paradigm. As discussed above, one measure that we consider to reflect enhanced approach is an increase in the number of central square entries in the open field. Data from our lab suggest that E$_2$ enhances approach in the open field. In support, rats that are reproductively senescent make fewer central entries to the open field (23$\pm$6) than do rats that are the same age (1 year old) but are reproductively competent (28$\pm$5, Figure 7.2, third bar), and are expected to have higher endogenous E$_2$ levels. Ovariectomized, compared to intact rats with high endogenous levels of E$_2$, enter significantly fewer central squares in the open field (Frye & Walf, 2004; Walf & Frye, 2005). Systemic or intrabrain (hippocampus or amygdala) administration of E$_2$ to ovariectomized rats significantly increases the number of central square entries in the open field, compared to vehicle administration (Frye & Walf, 2004; Walf & Frye, 2005, 2006). We have also seen that intact young, c57/Bl6 mice obtained from Jackson Laboratories show more central entries in the open field when E$_2$ is naturally elevated on proestrous (30$\pm$5), than when E$_2$ levels are lower on diestrous (1$\pm$1). Moreover, congenic c57/Bl6 mice, raised at SUNY Albany, that were intact but had low endogenous E$_2$ levels due to reproductive senescence (2 years of age), demonstrated fewer central entries than did the young mice described above (17$\pm$2), but the aged mice did have increased central entries in the open field with E$_2$ (65$\pm$5), over vehicle, administration.

The mechanisms through which E$_2$ may mediate approach–avoidance responses in the open field paradigm may involve actions of E$_2$ at the ERβ, rather than the ERα, isoform of the ER in the hippocampus. Wild-type c57 mice in proestrus spend more time in the center of the open field (30$\pm$5) than do diestrous mice (1$\pm$1); however, their ERβ knockout counterparts do not show this E$_2$-dependent estrous cycle increase in central entries in the open field (proestrous homozygous ERβ knockout-11$\pm$3; diestrous homozygous ERβ knockout-6$\pm$3). Systemic or intrahippocampal administration of SERMs

with selective actions at ERβ (DPN or coumestrol) increases central square entries in the open field, compared to vehicle or ERα-specific SERMs (PPT, 17α-E$_2$, Walf & Frye, 2005, 2006). Furthermore, E$_2$ administration to c57 wild-type mice, but not ERβ knockout mice, increases entries to the open field, over that seen with vehicle administration to either wild-type or knockout mice (Walf & Frye, 2006). These data suggest that E$_2$ can enhance approach behavior in the open field and that these effects may be due to actions at ERβ in the hippocampus. However, putative mechanisms other than ERs have not been extensively investigated and are the focus of ongoing studies in our laboratory.

Data from our lab suggest that E$_2$ enhances approach in the elevated plus maze, which as discussed above, we consider an increase in open arm time. In support, rats that are reproductively senescent spend less time (3$\pm$2 s) on the open arms of the elevated plus maze than do rats that are the same age (1 year old) but are reproductively competent and may have higher endogenous E$_2$ levels (20$\pm$3 s, Figure 7.2, fourth bar). Aged, intact, congenic c57/Bl6 mice that have low endogenous E$_2$ levels show increased open arm time in the plus maze with E$_2$ (70$\pm$24 s), but not vehicle (118$\pm$16 s), administration. Ovariectomized, young adult rats spend very little time on the open arms of the elevated plus maze compared to intact rats (Frye & Walf, 2004; Walf & Frye, 2005). Administration of E$_2$, either systemically or to the amygdala or hippocampus, increases the amount of time spent on the open arms, compared to vehicle administration (Frye & Walf, 2004; Walf & Frye, 2005, 2006).

E$_2$'s actions at ERβ may also underlie approach behavior in the elevated plus maze. Intact wild-type c57 mice in proestrus spend more time on the open arms of the elevated plus maze (18$\pm$3 s) than do diestrous mice (1$\pm$1 s); however, their ERβ-knockout counterparts do not show this E$_2$-dependent estrous cycle variation in open arm time in the elevated plus maze (proestrous homozygous ERβ knockout-5$\pm$1 s; diestrous homozygous ERβ knockout-1$\pm$1 s). Furthermore, E$_2$ administration to c57 wild-type mice, but not ERβ knockout mice, increases open arm time over that seen with vehicle administration to either wild-type or knockout mice (Walf & Frye, 2006). Consistent with these data, administration of the ERβ-selective SERMs, DPN and coumestrol, to ovx rats increases open arm time compared to vehicle or ERα-selective SERMs, PPT and 17α-E$_2$ (Walf & Frye, 2005). Hence, E$_2$'s actions at ERβ in the hippocampus may underlie some of its effects on approach behavior in the elevated plus maze. Investigations of other, nontraditional, mechanisms for these effects are ongoing.

Approach to a previously nonpreferred environment, as assessed in the conditioned place preference task, is also enhanced by E_2. E_2, but not vehicle, administration to ovariectomized rats paired with a nonpreferred environment switches preference to this environment (Frye & Rhodes, 2006). Our investigations of E_2's putative mechanisms have revealed that actions at ERs in the nucleus accumbens may underlie these effects. Blocking E_2's actions at ERs in the nucleus accumbens with a nonspecific ER antagonist (tamoxifen), a specific ER antagonist (ICI 182,780), or antisense oligonucleotides to ERs, attenuates E_2-induced conditioned approach to the originally nonpreferred side of the chamber (Walf et al., 2006). Thus, these data suggest that actions of E_2 at ERs in the nucleus accumbens mediate approach to a previously nonpreferred environment. Whether it is actions of E_2 at $ER\alpha$ or $ER\beta$ is the subject of ongoing investigations.

PROGESTINS AND APPROACH–AVOIDANCE

The effects of E_2 to enhance approach–avoidance responses involved in reproductive behavior are enhanced by P_4. As discussed above, removal of the primary source of endogenous estrogens and progestins, the ovaries, abolishes reproductive behavior of rodents in both standard and paced mating paradigms. Administration of P_4 or $3\alpha,5\alpha$-THP systemically or to the midbrain ventral tegmental area (VTA) of ovariectomized, E_2-primed rats, mice, or hamsters increases solicitation and approach behaviors of female rodents in response to a stimulus male (Frye & Vongher, 1999a,c, 2001). Ovariectomized, E_2-primed rats administered P_4 or $3\alpha,5\alpha$-THP, either systemically or to the VTA, also exhibit enhanced approach–avoidance responses in paced mating situations, as indicated by increased percent exits and return latencies following mating contacts (Frye, Bayon, Pursnani, & Purdy, 1998; Frye & Rhodes, 2006; Frye et al., 2006a). Notably, the effects of P_4 or $3\alpha,5\alpha$-THP to facilitate sexual behavior of rats are not attenuated by infusions of PR blockers to the VTA (Frye, Murphy, & Platek 2000; Frye & Vongher, 1999b). Similarly, intravenous infusions of P_4 can facilitate sexual behavior of PR knockout (PRKO) mice in a manner similar to that seen following P_4 to wild-type control mice (Frye et al., 2006b). Thus, actions of progestins to facilitate sexual receptivity may be somewhat independent of actions at PRs.

Additional data suggest that the mechanism of P_4's effects on approach–avoidance responses involved in reproductive behavior may be due to actions of $3\alpha,5\alpha$-THP, at $GABA_A$ receptors in the VTA. In support, blocking biosynthesis of, or metabolism to, $3\alpha,5\alpha$-THP,

attenuates solicitation and approach behaviors in both standard and paced mating paradigms (Frye, 2001; Frye et al., 1998; Frye et al., 2006a). Further, blocking actions of progestins at $GABA_A$ or dopamine type 1 receptors in the VTA significantly reduce P_4- and $3\alpha,5\alpha$-THP-induced solicitation and approach behaviors of female rodents (Frye, 2001; Frye et al., 2006a,b; Frye & Vongher, 1999; Sumida, Walf, & Frye, 2005). Together, these data suggest that P_4 influences approach–avoidance responses involved in reproductive behaviors and that these effects are likely due to actions of P_4's metabolite, $3\alpha,5\alpha$-THP, and its actions at $GABA_A$ or dopamine type 1 receptors in the VTA.

In addition to effects on approach–avoidance behaviors involved in reproductive processes, progestins also influence approach–avoidance in other paradigms of social behavior involving conspecifics. We have examined the duration of time spent by ovariectomized wild type, 5α-reductase deficient, or PRKO mice in a social interaction test with a conspecific that was introduced into their home-cage. Mice were administered P_4 (1 mg, SC) or propylene glycol vehicle and an hour later the frequency of prosocial behaviors (sniffing, grooming, following with contact) were observed. The number of social interactions was significantly increased in wild type (24.1 ± 0.8) and 5α-reductase (23.5 ± 0.8) deficient, but not PRKO (9.3 ± 1.8) mice administered P_4 compared to those administered vehicle control (15.8 ± 1.3). Together, these data suggest that progestins can enhance approach–avoidance behavior directed toward conspecifics and that some of these effects may be independent of metabolism and require actions at intracellular PRs.

Evidence from the open field tasks also supports a role of progestins in mediating approach. Ovariectomized rats, compared to intact rats with high E_2 and P_4 levels, exhibit decreased approach behavior in the open field, as indicated by fewer entries into the central squares and enhanced peripheral square entries. Administration of P_4 or $3\alpha,5\alpha$-THP, either systemically or to the amygdala, of ovariectomized rats or mice increases central square entries in the open field (Frye et al., 2006a; Frye & Walf, 2004; Frye, Walf, Rhodes, & Harney, 2004).

Investigations of P_4's putative mechanisms for modulation of approach–avoidance responses in the open field suggest that actions of $3\alpha,5\alpha$-THP may underlie some of these effects. Blocking formation of $3\alpha,5\alpha$-THP, systemically or in the hippocampus or amygdala, of proestrous or ovariectomized, progestin-primed rats significantly decreases approach responses in the open field (Rhodes & Frye, 2001; Frye & Walf, 2002, 2004; Walf, Sumida, & Frye, 2006). Additionally, systemic administration of P_4 to mice that are genetically unable to metabolize P_4 to $3\alpha,5\alpha$-THP (5α-reductase mice) does not increase central square entries in a manner similar to that seen following P_4 to wild-type mice (Frye et al., 2004). P_4 administration to mice that lack functional intracellular PRs has similar effects to enhance approach behaviors in the open field as is seen in P_4-administered mice with functional PRs, which suggests that P_4's effects may be due to actions of $3\alpha,5\alpha$-THP at substrates other than PRs (Frye et al., 2006b). Together, these data suggest that P_4, through actions of its metabolite, $3\alpha,5\alpha$-THP, at substrates other than intracellular PRs mediates approach–avoidance responses in the open field task.

One substrate to consider is whether some of progestins' effects occur in part through actions at the dopamine system. In support, P_4 administration to ovx, wild-type mice increases approach behavior in an open field compared to that observed with vehicle administration (Figure 7.3, left). However, dopamine transporter knockout mice administered P_4 exhibit approach behavior in the open field that is similar to that seen following vehicle administration to knockout mice (Figure 7.3, right) or their wild-type counterparts. Notably, knockout mice administered vehicle entered more total squares (305 ± 8) in this task compared to wild-type mice administered vehicle (202 ± 9) or P_4 (187 ± 10) or knockout mice administered P_4 (207 ± 9). The opposite patterns of effects of P_4 on these two measures suggest that it is unlikely that the effects observed were due only to differences in locomotor behavior among the groups.

Another model in which we have investigated progestins' effects on approach–avoidance responses is the elevated plus maze. Similar to data in the open field discussed above, ovariectomy reduces approach behaviors in the elevated plus maze, as indicated by less time spent on the open arms of the elevated plus maze. Systemic or intra-brain (hippocampus or amygdala) administration of P_4 or $3\alpha,5\alpha$-THP, but not vehicle, to ovariectomized E_2- or vehicle-primed rats or mice increases time spent on the open arms of the elevated plus maze, independent of total arm entries made (Frye et al., 2006a; Frye & Walf, 2004). Attenuating P_4's metabolism to $3\alpha,5\alpha$-THP, either pharmacologically or by administration of P_4 to 5α-reductase mice, significantly reduces time spent on the open arms of the elevated plus maze (Frye & Rhodes, 2001; Frye et al., 2004; Walf et al., 2006). Actions of P_4 at PRs do not appear to be necessary for enhanced approach as P_4 administration to mice lacking functional PRs increases time spent on the open arms of the elevated plus maze in a manner similar to that seen following P_4 administration to mice with functional PRs (Frye et al., 2006b). These data, together with above, suggest that progestins can modulate approach–avoidance responses in classic conflict tasks and that these effects may be due, at least in part, to actions of $3\alpha,5\alpha$-THP at nontraditional substrates, such as $GABA_A$ receptors.

We have also examined progestins' ability to mediate conditioned approach responses using the conditioned place preference paradigm. Ovariectomized rats that had vehicle administration paired with the originally non-preferred side do not switch their side preference on test day. However, pairing P_4 administration with the originally nonpreferred side of the conditioning chamber results in a conditioned approach to this side of the apparatus (i.e., more time spent on this side, Frye, 2007). Initial investigations of the mechanisms underlying this effect have revealed that actions at PRs are not necessary. P_4 administration to mice lacking functional PRs has similar effects to enhance conditioned approach as is seen following P_4 administration to mice with functional PRs (Frye, 2007). Together, these data suggest that P_4 can enhance approach to previously neutral stimuli and that these effects may be independent of actions at intracellular PRs.

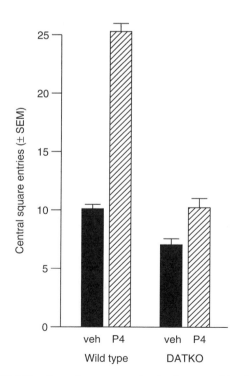

FIGURE 7.3 Central square entries in the open file of wild type (left) or DATKO (right) mice administered vehicle (solid bars) or P4 (striped bars).

ANDROGENS AND APPROACH–AVOIDANCE

Our laboratory has also investigated androgens' role in mediating approach–avoidance responses in reproductive behaviors.

Androgens enhance approach behavior of male and female rodents in the open field. In support, intact, aged congenic c57 mice demonstrate fewer entries in the center of the open field (12 ± 2) than do younger c57 counterparts (67 ± 20), which are expected to have higher endogenous androgen levels compared to the senescent mice. As well, administration of T to the aged c57 mice increases central entries (72 ± 7). Gonadectomy of male or female rats significantly reduces the number of central square entries compared to that of intact rats (Edinger & Frye, 2006; Frye & Lacey, 2001). Systemic or intrahippocampal administration of T or its 5α-reduced metabolites, DHT and 3α-diol, increases approach to aversive stimuli in the open field, as evidenced by increased central square entries compared to vehicle administration (Edinger & Frye, 2004, 2005, 2006; Frye & Edinger, 2004; Frye & Lacey, 2001; Frye & Seliga, 2001). Thus, androgens can enhance approach/exploration in the open field.

We have begun to investigate the mechanisms through which androgens may have their enhancing effects in the open field. To date, our data suggest that enhanced approach in the open field may be mediated, in part, by actions of 3α-diol in the hippocampus, independent of actions at intracellular ARs. Administration of 3α-diol to aged c57 mice is as effective as T to increase central entries (50 ± 7) over that produced by vehicle administration. Blocking T's metabolism to 3α-diol, systemically or in the hippocampus, attenuates T's enhancing effects on approach in the open field of rats (Frye & Edinger, 2004). Additionally, blocking T's actions at intracellular ARs in the hippocampus does not alter T's enhancing effects in the open field (Edinger & Frye, 2006). Together, these data suggest that androgens can enhance approach behavior in the open field task and that these effects may be due to actions of 3a-diol, independent of ARS in the hippocampus.

We have also examined androgens' effects on approach behavior in the elevated plus maze. There is an age-related decline in approach behavior in the elevated plus maze, such that intact, young adult Long-Evans rats (4 months) have increased open arm time ($34\pm5\,\text{s}$) compared to intact, midaged rats (12 months old; $16\pm5\,\text{s}$), which may be due to reduced central androgen levels of male rats with aging. A similar pattern of effects has been observed

in our laboratory with Fisher 344 rats, such that 4 month ($29\pm7\,\text{s}$) > 13 month ($3\pm1\,\text{s}$) > 24 month ($1\pm1\,\text{s}$) old rats spent a longer duration on the open arms. Additionally, administration of T (164 ± 19) or 3α-diol (242 ± 18) to aged c57 mice similarly increases open arm time and produces significant increases over that seen with vehicle administration (101 ± 29). Among male and female rats, gonadectomy significantly reduces the amount of time spent on the open arms of the elevated plus maze, compared to intact rats (Edinger & Frye, 2006; Frye & Lacey, 2001). Systemic or intrahippocampal administration of T, DHT, or 3α-diol to male or female rats significantly increases approach behavior in the elevated plus maze, as indicated by increased time spent on the open arms of the elevated plus maze (Edinger & Frye, 2004, 2005, 2006; Frye & Edinger, 2004; Frye & Lacey, 2001; Frye & Seliga, 2001).

Our investigations into the mechanisms through which androgens enhance approach behavior in the elevated plus maze have revealed that T's metabolism to 3α-diol in the hippocampus is necessary and that actions at ARs in the hippocampus are not necessary. Blocking T's metabolism to 3α-diol, systemically or in the hippocampus, attenuates T's enhancing effects open arm time in the elevated plus maze. This effect is not abrogated when T's actions at ARs are blocked in the hippocampus (Edinger & Frye, 2006). These data, together with the above, suggest that androgens have consistent effects and mechanisms to enhance approach behavior in two classic conflict paradigms.

We have also extensively investigated the effects and mechanisms of androgens to mediate approach behavior using the conditioned place preference model. Administration of T, DHT, or 3α-diol, either systemically or to the nucleus accumbens, enhances approach to a previously nonpreferred environment (Frye, Park, Tanaka, Rosellini, & Svare, 2001; Frye, Rhodes, Rosellini, & Svare, 2002; Rosellini, Svare, Rhodes, & Frye, 2001). Data from our lab suggest that androgen-mediated conditioned place preference occurs via actions of 3α-diol at $GABA_A$ receptors in the nucleus accumbens. Inhibiting formation of 3α-diol in the nucleus accumbens attenuates T-induced conditioned place preference (Frye, 2007). Further, blocking androgen action at $GABA_A$ receptors in the nucleus accumbens abrogates enhanced approach to a nonpreferred environment (Frye, 2007). As well, dopaminergic lesions to the nucleus accumbens abrogate the enhancing effects of androgens on conditioned place preference (Frye, 2007). Together, these data suggest that androgens can enhance approach behavior assessed in the conditioned place preference paradigm and that these effects likely involve actions of 3α-diol at GABA$_A$ receptors, which can alter dopamine function, in the nucleus accumbens.

POTENTIAL IMPLICATIONS FOR FUTURE RESEARCH

Although the above data implicate steroid hormones as having an important role in the modulation of approach–avoidance behavior, a critical question is the extent of their applicability to humans. Indeed, the value of much research these days lies in the ability for results to go "from bench to bedside." Because of the many intervening variables associated with humans (i.e., socioeconomic status, environment, previous experience, etc.) that cannot be controlled, it is imperative that basic research investigating the role of steroid hormones in modulating approach–avoidance be conducted.

As discussed previously, there are a number of animal models of approach–avoidance behavior that have been used to investigate effects of steroid hormones on these processes. There are also models of many neuropsychiatric disorders, including schizophrenia, which are characterized by deficits in social and affective functioning and appear to be influenced by hormones (Castner, Goldman-Rakic, & Williams, 2004; Frye & Walf, 2004; Laruelle, Kegeles, & Abi-Dargham, 2003). Many of these models of specific disorders have driven subsequent clinical studies. For instance, early research on the effects of the selective-serotonin-reuptake inhibitor, fluoxetine, on steroid hormone levels in rats revealed that fluoxetine, but not vehicle, administration to male rats increased central levels of 3α,5α-THP (Uzunov, Cooper, Costa, & Guidotti, 1996). Soon after, this same research group demonstrated that men with unipolar depression treated with fluoxetine had increased levels of 3α,5α-THP in cerebrospinal fluid that was positively correlated with improved symptomology (Uzunova et al., 1998). This is just one example in which animal models of neuropsychiatric disorders, which are characterized by impaired approach–avoidance processes, have been used to study effects of steroid hormones in mediating these processes and led to subsequent research and similar findings in a clinical population. There are of course, caveats that must be taken into account when considering the issue of applying research findings in lower animals to humans. First, there is no perfect animal model for approach–avoidance processes. For this reason, it is important to take advantage of the numerous models that are available to ascertain which models elicit consistent results. Second, one of the advantages of animal models, that outside factors can be controlled, is also a drawback. It is important to control as many outside factors as possible to begin to understand steroid hormones' effects on approach–avoidance; however, because of the rich environmental and experiential stimulation that humans receive, results from a 'clean' rodent model are somewhat limited in their generalizability to humans. Further, the models and results that we have discussed deal mainly with approach motivation/behavior, more extensive work is needed to acquire a comparable understanding of avoidance motivation/behavior.

As discussed above, E$_2$, progestins, and androgens can mediate these processes via multiple mechanisms in the brain. Notably, stress-induced steroid production can be disrupted in schizophrenia. A novel polymorphism and genetic mutation in the sequence encoding the gene for the mitochondrial benzodiazepine receptor (MBR), which is necessary for steroid biosynthesis in glial cells, has been demonstrated among some schizophrenics, and may create a predisposition to oversensitivity to stress (Kurumaji, Nomoto, Yoshikawa, Okubo, & Toru, 2000; Myin-Germeys, van Os, Schwartz, Stone, & Delespaul, 2001; Read, Perry, Moskowitz, & Connolly, 2001). As well, social isolation (an animal model of schizophrenia) decreases steroid biosynthesis in male mice (Dong et al., 2001). Further, effective pharmacotherapies for schizophrenia and depression alter metabolism enzymes necessary for production of estrogens, progestins, and androgens (Frye & Seliga, 2002, 2003; Griffin & Mellon, 1999; Marx, Duncan, Gilmore, Lieberman, & Morrow, 2000; Marx & Lieberman, 1998). Given these data, and the fact that many other neuropsychiatric disorders are associated with changes in steroid hormones, it is imperative that the effects and mechanisms of steroid hormones for approach–avoidance processes are further elucidated.

ACKNOWLEDGMENTS

This research is supported by the National Institute of Mental Health and the National Science Foundation. The substantive contributions of Alicia A. Walf (estrogen data), Kassandra Edinger (androgen data), Jason J. Paris (5α-reductase and PR knockout data), and Kanako Sumida (DATKO data) are greatly appreciated. As well, their valuable input on previous versions of this manuscript is appreciated.

REFERENCES

Andréen, L., Sundstrom-Poromaa, I., Bixo, M., Nyberg, S., & Backstrom, T. (2006). Allopregnanolone concentration and mood-a bimodal association in postmenopausal women treated with oral progesterone. *Psychopharmacology (Berl)*, *187*(2), 209–221.

Bäckström, T., Sanders, D., Leask, R., Davidson, D., Warner, P., & Bancroft, J. (1983). Mood, sexuality, hormones, and the menstrual cycle. II. Hormone levels and their relationship to the premenstrual syndrome. *Psychosomatic Medicine*, *45*(6), 503–507.

Balthazart, J., Cornil, C. A., Taziaux, M., Charlier, T. D., Baillien, M., & Ball, G. F. (2006). Rapid changes in production and behavioral action of estrogens. *Neuroscience*, *138*(3), 783–791.

Barbaccia, M. L., Serra, M., Purdy, R. H., & Biggio, G. (2001). Stress and neuroactive steroids. *International Review of Neurobiology, 46*, 243–272.

Baulieu, E. E., Robel, P., & Schumacher, M. (2001). Neurosteroids: Beginning of the story. *International Review of Neurobiology, 46*, 1–32.

Baulieu, E. E., Schumacher, M., Koenig, H., Jung-Testas, I., & Akwa, Y. (1996). Progesterone as a neurosteroid: Actions within the nervous system. *Cellular and Molecular Neurobiology*, *16*(2), 143–154.

Beach, F. A. (1976). Sexual attractivity, proceptivity, and receptivity in female mammals. *Hormones and Behavior*, *7*(1), 105–138.

Bernardi, F., Pluchino, N., Stomati, M., Pieri, M., & Genazzani, A. R. (2003). CNS: Sex steroids and serms. *Annals of the New York Academy of Sciences*, *997*, 378–388.

Bettini, E., & Maggi, A. (1992). Estrogen induction of cytochrome c oxidase subunit III in rat hippocampus. *Journal of Neurochemistry*, *58*(5), 1923–1929.

Bitran, D., Shiekh, M., & McLeod, M. (1995). Anxiolytic effect of progesterone is mediated by the neurosteroid allopregnanolone at brain GABAA receptors. *Journal of Neuroendocrinology*, *7*(3), 171–177.

Bronson, F. H., & Desjardins, C. (1982 Oct). Endocrine responses to sexual arousal in male mice. *Endocrinology*, *111*(4), 1286–1291.

Castner, S. A., Goldman-Rakic, P. S., & Williams, G. V. (2004). Animal models of working memory: Insights for targeting cognitive dysfunction in schizophrenia. *Psychopharmacology (Berl)*, *174*(1), 111–125.

Cunningham, G. R., Tindall, D. J., & Means, A. R. (1979). Differences in steroid specificity for rat androgen binding protein and the cytoplasmic receptor. *Steroids*, *33*(3), 261–276.

Day, J. R., Laping, N. J., Lampert-Etchells, M., Brown, S. A., O'Callaghan, J. P., McNeill, T. H., & Finch, C. E. (1993). Gonadal steroids regulate the expression of glial fibrillary acidic protein in the adult male rat hippocampus. *Neuroscience, 55*, 435–443.

Dong, E., Matsumoto, K., Uzunova, V., Sugaya, I., Takahata, H., Nomura, H., et al. (2001). Brain 5α-dihydroprogesterone and allopregnanolone synthesis in a mouse model of protracted social isolation. *Proceedings of the National Academy of Sciences of the United States of America*, *98*(5), 2849–2854.

Duenas, M., Luquin, S., Chowen, J. A., Torres-Aleman, I., Naftolin, F., & Garcia-Segura, L. M. (1994). Gonadal hormone regulation of insulin-like growth factor-I-like immunoreactivity in hypothalamic astroglia of developing and adult rats. *Neuroendocrinology*, *59*(6), 528–538.

Edinger, K. L., & Frye, C. A. (2004). Testosterone's analgesic, anxiolytic, and cognitive-enhancing effects may be due in part to actions of its 5α-reduced metabolites in the hippocampus. *Behavioral Neuroscience, 118*(6), 1352–1364.

Edinger, K. L., & Frye, C. A. (2005). Testosterone's anti-anxiety and analgesic effects may be due in part to actions of its 5α-reduced metabolites in the hippocampus. *Psychoneuroendocrinology*, *30*(5), 418–430.

Edinger, K. L., & Frye, C. A. (2006). Intrahippocampal administration of an androgen receptor antagonist, flutamide, can increase anxiety-like behavior in intact and DHT-replaced male rats. *Hormones and Behavior*, *50*(2), 216–222.

Etgen, A. M., (1984). Progestin receptors and the activation of female reproductive behavior: A critical review. *Hormones and Behavior*, *18*(4), 411–430.

Falkenstein, E., Tillmann, H. C., Christ, M., Feuring, M., & Wehling, M. (2000). Multiple actions of steroid hormones—a focus on rapid, nongenomic effects. *Pharmacological Reviews*, *52*(4), 513–556.

Fannon, S. A., Vidaver, R. M., & Marts, S. A. (2001). An abridged history of sex steroid hormone receptor action. *Journal of Applied Physiology (Bethesda, Md.: 1985)*, *91*(4), 1854–1859.

Ferreira, A., & Caceres, A. (1991). Estrogen-enhanced neurite growth: Evidence for a selective induction of Tau and stable microtubules. *The Journal of Neuroscience: The Official Journal of the Society for Neuroscience*, *11*(2), 392–400.

Fish, E. W., Faccidomo, S., DeBold, J. F., & Miczek, K. A. (2001). Alcohol, allopregnanolone and aggression in mice. *Psychopharmacology (Berl)*, *153*(4), 473–483.

Ford, C. S., & Beach, F. A. (1951). *Patterns of sexual behavior*. New York: Harper.

Forlano, P. M., Schlinger, B. A., & Bass, A. H. (2006). Brain aromatase: new lessons from non-mammalian model systems. *Front Neuroendocrinol.*, *27*(3), 247–274.

Frye, C. A., (2001). The role of neurosteroids and non-genomic effects of progestins and androgens in mediating sexual receptivity of rodents. *Brain Research. Brain Research Reviews*, *37*(1–3), 201–222.

Frye, C. A., (2007). Progestins influence motivation, reward, conditioning, stress, and/or response to drugs of abuse. *Pharmacology Biochemistry and Behavior, 86*(2), 209–219.

Frye, C. A., Bayon, L. E., Pursnani, N. K., & Purdy, R. H. (1998). Links the neurosteroids, progesterone and 3α,5α-THP, enhance sexual motivation, receptivity, and proceptivity in female rats. *Brain Research*, *808*(1), 72–83.

Frye, C. A., & Edinger, K. L. (2004). Testosterone's metabolism in the hippocampus may mediate its anti-anxiety effects in male rats. *Pharmacology Biochemistry and Behavior,* 78(3), 473–481.

Frye, C. A., & Lacey, E. H. (2001). Posttraining androgens' enhancement of cognitive performance is temporally distinct from androgens' increases in affective behavior. *Cognitive, Affective & Behavioral Neuroscience,* 1(2), 172–182.

Frye, C. A., McCormick, C. M., Coopersmith, C., & Erskine, M. S. (1996). Effects of paced and non-paced mating stimulation on plasma progesterone, 3α-diol and corticosterone. *Psychoneuroendocrinology,* 21(4), 431–439.

Frye, C. A., Murphy, R. E., & Platek, S. M. (2000). Anti-sense oligonucleotides, for progestin receptors in the VMH and glutamic acid decarboxylase in the VTA, attenuate progesterone-induced lordosis in hamsters and rats. *Behavioral Brain Research,* 115(1), 55–64.

Frye, C. A., & Orecki, Z. A. (2002a). Prenatal stress produces deficits in socio-sexual behavior of cycling, but not hormone-primed, Long-Evans rats. *Pharmacology, Biochemistry, and Behavior,* 73(1), 53–60.

Frye, C. A., & Orecki, Z. A. (2002b). Prenatal stress alters reproductive responses of rats in behavioral estrus and paced mating of hormone-primed rats. *Hormones and Behavior,* 42(4), 472–483.

Frye, C. A., Park, D., Tanaka, M., Rosellini, R., & Svare, B. (2001). The testosterone metabolite and neurosteroid 3α-androstanediol may mediate the effects of testosterone on conditioned place preference. *Psychoneuroendocrinology,* 26(7), 731–750.

Frye, C. A., & Rhodes, M. E. (2006). Infusions of 5a-pregnan-3a-ol-20-one (3a,5a-THP) to the ventral tegmental area, but not the substantia nigra, enhance exploratory, anti-anxiety, social and sexual behaviours and concomitantly increase 3a,5a-THP concentrations in the hippocampus, diencephalon and cortex of ovariectomised oestrogen-primed rats. *Journal of Neuroendocrinology,* 18(12), 960–975.

Frye, C. A., Rhodes, M. E., Petralia, S. M., Walf, A. A., Sumida, K., & Edinger, K. L. (2006a). 3α-hydroxy-5α-pregnan-20-one in the midbrain ventral tegmental area mediates social, sexual, and affective behaviors. *Neuroscience,* 138(3), 1007–1014.

Frye, C. A., Rhodes, M. E., Rosellini, R., & Svare, B. (2002). The nucleus accumbens as a site of action for rewarding properties of testosterone and its 5α-reduced metabolites. *Pharmacology, Biochemistry, and Behavior,* 74(1), 119–127.

Frye, C. A., & Seliga, A. M. (2001). Testosterone increases analgesia, anxiolysis, and cognitive performance of male rats. *Cognitive, Affective & Behavioral Neuroscience,* 1(4), 371–381.

Frye, C., & Seliga, A. (2002). Olanzapine and progesterone have dose-dependent and additive effects to enhance lordosis and progestin concentrations of rats. *Physiology and Behavior,* 76(1), 151–158.

Frye, C. A., & Seliga, A. M. (2003). Olanzapine's effects to reduce fear and anxiety and enhance social interactions coincide with increased progestin concentrations of ovariectomized rats. *Psychoneuroendocrinology,* 28(5), 657–673.

Frye, C. A., Sumida, K., Dudek, B. C., Harney, J. P., Lydon, J. P., O'Malley, B. W., et al. (2006b). Progesterone's effects to reduce anxiety behavior of aged mice do not require actions via intracellular progestin receptors. *Psychopharmacology (Berl),* 186(3), 312–322.

Frye, C. A., & Vongher, J. M. (1999a). Progesterone has rapid and membrane effects in the facilitation of female mouse sexual behavior. *Brain Research,* 815(2), 259–269.

Frye, C. A., & Vongher, J. M. (1999b). GABA(A), D1, and D5, but not progestin receptor, antagonist and anti-sense oligonucleotide infusions to the ventral tegmental area of cycling rats and hamsters attenuate lordosis. *Behavioural Brain Research,* 103(1), 23–34.

Frye, C. A., & Vongher, J. M. (2001). Ventral tegmental area infusions of inhibitors of the biosynthesis and metabolism of 3α,5α-THP attenuate lordosis of hormone-primed and behavioural oestrous rats and hamsters. *Journal of Neuroendocrinology,* 13(12), 1076–1086.

Frye, C. A., & Walf, A. A. (2002). Changes in progesterone metabolites in the hippocampus can modulate open field and forced swim test behavior of proestrous rats. *Hormones and Behavior,* 41(3), 306–315.

Frye, C. A., & Walf, A. A. (2004). Estrogen and/or progesterone administered systemically or to the amygdala can have anxiety-, fear-, and pain-reducing effects in ovariectomized rats. *Behavioral Neuroscience,* 118(2), 306–313.

Frye, C. A., & Vongher, J. M. (1999c). 3α,5α-THP in the midbrain ventral tegmental area of rats and hamsters is increased in exogenous hormonal states associated with estrous cyclicity and sexual receptivity. *Journal of Endocrinological Investigation,* 22(6), 455–464.

Frye, C. A., & Walf, A. A. (2002). Links Changes in progesterone metabolites in the hippocampus can modulate open field and forced swim test behavior of proestrous rats. *Hormones and Behaviour,* 41(3), 306–315.

Frye, C. A., Walf, A. A., & Petralia, S. M. (2006). Progestins' effects on sexual behaviour of female rats and hamsters involving D1 and GABA(A) receptors in the ventral tegmental area may be G-protein-dependent. *Behavioural Brain Research,* 172(2), 286–293.

Frye, C. A., Walf, A. A., Rhodes, M. E., & Harney, J. P. (2004). Progesterone enhances motor, anxiolytic, analgesic, and antidepressive behavior of wild-type mice, but not those deficient in type 1 5α-reductase. *Brain Research,* 1004 (1–2), 116–124.

Frye, C. A., & Wawrzycki, J. (2003). Effect of prenatal stress and gonadal hormone condition on depressive behaviors of female and male rats. *Hormones and Behavior,* 44(4), 319–326.

Gee, K. W. (1988). Steroid modulation of the GABA/benzodiazepine receptor-linked chloride ionophore. *Molecular Neurobiology,* 2(4), 291–317.

Gibbs, R. B. (1998). Levels of trkA and BDNF mrna, but not NGF mrna, fluctuate across the estrous cycle and increase in response to acute hormone replacement. *Brain Research,* 787(2), 259–268.

Gibbs, R. B. (1999). Treatment with estrogen and progesterone affects relative levels of brain-derived neurotrophic factor mrna and protein in different regions of the adult rat brain. *Brain Research, 844*(1–2), 20–27.

Gibbs, R. B., Hashash, A., & Johnson, D. A. (1997). Effects of estrogen on potassium-stimulated acetylcholine release in the hippocampus and overlying cortex of adult rats. *Brain Research, 749*(1), 143–146.

Gibbs, R. B., Wu, D., Hersh, L. B., & Pfaff, D. W. (1994). Effects of estrogen replacement on the relative levels of choline acetyltransferase, trka, and nerve growth factor messenger rnas in the basal forebrain and hippocampal formation of adult rats. *Experimental Neurology, 129*(1), 70–80.

Graham, J. M., & Desjardins, C. (1980). Classical conditioning: Induction of luteinizing hormone and testosterone secretion in anticipation of sexual activity. *Science, 210*(4473), 1039–1041.

Griffin, L. D., & Mellon, S. H. (1999). Selective serotonin reuptake inhibitors directly alter activity of neurosteroidogenic enzymes. *Proceedings of the National Academy of Sciences of the United States of America, 96*(23), 13512–13517.

Honda, K., Sawada, H., Kihara, T., Urushitani, M., Nakamizo, T., Akaike, A., et al. (2000). Phosphatidylinositol 3-kinase mediates neuroprotection by estrogen in cultured cortical neurons. *Journal of Neuroscience Research, 60*(3), 321–327.

Hull, E. M., Muschamp, J. W., & Sato, S. (2004). Dopamine and serotonin: Influences on male sexual behavior. *Physiology & behavior, 83*(2), 291–307.

Iswari, S., Colas, A. E., & Karavolas, H. J. (1986). Binding of 5α-dihydroprogesterone and other progestins to female rat anterior pituitary nuclear extracts. *Steroids, 47*(2–3), 189–203.

Kajantie, E., & Phillips, D. I. (2006). The effects of sex and hormonal status on the physiological response to acute psychosocial stress. *Psychoneuroendocrinology, 31*(2), 151–178.

Keenan, D. M., Veldhuis, J. D., & Yang, R. (1998). Joint recovery of pulsatile and basal hormone secretion by stochastic nonlinear random-effects analysis. *American Journal of Physiology, 275*(6 Pt 2), R1939–1949.

Kimura, D. (2002). Sex hormones influence human cognitive pattern. *Neuro Endocrinology Letters, 23*(4), 67–77.

Kirschbaum, C., & Hellhammer, D. H. (1999). Noise and stress—salivary cortisol as a non-Invasive measure of allostatic load. *Noise & Health, 1*(4), 57–66.

Kudielka, B. M., & Kirschbaum, C. (2005). Sex differences in HPA axis responses to stress: A review. *Biological Psychology, 69*(1), 113–132.

Kurumaji, A., Nomoto, H., Yoshikawa, T., Okubo, Y., & Toru, M. (2000). An association study between two missense variations of the benzodiazepine receptor (peripheral) gene and schizophrenia in a Japanese sample. *Journal of Neural Transmission (Vienna, Austria: 1996), 107*(4), 491–500.

Laruelle, M., Kegeles, L. S., & Abi-Dargham, A. (2003). Glutamate, dopamine, and schizophrenia: From pathophysiology to treatment. *Annals of the New York Academy of Sciences, 1003*, 138–158.

Linford, N., Wade, C., & Dorsa, D. (2000). The rapid effects of estrogen are implicated in estrogen-mediated neuroprotection. *Journal of Neurocytology, 29*(5–6), 367–374.

MacGregor, J. I., & Jordan, V. C. (1998). Basic guide to the mechanisms of antiestrogen action. *Pharmacological Reviews, 50*(2), 151–196

Macrae, C. N., Alnwick, K. A., Milne, A. B., & Schloerscheidt, A. M. (2002). Person perception across the menstrual cycle: Hormonal influences on social-cognitive functioning. *Psychological Science: A Journal of the American Psychological Society / Aps, 13*(6), 532–536.

Majewska, M. D., Harrison, N. L., Schwartz, R. D., Barker, J. L., & Paul, S. M. (1986). Steroid hormone metabolites are barbiturate-like modulators of the GABA receptor. *Science, 232*(4753), 1004–1007.

Marx, C. E., Duncan, G. E., Gilmore, J. H., Lieberman, J. A., & Morrow, A. L. (2000). Olanzapine increases allopregnanolone in the rat cerebral cortex. *Biological Psychiatry, 47*(11), 1000–1004.

Marx, C. E., & Lieberman, J. A. (1998). Psychoneuroendocrinology of schizophrenia. *The Psychiatric Clinics of North America, 21*(2), 413–434.

McCarthy, M. M., Felzenberg, E., Robbins, A., Pfaff, D. W., & Schwartz-Giblin, S. (1995). Infusions of diazepam and allopregnanolone into the midbrain central gray facilitate open-field behavior and sexual receptivity in female rats. *Hormones and Behavior, 29*(3), 279–295.

McMillan, P. J., Singer, C. A., & Dorsa, D. M. (1996). The effects of ovariectomy and estrogen replacement on trka and choline acetyltransferase mrna expression in the basal forebrain of the adult female Sprague-Dawley rat. *The Journal of Neuroscience: The Official Journal of the Society for Neuroscience, 16*(5), 1860–1865.

Melcangi, R. C., Magnaghi, V., Galbiati, M., & Martini, L. (2001). Formation and effects of neuroactive steroids in the central and peripheral nervous system. *International Review of Neurobiology, 46*, 145–176.

Migliaccio, A., Di Domenico, M., Castoria, G., de Falco, A., Bontempo, P., Nola, E., et al. (1996). Tyrosine kinase/p21ras/MAP-kinase pathway activation by estradiol-receptor complex in MCF-7 cells. *The Embo Journal, 15*(6), 1292–1300.

Murphy, D. D., & Segal, M. (2000). Progesterone prevents estradiol-induced dendritic spine formation in cultured hippocampal neurons. *Neuroendocrinology, 72*(3), 133–143.

Myin-Germeys, I., van Os, J., Schwartz, J. E., Stone, A. A., & Delespaul, P. A. (2001). Emotional reactivity to daily life stress in psychosis. *Archives of General Psychiatry, 58*(12), 1137–1144.

Nelson, R. (2005). *An Introduction to Behavioral Endocrinology*. Sinauer, Sunderland, Massachusetts.

N-Wihlback, A. C., Sundstrom-Poromaa, I., & Backstrom, T. (2006). Action by and sensitivity to neuroactive steroids in menstrual cycle related CNS disorders. *Psychopharmacology (Berl), 186*(3), 388–401.

O'Malley, B. W., & Means, A. R. (1974). Female steroid hormones and target cell nuclei. *Science, 183*, 610–620.

Papadopoulos, V. (2004). In search of the function of the peripheral-type benzodiazepine receptor. *Endocrine Research, 30*(4), 677–684.

Petralia, S. M., & Frye, C. A. (2004). In the ventral tegmental area, G-proteins and camp mediate the neurosteroid 3α,5α-THP's actions at dopamine type 1 receptors for lordosis of rats. *Neuroendocrinology, 80*(4), 233–243.

Penton-Voak, I. S., Perrett, D. I., Castles, D. L., Kobayashi, T., Burt, D. M., Murray, L. K., et al. (1999). Menstrual cycle alters face preference. *Nature, 399*(6738), 741–742.

Pfaff, D. W., Berrettini, W. H., & Joh, T. H. *Genetic Influences on Neural and Behavioral Functions.* 2000. New York: CRC Press.

Pfaff, D. W., & McEwen, B. S. (1983). Actions of estrogens and progestins on nerve cells. *Science, 219*, 808–814.

Pouliot, W. A., Handa, R. J., & Beck, S. G. (1996). Androgen modulates *N*-methyl-D-aspartate-mediated depolarization in CA1 hippocampal pyramidal cells. *Synapse (New York), 23*(1), 10–19.

Protopopescu, X., Pan, H., Altemus, M., Tuescher, O., Polanecsky, M., & McEwen, B., et al. (2005). Orbitofrontal cortex activity related to emotional processing changes across the menstrual cycle. *Proceedings of the National Academy of Sciences of the United States of America, 102*(44), 16060–16065.

Purvis, K., & Haynes, N. B. (1974). Short-term effects of copulation, human chorionic gonadotrophin injection and non-tactile association with a female on testosterone levels in the male rat. *The Journal of Endocrinology, 60*(3), 429–439.

Quetel, C. (1990). *History of Syphilis.* Baltimore, Maryland: John Hopkins Press.

Read, J., Perry, B. D., Moskowitz, A., & Connolly, J. (2001). The contribution of early traumatic events to schizophrenia in some patients: A traumagenic neurodevelopmental model. *Psychiatry, 64*(4), 319–345.

Reddy, D. S., O'Malley, B. W., & Rogawski, M. A. (2005). Anxiolytic activity of progesterone in progesterone receptor knockout mice. *Neuropharmacology, 48*(1), 14–24.

Rhodes, M. E., & Frye, C. A. (2001). Inhibiting progesterone metabolism in the hippocampus of rats in behavioral estrus decreases anxiolytic behaviors and enhances exploratory and antinociceptive behaviors. *Cognitive, Affective, and Behavioral Neuroscience, 1*(3), 287–296.

Rhodes, M. E., & Frye, C. A. (2006). ERb-selective SERMs produce mnemonic-enhancing effects in the inhibitory avoidance and water maze tasks. *Neurobiology of Learning and Memory, 85*(2), 183–191.

Roca, C. A., Schmidt, P. J., Altemus, M., Deuster, P., Danaceau, M. A., Putnam, K., et al. (2003). Differential menstrual cycle regulation of hypothalamic-pituitary-adrenal axis in women with premenstrual syndrome and controls. *The Journal of Clinical Endocrinology and Metabolism, 88*(7), 3057–3063.

Rosellini, R. A., Svare, B. B., Rhodes, M. E., & Frye, C. A. (2001). The testosterone metabolite and neurosteroid 3α-androstanediol may mediate the effects of testosterone on conditioned place preference. *Brain Research. Brain Research Reviews, 37*(1–3), 162–171.

Rupprecht, R. (2003). Neuroactive steroids: Mechanisms of action and neuropsychopharmacological properties. *Psychoneuroendocrinology, 28*(2), 139–168.

Rupprecht, R., & Holsboer, F. (2001). Neuroactive steroids in neuropsychopharmacology. *International Review of Neurobiology, 46*, 461–477.

Sanders, D., Warner, P., Backstrom, T., & Bancroft, J. (1983). Mood, sexuality, hormones and the menstrual cycle. I. Changes in mood and physical state: Description of subjects and method. *Psychosomatic Medicine, 45*(6), 487–501.

Schmidt, P. J., Nieman, L. K., Danaceau, M. A., Adams, L. F., & Rubinow, D. R. (1998). Differential behavioral effects of gonadal steroids in women with and in those without premenstrual syndrome. *The New England Journal of Medicine, 338*(4), 209–216.

Schmitz, C., Rhodes, M. E., Bludau, M., Kaplan, S., Ong, P., & Ueffing, I., et al. (2002). Depression: Reduced number of granule cells in the hippocampus of female, but not male, rats due to prenatal restraint stress. *Molecular Psychiatry, 7*(7), 810–813.

Selye, H. (1942). The antagonism between anesthetic steroid hormones and pentamethylenetetrazol (metrazol). *The Journal of Laboratory and Clinical Medicine, 27*, 1051–1053.

Shughrue, P. J., & Dorsa, D. M. (1993). Gonadal steroids modulate the growth-associated protein GAP-43 (neuromodulin) mrna in postnatal rat brain. *Brain Research. Developmental Brain Research, 73*(1), 123–132.

Singh, M., Meyer, E. M., & Simpkins, J. W. (1995). The effect of ovariectomy and estradiol replacement on brain-derived neurotrophic factor messenger ribonucleic acid expression in cortical and hippocampal brain regions of female Sprague-Dawley rats. *Endocrinology, 136*(5), 2320–2324.

Smith, H. E., Smith, R. G., Toft, D. O., Neergaard, J. R., Burrows, E. P., & O'Malley, B. W. (1974 Sep 25). Binding of steroids to progesterone receptor proteins in chick oviduct and human uterus. *The Journal of Biological Chemistry, 249*(18), 5924–5932.

Steiner, M., Dunn, E., & Born, L. (2003 Mar). Hormones and mood: From menarche to menopause and beyond. *Journal of Affective Disorders, 74*(1), 67–83.

Stone, D. J., Song, Y., Anderson, C. P., Krohn, K. K., Finch, C. E., & Rozovsky, I. (1998). Bidirectional transcription regulation of glial fibrillary acidic protein by estradiol in vivo and in vitro. *Endocrinology, 139*, 3202–3209.

Sumida, K., Walf, A. A., & Frye, C. A. (2005 Jun 3). Progestin-facilitated lordosis of hamsters may involve dopamine-like type 1 receptors in the ventral tegmental area. *Behavioural Brain Research, 161*(1), 1–7.

Toran-Allerand, C. D. (2000). Novel sites and mechanisms of oestrogen action in the brain. *Novartis Foundation Symposium, 230*, 56–69;

Uzunov, D. P., Cooper, T. B., Costa, E., & Guidotti, A. (1996). Fluoxetine-elicited changes in brain neurosteroid content measured by negative ion mass fragmentography. *Proceedings of the National Academy of Sciences of the United States of America, 93*(22), 12599–12604.

Uzunova, V., Sheline, Y., Davis, J. M., Rasmusson, A., Uzunov, D. P., Costa, E., et al. (1998). Increase in the cerebrospinal fluid content of neurosteroids in patients with unipolar major depression who are receiving fluoxetine or fluvoxamine. *Proceedings of the National Academy of Sciences of the United States of America*, *95*(6), 3239–3244.

Vasudevan, N., Kow, L. M., & Pfaff, D. (2005). Integration of steroid hormone initiated membrane action to genomic function in the brain. *Steroids*, *70*(5–7), 388–396.

Verhoeven, G., Heyns, W., & De Moor, P. (1975). Testosterone receptors in the prostate and other tissues. *Vitamins and Hormones*, *33*, 265–281.

Walf, A. A., Ciriza, I., Garcia-Segura, L. M., & Frye, C. A. (2008). Antisense oligodeoxynucleotides for estrogen receptor-beta and alpha attenuate estradiol's modulation of affective and sexual behavior, respectively, *Neuropsychopharmacology, 33*(2), 431–440.

Walf, A. A., & Frye, C. A. (2005). ERβ-selective estrogen receptor modulators produce antianxiety behavior when administered systemically to ovariectomized rats. *Neuropsychopharmacology: Official Publication of the American College of Neuropsychopharmacology*, *30*(9), 1598–1609.

Walf, A. A., & Frye, C. A. (2006). A review and update of mechanisms of estrogen in the hippocampus and amygdala for anxiety and depression behavior. *Neuropsychopharmacology: Official Publication of the American College of Neuropsychopharmacology*, *31*(6), 1097–1111.

Walf, A. A., Rhodes, M. E., Meade, J. R., Harney, J. P., & Frye, C. A. (2007). Estradiol-induced conditioned place preference may require actions at estrogen receptors in the nucleus accumbens. *Neuropsychopharmacology 32*(3), 522–530.

Walf, A. A., Sumida, K., & Frye, C. A. (2006). Inhibiting 5 alpha-reductase in the amygdala attenuates antianxiety and antidepressive behavior of naturally receptive and hormone-primed ovariectomized rats. *Psychopharmacology (Berl)*, *186*(3), 302–311.

Watters, J. J., Campbell, J. S., Cunningham, M. J., Krebs, E. G., & Dorsa, D. M. (1997). Rapid membrane effects of steroids in neuroblastoma cells: Effects of estrogen on mitogen activated protein kinase signalling cascade and c-fos immediate early gene transcription. *Endocrinology*, *138*(9), 4030–4033.

White, N. M., & Carr, G. D. (1985). The conditioned place preference is affected by two independent reinforcement processes. *Pharmacology, Biochemistry, and Behavior*, *23*(1), 37–42.

Wise, P. M., Dubal, D. B., Wilson, M. E., & Rau, S. W. (2000). Estradiol is a neuroprotective factor in in vivo and in vitro models of brain injury. *Journal of Neurocytology*, *29*(5–6), 401–410.

Zhou, Y., Watters, J. J., & Dorsa, D. M. (1996). Estrogen rapidly induces the phosphorylation of the camp response element binding protein in rat brain. *Endocrinology*, *137*(5), 2163.

Olfaction

8 Development of Olfactory Modulated Approach and Avoidance Motivated Behaviors

Regina M. Sullivan, Donna J. Toufexis, and Donald A. Wilson

CONTENTS

Approach and avoidance can be considered the fundamental building blocks of social behavior by either facilitating or attenuating interactions with conspecifics. Historically, the terms approach and avoidance have been associated with behavioral control through manipulation of pleasure and pain, as well as incentive to motivate behavior, and finally with cognition and learning, although mostly in isolation from one other. An integration of the concepts of approach and avoidance appears to have begun with Schneirla (Rosenblatt, Turkewitz, & Schneirla, 1969; Schneirla, 1966) who viewed approach and avoidance as important modes of behavior permitting animals to quickly adapt to environmental changes. Contrary to previous researchers, Schneirla did not view approach and avoidance as dependent on instinct or learning. Rather, he viewed control over behavior as a complex interaction between instinct and experience that blurred the distinction between nature and nurture.

Consistent with Schneirla's view of approach and avoidance as organizing forces for behavior, here we review two stages of development where approach and avoidance show dramatic changes, and where the lines between maturation and experience are blurred. Specifically, we describe olfactory control over infants' attachment to the mother and the mother's attachment to her infants. The neurobehavioral approach described here will highlight how approach and avoidance become distinct from the original pain and pleasure dichotomy, and take on a broader role as fundamental building blocks of social behavior.

BENEFITS OF OLFACTORY ASSESSMENT OF APPROACH–AVOIDANCE WITHIN A SOCIAL CONTEXT

The neurobiology of approach–avoidance social behaviors has been modeled extensively in rodents with a strong dependence on the olfactory system as the primary channel mediating those social behaviors. The reliance on olfaction has been fortuitous for researchers since it is a phylogenetically conserved and simplistic sensory system and provides an excellent model system for the study of motivated behaviors. Before discussing social olfactory cues and approach–avoidance behaviors, a brief description of the olfactory system and its connection to brain regions associated with cognitive and emotional processing will be given (for more in depth reviews of the olfactory system Doty, 2001; Wilson, Best, & Sullivan, 2004; Wilson & Stevenson, 2006).

The primary olfactory system includes the olfactory receptor sheet, the olfactory bulb containing the second-order neuron mitral cells, and the olfactory cortex. The olfactory cortex can be further subdivided into several regions including the piriform cortex, anterior olfactory nucleus, cortical nucleus of the amygdala, and olfactory tubercle. Both the olfactory bulb and olfactory cortex have direct connections to limbic structures such as the amygdala and entorhinal cortex. Finally, the olfactory system includes a thalamocortical loop, via piriform cortex projections to the dorsomedial nucleus of the thalamus which in turn projects to the orbitofrontal neocortex. Of particular relevance for the present discussion, the olfactory, limbic, and neocortical structures involved are connected reciprocally. Thus, for example, not only does olfactory information project to the amygdala and entorhinal cortex, but these areas also send significant projections back to the olfactory bulb and piriform cortex. This reciprocal feedforward and feedback system can permit experience, context, and behavioral state to modulate odor processing as early as the second-order neurons.

The olfactory system is in many ways the epitome of an associative network. Odor perception involves synthesis of components within complex molecular mixtures through associative connections and synaptic plasticity, resulting in formation of configural odor objects. Thus, coffee aroma, composed of literally hundreds of different species of volatile molecules, is experienced largely as a unitary percept. The olfactory system performs this feat through an initial highly analytical peripheral stage wherein olfactory receptors recognize specific molecules or molecular features, followed by a synthetic cortical stage wherein co-occurring features are merged together to form unique, associative objects. However, due to the anatomical triangulation with limbic and neocortical structures mentioned above, these odor objects can include and evoke strong multimodal, emotional, and memory-rich perceptions.

For example, the anterior piriform cortex appears to play a special role in the synthesis of co-occurring molecular features into patterns of network activity unique to the odor in which those features occur (Kadohisa & Wilson, 2006b; Gottfried, 2006; Wilson, 2000)—a process roughly similar to face selective neurons in inferotemporal visual cortex. Thus, from anterior piriform cortex processing, we know we smell a peach. The posterior piriform cortex expands on this associative synthesis and appears to encode a higher-order representation of odor quality, thus enabling us to know the smell of peach is fruity and similar in some way to other fruity smells (Gottfried, Winston, & Dolan, 2006; Kadohisa & Wilson, 2006a,b; Wilson, 2000). However, the posterior piriform cortex also receives a selectively strong input from the amygdala, which in turn has received input from the olfactory bulb and anterior piriform cortex. This suggests that encoding of this odor becomes highly intertwined, perhaps inextricably, with the emotional

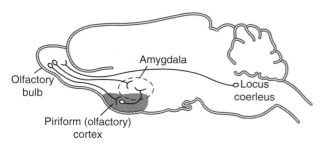

FIGURE 8.1 The flow of olfactory information begins in the nose, where odor molecules stimulate the receptors. This information is processed by the olfactory bulb and is directly relayed to the olfactory piriform cortex, where it is sent to other brain areas. The olfactory bulb also directly sends odor information to brain areas critical in emotional and cognitive processing of odors, such as the piriform "olfactory" cortex and the amygdala. The locus coeruleus (LC) projects to the olfactory bulb and is the bulb's sole source of norepinephrine (NE).

memories associated with that stimulus. In fact, as described below, neurons in the adult posterior piriform respond differentially to learned aversive odors compared to novel odors in both infancy and adulthood (Calu, Roesch, Stalnaker, & Schoenbaum, 2006; Sevelinges, Gervais, Messaoudi, Granjon, & Mouly, 2004).

This opportunity for mixing of basic odor encoding with memorial, emotional, and state-dependent associations, which can lead to expression of stimulus approach and avoidance behaviors, occurs through the central olfactory pathway. Next, we briefly review the main system components, which are illustrated in Figure 8.1.

OLFACTORY RECEPTORS AND THE OLFACTORY BULB

The olfactory receptor sheet is composed of receptor neurons that, as a population, express hundreds of different genes that encode olfactory G-protein coupled receptors, with each individual receptor neuron expressing a single receptor gene (Buck, 2004; Liberles & Buck, 2006; Mori, Takahashi, Igarashi, & Yamaguchi, 2006). Biological (including social) odors (either natural or learned) are generally complex and composed of many different molecules, with each molecule or section of that molecule, binding to a specific receptor. This results in a distribution of receptor activation that is usually spread across the receptor sheet, with different odorants activating different combinations of receptors. Thus, the olfactory receptors appear to deconstruct the odorant before synapsing with mitral/tufted cells, the primary output neurons of the olfactory bulb. The process of putting the social odor back together begins with the remarkably precise projection of olfactory receptor neuron axons to the olfactory bulb, with each glomerulus receiving homogeneous input from receptors expressing the same

receptor gene. The glomeruli are functional units of dense neuropil containing receptor neuron axons and dendrites of mitral and tufted cells and modulated by juxtaglomerular neurons (Chen & Shepherd, 2005; Greer, Stewart, Kauer, & Shepherd, 1981; Spors, Wachowiak, Cohen, & Friedrich, 2006; Willhite et al., 2006; Yang et al., 1998). The mitral cells appear to function largely as feature detectors, although the extensive interactions within and between glomeruli and via granule cells enhance contrast between similar features important in eventual resynthesis of the odor (Nagai, Sano, & Yokoi, 2005; Yokoi, Mori, & Nakanishi, 1995). The mitral/tufted cells project out of the olfactory bulb, but their activity is modulated at two levels within the bulb by intrinsic interneurons and centrifugal projections from the rest of the brain (Araneda & Firestein, 2006; Buonviso, Amat, & Litaudon, 2006; Duchamp-Viret & Duchamp, 1993; Hayar, Karnup, Shipley, & Ennis, 2004). The bulb receives descending input from myriad brain areas, but of particular importance here (discussed below) is the centrifugal input from the locus coeruleus (LC), which distributes norepinephrine (NE) to cells in both the granule cell and glomerular layers.

The important role of odors in controlling social behavior is reflected in the olfactory bulb's direct projection to brain areas important for cognition and emotional processing, which modulate approach and avoidance behaviors. Mitral cells that leave the olfactory bulb are glutamatergic neurons and project directly or indirectly to a wide range of brain areas, although of particular relevance for social approach–avoidance behaviors are the olfactory cortex, entorhinal cortex, hippocampus, amygdala, and hypothalamus (reviews, Breer, Fleischer, & Strotmann, 2006; Brennan & Kendrick, 2006; Gottfried, 2006; Wilson & Mainen, 2006; Wilson & Stevenson, 2006). As noted above, these cortical olfactory circuits further reconstruct the odor while integrating the olfactory information with other sensory systems, as well as the animal's state, context, and biological learned significance (Dardou, Datiche, & Cattarelli, 2006; Knafo et al., 2005; Moriceau, Wilson, Levine, & Sullivan, 2006; Otto & Giardino, 2001; Shionoya et al., 2006; Staubli, Ivy, & Lynch, 1984; Wiltgen, Sanders, Anagnostaras, Sage, & Fanselow, 2006; Wolff, Gibb, & Dalrymple-Alford, 2006).

The role of the hippocampal formation and the amygdala in memory for olfactory cues has been well described for adults (Schoenbaum, Chiba, & Gallagher, 1999; Sutherland, McDonald, Hill, & Rudy, 1989; Touzani & Sclafani, 2005). Throughout the olfactory system, there is strong modulation by neurotransmitter systems (Gomez et al., 2005) important in regulating social behaviors and plasticity. For example, NE from the nucleus locus coeruleus heavily innervates the olfactory bulb and cortex

(Bouret & Sara, 2002; Linster & Hasselmo, 2001; Tronel, Feenstra, & Sara, 2004) and, as is described below, has a critical function in mother–infant attachment in both the infant and mother. The olfactory bulb and cortex also receive cholinergic input from the horizontal limb of the diagonal band of Broca (HLDB). Interestingly, both the LC and the HLDB are responsive to olfactory input (Bouret & Sara, 2002; Linster & Hasselmo, 2001; Tronel et al., 2004) and illustrate a potentially interesting feedback loop where olfactory processing is itself partially under olfactory control.

Of particular importance when assessing the development of approach–avoidance behaviors is the maturation and functional ability of brain areas within the olfactory circuit and its interaction with the limbic system. Indeed, while the infant rat can smell, discriminate odors, and process these odors in a complex fashion (Fletcher, Smith, Best, & Wilson, 2005), the infant rat brain is still immature and does not have all brain areas available to the adult rat. While determining when specific brain areas become functional is difficult, anatomical development can provide guidance and certainly approximate an age when functional contribution to behavioral expression can occur. For example, in the infant rat, hippocampal output is probably not present until late in the second week of life (Crain, Cotman, Taylor, & Lynch, 1973; Nair & Gonzalez-Lima, 1999) and hippocampal dependent behaviors such as spatial learning do not seem to emerge until around weaning age (Brown, Pagani, & Stanton, 2005; Kim & Richardson, 2007; Ivkovich & Stanton, 2001; Rudy, 1994; Rudy & Morledge, 1994; Stanton, 2000). The frontal cortex development and its projections to the amygdala are also protracted with anatomical maturation and connections occurring between PN8 and 14 with the transition to the "adult-like" laminar cellular organization by PN13 (Bouwmeester, Smits, & Van Ree, 2002; Bouwmeester, Wolterink, & van Ree, 2002; Kolb & Cioe, 1996; Verwer, Van Vulpen, & Van Uum, 1996). Behaviors associated with frontal cortical behavior, such as extinction effects (i.e., partial reinforcement effects) on learning and expression, do not seem to emerge until after postnatal day (PN10) further suggesting protracted development (Nair & Gonzalez-Lima, 1999). The amygdala also continues to develop during the postnatal period. The basolateral complex first emerges at E17 with most neurons produced between E20 and PN7. Other amygdaloid nuclei lag behind the basolateral by a few days and continue to develop until adolescence (Berdel & Morys, 2000; Berdel, Morys, Maciejewska, & Dziewiatkowski, 1997; Dziewiatkowski et al., 1998; Morys, Berdel, Jagalska-Majewska, & Luczynska,

1999a; Morys, Berdel, Kowianski, & Dziewiatkowski, 1998; Morys, et al., 1999b). Olfactory information is received by the amygdala in the early neonatal period (Schwob, Haberly, & Price, 1984; Schwob & Price, 1984). Connections with other higher-order brain areas mature sequentially (Bouwmeester et al., 2002; Cunningham, Bhattacharyya, & Benes, 2002; Hunt, 1999; Hunt, Richardson, & Campbell, 1994; Nair, Berndt, Barrett, & Gonzalez-Lima, 2001), such that components of the fear response become incorporated into the behavior as pups mature (Hunt et al., 1994). Together, the protracted development of these brain areas suggests the neonate has a unique circuitry for odor-based approach and avoidance behavior, which is further discussed below.

MOTHER–INFANT INTERACTIONS: OLFACTORY MODULATION OF INFANT APPROACH AND AVOIDANCE BEHAVIOR

DEVELOPMENT OF APPROACH–AVOIDANCE BEHAVIOR IN INFANT RATS

The newborn infant rat must express approach behaviors at birth in order to survive (Galef & Kaner, 1980; Leon, 1992). Indeed, altricial pups are born hairless, with nonfunctional visual and auditory systems, and depend upon their approach to the mother for warmth, nutrition, and protection using the maternal odor. In the early days of life, the motorically immature pups remain in the nest and nurse almost continuously. Pups are occasionally displaced from the nest when the mother enters/leaves, a process sometimes associated with distress to pups when the dam drags still-attached pups across the nest and steps on others. Thus, pups' early life is generally spent within the confines of the nest exposed to maternal odor as they nurse and are groomed by the mother, but with occasional painful stimuli from the mother. It is important to note that pups feel pain, without pain threshold differences for the stimuli and ages that will be presented here, at least related to the development of the switch from approach to avoidance behaviors that will be described below (Collier & Bolles, 1980; Emerich, Scalzo, Enters, Spear, & Spear, 1985). We call this neonatal period of the pups' early life the sensitive period since, as described below, pups show unique learning ability that appears to enhance pups learning the maternal odor, which ends around PN10. Although some unique learning abilities continue in the more mature postsensitive period pups, the learning is more context dependent and it gradually becomes more "adult-like" by weaning at PN21–23. The postsensitive period represents a change in pups' environment as walking emerges, pups begin to nibble on food and have increased number of excursions outside the nest. These pups actually have a monumental transition to make from complete dependence on the mother during the sensitive period to complete independence at weaning. As will be outlined below, pups' olfactory guided behaviors such as approach and avoidance appears to accommodate the changing demands of life as pups make this transition from complete dependence to complete independence.

Pups respond to the maternal odor at birth with approach behaviors and nipple attachment (Pedersen & Blass, 1982; Polan & Hofer, 1999). Although we initially thought of maternal odor as a pheromone, it now appears the maternal odor is initially learned prenatally, and reinforced during the birth process and repeatedly throughout the postnatal period, presumably due to maternal diet altering the maternal odor (Cheslock, Varlinskaya, Petrov, & Spear, 2000; Pedersen, Williams, & Blass, 1982). While there is some risk in learning the odor required for a survival-dependent behavior, prenatal odor learning of the mother's amniotic fluid (mothers spread the amniotic fluid on their ventrum during the birth process) and rapid postnatal learning appear to provide pups with a system to ensure rapid and robust maternal odor learning.

INTENSITY BASED APPROACH–AVOIDANCE BEHAVIORS IN PUPS

The intensity of an odor seems important in determining approach/avoidance behavior in rat pups, which has been documented by Schneirla and his colleagues (Rosenblatt

et al., 1969; Schneirla, 1966). Rosenblatt has suggested that the incentive or motivational components of odors need to be learned by pups and are superimposed over this basic behavioral control. Indeed, even a fetal rat will exhibit aversive behaviors (face wiping) when presented with a strong odor (Robinson & Smotherman, 1994; Smotherman, Arnold, & Robinson, 1993).

LEARNING APPROACH AND AVOIDANCE RESPONSES TO ODORS IN PUPS

Pups show an enhanced ability for learning approach behaviors during the early life sensitive period. This heightened learning is not surprising since maternal odor learning is critical for survival and has been documented in many altricial species and clearly illustrated in imprinting, which is also viewed as a learning process by Lorenz. Infant rat pups rapidly learn olfactory guided approach behavior by simply pairing the odor with one of a variety of reinforcers, such as milk, tactile stimulation, or warmth (Figure 8.2A). During early life and most notably during the sensitive period (until PN10), pairing an odor with a painful stimulus (0.5 mA shock or tailpinch) also produces an odor preference (Figure 8.2B) although this changes as the sensitive period ends (Camp & Rudy, 1988; Moriceau & Sullivan, 2004; Roth & Sullivan, 2005; Sullivan, Brake, Hofer, & Williams, 1986; Sullivan, Landers, Yeaman, & Wilson, 2000). As discussed above, pups feel pain and respond to both shock and tailpinch with behaviors associated with pain such as escape and vocalization. Pups do not learn to approach the shock or tail-pinch and continue to show avoidance behaviors to these stimuli; rather, an approach

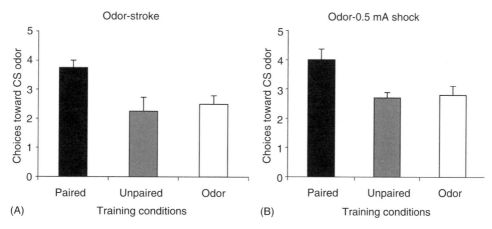

(A) Odor-stroke

(B) Odor-0.5 mA shock

FIGURE 8.2 During the sensitive period for learning, pairing an odor with either (A) tactile stimulation that mimics maternal licking of pups or with (B) painful 0.5 mA shock that mimics pain from the mother results in an odor preference to the odor. The day after conditioning, pups were tested in a Y-maze that required pups to choose either the conditioned odor or the familiar odor of clean bedding. After 10 days of age, the tactile stimulation does not support learning and the 0.5 mA shock will produce an aversion when paired with an odor.

response to the odor previously paired with pain is expressed. Our recent work has demonstrated this paradoxical odor preference learning following odor–pain association also occurs when the pain is induced by a stressed mother, who exhibits rough handling and transporting of pups without nursing (Roth & Sullivan, 2005), a paradigm developed in the Baram lab (Gilles, Schultz, & Baram, 1996). Thus, as discussed in the introduction, the historical framework of approach and avoidance becomes distinct from the simple pain and pleasure dichotomy and the motivation of approach and avoidance takes on a broader role as fundamental building blocks of social behavior.

Sensitive period pups can learn to avoid odors, although this appears to be associated with malaise and interoceptive distress rather than exteroceptive pain (Haroutunian & Campbell, 1979). Specifically, fetal rat pups can learn to avoid odors paired with malaise-producing LiCl (Smotherman, 1982). Additionally, very young postnatal pups can learn to avoid an odor paired with a 1.2 mA shock, although this level of shock appears to be supporting aversion learning via malaise since it produces gastrointestinal distress similar to LiCl (Coopersmith, Lee, & Leon, 1986; Kucharski & Spear, 1984; Miller, Molina, & Spear, 1990; Rudy & Cheatle, 1983; Shionoya et al., 2006; Smotherman, 1982). This early life odor–malaise aversion learning is present before the maturation of brain structures normally supporting such illness-induced aversion learning in adults. For example, the amygdala plays a critical role in adult odor–malaise conditioning (Touzani & Sclafani, 2005), yet as reviewed above, anatomical amygdala connections and synaptogenesis have not occurred in the fetus exhibiting odor–malaise learning. Indeed, recent work from our lab suggests odor–malaise learning (using LiCl) (Shionoya et al., 2006) (and using 1.2 mA shock) (Raineki, Shionoya, Moriceau, Sander, & Sullivan, 2007) uses a nonamygdala neural circuit for learning with engagement of the amygdala into the learning circuit shortly before weaning. As is discussed below, this is in sharp contrast to the engagement the amygdala using odor-0.5 mA fear conditioning with inclusion of the amygdala into the neural circuit occurring almost one week earlier (Moriceau & Sullivan, 2006; Moriceau et al., 2006). Together, this summary of pups' aversion learning clearly indicates neonatal rat pups can learn and express avoidance behaviors, although the neural circuitries supporting aversion and approach behaviors are not the same as that identified in the adult.

THE NEURAL BASIS OF PUP APPROACH–AVOIDANCE LEARNING

The sharp distinction between pups' learning of approach and avoidance behaviors from odor-0.5 mA shock during

the sensitive period and after the sensitive period is mirrored by dramatic changes in the neural circuit supporting this learning. As will be reviewed here, both odor preference and aversions appear coded by the olfactory bulb, although the anterior piriform is associated with odor preferences and the posterior piriform appears to be associated with odor aversions at least in pups.

Olfactory Bulb

During the sensitive period, odor learning appears to be coded by changes in the olfactory bulb response patterns and occurs with natural maternal odor, artificial odors experienced in the nest, and outside the nest in controlled learning experiments (Harley, Darby-King, McCann, & McLean, 2006; Leon & Johnson, 2003; Pedersen & Blass, 1982; Roth & Sullivan, 2005; Shionoya et al., 2006; Smotherman, 1982; Sullivan, Wilson, Wong, Correa, & Leon, 1990; Wilson & Leon, 1988; Woo, Oshita, & Leon, 1996; Yuan, Harley, Bruce, Darby-King, & McLean, 2000). The modified olfactory bulb response is characterized by immediate-early gene activity (c-fos), intrinsic optical imaging, enhanced 2-deoxyglucose (2-DG) uptake, and modified single-unit response patterns of the bulb's output neurons, mitral/tufted cells. Similarly to the behavioral changes in attachment, the olfactory bulb occurs during early life but is retained into adulthood (Woo & Leon, 1987). As pups mature, the olfactory bulb's ability to exhibit the associative learning-induced changes diminishes. While we had previously thought these learning associated olfactory bulb changes were limited to acquisition during early life (Woo & Leon, 1987), mating (Brennan, Kaba, & Keverne, 1990), and parturition (Levy, 2002), although prolonged odor training in adulthood also induces similar olfactory bulb plasticity (Ressler, personal communication).

Piriform Cortex

Recent work suggests this early life odor preference learning is also encoded in the piriform cortex, perhaps limited to the anterior olfactory cortex, while the posterior appears to encode pups' odor aversion (Moriceau & Sullivan, 2006; Moriceau et al., 2006; Roth & Sullivan, 2005). Physiologically and anatomically, the anterior and posterior piriform are distinct structures, with the anterior more strongly influenced by input from the olfactory bulb and the posterior more heavily influenced by intracortical connectivity and input from other limbic structures (Wilson & Stevenson, 2003). While both areas of the piriform have strong limbic system connections, there are particularly strong connections via the posterior piriform (Swanson & Petrovich, 1998). There is also an important role of the piriform cortex in adult odor learning (Bernabeu, Thiriet, Zwiller, & Di Scala, 2006; Brosh, Rosenblum, & Barkai, 2006;

Calu et al., 2006; Kadohisa & Wilson, 2006b; Martin, Gervais, Messaoudi, & Ravel, 2006; Ross & Eichenbaum, 2006; Schoenbaum et al., 1999; Sevelinges et al., 2004).

THE IMPORTANCE OF NE FROM THE LOCUS COERULEUS FOR PUPS' LEARNING

During the sensitive period, both approach and avoidance learning and its corresponding olfactory bulb learning-induced changes appear dependent on NE from the locus coeruleus (LC) (Harley et al., 2006; Sullivan, Stackenwalt, Nasr, Lemon, & Wilson, 2000; Sullivan & Wilson, 1994). NE is not intrinsic to the olfactory bulb but is received from the LC (McLean & Shipley, 1991). Diverse types of sensory stimulation that support sensitive period pup learning (e.g., 1 s stroking, shock) produce abundant NE release from the neonatal LC. Specifically, the presentation of a sensory stimulus causes a prolonged (20–30 s) LC response, which is in sharp contrast to the very brief millisecond response found in older pups and adults (Nakamura & Sakaguchi, 1990). This heightened LC activation is reflected in the copious release of NE within the olfactory bulb (Rangel & Leon, 1995). While this high level of NE is critical for olfactory preference conditioning in the young sensitive period pups, with maturation (>PN10) NE release from the LC is no longer sufficient to produce odor preference learning in postsensitive period pups (Harley et al., 2006; Moriceau & Sullivan, 2004; Sullivan et al., 2000; Sullivan & Wilson, 1994). This developmental change in the LC's NE release

is likely due to the functional emergence of the LC's inhibitory α2 noradrenergic autoreceptors as the sensitive period ends, which quickly terminate the LC's response to sensory stimuli (McGaugh, 2006; Nakamura & Sakaguchi, 1990). With this postsensitive period LC maturation, NE begins to plays a more modulatory role of enhancing or attenuating memories in a manner similar to adults (Ferry & McGaugh, 2000; McGaugh, 2006). Thus, while many neurotransmitters have a role in early olfactory learning in neonatal rats, NE appears to have a particularly important role.

LABILE INFANTILE APPROACH–AVOIDANCE BEHAVIORS: SWITCHING APPROACH TO AVOIDANCE

As mentioned above, odor-0.5 mA shock conditioning produces an odor preference in pups younger than PN10 but an odor aversion in pups PN10 and older (Camp & Rudy, 1988; Sullivan et al., 2000). A simplistic interpretation of the ability of odor-0.5 mA shock to produce an odor aversion is that the amygdala, a brain area important for adult fear conditioning (reviews, Davis, Walker, & Myers, 2003; Fanselow & Poulos, 2005; LeDoux, 2003), matures around PN10 and permits avoidance acquisition and fear conditioning. However, based on our ability to pharmacologically accelerate or retard the age pups learn to avoid odors, amygdala maturation is not the entire issue. Indeed, during the sensitive period, either increasing pups' corticosterone (CORT) or decreasing pups' opioids permit pups to learn an aversion from odor-0.5 mA shock conditioning (Figure 8.3).

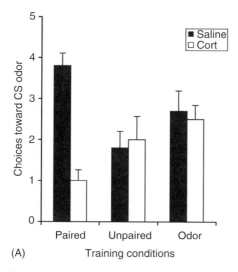

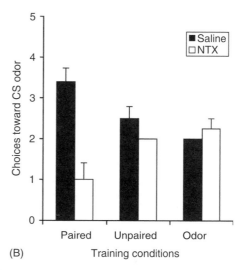

FIGURE 8.3 The age pups switch from sensitive-period learning to postsensitive period learning occurs by (A) increasing corticosterone (CORT) just before conditioning (Moriceau et al., 2004; Moriceau et al., 2006) or (B) blocking opioid receptors with Naltrexone just after conditioning (Roth & Sullivan, 2003). The day after conditioning, pups were tested in a Y-maze that required pups to choose either the conditioned odor or the familiar odor of clean bedding.

Both opioids and CORT are important in modulating pups' odor learning because they have been shown to strongly motivate infant rat behavior and appear to program pups' motivational and emotional development. Furthermore, maternal behaviors toward the pups influence pups' physiology and neurotransmitters, including opioids and CORT, suggesting the mother may modulate pup learning.

OPIOID MODULATION OF PUP APPROACH–AVOIDANCE

Pups have a fully functional opioid system. Nursing elevates pups' opioid levels, which serve to quiet pups, reduce pain threshold, and support nipple attachment (Blass, 1997; Blass, Shide, Zaw-Mon, & Sorrentino, 1995; Goodwin & Barr, 1997; Nelson & Panksepp, 1998; Petrov, Nizhnikov, Varlinskaya, & Spear, 2006; Shayit, Nowak, Keller, & Weller, 2003). Opioids are also important in pup learning since odor–morphine pairings support a conditioned odor preference that can be blocked with the opioid receptor antagonist naltrexone (Kehoe & Blass, 1986; Randall, Kraemer, Dose, Carbary, & Bardo, 1992; Roth & Sullivan, 2003, 2006; Shayit et al., 2003). These studies also indicate that blocking opioids (naltrexone) either during or after conditioning prevent odor learning in either a classical conditioning procedure (odor-stroking that mimics maternal licking) or natural interactions with the mother. Furthermore, mice lacking μ-opioid receptors do not demonstrate a preference toward maternal odor (Moles, Kieffer, & D'Amato, 2004). This critical role of opioids for pup learning of maternal odor is in sharp contrast to the important, albeit modulatory, role of opioids in adult learning (McGaugh & Cahill, 1997). Together, these results suggest that opioids, which are increased by nursing, facilitate the learning of the approach response to maternal odor.

An additional critical role for opioids in sensitive-period learning of approach responses is revealed when odor-0.5 mA shock conditioning is used (Roth, Moriceau, & Sullivan, 2006; Roth & Sullivan, 2006). Specifically, blocking opioid receptors during consolidation of memories resulted in pups learning to avoid the odor previously paired with shock. Furthermore, the blocking of opioids during consolidation appeared to prevent the neural changes in the olfactory bulb and engage the amygdala. Indeed, the site of opioid action controlling this posttraining switch from preference to aversion learning appears to be the amygdala since a naltrexone infusion directly into the amygdala posttraining causes the odor–shock conditioning to result in a learned odor aversion.

CORTICOSTERONE MODULATION OF PUP APPROACH–AVOIDANCE

Pups' sensitive period is coincident with stress hyporesponsivity known as the "stress hyporesponsive period" (SHRP) that is characterized by low basal CORT levels and the inability of most stressful stimuli (i.e., shock) to increase CORT (Levine, 2005). The hypothalamic–pituitary–adrenal axis (HPA), which releases CORT, is suppressed by the sensory stimuli pups received from the mother and removal of this sensory stimuli for as little as 1 h begins to cause activation of the HPA (Levine, 2001). Specifically, during the sensitive period, milk, nursing, and sensory stimulation from the mother keep pups' CORT levels low, although simple maternal presence can also lower CORT (Stanton, Wallstrom, & Levine, 1987; Suchecki, Rosenfeld, & Levine, 1993). One of the roles of CORT may be to attenuate learning aversions to the mother.

In early life, CORT levels appear to control pups' avoidance of predator odors with low levels of CORT preventing the freezing response to predator odor. Fear of predator odor appears to emerge around PN10 (Takahashi, 1996), which is coincident with the emergence of fear conditioning outlined above. Wiedenmayer and Barr (2001) extended these results and found amygdala activity, which is important in fear to predator odor, emerged ontogenetically concurrent with fear to predator odor. Takahashi has also shown that simply increasing CORT levels during the sensitive period pups show fear to predator odor by freezing (immobility) (Takahashi, 1996). A combined assessment of CORT, amygdala activity and fear to predator odor (Moriceau, Roth, Okotoghaide, & Sullivan, 2004) suggests CORT is implicated in amygdala (basolateral complex) activation, either directly or indirectly, to permit the expression of infant fear to predator odor. Specifically, we could prematurely activate the expression of freezing and activation of the basolateral/ lateral complex of the amygdala in neonates through exogenous injections of CORT. Additionally, we were also able to retard the developmental expression of fear to predator odor and amygdala activation through adrenalectomy, which eliminates the pups' source of CORT.

It should be noted that the role of the basolateral amygdala in unlearned (predator) fear may differ between pups and adults. The adult literature suggests the central nucleus, the basolateral complex of the amygdala, and the medial amygdala are involved in response to predator odor (Kemble, Blanchard, & Blanchard, 1990; Lang, Davis & Ohman, 2000; Li, Maglinao, & Takahahsi, 2004; Wallace & Rosen, 2001). There are also developmental changes in amygdala responses to predator odor: the central nucleus and the medial amygdala are not activated, at least by naturally fearful odors until after weaning when the avoidance (fleeing) response emerges (Wiedenmayer & Barr, 2001).

CORT is also important in modulating pup odor–shock learning, at least through the modulation of odor-0.5 mA shock conditioning. We have shown that increasing sensitive period CORT (systematic, amygdala) permits odor–shock conditioning to result in an odor aversion rather than the age typical odor preference; while preventing the CORT increase (adrenalectomy) prolongs the sensitive period in older pups. The CORT manipulation also modulates neural correlates of sensitive-period odor learning in a manner consistent with the behavior, including the olfactory bulb neural correlates of preference learning and amygdala (basolateral complex) participation in fear conditioning (Moriceau & Sullivan, 2006). Our working hypothesis is that low CORT levels prevent the amygdala from participating in odor–shock conditioning during the sensitive period and attenuate pups odor aversion learning.

Maternal presence can attenuate stress-induced CORT release even in postsensitive period pups. The presence of an anesthetized dam attenuates pups' response to shock and prevents normal novelty-induced increase in CORT (Stanton et al., 1987; Suchecki et al., 1993). Thus, we used maternal presence as a naturalistic method of reducing CORT in postsensitive period pups during odor–shock conditioning. Indeed, while postsensitive period pups readily learn to avoid odor previously paired with shock, the same conditioning done in the presence of the mother resulted in a learned odor preference. The important role of maternal suppression of shock-induced CORT release was verified by systemic and intra-amygdala CORT infusions, which permitted pups to learn odor aversions in the presence of the mother. Similar CORT attenuation by social cues has been found in other paradigms and has a dramatic modulatory effect on motivation within social attachments in both infancy and adulthood (Hennessy, Hornschuh, Kaiser, & Sachser, 2006).

Together, the research reviewed above suggests the control of infant approach behaviors, as well as the motivation and learning of those approach responses is a critical feature of early life. While many hormones and neurotransmitters work in concert to control infant behavior and its development, NE, opioids, and CORT appear to have a critical role in determining pup approach responses that are critical for survival in early life. Moreover, the mother's ability to increase pups opioids and NE, while decreasing pups CORT, may greatly

facilitate the learning and expression of pup approach responses to the mother.

MOTHER–INFANT INTERACTIONS: THE SWITCH FROM AVOIDANCE TO MATERNAL BEHAVIOR

Two mammalian species, the rat and the sheep, have been extensively used to describe the neural basis of maternal behavior with remarkable convergence between the two species. Extensive reviews of the behavioral and neural basis of maternal behavior are available (Insel, 2003; Numan, 1988, 2004, 2007; Pedersen & Boccia, 2002) and the present discussion will focus on the neuronal systems, hormones, and peptides that underlie the dramatic switch of pup odor aversion to pup odor approach behaviors seen at parturition.

When virgin female rats are exposed to pups, they ignore, avoid, or occasionally attack them. As will be detailed later on, the virgin female mediates these avoidant behaviors through the perception of pup odor as aversive. However, if exposed to well-fed pups over the course of 5–7 days this aversive response changes, and the virgin female starts to retrieve and groom the pups, build a nest, and display nursing behavior (Fleming & Luebke, 1981). This change in responsiveness from aversion to maternal behavior is called "sensitization," and involves a change in emotional valence toward pup odor. In contrast to this, a female rat that has just given birth for the first time (a primiparous female) shows instantaneous maternal behavior. The immediate onset of maternal behavior in first time mothers results from the activational effects exerted by gestational and steroid hormones in late pregnancy and during parturition (Numan, 2007). Indeed, administration of a similar hormone regime to virgin females hastens the onset of sensitization in these animals (Siegel, Doerr, & Rosenblatt, 1978; Siegel & Rosenblatt, 1975). However, it is important to note that sensitization occurs in virgin females who are ovariectomized (Rosenblatt, 1967), suggesting that these hormone changes prime a neural system that can also be activated through other avenues. Thus, studies examining the onset of maternal behavior pointed to the existence of a nodal brain area responsible for shifting the valence of pup-related odor stimuli from negative to positive and responsive to the priming effects of gestational hormones. Logically, such a brain region would control volitional types of maternal behavior that are appetitive in nature and require a change in motivational state, such as retrieving and grooming pups, and be less involved in other more reflexive responses like nursing behavior. Studies undertaken throughout the 1970s and 1980s by Michael Numan and colleagues indicate that the medial preoptic area (MPOA) of the hypothalamus and the immediately adjacent ventral portion of the bed nucleus of the stria terminalis (vBNST) constitute this pivotal brain region (see Numan, 2006 for a review).

THE MPOA/vBNST REGION MEDIATES THE CHANGE IN EMOTIONAL VALENCE OF MATERNAL BEHAVIOR

Bilateral damage to the MPOA/vBNST completely abolishes retrieval behavior and reduces, but does not eliminate, nursing behavior (Numan, Corodimas, Numan, Factor, & Piers, 1988). Moreover, motor activity, hording, and sexual behavior remain following MPOA/vBNST damage, demonstrating not only the specific effects of the lesion on maternal behavior, but also indicating that motor behavior that could be utilized to retrieve pups is left intact (Numan, 1974; Numan & Callahan, 1980; Numan & Corodimas, 1985; Numan et al., 1988).

In addition to the detriments in maternal behavior observed after MPOA/vBNST lesions, there are other lines of evidence implicating this brain region in the generation and control of voluntary maternal responses. For instance, the MPOA/vBNST contains receptors for the gestational hormone prolactin (Bakowska & Morrell, 1997) and for the gonadal steroids estrogen and progesterone (Numan et al., 1999; Shughrue, Lane, & Merchenthaler, 1997) mentioned above as integral as the genesis of maternal behavior in the primiparous female. Further, the injection of estrogen or prolactin directly into the MPOA/vBNST initiates maternal behavior in rats (Bridges et al., 1997; Bridges & Ronsheim, 1990). In addition, neurons in the MPOA/vBNST express the immediate-early gene product Fos protein during maternal behavior (Lonstein & De Vries, 2000). Both cFos and Fos B proteins are increased in females who are with pups and showing active maternal behavior. The level of these proteins decreases if females are separated from pups (Stack & Numan, 2000). In a corroborating experiment, parturient females showing a conditioned place preference for areas previously paired with the presence of pups show the induction of Fos in the MPOA/vBNST when in the conditioned area (Mattson & Morrell, 2005). The specificity of MPOA/vBNST activation in response to pup-related stimuli was demonstrated in an experiment showing that lesions of the MPOA/vBNST disrupted lever pressing to obtain pups, but not lever pressing to obtain food (Lee, Clancy, & Fleming, 2000).

BRAIN AREAS MEDIATING THE MOTHER'S AVOIDANCE OF PUP ODOR

By what mechanism does the MPOA/vBNST effect this change in emotional valence? In his important 2006 review, Michael Numan suggests that two complementary sequences of events are necessary. First, brain regions mediating aversive responses to pup odor must be dampened or suppressed while those mediating motivational responses must be heightened (Numan, 2006). First, we will consider the circuitry mediating the aversive responses.

As described above, naive virgin females initially find pups highly aversive. Moreover, this aversion to pups is mediated through olfaction in that virgin or early stage pregnant females avoid the odor of pups even though these same odors induce approach behaviors in the newly parturient female. Approach behavior in the parturient female has been also shown to occur in several other mammalian species (Brennan & Kendrick, 2006; Fleming et al., 2002; Gonzalez-Mariscal, 2001; Levy, 2002; Poindron, Nowak, Levy, Porter, & Schaal, 1993). Thus, similarly to that described for pups, a dramatic shift in the hedonic value of an odor is critical in supporting social behavior. It has been shown that rendering a virgin female anosmic enhances the sensitization of maternal behavior (Fleming & Rosenblatt, 1974; Fleming, Vaccarino, Tambosso, & Chee, 1979). There is substantial input from the olfactory bulb and the accessory olfactory bulb to the medial nucleus of the amygdala (MeA), and lesions of this portion of the amygdala also accelerate the onset of maternal behavior in virgin female rats (Fleming, Vaccarino, & Luebke, 1980; Numan, Numan, & English, 1993). Therefore, it is likely that the MeA and its efferent projections underlie the aversive response to pup odors. Among its many targets, the MeA projects to two areas that are particularly involved in producing fear and anxiety behaviors: the caudal anterior hypothalamic nucleus (cAHN)) and the periaqueductal grey (PAG) (Canteras, Simerly, & Swanson, 1995; Risold, Canteras, & Swanson, 1994). Disruptions of both of theses areas facilitate maternal behavior (Bridges, Mann, & Coppeta, 1999; Sheehan, Cirrito, Numan, & Numan, 2000; Sheehan, Paul, Amaral, Numan, & Numan, 2001; Sukikara, Mota-Ortiz, Baldo, Felicio, & Canteras, 2006), suggesting that it is these two projection regions of the MeA that activate aversive responses to pup odors in virgin females. With this in mind, studies by Michael and Marilyn Numan using the anterograde tracer PHAL, along with labeling for Fos activation, found that neurons in the MPOA/vBNST showed activation during maternal behavior where also those with projections to the cAHN and the PAG (Numan & Numan, 1996, 1997). It has been shown that a large number of the neurons in the MPOA/vBNST that are active during maternal behavior produce the enzyme needed to make GABA, the major inhibitory neurotransmitter in the brain (Lonstein & De Vries, 2000). Therefore, it seems likely that the MPOA/vBNST is inhibiting the aversive response to pup odor by inhibition of the cAHN and the PAG.

BRAIN REGIONS MEDIATING THE MOTIVATIONAL ASPECTS OF MATERNAL BEHAVIOR

Once maternal behavior has been established, additional sensory systems also become engaged and coordinate the dam's maternal behaviors expressed toward pups, with pup stimulation during nursing important in maintaining the maternal behavior. The process by which the female's avoidance from pup odor becomes approach has some processes that are similar to those already described in the pup. Indeed, the mother also shows increased opioid levels and has a CORT SHRP with an important role of the amygdala. This suggests that the neural control of social behaviors involving approach and avoidance may share some overlap in infants and mothers (Levy, Keller, & Poindron, 2004). However, the role of the mother in mother–infant interactions is more complex than that of pups, with a more intricate neural control.

The ascending dopaminergic (DA) projections arising from the ventral tegmental area (VTA) and the retrorubral field (RRF) are believed to control appetitive and positive motivational states (Berridge, 2004). A major target of this pathway is the shell of the nucleus accumbens (NA) (Berridge, 1996; Pecina, Smith, & Berridge, 2006; Stern & Lonstein, 2001). The NA also receives afferents from the cortex, the hippocampus, and the amygdala (Pennartz, Groenewegen, & Lopes da Silva, 1994), making it a good candidate as a center for the integration of emotional, cognitive, and appetitive information. Several studies implicate DA in the NA in maternal behavior. DA release is increased and Fos protein expression is induced in the NA during maternal behavior (Champagne et al., 2004; Lonstein, Simmons, Swann, & Stern, 1998; Stack, Balakrishnan, Numan, & Numan, 2002), and 6-hydroxy dopamine lesions of the NA will disrupt maternal behavior. This latter study found that certain aspects of maternal behavior like licking, grooming, and pup retrieval were predominately affected by these lesions, while nursing behavior was only marginally disrupted (Hansen, Harthon, Wallin, Lofberg, & Svensson, 1991b; Numan & Smith, 1984). Thus, DA from the VTA and RRF to the

NA may be involved in mediating volitional maternal responses. Indeed, lesions of the VTA disrupt these same features of maternal behavior (Hansen, Harthon, Wallin, Lofberg, & Svensson, 1991a) providing additional evidence for the involvement of this pathway. In fact, both the VTA and the RRF receive projections from the MPOA/vBNST, and therefore this circuitry may represent the major mechanism for the induction of the approach portion of the maternal response.

OTHER BEHAVIORAL CHANGES THAT LIKELY FACILITATE MATERNAL BEHAVIOR

In addition to the shift over from avoidance to approach that appears to be governed by activation of the MPOA/vBNST, other changes in the behavior of the parturient female include much that would lend itself to accommodating maternal behavior. For instance, levels of anxiety and related behavior are significantly dampened following birth. In most, however not all (Lonstein, 2005) studies, lactating rats show decreases in anxiety and fear. For example, lactating rats spend more time on the open arms in the elevated plus maze (Pereira, Uriarte, Agrati, Zuluaga, & Ferreira, 2005), more time in the center of the open field (Toufexis, Rochford, & Walker, 1999), increased punished drinking, and reduced shock-induced burying behavior (Ferreira, Hansen, Nielsen, Archer, & Minor, 1989), all indicating a reduction in emotional reactivity to anxiogenic stimuli during this period. In contrast, lactating rats show greatly increased aggression toward conspecifics that begins with parturition (Rosenblatt, 1989). Interestingly, maternal aggression in rats is related to a reduction in reactivity to the odor of the conspecifics which usually functions to inhibit attack (Mayer & Rosenblatt, 1993).

THE INVOLVEMENT OF SPECIFIC NEUROTRANSMITTERS IN MATERNAL APPROACH BEHAVIOR

While several neurotransmitters are involved in maternal behavior, either directly or indirectly, we focus here on oxytocin, NE, CORT, and opioids since considerable research has indicated a specific, direct role for maternal behavior.

Oxytocin

Oxytocin is probably the neuropeptide most associated with maternal behavior. It is released via the pituitary from neurosecretory neurons in the hypothalamic paraventricular nucleus (PVN) and produces uterine contractions at birth and suckling-induced milk ejection (Aono,

1990). In addition, oxytocin from the PVN functions as a neurotransmitter and is present in many neural systems throughout the brain (Caffe, Van Ryen, Van der Woude, & Van Leeuwen, 1989; Fliers, Guldenaar, van de Wal, & Swaab, 1986; Insel, Gingrich, & Young, 2001; McEwen, 2004), including those such as the MPOA/vBNST, VTA, and NA, which, as we have described above, are integral to the establishment of maternal approach behavior (Numan, 2006, 2007). It is well established that oxytocin is involved in mediating many aspects of social behavior that involve olfactory processes, including pair-bonding in monogamous animal species (Bielsky & Young, 2004), and aggression (Bosch, Meddle, Beiderbeck, Douglas, & Neumann, 2005; Ferris et al., 1992).

Studies indicate that the release of oxytocin is involved in the onset, but not the maintenance, of maternal behavior in the rat and the sheep (Insel & Shapiro, 1992; Neumann, 2003; Pedersen, 1997; Pedersen & Boccia, 2002; Pedersen, Caldwell, Peterson, Walker, & Mason, 1992). In rats, ICV injection of oxytocin facilitates (Pedersen, 1997; Pedersen, Ascher, Monroe, & Prange, 1982) and an oxytocin antagonist disrupts (Neumann, Koehler, Landgraf, & Summy-Long, 1994) the onset of maternal behavior in hormone-primed rats. However, oxytocin is not necessary for the maintenance of established maternal behavior (Fahrbach, Morrell, & Pfaff, 1985; van Leengoed, Kerker, & Swanson, 1987). In a similar vein, electrolytic lesions of the PVN inhibit the onset but not the continuance of on-going maternal behavior (Insel & Harbaugh, 1989). An oxytocin antagonist injected into the VTA or the MPAO/vBNST also inhibits the onset of maternal behavior, thus acting at sites important for stimulating approach behavior (Pedersen, Caldwell, Walker, Ayers, & Mason, 1994), and maybe critically important in initiating the motivational aspects of this behavior.

There is evidence that oxytocin is aiding the onset of maternal behavior by modulating olfactory input at the level of the olfactory bulb. Direct infusions of an oxytocin antagonist into the olfactory bulb at the beginning of parturition delay retrieval, the crouching over and grooming of pups, and nest building (Yu, Kaba, Okutani, Takahashi, & Higuchi, 1996b) while intrabulbar infusions of oxytocin induces maternal behavior in virgin female rats (Yu, Kaba, Okutani, Takahashi, Higuchi et al., 1996a). Moreover, electrical stimulation of oxytocin neurons in the PVN inhibits mitral cells and excites granule cells within the olfactory bulb, providing a possible mechanism for oxytocin's actions (Yu, Kaba, Okutani, Takahashi, & Higuchi, 1996).

In addition to its direct effect on olfaction, there is also data showing that oxytocin may be involved in reducing the response to aversive stimuli. For example, oxytocin in the central amygdaloid nucleus depresses fear and anxiety behavior (Bale, Davis, Auger, Dorsa, & McCarthy, 2001).

Norepinephrine

High levels of NE in the newly parturient mother has been shown in myriad species, although a causal relationship with learning about the new infant has only been well documented in the sheep and rodent (Dickinson & Keverne, 1988; Moffat, Suh, & Fleming, 1993; Thomas & Palmiter, 1997). Similar to neonatal rat pup learning, the increase in NE in the mother appears to be primarily from the LC. The olfactory bulb's sole source of NE is the LC and is a critical feature in the odor recognition described here in rodents and sheep in learning about their offspring. In rodents, which have large litters separated by burrows, the mother appears to learn an indiscriminant preference for pups' odor and will accept and nurse similar smelling pups from other litters. Increasing levels of NE facilitate this maternal learning (Moffat et al., 1993). The ewe, however, learns a specific attraction to one lamb, presumably to be able to locate the lamb within the herd (Levy, 2002), alien lambs that approach the mother are attacked. The role of NE in learning the lamb odor is extensive and has eloquently shown that the increasing NE levels within the olfactory bulb are important in mediating rapid, robust odor learning. It should be noted that there seems to be an ubiquitous role for NE in control of mating related social contact, including mating and pregnancy block, where the exposure to a novel male's odor blocks pregnancy (Brennan et al., 1990). In summary, the importance of NE in the social learning which occurs at birth maybe a conserved neural mechanism that is critical for rapid social learning throughout the life span.

Opiates

On the basis of manipulation of the opioid system through injections of morphine or the opioid receptor antagonist naltrexone, opioids have been shown to enhance pup acceptance (approach or reduction of aversion) by the mother (Mann, Kinsley, & Bridges, 1991; Rubin & Bridges, 1984). This work suggests this opioid effect is due, at least in part, to increasing the rewarding value of pups or the mother's motivational level to approach and seek pups, both of which are enhanced by morphine. Additionally, opioids have a more specific role in enhancing the mother's learning about her pups but also disrupt maternal behavior by shortening nursing bouts and disorganizing behavioral sequences of pup interactions.

Corticosterone

CORT, the most prevalent glucocorticoid in the rat, has a robust effect on the maternal response to pups and their odor (Catalani et al., 2002; Graham, Rees, Steiner, & Fleming, 2006; Rees, Panesar, Steiner, & Fleming, 2006). Due to the ubiquitous role of CORT in physiological function, a variety of techniques have been used to study the effects of CORT on maternal behavior that include removal of the source of CORT, the adrenal gland, CORT synthesis, as well as through injection of receptor agonists and antagonists. CORT does not appear important in the mother's learning about pups or initiating the onset of maternal behavior, although lowering CORT does attenuate some maternal behavior (Rees, Panesar, Steiner, & Fleming, 2004).

However, CORT does have an important function in modulating the mother's approach and avoidance behavior. The mother rat, as well as the human mother, exhibits an SHRP, that is the dam shows a blunted CORT response to stress (Deschamps, Woodside, & Walker, 2003). In general, this SHRP appears responsible for decreased fear, which probably contributes to increased approach to pups but also increased approach toward intruders and aggression. Indeed, the rat mother will attack a very large male, which is a predator to rat pups that enter the nest. Thus, increased approach behavior by the dam is not simply related to an increase in hedonic value of odors and represents a reduction in fearfulness. However, the mother's hyporesponsive period appears to be context dependent, with a rapid CORT response elicited in lactating females under specific conditions. Indeed, when pups are threatened, the mother does respond with an elevation in CORT. Specifically, lactating females were presented with a predator (novel male rat or other predator odor), which elicited a blunted response when pups were not present, although a robust response if pups were present (Deschamps, Woodside, & Walker, 2003).

It should also be noted that opioids, NE, and CORT all have a role in many social behaviors beyond mother–infant interactions, including pair bonding (Carter, 1998; Insel et al., 2001; Panksepp, Nelson, & Siviy, 1994). Additionally, myriad neurotransmitter systems and hormones, some of which interact with opioids and CORT, while others modify behavior independently, modify pup and maternal behavior. Maternal behavior between species differs greatly and suggests caution extrapolating specific neurobiological mechanisms of maternal behavior from one species to another. For example, rat and sheep maternal behavior is to some degree "hard-wired" at least in comparison to the primate, where experience is of paramount importance. Also, in sharp contrast to the aversion exhibited to infants by nulliporous rats and sheep, both human and nonhuman primates are strongly attracted to infants suggesting the approach avoidance issues discussed is likely not relevant. Finally, while rats form a bond to pups in general, sheep and primates form attachments to a specific individual.

SUMMARY

Mother–infant interactions represent a dynamic, intricate, and coordinated dance between the infant and mother. For rodents and sheep, both the infant and mother respond to one another's olfactory cues, which initially causes approach behaviors that initiate this coordination. Both NE and oxytocin appear to be important in the formation of this odor guided approach response. Once mother–infant contact is made, somatosensory stimuli appear to further guide the mother–infant dance, although odor cues continue to be important. The neural systems that guide the behavior of the mother and infant have some substrates in common, with suppression of amygdala function and blunting of the stress CORT response appearing to enhance the probability of approach behaviors. Opioids may facilitate this interaction by enhancing learning as well as enhancing the pleasure of this interaction.

We would like to end this brief summary of mother–infant social approach and avoidance with a note of caution. The neural control of social approach and avoidance in the infant and mother is both complex and controlled by the complex coordination of multiple brain areas, neurotransmitters, and hormones in a dynamic fashion. While we have stressed the overlap in the control of maternal and infant approach and avoidance, areas of divergence are well documented. The relative importance of experience versus "hard-wired" contributions of mother–infant attachment varies between species and primates do not show the switch from aversion to approach seen in rodents. Thus, we suggest emphasis should be placed on general principle when extrapolating information from one species or another concerning the neurobiological basis of these important social behaviors.

ACKNOWLEDGMENT

This work was supported by grants NIH-NICHD-HD33402, NSF-IOB-0544406, and OCAST Oklahoma Science and Technology HR05–114 to RMS; grants NIDCD-DC00866 and the National Alliance for Autism Research to DAW and The Center for Behavioral Neurosciences (NSF agreement IBN-9876754) RR00165 to the Yerkes National Primate center and NIH MH76869 to DJT.

REFERENCES

Aono, T. (1990). Hormonal control of lactation. *Nippon Sanka Fujinka Gakkai Zasshi*, *42*, 867–872.

Araneda, R. C., & Firestein, S. (2006). Adrenergic enhancement of inhibitory transmission in the accessory olfactory bulb. *Journal of Neuroscience*, *26*, 3292–3298.

Bakowska, J. C., & Morrell, J. I. (1997). Atlas of the neurons that express mRNA for the long form of the prolactin receptor in the forebrain of the female rat. *Journal of Comparative Neurology*, *386*, 161–177.

Bale, T. L., Davis, A. M., Auger, A. P., Dorsa, D. M., & McCarthy, M. M. (2001). CNS region-specific oxytocin receptor expression: Importance in regulation of anxiety and sex behavior. *Journal of Neuroscience*, *21*, 2546–2552.

Berdel, B., & Morys, J. (2000). Expression of calbindin-D28 k and parvalbumin during development of rat's basolateral amygdaloid complex. *International Journal of Developmental Neuroscience*, *18*, 501–513.

Berdel, B., Morys, J., Maciejewska, B., & Dziewiatkowski, J. (1997). Volume and topographical changes of the basolateral complex during the development of the rat's amygdaloid body. *Folia Morphologiica (Warszawa)*, *56*, 1–11.

Bernabeu, R., Thiriet, N., Zwiller, J., & Di Scala, G. (2006). Lesion of the lateral entorhinal cortex amplifies odor-induced expression of c-fos, junB, and zif 268 mRNA in rat brain. *Synapse*, *59*, 135–143.

Berridge, K. C. (1996). Food reward: Brain substrates of wanting and liking. *Neuroscience and Biobehavioral Review*, *20*, 1–25.

Berridge, K. C. (2004). Motivation concepts in behavioral neuroscience. *Physiology & Behavior*, *81*, 179–209.

Bielsky, I. F., & Young, L. J. (2004). Oxytocin, vasopressin, and social recognition in mammals. *Peptides*, *25*, 1565–1574.

Blass, E. M. (1997). Interactions between contact and chemosensory mechanisms in pain modulation in 10-day-old rats. *Behavioral Neuroscience*, *111*, 147–154.

Blass, E. M., Shide, D. J., Zaw-Mon, C., & Sorrentino, J. (1995). Mother as shield: Differential effects of contact and nursing on pain responsivity in infant rats—evidence for nonopioid mediation. *Behavioral Neuroscience*, *109*, 342–353.

Bosch, O. J., Meddle, S. L., Beiderbeck, D. I., Douglas, A. J., & Neumann, I. D. (2005). Brain oxytocin correlates with maternal aggression: Link to anxiety. *Journal of Neuroscience*, *25*, 6807–6815.

Bouret, S., & Sara, S. J. (2002). Locus coeruleus activation modulates firing rate and temporal organization of odour-induced single-cell responses in rat piriform cortex. *Journal of Neuroscience*, *16*, 2371–2382.

Bouwmeester, H., Smits, K., & Van Ree, J. M. (2002). Neonatal development of projections to the basolateral amygdala from prefrontal and thalamic structures in rat. *Journal of Comparative Neurology*, *450*, 241–255.

Bouwmeester, H., Wolterink, G., & van Ree, J. M. (2002). Neonatal development of projections from the basolateral amygdala to prefrontal, striatal, and thalamic structures in the rat. *Journal of Comparative Neurology*, *442*, 239–249.

Breer, H., Fleischer, J., & Strotmann, J. (2006). The sense of smell: Multiple olfactory subsystems. *Cellular and Molecular Life Sciences*, *63*, 1465–1475.

Brennan, P., Kaba, H., & Keverne, E. B. (1990). Olfactory recognition: A simple memory system. *Science*, *250*, 1223–1226.

Brennan, P. A., & Kendrick, K. M. (2006). Mammalian social odours: Attraction and individual recognition. *Philosophical Transactions of the Royal Society London B Biological Sciences*, *361*, 2061–2078.

Bridges, R. S., Mann, P. E., & Coppeta, J. S. (1999). Hypothalamic involvement in the regulation of maternal behaviour in the rat: Inhibitory roles for the ventromedial hypothalamus and the dorsal/anterior hypothalamic areas. *Journal of Neuroendocrinology*, *11*, 259–266.

Bridges, R. S., Robertson, M. C., Shiu, R. P., Sturgis, J. D., Henriquez, B. M., & Mann, P. E. (1997). Central lactogenic regulation of maternal behavior in rats: Steroid dependence, hormone specificity, and behavioral potencies of rat prolactin and rat placental lactogen I. *Endocrinology*, *138*, 756–763.

Bridges, R. S., & Ronsheim, P. M. (1990). Prolactin (PRL) regulation of maternal behavior in rats: Bromocriptine treatment delays and PRL promotes the rapid onset of behavior. *Endocrinology*, *126*, 837–848.

Brosh, I., Rosenblum, K., & Barkai, E. (2006). Learning-induced reversal of the effect of noradrenalin on the postburst AHP. *Journal of Neurophysiology*, *96*, 1728–1733.

Brown, K. L., Pagani, J. H., & Stanton, M. E. (2005). Spatial conditional discrimination learning in developing rats. *Developmental Psychobiology*, *46*, 97–110.

Buck, L. B. (2004). Olfactory receptors and odor coding in mammals. *Nutrition Review*, *62*, S184–188; discussion S224–141.

Buonviso, N., Amat, C., & Litaudon, P. (2006). Respiratory modulation of olfactory neurons in the rodent brain. *Chemical Senses*, *31*, 145–154.

Caffe, A. R., Van Ryen, P. C., Van der Woude, T. P., & Van Leeuwen, F. W. (1989). Vasopressin and oxytocin systems in the brain and upper spinal cord of Macaca fascicularis. *Journal of Comparative Neurology*, *287*, 302–325.

Calu, D. J., Roesch, M. R., Stalnaker, T. A., & Schoenbaum, G. (2006). Associative encoding in posterior piriform cortex during odor discrimination and reversal learning. *Cerebral Cortex*, *17*, 643–652.

Camp, L. L., & Rudy, J. W. (1988). Changes in the categorization of appetitive and aversive events during postnatal development of the rat. *Developmental Psychobiology*, *21*, 25–42.

Canteras, N. S., Simerly, R. B., & Swanson, L. W. (1995). Organization of projections from the medial nucleus of the amygdala: A PHAL study in the rat. *Journal of Comparative Neurology*, *360*, 213–245.

Carter, C. S. (1998). Neuroendocrine perspectives on social attachment and love. *Psychoneuroendocrinology*, *23*, 779–818.

Catalani, A., Casolini, P., Cigliana, G., Scaccianoce, S., Consoli, C., Cinque, C., et al. (2002). Maternal corticosterone influences behavior, stress response and corticosteroid receptors in the female rat. *Pharmacology, Biochemistry and Behavior, 73*, 105–114.

Champagne, F. A., Chretien, P., Stevenson, C. W., Zhang, T. Y., Gratton, A., & Meaney, M. J. (2004). Variations in nucleus accumbens dopamine associated with individual differences in maternal behavior in the rat. *Journal of Neuroscience, 24*, 4113–4123.

Chen, W. R., & Shepherd, G. M. (2005). The olfactory glomerulus: A cortical module with specific functions. *Journal of Neurocytology, 34*, 353–360.

Cheslock, S. J., Varlinskaya, E. I., Petrov, E. S., & Spear, N. E. (2000). Rapid and robust olfactory conditioning with milk before suckling experience: Promotion of nipple attachment in the newborn rat. *Behavioral Neuroscience, 114*, 484–495.

Collier, A. C., & Bolles, R. C. (1980). The ontogenesis of defensive reactions to shock in preweaning rats. *Developmental Psychobiology, 13*, 141–150.

Coopersmith, R., Lee, S., & Leon, M. (1986). Olfactory bulb responses after odor aversion learning by young rats. *Brain Research, 389*, 271–277.

Crain, B., Cotman, C., Taylor, D., & Lynch, G. (1973). A quantitative electron microscopic study of synaptogenesis in the dentate gyrus of the rat. *Brain Research, 63*, 195–204.

Cunningham, M. G., Bhattacharyya, S., & Benes, F. M. (2002). Amygdalo-cortical sprouting continues into early adulthood: Implications for the development of normal and abnormal function during adolescence. *Journal of Comparative Neurology, 453*, 116–130.

Dardou, D., Datiche, F., & Cattarelli, M. (2006). Fos and Egr1 expression in the rat brain in response to olfactory cue after taste-potentiated odor aversion retrieval. *Learning & Memory, 13*, 150–160.

Davis, M., Walker, D. L., Myers, K. M. (2003). Role of the amygdala in fear extinction measured with potentiated startle. *Annals of the New York Academy of Science, 985*, 218–232.

Deschamps, S., Woodside, B., & Walker, C. D. (2003). Pups presence eliminates the stress hyporesponsiveness of early lactating females to a psychological stress representing a threat to the pups. *Journal of Neuroendocrinology, 15*, 486–497.

Dickinson, C., & Keverne, E. B. (1988). Importance of noradrenergic mechanisms in the olfactory bulbs for the maternal behaviour of mice. *Physiology & Behavior, 43*, 313–316.

Doty, R. L. (2001). Olfaction. *Annual Review of Psychology, 52*, 423–452.

Duchamp-Viret, P., & Duchamp, A. (1993). GABAergic control of odour-induced activity in the frog olfactory bulb: Possible GABAergic modulation of granule cell inhibitory action. *Neuroscience, 56*, 905–914.

Dziewiatkowski, J., Berdel, B., Kowianski, P., Kubasik-Juraniec, J., Bobek-Billewicz, B., & Morys, J. (1998). The amygdaloid body of the rabbit—a morphometric study using image analyser. *Folia Morphologiica (Warszawa), 57*, 93–103.

Emerich, D. F., Scalzo, F. M., Enters, E. K., Spear, N. E., & Spear, L. P. (1985). Effects of 6-hydroxydopamine-induced catecholamine depletion on shock-precipitated wall climbing of infant rat pups. *Developmental Psychobiology, 18*, 215–227.

Fahrbach, S. E., Morrell, J. I., & Pfaff, D. W. (1985). Possible role for endogenous oxytocin in estrogen-facilitated maternal behavior in rats. *Neuroendocrinology, 40*, 526–532.

Fanselow, M., Poulos, A. M. (2005). The neuroscience of mammalian associative learning. *Annual Review of Psychology, 6*, 207–234.

Ferreira, A., Hansen, S., Nielsen, M., Archer, T., & Minor, B. G. (1989). Behavior of mother rats in conflict tests sensitive to antianxiety agents. *Behavioral Neuroscience, 103*, 193–201.

Ferris, C. F., Foote, K. B., Meltser, H. M., Plenby, M. G., Smith, K. L., & Insel, T. R. (1992). Oxytocin in the amygdala facilitates maternal aggression. *Annals of the New York Academy of Science, 652*, 456–457.

Ferry, B., & McGaugh, J. L. (2000). Role of amygdala norepinephrine in mediating stress hormone regulation of memory storage. *ACTA Pharmacologica Sinica (Beijing), 21*, 481–493.

Fleming, A., Vaccarino, F., Tambosso, L., & Chee, P. (1979). Vomeronasal and olfactory system modulation of maternal behavior in the rat. *Science, 203*, 372–374.

Fleming, A. S., Kraemer, G. W., Gonzalez, A., Lovic, V., Rees, S., & Melo, A. (2002). Mothering begets mothering: The transmission of behavior and its neurobiology across generations. *Pharmacology, Biochemistry and Behavior, 73*, 61–75.

Fleming, A. S., & Luebke, C. (1981). Timidity prevents the virgin female rat from being a good mother: Emotionality differences between nulliparous and parturient females. *Physiology & Behavior, 27*, 863–868.

Fleming, A. S., & Rosenblatt, J. S. (1974). Olfactory regulation of maternal behavior in rats. I. Effects of olfactory bulb removal in experienced and inexperienced lactating and cycling females. *Journal of Comparative Physiological Psychology, 86*, 221–232.

Fleming, A. S., Vaccarino, F., & Luebke, C. (1980). Amygdaloid inhibition of maternal behavior in the nulliparous female rat. *Physiology & Behavior, 25*, 731–743.

Fletcher, M. L., Smith, A. M., Best, A. R., & Wilson, D. A. (2005). High frequency oscillations are not necessary for simple olfactory discriminations in young rats. *Journal of Neuroscience, 25*, 792–798.

Fliers, E., Guldenaar, S. E., van de Wal, N., & Swaab, D. F. (1986). Extrahypothalamic vasopressin and oxytocin in the human brain; presence of vasopressin cells in the bed nucleus of the stria terminalis. *Brain Research, 375*, 363–367.

Galef, B. G., Jr., & Kaner, H. C. (1980). Establishment and maintenance of preference for natural and artificial olfactory stimuli in juvenile rats. *Journal of Comparative Physiological Psychology, 94*, 588–595.

Gomez, C., Brinon, J. G., Barbado, M. V., Weruaga, E., Valero, J., & Alonso, J. R. (2005). Heterogeneous targeting of centrifugal inputs to the glomerular layer of the main olfactory bulb. *Journal of Chemical Neuroanatomy, 29*, 238–254.

Gonzalez-Mariscal, G. (2001). Neuroendocrinology of maternal behavior in the rabbit. *Hormones and Behavior, 40,* 125–132.

Goodwin, G. A., & Barr, G. A. (1997). Evidence for opioid and nonopioid processes mediating adaptive responses of infant rats that are repeatedly isolated. *Developmental Psychobiology, 31,* 217–227.

Gottfried, J. A. (2006). Smell: Central nervous processing. *Advances in Otorhinolaryngology, 63,* 44–69.

Gilles, E. E., Schultz, L., Baram, T. Z. (1996). Abnormal corticosterone regulation in an immature rat model of continuous chronic stress. *Pediatric Neurology, 15,* 114–119.

Gottfried, J. A., Winston, J. S., & Dolan, R. J. (2006). Dissociable codes of odor quality and odorant structure in human piriform cortex. *Neuron, 49,* 467–479.

Graham, M. D., Rees, S. L., Steiner, M., & Fleming, A. S. (2006). The effects of adrenalectomy and corticosterone replacement on maternal memory in postpartum rats. *Hormones and Behavior, 49,* 353–361.

Greer, C. A., Stewart, W. B., Kauer, J. S., & Shepherd, G. M. (1981). Topographical and laminar localization of 2-deoxyglucose uptake in rat olfactory bulb induced by electrical stimulation of olfactory nerves. *Brain Research, 217,* 279–293.

Hansen, S., Harthon, C., Wallin, E., Lofberg, L., & Svensson, K. (1991a). Mesotelencephalic dopamine system and reproductive behavior in the female rat: Effects of ventral tegmental 6-hydroxydopamine lesions on maternal and sexual responsiveness. *Behavioral Neuroscience, 105,* 588–598.

Hansen, S., Harthon, C., Wallin, E., Lofberg, L., & Svensson, K. (1991b). The effects of 6-OHDA-induced dopamine depletions in the ventral or dorsal striatum on maternal and sexual behavior in the female rat. *Pharmacology, Biochemistry and Behavior, 39,* 71–77.

Haroutunian, V. & Campbell, B. A. (1979). Emergence of interoceptive and exteroceptive control of behavior in rats. *Science, 205,* 927–929.

Harley, C. W., Darby-King, A., McCann, J., & McLean, J. H. (2006). Beta1-adrenoceptor or alpha1-adrenoceptor activation initiates early odor preference learning in rat pups: Support for the mitral cell/cAMP model of odor preference learning. *Learning & Memory, 13,* 8–13.

Hayar, A., Karnup, S., Shipley, M. T., & Ennis, M. (2004). Olfactory bulb glomeruli: External tufted cells intrinsically burst at theta frequency and are entrained by patterned olfactory input. *Journal of Neuroscience, 24,* 1190–1199.

Hennessy, M. B., Hornschuh, G., Kaiser, S., & Sachser, N. (2006). Cortisol responses and social buffering: A study throughout the life span. *Hormones and Behavior, 49,* 383–390.

Hunt, P. S. (1999). A further investigation of the developmental emergence of fear-potentiated startle in rats. *Developmental Psychobiology, 34,* 281–291.

Hunt, P. S., Richardson, R., & Campbell, B. A. (1994). Delayed development of fear-potentiated startle in rats. *Behavioral Neuroscience, 108,* 69–80.

Insel, T. R. (2003). Is social attachment an addictive disorder? *Physiology & Behavior, 79,* 351–357.

Insel, T. R., Gingrich, B. S., & Young, L. J. (2001). Oxytocin: Who needs it? *Progress in Brain Research, 133,* 59–66.

Insel, T. R., & Harbaugh, C. R. (1989). Lesions of the hypothalamic paraventricular nucleus disrupt the initiation of maternal behavior. *Physiology & Behavior, 45,* 1033–1041.

Insel, T. R., & Shapiro, L. E. (1992). Oxytocin receptors and maternal behavior. *Annals of the New York Academy of Science, 652,* 122–141.

Ivkovich, D., & Stanton, M. E. (2001). Effects of early hippocampal lesions on trace, delay, and long-delay eyeblink conditioning in developing rats. *Neurobiology of Learning and Memory, 76,* 426–446.

Kadohisa, M., & Wilson, D. A. (2006a). Olfactory cortical adaptation facilitates detection of odors against background. *Journal of Neurophysiology, 95,* 1888–1896.

Kadohisa, M., & Wilson, D. A. (2006b). Separate encoding of identity and similarity of complex familiar odors in piriform cortex. *Proceeding of the National Academy of Science USA, 103,* 15206–15211.

Kehoe, P., & Blass, E. M. (1986). Central nervous system mediation of positive and negative reinforcement in neonatal albino rats. *Brain Research, 392,* 69–75.

Kemble, E. D., Blanchard, D. C. & Blanchard, R. J. (1990). Effects of regional amygdaloid lesions on flight and defensive behaviors of wild black rats (*Rattus rattus*). *Physiology & Behavior, 41,* 1–5.

Kim, J. H., & Richardson, R. (2007). A developmental dissociation of context and GABA effects on extinguished fear in rats. *Behavioral Neuroscience, 121,* 131–139.

Knafo, S., Barkai, E., Herrero, A. I., Libersat, F., Sandi, C., & Venero, C. (2005). Olfactory learning-related NCAM expression is state, time, and location specific and is correlated with individual learning capabilities. *Hippocampus, 15,* 316–325.

Kolb, B., & Cioe, J. (1996). Sex-related differences in cortical function after medial frontal lesions in rats. *Behavioral Neuroscience, 110,* 1271–1281.

Kucharski, D., & Spear, N. E. (1984). Conditioning of aversion to an odor paired with peripheral shock in the developing rat. *Developmental Psychobiology, 17,* 465–479.

Lang, P. J., Davis, M., & Ohman, A. (2000). Fear and anxiety: Animal models and human cognitive psychophysiology. *Journal of Affective Disorders, 61,* 137–159.

LeDoux, J. (2003). The emotional brain, fear, and the amygdala. *Cellular and Molecular Neurobiology, 23,* 727–38.

Lee, A., Clancy, S., & Fleming, A. S. (2000). Mother rats bar-press for pups: Effects of lesions of the mpoa and limbic sites on maternal behavior and operant responding for pup-reinforcement. *Behavioral Brain Research, 108,* 215–231.

Leon, M. (1992). Neuroethology of olfactory preference development. *Journal of Neurobiology, 23,* 1557–1573.

Leon, M., & Johnson, B. A. (2003). Olfactory coding in the mammalian olfactory bulb. *Brain Research Reviews, 42,* 23–32.

Levine, S. (2001). Primary social relationships influence the development of the hypothalamic–pituitary–adrenal axis in the rat. *Physiology & Behavior, 73,* 255–260.

Levine, S. (2005). Developmental determinants of sensitivity and resistance to stress. *Psychoneuroendocrinology, 30*, 939–946.

Levy, F. (2002). Neurobiological mechanisms involved in recognition of olfactory signature of the young in sheep. *Journal of Social and Biological Structures, 196*, 77–83.

Levy, F., Keller, M., & Poindron, P. (2004). Olfactory regulation of maternal behavior in mammals. *Hormones and Behavior, 46*, 284–302.

Li, A. B., Maglinao, C. D., Takahahsi, L. K. (2004). Medial amygdala modulation of predator odor-induced unconditioned fear in the rat. *Behavioral Neuroscience, 118*, 324–332.

Liberles, S. D., & Buck, L. B. (2006). A second class of chemosensory receptors in the olfactory epithelium. *Nature, 442*, 645–650.

Linster, C., & Hasselmo, M. E. (2001). Neuromodulation and the functional dynamics of piriform cortex. *Chemical Senses, 26*, 585–594.

Lonstein, J. S. (2005). Resolving apparent contradictions concerning the relationships among fear or anxiety and aggression during lactation: theoretical comment on D'Anna, Stevenson, and Gammie (2005). *Behavioral Neuroscience, 119*, 1165–1168.

Lonstein, J. S., & De Vries, G. J. (2000). Maternal behaviour in lactating rats stimulates c-fos in glutamate decarboxylase-synthesizing neurons of the medial preoptic area, ventral bed nucleus of the stria terminalis, and ventrocaudal periaqueductal gray. *Neuroscience, 100*, 557–568.

Lonstein, J. S., Simmons, D. A., Swann, J. M., & Stern, J. M. (1998). Forebrain expression of c-fos due to active maternal behaviour in lactating rats. *Neuroscience, 82*, 267–281.

Mann, P. E., Kinsley, C. H., & Bridges, R. S. (1991). Opioid receptor subtype involvement in maternal behavior in lactating rats. *Neuroendocrinology, 53*, 487–492.

Martin, C., Gervais, R., Messaoudi, B., & Ravel, N. (2006). Learning-induced oscillatory activities correlated to odour recognition: A network activity. *Journal of Neuroscience, 23*, 1801–1810.

Mattson, B. J., & Morrell, J. I. (2005). Preference for cocaine- versus pup-associated cues differentially activates neurons expressing either Fos or cocaine- and amphetamine-regulated transcript in lactating, maternal rodents. *Neuroscience, 135*, 315–328.

Mayer, A. D., & Rosenblatt, J. S. (1993). Contributions of olfaction to maternal aggression in laboratory rats (*Rattus norvegicus*): Effects of peripheral deafferentation of the primary olfactory system. *Journal of Comparative Psychology, 107*, 12–24.

McEwen, B. B. (2004). General introduction to vasopressin and oxytocin: Structure/metabolism, evolutionary aspects, neural pathway/receptor distribution, and functional aspects relevant to memory processing. *Advances in Pharmacology, 50*, 1–50, 655–708.

McGaugh, J. L. (2006). Make mild moments memorable: Add a little arousal. *Trends in Cognitive Science, 10*, 345–347.

McGaugh, J. L., & Cahill, L. (1997). Interaction of neuromodulatory systems in modulating memory storage. *Behav Brain Research, 83*(1–2), 31–38.

McLean, J. H., & Shipley, M. T. (1991). Postnatal development of the noradrenergic projection from locus coeruleus to the olfactory bulb in the rat. *Journal of Comparative Neurology, 304*, 467–477.

Miller, J. S., Molina, J. C., & Spear, N. E. (1990). Ontogenetic differences in the expression of odor-aversion learning in 4- and 8-day-old rats. *Developmental Psychobiology, 23*, 319–330.

Moffat, S. D., Suh, E. J., & Fleming, A. S. (1993). Noradrenergic involvement in the consolidation of maternal experience in postpartum rats. *Physiology & Behavior, 53*, 805–811.

Moles, A., Kieffer, B. L., & D'Amato, F. R. (2004). Deficit in attachment behavior in mice lacking the 5-opioid receptor gene. *Science, 304*, 1983–1986.

Mori, K., Takahashi, Y. K., Igarashi, K. M., & Yamaguchi, M. (2006). Maps of odorant molecular features in the mammalian olfactory bulb. *Physiological Reviews, 86*, 409–433.

Moriceau, S., Roth, T. L., Okotoghaide, T., & Sullivan, R. M. (2004). Corticosterone controls the developmental emergence of fear and amygdala function to predator odors in infant rat pups. *International Journal of Developmental Neuroscience, 22*, 415–422.

Moriceau, S., & Sullivan, R. M. (2004). Unique neural circuitry for neonatal olfactory learning. *Journal of Neuroscience, 24*, 1182–1189.

Moriceau, S., & Sullivan, R. M. (2006). Maternal presence serves as a switch between learning fear and attraction in infancy. *Nature Neuroscience, 9*, 1004–1006.

Moriceau, S., Wilson, D. A., Levine, S., & Sullivan, R. M. (2006). Dual circuitry for odor-shock conditioning during infancy: Corticosterone switches between fear and attraction via amygdala. *Journal of Neuroscience, 26*, 6737–6748.

Morys, J., Berdel, B., Jagalska-Majewska, H., & Luczynska, A. (1999a). The basolateral amygdaloid complex—its development, morphology and functions. *Folia Morphologiica (Warszawa), 58* (Suppl. 2), 29–46.

Morys, J., Berdel, B., Kowianski, P., & Dziewiatkowski, J. (1998). The pattern of synaptophysin changes during the maturation of the amygdaloid body and hippocampal hilus in the rat. *Folia Neuropathologia, 36*, 15–23.

Morys, J., Berdel, B., Kowianski, P., Majak, K., Tarnawski, M., & Wisniewski, H. M. (1999b). Relationship of calcium-binding protein containing neurons and projection neurons in the rat basolateral amygdala. *Neuroscience Letters, 259*, 91–94.

Nagai, Y., Sano, H., & Yokoi, M. (2005). Transgenic expression of Cre recombinase in mitral/tufted cells of the olfactory bulb. *Genesis, 43*, 12–16.

Nair, H. P., Berndt, J. D., Barrett, D., & Gonzalez-Lima, F. (2001). Maturation of extinction behavior in infant rats: Large-scale regional interactions with medial prefrontal cortex, orbitofrontal cortex, and anterior cingulate cortex. *Journal of Neuroscience, 21*, 4400–4407.

Nair, H. P., & Gonzalez-Lima, F. (1999). Extinction of behavior in infant rats: development of functional coupling between septal, hippocampal, and ventral tegmental regions. *Journal of Neuroscience, 19*, 8646–8655.

Nakamura, S., & Sakaguchi, T. (1990). Development and plasticity of the locus coeruleus: A review of recent physiological and pharmacological experimentation. *Progress in Neurobiology, 34*, 505–526.

Nelson, E. E., & Panksepp, J. (1998). Brain substrates of infant-mother attachment: Contributions of opioids, oxytocin, and norepinephrine. *Neuroscience and Biobehavioral Review, 22*, 437–452.

Neumann, I., Koehler, E., Landgraf, R., & Summy-Long, J. (1994). An oxytocin receptor antagonist infused into the supraoptic nucleus attenuates intranuclear and peripheral release of oxytocin during suckling in conscious rats. *Endocrinology, 134*, 141–148.

Neumann, I. D. (2003). Brain mechanisms underlying emotional alterations in the peripartum period in rats. *Depression and Anxiety, 17*, 111–121.

Numan, M. (1974). Medial preoptic area and maternal behavior in the female rat. *Journal of Comparative Physiological Psychology, 87*, 746–759.

Numan, M. (1988). Neural basis of maternal behavior in the rat. *Psychoneuroendocrinology, 13*, 47–62.

Numan, M. (2004). Maternal behaviors: Central integration or independent parallel circuits? Theoretical comment on Popeski and Woodside (2004). *Behavioral Neuroscience, 118*, 1469–1472.

Numan, M. (2006). Hypothalamic neural circuits regulating maternal responsiveness toward infants. *Behavioral and Cognitive Neuroscience Reviews, 5*, 163–190.

Numan, M. (2007). Motivational systems and the neural circuitry of maternal behavior in the rat. *Developmental Psychobiology, 49*, 12–21.

Numan, M., & Callahan, E. C. (1980). The connections of the medial preoptic region and maternal behavior in the rat. *Physiology & Behavior, 25*, 653–665.

Numan, M., & Corodimas, K. P. (1985). The effects of paraventricular hypothalamic lesions on maternal behavior in rats. *Physiology & Behavior, 35*, 417–425.

Numan, M., Corodimas, K. P., Numan, M. J., Factor, E. M., & Piers, W. D. (1988). Axon-sparing lesions of the preoptic region and substantia innominata disrupt maternal behavior in rats. *Behavioral Neuroscience, 102*, 381–396.

Numan, M., & Numan, M. (1996). A lesion and neuroanatomical tract-tracing analysis of the role of the bed nucleus of the stria terminalis in retrieval behavior and other aspects of maternal responsiveness in rats. *Developmental Psychobiology, 29*, 23–51.

Numan, M., & Numan, M. J. (1997). Projection sites of medial preoptic area and ventral bed nucleus of the stria terminalis neurons that express Fos during maternal behavior in female rats. *Journal of Neuroendocrinology, 9*, 369–384.

Numan, M., Numan, M. J., & English, J. B. (1993). Excitotoxic amino acid injections into the medial amygdala facilitate maternal behavior in virgin female rats. *Hormones and Behavior, 27*, 56–81.

Numan, M., Roach, J. K., del Cerro, M. C., Guillamon, A., Segovia, S., Sheehan, T. P., et al. (1999). Expression of intracellular progesterone receptors in rat brain during different reproductive states, and involvement in maternal behavior. *Brain Research, 830*, 358–371.

Numan, M., & Smith, H. G. (1984). Maternal behavior in rats: Evidence for the involvement of preoptic projections to the ventral tegmental area. *Behavioral Neuroscience, 98*, 712–727.

Otto, T., & Giardino, N. D. (2001). Pavlovian conditioning of emotional responses to olfactory and contextual stimuli: A potential model for the development and expression of chemical intolerance. *Annals of the New York Academy of Science, 933*, 291–309.

Panksepp, J., Nelson, E., & Siviy, S. (1994). Brain opioids and mother–infant social motivation. *Acta Paediatrica Supplement, 397*, 40–46.

Pecina, S., Smith, K. S., & Berridge, K. C. (2006). Hedonic hot spots in the brain. *Neuroscientist, 12*, 500–511.

Pedersen, C. A. (1997). Oxytocin control of maternal behavior. Regulation by sex steroids and offspring stimuli. *Annals of the New York Academy of Science, 807*, 126–145.

Pedersen, C. A., Ascher, J. A., Monroe, Y. L., & Prange, A. J., Jr. (1982). Oxytocin induces maternal behavior in virgin female rats. *Science, 216*(4546), 648–650.

Pedersen, C. A., & Boccia, M. L. (2002). Oxytocin links mothering received, mothering bestowed and adult stress responses. *Stress, 5*, 259–267.

Pedersen, C. A., Caldwell, J. D., Peterson, G., Walker, C. H., & Mason, G. A. (1992). Oxytocin activation of maternal behavior in the rat. *Annals of the New York Academy of Science, 652*, 58–69.

Pedersen, C. A., Caldwell, J. D., Walker, C., Ayers, G., & Mason, G. A. (1994). Oxytocin activates the postpartum onset of rat maternal behavior in the ventral tegmental and medial preoptic areas. *Behavioral Neuroscience, 108*, 1163–1171.

Pedersen, P. E., & Blass, E. M. (1982). Prenatal and postnatal determinants of the 1st suckling episode in albino rats. *Developmental Psychobiology, 15*, 349–355.

Pedersen, P. E., Williams, C. L., & Blass, E. M. (1982). Activation and odor conditioning of suckling behavior in 3-day-old albino rats. *Journal of Experimental Psychology: Animal Behavior Process, 8*, 329–341.

Pennartz, C. M., Groenewegen, H. J., & Lopes da Silva, F. H. (1994). The nucleus accumbens as a complex of functionally distinct neuronal ensembles: An integration of behavioural, electrophysiological and anatomical data. *Progress in Neurobiology, 42*, 719–761.

Pereira, M., Uriarte, N., Agrati, D., Zuluaga, M. J., & Ferreira, A. (2005). Motivational aspects of maternal anxiolysis in lactating rats. *Psychopharmacology (Berlin), 180*, 241–248.

Petrov, E. S., Nizhnikov, M. E., Varlinskaya, E. I., & Spear, N. E. (2006). Dynorphin A (1–13) and responsiveness of the newborn rat to a surrogate nipple: Immediate behavioral consequences and reinforcement effects in conditioning. *Behavioral Brain Research, 170*, 1–14.

Poindron, P., Nowak, R., Levy, F., Porter, R. H., & Schaal, B. (1993). Development of exclusive mother-young bonding in sheep and goats. *Oxford Review of Reproductive Biology*, *15*, 311–364.

Polan, H. J., & Hofer, M. A. (1999). Maternally directed orienting behaviors of newborn rats. *Developmental Psychobiology*, *34*, 269–279.

Raineki, C., Shionoya, K., Moriceau, S., Sander, K., & Sullivan, R. M. (2007). Behavioral and neural comparison of the ontogeny of olfactory fear and odor-LiCl learning in rat pups. *Society for Neuroscience Abstracts*, San Diego.

Randall, C. K., Kraemer, P. J., Dose, J. M., Carbary, T. J., & Bardo, M. T. (1992). The biphasic effect of morphine on odor conditioning in neonatal rats. *Developmental Psychobiology*, *25*, 355–364.

Rangel, S., & Leon, M. (1995). Early odor preference training increases olfactory bulb norepinephrine. *Develomental Brain Research*, *85*, 187–191.

Rees, S. L., Panesar, S., Steiner, M., & Fleming, A. S. (2004). The effects of adrenalectomy and corticosterone replacement on maternal behavior in the postpartum rat. *Hormones and Behavior*, *46*, 411–419.

Rees, S. L., Panesar, S., Steiner, M., & Fleming, A. S. (2006). The effects of adrenalectomy and corticosterone replacement on induction of maternal behavior in the virgin female rat. *Hormones and Behavior*, *49*, 337–345.

Risold, P. Y., Canteras, N. S., & Swanson, L. W. (1994). Organization of projections from the anterior hypothalamic nucleus: A *Phaseolus vulgaris*-leucoagglutinin study in the rat. *Journal of Comparative Neurology*, *348*, 1–40.

Robinson, S. R., & Smotherman, W. P. (1994). Behavioral effects of milk in the rat fetus. *Behavioral Neuroscience*, *108*, 1139–1149.

Rosenblatt, J. S. (1967). Nonhormonal basis of maternal behavior in the rat. *Science*, *156*(781), 1512–1514.

Rosenblatt, J. S. (1989). The physiological and evolutionary background of maternal responsiveness. *New Directions in Child Development*, *43*, 15–30.

Rosenblatt, J. S., Turkewitz, G., & Schneirla, T. C. (1969). Development of home orientation in newly born kittens. *Transactions of the New York Academy of Science*, *31*, 231–250.

Ross, R. S., & Eichenbaum, H. (2006). Dynamics of hippocampal and cortical activation during consolidation of a nonspatial memory. *Journal of Neuroscience*, *26*(18), 4852–4859.

Roth, T. L., Moriceau, S., & Sullivan, R. M. (2006). Opioid modulation of Fos protein expression and olfactory circuitry plays a pivotal role in what neonates remember. *Learning & Memory*, *13*, 590–598.

Roth, T. L., & Sullivan, R. M. (2003). Consolidation and expression of a shock-induced odor preference in rat pups is facilitated by opioids. *Physiology & Behavior*, *78*, 135–142.

Roth, T. L., & Sullivan, R. M. (2005). Memory of early maltreatment: Neonatal behavioral and neural correlates of maternal maltreatment within the context of classical conditioning. *Biological Psychiatry*, *57*, 823–831.

Roth, T. L., & Sullivan, R. M. (2006). Examining the role of endogenous opioids in learned odor–stroke associations in infant rats. *Developmental Psychobiology*, *48*, 71–78.

Rubin, B. S., & Bridges, R. S. (1984). Disruption of ongoing maternal responsiveness in rats by central administration of morphine sulfate. *Brain Research*, *307*, 91–97.

Rudy, J. W. (1994). Ontogeny of context-specific latent inhibition of conditioned fear: Implications for configural associations theory and hippocampal formation development. *Developmental Psychobiology*, *27*, 367–379.

Rudy, J. W., & Cheatle, M. D. (1983). Odor-aversion learning by rats following LiCl exposure: Ontogenetic influences. *Developmental Psychobiology*, *16*, 13–22.

Rudy, J. W., & Morledge, P. (1994). Ontogeny of contextual fear conditioning in rats: Implications for consolidation, infantile amnesia, and hippocampal system function. *Behavioral Neuroscience*, *108*, 227–234.

Schneirla, T. C. (1966). Behavioral development and comparative psychology. *Quarterly Review of Biology*, *41*, 283–302.

Schoenbaum, G., Chiba, A. A., & Gallagher, M. (1999). Neural encoding in orbitofrontal cortex and basolateral amygdala during olfactory discrimination learning. *Journal of Neuroscience*, *19*, 1876–1884.

Schwob, J. E., Haberly, L. B., & Price, J. L. (1984). The development of physiological responses of the piriform cortex in rats to stimulation of the lateral olfactory tract. *Journal of Comparative Neurology*, *223*, 223–237.

Schwob, J. E., & Price, J. L. (1984). The development of axonal connections in the central olfactory system of rats. *Journal of Comparative Neurology*, *223*, 177–202.

Sevelinges, Y., Gervais, R., Messaoudi, B., Granjon, L., & Mouly, A. M. (2004). Olfactory fear conditioning induces field potential potentiation in rat olfactory cortex and amygdala. *Learning & Memory*, *11*, 761–769.

Shayit, M., Nowak, R., Keller, M., & Weller, A. (2003). Establishment of a preference by the newborn lamb for its mother: The role of opioids. *Behavioral Neuroscience*, *117*, 446–454.

Sheehan, T., Paul, M., Amaral, E., Numan, M. J., & Numan, M. (2001). Evidence that the medial amygdala projects to the anterior/ventromedial hypothalamic nuclei to inhibit maternal behavior in rats. *Neuroscience*, *106*, 341–356.

Sheehan, T. P., Cirrito, J., Numan, M. J., & Numan, M. (2000). Using c-Fos immunocytochemistry to identify forebrain regions that may inhibit maternal behavior in rats. *Behavioral Neuroscience*, *114*, 337–352.

Shionoya, K., Moriceau, S., Lunday, L., Miner, C., Roth, T. L., & Sullivan, R. M. (2006). Development switch in neural circuitry underlying odor–malaise learning. *Learning & Memory*, *13*, 801–808.

Shughrue, P. J., Lane, M. V., & Merchenthaler, I. (1997). Comparative distribution of estrogen receptor-alpha and -beta mRNA in the rat central nervous system. *Journal of Comparative Neurology*, *388*, 507–525.

Siegel, H. I., Doerr, H. K., & Rosenblatt, J. S. (1978). Further studies on estrogen-induced maternal behavior in hysterectomized-ovariectomized virgin rats. *Physiology & Behavior*, *21*, 99–103.

Siegel, H. I., & Rosenblatt, J. S. (1975). Estrogen-induced maternal behavior in hysterectomized-overiectomized virgin rats. *Physiology & Behavior*, *14*, 465–471.

Smotherman, W. P. (1982). Odor aversion learning by the rat fetus. *Physiology & Behavior, 29*, 769–771.

Smotherman, W. P., Arnold, H. M., & Robinson, S. R. (1993). Responses to ecologically relevant stimuli in the rat fetus: Interactive effects of milk and an artificial nipple. *Developmental Psychobiology, 26*, 359–374.

Spors, H., Wachowiak, M., Cohen, L. B., & Friedrich, R. W. (2006). Temporal dynamics and latency patterns of receptor neuron input to the olfactory bulb. *Journal of Neuroscience, 26*, 1247–1259.

Stack, E. C., Balakrishnan, R., Numan, M. J., & Numan, M. (2002). A functional neuroanatomical investigation of the role of the medial preoptic area in neural circuits regulating maternal behavior. *Behav Brain Research, 131*, 17–36.

Stack, E. C., & Numan, M. (2000). The temporal course of expression of c-Fos and Fos B within the medial preoptic area and other brain regions of postpartum female rats during prolonged mother—young interactions. *Behavioral Neuroscience, 114*, 609–622.

Stanton, M. E. (2000). Multiple memory systems, development and conditioning. *Behavioral and Brain Research, 110*, 25–37.

Stanton, M. E., Wallstrom, J., & Levine, S. (1987). Maternal contact inhibits pituitary–adrenal stress responses in preweanling rats. *Developmental Psychobiology, 20*, 131–145.

Staubli, U., Ivy, G., & Lynch, G. (1984). Hippocampal denervation causes rapid forgetting of olfactory information in rats. *Proceeding of the National Academy of Science USA, 81*, 5885–5887.

Stern, J. M., & Lonstein, J. S. (2001). Neural mediation of nursing and related maternal behaviors. *Progress in Brain Research, 133*, 263–278.

Suchecki, D., Rosenfeld, P., & Levine, S. (1993). Maternal regulation of the hypothalamic–pituitary–adrenal axis in the infant rat: The roles of feeding and stroking. *Developmental Brain Research, 75*, 185–192.

Sukikara, M. H., Mota-Ortiz, S. R., Baldo, M. V., Felicio, L. F., & Canteras, N. S. (2006). A role for the periaqueductal gray in switching adaptive behavioral responses. *Journal of Neuroscience, 26*, 2583–2589.

Sullivan, R. M., Brake, S. C., Hofer, M. A., & Williams, C. L. (1986). Huddling and independent feeding of neonatal rats can be facilitated by a conditioned change in behavioral state. *Developmental Psychobiology, 19*, 625–635.

Sullivan, R. M., Landers, M., Yeaman, B., & Wilson, D. A. (2000). Good memories of bad events in infancy. *Nature, 407*, 38–39.

Sullivan, R. M., Stackenwalt, G., Nasr, F., Lemon, C., & Wilson, D. A. (2000). Association of an odor with activation of olfactory bulb noradrenergic beta-receptors or locus coeruleus stimulation is sufficient to produce learned approach responses to that odor in neonatal rats. *Behavioral Neuroscience, 114*, 957–962.

Sullivan, R. M., & Wilson, D. A. (1994). The locus coeruleus, norepinephrine, and memory in newborns. *Brain Research Bulletin, 35*(5–6), 467–472.

Sullivan, R. M., Wilson, D. A., Wong, R., Correa, A., & Leon, M. (1990). Modified behavioral and olfactory bulb responses to maternal odors in preweanling rats. *Developmental Brain Research, 53*, 243–247.

Sutherland, R. J., McDonald, R. J., Hill, C. R., & Rudy, J. W. (1989). Damage to the hippocampal formation in rats selectively impairs the ability to learn cue relationships. *Behavioral and Neural Biology, 52*, 331–356.

Swanson, L. W., & Petrovich, G. D. (1998). What is the amygdala? *Trends in Neuroscience, 21*, 323–331.

Takahashi, L. K. (1996). Glucocorticoids and the hippocampus. Developmental interactions facilitating the expression of behavioral inhibition. *Molecular Neurobiology, 13*, 213–226.

Thomas, S. A., & Palmiter, R. D. (1997). Disruption of the dopamine beta-hydroxylase gene in mice suggests roles for norepinephrine in motor function, learning, and memory. *Behavioral Neuroscience, 111*, 579–589.

Toufexis, D. J., Rochford, J., & Walker, C. D. (1999). Lactation-induced reduction in rats' acoustic startle is associated with changes in noradrenergic neurotransmission. *Behavioral Neuroscience, 113*, 176–184.

Touzani, K., & Sclafani, A. (2005). Critical role of amygdala in flavor but not taste preference learning in rats. *Journal of Neuroscience, 22*, 1767–1774.

Tronel, S., Feenstra, M. G., & Sara, S. J. (2004). Noradrenergic action in prefrontal cortex in the late stage of memory consolidation. *Learning & Memory, 11*, 453–458.

van Leengoed, E., Kerker, E., & Swanson, H. H. (1987). Inhibition of post-partum maternal behaviour in the rat by injecting an oxytocin antagonist into the cerebral ventricles. *Journal of Endocrinology, 112*, 275–282.

Verwer, R. W., Van Vulpen, E. H., & Van Uum, J. F. (1996). Postnatal development of amygdaloid projections to the prefrontal cortex in the rat studied with retrograde and anterograde tracers. *Journal of Comparative Neurology, 376*, 75–96.

Wallace, K. J., & Rosen, J. B. (2001). Neurotoxic lesions of the lateral nucleus of the amygdala decrease conditioned fear but not unconditioned fear of a predator odor: Comparison with electrolytic lesions. *Journal of Neuroscience, 21*, 3691–3627.

Wiedenmayer, C. P., & Barr, G. A. (2001). Developmental changes in c-fos expression to an age-specific social stressor in infant rats. *Behavioural Brain Research, 126*, 147–157.

Willhite, D. C., Nguyen, K. T., Masurkar, A. V., Greer, C. A., Shepherd, G. M., & Chen, W. R. (2006). Viral tracing identifies distributed columnar organization in the olfactory bulb. *Proceedings of the National Academy of Science USA, 103*, 12592–12597.

Wilson, D. A. (2000). Odor specificity of habituation in the rat anterior piriform cortex. *Journal of Neurosciencephysiol, 83*, 139–145.

Wilson, D. A., & Leon, M. (1988). Spatial patterns of olfactory bulb single-unit responses to learned olfactory cues in young rats. *Journal of Neurosciencephysiol, 59*, 1770–1782.

Wilson, D. A., Best, A. R., & Sullivan, R. M. (2004). Plasticity in the olfactory system: Lessons for the neurobiology of memory. *The Neuroscientist, 10*, 513–524.

Wilson, R. I., & Mainen, Z. F. (2006). Early events in olfactory processing. *Annual Review of Neuroscience*, *29*, 163–201.

Wilson, D. A., & Stevenson, R. J. (2003). Olfactory perceptual learning: The critical role of memory in odor discrimination. *Neuroscience and Biobehavioral Review*, *27*, 307–328.

Wilson, D. A., & Stevenson, R. J. (2006) *Learning to smell: olfactory perception from neurobiology to behavior*. Baltimore: John Hopkins Press.

Wiltgen, B. J., Sanders, M. J., Anagnostaras, S. G., Sage, J. R., & Fanselow, M. S. (2006). Context fear learning in the absence of the hippocampus. *Journal of Neuroscience*, *26*, 5484–5491.

Wolff, M., Gibb, S. J., & Dalrymple-Alford, J. C. (2006). Beyond spatial memory: The anterior thalamus and memory for the temporal order of a sequence of odor cues. *Journal of Neuroscience*, *26*, 2907–2913.

Woo, C. C., & Leon, M. (1987). Sensitive period for neural and behavioral response development to learned odors. *Brain Research*, *433*, 309–313.

Woo, C. C., Oshita, M. H., & Leon, M. (1996). A learned odor decreases the number of Fos-immunopositive granule cells in the olfactory bulb of young rats. *Brain Research*, *716*, 149–156.

Yang, X., Renken, R., Hyder, F., Siddeek, M., Greer, C. A., Shepherd, G. M., et al. (1998). Dynamic mapping at the laminar level of odor-elicited responses in rat olfactory bulb by functional MRI. *Proceeding of the National Academy of Science USA*, *95*, 7715–7720.

Yokoi, M., Mori, K., & Nakanishi, S. (1995). Refinement of odor molecule tuning by dendrodendritic synaptic inhibition in the olfactory bulb. *Proceedings of the National Academy of Science USA*, *92*, 3371–3375.

Yu, G. Z., Kaba, H., Okutani, F., Takahashi, S., & Higuchi, T. (1996a). The olfactory bulb: A critical site of action for oxytocin in the induction of maternal behaviour in the rat. *Neuroscience*, *72*, 1083–1088.

Yu, G. Z., Kaba, H., Okutani, F., Takahashi, S., Higuchi, T., & Seto, K. (1996b). The action of oxytocin originating in the hypothalamic paraventricular nucleus on mitral and granule cells in the rat main olfactory bulb. *Neuroscience*, *72*, 1073–1082.

Yuan, Q., Harley, C. W., Bruce, J. C., Darby-King, A., & McLean, J. H. (2000). Isoproterenol increases CREB phosphorylation and olfactory nerve-evoked potentials in normal and 5-HT-depleted olfactory bulbs in rat pups only at doses that produce odor preference learning. *Learning & Memory*, *7*, 413–421.

Part III

Basic Dispositions, Goals, and States

Basic Personality Dispositions

9 Basic Personality Dispositions Related to Approach and Avoidance: Extraversion/Neuroticism, BAS/BIS, and Positive/Negative Affectivity

Randy J. Larsen and Adam A. Augustine

CONTENTS

Many authors in this volume conceptualize approach and avoidance motivation in state terms, and focus on the various situational, biological, and social processes that influence these fundamental motivational states. However, approach and avoidance motivation can also be conceptualized in trait terms, and the interest here would focus on the personality processes that influence peoples' characteristic or typical levels of these fundamental motives. Although a perennial question in personality psychology concerns the nature and number of basic personality traits, the theoretical constructs of trait approach and trait avoidance are relatively new introductions, though they have been connected with established trait taxonomies. In this chapter we seek to apply a construct validity approach (Cronbach & Meehl, 1955) in order to understand the scientific meaning and utility of approach and avoidance as trait concepts. This involves examining the nomological

network of empirical associations established around these constructs. Our focus will be on other personality variables and various outcome and criterion variables that have been related to the constructs of approach and avoidance motivation in an individual differences perspective.

TRAIT DISPOSITIONS: EXTRAVERSION AND NEUROTICISM

In searching for basic personality traits, different taxonomies have emerged depending on which criteria the researchers apply. Two traits that emerge in almost every systematic taxonomy are, in some form or another, the traits of extraversion and neuroticism. Extraversion and neuroticism were documented quite early by Eysenck (1951) who used biological criteria (that fundamental traits should have a biological basis, should be at least partly genetic, and should be observable in other primates). The traits of extraversion and neuroticism also emerged in early trait taxonomies based on the lexical hypothesis (Digman, 1990). The lexical hypothesis holds that, if a personality trait were important to social functioning, then in the development of language humans would invent many words (mostly adjectives, some nouns) to describe people who had or did not have this trait. This lexical analysis of trait adjectives resulted in the so-called Big Five taxonomy (Norman, 1963), with extraversion and neuroticism emerging in every lexical-based taxonomy. Applied to the English language, such analyses have consistently revealed a remarkably replicable structure, with extraversion and neuroticism emerging as the two most consistent and powerful traits. Moreover, the analyses of other languages, from Japanese to Russian to German to Croatian, have resulted in a very similar structure, suggesting that different cultures have generated similar ways of talking about and linguistically encoding important individual differences (McCrae et al., 2005).

Of all the traits in the various taxonomies of personality, the traits of extraversion and neuroticism have perhaps received the most attention from researchers (Larsen & Buss, 2007). This is most likely due to the fact that Eysenck very early on proposed a causal theory of these traits that could be experimentally tested. Eysenck proposed that extraversion was linked to general cortical arousability (extraverts were less arousable than introverts and hence needed strong stimulation) and that neuroticism was linked to a lower threshold for activation in the limbic system. A vast amount of research has been done on these theoretical notions (Eysenck, 1998; Zelenski, 2007), some of which has been supportive and some of which pushes the theoretical notions in new directions. Eysenck's simple cortical arousal view of extraversion, which was proposed before we knew much about brain function, is almost certainly inaccurate or incomplete. Eysenck himself stated, "Clearly the concept of general physiological arousal… does not seem viable any longer [as an explanation of the extraversion–introversion dimension]" (Eysenck, 1998, p. 248). Moreover, "increased activation in the limbic system" seems too vague to give a complete or accurate account of the biological roots of neuroticism (Canli, 2006a; LeDoux, 1996). Although Eysenck's older biological theory of personality has not remained intact, the traits of neuroticism and extraversion do have robust biological correlates, both in the central nervous system (Canli, 2004) as well as the peripheral nervous system (DePascalis, 2004).

Although the biological theories of extraversion and neuroticism have undergone major revisions in the past several decades, they have nevertheless built up a substantial amount of evidence on the behavioral correlates of these dimensions. Although a review of the well-established correlates of extraversion and neuroticism is beyond the scope of this chapter, we mention this large research corpus as a potential explanation for why these traits emerge as the most powerful traits in various taxonomies. It may be that extraversion and neuroticism emerge as primary traits in, say, the lexical taxonomies, precisely because these traits predict a wide collection of important social behaviors, performance outcomes, and even clinically relevant phenomena. Researchers have recently related extraversion and neuroticism to tendencies to approach or avoid specific classes of stimuli. Eysenck even related these traits explicitly to affect, predicting that extraversion promoted a susceptibility to positive affect and neuroticism promoted a susceptibility to negative affect (Eysenck & Eysenck, 1985). We turn now to a discussion of research on dispositional affect.

AFFECTIVE DISPOSITIONS: POSITIVE AND NEGATIVE AFFECTIVITY

There is a great deal of evidence that emotion is also well represented by two broad and orthogonal dimensions (Larsen & Diener, 1992). One dimension is related to approach motivation and is elicited by appetitive stimuli (i.e., positive hedonic stimuli, reward cues, signals of safety). It is experienced as enthusiasm, interest, pleasantness, or relief and can be generically termed positive affect (PA). The other affect dimension is related to avoidance motivation or withdrawal and is elicited by aversive stimuli (i.e., negative hedonic stimuli, threat cues, punishment). It is experienced as a variety of negative emotions, ranging from anxiety, anger, and frustration, to disgust. We can generically refer to these aversively motivated states as representing the negative affect (NA) dimension.

Among researchers in emotion, there are two basic views on the conceptual nature of the affect domain. One view, the primary emotions view, holds that the domain of affect is best conceptualized as a set of discrete categorical or fundamental (by some criterion) emotions. Primary emotion theorists often propose lists of usually between five to nine basic emotions, defined by such criteria as unique facial expressions, distinct action tendencies, or adaptive significance from an evolutionary perspective. In contrast, a second viewpoint holds that the affect domain is represented by a small set of underlying dimensions, not distinct categories. This view is called the dimensional view and it is based on the idea that all emotional experiences are blends of a few superordinate emotion dimensions, e.g., valance and arousal, or positive and negative emotions (Larsen & Diener, 1992).

Zelenski and Larsen (2000) discuss how dimensional views of emotion are most useful for representing longer term or dispositional tendencies in affective experiences. These authors present evidence that, for example, people who have a lot of sadness in their daily lives also have a lot of anger. Zelenski and Larsen monitored people's emotions twice a day, every day, for one month and found that people who frequently had episodes of one kind of negative emotion (e.g., anger) also frequently had episodes of other negative emotions (e.g., guilt, sadness, etc.). People are rarely angry and sad *at the same time*. Nevertheless, people who are frequently angry are also frequently sad, and have other frequent negative emotions as well, over the long term. This is consistent with the dimensional view, which would posit an underlying dimension of general NA. Similar dimensional findings are reported for positive emotions. Indeed, Zelenski and Larsen argue that the dimensional view (i.e., PA and NA) provides a better fit to data based on emotions averaged over time than the categorical view. In other words, when it comes to representing dispositional affect, the two broad traits of PA and NA do a better job than a categorical view of emotion.

A dispositional approach to PA and NA emphasizes the trait-like characteristics of these dimensions. Dispositional affect is thought of as a person's average level, their typical amount of a given emotion. Certainly there are many causes of emotion (e.g., PA may increase upon receiving a compliment or winning the lottery), but what the trait view is concerned with is, other things being equal, what is the person's expected value? For example, if we averaged out all the momentary and situational influences on affect, what would be the person's set-point level of PA or NA?

Persons high in NA will exhibit, on average, higher levels of distress, anxiety, annoyance, irritability, hostility, worry, anxiety, fear, and dissatisfaction, and they tend to focus on the unpleasant characteristics of themselves, the world, the future, and other people (Larsen & Ketelaar, 1989, 1991). As such, high NA people are often viewed as "complainers" in the sense that they appear dissatisfied with their circumstances, with other people, with their own characteristics (e.g., they complain about health problems; Larsen, 1992). Moreover, high NA persons appear vigilant for impending problems and are pessimistic about the future (Necowitz & Roznowski, 1994; Schonfeld, 1996).

Persons who are high on the trait PA dimension are characterized by a high level of energy and engagement with the environment, particularly the social environment. Others see them as enthusiastic, optimistic, and actively involved with life. They tend to have optimistic expectations about the future and are highly sociable, preferring the company of others to isolation (Watson, 2000).

The dimensions of PA and NA, assessed as dispositional tendencies, are empirically orthogonal, and may in fact represent neurologically or at least psychologically distinct affective systems. When it comes to trait affect, PA and NA may be thought of as the Big Two (Tellegen, 1985). The measurement implications for assessing these two dimensions of affect in dispositional terms are discussed in more detail in Larsen and Diener (1992). A general guide to measuring affect, discussing the pros and cons of several methods, can be found in Larsen and Fredrickson (1999) and Larsen and Prizmic (2006).

Data are accumulating to also suggest that dispositional levels of PA and NA each have a modest heritability component (Baker, Cesa, Gatz, & Grodsky, 1992). For example, in a study of monozygotic and dizygotic twins reared apart, Lykken and Tellegen (1996) estimated heritability at 40% for PA and 55% for NA. Only PA showed a significant shared environment component, at 22%. These results are important because they imply that PA and NA are orthogonal even in genetic analyses, implying separate biological underpinnings.

Extraversion and neuroticism have been linked in correlational studies with trait measures of PA and NA, respectively (Costa & McCrae, 1980; Eysenck & Eysenck, 1985; McCrae & Costa, 1991). Indeed, over a dozen studies have reported correlations between extraversion and PA and neuroticism and NA (Rusting & Larsen, 1997) suggesting that these two traits have strong affective components. For example, Costa and McCrae (1980) measured E and N in their large longitudinal sample of adults in the Baltimore area. At a follow-up assessment 10 years later, they assessed average levels of PA and NA, and found that E predicted PA, and N predicted NA, 10 years later. In another study, Costa and McCrae used spouse-rated measures of personality and self-reported mood and again found the strong links between E-PA and N-NA.

The links between extraversion and neuroticism and PA and NA are often discussed in terms of *emotional reactivity*. That is, extraverts and high-neuroticism persons respond to stimuli with more intense emotions than introverts and low-neuroticism persons, as opposed to an indirect relationship between personality and affect (e.g., spending more time in positive or negative situations). Correlational data, however, cannot directly test the reactivity hypothesis. What is necessary is to conduct experimental studies, where extraverts and high-neuroticism subjects are subjected to mood inductions and differential reactivity to those inductions can be tested.

While many researchers have argued that E and N represent differential reactivity to PA and NA stimuli, respectively, correlational data do not provide conclusive evidence for such claims. For example, it could be that extraverts establish more supportive social networks than introverts, and these supportive social networks lead to the higher levels of PA found among extraverts. Experimental evidence is needed, where extraverts and introverts are exposed to identical levels of affective stimulation, and differences in emotional responding are examined. Larsen and his colleagues have gathered experimental data on E and N and differential reactivity to emotion inductions in the laboratory. In four separate studies to date (Larsen & Ketelaar, 1989, 1991; Rusting & Larsen, 1999; Zelenski & Larsen, 1999) this team has found that E relates to differential susceptibility to positive mood inductions and that N relates to negative mood inductions. For example, in Larsen and Ketelaar (1989) the pleasant and unpleasant moods were induced using false performance feedback (success and failure, respectively). PA and NA were assessed both before and after the mood induction. Extraversion predicted significant increases in PA to the success feedback, and neuroticism predicted significant increases in NA to the failure feedback. Such results provide support for the differential reactivity hypothesis. These results have replicated across experiments that employed a variety of laboratory mood induction techniques (e.g., false feedback, mental imagery, pictorial stimuli), combinations of different experimental designs, and different dependent variables. Extraverts consistently report more PA in response to positive-mood-inducing stimuli, and high-neuroticism persons report more NA in response to negative-mood-inducing stimuli. The main effect of personality (extraversion and neuroticism) on emotional reactivity, using standard laboratory mood induction procedures, has been replicated by others (Canli et al., 2001; Gomez, Cooper, & Gomez, 2000).

A review by Rusting (1998) also provides evidence for the direct effect of personality on affect-congruent cognition. For example, Rusting and Larsen (1998) found that extraverts were more likely to interpret auditorily presented homophones in a positive way (e.g., "sweet," as opposed to "suite"), and high-neuroticism persons were more likely to interpret homophones in a negative way (e.g., "die," as opposed to "dye"). In a story completion task (as part of the same study), extraverts responded with more positive stories, and high-neuroticism persons responded with more negative stories. Moreover, these effects persisted after controlling for mood state. Thus, personality appeared to have a direct effect on interpretations of ambiguous stimuli. This suggests that personality might also have a direct effect on other types of cognitive judgments.

Research also reveals that high-neuroticism persons spend more time focusing on their NA than do emotionally stable individuals (Kardum, 1999). When presented with a negative stimulus, the high-neuroticism individual will spend more time thinking about the impact of the negative stimulus and their reaction to the stimulus than would an emotionally stable individual. High-neuroticism persons are also less able to understand their emotions (King, 1998). Indeed, affect clarity (Salovey, Mayer, Goldman, Turvey, & Palfai, 1995), or the ability to understand affective experience, is negatively associated with neuroticism (Swinkels & Giuliano, 1995). It has also been demonstrated that extraverts are better able to understand and express their PA than introverts (King, 1998; Swinkels & Giuliano, 1995). This means that, for the introverted individual, the experience of PA may present a confusing or unfamiliar situation. The introvert may express his or her PA in a socially inappropriate way, such as laughing at a particularly inopportune moment. This would most likely result in negative social feedback and hinder the introvert's ability to maintain PA in social settings.

Extraversion and neuroticism are also related, in a somewhat counterintuitive way, to the excitation transfer effect applied to positive and NA. Bunce, Larsen, and Cruz (1993) examined the transfer of arousal to pleasant and unpleasant photographic images. Participants first provide baseline ratings of how a series of negative or positive images made them feel. Residual arousal was then induced by having participants pedal a bicycle ergometer until heart rates were over 120 beats per minute. Participants then rested in a chair and subjectively monitored their heart rates. When subjects reported being fully recovered from the exercise, their heart rates were actually almost 20 beats per minute over baseline. They then provided additional ratings of a set of emotional images. Excitation transfer was calculated as the increase in postexercise affect ratings attributed to emotional images, controlling for the preexercise ratings. Neuroticism predicted excitation transfer to the positive images, and extraversion predicted excitation transfer to the negative images. Results were interpreted as excitation transfer resulting from the need to interrogate bodily responses for emotions that were dispositionally unfamiliar to the person. That is, high-neuroticism persons are unfamiliar with PA, and so primarily look to their bodily states when asked to rate how positive stimuli make them feel. Similarly, extraverts are less familiar with NA, and so look to their bodily states for information regarding how they are reacting to negative stimuli.

Individual differences also exist in the temporal parameters of affective responding (affective chronometry, Davidson, 1998). Davidson (1998) suggests, for example, that some individuals may take longer to reach the highest intensity of an affective experience (rise time to peak). In addition, some individuals may require a longer period to return to an emotionally neutral state (i.e., recovery time). Hemenover (2003) found that high-neuroticism persons and introverts (vs. emotionally stables and extraverts, respectively) experience a slower decay rate of NA and a faster decay rate of PA in the absence of focused repair efforts.

Individual differences also exist in the ability to regulate affect (Larsen, 2000). In a series of studies, Shulman, Augustine, and Hemenover (2006) induced NA and then required participants to engage in randomly assigned repair strategies. When using a distraction strategy (a strategy known to be effective for affect repair), high-neuroticism persons (vs. emotionally stables) were less able to repair induced NA. Additionally, it was found that extraverts (vs. introverts) were better able to enhance their PA when using a reappraisal repair strategy.

Theories Relating Extraversion to Positive Affect

There is some debate concerning the core of the personality trait of extraversion. Data from Ashton, Lee, and Paunonen (2002) suggest that the core of extraversion is sociability, or the enjoyment of social activity. Alternatively, the central feature of extraversion may be reward sensitivity, which makes pleasant situations more stimulating for the extravert (Lucas & Diener, 2001). Regardless of which feature (sociability or reward sensitivity) forms the core of extraversion, the centrality of these constructs conveys the importance of approach-related behavior for the highly extraverted (vs. introverted). The extravert (vs. introvert) experiences greater benefits from participation in both generally pleasant situations and, more specifically, pleasant social situations. The increased PA from these situations leads to a general tendency for the extraverted individual to approach pleasant stimuli more than the introvert.

The relatively high level of approach behavior exhibited by the extravert often leads to affective benefits. Numerous data support a link between the extraverts' increased participation in pleasant social situations and the experience of positive hedonic tone. First, extraverts (vs. introverts) report more PA and less NA when they are engaged in a social situation (Diener, 1984; Emmons, Diener, & Larsen, 1986). Second, the correlation between extraversion and PA increases when PA is measured in a social setting (Emmons et al., 1986), suggesting that merely being in the presence of others increases the PA of a highly extraverted individual. Third, extraverts choose to spend more time engaging in social interactions (Emmons et al.), perhaps due to the affective benefits they accrue during such interactions. Fourth, the sociability facet (vs. all others) of extraversion correlates the highest with measures of PA (Emmons & Diener, 1986), indicating that the enjoyment of social interaction may be responsible for the higher levels of PA experienced by the extraverted individual. Finally, extraverts experience more positive life events when with friends and at work (Headey, Glowacki, Holmstrom, & Wearing, 1985), suggesting that for extraverts (vs. introverts) pleasant social interactions initiate a cascade of recursive pleasant feelings and experiences.

Although the affective benefits of social interaction are, perhaps, most obvious for the extraverted individual, pleasant social situations can also lead to a gain in PA for most individuals, regardless of their standing on the personality trait extraversion. For instance, Reis, Sheldon, Gable, Roscoe, and Ryan (2000) found that one's daily experience of PA covaries with one's feelings of relatedness to others. More specifically, pleasant social interactions directly contribute to PA levels, such that the more pleasant social interactions experienced on a given day, the higher levels of PA reported on that day. Additionally, one's levels of PA can be predicted chronologically: PA is highest on Friday and Saturday, the days during which more pleasant social interactions typically occur (Larsen & Kasimatis, 1990; Reis et al., 2000). These findings together indicate that PA is heightened through pleasant social interactions.

Pleasant social contact is also related to subjective well-being (composed primarily of high positive and low NA), with those higher in subjective well-being possessing more social resources (i.e., friends and close acquaintances). Indeed, satisfaction with social support networks positively correlates with subjective well-being (Diener, 1984), and intervention programs designed to increase quantity and quality of social support networks also increase positive and decrease NA (Fordyce, 1983). Moreover, Nezlek, Imbrie, and Shean (1994) found that people at high (vs. low) risk for clinical depression had fewer social interactions and even when they did, those social interactions were of less relative quality.

Additional evidence for a potential dissociation of trait extraversion from the relationship between pleasant social situations and PA comes from a series of studies conducted by Fleeson, Malanos, and Achille (2002). First, it was found that self-reports of extraversion can rapidly fluctuate over short periods (hours). Individual differences in extraversion covaried with fluctuations in PA such that, the more state extraversion one was displaying, the higher one's levels of PA. Additionally, it was found that all individuals, regardless of their trait level of extraversion, enjoyed acting extraverted. These findings indicate that, in terms of affective functioning, acting extraverted can put even the introvert into the positive affective states typically enjoyed by the extravert. Second, it was found that this first set of results replicated across a longer period (weeks). Finally, in an experimental manipulation of extraversion during social interaction where some individuals were instructed to act introverted and others to act extraverted, it was found that state, not trait, extraversion accounted for increases in PA during the interaction. Additionally, acting extraverted increased one's perceived pleasantness of the interaction (Fleeson et al., 2002).

Although extraversion does predict a tendency to approach pleasant situations, the participation in pleasant social situations itself seems to instill PA in most individuals. This increased experience of PA is also linked to an increase in approach-related behavior. Unlike NA, which demands cognitive interpretation (i.e., why am I feeling this way?), PA promotes exploratory behavior. Fredrickson's (1998) broaden and build model of PA suggests that once one is experiencing PA, one seeks to expand and continue that experience. The experience of joy encourages one to "play" with the environment and to seek others who wish to enjoy these experiences as well. The experience of interest encourages one to approach novel situations, ideas, and individuals that are related to the object of interest. The experience of love encourages one to play, explore, and savor important individuals, all involving approach behaviors.

Theories Relating Neuroticism to Negative Affect

Saying that neuroticism is a propensity to experience NA is almost a tautology; questionnaire measures of neuroticism inquire about a tendency to experience such negative emotions as anxiety, worry, and irritation. Nevertheless, several theories have been proposed to specify the mechanisms that underlie both neuroticism and trait NA. Because neuroticism and trait NA show a remarkable level of consistency over time (Conley, 1985), as well as a moderate degree of heritability (Goldsmith, Aksan, Essex, & Vandell, 2001), many theories have focused on biological bases of these constructs. As already mentioned, Eysenck's original theory of neuroticism implicated a tendency of the limbic system in the brain to become easily aroused in high-neuroticism per-

sons. Modern researchers have examined more specific areas of the brain for clues to the source of neuroticism. For example, Canli et al. (2001) had subjects view a large number of positive and negative images in alternating blocks while their brains were scanned using fMRI. In examining specific brain areas that showed increased activation to the negative images relative to positive images, these researchers found that neuroticism correlated with reduced activation in the left mid temporal gyrus and the left mid frontal gyrus. These results are consistent with earlier imaging studies of depressed persons (a condition linked to neuroticism), which identified reduced metabolism in the left frontal cortex associated with depression (Baxter et al., 1989).

More recently, Eisenberger, Lieberman, and Satpute (2005) reviewed theories suggesting that neuroticism is the result of an especially sensitive neural comparator, a mechanism that detects mismatches between actual and expected states of the world (Carver & Scheier, 1990). Neuroscientists have highlighted the importance of discrepancy detection for identifying incorrect responses. This function appears to be carried out by the dorsal anterior cingulated cortex (dACC). Eisenberger et al. (2005) used an oddball task, which is a discrepancy detection task known to activate the dACC. They found that activity in the dACC during the discrepancy detection task was positively correlated with self-reported neuroticism. As more brain researchers become interested in individual variability, it is likely that more specific theories will be developed and tested about the neural basis of neuroticism.

Other theories of neuroticism have emphasized cognitive contributions to increased NA reactivity. Several theorists have argued that neuroticism is caused by specific styles of information processing, e.g., perceiving, attending, thinking, and remembering that promotes NA. For example, Lishman (1972) reported that high-neuroticism persons were more likely, and faster, to recall unpleasant information than low-neuroticism persons, though there was no difference associated with the recall of pleasant information. Martin, Ward, and Clark (1983) had subjects study information about themselves and others. When later asked to recall this information, high-neuroticism subjects recalled more negative information about themselves, but did not recall more negative information about others. Many psychologists hold that emotional information is stored in memory, much like any other bit of information, and that each piece of information is linked to other pieces. Individuals may differ in the density of the associations that surround negative information, with high-neuroticism subjects having richer associational networks around negative information. Consequently, for them, unpleasant information is more accessible, leading to higher rates of activation and recall among high-neuroticism persons.

Other cognitive theories of neuroticism emphasize the encoding of negative information, and suggest that high-neuroticism subjects pay more attention to threats and unpleasant information in their environments (Dalgleish, 1995; Matthews, 2000; Matthews, Derryberry, & Siegle, 2000). These theories posit that high-neuroticism subjects are particularly vigilant for cues of threat and are constantly on the lookout for negative information in their environments that might be interpreted as menacing, unsafe, or foreboding. A common technique for assessing the capture of attention by negative information is the so-called emotional Stroop task. Like the original Stroop task, subjects are presented with words in various colors, and are instructed to ignore the words and name the color of the ink in which the word appears as quickly as possible. However, when people are exposed to single words presented in the visual field, the semantic meaning of those words is automatically activated. In the emotional Stroop task, the words consist of either threatening words (e.g., fear, murder, failure, grief, disease, etc.) or neutral words. A common finding is that people are slower to name the colors of threatening words than neutral words, and suggests that threatening information generally captures attention (Algom, Chajut, & Lev, 2004). However, many studies have also found that persons high on neuroticism or trait anxiety show an especially strong interference effect (slowing of RT to name the color) to the negative words (Williams, Mathews, & MacLeod, 1996).

MOTIVATIONAL DISPOSITIONS: BEHAVIORAL ACTIVATION AND BEHAVIORAL INHIBITION

In terms of theoretical explanations for why personality should relate to affect, perhaps the most relevant theory is that proposed by Gray (1990, 1994). This theory called Reinforcement Sensitivity Theory (or RST) is actually a revision of that proposed by Eysenck (1967). Both theories offer explanations for the biological basis of the two main dimensions of personality, i.e., extraversion and neuroticism. Gray proposed an alternative explanation by positing two separate brain mechanisms responsible for sensitivity to cues of reward and cues of punishment. Gray suggested that extraversion (Gray actually preferred the term "impulsivity") is related to an enhanced sensitivity to cues of reward. Extraverts are mainly

motivated by pleasure or reward, and so have a strong tendency to approach, even (or especially) in novel situations. Extraverts expect rewards, and are vigilant for possible sources of reward in the environment. Gray thus named the hypothesized neurological substrate for this individual difference the behavioral approach system (BAS). This system responds to rewards and incentives and it generates PA.

Gray hypothesized that neuroticism (Gray actually preferred the term "anxiety") was responsible for individual differences in response to cues of punishment or frustration. That is, high-neuroticism individuals are mainly motivated to avoid punishment and so have a strong tendency to inhibit their behavior, especially in novel environments. Gray thus named the hypothesized neurological substrate for this individual differences the behavioral inhibition system (BIS). Persons with a strong BIS are vigilant for signs of impending punishment or frustration in the environment and as such are sensitive to aversive stimuli. The BIS responds to punishment and aversive stimuli and is responsible for NA.

Gray's theory of personality (Reinforcement Sensitivity Theory; Gray, 1994; Pickering, Corr, & Gray, 1999) can be described as a causal model for the traits of extraversion and neuroticism (Rusting & Larsen, 1999). Gray has described two independent brain systems, the BAS and the BIS. Differences in the strength of these brain systems cause two personality traits which Gray has named impulsivity (strong BAS or reward sensitivity) and anxiety (strong BIS or punishment sensitivity). Furthermore, Gray has located his traits as rotations in the extraversion–neuroticism conceptual space. Some debate has focused on where exactly to locate BAS and BIS in this conceptual space (Gomez et al., 2000; Pickering et al., 1999; Rusting & Larsen, 1997, 1999; Zuckerman, Joireman, Kratl, & Kuhilan, 1999). Rusting and Larsen (1999) present empirical evidence that Gray's constructs of BAS and BIS lie on top of extraversion and neuroticism in personality space. Other data make it clear that reward sensitivity loads highly on extraversion markers, and punishment sensitivity loads highly on neuroticism markers (Zelenski & Larsen, 1999).

To the extent that BAS strength "causes" extraversion and BIS strength causes neuroticism, Gray's theory helps explain why extraverts respond to positive mood inductions with more positive moods, and why high-neuroticism respond to negative mood inductions with more negative moods. That is, it makes intuitive sense that a person sensitive to cues for reward (i.e., an extravert or someone with a strong BAS) would respond to such cues with more positive emotion, and that a person sensitive to cues for punishment (i.e., a high-N person, or someone with a strong BIS) would respond to such cues with more negative emotion.

Many other researchers in the area of emotion and personality have similarly used Gray's theory to account for their observations. First, Davidson and his colleagues have been working in the general area of affective neuroscience. Part of this research program focuses on affective dispositions and their neurological underpinnings. In terms of brain function, abundant evidence suggests a prefrontal cortical asymmetry in PA and NA (Cacioppo & Gardner, 1999). Assessed with EEG, PA is associated with left prefrontal cortex activation, whereas NA is associated with greater relative right prefrontal cortex activation (Davidson, 1993a; Davidson, Ekman, Saron, Senulis, & Friesen, 1990). Similar results have also been obtained in very young children (Fox & Davidson, 1986) using sweet and bitter solutions placed in the mouths of 10-month-old infants to produce pleasant and unpleasant "emotional" reactions. The infants showed more relative left than right prefrontal cortex activation to the sweet solution, and more right than left brain activation to the bitter solution.

Researchers have established that the cortical asymmetry associated with emotion appears to behave like a dispositional characteristic. For example, Fox, Bell, and Jones (1992) studied a group of infants at age 7 months and again at age 12 months, and found that the EEG measures of cortical asymmetry taken at those two periods were highly correlated. Davidson (1993b) reports similar results from adults, showing that measures of EEG asymmetry show test–retest correlations in the range of .66 to .73 across studies. These findings suggest that individual differences in cortical asymmetry related to PA and NA exhibit enough stability and consistency to consider them as indicative of some underlying biological disposition or trait.

Other studies suggest that EEG asymmetry in the prefrontal cortex indicates a dispositional vulnerability to positive or negative emotional states. Tomarken, Davidson, and Henriques (1990) and Wheeler, Davidson, and Tomarken (1993) examined the relation between individual differences in resting frontal asymmetry and later reactions to emotional film clips in normal participants. The hypothesis was that participants with greater right-side activation at rest (measured before watching the films) would report more intense *negative* emotional reactions to the fear and disgust films compared to those participants with relatively more left-side activation. The opposite prediction was made for participants with greater left-side activation. The predictions were essentially supported; cortical asymmetry measures taken *before* the films pre-

dicted participants' *subsequent* self-reported emotional reactions to the films. A study by Sutton and Davidson (1997) showed that dispositionally positive persons (assessed by Carver and White's [1994] BIS/BAS inventory, see below) showed greater relative left EEG asymmetry at cortical electrode sites at baseline, in the absence of emotional stimulation. Davidson (1998) explicitly draws on the concepts of approach and withdrawal to organize the literature on affective dispositions and brain function, finding great utility for the orthogonal concepts of approach/incentive/appetitive states and withdrawal/avoidance/aversive states, and their separable activation.

Another research group making extensive use of Gray's theory is that of Carver and his colleagues (Carver & White, 1994; Carver, Sutton, & Scheier, 1999). Carver and White developed and validated a scale to measure individual differences in the strength of the BIS and BAS. Carver et al. (1999) review Gray's theory emphasizing individual differences in approach or incentive motivation and individual differences in withdrawal or aversive motivation. They then go on to show how several programs of research can be integrated into the theme that humans appear to possess separate systems for responding to incentives with approach behavior and to threats with avoidance behavior. These two systems show reliable individual differences, they relate to major affective dispositions, they may be lateralized in our cortical architecture, they may have important and separable discrepancy feedback control loops, and they may relate to ideal self-concepts and ought self-concepts. Many points are brought to bear on the Big Two personality dimensions by Carver et al., such that the overall meaning of the constructs might best be captured by the general terms of approach and avoidance traits.

Larsen, Chien, and Zelenski (2008) used the BAS or BIS constructs in an experimental study involving performance under conditions of either reward or punishment. In this study participants were required to complete hundreds of trials of the Stroop color-word task, with a one-second response window on each trial. The response window made it an especially difficult task, and participants made errors on about half the trials. Participants were either in a "reward" group or a "punishment" group. In the reward group, subjects earned points that counted toward payment for each trial that was correct and within the time window. They received only reward feedback on correct trials; incorrect or responses that were too slow resulted in no feedback. In this condition, participants only had cues of reward that reinforced correct responses. Subjects earned $5 on average for participating in this 20 min study. Participants in the punishment condition began the study with $10 and were punished by loosing money after each incorrect or slow response. In this condition, participants only had cues of punishment for wrong responses; correct responses resulted in no feedback. Participants in this condition lost an average of $5. As such, participants in both conditions finished the experiment with $5, on average, but one group was rewarded on a trial-by-trial basis whereas the other group was punished on a trial-by-trial basis. Performance (average reaction time and percentage of correct responses on the last 100 trials) served as the dependent variable. In the reward condition, BAS scores (measured with Carver & White's 1994 inventory) predicted better performance, with high BAS persons working faster and becoming more accurate when they were working for reward. In the punishment condition, BIS scores best predicted performance, with the high-BIS persons responding faster and more accurately than the low-BIS persons. Such behavioral findings are consistent with Gray's model of BAS and BIS referring to differential sensitivity to cues of reward and punishment.

Other researchers are similarly drawing heavily on Gray's model and should be mentioned here. Depue (1996; Depue & Collins, 2000) uses Gray's theory to organize his research on dopamine and affective dispositions. Cacioppo and Gardner (1999) use aspects of Gray's theory to account for bivalent effects in the attitude literature. Cloninger (1987) draws on Gray's theory to account for genetically influenced susceptibilities to certain personality disorders and related behavioral patterns, e.g., alcohol abuse.

Gray's theory has many interesting implications. For example, let's say you want to motivate someone to engage in some behavior, say to quit smoking. You could present your arguments in terms of the rewards of quitting (e.g., food will taste better) or the aversive consequences of continuing (e.g., shortness of breath on exertion). For some persons (those with strong BAS) you should emphasize the rewards of quitting (food will taste better, they will feel healthier, they will live longer, etc.). On the other hand, with individuals who have a strong BIS, it might work better to emphasize the threatening or aversive aspects of not quitting (e.g., social ostracism, multiple diseases and health complications, early death). Any persuasive message can be framed in terms of the rewards or the costs (punishments), and so may differentially appeal to persons who are high or low on BIS or BAS sensitivity. Walker, Larsen, Zona, Govindan, and Fisher (2004) illustrate how appetitive and aversive urges separately predict smoking relapse in patients who have undergone lung cancer surgery. Some relapse because of the desire to regain the pleasurable aspects of smoking, and others relapse to avoid the pain of withdrawal.

Gray's theory suggests that dispositional affect (the Big Two of PA and NA) and personality (the Big Two of extraversion and neuroticism) have, at least in part, a biological basis that lies in circuits sensitive to cues of reward and punishment and that generate action tendencies to approach or avoid. If this is true, then we should see individual differences emerge very early in life, perhaps replicate in other primates, remain relatively stable over time, and we should be able to find some biological correlates of such individual differences, perhaps in the form of brain activation and genetic heritability.

INTEGRATION OF PERSONALITY CONSTRUCTS INTO APPROACH AND AVOIDANCE MOTIVATION

As discussed so far, there are many different individual difference variables that appear related to the approach and avoidance constructs. Zelenski and Larsen (1999) provide strong evidence that measures of these variables coalesce into composite factors that can be identified with approach and avoidance constructs. The Zelenski and Larsen study is noteworthy in that, in addition to self-report questionnaire personality measures, they examined individual differences in affective reactivity (to a laboratory mood induction procedure) as well as naturalistic affect (using experience sampling over a month-long period of daily report). The self-report measures examined by Zelenski and Larsen included the Eysenck Personality Questionnaire (EPQ; Eysenck, Eysenck, & Barrett, 1985), Cloninger's Temperament and Character Inventory (TCI; Cloninger, Svrakic, & Przybeck, 1993), the Generalized Reward and Punishment Expectancy Scales (GRAPES; Ball & Zuckerman, 1990), the BIS/BAS Scales (Carver & White, 1994), and the I7 Impulsivity Questionnaire (Eysenck, Pearson, Easting, & Allsopp, 1985). These scales were submitted to principle axis factor analysis, and three factors emerged, accounting for nearly 50% of the common variance. One factor clearly represented approach sensitivity (loading reward sensitivity, reward expectancy, extraversion, and BAS scales). Another factor clearly represented avoidance sensitivity (loading neuroticism, punishment sensitivity, harm avoidance, and BIS scales). A third factor emerged which loaded impulsivity items (impulsivity and psychoticism) and suggests that the term "impulsivity," which Gray often used to refer to the BAS construct, is a poor designation for approach motivation.

The results of this factor analysis are consistent with the idea that two broad traits underlie this collection of specific personality measures. Extraversion, reward sensitivity, reward expectancy, and BAS measures share a common core that appears related to a tendency to approach, whereas neuroticism, harm avoidance, punishment sensitivity, and BIS measures share a common core that appears to be related to avoidance motivation. Similar correlational results have been reported by others (Elliot & Thrash, 2002; Gable, Reis, & Elliot, 2003; Zuckerman et al., 1999). Lucas, Diener, Grob, Suh, and Shao (2000) focused on extraversion, and modeling data gathered from 39 different cultures, report that the core of extraversion appears to be reward sensitivity, not sociability, strengthening the inference that approach tendencies form the basis of extraversion.

Besides using factor analysis to identify the core components of approach and avoidance across a collection of related personality variables, Zelenski and Larsen (1999) then used those composite scores to predict responsiveness to laboratory mood inductions as well as average affective states over a month of daily reporting. The mood induction consisted of having subjects view a set of positive and negative images, displayed in alternating blocks. After each block, subjects rated how the images made them feel. The avoidance composite best predicted NA following the negative images, and the approach composite best predicted PA following the positive images. Similarly, after aggregating positive and NA scores over 28 consecutive days of thrice daily reporting, Zelenski and Larsen (1999) reported that the approach composite was the best predictor of aggregated PA and the avoidance composite was the best predictor of aggregated NA. More importantly, the composite scores, based on the latent factors identified in the factor analysis, better predicted the outcome variables (emotional reactivity and aggregated affect) than any of the single measures that went into the factor analysis.

All of the dispositional variables discussed in this chapter are related, in one way or another, to tendencies to either approach or avoid specific categories of stimuli or situations. Several findings provide more concrete evidence for this theme. Digman (1997) performed a secondary factor analysis of numerous correlational studies of the Big Five traits. This "super" factor analysis found that the Big Five traits reliably loaded on two super factors, one composed of neuroticism, (low)-conscientiousness, and (low)-agreeableness (an avoidance factor) and the other composed of extraversion and openness (an approach factor). Although Digman discussed the potential meanings of these super factors in terms of

socialization, personal growth, and emotionality, these factors might also be interpreted as related to general approach and avoidance tendencies. Neuroticism, as previously described, is related to NA. Negative affect itself can often serve as a motivator to avoid the further and future experience of NA (Frijda, 1994). For instance, experiencing fear may elicit actions necessary to avoid the fear experience itself. Conscientiousness is a trait of organization, both of items and relationships (Costa & McCrae, 1992). Although one could spend an afternoon organizing his or her closet (an approach-related behavior), the process of maintaining an organized life (which is indicative of this personality trait) is generally one of avoiding those things which lead to disorder. Agreeableness, a trait related to politeness, could also be thought of in terms of avoidance. The process of maintaining an air of politeness is generally one of avoiding impolite actions. Also as previously described, extraversion is an approach-related trait. Openness could similarly be considered a trait of approach-related behavior because it refers to the tendency to prefer new or unusual situations. Those high in openness have a tendency to approach novel stimuli.

Although Digman's (1997) super factors could be interpreted as representing general tendencies of approach and avoidance, this is just one interpretation. Elliot and Thrash (2002) provide direct evidence for the assertion that approach and avoidance tendencies represent the overlying structure of personality. In a series of seven programmatic confirmatory factor-analytic studies, Elliot and Thrash demonstrated that extraversion, BAS, and positive emotionality loaded on one general approach factor. This approach factor was predictive of a variety of approach-related performance and mastery goals. Neuroticism, BIS, and negative emotionality loaded on one general avoidance factor. This avoidance factor was predictive of a variety of avoidance-related performance and mastery goals. Given these findings, it seems that the superordinate structures, or the Big Two of personality, are the general tendencies to approach and avoid specifically rewarding or specifically punishing stimuli and situations.

Evidence from affective neuroscience and behavioral genetics suggests that the approach–avoidance superstructure of human personality is based, in part, on biological factors. With regards to approach-related constructs, individual differences in positive affective functioning can be predicted by individual differences in baseline activation of the left prefrontal cortex (Davidson, Jackson, & Kallin, 2000). Additionally, several brain areas differentially respond to positive affective stimuli as a function of extraversion (Canli, 2006b). The dopamine system also plays a role, with mesolimbic and mesocortical dopaminergic pathways showing greater activation during reward-directed behavior (Pickering & Gray, 1999). The heritability of approach-related personality traits may be due, in part, to the genetic structure underlying dopamine functioning. Plomin and Caspi (1999) found that differences in the structure of the DRD4 gene are associated with differential activation of the dopamine pathways. In other words, different genotypes of DRD4 may lead to differential levels of expressed novelty seeking and extraversion through the differential activation of dopaminergic pathways (Canli, 2006b). Thus, DRD4 is linked with extraversion, which in turn moderates activation of brain regions associated with PA and is linked to BAS. This gene may provide the basis for one of the fundamental factors of human personality, the tendency to approach.

With regards to avoidance-related behavior, glucose metabolism rates in the amygdala predict some aspects of negative affective reactions and predict the differential ability to understand NA (i.e., affect clarity). Additionally, individual differences in baseline activation of the right prefrontal cortex predict individual differences in negative affective functioning as well as behavioral inhibition and wariness (Davidson et al., 2000). Neuroticism (and depression) has been associated with the activation levels of the serotonin transporter gene 5-HT (Canli et al., 2006). This gene appears to moderate the effects of stress on depression, rumination, and activation of brain areas associated with NA. Thus, 5-HT may be linked with neuroticism, which is in turn linked with NA, the BIS system, and avoidance motivation. Although a less direct connection than that between approach and DRD4, 5-HT may represent a gene underlying the tendency to avoid.

CONCLUSION

The tendencies to approach and to avoid have been implicated, both on a theoretical and an empirical level, as two of the most fundamental dimensions underlying human personality, as well as individual differences in the behavior patterns of other mammals (Mehta & Gosling, 2006). Broad links between the personality traits of extraversion, positive affectivity, and the behavioral activation system suggest an underlying dispositional tendency to approach. Additionally, broad links between the personality traits of neuroticism, negative affectivity, and the behavioral inhibition system suggest an underlying dispositional tendency to avoid. Although these two super traits may not encapsulate all of human personality, findings from social psychology, affective neuroscience, and genomic science

all implicate the two constructs of dispositional approach and avoidance as central to our understanding of both the form and the function of personality.

ACKNOWLEDGMENT

Preparation of this chapter was supported in part by grant RO1-MH63732 from the National Institute of Mental Health.

REFERENCES

Algom, D., Chajut, E., & Lev, S. (2004). A rational look at the emotional Stroop phenomenon: A generic slowdown, not a Stroop effect. *Journal of Experimental Psychology: General, 133*, 323–338.

Ashton, M. C., Lee, K., & Paunonen, S. V. (2002). What is the central feature of extraversion? Social attention versus reward sensitivity. *Journal of Personality and Social Psychology, 83*, 245–252.

Baker, L. A., Cesa, I. L., Gatz, M., & Grodsky, A. (1992). Genetic and environmental influences on positive and negative affect: Support for a two-factor theory. *Psychology of Aging, 7*, 158–163.

Ball, S. A., & Zuckerman, M. (1990). Sensation seeking, Eysenck's personality dimensions and reinforcement sensitivity in concept formation. *Personality and Individual Differences, 11*, 343–353.

Baxter, L. R., Schwartz, J. M., Phelps, M. E., Mazziotta, J. C., Guze, B. H., Selin, C. E., et al. (1989). Reduction of prefrontal cortex glucose metabolism common to three types of depression. *Archives of General Psychiatry, 46*, 243–250.

Bunce, S. C., Larsen, R. J., & Cruz, M. (1993). Individual differences in the excitation transfer effect. *Personality and Individual Differences, 15*, 507–514.

Cacioppo, J. T., & Gardner, W. L. (1999). Emotion. *Annual Review of Psychology, 50*, 191–214.

Canli, T. (2004). Functional brain mapping of extraversion and neuroticism: Learning from individual differences in emotion processing. *Journal of Personality, 72*, 1105–1132.

Canli, T. (2006a). *The biology of personality and individual differences*. New York: The Guilford Press.

Canli, T. (2006b). Genomic imaging of extraversion. In T. Canli (Ed.), *Biology of personality and individual differences* (pp. 93–115). New York: The Guilford Press.

Canli, T., Qiu, M., Omura, K., Congson, E., Haas, B. W., Amin, Z., et al. (2006). Neural correlates of epigenesis. *Proceedings of the National Academy of Sciences, 103*, 16033–16038.

Canli, T., Zuo, Z., Kang, E., Gross, J., Desmond, J. E., & Gabrieli, J. D. (2001). An fMRI study of personality influences on brain reactivity to emotional stimuli. *Behavioral Neuroscience, 115*, 33–42.

Carver, C. S., & Scheier, M. F. (1990). Origins and functions of positive and negative affect: A control-process view. *Psychological Review, 97*, 19–35.

Carver, C. S., Sutton, S. K., & Scheier, M. F. (1999). Action, emotion, and personality: Emerging conceptual integration. *Personality and Social Psychology Bulletin, 26,* 741–751.

Carver, C. S., & White, T. L. (1994). Behavioral inhibition, behavioral activation, and affective responses to impending reward and punishment: The BIS/BAS scales. *Journal of Personality and Social Psychology, 67,* 319–333.

Cloninger, C. R. (1987). A systematic method of clinical description and classification of personality variants: A proposal. *Archives of General Psychiatry, 44,* 573–588.

Cloninger, C. R., Svrakic, D. M., & Przybeck, T. R. (1993). A psychobiological model of temperament and character. *Archives of General Psychiatry, 50,* 975–990.

Conley, J. J. (1985). Longitudinal stability of personality traits: A multitrait-multimethod-multioccasion analysis. *Journal of Personality and Social Psychology, 49,* 1266–1282.

Costa, P. T., & McCrae, R. R. (1980). Influence of extraversion and neuroticism on subjective well-being: Happy and unhappy people. *Journal of Personality and Social Psychology, 36,* 668–678.

Costa, P. T., & McCrae, R. R. (1992). *Revised NEO personality inventory (NEO-PI-R) and NEO five-factor inventory (NEO-FFI) professional manual.* Odessa, Florida: Psychological Assessment Resources.

Cronbach, L. J., & Meehl, P. (1955). Construct validity in psychological tests. *Psychological Bulletin, 52,* 281–302.

Dalgleish, T. (1995). Performance on the emotion Stroop task in groups of anxious, expert, and control subjects: A comparison of computer and card presentation formats. *Cognition and Emotion, 9,* 341–362.

Davidson, R. J. (1993a). The neuropsychology of emotion and affective style. In M. Lewis & J. M. Haviland (Eds.), *Handbook of emotions* (pp. 143–154). New York: The Guilford Press.

Davidson, R. J. (1993b). Parsing affective space: Perspectives from neuropsychology and psychophysiology. *Neuropsychology, 7,* 464–475.

Davidson, R. J. (1998). Affective style and affective disorders: Perspective from affective neuroscience. *Cognition and Emotion, 12,* 307–330.

Davidson, R. J., Ekman, P., Saron, C. D., Senulis, J. A., & Friesen, W. V. (1990). Approach/withdrawal and cerebral asymmetry: Emotional expression and brain physiology. *Journal of Personality and Social Psychology, 58,* 330–341.

Davidson, R. J., Jackson, D. C., & Kallin, N. H. (2000). Emotion plasticity, context and regulation: Perspectives from affective neuroscience. *Psychological Bulletin, 126,* 890–909.

DePascalis, V. (2004). On the psychophysiology of extraversion. In R. M. Stelmack (Ed.), *On the psychobiology of personality: Essays in honor of Marvin Zuckerman* (pp. 295–327). New York: Elsevier Science.

Depue, R. A. (1996). A neurobiological framework for the structure of personality and emotion: Implications for personality disorders. In J. F. Clarkin & M. F. Lenzenweger (Eds.), *Major theories of personality disorder* (pp. 347–390). New York: The Guilford Press.

Depue, R. A., & Collins, P. F. (2000). Neurobiology of the structure of personality: Dopamine, facilitation of incentive motivation, and extraversion. *Behavioral and Brain Sciences, 22,* 491–569.

Diener, E. (1984). Subjective well-being. *Psychological Bulletin, 95,* 542–575.

Digman, J. M. (1990). Personality structure: Emergence of the five-factor model. *Annual Review of Psychology, 41,* 417–440.

Digman, J. M. (1997). Higher order factors of the big five. *Journal of Personality and Social Psychology, 73,* 1246–1256.

Eisenberger, N. I., Lieberman, M. D., & Satpute, A. B. (2005). Personality from a controlled processing perspective: An fMRI study of neuroticism, extraversion, and self-consciousness. *Cognitive, Affective, and Behavioral Neuroscience, 5,* 169–181.

Elliot, A. J., & Thrash, T. M. (2002). Approach–avoidance motivation in personality: Approach and avoidance temperament goals. *Journal of Personality and Social Psychology, 82,* 804–818.

Emmons, R. A., & Diener, E. (1986). Influence of impulsivity and sociability on subjective well-being. *Journal of Personality and Social Psychology, 50,* 1211–1215.

Emmons, R. A., Diener, E., & Larsen, R. J. (1986). Choice and avoidance of everyday situations and affect congruence: Two models of reciprocal interactionism. *Journal of Personality and Social Psychology, 51,* 815–826.

Eysenck, H. J. (1951). The organization of personality. *Journal of Personality, 20,* 101–117.

Eysenck, H. J. (1967). *The biological bases of personality.* Springfield, IL: Charles C. Thomas.

Eysenck, H. J. (1998). *Dimensions of personality.* New Brunswick, NJ: Transaction Press.

Eysenck, H. J., & Eysenck, M. W. (1985). *Personality and individual differences.* New York: Plenum Press.

Eysenck, S. B. G., Eysenck, H. J., & Barrett, P. (1985). A revised version of the Psychoticism scale. *Personality and Individual Differences, 6,* 21–29.

Eysenck, S. B., Pearson, P. R., Easting, G., & Allsopp, J. F. (1985). Age norms for impulsiveness, venturesomeness and empathy in adults. *Personality and Individual Differences, 6,* 613–619.

Fleeson, W., Malanos, A. B., & Achille, N. M. (2002). An intraindividual process approach to the relationship between extraversion and positive affect: Is acting extraverted as "good" as being extraverted? *Journal of Personality and Social Psychology, 83,* 1409–1422.

Fordyce, M. W. (1983). A program to increase happiness: Further studies. *Journal of Counseling Psychology, 30,* 483–498.

Fox, N. A., Bell, M. A., & Jones, N. A. (1992). Individual differences in response to stress and cerebral asymmetry. *Developmental Neuropsychology, 8,* 165–184.

Fox, N. A., & Davidson, R. J. (1986). Taste-elicited changes in facial signs of emotion and the asymmetry of brain electrical activity in human newborns. *Neuropsychologia, 24,* 417–422.

Fredrickson, B. L. (1998). What good are positive emotions? *Review of General Psychology, 2,* 300–319.

Frijda, N. H. (1994). Emotions are functional, most of the time. In P. Ekman & R. J. Davidson (Eds.), *The nature of emotion: Fundamental questions* (pp. 112–122). New York: Oxford University Press.

Gable, S. L., Reis, H. T., & Elliot, A. J. (2003). Evidence for bivariate systems: An empirical test of appetition and aversion across domains. *Journal of Research in Personality, 37*, 349–372.

Goldsmith, H. H., Aksan, N., Essex, M., & Vandell, D. L. (2001). Temperament and socioemotional adjustment to kindergarten: A multi-informant perspective. In T. D. Wachs & G. A. Kohnstamm (Eds.), *Temperament in context* (pp. 103–138). Mahwah, NJ: Lawrence Erlbaum.

Gomez, R., Cooper, A., & Gomez, A. (2000). Susceptibility to positive and negative mood states: A test of Eysenck's, Gray's, and Newman's theories. *Personality and Individual Differences, 29*, 351–365.

Gray, J. A. (1990). Brain systems that mediate both emotion and cognition. *Motivation and Emotion, 4*, 269–288.

Gray, J. A. (1994). Personality dimensions and emotion systems. In P. Ekman & R. J. Davidson (Eds.), *The nature of emotion: Fundamental questions* (pp. 329–331). New York: Oxford University Press.

Headey, B., Glowacki, T., Holmstrom, E., & Wearing, A. (1985). Modeling change in perceived quality of life (PQOL). *Social Indicators Research, 17*, 267–298.

Hemenover, S. H. (2003). Individual differences in rate of affect change: Studies in affective chronometry. *Journal of Personality and Social Psychology, 85*, 121–131.

Kardum, I. (1999). Affect intensity and frequency: Their relation to mean level variability of positive and negative affect and Eysenck's personality traits. *Personality and Individual Differences, 26*, 33–47.

King, L. A. (1998). Ambivalence over emotional expression and reading emotions in situations and faces. *Journal of Personality and Social Psychology, 74*, 753–762.

Lang, P. J. (1995). The emotion probe: Studies of motivation and attention. *American Psychologist, 50*, 372–385.

Larsen, R. J. (1992). Neuroticism and selective encoding and recall of symptoms: Evidence from a combined concurrent-retrospective study. *Journal of Personality and Social Psychology, 62*, 480–488.

Larsen, R. J. (2000). Toward a science of mood regulation. *Psychological Inquiry, 11*, 129–141.

Larsen, R. J., & Buss, D. (2007). *Personality psychology: Domains of knowledge about human nature.* New York: McGraw-Hill.

Larsen, R. J., Chien, B. Y., & Zelenski, J. (2008). *Extraversion, neuroticism, reward, and punishment: Processing hedonic information in the emotion-word stroop task.* Manuscript under review.

Larsen, R. J., & Diener, E. (1992). Problems and promises with the circumflex model of emotion. *Review of Personality and Social Psychology, 13*, 25–59.

Larsen, R. J., & Fredrickson, B. L. (1999). Measurement issues in emotion research. In D. Kahneman, E. Diener, & N. Schwarz (Eds.), *Well-being: The foundations of hedonic psychology* (pp. 40–60). New York: Russell Sage Foundation.

Larsen, R. J., & Kasimatis, M. (1990). Individual differences in entrainment of mood to the weekly calendar. *Journal of Personality and Social Psychology, 58*, 164–171.

Larsen, R. J., & Ketelaar, T. (1989). Extraversion, neuroticism, and susceptibility to positive and negative mood induction procedures. *Personality and Individual Differences, 10*, 1221–1228.

Larsen, R. J., & Ketelaar, T. (1991). Personality and susceptibility to positive and negative emotional states. *Journal of Personality and Social Psychology, 61*, 132–140.

Larsen, R. J., & Prizmic, Z. (2006). Multimethod measurement of emotion. In M. Eid & E. Diener (Eds.), *Handbook of measurement: A multimethod perspective* (pp. 337–352). Washington, DC: American Psychological Association.

LeDoux, J. (1996). *The emotional brain: The mysterious underpinnings of emotional life.* New York: Simon & Schuster.

Lishman, W. A. (1972). Selective factors in memory. Part 1: Age, sex, and personality attributes. *Psychological Medicine, 2*, 121–138.

Lucas, R. E., & Diener, E. (2001). Understanding extraverts enjoyment of social situations: The importance of pleasantness. *Journal of Personality and Social Psychology, 81*, 343–356.

Lucas, R. E., Diener, E., Grob, A., Suh, E. M., & Shao, L. (2000). Cross-cultural evidence for the fundamental features of extraversion. *Journal of Personality and Social Psychology, 79*, 452–468.

Lykken, D., & Tellegen, A. (1996). Happiness is a stochastic phenomenon. *Psychological Science, 7*, 186–189.

Martin, M., Ward, J. C., & Clark, D. M. (1983). Neuroticism and the recall of positive and negative personality information. *Behaviour Research and Therapy, 21*, 495–503.

Matthews, G. (2000). Attention, automaticity, and affective disorder. *Behavior Modification, 24*, 69–93.

Matthews, G., Derryberry, D., & Siegle, G. J. (2000). Personality and emotion: Cognitive science perspectives. In S. E. Hampson (Ed.), *Advances in personality psychology* (Vol. 1, pp. 199–237). Philadelphia: Taylor & Francis.

McCrae, R. R., & Costa, P. T. (1991). Adding liebe und arbeit: The full five-factor model and well-being. *Personality and Social Psychology Bulletin, 17*, 227–232.

McCrae, R. R., Terracciano, A., et al. (2005). Universal features of personality traits from the observer's perspective: Data from 50 cultures. *Journal of Personality and Social Psychology, 88*, 547–561.

Mehta, P. H., & Gosling, S. D. (2006). How can animal studies contribute to research on the biological bases of personality? In T. Canli (Ed.), *Biology of personality and individual differences* (pp. 427–448). New York: The Guilford Press.

Necowitz, L. B., & Roznowski, M. (1994). Negative affectivity and job satisfaction: Cognitive processes underlying the relationship and effects on employee behaviors. *Journal of Vocational Behavior, 45*, 270–294.

Nezlek, J. B., Imbrie, M., & Shean, G. D. (1994). Depression and everyday social interaction. *Journal of Personality and Social Psychology, 67*, 1101–1111.

Norman, W. T. (1963). Toward an adequate taxonomy of personality attributes: Replicated factor structure in peer nomination personality ratings. *Journal of Abnormal Psychology, 66*, 574–583.

Pickering, A. D., Corr, P. J., & Gray, J. A. (1999). Reply to Rusting and Larsen (1999). *Personality and Individual Differences, 26*, 357–365.

Pickering, A. D., & Gray, J. A. (1999). The neuroscience of personality. In L. A. Pervin & O. P. John (Eds.), *Handbook of personality: Theory and research* (pp. 277–299). New York: The Guilford Press.

Plomin, R., & Caspi, A. (1999). Behavioral genetics and personality. In L. A. Pervin & O. P. John (Eds.), *Handbook of personality: Theory and research* (pp. 251–276). New York: The Guilford Press.

Reis, H. T., Sheldon, K. M., Gable, S. L., Roscoe, J., & Ryan, R. M. (2000). Daily well-being: The role of autonomy, competence, and relatedness. *Personality and Social Psychology Bulletin, 26*, 419–435.

Rusting, C. L. (1998). Personality, mood, and cognitive processing of emotional information: Three conceptual frameworks. *Psychological Bulletin, 124*, 165–196.

Rusting, C. L., & Larsen, R. J. (1997). Extraversion, neuroticism, and susceptibility to positive and negative affect: A test of two theoretical models. *Personality and Individual Differences, 22*, 607–612.

Rusting, C. L., & Larsen, R. J. (1998). Personality and cognitive processing of affective information. *Personality and Social Psychology Bulletin, 24*, 200–213.

Rusting, C. L., & Larsen, R. J. (1999). Clarifying Gray's theory of personality: A response to Pickering, Corr, and Gray. *Personality and Individual Differences, 26*, 167–172.

Salovey, P., Mayer, J. D., Goldman, S. L., Turvey, C., & Palfai, T. P. (1995). Emotional attention, clarity and repair: Exploring emotional intelligence using the Trait-Meta-Mood Scale. In J. W. Pennebaker (Ed.), *Emotion, disclosure and health* (pp. 125–154). Washington, DC: American Psychological Association.

Schonfeld, I. S. (1996). Relation of negative affectivity to self-reports of job stressors and psychological outcomes. *Journal of Occupational Health Psychology, 1*, 397–412.

Shulman, T. E., Augustine, A. A., & Hemenover, S. H. (2006). Studies in affect regulation: Linking affective chronometry and repair ability. In A. V. Clark (Ed.), *Psychology of Moods: New Research* (pp. 117–142). Hauppauge: Nova.

Sutton, S. K., & Davidson, R. J. (1997). Prefrontal brain asymmetry: A biological substrate of the behavioral approach and inhibition systems. *Psychological Science, 8*, 214–210.

Swinkels, A., & Giuliano, T. A. (1995). The measurement and conceptualization of mood awareness: Monitoring and labeling one's mood states. *Personality and Social Psychology Bulletin, 21*, 934–949.

Tellegen, A. (1985). Structures of mood and personality and their relevance to assessing anxiety, with an emphasis on self-report. In A. H. Tuma & J. D. Maser (Eds.), *Anxiety and the anxiety disorders* (pp. 681–706). Hillsdale, NJ: Erlbaum.

Tomarken, A. J., Davidson, R. J., & Henriques, J. B. (1990). Resting frontal brain asymmetry predicts affective responses to films. *Journal of Personality and Social Psychology, 59*, 791–801.

Walker, M. S., Larsen, R. J., Zona, D. M., Govindan, R., & Fisher, E. B. (2004). Smoking urges and relapse among lung cancer patients: Findings from a preliminary retrospective study. *Preventive Medicine, 39*, 449–457.

Watson, D. (2000). *Mood and temperament.* New York: The Guilford Press.

Wheeler, R. W., Davidson, R. J., & Tomarken, A. J. (1993). Frontal brain asymmetry and emotional reactivity: A biological substrate of affective style. *Psychophysiology, 30*, 82–89.

Williams, J. M. G., Mathews, A. & MacLeod, C. (1996). The emotion Stroop task and psychopathology. *Psychological Bulletin, 120*, 3–24.

Zelenski, J. M. (2007). Experimental approaches to individual differences and change: Exploring the causes and consequences of extraversion. In A. D. Ong & M. van Dulmen (Eds.), *Handbook of methods in Positive Psychology* (pp. 205–219). New York: Oxford University Press.

Zelenski, J. M., & Larsen, R. J. (1999). Susceptibility to affect: A comparison of three personality taxonomies. *Journal of Personality, 67*, 761–791.

Zelenski, J. M., & Larsen, R. J. (2000). The distribution of emotions in everyday life: A state and trait perspective from experience sampling data. *Journal of Research in Personality, 34*, 178–197.

Zuckerman, M., Joireman, J., Kratl, M., & Kuhilan, D. M. (1999). Where do motivational and emotional traits fit within three factor models of personality. *Personality and Individual Differences, 26*, 487–504.

Basic Dispositions in Nonhuman Animals

10 Individual Differences in Approach and Avoidance Motivation in Animals

Amanda C. Jones and Samuel D. Gosling

CONTENTS

Approach motivation may be defined as the tendency to direct behavior toward positive (e.g., rewarding) stimuli, and avoidance motivation as the tendency to direct behavior away from negative or undesirable (e.g., punitive) stimuli (Elliot, 2008). To survive, all animals, ranging from amoeba (Schneirla, 1959) to humans (Elliot & Thrash, 2002), must approach and avoid various situations, objects, and possibilities. The likelihood of an animal engaging in approach and avoidance behavior varies across situations and it also varies across individuals, with some individuals showing a greater propensity than others to engage in approach or avoidance behavior. In this chapter we focus on the latter case—individual differences in approach and avoidance—in nonhuman animals.

Individual differences in approach and avoidance motivation have been identified in a wide range of animal species, ranging from great tits (Both, Dingemanse, Drent, & Tinbergen, 2005; van Oers, Drent, de Goede, & van Noordwijk, 2003) and guppies (Budaev, 1997) to mice (Kazlauckas et al., 2005) and chimpanzees (Hebb, 1949). In this chapter we review the evidence for such individual differences in nonhuman animals. We focus on the benefits of using animal models to examine approach and avoidance and the major findings that animal studies have yielded.

LITERATURE REVIEW

Our discussion of animal research on approach and avoidance is based on a review of the literature. Previous studies differ in the terms they prefer with some using "personality" and others using "temperament." Although conceptual distinctions can be drawn between these two terms, the distinctions are not maintained clearly or consistently in the animal domain (Gosling, 2001; Jones & Gosling, 2005) so we treat the two terms as equivalent in the present chapter. Therefore, to identify relevant articles, we searched the PsycINFO and Biosis databases for articles containing the keywords "approach" and "avoidance," and either "personality" or "temperament".

An additional search was performed to find studies including "approach" and "avoidance", and "extraversion" and "neuroticism", because the personality traits of extraversion and neuroticism have been associated with approach behavior and avoidance behavior, respectively (Elliot & Thrash, 2002). Articles were included only if they focused on nonhuman animals and investigated approach or avoidance motivation as individual-difference variables. This review may have missed some relevant articles but the selected articles are sufficiently broad to illustrate the benefits of animal research and the findings that are emerging in this field.

The 28 articles identified in our search are summarized in Tables 10.1 through 10.3. The articles can be organized into three categories: Those that establish approach and avoidance as personality dimensions (summarized in Table 10.1), those that examine the antecedents of approach and avoidance motivation (Table 10.2), and those that examine the consequences of approach and avoidance motivation (Table 10.3). The categories are overlapping and some articles accomplish multiple goals, so some studies appear in more than one table. In each table, columns one through four present the basic details about each study. The main findings, particularly those relevant to approach or avoidance motivation, are summarized in column five. As we shall see, animal models afford several methodological benefits; the particular benefits exploited by each study are listed in columns six through nine.

EMPIRICAL STUDIES OF APPROACH AND AVOIDANCE MOTIVATION AS PERSONALITY DIMENSIONS IN ANIMALS

Here we explore the key features of the field represented in this sample, including the terminology, the methods used, the species studied, the sex of animals, the disciplines represented, and the goals of the research. This brief analysis is instructive in illustrating the diversity of research in this domain.

TABLE 10.1

Research Establishing Approach and Avoidance Motivation as Personality Dimensions

Study	Species	N	Sex	Main Finding(s)	Methodological Benefits			
					Experimental Control	Measure of Physiological Parameters	Naturalistic Observation	Accelerated Life History
Budaev (1997)	Guppies (*Poecilia reticulata*)	29	Males	PCA[a] of 83 behaviors shown during four test situations (open field test, predator inspection test, mirror test, schooling tendency test) revealed four dimensions: Activity exploration (AE), fear-avoidance, sociability, locomotion.	X	X	Some (high AE fish were caught first)	
Budaev (1998)[b]	Mice, paradise fish	775 mice, 120 paradise fish	Both	PCA[a] of mice and paradise fish behavior in two independent data sets revealed two dimensions: Fear-avoidance and activity exploration.	X			
Fairbanks (2001)	Vervet monkeys (*Cercopithecus aethiops sabaeus*)	128	Males	Vervet monkeys showed reliable individual differences in "impulsivity" in response to an intruder.	X			
Hebb (1949)	Chimpanzees	30	Both	Chimpanzees showed reliable individual differences in frequency of behaviors associated with avoidance, timidity, friendliness (approach), etc.	X			
Kazlauckas et al. (2005)[c]	Mice	79, reduced to 30	Males	Across time and situation, mice showed consistent exploratory behavior.	X			
Mather and Anderson (1993)	Octopuses (*Octopus rubescens*)	44	Not reported	Factor analysis of octopus behavior revealed three dimensions: Activity, reactivity, and avoidance.	X			
Mettke-Hofmann et al. (2005)	Sardinian warbler (*Sylvia melanocephala momus*), Garden warbler (*Sylvia borin*)	13 Garden warblers, 15 Sardinian warblers	Both	Sardinian warblers showed consistent, negatively correlated responses to neophobia and exploratory tests, but garden warblers failed to show consistent behavior (across time). Approach and avoidance may not be stable individual differences in garden warblers.	X			

(*continued*)

TABLE 10.1 (Continued)

Research Establishing Approach and Avoidance Motivation as Personality Dimensions

Study	Species	N	Sex	Main Finding(s)	Methodological Benefits			
					Experimental Control	Measure of Physiological Parameters	Naturalistic Observation	Accelerated Life History
Pollard et al. (1994)	Red deer (*Cervus elaphus*), red deer * Pere David Deer hybrids (*Cervus elaphus * Elaphurus davidianus*)	Study 1: 30 red deer; Study 2: 22 Hybrid and 34 red deer	Study 1: males; Study 2: Both	PCA[a] of deer behavior displayed during temperament testing reveals two dimensions: Fear (of humans) and exploratory behavior. Reliability across tests was low.	X	X		
Ray and Hansen (2004)	Rats	64	32 males, 32 females	PCA[a] of rats' behavior on hole board and canopy test revealed two dimensions: Harm avoidance and novelty seeking.	X	X		
Rèale et al. (2000)	Bighorn sheep (*Ovis canadensis*)	Variable (natural population)	Females	Docility and boldness (measured by tendency to be trapped and behavior when handled) were consistent within individuals.	X (limited)	X	X (included capture in wild)	
Sinn and Moltschaniwskyj (2005)	Dumpling squid (*Euprymna tasmanica*)	97	33 females, 64 males	Squids' behavior was not reliable across contexts (context-specific).	X	X		
Sinn et al. (2001)	Octopuses (*Octopus bimaculoides*)	73	Females	PCA[a] of octopuses' behavior displayed during the third week of life revealed four dimensions: Active engagement, arousal/readiness, aggression, and avoidance/disinterest.	X			X
Svartberg et al. (2005)	Dogs (*Canis familiaris*)	40–81; varied by test	Both	Dogs' behavior during testing was related to personality dimensions labeled as playfulness, chase-proneness, sociability, boldness, aggressiveness, and curiosity/fearfulness. All but aggressiveness and curiosity/fearfulness were reliable across test situations.	X			
van Oers et al. (2003)	Great tits (*Parus major*)	94 captured, 73 laboratory bred	Both	Risk-taking behavior is reliable in both wild-captured and laboratory-bred birds.	X			X (breeding)

Note: [a]   PCA, principle components analysis.

       [b]   Reanalysis of data from Royce, Poley, and Yeudall (1973) and Gervai and Csányi (1985).

       [c]   A number of studies fit in two or more categories of research; if so, they are listed in more than one table but the main findings summarized are restricted to those that are most pertinent to the category in which they are listed.

TABLE 10.2

Research on the Antecedents of Approach and Avoidance Motivation

Study	Species	N	Sex	Main Finding(s)	Experimental Control	Measure of Physiological Parameters	Naturalistic Observation	Accelerated Life History
Both et al. (2005)	Great tits (*Parus major*)	Varied by analysis	Both	Exploratory behavior is heritable.			X	X
Carere et al. (2005)	Great tits (*Parus major*)	34	18 Males, 16 females	Exploratory behavior is heritable.	X (including selective breeding)			X
Castanon and Mormède (1994)	Roman rats (2 strains)	Varied by analysis (range: 6–10/group)	Both	Genetic and maturational factors played a role in reactivity to stress in both rat strains, but the roles differed.	X (selective breeding, environment)	X		
Clarke and Lindburg (1993)	Cynomolgus macaques, lion-tailed macaques	5 Cynomolgus macaques, 5 lion-tailed macaques	Males	Lion-tailed macaques showed more interest in other animals, higher vigilance, more instrumental behavior, and greater readiness to enter a novel cage than Cynomolgus macaques. These were interpreted as greater boldness, curiosity, and instrumental behavior.	X			
Dulawa et al. (1999)	D4R+/+ (wild-type) and D4R–/– (dopamine D4 receptor knock-out) mice	Variable (range: 18–85/group)	Both	Dopamine influences novelty-related exploration. D4R–/– mice were less behaviorally responsive in all tests, indicating a decrease in novelty-related exploration.	X	X		
Fairbanks (2001)	Vervet monkeys (*Cercopithecus aethiops sabaeus*)	128	Males	Vervet monkeys' impulsivity scores peaked at age 4 (when monkeys leave their natal group) and showed relationships to dominance status.	X			
Herman et al. (1986)	Brattleboro rats (vasopressin-deficient, diabetic), Long-Evans rats	40 (20 of each strain, 10 of each from each supplier)	Males	Overall results indicate within- and between-strain differences (related to vasopressin deficiency) as well as between-colony differences in temperament-related behavior (i.e., approach/avoidance and avoidance learning).	X	X (vasopressin-deficient Brattleboro strain)		

(*continued*)

TABLE 10.2 (Continued)
Research on the Antecedents of Approach and Avoidance Motivation

Study	Species	N	Sex	Main Finding(s)	Methodological Benefits			
					Experimental Control	Measure of Physiological Parameters	Naturalistic Observation	Accelerated Life History
Ray and Hansen (2004)	Rats	64	32 Males, 32 females	Differences in rats' avoidance and novelty-seeking behavior were found based on sex, reproductive status, and (in females) estrus cycle phase.	X	X		
Réale et al. (2000)	Bighorn sheep (*Ovis canadensis*)	Variable (natural population)	Females	Mixed results on heritability of docility and boldness.	X (limited)	X	X (included capture in wild)	
Saetre et al. (2006)	Dogs (*Canis familiaris*) (breeds: German Shepherd Dogs and Rottweilers)	>10,000	Both	Greater than 50% of genetic variation could be explained by a single broad component (shyness–boldness); only aggression seems independently inherited.	X	X		
Sinn and Moltschaniwskyj (2005)	Dumpling squid (*Euprymna tasmanica*)	97	33 Females, 64 males	Squids' behavior was not predicted by sex or reproductive condition but was predicted by age.	X	X		
Sinn et al. (2001)	Octopuses (*Octopus bimaculoides*)	73	Females	Findings indicated significant changes in temperament as octopuses' age and significant effects of relatedness.	X			X
Shaklee (1963)	Firemouth (*Chichlasoma meeki*), Platy variatus	Variable	Both; variable by study and species	Firemouth and Platy variatus showed systematic light avoidance.	X			

Study	Species	Sample Size	Sex	Findings		
	(Xiphophorus variatus), Zebra fish (Brachydanio rerio), Goldfish (Carassius auratus)					
Markowitz et al. (1998)	Targhee sheep (Ovis aries)	96 (48 twin sets)	Not reported	Lambs fed by humans showed less avoidance of humans in temperament tests. Greatest effect was in lambs fed by humans at 1–3 days of age.	X	
Pollard et al. (1994)	Red deer (Cervus elaphus), red deer * Pere David Deer hybrids (Cervus elaphus *Elaphurus davidianus)	Study 1: 30 red deer; Study 2: 22 hybrid and 34 red deer	Study 1: males; Study 2: both	No strong effects of genotype.	X	X
Svartberg et al. (2005)	Dogs (Canis familiaris)	40–81; varied by test	Both	Aggressiveness and curiosity/fearfulness decreased from Test 1 to Test 2, indicating that these traits may be sensitive to novelty and experience.	X	
Utsurikawa (1917)	Rats	Not reported	Both	Inbred and outbred rats appear to show differences in temperament. Inbred rats generally appear more avoidant, fearful, and aggressive but less active.	X	
van Oers et al. (2003)	Great tits (Parus major)	94 Captured, 73 laboratory bred	Both	Risk taking is heritable.	X	X (breeding)

Note: A number of studies fit in two or more categories of research; if so, they are listed in more than one table but the main findings summarized are restricted to those that are most pertinent to the category in which they are listed.

TABLE 10.3

Research on the Consequences of Approach and Avoidance Motivation

Study	Species	N	Sex	Main Finding(s)	Methodological Benefits			
					Experimental Control	Measure of Physiological Parameters	Naturalistic Observation	Accelerated Life History
Both et al. (2005)	Great tits (*Parus major*)	Varied by analysis	Both	Reproductive success varied as a function of exploratory behavior, with most and least exploratory parents producing largest, healthiest offspring			X	X
Budaev and Zhuikov (1998)	Guppies (*Poecilia reticulata*)	23	Males	Guppies high in fear-avoidance and low in active exploration were fastest to learn active avoidance of shock; fear-avoidance was only influential in guppies low in active exploration.	X	X		
Carere et al. (2005)	Great tits (*Parus major*)	34	18 Males, 16 females	Birds categorized as "fast" explorers showed more consistent behavior across time and situation, whereas "slow" explorers appeared more reactive and showed more variation in behavior.	X (including selective breeding)			X
Clarke and Lindburg (1993)	Cynomolgus macaques, lion-tailed macaques	5 Cynomolgus macaques, 5 lion-tailed macaques	Males	Interest in other animals, vigilance, instrumental behavior, and readiness to enter a novel cage were seen as behavioral manifestations of boldness, curiosity, and instrumental behavior.	X			
Hebb (1949)	Chimpanzees	30	Both	Chimpanzees showed reliable individual differences in frequency of behaviors associated with avoidance, timidity, friendliness (approach), etc.	X			

Study	Species	N	Sex	Findings		
Kazlauckas et al. (2005)	Mice	79, reduced to 30	Males	Highly exploratory mice showed more aggression and higher cognitive ability.	X	
Mettke-Hofmann et al. (2005)	Sardinian warbler (*Sylvia melanocephala momus*), garden warbler (*Sylvia borin*)	13 garden warblers, 15 Sardinian warblers	Both	Sardinian warblers showed consistent, negatively correlated responses to neophobia and exploratory tests, but garden warblers failed to show consistent behavior (across time). Approach and avoidance may not be stable individual differences in garden warblers.	X	
Quinn and Cresswell (2005)	Chaffinches (*Fringilla coelebs*)	37	24 Males, 13 females	Higher activity was associated with greater predator avoidance, supporting a hypothesis of differing predation risk across individuals (due to personality).	X	
Svartberg et al. (2005)	Dogs (*Canis familiaris*)	40–81; varied by test	Both	Behaviors were related to personality dimensions of playfulness, chase-proneness, sociability, boldness, aggressiveness, and curiosity/fearfulness.	X	
Visser et al. (2003)	Horses (breed: Dutch Warmblood)	38 (reduced from 41)	24 Males, 14 females	A significant proportion of variability in show-jumping performance can be predicted from early personality tests. Furthermore, postures (e.g., tail elevation) previously thought indicative of nervousness were not correlated with avoidance behavior or heart rate.	X	X (e.g., heart rate)

Note: A number of studies fit in two or more categories of research; if so, they are listed in more than one table but the main findings summarized are restricted to those that are most pertinent to the category in which they are listed.

TERMINOLOGY

As described above, all of the studies in our review were identified by using the keywords "approach" and "avoidance". But even with this select set of articles, a variety of other, more specific terms were also used to discuss approach- and avoidance-related behaviors. For example, specific terms for describing avoidance-related behaviors and tendencies have included "neophobia" (Mettke-Hofmann, Ebert, Schmidt, Steiger, & Stieb, 2005) and "curiosity/fearfulness" (Svartberg, Tapper, Temrin, Radesäter, & Thorman, 2005). Terms used to describe approach-related behaviors and tendencies have included "exploratory behavior" (Mettke-Hofmann et al., 2005; Pollard et al., 1994), "novelty seeking" (Ray & Hansen, 2004), "risk-taking behavior" (van Oers et al., 2003), and "boldness" (Rèale, Gallant, LeBlanc, & Festa-Bianchet, 2000; Svartberg et al., 2005).

Most animal studies have not examined the degree to which approach and avoidance motivation are related. However, previous research on humans and animals suggests the dimensions are separable (Larsen & Augustine, 2008); several of the 28 studies reviewed here looked at approach alone (seven studies) or avoidance alone (two studies).

ASSESSMENT METHODS

In almost all of the studies reviewed, approach and avoidance motivation were assessed by observing animals' responses to novel situations or stimuli, whether potentially positive (e.g., food) or negative (e.g., predators). For example, to assess exploratory tendencies, Both et al. (2005) observed how rapidly great tits moved from branch to branch in a novel, tree-filled environment. Mettke-Hofmann et al. (2005) exposed Sardinian and garden warblers to novel objects (food, a mop head) to assess their neophobia (fear and avoidance of the novel objects) and exploratory behaviors. As these examples illustrate, approach motivation has generally been measured in terms of amount of exploratory ambulation (e.g., jumping from branch to branch, Both et al.; movement during an open field test, Garcia-Sevilla, 1984; tendency to approach and inspect a predator, Budaev, 1997). Avoidance motivation has typically been measured in terms of movement away from or failure to approach a stimulus (e.g., systematic light avoidance, Shaklee, 1963; predator avoidance, Quinn & Cresswell, 2005; avoidance of people, Rèale et al. 2000). Note that it is not the case that a single paradigm is associated with tests of either approach or avoidance; a single paradigm, like the predator-approach paradigm, can be used to detect approach (reflected in predator approach and inspection) or avoidance (reflected in movement away from or failure to approach a stimulus). In such contexts it may be difficult to assess approach and avoidance as separable dimensions.

SPECIES STUDIED

Approach and avoidance tendencies have been examined in a relatively broad array of taxa, as can be seen in column 2 of Tables 10.1 through 10.3. Animals represented include birds (e.g., great tits, Both et al., 2005; Carere, Drent, Privitera, Koolhaas, & Groothuis, 2005; van Oers et al., 2003; Sardinian and garden warblers, Mettke-Hofmann et al., 2005; chaffinches, Quinn & Cresswell, 2005), fish (e.g., guppies, Budaev, 1997; paradise fish, Budaev, 1998; Firemouth, Platy variatus, Zebra fish, Goldfish, Shaklee, 1963), cephalopods (squid, Sinn & Moltschaniwskyj, 2005; octopuses, Mather & Anderson, 1993), rodents (rats, Castanon & Mormède, 1994; mice, Dulawa, Grandy, Low, Paulus, & Geyer, 1999), and primates (Cynomolgus and lion-tailed macaques, Clarke & Lindburg, 1993; chimpanzees, Hebb, 1949; vervet monkeys; Fairbanks, 2001), among others.

SEX OF ANIMALS

Most of the studies included both sexes. However, a few studies failed to report the sex of their subjects, and many studies examining both males and females did not report how many animals of each sex were included. Of those that looked at only one sex, six studies (just over 21% of the studies in the review) looked at males only, and two looked at females only. Although both sexes have received attention, very little is known about sex-linked differences in approach and avoidance in animals. One of the few research programs to explore sex differences has focused on the sexually monomorphic species, dumpling squid; these studies revealed no sex differences in approach and avoidance behavior (Sinn, Apiolaza, & Moltschaniwskyj, 2006; Sinn, Gosling, & Moltschaniwskyj, in press; Sinn & Moltschaniwskyj, 2005).

DISCIPLINES LOOKING AT APPROACH AND AVOIDANCE MOTIVATION AS PERSONALITY DIMENSIONS

The studies included in this sample are drawn from two general areas of study: Biological or comparative psychology and animal behavior. This array of disciplines is somewhat narrower than those exploring personality in dogs, which included animal behavior, biology, psychology, animal welfare, and veterinary medicine

(Jones & Gosling, 2005), or animal personality more broadly, which included primatology, anthropology, animal behavior, psychology, veterinary medicine, and applied agriculture, among others (Gosling, 2001).

Weinstein, Capitanio, and Gosling (2006) identified three broad goals driving research on animal personality. The first goal is to understand animals in their own right, with the aim of elucidating the role of behavior in the species' ecology; comparisons across species and across ecologies can be used to inform broader questions about the evolutionary process shaping these traits. The second goal of animal research is to use animals as a model for furthering our understanding of human behavior; for example, animal studies have been used for many years to shed light on numerous basic psychological processes ranging from sensation and perception to learning and social behavior (Domjan & Purdy, 1995). The third goal is to examine personality with the aim of making practical use of animals (e.g., testing their suitability as guide dogs) or improving their welfare (e.g., reducing stress in animal shelters). The studies of approach and avoidance included in this review are primarily conducted with respect to the first and second of these goals.

Within these goals, a number of substantive findings have emerged from animal studies of approach and avoidance motivation. The findings tend to inform one of the two broad areas: The antecedents of approach and avoidance and the consequences of approach and avoidance. These distinctions drive the organization of the second half of our chapter, which will follow our discussion of the benefits of animal research.

WHAT ARE THE BENEFITS OF EXAMINING APPROACH AND AVOIDANCE MOTIVATION IN ANIMALS?

Animal studies derive benefits from the fact that they permit research that is difficult or impossible to do using human participants. In particular, animal research affords at least four basic types of benefits: (1) greater experimental control, (2) more options for measuring physiological parameters, (3) greater opportunity for naturalistic observation, and, in many species, (4) faster maturation and progression through life phases. In this section, we will illustrate each benefit using studies from the review and we will evaluate trends in the extent to which researchers have utilized these benefits.

BENEFIT 1: GREATER EXPERIMENTAL CONTROL

With nonhuman animals as subjects, researchers are able to perform manipulations that are difficult or impossible

with humans. Through these manipulations, studies of animals have the potential to shed new light on how such factors as experience, breeding, and genes are related to approach and avoidance motivation.

Environmental Manipulations (Control of Exposure/Experiences)

The environments and experiences of captive animals (e.g., those in laboratories or zoos) are largely controlled by the people who manage them. Thus, researchers studying captive animals can carefully manipulate the animals' environments and experiences, and record the animals' responses. For example, Markowitz, Dally, Gursky, and Price (1998) experimentally manipulated the age at which lambs experienced extensive handling and feeding by humans. The researchers were interested in determining how the timing of this early socialization experience affected the lambs' affinity for (approach toward) humans. Results indicated that lambs that have 40 min of positive interaction with a human during days 1–3 of life show greater approach behavior when compared with lambs that experienced positive contact with humans at later ages and than controls (who had minimal contact with humans). The lambs socialized from days 1–3 were quicker to contact people and spent more time in close proximity to people. Clearly, although such intrusive manipulations are powerful and highly informative, they would not be possible in human studies.

Selective Breeding of a Population

The degree to which nature (genetics) and nurture (environment) combine to shape behavior continues to intrigue researchers and laypeople alike. It is now clear that the two components interact in a complex manner, making it especially important to find ways to exercise experimental control over the genetic make-up and experiences of a population. Such control can be achieved through selective breeding of a population of animals so that they are genetically predisposed to demonstrate a particular behavior of interest; at the extreme, inbred strains are the clearest example, but with advances in cloning technology, studies using true genetic clones are also beginning to appear (Iguchi, Matsubara, & Hakoyama, 2001).

Carere et al. (2005) studied stability of great tits' approach and avoidance behavior within and across situations, looking at two different populations of great tits; one population was bred to be fast approachers (i.e., approach novel objects quickly, show a large amount of movement in an open field test), and the other was bred to be slow approachers (i.e., approach novel objects slowly, show a small amount of movement in an open field test). Among their results was the finding that fast birds tended to be more consistent in their approach and amount of movement than slow birds; slow birds showed greater behavioral plasticity, often becoming faster to approach novel objects over repeated testing.

Castanon and Mormède (1994) compared reactivity to stress in two strains of Roman rats that were selectively bred for their avoidance behavior: Roman low avoidance (RLA) and Roman high avoidance (RHA) rats. By utilizing two intentionally bred strains of rats, the researchers aimed to tease apart the role of genetics and of experience during maturation in shaping avoidance behavior. They found that the role of maturation varied across the two strains of rats, with maturation having a greater impact on RLA rats, indicating that changes during maturation may be more variable and genetic factors may be less plastic in some strains than in others.

Genetic Manipulations

A profoundly strong method for examining the impact of genetics on behavior is directly manipulating genes through knock out (where individuals are missing a specific gene) or transgenic (those in which a gene has been inserted) studies—methods clearly impossible to implement with human subjects. A behavior with great potential for exploration through this method is novelty seeking, or a tendency to approach stimuli not previously encountered. In personality-inventory studies of humans, novelty seeking has been linked to polymorphisms of the human dopamine D4 receptor (Benjamin, Patterson, Greenberg, Murphy, & Hamer, 1996; Ebstein et al., 1996). Researchers seeking to examine the mechanisms underlying this relationship have turned to mice models. For example, Dulawa et al. (1999) compared dopamine D4 receptor–knock-out mice (D4R−/−) and wild-type mice (D4R+/+) with the goal of examining whether D4R primarily influences the exploratory or anxious component of responses to the approach–avoidance conflict. To do this, the researchers used three tests: An open field test in which mice were placed in an open, novel, exposed area that forced exploratory behavior because there was no possible escape from novelty; an emergence test in which mice were able to either explore the open field or hide in a cylinder; and a novel object test in which mice were free to explore a novel object in a nonthreatening, familiar environment. They found that the knock-out mice were less exploratory in response to all three tests. The smallest differences between the groups were in the open field test, which elicits the most avoidance behavior. The largest differences were observed in the novel object test, which maximizes approach behavior.

Functional Genomics

The notion that genes and the environment exert independent effects on behavior has long been deemed simplistic and obsolete (Hamer, 2002; Robinson, 2004). Scientists now know that gene expression itself is influenced by both heredity and the environment. Variation in gene expression affects protein activity, brain processes, and ultimately, behavior. Through the development of new genomic techniques using animal models, investigators can measure gene expression by quantifying the amount of messenger RNA (mRNA) produced by a particular gene. The ability to measure gene expression through mRNA allows researchers to consider complex, dynamic models of gene–behavior relationships. Not only can researchers investigate how environmental and hereditary factors interact to influence gene expression, but also variation in gene expression can also be examined as a predictor of subsequent brain processes and behavior. Through research conducted in animals, psychologists have begun to understand the interplay between hereditary and environmental influences on genetic activity and individual differences (Gosling & Mollaghan, 2006). These methods have begun to illuminate neural mechanisms that underlie approach and avoidance behavior (Lindberg et al., 2005).

BENEFIT 2: GREATER OPPORTUNITIES TO MEASURE PHYSIOLOGICAL PARAMETERS

With animals as subjects, experimenters have unique opportunities to measure physiological parameters that may underlie approach and avoidance behavior. For example, some physiological measurements require decapitation and examination of brain areas, and others necessitate precise experimental control to allow for frequent, precisely timed sampling of the measure. These and other requirements point to the use of animal models.

Morphological Measurements

Although morphological measurements can be taken in humans, animal studies allow researchers to take particularly detailed measurements, especially when the animals can be sedated. These methods allow researchers to examine numerous indexes of fitness such as injury history or body mass (López, Hawlena, Polo, Amo, & Martín, 2005; Sinn & Moltschaniwskyj, 2005; Ward, Thomas, Hart, & Krause, 2004). For example, Rèale et al. (2000) recorded the body mass of wild bighorn ewes by capturing and sedating the sheep. They examined the relationship between body mass and the ewes' tendency to approach a food-baited trap. Results indicated no relationship between "boldness" and body mass.

Neurological Measurements

In the early 1960s, it was discovered that rats of a certain strain, diabetes insipidus Brattleboro rats, are unable to synthesize vasopressin in their brains; vasopressin was later implicated in approach behavior. The rats' inability to synthesize vasopressin is due to an autosomal genetic mutation (Valtin & Schroeder, 1964). The deficit cannot be restored through such manipulations as injection of vasopressin (Herman, Thomas, Laycock, Gartside, & Gash, 1986). Knowledge of the condition of diabetes insipidus Brattleboro rats allowed researchers to explore vasopressin's functioning in relation to approach and avoidance behavior. For example, Herman et al. (1986) examined variability in how normal (Long Evans) and diabetes insipidus (Brattleboro) rats acquire approach and avoidance behaviors. Results indicated that the two groups varied significantly such that vasopressin may shape behavior related to goal approach by affecting arousal, attentiveness, and memory, which may cause the rats' decreased ability to acquire approach and avoidance behaviors. The authors concluded that a vasopressin deficiency may lead to changes in temperament, including an increase in approach behavior due to a decreased tendency to attend to or remember aversive experiences.

BENEFIT 3: GREATER OPPORTUNITIES FOR OBSERVATION

To illustrate the observational opportunities in animal studies, consider a 4-year observational study of a large natural population of great tits that examined the relationship between reproductive success and exploratory behavior (Both et al., 2005). Researchers captured birds, tagged them, and tested their behavior in a novel environment. Exploration, arguably linked to boldness and approach behavior, was scored as the number of times a bird hopped between branches on a tree and flights between trees or perches during the brief test. The birds were then released back into their natural environments and their reproductive success was tracked. Naturalistic factors (e.g., habitat quality) were taken into account. Exploratory behavior was temporally stable and genetically heritable and affected reproductive success, with the most and least exploratory birds producing the largest, healthiest offspring.

With animals as subjects, experimenters have numerous opportunities for experimental and naturalistic observation. Animals can be observed for extended time periods, in great detail, and in virtually any situation or context. Over the last decade, a large array of tests have been developed to assess different elements of approach and avoidance behaviors. With advances in computing, the observation of many behaviors is becoming increasingly amenable to automation (Izquierdo, Wellman, & Holmes, 2006a; Izquierdo et al., 2006b; Millstein, Ralph, Yang, & Holmes, 2006). In fact, some variables (e.g., prepulse inhibition, Millstein et al., 2006) can only be measured by specially designed automated equipment. Other variables (e.g., freezing behavior) can be measured by automation, but are more accurately and reliably measured by human observation (Izquierdo et al., 2006a), and automation cannot observe all variables (e.g., a computer cannot accurately determine whether an animal is immobile because it froze or because it is sedated or dead). The greater opportunities for observation are particularly pronounced for animals in captivity, which can be observed for their entire lives; for example, Sinn et al. (in press) examined approach and avoidance behaviors in 41 dumpling squid tested every 3 weeks from birth through adulthood. Researchers may also observe animals in their natural environments. Naturalistic observation may be limited by various factors (e.g., how elusive the animal is), but is still likely to afford more observation than is practical in naturalistic studies of humans.

BENEFIT 4: ACCELERATED LIFE HISTORY

Given the short life spans of many species, studies of animals permit longitudinal studies that last the entire life course, from conception to natural death, in a relatively short time (e.g., weeks, for some species), and allow multigenerational studies (Sinn et al., 2006). This benefit allows researchers to examine the relationship between genes, experience, and approach and avoidance behavior by looking at an entire breeding season and the maturation of resulting offspring. Equivalent studies of humans would take decades, would be tremendously costly, and would be very challenging to conduct.

In species with short life spans, researchers can also selectively breed animals and then monitor the development of the offspring. For example, van Oers et al. (2003) bred great tits to demonstrate that risk-taking behavior had a genetic component. Because great tits reach sexual maturity relatively early (compared to humans) and because gestational periods are brief, the researchers were able to test birds' risk-taking tendencies, then selectively breed birds with high and low levels of risk-taking behavior for two generations.

Results indicated that the trait has a heritability of about 19% in great tits.

MAJOR FINDINGS FROM ANIMAL STUDIES OF APPROACH AND AVOIDANCE MOTIVATION

Studies of nonhuman animals have yielded numerous substantive findings relevant to individual differences in approach and avoidance motivation. In this section, we describe some of the major findings to emerge from the animal literature. We divide the review into three broad sections. The first section describes research establishing approach and avoidance as personality dimensions in animals, the second describes research on the antecedents of approach and avoidance, and the third describes studies of the consequences of approach and avoidance.

APPROACH AND AVOIDANCE MOTIVATION AS PERSONALITY DIMENSIONS

The first subset of studies in our review (summarized in Table 10.1) focused on establishing approach and avoidance motivation as personality dimensions. These studies have yielded three main findings: Individual animals' approach and avoidance behaviors are consistent over time, they can be found across a variety of environments and species, and they seem to reflect two relatively independent dimensions.

To examine the consistency across time of approach- and avoidance-related behaviors, Mettke-Hofmann et al. (2005) compared neophobic and exploratory behaviors of Sardinian and garden warblers during two different seasons in a year. Neophobia was tested by observing and recording birds' latency to approach their feeding dish when a novel object (a mop head) had been placed beside it. Exploratory behavior was tested by placing a different novel object (a tube) in the birds' environment and recording the birds' latency to approach and explore the tube. Birds were first tested at the end of their breeding season, then tested again 10 months later (in Spring). They found that only Sardinian warblers' behavior was consistent across the two tests. Their findings suggested that temporal consistence can be found but is not guaranteed. In a similar vein, Sinn et al. (in press) examined behavioral responses of dumpling squid to a threat stimulus (avoidance) and a feeding situation (approach) tested twice every 3 weeks from 3 to 16 weeks of age; the consistency with which individuals expressed avoidance and approach

behaviors varied across the lifespan and each trait showed a different pattern of consistency. Specifically, squid became more consistent in their responses through juvenile periods in both threat and feeding contexts but sexual maturity (weeks 9–12) brought a period of major behavioral reorganization, in which consistency virtually disappeared. After the maturation process (weeks 12–16) avoidance behavior stabilized but consistency in approach behavior was not regained over the 4 weeks measured in adulthood. Their findings suggest that maturation may impact the consistency with which individuals display approach and avoidance behaviors. Because they found that avoidance stabilized in adulthood but approach did not, their findings indicate that these two types of behaviors may not always show parallel patterns of stability and development.

The studies in our review also indicate that approach and avoidance dimensions can be found in species that occupy a broad array of ecologies, from octopuses (Mather & Anderson, 1993) and rats (Garcia-Sevilla, 1984) to great tits (van Oers et al., 2003) and deer (Pollard, Littlejohn, & Webster, 1994). Across these species, approach and avoidance are exhibited through a variety of behaviors, ranging from behavior during handling (Rèale et al., 2000) to response to a person in a unfamiliar costume (Svartberg et al., 2005) and systematic light avoidance (Shaklee, 1963). By examining the behavior of mice and paradise fish in parallel, Budaev (1998) provides further evidence that analogous patterns of approach and avoidance behavior can be found in species that occupy very different ecologies. He used factor analysis to identify the major dimensions underlying behavior in mice and paradise fish, removing any unique variables (or specific behaviors) that did not appear to be correlated with other variables examined. A set of two parallel factors were found to underlie behavior in the two species, despite substantial differences between the species, their ecological niches, and the behavioral testing conditions. When these factors were compared with those from other studies (Budaev, 1997), they were found to be consistent with the previously labeled factors, activity-exploration and fear-avoidance.

Researchers have also addressed the question of whether approach and avoidance should be considered as the two poles of a single dimension or as independent dimensions. For example, Mettke-Hofmann et al. (2005) found that neophobia and exploratory behavior were negatively correlated in Sardinian warblers, but independent in garden warblers. Garcia-Sevilla (1984) investigated the relationship between movement (linked to approach) and defecation (linked to avoidance) in rats.

Rats placed in a minimally frightening environment showed consistent individual differences in how much they moved around the environment but showed no significant patterns of defecation; the two types of behaviors were independent.

Other researchers have used factor analyses of animals' performance on behavioral tests to determine the extent to which approach and avoidance should be considered independent factors in animals (Mather & Anderson, 1993; Pollard et al., 1994; Ray & Hansen, 2004; Sinn, Perrin, Mather, & Anderson, 2001). For example, Pollard et al. collected behavioral data from multiple administrations of personality tests in 30 newly weaned, male red deer calves. Calves were tested in two groups of 15 on various personality tests, including latency to eat in the presence of a human, latency to sniff a novel object, aggression during feeding, and behavior during various confinement conditions (e.g., with or without a human). The calves' scores on each test were rank ordered. Principle components analysis (PCA) of the data revealed two underlying factors driving behavior across the various types of personality tests: Exploratory behavior and fear of humans. Thus, findings derived from correlations of small numbers of behavior as well as PCAs of larger arrays of behavior converge to suggest that approach and avoidance tend to reflect largely independent dimensions, although there are some exceptions.

There is clearly much psychometric and structural work to be done but the findings to date suggest three broad conclusions. First, approach and avoidance often demonstrate temporal consistency, although such consistency is by no means guaranteed. Second, approach and avoidance dimensions can be found across a wide range of species, despite differences between species in how the behaviors are expressed, the ecological niches in which they live, and how the dimensions were tested. Third, and consistent with findings from the human domain, approach and avoidance motivation are best conceived as two separable dimensions.

ANTECEDENTS OF APPROACH AND AVOIDANCE MOTIVATION

Studies of the antecedents that may underlie individual differences in approach and avoidance motivation are summarized in Table 10.2.

Approach and Avoidance Motivation Have a Genetic Basis

Several animal studies of approach and avoidance motivation have examined the role of genetics. All but one of

the studies reviewed here indicate a genetic basis for approach and avoidance behavior. For example, rats have been selectively bred to form strains that differ in their reactivity to stress (Castanon & Mormède, 1994), which is thought to be related to and possibly form a basis for avoidance behavior. Even without selective breeding for the trait, rat littermates show similar levels of ambulation (Garcia-Sevilla, 1984), which is linked to exploratory behavior. However, it is possible that these differences are driven by differences in the animals' environments or their interactions with their parents. Studies of great tits also provide evidence for a genetic basis for exploratory and risk-taking behavior but by using hand rearing they reduce the potential roles of environment and rearing. For example, van Oers et al. (2003) captured, hand reared, and then individually housed great tits before testing their exploratory and risk-taking behavior. They used scores from these tests to selectively breed high- and low-risk-taking birds, which were then tested for exploratory and risk-taking behaviors. Strong relationships between parents' and offsprings' risk-taking behavior were identified. These relationships are thought to be based on genetics, not environment or experience, because the birds were hand reared and thus did not learn exploratory tendencies from their parents. Kinship is also a significant factor in determining Sardinian warblers' responses to novelty and to exploratory tests (Mettke-Hofmann et al., 2005) and octopuses' responses to tests of approach and avoidance (Sinn et al., 2001). Similarly, Saetre et al. (2006) found that the heritability of boldness (reflecting approach behavior) was high in German shepherd dogs and Rottweilers. The one exception in this pattern of findings was Rèale and colleagues' (2000) studies of a natural population of bighorn sheep ewes, which found mixed results for the heritability of approach and avoidance tendencies. Despite this exception, the majority of studies found evidence for a substantial genetic component driving individual differences in approach and avoidance motivation.

Physiology Influences Approach and Avoidance Motivation

Several studies have focused on the roles of endocrinology and neurology in approach and avoidance motivation. Herman et al. (1986) found that vasopressin deficiency may be related to an increase in fearfulness (e.g., defecation) in the diabetes insipidus Brattleboro rat, although diabetes insipidus rats also showed a decreased tendency to remember aversive events. Variations in neurological receptors also shape behavioral reactivity by controlling how much of a neurotransmitter is used. For example, dopamine D4R knock-out mice, which are less responsive to dopamine, show less approach toward novel objects when compared to normal, wild mice (Dulawa et al., 1999). In these examples, the animal literature implicates vasopressin as related to increased avoidance behavior, and dopamine as related to approach behavior. More broadly, animal research indicates that endocrine and neurological variations can have direct ties to animals' approach and avoidance behavior. It may be possible that these systems operate by changing the animals' subjective experience of stimuli; for example, perhaps animals which are highly sensitive to dopamine experience surges of pleasure when they venture into new territory as a result of dopamine that is released. Differences in this reward pathway in the brain may play a fundamental role in explaining individual differences in approach behaviors (Depue & Collins, 1999).

Experience Influences Approach and Avoidance Behaviors

Although personality has a strong genetic basis, it is also influenced by experience. Several animal studies have supported the role of experience in shaping approach and avoidance behavior. For example, as noted above, Markowitz et al. (1998) found that lambs socialized to humans at 1–3 days of age were subsequently more sociable with humans than were controls or lambs socialized at other ages. Evidence from a study of dogs suggests that even brief experiences can affect approach and avoidance behavior. Svartberg et al. (2005) found that dogs, aged 12–24 months assessed twice approximately a month apart, were more curious or fearless on their second test than their first. That is, dogs scored higher on a curiosity or fearlessness factor, which encompasses a variety of approach behaviors, including avoidance of startling stimuli and exploration in potentially frightening situations (e.g., in which someone suddenly appears, startling noises are made; Svartberg & Forkman, 2002). Svartberg and colleagues posit that dogs' curiosity and fearlessness may be extremely sensitive to experience. On closer investigation, the authors found that this change in response from Test 1 to Test 2 is dependent on individual differences in the dogs' scores at Test 1: Dogs that were more fearful on the first test subsequently showed less fear after even a single experience of the test. Together, these studies suggest that approach and avoidance behavior may be particularly sensitive to various types of experiences (e.g., early socialization, desensitization), but they also suggest there may be sensitive periods when socialization is more effective, and that some individuals may be more strongly impacted by experience.

Age Influences Approach and Avoidance Behaviors

As in studies of humans, some animal studies provide support for mean-level changes in personality with increases in age. It has been suggested that, in humans, avoidance motivation increases with age (Elliot, 1999). Other patterns may also exist, particularly in nonhuman animals. For example, Fairbanks (2001) found that monkeys' showed individual differences in impulsivity, but that across individuals, impulsivity peaked when the monkeys were ready to leave the natal group (about 4-years-old). Such increases in impulsivity may prepare the monkeys to leave their natal groups. These studies suggest the relationship between approach behavior and age may facilitate successful completion of necessary life tasks (e.g., leaving the natal group, mating). The findings raise the possibility that changes in human approach and avoidance motivation could be associated with challenges in the human life course. Perhaps, for example, an increase in anxiety and conscientiousness helps new parents care for infants.

CONSEQUENCES OF APPROACH AND AVOIDANCE MOTIVATION

The effects of approach and avoidance motivation are broad reaching, touching on outcomes as diverse as levels of stress, and the development of different types of diets. Approach and avoidance motivation have also been found to impact many aspects of health, including the ultimate measure of health, production of viable offspring. Here we review some of the main findings to emerge from the animal literature (Table 10.3).

Avoidance Motivation Affects Stress and Physical Health

Individuals higher in avoidance motivation are more likely than those lower in avoidance motivation to find situations stressful. This increased sensitivity could be beneficial by increasing the likelihood that an individual will be able to mobilize resources in time to avoid a negative situation (e.g., a predator), but it could be detrimental in captive animals which, for example, might be stressed by their daily environments or caretakers. Over-activating stress responses can have deleterious side effects on physical and mental health. Decreasing individuals' experience of avoidance motivation, whether through experience or changes in the environment, would be likely to improve their overall welfare. For different individuals, this requires different measures, because some are more prone to avoidance motivation and because individuals may differ in their reaction to certain stimuli. For example, Visser et al. (2003) found that some horses show behaviors linked to nervousness and stress during show-jumping performances. Horses showing these nervous and stressed behaviors are less likely to perform well than horses which do not show nervous and stressed behaviors. Visser et al. suggest that horses which experience a great amount of stress during show jumping should be considered for removal from training and placed in roles more suited to their personalities. However, assignment of individuals to situations based on their personalities may not be the only way to manage stress and improve welfare. As discussed above, Markowitz et al. (1998) found that early socialization of lambs can serve to decrease the avoidance behavior exhibited in response to typical stressors (e.g., people). Also discussed above, Svartberg et al. (2005) found that some individuals (those higher in fearfulness during initial assessments) may be especially sensitive to experience, showing a greater decrease in fear than animals which were more curious or fearless during initial assessments. Such work has direct practical applications; by considering both individual differences and the effects of experience, people keeping domesticated animals may be able to reduce their stress levels. Specifically, the findings could inform decisions on the placement of animals in environments so that environments most suitable to an animal's approach and avoidance levels are found, and by informing socialization choices so that animals are desensitized to stressors they will experience later. It is likely that the lessons learned about reducing stress in animals will also have uses in the human domain.

Avoidance Motivation Affects Predation Risk

In the animal kingdom, one obvious way to maintain health is to avoid predators. There is evidence that both approach and avoidance are relevant to this crucial task. Avoidance of predators can be facilitated by a highly sensitive startle response (probably related to avoidance motivation and general fearfulness), and also by maintaining a high level of activity (probably related to exploring and to approach motivation).

Quinn and Cresswell (2005) found a relationship between activity level and predator avoidance behaviors in chaffinches, such that active birds (generally showing more approach-linked behaviors) were less likely than inactive birds to be preyed upon. Budaev (1997) found individual differences in fear-avoidance of predators in guppies. Thus, different species, and indeed different individuals within a species, may draw on different motivational systems to avoid predators. And the local ecological conditions would influence the optimal level of approach and avoidance behaviors—highly avoidant animals would avoid predators but may incur costs such as opportunities for foraging and mating.

Approach and Avoidance Motivation Affect Production of Offspring

From an evolutionary standpoint, production of a large number of healthy, viable offspring to pass on an individuals' genetic material can be considered the ultimate measure of an individual's health. Animal studies suggest that approach and avoidance behaviors play a role in the production of viable offspring. For example, Both et al. (2005) found that approach and avoidance behaviors in great tits played significant roles in reproductive success. Neither the birds with the strongest tendencies to approach stimuli quickly nor those which are extremely cautious and slow to approach are the most successful. Rather, great tits which have either extreme of personality exhibit the most reproductive success. This study suggests that highly different personalities can be similarly beneficial in the great tits' environment. Both et al. suggest that fast- and slow-exploring great tits evolved so that they could fill different ecological niches. Fast-exploring males tended to occupy better territories and better nests, and slow-exploring birds make better parents because they are better adapted to finding food in inconsistent foraging conditions, being more likely to find, eat, and feed alternative foods. The use of alternative foods is particularly beneficial because slow-exploring birds are likely to live in lower quality territories where less food is available. Having fast- and slow-exploring great tits suited to different environments permits the coexistence of a greater number of individuals than would be possible if they all followed the same strategy. Together, studies of approach and avoidance and reproductive success suggest there is some variability across species and environments in which types of behaviors are best suited to mating and leaving viable offspring. No single set of approach and avoidance tendencies is universally superior to all others. The fact that different strategies are better at different times may help drive and maintain the evolution of individual differences in approach and avoidance tendencies (Dall, Houston, & McNamara, 2004; Nettle, 2006; Sih, Bell, & Johnson 2004a; Sih, Bell, Johnson, & Ziemba, 2004b; Wilson, 1998).

Approach Motivation Affects Behavioral Experimentation

Approach and avoidance motivation may affect the development and acquisition of not only short-term behaviors (e.g., predator avoidance), but also long-term behaviors (e.g., dietary choices). Clarke and Lindburg (1993) suggest that approach and avoidance motivation differences between lion-tailed and Cynomolgus macaques may underlie differences in their tool use and diet. Male Cynomolgus macaques show passive and reserved behavior compared to the lion-tailed macaques, which are described as showing bold, curious, and instrumental behaviors (e.g., interest in other animals and willingness to enter novel cages). The lion-tailed macaque also has a more omnivorous diet and developed an ability to manufacture and use tools. This study suggests that having a general tendency to approach novelty may encourage animals to try new things (e.g., foods, uses of objects), allowing for more diverse behavior. Future studies could investigate this possibility by examining the connection between approach prevalence and avoidance tendencies and the ecological niches in which these species (or their ancestors) lived.

Avoidance Motivation Affects Learning

It has long been suggested that fearful, avoidant animals might be quicker to acquire avoidance responses because they are already prone to avoidance. However, some studies have found no differences between high and low avoidance animals in terms of speed of learning. For example, Ray and Lenz (1968) hypothesized that more aroused and emotional rats would have greater difficulty acquiring a conditioned avoidance response than would less aroused, less emotional rats. To test their hypothesis, Ray and Lenz compared rats whose unconditioned stimulus was a relatively mild release of air (£25 per square inch [psi]) to those whose stimulus was a more intense release of air (40 psi). The rats exposed to 40 psi were more "emotional," as indicated by increased urination and defecation, but the two groups showed no difference in acquisition of the avoidance response. Other researchers have suggested that avoidant animals are slower to acquire avoidance responses because their fear or emotionality interferes with their learning of the response. However, animal studies of approach and avoidance behavior fail to provide a clear answer. In studies of guppies, Budaev and Zhuikov (1998) found that fishes with high levels of fear-avoidance and low levels of active exploration were faster to learn shock avoidance tasks. In a very different study, Visser et al. (2003) found that horses' performance on an avoidance-learning task, among other tests, negatively predicted later show-jumping performance. That is, highly avoidant horses performed worse than horses that did not show much avoidance behavior. Together, these two studies dispute Ray and Lenz's findings, but tentatively support the suggestion that avoidant animals may perform worse on potentially stress-inducing tasks.

Approach and Avoidance Motivation Affect Migration and Movement

Animal studies also suggest that approach and avoidance tendencies may play a role in animals' large-scale patterns of movement (e.g., migration; Dingemanse, Both, van Noordwijk, Rutten, & Drent, 2003; Fraser, Gilliam, Daley, Le, & Skalski, 2001). As mentioned above researchers have found that vervet monkeys' impulsivity scores peak around age 4 (Fairbanks, 2001), which is when they leave their natal groups, venturing out on their own without the safety and protection of their group. It is possible that the increase in impulsivity is necessary for vervet monkeys to make such a profound and potentially dangerous life change. In addition (nonmigratory) Sardinian warblers are less neophobic and more exploratory than (migratory) garden warblers (Mettke-Hofmann et al., 2005), further suggesting that the differing lifestyles, including migratory habits, of garden and Sardinian warblers require different levels of approach and avoidance. For example, living in a single location year round may require more approach behavior (especially exploration) to enable an individual to find enough food sources when food is scarce. In both the vervet monkey and the Sardinian warbler, it seems that high levels of approach motivation are related to exploratory behavior and these behaviors are consistent with the ecological challenges faced by each species.

CONCLUSION

Our review of the literature revealed that animal studies are taking advantage of the numerous benefits associated with animal research. Relatively few studies have examined approach and avoidance motivation as personality dimensions, but those which have done so are yielding important discoveries, both about topics that are typically examined in human studies (e.g., relationships between personality and age), and about topics that are not (e.g., evolution). However, research has only just begun to tap the seemingly limitless number of questions to be addressed. Many questions remain, and many more questions will surface as more is learned and as new techniques (e.g., automated observations) are developed.

We suggest that researchers studying approach and avoidance in humans may find it useful to consider the parallel animal literature. However, we also urge animal researchers to draw on findings from studies of other animal species, including humans. By integrating work in the animal and human domains, we anticipate that great advances will be made over the coming years in understanding approach and avoidance tendencies. Studies on the biological bases and health consequences of approach and avoidance are particularly amenable to a comparative approach and, we suspect, are particularly likely to benefit from a combined human–animal approach.

ACKNOWLEDGMENTS

Preparation of this chapter was supported by a National Science Foundation Graduate Research Fellowship to Amanda C. Jones. We are indebted to David Sinn for his valuable comments on an earlier draft of this chapter.

REFERENCES

Benjamin, J., Li, L., Patterson, C., Greenberg, B. D., Murphy, D. L., & Hamer, D. H. (1996). Population and familial association between the D4 dopamine receptor gene and measures of novelty seeking. *Nature genetics*, *12*, 81–84.

Both, C., Dingemanse, N. L., Drent, P. J., & Tinbergen, J. M. (2005). Pairs of extreme avian personalities have highest reproductive success. *Journal of Animal Ecology*, *74*, 667–674.

Budaev, S. (1997). "Personality" in the Guppy (*Poecilia reticulate*): A correlational study of exploratory behavior and social tendency. *Journal of Comparative Psychology*, *111*, 399–411.

Budaev, S. (1998). How many dimensions are needed to describe temperament in animals: A factor reanalysis of two data sets. *International Journal of Comparative Psychology*, *11*, 17–29.

Budaev, S., & Zhuikov, A. Y. (1998). Avoidance learning and "Personality" in the Guppy (*Poecilia reticulate*). *Journal of Comparative Psychology*, *112*, 92–94.

Carere, C., Drent, P. J., Privitera, L., Koolhaas, J. M., & Groothuis, G. G. (2005). Personalities in great tits, *Parus major*: Stability and consistency. *Animal Behaviour*, *70*, 795–805.

Castanon, N., & Mormède, P. (1994). Psychobiogenetics: Adapted tools for the study of coupling between behavioral and neuroendocrine traits of emotional reactivity. *Psychoneuroendocrinology*, *19*, 257–282.

Clarke, A. S., & Lindburg, D. G. (1993). Behavioral contrasts between male cynomolgus and lion-tailed macaques. *American Journal of Primatology*, *29*, 49–59.

Dall, S. R. X., Houston, A. I., & McNamara, J. M. (2004). The behavioural ecology of personality: Consistent individual differences from an adaptive perspective. *Ecology Letters*, *7*, 734–739.

Depue, R. A., & Collins, P. F. (1999). Neurobiology of the structure of personality: Dopamine, facilitation of incentive motivation, and extraversion. *Behavioral and Brain Sciences*, *22*, 491–569.

Dingemanse, N. J., Both, C., van Noordwijk, A. J., Rutten, A. L., & Drent, P. J. (2003). Natal dispersal and personalities in great tits (*Parus major*). *Proceedings of the Royal Society of London, Series B*, *270*, 741–747.

Domjan, M., & Purdy, J. E. (1995). Animal research in psychology: More than meets the eye of the general psychology student. *American Psychologist*, *50*, 496–503.

Dulawa, S. C., Grandy, D. K., Low, M. J., Paulus, M. P., & Geyer, M. A. (1999). Dopamine D4 receptor–knock-out mice exhibit reduced exploration of novel stimuli. *The Journal of Neuroscience*, *19*, 9550–9556.

Ebstein, R. P., Novick, O., Umansky, R., Priel, B., Osher, Y., Blaine, D., et al. (1996). Dopamine D4 receptor (D4DR) exon III polymorphism associated with the human personality trait of novelty seeking. *Nature genetics*, *12*, 78–80.

Elliot, A. J. (2008). Approach and avoidance motivation. In A. J. Elliot (Ed.), *Handbook of Approach and Avoidance Motivation* (pp. 3–14). Boca Raton, Florida: Taylor & Francis.

Elliot, A. J. (1999). Approach and avoidance motivation and achievement goals. *Educational Psychologist*, *34*, 169–189.

Elliot, A. J., & Thrash, T. M. (2002). Approach–avoidance motivation in personality: Approach and avoidance temperaments and goals. *Journal of Personality and Social Psychology*, *82*, 804–818.

Fairbanks, L. A. (2001). Individual differences in response to a stranger: Social impulsivity as a dimension of temperament in vervet monkeys (*Cercopithecus aethiops sabaeus*). *Journal of Comparative Psychology*, *115*, 22–28.

Fraser, D. F., Gilliam, J. F., Daley, M. J., Le, A. N., & Skalski, G. T. (2001). Explaining leptokurtic movement distributions: Intrapopulation variation in boldness and exploration. *The American Naturalist*, *158*, 124–135.

Garcia-Sevilla, L. (1984). Extraversion and neuroticism in rats. *Personality and Individual Differences*, *5*, 511–532.

Gervai, J., & Csányi, V. (1985). Behavior-genetic analysis of the paradise fish, *Macropodus opercularis*. I. Characterization of the behavioral responses of inbred strains in novel environments: A factor analysis. *Behavior Genetics*, *15*, 503–519.

Gosling, S. D. (2001). From mice to men: What can we learn about personality from animal research? *Psychological Bulletin*, *127*, 45–86.

Gosling, S. D., & Mollaghan, D. M. (2006). Animal research in social psychology: A bridge to functional genomics and other unique research opportunities. In P. A. M. van Lange (Ed.), *Bridging social psychology: Benefits of transdisciplinary approaches* (pp. 123–128). Mahweh NJ: Erlbaum.

Hamer, D. (2002). Genetics. Rethinking behavior genetics. *Science*, *298*, 71–72.

Hebb, D. O. (1949). Temperament in chimpanzees: I. Method of analysis. *Journal of Comparative and Physiological Psychology*, *42*, 192–206.

Herman, J. P., Thomas, G. J., Laycock, J. F., Gartside, I. B., & Gash, D. M. (1986). Behavioral variability within the

Brattleboro and Long-Evans rat strains. *Physiology & Behavior, 36,* 713–721.

Iguchi, K., Matsubara, N., & Hakoyama, H. (2001). Behavioural individuality assessed from two strains of cloned fish. *Animal Behaviour, 61,* 351–356.

Izquierdo, A., Wellman, C. L., & Holmes, A. (2006a). Brief uncontrollable stress causes dendritic retraction in infralimbic cortex and resistance to fear extinction in mice. *The Journal of Neuroscience, 26,* 5733–5738.

Izquierdo, A., Wiedholz, L. M., Millstein, R. A., Yang, R. J., Bussey, T. J., Saksida, L. M., et al. (2006b). Genetic and dopaminergic modulation of reversal learning in a touch-screen-based operant procedure for mice. *Behavioural Brain Research, 171,* 181–188.

Jones, A. C., & Gosling, S. D. (2005). Temperament and personality in dogs (*Canis familiaris*): A review and evaluation of past research. *Applied Animal Behaviour Science, 95,* 1–53.

Kazlauckas, V., Schuh, J., Dall'Igna, O. P., Pereira, G. S., Bonan, C. D., & Lara, D. R. (2005). Behavioral and cognitive profile of mile with high and low exploratory phenotypes. *Behavioural Brain Research, 162,* 272–278.

Larsen, R. J., & Augustine, A. A. (2008). Basic personality dispositions related to approach and avoidance: Extraversion/neuroticism, BAS/BIS, and positive/negative affectivity. In A. J. Elliot (Ed.), *Handbook of approach and avoidance motivation* (pp. 151–164). Boca Raton, Florida: Taylor & Francis.

Lindberg, J., Björnerfeldt, S., Saetre, P., Svartberg, K., Seehuus, B., Bakken, M., et al. (2005). Selection for tameness has changed brain gene expression in silver foxes. *Current Biology, 15,* R915–R916.

López, P., Hawlena, D., Polo, V., Amo, L., & Martín, J. (2005). Sources of individual shy-bold variations in antipredator behaviour of male Iberian rock lizards. *Animal Behaviour, 69,* 1–9.

Markowitz, T. M., Dally, M. R., Gursky, K., & Price, E. O. (1998). Early handling increases lamb affinity for humans. *Animal Behaviour, 55,* 573–587.

Mather, J. A., & Anderson, R. C. (1993). Personalities of octopuses (*Octopus rubescens*). *Journal of Comparative Psychology, 107,* 336–340.

Mettke-Hofmann, C., Ebert, C., Schmidt, T., Steiger, S., & Stieb, S. (2005). Personality traits in resident and migratory warbler species. *Behaviour, 142,* 1357–1375.

Millstein, R. A., Ralph, R. J., Yang, R. J., & Holmes, A. (2006). Effects of repeated maternal separation on prepulse inhibition of startle across inbred mouse strains. *Genes, Brain and Behavior, 5,* 346–354.

Nettle, D. (2006). The evolution of personality variation in humans and other animals. *American Psychologist, 61,* 622–631.

Pollard, J. C., Littlejohn, R. P., & Webster, J. R. (1994). Quantification of temperament in weaned deer calves of two genotypes (*Cervus elaphus* and *Cervus elaphus* × *Elaphurus davidianus* hybrids). *Applied Animal Behaviour Science, 41,* 229–241.

Quinn, J. L., & Cresswell, W. (2005). Personality, anti-predation behaviour and behavioural plasticity in the chaffinch *Fringilla coelebs. Behaviour, 142,* 1377–1402.

Ray, A. J. Jr., & Lenz, P. (1968). Pressurized air shuttle avoidance and emotionality. *The Journal of Genetic Psychology, 112,* 43–48.

Ray, J., & Hansen, S. (2004). Temperament in the rat: Sex differences and hormonal influence on harm avoidance and novelty seeking. *Behavioral Neuroscience, 118,* 488–497.

Rèale, D., Gallant, B. Y., LeBlanc, M., & Festa-Bianchet, M. (2000). Consistency of temperament in bighorn ewes and correlates with behaviour and life history. *Animal Behaviour, 60,* 589–597.

Robinson, G. E. (2004). Genomics. Beyond nature and nurture. *Science, 304,* 397–399.

Royce, J. R., Poley, W., & Yeudall, L. T. (1973). Behavior-genetic analysis of mouse emotionality: I. Factor analysis. *Journal of Comparative and Physiological Psychology, 83,* 36–47.

Saetre, P., Strandberg, E., Sundgren, P. E., Pettersson, U., Jazin, E., & Bergström, T. F. (2006). The genetic contribution to canine personality. *Genes, Brain and Behavior, 5,* 240–248.

Schneirla, T. (1959). An evolutionary and developmental theory of biphasic processes underlying approach and withdrawal. In *Nebraska Symposium on motivation* (pp. 1–42). Lincoln, Nebraska: University of Nebraska Press.

Shaklee, A. B. (1963). Comparative studies of temperament: Fear responses in different species of fish. *The Journal of Genetic Psychology, 102,* 295–310.

Sih, A., Bell, A., & Johnson, J. C. (2004a). Behavioral syndromes: An ecological and evolutionary overview. *Trends in Ecology and Evolution, 19,* 372–378.

Sih, A., Bell, A. M., Johnson, J. C., & Ziemba, R. E. (2004b). Behavioral syndromes: An integrative overview. *Quarterly Review of Biology, 79,* 241–277.

Sinn, D. L., Apiolaza, L. A., & Moltschaniwskyj, N. A. (2006). Heritability and fitness-related consequences of squid personality traits. *Journal of Evolutionary Biology, 19,* 1437–1447.

Sinn, D. L., Gosling, S. D., & Moltschaniwskyj, N. A. (in press). Lifetime development of shy/bold behaviour in squid: Consistency and change through the time and across contexts. *Animal Behavior.*

Sinn, D. L., & Moltschaniwskyj, N. A. (2005). Personality traits in dumpling squid (*Euprymna tasmanica*): Context-specific traits and their correlation with biological characteristics. *Journal of Comparative Psychology, 119,* 99–110.

Sinn, D. L., Perrin, N. A., Mather, J. A., & Anderson, R. C. (2001). Early temperamental traits in an octopus (*Octopus bimaculoides*). *Journal of Comparative Psychology, 115,* 351–364.

Svartberg, K., & Forkman, B. (2002). Personality traits in the domestic dog (*Canis familiaris*). *Applied Animal Behaviour Science, 79,* 133–155.

Svartberg, K., Tapper, I., Temrin, H., Radesäter, T., & Thorman, S. (2005). Consistency of personality traits in dogs. *Animal Behaviour, 69,* 283–291.

Utsurikawa, N. (1917). Temperamental differences between outbred and inbred strains of the albino rat. *The Journal of Animal Behavior, 7*, 111–129.

Valtin, H., & Schroeder, H. A. (1964). Familial hypothalamic diabetes insipidus in rats (Brattleboro strain). *American Journal of Physiology, 206*, 425–430.

van Oers, K., Drent, P. J., de Goede, P., & van Noordwijk, A. J. (2003). Realized heritability and repeatability of risk-taking behavior in relation to avian personalities. *Proceedings of the Royal Society of London, B, 271*, 65–73.

Visser, E. K., van Reenan, C. G., Engel, B., Schilder, M. B. H., Barnevald, A., & Blokhuis, H. J. (2003). The association between performance in show-jumping and personality traits earlier in life. *Applied Animal Behaviour Science, 82*, 279–295.

Ward, A. J. W., Thomas, P., Hart, P. J. B., & Krause, J. (2004). Correlates of boldness in three-spined sticklebacks (*Gasterosteus aculeatus*). *Behavioral Ecology and Sociobiology, 55*, 561–568.

Weinstein, T., Capitanio, J. P., & Gosling, S. D. (2006). Animal studies of personality. In O. P. John, R. W. Robins, & L. A. Pervin (Eds.), *Handbook of personality theory and research*. New York: Guilford.

Wilson, D. S. (1998). Adaptive individual differences within single populations. *Philosophical Transactions of the Royal Society of London, Series B, 353*, 199–205.

Behavioral Genetics

11 Genetic Influences on Individual Differences in Approach and Avoidance

H. Hill Goldsmith and Kathryn Lemery-Chalfant

CONTENTS

The notions of approach and avoidance hold tremendous potential for linking disparate concepts and subdisciplines of biobehavioral science, as contributions to this volume amply demonstrate. Genetic research tends not to be an initial line of inquiry in research on approach and avoidance, but we can readily assimilate approach and avoidance to concepts that have been investigated from a genetic perspective. For instance, we can link approach and avoidance to temperament and emotion regulation, domains where the behavior-genetic approach has been employed.

In doing so, we adopt a developmental perspective and focus mainly on research with children in this chapter.

The organizational plan for the chapter is first to specify the domains of individual differences that we will treat. The main body of the chapter is organized around four topics: inferences from twin studies, candidate gene studies, endophenotypes, and gene–environment interactions. After a brief explanation of methods or concepts subsumed by these four topics, we present illustrative research related to approach or avoidance tendencies, or their regulation. We emphasize human twin research because the bulk of relevant research uses twin methodology. Then, we treat some added complexities of genetic analysis. We close with a forecast of how a genetic perspective can help refine our understanding of approach and avoidance motivation.

The behavior-genetic framework continually evolves; it incorporates any method of linking genetic influences to behavior, and it involves synergistic connections between human and nonhuman (mostly mouse) research strategies (Goldsmith, 2003). In broad perspective, human behavior-genetic approaches can be divided into quantitative genetic approaches (or genetic epidemiology) and molecular genetic approaches (mainly linkage and association studies). Prospects are brightening for widespread integration of molecular and quantitative genetic approaches and for dealing with complex, nonlinear systems from a genetic perspective. However, most of the emphasis in this chapter is on human quantitative genetic approaches.

Behavior-genetic analysis is about individual differences. Thus, the relevant perspectives on approach and avoidance for behavior-genetic analyses are those that focus on individual differences, such as those overviewed by Larsen (chapter 9, this volume). Larsen makes the case that the broad personality dimension of extraversion, or positive affect, can be aligned with approach motivation; similarly, neuroticism, or negative affect, is strongly linked to avoidance motivation (Elliot & Thrash, 2002). With some translation to children, we shall use the personality/temperament dimensions and scales designated by Larsen as falling under the approach or avoidance rubrics to define the pool of exemplars for our illustrations of behavior-genetic approaches.

At the outset, we assert that no plausible "genetic level" definition of approach or avoidance motivation exists, nor should it. Rather, genetic questions can be posed regarding approach and avoidance defined at a behavioral level. Features of behavioral definitions of approach and avoidance that optimize the chances of fruitful genetic investigation include (1) centrality of individual differences, (2) links with biological processes, and (3) feasibility of assessment in large samples. For many of the measures used in genetic studies, it would be very difficult to distinguish basic "reactive" tendencies to approach or avoid from the regulation of this reactivity. The plausibility of validly distinguishing reactive from regulatory concepts in questionnaire measures is particularly dim. Regulation of approach and avoidance tendencies is closely tied conceptually to affect regulation. Thus, in this chapter, we also consider affect regulation.

The regulation of affect has become a field of intensive study (Fox, 1994; Gross, 2007). Regulatory processes allow the individual to adjust to situational changes and modulate emotional responses. Multiple goals, sometimes within the same situation, may elicit different and sometimes incongruent forms of emotion regulation (Thompson & Calkins, 1996). During early infancy, when intrinsic emotion regulation abilities are limited, caregiver behavior may provide exogenous emotion regulation for the infant. As early development proceeds, individual differences in emotion regulation are likely influenced by biological differences in executive attentional systems in the anterior attention network in the prefrontal cortex (Rueda, Posner, & Rothbart, 2004). The instrumental behaviors being regulated are often approach or avoidance.

Affect regulation is integral to conceptualizations of temperament (Derryberry & Rothbart, 1997; Goldsmith, Lemery, Aksan, & Buss, 2000). The rubric of temperament, in turn, subsumes approach and avoidance tendencies. Thus, studies of the genetics of approach and avoidance, at least during infancy and childhood, are alternately construed as studies of the genetics of temperament. Temperament can be defined as individual differences in emotional reactivity (Goldsmith & Campos, 1982), and approach and avoidance are often instrumental manifestations of that reactivity. Contemporary researchers understand temperament to be dynamic rather than static; its reactive and regulatory components are manifested differentially across the first years of life (Rothbart & Bates, 2006).

With this background, we now turn to a sample of methods and concepts from behavioral genetics that can be used to analyze approach and avoidance.

TWIN METHOD: CONCEPTS AND APPLICATION TO APPROACH AND AVOIDANCE

At the outset, it is important to realize that no single method such as twin studies stands alone in the behavior-genetic framework as a basis for inference. Most behavior-genetic designs are quasi-experimental or correlational, and each has its strengths and shortcomings. Confident inferences depend on replication within and confirmation across methods.

KEY CONCEPTS: HERITABILITY AND ENVIRONMENTAL VARIANCE

The relative strength of various classes of genetic and environmental factors can be inferred from patterns of covariation among family members who have varying degrees of genetic overlap and shared environments. The heritability statistic estimates the association between genetic overlap and similarity on behavioral traits. The heritable component can be divided into additive and nonadditive effects, and the environmental component can be divided into effects shared versus nonshared by relatives. Figure 11.1 depicts a twin model that decomposes the variance in a given phenotype into additive genetic (A), shared environmental (C), and nonshared environmental (E) latent effects. The correlation between A_1 and A_2 for identical or monozygotic (MZ) twins is set to 1.00 because they share 100% of their genes; whereas the correlation between A_1 and A_2 for fraternal or dizygotic (DZ) twins is set to 0.50 because they share on average 50% of their segregating genes. The correlation between C_1 and C_2 is set to 1.00 for both types of twins growing up in the same home, whereas E_1 and E_2 are not correlated between cotwins. This basic biometric model can be expanded for longitudinal, multivariate analysis (Neale & Cardon, 1992).

The concept of heritability has many interpretive limitations. Heritability applies only to differences among persons within populations, not to the development of single individuals or to differences between populations. Heritability may also change during the lifespan, due to the dynamic nature of gene action, changes in the effects of environmental factors, changes in the nature of the trait being measured, or other constellations of factors (Carey, 1988). Because heritability is a ratio involving both genetic and environmental effects, a relevant environment—perhaps something like family stress—that varies widely across a population will reduce heritability whereas more nearly uniform environmental conditions increase it (Falconer, 1989). Another caveat is that similar heritability estimates for two traits, even conceptually related traits, do not imply common genetic underpinnings. In fact, the great majority of reliable heritability estimates for human behavioral traits lie in a 30–70% range although weakly heritable or nonheritable exceptions do exist; examples include early positive emotionality (Goldsmith, 2003) and security of parent–child attachment (Bokhorst et al., 2003).

The developmental implications of simple heritability estimates are also limited. Classic behavior-genetic inferences are confined to genetic and environmental *effects on phenotypic variance*, not gene action and the direct action of environmental influences per se. Genes exert their effects on behavior via complex pathways that involve feedback loops, rate-limiting processes, and other nonlinear mechanisms. Environments undoubtedly also exert many of their effects in inherently nonlinear ways. Nevertheless, analyzing individual differences by linear regression of outcome on sources of variation can be informative, even when the individual differences result from highly contingent, interactive developmental processes operating in the lives of individuals. Such linear models relating predictors and outcomes are used profitably in other fields, such as economics and decision making (Dawes & Corrigan, 1974), where the underlying processes involved are also complex and interactive.

Environmental effects are also subject to behavior-genetic analysis. Environmental effects can be shared or nonshared by a particular set of family members. Shared environmental effects explain similarity between twins and relatives in addition to that accounted for by common genes. Shared environmental variance also accounts for the similarity of genetically unrelated individuals who are reared together. The nonshared environmental variance is the remainder of the variance not explained by genes or shared environment (see Turkheimer & Waldron, 2000, for a conceptual review). It includes the effects of experiences that are unique to each individual and independent of genetic factors. Nonshared environmental variance can be directly estimated from differences between MZ cotwins. The estimate of nonshared environment is often confounded with measurement error.

A common misunderstanding is that environmental effects are "what is left over" after genetic effects are estimated. Typical behavior-genetic methods treat genetic and shared environmental effects in an even-handed manner, given the assumptions about how these effects can be partitioned. The more cogent criticism is that the genetic partitioning is based on sound theories of Mendelian inheritance whereas the environmental partitioning is based on familial units that might not be the most important markers of environmental influence. Despite extensive explication of the issue (Plomin & Daniels, 1987), the meaning of "shared" and "nonshared" environments continues to create confusion. The variance component referred to as shared environment can differ from one kinship design to the next. That is, the environment shared by cotwins has a somewhat different quality from the environment shared by ordinary siblings or adopted siblings, and is certainly different from the environment shared by parents and offspring. Of course, these differences in the quality of the shared environment might well be irrelevant to the behavior under study. Fortunately, many of these issues can be subjected to empirical tests, which generally support the twin method (Martin, Boomsma, & Machin, 1997).

Parents can exert strong experiential effects on their offspring behavior in the absence of a shared environmental factor in biometric analyses. For example, hypothetically, aggressive fathers might induce inhibited behavior in children of a certain age. Such a hypothetical effect would not emerge in a univariate analysis of parent–offspring data of either aggressiveness or inhibition. Part of the solution to problems like this is use of multivariate analysis (McArdle & Goldsmith, 1990; Neale & Cardon, 1992). A more important part of the solution is integrating theories of how the environment works into these multivariate designs. In summary, the distinctions between shared and non-shared environmental effects and transmitted environmental effects in behavior-genetic designs do not map well onto some issues concerning the nature and effects of interaction among family members (Hoffman, 1991). Testing for environmental risk and protective factors in ways that are also sensitive to genetic factors requires programmatic application of several research strategies (Rutter, Pickles, Murray, & Eaves, 2001).

We shall illustrate the investigation of genetic and environmental variance with data gathered using the classical twin method, wherein the phenotypic similarity of MZ and DZ pairs is contrasted. The assumptions of the twin method, principally twin representativeness of nontwins and equal environments of MZ and DZ twins, are portrayed carefully in textbooks (Plomin, DeFries, McClearn, & McGuffin, 2003).

ILLUSTRATION OF THE TWIN METHOD: ANALYSES OF AFFECT REGULATION

To illustrate use of the twin method, we provide an extended treatment of data on affect regulation from an ongoing project, with details of the univariate analyses treated in Lemery-Chalfant, Doelger, and Goldsmith (in press), and longitudinal analyses unique to this chapter.

Sample and Procedures

The sample consisted of twin pairs participating in the longitudinal Wisconsin Twin Project (WTP), a population-based sample of young twins born in the state of Wisconsin (Goldsmith, Lemery-Chalfant, Schmidt, Arneson, & Schmidt, 2007; Lemery-Chalfant, Goldsmith, Schmidt, Arneson, & Van Hulle, 2006). We selected twin pairs (average age = 7.58; SD = 1.00) who had parent-report and observer assessment of affect regulation (N = 563 pairs). Additionally, 283 pairs had another parent-report assessment on average 2 years earlier

(average age = 5.5; SD = 1.30); these earlier assessments are included to allow illustration of longitudinal twin analyses. The sample was 51% female, and families were predominately Caucasian, with a fairly wide distribution of SES. For example, 31% of fathers had a high school education or less, and 32% were college graduates.

Mothers and fathers completed temperament questionnaires independently when the twins were approximately 5 years old, and again when they were approximately 7 years old. At 7 years, the twins also participated in a 4-hr, home-based assessment. The two experimenters who administered tasks to the twins during the home visit independently completed measures of the twin's temperament after reviewing videotapes within a week of the visit. Several of the observer ratings and parent-report questionnaire scales were related to affect regulation. The *Children's Behavior Questionnaire* (CBQ, Rothbart, Ahadi, Hershey, & Fisher, 2001) was our parent-report measure; the relevant CBQ factor was Effortful Control. Effortful Control is defined as "the efficiency of executive attention, including the ability to inhibit a dominant response or to activate a subdominant response, to plan, and to detect errors" (Rothbart & Bates, 2006, p. 129). These processes modulate temperamental reactivity and behaviors. We computed the mean for correlated mother and father reports of Effortful Control for both occasions of assessment. The observers who visited the home completed three 5-point rating scales relevant to attentional control (adaptation to change in test materials, attention to tasks, and persistence in completing tasks items). These ratings were based on the child's behavior throughout the visit, including transitions from one task to the next. The three correlated items were averaged and the averages were then aggregated across observers. For all analyses, parent and observer reports were treated separately because we regarded the parental report as a measure of enduring trait regulation and the observer report as more a state measure of regulation and control.

Key Results: Twin Similarity

Girls scored significantly higher than boys on all variables, which raised the possibility that analyses would need to be done separately by gender. Table 11.1 shows the intraclass correlations for the different twin types. For girls and boys across both variables, MZ twins were more similar than DZ twins, signaling significant heritability. For parental report, the DZ correlations were lower than what would be expected under an additive genetic model (i.e., DZ twins should be somewhat similar on heritable traits as they

TABLE 11.1

Twin Intraclass Correlations and Standardized Estimates for Best-Fitting Biometric Models

	Female MZ	Female DZ	Male MZ	Male DZ	Opposite-Sex DZ	H^2	e^2
Age 5 parent-report Effortful Control	.65	.27	.71	−.11	.04	.68	.32
Age 7 parent-report Effortful Control	.75	.32	.67	.03	.04	.79 girls, .71 boys	.21 girls, .29 boys
Age 7 observed attentional control	.82	.50	.82	.44	.52	.83	.17

Note: MZ = monozygotic (identical) twins; DZ = dizygotic (fraternal) twins; H^2 = broad sense heritability (additive + nonadditive genetic influence); e^2 = nonshared environmental influence. There were no significant shared environmental influences. Both parent-report measures are composites of mother and father report; observed attentional control is a composite of observer 1 and observer 2 ratings.

share approximately 50% of their genes in common), suggesting possible rater contrast effects. On the basis of the notion that contrasting twins in the same family during the rating process would distort equality of variances across twin pairs, we can test for this bias (Saudino, McGuire, Reiss, Hetherington, & Plomin, 1995). There were no consistent differences in variances by sex and zygosity group across the two twin samples for any of the measures, so contrast effects were not considered further.

Key Results: Model-Fitting

The next phase of a twin analysis is generally to fit a univariate biometric model of the type previously shown in Figure 11.1. We did this with one added feature; we tested whether the magnitude of genetic and environmental influences differed between boys and girls, and there was evidence of gender differences in magnitude for parent report of Effortful Control at 7 years. The parameter estimates that resulted from fitting the univariate models are shown in the right hand side of Table 11.1. Individual differences in parent report of Effortful Control reflected 68–79% broad sense heritability (which includes both additive and nonadditive genetic influences) with no significant influence of the shared environment. Similarly, heritability of observer report attentional control was estimated at 83%, with the remainder of the variance due to the nonshared environment.

Table 11.2 gives the phenotypic correlations among the variables, separately for boys and girls. As expected, parental report of Effortful Control at both ages was highly correlated, so we fit a longitudinal model to determine genetic and environmental influences on stability of this trait from 5 to 7 years of age. Estimates significantly differed in magnitude by gender; that is, a model constraining estimates across gender did not fit as well. The best-fitting longitudinal model is depicted in Figure

11.2, showing one twin for clarity. The paths decomposing the covariance extend from the latent variables on the left to Effortful Control at age 7 on the right. Both genetic and nonshared environmental influences accounted for the covariance, with the genetic component larger for girls, and the environmental component larger for boys. For both genders, there were substantial new genetic influences on age 7 Effortful Control (represented by the genetic latent variable on the right) that were not shared with age 5 Effortful Control.

Key Results: Substantive Interpretation

Considered individually, genetic influences accounted for the majority of the variance in both parent-report Effortful

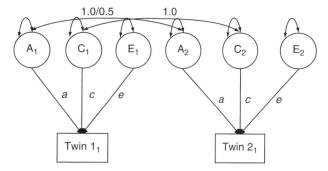

FIGURE 11.1 Univariate twin model for a measured variable, allowing additive genetic (A), shared environmental (C), and nonshared environmental effects (E) to predict scores for twin 1 and twin 2. The correlation between A_1 and A_2 is set to 1.0 for monozygotic (MZ) twin pairs, and 0.5 for dizygotic (DZ) twin pairs. The correlation between C_1 and C_2 is set to 1.0 for both twin types. The variances for each of the latent factors are set to 1.0. Finally, a^2, c^2, and e^2 are the percentage of variance in the measured variables accounted for by genetic, shared environmental, and nonshared environmental influences, respectively.

TABLE 11.2
Phenotypic Correlations among Parent and Observer Report of Effortful and Attentional Control

Variable	1	2	3
1. Age 5 parent-report Effortful Control	—	.68**	.31*
2. Age 7 parent-report Effortful Control	.69**	—	.22**
3. Age 7 observed attentional control	.21	.28**	—

Note: *p < .05. **p < .01. Correlations for girls are displayed above the diagonal and correlations for boys are displayed below the diagonal. Parent report is a composite of mother and father report; observed attentional control is a composite of observer 1 and observer 2 ratings.

Control and observed Attentional Control, with no significant effects of the shared environment. High heritability is consistent with results from molecular genetic studies, where behavioral measures of executive attention have been associated with the long repeat form of the dopamine D4 receptor gene and variants of the monoamine oxidase A gene associated with lower enzyme expression (Fossella, Posner, Fan, Swanson, & Pfaff, 2002). With our longitudinal model, results suggested that genetic

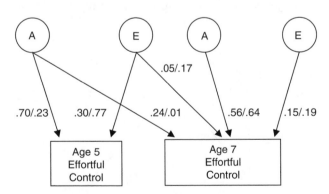

FIGURE 11.2 Longitudinal genetic model decomposing the variances and covariance between parent-report Effortful Control at 5 and 7 years of age into additive genetic (A) and nonshared environmental (E) components. There was no significant influence of the shared environment. The factor loadings are squared standardized parameter estimates, representing the variance accounted for in the measured variable by the latent factor, with estimates given for girls first, then boys. Because the estimates are the same for twin 1 and twin 2, only estimates for twin 1 are displayed. This final reduced model fit the data well [−2LL (1342) = 2709.75; $\chi^2_\Delta(6)$ = 2.72, p = .84, AIC = −9.28].

influences on Effortful Control in middle childhood are dynamic, and new genes may influence the trait at 7 years that do not influence it at 5 years. This is the first biometric decomposition of Effortful Control measured longitudinally and will need to be replicated.

With this detailed presentation of one set of twin study results as background, we turn to a broader characterization of twin studies related to approach and avoidance.

SELECTED LITERATURE ON TWIN STUDIES CONCERNING APPROACH AND AVOIDANCE

The literature in this field is substantial. As noted by Larsen (this volume), approach and avoidance neatly match the two major factors in adult personality inventories, Extraversion and Neuroticism (see also Elliot & Thrash, 2002). The process of matching adult personality traits with childhood temperament traits now has a substantial empirical basis (Caspi, Roberts, & Shiner, 2005). Here, we provide overviews of the genetic studies on childhood phenotypes related to approach and avoidance.

Anxiety

In the area of avoidance, we confine our summary to symptoms of anxiety, perhaps one of the most direct manifestations of avoidance tendencies. Twin studies almost uniformly support genetic influences on anxiety symptoms in children and adolescents. Eaves et al. (1997) estimated heritability of 60% for parent-reported anxiety symptoms. Topolski et al. (1997) reported heritability estimates ranging from .23 to .45 in male and .42 to .47 in female twins aged 8 to 16. In some studies, shared environmental factors influence anxiety more in boys than in girls (Eley & Stevenson, 1999). Feigon, Waldman, Levy, and Hay (2001) reported that shared environment accounted for 51% of the variation in boys versus 21% in girls and that heritability increased with age; however, other twin studies do not find age-related changes (Eley & Stevenson, 1999; Legrand, McGue, & Iacono, 1999). Using a diagnostic interview (DSM-IV criteria), heritability was high for a diagnosis of separation anxiety (73%) and specific phobia (60%) in a community sample of 6-year-old twins (Bolton et al., 2006). Genetic influences may differ for discrete anxiety disorders: greater for generalized anxiety symptoms (Goldsmith & Lemery, 2000) and weaker for separation anxiety (Topolski et al., 1997). Genetic influences on specific phobias may be unrelated to those for other anxiety disorders (Hettema, Prescott, Myers, Neale, & Kendler, 2005).

Parental ratings of anxiety/depression in the large, longitudinal Netherlands Twin Register indicated that

(a) heritability did not differ by gender, (b) heritability dropped with increasing age (76% at 3 years to 48% at 12 years), and (c) shared environmental influence increased with age (Boomsma, van Beijsterveldt, & Hudziak, 2005). With a different sample, the stability in internalizing symptoms at the ages of 7, 8, 9, 10, 11, and 12 years was due to the transmission of earlier genetic influences, whereas change could be attributed to nonshared environment and age-specific genetic influences (Haberstick, Schmitz, Young, & Hewitt, 2005). With lifetime diagnoses in a combined sample of Australian and Dutch adult twins and siblings, heritability estimates ranged from 36% for major depression to 50% for social phobia (Middeldorp et al., 2005), supporting the view that heritability of internalizing disorders decreases with age.

ADHD and Conduct Problems

In the area of approach motivation, we confine our summary to two symptom groups that represent approach tendencies in childhood (ADHD and conduct problems) although both of these symptom groups reflect maladaptive approach. The extensive literature on the genetics of attention deficit hyperactivity disorder (ADHD) holds some complexities, but more than a dozen twin studies, plus studies using other genetically informative designs, suggest substantial genetic contributions (heritabilities in the .60s) to the liability to ADHD. Despite some twin studies that show a subtype to be less heritable (e.g., the hyperactive-impulsive group in Willcutt, Pennington, & DeFries, 2000) or a particular method of assessment to yield weak genetic effects (e.g., self-report from adolescent twins in Martin, Scourfield, & McGuffin, 2002), the conclusion that genetic factors contribute to ADHD seems firm. Recent twin studies have systematically accounted for age, gender, and informant effects (Rietveld, Posthuma, & Dolan, 2003) and examined whether comorbid conditions share genetic underpinnings with ADHD, with evidence of shared genetic influences for comorbid conduct problems (Nadder, Rutter, & Silberg, 2002). Some evidence both from twin studies and molecular genetic studies indicates that the diagnostic features of ADHD may have different genetic underpinnings (Waldman et al., 1998), which suggests the utility of dividing ADHD into more homogeneous subgroups (Nigg, Goldsmith, & Sachek, 2004).

The literature on genetics of oppositional behavior, conduct problems, more overt antisocial behavior, and disinhibitory psychopathology, more generally, is even more complex than the ADHD literature, as our prior reviews on the topic have emphasized (Goldsmith & Gottesman, 1996; Nigg & Goldsmith, 1998). A study of 1116 pairs of 5-year-old British twins yielded perhaps the strongest evidence yet for genetic effects on early antisocial behavior. Arseneault et al. (2003) estimated 82% heritability for a common factor derived from mother, teacher, observer, and self-report measures. In another recent study, the stability in externalizing symptoms at the ages of 7, 8, 9, 10, 11, and 12 years was due to a common genetic factor, as well as to a nonshared environmental factor that was transmitted across ages (Haberstick et al., 2005). Change could be attributed to age-specific genetic and nonshared environmental influences. In an American sample, shared environment contributed to the comorbidity of ADHD, ODD, and CD common to mother and 11-year-old child report, whereas comorbidity unique to each rater was genetic or nonshared environmental in nature (Burt, McGue, Krueger, & Iancono, 2005). In 14-year-old Finnish twins, genetic factors accounted for most of the comorbidity among ADHD, ODD, and CD, but submodels suggested that some unique genetic factors were also required (Dick et al., 2005). In 17-year-old twins, the trait of Impulsive Antisociality was associated with increased genetic risk for externalizing disorders (Blonigen, Hicks, Krueger, Patrick, & Iancono, 2005).

This overview establishes strong genetic factors for the occurrence and continuity of ADHD and conduct problems. It also implicates environmental factors in several ways.

LINKAGE AND ASSOCIATION STUDIES

CONCEPTS AND METHODS

Identifying individual genes involved in etiology is currently feasible although still in early stages for approach and avoidance. This task of identifying genes inevitably follows from the results of the Human Genome Project and the succeeding HapMap projects (International HapMap Consortium, 2005). Here, our attention is focused on "complex inheritance," which encompasses polygenic inheritance (many genes, each having a small effect and coupled with environmental effects); single genes of discernible effect operating in a background of both polygenic and environmental effects; genetic heterogeneity (different genes influencing the behavior of interest in different subsets of individuals); and presence of phenocopies (environmentally molded phenotypes that resemble genetically influenced ones).

The methods that are applicable to complex inheritance are varieties of linkage analysis and association studies (see Sham, 1998, for a more technical treatment).

In general, these methods were developed to study the genetic basis of diseases, for which an individual can be considered as affected or not. However, most of the methods can be adapted to study trait variation that is not "all or none," as exemplified by approach or avoidance tendencies. Linkage methods include classic pedigree analysis in which statistical transmission models are tested in large families. A class of nonparametric analyses called "allele-sharing methods" (Lander & Schork, 1994) examine affected relatives, such as siblings who both have a disease, to determine whether a genetic marker is shared via inheritance by these affected relatives more frequently than expected. The most common implementation of allele-sharing methodology is the analysis of affected sibling pairs in "genome scans," often with a finer-grained scan following an initial scan. In a genome scan, linkage analysis is conducted using a series of anonymous polymorphisms, or genetic probes, spaced at relatively constant intervals over the entire genome—about 350 markers with an average spacing of 10 centi-Morgans (cM) in the late 1990s and early 2000s, but much more closely in recent research. The results of the scan are used to identify candidate chromosomal regions that are shared at rates greater than 50% (the rate expected for randomly selected markers for full siblings). Recently, in addition to using many more genetic markers (usually single nucleotide polymorphisms, or SNPs), parent–parent–child trios rather than sib pairs have been studied, and highly discordant in addition to concordant pairs of relatives have been considered. This genome scan approach offers the potential of identifying genes previously unsuspected of having an influence on the phenotype of interest. Genome scans are complicated by several factors, including these: (1) instead of a single test for linkage, one must conduct multiple tests across the entire genome; and (2) genetic heterogeneity and phenotyping mistakes (e.g., mis-diagnosis) can seriously distort results. Both linkage and association benefit from technologies such as gene chips and expressed sequence arrays (Kelsoe, 2004; Watson & Akil, 1999), which can detect structural DNA differences or differences in expression (in mRNA) of thousands of genes on a single chip.

The most common method used for studying approach and avoidance tendencies is the allelic association study. These studies compare the frequency of a genetic marker in two samples (e.g., an inhibited versus a noninhibited group). A classic association is between the blood group O and duodenal ulcer. Unless the genetic marker and the actual gene responsible for the disorder are very tightly linked, results from properly conducted association studies will be negative. Of course, the goal of association studies is to test candidate genes that might themselves be responsible for a phenotype. A key limitation of association studies is that spurious association can occur due to population stratification; that is, the samples studied might come from a population that contains groups with differing frequencies of the allele under study. If these groups differ for any reason in occurrence of a phenotype, then a spurious association of allele and the phenotype may result. Some association studies have been conducted with genetic probes that systematically cover large expanses of the genome, thus allowing a search for association with quantitative trait loci (QTLs). QTLs are genetic regions responsible for small but discernible quantitative effects on a phenotype. The smallest QTL effect that can be detected by association with a marker depends on the distance from the marker to the QTL, the size of population, and the heritability of the trait or disorder. In plant genetics, QTLs accounting for as little as 0.3% of the phenotypic variance have been reported, as reviewed by Tanksley (1993).

It might seem straightforward to compare extreme groups (e.g., children with strong versus weak approach tendencies) for different frequencies of a candidate gene or QTL. However, strong approach in one subset of individuals might have different roots than similarly strong approach in another subset. This trait heterogeneity problem haunts current attempts to associate behavior with specific genes (Cardon, 2006). There are other practical difficulties in this genre of research. For instance, individuals at the extreme of the distribution might possess several alleles promoting higher trait values. The effect of any one allele may be more difficult to discern against this "high value" genetic background than in more typical genetic backgrounds.

In conceptualizing genes that have only small effects on the phenotype, it is important to realize that they might be related to major genes of large effect. That is, if a major gene leading to qualitative dysfunction is identified, other alleles at the same locus could affect more subtle quantitative variation. The allele that leads to qualitative dysfunction could code for an inactive protein whereas a different allelic variant of the same gene might lead to an active but physiologically nonoptimal protein.

EXAMPLE: GENE ASSOCIATION WITH AN AVOIDANCE-RELATED BEHAVIOR

A prototypic example of an allelic association with an avoidance-related trait in humans concerned a polymorphism in a promoter of the serotonin transporter gene on chromosome 17q, which accounted for 3–4% of the variance in self-reported anxiety proneness, a marker of avoidance. This finding held in two samples totaling 505 individuals, and the allele in question also differentiated affected from unaffected siblings (Lesch et al., 1996). Serotonin is, of course, involved in neurotransmission in regions of the limbic system and cortex associated with anxious behavior, and some antidepressant and antianxiety drugs inhibit uptake of serotonin. The serotonin transporter is a protein that helps "fine-tune" this neurotransmission. The allele of the serotonin transporter promoter that leads to decreased transporter activity—at least in lymphoblast cell lines—occurred at a high frequency, 43%, in the samples studied (Lesch et al., 1996). Persons with this allele would be expected to show increased serotonergic transmission, and they report higher neuroticism scores (but are not different on the other factors of the Big Five personality traits). Lesch et al. (1996) cautioned that their results, from a normal sample, may not generalize as a cause of clinically significant levels of anxiety in patients. Although replications have been reported, some comprehensive failures to replicate these results have also been reported (Willis-Owen et al., 2005).

Another issue in this line of research is the nonspecificity of findings from candidate gene studies where the gene affects functioning in key pathways regulating neurotransmitters. Such a lack of specificity is perhaps unsurprising for genes mediating neurotransmitter function in circuitry central to affective processing. Population stratification is also a concern in these studies because Gelernter, Cubells, Kidd, Pakstis, and Kidd (1999) showed that the frequency of the serotonin transporter promoter allele under study in this research varies widely (from .29 to .89) in eight geographically distinct ethnic groups.

EXAMPLE: GENE ASSOCIATION WITH APPROACH-RELATED BEHAVIORS

In addition to alleles coding for genes related to serotonin function, numerous studies have examined the association of emotion-related traits and disorders with genes for dopamine receptors and transporters. For instance, two studies in 1996 showed an association of the personality trait of novelty seeking with the 7-repeat allele of the dopamine receptor D4 (DRD4) gene (Benjamin et al., 1996; Ebstein, Novick, Umansky, Priel, & Osher, 1996). However, a meta-analysis that includes eight subsequent studies, with varying characteristics, casts doubt on the validity or at least the generalizability of the association (Wahlsten, 1999). The literature on this association has grown, with both replications and nonreplications (Strobel, Spinath, Angleitner,

Riemann, & Lesch, 2003); more DRD4 polymorphisms have been examined, and interactions both with other genes and with other behaviors have been considered.

DRD4 receptor allele have also been associated with ADHD in four studies and not confirmed in one as of 2000 (see Swanson et al., 2000b, for review). A study that broke new methodological ground used this association as the basis for dividing severely affected ADHD children into subtypes based on presence of the specific DRD4 allele that appears to be a susceptibility gene (Swanson, et al., 2000a). Then, those subjects (41%) who had at least one copy of the target allele were compared with subjects who had the allele absent. The comparison was on three neuropsychological tests intended to probe the functioning of three cortical regions implicated in attentional deficits in ADHD (anterior cingulate, right dorsolateral prefrontal, and posterior parietal). Compared with non-ADHD controls, the entire ADHD group showed slow and inefficient processing. However, the ADHD subgroup characterized by presence of the susceptibility allele (the 7-repeat allele of the DRD4-III gene) showed no attentional deficits, leading the authors to speculate that this allele marked cases of ADHD with an affective phenotype predisposing to the development of ADHD.

Of course, DRD4 is not the only gene that has been examined for association with approach behavior. For example, genetic variants in noradrenergic receptors have been examined for association with the irritability, hostility, and impulsivity domains (Comings et al., 2000). In this study, as in others, variation in a single gene accounted for only a few percent of the phenotypic variance.

An obvious conclusion from this line of research is that all findings require replication and tests of generalization. Small samples, multiple tests, genetic heterogeneity, and "cheap phenotyping" via questionnaire are likely culprits in accounting for inconsistencies. One challenge for behavioral scientists is to take a larger role in genetic association and linkage studies so that the assessment of the phenotype incorporates developmental concerns and any available indicators from cognitive or affective neuroscience. In other words, the behavioral side of the investigation should be at least as sophisticated as the genetic side.

GENE–ENVIRONMENT INTERACTION

CONCEPTS AND METHODS

Upon first exposure to behavioral genetics, scientists often question how mutual or interactive processes are treated. The concept of gene–environment (GxE)

interaction provides one partial answer. Both historically (Erlenmeyer-Kimling, 1972) and more recently (Rutter, Moffitt, & Caspi, 2006), scientists have promoted the notion of GxE interaction to understand the origins of complex behavioral patterns, such as childhood withdrawal tendencies. As attractive as the idea of GxE interaction is for nondeterministic views of etiology, these interactions can be difficult to operationalize. On the genetic side, it is currently impossible in human studies to quantify the full genetic effect in a specific way. That is, we know the identity of only a few genes associated with any given complex human phenotype, and thus can only test for interaction of a fraction of the "genotypic risk" with experience. Results using these already-identified genes (the "low-hanging fruit") may prove nonrepresentative. One solution is to infer the genotype from the phenotypes of genetic relatives, which is the tradition of genetic epidemiology. However, this genetic risk assessment is indirect, and it fails to suggest specific genetic mechanisms. On the environmental side, the chief difficulty lies in conceptualizing risk factors that are fully independent of genetic influence. That is, genotype and environmental risk factors are often correlated, which means that GxE interactions must be detected in the presence of genotype by environment correlations. From a statistical perspective, this means that interaction must be detected in the presence of multicollinearity. Three other statistical/methodological problems plague the field. First is the possibility of selective reporting of positive findings, a problem that looms large with the recent feasibility of testing thousands of genes. Second is the well-known scaling problem: observed ordinal interactions can often be eliminated by scale transformations (Cohen, Cohen, West, & Aiken, 2003). Third, and more tentatively, some GxE interactions reported in the literature could represent statistical artifacts rather than describe developmental phenomena (Eaves, 2006). Given the difficulties in studying GxE interaction, consistent results across different methods are needed to confidently assert its existence for a given pairing of G and E.

EXAMPLE: A RISK ALLELE BY EXPERIENCE INTERACTION FOR AVOIDANCE-RELATED BEHAVIOR

An example of GxE interaction is the demonstration that a polymorphism in the promoter region of the gene for the serotonin transporter (5-HTT) interacts with maternal reports of social support to predict inhibited behavior with unfamiliar peers in middle childhood (Fox et al., 2005). Children who possessed the short 5-HTT allele

and whose mothers had low social support showed higher rates of behavioral inhibition in middle childhood.

EXAMPLE: A GENETIC RISK BY EXPERIENCE INTERACTION FOR AVOIDANCE-RELATED BEHAVIOR

In our own laboratory, we attempted a systematic approach to the issue of GxE interaction (Vendlinski, Lemery-Chalfant, Essex, & Goldsmith, 2007). The three methods that we used represent quasi-experimental, quantitative genetic techniques. Note that we refer to a test of "genetic risk by experience interaction" rather than "gene by environment interaction." This terminology acknowledges possible nonindependence of genetic risk (G-risk) and experiential risk (E-risk). We were attempting to predict children's internalizing problems in a sample of 8-year-old twins from the WTP (Goldsmith et al., 2007; Lemery-Chalfant et al., 2006). Multi-instrument composites were used to characterize both parent and child internalizing and five individual experiential risk factors were combined to form a cumulative risk index. We quantified genetic risk in two ways: by the cotwin's phenotype and by the parents' averaged phenotype for internalizing problems (mainly anxiety and depression). We also asked whether the heritability was different in twins growing up in families who experienced notable stress versus those growing up in families with average or low stress. We found consistent evidence for GxE interaction in child internalizing with significant interaction effects emerging within each of the three methods. The direction of interaction was such that associations between experiential risk and internalizing were strongest for children at elevated genetic risk. In addition, child internalizing problems were more heritable for children at low experiential risk than those from high risk family contexts. The effect sizes indicated that the main effects of genetic and experiential risk were much better predictors of child internalizing than was their interaction.

In conclusion, recent literature supports modest GxE interaction for individual differences in childhood avoidance tendencies. Approach tendencies are largely uninvestigated in this arena although an initial analysis in our laboratory suggests that they may be less prevalent than in the avoidance domain.

ENDOPHENOTYPES

THE ENDOPHENOTYPE CONCEPT

The basic reductionist paradigm for understanding the etiology of behavior can be depicted as Genetics →

Neuroscience → Behavior. The term "neuroscience" in this pathway denotes a host of intervening variables between the genetic and behavioral levels of analysis; it can be termed the endophenotypic level of analysis. That is, the endophenotype is, roughly speaking, intermediate between the genotype and the organism's "behavioral surface" that we can observe. Of course, the implied causal pathway is likely to be affected by feedback loops, regulatory mechanisms, and other network effects, as well as nongenetic sources of influence.

The demonstration of genetic effects in quantitative genetic studies encourages the search for endophenotypic markers (Gottesman & Gould, 2003). This is different from simply searching for biological markers—also a useful exercise—because successfully identified endophenotypes facilitate multilevel, simultaneous study of genes, biology, and behavior. Among the desirable properties of a good endophenotype for genetic analysis are (1) an etiologic association with the complex behavioral phenotype, (2) presence in some unaffected relatives, and (3) being amenable to objective measurement. Endophenotypes can be biochemical, neurological, anatomical, psychophysiological, endocrine, sensorimotor, perceptual, cognitive, or affective in nature.

From a genetic perspective, the chapters in part II of this volume explain possible endophenotypes for approach and avoidance. The diversity of the biological measures described in the part II chapters suggests the richness of potential endophenotypes for genetic analyses of approach and avoidance. This is particularly true for anxiety-related phenotypes (Bakshi & Kalin, 2000), which have been subjected to genetic analysis mainly in mice to the present time.

The endophenotype concept has proven quite useful, despite the observation that biological measures tend not to be more heritable than behavioral characterization of disorders (Flint & Munafo, 2007). Complex behavioral phenotypes such as approach and avoidance do not yield readily to genetic analysis. The same is true for complex medical disorders such as coronary artery disease and idiopathic generalized epilepsies, but including endophenotypic indicators has aided gene identification for these disorders (Durner et al., 2001; Greenberg et al., 2000; Klos et al., 2001). These and other medical examples (Wang, Chang, Chang, Curb, Ho, & Hsiung, 2006) suggest that a greater understanding of the disease processes yields endophenotypes that can themselves become foci of genetic analysis. For behavioral approach and avoidance, this level of analysis remains largely a future goal.

EXAMPLE: GENETIC ANALYSIS OF BASAL CORTISOL LEVELS

A complicated and somewhat inconsistent literature suggests that cortisol hormone levels are associated with measures of both avoidance (higher cortisol) and approach (lower cortisol). If this is so, then cortisol level is a reasonable candidate for endophenotypic analysis. An initial step in this analysis is the estimation of the heritability of cortisol measures, which we review here.

There is good reason to suspect genetic effects on cortisol levels. Genes related to the corticotropin releasing hormone (CRH), its receptors, and peptides have been implicated in animal models of behavior inhibition (Bakshi & Kalin, 2000). CRH is a peptide that mediates the HPA axis stress response, a major component of which is pulses of cortisol production. Polymorphisms in the regulatory region of the CRH gene have been identified and their relationships to cortisol activity and behavior inhibition are being investigated. Recently, researchers have found a link between the CRH gene and behavioral inhibition in children of a parent with panic disorder (Smoller et al., 2003; Smoller et al., 2005). In addition, polymorphisms in cortisol-receptor genes that may have important implications for HPA axis regulation have been identified (Wüst et al., 2004).

From a quantitative perspective, genetic and environmental influences on basal cortisol have been shown to vary throughout the day (Linkowski et al., 1993). Studies have demonstrated significant genetic influence on cortisol during the awakening period but not on cortisol collected later in the day (Bartels, de Geus, Kirschbaum, Sluyter, & Boomsman, 2003; Kupper et al., 2005; Wust, Federenko, Hellhammer, & Kirschbaum, 2000). Measures of reactive cortisol response to a social stress test are also moderately heritable (Federenko, Nagamine, Hellhammer, Wadhwa, & Wust, 2004; Kirschbaum, Wust, Faig, & Hellhammer, 1992). Interestingly, heritability estimates increased substantially upon repeated exposure to the same social stressor, suggesting that the genetically influenced "trait" component of the cortisol response becomes more apparent (Federenko et al., 2004). In a pair of large samples, our research group recently demonstrated that late afternoon cortisol levels are similar among family members, but not heritable (Schreiber et al., 2006). Thus, late afternoon cortisol might be a relevant biomarker but not an endophenotype.

In summary, the genetic analysis of cortisol measures using both molecular and quantitative approaches illustrates components of an endophenotypic approach to behavior, with particular relevance to avoidance-related behavior.

GENETIC COMPLEXITIES

This is a short chapter and genetics is a big topic. We now mention some issues in genetic analysis of behavior that complicate and enrich the topic. The first topic is genetic heterogeneity, the circumstance in which subsets of persons with a putatively unitary clinical disorder have different genetic roots of the disorder. Genetic heterogeneity, which we previously mentioned, applies not only to disorders but also more generally to traits. That is, it is possible that different genes affect traits in the low, medium, and high ranges of trait values. Also, different combinations of genes can result in the same trait phenotype in different individuals or different subgroups of the population. Kendler et al. (1996) studied depression in a large population-based sample of female adult twins. Depression, of course, has been related to low approach behavior in the hedonically positive domain (Watson, Clark, & Carey, 1988). According to Kendler et al. (1996), concordant twin pairs had the same depressive syndrome (seven classes, of which three represent the clinical syndromes of mild typical depression, atypical depression, and severe typical depression) more often than chance, and resemblance was greater in MZ than DZ twin pairs. In other words, certain clinical features of depression "ran true" in families (twins in this case), suggesting genetically based heterogeneity within depression.

A second complexity is developmental change in genetic influences. It is especially important to consider the potential changing influences of genes and the environment across developmental transitions, when reorganization in one system is often followed by reorganization in another (e.g., locomotor and cognitive changes during infancy). It is also important to note that the tendency to equate genetics or biology with "constraint" and experience with "possibility," while perhaps holding some validity, should probably be resisted. At best, these equations are over-simplifications.

A whole class of complexities in genetics is non-Mendelizing genetic influences (see Goldsmith, 2003, for details). These influences might not be revealed by the standard quantitative (e.g., twin study) and molecular genetic (e.g., candidate gene study) approaches that we have discussed. A list of non-Mendelian mechanisms would include mitochondrial inheritance (influence by non-nuclear DNA), imprinting (wherein a gene's expression is modulated based on whether it is transmitted from the father or the mother, as in Prader–Willi and Angelman syndromes), progressive amplification (repeated duplication of DNA segments across generations, as in Fragile X and Huntington disease), and the degree of homozygosity (which may reduce an organism's metabolic buffering and thus render it susceptible to insult from environmental perturbations). Developmental instability, possibly related to homozygosity, is an especially promising area for investigation of behavioral variability (Yeo, Gangestad, Thoma, Shaw, & Repa, 1997). Other exciting developments in human genetics are tracing clinical outcomes to variations in the number of copies of genes within the genotype (Sharp et al., 2006) and in the pattern of DNA methylation and de-methylation that inactivates or activates gene expression (Reik, Dean, & Walter, 2001).

SUMMARY AND PROSPECTS FOR INTEGRATION

Quantitative genetic research (twin, family, and adoption studies) has been undertaken increasingly over the past two decades, and projects are currently being extended longitudinally. Heritability seldom rises above a figure of about 70% of the observed variance. In longitudinal analyses, much of the stability—in some cases practically all the stability—of these traits is due to the stability of genetic influences rather than stability of environmental factors. Both genes and environments seem to influence change in most traits related to approach or avoidance. Adoption and step-family evidence still needs to be integrated more fully with the more widely available twin results. A continuing need in quantitative genetic studies is for assessment other than self- or parental-report of approach or avoidance-related phenotypes. Some laboratory-based assessment of temperament/emotionality has occurred in twin and adoption studies, but much more is needed. Classic twin and family studies need to continue the present trend of becoming highly multivariate, incorporating both dimensional (e.g., temperament trait) and categorical (e.g., diagnosis) variables, and multiple, theoretically relevant occasions of study. Our brief treatment of more complex genetic issues, including non-Mendelizing genetic effects, caution us not to become paradigm-bound—even to useful paradigms such as the twin design and candidate gene studies—if we wish to discern the entire panorama of genetic influences on behavior.

Nevertheless, anticipating that genetic underpinnings of approach and avoidance can be established, such knowledge feeds back to affect our thinking about fundamental issues in at least two major ways. First, if we find that the genetic underpinnings of approach and avoidance are shared with other behavioral phenotypes in the cognitive, perceptual, motoric, social, or affective domains, then some reconceptualization of the boundaries of concepts may be indicated. Second, if genetic effects are strong, it becomes difficult to defend learning-based accounts of approach and avoidance that do not recognize individual differences in propensity or susceptibility to learning.

Another need in this area is integration of assessment of specific genetic and experiential processes into the twin and adoption studies to "actualize" the genetic and environmental components of the observed variation. Synthetic data analytic approaches exist for measuring specific genes within such classic quantitative designs (Fulker, Cherny, Sham, & Hewitt, 1999). On the social side of the environment, measures of specific interactional processes need to be refined and incorporated into studies. Environmental assessment needs to extend into the realm of biological measures as well. Identified environmental factors should be quantified (e.g., in terms of increases in relative risk) and compared with other known risk factors to evaluate their importance. On the genetic side, variation is "actualized" by detecting specific genes associated with the trait.

There is a question of whether investigation will more profitably be gene (wherein the behavioral correlates of identified genes are sought) or behavior-centered (wherein the investigator begins with a phenotype and searches for associated genetic markers). These efforts promise a new synergism with animal research, where gene function in the neurophysiological sense is more easily investigated.

Finally, genetic research on approach and avoidance may be one of the "missing links" in psychiatric epidemiology. Psychiatric epidemiology has yielded quite clear evidence of genetic input to common clinical phenotypes such as schizophrenia, bipolar affective disorder, unipolar depression, antisocial personality disorder, and ADHD. Other clinical phenotypes are less well studied. An alternate route to analyzing these disorders is to examine likely dimensional underpinnings, such as poor impulse control, activity level, anger and emotional aggressiveness, inhibition, and sadness, all of which map onto the approach and avoidance framework.

Progress in understanding the genetics of approach and avoidance is dependent on interdisciplinary research, involving the disciplines represented in this *Handbook* and others such as epidemiology and medical specialties. The effect sizes in the prediction of most emotion-related behavior are modest, thus allowing ample room for multiple predictors from different domains. *Different* explanatory factors are not always *competing* explanatory factors. Enthusiasm for reductionistic explanations based on genetics for the origins of the neural underpinnings of approach and avoidance should not overshadow the appreciation of developmental plasticity in their manifestation.

REFERENCES

Arseneault, L., Moffitt, T. E., Caspi, A., Taylor, A., Rijsdijk, F. V., Jaffee, S. R., et al. (2003). Strong genetic effects on cross-situational antisocial behaviour among 5-year-old children according to mothers, teachers, examiner-observers, and twins' self-reports. *Journal of Child Psychology and Psychiatry*, 44, 832–848.

Bakshi, V. P. & Kalin, N. H. (2000). Corticotropin-releasing hormone and animal models of anxiety: Gene–environment interactions. *Biological Psychiatry*, 48, 1175–1198.

Bartels, M., de Geus, E. J., Kirschbaum, C., Sluyter, F., & Boomsma, D. I. (2003). Heritability of daytime cortisol levels in children. *Behavior Genetics*, 33, 421–433.

Benjamin, L., Li, L., Patterson, C., Greenberg, B. D., Murphy, D. L., & Hamer, D. H. (1996). Population and familial association between the D4 dopamine receptor gene and measures of novelty seeking. *Nature Genetics*, 12, 81–84.

Blonigen, D. M., Hicks, B. M., Krueger, R. F., Patrick, C. J., & Iacono, W. G. (2005). Psychopathic personality traits: Heritability and genetic overlap with internalizing and eternalizing psychopathology. *Psychological Medicine*, 35, 637–648.

Bokhorst, C. L., Bakermans-Kranenburg, M. J., Fearon, R. M., van IJzendoorn, M. H., Fonagy, P., & Schuengel, C. (2003). The importance of shared environment in mother-infant attachment security: A behavioral genetic study. *Child Development*, 74, 1769–1782.

Bolton, D., Eley, T. C., O'Connor, T. G., Perrin, S., Rabe-Hesketh, S., Rijsdijk, F., et al. (2006). Prevalence and genetic and environmental influences on anxiety disorders in 6-year-old twins. *Psychological Medicine*, 36, 335–344.

Boomsma, D. I., van Beijsterveldt, C. E., & Hudziak, J. J. (2005). Genetic and environmental influences on anxious/depression during childhood: A study from the Netherlands Twin Register. *Genes, Brain, and Behavior*, 4, 466–481.

Burt, S. A., McGue, M., Krueger, R. F., & Iacono, W. G. (2005). Sources of covariation among the child-externalizing disorders: Informant effects and the shared environment. *Psychological Medicine*, 35, 1133–1144.

Cardon, L. R. (2006). Genetics delivering new disease genes. *Science*, 314, 1403–1405.

Carey, G. (1988). Inference about genetic correlations. *Behavior Genetics*, 18, 329–338.

Caspi, A., Roberts, B. W., & Shiner, R. L. (2005). Personality development: Stability and change. *Annual Review of Psychology*, 56, 453–484.

Cohen, J., Cohen, P., West, S. G., & Aiken, L. S. (2003). *Applied multiple regression/correlation analysis for the behavioral sciences* (3rd ed.), Mahwah, NJ: Lawrence Erlbaum Associates.

Comings, D. E., Johnson, J. P., Gonzalez, N. S., Huss, M., Saucier, G., McGue, M., et al. (2000). Association between the adrenergic alpha 2A receptor gene (ADRA2A) and measures of irritability, hostility, impulsivity and memory in normal subjects. *Psychiatric Genetics*, 10, 39–42.

Dawes, R. M., & Corrigan, B. S. (1974). Linear models in decision making. *Psychological Bulletin*, 81, 95–106.

Derryberry, D., & Rothbart, M. K. (1997). Reactive and effortful processes in the organization of temperament. *Development and Psychopathology*, *9*, 633–652.

Dick, D. M., Viken, R. J., Kaprio, J., Pulkkinen, L., & Rose, R. J. (2005). Understanding the covariation among childhood externalizing symptoms: genetic and environmental influences on conduct disorder, attention deficit hyperactivity disorder, and oppositional defiant disorder symptoms. *Journal of Abnormal Child Psychology*, *33*, 219–229.

Durner, M., Keddache, M. A., Tomasini, L., Shinnar, S., Resor, S. R., Cohen, J., et al. (2001). Genome scan of idiopathic generalized epilepsy: Evidence for major susceptibility gene and modifying genes influencing the seizure type. *Annals of Neurology*, *49*, 328–335.

Eaves, L. J. (2006). Genotype X environment interaction in psychopathology: Fact or artifact? *Twin Research and Human Genetics*, *9*, 1–8.

Eaves, L. J., Silberg, J. L., Meyer, J. M., Maes, H. H., Siminoff, E., Pickles, A., et al. (1997). Genetics and developmental psychopathology: 2. The main effects of genes and environment on behavioral problems in the Virginia Twin Study of Adolescent Behavioral Development. *Journal of Child Psychology and Psychiatry*, *38*, 965–980.

Ebstein, R. P., Novick, O., Umansky, R., Priel, B., & Osher, Y. (1996). Dopamine D4 receptor (D4DR) exon III polymorphism associated with the human personality trait of novelty seeking. *Nature Genetics*, *12*, 78–80.

Eley, T., & Stevenson, J. (1999). Exploring the covariation between anxiety and depression. *Journal of Child Psychology and Psychiatry*, *40*, 1273–1282.

Elliot, A. J., & Thrash, T. M. (2002). Approach–avoidance motivation in personality: Approach and avoidance temperament and goals. *Journal of Personality and Social Psychology*, *82*, 804–818.

Erlenmeyer-Kimling, L. (1972). Gene–environment interactions and the variability of behavior. In L. Ehrman, G. S. Omenn, & E. Caspari (Eds.), *Genetics, environment, and behavior* (pp. 181–208). New York: Academic Press.

Falconer, D. S. (1989). *Introduction to quantitative genetics* (3rd ed.), New York: Longman.

Federenko, I. S., Nagamine, M., Hellhammer, D. H., Wadhwa, P. D., & Wust, S. (2004). The heritability of hypothalamus pituitary adrenal axis responses to psychosocial stress is context dependent. *Journal of Clinical Endocrinology and Metabolism*, *89*, 6244–6250.

Feigon, S. A., Waldman, I. D., Levy, F., & Hay, D. A. (2001). Genetic and environmental influences on separation anxiety disorder symptoms and their moderation by age and sex. *Behavior Genetics*, *3*, 403–411.

Flint, J., & Munafo, M. R. (2007). The endophenotype concept in psychiatric genetics. *Psychological Medicine*, *37*, 163–180.

Fossella, J., Posner, M. I., Fan, J., Swanson, J. M., & Pfaff, D. W. (2002). Attentional phenotypes for the analysis of higher mental function. *Scientific World Journal*, *2*, 217–223.

Fox, N. A. (Ed.) (1994). The development of emotion regulation: Biological and behavioral considerations. *Monographs of the Society for Research in Child Development*, *59*(2–3, Serial No. 240).

Fox, N. A., Nichols, K. E., Henderson, H. A., Rubin, K., Schmidt, L., Hamer, D., Ernst, M., & Pine, D. S. (2005). Evidence for a gene-environment interaction in predicting behavioral inhibition in middle childhood. *Psychological Science*, *16*, 921–926.

Fulker, D. W., Cherny, S. S., Sham, P. C., & Hewitt, J. K. (1999). Combined linkage and association sib-pair analysis for quantitative traits. *American journal of Human Genetics*, *64*(1), 259–267.

Gelernter, J., Cubells, J. F., Kidd, J. R., Pakstis, A. J., & Kidd, K. K. (1999). Population studies of polymorphisms of the serotonin transporter protein gene. *American Journal of Medical Genetics*, *88*, 61–66.

Goldsmith, H. H. (2003). Genetics of emotional development. In R. J. Davidson, K. Scherer, & H. H. Goldsmith (Eds.), *Handbook of affective sciences* (pp. 300–319). New York: Oxford University Press.

Goldsmith, H. H., & Campos, J. J. (1982). Toward a theory of infant temperament. In R. N. Emde & R. J. Harmon (Eds.), *The Development of attachment and affiliative systems* (pp. 161–193). New York: Plenum Press.

Goldsmith, H. H., & Gottesman, I. I. (1996). Heritable variability and variable heritability in developmental psychopathology. In M. F. Lenzenweger & J. Haugaard (Eds.), *Frontiers in psychopathology* (pp. 5–43). New York: Oxford University Press.

Goldsmith, H. H., & Lemery, K. S. (2000). Linking temperamental fearfulness and anxiety symptoms: A behavior-genetic perspective. *Biological Psychiatry*, *48*, 1199–1209.

Goldsmith, H. H., Lemery, K., Aksan, N., & Buss, K. A. (2000). Temperamental substrates of personality development. In D. Molfese & V. Molfese (Eds.), *Temperament and personality development across the lifespan* (pp. 1–32). Mahwah, NJ: Erlbaum.

Goldsmith, H. H., Lemery-Chalfant, K., Schmidt, N. L., Arneson, C. L., & Schmidt, C. K. (2007). Longitudinal analyses of affect, temperament, and childhood psychopathology. *Twin Research and Human Genetics*, *10*, 118–126.

Gottesman, I. I., & Gould, T. D. (2003). The endophenotype concept in psychiatry: Etymology and strategic intentions. *American Journal of Psychiatry*, *160*, 636–645.

Greenberg, D. A., Durner, M., Keddache, M., Shinnar, S., Resor, S. R., Moshe, S. L., et al. (2000). Reproducibility and complications in gene searches: Linkage on chromosome 6, heterogeneity, association, and maternal inheritance in juvenile myoclonic epilepsy. *American Journal of Human Genetics*, *66*, 508–516.

Gross, J. J. (Ed.) (2007). *Handbook of emotion regulation*. New York: Guildford Press.

Haberstick, B. C., Schmitz, S., Young, S. E., & Hewitt, J. K. (2005). Contributions of genes and environments to stability and change in externalizing and internalizing problems during elementary and middle school. *Behavior Genetics*, *35*, 381–396.

Hettema, J. M., Prescott, C. A., Myers, J. M., Neale, M. C., & Kendler, K. S. (2005). The structure of genetic and environmental risk factors for anxiety disorders in men and women. *Archives of General Psychiatry, 62,* 182–189.

Hoffman, L. W. (1991). The influence of the family environment on personality: Accounting for sibling differences. *Psychological Bulletin, 110,* 187–203.

International HapMap Consortium. (2005). A haplotype map of the human genome. *Nature, 437,* 1299–1320.

Kelsoe, J. R. (2004). Genomics and the Human Genome Project: Implications for psychiatry. *International Review of Psychiatry, 16,* 294–300.

Kendler, K. S., Eaves, L. J., Walters, E. E., Neale, M. C., Heath, A. C., & Kessler, R. C. (1996). The identification and validation of distinct depressive syndromes in a population-based sample of female twins. *Archives of General Psychiatry, 53,* 391–399.

Kirschbaum, C., Wust, S., Faig, H. G., & Hellhammer, D. H. (1992). Heritability of cortisol responses to human corticotropin-releasing hormone, ergometry, and psychological stress in humans. *Journal of Clinical Endocrinology and Metabolism, 75,* 1526–1530.

Klos, K. L., Kardia, S. L. R., Ferrell, R. E., Turner, S. T., Boerwinkle, E., & Sing, C. F. (2001). Genome-wide linkage analysis reveals evidence of multiple regions that influence variation in plasma lipid and apolipoprotein levels associated with risk of coronary heart disease. *Arteriosclerosis Thrombosis and Vascular Biology, 21,* 971–978.

Kupper, N., de Geus, E. J., van den Berg, M., Kirschbaum, C., Boomsma, D. I., & Willemsen, G. (2005). Familial influences on basal salivary cortisol in an adult population. *Psychoneuroendocrinology, 30,* 857–868.

Lander, E. S., & Schork, N. J. (1994). Genetic dissection of complex traits. *Science, 265,* 2037–2048.

Legrand, L. N., McGue, M., & Iacono, W. G. (1999). A twin study of state and trait anxiety in childhood and adolescence. *Journal of Child Psychology and Psychiatry, 40,* 953–958.

Lemery-Chalfant, K., Doelger, L., & Goldsmith, H. H. (in press). Genetic relations between effortful and attentional control and symptoms of psychopathology in middle childhood. *Infant and Child Development.*

Lemery-Chalfant, K., Goldsmith, H. H., Schmidt, N. L., Arneson, C. L., & Van Hulle, C. A. (2006). Wisconsin Twin Project: Current directions and findings. *Twin Research and Human Genetics, 9,* 1030–1037.

Lesch, K. P., Bengel, D., Heils, A., Sabol, S. Z., Greenberg, B. D., Petri, S., et al. (1996). Association of anxiety-related traits with a polymorphism in the serotonin transporter gene regulatory region. *Science, 274,* 1527–1531.

Linkowski, P., Van Onderbergen, A., Kerkhofs, M., Bosson, D., Mendlewicz, J., & Van Cauter, E. (1993). Twin study of the 24-h cortisol profile: Evidence for genetic control of the human circadian clock. *American Journal of Physiology, 264*(2 Pt 1), E173–181.

Middeldorp, C. M., Birley, A. J., Cath, D. C., Gillespie, N. A., Willemsen, G., Statham, D., et al. (2005). Familial clustering of major depression and anxiety disorders in Australian and Dutch twins and siblings. *Twin Research and Human Genetics, 8,* 609–615.

Martin, N., Boomsma, D., & Machin, G. (1997). A twin-pronged attack on complex traits. *Nature Genetics, 17,* 387–392.

Martin, N., Scourfield, J., & McGuffin, P. (2002). Observer effects and heritability of childhood attention-deficit hyperactivity disorder symptoms. *British Journal of Psychiatry, 180,* 260–265.

McArdle, J. J., & Goldsmith, H. H. (1990). Alternative common factor models for multivariate biometric analyses. *Behavior Genetics, 20,* 569–608.

Nadder, T. S., Rutter, M., & Silberg, J. L. (2002). Genetic effects on the variation and covariation of attention deficit-hyperactivity disorder (ADHD) and oppositional-defiant disorder/conduct disorder (OCD/CD) symptomatologies across informant and occasion of measurement. *Psychological Medicine, 32,* 39–53.

Neale, M. C., & Cardon, L. R. (1992). *Methodology for genetic studies of twins and families.* Dordrecht, The Netherlands: Kluwer.

Nigg, J. T., & Goldsmith, H. H. (1998). Recent developments in behavioral genetics and developmental psychopathology. *Human Biology, 70,* 387–412.

Nigg, J. T., Goldsmith, H. H., & Sachek, J. (2004). Temperament and attention deficit hyperactivity disorder: The development of a multiple pathway model. *Journal of Clinical Child and Adolescent Psychology, 33,* 42–53.

Plomin, R., & Daniels, D. (1987). Why are children in the same family so different from each other? *Behavioral and Brain Sciences, 10,* 1–16.

Plomin, R., DeFries, J. C., McClearn, G. E., & McGuffin, P. (2003). *Behavioral genetics* (4th ed.). New York: Worth Publishers.

Reik, W., Dean, W., & Walter, J. (2001). Epigenetic reprogramming in mammalian development. *Science, 293,* 1089–1093.

Rietveld, M. J. H., Posthuma, D., & Dolan, C. V. (2003). ADHD: Sibling interactions or dominance: An evaluation of statistical power. *Behavior Genetics, 33,* 247–255.

Rothbart, M. K., & Bates, J. E. (2006). Temperament. In W. Damon (Series Ed.) & N. Eisenberg (Vol. Ed.) (Eds.), *Handbook of child psychology. Vol. 3. Social, emotional, personality development* (6th ed.) (pp. 99–166). New York: Wiley.

Rothbart, M. K., Ahadi, S. A., Hershey, K. L., & Fisher, P. (2001). Investigations of temperament at three to seven years: The Children's Behavior Questionnaire. *Child Development, 72,* 1394–1408.

Rueda, M. R., Posner, M. I., & Rothbart, M. K. (2004). Attentional control and self-regulation. In R. F. Baumeister & K. D. Vohs (Eds.), *Handbook of self-regulation: Research, theory, and applications* (pp. 283–300). New York: Guilford Press.

Rutter, M., Moffitt, T. E., & Caspi, A. (2006). Gene–environment interplay and psychopathology: Multiple varieties but real effects. *Journal of Child Psychology and Psychiatry, 47,* 226–261.

Rutter, M., Pickles, A., Murray, R., & Eaves, L. (2001). Testing hypotheses on specific environmental causal effects on behavior. *Psychological Bulletin, 127,* 291–324.

Saudino, K. J., McGuire, S., Reiss, D., Hetherington, E. M., & Plomin, R. (1995). Parent ratings of EAS temperaments in twins, full siblings, half siblings, and step siblings. *Journal of Personality and Social Psychology, 68,* 723–733.

Schreiber, J. E., Shirtcliff, E., Van Hulle, C., Lemery-Chalfant, K. S., Klein, M. H., Kalin, N. H., et al. (2006). Environmental influences on family similarity in afternoon cortisol levels: Twin and parent–offspring designs. *Psychoneuroendocrinology, 31,* 1131–1137.

Sham, P. (1998). *Statistics in human genetics.* London: Arnold.

Sharp, A. J., Hansen, S., Selzer, R. R., Cheng, Z., Regan, R., Hurst, J. A., et al. (2006). Discovery of previously unidentified genomic disorders from the duplication architecture of the human genome. *Nature Genetics, 38,* 1038–1042.

Smoller, J. W., Rosenbaum, J. F., Biederman, J., Kennedy, J., Dai, D., Racette, S. R., et al. (2003). Association of a genetic marker at the corticotropin-releasing hormone locus with behavioral inhibition. *Biological Psychiatry, 54,* 1376–1381.

Smoller, J. W., Yamaki, L. H., Fagerness, J. A., Biederman, J., Racette, S., Laird, N. M., et al. (2005). The corticotropin-releasing hormone gene and behavioral inhibition in children at risk for panic disorder. *Biological Psychiatry, 57,* 1485–1492.

Strobel, A., Spinath, F. M., Angleitner, A., Riemann, R., & Lesch, K. P. (2003). Lack of association between polymorphisms of the dopamine D4 receptor gene and personality. *Neuropsychobiology, 47,* 52–56.

Swanson, J., Oosterlaan, J., Murias, M., Schuck, S., Flodman, P., Spence, M. A., et al. (2000a). Attention deficit/hyperactivity disorder children with a 7-repeat allele of the dopamine receptor D4 gene have extreme behavior but normal performance on critical neuropsychological tests of attention. *Proceedings of the National Academy of Sciences, 97,* 4754–4759.

Swanson, J. M., Flodman, P., Kennedy, J., Spence, M. A., Moyzis, R., Schuck, S., et al. (2000b). Dopamine genes and ADHD. *Neuroscience and Biobehavioral Reviews, 24,* 21–25.

Tanksley, S. D. (1993). Mapping polygenes. *Annual Review of Genetics, 27,* 205–233.

Thompson, R. A., & Calkins, S. (1996). The double-edged sword: Emotional regulation for children at risk. *Development and Psychopathology, 8,* 163–182.

Topolski, T. D., Hewitt, J. K., Eaves, L. J., Silberg, J. L., Meyer, J. M., Rutter, M., et al. (1997). Genetic and environmental influences on child reports of manifest anxiety, and symptoms of separation anxiety and overanxious disorders: A community-based twin study. *Behavior Genetics, 27,* 15–28.

Turkheimer, E., & Waldron, M. C. (2000). Nonshared environment: A theoretical, methodological, and quantitative review. *Psychological Bulletin, 126,* 78–108.

Vendlinski, M. K., Lemery-Chalfant, K., Essex, M. J., & Goldsmith, H. H. (2007). A systematic approach for detecting genetic risk by experience interaction for childhood internalizing problems. Under editorial review.

Wahlsten, D. (1999). Single-gene influences on brain and behavior. *Annual Review of Psychology, 50,* 599–624.

Waldman, I. D., Rowe, D. C., Abramowitz, A., Kozel, S. T., Mohr, J. H., Sherman, S. L., et al. (1998). Association and linkage of the dopamine transporter gene and attention-deficit hyperactivity disorder in children: heterogeneity owing to diagnostic subtype and severity. *American Journal of Human Genetics, 63,* 1767–1776.

Wang, W. C., Chang, I. S., Chang, C. H., Curb, D., Ho, L. T., & Hsiung, C. A. (2006). Incorporating endophenotypes into allele-sharing based linkage tests. *Genetic Epidemiology, 30,* 133–142.

Watson, D., Clark, L. A., & Carey, G. (1988). Positive and negative affectivity and their relation to anxiety and depressive disorders. *Journal of Abnormal Psychology, 97,* 346–353.

Watson, S. J., & Akil, H. (1999). Gene chips and arrays revealed: A primer on their power and their uses. *Biological Psychiatry, 45,* 533–543.

Willcutt, E. G., Pennington, B. F., & DeFries, J. C. (2000). Etiology of inattention and hyperactivity/impulsivity in a community sample of twins with learning difficulties. *Journal of Abnormal Child Psychology, 28,* 149–159.

Willis-Owen, S. A., Turri, M. G., Munafo, M. R., Surtees, P. G., Wainwright, N. W., Brixey, R. D., et al. (2005). The serotonin transporter length polymorphism, neuroticism, and depression: A comprehensive assessment of association. *Biological Psychiatry, 58,* 451–466.

Wust, S., Federenko, I., Hellhammer, D. H., & Kirschbaum, C. (2000). Genetic factors, perceived chronic stress, and the free cortisol response to awakening. *Psychoneuroendocrinology, 25,* 707–720.

Wüst, S., Federenko, I. S., van Rossum, E. F., Koper, J. W., Kumsta, R., Entringer, S., Hellhammer, D. H. (2004). A psychobiological perspective on genetic determinants of hypothalamus-pituitary-adrenal axis activity. *Annals of the New York Academy of Sciences, 1032,* 52–62.

Yeo, R. A., Gangestad, S. W., Thoma, R., Shaw, P., & Repa, K. (1997). Developmental instability and cerebral lateralization. *Neuropsychology, 11,* 552–562.

Social Motives and Goals

12 Making Connections and Avoiding Loneliness: Approach and Avoidance Social Motives and Goals

Shelly L. Gable and Elliot T. Berkman

CONTENTS

Science has documented, and personal experience confirms, that social relationships entail both pleasure and pain. Potential social incentives include affiliation, affection, intimacy, friendship, and love. The benefits garnered by positive social relationships are numerous and increasingly well documented. For example, Diener and Seligman (2002) identified the happiest people (i.e., top 10%) using multiple converging reports. The one aspect of their lives they all had in common was that they had strong positive social relationships. And, perceiving that one has supportive ties with others has been associated with numerous health benefits, including stronger immune responses and improved cardiovascular functioning (see Uchino, Cacioppo, & Kiecolt-Glaser, 1996, for a review). Finally, close relationships are cited by most people as a source of meaning in their lives (Klinger, 1977).

Equally potent though are the potential threats inherent in relationships, including conflict, rejection, humiliation, competition, and jealousy. Relationship woes are, more often than not, the primary reason people cite when seeking out psychotherapy (Pinsker, Nepps, Redfield, & Winston, 1985). Physiologically, the threat of social evaluation and rejection has been repeatedly associated with cortisol production (Dickerson & Kemeny, 2004); and negative emotional exchanges in close relationships have also been associated with increased ambulatory blood pressure, a precursor to cardiovascular disease (Holt-Lunstad, Uchino, Smith, Olson-Cerny, & Nealey-Moore, 2003). Sadly, violence in close relationships extorts a direct effect on mental or physical health at alarmingly high rates—the 1996 National Violence Against Women Survey found that 22% of women and 7% of men have experienced violence at the hands of an intimate partner (Tjaden & Thoennes, 2000).

One strategy might be to pass up the potential incentives of relationships in order to eliminate the risks. However, for centuries we have known that social isolation is not a viable alternative. Aristotle once wrote "Without friends no one would choose to live, though he had all other goods." In 1897 Emile Durkheim published findings examining the links between social ties and suicide through a variety of archival data such as church records. These records showed those with the fewest ties to church, family, and community were most at risk for taking their own lives. The risk of social isolation is not limited to self-inflicted mortality, as was illustrated in a prominent review by House, Landis, and Umberson (1988). The authors found that failing to maintain minimal social ties has a mortality risk similar to heavy smoking. Recent work by Cacioppo and colleagues has shown that loneliness is linked to various processes associated with increased morbidity and mortality such as poorer cardiovascular function and reduced sleep quality (Cacioppo, Hawkley, & Bernston, 2003). Given our evolutionary history of small group living, it should not surprise us that strong social bonds are so closely tied to survival (Bugental, 2000). The fitness advantage of strong social bonds has also been found in other primate species, such as the finding that the sociality of adult baboons was positively correlated with the survival of their infants; and this effect was independent of the dominance ranking of the adult female and environmental conditions (Silk, Alberts, & Altmann, 2003).

Thus, despite the precarious balance of social incentives and threats, people (and other primates) are tenaciously motivated to form and maintain strong and stable social bonds. Although there is a lot of evidence that people have a *need* for close social attachments (see Baumeister & Leary, 1995 and Reis, Collins, & Berscheid, 2000 for reviews), proportionally little work has investigated the processes involved in establishing, maintaining, and dissolving social bonds from a motive or goal theory perspective. Moreover, because of the documented

incentives and threats that are inherent in interpersonal relationships an approach–avoidance model of social motivation has great potential. That is, social motives and goals can be focused on a rewarding, desired end-state (approach); or social motives and goals can be focused on a punishing, undesired end-state (avoidance); and our understanding of both foci are crucial for understanding relational thought and behavior.

However, research on social bonds and close relationships has been concerned with *either* the rewarding aspects (e.g., companionship, love) or the punishing aspects (e.g., rejection, insecurity), and rarely has examined them in tandem. Given that interpersonal relationships present us with both threats and incentives, research on motives, goals, and the regulation of social behavior needs to simultaneously address the approach dimension and the avoidance dimension. Our objective for this chapter is to integrate work from the divergent fields of close relationships and approach and avoidance motives and goals, with the hope of enhancing our understanding of both. To accomplish this we will first review previous work on social motivation and discuss existing theories and findings in the field of close relationships in light of an approach and avoidance perspective. Then we will present our model of approach and avoidance social motivation and empirical evidence for the links between approach and avoidance social motives and goals and outcomes, focusing on a set of mediating mechanisms which we feel hold promise for understanding these links.

EARLY EXAMINATIONS OF APPROACH AND AVOIDANCE SOCIAL MOTIVATION

As the very existence of this book suggests, viewing motives to move toward desired end-states (appetitive or approach) and motives to avoid undesired end-states (aversive or avoidance) as independent and distinct motivations has been recognized for quite some time and across a variety of domains (e.g., Atkinson, 1958; Lewin, 1935; Miller, 1959; Pavlov, 1927; Schneirla, 1959; also see Elliot, this volume). The distinction has continued to garner support from contemporary theories of motivation and behavioral self-regulation. In addition, the appetitive–aversive distinction has been noted in a variety of areas outside of motivation, including affect, attitude, and coping processes (Cacioppo & Gardner, 1999; Gable, Reis, & Elliot, 2003; Gray, 1990; Moos, 1997; Tellegen, Watson, & Clark, 1999). The theoretical and empirical attention paid to social and relational motivation over the years has been far less than the attention given to other motives, such as achievement and autonomy.

AFFILIATION MOTIVATION

Relationship-relevant motives have been examined intermittently over the last half century and a review of this work reveals the early emergence of the approach–avoidance distinction. Among Murray's (1938) human needs relevant to social bonds, the need for affiliation (nAff) has received the most empirical attention. Some of the earliest work employed the Thematic Apperception Test pictures (TAT; Morgan & Murray, 1935). For example, Shipley and Veroff (1952) defined the need for affiliation as stemming from insecurity and rejection. TAT stories from control subjects were compared to stories from subjects who had recently been rejected by a fraternity or judged on likability by other members of their fraternity. Shipley and Veroff found that picture stories from the experimental subjects contained significantly more statements about actual or possible separation from others and thus concluded that affiliation motivation was "activated" in these subjects. The researchers then constructed a scoring scheme similar to the one created by McClelland and his colleagues to measure the need for achievement (McClelland, Clark, Roby, & Atkinson, 1949) to measure the strength of the need for affiliation with the TAT.

Also using the TAT, McKeachie, Lin, Milholland, and Isaacson (1966) found that students who scored high on need for affiliation performed better in courses led by instructors who were high in warmth and concern for others than students who were low on need for affiliation. Boyatzis (1968; as cited in Boyatzis, 1973) found that high and low need for affiliation people benefited less from a small groups course in achievement motivation training than people with moderate needs for affiliation. The author surmised that people higher in need for affiliation became focused on the interpersonal aspects of the training course (i.e., small group format) whereas people low in affiliation motivation were put off by the same interpersonal aspects of the group. Lansing and Heyns (1959) found that people with a high need for affiliation made more personal phone calls at work and wrote more letters than those with low affiliative needs.

Atkinson, Heyns, and Veroff (1954) expanded the definition of need for affiliation to include thoughts concerned with "establishing, maintaining, or restoring a positive affective relationship with another person(s)" (p. 405). They found that need for affiliation was positively correlated with approval-seeking behavior and confidence. Interestingly, need for affiliation (as measured by TAT responses) was negatively correlated with popularity. In their interpretation of their results, Atkinson et al. (1954) suggested that the arousal conditions activated two types of needs for affiliation: a hope of affiliation (approach) and a fear of rejection (avoidance). Subsequently, deCharms (1957) coded TAT imagery concerned with positive relationships and attaining affiliation as approach affiliation (+Aff) and TAT imagery concerned with separation and rejection as avoidance affiliation (−Aff) in a study of task performance in groups. The results showed that those high on −Aff were significantly more productive in competitive groups and less productive in cooperative groups than people with low −Aff.

Relying on expectancy theories, Mehrabian (1976) also distinguished approach affiliation motives from avoidance affiliation motives (Mehrabian & Ksionzky, 1972; Russell & Mehrabian, 1978). In this model, affiliation motives were based on expectations of positive and negative reinforcers in interpersonal relationships (Mehrabian & Ksionzky, 1972). Breaking from the traditional reliance on the TAT to study affiliation motives, he developed and validated two self-report measures of affiliative behavior, affiliative tendency and sensitivity to rejection (Mehrabian, 1976). He found that people high on affiliative tendency were less anxious, elicited more positive affect from others, were more self-confident, and saw themselves as similar to others. People high in sensitivity to rejection were less confident, more anxious, and were judged less positively by others than people low on sensitivity to rejection. These results marked one of the first taxonomies of affiliative characteristics in terms of a two-dimensional scheme based on expectations of positive and negative reinforcers in interpersonal relationships (Mehrabian & Ksionzky, 1972).

In 1973, Boyatzis conducted a review of the work on affiliation motivation, and noted that much of the work was empirically based on Shipley and Veroff's (1952) original idea that the need for affiliation was activated primarily in response to experiences of separation, rejection, or social evaluation. The other commonality of this work was the conceptualization of affiliation motivation as a classic deficit model (Murray, 1938) or as part of a drive reduction conflict (Miller, 1959). Boyatzis argued that an approach need for affiliation did not fit with these models because the existence of close relationships should not decrease affiliation motivation (as predicted by a deficit model), but rather the presence of relationships should stimulate further approach motivation. Boyatzis reasoned that individuals with high-approach motivation will: "(1) be relaxed, spontaneous and open in [his/her] behavior with others; (2) take steps to provide [himself/herself] with the opportunity to relate to others but not actively pursue others; and (3) be genuinely interested in others" (p. 272).

Boyatzis (1973) also argued that the distinction between approach and avoidance affiliation motivation was similar to Maslow's (1968) distinction between growth motivation and deficiency motivation. Thus, approach and avoidance affiliation motivation should be related to different outcomes. Boyatzis speculated that approach social motives should be positively related to outcomes such as sincerity, sensitivity, and popularity. Not only were these particular close relationship-relevant outcomes rarely examined, but also the majority of previous research focused on *nonsocial* outcomes, such as productivity in competitive groups and performance in achievement training courses. Moreover, none of the prior work examined the establishment, maintenance, or dissolution of real social bonds (i.e., outside of relationships created in the experimental laboratory).

The theoretical position offered by Boyatzis over 30 years ago is consistent with the contemporary idea that there are separate approach and avoidance systems, likely based on different neurobiological systems (Gray, 1987, 1990) which operate through independent processes. The approach social motive is focused on obtaining positive outcomes, such as closeness and intimacy, whereas the avoidance social motive seems focused on a negative outcome, avoiding rejection or loneliness. As noted by Higgins (1998), a fundamental principle of human motivational processes is approaching pleasure and avoiding pain. However, pleasure can refer to the presence of positive outcomes or the absence of negative outcomes, whereas pain can refer to the presence of negative outcomes or the absence of positive outcomes. Applying this principle to an approach affiliation motive, pleasure may come from obtaining closeness in personal relationships and pain may come from not being able to obtain the desired closeness. Regarding avoidance affiliation motivation, pleasure may come from avoiding rejection and insecurity and pain may come from failing to avoid rejection.

INTIMACY MOTIVATION

The vast majority of research on social motives has focused on affiliation and rejection motives. McAdams (1982) however, distinguished affiliation motives from intimacy motives by creating an additional scoring protocol for the TAT. He viewed intimacy motives as stemming from a more passive social orientation. McAdams thought interactions that resulted from intimacy motives would be reciprocal, harmonious, and disclosing. He conducted an experience sampling study and found that intimacy motivation positively predicted the frequency of positive emotions in interpersonal situations

and negatively predicted the desire to be alone during interpersonal interactions. Affiliation motives and intimacy motives were both correlated with time spent in verbal and written communications with others. Affiliation motives (but not intimacy motives) predicted desire to be interacting with others when alone (McAdams & Constantian, 1983). In a subsequent study, intimacy motivation predicted self-disclosure to and concern for the well-being of friends (McAdams, Healy, & Krause, 1984). More recent work by Sanderson and Cantor (1997) found that individuals with a strong focus on intimacy in dating relationships experienced greater relationship satisfaction and were more likely to maintain their relationship over time.

The work on intimacy motives is exciting because it examines social motives beyond affiliation and rejection. For example, intimacy motives are a form of social motivation particularly relevant to ongoing close relationships. However, it is unclear whether intimacy motivation is an approach motive or an avoidance motive. It is possible for intimacy motives to be focused on desired end-states (e.g., hope to obtain intimacy) or undesired end-states (e.g., fear of detachment). Work that examines a range of motives and goals in meaningful social relationships using an approach and avoidance perspective is still needed because it is clear that the strong links between social bonds and health and well-being are rooted in kinships, friendships, and romantic relationships.

INCENTIVES AND THREATS IN INTERPERSONAL RELATIONSHIPS

Although researchers and theorists in the field of close relationships have rarely used a motivational perspective in their work, they have touched upon processes related to approaching incentives or avoiding threats and punishments. It is interesting to note that almost all of this work addresses either incentives *or* threats and fails to examine them in tandem. In the following sections we review some of this work as preliminary evidence for the importance of establishing and testing a coherent model of incentive- and threat-based social and relationship motivation.

THREATS IN RELATIONSHIPS

One of the most influential theoretical perspectives in close relationships research in the last two decades is attachment theory (Bowlby, 1969). Recent applications of attachment theory in close relationships have focused largely on individual differences in sensitivities to threats.

The measure most commonly used at present is based on a two-dimensional model: One dimension is anxiety about abandonment and the second dimension is avoidance of closeness (Brennan, Clark, & Shaver, 1998). Individual differences in these two attachment dimensions have been linked to many relationship processes, including cognitive processing (Mikulincer, 1998), caregiving (Collins & Feeney, 2004), and sexual behavior (Davis, Shaver, & Vernon, 2004). It is interesting to note that contemporary researchers have focused almost entirely on threat management, and this has been quite fruitful in terms of advancing knowledge of close relationship processes. However, Bowlby originally also described exploration processes, which seem to us to be more in-line with incentive-based motivations.

Downey and colleagues have also described a construct called rejection sensitivity (Downey, Freitas, Michaelis, & Khouri, 1998). They define rejection sensitivity as the tendency to anxiously expect and intensely react to rejection by significant others. Individual differences in rejection sensitivity have also been associated with relationship processes, such as behavior during problem-solving discussions, negative emotions following conflicts with a romantic partner, and violence in relationships (Ayduk et al., 1999; Downey et al., 1998; Downey, Feldman, & Ayduk, 2000).

Biologically oriented studies of dyadic interaction have also focused largely on threats and punishing possible outcomes, such as rejection and conflict. These studies have documented harmful effects such as diminished immunological competence, heightened sympathetic activation, and increased neuroendocrine reactivity during interpersonal conflict or threats of rejection (see Kiecolt-Glaser, 1999, for a review). Studies on immune responses to social threats and rejection have been particularly insightful. Dickerson and others have highlighted the relationship between social evaluation (with the possibility of rejection) and the physiological stress response (Dickerson & Kemeny, 2004). A series of follow-up studies specified the connection from social rejection to shame experiences, and from shame to deleterious responses such as increased proinflammatory cytokine activity (Dickerson, Gruenewald, & Kemeny, 2004) and a heightened cortisol stress response (Dickerson & Kemeny, 2004; Gruenewald, Kemeny, Aziz, & Fahey, 2004). Social Self Preservation Theory (SSPT; Dickerson, Gable, Kemeny, Aziz, & Irwin, 2005) attempts to bring this work together by building a biopsychosocial model of social threats. According to SSPT, threats to status or self-esteem such as social rejection produce feelings of shame and humiliation, which in turn initiate a cascade of biological responses including hypothalamic-pituitary-adrenal axis hormone and proinflammatory cytokine release. This line of work is a first step toward uncovering pathways from social threats to disease outcomes.

Using functional magnetic resonance imaging (fMRI) to measure central nervous system activity, Eisenberger and colleagues have shown that one experience of social pain—rejection—recruits some of the same neural regions as physical pain (Eisenberger, Lieberman, & Williams, 2003; Eisenberger & Lieberman, 2004). Further investigations from that group have also shown that reports of social isolation during an experience sampling study are associated with activation in pain areas such as the dorsal anterior cingulate cortex, amygdala, and periaqueductal gray (Eisenberger, Jarcho, Lieberman, & Naliboff, 2006). An independent neuroimaging laboratory has confirmed these observations, adding that pain regions (e.g., dACC) are also active when participants imagine negative relationship scenarios (Gillath, Bunge, Shaver, Wendelken, & Mikulincer, 2005).

The biological evidence converges on the connection between social threats and deleterious outcomes ranging from negative affect and stress to immune responses and activation of the pain matrix in the brain. Given all of the links between social threats, social pain, and biological outcomes, it is not hard to understand the findings relating loneliness and isolation to poor health indicators (Hawkley, Burleson, Berntson, & Cacioppo, 2003), disease (Cohen & Hamrick, 2003), and even death (Berkman & Syme, 1979; House, Landis, & Umberson, 1988).

INCENTIVES IN RELATIONSHIPS

As we noted above, most of the research into the biology of social processes has focused on social threats. However, the existence of a parallel circuitry for a social motivational or attachment system regulating social rewards and social threats in mammals and humans has recently been posited (Insel, 2000; Panksepp, 1998). As in humans, the literature on animal social neurobiology, which has traditionally focused on the separation-distress system, is starting to turn to a social reward system (DePue & Morrone-Stupinsky, 2005; Panksepp, Nelson, & Bekkedal, 1997). Recent work on both animals and humans suggests that specific neuropeptides, such as oxytocin, are involved in the social attachment system (Carter, 1996; Taylor et al., 2000). Most relevant to the present discussion of incentive-based processes is the consistent finding that positive social interactions, notably those entailing affectionate contact, are associated with increases in oxytocin level (Carter, 1998), and in turn, oxytocin appears to stimulate affectionate contact, as well as affiliation (Insel, 2003) and nurturance (Taylor et al., 2000) in both humans and animals. Other recent work with humans also links oxytocin to trust. Specifically, Zak and colleagues (Kosfeld, Heinrichs, Zak, Fischbacher, & Fehr, 2005; Zak, Kurzban, & Matzner, 2005) have demonstrated that oxytocin levels increase following a gesture of trust from a partner, and that intranasal administration of oxytocin increases trust behavior in an investment game. Taken together with research connecting oxytocin to affiliation and affection, this work provides evidence that oxytocin is part of a social approach system in humans.

Furthermore, investigations using functional neuroimaging suggest that socially rewarding experiences activate brain regions associated with pleasure. Bartels and Zeki (2000, 2004) scanned new mothers while they viewed images of their infants and other familiar babies. A comparison of the two conditions revealed increases in the caudate, putamen, and nucleus accumbens in own-child relative to other-child picture viewing. Another study found activity in these same ventral striatum regions during amphetamine-induced euphoria (Drevets et al., 2001). It is not surprising that the ventral striatum is associated with rewarding social experiences since it is part of the dopamine reward system (Depue & Collins, 1999; Koob, 1999) and also rich in oxytocin receptors (Schlaepfer et al., 1998). Thus, we believe there is growing evidence that humans are biologically wired to desire social incentives. Our close relationships fulfill that desire. In light of the tight link between social incentives and biological processes, it is not surprising that relationship health seems to be coupled to the social incentives derived therein.

Aron and colleagues' work on the role of shared fun and recreation in close relationships is an excellent example of incentive-based processes. Studies by Aron, Norman, Aron, McKenna, and Heyman (2000) show relationship quality was improved by joint participation in novel, arousing activities. In a series of experiments, spouses were asked to complete strange tasks together such as traversing an obstacle course as fast as possible while holding a soft object between them without using their hands, arms, or teeth. When participants did these activities separately or did other arousing and novel activities alone, there was not a beneficial effect on relationship well-being. Shared recreation may benefit couple well-being because of the rewarding aspects of shared positive emotions.

Another example of incentive-based work in close relationships comes from research on love and affection. Some researchers have argued that the role that the emotion love plays in ongoing relationships is limited and that processes such as conflict management and the regulation of negative emotions is far more important (e.g., Gottman). However, research has shown that these presumably incentive-based relationship processes play an important role in the maintenance of close bonds. For example, in their longitudinal study of rural Pennsylvania newlyweds, Huston and Vangelisti (1991) showed that expressions of affection, especially by husbands, accounted for significant variance in marital satisfaction assessed two years later. Similarly, overt affection and expressions of love in the first two years of marriage predicted fewer divorces in a 13-year follow-up (Huston, Caughlin, Houts, Smith, & George, 2001).

AN APPROACH AND AVOIDANCE MODEL OF SOCIAL MOTIVES AND GOALS

Our recent work has focused on the link between approach and avoidance social motives and goals and social and relationship outcomes (e.g., loneliness and relationship satisfaction). This work is based on a hierarchical model of approach–avoidance motivation (Elliot, 2006; Gable, 2006) depicted in Figure 12.1. The model concurrently addresses the influence of dispositional individual differences (i.e., social motives), environmental factors (e.g., recent events in a particular close relationship), and short-term strivings (i.e., social goals) on behavior outcomes. The basic model can be applied to general social motives and goals (e.g., to make friends; to not be lonely), or it can be applied to motives and goals within specific relationships (e.g., to increase intimacy with my spouse; to not anger my spouse). As outlined in the model, approach social motives and the current incentives in the social environment predispose people to adopt short-term approach social goals; and avoidance social motives and current threats in the social environment predispose people to adopt avoidance social goals. For example, in a discussion on household chores, a husband who has strong approach social motives and recently has had several fun interactions with his wife will be more likely to adopt approach goals, such as "I want us to have an easy discussion and for both of us to be happy with the outcome"; whereas a husband who has strong avoidance motives and has had a series of conflicts with his wife in the last week will be more likely to adopt avoidance goals, such as "I want to avoid an argument and for neither of us to be dissatisfied with the outcome." Or, moving

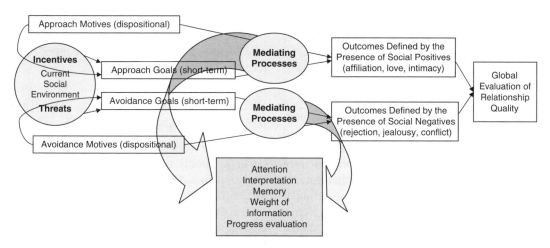

FIGURE 12.1   An approach–avoidance model of social motivation and social goals.

to a new town, a person who has strong approach social motives or who has had pleasant first encounters with new neighbors will be more likely to adopt approach goals when going to neighborhood block party, such as "I want to meet new people and make a good impression"; whereas someone who has strong avoidance motives or whose first encounters with new neighbors have been cold or hostile will be more likely to adopt avoidance goals, such as "I don't want to stand there alone or make a fool of myself."

Approach and avoidance motives and goals should be linked to different social outcomes (just as predicted three decades earlier by Boyatsis). Approach social goals will be strongly associated with outcomes defined by the presence of social rewards, such as affiliation and intimacy. For individuals who are largely approach oriented or find themselves in a reward-rich environment, pleasing interactions and relationships are defined as those which provide such rewards as companionship and understanding; painful relationships are those that fail to provide these rewards. Avoidance social goals will be strongly associated with outcomes defined by the presence of punishment, such as rejection and conflict. For individuals who are primarily avoidance oriented or find themselves in a threat-rich environment, pleasing interactions and relationships are defined as those that lack uncertainty, disagreements, and anxiety; painful relationships are those that possess these negative qualities. These social outcomes (i.e., intimacy, conflict) are predicted to combine and form global feelings about social bonds and relationship quality. It is also hypothesized that different processes mediate the relationship between approach goals and social outcomes and between avoidance goals and

social outcomes (we return to the question of mediating processes below).

Finally, two important components of the model are not easily captured in a figure: the special dyadic and temporal properties of social goals in the context of a relationship. Previous investigations into motivation (e.g., achievement) have focused on the individual as the unit of analysis. In the context of a relationship it is crucial to investigate not only the goals and motives of the individual, but also those of the partner, and perhaps even more importantly, the unique interaction of the two. Examining dyadic interactions in the laboratory provides an ideal way of capturing the richness of the interplay of the partners' social motives and goals in a relationship context. However, as sophisticated as one interaction may be, it still does not provide a complete picture. Social motives and goals are expected to fluctuate dynamically over time in a relationship, responding to progress assessments and changes in the partner and the larger social environment. Thus it is crucial to employ repeated assessments of both individual- and relationship-level factors. We believe that social motives and goals are connected to important outcomes, particularly in the context of close relationships. However, the potential of the model can likely only be fully realized with both dyadic and longitudinal methodologies. Research employing this model has established the links between social motives, goals, and outcomes. First, three recent studies by Gable (2006) found that individual differences in distal motives predicted more proximal goals. Specifically, individuals with strong approach motives were more likely to adopt short-term approach social goals (e.g., "Make new friends," "Be considerate to my family") and those with strong avoidance motives were more likely to adopt short-term avoidance social goals ("To not be lonely," "Avoid conflicts with my parents"; Gable, 2006). Moreover, as predicted by the model depicted in Figure 12.1, these motives and goals were associated with different social outcomes. Specifically, approach motives and goals were associated with positive social attitudes and more satisfaction with social bonds. Avoidance motives and goals were associated with more negative social attitudes and relationship insecurity. Both approach and avoidance motivation predicted loneliness, an outcome that features both incentives and threats (Gable, 2006). The effects of social motives and goals remained significant when controlling for general sensitivity to reward and punishment (e.g., individual differences in behavioral activation system (BAS) and behavioral inhibition system (BIS) sensitivities).

In subsequent research, Elliot, Gable, and Mapes (2006) created a brief measure of approach and avoidance goals that focused on friendships. They found that those with strong approach friendship goals reported more satisfaction with their social lives, and less loneliness than those with weaker approach social goals (Study 1). They also found that the strength of avoidance motives (fear of rejection) predicted the strength of avoidance friendship goals and that strength of approach motives (need for affiliation) predicted the strength of approach friendship goals. Finally, approach friendship goals were associated with positive changes in well-being over time and avoidance friendship goals were associated with increased physical symptoms over time.

Links between motives and outcomes have also been examined in specific relationships. Impett and colleagues (Impett, Gable, & Peplau, 2005; Impett, Peplau, & Gable, 2005) examined approach and avoidance motives in ongoing romantic relationships. Romantic couples' motives for everyday relationship sacrifices (enacting a behavior that is not preferred; such as accompanying a partner to a dull work function, not spending time with friends, and having sex when "not in the mood") were studied in a daily experience study that included a longitudinal component. The results showed that on days individuals sacrificed for approach motives (e.g., to promote intimacy), they reported greater positive affect and relationship satisfaction. But, on days when they enacted the same behaviors for avoidance motives (e.g., to avoid conflict), they reported greater negative affect, lower relationship satisfaction, and more conflict. Sacrificing for avoidance motives was particularly harmful to the maintenance of relationships over time: The more individuals sacrificed for avoidance motives over the course of the

study, the less satisfied they were with their relationships 6 weeks later and the more likely they were to have broken up. These results remained when controlling for initial levels of satisfaction.

PROCESSES MEDIATING SOCIAL MOTIVES AND GOALS AND OUTCOMES

Much of the work on approach and avoidance motivation either implicitly or explicitly posits that they are relatively independent systems. This also means that each system likely operates through somewhat different processes. For example, in a series of three studies on general approach and avoidance motivational dispositions (BAS/BIS) and reactions to daily events, Gable, Reis, and Elliot (2000) found that strong avoidance motives were associated with more daily negative affect (NA) and strong approach motives were predictive of increased daily positive affect (PA). More importantly, the relationship between approach motivation and PA was explained by varying levels of exposure whereas the relationship between avoidance motivation and NA was explained by varying levels of sensitivity. People with stronger approach motives experienced more daily PA because they experienced more frequent and more important positive events (exposure) than those with weaker approach motives. People with stronger avoidance motives did not report experiencing negative events more frequently or see negative events as more important, however, they reacted more strongly to the occurrence of negative events (reactivity) than those with weaker avoidance motives.

We have also recently found evidence for these different mediating processes in the social domain. Specifically, Gable (2006) found that approach social motives and goals were associated with increased exposure to positive events, such that approach motives and goals predicted increased frequency of the occurrence of positive social events (but not frequency of negative social events), which mediated the link between approach motives and outcomes. In addition, avoidance motives and goals were correlated with increased reactivity to negative social events (Elliot, Gable, & Mapes, 2006; Gable, 2006). Thus, there is tentative evidence that approach and avoidance motives are linked to social outcomes through different processes (Gable et al., 2000). The next step in the research linking social motives and goals to social outcomes is examination of specific perceptual, cognitive, and affective processes that mediate these links. Below we outline five processes we believe are likely to serve as mediators in our model.

ATTENTION

One mechanism linking motives and goals to outcomes is likely to occur very early in the processing chain, attention. Before reacting or responding to social incentives and threats, individuals must first attend to them. Work on general approach and avoidance motives has shown that individual differences in these motives predict increased attentional focus toward rewarding and threatening stimuli, respectively. For example, using the BAS and BIS scales as measures of approach and avoidance motivation, Avila and Parcet (2002) showed that participants higher in BAS (compared to those lower in BAS) were more attentive to targets when they were primed with a positive incentive cue than no cue.

In addition, numerous studies on anxiety disorders and phobias have shown that high trait anxiety (which is closely linked to avoidance motivation; Gable, Reis, Impett, & Asher, 2004) is associated with increased attention to threatening cues (Mathews & MacLeod, 1994). The emotional Stroop task has been used most frequently to study anxiety and attention. Subjects are presented with a word printed in colored ink. They are asked to name the color of a word, and if the word is threatening, people who are highly anxious—either dispositionally or situationally induced—are slower to respond to the threatening word. These delays are thought to reflect enhanced attention to the threatening word (MacLeod & Mathews, 1988) because people are unable to take their attention off the threatening word and attend to the color of the ink. The paradigm has also been used to study attention to rewards; for example, optimists show more interference on positive words (Segerstrom, 2001). There is also excellent evidence for domain specificity; spider phobic subjects were slower to respond to spider-related threatening words than nonspider phobics, but the two groups did not differ in their responses to other threatening words (William, Mathews, & MacLeaod, 1996).

Another technique used to study systematic patterns in attention is the dot-probe task. In this paradigm two words are simultaneously presented on a computer screen (e.g., a threatening word and a neutral word). After a 500 ms delay the words disappear and a dot appears where one of the words previously was located, and participants press a key indicating the dot's location. Using this technique, Derryberry and Reed (1994) have shown that individuals with strong approach motivation (defined by high extraversion [E] and low neuroticism [N]) were slower to shift attention away from locations indicating a positive incentive, whereas those with strong avoidance motivation (low E and high N) were slower to shift attention away from locations indicating a punishment. In addition, MacLeod and Mathews (1988) found that chronically anxious people are faster at responding to the dot when it appears in the threatening word space than in the neutral word space, whereas nonanxious people do not show this bias.

Thus, there is good evidence from research using the dot-probe technique and the emotional Stroop task that individual differences in motives and goals influence attention. However, none of this work has directly examined social motives and goals or social incentives or threats, nor does any of this work examine attention in existing relationships. In our lab we have begun a series of studies to examine social motives and attention biases. Although the results are preliminary, we have found that approach goals are significantly positively correlated with attention biases for positive social stimuli using human face stimuli in both the dot-probe task and the emotional Stroop task (Gable & Berkman, 2008). These results are promising even though more work needs to be done.

MEMORY

Another important cognitive process that is likely to mediate the association between motives or goals, and outcomes is memory. That is, social information that is attended to can influence expectations and future interactions only if it is stored in memory. Social memory and expectancies are important in ongoing social interaction because expectancy-confirmation processes have an effect on future interactions by influencing how new information is gathered from the target, behavior toward the target, interpretation of ambiguous signals, and through behavior elicited from the target (Neuberg, 1996). This seems especially important in ongoing close relationships as memories from repeated interactions with an individual likely lead to strong or elaborate expectancies.

Strachman and Gable (2006) found evidence for memory biases associated with social goals. Specifically, two studies examined the influence of approach and avoidance social goals on memory for ambiguous social information. In one study people with strong avoidance social goals had better memory of negative information of ambiguous social cues (Strachman & Gable, Study 1). Accordingly, they also had a more negative evaluation of the social actors. In another study, social goals for an upcoming interaction with a stranger were experimentally manipulated. Those in the avoidance goal condition remembered more negative information about the other person than those in the approach goal condition. They also expressed more dislike for the stranger in the avoidance condition than in the approach condition. These results suggest that goals bias memory of social information, however, the studies focused on social interactions created in the laboratory and not existing close relationships. Future work is needed to examine whether these memory biases exist in long-term close relationships.

INTERPRETATION OF AMBIGUOUS SOCIAL INFORMATION

Another process through which approach and avoidance motives and goals are expected to influence social outcomes is the interpretation of ambiguous stimuli. This is especially relevant in interpersonal relationships because social behavior is complex and multifaceted. Thus, there are often multiple interpretations of social cues and no definitive roadmap with which to judge another's behavior in an interaction. Many social events are subjective; a spouse's distance can be the beginnings of a bad cold or dissatisfaction with you; a stranger's smile can be flirtatious or polite. Strachman and Gable (2006) also analyzed the interpretation of ambiguous information. They found that those with strong avoidance goals were more likely to interpret seemingly neutral social information with a negative spin than those with weaker avoidance goals. For example, when told a man picked up his date at 10:00, those with strong avoidance goals were likely to state that the man was late picking up his date, even though there was no mention of him being late in the original scenario. Again, more research is needed to determine the role that goal-related interpretation biases play in ongoing intimate relationships. However, the implications of negatively interpreting neutral or even positive behavior from one's partner have for the health of a close relationship are clear (i.e., clearly bad).

WEIGHT OF SOCIAL INFORMATION

Once social information is attended to, interpreted, and remembered, it may or not be used in making global evaluations. That is, a series of negative interactions in a marriage may be interpreted and remembered equally by both spouses. However, one spouse may deem these interactions as irrelevant to her overall marital satisfaction whereas the other spouse may view them as an integral component of his overall marital satisfaction. Approach and avoidance social goals may systematically influence the type of social information that is used in global evaluations. Specifically, those with strong approach social goals should weigh the presence of

positive social information and interactions more heavily in global evaluations than those with weaker approach social goals. And, those with strong avoidance social goals should place more weight on the presence of negative social information and interactions when making global evaluations than those with weaker avoidance social goals.

Although we have not yet examined these ideas in the context of social motives and goals, Updegraff, Gable, and Taylor (2004) did examine this in the context of general approach and avoidance motivation and positive and negative emotions. Specifically, a lab study and a signal-contingent daily experience study found that high-approach participants (BAS) made satisfaction ratings that were more strongly tied to PA as compared to low-approach participants. Although avoidance motivation (BIS) was positively associated with the experience of NA, it did not predict the weighting of negative emotions in life satisfaction judgments. If we found parallel results in close relationships, differences in motivation and goals would influence how different qualities of relationships (e.g., intimacy, trust) are weighted in overall satisfaction. Specifically, approach motives and goals should be positively correlated with appetitive-relevant outcomes, such as passionate love, and avoidance motives and goals will be negatively correlated with aversive-relevant outcomes, such as security; and that those high on approach motives and goals will weigh appetitive outcomes more in overall satisfaction. These global evaluations of satisfaction are likely to be very important to relationship stability and decisions regarding staying or leaving a relationship.

EVALUATION OF PROGRESS ON GOALS

As noted above, a unique characteristic of close relationship is that they persist over time. Thus, it is very likely that progress on goals in interpersonal relationships is assessed and reassessed over time. On the basis of predictions from Carver and Scheier's (1982, 1990) Control-Process model, it is also very likely that a fundamental contributor to emotional experience will be the evaluation of goal progress. Specifically, this model outlines that individuals compare their current level of goal attainment to some standard; if progress exceeds the standard, PA is experienced; if progress falls short of the standard, NA is experienced; and if progress is equal to the standard, no affect is experienced. Moreover, the focus of the goal (approach or avoidance) also influences which emotions are experienced. When progress exceeds the standards in an avoidance goal framework, relief is experienced. When progress exceeds the standards in an approach goal framework, joy is experienced. When progress falls short in an avoidance goal framework, anxiety is the primary emotion. And, when progress falls short in an approach goal framework, disappointment is the primary emotion (Carver, 2004; Higgins, 1997; Mowrer, 1960). Relationship quality and emotional experience can be examined as a function of rate of progress on approach and avoidance goals in one's romantic relationship. Moreover, the cues for goal progress are likely to be different in approach and avoidance frameworks. For example, someone who has the goal of not being rejected by his partner is only one rebuff away from failure at any given time, regardless of how many accepting interactions he experiences with his partner. However, someone who has an approach goal of growing more intimate with his partner grows closer to his goal with each mutual disclosing interaction. We are not aware of any research that specifically examines goal progress in social relationships, but this is likely a fruitful topic for research.

CONCLUSION

In this chapter, we have outlined a model of social goals and motives and their impact on important outcomes such as relationship satisfaction and affect. This model grew out of our observations that previous work on social motives had focused on either incentives (e.g., affiliation) or threats (e.g., rejection), but never both in tandem. We believe our model is the first to consider both social incentives and threats simultaneously, working through different pathways, and relating to different outcomes. Unique features of social motivation in the context of ongoing relationships that may prove challenging to future research are the dyadic interaction of the motives and goals of both partners and the necessity of following relationships across time. However, our recent work investigating the social and cognitive processes linking goals to social processes indicates that the model may yield useful and important insights into our understanding of both close relationships and individual motivation.

ACKNOWLEDGMENTS

Preparation of this chapter was facilitated by CAREER Grant #BCS 0444129 from the National Science Foundation awarded to the first author.

REFERENCES

Aron, A., Norman, C. C., Aron, E. N., McKenna, C., & Heyman, R. E. (2000). Couples' shared participation in novel and arousing activities and experienced relationship quality. *Journal of Personality and Social Psychology*, 78(2), 273–284.

Atkinson, J. W. (Ed.) (1958). *Motives in fantasy, action, and society*. Princeton, NJ: Van Nostrand.

Atkinson, J. W., Heyns, R. W., & Veroff, J. (1954). The effect of experimental arousal of the affiliation motive on thematic apperception. *Journal of Abnormal and Social Psychology*, 49(3), 405–410.

Avila, C., & Parcet, M. A. (2002). Individual differences in reward sensitivity and attentional focus. *Personality and Individual Differences*, 33, 979–996.

Ayduk, O., Downey, G., Testa, A., Yen, Y., & Shoda, Y. (1999). Does rejection elicit hostility in rejection sensitive women? *Social Cognition Special Issue: Social Cognition and Relationships*, 17(2), 245–271.

Bartels, A., & Zeki, S. (2000). The neural basis of romantic love. *Neuroreport*, 11(17), 3829–3834.

Bartels, A., & Zeki, S. (2004). The neural correlates of maternal and romantic love. *Neuroimage*, 21(3), 1155–1166.

Baumeister, R. F., & Leary, M. R. (1995). The need to belong: Desire for interpersonal attachments as a fundamental human motivation. *Psychological Bulletin*, 117, 497–529.

Berkman, L. F., & Syme, S. L. (1979). Social networks, hos resistance, and mortality: A nine-year follow-up study of Alameda County residents. *American Journal of Epidemiology*, 109(2), 186–204.

Bowlby, J. (1969). *Attachment and loss: Vol 1. Attachment*. New York: Basic Books.

Boyatzis, R. E. (1968). The influence of need for affiliation on achievement motivation training. Unpublished paper, Harvard University.

Boyatzis, R. E. (1973). Affiliation motivation. In D. C. McClelland & R. S. Steele, (Eds.), *Human motivation: A book of readings* (pp. 252–276). Morristown, NJ: General Learning Press.

Brennan, K. A., Clark, C. L., & Shaver, P. R. (1998). Self-report measures of adult attachment: An integrative overiew. In J. A. Simpson & W. S. Rholes (Eds.), *Attachment theory and close relationships* (pp. 46–76). New York: Guilford Press.

Bugental, D. P. (2000). Acquisition of the algorithms of social life: A domain-based approach. *Psychological Bulletin*, 126, 187–219.

Cacioppo, J. T., & Gardner, W. L. (1999). Emotions. *Annual Review of Psychology*, 50, 191–214.

Cacioppo, J. T., Hawkley, L. C., & Bernston, G. G. (2003). The anatomy of loneliness. *Current Directions in Psychological Science*, 12(3), 71–74.

Carter, C. S. (1996). Neuroendocrine perspectives on social attachment and love. *Psychoneuroendocrinology*, 23, 779–818.

Carter, C. S. (1998). Neuroendocrine perspectives on social attachment and love. *Psychoneuroendocrinology*, *23*(8), 779–818.

Carver, C. S. (2004). Negative affects deriving from the behavioral approach system. *Emotion*, *4*, 3–22.

Carver, C. S., & Scheier, M. F. (1982). Control theory: A useful conceptual framework for personality-social, clinical, and health psychology. *Psychological Bulletin*, *92*, 111–135.

Carver, C. S., & Scheier, M. F. (1990). Origins and functions of positive and negative affect: A control-process view. *Psychological Review*, *97*, 19–35.

Cohen, S., & Hamrick, N. (2003). Stable individual differences in physiological response to stressors: Implications for stress-elicited changes in immune related health. *Brain, Behavior and Immunity*, *17*(6), 407–414.

Collins, N. L., & Feeney, B. C. (2004). A safe haven: An attachment theory perspective on support seeking and caregiving in romantic relationships. *Journal of Personality and Social Psychology*, *78*, 1053–1073.

Davis, D., Shaver, P. R., & Vernon, M. L. (2004). Attachment style and subjective motivations for sex. *Personality and Social Psychology Bulletin*, *30*, 1076–1090.

deCharms, R. (1957). Affiliation motivation and productivity in small groups. *Journal of Abnormal and Social Psychology*, *55*(2), 222–226.

Depue, R. A., & Collins, P. F. (1999). Neurobiology of the structure of personality: Dopamine, facilitation of incentive motivation, and extraversion. *The Behavioral and Brain Sciences*, *22*(3), 491–517.

Depue, R. A., & Morrone-Strupinsky, J. V. (2005). A neurobehavioral model of affiliative bonding: Implications for conceptualizing a human trait of affiliation. *The Behavioral and Brain Sciences*, *28*(3), 313–350.

Derryberry, D., & Reed, M. A. (1994). Temperament and attention: Orienting toward and away from positive and negative signals. *Journal of Personality and Social Psychology*, *66*, 1128–1139.

Dickerson, S. S., Gable, S. L., Kemeny, M. E., Aziz, N., & Irwin, M. R. (2005). *Social-evaluative threat and proinflammatory cytokine activity: An experimental laboratory investigation.* Paper presented at the Annual Meeting of the American Psychosomatic Society, Vancouver, CA.

Dickerson, S. S., Gruenewald, T. L., & Kemeny, M. E. (2004). When the social self is threatened: Shame, physiology, and health. *Journal of Personality*, *72*(6), 1191–1216.

Dickerson, S. S., & Kemeny, M. E. (2004). Acute stressors and cortisol responses: A theoretical integration and synthesis of laboratory research. *Psychological Bulletin*, *130*(3), 355–391.

Diener, E., & Seligman, M. E. P. (2002). Very happy people. *Psychological Science*, *13*(1), 81–84.

Downey, G., Feldman, S., & Ayduk, O. (2000). Rejection sensitivity and male violence in romantic relationships. *Personal Relationships*, *7*(1), 45–61.

Downey, G., Freitas, B. L., Michaelis, B., & Khouri, H. (1998). The self-fulfilling prophecy in close relationships: Rejection sensitivity and rejection by romantic partners. *Journal of Personality and Social Psychology*, *75*, 545–560.

Drevets, W. C., Gautier, C., Price, J. C., Kupfer, D. J., Kinahan, P. E., Grace, A. A., et al. (2001). Amphetamine-induced dopamine release in human ventral striatum correlates with euphoria. *Biological Psychiatry*, *49*(2), 81–96.

Eisenberger, N. I., Jarcho, J. M., Lieberman, M. D., & Naliboff, B. D. (2006). An experimental study of shared sensitivity to physical pain and social rejection. *Pain*, *126*, 132–138.

Eisenberger, N. I., & Lieberman, M. D. (2004). Why rejection hurts: A common neural alarm system for physical and social pain. *Trends in Cognitive Sciences*, *8*(7), 294–300.

Eisenberger, N. I., Lieberman, M. D., & Williams, K. D. (2003). Does rejection hurt? An FMRI study of social exclusion. *Science*, *302*(5643), 290–292.

Elliot, A. J. (2006). A hierarchical model of approach and avoidance motivation. *Motivation and Emotion*, *30*, 111–116.

Elliot, A. J., Gable, S. L., & Mapes, R. R. (2006). Approach and avoidance motivation in the social domain. *Personality and Social Psychology Bulletin*, *32*, 378–391.

Gable, S. L. (2006). Approach and avoidance social motives and goals. *Journal of Personality*, *71*, 175–222.

Gable, S. L., & Berkman, E. T. (2008). Which face in the crowd? Social goals and biases in attention. Manuscript under review.

Gable, S. L., Reis, H. T., & Elliot, A. J. (2000). Behavioral activation and inhibition in everyday life. *Journal of Personality and Social Psychology*, *78*, 1135–1149.

Gable, S. L., Reis, H. T., & Elliot, A. J. (2003). Evidence for bivariate systems: An empirical test of appetition and aversion across domains. *Journal of Research in Personality*, *37*(5), 349–372.

Gable, S. L., Reis, H. T., Impett, E. A., & Asher, E. R. (2004). What do you do when things go right? The intrapersonal and interpersonal benefits of sharing positive events. *Journal of Personality and Social Psychology*, *87*(2), 228–245.

Gillath, O., Bunge, S. A., Shaver, P. R., Wendelken, C., & Mikulincer, M. (2005). Attachment-style differences in the ability to suppress negative thoughts: Exploring the neural correlates. *Neuroimage*, *28*(4), 835–847.

Gottman, J. M., Coan, J., Carrere, S., & Swanson, C. (1998). Predicting marital happiness and stability from newlywed interactions. *Journal of Marriage & the Family*, *60*, 5–22.

Gray, J. A. (1987). *The psychology of fear and stress* (2nd ed.). New York: Cambridge University Press.

Gray, J. A. (1990). Brain systems that mediate both emotion and cognition. *Cognition and Emotion*, *4*, 269–288.

Gruenewald, T. L., Kemeny, M. E., Aziz, N., & Fahey, J. L. (2004). Acute threat to the social self: Shame, social self-esteem, and cortisol activity. *Psychosomatic Medicine*, *66*(6), 915–924.

Hawkley, L. C., Burleson, M. H., Berntson, G. G., & Cacioppo, J. T. (2003). Loneliness in everyday life: Cardiovascular activity, psychosocial context, and health behaviors. *Journal of Personality and Social Psychology*, *85*(1), 105–120.

Higgins, E. T. (1997). Beyond pleasure and pain. *American Psychologist*, *52*, 1280–1300.

Higgins, E. T. (1998). Promotion and prevention: Regulatory focus as a motivational principle. *Advances in Experimental Social Psychology, 30,* 1–46.

Holt-Lunstad, J., Uchino, B. N., Smith, T. W., Olson-Cerny, C., & Nealey-Moore, J. B. (2003). Social relationships and ambulatory blood pressure: Structural and qualitative predictors of cardiovascular function during everyday social interactions. *Health Psychology, 22*(4), 388–397.

House, J. S., Landis, K. R., & Umberson, D. (1988). Social relationships and health. *Science, 241,* 540–545.

Huston, T. L., Caughlin, J. P., Houts, R. M., Smith, S. E., & George, L. J. (2001). The connubial crucible: Newlywed years as predictors of marital delight, distress, and divorce. *Journal of Personality and Social Psychology, 80*(2), 237–252.

Huston, T. L., & Vangelisti, A. L. (1991). Socioemotional behavior and satisfaction in marital relationships: A longitudinal study. *Journal of Personality and Social Psychology, 61*(5), 721–733.

Impett, E., Gable, S. L., & Peplau, L. A. (2005). Giving up and giving in: The costs and benefits of daily sacrifice in intimate relationships. *Journal of Personality and Social Psychology, 89,* 327–344.

Impett, E., Peplau, L. A., & Gable, S. L. (2005). Approach and avoidance sexual motives: Implications for personal and interpersonal well-being. *Personal Relationships, 12,* 465–482.

Insel, T. R. (2000). Toward a neurobiology of attachment. *Review of General Psychology, 4,* 176–185.

Insel, T. R. (2003). The neurobiology of affiliation: Implications for autism. In R. J. Davidson, K. R. Scherer, & H. H. Goldsmith (Eds.), *Handbook of affective sciences* (pp. 1010–1020). New York: Oxford University Press.

Kiecolt-Glaser, J. K. (1999). Stress, personal relationships, and immune function: Health implications. *Brain, Behavior and Immunity, 13*(1), 61–72.

Klinger, E. (1977). *Meaning & void: Inner experience and the incentives in people's lives.* Minneapolis, MN: University of Minnesota Press.

Koob, G. F. (1999). Cocaine reward and dopamine receptors: Love at first sight. *Archives of General Psychiatry, 56*(12), 1107–1108.

Kosfeld, M., Heinrichs, M., Zak, P. J., Fischbacher, U., & Fehr, E. (2005). Oxytocin increases trust in humans. *Nature, 435*(7042), 673–676.

Lansing, J. B., & Heyns, R. W. (1959). Need affiliation and frequency of four types of communication. *Journal of Abnormal and Social Psychology, 58*(3), 365–372.

Lewin, K. (1935). *A dynamic theory of personality.* New York: McGraw-Hill.

MacLeod, C., & Mathews, A. (1988). Anxiety and the allocation of attention to threat. *Quarterly Journal of Experimental Psychology: Human Experimental Psychology, 40,* 653–670.

Maslow, A. H. (1968). *Toward a psychology of being* (2nd ed.). Princeton, NJ: Van Nostrand.

Mathews, A., & MacLeod, C. (1994). Cognitive approaches to emotion and emotional disorders. *Annual Review of Psychology, 45,* 25–50.

McAdams, D. P. (1982). Intimacy Motivation. In A. J. Stewart (Ed.), *Motivation and society* (pp. 133–171). San Francisco: Jossey-Bass Publishers.

McAdams, D. P., & Constantian, C. A. (1983). Intimacy and affiliation motives in daily living: An experience sampling analysis. *Journal of Personality and Social Psychology, 45*(4), 851–861.

McAdams, D. P., Healy, S., & Krause, S. (1984). Social motives and patterns of friendship. *Journal of Personality and Social Psychology, 47,* 828–838.

McClelland, D. C., Clark, R. A., Roby, T. B., & Atkinson, J. W. (1949). The projective expression of needs. IV. The effect of the need for achievement on thematic apperception. *Journal of Experimental Psychology, 39*(2), 242–255.

McKeachie, W. J., Lin, Y.-G., Milholland, J., & Isaacson, R. (1966). Student affiliation motives, teacher warmth, and academic achievement. *Journal of Personality and Social Psychology, 4*(4), 457–461.

Mehrabian A. (1976). Questionnaire measures of affiliative tendency and sensitivity to rejection. *Psychological Reports, 38,* 199–209.

Mehrabian, A., & Ksionzky, S. (1972). Some determiners of social interaction. *Sociometry, 35*(4), 588–609.

Mikulincer, M. (1998). Attachment working models and the sense of trust: An exploration of interaction goals and affect regulation. *Journal of Personality and Social Psychology, 74,* 1209–1224.

Miller, N. E. (1959). Liberalization of basic S-R concepts: Extensions to conflict behavior, motivation, and social learning. In S. Koch (Ed.), *Psychology: A study of science, Study 1* (pp. 198–292). New York: McGraw-Hill.

Moos, R. H. (1997). Assessing approach and avoidance: Coping skills and their determinants and outcomes. *Indian Journal of Clinical Psychology, 24*(1), 58–64.

Morgan, C. D., & Murray, H. H. (1935). A method for investigating fantasies: The thematic apperception test. *Archives of Neurology and Psychiatry (Chicago), 34,* 289–306.

Mowrer, O. (1960). *Learning theory and behavior.* New York: Wiley.

Murray, H. A. (1938). *Explorations in personality.* Oxford, England: Oxford Univ. Press.

Neuberg, S. L. (1996). Expectancy influences in social interaction: The moderating role of social goals. In P. M. Gollwitzer & J. A. Bargh (Eds.), *The psychology of action: Linking cognition and motivation to behavior* (pp. 529–552). New York: Guilford Press.

Panksepp, J. (1998). *Affective neuroscience: The foundations of human and animal emotions.* London: Oxford University Press.

Panksepp, J., Nelson, E., & Bekkedal, M. (1997). Brain systems for the mediation of social separation-distress and social-reward. Evolutionary antecedents and neuropeptide intermediaries. In C. S. Carter & I. I. Lederhendler (Eds.), *The integrative neurobiology of affiliation. Annals of the New York Academy of Sciences* (Vol. 807, pp. 78–100). New York: New York Academy of Science.

Pavlov, I. P. (1927). *Conditional reflexes: An investigation of the physiological activity of the cerebral cortex*. Oxford, England: Oxford University Press.

Pinsker, H., Nepps, P., Redfield, J., & Winston, A. (1985). Applicants for short-term dynamic psychotherapy. In A. Winson (Ed.), *Clinical and research issues in short-term dynamic psychotherapy* (pp. 104–116). Washington, DC: American Psychiatric Association.

Reis, H. T., Collins, W. A., & Berscheid, E. (2000). The relationship context of human behavior and development. *Psychological Bulletin, 126*, 844–872.

Russell, J. A., & Mehrabian, A. (1978). Approach–avoidance and affiliation as functions of the emotion-eliciting quality of an environment. *Environment and Behavior, 10*(3), 355–387.

Sanderson, C. A., & Cantor, N. (1997). Creating satisfaction in steady dating relationships: The role of personal goals and situational affordances. *Journal of Personality and Social Psychology, 73*(6), 1424–1433.

Schlaepfer, T. E., Strain, E. C., Greenberg, B. D., Preston, K. L., Lancaster, E., Bigelow, G. E., et al. (1998). Site of opioid action in the human brain: mu and kappa agonists' subjective and cerebral blood flow effects. *The American Journal of Psychiatry, 155*(4), 470–473.

Schneirla, T. C. (1959). An evolutionary and developmental theory of biphasic processes underlying approach and withdrawal. *Nebraska Symposium on Motivation* (Vol. 7, pp. 1–43). Lincoln, NE: University of Nebraska Press.

Segerstrom, S. C. (2001). Optimism and attentional bias for negative and positive stimuli. *Personality and Social Psychology Bulletin, 27*, 1334–1343.

Shipley, T. E., Jr., & Veroff, J. (1952). A projective measure of need for affiliation. *Journal of Experimental Psychology, 43*(5), 349–356.

Silk, J. B., Alberts, S. C., & Altmann, J. (2003). Social bonds of female baboons enhance infant survival. *Science, 302*(5648), 1231–1234.

Strachman, A., & Gable, S. L. (2006). What you want (and don't want) affects what you see (and don't see): Avoidance social goals and social events. *Personality and Social Psychology Bulletin, 32*, 1446–1458.

Taylor, S. E., Klein, L. C., Lewis, B. P., Gruenewald, T. L., Gurung, R. A. R., & Updegraff, J. A. (2000). Biobehavioral responses to stress in females: Tend-and-befriend, not fight-or-flight. *Psychological Review, 107*, 411–429.

Tellegen, A., Watson, D., & Clark, L. A. (1999). On the dimensional and hierarchical structure of affect. *Psychological Science, 10*(4), 297–303.

Tjaden, P., & Thoennes, N. (2000). Prevalence and consequences of male-to-female and female-to-male intimate partner violence as measured by the National Violence Against Women Survey. *Violence Against Women, 6*(2), 142–161.

Uchino, B. N., Cacioppo, J. T., & Kiecolt-Glaser, J. K. (1996). The relationship between social support and physiological processes: A review with emphasis on underlying mechanisms and implications for health. *Psychological Bulletin, 119*(3), 488–531.

Updegraff, J. A., Gable, S. L., & Taylor, S. E. (2004). What makes experiences satisfying? The interaction of approach–avoidance motivations and emotions in well-being. *Journal of Personality and Social Psychology, 86*, 496–504.

William, J. M. G., Mathews, A., & MacLeaod, C. (1996). The emotional stroop task and psychopathology. *Psychological Bulletin, 120*, 3–24.

Zak, P. J., Kurzban, R., & Matzner, W. T. (2005). Oxytocin is associated with human trustworthiness. *Hormones and Behavior, 48*(5), 522–527.

Achievement Motives and Goals

13 Approach and Avoidance Motivation in the Achievement Domain: Integrating the Achievement Motive and Achievement Goal Traditions

Todd M. Thrash and Anne L. Hurst

CONTENTS

In this chapter, we provide a historical and conceptual overview of the use of the approach–avoidance distinction in the achievement motivation literature. We begin with a few definitions that will constrain and delimit the domain of achievement motivation. The term *motivation* is often used to refer to the energization and direction of behavior (Deci & Ryan, 1985; Elliot, 1997; see also McClelland, 1987). Following Elliot and Dweck (2005), we define *achievement* as the attainment of competence or the avoidance of incompetence. Accordingly, *achievement motivation* may be defined as the energization and direction of behavior that is oriented toward the attainment of competence or the avoidance of incompetence.

The distinction between approach and avoidance forms of achievement motivation concerns whether behavior is energized by or directed toward positive possibilities (i.e., competence) or is energized by or directed toward negative possibilities (i.e., incompetence; Elliot, 2005, 2006).

The achievement motivation literature encompasses a number of approaches, including the level of aspiration approach (Lewin, Dembo, Festinger, & Sears, 1944), the achievement motive approach (McClelland, Atkinson, Clark, & Lowell, 1953), the test anxiety approach (Mandler & Sarason, 1952), the risk-taking model (Atkinson, 1957), attribution theory (Weiner & Kukla, 1970), the achievement goal approach (Dweck & Elliot,

1983), and the hierarchical model of achievement motivation (Elliot & Church, 1997). We focus primarily on the achievement motive and achievement goal approaches, which have been the most prominent historically, as well as the hierarchical model, a recent approach that uses the approach–avoidance distinction as a framework for integrating the achievement motive and achievement goal traditions. However, before turning to these literatures, we begin with a brief introduction to the classic level of aspiration literature. The early writings in this literature foreshadowed many of the important themes that later emerged in the achievement motive, achievement goal, and hierarchical model literatures.

LEVEL OF ASPIRATION TRADITION

Programmatic research on achievement motivation began with a demonstration in Kurt Lewin's laboratory that feelings of success and failure depend on one's *level of aspiration* (LA), the performance standard or goal to which one aspires (Hoppe, 1930). A given level of performance is experienced as a success if it exceeds one's LA, or as a failure if it falls short of one's LA. In an effort to explain goal-setting behavior, Hoppe argued that the adoption of a particular LA is determined in part by ego-related needs, including a need to keep the LA high (i.e., the need to achieve success, an approach need) and a need to keep the LA low (i.e., the need to avoid failure, an avoidance need; see Gould, 1939, footnote 2). Frank (1935) posited the existence of these same needs, but he argued that they influence the *goal discrepancy*, that is, one's LA relative to one's past level of performance, rather than one's LA per se.

A monograph by Gould (1939) suggested a need for greater nuance in the interpretation of LA data. Whereas previous theorists had implicitly treated the need for success and the fear of failure as mutually exclusive or as opposite ends of a continuum, Gould argued that these needs represent separate and independently varying dimensions. Gould also challenged the tendency to treat LA behavior as directly indicative of underlying needs. "It is psychologically not implausible that quite different inner motivations will, under certain circumstances, make for apparently similar overt behavioral responses, and as a corollary, similar inner motivations and needs will produce apparently opposite behavior reactions" (p. 36). Drawing on quantitative LA data and accompanying interview data, Gould argued that both the need to achieve success and the fear of failure may be manifested as positive or negative goal discrepancies. For instance, fear of failure may lead an individual to adopt an LA well below his or her past level of performance, thus ensuring

success; alternatively, it may lead an individual to adopt an LA well above his or her past level of performance, thus providing an excuse for failure.

Often regarded as the first theory of achievement motivation, the *resultant valence theory* was developed by Escalona (1940) and extended by Festinger (1942) and Lewin et al. (1944). Lewin et al. theorized that, when faced with a task having different levels of difficulty, an individual's choice of LA is a joint function of separate tendencies to approach success and avoid failure. The positive valence (i.e., value) of success is posited to increase with task difficulty, whereas the probability of success decreases with difficulty. The weighted valence of success for a given difficulty level is computed as the product of the positive valence of success and the probability of success; this variable represents the approach tendency at the specified level of difficulty. The negative valence (i.e., aversiveness) of failure is posited to decrease with task difficulty, whereas the probability of failure increases with difficulty. The weighted valence of failure for a given difficulty level is computed as the product of the negative valence of failure and the probability of failure; this variable represents the avoidance tendency at the specified level of difficulty. On the basis of an assumption that approach and avoidance processes have opposite effects, Lewin et al. computed the resultant valence for a given difficulty level as the weighted valence of success minus the weighted valence of failure. The individual was theorized to choose the difficulty level at which the resultant valence is maximized.

Although the variables that influence LA were posited to be situation specific, Lewin et al. also addressed the issue of individual differences in need strength. "Great differences exist among people in regard to the degree to which they are ruled by the tendency to avoid failure or by the tendency to seek success" (p. 366). Such individual differences were posited to influence the situation-specific valences; for instance, an individual high in fear of failure was posited to have stronger negative valences of failure across levels of task difficulty, generally leading to a resultant valence tendency that is maximized at lower levels of difficulty. Lewin et al. stated that this prediction is consistent with the observation that individuals with low goal discrepancies tend to be high in fear of failure. Although lacking some of the nuance of Gould's model, the Lewin et al. model has been particularly influential (Atkinson, 1957), likely because it is parsimonious and makes specific, readily refutable predictions about achievement behavior.

These early developments in the LA literature foreshadowed several important themes that would recur in the achievement motivation literature. First, achievement-related outcomes are influenced by the *goals* (e.g., LA) that the individual adopts in achievement settings. Second, a full understanding of achievement-related behavior and outcomes requires attention not only to the individual's goals, but also to the underlying needs that they serve. Third, a fundamental distinction—perhaps the most fundamental distinction—among need and goal constructs is whether the need or goal orients the individual toward the possibility of positive or negative outcomes; a construct may involve approach toward positive outcomes or avoidance of negative outcomes. We turn next to the need (motive) tradition, which was influenced by the Lewinian approach but which also had deep roots in the clinical literature.

ACHIEVEMENT NEED (MOTIVE) TRADITION

HENRY MURRAY AND COLLEAGUES

The contemporary concept of need or motive is generally traced to the writings of Henry Murray, who drew inspiration from Freud, McDougal, Jung, Adler, and Lewin. In conjunction with his colleagues at the Harvard Psychological Clinic, Murray (1938) published the landmark *Explorations in Personality*, in which he offered a theory and catalog of human needs. Convinced of the purposiveness of human behavior, Murray found directional tendencies to be better characterized in terms of the effects that are produced than in terms of physical movements or behaviors (actones), which had been emphasized by some instinct theorists. For example, Murray noted that the behaviors of putting food in the mouth and putting poison in the mouth are similar but have different effects; conversely, the behaviors of putting poison in the mouth and pulling the trigger of a revolver are different but may have the same effect. As illustrated in these examples, Murray argued that human behavior is more explicable in terms of the ends that are sought than in terms of specific behavioral acts.

Murray explained the directedness of human behavior in terms of underlying needs. Murray (1938) defined *need* as follows:

> A need is a construct (a convenient fiction or hypothetical concept) which stands for a force (the physicochemical nature of which is unknown) in the brain region, a force which organizes perception, apperception, intellection, conation, and action in such a way as to transform in a certain direction an existing, unsatisfying situation (pp. 123–124).

Murray conceptualized needs as operating dynamically. A need may be aroused either by internal stimuli (e.g., sensations produced by food deprivation) or by the press of external stimuli (e.g., the sight of a pizza). Murray portrayed need arousal as unpleasant and as enduring until a particular effect is achieved, typically as a result of motivated behavior that brings about the desired effect. Whereas the bulk of Murray's theoretical attention focused on the dynamic functioning of needs, he also employed the term *need* to describe individual differences. In this sense, a need indicates a potentiality or readiness to respond toward a particular end under particular stimulus conditions.

Murray distinguished between *viscerogenic needs*, which involve bodily tensions and satisfactions (e.g., the need for food), and *psychogenic needs*, which involve psychological tensions and satisfactions (e.g., the need for affiliation). Murray also drew an explicit approach–avoidance distinction. Among viscerogenic needs, Murray distinguished *positive needs* (e.g., need for food) from *negative needs* (e.g., need for noxavoidance, or need to avoid or rid oneself of noxious stimuli). "The positive needs are chiefly characterized subjectively by a desire to reach the (end state), whereas the negative needs are chiefly characterized by a desire to get away from the (beginning state)" (Murray, 1938, p. 80). Murray drew a similar distinction with respect to psychogenic needs. "On the basis of whether they lead a subject to approach or separate himself from an object, these (psychogenic) needs may be divided into those which are positive and those which are negative, respectively" (p. 84). Murray further classified positive psychogenic needs as being either *adient* or *contrient*. Adient needs are those that cause a person to approach a liked object (e.g., need for affiliation), whereas contrient needs are those that cause a person to approach a disliked object (e.g., need for aggression). Murray also used the term *abient needs* to describe negative needs (cf. Holt, 1931).

Although all needs are potentially operative in achievement settings, an achievement need or motive is one that explicitly concerns competence. Two of Murray's psychogenic needs meet this criterion.* The *need for achievement* (nAch), an adient need, involves the following desires and effects:

> To accomplish something difficult. To master, manipulate, or organize physical objects, human beings, or ideas. To do this as rapidly, and as independently as possible.

---

* A third need, the need for Counteraction, also concerns competence. Murray noted that this need has the following desires and effects: "To master or make up for a failure by restriving. To obliterate an humiliation by resumed action. To overcome weaknesses, to repress fear. To efface a dishonor by action. To search for obstacles and difficulties to overcome. To maintain self-respect and pride on a high level" (p. 195). However, after conducting his research, Murray decided that this need represents a combination of nAch and the need for Inviolacy, which is not achievement related. Accordingly, we have not classified the need for Counteraction as a separate achievement need.

> To overcome obstacles and attain a high standard. To excel one's self. To rival and surpass others. To increase self-regard by the successful exercise of talent (p. 164).

In contrast, the *need for infavoidance* (nInf), an abient need, involves the following desires and effects:

> To avoid humiliation. To quit embarrassing situations or to avoid conditions which may lead to belittlement: the scorn, derision, or indifference of others. To refrain from action because of the fear of failure (p. 192).

Murray argued that needs may be conscious or unconscious and that conscious needs may be reported accurately or inaccurately. Accordingly, Murray supplemented self-reports of need strength with other, diverse methods, including clinical observation and use of a picture-story exercise (PSE) called the Thematic Apperception Test (TAT; Morgan & Murray, 1935). The TAT methodology, for which Murray is perhaps best known, involved asking participants to tell stories about each of a set of pictures and then interpreting the thematic content of the stories. "One of its chief virtues," argued Murray (1938) of the TAT, "is that the subject reveals some of his innermost fantasies without being aware that he is doing so" (p. 545). Although Murray (1938) provided a rudimentary quantitative coding system for optimism–pessimism, interpretation of TAT stories for nAch, nInf, and other needs was based largely on the psychologist's subjective impression of the dominant or recurrent story themes.

DAVID MCCLELLAND AND COLLEAGUES

Murray's need tradition was carried on by David McClelland and his colleagues. McClelland (1951) embraced Murray's distinction between underlying needs and the means through which they are fulfilled but argued that Murray did not go far enough in consistently maintaining this distinction. "It would simplify matters if Murray's needs were conceived always in terms of the inferred goals of behavior rather than in terms of the behavioral trends usually characterizing the means of attaining them. In this way they would fulfill the purpose of the motive concept in psychological theory more closely which ... is to group together a variety of different behavioral trends around a common cause or a common goal" (McClelland, 1951, p. 407).

On the basis of an analysis of the clinical and experimental literatures on motivation, McClelland (1951) made the approach–avoidance distinction a central part of his conceptualization of motives. McClelland (1951) defined *motive* as "a strong affective association, characterized

by an anticipatory goal reaction, and based on past association of certain cues with pleasure or pain" (p. 466). McClelland et al. (1953) theorized that positive affect (pleasure) and negative affect (pain) are primary or unlearned states. Internal or environmental cues that are present while experiencing positive or negative affect become associated with the affective state; subsequently, those cues will redintegrate (activate) an affective state similar to the primary affect but anticipatory in nature. For instance, cues associated with shame experiences may subsequently redintegrate an anticipatory fear state. The affectively charged anticipatory state energizes either approach processes (when positive affect is anticipated) or avoidance processes (when negative affect is anticipated). McClelland et al. used the terms approach and avoidance with respect to the genotypic, motive level of analysis and noted that the phenotypic manifestation of a motive sometimes involves a directional tendency of the opposite valence. For instance, McClelland argued that an avoidance motive could motivate approach toward and removal of an aversive stimulus (cf. Murray, 1938).

Within the achievement domain, McClelland (1951) drew a conceptual distinction between the approach-based nAch and the avoidance-based fear of failure (FF), which correspond to Murray's nAch and nInf. "Thus we speak of *n* achievement when the person's primary goal is to enjoy the glories of success, and of *f* failure when a person's primary goal is to avoid the misery and disgrace of failure" (McClelland, 1951, p. 468). Atkinson (1957), similarly, conceptualized nAch as the capacity to experience pride upon success and FF as the capacity to experience shame upon failure. Most conceptualizations of nAch tend to emphasize the natural incentives (e.g., variety or effectance) that underlie the joy or pride of success (Elliot, McGregor, & Thrash, 2002; McClelland, 1987), whereas most conceptualizations of FF tend to emphasize the role of affiliative concerns in rendering failure a painful or shameful event (Birney, Burdick, & Teevan, 1969; Conroy, 2003; Elliot & Thrash, 2004; McGregor & Elliot, 2005; for an alternative perspective, see Schultheiss & Brunstein, 2005).

McClelland lauded Murray's multi-method approach to the assessment of personality but argued that fantasy measures (e.g., PSEs) provide the most direct access to the affective associative networks that comprise motives (McClelland, 1951, 1987). Accordingly, McClelland refined Murray's TAT assessment procedure and developed an objective system for coding nAch. McClelland et al. (1953) noted that their theory of motives, including the approach–avoidance distinction, was not fully in place when they developed their coding system for nAch.

Indeed, in their initial empirical work, McClelland and his colleagues conceptualized nAch as a unitary form of motivation analogous to the hunger drive. In a preliminary study, Atkinson and McClelland (1948) surreptitiously manipulated the duration of time since participants had eaten their last meal, administered a PSE, and examined ways in which the stories differed as a function of food deprivation. Atkinson and McClelland found that participants who had gone longer since their last meal included more references to instrumental activities directed at getting food. In fact, story content was found to be more reflective of the duration of food deprivation than were participants' self-reports of hunger, thus supporting the utility of the PSE approach to the assessment of motivation. McClelland, Clark, Roby, and Atkinson (1949) reasoned that if psychogenic needs operate in the same manner as viscerogenic needs, then nAch may be aroused by exposing participants to failure on an achievement task, much as the need for food had been aroused by depriving individuals of food. Accordingly, McClelland et al. (1949) developed a preliminary coding system for nAch based on differences between stories told under relaxed and failure conditions. However, doubts were raised about the appropriateness of manipulating nAch through failure experiences (McArthur, 1953; McClelland et al.).

In revising their coding system, McClelland and his colleagues focused on differences among stories written under relaxed, neutral, and achievement conditions, which differed according to the importance placed on a good performance on a set of achievement-relevant tasks (McClelland et al., 1953). This approach, like their original approach, was guided by a unitary conceptualization of the achievement motive. Participants in the achievement condition told stories rich in achievement imagery (imagery concerning competition with a standard of excellence, unique accomplishment, or long-term investment) and elaborated such imagery by, for instance, referring to achievement needs, positive or negative instrumental activities, and positive or negative anticipatory goal states. These and other story features became the basis of McClelland's final coding system (Version C) for nAch (McClelland et al.).

Once the nAch coding system was derived based on the study of manipulated motivational states, it was extended to the assessment of individual differences in motive dispositions. If, in the absence of experimental manipulation, a given individual tends to write stories with richly elaborated achievement imagery (i.e., stories that resemble those written by most individuals after an achievement arousal manipulation), then he or she was presumed to have a dispositionally high nAch. McClelland et al. (1953) reported a number of findings in support of the validity of their PSE as a measure of individual differences in achievement motivation. For instance, individuals high in nAch were found to improve more quickly on a scrambled word task, receive higher grades in college, and recall more incompleted tasks (McClelland et al.). Subsequent research has shown that nAch is predicted by socialization practices emphasizing independent achievement at an early age (McClelland & Pilon, 1983), and that it predicts preference on moderately challenging tasks (deCharms & Carpenter, 1968) and successful entrepreneurial activity (McClelland, 1965). An index of cultural nAch scored from children's literature has been found to predict the rise and fall of U.S. patents (deCharms & Moeller, 1962). More detailed reviews of the correlates of nAch are available elsewhere (Heckhausen, 1991; Koestner & McClelland, 1990; McClelland, 1987; Schultheiss & Brunstein, 2005; Spangler, 1992).

In the course of validating the nAch measure, McClelland et al. (1953) discovered signs that their measure may conflate an approach-based *hope of success* (HS; which McClelland, 1951, had called need for achievement) and an avoidance-based FF, such that HS is highest among individuals near the top of the nAch distribution and FF is highest among individuals in the middle (or the lower half; e.g., Atkinson, 1953) of the nAch distribution. In a study of recognition thresholds, for instance, McClelland and Liberman (1949) found that participants in the upper third of the nAch distribution were the fastest to recognize success-related words (e.g., success, mastery), and participants in the middle third of the distribution were the slowest to recognize failure-related words (e.g., failure, unable). The conclusion that nAch may conflate HS and FF was perhaps inevitable in light of the undifferentiated conceptualization of the achievement motive on which their instrument development process was based. McClelland et al. reported that they attempted, without success, to develop independent coding systems for HS and FF. Other early attempts were reported by Clark, Teevan, and Ricciuti (1956), Moulton (1958), Anderson (1962), and deCharms and Davé (1965). Atkinson opted to abandon fantasy as a means of measuring FF and instead operationalized FF as self-reported test anxiety, while continuing to use fantasy-based measures of nAch (Atkinson, 1987; Atkinson & Litwin, 1960).

A well-validated PSE measure of FF was developed by Birney et al. (1969). According to Birney et al., FF is manifest in participants' stories not as overt expressions of fear of failure, but rather as depictions of a hostile or threatening environment (hostile press), including reprimands for personal actions, legal retaliation, or deprivation of affiliative relationships. Birney et al. conducted a series of validation studies based on an alternative manifestations model similar to that of Gould (1939). These researchers reported that individuals high in FF tend to avoid participating in achievement tasks. If engaged in an achievement task, these individuals tend to adopt excessively high, excessively low, or otherwise erratic LA behavior patterns, as if avoiding meaningful task engagement. Individuals high in FF tend to perform poorly when the task is threatening (e.g., unfamiliar, complex, or timed) but may perform well when the task is not threatening. Independently of Birney et al., Heckhausen (1963) developed a coding system for both HS and FF using German-language materials. McClelland's nAch and Heckhausen's HS are so highly correlated that they are generally regarded as alternative indicators of the same, approach-based motive (McClelland, 1987). HS and FF tend to be weakly negatively related, indicating that they are largely independent dimensions, rather than opposite ends of a continuum or facets of a superordinate construct. Heckhausen (1991) reviewed additional evidence of the discriminant validity of these dimensions. Heckhausen's coding system has been translated into English (Schultheiss, 2001) and has been used successfully with U.S. participants (Thrash, Elliot, & Schultheiss, 2007).

Implicit and Explicit Achievement Motives

Beginning with Murray (1938), a number of researchers have developed questionnaires intended to assess nAch (Edwards, 1959; Jackson, 1974) or FF (Conroy, 2001; Hermans, 1990). deCharms, Morrison, Reitman, and McClelland (1955) reported that PSE and questionnaire measures of nAch were significantly but only weakly correlated, a finding corroborated by a more recent meta-analysis ($r = .09$; Spangler, 1992). The poor convergence and other findings have led some researchers to claim that PSE measures are invalid (Entwisle, 1972). However, McClelland has made a persuasive case that the poor convergence reflects the fact that PSEs and questionnaires assess different constructs. McClelland, Koestner, and Weinberger (1989) referred to the constructs assessed by PSE measures as *implicit motives*, and they referred to the constructs assessed by questionnaires as *self-attributed motives*. Hereafter, we refer to self-attributed motives as *explicit motives*.

Theorists have identified a variety of ways in which implicit and explicit motives differ. The majority of such theorizing has focused on implicit and explicit nAch or other approach motives. In an influential article, McClelland et al. (1989) reviewed evidence of the discriminant validity of implicit and explicit motives, including nAch. McClelland et al. argued that implicit nAch tends to predict spontaneous behavioral trends over time (operant behavior), whereas explicit nAch tends to predict immediate choices or responses to specific situations (respondent behavior). Implicit nAch was theorized to be activated in the presence of activity-based incentives (e.g., optimal challenges), whereas explicit nAch was theorized to be activated by explicit social incentives or demands (e.g., verbal requests to perform as well as possible). Implicit nAch was posited to be grounded in early, affect-based learning experiences, whereas explicit nAch was posited to be derived from verbally-mediated learning once the self-schema has developed. Finally, one's level of implicit nAch was presumed not to be consciously accessible, whereas one's level of explicit nAch was posited to be reflected in one's consciously held values. Empirical studies have provided strong support for the discriminant validity of implicit and explicit nAch and have generally supported McClelland et al.'s arguments (Brunstein & Maier, 2005; Koestner, Weinberger, & McClelland, 1992; Spangler, 1992).

Research on the discriminant validity of implicit and explicit motives has paved the way for a second generation of research focused on the consequences and predictors of *motive congruence*, the degree of correspondence between implicit and explicit motives. Incongruence between implicit and explicit nAch has been found to predict volitional depletion (Kehr, 2004) and decrements in subjective well-being (Baumann, Kaschel, & Kuhl, 2005; Kehr, 2004; for related research on motive–goal congruence, see Brunstein, Schultheiss, & Grässmann, 1998; Hofer & Chasiotis, 2003). Other researchers have sought to identify factors that predict motive congruence. As an organizational framework, Thrash and Elliot (2002) identified three potential classes of such factors: (1) motive characteristics (e.g., approach versus avoidance), (2) trait- or state-level moderating variables, and (3) methodological factors. The first set of factors has not yet been examined systematically, but researchers have begun to investigate the latter two sets of factors.

Regarding the second class of factors, Thrash and Elliot (2002) examined the moderating role of *self-determination*, which refers to autonomy or authenticity (Deci & Ryan, 1985; Sheldon & Deci, 1996). Thrash and Elliot argued that feelings of self-determination may reflect, at least in part, the development of explicit values that are well aligned with one's more deeply grounded implicit motivational proclivities. As predicted, self-determination interacted with implicit nAch in the prediction of explicit nAch, such that implicit nAch was a robust predictor of explicit nAch among individuals high in self-determination ($r = .40$, $p < .01$) but failed to predict explicit nAch among individuals low in self-determination ($r = -.07$, ns).

In a second study, Thrash et al. (2007) examined three additional trait moderators: *private body consciousness*, a sensitivity to internal bodily processes (Miller, Murphy, & Buss, 1981), *self-monitoring*, a tendency to monitor the social environment and adjust one's behavior or attitudes accordingly (Snyder & Gangestad, 1986), and *preference for consistency*, a tendency to seek consistency among cognitions (Cialdini, Trost, & Newsom, 1995). Thrash et al. proposed that private body consciousness may promote congruence, because the effects of implicit motive arousal are embodied and may be perceptible as gut feelings (see also Katkin, Wiens, & Öhman, 2001). Self-monitoring was posited to impede congruence, because the achievement values internalized from the social environment are less likely to correspond to one's implicit motives than are internally-generated values. Preference for consistency, finally, was expected to predict greater congruence, because individuals high in this trait would be more motivated to reconcile discrepancies between explicit motives and any rudimentary knowledge of one's implicit motives. Results showed that all three traits uniquely moderated the relationship between implicit and explicit nAch, suggesting that multiple, distinct processes are responsible for motive congruence. These three moderation findings corroborate, in a more differentiated fashion, the earlier findings of Thrash and Elliot (2002), in that self-access, resistance to heteronomous external influences, and personality integration are all core aspects of what it means to be self-determined (Deci & Ryan, 1985).

In related research on the congruence between implicit motives and explicit goals, Brunstein (2001) found that state-oriented (as opposed to action-oriented) individuals tend to adopt goals that are incongruent with implicit motives. More recently, Baumann et al. (2005) proposed that state orientation represents a vulnerability factor, rather than a direct cause, of incongruence. These researchers reported that state orientation interacted with stress to predict incongruence between implicit and explicit nAch, such that state orientation predicted incongruence under high but not low stress. In addition, motive incongruence led to lower well-being and partially mediated the effect of the state orientation × stress interaction on well-being.

Regarding the third set of factors, Thrash et al. (2007) examined a methodological factor that may impact implicit–explicit congruence. Thrash et al. argued that the correlation between implicit and explicit nAch may have been underestimated in past research due to a lack of correspondence of content between implicit and explicit measures (cf. Ajzen & Fishbein, 1977). Three existing measures of explicit nAch were found to be unrelated to implicit nAch, as assessed using Heckhausen's coding system for HS (r's = .00, .00, and .02). In contrast, a new measure of explicit nAch (Schultheiss & Murray, 2002), with item content that directly corresponds to the categories of Heckhausen's coding system, was found to be significantly related to implicit nAch ($r = .17$, $p < .05$). This finding, together with findings reviewed above, indicates that implicit and explicit motives are not statistically independent. Implicit and explicit nAch tend to share some variance, particularly when content-matched measures are used, and the extent of shared variance varies systematically as a function of moderator variables.

An important direction for future research is to identify variables that moderate congruence between implicit and explicit avoidance motives. In the study by Thrash and Elliot (2002), self-determination failed to emerge as a significant moderator of congruence between implicit and explicit FF, and we are aware of no studies that have successfully documented a moderator of the relation between these variables or other avoidance motives. The factors that moderate congruence for avoidance motives may not be the same as those that moderate congruence for approach motives. It would be worthwhile to explore the possibility that defense mechanisms (Baumeister, Dale, & Sommer, 1998; Egloff & Krohne, 1996; Vaillant, 2000) disrupt congruence for FF and other motives that threaten the ego, using rigorous methods for the assessment of nonconscious (implicit) motives that were not available in Freud's time (for primers on the use of PSEs in research, see Schultheiss & Pang, 2007; Smith, Feld, & Franz, 1992).

ACHIEVEMENT GOAL TRADITION

The achievement motive tradition gave rise to two influential theoretical traditions prior to the emergence of the achievement goal approach. The first was Atkinson's (1957) risk-taking model. Atkinson combined Lewin et al.'s (1944) resultant valence theory and the achievement motive approach by removing the contribution of individual differences from Lewin et al.'s valence terms and reintroducing individual differences in the form of separate motive variables (implicit nAch and explicit FF), which were posited to combine multiplicatively with the corresponding valence and probability variables. The second tradition was Weiner's (Weiner & Kukla, 1970) attributional approach. Weiner reconceptualized achievement motives as tendencies to make particular patterns of causal attributions for success and failure. Both approaches, as well as the achievement goal tradition that followed, reflected a broader cognitive revolution in psychology that had begun to take hold in the late 1950s (Cofer, 1981; Dember, 1974; Weiner, 1990).

The achievement goal approach emerged during the late 1970s and early 1980s. As reviewed by Thrash and Elliot (2001), achievement goal researchers articulated a number of critiques of the motive tradition, particularly McClelland's implicit nAch tradition. Most notably, achievement goal researchers argued that the implicit nAch construct is ill-suited for accounting for the specific ends toward which individuals strive in particular situations or contexts (Dweck & Leggett, 1988). Although a number of researchers have made important contributions to the achievement goal tradition, in the following we discuss the theories of Carol Dweck and John Nicholls, who are generally regarded as the most prominent pioneers of the achievement goal approach (see also Ames, 1984; Maehr, 1983). We then discuss Andrew Elliot's more recent contributions in critiquing and extending the achievement goal framework.

DWECK'S ACHIEVEMENT GOAL APPROACH

Dweck's goal conceptualization emerged from her studies of helplessness in elementary school children. In a series of studies, Dweck and her colleagues demonstrated that children of equal ability respond differently to failure (Diener & Dweck, 1978; Dweck, 1975; Dweck & Reppucci, 1973). Some children respond to failure with an adaptive *mastery* pattern characterized by attributions to insufficient effort, positive affect, sustained persistence and performance, and pursuit of challenge. Other children respond to failure with a maladaptive *helpless* pattern characterized by attributions to insufficient ability, negative affect, decrements in persistence and performance, and avoidance of challenge.

In order to account for these divergent response patterns, Dweck (Dweck, 1986; Dweck & Elliott, 1983) argued that children may pursue qualitatively different goals in an achievement situation, and that the type of goal pursued provides a framework that organizes affective, cognitive, and behavioral responses to failure. Dweck identified two types of achievement goals: *learning goals*, in which one aims to develop competence or master a task, and *performance goals*, in which one seeks to demonstrate one's competence. In the context provided by a learning goal, failure indicates that a new strategy or additional effort is needed, and therefore the adaptive mastery response pattern was posited to follow. In contrast, in the context provided by a performance goal, failure suggests a lack of ability and therefore creates a vulnerability to the helpless response pattern. This vulnerability to helplessness was posited to become manifest particularly among children low in perceived competence (Elliott & Dweck, 1988).

Dweck proposed the concept of implicit theories of intelligence to address the issue of individual differences in goal pursuit (Dweck, Chiu, & Hong, 1995; Dweck & Elliott, 1983; Dweck & Leggett, 1988). *Incremental theorists*, who believe that intelligence is a malleable quality that may be increased, were posited to adopt learning goals. In contrast, *entity theorists*, who believe that intelligence is a fixed entity, were posited to adopt performance goals. Thus, Dweck's full model consisted of implicit theories as antecedents of achievement goals, which, in interaction with perceptions of ability, are the proximal predictors of response patterns upon failure.

NICHOLLS'S ACHIEVEMENT GOAL APPROACH

Nicholls's achievement goal approach emerged from his investigations of developmental changes in children's conceptions of ability (Nicholls, 1989). Nicholls described these changes as a process of differentiation, in which children gradually come to understand that ability is distinct from other concepts such as effort. The typical 5-year-old, who has an *undifferentiated* conception of ability, feels competent simply as a result of learning or mastering a task. Ability in the undifferentiated sense is experienced immediately and subjectively as the gaining of insight or task mastery (Nicholls, 1984b). Feelings of ability in the undifferentiated sense are enhanced when a high degree of effort is required to conquer a challenging task. Effort implies that the task is difficult and, in turn, that one is able. By the age of 12 or 13, however, the child develops a *differentiated* conception of ability as an abstracted capacity. A valid inference about one's ability in the differentiated sense requires that one takes into account social performance norms and effort expenditure. For instance, one infers ability in the differentiated sense when one performs as well as others with less effort, or performs better than others with equal or less effort. Accordingly, task-derived feelings of competence may be overridden by the more sophisticated cognitive processes used in making an objective, comparative judgment of one's ability.

In applying his developmental work to the issue of adolescent and adult achievement motivation, Nicholls

(1984a) assumed that each person's purpose in an achievement setting is to demonstrate ability, but argued that individuals may aim for ability in either the differentiated or undifferentiated sense. Nicholls argued that under neutral conditions, one seeks ability in the undifferentiated sense. However, certain situations, such as interpersonal competition, promote use of the differentiated conception. Nicholls used the term *task-involvement* to describe the state associated with the aim of acquiring ability in the undifferentiated sense, and he portrayed task-involvement as an intrinsically motivated state. The term *ego-involvement* refers to the state in which one seeks ability in the differentiated sense, and Nicholls described this state in terms of preoccupation with the self and its adequacy. Nicholls has linked task-involvement to a positive pattern of achievement-related affect, cognition, and behavior. Ego-involvement, on the other hand, is linked to a nonoptimal pattern of responses; however, ego-involvement is posited to interact with perceptions of ability, such that ego-involvement is deleterious primarily for individuals with low perceptions of their ability. Individual differences in the tendencies to experience task- and ego-involvement were described by Nicholls as *task-orientation* and *ego-orientation*, respectively (Nicholls, Cheung, Lauer, & Patashnick, 1989).

Many similarities are apparent in the conceptualizations presented by Dweck and Nicholls, in particular the delineation of two qualitatively different types of achievement goals or states, one focused on the development of competence or task mastery (i.e., learning goal, task-involvement), the other focused on proving or demonstrating ability (i.e., performance goal, ego-involvement). Ames and Archer (1987, 1988) argued that the constructs proposed by Dweck, Nicholls, and other theorists (Ames, 1984; Ryan, 1982) are similar enough to warrant theoretical integration. Accordingly, they identified two types of achievement goals, which they called *mastery* and *performance* goals. Reflecting their numerous influences, Ames and Archer conceptualized goals as broad networks or frameworks that include the various goal contents discussed by Dweck, Nicholls, and other theorists.

Ames and Archer's theoretical integration likely contributed to a flurry of research on achievement goals that occurred during the late 1980s and throughout the 1990s. The conclusion that many drew from this body of research was that mastery goal adoption leads to a variety of positive outcomes, whereas performance goal adoption leads to a variety of negative outcomes. However, some researchers questioned the consistency of the finding that performance goals are maladaptive (Harackiewicz & Elliot, 1993; Harackiewicz & Sansone, 1991). The

performance goal construct apparently was in need of greater theoretical scrutiny.

ELLIOT'S TRICHOTOMOUS AND 2 × 2 ACHIEVEMENT GOAL FRAMEWORKS

Andrew Elliot proposed that the approach–avoidance distinction, which had been neglected in the achievement goal literature, may help account for the inconsistencies in the effects of performance goals. The approach–avoidance distinction had been given some nascent attention in the early achievement goal literature (Dweck & Elliott, 1983; Nicholls, 1984a), but subsequently this distinction was abandoned (Elliot, 2005). Dweck tended to treat both mastery and performance goals as appetitive (Dweck & Leggett, 1988) or treated performance goals as an omnibus category that included both the seeking of positive judgments of ability and the avoidance of negative judgments (Elliott & Dweck, 1988), and Nicholls portrayed task- and ego-involvement as forms of approach motivation (Nicholls, Patashnick, Cheung, Thorkildsen, & Lauer, 1989).

In the literature review of his dissertation, Elliot (1994) classified published experimental studies based on whether the performance goal manipulation drew participants' attention to the possibility of positive outcomes (which imply the elicitation of approach motivation) or negative outcomes (which imply the elicitation of avoidance motivation). Elliot found that the former tended to produce a positive set of processes and outcomes, whereas the latter tended to produce a negative set of processes and outcomes. An analysis of existing field studies led to the same conclusion (Elliot, 1994; see Rawsthorne & Elliot, 1999, for a meta-analytic review that supported Elliot's (1994) observations). Accordingly, Elliot (1994) proposed that the performance goal construct be bifurcated into separate performance-approach and performance-avoidance constructs. The resulting *trichotomous achievement goal framework* thus comprises three types of achievement goals. As conceptualized by Elliot, *mastery goals* are focused on the development of competence or the attainment of task mastery; *performance-approach goals* are focused on the attainment of normative competence (i.e., outperforming others); and *performance-avoidance goals* are focused on the avoidance of normative incompetence (i.e., not performing worse than others). Elliot (1994) confirmed the utility of the trichotomous framework using experimental methods (Elliot & Harackiewicz, 1996), and Elliot and Church (1997) further established the utility of this framework using classroom field data. As an illustrative finding, Elliot and Church (1997)

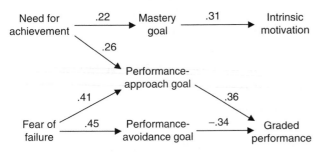

FIGURE 13.1 Hierarchical model reported by Elliot and Church (1997). Coefficients in the figure are standardized regression coefficients. All coefficients are significant at $p < .05$. Competence expectancy (not shown) was included as a predictor of mastery goal ($\beta = .34$), performance-approach goal ($\beta = .21$), and performance-avoidance goal ($\beta = -.14$).

reported that the adoption of mastery goals enhanced intrinsic motivation; the adoption of performance-approach goals enhanced graded performance; and the adoption of performance-avoidance goals led to a decrement in both intrinsic motivation and graded performance (see the right half of Figure 13.1). These findings were documented while competence expectancies were controlled. Numerous subsequent studies have attested to the utility of the trichotomous achievement goal framework (for reviews, see Elliot, 2005; Elliot & Moller, 2003).

The three goals of Elliot's trichotomous framework may be distinguished based on how competence is defined and how it is valenced (Elliot, 1999, 2005). The mastery-performance distinction concerns whether competence is defined in terms of self- and task-based standards (mastery goals) or normative standards (performance-approach and performance-avoidance goals). The approach–avoidance distinction concerns whether competence is positively valenced (mastery and performance-approach goals) or negatively valenced (performance-avoidance goals). Accordingly, the three goals of Elliot's trichotomous framework may be conceptualized as occupying three of the quadrants of a two-dimensional space defined by how the goal of competence is defined and valenced. Elliot (1999) and Elliot and McGregor (2001) argued that the empty cell of this 2 × 2 conceptual space represents an overlooked but important type of goal called *mastery-avoidance*, in which one avoids self- or task-based incompetence (e.g., not losing one's skills or not misunderstanding material). The addition of the mastery-avoidance goal construct results in four distinct goal types that compose the 2 × 2 *achievement goal framework*: mastery-approach (formerly called mastery goals), mastery-avoidance, performance-approach, and performance-avoidance. Elliot and McGregor (2001)

demonstrated that all four types of goals have distinct nomological networks. A number of subsequent studies have further established the utility of the 2 × 2 framework (for reviews, see Cury, Elliot, Da Fonseca, & Moller, 2006; Moller & Elliot, 2006).

HIERARCHICAL MODEL OF APPROACH AND AVOIDANCE ACHIEVEMENT MOTIVATION

PRIOR THEORY AND RESEARCH ON THE HIERARCHICAL MODEL

Elliot's second major contribution to the achievement motivation literature, in addition to introducing the approach–avoidance distinction to the achievement goal tradition, was to integrate the achievement motive and achievement goal traditions. Elliot and his colleagues (Elliot, 1997; Elliot & Church, 1997; Elliot & Thrash, 2001; Thrash & Elliot, 2001) argued that both traditions have strengths and weaknesses and that the strengths of one tradition tend to correspond to the weaknesses of the other. For instance, Elliot (1997) argued that achievement motive constructs are well-suited for explaining the *energization* of achievement-related behavior. An individual high in nAch, for example, engages in an achievement task because it arouses in him or her an anticipatory affective state that signifies a potentially satisfying affective experience. Although motives explain the energization of behavior, they are ill-suited for precisely predicting the *direction* of behavior in particular contexts, given that they are conceptualized and assessed as dispositional, global constructs. Achievement goal researchers had responded by developing context-specific goal constructs that were well-suited for making precise predictions about behavior and outcomes. However, in focusing on the goals that direct behavior, achievement goal researchers tended to neglect the issue of how goals are energized. Given these and other complementary strengths and weaknesses of the achievement motive and achievement goal traditions, Elliot argued that the best evolutionary option for the field was theoretical integration across traditions, rather than replacement of motive constructs with goal constructs.

Integrating achievement motive and goal constructs into a single model required a less expansive conceptualization of goal than had been typical in the achievement goal literature. On the basis of the traditional usage of the goal concept within and beyond psychology, Elliot and Fryer (2007) defined goal as a "cognitive representation of a future object that the organism is committed to approach or avoid" (for earlier approximations of this definition, see Elliot, 1997; Elliot & Church, 1997; Elliot & Thrash, 2001; Thrash & Elliot, 2001). In contrast, most achievement goal theorists have tended to define goals more broadly as the individual's *purpose* for engaging in achievement behavior (Dweck, 1996; Maehr, 1989) or as a broad cognitive *network* or framework that is defined in terms of a series of characteristics (Ames & Archer, 1988; Anderman & Maehr, 1994). On the basis of a review of the achievement goal literature, Thrash and Elliot (2001) showed that achievement goal constructs tend to encompass not only phenotypic *ends* or goals per se (e.g., performing well relative to others) but also the individual's genotypic *reason* for pursuing those goals (e.g., in order to demonstrate one's adequacy). These theorists argued that the expansion of the goal construct to encompass underlying reasons for achieving had been necessary in order for goal constructs to cover some of the conceptual space that previously had been covered by motive constructs. However, with the integration of the motive and goal traditions, it was no longer necessary, nor desirable, to use an expanded goal construct (Elliot & Thrash, 2001; Thrash & Elliot, 2001). Thus, Elliot's goal constructs, in both the trichotomous and 2 × 2 frameworks, have been conceptualized straightforwardly as represented objectives or ends (i.e., competence or incompetence, variously defined) that are sought or avoided.

Within Elliot's (1997) hierarchical model of achievement motivation, nAch and FF, whether implicit or explicit, are conceptualized as affectively-based dispositions that energize achievement activity and orient individuals toward the possibility of success or failure, respectively. The rudimentary sense of direction provided by motive arousal is insufficiently precise to regulate behavior effectively. However, motive arousal is posited to prompt the selection and adoption of achievement goals, which serve as concrete surrogates for their underlying motives and direct motive-derived energy toward specific ends. Thus, dispositional achievement motives are posited to exert a distal, indirect effect on achievement-relevant outcomes, with motive-charged achievement goals serving as the direct regulators of behavior and the proximal predictors of achievement-relevant outcomes. Similar ideas had been proposed by Nuttin (1984), who described goals as "concretized needs" and "cognitive-dynamic carriers," and by Emmons (1989), who portrayed personal strivings as "instantiations" of underlying motive dispositions.

The original presentation of the hierarchical model was based on the trichotomous achievement goal framework (Elliot & Church, 1997). Elliot and Church (1997) theorized that motives tend to orient individuals toward like-valenced goals; in particular, nAch was posited to

predict the adoption of mastery (i.e., mastery-approach) and performance-approach goals, and FF was posited to predict the adoption of performance-avoidance goals. Elliot and Church further theorized that FF would additionally predict the adoption of performance-approach goals as an alternative self-regulatory strategy, in which an individual strives to prevent failure by attaining normatively-defined success. This proposal is consistent with McClelland et al.'s (1953) argument, discussed above, that the valence of a motive need not match the valence of its phenotypic manifestation. On the basis of explicit motive measures and classroom goal data, the predicted pattern of motive–goal relationships was fully supported (Elliot & Church, 1997). Moreover, motives exerted only indirect effects on achievement outcomes; achievement goals functioned as the direct, proximal predictors of achievement outcomes (Figure 13.1).

Other studies have extended Elliot and Church's hierarchical model in various ways. Elliot and McGregor (1999) demonstrated that performance-approach and performance-avoidance goals are predicted by implicit FF, as well as explicit FF, and that state test anxiety mediates the negative effect of performance-avoidance goals on graded performance. Thrash and Elliot (2002) used structural equation modeling to demonstrate that superordinate nAch and FF latent variables, based on both implicit and explicit observed variables, predict achievement goals in the manner documented by Elliot and Church (1997). Studies of Asian-American students and Japanese students replicated the finding that the effects of explicit motives on outcomes are mediated by achievement goals, although some of the motive–goal and goal–outcome linkages were different than those based on general U.S. student samples (Tanaka & Yamauchi, 2000, 2001; Zusho, Pintrich, & Cortina, 2005). Elliot and McGregor (2001) extended the hierarchical model, using the newer 2 × 2 achievement goal framework as its foundation. Finally, Conroy and Elliot (2004) showed that explicit FF tends to predict change in achievement goals across time, whereas achievement goals tend not to predict change in explicit FF. This finding suggests that the relationships between motives and goals do not simply reflect overlapping construct or method variance, and it further suggests that motives exert a causal influence on goal adoption.

NEW DIRECTIONS FOR RESEARCH ON THE HIERARCHICAL MODEL

We conclude this chapter by pointing to several promising areas for future research on the hierarchical model of achievement motivation. Several of our suggestions concern the elaboration and extension of what we regard as the most important principles embodied in the model: *alternative manifestations* of motives and *alternative dynamics* of goals (see also Frenkel-Brunswik, 1942). The hierarchical model specifies that a given motive may underlie more than one type of goal (e.g., nAch underlies both mastery-approach and performance-approach goals) and that a given type of goal may be undergirded by more than one motive (e.g., performance-approach is undergirded by nAch and FF). This model nicely captures the non-1-to-1 correspondence between genotypic (motive) and phenotypic (goal) processes that, as we have seen, is a central tenet (if not the sine qua non) (McClelland, 1951) of theories of human motivation (Frenkel-Brunswik, 1942; Gould, 1939; McClelland et al., 1953; Murray, 1938; Thrash & Elliot, 2001).

To date, the nonnested hierarchical (lattice) structure implied by the principles of alternative manifestations and alternative dynamics has typically been tested using multiple regression, path modeling, or structural equation modeling. A limitation of these variable-focused analytic strategies in testing the lattice structure is that it is often not clear whether the alternative manifestations of a given motive are manifest in the same individuals or in different individuals. For instance, the fact that nAch uniquely predicts both mastery-approach goals and performance-approach goals may indicate that a high nAch leads individuals to adopt both types of goals; alternatively, it may indicate that a high nAch leads some individuals to adopt mastery-performance goals and leads others to adopt performance-approach goals. This is not a trivial distinction. For instance, in the former but not in the latter case, nAch would predispose individuals to what may be the optimal achievement goal profile—the simultaneous pursuit of performance-approach and mastery-approach goals. A related question is whether an individual high in a given motive is able to move flexibly among different goal manifestations as the prospects of reaching a given goal vary across time or contexts (see also Lewin's, 1935, concept of substitutability). For instance, if an individual high in nAch encounters difficulty in reaching a performance-approach goal, may the same motive energy be rechanneled toward mastery-approach, as an alternative means of motive satisfaction? It would be valuable in future research to supplement between-person, variable-focused research strategies with other, diverse analytic strategies (e.g., cluster analysis, multilevel modeling) and methods in order to learn more about how achievement motives and goals are configured within particular individuals (see also Block & Ozer, 1982; Frenkel-Brunswik, 1942; Magnusson, 1998; McClelland, 1992; Van Yperen, 2006) and across time

(for recent research on various forms of goal change, see Fryer & Elliot, 2007).

A second and related area in need of research concerns the factors that moderate relationships between motives and goals or that produce particular motive–goal configurations. The argument that a given motive may have alternative manifestations has an appealing richness; however, this richness could be construed as indeterminacy if the factors that influence the choice of a particular goal manifestation are not specified (Frenkel-Brunswik, 1942; Popper, 1965). We speculate that the choice of a particular outlet for a particular motive is a function of determining tendencies within the motive itself (e.g., FF may lead most spontaneously to performance-avoidance goals) and factors extrinsic to the motive, such as self-regulatory processes (e.g., a deliberate reorientation toward performance-approach goals) and environmental cues and affordances (e.g., a classroom atmosphere that promotes the adoption of performance-approach goals). It may be valuable to extend existing theories and research on motive–goal congruence (Schultheiss & Brunstein, 1999) and implicit–explicit motive congruence (Thrash et al., 2007) to the specific motive–goal links within the hierarchical model.

Third, research is needed on the consequences of particular motive–goal configurations. Certain manifestations of a given motive may lead to better outcomes than others, and a goal may lead to better outcomes if it is energized by certain motives rather than others. Moreover, certain motive–goal combinations may be particularly beneficial or detrimental, even if the motive did not give rise to the goal. For instance, nAch may have virtually no causal effect on the adoption of performance-avoidance goals; nevertheless, by chance alone, some individuals would be high in both nAch and performance-avoidance goals, and the adoption of performance-avoidance goals may provide a context that influences the way in which nAch is channeled or expressed. Likewise, implicit motives may tend to be relatively weak predictors of explicit goals; nevertheless, explicit goals may influence the expression of implicit motives (McClelland et al., 1989). The issue that we are addressing is distinct from that of the main effects of motives or goals, which does not take into consideration motive–goal fit or compatibility. A number of statistical options are available to address this issue, such as cluster analysis and motive × goal interactions in single-level or multilevel models. For instance, multilevel modeling could be used to examine whether the within-person relationship between goal endorsement and an achievement outcome varies as a function of individual differences in motives or motive profiles.

Fourth, whereas past presentations of the hierarchical model have emphasized the idea that cognition (goals) operates in the service of underlying affective and motivational impulses (motives), it would also be valuable to explore ways in which cognitive processes may recruit motivational energy. Research on inspiration, for instance, indicates that the approach temperament motivational system (Elliot & Thrash, 2002, in press) is "awakened" through experiences of illumination or insight and thereafter provides the motivational impetus for action (Thrash & Elliot, 2003, 2004). We speculate, similarly, that some instances of inspiration involve the instilling of new achievement goals that successfully awaken or recruit energy from nAch (e.g., implicit nAch), particularly among individuals whose nAch had been dormant or had not found adequate expression in the form of goal pursuit. Witnessing the beauty of mastery, including others' demonstrations of task mastery, as well as mastery-oriented imagery contained in one's own creative insights, may be particularly effective in inspiring the adoption of mastery-approach goals and in awakening a dormant nAch.

Finally, we should bear in mind that, as Murray (1938) emphasized, constructs are hypothetical and should not be reified. As we have discussed previously (Elliot & Thrash, 2001; Thrash & Elliot, 2001), empirical studies of the hierarchical model have assessed motives as latent dispositions and goals as context-specific aims, an approach that nicely emphasizes the conceptual distinction between genotypic and phenotypic levels of analysis but that does not capture a functionally integrated construct as well as it might. Rather than conceptualizing the energizational aspect as an abstraction residing at the person level (i.e., a motive) which is then made available to specific goals or aims in a particular situation or context, it may be desirable to view goal adoption as the creation of a new, context-specific cognitive-dynamic entity, called a *goal complex*. Murray (1938; see also Murray, 1936) provided an early precedent: "One might say that traces (images) of cathected objects in familiar settings become integrated in the mind with the needs and emotions which they customarily excite, as well as with images of preferred modes. A hypothetical compound of this sort may be called a *need integrate*, or *complex*" (p. 110). Allport (1937) noted, "Now, this conception of a need integrate is a great improvement over the skeleton need. It fulfills well our demand for a unit of analysis that is concrete, life-like, and personal" (pp. 241–242).

The methodologies of the motive and goal traditions may both prove useful in operationalizing this type of construct. For instance, whereas PSE methodologies are often optimized for assessing individual differences in achievement motivation across a variety of achievement contexts, the methodology could be adapted to study context-specific, implicit goal complexes. Specifically, the researcher could select context-specific rather than diverse pictures, and coding categories based on the 2 × 2 achievement goal framework could be integrated into the traditional nAch and FF coding systems. As a second approach, researchers are beginning to operationalize the end and reason components of achievement goals discussed by Thrash and Elliot (2001; Elliot & Thrash, 2001), using explicit, self-report methodologies (Fryer, Zahn, & Elliot, 2007; Urdan & Mestas, 2006; see also Grant & Dweck, 2003). Both the PSE approach and the explicit self-report approach permit the context-specific assessment of motivational variables, and both allow the independent operationalization of genotypic and phenotypic motivational processes. As in the motive literature, we suspect that these two methodological approaches to the assessment of goal complexes would yield largely independent, but partially overlapping, constructs. Accordingly, the issue of congruence between implicit and explicit constructs may prove to be a critically important research question in the goal complex literature, as it has been in the motive literature. In the spirit of Elliot's continual efforts at theoretical integration, we have offered these five recommendations in the hope that the hierarchical model of achievement motivation may stretch more deeply into the field's psychodynamic past while pushing the frontier with increasingly useful and veridical constructs, operationalizations, and analytic strategies.

REFERENCES

Ajzen, I., & Fishbein, M. (1977). Attitude–behavior relations: A theoretical analysis and review of empirical research. *Psychological Bulletin, 84,* 888–918.

Allport, G. W. (1937). *Personality: A psychological interpretation.* New York: Henry Holt and Company.

Ames, C. (1984). Competitive, cooperative, and individualistic goal structures: A cognitive-motivational analysis. In R. Ames & C. Ames (Eds.), *Research on motivation in education: Vol. 1. Student motivation* (pp. 177–207). New York: Academic Press.

Ames, C., & Archer, J. (1987). Mothers' beliefs about the role of ability and effort in school learning. *Journal of Educational Psychology, 79,* 409–414.

Ames, C., & Archer, J. (1988). Achievement goals in the classroom: Students' learning strategies and motivation processes. *Journal of Educational Psychology, 80,* 260–267.

Anderman, E. M., & Maehr, M. L. (1994). Motivation and schooling in the middle grades. *Review of Educational Research, 64,* 287–309.

Anderson, R. C. (1962). Failure imagery in the fantasy of induced arousal. *Journal of Educational Psychology, 53,* 293–298.

Atkinson, J. W. (1953). The achievement motive and recall of interrupted and completed tasks. *Journal of Experimental Psychology, 46*, 381–390.

Atkinson, J. W. (1957). Motivational determinants of risk-taking behavior. *Psychological Review, 64*, 359–372.

Atkinson, J. W. (1987). Michigan studies of fear of failure. In F. Halisch & J. Kuhl (Eds.), *Motivation, intention, and volition.* New York: Springer-Verlag.

Atkinson, J. W., & Litwin, G. H. (1960). Achievement motive and test anxiety conceived as motive to approach success and motive to avoid failure. *Journal of Abnormal and Social Psychology, 60*, 52–63.

Atkinson, J. W., & McClelland, D. C. (1948). The effects of different intensities of the hunger drive on thematic apperception. *Journal of Experimental Psychology, 38*, 643–658.

Baumann, N., Kaschel, R., & Kuhl, J. (2005). Striving for unwanted goals: Stress-dependent discrepancies between explicit and implicit achievement motives reduce subjective well-being and increase psychosomatic symptoms. *Journal of Personality and Social Psychology, 89*, 781–799.

Baumeister, R. F., Dale, K., & Sommer, K. L. (1998). Freudian defense mechanisms and empirical findings in modern social psychology: Reaction formation, projection, displacement, undoing, isolation, sublimation, and denial. *Journal of Personality, 66*, 1081–1124.

Birney, R. C., Burdick, H., & Teevan, R. C. (1969). *Fear of failure.* New York: Van Nostrand-Reinhold.

Block, J., & Ozer, D. J. (1982). Two types of psychologists: Remarks on the Mendelsohn, Weiss, and Feimer contribution. *Journal of Personality and Social Psychology, 42*, 1171–1181.

Brunstein, J. C. (2001). Persönliche Ziele und Handlungs-versus Lageorientierung: Wer bindet sich an realistische und bedürfniskongruente Ziele? [Personal goals and action versus state orientation: Who builds a commitment to realistic and need-congruent goals?]. *Zeitschrift für Differentielle und Diagnostische Psychologie, 22*, 1–12.

Brunstein, J. C., & Maier, G. W. (2005). Implicit and self-attributed motives to achieve: Two separate but interacting needs. *Journal of Personality and Social Psychology, 89*, 205–222.

Brunstein, J. C., Schultheiss, O. C., & Grässmann, R. (1998). Personal goals and emotional well-being: The moderating role of motive dispositions. *Journal of Personality and Social Psychology, 75*, 494–508.

Cialdini, R. B., Trost, M. R., & Newsom, J. T. (1995). Preference for consistency: The development of a valid measure and the discovery of surprising behavioral implications. *Journal of Personality and Social Psychology, 69*, 318–328.

Clark, R. A., Teevan, R., & Ricciuti, H. N. (1956). Hope of success and fear of failure as aspects of need for achievement. *The Journal of Abnormal and Social Psychology, 53*, 182–186.

Cofer, C. N. (1981). The history of the concept of motivation. *Journal of the History of the Behavioral Sciences, 17*, 48–53.

Conroy, D. E. (2001). Progress in the development of a multi-dimensional measure of fear of failure: The performance failure appraisal inventory (PFAI). *Anxiety, Stress, and Coping, 14*, 431–452.

Conroy, D. E. (2003). Representational models associated with fear of failure in adolescents and young adults. *Journal of Personality, 71*, 757–783.

Conroy, D. E., & Elliot, A. J. (2004). Fear of failure and achievement goals in sport: Addressing the issue of the chicken and the egg. *Anxiety, Stress, and Coping: An International Journal, 17*, 271–285.

Cury, F., Elliot, A. J., Da Fonseca, D., & Moller, A. C. (2006). The social-cognitive model of achievement motivation and the 2 × 2 achievement goal framework. *Journal of Personality and Social Psychology, 90*, 666–679.

Deci, E. L., & Ryan, R. M. (1985). *Intrinsic motivation and self-determination in human behavior.* New York: Plenum.

deCharms, R., & Carpenter, V. (1968). Measuring motivation in culturally disadvantaged school children. In H. J. Klausmeirer & G. T. O'Hearn (Eds.), *Research and development toward the improvement of education.* Madison, WI: Educational Research Services.

deCharms, R., & Davé, P. N. (1965). Hope of success, fear of failure, subjective probability, and risk-taking behavior. *Journal of Personality and Social Psychology, 1*, 558–568.

deCharms, R., & Moeller, G. H. (1962). Values expressed in American children's readers: 1800–1950. *Journal of Abnormal and Social Psychology, 64*, 136–142.

deCharms, R., Morrison, H. W., Reitman, W., & McClelland, D. C. (1955). Behavioral correlates of directly and indirectly measured achievement motivation. In D. C. McClelland (Ed.), *Studies in motivation* (pp. 414–423). New York: Appleton-Century-Crofts.

Dember, W. N. (1974). Motivation and the cognitive revolution. *American Psychologist, 29*, 161–168.

Diener, C. I., & Dweck, C. S. (1978). An analysis of learned helplessness: Continuous changes in performance, strategy and achievement cognitions following failure. *Journal of Personality and Social Psychology, 36*, 451–462.

Dweck, C. S. (1975). The role of expectations and attributions in the alleviation of learned helplessness. *Journal of Personality and Social Psychology, 31*, 674–685.

Dweck, C. S. (1986). Motivational processes affecting learning. *American Psychologist, 41*, 1040–1048.

Dweck, C. S. (1996). Capturing the dynamic nature of personality. *Journal of Research in Personality, 30*, 348–362.

Dweck, C. S., Chiu, C., & Hong, Y. (1995). Implicit theories and their role in judgments and reactions: A world from two perspectives. *Psychological Inquiry, 6*, 267–285.

Dweck, C. S., & Elliott, E. S. (1983). Achievement motivation. In P. H. Mussen (Gen. Ed.) & E. M. Hetherington (Vol. Ed.), *Handbook of child psychology: Vol. IV. Socialization, personality, and social development* (4th ed., pp. 643–691). New York: John Wiley & Sons.

Dweck, C. S., & Leggett, E. L. (1988). A social-cognitive approach to motivation and personality. *Psychological Review, 95*, 256–273.

Dweck, C. S., & Reppucci, N. D. (1973). Learned helplessness and reinforcement responsibility in children. *Journal of Personality and Social Psychology, 25,* 109–116.

Edwards, A. L. (1959). *Edwards personality preference schedule manual—revised.* Cleveland, OH: Psychological Corporation.

Egloff, B., & Krohne, H. W. (1996). Repressive emotional discreteness after failure. *Journal of Personality and Social Psychology, 70,* 1318–1326.

Elliot, A. J. (1994). *Approach and avoidance achievement goals: An intrinsic motivation analysis.* Unpublished doctoral dissertation, University of Wisconsin, Madison, WI.

Elliot, A. J. (1997). Integrating the "classic" and "contemporary" approaches to achievement motivation: A hierarchical model of approach and avoidance achievement motivation. In M. L. Maehr & P. R. Pintrich (Eds.), *Advances in motivation and achievement* (Vol. 10, pp. 143–179). Greenwich, CT: JAI Press.

Elliot, A. J. (1999). Approach and avoidance motivation and achievement goals. *Educational Psychologist, 34,* 149–169.

Elliot, A. J. (2005). A conceptual history of the achievement goal construct. In A. Elliot & C. Dweck (Eds.), *Handbook of competence and motivation* (pp. 52–72). New York: Guilford Press.

Elliot, A. J. (2006). The hierarchical model of approach–avoidance motivation. *Motivation and Emotion, 30,* 111–116.

Elliot, A. J., & Church, M. A. (1997). A hierarchical model of approach and avoidance achievement motivation. *Journal of Personality and Social Psychology, 72,* 218–232.

Elliot, A. J., & Dweck, D. S. (2005). Competence as the core of achievement motivation. In A. Elliot & C. Dweck (Eds.), *Handbook of competence and motivation* (pp. 3–12). New York: Guilford Press.

Elliot, A. J., & Fryer, J. W. (2007). The goal construct in psychology. In J. Shah & W. Gardner (Eds.), *Handbook of motivational science* (pp. 235–250). New York: Guilford Press.

Elliot, A. J., & Harackiewicz, J. M. (1996). Approach and avoidance achievement goals and intrinsic motivation: A mediational analysis. *Journal of Personality and Social Psychology, 70,* 461–475.

Elliot, A. J., & McGregor, H. A. (1999). Test anxiety and the hierarchical model of approach and avoidance achievement motivation. *Journal of Personality and Social Psychology, 76,* 628–644.

Elliot, A. J., & McGregor, H. A. (2001). A 2 × 2 achievement goal framework. *Journal of Personality and Social Psychology, 80,* 501–519.

Elliot, A. J., McGregor, H. A., & Thrash, T. M. (2002). The need for competence. In E. Deci & R. Ryan (Eds.), *Handbook of self-determination Theory* (pp. 361–387). Rochester: University of Rochester Press.

Elliot, A. J., & Moller, A. (2003). Performance-approach goals: Good or bad forms of regulation? *International Journal of Educational Research, 39,* 339–356.

Elliot, A. J., & Thrash, T. M. (2001). Achievement goals and the hierarchical model of achievement motivation. *Educational Psychology Review, 12,* 139–156.

Elliot, A. J., & Thrash, T. M. (2002). Approach–avoidance motivation in personality: Approach and avoidance temperaments and goals. *Journal of Personality and Social Psychology, 82,* 804–818.

Elliot, A. J., & Thrash, T. M. (2004). The intergenerational transmission of fear of failure. *Personality and Social Psychology Bulletin, 30,* 957–971.

Elliot, A. J., & Thrash, T. M. (in press). Approach and avoidance temperaments. In G. J. Boyle, G. Matthews, & D. H. Saklofske (Eds.), *The Sage handbook of personality theory and assesment: Vol. 1. Personality theories and models.* Thousand Oaks, CA: Sage Publications.

Elliott, E. S., & Dweck, C. S. (1988). Goals: An approach to motivation and achievement. *Journal of Personality and Social Psychology, 54,* 5–12.

Emmons, R. A. (1989). The personal striving approach to personality. In L. A. Pervin (Ed.), *Goal concepts in personality and social psychology* (pp. 87–126). Hillsdale, NJ: Lawrence Erlbaum Associates.

Entwisle, D. R. (1972). To dispel fantasies about fantasy-based measures of achievement motivation. *Psychological Bulletin, 77,* 377–391.

Escalona, S. K. (1940). The effect of success and failure upon the level of aspiration and behavior in manic-depressive psychoses. *University of Iowa, Studies in Child Welfare, 16,* 199–302.

Festinger, L. (1942). A theoretical interpretation of shifts in level of aspiration. *Psychological Review, 49,* 235–250.

Frank, J. D. (1935). Some psychological determinants of the level of aspiration. *American Journal of Psychology, 47,* 285–293.

Frenkel-Brunswik, E. (1942). Motivation and behavior. *Genetic Psychology Monographs, 26,* 121–265.

Fryer, J. W., & Elliot, A. J. (2007). Stability and change in achievement goals. *Journal of Educational Psychology 99,* 700–714.

Fryer, J. W., Zahn, I., & Elliot, A. J. (2007, April). *The reasons behind achievement goal endorsement: A qualitative analysis.* Paper presented at the annual meeting of the American Educational Research Association, Chicago, IL.

Gould, R. (1939). An experimental analysis of "level of aspiration." *Genetic Psychology Monographs, 21,* 3–115.

Grant, H., & Dweck, C. S. (2003). Clarifying achievement goals and their impact. *Journal of Personality and Social Psychology, 85,* 541–553.

Harackiewicz, J. M., & Elliot, A. J. (1993). Achievement goals and intrinsic motivation. *Journal of Personality and Social Psychology, 65,* 904–915.

Harackiewicz, J. M., & Sansone, C. (1991). Goals and intrinsic motivation: You can get there from here. In M. Maehr & P. Pintrich (Eds.), *Advances in motivation and achievement* (Vol. 7, pp. 21–49). Greenwich, CT: JAI Press.

Heckhausen, H. (1963). *Hoffnung und Furcht in der Leistungsmotivation.* Meisenheim/Glan: Hain.

Heckhausen, H. (1991). *Motivation and action.* Berlin: Springer-Verlag.

Hermans, W. (1990). Fear of failure as a distinctive personality trait measure of test anxiety. *Journal of Research and Development in Education, 23*, 180–185.

Hofer, J., & Chasiotis, A. (2003). Congruence of life goals and implicit motives as predictors of life satisfaction: Cross-cultural implications of a study of Zambian male adolescents. *Motivation and Emotion, 27*, 251–272.

Holt, E. B. (1931). *Animal drive and the learning process: An essay toward radical empiricism.* New York: Holt and Company.

Hoppe, F. (1930). Untersuchungen zur Handlungs- und Affektpsychologie. IX. Erfolg und Mißerfolg [Psychological studies of action and affect. IX. Success and failure]. *Psychologische Forschung, 14*, 1–63.

Jackson, D. N. (1974). *Manual for the personality research form.* Goshen, New York: Research Psychology Press.

Katkin, E. S., Wiens, S., & Öhman, A. (2001). Nonconscious fear conditioning, visceral perception, and the development of gut feelings. *Psychological Science, 12*, 366–370.

Kehr, H. M. (2004). Implicit/explicit motive discrepancies and volitional depletion among managers. *Personality and Social Psychology Bulletin, 30*, 315–327.

Koestner, R., & McClelland, D. C. (1990). Perspectives on competence motivation. In L. A. Pervin (Ed.), *Handbook of personality: Theory and research* (pp. 527–548). New York: Guilford Press.

Koestner, R., Weinberger, J., & McClelland, D. C. (1992). Task-intrinsic and social-extrinsic sources of arousal for motives assessed in fantasy and self-report. *Journal of Personality, 59*, 57–82.

Lewin, K. (1935). *A dynamic theory of personality: Selected papers.* New York: McGraw-Hill.

Lewin, K., Dembo, T., Festinger, L., & Sears, P. S. (1944). Level of aspiration. In J. M. Hunt (Ed.), *Personality and the behavior disorders: A handbook based on experimental and clinical research* (pp. 333–378). New York: Ronald Press Company.

Maehr, M. L. (1983). On doing well in science: Why Johnny no longer excels; Why Sarah never did. In S. G. Paris, G. M. Olson, & H. W. Stevenson (Eds.), *Learning and motivation in the classroom* (pp. 179–210). Hillsdale, NJ: Lawrence Erlbaum Associates.

Maehr, M. L. (1989). Thoughts about motivation. In C. Ames & R. Ames (Eds.), *Research on motivation in education: Vol. 3. Goals and cognitions* (pp. 299–315). New York: Academic Press.

Magnusson, D. (1998). The logic and implications of a person-oriented approach. In R. B. Cairns, L. R. Bergman, & J. Kagan (Eds.), *Methods and models for studying the individual* (pp. 33–64). Thousand Oaks, CA: Sage.

Mandler, G., & Sarason, S. B. (1952). A study of anxiety and learning. *Journal of Abnormal and Social Psychology, 47*, 166–173.

McArthur, C. (1953). The effects of need achievement on the content of TAT stories: A re-examination. *The Journal of Abnormal and Social Psychology, 48*, 532–536.

McClelland, D. C. (1951). *Personality.* New York: Sloane.

McClelland, D. C. (1965). N Achievement and entrepreneurship: A longitudinal study. *Journal of Personality and Social Psychology, 1*, 389–392.

McClelland, D. C. (1987). *Human motivation.* New York: Cambridge.

McClelland, D. C. (1992). Motivational configurations. In C. P. Smith (Ed.), *Motivation and personality: Handbook of thematic content analysis* (pp. 87–99). Cambridge: Cambridge University Press.

McClelland, D. C., Atkinson, J. W., Clark, R. A., & Lowell, E. L. (1953). *The achievement motive.* New York: Appleton-Century-Crofts.

McClelland, D. C., Clark, R. A., Roby, T. B., & Atkinson, J. W. (1949). The effect of the need for achievement on thematic apperception. *Journal of Experimental Psychology, 37*, 242–255.

McClelland, D. C., Koestner, R., & Weinberger, J. (1989). How do self-attributed and implicit motives differ? *Psychological Review, 96*, 690–702.

McClelland, D. C., & Liberman, A. M. (1949). The effect of need for achievement on recognition of need-related words. *Journal of Personality, 18*, 236–251.

McClelland, D. C., & Pilon, D. A. (1983). Sources of adult motives in patterns of parent behavior in early childhood. *Journal of Personality and Social Psychology, 44*, 564–574.

McGregor, H. A., & Elliot, A. J. (2005). The shame of failure: Examining the link between fear of failure and shame. *Personality and Social Psychology Bulletin, 31*, 218–231.

Miller, L. C., Murphy, R., & Buss, A. H. (1981). Consciousness of body: Private and public. *Journal of Personality and Social Psychology, 41*, 397–406.

Moller, A. C., & Elliot, A. J. (2006). The 2 × 2 achievement goal framework: An overview of empirical research. In A. V. Mitel (Ed.), *Focus on educational psychology* (pp. 307–326). New York: Nova Science Publishers.

Morgan, C. D., & Murray, H. M. (1935). A method for investigating fantasies: The thematic apperception test. *Archives of Neurology and Psychiatry, 34*, 289–306.

Moulton, R. W. (1958). Notes for a projective measure of fear of failure. In J. W. Atkinson (Ed.), *Motives in fantasy, action, and society: A method of assessment and study* New York: D. Van Nostrand Co.

Murray, H. A. (1936). Facts which support the concept of need or drive. *The Journal of Psychology, 3*, 27–42.

Murray, H. A. (1938). *Explorations in personality.* New York: Oxford University Press.

Nicholls, J. G. (1984a). Achievement motivation: Conceptions of ability, subjective experience, task choice, and performance. *Psychological Review, 91*, 328–346.

Nicholls, J. G. (1984b). Conceptions of ability and achievement motivation. In R. Ames & C. Ames (Eds.), *Research on motivation in education: Vol. 1. Student motivation* (pp. 39–73). New York: Academic Press.

Nicholls, J. G. (1989). *The competitive ethos and democratic education.* Cambridge, MA: Harvard University Press.

Nicholls, J. G., Cheung, P. C., Lauer, J., & Patashnick, M. (1989). Individual differences in academic motivation: Perceived ability, goals, beliefs, and values. *Learning and Individual Differences, 1*, 63–84.

Nicholls, J. G., Patashnick, M., Cheung, P., Thorkildsen, T., & Lauer, J. (1989). Can achievement motivation succeed with only one conception of success? In F. Halisch & J. Van den Beroken (Eds.), *Competence considered* (pp. 187–204). Lisse, The Netherlands: Swets & Zeitlinger.

Nuttin, J. (1984). *Motivation, planning, and action: A relational theory of behavior dynamics.* (R. P. Lorion & J. E. Dumas, Trans.). Hillsdale, NJ: Lawrence Erlbaum Associates.

Popper, K. (1965). *Conjectures and refutations* (rev. ed). London: Routledge and Kegan Paul.

Rawsthorne, L. J., & Elliot, A. J. (1999). Achievement goals and intrinsic motivation: A meta-analytic review. *Personality and Social Psychology Review, 3*, 326–344.

Ryan, R. M. (1982). Control and information in the interpersonal sphere: An extension of cognitive evaluation theory. *Journal of Personality and Social Psychology, 43*, 450–461.

Schultheiss, O. C. (2001). *Manual for the assessment of hope of success and fear of failure (English translation of Heckhausen's need for achievement measure).* Unpublished manuscript, University of Michigan at Ann Arbor.

Schultheiss, O. C., & Brunstein, J. C. (1999). Goal imagery: Bridging the gap between implicit motives and explicit goals. *Journal of Personality, 67*, 1–38.

Schultheiss, O. C., & Brunstein, J. C. (2005). An implicit motive approach to competence. In A. J. Elliot & C. S. Dweck (Eds.), *Handbook of competence and motivation* (pp. 31–51). New York: Guilford Press.

Schultheiss, O. C., & Murray, T. (2002). *Hope of success/fear of failure questionnaire.* Ann Arbor: Department of Psychology, University of Michigan.

Schultheiss, O. C., & Pang, J. S. (2007). Measuring implicit motives. In R. W. Robins, R. C. Fraley, & R. F. Krueger (Eds.), *Handbook of research methods in personality psychology* (pp. 322–344). New York: Guilford Press.

Sheldon, K. M., & Deci, E. L. (1996). *The self-determination scale.* Unpublished manuscript, University of Rochester at New York.

Smith, C. P., Feld, S. C., & Franz, C. E. (1992). Methodological considerations: Steps in research employing content analysis systems. In C. P. Smith (Ed.), *Motivation and personality: Handbook of thematic content analysis* (pp. 515–536). Cambridge: Cambridge University Press.

Snyder, M., & Gangestad, S. (1986). On the nature of self-monitoring: Matters of assessment, matters of validity. *Journal of Personality and Social Psychology, 51*, 125–139.

Spangler, W. D. (1992). Validity of questionnaire and TAT measures of need for achievement: Two meta-analyses. *Psychological Bulletin, 112*, 140–154.

Tanaka, A., & Yamauchi, H. (2000). Causal models of achievement motive, goal orientation, intrinsic interest, and academic achievement in the classroom. *Japanese Journal of Psychology, 71*, 317–324 [in Japanese].

Tanaka, A., & Yamauchi, H. (2001). A model for achievement motives, goal orientations, intrinsic interest, and academic achievement. *Psychological Reports, 88*, 123–135.

Thrash, T. M., & Elliot, A. J. (2001). Delimiting and integrating achievement motive and goal constructs. In A. Efklides, J. Kuhl, & R. M. Sorrentino (Eds.), *Trends and prospects in motivation research* (pp. 3–21). Boston: Kluwer.

Thrash, T. M., & Elliot, A. J. (2002). Implicit and self-attributed achievement motives: Concordance and predictive validity. *Journal of Personality, 70*, 729–755.

Thrash, T. M., & Elliot, A. J. (2003). Inspiration as a psychological construct. *Journal of Personality and Social Psychology, 84*, 871–889.

Thrash, T. M., & Elliot, A. J. (2004). Inspiration: Core characteristics, component processes, antecedents, and function. *Journal of Personality and Social Psychology, 87*, 957–973.

Thrash, T. M., Elliot, A. J., & Schultheiss, O. C. (2007). Methodological and dispositional predictors of congruence between implicit and explicit need for achievement. *Personality and Social Psychology Bulletin, 33*, 961–974.

Urdan, T., & Mestas, M. (2006). The goals behind performance goals. *Journal of Educational Psychology, 98*, 354–365.

Vaillant, G. E. (2000). Adaptive mental mechanisms: Their role in a positive psychology. *American Psychologist, 55*, 89–98.

Van Yperen, N. W. (2006). A novel approach to assessing achievement goals in the context of the 2×2 framework: Identifying distinct profiles of individuals with different dominant achievement goals. *Personality and Social Psychology Bulletin, 32*, 1432–1445.

Weiner, B. (1990). History of motivational research in education. *Journal of Educational Psychology, 82*, 616–622.

Weiner, B., & Kukla, A. (1970). An attributional analysis of achievement motivation. *Journal of Personality and Social Psychology, 15*, 1–20.

Zusho, A., Pintrich, P. R., & Cortina, K. S. (2005). Motives, goals, and adaptive patterns of performance in Asian American and Anglo American students. *Learning and Individual Differences, 15*, 141–158.

Motivational States

14 Activation and Measurement of Motivational States

Ronald S. Friedman and Jens Förster

CONTENTS

Perhaps to a unique extent within the field of psychology, social cognitive researchers have adopted as a major aim the elucidation of the mechanisms by which motivation influences cognition (Higgins & Sorrentino, 1990; Sorrentino & Higgins, 1996). Accordingly, over the last few decades, social cognitivists have produced a wide range of findings casting new light upon the way in which motivational orientations affect the processing and storage of information (Gollwitzer, Heckhausen, & Steller, 1990; Higgins & Tykocinski, 1992; Kuhl & Kazén 1999; Moskowitz, Gollwitzer, Wasel, & Schaal, 1999), problem solving (Elliot & McGregor, 2001; Mueller & Dweck, 1998), decision making (Shah, Kruglanski, & Friedman, 2002; Trope & Liberman, 2003), and social judgment (Fein & Spencer, 1997; Kunda & Spencer, 2003). Inspiration for modern investigations of the motivation-cognition interface has been drawn from a range of earlier conceptual advancements. Among the most influential of these is Easterbrook's (1959) classic notion that "...arousal [reduces]...the range of cues that an organism uses...." As it has typically been construed, this "Easterbrook hypothesis" suggests that the affective tension associated with avoidance motivational states constricts the span of perceptual attention, promoting focus upon local as opposed to global details in visual space (Burke, Heuer, & Reisberg, 1992; Cacioppo,

Berntson, & Crites, 1996). This proposition has been supported by a number of studies suggesting, for instance, that tense arousal (i.e., anxiety) increases attention to local components of visual stimuli as opposed to their global configuration (Tyler & Tucker, 1982; cf. Reeves & Bergum, 1972; Weltman, Smith, & Edstrom, 1971).

Of course, while it offers a useful starting point for understanding the impact of motivation on cognitive processing, the Easterbrook hypothesis is only of limited utility as a predictive framework. First, assuming the "arousal" to which Easterbrook refers is restrictively defined as an affective concomitant of avoidance motivational states, his hypothesis remains silent with regard to how the states of affective excitation associated with approach motivational states (e.g., elation) influence the scope of perception. Second, the Easterbrook hypothesis does not directly make predictions regarding how arousal states, irrespective of whether they are associated with aversive or appetitive motivation, not only affect perceptual, but also conceptual performance (e.g., ability to solve creative or analytical reasoning problems).

Addressing these limitations, Tucker and his colleagues (Tucker & Williamson, 1984; see also, Derryberry & Reed, 1998; Derryberry & Tucker, 1994; Luu, Tucker, & Derryberry, 1998) have put forth an elaborate neuropsychological model that integrates the Easterbrook hypothesis in the course of offering a refined and expanded account of the link between motivation and attention. On the functional level, Tucker essentially argues that aversive arousal not only constricts the scope of perceptual attention (i.e., the extent to which attention is trained upon local versus global details), but also analogously reduces the scope of what might be termed *conceptual attention,* the attentional selection of stored mental representations in long-term memory as opposed to the selection of sensory-based percepts (cf. Anderson & Neely, 1996). Just as a narrower scope of perceptual attention entails focusing upon a smaller number of external percepts, a narrower scope of conceptual attention entails cognitive activation of fewer constructs in memory (typically those with the highest a priori level of accessibility in a particular context). So, for instance, although contextually priming the homograph "bank" might cognitively activate dominant (e.g., money) as well as subordinate (e.g., river) semantic associates of this concept, according to Tucker's model (Derryberry & Tucker, 1994), aversive arousal should reduce the accessibility of the latter class of associates.

Beyond their extension of the Easterbrook hypothesis to predict effects of arousal on conceptual selection, Tucker and his colleagues also suggest that not all forms of arousal are created equal—unlike aversive arousal, arousal associated with approach motivational states (e.g., elation) will broaden, as opposed to narrow, both perceptual and conceptual attentional scope. More specifically, elated arousal is predicted to bias attention to global form and to facilitate detection of peripheral cues on the perceptual level, whereas it is posited to promote activation of mental representations with lower a priori accessibility (e.g., subordinate semantic associates) on the conceptual level.

Beyond these functional predictions, Tucker and his associates propose that the attentional "tuning" effects of "elated" and "tense" arousal states flow from their origins in distinct brain systems (Derryberry & Tucker, 1994; Tucker & Williamson, 1984). The *phasic* system associated with appetitive arousal is conceived of as right lateralized. In the face of approach-worthy incentives it automatically elicits a *habituation bias,* expanding attentional scope and enabling access to perceptually peripheral or cognitively inaccessible information. In contrast, the *tonic* system associated with aversive arousal is proposed to reside in the left hemisphere. Upon exposure to threat cues, it automatically elicits a *redundancy bias,* constricting the scope of attention and "choking off" access to "remote" stimuli and constructs. It is suggested that the connection between appetitive and aversive arousal states and these information processing biases is hard-wired.

Numerous studies have produced evidence consistent with the predictions of Tucker's attentional tuning model. For instance, two recent experiments conducted by Gasper (Gasper, 2004; Gasper & Clore, 2002) have shown that individuals induced to feel happiness (i.e., elated arousal) were relatively likely to categorize complex figures (e.g., a set of small triangles arranged in the shape of a square or a set of small squares arranged in the form of a triangle) on the basis of their global structure as opposed to their local components. Likewise, Basso, Schefft, Ris, and Dember (1996) found that trait happiness was associated with a tendency to rely on global as opposed to local structure in perceiving figures. These studies support Tucker and his colleagues' contention that arousal states associated with appetitive motivation broaden the span of perception, here, by leading individuals to focus on the "forest" at the expense of the "trees."

The predictions of the attentional tuning model regarding the effects of arousal on conceptual attention are also supported by a range of studies. For instance, Isen and Daubman (1984) asked participants to rate the goodness-of-fit of a set of weak exemplars to their overarching categories (e.g., the extent to which a "camel" was a member of the category "modes of transportation"). They found that positive mood (i.e., elated arousal) gave rise to a tendency to more readily accept atypical items into the given categories. This ostensibly supports the notion that approach-related arousal states broaden the scope of conceptual attention, enabling access to features shared between rated exemplars and more prototypical category members and thereby permitting online formation of more inclusive mental categories. In addition, Isen and her colleagues (Isen, 2000) have put forth a wide range of evidence suggesting that mild states of positive affective arousal bolster creativity. For instance, they have shown that happy mood reduces functional fixity (i.e., the inability to find a novel use for an object with a previously established function) and that it engenders a propensity to generate relatively unusual free associations (Isen, Daubman, & Nowicki, 1987; Isen, Johnson, Mertz, & Robinson, 1985). Presumably, the processes of "insight" required to escape functional fixity as well as those involved in generating a relatively "remote" free associate require access to information with relatively low a priori accessibility in long-term memory. As such, it is possible that the elated arousal states elicited in these studies broadened the scope of conceptual attention, permitting greater activation of the comparatively inaccessible material required for enhanced creativity (cf. Martindale, 1995; Mednick, 1962).

Complementing these findings regarding approach-related arousal, Mikulincer and his associates have adduced evidence consistent with the notion that aversive arousal diminishes the scope of conceptual attention. Specifically, using a design similar to that employed by Isen and Daubman (1984), Mikulincer, Kedem, and Paz (1990a; see also, Mikulincer, Paz, & Kedem, 1990b) found that both state and trait anxious individuals were more, rather than less, likely to bar prospective exemplars from inclusion in a given category. As such, this suggests that aversive arousal may indeed constrict the internal "spotlight" of attention impeding cognitive access to features that atypical exemplars hold in common with more prototypical items (e.g., that both a camel and an automobile make groaning noises and emit foul odors).

However, despite such supportive evidence, other findings cast doubt upon the ability of Tucker's model to comprehensively account for the link between motivation, attention, and task performance. First, Tucker and his colleagues (Derryberry & Tucker, 1994) essentially predict a main effect of the valence of emotional arousal on attentional scope, with elated arousal states broadening and tense states constricting selection of percepts or concepts. As such, in terms of ultimate performance, tasks requiring broadened attentional scope should benefit from elated arousal and those requiring narrowed scope should benefit from tense arousal. However, recent research in support of Martin's (2001) "mood as input" theory has suggested that effects of emotional arousal on task performance are less dependent upon attentional processes than on sheer productivity and are more interactive in nature than Tucker's model would suggest. Specifically, according to the mood as input framework, the information conveyed by pleasant and unpleasant affective states can lead to either increased or decreased processing effort, depending upon which "stop rule" is adopted during task engagement. When participants are provided with enjoyment-based stop rules (e.g., "Stop when you no longer feel like continuing."), those in pleasant moods misattribute their feelings to their enjoyment of the task and exert more effort than those in unpleasant moods, who misattribute their feelings to low task enjoyment. In corresponding fashion, when they are given performance-based stop rules (e.g., "Stop when you think you've done enough."), individuals in pleasant moods misattribute their feelings to having made sufficient progress on the task and withdraw processing effort sooner than do participants in unpleasant moods, who misattribute their feelings to insufficient task progress. Critically, such interactive effects on effort have been shown to influence creative generation, with individuals in pleasant, relative to unpleasant, affective states producing more original alternatives under enjoyment-based stop rules and fewer original alternatives under performance-based rules

(Martin & Stoner, 1996; see also, Friedman, Förster, & Denzler, 2007; Hirt, Levine, McDonald, Melton, & Martin, 1997). These results suggest that earlier findings of increased creativity under elated arousal states (Isen et al., 1985) may not have reflected broadened conceptual attention so much as increased effort on "fun" tasks (e.g., free association) for which enjoyment stop rules were likely to have been adopted by default.

Another challenge to the attentional tuning model has come from psychophysiological research. Here, the majority of findings have suggested that states of appetitive and aversive arousal are associated with patterns of hemispheric activation that are largely the opposite of those predicted by Tucker and his associates (Derryberry & Tucker, 1994; Tucker, Antes, Stenslie, & Barnhardt, 1978; Tucker & Williamson, 1984). More specifically, a veritable sea of findings has documented that elated arousal states (as well as personality traits associated with such states, e.g., extraversion, BAS sensitivity) predict greater relative left, rather than right, hemispheric activation. Correspondingly, numerous studies have demonstrated that tense arousal states (as well as traits associated with such states, e.g., neuroticism, BIS sensitivity) are predictive of greater relative right, as opposed to left, hemispheric activation (Davidson, 1992, 1995; Davidson & Tomarken, 1989; see Coan & Allen, 2003, for a review). Such findings quite starkly call into question the validity of the neuropsychological predictions advanced by Tucker and his associates and thereby undermine the overall viability of the attentional tuning model.

PROPOSED MODIFICATION OF ATTENTIONAL TUNING THEORY

In fairness, it is possible that a heretofore empirically unverified main effect of arousal valence on attentional scope may coexist with the robust interactive effects of affective experience on task performance documented by mood as input researchers. Moreover, despite the prevailing view, not all psychophysiological evidence is discordant with the predictions of Tucker and colleagues regarding associations between elated and tense arousal and hemispheric lateralization (Baxter, et al., 1987; Buchsbaum et al., 1985; Carter, Johnson, & Borkovec, 1986). However, given the difficulties posed to the attentional tuning model by recent findings, the question arises as to whether it would be possible to modify Tucker's model to salvage the bulk of its innovative predictions while rendering it more compatible with extant evidence regarding the link between affective arousal, motivation, and cognition.

One possibility is that the attention tuning effects posited by Tucker and colleagues are not the result of the arousal states that accompany approach or avoidance motivational orientations, but rather, flow from the sheer focus on approaching a desired end-state or avoiding an undesired end-state. According to regulatory focus theory (RFT) (Higgins, 2000; Higgins, Shah, & Friedman, 1997), when individuals pursuing approach goals subjectively perceive that they are succeeding (i.e., that there is a relatively small discrepancy between their current state and goal state) this arouses in them cheerfulness-related emotions, whereas when they subjectively perceive that they are failing (i.e., that there is a large discrepancy between their current state and goal state) this engenders dejection-related emotions. Correspondingly, when individuals pursuing avoidance goals perceive that they are succeeding, they are posited to feel quiescence-related affect, whereas when they perceive that they are failing, they are posited to experience agitation-related affect (cf. Carver, Sutton, & Scheier, 2000). However, RFT suggests that these distinct qualities of emotional arousal are only keenly felt when the individual is provided with or reminded of feedback concerning goal progress. As such, the sheer cognitive anticipation of appetitive or aversive end-states (i.e., regulatory focus) during the course of self-regulation may entail little in the way of conscious affective experience. Although emotional arousal is a by-product of approach and avoidance motivational states, these states are elicited, and at least initially guide action, in the absence of emotional experience.

RFT's conceptual decoupling of arousal and motivational orientation opens the door to another core prediction of the theory: approach and avoidance goals elicit distinct strategic tendencies and do so *independent of emotional arousal*.* These tendencies are described in signal detection terms (Crowe & Higgins, 1997; Förster, Higgins, & Taylor Bianco, 2003; Higgins, 2000; see also, e.g., Tanner & Swets, 1954). Approach goals are posited to engender a proclivity to maximize "hits" and minimize errors of omission (misses) inasmuch as the latter symbolically represent gains and nongains, outcomes to which approach-oriented (i.e., *promotion-focused*) individuals are sensitized. Likewise, avoidance goals are posited to engender a strategic tendency to maximize "correct rejections" and minimize errors of commission (false alarms), which represent the nonlosses and losses to which avoidance-oriented (i.e., *prevention-focused*) individuals are sensitized.

Substantial evidence has been marshaled in support of these proposed strategic biases. For instance, in one study by Crowe and Higgins (1997), participants were told that they would initially work on a test of recognition memory and that this would be followed by a second task. They were informed that there were two potential alternatives for this second task, either an activity that had earlier been rated by the participant as well-liked or one that had earlier been rated as disliked. Participants in the promotion framing conditions were told that their performance on the memory task would determine whether or not they would get to work on the *liked* task next. In contrast, those in the prevention framing conditions were told that their performance would determine whether or not they would have to work on the *disliked* task next. In this way, the same objective contingency was used to orient participants toward either approaching a desired end-state or avoiding an undesired end-state. Performance on the initial recognition memory task was subjected to a signal detection analysis. As predicted by RFT, approach-oriented participants exhibited a yea-saying bias leading to a greater number of hits as well as false alarms in recognition, whereas avoidance-oriented participants exhibited a nay-saying bias, leading to a greater number of correct rejections and misses. Critically, in this study and myriad subsequent conceptual replications (Förster, Higgins, & Idson, 1998; Förster et al., 2003; Seibt & Förster, 2004; Shah, Higgins, & Friedman, 1998), task framing manipulations used to elicit distinct motivational orientations were not found to elicit significant changes in self-reported affective arousal.

Returning to attentional tuning theory, given that the sheer cognitive orientation toward desired versus undesired end-states appears to alter response biases independent of emotional experience, it raises the possibility that self-regulatory focus also instigates the changes in attentional scope originally posited by Tucker and colleagues to accompany elated versus tense arousal states. Although speculative, such differential tuning of the scope of attention in approach versus avoidance motivational states might be adaptive: When motivated to avoid a potential threat, narrow attention (e.g., on the source of threat and "tried and true" means to escape it) may be essential in averting loss (e.g., bodily harm). However, when motivated to approach a potential incentive, such attentional constraints may be unnecessary inasmuch as failure to avoid a threat is subjectively more vital than failure to attain an incentive (Kahneman & Tversky, 1979; cf. Idson, Liberman, & Higgins, 2000). In fact, narrowed attention during the course of approach-based self-regulation may be maladaptive inasmuch as a broader scope of perceptual

---

* As discussed by Winkielman and Berridge (2004), the existence and nature of unconscious emotion remains a matter of debate. Therefore, for the sake of parsimony, the term "arousal" is used at present to refer solely to conscious affective experience (e.g., elation or tension).

attention may enable detection of novel incentives and broader conceptual attention may enable access to information promoting development of novel means of goal attainment. While these benefits might also be of use during avoidance-based self-regulation, they may not outweigh the costs of distraction from the object or state to be averted or those of departing from time-tested plans of coping. In any case, it seems plausible that attentional narrowing in avoidance states and attentional broadening in approach states may be adaptive for self-regulation. Moreover, there is little reason to assume that elated or tense arousal should be required for elicitation of these attentional patterns. Rather, these tendencies may be particularly adaptive for the very reason that they weather the ebb and flow of affective arousal that occurs during the course of goal striving.

The notion that attentional tuning effects are based on regulatory focus as opposed to arousal may also help account for discrepancies between the neuropsychological predictions of Tucker's model and leading views regarding the hemispheric substrates of arousal. As noted earlier, attentional tuning theory proposes that the constriction of attention scope associated with tense arousal largely relies on right hemispheric processing whereas the expansion of scope associated with elated arousal largely relies on left hemispheric processing; yet, most research has suggested that these arousal states are associated with the very opposite pattern of relative hemispheric activation. However, if attentional tuning is associated with regulatory focus rather than emotional arousal, Tucker and his colleagues' predictions may not be at all incompatible with extant neuropsychological evidence: Heller has recently theorized that tense arousal (i.e., anxiety) may be subdivided into a somatic component, reflecting the physiological excitation associated with avoidance motivational states (i.e., panic), as well as a cognitive component, reflecting the anticipation of threats (i.e., worry). Moreover, she and her colleagues have put forth evidence suggesting that the cognitive component is associated with greater relative left hemispheric activation than is the somatic component (Heller, Koven, & Miller, 2003; Heller & Nitschke, 1998; Heller, Nitschke, Etienne, & Miller, 1997; Nitschke, Heller, Palmieri, & Miller, 1999). Assuming that the cognitive component of anxiety to which Heller refers is akin to a prevention focus, a focus on the prospect of undesired outcomes (Higgins, 2000; Higgins et al., 1997), it is therefore possible that avoidance motivational states may indeed shunt activation toward the left hemisphere as proposed by attentional tuning theory (see Derryberry & Reed, 1998, for an analogous proposition). Following this

reasoning, it is likewise possible that approach-related states, or more specifically the promotion foci associated with these states, engender diminished relative left (increased relative right) hemispheric activation, consistent with Tucker's hypotheses.

In the sections that follow, we discuss the results of a program of behavioral research conducted over the last several years, the results of which may be viewed as supportive of the regulatory focus-based modification of attentional tuning theory offered at present. We begin with evidence suggesting that promotion and prevention foci, as well as behaviors associated with these foci, alter the scope of perceptual and conceptual attention in a manner consistent with the revised tuning model. Afterward, we present preliminary evidence that regulatory foci shift the balance of hemispheric activation in a manner consistent with this model and, moreover, that these shifts in activation may at least partially mediate observed variations in attentional scope.

EFFECTS OF RUDIMENTARY PROMOTION AND PREVENTION FOCI ON ATTENTIONAL SCOPE

As discussed earlier, the cognitive focus on approaching desired outcomes (i.e., promotion focus) versus preventing undesired outcomes (i.e., prevention focus) has been manipulated in scores of previous studies by informing participants that either desired or undesired outcomes were contingent upon their task performance (Crowe & Higgins, 1997; Higgins et al., 1997; Shah et al., 1998; cf. Higgins, Roney, Crowe, & Hymes, 1994). By-and-large, postmanipulation self-report measures have failed to detect reliable effects of such regulatory focus framing manipulations on affective experience. Moreover, all reported effects of these manipulations on response biases have remained reliable when statistically controlling for transient affectivity. However, given that these manipulations entail pursuit of personally relevant goals (e.g., attempts to ensure that a subsequent task will be enjoyable/not unenjoyable), it seems possible that they may elicit more emotional arousal than measures have yet detected (due, for instance, to insensitivity or reactivity in measurement). Therefore, given the theoretical importance of dissociating the cognitive and somatic states associated with approach and avoidance motivational orientations, instead of relying on extant regulatory focus framing manipulations, we invented a new regulatory focus manipulation that stood to further reduce the potential for emotional arousal (Friedman & Förster, 2001). Specifically, in the promotion framing condition, we simply had participants complete an easily-solvable paper and pencil maze in which they were asked to lead a cartoon mouse depicted in the center of the maze to a piece of cartoon cheese located outside the maze. Correspondingly, in the prevention condition, participants completed an analogous maze in which they were to lead out of the maze to escape a cartoon owl. These rudimentary tasks were meant to elicit a sheer focus on attaining a desired end-state or avoiding an undesired end-state, respectively. However, inasmuch as these "virtual" regulatory foci either involved leading a cartoon rodent to cartoon cheese or away from a cartoon predator, we assumed that maze completion should generate even less emotional arousal than "standard" framing manipulations, which again, entail self-regulation vis-à-vis actual (dis)incentives.

To assess the construct validity of these maze tasks as manipulations of regulatory focus we conducted a study (Friedman & Förster, 2001) in which we used the mazes to assess the central prediction of RFT that promotion, relative to prevention, foci will engender a "risky" decision-making bias. Specifically, we conceptually replicated the procedure of Crowe and Higgins (1997), asking participants to perform a recognition memory task in which they had to first encode a series of words and then later decide ("yes" or "no") whether each of these words, as well as an equal number of unpresented distracter words, had been seen earlier. Immediately prior to the recognition test, participants were given two minutes to complete either the "cheese" (promotion condition) or "owl" (prevention condition) maze, as part of what was ostensibly a separate study. As predicted, signal detection analyses revealed that although the mazes did not involve personal approach or avoidance goals, completion of the promotion, relative to the prevention, maze produced a yea-saying bias in recognition (i.e., a tendency to attain hits at the expense of false alarms). Furthermore, as expected, there were no effects of the maze manipulation on self-reported emotional arousal. In sum, these findings suggest that despite the fact they merely entail "virtual" self-regulation, completion of the cheese and owl mazes is sufficient to elicit distinct regulatory foci.

Assuming the validity of the manipulation, at least two recent maze completion studies are consistent with the view that promotion, relative to prevention, foci elicit a broader scope of perceptual attention. In the first of these studies (Förster, Friedman, Özelsel, & Denzler, 2006, Experiment 1), following either cheese or owl maze completion, participants were presented on a computer screen with a series of large capital letters comprised of small capital letters (Derryberry & Reed, 1998; Navon, 1977; Pomerantz, 1983). On a given trial, participants

were first presented with a fixation cross (+) in the center of the screen for 500 ms. Afterward, they were randomly presented with one of the eight composite letters and asked to press one response key if the stimulus contained the letter "H" and another if it contained the letter "L." Four of the stimuli included global target letters (e.g., a large L made of small Ts), whereas four included local target letters (e.g., a large T made of small Ls). Participants were asked to respond as quickly as possible. In this task, a broader scope of perceptual attention should be reflected in relatively fast responses to global targets whereas narrower perceptual scope should be reflected in relatively fast responses to local targets. In line with predictions, participants in the promotion framing condition were indeed significantly faster to respond to global than to local targets, indicating an expansion of attention enabling them to "see the forest for the trees." In contrast, prevention-focused individuals were faster to respond to local than to global targets, suggesting that their perceptual attention was narrowed upon the "trees" at the expense of the "forest" (see also, Förster & Higgins, 2005).

In another perceptual study, a between-participants manipulation of regulatory focus using the mazes was followed by administration of the first half of the Snowy Pictures Test (SPT) (Ekstrom, French, Harman, & Dermen, 1976) as part of an ostensibly separate experiment. In the SPT, participants are presented with a set of drawings of familiar objects (e.g., a rowboat, a hand) hidden within patterns of visual noise or "snow" and are required to identify each of the obscured objects. On these tasks, the visual system receives only fragmented cues from which to generate a distinctly identifiable percept. A broader focus of visual attention presumably allows a greater number of cues to enter visuospatial working memory, providing more information for use in object perception and bolstering SPT performance (cf. Miyake, Witzki, & Emerson, 2001). In corresponding fashion, narrower attentional scope should impair SPT performance by permitting access to visual working memory of only a relatively limited subset of the cues in the visual scene. Accordingly, individuals in a promotion focus, which is predicted to expand the scope of perceptual attention, were able to correctly identify significantly more SPT images than were those in a prevention focus (Friedman & Förster, 2001, Experiment 1).

Beyond these results vis-à-vis perceptual scope, a growing number of findings using our "virtual" regulatory focus manipulation appear to support the notion that promotion foci expand and that prevention foci constrict the scope of conceptual attention. In one study (Friedman & Förster, 2001, Experiment 4), after completing the maze tasks, our German participants were administered a word-fragment completion task. Here, 15 word fragments (e.g., FL_CH) were printed twice, once in one column and again in an adjacent column. Each fragment could be solved in at least two ways to produce different German words (e.g., *flach* [shallow] and *Fluch* [curse]). Participants were given 30 seconds to complete as many rows as possible. Presumably, when solving tasks of this ilk, the first solution offered for a given word fragment is that with the highest level of a priori cognitive accessibility. Generating a second solution to the same fragment should therefore require a broadening of conceptual attention to access more cognitively "remote" solutions (particularly since recall of the first solution may serve to "fixate" conceptual attention on this initially accessible response; see Smith, 1995). Based on this reasoning, it was predicted that a promotion, relative to a prevention, focus should enable completion of more fragments in the second column (i.e., those for which a first solution had already been offered). This prediction was strongly borne out (see Förster, Friedman, Özelsel, & Denzler, 2006, Experiment 3, for a closely related finding).

According to a number of theorists (Förster, Friedman, & Liberman, 2004; Friedman, Fishbach, Förster, & Werth, 2003; Martindale, 1995), one of the ultimate benefits of a broadened scope of conceptual attention is enhanced creativity. As famously proposed by Mednick (1962), generating innovative solutions presumably requires activating relatively inaccessible material (i.e., remote associates) in long-term memory. As such, the expanded attentional scope engendered by promotion, relative to prevention, foci should improve creative generation by increasing the likelihood that such material becomes available for use in problem solving. In a study bearing on this prediction (Friedman & Förster, 2001, Experiment 2), participants who had completed the cheese and owl mazes were subsequently administered a variant of a well-established creativity task, the alternative uses test (Guilford, Christensen, Merrifield, & Wilson, 1978). Specifically, they were given one minute to generate as many creative uses for a brick as they could think of, refraining to the extent possible from typical uses or uses that were virtually impossible. Responses were coded for creativity by several independent judges. An example of a relatively creative response was "to crush it and use to draw pictures on the sidewalk," whereas an example of a less creative response was "to build a house with it." Analyses indeed revealed that responses generated by promotion-focused individuals were more creative than those produced by prevention-focused individuals. These findings were not due to differences in sheer fluency (i.e., the raw number of items produced), which did not differ between conditions. This suggests that increased creativity did not simply result from increased quantity, but quality of responses. Again, this quality difference was presumably due to relative differences in the breadth of conceptual attention. Critically, as in all studies using the "virtual" regulatory focus manipulation, the effects at hand were statistically independent of emotional arousal (as gauged via self-report). As such, they are again consistent with the notion that the attentional tuning effects posited by Tucker and his colleagues to accompany approach and avoidance motivational states may be more associated with the cognitive than the somatic components of these states.

EFFECTS OF APPROACH AND AVOIDANCE MOTOR ACTIONS ON ATTENTIONAL TUNING

While the aforementioned findings using the maze manipulation offer the most compelling evidence in support of a regulatory focus-based reinterpretation of attentional tuning theory, the results of another line of research are also consistent with this view. In this work, participants were either asked to press their palms upward against a surface, leading them to enact a motor action typically, if not invariably, used to pull desired objects toward the body, or asked to press their palms downward against a surface, leading them to enact a motor action usually associated with pushing undesired objects away from the body (Cacioppo, Priester, & Berntson, 1993; Centerbar & Clore, 2006; Chen & Bargh, 1999; Neumann & Strack, 2000; cf. Markman & Brendl, 2005). Inasmuch as these behaviors are indeed enacted when individuals want something or want to avoid something, they should typically be associated either with a cognitive focus on desired end-states (i.e., promotion focus) or a focus on undesired end-states (i.e., prevention focus), respectively. As such, it is possible that by dint of this habitual association, enactment of these approach and avoidance motor actions is conditioned to modify attentional scope in the manner posited by attentional tuning theory to accompany approach versus avoidance motivational states (see also, Förster et al., 1998).

In one study bearing on this hypothesis, participants were led to enact approach or avoidance motor actions by having them press their dominant (right) hands upward or downward against a countertop, respectively (Friedman & Förster, 2000, Experiment 2). To draw participants' attention away from the meaning of their motor actions (i.e., as pulling/pushing or wanting/not wanting) and thereby mitigate self-perception effects on performance (Bem, 1972; Olson & Hafer, 1990), participants were provided with a cover story suggesting that the actions requested of them constituted a standard means of activating the contralateral (left) brain hemisphere. While engaging in these motor actions under this pretext, participants completed the SPT, announcing their responses to the experimenter vocally while their dominant hands were otherwise occupied. As discussed earlier, the SPT gauges the ability to perceptually "close" a series of partially obscured figures and may be viewed as benefiting from a relatively broad scope of visual attention. Conceptually replicating findings using the cheese and owl mazes (Friedman & Förster, 2001, Experiment 1), it was found that individuals who engaged in the presumed approach, relative to avoidance, motor action were able to perceive significantly more of the SPT images.

These results were themselves conceptually replicated using another measure of perceptual closure, the Gestalt Completion Task (GCT) (Ekstrom et al., 1976). Images in the GCT are not obscured by visual "snow," but are merely incomplete, requiring individuals to piece together a perceptual "Gestalt" from a partial set of visual cues. Therefore, GCT performance may be viewed as benefiting from expanded visual attention to the fragmented images, enabling concurrent working memory access to a greater number of cues from which to generate a distinctly identifiable percept. Accordingly, as found using the SPT, enactment of approach, relative to avoidance motor actions, bolstered task performance (Friedman & Förster, 2000, Experiments 3 & 4). Again, assuming that approach motor actions are associatively linked to a promotion focus and avoidance motor actions linked to a prevention focus, these findings provide additional support for the notion that promotion, relative to prevention, foci expand the scope of perceptual attention (see also, Friedman & Förster, 2000, Experiment 1).

Complementing the aforementioned findings regarding perceptual scope, evidence also suggests that approach and avoidance motor actions moderate the breadth of conceptual attention. One recent experiment investigated the influence of these motor actions on conceptual scope using a part-list cuing paradigm (Anderson & Neely, 1996; Nickerson, 1984; Roediger & Neely, 1982). In part-list cuing tasks, individuals typically memorize categorized word lists, in which each word belongs to one of a limited number of semantic categories (e.g., fish, trees). After encoding the list, participants are presented with a certain number of words from each category and asked to use these words as cues to help them retrieve the remaining words from the categorized list. Numerous studies

have found that participants recall fewer words from a given category when a greater number of words from that category are presented as retrieval cues (Rundus, 1973; Slamecka, 1968; Watkins, 1975). One account for this effect, advanced by Anderson and his colleagues (Anderson & Neely, 1996; Anderson & Spellman, 1995), is that when part-list cues are provided for use in retrieval, individuals first retrieve the stored mental representation of the cue, a process entailing the narrowing of conceptual selection upon this representation. According to Anderson's model, this constriction of attention acts to inhibit cognitive activation of noncue items from the same category (a special case of *retrieval-induced forgetting*).

Based on this reasoning, it is possible that the enactment of approach and avoidance motor actions may either mitigate or exacerbate this retrieval blocking effect by broadening or narrowing the scope of conceptual attention, respectively. More specifically, promotion-related action should expand conceptual scope, operating against the inhibitory force of selective attention engendered by cue retrieval, and thereby bolstering retrieval of noncue items within the same category. Correspondingly, prevention-related action should constrict the scope of conceptual selection, honing the internal spotlight of attention upon cue representations, and thereby impairing recall of noncue category items.

To test this, Förster and his colleagues (2006; Experiment 2) had participants encode three different sets of categorized word lists, each comprised of items from four distinct categories (e.g., cookware, fish, insects, and trees). For a given list, words to be encoded were sequentially presented in fixed-random order for three seconds apiece with the category label for each word appearing beneath it on screen. After each list was encoded a delay period ensued, followed by a test of free recall. For each category on a particular list, either one or four part-list cues (i.e., originally presented words from that category) were printed on the recall sheet. These words were billed as "examples of correct answers," thereby prompting individuals to use them as retrieval cues. Critically, while recalling the contents of each list in this way, participants were asked to engage in the arm actions to which they had been randomly assigned (i.e., approach, avoidance, or neither).

In terms of predictions, in line with earlier findings, it was expected that presentation of four, relative to one, part-list cues would undermine the ability to recall remaining category (i.e., noncue) items. To reiterate, this prediction flows from the idea that processing of part-list cues narrows conceptual attention upon the mental representations of these cues, inhibiting activation of noncue words. The greater the number of part-list cues that are processed, the more inhibition is directed at remaining category items, diminishing their accessibility to consciousness. Beyond replicating the "classic" part-list cuing effect, we predicted that enactment of approach, relative to avoidance, behavior would mitigate attentional narrowing upon cue item representations. This would presumably allow the "spotlight" of conceptual attention to encompass noncue items, enabling their retrieval and thereby diminishing part-list cuing inhibition (i.e., reducing deficits in recall when multiple cues were presented). Indeed, results revealed that while recall was uniformly high in the single-cue condition, when four cues were presented, individuals who performed avoidance motor actions showed the poorest recall of noncue items and those in the control group showed only slightly better recall. In both cases, the part-list cuing effect, operationalized as the difference between recall of noncue items in the single and multiple cue conditions, was statistically reliable. However, when participants performed approach motor actions, there was virtually no part-list cuing inhibition, suggesting that these actions expanded the scope of conceptual attention to encompass items that would otherwise be inhibited (cf. Kuhl & Kazén, 1999).

Using this manipulation of approach and avoidance motor actions, we have also replicated a number of previously mentioned effects of regulatory focus framing on the scope of conceptual attention. For instance, approach, relative to avoidance, motor actions have been found to bolster the ability to complete word fragments for which an initial solution has been tendered (Friedman & Förster, 2002, Experiments 3 & 4) and to enhance the ability to generate creative alternative uses for a common object (Friedman & Förster, 2002, Experiment 2). Notably, it has also been found that approach, relative to avoidance, motor actions impair rather than enhance performance on analytical reasoning problems (Friedman & Förster, 2000, Experiment 7). This is consistent with the attentional tuning view espoused at present: Unlike word fragment completion and creative generation tasks, analytical reasoning problems require narrowed attention upon the information provided (e.g., logical premises) as opposed to expanded access to remote associates. Activation of constructs low in a priori accessibility may, if anything, stand to distract attention from essential problem elements and thereby undermine performance. The finding that avoidance motor actions bolster analytical reasoning is particularly significant because it helps rule out the possibility that

the facilitative effects of approach motor actions are due to enhanced motivation as opposed to differential attentional processing.*

In sum, a range of studies support the contention that motor actions associatively linked to regulatory foci moderate the breadth of perceptual and conceptual attention, with enactment of promotion-related, relative to prevention-related, behaviors expanding attentional scope. Notably, although the arm contractions used to operationalize approach behaviors (i.e., pulling upward) are occasionally reported to be more effortful than those used to operationalize avoidance behaviors (i.e., pushing downward), all findings using these manipulations have remained reliable statistically controlling for self-reported strain or discomfort. Furthermore, these arm contractions have not been found to reliably engender differential affective arousal (Neumann & Strack, 2000). As such, the aforementioned results are consistent with the notion that the effects of motivational states on attentional tuning are more "cognitive" than "somatic" in origin (cf. Derryberry & Reed, 1998).

EFFECTS OF "VIRTUAL" REGULATORY FOCI ON HEMISPHERIC ACTIVATION

As discussed earlier, according to Tucker and his colleagues (Derryberry & Tucker, 1994; Tucker & Williamson, 1984), elated arousal, and the habituation bias it entails, is right lateralized, whereas tense arousal, and the redundancy bias it entails, is left lateralized. Again, this position is at odds with the majority of findings regarding the link between emotional arousal and hemispheric activation. However, assuming that the attentional tuning effects of motivational state are driven

---

* At first glance, it may appear surprising that states associated with a cognitive focus on avoiding undesired end-states should bolster analytical problem solving. Countless studies suggest that worry, a ruminative focus upon prospective undesired end-states, often impairs analytical performance (see Sarason, Pierce, & Sarason, 1996, for a review). Such studies have primarily revealed that worry disrupts performance by promoting off-task thinking (e.g., rumination regarding the consequences of failure). However, although habitually associated with pursuit of avoidance goals, engagement in avoidance motor actions does not involve actual self-regulation and thereby does not introduce the potentially worrisome prospect of failure. As such, these rudimentary actions should provide little, if any, basis for disruptive off-task rumination. Rather, the narrowed scope of attention elicited by avoidance motor actions, via their association with prevention foci, should intensify focus upon the contents of the problem at hand (i.e., promote on-task thinking), thereby facilitating, as opposed to undermining, analytical performance.

by regulatory focus as opposed to arousal, Tucker's predictions may be consistent with research suggesting that the cognitive component of avoidance motivational states (presumably akin to a prevention focus) is left, as opposed to right, lateralized (Heller et al., 2003). Of course, this raises the empirical question: Do prevention, relative to promotion, foci engender greater relative left (diminished relative right) hemispheric activation?

Preliminary evidence bearing on this issue was provided by a recent study in which regulatory focus and emotional arousal were separately manipulated and relative hemispheric activation was behaviorally assessed (Friedman & Förster, 2005, Experiment 3). Specifically, participants were either administered the "standard" cheese or owl mazes (meant to induce a promotion or prevention focus, respectively), or a variant of the maze tasks meant to elicit affective arousal. In the appetitive arousal group, participants were asked to look at the cheese maze and imagine the mouse gradually approaching the cheese and eventually eating it. They were then given ten minutes to write a vivid story from the perspective of the mouse, to be entitled, "The Happiest Day in the Life of the Mouse." Those in the aversive arousal group were asked to look at the owl maze and to imagine the mouse attempting to escape the owl, but eventually getting caught, killed, and eaten. The title of their story was to be "The Terrible Death of the Mouse." A manipulation check revealed a significant effect of this writing manipulation on affective arousal (i.e., current mood), whereas in line with earlier studies, there was no effect of the standard maze manipulation on self-reported affectivity.

Following these manipulations, participants completed a variant of the Milner line bisection task (Milner, Brechmann, & Pagliarini, 1992). In this task, participants are presented with a series of horizontal lines and asked to mark the center of each line. On average, participants commit a leftward error in bisection. This indicates an attentional bias toward the left visual field (LVF), engendering attentional neglect of the rightward extension of the line. Theoretically speaking, this LVF bias reflects greater relative right hemispheric activation; however, the extent of the bias varies enabling assessment of transient differences in the relative activation of the right versus left hemispheres (Baumann, Kuhl, & Kazén, 2005; Morton, 2003; Shrira & Martin, 2005).

In terms of results, consistent with scores of previous findings (see Coan & Allen, 2003, for a review), within the emotional arousal condition, those in whom appetitive arousal was induced demonstrated significantly greater relative left hemispheric activation than those in the aversive arousal group. In multiple regression analyses,

the reliability of this effect was reduced by the inclusion as a statistical covariate of the manipulation check assessing current mood. This reinforces the assumption that this effect was mediated by induced differences in emotional arousal. In contrast, following predictions, within the regulatory focus condition, a prevention focus was associated with greater relative left hemispheric activation than was a promotion focus. This suggests that the sheer cognitive orientation toward desired versus undesired end-states may indeed entail a pattern of hemispheric activation that is essentially the opposite of that associated with appetitive versus aversive emotional arousal (see also, Friedman & Förster, 2005, Experiments 1 & 2; Förster & Friedman, in press).

As discussed earlier, according to the original attentional tuning model (Derryberry & Tucker, 1994; Tucker & Williamson, 1984), the narrowing of attention associated with tense arousal states predominantly relies upon left hemispheric processing, whereas the broadening of attention associated with elated arousal states relies upon right hemispheric processing. However, assuming that the changes in hemispheric activation posited by Tucker are driven by regulatory focus, the question then arises: Are the effects of promotion and prevention foci on attentional tuning mediated by the variations in relative hemispheric activation these foci appear to elicit? Addressing this issue, in one study (Friedman & Förster, 2005, Experiment 4), participants who completed the maze manipulation of regulatory focus were administered a variant of the aforementioned Milner line bisection task followed by two tasks, one on which performance benefits from broadened conceptual scope (generating creative alternative uses for a brick; see above) and another on which performance benefits from narrowed conceptual scope (an analytical reasoning test; see above). Replicating previous results, promotion, relative to prevention, focus was associated with increased creativity and impaired analytical reasoning. (Again, this pattern presumably reflects an expanded scope of attention on the conceptual level.) Moreover, a promotion focus was again associated with lesser relative left (i.e., greater relative right) hemispheric activation than was a prevention focus. Finally, multivariate analyses indeed suggested that the effects of regulatory focus on attentional scope (as operationalized via creative and analytical reasoning performance) were mediated to a statistically significant extent by variations in relative hemispheric activation. As such, there is at least preliminary evidence consistent with Tucker's overarching assertion that approach and avoidance motivational states (if perhaps their "cognitive" as opposed to "somatic" components) tune the scope of attention by differentially allocating processing demands to the left versus right hemispheres.

CONCLUSION

To conclude, we have collected a range of evidence suggesting that promotion, relative to prevention, foci expand the scope of attention on both the perceptual and conceptual levels. Our results also suggest that the effects of regulatory focus on attentional scope may be mediated by differential allocation of processing demands to the left versus right hemispheres. This is consistent with Tucker's assertion that the left hemispheric processing elicited by appetitive motivational states is characterized by a redundancy bias that constricts the scope of attention, whereas the right hemispheric processing elicited by aversive states is characterized by a habituation bias that expands attentional scope (Derryberry & Tucker, 1994; Tucker & Williamson, 1984). However, our results suggest that it is the sheer self-regulatory focus on desired versus undesired end-states, as opposed to the elicitation of elated versus tense arousal, that drives these effects of motivational state on relative hemispheric activation and attentional scope.

Of course, while these findings are encouraging with respect to the viability of the proposed modification of attentional tuning theory, they are far from conclusive due to limitations in both the manipulations and measures employed. For instance, all presently reported studies using the maze manipulation of regulatory focus entailed pursuit of the same "virtual" goals, either helping a mouse find her way to cheese or away from an owl. While studies administering analogous maze tasks have used different goal contents to manipulate regulatory focus (e.g., helping a driver find a free parking space [promotion] versus avoid a ticket [prevention]; Werth & Förster, in press; see also, Fazio, Eiser, & Shook, 2004), these studies have not gauged attentional scope. As such, to ensure external validity, the present findings must be conceptually replicated using manipulations involving alternative "virtual" self-regulatory scenarios.

In terms of measures, one obvious shortcoming of the reported research is that only behavioral indices of relative hemispheric activation were employed. While such indices may indeed respond to chronic or transient variation in brain activation, they are undoubtedly lower in construct validity, as well as reliability, than psychophysiological measures. Furthermore, indirect measures such as the Milner line bisection task provide little or no information regarding absolute patterns of hemispheric activation. Therefore, findings using these measures cannot confirm whether the behavioral response patterns (e.g., bisection errors) obtained reflect diminished activation of one hemisphere, increased activation of the opposing hemisphere, or both. As a result, diagnostic evaluation of the basic neuropsychological predictions of the modified attentional tuning model must await direct measurement of absolute hemispheric activation, for instance, via EEG.

Assuming that the shortcomings of our research program can be resolved, the present model may be applicable to numerous domains of social behavior. For instance, with respect to human communication, myriad aspects of language comprehension, including the ability to interpret jokes and metaphors as well the ability to, resolve lexical ambiguity may be viewed as requiring broadened conceptual attention (i.e., activation of constructs with low a priori accessibility, including alternative or normatively subordinate word meanings; see, e.g., Beeman, 1998). Correspondingly, with respect to person perception, interpretation of facial expressions (e.g., their emotional content), as well as sheer face recognition, may benefit from broadened perceptual attention inasmuch as this should enhance the processing of configural relations between facial features (Schooler, 2002). Altogether, this suggests that by dint of its impact upon the breadth of attention, regulatory focus should play a moderating role in a variety processes essential to social interaction.

In closing, a great deal of additional research will be required to validate the proposed integration of attentional tuning theory and RFT. If the proposal at hand remains viable in light of subsequent findings, it will help resolve a number of inconsistencies in the literature and offer an expanded basis for formulating predictions regarding the psychological impact of distinct self-regulatory foci. More generally, it will reinforce the notion, most strongly enunciated by Higgins (2000), that approach and avoidance motivational states are multifaceted, and that the potentially unique effects of each facet must be empirically isolated in order to elucidate the complex interplay between motivation and cognition.

REFERENCES

Anderson, M. C., & Neely, J. H. (1996). Interference and inhibition in memory retrieval. In E. L. Bjork & R. A. Bjork (Eds.), *Memory* (pp. 237–313). New York: Academic Press.

Anderson, M. C., & Spellman, B. A. (1995). On the status of inhibitory mechanisms in cognition: Memory retrieval as a model case. *Psychological Review, 102*, 68–100.

Basso, M. R., Schefft, B. K., Ris, M. D., & Dember, W. N. (1996). Mood and global–local visual processing. *Journal of the International Neuropsychological Society, 2*, 249–255.

Baumann, N., Kuhl, J., & Kazén, M. (2005). Left-hemispheric activation and self-infiltration: Testing a neuropsychological model of internalization. *Motivation and Emotion*, *29*(3), 135–163.

Baxter, L. R., Phelps, M. E., Mazziotta, J. C., Guze, B. H., Schwartz, J. M., & Selin, C. E. (1987). Local cerebral glucose metabolic rates in obsessive-compulsive disorder. *Archives of General Psychiatry*, *44*, 211–218.

Beeman, M. (1998). Coarse semantic coding and discourse comprehension. In M. Beeman & C. Chiarello (Eds.), *Right hemisphere language comprehension: Perspectives from cognitive neuroscience* (pp. 255–284). Mahwah, NJ: Erlbaum.

Bem, D. J. (1972). Self-perception theory. In L. Berkowitz (Ed.), *Advances in experimental social psychology* (*Vol. 6*, pp. 1–62). New York: Academic Press.

Buchsbaum, M. S., Hazlett, E., Sicotte, N., Stein, M., Wu, J., & Zetin, M. (1985). Topographic EEG changes with benzodiazepine administration in generalized anxiety disorder. *Biological Psychiatry*, *20*, 832–842.

Burke, A., Heuer, F., & Reisberg, D. (1992). Remembering emotional events. *Memory and Cognition*, *20*, 277–290.

Cacioppo, J. T., Berntson, G. G., & Crites, S. L. Jr. (1996). Social neuroscience: Principles of psychophysiological arousal and response. In E. T. Higgins & A. W. Kruglanski (Eds.), *Social psychology: Handbook of basic principles* (pp. 72–101). New York: Guilford.

Cacioppo, J. T., Priester, J. R., & Berntson, G. G. (1993). Rudimentary determinants of attitudes II: Arm flexion and extension have differential effects on attitudes. *Journal of Personality and Social Psychology*, *65*, 5–17.

Carter, W. R., Johnson, M. C., & Borkovec, T. D. (1986). Worry: An electrocortical analysis. *Advances in Behavioral Research and Therapy*, *8*, 193–204.

Carver, C. S., Sutton, S. K., & Scheier, M. F. (2000). Action, emotion, and personality: Emerging conceptual integration. *Personality and Social Psychology Bulletin*, *26*, 741–751.

Centerbar, D., & Clore, G. L. (2006). Do approach–avoidance actions create attitudes? *Psychological Science*, *17*, 22–29.

Chen, M., & Bargh, J. A. (1999). Consequences of automatic evaluation: Immediate behavioral predispositions to approach or avoid the stimulus. *Personality and Social Psychology Bulletin*, *25*, 215–224.

Coan, J. A., & Allen, J. J. B. (2003). The state and trait nature of frontal EEG asymmetry in emotion. In K. Hugdahl & R. J. Davidson (Eds.), *The asymmetrical brain* (pp. 565–615). Cambridge, MA: MIT Press.

Crowe, E., & Higgins, E. T. (1997). Regulatory focus and strategic inclinations: Promotion and prevention in decision making. *Organizational Behavior and Human Decision Processes*, *69*, 117–132.

Davidson, R. J. (1992). Anterior cerebral asymmetry and the nature of emotion. *Brain and Cognition*, *20*, 125–151.

Davidson, R. J. (1995). Cerebral asymmetry, emotion, and affective style. In R. J. Davidson & K. Hugdahl (Eds.), *Brain asymmetry* (pp. 361–387). Cambridge, MA: MIT Press.

Davidson, R. J., & Tomarken, A. J. (1989). Laterality and emotion: An electrophysiological approach. In F. Boller & J. Grafman (Eds.), *Handbook of neuropsychology* (pp. 419–441). Amsterdam: Elsevier.

Derryberry, D., & Reed, M. A. (1998). Anxiety and attentional focusing: Trait, state and hemispheric influences. *Personality and Individual Differences*, *25*, 745–761.

Derryberry, D., & Tucker, D. M. (1994). Motivating the focus of attention. In P. M. Niedenthal & S. Kitayama (Eds.), *Heart's eye: Emotional influences in perception and attention* (pp. 167–196). New York: Academic Press.

Easterbrook, J. A. (1959). The effect of emotion on cue utilization and the organization of behavior. *Psychological Review*, *66*, 183–201.

Ekstrom, R. B., French, J. W., Harman, H. H., & Dermen, D. (1976). Manual for kit of factor-referenced cognitive tests. Princeton, NJ: Educational Testing Service.

Elliot, A. J., & McGregor, H. A. (2001). A 2 × 2 achievement goal framework. *Journal of Personality and Social Psychology*, *80*(3), 501–519.

Fazio, R. H., Eiser, J. R., & Shook, N. J. (2004). Attitude formation through exploration: Valence asymmetries. *Journal of Personality and Social Psychology*, *87*, 293–311.

Fein, S., & Spencer, S. J. (1997). Prejudice as self-image maintenance: Affirming the self through derogating others. *Journal of Personality and Social Psychology*, *73*, 31–44.

Förster, J., & Friedman, R. S. (in press). Expression entails anticipation: Toward a self-regulatory model of bodily feedback effects. In G. R. Semin & E. R. Smith (Eds.), *Embodied grounding: Social, cognitive, affective, and neuroscientific approaches*. New York: Cambridge.

Förster, J., Friedman, R., & Liberman, N. (2004). Temporal construal effects on abstract and concrete thinking: Consequences for insight and creative cognition. *Journal of Personality and Social Psychology*, *87*, 177–189.

Förster, J., Friedman, R. S., Özelsel, A., & Denzler, M. (2006). Enactment of approach and avoidance behavior influences the scope of perceptual and conceptual attention. *Journal of Experimental Social Psychology*, *42*, 133–146.

Förster, J., & Higgins, E. T. (2005). How global vs. local processing fits regulatory focus. *Psychological Science*, *16*, 631–636.

Förster, J., Higgins, E. T., & Idson, L. C. (1998). Approach and avoidance strength during goal attainment: Regulatory focus and the "goal looms larger" effect. *Journal of Personality and Social Psychology*, *75*, 1115–1131.

Förster, J., Higgins, E. T., & Taylor Bianco, A. (2003). Speed/accuracy in performance: Tradeoff in decision making or separate strategic concerns?. *Organizational Behavior and Human Decision Processes*, *90*(1), 148–164.

Friedman, R., Fishbach, A., Förster, J., & Werth, L. (2003). Attentional priming effects on creativity. *Creativity Research Journal*, *15*, 277–286.

Friedman, R. S., & Förster, J. (2000). The effects of approach and avoidance motor actions on the elements of creative insight. *Journal of Personality and Social Psychology*, *79*, 477–492.

Friedman, R. S., & Förster, J. (2001). The effects of promotion and prevention cues on creativity. *Journal of Personality and Social Psychology*, *81*, 1001–1013.

Friedman, R. S., & Förster, J. (2002). The influence of approach and avoidance motor actions on creative cognition. *Journal of Experimental Social Psychology*, *38*, 41–55.

Friedman, R. S., & Förster, J. (2005). The influence of approach and avoidance cues on attentional flexibility. *Motivation and Emotion*, *29*, 69–81.

Friedman, R. S., Förster, J., & Denzler, M. (2007). Interactive effects of mood and task framing on creative generation. *Creativity Research Journal*, *19*, 141–162.

Gasper, K. (2004). Do you see what I see? Affect and visual information processing. *Cognition and Emotion*, *18*, 405–421.

Gasper, K., & Clore, G. (2002). Attending to the big picture: Mood and global versus local processing of visual information. *Psychological Science*, *13*, 34–40.

Gollwitzer, P. M., Heckhausen, H., & Steller, B. (1990). Deliberative vs. implemental mind-sets: Cognitive tuning toward congruous thoughts and information. *Journal of Personality and Social Psychology*, *59*, 1119–1127.

Guilford, J. P., Christensen, P. R., Merrifield, P. R., & Wilson, R. C. (1978). *Alternate uses manual.* Orange, CA: Sheridan Psychological Services.

Heller, W., Koven, N. S., & Miller, G. A. (2003). Regional brain activity in anxiety and depression, cognition/emotion interaction, and emotion regulation. In K. Hugdahl & R. J. Davidson (Eds.), *The Asymmetrical Brain* (pp. 533–564). Cambridge, MA: MIT Press.

Heller, W., & Nitschke, J. B. (1998). The puzzle of regional brain activity in depression and anxiety: The importance of subtypes and comorbidity. *Cognition and Emotion*, *12*, 421–447.

Heller, W., Nitschke, J. B., Etienne, M. A., & Miller, G. A. (1997). Patterns of regional brain activity differentiate types of anxiety. *Journal of Abnormal Psychology*, *106*, 376–385.

Higgins, E. T. (2000). Beyond pleasure and pain. In E. T. Higgins & A. W. Kruglanski (Eds.), *Motivational science: Social and personality perspectives* (pp. 231–255). Philadelphia: Taylor & Francis.

Higgins, E. T., Roney, C., Crowe, E., & Hymes, C. (1994). Ideal versus ought predilections for approach and avoidance: Distinct self-regulatory systems. *Journal of Personality and Social Psychology*, *66*, 276–286.

Higgins, E. T., Shah, J., & Friedman, R. (1997). Emotional responses to goal attainment: Strength of regulatory focus as moderator. *Journal of Personality and Social Psychology*, *72*, 515–525.

Higgins, E. T., & Sorrentino, R. M. (Eds.) (1990). *The handbook of motivation and cognition: Foundations of social behavior (Vol. 2)*. New York: Guilford.

Higgins, E. T., & Tykocinski, O. (1992). Self-discrepancies and biographical memory: Personality and cognition at the level of psychological situation. *Personality & Social Psychology Bulletin*, *18*, 527–535.

Hirt, E. R., Levine, G. M., McDonald, H. E., Melton, R. J., & Martin, L. L. (1997). The role of mood in quantitative and qualitative aspects of performance: Single or multiple mechanisms? *Journal of Experimental Social Psychology*, *33*, 602–629.

Idson, L. C., Liberman, N., & Higgins, E. T. (2000). Distinguishing gains from nonlosses and losses from nongains: A regulatory focus perspective on hedonic intensity. *Journal of Experimental Social Psychology*, *36*, 252–274.

Isen, A. M. (2000). Positive affect and decision making. In M. Lewis & J. Haviland-Jones (Eds.) (2nd ed., pp. 417–435). *Handbook of emotions.* New York: Guilford.

Isen, A. M., & Daubman, K. A. (1984). The influence of affect on categorization. *Journal of Personality and Social Psychology*, *47*, 1206–1217.

Isen, A. M., Daubman, K. A., & Nowicki, G. P. (1987). Positive affect facilitates creative problem solving. *Journal of Personality and Social Psychology*, *52*, 1122–1131.

Isen, A. M., Johnson, M. M. S., Mertz, E., & Robinson, G. F. (1985). The influence of positive affect on the unusualness of word associations. *Journal of Personality and Social Psychology*, *48*, 1413–1426.

Kahneman, D., & Tversky, A. (1979). Prospect theory: An analysis of decisions under risk. *Econometrica*, *47*, 313–327.

Kuhl, J., & Kazén, M. (1999). Volitional facilitation of difficult intentions: Joint activation of intention memory and positive affect removes Stroop interference. *Journal of Experimental Psychology: General*, *128*, 382–399.

Kunda, Z., & Spencer, S. J. (2003). When do stereotypes come to mind and when do they color judgment? A goal-based theoretical framework for stereotype activation and application. *Psychological Bulletin*, *129*, 522–544.

Luu, P., Tucker, D. M., & Derryberry, D. (1998). Anxiety and the motivational basis of working memory. *Cognitive Therapy and Research*, *22*, 577–594.

Markman, A. B., & Brendl, C. M. (2005). Constraining theories of embodied cognition. *Psychological Science*, *16*, 6–10.

Mednick, S. A. (1962). The associative basis of the creative process. *Psychological Review*, *69*, 220–232.

Martin, L. L. (2001). Mood as input: A configural view of mood effects. In L. L. Martin & G. L. Clore (Eds.), *Theories of mood and cognition: A user's guidebook* (pp. 135–157). Mahwah, NJ: Erlbaum.

Martin, L. L., & Stoner, P. (1996). Mood as input: What we think about how we feel determines how we think. In L. L. Martin & A. Tesser (Eds.), *Striving and feeling: Interactions among goals, affect, and self-regulation* (pp. 279–301). Hillsdale, NJ: Erlbaum.

Martindale, C. (1995). Creativity and connectionism. In S. M. Smith, T. B. Ward, & R. A. Finke (Eds.), *The creative cognition approach* (pp. 249–268). Cambridge, MA: Bradford.

Mikulincer, M., Kedem, P., & Paz, D. (1990a). Anxiety and categorization—1. The structure and boundaries of mental categories. *Personality and Individual Differences*, *11*, 805–814.

Mikulincer, M., Paz, D., & Kedem, P. (1990b). Anxiety and categorization—2. Hierarchical levels of mental categories. *Personality and Individual Differences*, *11*, 815–821.

Milner, A. D., Brechmann, M., & Pagliarini, L. (1992). To halve and to halve not: An analysis of line bisection in normal subjects. *Neuropsychologia, 30,* 515–526.

Miyake, A., Witzki, A. H., & Emerson, M. J. (2001). Field dependence–independence from a working memory perspective: A dual-task investigation of the Hidden Figures Test. *Memory, 9,* 445–457.

Morton, B. E. (2003). Two-hand line-bisection task outcomes correlate with several measures of hemisphericity. *Brain and Cognition, 51,* 305–316.

Moskowitz, G. B., Gollwitzer, P. M., Wasel, W., & Schaal, B. (1999). Preconscious control of stereotype activation through chronic egalitarian goals. *Journal of Personality and Social Psychology, 77,* 167–184.

Mueller, C., & Dweck, C. (1998). Praise for intelligence can undermine children's motivation and performance. *Journal of Personality & Social Psychology, 75*(1), 33–52.

Navon, D. (1977). Forest before trees: The precedence of global features in visual perception. *Cognitive Psychology, 9,* 353–383.

Neumann, R., & Strack, F. (2000). Approach and avoidance: The influence of proprioceptive and exteroceptive cues on encoding of affective information. *Journal of Personality & Social Psychology, 79,* 39–48.

Nickerson, R. S. (1984). Retrieval inhibition from part-set cuing: A persisting enigma in memory research. *Memory and Cognition, 12,* 531–552.

Nitschke, J. B., Heller, W., Palmieri, P. A., & Miller, G. A. (1999). Contrasting patterns of brain activity in anxious apprehension and anxious arousal. *Psychophysiology, 36,* 628–637.

Olson, J. M., & Hafer, C. L. (1990). Self-inference processes: Looking back and ahead. In J. M. Olson & M. P. Zanna (Eds.), *Self-inference processes: The Ontario symposium* (Vol. 6, pp. 293–320). Hillsdale, NJ: Erlbaum.

Pomerantz, J. R. (1983). Global and local precedence: Selective attention in form and motion perception. *Journal of Experimental Psychology: General, 112,* 516–540.

Reeves, F. B., & Bergum, B. O. (1972). Perceptual narrowing as a function of peripheral cue relevance. *Perceptual and Motor Skills, 35,* 719–724.

Roediger, H. L., & Neely, J. H. (1982). Retrieval blocks in episodic and semantic memory. *Canadian Journal of Psychology, 36,* 213–242.

Rundus, D. (1973). Negative effects of using list items as retrieval cues. *Journal of Verbal Learning and Verbal Behavior, 12,* 43–50.

Sarason, I. G., Pierce, G. R., & Sarason, B. R. (Eds.) (1996). *Cognitive interference: Theories, methods, and findings.* Hillsdale, NJ: Erlbaum.

Schooler, J. W. (2002). Verbalization produces a transfer inappropriate processing shift. *Applied Cognitive Psychology, 16,* 989–997.

Seibt, B., & Förster, J. (2004). Risky and careful processing under stereotype threat: How regulatory focus can enhance and deteriorate performance when self stereotypes are active. *Journal of Personality and Social Psychology, 87,* 38–56.

Shah, J., Higgins, E. T., & Friedman, R. S. (1998). Performance incentives and means: How regulatory focus influences goal attainment. *Journal of Personality and Social Psychology, 74,* 285–293.

Shah, J. Y., Kruglanski, A. W., & Friedman, R. (2002). A goal systems approach to self-regulation. In M. P. Zanna, J. M. Olson, & C. Seligman (Eds.), *The Ontario Symposium on Social Psychology* (pp. 247–276). New Jersey: Erlbaum.

Shrira, I., & Martin, L. L. (2005). Stereotyping, self-affirmation, and the cerebral hemispheres. *Personality & Social Psychology Bulletin, 31*(6), 846–856.

Slamecka, N. J. (1968). An examination of trace storage in free recall. *Journal of Experimental Psychology, 76,* 504–513.

Smith, S. M. (1995). Fixation, incubation, and insight in memory, problem solving, and creativity. In S. M. Smith, T. B. Ward, & R. A. Finke (Eds.), *The creative cognition approach* (pp. 135–155). Cambridge, MA: MIT Press.

Sorrentino, R. M., & Higgins, E. T. (Eds.) (1996). *The handbook of motivation and cognition: The interpersonal context (Vol. 3).* New York: Guilford.

Tanner, W. P., & Swets, J. A. (1954). A decision-making theory of visual detection. *Psychological Review, 61,* 401–409.

Trope, Y., & Liberman, N. (2003). Temporal construal. *Psychological Review, 110,* 401–442.

Tucker, D. M., Antes, J. R., Stenslie, C. E., & Barnhardt, T. M. (1978). Anxiety and lateral cerebral function. *Journal of Abnormal Psychology, 87,* 380–383.

Tucker, D. M., & Williamson, P. A. (1984). Asymmetric neural control systems in human self-regulation. *Psychological Review, 91,* 185–215.

Tyler, S. K., & Tucker, D. M. (1982). Anxiety and perceptual structure: Individual differences in neuropsychological function. *Journal of Abnormal Psychology, 91,* 210–220.

Watkins, M. J. (1975). Inhibition in recall with extralist "cues." *Journal of Verbal Learning and Verbal Behavior, 14,* 294–303.

Weltman, G., Smith, J. E., & Edstrom, G. H. (1971). Perceptual narrowing during pressure-chamber exposure. *Human Factors, 13,* 99–107.

Werth, L., & Förster, J. (in press). The effects of regulatory focus on braking speed. *Journal of Applied Social Psychology, 37,* 2764–2787.

Winkielman, P., & Berridge, K. C. (2004). Unconscious Emotion. *Current Directions in Psychological Science, 13,* 120–123.

Part IV

Evaluative Processes

Evolution of Evaluative Processes I

15 Internal Regulatory Variables and the Design of Human Motivation: A Computational and Evolutionary Approach

John Tooby, Leda Cosmides, Aaron Sell, Debra Lieberman, and Daniel Sznycer

CONTENTS

THE NEXT COGNITIVE REVOLUTION: THE ADAPTATIONIST INTEGRATION OF MOTIVATION AND COGNITION

The discovery by biologists and physicists that natural selection is the only antientropic force that builds functional machinery into organisms led to an important insight: Natural selection provides the underlying theories explaining why functional mechanisms in the species-typical architecture of the brain have the designs that they do (Tooby, Cosmides, & Barrett, 2003). This connects the evolutionary sciences to psychology and neuroscience directly. Models of selection pressures (adaptive problems) faced by a species provide the design criteria that a species' mechanisms evolved to solve. Mechanisms evolved their design features—their functional properties—as methods for solving these adaptive problems.

Evolutionary psychology as a framework emerged because of the scientific benefits of employing these facts explicitly in research (Buss, 2005; Tooby & Cosmides, 1992). It proceeds by (1) deriving models of adaptive problems from evolutionary biology and our knowledge of the structure of the ancestral world, and then (2) using these models to design critical empirical tests of competing theories about the architecture of the mechanisms (if any) that evolved to solve them.

An equally essential element of evolutionary psychology is its participation in the cognitive revolution. The brain's properties as a physical system were organized by natural selection so that they function as an information processing system or organ of computation. It takes information as input, performs operations on it, and uses the output to regulate behavior so that it solves adaptive problems more effectively than the organism could in the absence of those procedures.

The ability to describe the functional properties of psychological mechanisms in terms of their computational operations gives us the appropriate language for characterizing their designs in terms of their evolved functions—functions that are, by their nature, inherently computational and regulatory. In short, the brain contains, not metaphorically but actually, evolved programs designed by natural selection to compute the solutions to adaptive information-processing problems involving the regulation of behavior.

Because humans, like other organisms, were challenged over their evolution by a rich diversity of adaptive problems (e.g., disease avoidance, mate selection), successful behavior regulation favored the evolution of a multiplicity of programs to solve them (e.g., disgust,

sexual attraction). As we will demonstrate with two main examples—kin detection and anger—the structure of an evolved program can be discovered to embody a computational problem-solving strategy whose circuit logic exploits the ancestral structure of the adaptive problem. For example, the structure of ancestral hunter-gatherer life provided stably informative cues to genetic relatedness that our kin detection system evolved to target (see below; Lieberman, Tooby, & Cosmides, 2007).

Although there is a great emphasis in the traditional cognitive sciences on how organisms perceive and understand the world, there is astonishingly little cognitive work mapping how motivation and valuation work to regulate action. Because cognitive science descended from philosophy, cognitive scientists often treat the mind as if it exists solely to discover truths (as with perception, learning, and reasoning) rather than to regulate action adaptively. Fodor, for example, expresses this view when he says that the function of cognition is "the fixation of true beliefs" (Fodor, 2000, p. 68). Of course, true beliefs may be one useful element in the adaptive regulation of behavior. But as Hume was the first to point out, true beliefs by themselves have no implications for how to behave— what to approach, what to avoid, what to value, how to feel, what to do (Tooby, Cosmides, & Barrett, 2005). Encyclopedias have no motivations. As Hume understood, value is not an objective property of the external world, there to be observed. A man may be sexually attractive to many women, but sexually repulsive to his sister—so which is he "really"? In reality, value information must be internally computed and, unlike true beliefs, may validly differ across individuals. Moreover, value information is an indispensable component of almost every decision about how to behave. We argue in this chapter that there is a large and often overlooked class of neurocomputational programs that evolved to compute adaptive valuations (and their inputs)—valuations that are incapable of being either true or false.

Fodor (2000) justifies cognitive scientists' neglect of so-called conative processes (processes governing preferences, approach, avoidance, motivation, and valuation) by arguing that cognitive and conative mechanisms are separate; therefore, cognitive science can neglect motivation without being deformed in the process. In contrast, we think the cognitive sciences have been impaired by this artificial division. As we explore below with two case studies—kin detection and anger—computational elements for fact and value are often inextricably joined within the same cognitive adaptations, and so must be studied together.

The purpose of this chapter is to sketch out a new framework for thinking about motivation that is not only computational and grounded in evolutionary biology, but also shows how motivational elements articulate with the rest of the cognitive architecture as part of a single, coevolved functional system. Findings in the evolutionary sciences imply the existence of a large number of adaptive problems—including problems in social interaction—for which there exist no corresponding motivational theories. We will illustrate this computational approach to motivation with several of these adaptive problems, including incest avoidance, kin selection, power-based bargaining, and reciprocity.

In order to construct a theoretical framework capable of incorporating this new range of cases, we need to introduce a new class of computational elements that have no present counterpart in the cognitive sciences. We think serious analysis of how the human brain accomplishes certain tasks involving valuation and behavior-regulation forces us to posit such entities. Indeed, not only do we think they are theoretically mandated, but we are involved in a series of research programs to demonstrate that they are psychologically and neurally real. We call these computational elements "internal regulatory variables."

INTERNAL REGULATORY VARIABLES AND MOTIVATION

For both theoretical and empirical reasons, we expect that the architecture of the human mind is by design full of registers for evolved variables whose function is to store summary magnitudes (or parameters) that allow value computation to be integrated into behavior regulation (Kirkpatrick & Ellis, 2001; Lieberman et al., 2007). These internal regulatory variables are not traditional theoretical entities such as concepts, representations, goal states, beliefs, or desires. Instead, they are indices that acquire their meaning by the evolved behavior-controlling and motivation-generating procedures that access them. That is, each has a location embedded in the input–output relations of our evolved programs, and their function inheres in the role they play in the decision flow of these the programs. We have evolved specializations designed to compute them and to output them to critical junctures in our evolved decision-making systems.

To take a (seemingly) simple example, it is not enough to know that mongongo nuts belong to the category "food" and are therefore to be approached. Studies of the foraging behavior of living hunter-gatherers show that the decision to look for and pick up any given food resource is based on complex calculations that combine several variables (Smith & Winterhalder, 1992;

Winterhalder & Smith, 2000). These variables include (at minimum) the calories per gram of each food resource, its average package size (grams per unit caught or gathered), its average search time (how long it takes to find it), and its average handling time (how long it takes to capture it and convert it into edible form—cracking the nuts, butchering the animal, cooking it, and so on). Models using all four variables predict more variance in what foragers actually look for and take than ones based on caloric value alone. These models predict foraging motivations—which foods people actively search for when they go out foraging, which foods they do not bother with even when they come across them, and which they decide are worth the effort of capturing/extracting/gathering and hauling back to camp.

These mathematical models have implications for the computational architecture of the motivational systems that regulate approach and avoidance while foraging. That these models successfully predict behavior implies that the brain has programs that compute, for each food, the value of these four variables (or of proxy variables correlated with them). Each computed value has a magnitude that represents, respectively, how calorie rich, how big, how difficult to find, and how difficult to obtain and prepare each food resource is. A different constellation of these four values will be computed for each food resource, and the constellation applying to a given animal or plant needs to be stored and retrieved in tandem when deciding whether to forage for it. For !Kung foragers, the values that apply to mongongo nuts need to be stored in a separate mental file folder from those that apply to acacia beetles, Grewia berries, ivory palm, Tsama melons, hartebeest meat, and hundreds of other foods. Functionally, one would expect the evolution of a foraging-specialized data format consisting of (at least) four registers, each dedicated to indexing one of the four variables. When foraging, the values of these variables are accessed by a program that combines them, producing motivations expressed in choices. As a result, we observe foragers seeking foods with better joint combinations of package size, search time, calorie density, and handling time, over worse combinations, according to the algorithm in the motivational system that integrates them. Because foraging motivations are regulated by the magnitudes of these four variables, they are examples of internal regulatory variables.

Internal regulatory variables are not an exotic feature of human motivational systems; they are key features of every feedback-regulated process in multicellular organisms. Exquisitely designed regulatory systems permeate the human body, producing functional outcomes by entraining processes at all levels of organization, from gene activation and protein synthesis to organ function to behavior. Motivational systems are simply one class of regulatory system. They differ from regulatory systems like the Krebs cycle primarily in that their adaptive function—the problem they were organized by natural selection to solve—is to regulate behavior rather than metabolism. Even this divide is not sharp—many metabolic regulatory systems require behavior-regulating motivational systems (e.g., glucose delivery and hunger, electrolyte balance and thirst), and many motivational systems cannot do their job without regulating metabolism as well as behavior (e.g., predator evasion and the flight–fight response).

Our working hypothesis is that motivational systems, like other regulatory systems, are interpenetrated by networks of internal regulatory variables designed by selection. This is known to be true for the motivational systems regulating fluid balance (for thirst), energy reserves (for hunger), body temperature (for thermoregulation), and carbon dioxide levels (for breathing). We think it is equally true for motivational systems regulating social interaction. Just as there are internal regulatory variables that register the caloric value of a food resource or the level of glucose in the blood, there should be internal regulatory variables that register those properties of persons, acts, and situations that are needed to compute adaptive motivations. Examples include how much a particular person is willing to sacrifice his or her own welfare for yours (a welfare trade-off ratio), how valuable a particular person would be to you as a sexual partner (a sexual value index), how much harm a person could inflict on you in a fight (a formidability index), how genetically related a person is to you (a kinship index), and so on.

According to this view, internal regulatory variables evolved to track those narrow, targeted properties of the body, the social environment, and the physical environment whose computation provided inputs needed by evolved decision-making programs in order to generate motivations to action. Internal regulatory variables have magnitudes or discrete parameter values. They encode value, provide formatted input to mechanisms that compute value, or provide parameter values to decision-making circuits.

FELT EXPERIENCE AND INTERNAL REGULATORY VARIABLES

Because we are subjectively aware of a rich world of feeling involved in motivations, it may seem odd, even bloodless, to talk about a computational approach to motivation, where behavior is regulated by internal variables. After all, every one of us has felt the pushes and pulls of motivation—the impulse to help a friend, to yell at a bully, to discharge an obligation, to express gratitude for an unexpected act of kindness. We all have phenomenal experiences, and their existence raises many interesting and unsolved philosophical puzzles (Dennett, 1988; Tye, 2003). But the success of vision science shows that scientific progress can be made nevertheless, by investigating the computational processes that generate experiences. Before proceeding, we would like to explain how the intuitive clarity of felt experience neither contradicts nor pre-empts the need for a computational account of motivation.

In discussing the relationship between computation and conscious experience, Jackendoff (1987) points out that differences in perceived color—the experience of yellow versus blue—can be thought as a data format by which the mind represents differences in the reflectant properties of surfaces. The computed products of lower level visual processing are represented in data formats that cannot be consciously accessed; they are accessed only by mechanisms internal to the visual system. In contrast, the data format we experience as color can be accessed by a wide variety of behavior-regulating systems. We suspect a similar view of felt experiences will emerge from a computational approach to motivation. Some felt experiences may be a data format by which the mind broadcasts, in a way that is accessible to many other mechanisms, the magnitude of certain internal regulatory variables (Tooby & Cosmides, 2008). In other cases, a felt experience may be the output of a motivational system, with its felt intensity regulated by the (nonconscious) magnitude of the internal regulatory variables it accesses while performing its computations. That is, differences in the magnitudes of these variables cause increases or decreases in your impulse to help or harm, your feelings of sexual attraction, disgust, gratitude, guilt, shame, obligation, pride, entitlement, and so on.

Representing the outputs of motivational systems in the broadly accessible data format of felt experience may be one key to the human ability to improvise novel solutions to adaptive problems (Cosmides & Tooby, 2000a, 2001). Imagined alternatives can be evaluated by how they change the intensity of these felt experiences—an internal feedback system that steers behavioral responses toward adaptive outcomes.

Felt experience is so central to folk theories of motivation that it can blind us to the need for computational accounts, just as the immediacy of perceptual experience blinded vision scientists of the 1960s to the need for computational accounts of vision (Marr, 1982). So before turning to social motivation, we would like to pause briefly to consider the ways in which felt experience may be related to internal regulatory variables and computation.

Conscious and Nonconscious Access to Internal Regulatory Variables

Sometimes the operation of internal regulatory variables is entirely nonconscious. For example, the kidneys are equipped with an internal regulatory variable that registers levels of oxygen in the blood. When blood oxygen falls below a certain threshold value, this stimulates the production of erythropoietin, a hormone that triggers maturation of red blood cells in the bone marrow. This is unaccompanied by any felt experience—the brain does not seem to have any design feature capable of consciously representing levels of erythropoietin or blood oxygen. Blood oxygen level is not represented as a felt experience even when it is dangerously low: Only the consequences of hypoxia, as it damages organ systems, are felt, causing headache, nausea, breathlessness, and other aversive experiences.

In contrast, some motivational systems are designed to produce felt experiences as a result of having processed an internal regulatory variable, and those felt experiences guide behavior in a direct and adaptive fashion. The suffocation alarm system is a familiar example. There is an internal regulatory variable that registers carbon dioxide to oxygen levels in circulation. When this ratio increases too quickly, the suffocation alarm system is triggered. It downregulates motivations to pursue ongoing activities (e.g., we stop reading under the covers), upregulates motivations to change position, and produces the felt experience of suffocation. That felt experience guides our movements: We change position, sometimes frantically, following any experienced decline in the sense of suffocation until the awful felt experience ceases entirely—which happens when the regulatory variable reaches a normal level again. Ondine's curse, a disorder of the CO_2/O_2 regulatory variable or its ability to trigger the alarm system, is usually fatal: children born with this disorder suffocate in their sleep.

The felt experience of suffocation could be considered a readout of the magnitude of the CO_2/O_2 regulatory variable—a data format that allows movement programs to access changes in its value on a second-by-second basis, until its value falls below threshold again. That is, changes in the intensity of a given felt experience can be thought of as a special data format, one that makes changes in the magnitude of an internal regulatory variable accessible to a broad array of behavior-regulating mechanisms.

Differences between stimuli in key properties—fat content of foods, for example—should produce different values for the regulatory variable associated with each stimulus; the magnitude of these values can, in turn, be represented as different intensities of felt experience. A chocolate truffle generates a more intense felt experience of richness than a celery stick, whether you are eating them or just imagining eating them, and that intensity reflects their relative caloric content. That these felt experiences can be generated by imagination alone suggests that values for an internal regulatory variable registering the caloric content of each were previously stored; imagining oneself seeing and eating them initiates a process that transforms their magnitudes into a data format of felt experience.

Tracking different properties of the world—caloric content versus handling time, for example—clearly requires distinct regulatory variables. But if felt experience is functional—allowing imagination-based planning, for example—then the data formats by which distinct variables are experienced need to be different from one another, and qualitatively different to the extent they need to encode different types of information. Different regulatory variables need to be associated with distinct types of *qualia*, to use the philosophers' term (Tye, 2003). So the output of different regulatory variables into consciousness feels qualitatively different. In order to make decisions, however, at some level in the architecture (conscious or nonconscious) these different data types need to be tagged with a kind of information that makes them comparable—payoff information.

Accordingly, the felt experience of richness is qualitatively distinct from the felt experience of effort—or of anticipated effort, for that matter. Watching an ice cream commercial in the kitchen can activate the felt intensity of richness associated with ice cream, exerting a motivational pull. But this pull can be trumped by the (quite different) felt experience of anticipated effort that arises as you imagine trekking across town to get it, especially when you are already tired. Algorithms in the foraging motivation system combine the magnitudes of both variables (caloric value and anticipated effort) and others as well; you experience the output of these algorithms as a motivation to action—either to go for the ice cream or just stay home.

An internal regulatory variable may have no associated felt experience, yet increase or decrease the felt experiences produced by various motivation systems. An example we will discuss later is the kinship index, a regulatory variable whose magnitude represents an estimate of a familiar other's degree of genetic relatedness to oneself (Lieberman et al., 2007). There does not seem to be a felt experience uniquely associated with its value. But the magnitude of the kinship index up- and downregulates distinct types of felt experiences. A high kinship index produces feelings of disgust when accessed by the sexual motivation system at the possibility of sexual contact with the person, and impulses to help when accessed by the system regulating altruistic motivations.

Obviously the value of an internal variable can be stored without being transformed into a felt experience, just as episodes from one's life can be stored without being transformed into a remembered experience of the past—a transformation that requires the operation of particular computations at retrieval (Klein, German, Cosmides, & Gabriel, 2004). In many cases, especially those requiring fast action, the computational systems that produce motivations may be able to access the values of internal regulatory variables without their having first been processed and reformatted as a felt experience. Indeed, there should be principles of good design determining when stored values and summary conclusions are accessed directly rather than being first transformed into felt experiences (Klein, Cosmides, Tooby, & Chance, 2002). For example, if foraging algorithms have repeatedly registered a particular food as calorie poor, hard to find, and difficult to prepare, and repeatedly performed calculations on those variables, the motivational implications for action—"don't bother with food X"—might simply be stored as a summary conclusion and quickly retrieved, without any accompanying affect.

Transforming the magnitude of regulatory variables into felt experience may be necessary, however, when we are faced with a choice but have no precomputed summary conclusion. It may also be necessary when the computations of two or more regulatory systems produce motivations to action that are in direct conflict with one another. Indeed, this last case may be when it is most important to make the information stored in regulatory variables available to a broad array of mechanisms through felt experience. Imagining situations in a quasi-perceptual way can activate felt experiences, ones reflecting the magnitude of stored regulatory variables and ones reflecting the output of the motivational systems these variables feed (Cosmides & Tooby, 2000b; Tooby & Cosmides, 1990). But it does so in a way that is decoupled from action—a design feature that allows us to simulate how we would *feel* about the outcomes of actions, which is pivotal for choosing between alternative courses of action and planning for the future (Cosmides & Tooby, 2000a; Tooby & Cosmides, 2001). Seen in this way, the ability to transform the magnitudes of internal regulatory variables and their motivational outputs into felt experience is a crucial facet not just of improvisational intelligence, but of human foresight and choice, allowing

us to not only simulate what would happen, but how we would feel about what would happen.

Our point is this: There should be principled relationships between internal regulatory variables and felt experience. The fact that we experience ourselves as motivated by feelings and impulses does not render a computational account of motivation unnecessary, any more than our experience of seeing the world renders a computational account of vision unnecessary.

DISCOVERING INTERNAL REGULATORY VARIABLES: THE ROLE OF THEORIES OF ADAPTIVE FUNCTION

If we are to discover internal regulatory variables that govern social motivations, we need to properly understand the adaptive problems of social life that these variables evolved to solve. But from an evolutionary perspective, what is social interaction for? What problems of survival, reproduction, and fitness promotion do individuals face when they live socially, and what behavioral responses count as adaptive solutions to these problems? We cannot rely on intuition to answer these questions because the history of the behavioral and biological sciences shows that, until the 1970s, many of the most prominent behavioral theories were based on serious misunderstandings of how natural selection works (Williams, 1966; see also Tooby & Cosmides, 1992).

Fortunately, over the last 40 years, evolutionary researchers have carefully analyzed how natural selection shapes the social interactions of many species. As a result, they have developed formal theories defining a series of specific adaptive problems arising from social life—theories that also specify what behavioral patterns constitute adaptive solutions. These models have been validated using the behavior of thousands of species. For example, the theory of kin selection analyzes selection on altruism within the family. This theory specifies how human motivational adaptations should be designed to make decisions about, for example, when to help siblings and when siblings will be in conflict with their parents and each other over how parents allocate investments of time, effort, and resources among them (Hamilton, 1964; Trivers, 1974). Analyses of the selection pressures posed by deleterious recessives and coevolving pathogens lead to predictions about motivational systems regulating inbreeding avoidance (Lieberman et al., 2007; Tooby, 1982). Theories of sexual selection define adaptive problems and solutions posed by courtship and mating (Buss & Schmitt, 1993; Daly & Wilson, 1983; Symons, 1979; Trivers, 1972; Williams, 1966). The asymmetric war of attrition is a game theoretic model of the selection pressures shaping bargaining, aggression, dominance, and resource division (Hammerstein & Parker, 1982; Huntingford & Turner, 1987). The banker's paradox model of deep engagement relationships (Tooby & Cosmides, 1996) and risk-buffering models of sharing (Gurven, Allen-Arave, Hill, & Hurtado, 2000) describe adaptive problems that friendships and within-group sharing solve. Theories of reciprocal altruism and social exchange illuminate selection pressures shaping two-person exchange (Axelrod & Hamilton, 1981; Boyd, 1988; Cosmides & Tooby, 1989; Trivers, 1971). Models of the evolution of n-person cooperation illuminate the problems that must be solved for coalitional alliances and group cooperation to be evolutionarily stable (Boyd & Richerson, 1992; Tooby, Cosmides, & Price, 2006).

To map certain components of the evolved psychological architecture of our species, we have found it useful to start with a task analysis of the adaptive problems defined by these models. This helps to specify what properties computational systems capable of solving them would need. In doing this, it rapidly became clear that the computational systems that produce social motivations would need internal regulatory variables. They are necessary in order to track those properties and actions of persons that are relevant to computing the adaptive solutions specified by these theories.

But this poses an interesting problem for systems regulating approach and avoidance motivations. For certain stimuli, the value of an internal regulatory variable can be computed in a way that takes no account of the properties of the individual doing the computing: The number of calories per gram of mongongo nuts is the same, regardless of who will be eating them. In contrast, the value of a person as a social partner sensitively depends on the circumstances and properties of the valuer. For example, if you and I are both looking for a sexual partner, the fact that the attractive person walking by is my sibling renders them sexually valueless to me, but not to you; on the other hand, if we are both sick and need care, that same sibling is likely to be more valuable to me than to you.

In other words, a social partner cannot have an invariant value that makes them a stimulus eliciting approach or avoidance; their value depends on who they are interacting with and what type of interaction is at issue. For this reason, there should be programs that compute and represent the magnitude of each internal regulatory variable in a way that is indexed to the self: person i's value as a sexual partner to me, their genetic relatedness to me, their aggressive formidability relative to mine, their status relative to mine, their value as a cooperative partner to me, how much of their own welfare they are willing to sacrifice to enhance my welfare, and so on.

We will illustrate this first with genetic relatedness, and then with the motivational system that produces anger.

THE COMPUTATIONAL ARCHITECTURE OF SIBLING DETECTION IN HUMANS

Oysters never know their siblings. Their parents release millions of gametes into the sea, most of which are eaten. Only a few survive to adulthood, and these siblings are so dispersed that they are unlikely to ever meet, let alone interact. The ecology of many species causes siblings to disperse so widely that they never interact as adults, and siblings in species lacking parental care typically do not associate as juveniles either. Humans, however, lie at the opposite end of this spectrum. Hunter-gatherer children typically grow up in families with parents and siblings, and live in bands that often include grandparents, uncles, aunts, and cousins. The uncles, aunts, and cousins are there because human siblings also associate as adults—like most people in traditional societies, adult hunter-gatherers are motivated to live with relatives nearby, if that is an option.

That close genetic relatives frequently interacted ancestrally is an important fact about our species. Some of the best established models in evolutionary biology show that genetic relatedness is an important factor in the social evolution of such species (Hamilton, 1964; Williams & Williams, 1957). Genetic relatedness refers to the increased probability, compared to the population average, that two individuals will both carry the same randomly sampled gene, given information about common ancestors. The relatedness between two individuals is typically expressed by a measure, the degree of relatedness, r_{ij}, expressed as a probability. This is a continuous variable that for humans usually has an upper bound around 0.5 (with full siblings, parents and offspring) and a lower bound of zero (with nonrelatives). Two different social motivation systems require an internal regulatory variable that tracks genetic relatedness: one governing sexual attraction/aversion, the other governing altruism. We first describe the selection pressures that should have shaped these motivational programs, then turn to computational models of the motivational programs that these selection pressures led us to propose and test.

DEGREE OF RELATEDNESS AND INBREEDING DEPRESSION: SELECTION PRESSURES

Animals are highly organized systems (hence "organisms"), whose functioning can easily be disordered by random changes. Mutations are random events, and they occur every generation. Many of them disrupt the functioning of our tightly engineered regulatory systems. A single mutation can, for example, prevent a gene from being transcribed (or from producing the right protein). Given that our chromosomes come in pairs (one from each parent), a nonfunctional mutation need not be a problem for the individual it appears in. If it is found on only one chromosome of the pair and is recessive, the other chromosome will produce the right protein and the individual may be healthy. But if the same mutation is found on both chromosomes, the necessary protein will not be produced by either. The inability of an organism to produce one of its proteins can impair its development or kill it.

Such genes, called "deleterious recessives," are not rare. They accumulate in populations precisely because they are not harmful when heterozygous—that is, when it is matched with an undamaged allele. Their harmful effects are expressed, however, when they are homozygous—that is, when the same impaired gene is supplied from both parents. Each human carries a large number of deleterious recessives, most of them unexpressed. When expressed, they range in harmfulness from mild impairment to lethality. A "lethal equivalent" is a set of genes whose aggregate effects, when homozygous, completely prevent the reproduction of the individual they are in (as when they kill the bearer before reproductive age). It is estimated that each of us has at least one to two lethal equivalents worth of deleterious recessives (Bittles & Neel, 1994; Lieberman, 2004). However, the deleterious recessives found in one person are usually different from those found in another.

These facts become socially important when natural selection evaluates the fitness consequences of mating with a nonrelative versus mating with a close genetic relative (for example, a parent or sibling). In reproduction, each parent places half of its genes into a gamete, which then meet and fuse to form the offspring. For parents who are genetically unrelated, the rate at which harmful recessives placed in the two gametes are likely to match and be expressed is a function of their frequency in the population. If (as is common) the frequency in the population of a given recessive is 1/1000, then the frequency with which it will meet itself (be homozygous) in an offspring is only 1 in 1,000,000.

In contrast, if the two parents are close genetic relatives, then the rate at which deleterious recessives are rendered homozygous is far higher. The degree of relatedness between full siblings, or parents and offspring is ½. Therefore, each of the deleterious recessives one sibling inherited from her parents has a 50% chance of being in her brother. Each sibling has a further 50% chance of placing any given gene into a gamete, which means that for any given deleterious recessive found in one sibling, there is a ⅛ chance that a brother and sister will pass two copies to their joint offspring (a ½ chance both siblings have it times a ½ chance the sister places it in the egg times a ½ chance the brother places it in the sperm). Therefore, incest between full siblings renders one-eighth of the loci homozygous in the resulting offspring, leading to a fitness reduction of 25% in a species carrying two lethal equivalents (two lethal equivalents per individual × ⅛ expression in the offspring = 25%). This is a large selection pressure—the equivalent of killing one quarter of one's children. Because inbreeding makes children more similar to their parents, it also defeats the function of sexual reproduction, which is to produce genetic diversity that protects offspring against pathogens that have adapted to the parents' phenotype (Tooby, 1982).

The decline in the fitness of offspring (in their viability and consequent reproductive rate) resulting from matings between close genetic relatives is called *inbreeding depression*. Incest is rare, but it sometimes happens, and studies of children produced by inbreeding versus outbreeding allow researchers to estimate the magnitude of inbreeding depression in humans. For example, in one study it was possible to compare children fathered by first degree relatives (brothers and fathers) to children of the same women who were fathered by unrelated men. The rate of death, severe mental handicap, and congenital disorders was 54% in the children of first degree relatives, compared to 8.7% in the children born of nonincestuous matings (Seemanova, 1971; see also Adams & Neel, 1967).

Both selection pressures—deleterious recessives and pathogen-driven selection for genetic diversity—have the same reproductive consequence: Individuals who avoid mating with close relatives will leave more descendants than those whose mating decisions are unaffected by relatedness. This means that mutations that introduce motivational design features that cost-effectively reduce the probability of incest will be strongly favored by natural selection. For species in which close genetic relatives who are reproductively mature are commonly exposed to each other, an effective way of reducing incest is to make cues of genetic relatedness reduce sexual attraction. Indeed, incest is a major fitness error, and so the prospect of sex with a sibling or parent should elicit sexual disgust or revulsion—an avoidance motivation.

DEGREE OF RELATEDNESS AND ALTRUISM: SELECTION PRESSURES

In species that live socially, conflicts of interest are ubiquitous. If I use a resource, you cannot; if I see a predator and warn you, allowing you to escape, you will benefit but the predator's attention will be drawn to me; if you successfully court an attractive person, that person becomes unavailable to me. That is, situations frequently arise in which you can take an action that will benefit you, but impose a cost on me; equally, there will be situations in which you do something that will benefit me, but at some cost to yourself. From a selectionist perspective, to what extent should your decisions take my welfare into account, and vice versa? When should you trade off some of your welfare to enhance mine? The theory of kin selection showed that selection favors one organism weighting the welfare of another to some extent when the two are genetically related (Hamilton, 1964; Williams & Williams, 1957).

Making Welfare Trade-Offs

To capture this notion of a trade-off, let us define a variable: a "welfare trade-off ratio" or $WTR_{actor, j}$ (Tooby & Cosmides, 2008). By hypothesis, this is an internal regulatory variable signifying how much weight an individual actor places on j's welfare relative to the actor's own. What we want to know is how natural selection will set the value of this variable. Equations 15.1 and 15.2 express decision rules for situations in which one's interests conflict with those of individual j. They are generalizations of standard formulas in evolutionary biology, in which benefits and costs (welfare) are defined as increases and decreases in an individual's reproduction. (Evolutionary models assume that humans, like other animals, have mechanisms for reckoning the benefits and costs of actions to self and others, and that these evolved because they reflect the average reproductive consequences of choices in our ancestral past.)

Given the possibility of taking an action, $\underline{A}$, that benefits one's self while imposing a cost on individual j, take beneficial action $\underline{A}$ when Equation 15.1 is satisfied, but not otherwise:

$$B_{self} > (WTR_{self, j}) (C_j), \text{ that is, when } B_{self}/C_j > WTR_{self, j}. \tag{15.1}$$

Given the possibility of taking an action, A, that benefits j at some cost to the self, take costly action A when Equation 15.2 is satisfied, but not otherwise:

$$C_{self} < (WTR_{self, j}) (B_j), \text{ that is, when } C_{self}/B_j > WTR_{self, j}. \tag{15.2}$$

If $WTR_{self, j} = 0$, that means you place no weight on j's welfare: Equation 15.1 means you will take self-beneficial actions no matter how large a cost they impose on j, and Equation 15.2 means you will never incur a cost to benefit j. If $WTR_{self, j} = 1$, that means you are as concerned with j's welfare as your own: you will not take a beneficial action unless the cost it imposes on j is less than the benefit you gain (Equation 15.1), and you will help j whenever the cost to you is smaller than the benefit j gains (Equation 15.2).

So what WTR function will natural selection favor? That depends on many factors, some of which are important to our discussion of anger later in this chapter. For example, if j is a trustworthy cooperative partner who reciprocates favors often, then selection might favor a WTR toward j that is higher than to an unreliable partner (Trivers, 1971). If you have no cooperative relationship, then your WTR toward j may be set by your relative ability to harm one another: If you and j both value a resource equally, but j can easily injure you in a fight, then you will be better off ceding the resource to j than engaging in a fight that damages you more than the resource gain would benefit you. This is the insight behind the *asymmetric war of attrition* (Hammerstein & Parker, 1982), a game theoretic model that explains why animals in many species engage in displays of their ability to harm one another, and why they settle on stable dominance hierarchies in which low ranking individuals cede resources to higher ranking ones without a fight (Huntingford & Turner, 1987). One way of expressing this is that your WTR toward j will be a function, at least in part, of your relative ability to injure one another—lower when you are the better fighter, higher when j is the better fighter.

The insight of kin selection theory is that natural selection should set your WTR toward j to be a function, at least in part, of your genetic relatedness to j (Hamilton, 1964; Williams & Williams, 1957). To make the insight clearer, let us leave aside factors such as reciprocation and the ability to cause injury, and consider two alternative motivational designs. The first design sets $WTR_{self, j} = 0$, even when j is a genetic relative. The second design is a recent mutation in the population, which sets $WTR_{self, j} = r_{self, j}$, the self's degree of relatedness to j. Which WTR setting will spread by natural selection?

Biologists recognize that the second design is strongly favored by selection in species, such as humans, where close genetic relatives frequently interact. If you inherited this design from your ancestors, $r_{self, j}$ expresses the probability that your genetic relative also inherited that same mutation from the same ancestors. That means the new design can promote its own reproduction by making trade-offs between your reproduction and the reproduction of your close relatives—trade-offs reflecting the probability that your close relatives also have this new design.

When $WTR_{self,j} = r_{self,j}$, then Equation 15.2 reduces to Hamilton's rule: help j, but only when $C_{self} < (r_{self,j}) (B_j)$, that is, when the costs to your own reproduction are outweighed by the benefits to j's reproduction, discounted by the probability, $r_{self,j}$, that j has inherited the same mutant design from a recent common ancestor. The altruistic design will also refrain from self-beneficial actions that are too costly to the reproduction of relatives: It will not take actions where $B_{self} < (r_{self,j}) (C_j)$, Equation 15.1. These choices promote the replication of the design itself, by sometimes sacrificing your reproduction to enhance that of your genetic relatives. (As with deleterious recessives, you can see that whether this design spreads is a function of the probability that the same design is present in the genetic relative—not the total proportion of genes held in common.)

In comparison, the design that sets $WTR_{self,j}$ equal to zero is at a competitive disadvantage. An actor equipped with a $WTR_{self,j} = 0$ design will take self-beneficial actions, even when the benefit to the actor's own reproduction is minute and the cost to a relative's reproduction is huge. This means it indiscriminately imposes costs on the reproduction of relatives, who carry the same design with a probability equal to $r_{self,j}$. The design also loses opportunities to replicate itself by failing to take any action that is individually costly—even those that would provide a large benefit to the reproduction of a relative at a minor cost to the self.

The selection pressure described by Hamilton's rule does not mean that $WTR_{self,j}$ (henceforth: WTR_j) should be never be higher than $r_{self,j}$—your full sib might also be a great reciprocation partner, or powerful enough to extort you into sacrificing your welfare for his. It means that the designs favored by selection should use genetic relatedness between self and j to place a lower boundary on WTR_j, causing you to help in accordance with Hamilton's rule even when there is no chance the favor will be reciprocated and no chance of extortion. It also means that selection should shape motivation so that the tendency to exploit is restrained by the detection of genetic relatedness (see Equation 15.1).

This analysis predicts that natural selection should have designed the human motivational architecture to embody programs determining how high one's welfare trade-off ratio toward other individuals should be set. These programs should take many variables into account, such as aggressive formidability or value as a cooperative partner. However, kin selection theory tells us that, all else equal, WTR should be upregulated for close genetic relatives, motivating us to help kin more and harm them less than we otherwise would.

THE KINSHIP INDEX AS AN INTERNAL REGULATORY VARIABLE

What might a computational approach to social motivation look like—what kind of internal regulatory variables are needed, and how they might regulate each other and behavior? The selection pressures just discussed suggested a number of hypotheses about the design of motivational systems. Our research has been testing the model shown in Figure 15.1. The key internal regulatory variables in this model are a sexual value index (SV_j), a welfare trade-off ratio (WTR_j) and, most importantly, a kinship index (KI_j).

The importance of degree of relatedness for inbreeding avoidance and altruism led us to expect that the human brain reliably develops a kin detection system. For each familiar individual j, this neurocomputational system would need to compute and update a continuous variable, the *kinship index*, KI_j. KI_j is an internal regulatory variable whose magnitude reflects the kin detection system's pairwise estimate of the degree of relatedness between self and j. The kinship index should serve as input to at least two different motivational systems: one regulating feelings of sexual attraction and revulsion and another regulating altruistic impulses. Each has its own proprietary regulatory variables.

Sexual Motivation System

Proprietary to the system-motivating sexual attraction is the sexual value index, SV_j. SV_j is a regulatory variable whose magnitude reflects j's value as a sexual partner for the self (note that value as a sexual partner is not equivalent to value as a long-term mate). The sexual value estimator is a system designed to compute SV_js based on many inputs, including cues that were correlated with fertility and health among our hunter-gatherer ancestors (for review, see Sugiyama, 2005). The kinship index associated with j is one of the variables that the sexual value estimator uses. When the magnitude of $KI_j = 0$, the magnitude of SV_j should be a function of all the other cues the sexual value estimator takes as input. But when the magnitude of KI_j is high, this should decrease the magnitude of SV_j dramatically. That is, the sexual value estimator's internal algorithms should be designed to weight a high KI_j more heavily than other inputs.

Cues—real or internally generated through imagination—signaling the possibility of sexual contact with j should activate the sexual motivation system. When this happens, the value of SV_j should be transformed into a felt experience. A high value of SV_j should be transformed into the felt experience of sexual attraction; a low

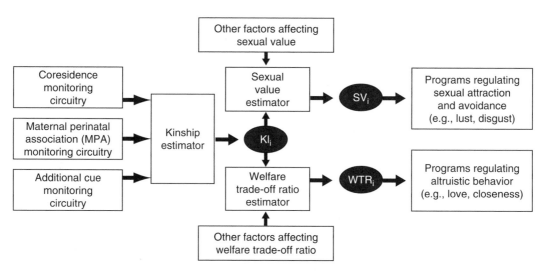

FIGURE 15.1 Model of the human kin detection system, and the internal regulatory variables (black ovals) it computes and regulates. Monitoring circuitry registers cues ancestrally correlated with genetic relatedness (e.g., coresidence duration, MPA). A "kinship estimator" transforms these inputs into a kinship index (KI_i) for each familiar individual i. The kinship index is used by downstream systems to compute two other regulatory variables: a sexual value index (SV_i) and a welfare trade-off ratio index (WTR_i). These serve as input to two motivational systems, one that regulates the allocation of mating effort and another that regulates altruism.

value of SV_j should be transformed into the felt experience of sexual disgust. There does not seem to be a felt experience associated with KI_j per se, only with the variables it regulates.

Altruistic Motivation System

According to the model in Figure 15.1, the welfare trade-off ratio, WTR_j, is an internal regulatory variable expressing how much you value j's welfare relative to your own. Its value is nonconsciously expressed in many decisions you make throughout the day—how much chocolate you leave for j, how loud to play your music when j is trying to work, whether to clean up the mess or leave it for j, whether to call home to let j know you will be late. It is computed by a system, the welfare trade-off ratio estimator, that takes into account a specific array of relevant variables (cooperation, formidability, etc.), as discussed above. KI_j should be one of these variables: Higher magnitudes of KI_j should result in higher computed magnitudes for WTR_j. Conflicts of interest should activate decision rules that implement Equations 15.1 and 15.2 (above). The output of these decision rules can be represented in the data format of a felt experience—the impulse to help j (Equation 15.2) or to avoid harming j (Equation 15.1). When events trigger a recomputation of WTR_j, setting it at a higher or lower value, the newly recomputed value of WTR_j may itself be transformed, at least temporarily, into the data format of a felt experience: an increase

or decrease in a feeling of warmth, love, or caring toward j. The felt experience makes the new WTR_j value broadly accessible, allowing many mechanisms to recalibrate the extent to which they take j's welfare into account.

Triangulating the Kinship Index

That a kinship index should regulate two independent systems—altruism and sexual aversion—provides a method for determining which cues the kin detection system uses to compute the kinship index. If a computational element corresponding to KI_j exists, then any input to the kin detection system that increases the magnitude of KI_j should have two independent but co-ordinated effects: It should increase WTR_j and decrease SV_j. When asked to imagine the right activating situations, the magnitudes of these regulatory variables should be transformed into intensities of felt experience: A low SV_j should be represented as a high felt intensity of disgust at the thought of sex with j, and a high WTR_j should produce stronger impulses to help j than a lower WTR_j. This leads to a specific prediction: Inputs to the kin detection system that regulate feelings of altruism toward j should also regulate degree of sexual aversion toward j.

By triangulation, therefore, we were able to infer which cues the kin detection system uses. People vary in their exposure to potential kinship cues, so variation in exposure to specific cues for a given sibling can be quantitatively matched to variation in the subject's feelings of sexual aversion and altruism toward that sibling. If a cue is used in computing the kinship index, then it should regulate sexual aversion and altruism toward j, and the pattern of cue use should be the same for both motivational systems. Using this logic, we were also able to discover how the kinship estimator combines cues to compute a kinship index for siblings. Methods and details of the results we discuss below can be found in Lieberman et al. (2007).

COMPUTING THE KINSHIP INDEX FOR SIBLINGS

Detecting genetic relatedness is a major adaptive problem, but not an easy one to solve. Neither we nor our ancestors can see another person's DNA directly and compare it to our own, in order to determine genetic relatedness. Nor can the problem of detecting genetic relatives be solved by a domain-general learning mechanism that picks up local, transient cues to genetic relatedness: To deduce which cues predict relatedness locally, the mechanism would need to already know the genetic relatedness of others—the very information it lacks and needs to find. So the best evolution can do is to design a kin detection system that uses cues that were reliably correlated with genetic relatedness in the ancestral past to compute the magnitude of a kinship index. This requires *monitoring circuitry*, which is designed to register cues that are relevant in computing relatedness. It also requires a computational unit, the "kinship estimator," whose procedures were tuned by a history of selection to take these registered inputs and transform them into a kinship index. So, what cues does the monitoring circuitry register, and how does the kinship estimator transform these into a kinship index?

By considering the statistical information about genetic relatedness that was built into the structure of hunter-gatherer life, we predicted that the kin detection system would use two independent cues as the source of its information about relatedness of siblings: maternal perinatal association, and duration of coresidence during the period of parental investment.

Olders Detecting Younger Siblings

As mammals, human mothers nurse and care for their newborn infants, so seeing your own mother care for a newborn is a reliable cue that this baby is your sibling. We call this the "maternal perinatal association cue," or MPA. Our data show that levels of altruism and sexual aversion toward a particular younger sibling are high for subjects who have been exposed to the MPA cue—that is for subjects who are older than their siblings and were present in

the home when their biological mother was caring for that new baby. This is true no matter how long the subject and younger sibling subsequently coreside in the same household.

Youngers Detecting Older Sibs

If you are younger, the maternal perinatal association cue will not work, because you did not exist at the time your older sibling was born. So to detect older siblings, the mind defaults to a different but weaker cue: How long you coresided with this child during the period of parental investment, from your birth until late adolescence. Hunter-gatherer bands are composed of several nuclear and extended families; as conditions change, these bands fission into smaller groups and later fuse back together again. But when they fission, they do so along family lines, with children staying with parents (especially mothers). Under such conditions, the more time one child spends with another, the more closely related they are likely to be. (We found that duration of childhood coresidence is still highly correlated ($r = \sim.70$) with relatedness (i.e., with a sibling being full, half, or unrelated step), even among the postindustrial subjects in our study.)

When the MPA cue is absent, our data show that levels of altruism and sexual aversion toward a particular sibling are set by duration of childhood coresidence. It takes 14–18 years of coresidence to produce levels of altruism and sexual aversion toward siblings that are as high as those produced by being exposed to the MPA cue. The group of people who are not exposed to the MPA cue includes all youngers detecting older siblings, all subjects with step and adoptive siblings, and about 12% olders with younger siblings.

Our data indicate that the kinship estimator computes kinship indexes nonconsciously, and independently of consciously held beliefs about genetic relatedness. A striking example of this from our research involves siblings who are step or adoptive—that is, siblings who the subject knows are not genetically related. Duration of coresidence predicts altruism and sexual aversion toward step and adoptive siblings, just as it does for youngers detecting older siblings. This shows that when conscious beliefs conflict with the output of the kin detection system, the criteria used by the kin detection system prevail.

Cue Integration by the Kinship Estimator

If the effects of MPA and coresidence duration were additive, this would be consistent with a model in which data from the monitoring circuitry were being fed directly into each of the two motivational systems (sexual and altruism), with no intervening regulatory variable—that is, with no kinship index. But their effects were not additive: There is an interaction between the two cues. When the MPA cue is present, levels of altruism and sexual aversion toward that sibling are high, and long coresidence durations do not result in any increase in their levels. Coresidence duration affects levels of altruism and sexual aversion only when the MPA cue is absent.

That is, the effects of coresidence duration are conditional on the presence or absence of the MPA cue. For cues to be combined in this nonadditive way, there needs to be a mechanism that does the combining. This is evidence for the existence of the kinship estimator program. The data showing conditional cue use indicate that in computing kinship indexes, the kinship estimator employs an algorithm that combines the two cues in a noncompensatory way (as in a decision tree).

Importantly, the pattern of conditional cue use is the same, whether the dependent measure assesses levels of altruism (number of favors done for sibling j in the last month; willingness to donate a kidney to sibling j), levels of disgust at the thought of sex with sibling j, or degree of moral opposition to third party sibling incest (an unobtrusive measure of sexual aversion, which can be used in assessments of subjects with only one opposite sex sibling). This is important converging evidence for the model in Figure 15.1: Sibling altruism, sibling sexual aversion, and moral opposition to third party sibling incest—wildly disparate kin-relevant behaviors—are all being regulated by the same developmental cues, MPA and coresidence duration, combined in the same way. It is a surprising finding, predicted by no other theory. Yet it is precisely what one would expect if the same internal regulatory variable, a kinship index, serves as input to two different motivational systems.

ANGER AS A RECALIBRATIONAL EMOTION

If internal regulatory variables are psychologically and neurally real, then selection could build adaptations whose function is recalibrate them advantageously. We have been testing the hypothesis that the adaptive function of certain emotion programs—anger, gratitude, and guilt, for example—is to recalibrate internal regulatory variables in one's own brain and in the brains of other people (Sell, 2005; Sell, Tooby, & Cosmides, in prep. a, b; Tooby & Cosmides, 2008; Sznycer, Price, Tooby & Cosmides, in prep.). Indeed, we think the WTR regulatory variable lies at the core of each of these emotion programs. We will use anger to illustrate the usefulness of framing emotions as programs that use and operate on regulatory variables.

Specifically, we propose that anger is the expression of a neurocomputational system that evolved to adaptively regulate behavior in the context of resolving conflicts of interest in favor of the angry individual. It evolved as an instrument of social negotiation. Its primary functional goal is to upregulate the WTR in the brain of the target of the anger, so that the target places more weight on the welfare of the angered individual. The anger program is designed to bargain for better treatment by deploying two negotiative tools: (1) in cooperative relationships, threats to withdraw benefits (or actually withdrawing them), and (2) in neutral or antagonistic relationships, threats to inflict costs (or actually inflicting them). The computational logic of anger orchestrates the advertisement of these contingencies through emotional display (e.g., anger face), verbal communication (e.g., threats), or action (e.g., striking, abandoning a relationship).

Before proceeding, it is important to recognize that the programs in an organism should be designed to trade-off its welfare differently when the organism is being observed than when it is not. When one's acts are being monitored by an individual whose welfare is affected, that individual can respond by retaliating or rewarding the actor. But when one's acts are private and will not be known to impacted individuals, selection should produce a system that weights their welfare only insofar as it is in the actor's intrinsic interest to do so. Hence, there should be algorithms that compute two parallel, independent WTRs for each social other: (1) an intrinsic WTR, which sets a lower boundary on how much weight the actor places on the other party's welfare even when the actor's choices are not being observed; and (2) the public or monitored WTR, which guides an individual's actions when the recipient (or relevant others) can observe them. The kinship index is one variable that sets intrinsic WTRs. Monitored WTRs are set by aggressive intimidation and reciprocity. Anger is designed to modify monitored WTRs.

RAISING OTHERS' WTRs TOWARD YOU

Equations 15.1 and 15.2 express decision rules that should guide behavior when there is a conflict of interest. An implication of these equations is that any person, P, will treat you better when P's welfare trade-off ratio toward you is higher (see Figure 15.2). For example, Equation 15.1 says that if person P's WTR toward you is 1, P values your welfare as much as his (or her) own; accordingly, P will refrain from taking any action that imposes a cost on you (C_{you}) that is greater than the benefit

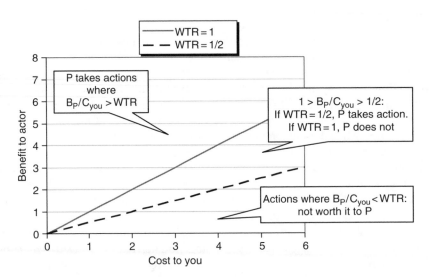

FIGURE 15.2 An actor's welfare trade-off ratio (WTR) toward you can be inferred by observing how large a cost that individual is willing to impose on you for how small a benefit gained. The gray line represents a WTR of 1, meaning that the actor values your welfare as heavily as his or her own. The black dashed line represents a WTR of ½, meaning the actor values your welfare only half as much as his or her own. The area between these two lines represents the set of cost-imposing actions an actor would take if his or her WTR toward you were ½, but not if it were 1. Raising an individual's WTR toward you allows you to avoid these costs.

it provides to P (B_P)—that is, P will refrain when B_P/C_{you} < 1. But if P's WTR toward you is ½, P values your welfare only half as much as his own; that is, P will take actions for which B_P/C_{you} > ½. This means there is a set of cost-imposing actions, ones for which ½ < B_P/C_{you} < 1, that P will take when his WTR_{you} = ½, but not when his WTR_{you} = 1 (see Figure 15.2). You will be spared more of these costs to the extent there is some way of raising P's WTR toward you.

But why should P raise his WTR toward you, when this reduces the set of self-beneficial actions that he will be willing to take? Humans, unlike most species, engage in many forms of cooperation: dyadic reciprocation (Cosmides & Tooby, 2005; Gurven, 2004; Trivers, 1971), coalitional (group) cooperation (Tooby et al., 2006), food sharing as a form of risk pooling (Kaplan & Hill, 1985), and deep engagement relationships (Tooby & Cosmides, 1996). If P does not raise his WTR toward you—that is, if he does not treat you better—then he may lose you as a cooperative partner.

If you are a good and reliable reciprocator, for example, then P benefits from having you as a cooperative partner. If your motivational system is designed to make your level of cooperation contingent on how well P treats you, then P might be able to increase your level of cooperation by treating you better, by raising P's own WTR_{you}. But P pays a price by increasing his WTR_{you}: A higher WTR_{you} means P will be sacrificing his own

welfare more often for you, and refraining from a larger set of self-beneficial actions. So what price, in the form of a higher WTR_{you}, should P be willing to pay to maintain or increase your cooperation toward him?

There is an equilibrium WTR value, at which the marginal increase in price P would pay, in the form of a higher WTR_{you}, is exactly offset by the marginal increase in benefits P would gain by doing so, through increased cooperation from you. If P's WTR toward you is below this equilibrium value, the marginal decrease in your cooperation that this elicits will make P worse off than he could be. When this is true, there is the possibility of raising P's WTR toward you. By threatening to lower your level of cooperation with P—or even withdraw it by switching to a partner who values your welfare more highly (i.e., whose WTR toward you is higher)—it should be possible to raise P's WTR_{you} to a value closer to P's equilibrium point.

Another reason P might raise his WTR toward you is that you will inflict costs on him if he does not. Like most other species, humans sometimes use aggression to induce others to sacrifice their own welfare for the aggressor's. Using variables such as the relative value of a resource to two contestants and their relative fighting ability, game theoretic models such as the Asymmetric War of Attrition (AWA) specify conditions under which a contestant should cede a resource or fight for it (Hammerstein & Parker, 1982; Maynard Smith, & Parker, 1976). The

AWA predicts that, if Y does not relinquish a resource, X will fight Y when $v(X)/v(Y) > k(X)/k(Y)$, that is, when the relative value (v) of the resource to X exceeds the relative costs (k) that X will incur by fighting Y. More specifically, $k(X)$ is the rate at which X will incur injuries if a fight between X and Y ensues, which is a function of their relative fighting ability. Behavior consistent with the AWA requires programs that compute one's formidability relative to others, and use this information to adaptively regulate responses to resource conflict. For example, if you and person P value a resource equally and both of you know that P is more aggressively formidable than you are, the AWA predicts that P will try to take the resource and you will relinquish it rather than risk injury in a fight.

This means that, all else equal, more formidable individuals will be more willing to initiate resource contests than less formidable ones, and less formidable individuals will defer to these demands. If cooperation (and so forth), is not an issue, then there is an equilibrium WTR value toward you, based on your formidability relative to P, where the benefits to P of getting or keeping a resource of value V_P are exactly offset by the costs P will suffer by fighting you for it.

If P's current WTR toward you is below this equilibrium value, there is the possibility of raising it by threatening to aggress against P. Dominance hierarchies in species lacking cooperation are the result of such negotiations. In the absence of any contested resource, individual animals aggressively display toward one another, assessing who can hurt whom. Having determined this, injurious fights become unnecessary: Weaker individuals cede resources to stronger ones, whenever the relative value of the resource to the weaker one is less than the value of a regulatory variable expressing their relative formidability.

The AWA, Hamilton's rule, and reciprocal altruism theory each express how selection should shape an equilibrium WTR based on a single factor (formidability, genetic relatedness, or value as a reciprocator, respectively). But humans engage in cooperation as well as aggression, and we live in the presence of kin as well as nonkin. This should select for a welfare trade-off ratio estimator equipped with algorithms that compute equilibrium WTRs based on the values of several different regulatory variables: ones expressing an individual's value as a reciprocator, coalition mate, sexual partner, and friend, as well as the kinship index associated with that individual and a variable expressing that individual's formidability relative to one's own. Indeed, your welfare trade-off ratio estimator should be designed by selection

to compute two sets of WTRs: the WTRs that should regulate your behavior toward others, and the equilibrium WTRs that others should express toward you.

If P knows that you will not respond by threatening to withdraw benefits or inflict costs, then P can benefit by having a WTR toward you that is lower than the equilibrium value would be if you were to respond. What can raise P's WTR_{you} nearer to the equilibrium value is your ability to monitor P's actions to see what WTR_{you} they express, and respond. Anger, we propose, is the activation of a response system designed to negotiate the value of the offending person's WTR toward you. We call this proposal the recalibrational theory of anger (Sell, 2005; Sell, Tooby, & Cosmides, in prep. a, b).

ANGER AS A NEGOTIATION OVER WTR VALUES

Social behavior publicly advertises WTRs. Given the ability to estimate the consequences of actions on welfare—the costs and benefits they impose on oneself and others—one can infer one person's WTR toward another from his or her actions. For example, assume that you observe a person named Aaron taking an action that inflicts a cost of 4 (notional) units on you to gain a benefit of 1 unit for himself. From this, you can infer that Aaron's $WTR_{you} \leq \frac{1}{4}$. ($B_{Aaron}/C_{you} = \frac{1}{4}$; Equation 15.1 means Aaron would take this action only if $B_{Aaron}/C_{you} \geq WTR_{you}$.)

Most theories of anger recognize that humans typically get angry when someone imposes a cost on them; and, all else equal, the larger the cost, the more angry the person becomes. But the recalibrational theory of anger further predicts that being harmed will not be sufficient to trigger anger. If anger is the expression of a system designed to negotiate WTRs, then it should be triggered when the offending person's action expresses a WTR_{you} that is too low—below what you feel entitled to or, more specifically, below what your WTR estimator has computed as the appropriate equilibrium value. (Thus, humans may become angry when they are benefited—but less than they feel entitled to.) This leads to a counterintuitive prediction: Holding the cost imposed constant, more anger will be triggered when the offending person imposed that cost to gain a small benefit than to gain a large one.

Assume that your WTR estimator has computed, based on the nature of your relationship, that Aaron's equilibrium WTR toward you should be $\frac{1}{2}$. You then see him ruin your expensive scarf, imposing a cost of 4 units on you. According to the recalibrational framework, whether you become angry should depend on how much Aaron benefited by using your scarf. If the benefit he got was only 1 unit—let us say Aaron ruined your scarf by using it to wipe ketchup off his face—then this action expresses a $WTR_{you} \leq \frac{1}{4}$. This is less than the equilibrium value of $\frac{1}{2}$, and so should trigger anger. But if Aaron ruined your scarf while using it to make a tourniquet to stop blood spurting from his child's arm, then the benefit he got was great—e.g., 24 units. This action should not trigger anger in you, despite the fact that it inflicts the same cost: In this case, Aaron's action is still consistent with a WTR_{you} of $\frac{1}{2}$. Indeed, the benefit to Aaron relative to the cost to you is consistent with Aaron having a WTR toward you as high as six ($B_{Aaron}/C_{you} = 24/4 = 6$). This means that Aaron would have taken this action even if his WTR_{you} was very high—even if he valued your welfare almost six times as much as his own. The anger system should not be activated under such circumstances, because the events do not reveal a WTR that needs to be recalibrated.

With these predictions in mind, we conducted experiments that held the cost imposed on the subject constant, while varying the size of the benefit the offending individual expected to gain by imposing it. Learning that the offending action was taken to procure a large monetary benefit made subjects less angry; learning that it was taken to procure a small one made them more angry (Sell, 2005; Sell, Tooby, & Cosmides, in prep. a).

According to the recalibrational theory of anger, the program monitoring WTRs is activated when someone imposes a cost on you (or fails to provide an expected benefit). If the detection component inside the anger program infers that this person's monitored WTR_{you} is below an estimate of the appropriate equilibrium value, then the anger system is triggered. The detection system sends an "anger signal" that regulates two downstream motivational systems as negotiative tools—one regulating cooperation, the other regulating aggression.

The Anger Program Orchestrating Cooperation

Assume, for this example, that Aaron is a cooperative partner of yours—a friend or colleague—and you observe him taking an action that imposes a large cost on you for a small benefit. Your detection system infers that this action expresses a WTR_{you} of B_{Aaron}/C_{you}. This value is lower than the equilibrium value your welfare trade-off ratio estimator had computed as reasonable based on the benefits Aaron gains by your association, so your detection system sends asignal activating the anger program and its regulation of cooperation. This program structures arguments and other communicative acts according to a functional logic of anger, each of whose features is designed to solve a different recalibrational problem.

Problem 1: Aaron may not realize that his action imposed a cost on anyone; alternatively, he may realize his action very likely imposed a cost on someone, but the fact that it imposed a cost on you may be something he did not realize or intend.

Solution: The anger program activates two specific motivational goals: to tell Aaron that the offending action imposed a cost on *you*, and to find out if Aaron realized his action would have this consequence before taking it. (If he could not have known his action would impose a cost on you, it does not imply his WTR_{you} is too low; discovering this should deactivate your anger system.)

Problem 2: Aaron may have misestimated the magnitudes of the cost imposed for benefit gained.

Solution: The anger program activates the goal of recalibrating those estimates, motivating you to argue that the cost imposed on you was higher or the benefit Aaron gained was lower than he thinks.

Problem 3: Aaron has underestimated your WTR_{Aaron}, resulting in an equilibrium WTR_{you} that is too low. (All else equal, Aaron—like everyone else—is better off associating with individuals whose WTR toward him is high rather than low, because such individuals will impose fewer costs on him and provide more benefits to him.)

Solution: The anger program's search engines scour episodic memory for examples of times when you sacrificed your welfare for his (i.e., incurred high costs to provide even small benefits), as these imply that your WTR_{Aaron} is high. Retrieval of these episodes will be accompanied by an intense desire to remind Aaron of these acts.

Problem 4: Aaron has underestimated how much he benefits from having you as a cooperative partner, resulting in an equilibrium WTR_{you} that is too low. (This is different from Problem 3: Even if your WTR toward Aaron is low, you could be in a position to help and support him (at low cost to yourself), by virtue of your status, connections, or special skills.)

Solution a: The anger program's search engines scour your episodic memory for examples of times you helped Aaron, providing important benefits to him. Such episodes should be easily retrieved, and accompanied by an intense desire to remind Aaron of these acts.

Solution b: The anger program activates a specific motivation: to threaten to withdraw cooperation, accompanied by the desire to vividly describe how this will cause Aaron to suffer. Aaron's equilibrium WTR_{you} should increase if either response convinces him that the future benefits he will obtain from your association are high; Solution b adds the threat that he will be losing these future benefits if he does not treat you better.

Trying to solve problems 1–4 will elicit an information exchange. Aaron might come to agree with you and apologize. On the recalibrational theory of anger, a sincere apology expresses the offending person's willingness to place more weight on your welfare in the future, by recalibrating his WTR_{you} upwards or by recalibrating his misestimates of costs and benefits to self and to you. A sincere apology is a signal that the anger system's recalibrational function has been accomplished, so it should deactivate the anger program, returning the cooperation system to normal mode and deactivating the aggression system. (In normal mode, the cooperation system motivates goals consistent with social exchange, providing help, and soliciting help; Cosmides & Tooby, 2005; Tooby & Cosmides, 1996.)

Alternatively, Aaron might respond that your variables need recalibrating: that you are exaggerating the cost he imposed, underestimating the benefits he gained, attributing bad intentions when he had none, exaggerating how much you have helped him in the past (overestimating your value to him) and at what personal cost (overestimating your WTR_{Aaron}), or forgetting how often he has come through for you and at what personal cost (i.e., your WTR_{Aaron} is lower than he deserves, justifying his lower WTR_{you}). If you come to agree with his points, this too should deactivate your anger program because you will no longer see his action as expressing a WTR_{you} that is too low. A complete meeting of the minds on all points is unnecessary to dispel your anger: Adjustment of variables sufficient to indicate that Aaron's WTR_{you} is not too low should be enough. But what if this does not happen?

Problem 5: Aaron's estimates of the costs and benefits associated with his action agree with yours, and so does his estimate of the appropriate equilibrium value for his WTR_{you}. But he believes you will not respond when his actions express a WTR_{you} below equilibrium.
Solution: The anger program activates a specific motivation: to threaten to withdraw cooperation from Aaron. Demonstrating that you are monitoring his WTR_{you} and are willing to respond by downregulating your cooperation is a way of increasing his monitored WTR_{you} to nearer his equilibrium value.

Problem 6: After all this, Aaron does not apologize; indeed, he indicates that he has no intention of raising his WTR_{you}.
Solution: The anger program recalibrates the value of your equilibrium WTR_{Aaron}, lowering it to reflect the fact that he places less weight on your welfare than you had

expected. The functional product of this will be to down-regulate your levels of cooperation toward Aaron, economizing on unrewarding social outlays.

In cooperative relationships, lowering—or threatening to lower—your WTR toward someone has functional consequences: Threatening to lower it motivates reform in insufficient reciprocators; actually lowering it cuts losses with cheaters.

Research testing for these specific anger responses as solutions to problems 1–7 is still in progress, but we have already confirmed a number of them, using vignette experiments and naturally occurring arguments collected from subjects. These experiments and results are reported in Sell (2005), Sell et al. (in prep. a), and Sznycer et al. (in prep.).

The Anger Program Orchestrating Aggression

Another way to negotiate WTRs is by threatening harm, so there are circumstances in which the anger program will regulate aggression. However, if aggression is used exploitatively inside a cooperative relationship, then the cooperative partner should avoid the exploiter (when possible), dissolving the relationship. Withdrawal of cooperation is a less expensive bargaining tool than aggression. In contrast, non-cooperators have no cooperation to threaten to withdraw. Hence, threats of aggression should be more common in noncooperative relationships, while threats of downregulating cooperation should be more common in cooperative ones.

Threatening harm is a more effective tactic the more capable the threatener is of inflicting harm at low relative cost. Therefore, anger should more easily trigger aggression as a negotiative tool in more formidable individuals than in weaker ones. This effect should be particularly pronounced in men, because in humans, males are stronger and tend to pre-empt force as a social tool. Although absolute levels of aggression vary between cultures, within cultures women are far less likely than men to resolve conflicts by using physical force (Campbell, 2002; Daly & Wilson, 1988).

Now, assume that circumstances force you and Aaron to interact, but you do not have a cooperative relationship. Moreover, Aaron's WTR_{you} is low because he has a low estimate of your formidability relative to his. He communicates this to you and others through insults: comments impugning your willingness to fight, disparaging your strength, advertising a flippant disregard for your distress, and other forms of disrespect—claims or demonstrations that he can treat you badly without fear of harm from you. If his estimate of your formidability is correct, you may need to accept a low WTR from Aaron. If it is not correct, insults and actions expressing a low WTR_{you} should activate the anger system in its aggressive mode. When this happens, the anger program should motivate specific actions and goals, each designed to solve a recalibrational problem. For example:

Problem 7:   Aaron's estimate of your relative ability to inflict costs on him—his formidability index with respect to you (FI_{you})—is too low.
Solution: The anger program activates a specific goal: to recalibrate the FI_{you} regulatory variable in Aaron's brain. It should motivate actions that demonstrate your ability to harm him, displays such as chest thrusting, pushing, or breaking things.

If these demonstrations are successful, they should raise Aaron's FI_{you} and his WTR_{you}, because his WTR should be based, at least in part, on his assessment of your formidability (see discussion of the AWA, above) and that of your coalitional allies. (Your coalition-derived formidability should be registered by a distinct regulatory variable in Aaron's motivational architecture, not merely by FI_{you}, which indexes your individual formidability.)

Note that these displays can also serve a parallel function: to signal how much you value a resource, or how large a cost Aaron's action imposed on you. That is, they can serve a communicative function as well, providing a solution to Problem 2 above (Aaron's mis-estimate of costs imposed or benefits gained). In nonverbal animals, escalating displays and an unwillingness to back down are means used to signal how much one values a contested resource (Austad, 1983; Enquist & Leimar, 1987).

Problem 8:   Despite your displays, Aaron does not adjust his FI_{you} (and WTR_{you}) or his estimates of the costs imposed for benefits gained: He refuses to signal deference, submission, or respect. Indeed, he makes clear his belief that you will not respond with aggression when his actions express a monitored WTR below equilibrium.
Solution: The anger program should activate a specific motivation: to threaten to harm Aaron. The harm can be physical or social.

Threatening physical harm carries the risk that Aaron will consider it a bluff. Therefore, this motivation is more likely to be activated when you actually are more formidable than Aaron, or when external constraints would prevent a fight from actually breaking out (e.g., friends or authorities are present who will hold you back).

Indeed, the logic of negotiation through the threat or actuality of inflicting costs is general, regardless of whether the costs are inflicted through violence, social manipulation, or other means. Different kinds of power

have different effects, and so we expect them to be encoded by different regulatory variables (formidability being different from status, for example).

When the anger program is orchestrating aggression, it should activate the motivation to escalate the displays and threats until one of you backs down. But what if neither of you backs down?

Problem 9:   Despite your threats, Aaron does not back down: The threats do not cause him to recalibrate his FI_{you} (and WTR_{you}) upwards.
Solution: The anger program activates the goal of actually harming Aaron. This may lead to a fight, which will end when its informational function has been accomplished—that is, when it becomes clear that one of you can, in fact, inflict more injury on the other. The function of this escalation—from insults to threats to aggression—is to cause formidability-based WTR recalibration, not to kill, but on rare occasions people die from injuries incurred during this negotiation. Of the homicides that do occur, a large number result from the escalation of what police call a trivial altercation—a public confrontation between two men over face or respect (Daly & Wilson, 1988).

Note two implications of this analysis of the role of aggression in negotiating WTRs. First, the anger program should be easier to trigger in people who are stronger (more formidable) because they can physically inflict more costs than weaker people can, enforcing a higher WTR toward themselves. Second, because they can inflict more injury at lower cost to themselves, aggressively formidable people should expect a higher equilibrium WTR from others, one where the benefits of not being harmed by the formidable person are exactly offset by the price of the higher WTR. All else equal, stronger, more formidable individuals should feel more entitled to deference and respect, more entitled to having other people's actions take their interests into account.

According to the recalibrational theory, anger is triggered by actions expressing a WTR below the equilibrium value the angered individual expected from others (based on an implicit computation of a power- or reciprocity-based equilibrium). This means that those who expect a higher WTR will be provoked by a larger set of actions than those who expect a lower WTR. For example, the set of actions between the two curves in Figure 15.2 should trigger anger in someone expecting a WTR of 1, but not in someone expecting a WTR of ½.

If more aggressively formidable people expect a higher equilibrium WTR from others, then there is a set of cost-imposing actions that will trigger anger in them, but would not trigger anger in someone expecting a lower

WTR. This leads to another surprising prediction that we have confirmed (Sell, 2005; Sell et al., in prep. b): Men who are physically stronger (as measured by lifting strength at the gym) are more prone to anger, feel more entitled to having their way, and have greater success resolving conflicts of interest in their favor. They have also been in more fights and believe more in the efficacy of aggression to settle conflicts. Interestingly, this belief in the efficacy of aggression reflects more than a rational assessment of their ability to win fights: It extends to international conflicts, where their personal strength could not possibly make a difference. We had predicted this in advance, on the grounds that modern humans think about conflicts between nation states with a mind designed for the ancestral world of hunter-gatherers. In that smaller world, a man's personal strength would be an important factor contributing to the formidability of the small coalitions (two to five individuals) in which he takes part (Tooby et al., 2006).

Approach Motivations in Anger

A common way of conceptualizing approach–avoidance motivation is to view positive stimuli as eliciting approach and negative stimuli as eliciting avoidance (Elliot, 2006). But in anger, a very negative stimulus—someone who has placed too little weight on your welfare—elicits approach, not avoidance. Indeed, the motivation for "approach" when you are angry can be overwhelming—so much so that when circumstances prevent you from expressing your feelings to the person you are angry with, the sense of frustration can be intense.

Nor is there a single way of characterizing approach in anger. When the anger program orchestrates cooperation, the approach response is to exchange information, argue, and, if necessary, withdraw cooperation, or even terminate the relationship and avoid the individual. When the anger program orchestrates aggression, the approach response is to demonstrate formidability, threaten harm, and, if necessary, actually injure the antagonist. "Approach" is a very rough way of characterizing behavioral responses. Like anger, foraging, courtship, and helping all involve approaching stimuli, yet the motivational systems regulating these activities have little in common with one another, and the approach behaviors they produce are unrecognizably different.

CONCLUSIONS

We can only move toward or away from things, so "approach" and "avoidance" capture a lot of what we do in life. The great appeal of describing responses in this way is that it characterizes behavior at an abstract level,

allowing generalizations that apply across many different concrete situations. What we have been trying to show, however, is that a satisfying level of abstraction can still be achieved while providing fine-grained descriptions of behavioral responses. The recalibrational theory of anger, for example, contains a fine-grained description of the specific content of arguments, yet these are described at an abstract level that applies to countless concrete situations (*You inflicted [a large cost] on me! You did it on purpose! You did it for [a trivial benefit] for yourself! I've been so good to you! I've sacrificed for you! If you're going to continue to treat me this way, I won't treat you so well in the future!*).

The key to achieving abstract yet detailed characterizations of social motivations lies in taking an evolutionary and computational approach to motivation. Internal regulatory variables are by their nature abstract: They may use concrete situations as input—acts of sacrifice for welfare trade-off ratios, duration of coresidence, and observations of one's own mother caring for an infant for kinship indexes—but they use these concrete situations to compute the magnitude of a variable, abstracted from those situations. These values are used by motivational systems, which activate abstract goals (make X suffer; put more weight on Y's welfare) that get filled in with concrete content depending on the situation.

Just as psychophysics allowed the principled study of perception, this framework opens a principled gateway into the scientific study of feeling—a previously intractable topic. According to this approach, conscious focus on a situation feeds new information through the architecture that triggers procedures designed to register or recalibrate the array of regulatory variables the new information is relevant to (Tooby & Cosmides, 2008). Next, signals of the significant changes in (some of) these variables are fed back into conscious awareness—presumably as a method to broadcast them to other programs they are relevant to. This cycle often appears to lead to chain reactions (as with grief, anger, and betrayal), where downstream programs are set off in their turn by receipt of further recalibrational information, triggering them then to broadcast their own contributions into conscious awareness. That is, the tapestry of felt experience that is directly elicited by the objects of awareness are, we think, annotations and evaluations about those objects in terms of changes in the internal regulatory variables relevant to them (that person is stronger than I thought; my sister is dead; this person was surprisingly kind to me; acacia beetles taste better than I thought). The demand for feeling computation often exceeds available bandwidth. When this happens, the individual spends time engaging in a particular form of behavior designed to maximize feeling computation, by suspending other activities that would distract from attention to the internal panorama of endogenous responses to new information. In short, feeling is a form of computation in which the values of regulatory variables are set, recalibrated, broadcast through the architecture, and output into awareness so that they can be fed into other programs designed to use them.

Finally, models provided by evolutionary biology can help identify internal regulatory variables whose computational role in our evolved motivational architecture we might not otherwise suspect. Indeed, they provide us with the experimental guidance necessary for constructing abstract yet fine-grained maps of the responses our motivational systems were evolutionarily designed to produce.

ACKNOWLEDGMENTS

We thank Howard Waldow and the NIH Director's Pioneer Award (LC) for making this research possible.

REFERENCES

Adams, M. S., & Neel, J. V. (1967). Children of incest. *Pediatrics, 40*, 55–62.

Austad, S. (1983). A game theoretical interpretation of male combat in the bowl and doily spider. *Animal Behaviour, 31*, 59–73.

Axelrod, R., & Hamilton, W. D. (1981). The evolution of cooperation. *Science, 211*, 1390–1396.

Bittles, A., & Neel, J. (1994). The costs of human inbreeding and their implications for variation at the DNA level. *Nature Genetics, 8*, 117–121.

Boyd, R., & Richerson, P. (1992). Punishment allows the evolution of cooperation (or anything else) in sizeable groups. *Ethology and Sociobiology, 13*, 171–195.

Boyd, R. (1988). Is the repeated prisoner's dilemma a good model of reciprocal altruism? *Ethology and Sociobiology, 9*, 211–222.

Buss, D. (2005). *The handbook of evolutionary psychology.* New York: Wiley.

Buss, D. M., & Schmitt, D. P. (1993). Sexual strategies theory: An evolutionary perspective on human mating. *Psychological Review, 100*, 204–232.

Campbell, A. (2002). *A mind of her own: The evolutionary psychology of women.* London: Oxford University Press.

Cosmides, L., & Tooby, J. (1989). Evolutionary psychology and the generation of culture, Part II. case study: A computational theory of social exchange. *Ethology & Sociobiology, 10*, 51–97.

Cosmides, L., & Tooby, J. (2000a). Consider the source: The evolution of adaptations for decoupling and metarepresentation. In D. Sperber (Ed.), *Metarepresentations: A multidisciplinary perspective.* (pp. 53–115.) Vancouver Studies in Cognitive Science. New York: Oxford University Press.

Cosmides, L., & Tooby, J. (2000b). Evolutionary psychology and the emotions. In M. Lewis & J. M. Haviland-Jones (Eds.), *Handbook of emotions, 2nd edition* (pp. 91–115). New York: Guilford.

Cosmides, L., & Tooby, J. (2001). Unraveling the enigma of human intelligence: Evolutionary psychology and the multimodular mind. In R. J. Sternberg & J. C. Kaufman (Eds.), *The evolution of intelligence* (pp. 145–198). Hillsdale, New Jersey: Erlbaum.

Cosmides, L., & Tooby, J. (2005). Neurocognitive adaptations designed for social exchange. In D. M. Buss (Ed.), *The handbook of evolutionary psychology* (pp. 584–627). Hoboken, New Jersey: Wiley.

Daly, M., & Wilson, M. (1983). *Sex, evolution, and behavior, 2nd edition.* Boston: Willard Grant.

Daly, M., & Wilson, M. (1988). *Homicide.* Chicago: Aldine.

Dennett, D. (1988). Quining qualia. In A. Marcel & E. Bisiach (Eds.), *Consciousness in modern science.* New York: Oxford University Press.

Elliot, A. (2006). The hierarchical model of approach–avoidance motivation. *Motivation and Emotion, 30*, 111–116.

Enquist, M., & Leimar, O. (1987). Evolution of fighting behaviour: The effect of variation in resource value. *Journal of Theoretical Biology, 127*, 187–205.

Fodor, J. (2000). *The mind doesn't work that way.* Cambridge, MA: MIT Press.

Gurven, M. (2004). To give or not to give: An evolutionary ecology of human food transfers. *Behavioral and Brain Sciences, 27*, 543–583.

Gurven, M., Allen-Arave, W., Hill, K., & Hurtado, M. (2000). It's a wonderful life: Signaling generosity among the Ache of Paraguay. *Evolution and Human Behavior, 21*, 263–282.

Hamilton, W. D. (1964). The genetical evolution of social behavior, I and II. *Journal of Theoretical Biology, 7*, 1–52.

Hammerstein, P., & Parker, G. A. (1982). The asymmetric war of attrition. *Journal of Theoretical Biology, 96*, 647–682.

Huntingford, F. A., & Turner, A. K. (1987). *Animal conflict.* New York: Chapman & Hall.

Jackendoff, R. (1987). *Consciousness and the computational mind.* Cambridge, MA: MIT Press.

Kaplan, H., & Hill, K. (1985). Food sharing among ache foragers: Tests of explanatory hypotheses. *Current Anthropology, 26*, 223–239.

Kirkpatrick, L. A., & Ellis, B. J. (2001). An evolutionary-psychological approach to self-esteem: multiple domains and multiple functions. In G. J. O. Fletcher & M. S. Clark (Eds.), *Blackwell handbook of social psychology: Interpersonal processes* (pp. 411–436). Oxford, UK: Blackwell Publishers.

Klein, S., Cosmides, L., Tooby, J., & Chance, S. (2002). Decisions and the evolution of memory: Multiple systems, multiple functions. *Psychological Review, 109*, 306–329.

Klein, S., German, T., Cosmides, L., & Gabriel, R. (2004). A theory of autobiographical memory: Necessary components and disorders resulting from their loss. *Social Cognition, 22*(5), 460–490.

Lieberman, D. (2004). Mapping the cognitive architecture of systems for kin detection and inbreeding avoidance: The

Westermarck hypothesis and the development of sexual aversions between siblings. Lieberman, Debra Lyn; Dissertation Abstracts International: Section B. *The Sciences & Engineering, 64*(8–B), 4110.

Lieberman, D., Tooby, J., & Cosmides, L. (2007). The architecture of human kin detection. *Nature, 445*, 727–731.

Marr, D. (1982). *Vision: A computational investigation into the human representation and processing of visual information.* San Francisco: Freeman.

Maynard Smith, J., & Parker, G. A. (1976). The logic of asymmetric contests. *Animal Behavior, 24*, 159–175.

Seemanova, E. (1971). A study of children of incestuous matings. *Human Heredity, 21*, 108–128.

Sell, A. (2005). Regulating welfare trade-off ratios: Three tests of an evolutionary-computational model of human anger. Doctoral dissertation.

Sell, A., Tooby, J., & Cosmides, L. (in prep.) Anger and welfare tradeoff ratios: Mapping the computational architecture of a recalibrational emotion system.

Sell, A., Tooby, J., & Cosmides, L. (in prep.) The logic of anger: Men, formidability and conflict.

Smith, E. A., & Winterhalder, B. (1992). *Evolutionary ecology and human behavior.* New York: Walter de Gruyter.

Sugiyama, L. S. (2005). Physical attractiveness in adaptationist perspective. In D. M. Buss (Ed.), *The handbook of evolutionary psychology* (pp. 292–343). New York: Wiley.

Symons, D. (1979). *The evolution of human sexuality.* New York: Oxford.

Sznycer, D., Price, J. G., Tooby, J., & Cosmides, L. (in prep.) Recalibrational emotions and welfare trade-off ratios: Cooperation in anger, guilt, gratitude, pride, and shame.

Tooby, J. (1982). Pathogens, polymorphism, and the evolution of sex. *Journal of Theoretical Biology, 97*, 557–576.

Tooby, J., & Cosmides, L. (1990). The past explains the present: Emotional adaptations and the structure of ancestral environments. *Ethology and Sociobiology, 11*, 375–424.

Tooby, J., & Cosmides, L. (1992). The psychological foundations of culture. In J. Barkow, L. Cosmides, & J. Tooby (Eds.), *The adapted mind: Evolutionary psychology and the generation of culture.* New York: Oxford University Press.

Tooby, J., & Cosmides, L. (1996). Friendship and the Banker's Paradox: Other pathways to the evolution of adaptations for altruism. In W. G. Runciman, J. Maynard Smith, &

R. I. M. Dunbar (Eds.), *Evolution of social behaviour patterns in primates and man. Proceedings of the British Academy, 88*, 119–143.

Tooby, J., & Cosmides, L. (2001). Does beauty build adapted minds? Toward an evolutionary theory of aesthetics, fiction and the arts. *SubStance, Issue 94/95, 30*(1), 6–27.

Tooby, J., & Cosmides, L. (2008). The evolutionary psychology of emotions and their relationship to internal regulatory variables. In M. Lewis & J. Haviland-Jones (Eds.), *Handbook of emotions, 3rd edition.* New York: Guilford.

Tooby, J., Cosmides, L., & Barrett, H. C. (2003). The second law of thermodynamics is the first law of psychology: Evolutionary developmental psychology and the theory of tandem, coordinated inheritances. *Psychological Bulletin, 129*(6), 858–865.

Tooby, J., Cosmides, L., & Barrett, H. C. (2005). Resolving the debate on innate ideas: Learnability constraints and the evolved interpenetration of motivational and conceptual functions. In P. Carruthers, S. Laurence, & S. Stich (Eds.), *The innate mind: Structure and content* (pp. 305–337). New York: Oxford University Press.

Tooby, J., Cosmides, L., & Price, M. (2006). Cognitive adaptations for n-person exchange: The evolutionary roots of organizational behavior. *Managerial and Decision Economics, 27*, 103–129.

Trivers, R. (1971). The evolution of reciprocal altruism. *Quarterly Review of Biology, 46*, 35–57.

Trivers, R. (1972). Parental investment and sexual selection. In B. Campbell (Ed.), *Sexual selection and the descent of man: 1871–1971* (pp. 136–179). Chicago: Aldine.

Trivers, R. (1974). Parent-offspring conflict. *American Zoologist, 14*, 249–264.

Tye, M. (2003). Qualia. *Stanford Encyclopedia of Philosophy.* www.plato.stanford.edu/entries/qualia.

Williams, G. (1966). *Adaptation and Natural Selection.* Princeton, New Jersey: Princeton University Press.

Williams, G. C., & Williams, D. C. (1957). Natural selection of individually harmful social adaptations among sibs with special reference to social insects. *Evolution, 17*, 249–253.

Winterhalder, B., & Smith, E. A. (2000). Analyzing adaptive strategies: Human behavioral ecology at twenty-five. *Evolutionary Anthropology, 9*, 51–72.

Evolution of Evaluative Processes II

16 Approach and Avoidance Motivation(s): An Evolutionary Perspective

Douglas T. Kenrick and Michelle N. Shiota

CONTENTS

Consider the following:

- The refreshments table at a party, loaded with meats, cheeses, potato chips, nuts, and desserts full of sugar and saturated fat;
- A physically attractive member of your preferred sex;
- An adorable kitten, mewing for attention; and
- Your parents.

Now consider this second list:

- A scorpion on the living room rug;
- A full glass of rotten, smelly milk;
- A driver who cuts you off on the freeway, making an obscene hand gesture; and
- Your romantic partner, laughing with his or her extremely attractive ex.

At first glance, all of the items on the first list are desirable, things or people we might want to approach, and those on the second list are undesirable, things or people we might want to avoid. At first, the utility of approach and avoidance in each case might seem obvious. However, closer examination of the lists challenges first impressions. First, our instinctive response to some of these situations can be quite alarming. For example, one might justifiably want to chase after the offending driver at high speed, return the hand gesture, and possibly ram into the back of his or her car. How can we explain the common impulse to do something so dangerous and foolish? A more subtle example lies in the cholesterol-laden refreshment table. Most humans find these kinds of foods extremely desirable in terms of taste; unfortunately, these foods are also strongly linked with many of the current major causes of death and disease in the developed world.

On closer examination, the differences among items in each list also become more salient. For example, you might want to approach the refreshments table, the potential romantic partner, and your parents, but not (we hope) in exactly the same way. Similarly, the strategy appropriate to avoid a glass of rotten milk is quite different from one that will prevent your partner's renewed interest in a former mate. From this perspective, the concepts of "approach" and "avoidance" are far from unidimensional.

Yet a third issue emerges when we consider the context surrounding one's experience of each item, including combinations of the items on the two lists. For example, your reaction to an attractive man or woman might depend, at least partly, on whether you are currently "spoken for" or not. If you are currently involved with someone else, you could still approach, but you might risk damaging your current relationship. Consider also the kitten walking toward a scorpion on the living room rug, preparing to play with it. You run toward the scorpion, push the kitten away, and step on the threat. Approach and avoidance are even more intertwined now—you have just physically moved toward the threat and distanced yourself from the desirable object, risking harm to yourself in the service of avoiding harm to a loved one.

EVOLUTIONARY PERSPECTIVE ON APPROACH AND AVOIDANCE MOTIVATION

In this chapter, we contend that an evolutionary perspective on approach and avoidance motivation helps make sense of each of these complications. Our discussion will incorporate three key features of an evolutionary perspective on behavior: functionality, domain-specificity, and trade-offs. We will argue that approach and avoidance are most usefully conceptualized in terms of end

states, rather than behaviors, and that many end-states people consistently approach and avoid are best understood in terms of their fitness implications in ancestral environments (Elliot, 2006). We will argue further that mechanisms of approach and avoidance are many and varied, differing in qualitative ways depending on the particular problem domain one currently confronts. Last, we will suggest that there are few cases of stimuli that are simply "approachable" or "avoidable." An evolutionary perspective helps us to predict the "trade-offs" individuals will make in various situations, according to individual ecological factors, individual differences, and the actor's developmental phase. Thus, an evolutionary perspective distinguishes between approach and avoidance at multiple levels of analysis (e.g., function, behavior), and offers more finely grained predictions about particular approach and avoidance behaviors in various situations. We will discuss the implications of this perspective for future research on approach and avoidance.

FUNCTIONALITY: WHAT ARE THE ADAPTIVE PURPOSES OF APPROACH AND AVOIDANCE?

From an evolutionary perspective, the first question one asks about a general behavioral tendency is: How might this tendency have increased the chance that our ancestors would survive and reproduce, increasing their representation in the gene pool of the future? Most psychologists are functionalists at some level, but we often think about "function" in nonevolutionary terms. For example, psychologists often talk about motivations to feel good, avoid discomfort, raise self-esteem, or help make the world a better place. Such analyses emphasize function at the level of the pleasantness of immediate experience, or long-term sociological consequences. An evolutionary analysis also recognizes that feelings are functional, but goes one critical step further by asking what feels good when, and how might that have served to pass one's genes on to future generations more successfully? (Alcock, 1993).

From an evolutionary perspective, one begins with the presumption that any category of end-state that people reliably approach was likely associated with opportunities for enhancing inclusive fitness—the representation of your genes in future generations either through your own offspring, or those of your genetic relatives—in ancestral environments. These opportunities ultimately come down to a few simple categories: (1) obtaining food and water, and other survival essentials; (2) finding a mate or mates; and (3) nurturing offspring (and genetic relatives capable of reproducing), so they can reproduce in turn. Conversely, any category of end-states that people reliably avoid was presumably associated with threats to inclusive fitness, such as (1) danger of death or serious bodily harm that would interfere with reproduction; (2) loss of survival essentials; (3) loss of mating opportunities, including the loss of an existing mate through death, abandonment, or poaching; and (4) death of offspring (or genetic relatives capable of reproducing). In order to explain any species-typical propensity to approach or avoid a category of targets, an evolutionary perspective links that propensity back to one or more of these proximal opportunities or threats.

One could think about approach and avoidance as behavioral tropisms, literally movements toward desirable stimuli and away from undesirable stimuli. Simple living organisms are equipped with unconditional tropic responses, such as a plant's tendency to grow toward light or to extend its roots toward water. In thinking about complex mobile organisms, however, it makes more sense to think of approach and avoidance in terms of strategies for attaining *goals*—sets of responses that increase the probability of a desired outcome, or decrease the probability of a negative outcome. Thinking in terms of goals makes it easier to see why one might functionally avoid some threat by moving toward its source (as in the case of the kitten and the scorpion), or why one might approach some opportunity by maintaining distance or temporarily moving in the opposite direction.

According to an evolutionary perspective, functionality is defined in terms of adaptive outcomes (on average) in ancestral environments, which may or may not translate into functionality in any given current environment (Crawford, 1998). Consider the common automatic response to the rude driver mentioned at the beginning of the chapter—anger, sometimes to the point of pursuing the driver and making threatening gestures of one's own. This is unlikely to produce any adaptive benefit, and on rare occasions, the outcome is highly maladaptive—an arrest for reckless driving, damage to your car, even death. Throughout most of our evolutionary history, however, angry displays at other people who wantonly insulted us or treated us unfairly would have served, on average, to ensure that one's status within the group was not compromised, and status comes with serious fitness benefits in terms of food, territory, and mates. Our ancestors did not have frequent anonymous interactions with strangers, and the potential for a high speed auto accident or police intervention was not part of the picture then, so it does not get factored into our instinctive reactions.

The impulse to chase someone down and let them know how angry you are is still there, however. Even in ancestral environments, such a response would have been

adaptive if it resulted in average positive outcomes, even if it occasionally resulted in losses (demonstrating anger always carried a cost of reciprocal aggression, even before SUVs). However, such demonstrations are common (in humans and in other animals) because they presumably resulted in net benefits sufficient to balance the risks. Thus, an evolutionary perspective helps us to explain and predict a number of behavioral tendencies that seem absurd or even harmful in the present environment.

Two key questions to ask, if one adopts an evolutionary perspective on approach–avoidance motivation, are (1) which categories of situations would our ancestors have needed to approach (i.e., recurrent opportunities) and (2) which would they have needed to avoid (i.e., recurrent threats), to reproduce more successfully on average?

DOMAIN-SPECIFICITY: WHY APPROACH AND AVOIDANCE STRATEGIES VARY

From an evolutionary perspective, general motivations to "feel good" or "avoid feeling bad" are inadequate to solving the very different problems humans face in different domains. Different goals require different actions, as in the examples of approaching the food, the potential romantic partner, and one's parents discussed earlier. Goals predict behavior better than available targets—the same target person may be approachable for some goals, but not for others. For example, it "feels better" to share material resources with one's sibling as opposed to a stranger, but the reverse is true for sharing sexual favors (Ackerman, Kenrick, & Schaller, 2007; Lieberman, Tooby, & Cosmides, 2007). Evolutionary psychologists use the terms "domain-specificity" or "modularity" to indicate the presumption that evolved behavioral mechanisms are functionally and neurologically discrete (Tooby & Cosmides, 2005).

Before researchers began to think about human behavior in evolutionary terms, it was presumed that there are an infinite and unconstrained number of possible approach or avoidance responses, contingent only on the idiosyncrasies of one's particular learning history. One could learn to associate any stimulus with sensory pleasure or pain, and thus any stimulus could acquire the properties of a goal. For example, Rachman and Hodgson (1968) conducted a study that involved conditioning sexual arousal to a pair of knee-length boots, on the general assumption that sexual arousal could be conditioned to whatever random stimuli happened to be present during genital stimulation. On this view, the potential associations between specific characteristics of the environment and a sense of reward or punishment are unlimited. Not only can individual features of the environment become linked to reward or punishment, but interactions between multiple features can as well. Implications of this can be daunting to contemplate, as Cronbach (1975) observed:

"Every second-order interaction is moderated by third order interactions, which in turn are moderated by higher order interactions. Once we attend to interactions, we enter a hall of mirrors that extends to infinity" (Cronbach, 1975, p. 119).

On entering any social situation, for example, one is presented with an overwhelming number of potentially important cues—there are several people, wearing different colored clothing and speaking with different accents, differing in height, standing or sitting, interacting with different people, and so on. If one has an unpleasant experience that "feels bad" in this situation, what can one learn from it? To avoid food in other people's houses? To avoid people? To avoid people in red shirts? To avoid tall people? To avoid people with a certain accent, or those sitting down? Some of these cues may actually be relevant to the cause of the unpleasant experience. For example, if the people in red shirts are members of a competing sports team, it might in fact be a good marker of potential hostility. At the same time, the relevance of a given cue may depend on more or less transitory factors (the social event is a party at the home of an opposing team member, and the opposing team wears red), and many cues will

be useless in predicting future outcomes regardless of context. Trying to decode which of this myriad of cues is the one actually associated with some desired or aversive outcome would be completely overwhelming with no limitations or guidance.

Thinking in evolutionary terms can help researchers discover a pathway out of this hall of mirrors (Kenrick, et al., 2002). Evolutionary reasoning—bolstered by neurophysiological evidence (Panksepp, 1982)—suggests a finite set of fundamental human goals, each linked to an adaptive problem posed by the environments in which ancestral humans lived. On the basis of several reviews of literature related to this question (Bugental, 2000; Buss, 1999; Fiske, 1992; Kenrick, Li, & Butner, 2003), we have suggested several key goals confronting humans living in social groups. For social mammals, these include alliance formation (getting along with other group members), self-protection (avoiding predation and conflict with other organisms who want the same resources), enhancing status (gaining preferential access to resources and mates), finding mates (choosing desirable mating partners), maintaining long-term mating bonds (hanging on to desirable partners), and offspring/kin care (contributing to the successful development of one's own offspring and other close genetic relatives).

Each of these goals involves different core opportunities (things to approach) and threats (things to avoid) (Schaller, Park, & Kenrick, 2007). We summarize these in Table 16.1; and also include distinct opportunities and threats in nonsocial contexts (e.g., finding edible food and

TABLE 16.1

Fundamental Goals and Associated Opportunities and Threats

Goal	Opportunities to Approach	Threats to Avoid
Essential resource acquisition	Food	Loss
	Water	Stealing or cheating by conspecifics
Self-protection	Shelter	Predators
	Parents and other adult caregivers (usually kin)	Violent conspecifics
	Trusted nonkin (especially in groups)	Toxins
Co-operative alliance formation	Sharing with alliance members	Rejection
	Play (co-ordination, bonding with alliance members)	Violation of group etiquette
Status enhancement	Socially valued accomplishments	Failure on socially valued tasks
	Conspicuous resource display	Insults by group members
	Connections with high-status group members	Connections with low-status group members
Finding mate	High-fitness potential mates	Same-sex competitors
Maintain mate	Fulfilling mate's needs	Illness or death of mate
		Sexual infidelity/mate-poaching
Offspring/kin care	Fulfilling offspring/kin needs	Illness or death of offspring/kin

avoiding toxins). Satisfying any one of these goals may facilitate others, or be facilitated by them. For example, forming social alliances may help one to acquire survival essentials such as food, and to protect oneself from threats from predators and out-group conspecifics. However, all of the goals ultimately come back to those listed earlier as fundamental, and the particular problems posed by the specific tasks of finding a mate, finding food, avoiding an enemy, and so on require different skills than those involved in finding a friend.

We briefly consider each of these goals below, with particular attention to what people generally approach, and hope to avoid, in each larger goal.

(1) *Essential resource acquisition*. Before even worrying about whether one is getting enough respect or affection, one needs to satisfy a number of basic bodily needs. Opportunities to acquire food and water are essential to attaining this goal, as is avoiding threats to these resources through loss, stealing, or other catastrophes.

(2) *Self-protection*. Human beings are vulnerable to a wide range of threats to physical well-being. We can be attacked by predators, or by violent conspecifics who want our possessions or our territory. We can ingest potentially lethal toxins, including spoiled food. These threats must be avoided. Fortunately, we can also approach stimuli that provide opportunities for protection. At the simplest level, this includes safe shelter. However, protection is often offered by conspecifics, both close kin (especially relevant for young and vulnerable individuals, who rely on parents and other adult kin for protection), and trusted nonkin within one's group. In the next section, we discuss the particular motivational system involved in forming and maintaining in-group alliances. There may, however, be distinct mechanisms involved in approaching groups of friends when one is concerned about threats (Taylor et al., 2000). Under these circumstances, for example, one might be inclined to prefer relatively larger aggregations of friends than might be desirable for a shared meal or a conversation in which intimate information is exchanged.

(3) *Co-operative alliance formation*. Essential resource acquisition and self-protection can be accomplished by individuals, but humans accomplish these tasks far more effectively in coalitions marked by co-operation and mutual exchange of resources (Cosmides & Tooby, 1992; Eibl-Eibesfeldt, 1975; Hrdy, 1999; de Waal, 1996). On the approach side, this coalitional goal may be linked to motivations toward sharing and play with alliance members. On the avoidance side, one must avoid threats of rejection by the alliance, and behaviors that might lead to rejection (such as violation of group etiquette).

(4) *Status enhancement*. For both sexes, there are tremendous fitness advantages to gaining and maintaining social status, including greater access to material resources and mating opportunities, and extended social alliances (de Waal, 1996; Fiske, 1991; Keltner, Gruenfeld, & Anderson, 2003). Because females use male status as a cue for mate selection, males are especially likely to be concerned with enhancement and potential loss of status (Buss, 1999; Kenrick & Luce, 2000). On the approach side, status enhancement can be achieved through socially valued accomplishments, through the conspicuous display of possessions, and through connections with those higher in the group hierarchy. This goal is also associated with a set of situations to avoid, including failing at socially valued tasks, being insulted or snubbed by other group members, and obvious relationships with those lower in the group hierarchy.

(5) *Finding mates*. Access to high-quality mates is essential to reproductive success, so people are likely to selectively attend to features connoting reproductive viability, and to pursue those people. Because of inherent differences in amount and type of parental investment, males and females are likely to approach and avoid somewhat distinct sets of features in potential mates. For instance, women place more value on indications of status than do men (Kenrick, Sundie, Nicastle, & Stone, 2002; Li & Kenrick, 2006; Sadalla, Kenrick, & Vershure, 1987). Compared with women, men place more value on age and other indicators of fertility (Kenrick & Keefe, 1992). In addition, because females make a much greater investment than males in child-bearing, females are more likely than males to prefer partners interested in long-term commitment; the reverse is true for short-term encounters (Clark & Hatfield, 1989; Haselton & Buss, 2000; Kenrick, Sadalla, Groth, & Trost, 1990).

Because biparental care requires a number of shared inputs from both parents, however, there are a number of features that both sexes seek in partners, such as co-operativeness (Li & Kenrick, 2006). Features associated with health and "good genes" are also considered attractive by both men and women (Gangestad & Simpson, 2000). On the avoidance side, both men and women must deter threats posed by same-sex competitors for mates, although men's and women's most dangerous rivals have somewhat different characteristics. Men are more concerned about competition from other men who are high in status, and women are more concerned about other women who display signs of fertility and physical attractiveness (Buunk, Massar, & Dijkstra, 2007; Gutierres, Kenrick, & Partch, 1999).

(6) *Maintain mate*. Because human infants are helpless and slow to develop, their survival is enhanced by the presence and support of multiple adults, and both biological parents have the greatest investment in the child's survival. Thus, long-term co-operative mating relationships would have been highly adaptive for our ancestors (Geary, 1998). Keeping a partner involves a distinct set of problems from finding a mate, however. Once a committed relationship is forged, demonstrations of one's attractiveness likely become somewhat less important than demonstrations of one's co-operativeness, generosity, and emotional stability. For this reason, it behooves one to approach opportunities to provide material support, emotional nurturance, and generally make sure one's mate's needs are fulfilled. One certainly needs to avoid any threats to the mate's life and physical health, as well as signs of potential infidelity or mate poaching.

(7) *Offspring/kin care*. The ultimate reason that human parents maintain long-term bonds is for offspring care. In 95% of other mammalian species, parental care is provided exclusively by the female without assistance from the male (Geary, 1998). Unlike other mammals, whose offspring are precocial and tend to be well-developed and somewhat mobile at birth, human offspring are altricial, or helpless at birth. In this way humans are more like a typical bird species than a typical mammalian species. Also like birds, humans have evolved a mating system that involves biparental care for their helpless offspring.

The problems involved in caring for offspring are different from those involved in getting along with nonkin alliance members or mates. The usual rules of social exchange, for example, do not apply in relationships between children and their parents (Kenrick, Sundie, & Kurzban, in press). Instead, parents provide benefits for children with little or no expectation of reciprocation, all the while welcoming new opportunities to fulfill the offsprings' needs and protect them from harm. This is not to say that parental provisioning is noncontingent; factors such as the parent's remaining reproductive potential, the number of other offspring, and the particular child's health are all critical determinants of differential parental care (Daly & Wilson, 1998; Geary, 1998; Hrdy, 1999; Kenrick, Sundie, & Kurzban, in press). There are design features built into parents to ensure parental care, including the familiar mechanisms of bonding (Bowlby, 1979; Zeifman & Hazan, 1997). There are also design features built into the children, who come preequipped with attachment mechanisms designed to direct and exploit parental investment—by crying when they are alone, hungry, or in pain, and cooing and smiling when parental attention is adequately monopolized (Bowlby, 1979; Eibl-Eibesfeldt, 1975). Besides investing directly in one's offspring, humans live in familial groups, and often care for their siblings, nephews and nieces, and their grandchildren. Again, those investments are not noncontingent, but finely tuned to factors such as the existence of other more closely related children (Laham, Gonsalkorale, & von Hippel, 2005).

Meaning of Domain-Specificity

We have argued that human approach and avoidance motivations and their associated behaviors are largely domain-specific, rather than global. It is important to distinguish between "domain-specificity" in the sense of specific goal content from "domain-specificity" in the sense of input format—an evolutionary perspective implies the former, but not necessarily the latter (Barrett & Kurzban, 2006). Domain-specific mechanisms are attuned to particular arrangements of input cues, but can occasionally be triggered by stimulus arrays mimicking those cues. For example, other young mammals (puppies and kittens, for example) have many of the same features that trigger parental sympathy, such as large heads and eyes, as well as high pitched whimpering cries (Eibl-Eibesfeldt, 1975). This is important in explaining both the situations in which some adaptation is clearly functional, and those in which a false alarm is likely. This distinction is also important in explaining why some modules can be content-general while still performing a fairly specific type of information processing, such as the module for working memory that briefly stores numbers, words, events, and information in a number of other formats.

It is also important to note that although domain-specificity does imply some degree of modularity in brain processes, most modern evolutionary theorists do not rigidly accept all the criteria for a module that Fodor suggested 25 years ago (Barrett & Kurzban, 2006; Carruthers, 2005). Fodor's (1983) criteria for modularity included domain-specificity, encapsulation, automaticity, inaccessibility to consciousness, speed, shallow inputs, neural localization, and specific breakdown patterns. As Barrett and Kurzban (2006) note in a recent review of the concept of modularity, the evidence accumulated in the intervening years suggests that not every domain-specific process meets each of the above criteria.

For example, early views of mental modules presumed that each functional unit would be represented in a "spatial chunk" of brain tissue (Barrett & Kurzban, 2006, p. 641). Evidence suggests instead that functional units may in some cases be neural networks distributed across different parts of the brain. This leads to an asymmetry in the implications of fMRI findings: differing regions of activation for two processes suggests different modules, but activation of the same region for two processes does not necessarily imply a single module. Two possible solutions for this dilemma include (1) eventually increasing the spatial resolution of scanning, or, more likely; (2) applying new factor analytic techniques for examining networks of activation across the brain, rather than individual voxels or larger subregions of neural tissue (Alexander & Moeller, 1994; Moeller, Strother, Sidtis, & Rottenberg, 1987).

Similarly, evidence suggests some degree of encapsulation in mental mechanisms—the existence of separate processes for handling different types of stimuli—but that encapsulation is incomplete. In the current understanding of psychological modularity, inputs from any given system can be sensitive to output from other systems. For example, simple memory processes for human faces are influenced by the perceiver's emotional state, and the emotional state on the target's face, although the modules for face recognition, emotion detection, and emotional experience are distinct (Ackerman et al., 2006; Becker, Kenrick, Neuberg, Blackwell, & Smith, 2007).

Summary

Very different rules apply to approaching different types of desirable opportunities relevant to different kinds of goals (food versus mates versus parents, for example). Likewise, different sets of rules apply to avoiding specific threats relevant to different kinds of goals (poisonous foods as opposed to mating rivals). Although much about

modularity is yet to be understood, there is overwhelming evidence that a simple distinction between approach and avoidance systems is inadequate.

Functional Trade-Offs in Approach and Avoidance Motivation

Recall the dilemma posed at the beginning of the chapter, of the individual deciding whether to approach an attractive potential partner, knowing that to do so threatens his or her relationship with an existing mate. Replace the kitten in the scorpion scenario with your own child and you have another dilemma—keep a safe distance from the threat, or approach the threat in the interests of protecting your offspring? Even the refreshment table poses a quandary. If you approach and heartily enjoy the food too often, you risk becoming less attractive to current or potential mates. All of these scenarios illustrate a third principle of evolutionary perspectives on approach and avoidance: few situations involve only a single goal, so trade-offs between opportunities and threats are inevitable.

Because approach–avoid decisions typically involve such trade-offs, which strategy is most functional at any time depends on a number of situational details. Thus, evolved psychological mechanisms in approach and avoidance are more likely to provide "if-then" algorithms or decision rules, taking the broader environment into consideration, than stereotyped behaviors (Kenrick, Li, & Butner, 2003; Kenrick, 2006a). At a broad level of analysis, different ecological factors may lead to very different approach and avoidance strategies within a species. For example, humans may mate polyandrously (one female with multiple males) when resources are very scarce, as brothers will fare better if they share investment in a small number of offspring (Crook & Crook, 1988). Extreme polygyny (one male with multiple females) is found under conditions where resources are rich but variable, and there are steep social hierarchies, such that some families can accumulate much more than others. In such circumstances a female's offspring may fare better if she mates polygynously with a member of a wealthy family than they would do if she mated monogamously with a poorer man. The circumstances predicting these variations in humans also predict variations in mating arrangements in bird species.

One appealing aspect of evolutionary psychology is its links with other disciplines, particularly biology and anthropology. Evolutionary theorists taking a broad perspective on different species and different human societies have developed some useful theoretical tools for thinking about human behavior that would not necessarily arise from considering only the people living in a particular culture at a particular time. Life history theory is one broad set of concepts for considering how a particular species solves its particular problems of surviving and reproducing, and is particularly germane to the issue of trade-offs (Partridge & Harvey, 1988; Kenrick & Luce, 2000; Kaplan & Gangestad, 2005; Stearns, 1976). Life-history theorists begin with the presumption that organisms are involved in a struggle to acquire and efficiently allocate limited energy resources. All mammals, for example, must allocate resources to (a) somatic development, (b) mating effort, and (c) parenting effort. Allocation of resources to one category necessarily involves trade-offs—searching for an additional mate means less time for parenting, feeding one's own body means less resources for one's offspring, and so on (Kaplan & Gangestad, 2005).

One implication of life-history theory for our purposes is that the outcome of trade-off situations can be predicted by knowing the actor's species and stage of life. Different species make very different allocations to the different life phases. For example, oak trees spend many years developing before they begin reproducing, but then they produce thousands of seeds, and continue reproducing for decades. Salmon spend 2 or 3 years developing, then reproduce in a single burst of reproductive effort, producing hundreds or thousands of eggs and then dying. Neither of these species devotes much effort to parenting. Elephants, on the other hand, are like oak trees in that they devote many years to somatic development and continue to reproduce for decades, but unlike oaks in that they have a very small number of offspring, and invest tremendous amounts of parental resources in each one.

There are also variations within species in life-history strategies. In most vertebrates, for example, females and males have different life histories. Human females, for example, mature earlier than males, invest several years in choosing a mate, and necessarily invest very high amounts of resources in each offspring. Human males can in theory, and sometimes in practice, have many more offspring, and need not invest as much in each offspring.

Punchline for Approach–Avoidance Motivation

Given that there are trade-offs everywhere in nature, nothing is purely and simply approachable, or purely and simply avoidable. Approaching a desirable potential mate is likely to bring costs and risks, such as life-threatening competition with other suitors, or loss of a current relationship. Similarly, the obvious self-protection strategy of running away from a dangerous predator (avoidance) may also have associated opportunity costs, such as leaving one's relatives at risk, or sacrificing valuable resources.

RESEARCH ADOPTING AN EVOLUTIONARY PERSPECTIVE ON APPROACH AND AVOIDANCE

Our discussion thus far has suggested that the processes involved in approach and avoidance should vary in functional ways depending on what fundamental motivational domain is currently active, and depending on individual differences in key life-history factors that affect decision trade-offs. In this section, we will briefly review some research following from this perspective, considering some classic research as well as several recent research findings from our own labs.

SAME TARGET MAY ELICIT APPROACH OR AVOIDANCE, DEPENDING ON THE GOAL

Social psychological models of close relationships traditionally involved a search for domain-general processes underlying all categories of intimacy. For example, reinforcement-affect theory (Clore & Byrne, 1974) posited that our feelings about a given target person were a function of the ratio of rewards to punishments that we had experienced in that person's company. The result of a history of rewards associated with a target person would incline us to be attracted toward that person, and the model presumed that we were inclined to approach those to whom we were attracted. Traditional exchange-based models presumed a slightly different domain-general process underlying attraction toward another person, emphasizing the expected ratio of benefits to costs in interactions with that person as compared to available alternatives (Thibaut & Kelley, 1959; Walster, Walster, & Berscheid, 1978). In their traditional formulations, such models did not explicitly differentiate between different categories of intimate relationships, such as friends versus kin versus romantic partners, although they would have presumed that a greater frequency of interactions had the potential to yield a greater number of benefits.

Considered in evolutionary context, the qualitative differences between approach responses in relationships with friends, mates, and close kin are more apparent. It is true that brothers and sisters have generally experienced a large number of rewarding interactions with one another, and people are especially likely to desire to affiliate with close kin throughout their lives (Daly, Salmon, & Wilson, 1997). Exchange relationships with kin tend to be biased in favorable ways (Ackerman et al., 2007). At the same time, the "positive affect" felt toward first-degree kin does not generally extend to the sexual domain. Instead, people asked to imagine romantic or sexual contact with their brothers or sisters report strongly negative affective reactions (Ackerman et al.; Lieberman et al., 2007).

From an evolutionary perspective, it is generally presumed that this uniquely negative response to approaching kin for mating goals is linked to the potential dangers of combining harmful recessive genes. Although deleterious recessive genes are normally rare, the probability they will be shared by a brother and sister are high enough to make the costs of intra-familial mating outweigh the benefits (Lieberman et al., 2007; Van den Berghe, 1983). Another possible mechanism for preferring distant relatives as mates involves resistance to disease, which is decreased by mating with close relatives. Other species, not subject to human cultural norms, also disfavor sexual contact with close relatives, and will avoid mating with siblings (Lieberman et al.), even when they were not raised together.

Aversion to incestuous mating does not seem to depend on cultural taboos against incest, but is instead linked to biological mechanisms operating outside human consciousness. Humans appear to rely on childhood coresidence as a cue of relatedness, triggering a mechanism evolved to prevent incest (Lieberman et al., 2007), even when cultural norms encourage those children to mate. In a massive social experiment, children on Israeli kibbutzim were raised in small groups of boys and girls born around the same time. There were no social norms discouraging romantic or sexual involvements between "pod-mates", and such involvements were even encouraged. However, Shepher (1971) examined several thousand marriages among these individuals and found that, although the pod-mates became life-long friends, they rarely married one another. This finding is particularly interesting because of the wealth of data suggesting that people prefer to marry their neighbors (Bossard, 1932), and Israeli children were likely to marry others raised on the same commune, but not in the same pod. Similarly, the common practice in China of raising very young girls in the same household as their future husbands has been associated with low fertility and high marital dissatisfaction and dissolution, with greater problems found when the children had been raised together from an early age (Wolf, 1993).

ACTIVATING DIFFERENT FUNDAMENTAL MOTIVES TRIGGERS APPROACH OR AVOIDANCE OF THE SAME TARGET

In a number of studies conducted with our colleagues, we have been activating different motivational states associated with the goals described in Table 16.1; and observing the consequences for cognitive and affective responses to various social situations (Griskevicius, Cialdini, & Kenrick, 2006a; Maner et al., 2005). The results of these experiments suggest that approach and avoidance inclinations toward a particular social stimulus can change dramatically, depending on the judge's current motivational state. For instance, a person with an otherwise neutral facial expression may be perceived as feeling anger by judges who are themselves feeling fear, if the target is a male member of a discriminable outgroup (Maner et al., 2005; Schaller, Park, & Mueller, 2003). Other research suggests that people are quicker and more accurate in detecting facial expressions of anger on males than on females, and that this process reflects physiognomic features of the male face rather than culturally recognized signs of gender (Becker et al., 2007). This "functional projection" makes sense given that threats to physical safety are more likely to come from strange males than strange females.

In another series of studies examining motivation-driven variations in approach and avoidance behaviors, participants were exposed to manipulations inducing either self-protective or mating motivation (e.g., by reading scenarios involving being alone in a dark house at night and overhearing sounds of someone breaking in, as opposed to imagining a romantic encounter with an attractive and desirable person). After these inductions, participants encountered another judgment task in which they got information regarding the opinions of other group members. Results indicated that both men and women were more likely to conform to group opinion after self-protective goals had been primed than in a neutral prime condition. Activating mating motives, however, generally had opposite effects on male and female participants. Whereas females in a romantic frame of mind again conformed more (compared to a neutral control group), men did the opposite—actually going against group opinion (Griskevicius, Goldstein, Mortensen, Cialdini, & Kenrick, 2006b).

These results fit precisely with two separate sets of evolution-based predictions about the adaptive functions of conformity and counter-conformity for achieving different goals. Under conditions of threat from potentially dangerous strangers, both men and women profit from group cohesion. On the other hand, there is a sex difference in the mating consequences of displaying independence from group opinion. Throughout the animal kingdom, males are generally more likely to compete with one another in an attempt to draw attention to their unique characteristics than are females. This difference is linked to differences in sexual selection and parental investment (Griskevicius et al., 2006a). The principle is well demonstrated by exceptions to the normal gender differences in life-history—when males contribute more to offspring than females do, as in phalaropes (a sandpiper-like bird), then females are more showy and competitive, and males are more selective.

SAME TARGET MAY ELICIT SIMULTANEOUS APPROACH AND AVOIDANCE RESPONSES

In another series of studies, Ackerman and his colleagues (2006) found that the normal tendency for people to homogenize members of out-groups was erased if the out-group members were males with angry facial expressions. This fits with the rationale we discussed above that angry males from outgroups are likely to pose a physical threat. Given this effect, we had expected to find that people pay particular attention to such individuals. However, findings from eye-tracking studies have tended to show the reverse—with participants looking at out-group males, and at angry faces, for less time than they look at other targets (Kenrick, Delton, Robertson, Becker, & Neuberg, 2007). Yet the same studies find higher-than-expected memory for those same targets. This disjunction between visual attention and later memory makes some functional sense—staring at an angry stranger is probably not something one wants to do, given that stares are themselves seen as threat gestures. At the same time, one does not want to forget potentially dangerous individuals, and so they seem to show the effects of emotional memory enhancement (Cahill, Prins, Weber, & McGaugh, 1994). A fascinating implication of this research is that not looking does not mean not attending.

Other research from our labs has indicated an opposite disjunction between visual attention and subsequent cognitive processing. Although both sexes look at, encode, and later remember beautiful women, women look at handsome men, but do not remember them for more than a few seconds (Becker, Kenrick, Guerin, & Maner, 2005; Maner et al., 2003). The suppression effect for handsome male strangers seems less intuitively sensible at first, but does fit well with findings on women's criteria for mate choice. Several evolutionary psychologists have provided evidence to suggest that male physical attractiveness is associated with so-called good genes (Gangestad, Thornhill, & Garver, 2002). Hence, it makes sense handsome men's faces elicit initial attention from women. Consistently, we found more visual fixations for handsome men amongst women who are ovulating, who are unrestricted, or who are in a romantic frame of mind. However, even if a woman is interested in a short-term relationship, it is unlikely that that relationship will be with a man who has not stayed around long enough to pass several levels of initial screening. Before committing to a relationship with a man, women generally require additional information, including reliable information about the man's social status or financial status (Buunk, Dijkstra, Fetchenhauer, & Kenrick, 2002; Kenrick, Sundie, Nicastle, & Stone, 2001; Li, Bailey, Kenrick, & Linsenmeier, 2002). Clark and Hatfield (1989) found in two studies conducted across two decades that not a single woman accepted an offer of a sexual liaison with a strange man, even though about half were willing to go on a date with him.

EMOTIONS FACILITATE APPROACHING OR AVOIDING PARTICULAR STIMULI, AND NOT OTHERS

According to an evolutionary approach to emotion, emotions prioritize particular fundamental goals and activate motivations to approach specific opportunities and avoid specific threats (Frijda, 1986; Lazarus, 1991; Plutchik, 1980). For example, compassion highlights offspring/kin care goals and associated nurturant motives, whereas pride highlights status enhancement goals and motives to advertise achievements and resources (Keltner, Haidt, & Shiota, 2006). Neuroscience research does support the existence of a system broadly facilitating reward anticipation and acquisition (Ghitza, Fabbricatore, Prokopenko, Pawlak, & West, 2003; Knutson, Taylor, Kaufman, Peterson, & Glover, 2005). However, this system is likely to interact with other systems in mediating particular positive emotions and associated motivations (Young & Wang, 2004). Thus, an evolutionary perspective on approach and avoidance motivation strongly suggests the existence of neurologically discrete positive and negative emotions (Tooby & Cosmides, 2005).

In one series of studies, we have considered how this approach might be relevant to consumer choices of various products. According to the affect infusion model (Forgas, 1995), people should learn to associate stimuli in the environment with their current mood state, such that an object or message encountered while one is in a positive mood will be "infused" with positive connotations but infused with negative connotations if encountered while one is in a negative mood. Previous studies of emotion and product attractiveness have supported this model, concluding that positive emotion generally enhances one's perception of product attractiveness (Batra & Stayman, 1990; Edell & Burke, 1987). An evolutionary approach, however, would suggest that specific positive emotions, facilitating approach of opportunities relevant to different goals, would only affect perceived attractiveness of goal-relevant categories of products.

Results reveal that, relative to a neutral condition, experimentally elicited pride increases the attractiveness of conspicuous, "public" items but not of inconspicuous household items of roughly the same value; contentment increases attractiveness of inconspicuous items but not conspicuous ones; and compassion has no effect on product attractiveness at all (Griskevicius, Shiota, & Nowlis, 2007). These findings suggest that positive emotions do not generally facilitate approach, but rather that they facilitate approaching objects that satisfy the specific goals activated by the emotion.

Much about the extent of modularity in human emotion is still unknown. For example, it is unclear whether there are separate modular systems designed to deal with fears of predators, fears of violent conspecifics, and fears of social disapproval, or whether these are all mediated by the same circuitry (Öhman & Mineka, 2001). Similarly, it is unclear whether the disgust systems involved in responding to noxious food substances share some or all their underlying machinery with systems mediating moral disgust (Haidt, 2001). Still, an evolutionary approach provides guidance in developing hypotheses and research paradigms for these and similar questions.

IMPLICATIONS OF AN EVOLUTIONARY PERSPECTIVE: FUTURE DIRECTIONS FOR RESEARCH

Adopting an evolutionary perspective on approach and avoidance raises a number of specific research questions. At the simplest level, it raises questions about the degree of modularity in the human mind. It seems functionally implausible that the same general mechanism is used for all forms of approach or for all forms of avoidance, and indeed there is evidence for this assumption (Garcia & Koelling, 1966; Sherry & Schacter, 1987; Wilcoxon, Dragoin, & Kral, 1972). Yet many questions remain about exactly how the mind works with regard to these processes. How many distinct approach and avoidance systems there are at the neurological level? How much sharing is there of subprograms between different modules? To what extent are these systems localized versus physically diffuse?

SPECIFIC RESEARCH QUESTIONS SUGGESTED BY THE EVOLUTIONARY PERSPECTIVE

A particular, largely unexplored research area suggested by an evolutionary perspective on approach motivation is distinguishing among multiple, potentially discrete positive emotions (Shiota, Campos, Keltner, & Hertenstein,

2004; Shiota, Keltner, & John, 2006). An evolutionary approach suggests the existence of discrete positive emotions that help us take advantage of specific kinds of opportunities in the environment, as well as discrete negative emotions that help us respond adaptively to different kinds of threats. Preliminary findings suggest that different positive emotions are associated with distinct facial and upper-body displays (Shiota, Campos, & Keltner, 2003; Tracy & Robins, 2004), and distinct effects on information processing (Griskevicius & Shiota, 2007), and that different positive emotion dispositions are differentially associated with several core personality processes (Shiota et al., 2006). Still, much research applying a discrete emotion perspective to positive emotion is yet to be done.

We also reviewed the broad literature on life history strategies, which suggests that every decision made by every organism involves trade-offs between different potential allocations of effort, particularly between bodily development and health versus mating opportunities versus offspring care. That perspective suggested that there are reliable links between individual development and life-history allocations, and that those links are reliably mediated by ecological factors. Despite the power of this perspective in explaining the behavior of animals, very little research on humans has been elucidated by this perspective, and most of that research has been conducted by anthropologists. Psychological research techniques could be immensely helpful in understanding how people approach and avoid different survival, mating, and kin care opportunities at different phases of their lives, and how such processes are affected by ecological factors and individual differences (Gangestad & Simpson, 2000).

GENERAL IMPLICATIONS OF AN EVOLUTIONARY APPROACH FOR THE PROCESS OF RESEARCH

An evolutionary approach to behavior has a number of distinct advantages. One of these is theoretical cohesiveness, in that adopting an explicitly evolutionary perspective helps us understand how proximate cognitive, affective, and behavioral processes make sense in light of general principles that apply across human cultures and across species. One common misconception is that the search for universal principles underlying diverse behavioral phenomena implies the absence of culture- or species-specific factors influencing behavior. Evolutionary theorists, whether they are studying humans or any other animal, are actually quite interested in the specifics characterizing that species, as well as in homologous processes. Evolutionary theorists studying human behavior are also interested in cultural variability as well as cultural constants (Ekman & Friesen, 1971; Gangestad, Haselton, & Buss, 2006; Kenrick, Nieuweboer, & Buunk, 2007; Norenzayan, Schaller, & Heine, 2006). At the same time, an evolutionary perspective counsels that the particulars of behavior within a given species or within a particular culture are not likely to be the products of general processes incompatible with the laws of natural selection (Kenrick, 2006b; Tooby & Cosmides, 2005).

There are numerous examples of cultural variation in what is desirable or undesirable that are still consistent with explanations rooted in evolutionary mechanisms. Mating preferences offer an excellent example of this phenomenon. As we noted earlier, some societies, such as the modern United States, regard polygamy as undesirable, if not evil; other societies have regarded it as normative, if not a positive good. We also noted that variations in the acceptance and prevalence of polygyny as well as polyandry seem to vary across human societies according to some of the same conditions influencing their prevalence in other animal species (Crook & Crook, 1988).

Consider another example, cultural variability in age preferences for mates. Because human females universally undergo menopause, and males continue to be able to have children into their later years, an evolutionary life-history model predicts a universal tendency for men, as they age, to prefer women relatively younger than themselves. This preference for relative youth is not presumed to follow from sex differences in social power or status, but from an attraction toward fertility cues. Teenage boys, for example, who have very little social status and power, report being attracted primarily to women several years older than themselves, though they do not believe those women are likely to reciprocate their interest (Kenrick, Gabrielidis, Keefe, & Cornelius, 1996). For very young men, it is older rather than younger women who are likely to manifest stronger fertility cues. However, men in their forties and fifties are attracted to women much younger than themselves, and this tendency appears to be universal (Kenrick & Keefe, 1992; Campos, Otta, & de Oliveira Siqueira, 2002).

The Tiwi society might appear to be an exception to this pattern, in that men in their twenties all marry older widows (Hart & Pillig, 1960). On closer examination, however, Tiwi men are attracted to younger women, but powerful older men have managed to monopolize all the young brides for themselves. This polygynous society requires all females to be married, whether they are young children or widows. Older men bequeath their own daughters at birth to another older male to whom they owe a favor, including having previously received one of his daughters as a bride. Because the older men

are not interested in widows, young men are free to marry them; by so doing they may elevate their position in society, and also curry future favors from the widow's male relatives. Thus, Tiwi society represents a novel and unusual dynamic arrangement of norms that nevertheless reflects human nature. Men everywhere are attracted to relatively young, fertile females, men everywhere compete for power, and in many cases, men's power is converted directly into a monopoly on desirable mates (Kenrick, Nieuweboer, & Buunk, 2007). Exactly how this plays out in a given society depends a great deal on the larger economic and social structure, but the principles are the same.

Another misconception about evolutionary approaches, less prevalent but still persisting in some corners, is that evolutionary researchers search for particular cases in which an animal demonstrates a "human-like" behavior pattern, and then quickly jump to the conclusion that the two patterns are manifestations of homologous processes. Instead, good comparative research is attentive to the particular functional connections between adaptations and eliciting ecological factors, and generates hypotheses accordingly. For example, cats are among those species that are not responsive to the taste of sugar, whereas humans are among those species that are. Sweetness is a feature evolved to attract fruit-eating animals to plants at the time when the fruit is fully ripe, and when the plant can most benefit from seed dispersal. Thus, it would only be noticed by plant-eaters, and we might hypothesize than herbivores and omnivores, but not carnivores, would find the taste of sugar pleasant. Similarly, if the function of embarrassment/shame is to prevent aggression by group members after you have violated a social norm (Keltner & Buswell, 1997), then we should expect to see shame-like behavior in highly social mammals that live in "packs," such as humans and dogs, but not in more solitary mammals such as cats.

CONCLUSION

An evolutionary perspective suggests that there are multiple approach and avoidance systems at the functional and neurological levels, designed to deal with the unique problems regularly encountered by ancestral humans. Particular approach or avoidance mechanisms are likely to be triggered by functionally relevant factors in the immediate environment, and by chronic ecological factors in interaction with individual differences linked to gender, age, and other physical factors. An evolutionary perspective offers a strong theoretical foundation for empirical research on domain-specific approach and avoidance motivation, and although we have reviewed a number of empirical findings emerging from this perspective, much territory remains uncharted.

ACKNOWLEDGMENT

The authors thank Vladas Griskevicius for his helpful comments on an earlier draft of this manuscript.

REFERENCES

Ackerman, J., Kenrick, D. T., & Schaller, M. (2007). Is friendship akin to kinship? *Evolution and Human Behavior, 28,* 365–374.

Ackerman, J., Shapiro, J. R., Neuberg, S. L., Kenrick, D. T., Schaller, M., Becker, D. V., et al. (2006). They all look the same to me (unless they're angry): From out-group homogeneity to out-group heterogeneity. *Psychological Science, 17,* 836–840.

Alcock, J. (1993). *Animal behavior* (5th ed.). Sunderland, MA: Sinauer.

Alexander, G. E., & Moeller, J. R. (1994). Application of the scaled subprofile model to functional imaging in neuropsychiatric disorders: A principal component approach to modeling regional patterns of brain function in disease. *Human Brain Mapping, 2,* 79–94.

Barrett, H. C., & Kurzban, R. (2006). Modularity in cognition: Framing the debate. *Psychological Review, 113,* 628–647.

Batra, R., & Stayman, D. M. (1990). The role of mood in advertising effectiveness. *Journal of Consumer Research, 17,* 203–214.

Becker, D. V., Kenrick, D. T., Guerin, S., & Maner, J. K. (2005). Concentrating on beauty: Sexual selection and sociospatial memory. *Personality and Social Psychology Bulletin, 31,* 1643–1652.

Becker, D. V., Kenrick, D. T., Neuberg, S. L., Blackwell, K. C., & Smith, D. M. (2007). The confounded nature of angry men and happy women. *Journal of Personality and Social Psychology, 92,* 179–190.

Bossard, J. H. S. (1932). Residential propinquity in marriage selection. *American Journal of Sociology, 38,* 219–224.

Bowlby, J. (1979). *The making and breaking of affectional bonds.* London: Tavistock.

Bugental, D. B. (2000). Acquisition of the algorithms of social life: A domain-based approach. *Psychological Bulletin, 126,* 187–219.

Buss, D. M. (1999). *Evolutionary psychology: The new science of the mind.* Boston, MA: Allyn and Bacon.

Buunk, B. P., Dijkstra, P., Fetchenhauer, D., & Kenrick, D. T. (2002). Age and gender differences in mate selection criteria for various involvement levels. *Personal Relationships, 9,* 271–278.

Buunk, A. P., Massar, K., & Dijkstra, P. (2007). A social cognitive evolutionary approach to jealousy: The automatic evaluation of one's romantic rivals. In J. P. Forgas, M. Haselton, & W. Von Hippel (Eds.), *Evolution and the social mind: Evolutionary psychology and social cognition* (pp. 213–248). New York: Psychology Press.

Cahill, L., Prins, B., Weber, M., & McGaugh, J. L. (1994). β-adrenergic activation and memory for emotional events. *Nature, 371,* 702–704.

Campos, L. D., Otta, E., & de Oliveira Siqueira, J. (2002). Sex differences in mate selection strategies: Content analyses and responses to personal advertisements in Brazil. *Evolution and Human Behavior, 23*(5), 395–406.

Carruthers, P. (2005). The case for massively modular models of mind. In R. Stainton (Ed.), *Contemporary debates in cognitive science* (pp. 205–225). Oxford, England: Blackwell.

Clark, R. D., & Hatfield, E. (1989). Gender differences in receptivity to sexual offers. *Journal of Psychology and Human Sexuality, 2,* 39–55.

Clore, G. L., & Byrne, D. (1974). A reinforcement affect model of attraction. In T. L. Huston (Ed.), *Foundations of interpersonal attraction* (pp. 143–170). New York: Academic Press.

Cosmides, L., & Tooby, J. (1992). Cognitive adaptations for social exchange. In J. H. Barkow, L. Cosmides, & J. Tooby (Eds.), *The adapted mind* (pp. 163–228). New York: Oxford University Press.

Crawford, C. (1998). The theory of evolution in the study of human behavior: An introduction and overview. In C. Crawford & D. L. Krebs (Eds.), *Handbook of evolutionary psychology: Ideas, issues, and applications* (pp. 3–42). Mahwah, NJ: Erlbaum.

Cronbach, L. J. (1975). Beyond the two disciplines of scientific psychology. *American Psychologist, 30,* 116–127.

Crook, J. H., & Crook, S. J. (1988). Tibetan polyandry: Problems of adaptation and fitness. In L. Betzig, M. Borgerhoff-Mulder, & P. Turke (Eds.), *Human reproductive behavior: A Darwinian perspective* (pp. 97–114). Cambridge, MA: Cambridge University Press.

Daly, M., Salmon, C., & Wilson, M. (1997). Kinship: the conceptual hole in psychological studies of social cognition and close relationships. In J. A. Simpson, & D. T. Kenrick (Eds.), *Evolutionary social psychology* (pp. 265–296). Mahwah, NJ: Erlbaum.

Daly, M., & Wilson, M. (1998). *The truth about Cinderella: A darwinian view of parental love.* New Haven, CT: Yale University Press.

de Waal, F. (1996). *Good natured: The origins of right and wrong in humans and other animals.* Cambridge, MA: Harvard University Press.

Edell, J., & Burke, M. C. (1987). The power of feelings in understanding advertising effects. *Journal of Consumer Research, 14,* 421–433.

Eibl-Eibesfeldt, I. (1975). *Ethology: The biology of behavior* (2nd ed.). New York: Holt, Rinehart, and Winston.

Ekman, P., and Friesen, W. V. (1971). Constants across cultures in the face and emotion. *Journal of Personality and Social Psychology, 17,* 124–129.

Elliot, A. J. (2006). The hierarchical model of approach–avoidance motivation. *Motivation and Emotion, 30,* 111–116.

Fiske, A. P. (1991). *Structures of social life.* New York: Free Press.

Fiske, A. P. (1992). The four elementary forms of sociality: Framework for a unified theory of social relations. *Psychological Review, 99,* 689–723.

Fodor, J. (1983). *The modularity of mind.* Cambridge, MA: MIT Press.

Forgas, J. P. (1995). Mood and judgment: The affect-infusion model. *Psychological Bulletin, 117,* 39–66.

Frijda, N. H. (1986). *The emotions.* New York: Cambridge University Press.

Gangestad, S. W., & Simpson, J. A. (2000). The evolution of human mating: Trade-offs and strategic pluralism. *Behavioral and Brain Sciences, 23,* 675–687.

Gangestad, S. W., Haselton, M. G., & Buss, D. M. (2006). Evolutionary foundations of cultural variation: Evoked culture and mate preferences. *Psychological Inquiry, 17,* 75–151.

Gangestad, S. W., Thornhill, R., & Garver, C. E. (2002). Changes in women's sexual interests and their partners' mate retention tactics across the menstrual cycle: Evidence for shifting conflicts of interest. *Proceedings of the Royal Society of London B, 269,* 975–982.

Garcia, J., & Koelling, R. A. (1966). Relation of cue to consequence in avoidance learning. *Psychonomic Science, 4,* 123–124.

Geary, D. C. (1998). *Male, female: The evolution of human sex differences.* Washington, DC: American Psychological Association.

Ghitza, U. E., Fabbricatore, A. T., Prokopenko, V., Pawlak, A. P., & West, M. O. (2003). Persistent cue-evoked activity of accumbens neurons after prolonged abstinence from self-administered cocaine. *Journal of Neuroscience, 23*(19), 7239–7245.

Griskevicius, V., Cialdini, R. B., & Kenrick, D. T. (2006a). Peacocks, picasso, and parental investment: The effects of romantic motives on creativity. *Journal of Personality and Social Psychology, 91,* 63–76.

Griskevicius, V., Goldstein, N., Mortensen, C., Cialdini, R. B., & Kenrick, D. T. (2006b). Going along versus going alone: When fundamental motives facilitate strategic (non) conformity. *Journal of Personality and Social Psychology, 91,* 281–294.

Griskevicius, V., & Shiota, M. N. (2007). Different positive emotions have distinct effects on persuasive message processing. Manuscript in preparation.

Griskevicius, V., Shiota, M. N., & Nowlis, S. (2007). Differential effects of pride, contentment, and compassion on product attractiveness. Manuscript in preparation.

Gutierres, S. E., Kenrick, D. T., & Partch, J. J. (1999). Beauty, dominance, and the mating game: Contrast effects in self-assessment reflect gender differences in mate selection. *Personality and Social Psychology Bulletin, 25,* 1126–1135.

Haidt, J. (2001). The emotional dog and its rational tail: A social intuitionist approach to moral judgment. *Psychological Review, 108,* 814–834.

Hart, C. W., & Pillig, A. R. (1960). *The Tiwi of North Australia.* New York: Holt, Rinehart, & Winston.

Haselton, M. G., & Buss, D. M. (2000). Error management theory: A new perspective on biases in cross-sex mind reading. *Journal of Personality and Social Psychology, 78,* 81–91.

Hrdy, S. H. (1999). *Mother nature: A history of mothers, infants, and natural selection.* New York: Pantheon.

Kaplan, H. S., & Gangestad, S. W. (2005). Life history and evolutionary psychology. In D. M. Buss (Ed.), *Handbook of evolutionary psychology* (pp. 68–95). New York: Wiley.

Keltner, D., & Buswell, B. N. (1997). Embarrassment: Its distinct form and appeasement functions. *Psychological Bulletin, 122*(3), 250–270.

Keltner, D., Gruenfeld, D. H., & Anderson, C. (2003). Power, approach, and inhibition. *Psychological Review, 110*(2), 265–284.

Keltner, D., Haidt, J., & Shiota. M. N. (2006). Social functionalism and the evolution of emotions, In M. Schaller, J. Simpson, & D. Kenrick (Eds.), *Evolution and social psychology* (pp. 115–142). New York: Psychology Press.

Kenrick, D. T. (2006a). A dynamical evolutionary view of love. In R. J. Sternberg & K. Weis, (Eds.), *Psychology of love* (2nd ed., pp. 15–34). New Haven, CT: Yale University Press.

Kenrick, D. T. (2006b). Evolutionary psychology: Resistance is futile. *Psychological Inquiry, 17,* 102–108.

Kenrick, D. T., Delton, A. W., Robertson, T., Becker, D. V. & Neuberg, S. L. (2007). How the mind warps: Processing disjunctions may elucidate ultimate functions. In J. P. Forgas, M. G. Haselton, & W. Von Hippel (Eds.), *The evolution of the social mind: Evolution and social cognition* (pp. 49–68). New York: Psychology Press.

Kenrick, D. T., Gabrielidis, C., Keefe, R. C., & Cornelius, J. (1996). Adolescents' age preferences for dating partners: Support for an evolutionary model of life-history strategies. *Child Development, 67,* 1499–1511.

Kenrick, D. T., Maner, J. K., Butner, J., Li, N. P., Becker, D. V., & Schaller, M. (2002). Dynamic evolutionary psychology: Mapping the domains of the new interactionist paradigm. *Personality and Social Psychology Review, 6,* 347–356.

Kenrick, D. T., & Keefe, R. C. (1992). Age preferences in mates reflect sex differences in human reproductive strategies. *Behavioral and Brain Sciences, 15,* 75–133.

Kenrick, D. T., Li, N. P., & Butner, J. (2003). Dynamical evolutionary psychology: Individual decision-rules and emergent social norms. *Psychological Review, 110,* 3–28.

Kenrick, D. T., & Luce, C. L. (2000). An evolutionary life-history model of gender differences and similarities. In T. Eckes & H. M. Trautner (Eds.), *The developmental social psychology of gender* (pp. 35–64). Hillsdale, NJ: Erlbaum.

Kenrick, D. T., Nieuweboer, S., & Buunk, A. P. (in press). Universal mechanisms and cultural diversity: Replacing the blank slate with a coloring book. Chapter to appear in M. Schaller, S. Heine, A. Norenzayan, T. Yamagishi, & T. Kameda (eds.) *Evolution, culture, and the human mind.* Mahwah, NJ: Lawrence Erlbaum Associates.

Kenrick, D. T., Sadalla, E. K., Groth, G., & Trost, M. R. (1990). Evolution, traits, and the stages of human courtship: Qualifying the parental investment model. *Journal of Personality*, *53*, 97–116.

Kenrick, D. T., Sundie, J. M. & Kurzban, R. (2008). Cooperation and conflict between kith, kin, and strangers: Game theory by domains. In C. Crawford & D. Krebs (Eds.), *Foundations of Evolutionary Psychology* (pp. 351–367). Mahwah, NJ: Erlbaum.

Kenrick, D. T., Sundie, J. M., Nicastle, L. D., & Stone, G. O. (2001). Can one ever be too wealthy or too chaste? Searching for nonlinearities in mate judgment. *Journal of Personality and Social Psychology*, *80*, 462–471.

Knutson, B., Taylor, J., Kaufman, M., Peterson, R., & Glover, G. (2005). Distributed neural representation of expected value. *Journal of Neuroscience*, *25*(19), 4806–4812.

Laham, S. M., Gonsalkorale, K., & von Hippel, W. (2005). Darwinian grandparenting: Preferential investment in more certain kin. *Personality and Social Psychology Bulletin*, *31*, 63–72.

Lazarus, R. S. (1991). *Emotion and adaptation*. New York: Oxford University Press.

Li, N. P., Bailey, J. M., Kenrick, D. T., & Linsenmeier, J. A. (2002). The necessities and luxuries of mate preferences: Testing the trade-offs. *Journal of Personality and Social Psychology*, *82*, 947–955.

Li, N. P., & Kenrick, D. T. (2006). Sex similarities and differences in preferences for short-term mates: What, whether, and why. *Journal of Personality and Social Psychology*, *90*, 468–489.

Lieberman, D., Tooby, J., & Cosmides, L. (2007). The architecture of human kin detection. *Nature*, *445*, 727–731.

Maner, J. K., Kenrick, D. T., Becker, D. V., Delton, A. W., Hofer, B., Wilbur, C. J., et al. (2003). Sexually selective cognition: Beauty captures the mind of the beholder. *Journal of Personality and Social Psychology*, *6*, 1107–1120.

Maner, J. K., Kenrick, D. T., Becker, D. V., Robertson, T. E., Hofer, B., Neuberg, S. L., et al. (2005). Functional projection: How fundamental social motives can bias interpersonal perception. *Journal of Personality and Social Psychology*, *88*, 63–78.

Moeller, J. R., Strother, S. C., Sidtis, J. J., & Rottenberg, D. A. (1987). Scaled subprofile model: A statistical approach to the analysis of functional patterns in positron emission tomographic data. *Journal of Cerebral Blood Flow and Metabolism*, *7*, 649–658.

Norenzayan, A., Schaller, M., & Heine, S. J. (2006). Evolution and culture. In M. Schaller, J. Simpson, & D. Kenrick (Eds.), *Evolution and social psychology* (pp. 343–366). New York: Psychology Press.

Öhman, A., & Mineka, S. (2001). Fears, phobias, and preparedness: Toward an evolved module of fear and fear learning. *Psychological Review*, *108*, 483–522.

Panksepp, J. (1982). Toward a general psychobiological theory of emotions. *Behavioral and Brain Sciences*, *5*, 407–67.

Partridge, L., & Harvey, P. H. (1988). The ecological context of life history evolution. *Science*, *241*, 1449–55.

Plutchik, R. (1980). A general psychoevolutionary theory of emotion. In R. Plutchik & H. Kellerman (Eds.), *Emotions: Theory, research, and experience*. (Vol. 1). New York: Academic Press.

Rachman, S., & Hodgson, R. J. (1968). Experimentally induced "sexual fetishism"; replication and development. *Psychological Record*, *18*, 25–27.

Sadalla, E. K., Kenrick, D. T., & Vershure, B. (1987). Dominance and heterosexual attraction. *Journal of Personality and Social Psychology*, *52*, 730–738.

Schaller, M., Park, J. H., & Kenrick, D. T. (2007). Human evolution and social cognition. In R. I. M. Dunbar & L. Barrett (Eds.), *Oxford handbook of evolutionary psychology* (pp. 491–504). Oxford, England: Oxford University Press.

Schaller, M., Park, J. H., & Mueller, A. (2003). Fear of the dark: Interactive effects of beliefs about danger and ambient darkness on ethnic stereotypes. *Personality and Social Psychology Bulletin*, *29*, 637–649.

Shepher, J. (1971). Mate selection among second generation kibbutz adolescents and adults: Incest avoidance and negative imprinting. *Archives of Sexual Behavior*, *1*, 293–307.

Sherry, D. F. & Shachter, D. L. (1987). The evolution of multiple memory systems. *Psychological Review*, *94*, 439–454.

Shiota, M. N., Campos, B., & Keltner, D. (2003). The faces of positive emotion: prototype displays of awe, amusement, and pride. *Annals of the New York Academy of Sciences*, *1000*, 296–299.

Shiota, M. N., Campos, B., Keltner, D., & Hertenstein, M. J. (2004). Positive emotion and the regulation of interpersonal relationships. In P. Philippot & R. S. Feldman (Eds.), *The regulation of emotion* (pp. 127–155). Mahwah, NJ: Lawrence Erlbaum.

Shiota, M. N., Keltner, D., & John, O. P. (2006). Positive emotion dispositions differentially associated with big five personality and attachment style. *Journal of Positive Psychology*, *1*(2), 61–71.

Stearns, S. C. (1976). Life history tactics: A review of the ideas. *The Quarterly Review of Biology*, *51*, 3–47.

Taylor, S. E., Klein, L. C., Lewis, B. P., Gruenewald, T. L., Gurung, R. A. R., & Updegraff, J. A. (2000). Biobehavioral responses to stress in females: Tend-and-befriend, not fight-or-flight. *Psychological Review*, *107*, 411–429.

Thibaut, J. W., & Kelley, H. H. (1959). *The social psychology of groups*. New York: Wiley.

Tooby, J., & Cosmides, L. (2005). Conceptual foundations of evolutionary psychology. In D. M. Buss (Ed.), *Handbook of evolutionary psychology* (pp. 5–67). New York: Wiley.

Tracy, J. L., & Robins, R. W. (2004). Show your pride: Evidence for a discrete emotion expression. *Psychological Science*, *15*(3), 194–197.

Van den Berghe, P. L. (1983). Human inbreeding avoidance: Culture in nature. *Behavioral and Brain Sciences*, *6*, 91–123.

Walster, E., Walster, G. W., & Berscheid, E. (1978). *Equity: Theory and Research*. Boston, MA: Allyn & Bacon.

Wilcoxon, H., Dragoin, E., & Kral, P. (1972). Illness-induced aversion in rats and quail. In M. E. P. Seligman & J. L. Hager (Eds.), *Biological boundaries on learning*. New York: Appleton-Century-Crofts.

Wolf, A. P. (1993). Westermarck redivivus. *Annual Review of Anthropology, 22*, 157–175.

Young, L. J., & Wang, Z. (2004). The neurobiology of pair bonding. *Nature Neuroscience, 7*(10), 1048–1054.

Zeifman, D., & Hazan, C. (1997). Attachment: The pair in pair bonds. In J. A. Simpson & D. T. Kenrick (Eds.), *Evolutionary social psychology* (pp. 237–264). Mahwah, NJ: Lawrence Erlbaum Associates.

Immediacy and Automaticity of Evaluation

17 Evaluative Readiness: The Motivational Nature of Automatic Evaluation

Melissa J. Ferguson and John A. Bargh

CONTENTS

The determinants and implications of people's likes and dislikes for stimuli in their environment have been a central topic of study over the 100 years since empirical psychology began (Allport, 1935; Brown, 1998; Eagly & Chaiken, 1993; Higgins & Brendl, 1996; McGuire, 1969, 1985; Osgood, Suci, & Tannenbaum, 1957; Rosenberg, 1965; Tesser & Martin, 1996; Zajonc, 2000). Throughout most of this period, researchers have studied people's likes and dislikes (i.e., attitudes, evaluations, preferences) by simply asking them to report them (Himmelfarb, 1993; Krosnick, Judd, & Wittenbrink, 2005). For example, a typical methodological strategy is to ask respondents to indicate on an 11-point scale how much they like a variety of stimuli. In this way, researchers have typically examined how people's explicitly (i.e., consciously, intentionally) generated evaluations predict their behavior across a range of circumstances, change after learning about new information or experiencing persuasive appeals, and compare to other people's evaluations (for reviews see Albarracín, Johnson & Zanna, 2005; Eagly & Chaiken, 1993). This approach has yielded valuable insight into the questions of how, when, why, and to what effect people evaluate stimuli as good versus bad.

Over the last two decades, however, there has been a remarkable shift in researchers' assumptions about the ways in which people generate likes and dislikes in response to stimuli. A considerable amount of data now show that people's evaluative processes are not limited or constrained to those times during which they are consciously and deliberately reflecting on a given stimulus. Instead, people evaluate the stimuli in their environment effortlessly, spontaneously, quickly, and often without realizing they have done so (Bargh, Chaiken, Govender, & Pratto, 1992; Fazio, 2001; Fazio, Sanbonmatsu, Powell, & Kardes, 1986; Greenwald, Klinger, & Liu, 1989; Greenwald, McGhee, & Schwartz, 1998; Zajonc, 1980). That is, on the mere perception of a stimulus, people invariably evaluate the stimulus in terms of being positive or negative, and they do so without being aware of it, intending to do so, or exerting any appreciable effort to do so (Bargh, 1994; for evidence of effortlessness, see Hermans, Crombez, & Eelen, 2000). For example, people are able to assess whether a facial expression is positive or negative on the basis of an exposure less than 10 ms in duration (Murphy & Zajonc, 1993; Niedenthal, 1990; Öhman, 1986), a time span almost 15 times shorter than the average human eye blink. Moreover, these immediate and effortless evaluations occur for a whole range of stimuli, including words, letters, pictures, drawings, people, faces, and even odors (for a review see Ferguson, 2007a; Musch & Klauer, 2003).

These findings have demonstrated the phenomenon of *automatic evaluation*—evaluations that are unintentionally generated on the mere perception of the respective stimuli. The examination of such evaluations has consumed a sizable portion of attitude research over the last 20 years, and especially over the last 5 years. In this chapter, we consider the motivational basis of this mode of evaluation. We first review theory suggesting that motivations and goals should be expected to be closely related with one another. We then describe several lines of recent research that provide empirical support for the notion that automatic evaluations are contingent or *conditional* on current and chronic goals and motivations. But first, we need to lay the groundwork for these substantive sections with a discussion of the terminology and methodology that characterize this area of research.

NOTES ON TERMINOLOGY

ATTITUDE VERSUS EVALUATION

Researchers have used a variety of terms to describe people's likes and dislikes, the two most common being *attitudes* and *evaluations*. Attitudes have been traditionally defined as consisting of affective, cognitive, and behavioral reactions to stimuli (Albarracín et al., 2005; Allport, 1935; Doob, 1947; Eagly & Chaiken, 1993; Osgood et al., 1957; Sarnoff, 1960; Smith, Bruner, &

White, 1956; Thurstone, 1931). However, they have more recently been defined simply as the evaluations associated with objects in memory (Fazio, 1986; Fazio, Chen, McDonel, & Sherman, 1982). In this way, *attitude* is virtually indistinguishable from *evaluation*, which is a less technical (i.e., academic) term referring simply to the assessment of whether a given stimulus is good or bad (Tesser & Martin, 1996). We use both of these terms freely throughout the chapter, while ascribing to the definition of an attitude as the evaluative information associated with a given object representation in memory.

Another critical notion in the attitude literature is the concept of *attitude object* (Allport, 1935; Bargh et al., 1992; Fazio, 2001; Fazio et al., 1986; Sarnoff, 1960; Smith et al., 1956; Thurstone, 1931). This is a general term referring to any stimulus toward which a person holds an attitude, and includes any conceptual or perceptual stimulus that can be discriminated (Eagly & Chaiken, 1993; Thurstone, 1927). Even though most of the research in this area has examined automatic attitudes toward graspable, or physical, objects, such as people (e.g., blacks, elderly, women), animals (e.g., cockroach, puppy), and everyday objects (e.g., consumer products, trees), people also automatically evaluate more abstract concepts such as ideals, values, and goals (Ferguson, 2007b).

It is also worthwhile to note that other theoretical constructs in social and cognitive psychology are related to people's preferences even though they do not regularly show up in the attitude literature per se. For example, Damasio (1999) and colleagues have argued that people immediately and unintentionally generate *somatic markers* in response to stimuli. These somatic markers essentially denote the anticipated emotional reaction to the corresponding stimulus, a definition that is roughly equivalent to how attitudes have been conceptualized over the past two decades. In addition, behavioral economists as well as sociologists use the term *tastes* to refer to people's preferences for stimuli. In economics, a person's tastes are assumed to be based on the degree to which the corresponding objects or stimuli can bring enjoyment, satisfaction, utility, or happiness to that person, so that the economic concept of *taste* is essentially equivalent to the notions of preferences, likes and dislikes, evaluations, and attitudes.

AFFECT AND EVALUATION

It is also useful to draw a distinction between evaluations and affective states, and we consider two points of discussion to this end. The first is whether evaluations necessarily involve affective processing in terms of the involvement of brain regions traditionally implicated in emotional and mood states (Davidson, Scherer, & Goldsmith, 2003). This would at first glance seem to be true given that many researchers commonly assume that evaluations involve *affective* reactions (Albarracín et al., 2005; Clore & Schnall, 2005; Eagly & Chaiken, 2003; Forgas, 2003), as mentioned earlier. Also, some scholars consider an automatic evaluation to be the initial spark of an eventual, comprehensive affective or emotional state (Damasio, 1999; LeDoux, 1996). However, we should note that there is no research as of yet that convincingly demonstrates that the types of evaluations that we talk about here—those that are unintentionally and immediately generated in response to stimuli—*necessarily* depend on the brain and physiological systems typically characterized as affective. Future research will undoubtedly continue to address the extent to which automatic evaluations recruit those brain regions typically identified with affective experiences, as well as the circumstances under which this occurs.

The second point of discussion regards the conceptual differences between evaluations and affect. For example, how are evaluations different from emotions? One classic distinction is that although both evaluations and emotional states occur in reaction to a particular stimulus or event, the latter are generally more durable, long lasting, and subjectively involving than the former (Tesser & Martin, 1996). Additionally, an evaluation is assumed to be a simple classification as positive versus negative, whereas emotions consist of shades of positive (e.g., elation, surprise) and negative (e.g., sadness, anger, anxiety) affect. Furthermore, emotional states are also classically defined as conscious experiences (Davidson et al., 2003), whereas evaluations, as mentioned previously, can occur nonconsciously.

How might evaluations differ from mood states? Mood states are assumed to be less introspectively linked to any one stimulus, and are consciously felt (Davidson et al., 2003; though see Winkielman, Berridge, Wilbarger, 2005), diffuse, and somewhat persistent (i.e., not fleeting, lasting more than 5 min). In contrast, evaluations are generated in direct response to stimuli, and are usually fleeting. Yet, the line demarcating these theoretical constructs is not always sharp. In particular, especially if the nascent evidence for nonconscious mood states increases, the putative qualitative difference between a nonconscious evaluation of a given conceptual or perceptual stimulus, and a nonconscious mood state resulting from some incidental event, will become obscured.

AUTOMATIC VERSUS IMPLICIT

In terms of the characteristic of *automatic*, we again consider two points of clarification. Firstly, although evaluations and attitudes are often referred to as automatic or implicit (e.g., automatic attitudes, automatic evaluations),

the terms automatic and implicit refer to the *measure* rather than the *construct* being measured. This is an important distinction as the latter would suggest that there are two qualitatively different evaluations—those that are automatic and those that are not. Although this is a possibility, research concerning it is ongoing and not yet conclusive (Fazio & Olson, 2003; Hofmann, Gawronski, Gschwendner, Le, & Schmitt, 2005; Nosek, 2005; Wilson, Lindsey, & Schooler, 2000).

The second point of clarification concerns the meaning of the terms *automatic* and *implicit*. The term automatic has been used to describe processes that unfold without the person's awareness, intention, effort, or control (Bargh, 1994; Moors & De Houwer, 2006). However, a process does not need to meet all four of these criteria in order to be designated as automatic (very few do at the level of complexity typically of interest to social and motivational psychology), and in this way the term is not very specific. Therefore, it is useful when using the term to specify exactly what criteria are implied for a particular process (Bargh, 1989). With regard to the literature on evaluations, the term "automatic" usually refers to the fact that they can be generated without the person's intention. Although some research has shown that evaluations can be generated without the person's awareness of the stimuli themselves, most of the research employs measures in which the person is aware of the stimulus that is being evaluated but is unaware that their evaluation is being measured (for a review see Ferguson, 2007a). We use the term automatic in this chapter to refer to evaluations that are generated without the person's intentions and usually without their awareness.

We also offer the caution that the meaning of the term *implicit* as used in social psychology (Greenwald & Banaji, 1995) is somewhat different from how it is used in much of the cognitive science literature (De Houwer, 2005; Fazio & Olson, 2003). In cognitive psychology the term implicit refers to knowledge or memory that can influence processing but that cannot be introspectively identified, even when the person tries to do so. For example, a classic case of implicit priming is the influence of a previously studied word on word-fragment completion even when the respondent has no memory of encountering the word during the study phase (Roediger, 1990; Squire & Kandel, 1999; Tulving & Craik, 2000). In social psychology, however, the term implicit is often used to describe evaluations that are generated without the person intending to do so, even if that person would be able to identify her or his evaluation of a given stimulus if asked to do so. For example, people would probably be able to easily identify their evaluation of many of the stimuli that are presented in implicit attitude measures, and at least some of the time these intentional (explicit) evaluations will line up with their unintentional (implicit) ones (Nosek, 2005). We return to this issue of *dissociation* between implicit and explicit evaluations later in this chapter.

NOTES ON MEASUREMENT

Throughout most of the last century of empirical psychology, researchers have measured people's preferences in the straightforward manner of just asking for them. For example, in order to find out how much people like elderly people, they would ask people to circle a number on an 11-point scale with 1 indicating extreme disliking and 11 representing extreme liking. As Schwarz and Bohner (2001) and others have noted, this type of measurement is highly susceptible to a range of contextual factors, that is, factors that are unrelated to the attitude but that nevertheless influence how the person responds. These factors can include mood states, response biases, demand effects, and impression maintenance (for a review see Schwarz & Bohner, 2001). Because of these factors, it is difficult to precisely and accurately interpret the meaning of a respondent's answer on an explicit attitude measure.

One area of research where the difficulty of interpretation is especially clear is intergroup attitudes. Given societal norms for egalitarianism and fairness toward other (especially stigmatized) groups, people may feel social pressure to keep hidden any negative feelings and evaluations they may harbor about other groups of people (Dovidio, Mann, & Gaertner, 1989; Jones & Sigall, 1971; Katz & Hass, 1988; McConahay, 1986; Sears, 1988). This means that explicit measures of prejudice can underestimate the actual amount of prejudice the respondent holds toward others. To attempt to circumvent this problem, researchers began to develop indirect, and less obtrusive, and reactive measures of attitudes. For example, in the Bogus Pipeline research (Jones & Sigall, 1971), participants were hooked up to an apparatus that was supposed to be capable of detecting their attempts at deception. Given this possibility of detection, participants did admit to greater levels of prejudice when using this measure compared to other explicit, traditional measures of the kind described above.

Although indirect (but explicit nonetheless) measures of this sort were an improvement, researchers continued to be interested in developing a method to assess a person's unintended and nonconscious evaluative responses to stimuli. Given the covert nature of the implicit methodologies developed by cognitive psychologists, social psychological researchers began to modify them in order to address social psychological issues and phenomena.

With regard to attitudes and evaluations, the two most common measures include the evaluative priming paradigm (Fazio et al., 1986) and the Implicit Association Test (Greenwald et al., 1998), among others (Brendl, Markman, & Messner, 2005; De Houwer, 2003; De Houwer & Eelen, 1998; Dovidio, Kawakami, Johnson, Johnson, & Howard, 1997; Koole, Dijksterhuis, & van Knippenberg, 2001; Niedenthal, 1990; Nosek & Banaji, 2001; Payne, Cheng, Govorun, & Stewart, 2005; von Hippel, Sekaquaptewa, & Vargas, 1997). These methods are summarized briefly in the next section.

EVALUATIVE PRIMING PARADIGM

Sequential priming paradigms were originally developed by cognitive psychologists to assess the degree to which memory locations related to a given stimulus become activated automatically on perception of that stimulus (Logan, 1980; Meyer & Schvaneveldt, 1971; Neely, 1976, 1977; Posner & Snyder, 1975; Shiffrin & Schneider, 1977). In such a paradigm the "prime" stimulus of interest (e.g., butter) is presented on a computer screen for a fraction of a second and is followed by a "target" stimulus that is either related to it (bread) or not (chimney), and to which the participant must make some kind of response or judgment (e.g., lexical decision). The common finding is that people can respond significantly more quickly to the targets when they are preceded by related versus unrelated primes. This suggests that quickly following the perception of a given stimulus, such as butter, the knowledge that is semantically or lexically related to butter, such as bread, becomes automatically activated in memory. This activation makes *bread* more accessible in memory (i.e., more likely to be applied to incoming stimuli; Higgins, 1996), and thus facilitates the perception and assessment of it during the target response. A key finding from research using this paradigm is that related knowledge becomes activated without the perceiver's intention, awareness, or control (Neely, 1977).

Fazio and colleagues (Fazio et al., 1986; see also Fiske, 1982) applied this finding to the question of whether evaluative knowledge also becomes activated automatically on the perception of a stimulus. For example, does a positive evaluation (i.e., "good") become activated as soon as someone reads the word *puppy*? To test this, the researchers developed an evaluative sequential priming paradigm in which primes that were either positive or negative were paired with targets that were either positive or negative but otherwise semantically unrelated to the primes. They found evidence for *evaluative priming*, such that people were faster at responding to the targets when they were preceded by evaluatively consistent versus inconsistent primes, even though the primes and targets were not otherwise related semantically. Since this first evidence was published, other researchers have replicated and extended the evaluative priming effect, and various alternatives have been offered concerning the underlying mechanisms of the effect (Castelli, Zogmaister, Smith, & Arcuri, 2004; Chaiken & Bargh, 1993; Fazio, 1993; Klauer & Musch, 2003; Klauer & Stern, 1992; Klinger, Burton, & Pitts, 2000; Wentura, 1999, 2000).

Importantly, the evaluative priming paradigm can be used as a way to implicitly assess the evaluation of a prime stimulus simply by gauging whether the mere perception of the prime facilitates positive versus negative targets, compared to baseline responding to each kind of target (Fazio, Jackson, Dunton, & Williams, 1995; Ferguson, 2007b; Ferguson & Bargh, 2004; Wittenbrink, Judd, & Park, 1997, 2001). For example, it is possible to present pictures of members of a certain group as the prime stimuli and measure whether the perception of a face facilitates responding to positive versus negative targets (Fazio et al., 1995). In fact, this kind of paradigm is one of the two most popular measures of automatic evaluations. One important characteristic of this paradigm is that participants' evaluations of the prime stimuli are assessed without their awareness, and participants are assumed to be unable to exert strategic control over the latency of their responses to the targets as a function of the nature of the primes.

Implicit Association Test

The other widely popular measure of automatic attitudes is the implicit association test (IAT; Greenwald et al., 1998). This paradigm also measures the degree to which people tend to associate a particular stimulus with positivity versus negativity, but does so in a different manner. In this case, participants are first asked to practice deciding on a computer whether a given stimulus belongs to one of two categories (e.g., young versus old people). For example, a word related to elderly people might appear on the screen and the respondent would have to press the key associated with elderly rather than the key associated with youth. In a second task, participants would have to judge each of a series of stimuli in terms of belonging to either positive or negative words (e.g., happy).

In the next phase of the measure, participants would be asked to accomplish these sorting tasks simultaneously using two response keys. In this way, they would have to press one key if the stimulus that appears on the screen is either elderly or positive, and would have to press another key if the stimulus is either young or negative.

The pairing of the categories would then be switched in the next task such that participants would have to press one key if the stimulus is elderly or negative, and another key if it is young or positive. The main analysis of these data consists of whether participants are faster at the first versus second sorting task. If they are faster on average at the second task, this implies that they have an easier time associating the elderly with negative things (and/or the young with positive things).

The IAT has generated an incredible amount of research, spanning attitudes toward various groups, individuals, the self, and products (Greenwald & Farnham, 2000; Greenwald, Banaji, Rudman, Farnham, Nosek, & Mellott 2002; Jordan, Spencer, & Zanna, 2003; Marsh, Johnson, & Scott-Sheldon, 2001; Nosek, Banaji, & Greenwald, 2002). This task is implicit in nature because participants are not being asked to report their attitudes. Also, as in the evaluative priming task, the data from the IAT consist of the speed of participants' responses. This means that it is very difficult for participants to manage or strategically conceal their underlying attitudes as this would require them to both detect differences in the speed with which they respond to targets across conditions, and to control their responses based on preconceived notions of appropriate responding. Moreover, also like the evaluative priming paradigm, the IAT demands quick responding and therefore does not give participants the necessary time to strategically edit their responses.

MOTIVATIONAL NATURE OF AUTOMATIC EVALUATION

What is the relationship between a person's current goal pursuits and the *automatic* evaluations they make? To answer this question, first consider how researchers have understood the relationship between motivations and goals, on the one hand, and conscious or intentional evaluations on the other. Researchers across areas of psychology have long assumed a close correspondence between people's preferences for stimuli and their motivations regarding those stimuli (Arnold, 1960; Bogardus, 1931; Chen & Bargh, 1999; Corwin, 1921; Doob, 1947; Frijda, 1986; Lang, 1984; Lazarus, 1991; Lewin, 1935; Mowrer, 1960; Osgood, 1953; Thurstone, 1931; Young, 1959). After all, one of the most fundamental axioms of motivation is the pleasure principle, or the notion that people approach things that make them feel good, and avoid those things that make them feel bad. As Bentham famously stated in 1789, "Nature has placed mankind under the governance of two sovereign masters: pain and pleasure. It is for them alone to point out what we ought to do, as well as to determine what we shall do." Given that attitudes reflect the person's assessment of whether the corresponding stimuli are good or bad, attitudes are therefore direct indications of our motivations toward those stimuli.

But what about *automatic* (nonconscious and unintended) evaluations? Is the relationship between automatic evaluations and goals different in an interesting way from that between conscious evaluations and goals? Indeed, numerous researchers over the last couple of decades have argued just that: automatic, more than conscious, evaluations seem especially tied to people's motivations because they facilitate people's general goals of securing rewards and avoiding dangers and threatening stimuli (Chen & Bargh, 1999; Damasio, 1999; Duckworth, Bargh, Garcia, & Chaiken, 2002; Fazio, 1989; Ferguson & Bargh, 2002, 2004; Lang, Bradley, & Cuthbert, 1990; LeDoux, 1996; Öhman, 1986; Pratkanis, Breckler, & Greenwald, 1989; Roskos-Ewoldsen & Fazio, 1992; Smith et al., 1956). They do so by *quickly* providing needed and important information about the nature of the stimuli in a person's environment. The nearly instantaneous delivery of this kind of relevant information can enable people to prepare to act and react to the objects in their surroundings in an adaptive, goal-consistent manner.

Automatic evaluations are functional also because they direct people toward those stimuli that have the most goal-relevance for them. For instance, Roskos-Ewoldsen and Fazio (1992) presented participants with a series of displays of line drawings of everyday objects (e.g., elephant, bug, bike) for very brief amounts of time. Using recall paradigms, they found that participants automatically attended, visually, to those objects toward which they possessed strong, automatically activated attitudes. In this way, people are immediately alerted to those objects that hold the most potential for their goals, either in terms of reward or danger. There exists substantial research showing how automatically activated attitudes facilitate judgment and decision making, and serve as reliable, effective guides toward goal-relevant behavior (Fazio, 1989, 1990; Fazio & Williams, 1986; Petty & Krosnick, 1995).

However, this conclusion regarding the motivational property of automatic evaluations is based on a single processing characteristic of how quickly they are generated, rather than anything about their content, or their relative intensity across situations. Does the content or intensity of automatic evaluations reflect anything about people's current goals? If the way in which people automatically evaluate stimuli reflects something about their

motivational stance toward the objects, then the content of automatic evaluations (i.e., good vs. bad) should fluctuate along with the person's goals regarding the objects. That is, they should reflect what the person wants at the moment (Lewin, 1926). Positive automatic evaluations should emerge when the person currently possesses an approach stance toward the objects, and negative automatic evaluations should automatically emerge when the person holds an avoidant stance toward the objects. Moreover, there should be some correspondence between people's chronic goals toward objects, and their automatic evaluations toward them. We now turn to several recent lines of empirical support for these propositions.

AUTOMATIC EVALUATIONS AND CURRENTLY ACCESSIBLE, CONSCIOUS GOALS

Recently, several lines of research have examined whether a person's currently accessible, conscious goals influence the way in which that person automatically evaluates the stimuli in their environment. Sherman, Presson, Chassin, Rose, and Koch (2003) examined the role of people's goal to smoke and their automatic evaluations toward smoking paraphernalia (e.g., cigarettes). All participants were instructed to refrain from smoking before arriving at the lab. Whereas some participants were allowed to smoke for a few minutes before completing the experiment, others were not allowed to smoke. This manipulation ensured that some participants had the goal to smoke whereas others had just satisfied their need. All participants then completed a measure of their implicit evaluations, and the results showed that those who had the current need to smoke evaluated the smoking-related stimuli as relatively more positive than those who had just fulfilled their need. These findings demonstrate that automatic evaluations seem to reflect the degree to which the perceiver currently wants to approach the respective stimuli.

In another line of studies, we (Ferguson & Bargh, 2004) examined the goals of achievement, thirst, and athleticism. We wanted to test whether the desire for, versus fulfillment of, a variety of goals would dictate people's immediate evaluations of stimuli related to those goals. In the first experiment, participants were asked to play a word game and they were told either that the game measured their verbal skills or that it was being developed for use in future research. They were instructed that in the game, they would earn a point for every word they could create out of a given set of letters, would earn extra points if the word was a noun, and still more points if the word was a noun that started with the letter "c." They then played the game for about 5 min, and then completed a measure of their automatic evaluations. At that point, half of the participants believed that they were finished with the word game, whereas the other half of the participants believed that they were going to be playing a second round of the game after the computer task (i.e., the automatic evaluation measure). In this manner we manipulated whether the task goal was still active or "turned off" because the task and goal pursuit had been completed (Lewin, 1926). We then measured the participants' automatic evaluations toward stimuli related to the game (e.g., *points*, *achieve*, *nouns*, *c*, *create*).

The main finding was that the content of participants' automatic evaluations toward game-related stimuli was a function of how much they cared about their performance in the game, and also whether they thought they would be playing the game again. Only those who thought that their verbal skills were being measured, and who believed that they would be playing again, produced positive automatic evaluations of the words. The findings from this experiment suggest that one's *current* (rather than recently fulfilled) achievement goal can influence automatic evaluations both of stimuli that have recently been designated as goal-relevant (e.g., noun, c, game) as well as stimuli that are chronically relevant to achievement (e.g., achieve, win).

Does the positivity of automatic evaluations depend on the extent to which a stimulus is related to the person's current goal? For example, are stimuli that are strongly versus weakly related to a current goal automatically evaluated in a more positive way? This would suggest the prediction, on functional grounds, that those stimuli that are most able to fulfill a goal are immediately evaluated as the most desirable. Our second experiment tested this hypothesis. Participants were instructed to refrain from drinking anything for three hours before arriving at the experiment, and thus they were all thirsty. Participants were then asked to sample either a variety of bottled waters, or a variety of dry, salty, sourdough pretzels. Whereas the thirst of those who sampled the water was sated, it was exacerbated for those who had to sample the pretzels. In this way, the goal of quenching one's thirst was recently fulfilled for some participants but was still active for the others.

All participants then completed a measure of their automatic evaluations of stimuli varying in their relevance to the goal. Based on pretest data, the stimuli were strongly (e.g., water, juice, drinking), indirectly (e.g., glass, bottle), weakly (e.g., coffee, beer), or not at all (e.g., chair, window) relevant to the thirst goal. Those

who were thirsty at the time of the measure gave automatic evaluations of the strongly relevant stimuli that were significantly more positive than their evaluations of the other stimuli, as well as significantly more positive than made by the nonthirsty participants. These findings demonstrate that automatic evaluations are *prospective* in that they reflect the upcoming or immediate utility of the stimuli, rather than only their recently experienced utility. Also, the results show that automatic evaluations are sensitive to the degree to which a certain stimulus can facilitate the perceiver's current goal.

A final question that we examined was whether participants' automatic evaluations would be sensitive to the strength of the perceiver's current goal. In this experiment, all participants were self-described athletes, in that they played athletics regularly and cared about their identity as an athlete. However, those who were varsity athletes cared more than those who were intramural (and nonvarsity) athletes. Participants were asked to describe either a recent failure or success in athletics, or were asked to describe their academic schedule. Based on self-completion theory (Wicklund & Gollwitzer, 1982), we expected that those who were asked to describe a recent athletic failure experience would be the most motivated to reclaim and reestablish their athletic identity, compared with those in the control condition and also compared to those who wrote about success. We then assessed participants' automatic evaluations of stimuli that were either relevant to the athletic goal (e.g., agile, athletic) or irrelevant to the goal (e.g., chair, smart). The results showed that those who cared most about the goal—the varsity athletes—displayed the most positive automatic evaluations toward the goal-relevant stimuli, relative to the intramural athletes, and also compared to the goal-irrelevant stimuli.

Together, the findings of Sherman et al. (2003) and Ferguson and Bargh (2004) demonstrate that people's currently accessible, conscious goals cause them to automatically evaluate the stimuli in their environment as a function of whether those stimuli can enable them to reach the goal. This suggests that automatic evaluations are motivational (and functional) in nature because they both provide information that is important to people's goals *quickly*, and also because they *reflect* people's current motivational priorities. In other words, the motivational nature of automatic evaluations goes beyond a single processing characteristic of the evaluations—the speed with which they are made—to their content and intensity within goal-relevant conditions. We now consider some implications and extensions of these findings.

AUTOMATIC EVALUATIONS AND CURRENTLY ACCESSIBLE, NONCONSCIOUS GOALS

The findings from the experiments described above suggest that automatic evaluations reflect the perceiver's *currently* rather than *recently* active goals. Motivational influences on automatic evaluations are also moderated by the strength or importance of the goal to the individual, as well as by the relevance of the evaluated stimulus for reaching that goal. An important remaining question is whether the goal has to be pursued in a conscious, intentional, verbally reportable manner for these effects to occur. In each of the studies reviewed above, the participants were consciously induced into the goal state, and could easily have been knowingly and intentionally thinking about how they might want to fulfill it. For those in the Sherman et al. (2003) studies, the cigarette-deprived smokers could well have been thinking about how good a cigarette would taste. For those in the Ferguson and Bargh (2004) studies, the thirsty participants could have been thinking about several things: achieving and scoring points with nouns (Experiment 1), wanting some water (Experiment 2), or improving their athletic performance (Experiment 3). Thus, it remains possible that the effects of goals on the automatic evaluation of goal-relevant stimuli are contingent on the perceiver consciously thinking about those objects.

Do goals influence automatic evaluations even when those goals are nonconsciously induced? There are several demonstrations now that goals can be activated from memory and influence behavior without the person's awareness or intentions (Aarts, Gollwitzer, & Hassin, 2004; Bargh, 2007; Bargh, Gollwitzer, Lee-Chai, Barndollar, & Troetschel, 2001; Chartrand & Bargh, 1996; Fishbach, Friedman, & Kruglanski, 2003; Fitzsimons & Bargh, 2003; Shah, 2003; Shah, Kruglanski, & Friedman, 2002). For instance, the goal to attain high performance on a given task can be activated merely by reading words related to achievement, with positive effects on participants' success and persistence on the assigned task (Bargh et al., 2001). Thus, one might expect other effects of a nonconsciously activated goal, such as on the individual's immediate and spontaneous evaluations of the goal-relevant stimuli in their environment. If goals automatically influence how people evaluate the stimuli in their environment, then even a nonconsciously activated goal should lead to the kinds of motivational effects on evaluation as with the studies, described above, involving conscious goal pursuit. Another relevant question is whether such motivational influences on automatic evaluations are functional for

the individual. We have been assuming here that if one's currently active goal fosters positive automatic evaluations of goal-helpful stimuli, the probability of one's attaining the goal will be enhanced. But is this actually the case? None of the experiments described so far have directly examined this question. One way to approach it would be to examine whether those participants who are the most skilled and successful in a goal domain are also the most likely to show the effects of goal activation on automatic evaluations. Thus, for example, when the goal of academic achievement has been activated in memory, those who are skilled in that domain should be the most likely to show more positive automatic (immediate, unintended) evaluations of the goal-friendly stimuli in that domain.

Some very recent research has addressed these questions (Ferguson, 2007c). In one experiment, participants were nonconsciously induced into either an academic goal, a goal unrelated to academics (i.e., a social goal), or no goal. Participants completed a scrambled sentence task (Srull & Wyer, 1979) wherein they were asked to make grammatically correct sentences out of sets of five words each. Presented in some of the sentences were words related to the academic goal (e.g., study, school, smart) or to the social goal (e.g., friends, laughing, social), depending on the condition to which participants had been randomly assigned. In the control condition, none of the words in the sentences were related to the focal goals. This method has been used previously to activate a construct out of participants' awareness, and indeed, none of the participants in this study reported any awareness of pursuing the primed goals. Once participants had been primed with a goal construct (or not), they completed a measure of their automatic evaluations of both words related to the academic goal (e.g., grades, graduation), and unrelated to the goal (e.g., chair, window).

From the above considerations, it was predicted that those participants nonconsciously primed with an academic goal should automatically evaluate the academic stimuli as most positive, relative to the irrelevant stimuli; further, the academic goal-primed participants were predicted to evaluate the academic stimuli more positively than would those participants who had been primed with a goal unrelated to academics (the social goal condition) or no goal at all. The results supported these predictions. Those in the academic-goal condition automatically evaluated the academic stimuli as most positive, compared to the other relevant cells. It was further predicted that those who are most skilled in the academic domain should be the most likely to show these kinds of effects, and this too was confirmed: those participants with the highest grade point average (GPA) were the most likely to show the academic-goal priming effect on the automatic evaluation of academic-related stimuli.

Taken together, this set of findings suggests that a goal can influence how people automatically evaluate the stimuli in their surroundings even when the goal has been activated and is operating nonconsciously. In addition, this effect seems to emerge particularly for those who are skilled in that goal domain, in harmony with the notion that motivational influences on evaluation are functional for the individual. The mere activation of the goal, even via minimal processing and awareness, is enough to change the way in which the perceiver sees and responds to the environment.

In our view, this effect of active goals on evaluation is the affective equivalent of Bruner's (1957) notion of "perceptual readiness," in which active goals cause goal-related mental representations to become more accessible or ready to be activated by relevant environmental stimuli. Just as we become, during goal pursuit, perceptually ready to see and hear goal-relevant objects and events in our environment, the recent research described above shows us to become "evaluatively ready" to positively evaluate and behaviorally approach those things that will facilitate the pursuit of the goal.

Another interesting aspect of these findings is that those skilled people primed with the academic goal automatically evaluated the academic-related stimuli as more positive than those who had been primed with the social goal. Previous research suggests that when people skilled at a certain goal perceive a temptation (e.g., TV) that is deleterious to that goal, the skilled-goal increases in accessibility and strength (Fishbach et al., 2003). This work might suggest that those primed with a social goal should evaluate academic-related stimuli just as positively as those primed with the academic goal itself, and yet this did not happen. However, there is an important difference between distractions and temptations to a goal, on the one hand, and reminders of an equally important competing goal, on the other. In the social goal condition described above (Ferguson, 2007c), participants were not primed with social temptations—rather they were primed with the goal of being with friends, one of the most basic and fundamental goals in human nature (Baumeister & Leary, 1995; Brewer, 1991). Based on the above results, we would suggest that skilled people are not "blind" to the importance of other competing goals than the one at which they are skilled. Instead, their implicit readiness to approach that goal can be deactivated when it conflicts with another important goal that is currently active (see Morsella, 2005; Oettingen et al., 2006, for more on how such goal conflicts are resolved nonconsciously.).

Although these findings suggest that nonconscious goals can influence automatic evaluations of goal-relevant stimuli in the environment, the effect seems limited to those stimuli that can *help* them achieve the goal. What about those stimuli that might distract or tempt the person away from the focal goal? Although it is surely helpful for a person's currently accessible goal to render as positive those things that can enable the pursuit of that goal, it must also be functional for the goal to render as negative those things that might undermine or distract the pursuit of the focal goal. If such an effect emerged, it would provide support for a kind of "evaluative goal shielding" as discussed by Shah, Friedman, & Kruglanski (2002). That is, the focused pursuit of a given goal might be protected or enhanced by the negative automatic evaluation of distractions to that goal pursuit.

This question was tested in another experiment (Ferguson, 2007c) in which participants were subliminally primed (or not) with the goal of academic achievement. They then completed an automatic evaluation measure of stimuli, some of which were temptations to the academic goal (e.g., TV) and some which were not. The results showed that those who were primed with the academic goal automatically evaluated the social temptations as more negative than the other stimuli; also, the academic-primed participants showed more negative automatic evaluations of the social temptations than did the nonprimed participants. Importantly, this effect emerged only for those with a high GPA (a marker of academic goal-skill), again showing the functional benefits of motivational influences on automatic evaluation.

These preliminary findings suggest that even goals that are nonconsciously activated in memory can influence the way in which people automatically evaluate the stimuli in their environment. Thus, the empirical findings described above regarding the effect of conscious goal pursuit on evaluations (Ferguson & Bargh, 2004; Sherman et al., 2003) are not contingent on people intentionally thinking and deliberating about how they might accomplish that goal. Furthermore, these more recent findings (Ferguson, 2007c) extend the evaluative reach of currently (and nonconsciously) accessible goals to those stimuli that would undermine the pursuit of that primed goal, especially in the case of people who are skilled at pursuing that goal.

We now consider the extent to which automatic evaluations are influenced by the person's chronically accessible (latent) goals, even when these are not currently active.

Automatic Evaluations and Chronically Accessible Goals

Although the recent research described above suggests that people's currently accessible goals can influence their automatic evaluations toward stimuli relevant to the goal, the motivational influence on evaluations may not be limited to those goals that are currently active. Surely people still automatically evaluate stimuli as good or bad even when those stimuli are unrelated to what the person is currently trying to accomplish. Indeed, it would seem dysfunctional to not do so (Chen & Bargh, 1999; Duckworth et al., 2002; Fazio, 1989; Ferguson & Bargh, 2002, 2004; Lang et al., 1990; LeDoux, 1996; Öhman, 1986; Pratkanis et al., 1989; Roskos-Ewoldsen & Fazio, 1992; Smith et al., 1956). We argue here that one's automatic evaluation of stimuli should, on average, reflect the typical importance of that stimulus for someone's goals. In this way, people may automatically evaluate puppies as relatively positive on average because they are typically always appealing (and nonthreatening), and cockroaches as relatively negative on average because they are typically always aversive and disgusting. This reasoning implies that just because an athlete's automatic evaluation of *agile* becomes more positive when she or he is currently concerned with that goal, it should still be relatively more positive on average than for someone for whom the athletic goal is unimportant.

In support of this claim, there is considerable evidence that people's automatic evaluations toward a range of stimuli on average predict their approach versus avoidance behaviors toward those stimuli (Blair, 2002; Chen & Bargh, 1999; Dovidio, Kawakami, & Gaertner, 2002; Dovidio et al., 1997; Duckworth et al., 2002; Epley & Caruso, 2004; Fazio et al., 1995; Haidt, 2001, 2003; Kawakami & Dovidio, 2001; Lambert, Payne, Ramsey, & Shaffer, 2005; McConnell & Leibold, 2001; Nosek et al., 2002). Someone who displays a positive automatic attitude toward stereotypically black names, for instance, is more likely to display warmth and friendliness to black people compared with someone who displays a negative attitude toward the same group (for a review see Fazio & Olson, 2003). Automatic evaluations have been found to be particularly predictive of those behaviors that are spontaneous and difficult to control, more so than of obvious and overt behaviors (Blair, 2002; Dovidio et al., 2002; Dovidio et al.; Ferguson, 2007b; Kawakami & Dovidio, 2001). Overall, this body of research indicates that people's automatic evaluations of stimuli are generally predictive of how they will tend to act toward those stimuli across time and situations. Because people's

approach and avoidance behaviors toward stimuli reflect their motivations toward those stimuli, automatic evaluations can be understood as reflections of motivations.

Interestingly, almost the entire literature on the predictive validity of automatic evaluations has focused on people's immediate evaluative responses to graspable stimuli, or those stimuli toward or away from one can physically move. For instance, almost all of the literature on how automatic evaluations toward groups predict behavior with group members has used stimuli such as group names, group labels, or faces of group members (Fazio & Olson, 2003). And yet, what about the more abstract values, goals, and ideals that undoubtedly predict people's behavior across physical targets and situations? If automatic evaluations reflect the perceiver's tendency to approach the respective stimuli, then automatic evaluations toward abstract goals, such as equality, should reflect the perceiver's tendency to approach—or pursue—that goal. The more one immediately and unintentionally evaluates the word *equality* with positivity, the more that person should be expected, on average, to demonstrate egalitarian behavior toward others.

How will such automatic evaluations of abstract concepts compare with what is known about how people evaluate concrete, graspable stimuli? The first thing to note is that the influence of any evaluation will depend on the accessibility of its referent (i.e., the respective attitude object). The more the referent is accessible in memory, the more its corresponding attitude should influence behavior toward that referent (Higgins, 1996). In addition, research also shows that the accessibility of abstract versus concrete memories fluctuates across circumstances (Trope & Liberman, 2003; Vallacher & Wegner, 1987; Wegner, Vallacher, Kiersted, & Dizadji, 1986). Thus, there is some reason to expect that automatic evaluations of abstract goals might sometimes be more influential on behavior than automatic evaluations toward concrete stimuli related to that goal.

Ferguson (2007b) examined the above questions in a series of experiments. In the first of these, participants arrived at the lab and completed an automatic evaluation measure of stimuli related to the goal to be thin, and also provided their explicit attitudes toward the goal and the strength of their current desire to reach the goal. Participants were then contacted about a week later through e-mail, and asked to indicate how many times over the past week they had engaged in each of a variety of behaviors, and also how many times they planned to engage in those same behaviors during the upcoming week. Among the behaviors was "resisting tempting food"—a behavior that had been rated in a pilot study as the most effective way to meet the goal of being thin. The results showed that participants' immediate, unintentional evaluations of the goal significantly predicted their reported successful goal pursuit, and did so above and beyond their explicit ratings of the desirability of the goal, and their explicit attitude toward the goal.

What about automatic evaluations of the goal to be thin versus the tempting foods that need to be avoided in order to meet the goal? This comparison was examined in the next experiment. Participants arrived at the lab and indicated how often they regulated their intake of fattening foods. Then between 3 and 5 weeks later they came back to the lab and completed a measure of their automatic evaluations of the goal to be thin, as well as a variety of tempting foods related to the goal. The results showed that participants' automatic evaluations of the goal significantly predicted their reported goal pursuit, while their automatic evaluations of the tempting foods did not. This set of findings indicates that automatic evaluations of goals are sometimes more predictive of goal pursuit than the concrete stimuli toward which goal-relevant behavior is directed.

In the above two experiments, however, participants merely reported goal pursuit rather than demonstrated actual goal pursuit. To test whether automatic evaluations of the goal to be thin would predict how much of a tempting food one would eat, participants arrived at the lab and were told that they would sample and comment on products as part of a marketing study. They were assigned to taste either goal-relevant, fattening (cookies) or goal-irrelevant, nonfattening (low-calorie mints) snacks. Right before they were asked to sample the food, they completed an automatic evaluation measure in which their evaluations toward the goal, as well as the goal-relevant target of behavior (cookies), were measured. The results showed that their automatic evaluations of the goal predicted their consumption of the goal-relevant snack, but not the goal irrelevant snack. Their automatic evaluations of the target of behavior (cookie) did not predict their consumption of the snack, however.

Finally, in the last experiment, the participant's automatic and explicit evaluations of an abstract goal, along with concrete stimuli related to that goal, were measured. Moreover, participants' overt as well as subtle goal-relevant behaviors were assessed. In particular, participants' automatic evaluations toward the goal of egalitarianism and a relatively more concrete target of egalitarian behavior— elderly people—were measured. Participants then provided their explicit attitudes toward the goal and the concrete goal-relevant stimulus. Finally, they were asked to express their support for a number of federal and state

sponsored policies and programs. Included in this list of policies was Medicare, the federal program that provides financial assistance to elderly people. Previous research has suggested that subtle prejudice toward a group is related to decreased support for programs that target that group (Dovidio, Glick, & Rudman, 2005; Levy & Schlesinger, 2005; McConahay, 1983, 1986; Swim, Aiken, Hall, & Hunter, 1995), and thus it was expected that participants' automatic evaluation of the goal of equality would predict their subtle prejudice toward the elderly, in terms of their support of Medicare. Participants also were explicitly asked to what extent a negative stereotypical trait of the elderly (i.e., rigidity) was true of elderly people in general; this constituted the blatant or overt indication of prejudice toward the elderly.

It was expected that their automatic evaluation of the goal might be less effective at predicting this overt expression of prejudice, in line with previous research (Asendorpf, Banse, & Mücke, 2002; Devine, 1989; Dovidio et al., 1997, 2002; Egloff & Schmukle, 2002; Fazio, 1990; Wilson et al., 2000). Indeed, the results suggested that their automatic evaluations toward the goal predicted their subtle expression of prejudice but not their overt expression of prejudice. However, their explicit attitude toward the group did predict their overt expression of prejudice toward the group. The pattern of findings thus replicated the main result from the previous experiments that people's automatic evaluations of a goal do seem to reliably predict their actual behavioral pursuit of that goal. Also, this may be particularly true for subtle versus blatant goal-relevant behaviors. This experiment also again suggests that automatic evaluations of goals can prove more predictive of goal pursuit than automatic evaluations of concrete stimuli related to the goal.

Together, the results from this line of experiments suggest that automatic evaluations of goals may on average reflect the importance of the goals to the perceiver. But, when should such implicit evaluations out-predict more explicit motivations? Firstly, automatic evaluations should out-predict explicit motivations when it is difficult for the person to accurately introspect on how much they want to reach the goal. Note that it may be very easy for people to say whether they want, versus do not want, a particular goal, but it might be more difficult for them to precisely know just *how* much they want that goal. In such a case it may be that the degree of people's unintentional, and immediately generated, positivity to words related to the goal ends up being a more accurate index of how much they, on average, pursue and want the goal. For example, the participants in the above research might have known that they cared about being egalitarian, but not been able to exactly pinpoint the degree of their commitment to the goal.

Secondly, automatic evaluations of goals should also better predict actual goal pursuit behavior than should explicit ratings of the strength of those motivations when the particular goal is accompanied by normative social or impression management pressures to explicitly respond in a certain way. For instance, there is considerable social pressure to espouse and endorse the goal of being egalitarian, and it may be that people's explicit commitment to this kind of goal is a poor reflection of how much they actually care about it. Again, in such a case it may be that people's spontaneous evaluation of words related to equality ends up being a better indication of how likely they are to pursue that goal in future circumstances.

When should automatic evaluations of goals out-predict automatic evaluations of more concrete stimuli? This question can essentially be translated into the question of when concrete versus abstract knowledge is likely to be most accessible in memory. There is a burgeoning literature on this topic, and researchers have identified a number of determinants, including temporal distance from an event being judged or evaluated (Trope & Liberman, 2003), the difficulty or familiarity of an action (Vallacher & Wegner, 1987), psychological distance (Trope & Liberman, 2003), spatial distance (Henderson, Fujita, Trope, & Liberman, 2006), and power (Smith & Trope, 2006).

For example, Vallacher and Wegner (1987) argued that when an action is familiar, and when both concrete and abstract knowledge related to the action exists in memory, the abstract knowledge is likely to be more accessible in memory than the concrete knowledge. Thus, when a person is climbing a tree and is asked what he or she is doing, the person is likely to say something about having fun (an abstract answer) rather than about holding onto tree limbs and branches (a concrete answer). In other words, the *why*, or high level, knowledge tends to be more accessible than the *how*, or low level, knowledge. In such cases, the evaluative information that is associated with the abstract knowledge (e.g., goals) should also be more accessible, and thus more influential and predictive, than the evaluative information associated with the concrete knowledge. In the experiments described above (Ferguson, 2007b) in which people's automatic evaluations of goals tended to be more predictive of their goal pursuit compared with their evaluations of relatively more concrete stimuli, it might have been the case that people were relatively familiar with those goal domains, and familiar with their strategies of

goal pursuit and self-regulation. Thus, their abstract knowledge (including knowledge about goals and values) may simply have been more accessible than their knowledge about the particular concrete items and objects relevant to the goal.

We now turn to a discussion of how automatic evaluations might be especially contingent on a person's goals and motivations.

MOTIVATION NATURE OF AUTOMATIC VERSUS EXPLICIT EVALUATIONS

Earlier in the chapter we discussed how automatic evaluations have been considered to be tied to motivations based on the speed with which they deliver important information to the perceiver. We argued that the motivational perspective of such evaluations can be considerably broadened in that automatic evaluations should actually reflect the content as well as intensity of the perceiver's current and chronic goals. However, how does this characteristic of automatic evaluations compare with the operation of explicit evaluations? That is, whereas automatic evaluations are clearly more functional than explicit evaluations at least in terms of the speed with which they are generated, are they ever more reflective of people's goals?

On the one hand, people's explicit evaluations can be clearly and directly reflective of what they want. People's explicit evaluations of the stimuli in their surroundings do fluctuate with their current goals regarding those stimuli. In fact, people's expressed desires for certain stimuli are often considered as a classic signature of a particular goal. When people (explicitly) express desire for food and drink, they are considered to have the goals of hunger and thirst, respectively (Cabanac, 1971). When people express their desire for meaningful relationships with others, they are understood as having the goal of belongingness. There is a long history in psychology of the tight connection between what people say they like and dislike, and what they say their goals and motivations are (Ajzen, 1991; Bandura, 1986; Cabanac, 1971; Deci & Ryan, 1985; Locke & Latham, 1990).

However, on the other hand, as mentioned earlier, there are reasons why what people say they want does not always match up well with what they actually do in terms of motivational behavior (approach versus avoiding). Because people might not be able to always accurately introspect on the intensity of their goals, perhaps especially across situations, there may be times when their automatic evaluation of a goal is more predictive of their goal-relevant behavior, as we have discussed. Furthermore, because people might be reluctant to express their true inclination toward some goal (either to others or to themselves), their automatic (unintentional) evaluations of goals might at times be more accurate indications of how they will act in actual goal-relevant situations (this should be especially true under time pressure or in complex, information-rich environments). Finally, people may simply be unwilling to exert the control necessary to act in line with their expressed preferences. There is considerable empirical support in the self-regulation literature for the dissociation between what people say they like and dislike, and what they in fact do (for reviews see Baumeister & Vohs, 2004; Carver & Scheier, 1981, 1998; Loewenstein, 1996). People's expressed preferences in domains of self-control and regulation are often at odds with how they actually behave.

Moreover, there is also evidence for the dissociation between expressed preferences and behavior in recent research on automatic evaluations and goals. In the work by Ferguson and Bargh (2004), in the first experiment that examined the effect of the achievement goal on automatic evaluations, participants were also asked to indicate their explicit evaluations toward the stimuli. The results showed that whereas the goal and timing conditions influenced participants' automatic evaluations as described earlier, they did not influence their explicit evaluations. This is some preliminary evidence that people may not always be able or perhaps willing to adjust their explicit evaluations toward their currently active goal, in line with our discussion here.

Another line of evidence suggesting a possible dissociation between people's explicit evaluations and their goal pursuit comes from the recent work on automatic evaluations of end-states (Ferguson, 2007b). In two experiments, people's explicit attitudes toward the abstract end-states did not reliably predict their behavior relevant to the end-state. In one experiment, their explicit attitude toward the goal of being thin did not predict their pursuit of this goal over the following week. In the other experiment, participants' explicit goal of equality did not predict their subtle expression of prejudice toward the elderly. In both cases, this disconnect may have emerged either because the participants were unable to introspect accurately on their desire for the goal, or were unwilling to do so. Future research is expected to continue to address the correspondence between people's goals, and their automatic versus explicit attitudes, but at this juncture we argue that automatic evaluations may be especially reflective of, and therefore predictive of, people's underlying motivations and goals.

CONCLUSIONS

In this chapter, we considered the motivational nature of automatic evaluations. We first considered the extent to which evaluations in general are closely tied to motivational behavior given the classic definitions of motivation and evaluations. We then reviewed recent research that examined questions relevant to this topic. Namely, we reviewed findings showing that a person's currently accessible, conscious goal influences how that person automatically evaluates the stimuli in her or his environment: people evaluate as positive those stimuli that can help them achieve the goal. Additionally, a goal does not have to reside in conscious awareness in order for it to influence automatic evaluations. Nonconsciously induced goals also can influence the automatic evaluation both of stimuli that can help the activated goal, as well as stimuli that can harm the activated goal. Recent findings also suggest that the effect of goals on automatic evaluations is functional in that it seems to emerge most strongly for those who are skilled at the particular goal domain. We also speculated that automatic evaluations might be more closely tied to goals and motivations than are explicit attitudes, and considered some new findings relevant to this matter. Overall, the evidence supports concluding in favor of a strong and direct influence of motivational states on how people naturally and nonconsciously evaluate the objects, people, events, and even abstract concepts and issues that make up their psychological environment.

REFERENCES

Aarts, H., Gollwitzer, P. M., & Hassin, R. (2004). Goal contagion: Perceiving is for pursuing. *Journal of Personality and Social Psychology, 87*, 23–37.

Ajzen, I. (1991). The theory of planned behavior. *Organizational Behavior and Human Decision Processes*, 50(2), 179–211.

Albarracín, D., Johnson, B. T., & Zanna, M. P. (2005). *The handbook of attitudes*. Mahwah, NJ: Erlbaum.

Allport, G. W. (1935). Attitudes. In C. Murchison (Ed.), *Handbook of social psychology* (pp. 798–844). Worcester, MA: Clark University Press.

Arnold, M. B. (1960). *Emotion and personality*. New York: Columbia University Press.

Asendorpf, J. B., Banse, R., Mücke, D. (2002). Double dissociation between implicit and explicit personality self-concept: the case of shy behavior. *Journal of Personality and Social Psychology, 83*, 380–393.

Bandura, A. (1986). *Social foundations of thought and action: A social cognitive theory*. Upper Saddle River, NJ: Prentice-Hall.

Bargh, J. A. (1989). Conditional automaticity: Varieties of automatic influence in social perception and cognition. In J. S. Ulerman & J. A. Bargh (Eds.), *Unintended thought* (pp. 3–51). New York: Guilford Press.

Bargh, J. A. (1994). The four horsemen of automaticity: Awareness, intention, efficiency, and control in social cognition. In R. J. Wyer & T. K. Srull (Eds.), *Handbook of social cognition* (pp. 1–40). Hillsdale, NJ: Lawrence Erlbaum Associates, Inc.

Bargh, J. A. (2007). *Social psychology and the unconscious: The automaticity of higher mental processes.* New York: Psychology Press.

Bargh, J. A., Gollwitzer, P. M., Lee-Chai, A., Barndollar, K., & Troetschel, R. (2001). The automated will: Nonconscious activation and pursuit of behavioral goals. *Journal of Personality and Social Psychology, 81,* 1014–1027.

Baumeister, R., & Leary, M. R. (1995). The need to belong: Desire for inter-personal attachments as a fundamental human motivation. *Psychological Bulletin, 117,* 497–529.

Baumeister, R. F., & Vohs, K. D. (Eds.). (2004). *Handbook of self-regulation: Research, theory, and applications.* New York: Guilford Press.

Blair, I. (2002). The malleability of automatic stereotypes and prejudice. *Personality and Social Psychological Review, 6,* 242–261.

Bogardus, E. (1931). *Fundamentals of social psychology* (2nd ed.). New York: Appleton-Century-Crofts.

Brendl, C. M., Markman, A. B., & Messner, C. (2005) Indirectly measuring evaluations of several attitude objects in relation to a neutral reference point. *Journal of Experimental Social Psychology, 41*(4), 346–368.

Brewer, M. B. (1991). The social self: On being the same and different at the same time. *Personality and Social Psychology Bulletin, 17,* 475–82.

Brown, J. D. (1998). *The self.* New York: McGraw-Hill.

Bruner, J. S. (1957). On perceptual readiness. *Psychological Review, 64*(2), 123–152.

Cabanac, M. (1971). Physiological role of pleasure. *Science, 173,* 1103–1107.

Carver, C. S., & Scheier, M. F. (1981). *Attention and self-regulation: A control-theory approach to human behavior.* New York: Springer.

Carver, C. S., & Scheier, M. F. (1998). *On the self-regulation of behavior.* New York: Cambridge University Press.

Castelli, L., Zogmaister, C., Smith, E. R., & Arcuri, L. (2004). On the automatic evaluation of social exemplars. *Journal of Personality and Social Psychology, 86,* 373–387.

Chaiken, S., Bargh, J. A. (1993). Occurrence versus moderation of the automatic attitude activation effect: Reply to Fazio. *Journal of Personality and Social Psychology, 64,* 759–765.

Chartrand, T. L., & Bargh, J. A. (1996). Automatic activation of impression formation and memorization goals: Nonconscious goal priming reproduces effects of explicit task instructions. *Journal of Personality and Social Psychology, 71,* 464–478.

Chen, M., & Bargh, J. A. (1999). Consequences of automatic evaluation: Immediate Behavioral predispositions to approach and avoid the stimulus. *Personality and Social Psychology Bulletin, 25,* 215–224.

Clore, G. L., & Schnall, S. (2005). The influence of affect on attitude. In D. Alabarracín, B. T. Johnson, & M. P. Zanna (Eds.), *The handbook of attitudes* (pp. 437–492). Mahwah, NJ: Erlbaum.

Corwin, G. (1921). Minor studies from the psychological laboratory of Cornell University. *American Journal of Psychology, 32,* 563–570.

Damasio, A. R. (1999). *The feeling of what happens: Body and emotion in the making of consciousness.* Orlando, FL: Harcourt.

Davidson, R., Scherer, K., & Goldsmith, H. (2003). *Handbook of affective sciences.* New York: Oxford University Press.

Deci, E. L., & Ryan, R. M. (1985). *Intrinsic motivation and self-determination in human behavior.* New York: Plenum.

De Houwer, J. (2003). The extrinsic affective Simon task. *Experimental Psychology, 50,* 77–85.

De Houwer, A. (2005). Early bilingual acquisition: Focus on morphosyntax and the separate development hypothesis. In J. Kroll & A. De Groot (Eds.), *The handbook of bilingualism* (pp. 30–48). Oxford, UK: Oxford University Press.

De Houwer, J., & Eelen, P. (1998). An affective variant of the Simon paradigm. *Cognition and Emotion, 8,* 45–61.

Devine, P. G. (1989). Stereotypes and prejudice: Their automatic and controlled components. *Journal of Personality and Social Psychology, 56,* 5–18.

Doob, L. W. (1947). The behavior of attitudes. *Psychological Review, 54,* 135–156.

Dovidio, J. F., Kawakami, K., & Gaertner, S. L. (2002). Implicit and explicit prejudice and interracial interaction. *Journal of Personality and Social Psychology, 82,* 62–68.

Dovidio, J. F., Mann, J., & Gaertner, S. L. (1989). Resistance to affirmative action: The implications of aversive racism. In F. A. Blanchard & F. J. Crosby (Eds.), *Affirmative action in perspective* (pp. 83–102). New York: SpringerVerlag.

Dovidio, J. F., Glick, P., & Rudman, L. (2005). *On the nature of prejudice: Fifty years after Allport.* Oxford, UK: Blackwell.

Dovidio, J. F., Kawakami, K., Johnson, C., Johnson, B., & Howard, A. (1997). On the nature of prejudice: Automatic and controlled processes. *Journal of Experimental Social Psychology, 33,* 510–540.

Duckworth, K. L., Bargh, J. A., Garcia, M., & Chaiken, S. (2002). The automatic evaluation of novel stimuli. *Psychological Science, 13,* 513–519.

Eagly, A. H., & Chaiken, S. (1993). *The psychology of attitudes.* Fort Worth, TX: Harcourt Brace Jovanovich College.

Epley, N., & Caruso, E. M. (2004). Egocentric ethics. *Social Justice Research, 17,* 171–187.

Egloff, B., & Schmukle, S. C. (2002). Predictive validity of an Implicit Association Test for assessing anxiety. *Journal of Personality and Social Psychology, 83,* 1441–1455.

Fazio, R. H. (1986). How do attitudes guide behavior? In R. M. Sorrentino & E. T. Higgins (Eds.), *Handbook of motivation and cognition: Foundations of social behavior* (pp. 204–243). New York: Guilford.

Fazio, R. H. (1989). On the power and functionality of attitudes: The role of attitude accessibility. In A. R. Pratkanis, S. J. Breckler, & A. G. Greenwald (Eds.), *Attitude structure and function* (pp. 153–179). Hillsdale, NJ: Erlbaum.

Fazio, R. H. (1990). Multiple processes by which attitudes guide behavior: The MODE model as an integrative framework. In M. P. Zanna (Ed.), *Advances in experimental social psychology* (Vol. 23, pp. 75–109). New York: Academic Press.

Fazio, R. H. (1993) Variability in the likelihood of automatic attitude activation: Data reanalysis and commentary on Bargh, Chaiken, Govender, and Pratto (1992). *Journal of Personality and Social Psychology*, 64, 753–758.

Fazio, R. H. (2001). On the automatic activation of associated evaluations: An overview. *Cognition and Emotion*, 14, 1–27.

Fazio, R. H., Chen, J., McDonel, E. C., & Sherman, S. J. (1982). Attitude accessibility, attitude–behavior consistency and the strength of the object-evaluation association. *Journal of Experimental Social Psychology*, 18, 339–357.

Fazio, R. H., & Olson, M. A. (2003). Implicit measures in social cognition research: Their meaning and use. *Annual Review of Psychology*, 54, 297–327.

Fazio, R. H., & Williams, C. J. (1986). Attitude accessibility as a moderator of the attitude-perception and attitude–behavior relations: An investigation of the 1984 presidential election. *Journal of Personality and Social Psychology*, 51, 505–514.

Fazio, R. H., Jackson, J. R., Dunton, B. C., & Williams, C. J. (1995). Variability in automatic activation as an unobtrusive measure of racial attitudes: A bona fide pipeline? *Journal of Personality and Social Psychology*, 69, 1013–1027.

Fazio, R. H., Sanbonmatsu, D. M., Powell, M. C., & Kardes, F. R. (1986). On the automatic activation of attitudes. *Journal of Personality and Social Psychology*, 50, 229–238.

Ferguson, M. J. (2007a). The automaticity of evaluation. Invited chapter in J. A. Bargh (Ed.), *Social psychology and the unconscious: The automaticity of higher mental processes* (pp. 219–264). Psychology Press.

Ferguson, M. J. (2007b). On the automatic evaluation of end-states. *Journal of Personality and Social Psychology, 92,* 596–611.

Ferguson, M. J. (2007c). On becoming ready to pursue a goal you don't know you have: Effects of nonconscious goals on evaluative readiness. Unpublished manuscript.

Ferguson, M. J., & Bargh, J. A. (2002). Sensitivity and flexibility: Exploring the knowledge function of automatic attitudes. In L. F. Barrett & P. Salovey (Eds.), *The wisdom in feeling: Psychological processes in emotional intelligence* (pp. 383–405). New York: Guilford Press.

Ferguson, M. J., & Bargh, J. A. (2004). Liking is for doing: Effects of goal pursuit on automatic evaluation. *Journal of Personality and Social Psychology*, 88, 557–572.

Fiske, S. T. (1982). Schema-triggered affect: Applications to social perception. In M. S. Clark & S. T. Fiske (Eds.), *Affect and cognition: The 17th annual Carnegie Symposium on cognition* (pp. 55–78). Hillsdale, NJ: Erlbaum.

Fitzsimons, G. M., & Bargh, J. A. (2003). Thinking of you: Nonconscious pursuit of interpersonal goals associated with relationship partners. *Journal of Personality and Social Psychology*, 84(1), 148–163.

Fishbach, A., Friedman, R., & Kruglanski, A. W. (2003). Leading us not unto temptation: Momentary allurements elicit automatic goal activation. *Journal of Personality and Social Psychology*, 84, 296–309.

Forgas, J. (2003). Affective influences on attitudes and judgments. In R. Davidson, K. Scherer, & H. Goldsmith (Eds.), *Handbook of affective sciences* (pp. 596–618). New York: Oxford University Press.

Frijda, N. (1986). *The Emotions.* Cambridge, MA: University Press.

Greenwald, A. G., & Banaji, M. R. (1995). Implicit social cognition: Attitudes, self-esteem, and stereotypes. *Psychological Review*, 102, 4–27.

Greenwald, A. G., Banaji, M. R., Rudman, L. A., Farnham, S. D., Nosek, B. A., & Mellott, D. S. (2002). A unified theory of implicit attitudes, stereotypes, self-esteem, and self-concept. *Psychological Review, 109,* 3–25.

Greenwald, A. G., & Farnham, S. D. (2000). Using the Implicit Association Test to measure self-esteem and self-concept. *Journal of Personality and Social Psychology*, 79, 1022–1038.

Greenwald, A. G., Klinger, M. R., & Liu, T. J. (1989). Unconscious processing of dichoptically masked words. *Memory and Cognition*, 17, 35–47.

Greenwald, A. G., McGhee, D. E., & Schwarz, J. L. K. (1998). Measuring individual differences in implicit cognition: The Implicit Association Test. *Journal of Personality and Social Psychology*, 74, 1464–1480.

Greenwald, A. G., Banaji, M. R., Rudman, L. A., Farnham, S. D., Nosek, B. A., Mellott, D. S. (2002). A unified theory of implicit attitudes, stereotypes, self-esteem, and self-concept. *Psychological Review*, 109, 3–25.

Haidt, J. (2001). The emotional dog and its rational tail: A social intuitionist approach to moral judgment. *Psychological Review*, 108, 814–834.

Haidt, J. (2003). The moral emotions. In R. J. Davidson, K. R. Scherer, & H. H. Goldsmith (Eds.), *Handbook of affective sciences* (pp. 852–870). Oxford: Oxford University Press.

Henderson, M., Fujita, K., Trope, Y., & Liberman, N. (2006). Transcending the "here:" The effect of spatial distance on social judgment. *Journal of Personality and Social Psychology*, 91(5), 845–856.

Hermans, D., Crombez, G., & Eelen, P. (2000). Automatic attitude activation and efficiency: The fourth horseman of automaticity. *Psychologica Belgica*, 40, 3–22.

Higgins, E. T. (1996). Knowledge activation: Accessibility, applicability, and salience. In E. T. Higgins & A. W. Kruglanski (Eds.), *Social psychology: Handbook of basic principles* (pp. 133–168). New York: Guilford Press.

Higgins, E. T. & Brendl, C. M. (1996). Principles of judging valence: What makes events positive or negative? In M. P. Zanna (Ed.), *Advances in experimental social psychology* (Vol. 28, pp. 95–160). San Diego, CA: Academic Press.

Himmelfarb, S. (1993). The measurement of attitudes. In A. H. Eagly, & S. Chaiken (Eds.), *The psychology of attitudes* (pp. 23–84). Fort Worth, TX: Harcourt Brace Jovanovich College.

Hofmann, W., Gawronski, B., Gschwendner, T., Le, H., & Schmitt, M. (2005). A meta-analysis on the correlation between the Implicit Association Test and explicit self-report measures. *Personality and Social Psychology Bulletin, 31*(10), 1369–1385.

Jones, E. E., & Sigall, H. (1971). The bogus pipeline: A new paradigm for measuring affect and attitude. *Psychological Bulletin, 76*, 349–364.

Jordan, C. H., Spencer, S. J., & Zanna, M. P. (2003). "I love me … I love me not:" Implicit self-esteem, explicit self-esteem, and defensiveness. In S. J. Spencer, S. Fein, M. P. Zanna, & J. M. Olson (Eds.), *Motivated social perception: The Ontario Symposium* (Vol. 9, pp. 117–145). Mahwah, NJ: Lawrence Erlbaum Associates.

Katz, I., & Hass, R. G. (1988). Racial ambivalence and American value conflict: Correlational and priming studies of dual cognitive structures. *Journal of Personality and Social Psychology, 55*, 893–905.

Kawakami, K., & Dovidio, J. F. (2001). Implicit stereotyping: How reliable is it? *Personality and Social Psychology Bulletin, 27*, 212–225.

Klauer, K. C., & Musch, J. (2003). Affective priming: Findings and theories. In J. Musch & K. C. Klauer (Eds.), *The psychology of evaluation: Affective processes in cognition and emotion* (pp. 7–49). Mahwah, NJ: Lawrence Erlbaum.

Klauer, K. C., & Stern, E. (1992). How evaluations guide memory-based judgments: A two-process model. *Journal of Experimental Social Psychology, 28*, 186–206.

Klinger, M. R., Burton, P. C., & Pitts, G. S. (2000). Mechanisms of unconscious priming: I. Response competition, not spreading activation. *Journal of Experimental Psychology: Learning, Memory, and Cognition, 26*, 441–455.

Koole, S. K., Dijksterhuis, A., & van Knippenberg, A. (2001). What's in a name: Implicit self-esteem. *Journal of Personality and Social Psychology, 80*, 614–627.

Krosnick, J. A., Judd, C. M., & Wittenbrink, B. (2005). The measurement of attitudes. In D. Albarracín, B. T. Johnson, & M. P. Zanna (Eds.), *The handbook of attitudes* (pp. 21–76). Mahwah, NJ: Erlbaum.

Lambert, A. J., Payne, B. K., Ramsey, S., & Shaffer, L. M. (2005). On the predictive validity of implicit attitude measures: The moderating effect of perceived group variability. *Journal of Experimental Social Psychology, 41*, 114–128.

Lang, P. J. (1984). Cognition in emotion: Concept and action. In C. Izard, J. Kagan, & R. Zajonc (Eds.), *Emotion, Cognition and Behavior* (pp. 196–226). New York: Cambridge University Press.

Lang, P. J., Bradley, M. M., & Cuthbert, B. N. (1990). Emotion, attention, and the startle reflex. *Psychological Review, 97*, 377–395.

Lazarus, R. S. (1991). Progress on a cognitive-motivational-relational theory of emotion. *American Psychologist, 46*, 819–834.

LeDoux, J. (1996). *The emotional brain*. New York: Touchstone.

Levy, B. R., & Schlesinger, M. J. (2005). When self-interest and age sterotypes collide: elders opposing increased funds for programs benefiting themselves. *Journal of Aging & Social Policy, 17*(2), 25–39.

Lewin, K. (1926). Vorsatz, Wille, und Bedürfnis [Intention, will, and need]. *Psychologische Forschung, 7*, 330–385.

Lewin, K. (1935). *A dynamic theory of personality*. New York: McGraw-Hill.

Locke, E. A., & Latham, G. P. (1990). *A theory of goal setting and task performance*. Englewood Cliffs, NJ: Prentice Hall.

Loewenstein, G. (1996). Out of control: Visceral influences on behavior. *Organizational Behavior and Human Decision Processes, 65*(3), 272–292.

Logan, G. D. (1980). Attention and automaticity in Stroop and priming tasks: Theory and data. *Cognitive Psychology, 12*, 523–553.

Marsh, K. L., Johnson, B. T., & Scott-Sheldon, L. A. J. (2001). Heart versus reason in condom use: Implicit versus explicit attitudinal predictors of sexual behavior. *Zeitschrift für Experimentelle Psychologie, 48*, 161–175.

McConahay, J. B. (1983). Modern racism and modern discrimination: The effects of race, racial attitudes, and context on simulated hiring decisions. *Personality and Social Psychology Bulletin, 9*, 551–558.

McConahay, J. (1986). Modern racism, ambivalence, and the Modern Racism scale. In J. Dovidio (Ed.), *Prejudice, discrimination, and racism* (pp. 91–125). San Diego, CA: Academic Press.

McConnell, A. R., & Leibold, J. M. (2001). Relations among the Implicit Association Test, discriminatory behavior, and explicit measures of racial attitudes. *Journal of Experimental Social Psychology, 37*, 435–442.

McGuire, W. J. (1969). The nature of attitudes and attitude change. In G. Lindzey & E. Aronson (Eds.), *Handbook of social psychology* (2nd ed., Vol. 3, pp. 136–314). Reading, MA: Addison-Wesley.

McGuire, W. J. (1985). Attitudes and attitude change. In G. Lindzey & E. Aronson (Eds.), *Handbook of social psychology* (3rd ed., Vol. 2, pp. 233–346). New York: Random House.

Meyer, D. E., & Schvaneveldt, R. W. (1971). Facilitation in recognizing pairs of words: Evidence of a dependence between retrieval operations. *Journal of Experimental Psychology, 90*, 227–234.

Moors, A., & De Houwer, J. (2006). Automaticity: A theoretical and conceptual analysis. *Psychological Bulletin, 132*(2), 297–326.

Morsella, E. (2005). The function of phenomenal states: Supramodular interaction theory. *Psychological Review, 112*(4), 1000–1021.

Mowrer, O. H. (1960). *Learning theory and behavior*. New York: Wiley.

Murphy, S. T., & Zajonc, R. B. (1993). Affect, cognition, and awareness: Affective priming with optimal and suboptimal stimulus exposures. *Journal of Personality and Social Psychology, 64*, 723–739.

Musch, J., & Klauer, K. C. (2003). *The psychology of evaluation: Affective processes in cognition and emotion*. Mahwah, NJ: Lawrence Erlbaum.

Neely, J. H. (1976). Semantic priming and retrieval from lexical memory: Evidence for faciliatory and inhibitory processes. *Memory and Cognition*, *4*, 648–654.

Neely, J. H. (1977). Semantic priming and retrieval from lexical memory: Roles of inhibitionless spreading activation and limited-capacity attention. *Journal of Experimental Psychology: General*, *106*, 225–254.

Niedenthal, P. M. (1990). Implicit perception of affective information. *Journal of Experimental Social Psychology*, *26*, 505–527.

Nosek, B. A. (2005). Moderators of the relationship between implicit and explicit evaluation. *Journal of Experimental Psychology: General*, *134*, 565–584.

Nosek, B. A., & Banaji, M. R. (2001). The go/no-go association task. *Social Cognition*, *19*(6), 625–666.

Nosek, B. A., Banaji, M. R., & Greenwald, A. G. (2002). Math = Male, Me = Female, therefore Math = / = me. *Journal of Personality and Social Psychology*, *83*, 44–59.

Öhman, A. (1986). Face the beast and fear the face: Animal and social fears as prototypes for evolutionary analysis of emotion. *Psychophysiology*, *23*, 123–145.

Osgood, C. E. (1953). *Method and theory in experimental psychology*. New York: Oxford University Press.

Osgood, C. E., Suci, G. J., & Tannenbaum, P. H. (1957). *The measurement of meaning*. Chicago: University of Illinois Press.

Oettingen, G., Grant, H., Smith, P. K., Skinner, M., & Gollwitzer, P. M. (2006). Nonconscious goal pursuit: Acting in an explanatory vacuum. *Journal of Experimental Social Psychology, 42,* 668–675.

Payne, B. K., Cheng, C. M., Govorun, O., & Stewart, B. (2005). An inkblot for attitudes: Affect misattribution as implicit measurement. *Journal of Personality and Social Psychology*, *89*, 277–293.

Pratkanis, A. R., Breckler, S. J., & Greenwald, A. G. (1989). *Attitude structure and function*. New Jersey: Erlbaum.

Petty, R. E., & Krosnick, J. A. (1995). *Attitude Strength: Antecedents and Consequences*. Mahway, NJ: Erlbaum.

Posner, M. I., & Snyder, C. R. R. (1975). Attention and cognitive control. In R. L. Solso (Ed.), *Information processing and cognition: The Loyola symposium* (pp. 55–85). Hillsdale, NJ: Erlbaum.

Roediger, H. L. (1990). Implicit memory: Retention without remembering. *American Psychologist*, *45*(9), 1043–1056.

Rosenberg, M. (1965). *Society and the adolescent self-image*. Princeton University Press: Princeton, NJ.

Roskos-Ewoldsen, D. R., & Fazio, R. H. (1992). On the orienting value of attitudes: Attitude accessibility as a determinant of an object's attraction of visual attention. *Journal of Personality and Social Psychology*, *63*, 198–211.

Sarnoff, I. (1960). Psychoanalytic theory and social attitudes. *Public Opinion Quarterly*, *24*, 251–279.

Sears, D. O. (1988). Symbolic racism. In P. A. Katz & D. A. Taylor (Eds.), *Eliminating racism:Profiles in controversy* (pp. 53–84). New York: Plenum.

Schwarz, N., & Bohner, G. (2001). The construction of attitudes. In A. Tesser & N. Schwarz (Eds.), *Blackwell handbook of social psychology: Intraindividual processes* (Vol. 1, pp. 436–457). Oxford, UK: Blackwell.

Shah, J. (2003). The motivational looking glass: How significant others implicitly affect goal appraisals. *Journal of Personality and Social Psychology*, *85*(3), 424–439.

Shah, J. Y., Friedman, R., & Kruglanski, A. W. (2002). Forgetting all else: On the antecedents and consequences of goal shielding. *Journal of Personality & Social Psychology, 83*(6), 1261–1280.

Shah, J. Y., Kruglanski, A. W., & Friedman, R. (2002). A goal systems approach to self-regulation. In M.P. Zanna, J. M. Olson, & C. Seligman (Eds.), *The Ontario symposium on personality and social psychology* (pp. 247–276). Mahwah, NJ: Erlbaum.

Sherman, S. J., Presson, C. C., Chassin, L., Rose, J. S., & Koch, K. (2003). Implicit and explicit attitudes toward cigarette smoking: The effects of context and motivation. *Journal of Social and Clinical Psychology*, *22*, 13–39.

Shiffrin, R. M., & Schneider, W. (1977). Controlled and automatic human information processing. *Psychological Review*, *84*, 127–190.

Smith, P. K., & Trope, Y. (2006). You focus on the forest when you're in charge of the trees: Power priming and abstract information processing. *Journal of Personality and Social Psychology*, *90*(4), 578–596.

Smith, M. B., Bruner, J. S., & White, R. W. (1956). *Opinions and personality*. New York: Wiley.

Squire, L. R., & Kandel, E. R. (1999). *Memory: From mind to molecules*. New York: W.H. Freeman & Co.

Srull, T. K., & Wyer, R. S. (1979). The role of category accessibility in the interpretation of information about persons: Some determinants and implications. *Journal of Personality and Social Psychology*, *37*(10), 1600–1672.

Swim, J. K., Aiken, K. J., Hall, W. S., & Hunter, B. A. (1995). Sexism and racism: Old-fashioned and modern prejudices. *Journal of Personality and Social Psychology*, *68*, 199–214.

Tesser, A., & Martin, L. (1996). The psychology of evaluation. In E. T. Higgins, & A. W. Kruglanski (Eds), *Social psychology: Handbook of basic principles* (pp. 400–432). New York: Guilford Press.

Thurstone, L. L. (1927). Psychological analysis. *American Journal of Psychology*, *38*, 368–398.

Thurstone, L. L. (1931). Measurement of social attitudes. *Journal of Abnormal and Social Psychology*, *26*, 249–269.

Trope, Y., & Liberman, N. (2003). Temporal construal. *Psychological Review*, *110*(3), 403–421.

Tulving, E., & Craik, F. I. M. (2000). *Handbook of memory*. Oxford, UK: Oxford University Press.

Vallacher, R. R., & Wegner, D. M. (1987). What do people think they're doing? Action identification and human behavior. *Psychological Review*, *94*, 3–15.

von Hippel, W., Sekaquaptewa, D., & Vargas, P. (1997). The Linguistic Intergroup Bias as an implicit indicator of prejudice. *Journal of Experimental Social Psychology*, *33*, 490–509.

Wegner, D. M., Vallacher, R. R., Kiersted, G., & Dizadji, D. (1986). Action identification in the emergence of social behavior. *Social Cognition*, *4*, 18–38.

Wentura, D. (1999). Activation and inhibition of affective information: Evidence for negative priming in the evaluation task. *Cognition and Emotion, 13*, 65–91.

Wentura, D. (2000). Dissociative affective and associative priming effects in the lexical decision task: *Yes* versus *no* responses to word targets reveal evaluative judgmental tendencies. *Journal of Experimental Psychology: Learning, Memory, and Cognition, 26,* 456–469.

Wicklund, R. A., & Gollwitzer, P. M. (1982). *Symbolic self-completion*. Hillsdale, NJ: Erlbaum.

Wilson, T. D., Lindsey, S., & Schooler, T. Y. (2000). A model of dual attitudes. *Psychological Review, 107*, 101–126.

Winkielman, P., Berridge, K. C., & Wilbarger, J. L. (2005). Unconscious affective reactions to masked happy versus angry faces influence consumption behavior and judgments of value. *Personality and Social Psychology Bulletin, 31*(1), 121–135.

Wittenbrink, B., Judd, C. M., & Park, B. (1997). Evidence for racial prejudice at the implicit level and its relationship with questionnaire measures. *Journal of Personality and Social Psychology, 72*, 262–274.

Wittenbrink, B., Judd, C. M., & Park, B. (2001). Spontaneous prejudice in context: Variability in automatically activated attitudes. *Journal of Personality and Social Psychology, 81*, 815–827.

Young, P. T. (1959). The role of affective processes in learning and motivation. *Psychological Review, 66*, 104–125.

Zajonc, R. B. (1980). Feeling and thinking. Preferences need no inferences. *American Psychologist, 35*, 151–175.

Zajonc, R. B. (2000). Feeling and thinking: Closing the debate over the independence of affect. In J. P. Forgas (Ed.), Feeling and thinking: The role of affect in social cognition (pp. 31–58). Cambridge, UK: Cambridge University Press.

Structure of Evaluation

18 The Functional Neuroarchitecture of Evaluative Processes

Gary G. Berntson and John T. Cacioppo

CONTENTS

FUNCTIONAL NEUROARCHITECTURE OF EVALUATIVE PROCESSES

A fundamental computation performed by humans is the differentiation between hostile and hospitable stimuli. Survival depends on the ability to perform this computation and adapt one's behavior accordingly. Evaluative processes refer to the operations supporting the computation, or set of computations, that are involved in the differentiation of hostile from hospitable stimuli. In this chapter, we review evidence that evaluative processes are fundamental to survival, are universal in humans and other animals, are manifest across the span of ontogeny as well as phylogeny, and represent multifarious computational operations, which differ predictably across levels of the neuraxis.

Traditionally in psychology, this computation was conceived as a unitary operation or process, with the outcome including a positioning of the stimulus at a point along the dimension of valence (Osgood, Suci, & Tannenbaum,

1957). Allport (1935) went so far as to ascribe to this computation a mental representation, a neural locus, and a behavioral predisposition: "a mental and neural state of readiness, organized through experience, exerting a directive or dynamic influence upon the individual's response to all objects and situations with which it is related." This was said to promote acceptance of, approval of, support of, or approach toward hospitable stimuli, and that promote rejection of, disapproval of, opposition to, or withdrawal from hostile stimuli. Allport (1967) and Osgood et al. (1957) wrote about what today would fall under the rubric of explicit evaluative processes—computations that are amenable to self-awareness and self-report. In recent years, notions about the computations of stimulus hospitability or hostility have been expanded to include implicit as well as explicit evaluative processes (Greenwald et al., 2002). Implicit evaluative processes represent the positioning of the stimulus along the valence dimension that, although reliably measurable, is not easily amenable to self-awareness, self-report, or self-control. Implicit evaluative processes can also differ in the specific information that is activated, but they too are generally conceived as instantiated in a unitary computation in which the positioning of the stimulus along a valence dimension accords with the probability distribution of what the same or similar stimuli have turned out to be in the past history of the species and the individual.

Evaluative processes are considerably more diverse than suggested by the simple implicit or explicit dichotomy. Evaluative processes encompass the broad range of operations and mechanisms that allow an organism to appraise the adaptive significance of stimuli or contexts, and to respond accordingly. Because of their critical survival functions, primitive (implicit) evaluative mechanisms have been highly conserved through evolution and more sophisticated; higher-level (explicit) evaluative processes have been hierarchically overlaid on these primitive substrates through evolution (Jackson, 1884/1958; MacLean, 1977, 1985). The influential 19th century neurologist, Jackson, noted that this entails the elaboration and "re-representation" of functions across levels of the neuraxis—from lower spinal systems to higher cortical association areas. This is echoed in MacLean's concept of the *triune brain* and its reptilian, paleomammalian, and neomammalian components. This neuroarchitectural hierarchy underlies and constrains evaluative processes. The present chapter will consider the structural and functional organization of evaluative systems and the psychological and behavioral implications of the multiple levels of function in evaluative mechanisms.

The terms *level* and *multilevel* have been used to distinguish between the levels of organization (e.g., the hierarchical organization in neural systems) as well as the levels of analysis or explanation (e.g., molecular, cellular, behavioral, social) at which a phenomenon can be explicated (Berntson & Cacioppo, 2004; Cacioppo & Tassinary, 1990; Cacioppo, Berntson, Sheridan, & McClintock, 2000; Larson et al., in press). These are not orthogonal dimensions, however, and multilevel approaches often encompass both. The present chapter will focus on the multilevel organization in evaluative systems, across levels of analysis.

LEVELS OF ORGANIZATION IN THE NERVOUS SYSTEM

In his essay "Evolution and dissolution of the nervous system," Jackson, emphasized the multilevel structure of

brain organization and function (Jackson, 1884/1958). In contrast to the view that the evolutionary emergence of higher levels of the neuraxis come to replace or bypass lower-level organizations and functions, Jackson noted that evolution results in a progressive neurological layering, or multilevel re-representation of functions. The higher-level functional re-representations are characterized by elaborated networks with progressively greater flexibility and sophistication. But rather than replacing lower mechanisms, re-representative systems extensively interact with and depend upon lower substrates in a hierarchical-like fashion.

NEURAL HIERARCHIES

Functional hierarchies are ubiquitous in neural systems. An example can be found in motor systems, which control somatic muscles of skeletal movement. As documented by early investigators, such as Sherrington (1906), basic somatomotor control is effected at the level of the spinal cord, with spinal reflexes representing the lowest central level in somatomotor control systems. Spinal reflex circuits are relatively simple and may be comprised of a single central synapse. The monosynaptic stretch reflex, exemplified by the knee jerk reflex to the physician's rubber mallet, is one example. This reflex entails an afferent somatosensory link arising from muscle stretch receptors that synapse directly on the lower motor neurons controlling that muscle. This simple circuit (Figure 18.1) provides for a reflexive

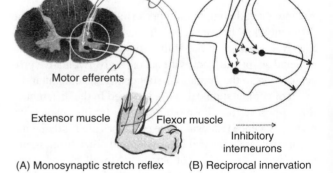

FIGURE 18.1 (A) Stretch reflex. Basic parallel circuits of the flexor and extensor stretch reflex. (B) Reciprocal innervation, an example of Sherrington's alliance of reflexes. Dotted lines represent inhibitory interneurons which achieve a level of reciprocal integration between flexor and extensor motor neuron pools.

contraction of the stretched muscle, which tends to compensate for the perturbing stretch. Stretch reflexes exist in all major classes of somatic muscles, including flexor muscles (which generally adduct or bring limbs toward the body) and extensor muscles (which generally abduct, or draw limbs away from the center of mass).

Opponent flexor (e.g., biceps) and extensor (e.g., triceps) reflexes antagonize one another and promote opposite outcomes for the limb (flexion and extension, respectively). The basic neural circuits of these reflexes are independent and organized in parallel, and they have limited inputs and outputs, allowing for rapid, efficient processing (Sherrington, 1906). The cost of this efficiency, however, is that lower-level systems have limited integrative capacity. Moreover, they can be in conflict. Simultaneous stretch of both the flexor and extensor muscle may lead to a reflexive increase in muscle tension in both muscles, but because they are opposed in their actions, there may be no resultant limb movement.

Greater levels of integration in motor systems are achieved by hierarchical circuits that promote coordination among the basic spinal reflexes—what Sherrington (1906) referred to as the *alliance of reflexes*. In our flexor and extensor example, this entails a collateral projection of the stretch receptor afferents onto inhibitory interneuron circuit elements, which in turn project to and inhibit the motor neuron for the opposing muscle. Stretching the flexor muscle, for example, results not only in activation of the flexor motor neurons (stretch reflex), but also inhibition of the opposing motor neurons via the inhibitory pathway illustrated in Figure 18.1B. This exemplifies a general principle of neural organization articulated by Sherrington (1906), the principle of *reciprocal innervation*, which stipulates that neural systems promote specific outcomes by activating the mechanisms for the target response while at the same time inhibiting opposing responses.

Consider the fate of a hungry donkey sitting equidistant between two equivalent piles of hay to which it was equally attracted. Would the donkey starve, being unable to select from these equally attractive goals? Lore has it that the philosopher Burdan contemplated this issue (sometime referred to as the parable of *Burdan's ass*). Burdan's contemplation notwithstanding, the answer is no. This type of approach–approach conflict is readily resolved (Miller, 1951), as noise or random variations in orientation or the approach disposition toward one of the choices would be associated with inhibition of the opposing disposition, in accord with the principle of reciprocal innervation. This principle of organization is not limited to the motor domain, but manifests broadly in psychological and cognitive processes, including evaluative processes and conflicts. We will return to these issues below.

Sherrington's alliance of reflexes does not stop with reciprocal innervation. As hierarchical levels are layered on the motor control system, progressively higher levels receive a wider array of inputs, have greater circuit complexity and computation capacity, and can achieve a broader and more flexible range of outputs. At the highest levels, beyond the primary motor cortex, cerebral systems must process a tremendous amount of sensory information, integrate this information with associative networks, emotional and motivational substrates, and expectancies, in the contexts of strategic goals and tactical plans. This requirement for enhanced information processing can impose a processing bottleneck that necessitates a slower, more serial mode of processing and selective attentional mechanisms (Shiffrin & Schneider, 1984). Although it is these highest level systems that confer the greatest cognitive and behavioral capacity, they do not operate in isolation but depend upon and interact with lower levels in the hierarchy.

NEURAL HETERARCHIES

Hierarchical dimensions of central nervous system organization can be demonstrated anatomically as well as functionally (Berntson, Boysen, & Cacioppo, 1993). The simple hierarchy depicted in Figure 18.2, however, belies the true complexity of neurobehavioral substrates, as long ascending and descending pathways can bypass intermediate levels of hierarchical organization and interconnect across widely separated neural levels. Cortical motor neurons project not only to intermediate-level somatomotor networks, but also directly onto spinal motor neurons through long descending pathways (Edgley et al., 1997; Porter, 1987). The long ascending and descending pathways in neural hierarchies, together with the existence of lateral interactions among elements (such as those that underlie reciprocal innervation), yield what has been termed a heterarchical organization (Berntson et al., 1993; Berntson & Cacioppo, 2007). The outputs of a strict hierarchical system are coherent, as all levels are linked by intermediate regulatory levels, and all outputs are by final common pathways. In a heterarchical organization, however, higher levels can directly access output mechanisms independent of intermediate levels. This organizational feature allows for concurrent expression of multiple re-representative systems, which can increase

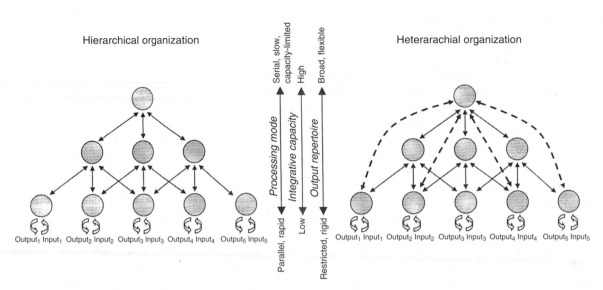

FIGURE 18.2 Hierarchical and heterarchical organizations. A heterarchy differs from a hierarchy in the existence of long ascending and descending pathways that span intermediate levels. Properties of the levels in both classes of organizations lie along the illustrated continua of *processing mode, integrative capacity, and output repertoire.* Heterarchical organizations, however, have greater integrative capacity and output flexibility as the long ascending and descending projections provide inputs and outputs that are not constrained by intermediate levels.

behavioral complexity but can also lead to functional conflicts. By volitionally stiffening the leg, for example, higher-level systems can mask the stretch reflex and usurp control of motor neuron pools.

RE-REPRESENTATION AND ORGANIZATION OF EVALUATIVE SUBSTRATES

LOWER LEVELS AND PRE-MOTIVATIONAL FUNCTIONS

Paralleling the pattern for somatic motor control, adaptive and protective reflexes and mechanisms are organized at all levels of the neuraxis. The pain withdrawal reflex, for example, is organized at the level of the spinal cord and can be seen even after spinal transections that isolate the cord from higher brain systems. Pain withdrawal reflexes are protective reactions that arise from somatosensory afferents, carrying nociceptive signals, which anatomically link to flexor neuron pools by a multisynaptic spinal pathway. Through this spinal reflex circuit, noxious stimuli yield a protective flexor withdrawal response. Likely because of their adaptive value, pain withdrawal reflexes are among the earliest to develop and the most resistant to disruption. Although pain withdrawal reflexes at the level of the cord may not require the invocation of a construct of emotion or affect, they represent an important low level evaluative mechanism for escape from noxious stimuli. Moreover, despite their neural simplicity, these circuits can show operant conditioning of

escape which can support not only escape from, but active *avoidance* of, pain stimuli (Grau et al., 2006).

In contrast to the primitive avoidance system associated with flexor reflexes, separate mechanisms exist at the level of the cord for opposing extensor responses which promote engagement with the environmental stimuli. Reflexes such as the extensor reflex in response to nonpainful cutaneous stimulation of the palm or the sole of the foot contribute to postural, locomotory, and grasping responses that serve to engage the organism with the environment.

As considered above, flexor and extensor reflexes are organized largely in parallel, as they control distinct motor neuron pools for opposing muscles. Nevertheless, they do interact. These lower reflex substrates are integrated by higher-level circuits, such as those that implement reciprocal innervation, which tends to reduce concurrent activation. They are also impacted by even higher systems that contribute to volitional actions and confer a greater degree of flexibility and control over flexor and extensor motor neuron pools and lower reflex substrates. Thus, we can volitionally contract both flexor and extensor muscles (e.g., in stiffening the arm) which can overcome the lower-level reciprocal innervation, and we are able to override or suppress flexor pain withdrawal reflexes (e.g., to remove a sliver from the finger). Beyond these neural interactions, there are simple mechanical constraints on the expression of activation of flexor and extensor muscles. For example, the biceps and the triceps muscles control the same joint, and yield opposite flexion and extension movements of the forearm. Flexion and extension movements are incompatible and cannot be expressed concurrently. Consequently, one might conceptualize the flexor–extensor movements along a bipolar continuum from maximal flexion to maximal extension. From a strictly behavioral standpoint, this may provide an accurate description of flexor and extensor movements, but it belies the fundamentally bivariate (although interacting) neural organizations that regulate flexor and extensor muscles, and it is inadequate in terms of mapping unequivocally onto underlying mechanisms.

INTERMEDIATE LEVELS: INTAKE AND REJECTION RESPONSES AND TASTE HEDONICS

Systems for evaluative processes and approach–avoidance reactions are further elaborated at the level of the brainstem. Decerebrate organisms, with no neural tissue above the level of the brainstem, show highly organized escape, avoidance, and defensive behaviors in response to aversive stimuli as well as approach/ingestive responses to palatable tastes (Berntson et al., 1993; Berntson & Micco, 1976). As was the case for flexor and extensor reflexes of the spinal cord, the basic brainstem substrates for approach and avoidance appear to be distinct and at least partially independent (Berntson et al.; Berridge & Grill, 1984; Steiner, Glaser, Hawilo, & Berridge, 2001).

An illustration of the organization of brainstem approach and avoidance systems comes from work on taste hedonics and intake and rejection responses in surgically decerebrated animals and tragic failures of neurodevelopmental cell migration in human anencephalic and hydranencephalic infants (for reviews see Berridge, 2004; Steiner et al., 2001). Both humans and other animals display stereotyped orofacial responses reflecting positive affective expression and ingestion (e.g., smiling, licking, swallowing) to palatable sweet solutions, and aversive-like facial expressions and ejection responses (e.g., gaping, tongue protrusion) to bitter or other unpalatable tastes. These responses emerge early in ontogeny and can be seen in both intact organisms and decerebrates, suggesting that these positive and negative hedonic reactions to gustatory stimuli reflect opposing patterns of approach and avoidance that are organized at brainstem levels and are highly conserved across ontogeny and phylogeny.

The behavioral manifestations of these opposing intake and rejection responses might be interpreted to reflect a bipolar hedonic continuum extending from highly positive or ingestion, through neutral, and to highly negative or rejection. Additional findings, however, suggest that the gustatory approach and withdrawal systems are at least partially independent, and do not converge on a single hedonic integrator (Berridge & Grill, 1984). Although intake and rejection responses tend to oppose each other, they are not entirely incompatible. Increasing the concentration of a bitter adulterant in an otherwise positive sucrose solution, for example, can increase the probability of rejection responses without decreasing the probability of intake responses. Moreover, increasing the concentration of both sweet and bitter tastes was found to increase both intake and rejection responses (Berridge & Grill, 1984). Positive and negative responses in such cases may co-occur and display a rapid alternation. Consequently, equal taste preference, as measured by behavioral consumption, does not necessarily imply an equivalent hedonic state. This is not to suggest that there is no interaction between these approach and avoidance responses, there probably is, but it is clear that mixing positive and negative hedonic stimuli does not yield a middling hedonic state of indifference. Rather, gustatory approach and avoidance reactions appear to reflect, at least in part, the separate activations of positive and negative hedonic dimensions (Berridge & Grill, 1984). A single overt behavioral measure of intake and rejection, such as the quantity of consumption, might be adequately described along a continuum from total rejection to total consumption. As was the case with flexor and extensor responses, however, this bipolar description again belies the underlying bivariate structure of the basic hedonic mechanisms.

HIGHER NEURAL LEVELS AND THE ELABORATION OF EVALUATIVE PROCESSES

The evaluative processes of brainstem origin are manifestations of what MacLean termed the reptilian brain, which was considered the evolutionarily conserved repository of primitive survival mechanisms associated with fight or flight (MacLean, 1985). It is not until the development of the paleomammalian brain (limbic system and archicortex) and the neomammalian brain (neocortex) that we see the full elaboration of evaluative processes (MacLean, 1985). As we have considered above, systems of the reptilian brain implement basic evaluative reactions, such as those associated with gustatory hedonics. The behavior of decerebrates, however, is largely reactive, stimulus-bound, and related to simple nonrelational dimensions of the environment.

Although decerebrates will ingest palatable foods, they do not show typical goal seeking in the absence of food stimuli (Berntson et al., 1993; Berntson & Micco, 1976). They could be likened to be prisoners of the momentary environmental context. Although they can display associative learning and may develop dispositions based on prior experience, the manifestation of these dispositions again is largely controlled by the immediate external context. The behavioral repertoire of the decerebrate is rigid and stereotyped, lacking the variability, flexibility, and spontaneity of intact organisms. The reptilian brain is sensitive to hedonics and responds to rewards and punishments, in a fashion reminiscent of the early drive reduction models of motivation (Hull, 1952). The early drive theories focused largely on biological homeostatic needs, and had limited applicability to more complex human behavior and social and cognitive contributions to motivation. The emerging incentive-based theories were more comprehensive in emphasizing the importance of anticipatory processes, expectancies, goal-striving, and higher-level motivations in guiding thought and action (Bolles, 1967). It is these latter aspects of motivation that the reptilian brain seems to lack, likely because they depend importantly on structures and systems that evolved above the level of the brainstem.

A general trend from lower to higher neuraxial levels of representation includes the gradient extending from simple circuits of limited dimensions and flexibility, with parallel automatic processing on the one hand, to more flexible systems comprised of complex networks of interacting systems supporting the integrative processing of more complex motivational phenomena. The latter entail multiple distributed networks for distinct but interacting aspects of evaluative processing that integrate perceptual, memorial, anticipatory, and affective functions. These systems integrate a vast amount of information and consequently may display a more serial controlled mode of processing, but one that supports the highest level of evaluative cognition.

Because of the evolutionary elaboration and increasing complexity of higher-level evaluative substrates, basic approach and withdrawal systems are not as discrete as at lower neuraxial levels. Indeed, both dispositional systems depend on common processing substrates associated, for example, with perceptual, attentional, and associative networks. Moreover, both may utilize the same cognitive and motor systems to implement their outcomes (e.g., running toward a goal or away from a threat). In addition, distinct dimensions of evaluative systems may show progressive differentiation. At a spinal cord level, approach and withdrawal systems are hardwired into parallel circuits that have separate sensory inputs and motor (extensor and flexor) outputs. The extent of neural activity in these circuits offers an adequate characterization of the associated action disposition, so, as noted above, constructs such as arousal, motivation, or emotion generally need not be invoked for their explication.

The complexity of higher circuits precludes this simplistic characterization. An example comes from recent work on the nucleus accumbens (nACC). The nACC has been long recognized as an important nodal point in rostral substrates for reward and positive hedonics. Virtually any stimulus or condition associated with pleasure, reward, or positive affect triggers dopamine release in the nACC, and administration of dopamine potentiating agents into this structure has been shown to be rewarding (Hoebel, Rada, Mark, & Pothos, 1999; Robinson & Berridge, 2003; Wise, 2006). Conversely, rewards and positive hedonic states are reduced by lesions of the nACC or pharmacological blockade of dopamine receptors in this structure (Hoebel et al., 1999; Robinson & Berridge, 2003; Wise, 2006). In addition to dopamine, endogenous opiate systems play an important potentiating role for positive affect in the nACC and the associated ventral pallidum (Pecina, Smith, & Berridge, 2006).

At these higher levels of organization, however, positive affective processes are not as monolithic as spinal reflex approach and withdrawal systems. Berridge (1996) has drawn an important distinction between what he terms "wanting" (incentive salience, goal-striving) and "liking" (positive hedonic effect, reward) dimensions of motivation. These dimensions are differentiated not only behaviorally, but have a distinct anatomy and pharmacology within the nACC and ventral pallidum as well (Pecina, et al., 2006). Findings such as this illustrate the complexity of rostral evaluative networks, and caution against attempts to define a punctuate localization of positive and negative substrates at higher levels of the neuraxis. Despite these complexities, however, it is clear that higher positive and negative evaluative substrates continue to be at least partially separable.

Higher-level approach and withdrawal systems are more distributed, and may share common circuits for perceptual, attentional, and memorial functions, but the affective mechanisms remain at least partially separable. At the most global organizational level, this is apparent in laterality of representations. Although the right hemisphere may have a greater overall affective representation than the left (Cacioppo & Gardner, 1999), considerable research indicates that the right hemisphere is preferentially involved in aversive or withdrawal motivation, whereas the left may be more involved in positive states. Positive emotional stimuli have been reported to induce greater left than right cortical activation whereas the opposite pattern is seen with negative stimuli (Canli, Desmond, Zhao, Glover, & Gabrieli, 1998; Davidson,

1998, 2004; Lee et al., 2004; Nitschke, Sarinopoulos, Mackiewicz, Schaefer, & Davidson, 2006; Pizzagalli, Sherwood, Henriques, & Davidson, 2005). In addition, individual differences in affective disposition have been reported to be associated with corresponding lateral activation asymmetries, and left hemisphere lesions are more likely to result in depression and negative affective consequences (Davidson, 1998). Efferent outputs also evidence an asymmetrical representation that is consistent with this hemispheric laterality model. Right insula stimulation, for example, yields larger sympathetic cardiac activation than does the left, the latter being more likely to induce parasympathetic cardiac changes (Oppenheimer, 1993, 2006; Oppenheimer, Gelb, Girvin, & Hachinski, 1992). Similarly, somatic outputs including affective facial expressions and manual reaction times to positive and negative stimuli show lateral asymmetries consistent with a right hemisphere bias for negative affect and a left hemisphere bias for positive affect (Davidson, Shackman & Maxwell, 2004; Root, Wong, & Kinsbourne, 2006). This right hemisphere bias toward negative affect has been attributed to a right lateralize visceral/nociceptive projection system, which is in turn associated with a peripheral asymmetry in sympathetic autonomic control and visceral/nociceptive afferent signaling (Craig, 2005).

The finding of laterality differences has not been universal as revealed by a meta-analytic study (Murphy, Nimmo-Smith, & Lawrence, 2003), although this should not be surprising in view of the complexity of affective processes and the wide variety of paradigms that may be tapping disparate aspects or dimensions of evaluative processes. Laterality differences, for example, may be more consistent with a distinction in (approach or withdrawal) action dispositions than with a simple positive versus negative emotion differentiation (Harmon-Jones, Vaughn, Mohr, Sigelman, & Harmon-Jones, 2004).

In view of the complexity of rostral neural systems and of higher-level evaluative processes, we are less likely to find simple mappings between affective processes (psychological domain) and neural substrates (biological domain). Progress toward this goal will require interdisciplinary, multilevel analyses (Cacioppo et al., 2000), and such efforts are currently underway. One important outcome of these studies is the recognition of the need for finer grained analyses of neural circuits.

As outlined above, the nACC is a structure that has been solidly established as a neural player in reward and positive incentives. Nevertheless, the nACC has been reported to also be activated in some negative states (Reynolds & Berridge, 2002, 2003). Although this has been suggested to question the separability of positive and negative evaluative substrates, a finer grained analysis of nACC systems yields a different picture. Although the nACC has an historical anatomical identity, it is actually comprised of multiple anatomically and functionally differentiated regions (Pecina et al., 2006; Zahm, 1999). Using local drug infusions, for example, Reynolds and Berridge (2002, 2003) report a rostrocaudal differentiation of nACC sites that trigger approach and feeding responses and avoidance and negative taste reactions, respectively. As was the case for intake and rejection responses at the level of the brainstem, this approach–avoidance dichotomy does not reflect a simple continuum extending from positive to negative. Activation of intermediate regions of the nACC were found to produce concurrent positive and negative reactions. Interactions between the positive and negative systems could be observed in some zones, for example, where activation resulted in a decrease in the aversive reactions to a bitter taste such as quinine (Pecina et al.). Importantly, these zones were not coextensive with those yielding an increase in positive hedonics, but appeared to constitute a separate inhibitory area.

The nACC provides a rather clear example of the anatomical and functional differentiation of positive and negative forebrain evaluative systems, likely because of the distinct behavioral correlates (intake and rejection, approach and avoidance). With other emotional states, action dispositions may not simply map onto positive and negative affect. Anger, for example, may lead to withdrawal or to approach and attack. Moreover, because of the complexity of higher neuropsychological systems, a given anatomical structure or system may implement only a dimension or aspect of evaluative processes. An example is the amygdala, which has long been implicated in fear and negative affect (LeDoux, 2003; Phelps, 2006). Imaging studies have reported amygdala activation during emotion, especially with negative emotions (Critchley et al., 2005; Irwin et al., 1996; Lane, Fink, Chau, & Dolan, 1997; Norris, Chen, Zhu, Small, & Cacioppo, 2004; Sabatinelli, Bradley, Fitzsimmons, & Lang, 2005; Zald & Pardo, 1997). Amygdala activation is seen during fear conditioning (LaBar et al., 1998), and lesions of this structure have been reported to disrupt fear conditioning (Bechara et al., 1995; LaBar & Cabeza, 2006; LeDoux, 2003; Phelps, 2006) and the perception of potential danger (Bauman, Lavenex, Mason, Capitanio, & Amaral, 2004). Patients with amygdala damage have been reported to display less intense negative, compared to positive, emotions (Tranel, Gullickson, Koch, & Adolphs, 2006); to show deficits in episodic or

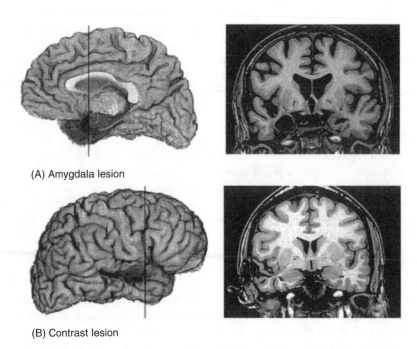

(A) Amygdala lesion

(B) Contrast lesion

FIGURE 18.3 (A) Amygdala and control lesions. Bilateral lesion of the amygdala secondary to Herpes Simplex Encephalitis. Although only two of the six patients in the amygdala group had bilateral lesions, the lesions of this patient illustrate the range of completeness of unilateral damage to the amygdala in other patients. (B) Illustration of one of the smaller lesions in the lesion contrast group. Adapted from "Amygdala contributions to selective dimensions of emotion," by G. G. Berntson, A. Bechara, H. Damasio, D. Tranel, & J. T. Cacioppo, 2007, *Social, Cognitive & Affective Neuroscience*, 2, p. 123.

autobiographical emotion-related memories (Buchanan, Tranel, & Adolphs, 2006; LaBar & Cabeza, 2006; Phelps, 2006; Phelps & LeDoux, 2005) and to evidence reduced emotional potentiation of memory (Cahill, Babinsky, Markowitsch, & McGaugh, 1995; McGaugh, 2004).

These and other findings clearly implicate the amygdala in negative affective processes (Phelps, 2006; Phelps & LeDoux, 2005), although the precise role of this structure remains to be fully elucidated. Although the amygdala appears to have a predominant role in negative emotions, it has also been suggested to be important in appetitive conditioning and positive affect (Everitt, Cardinal, Parkinson, & Robbins, 2003; Hamann, Ely, Hoffman, & Kilts, 2002; Mather et al., 2004). Although this might be suggested to question the separability of positive and negative substrates, it is also possible that the amygdala codes some aspect or dimension of emotion, such as emotional intensity or arousal rather than, or in addition to, emotional valence (Adolphs, Russell, & Tranel, 1999; Anderson et al., 2003; Bauman et al., 2004; Glascher & Adolphs, 2003; Kensinger & Schacter, 2006; Winston, Gottfried, Kilner, & Dolan, 2005).

We examined this question further, in a study of patients with amygdala damage and a clinical contrast

group with lesions that spared the amygdala (Figure 18.3). A series of pictures from the International Affective Picture Series were presented and participants were instructed to rate the slides separately on positivity, negativity, and arousal. Slides were selected based on normative ratings to be highly positive, moderately positive, neutral, moderately negative, and highly negative, with corresponding positive and negative pictures matched on arousal. As illustrated in Figure 18.4, patients with amygdala lesions rated both the positive and negative valence of the pictures comparably to the lesion control group and to the normative sample from young adults. Clearly these amygdala patients were able to recognize and appropriately categorize the positive and negative features of the picture stimuli. They differed dramatically, however, on arousal ratings. Control patients and the normative group showed a progressive increase in arousal ratings for more positive stimuli as well as the more negative stimuli. Although the amygdala patients showed the typical increase in arousal for progressively more positive stimuli, they failed to show an arousal gradient to the negative stimuli (Figure 18.4). That is, the patient group was deficient selectively in the arousal dimension of evaluative judgments.

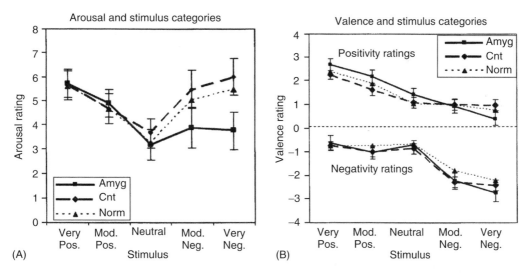

FIGURE 18.4 Evaluative ratings. Mean (s.e.m.) arousal (A) and valence (B) ratings across stimulus categories, for patients with amygdala lesions (Amyg) compared to the clinical contrast group (Cnt) and a normative control data (Norm). All groups effectively discriminated the stimulus categories and applied valance ratings accordingly. All groups also displayed comparable arousal functions to positive stimuli, but the amygdala group showed diminished arousal selectively to the negative stimuli. Adapted from "Amygdala contributions to selective dimensions of emotion," by G. G. Berntson, A. Bechara, H. Damasio, D. Tranel, & J. T. Cacioppo, 2007, *Social, Cognitive & Affective Neuroscience*, 2, p. 123.

EVALUATIVE SPACE MODEL AND THE NEUROARCHITECTURE OF EVALUATIVE PROCESSES

The ultimate expression of neural representation is embodied in cerebral cortical systems. It is these cortical systems that provide for the most sophisticated sensory and perceptual analyses, access to associative networks, attentional focus, conversant awareness, strategic planning, response selection, and outcome monitoring. These processes are central to the strategic organization of behavior—for anticipatory planning, cognitive simulations, and counterfactual reasoning; the establishment of self-awareness, actual–ideal self-discrepancies, and social alliances; and for adaptive, flexible, and creative responses to challenge. Although these higher processes are often most salient in social psychology, in fact they ultimately derive from and interact with lower-level neural representations. As re-represented systems do not supplant lower systems, there is also the opportunity for interactions and conflicts among approach and avoidance systems and across levels of organization.

Since Thurstone (1931) it has been common to consider affective states to extend along a bipolar continuum from positive to negative, or from happy to sad, or from liking to disliking, etc. (Russell & Carroll, 1999). On the basis of neural and behavioral evidence, however, Cacioppo and Berntson have argued that this is an overly restrictive

model of affective structure, and have proposed a more comprehensive bivariate model of affect (Cacioppo & Berntson, 1994; Cacioppo, Gardner & Berntson, 1997; Cacioppo, Larsen, Smith & Berntson, 2004). As illustrated in Figure 18.5, the bivariate model is comprised of separate dimensions that correspond to the separable functional and neural substrates for positive and negative states, and can vary at least partially independently. This model subsumes the bipolar concept as the reciprocal axis, as illustrated in Figure 18.5. It offers a more comprehensive account of affective states, however, and permits a representation of concurrent activation of positive and negative dimensions, as in the concurrent activation of intake and rejection responses considered above (Reynolds & Berridge, 2002, 2003). Thus, among other advantages, the evaluative space model can account for states of ambivalence or mixed feelings and for the low correlation sometimes observed between positive and negative feelings. For example, good outcomes that could have been better (i.e., disappointing wins) and bad outcomes that could have been worse (i.e., relieving losses) are typically given middling ratings on bipolar emotion scales which can only represent positive and negative along a single dimension. The use of separate positive and negative rating scales, however, reveals that the affective state is characterized not so much by indifference as a concurrent (coactivated) mix of positive and negative reactions (Larsen, McGraw, Mellers, & Cacioppo, 2004).

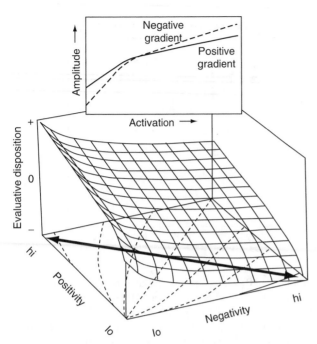

FIGURE 18.5 Evaluative space model. Bivariate evaluative space and its associated affective response surface. This surface represents the net disposition of an individual toward (+) or away from (–) the target stimulus. This disposition is expressed in relative units and the axis dimensions are in relative units of activation. The point on the surface overlying the left axis intersection represents a maximally positive disposition, and the point on the surface overlying the right axis intersection represents a maximally negative disposition. The two headed arrow (heavy line) illustrates the more limited bipolar model of affect, which can be represented by a single line. Each of the points overlying the dashed diagonal extending from the back to the front axis intersections represents a middling disposition. The nonreciprocal diagonal on the evaluative plane which represents different evaluative processes (e.g., neutral to ambivalence) yields the same middling expression on the affective response surface. Dashed lines (including the coactivity diagonal) represent isocontours on the evaluative plane, which depict many-to-one mappings between the affective response surface and the underlying evaluative space. These isocontours are illustrative rather than exhaustive. Inset: the activation functions depicted separately for positivity and negativity. Adapted from "Relationship between Attitudes and Evaluative Space," a critical review, with emphasis on the separability of positive and negative substrates, by J. T. Cacioppo and G. G. Berntson, 1994, *Psychological Bulletin,* 115, pp. 401–423. Reprinted with permission.

This is not to suggest there are no interactions between positive and negative evaluative processes. One source of interaction arises from simple mechanical constraints associated, for example, with incompatible response dispositions. The extensor and flexor reflexes of the cord serve the distinct and opposing functions of approach and avoidance, and are embodied in distinct neural circuits, according to what has been termed the *cardinal principle of evaluative bivalence* (Berntson et al., 1993). Despite their distinct neurological identities, however, flexor and extensor reflexes may control the same joint (e.g., the biceps and triceps that flex and extend the forearm). The forearm cannot flex and extend at the same time, of course, as these movements are opposite and incompatible. Based simply on behavioral observation, one might appropriately characterize flexion and extension on a bipolar scale. This bipolar representation, however, belies the more fundamental bivariate neural organization underlying limb control. With more sophisticated measurement techniques (e.g., muscle action potentials or EMG measures), one can observe concurrent variations in flexor and extensor activity (e.g., in volitional stiffening of the arm) that reveal flexor and extensor muscle coactivation. This may occur with a net flexor movement, a net extensor movement, or even in the complete absence of movement.

This is not the only source of interactions or constraints among flexor and extensor reflexes. As noted above, Sherrington's alliance of reflexes promotes coordination and integration among opposing neural systems, so a pattern of reciprocal innervation tends to minimize opposing actions. What is important to note, however, is that dual, bivariate (e.g., positive vs. negative) interacting systems may have very different functional properties, operating characteristics, and range of outputs than a single bipolar mechanism with an obligatory reciprocal structure. Mutual interference, be it mechanical or neural, may promote a more reciprocal-looking function, but unless that interactions and functional correlations between the dual systems are precisely reciprocal and 1:1, the range of functional states of that system will extend beyond a bipolar dimension.

FINE FEATURES OF THE EVALUATIVE SPACE MODEL

Higher evaluative mechanisms are not as strictly tied to a restricted set of motor outputs, but can achieve a wider array of behavioral responses (e.g., freezing, fleeing, or attacking in the face of threat). Behavioral dispositions arising from higher positive and negative evaluative processes may still evidence an output coupling, however, there may be final common pathways for behavioral output. The same response (e.g., walking) may be motivated by an approach disposition (walking toward a desired object) or an avoidance disposition (walking away from a feared object). One cannot walk toward and away from an object at the same time, however, even if approach and withdrawal dispositions are activated simultaneously. What may be seen under such conditions is a temporal vacillation between approach and withdrawal reactions, whether they be motor or cognitive (e.g., decision whether or not to buy a particular car).

In a classical series of studies, Miller used a variety of measures of motivation disposition (e.g., strength of pull on a tether to approach a reward or to avoid a noxious stimulus) to study conflicts in animals (Miller, 1958, 1959, 1961). In one series of studies, Miller measured the approach disposition to a food reward as a function of the proximity of the animal to the goal box (Figure 18.6). He then measured the avoidance disposition away from an electrified grid in the goal box, also as a function of proximity. As illustrated in Figure 18.6, Miller generally observed that the slope of the avoidance gradient was steeper than that of the approach gradient, such that at remote distances the approach disposition was greater than the avoidance disposition, whereas the reverse was the case when the animal was close to the goal box. In accord with the bivariate model of evaluative processing, when the food reward and the electrified grid were presented simultaneously, Miller found that the net approach and avoidance disposition was a simple summation of the two dispositions. When the animal was far away from the goal, where the approach gradient was greater than the

avoidance gradient, the animal tended to approach the goal. As the animal approached, however, and the steeper avoidance gradient was now greater than the approach gradient, the animal moved away from the goal. This is what Miller referred to as a stable equilibrium, as the animals tended to stay around the middle region where the approach and avoidance gradients were equal (but imparted opposite approach and avoidance dispositions). The animals seemed far from neutral or indifferent, however, but tended to vacillate, sometimes moving toward the goal box, then turning and moving away as the avoidance gradient became greater than the approach gradient.

How are these findings to be understood? The adaptive advantage of separable approach and avoidance substrates is that evolutionary pressures can adaptively sculpt these processes independently. Negative or threatening stimuli or conditions may pose a serious survival hazard, and selection pressures would likely favor the development and precedence of avoidance responses, especially when those stimuli are proximate. As noted above, this can be seen at the level of spinal reflexes, where the prepotency of flexor reflexes to noxious stimuli is readily apparent. This *negativity* bias can also be seen in higher evaluative processes. The magnitude of response to negative stimuli has been suggested to be generally larger than to positive stimuli (Baumeister, Bratslavsky, Finkenauer, & Vohs, 2001; Pratto & John, 1991). This can be seen in diverse attentional paradigms such as identification of negative versus positive emotional faces, and in event-related potential markers of the early stages of evaluative processing (Cacioppo et al., 2004; Öhman, Lundqvist, & Esteves, 2001). This negativity bias is reflected in the steeper slope of the negativity function of Figure 18.5. Although the negativity bias is firmly engrained at the level of flexor reflexes, and has been considered obligatory (Pratto & John, 1991), it may be subject to modulation by higher-level evaluative processes and the affective context (Smith et al., 2006).

In addition to the negativity bias associated with the steeper slope of the avoidance gradient, Miller observed what has been termed a *positivity offset*, reflecting the greater height of approach gradient as one moves further away from the goal (see Figure 18.5, and the insert in Figure 18.6). This, too, may have adaptive value for the organism and may reflect a feature engrained through evolution. Avoiding danger may be more adaptively significant in the near term, when the threat is imminent, but exploration and approach behaviors are essential in acquiring food, water, and in establishing a cognitive map of the environment and its positive attributes. A net positive

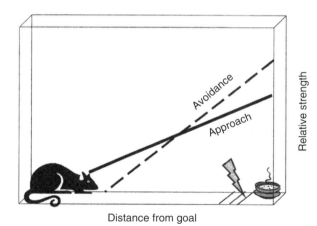

FIGURE 18.6 Miller's approach–avoidance conflict. Approach (solid line) and avoidance (dashed line) strength as a function of distance from the goal. Goal items include food (positive incentive) and shock (negative incentive). The avoidance gradient has a steeper slope, and predominates proximate to the goal box (negativity bias), whereas at more remote loci, the approach gradient is higher than the avoidance gradient (positivity offset).

approach disposition, especially when threats are minimal or remote, would enhance the likelihood of survival. Although negative stimuli may be more attention grabbing, especially at close proximity and high arousal levels, event-related potential studies suggest that positive stimuli may receive greater preferential processing at lower levels of activation (Herbert, Kissler, Junghofer, Peyk, & Rockstroh, 2006). The positivity offset is also apparent in the mere exposure effect on attitude formation, where familiarity with a novel object tends to promote a positive attitude in the absence of explicit positive or negative manipulations (Zajonc, 1968). Although organisms may be naturally wary of unfamiliar stimuli, in the absence of negative outcomes, there results a shift toward a positive disposition to those stimuli (Robinson & Elias, 2005). The positivity offset is represented in Figure 18.5 by the higher intercept of the positivity function, despite its lower slope.

It is important to note that Figure 18.5 depicts only one level of organization in the re-representative systems underlying evaluative processes. We have focused on the neomammalian representation in the evaluative space model, although evaluative processes have representations also at paleomammalian and reptilian brain levels. To fully conceptualize a heterarchical system an additional dimension would be needed to depict the separate evaluative space functions for different levels of organization. As discussed above for flexion and extension, the coupling between evaluative processes and behavioral outputs may differ across levels of organization. At the spinal level for example, flexion is associated with avoidance, whereas at a higher cognitive level, flexion may be associated with approach. The relations between central states and flexion and extension responses thus depend on what level is manifesting in behavioral control, and this may change over time and across contexts. Indeed, one of the important questions raised by the evaluative space model is how different levels interact and achieve expression in behavior. The importance of the evaluative space model is that it provides a quantitative model whereby such issues can be addressed.

SUMMARY

Conceptualizations of social motivation grounded in solid evidence regarding genetic and neural organization and function have the potential to improve the veracity and precision of evaluative concepts and processes, generate new and testable behavioral hypotheses, and broaden the scope and impact of social psychological theories. We here summarize the evaluative space model, derived from evidence spanning three centuries of research on the heterarchical organization of the central nervous system and its implications for implicit and explicit processes underlying approach and withdrawal. This model illustrates the potential utility of neuroscientific perspectives for social psychological processes, and the broadened perspective that can arise from multilevel research and the integration of social psychology and neuroscience.

REFERENCES

Adolphs, R., Russell, J. A., & Tranel, D. (1999). A role for the human amygdala in recognizing emotional arousal from unpleasant stimuli. *Psychological Science, 10*, 167–171.

Allport, G. (1967). Gordon Allport. In E. Boring & G. Lindzey (Eds.), *A history of psychology in autobiography* (Vol. 6, pp. 3–25). New York: Appleton-Century-Crofts.

Allport, G. W. (1935). Attitudes. In C. Murchison (Ed.), *Handbook of social psychology* (Vol. 2). Worchester, MA: Clark University Press.

Anderson, A. K., Christoff, K., Stappen, I., Panitz, D., Ghahremani, D. G., Glover, G., et al. (2003). Dissociated neural representations of intensity and valence in human olfaction. *Nature Neuroscience, 6*, 196–202.

Bauman, M. D., Lavenex, P., Mason, W. A., Capitanio, J. P., & Amaral, D. G. (2004). The development of mother–infant interactions after neonatal amygdala lesions in rhesus monkeys. *Journal of Neuroscience, 24*, 711–21.

Baumeister, R. F., Bratslavsky, E., Finkenauer, C., & Vohs, K. D. (2001). Bad is stronger than good. *Review of General Psychology, 5*, 323–370.

Bechara, A., Tranel, D., Damasio, H., Adolphs, R., Rockland, C., & Damasio, A. R. (1995). Double dissociation of conditioning and declarative knowledge relative to the amygdala and hippocampus in humans. *Science, 269*, 1115–1118.

Berntson, G. G., Bechara, A., Damasio, H., Tranel, D., & Cacioppo, J. T. (2007). Amygdala contributions to selective dimensions of emotion. *Social, Cognitive & Affective Neuroscience, 2*, 123–129.

Berntson, G. G., & Cacioppo, J. T. (2004). Multilevel analyses and reductionism: Why social psychologists should care about neuroscience and vice versa. In J. T. Cacioppo & G. G. Berntson (Eds.), *Essays in social neuroscience* (pp. 107–120). Cambridge, MA: MIT Press.

Berntson, G. G., & Cacioppo, J. T. (2007). Integrative physiology: Homeostasis, allostasis and the orchestration of systemic physiology. In Cacioppo, J. T., Tassinary, L. G., & Berntson, G. G. (Eds.). *Handbook of psychophysiology*, 3rd edition, (pp. 433–452). Cambridge, UK: Cambridge University Press.

Berntson, G. G., Boysen, S. T., & Cacioppo, J. T. (1993). Neurobehavioral organization and the cardinal principle of evaluative bivalence. *Annals of the New York Academy of Science, 702*, 75–102.

Berntson, G. G., & Micco, D. J. (1976). Organization of brainstem behavioral systems. *Brain Research Bulletin, 1*, 471–483.

Berridge, K. C. (1996). Food reward: Brain substrates of wanting and liking. *Neuroscience and Biobehavioral Reviews, 20,* 1–25.

Berridge, K. C. (2004). Motivation concepts in behavioral neuroscience. *Physiology & Behavior, 81,* 179–209.

Berridge, K. C., & Grill, H. J. (1984). Isohedonic tastes support a two-dimensional hypothesis of palatability. *Appetite, 5,* 221–231.

Bolles, R. C. (1967). *Theory of motivation.* New York: Harper & Row.

Buchanan, T. W., Tranel, D., & Adolphs, R. (2006). Memories for emotional autobiographical events following unilateral damage to medial temporal lobe. *Brain, 129,* 115–127.

Cacioppo, J. T., & Berntson, G. G. (1994). Relationship between attitudes and evaluative space: A critical review with emphasis on the separability of positive and negative substrates. *Psychological Bulletin, 115,* 401–423.

Cacioppo, J. T., & Gardner, W. L. (1999). Emotion. *Annual Review of Psychology, 50,* 191–214.

Cacioppo, J. T., Gardner, W. L., & Berntson, G. G. (1997). Beyond bipolar conceptualizations and measures: The case of attitudes and evaluative space. *Personality and Social Psychology Review, 1,* 3–25.

Cacioppo, J. T., Berntson, G. G., Sheridan, J. F., & McClintock, M. K. (2000). Multi-level integrative analyses of human behavior: The complementing nature of social and biological approaches. *Psychological Bulletin, 126,* 829–843.

Cacioppo, J. T., Larsen, J. T., Smith, N. K., & Berntson, G. G. (2004). The affect system: What lurks below the surface of feelings. In Manstead, A. S. R., Frijda, N., & Fischer, A. (Eds.). *Feelings and emotions* (pp. 221–240). Cambridge, UK: Cambridge University Press.

Cacioppo, J. T., & Tassinary, L. G. (1990). Inferring psychological significance from physiological signals. *American Psychologist, 45,* 16–28.

Cahill, L., Babinsky, R., Markowitsch, H. J., & McGaugh, J. L. (1995). The amygdala and emotional memory. *Nature, 377,* 295–296.

Canli, T., Desmond, J. E., Zhao, Z., Glover, G., & Gabrieli, J. D. (1998). Hemispheric asymmetry for emotional stimuli detected with fmri. *Neuroreport, 9,* 3233–3239.

Craig, A. D. (2005). Forebrain emotional asymmetry: A neuroanatomical basis? *Trends in Cognitive Sciences, 9,* 566–571.

Critchley, H. D., Taggart, P., Sutton, P. M., Holdright, D. R., Batchvarov, V., Hnatkova, K., et al. (2005). Activity in the human brain predicting differential heart rate responses to emotional facial expressions. *Neuroimage, 24,* 751–762.

Davidson, R. J. (1998). Anterior electrophysiological asymmetries, emotion, and depression: Conceptual and methodological conundrums. *Psychophysiology, 35,* 607–614.

Davidson, R. J. (2004). What does the prefrontal cortex "do" in affect: Perspectives on frontal EEG asymmetry research. *Biological Psychology, 67,* 219–233.

Davidson, R. J., Shackman, A. J., & Maxwell, J. S. (2004). Asymmetries in face and brain related to emotion. *Trends in Cognitive Sciences, 8,* 389–391.

Edgley, S. A., Eyre, J. A., Lemon, R. N., & Miller, S. (1997). Comparison of activation of corticospinal neurons and spinal motor neurons by magnetic and electrical transcranial stimulation in the lumbosacral cord of the anaesthetized monkey. *Brain, 120,* 839–853.

Everitt, B. J., Cardinal, R. N., Parkinson, J. A., & Robbins, T. W. (2003). Appetitive behavior: Impact of amygdala-dependent mechanisms of emotional learning. *Annals of the New York Academy of Sciences, 985,* 233–250.

Glascher, J., & Adolphs, R. (2003). Processing of the arousal of subliminal and supraliminal emotional stimuli by the human amygdala. *Journal of Neuroscience, 23,* 10274–10282.

Grau, J. W., Crown, E. D., Ferguson, A. R., Washburn, S. N., Hook, M. A., & Miranda, R. C. (2006). Instrumental learning within the spinal cord: Underlying mechanisms and implications for recovery after injury. *Behavioral and Cognitive Neuroscience Reviews, 5,* 191–239.

Greenwald, A. G., Banaji, M. R., Rudman, L. A., Farnham, S. D., Nosek, B. A., & Mellott, D. S. (2002). A unified theory of implicit attitudes, stereotypes, self-esteem, and self-concept. *Psychological Review, 109,* 3–25.

Hamann, S. B., Ely, T. D., Hoffman, J. M., & Kilts, C. D. (2002). Ecstasy and agony: Activation of human amygdala in positive and negative emotion. *Psychological Science, 13,* 135–141.

Harmon-Jones, E., Vaughn, K., Mohr, S., Sigelman, J., & Harmon-Jones, C. (2004). The effect of manipulated sympathy and anger on left and right frontal cortical activity. *Emotion, 4,* 95–101.

Herbert, C., Kissler, J., Junghofer, M., Peyk, P., & Rockstroh, B. (2006). Processing of emotional adjectives: Evidence from startle EMG and erps. *Psychophysiology, 43,* 197–206.

Hoebel, B. G., Rada, P. V., Mark, G. P., & Pothos, E. N. (1999). Neural systems for reinforcement and inhibition of behavior: Relevance to eating, addiction, and depression. In D. Kahneman, E. Diener, & N. Schwarz (Eds.), *Well-being: The foundations of hedonic psychology* (pp. 558–72). New York: Russell Sage Foundation.

Hull, C. L. (1952). *A behavior system: An introduction to behavior theory concerning the individual organism.* New Haven: Yale University Press.

Irwin, W., Davidson, R. J., Lowe, M. J., Mock, B. J., Sorenson, J. A., & Turski, P. A. (1996). Human amygdala activation detected with echo-planar functional magnetic resonance imaging. *NeuroReport, 7,* 1765–1769.

Jackson J. H. (1884/1958) Evolution and dissolution of the nervous system (Croonian lecture, 1884). In J. Taylor (Ed.) *Selected writings of John Hughlings Jackson,* (Vol. 2), New York, Basic Books.

Kensinger, E. A., & Schacter, D. L. (2006). Processing emotional pictures and words: Effects of valence and arousal. *Cognitive, Affective and Behavioral Neuroscience, 6,* 110–126.

LaBar, K. S., & Cabeza, R. (2006). Cognitive neuroscience of emotional memory. *Nature Reviews Neuroscience, 7,* 54–64.

LaBar, K. S., Gatenby, J. C., Gore, J. C., LeDoux, J. E., & Phelps, E. A. (1988). Human amygdala activation during conditioned fear acquisition and extinction: a mixed-trial fMRI study. *Neuron, 20*, 937–945.

Lane, R. D., Fink, G. R., Chau, P. M., & Dolan, R. J. (1997). Neural activation during selective attention to subjective emotional responses. *Neuroreport, 8*, 3969–3972.

Lane, R. D., Reiman, E. M., Bradley, M. M., Lang, P. J., Ahern, G. L., Davidson, R. J., et al. (1997). Neuroanatomical correlates of pleasant and unpleasant emotion. *Neuropsychologia, 35*, 1437–1444.

Larsen, J. T., Berntson, G. G., Poehlmann, K. M., Ito, T. A., & Cacioppo, J. T. (in press). *The psychophysiology of emotion.* In R. Lewis, J. M. Haviland-Jones, & L. F. Barrett (Eds.), The handbook of emotions, 3rd ed. New York: Guilford.

Larsen, J. T., McGraw, A. P., Mellers, B. A., & Cacioppo, J. T. (2004). The agony of victory and thrill of defeat: Mixed emotional reactions to disappointing wins and relieving losses. *Psychological Science, 15*, 325–330.

LeDoux, J. (2003). The emotional brain, fear, and the amygdala. *Cellular and Molecular Neurobiology, 23*, 727–738.

Lee, G. P., Meador, K. J., Loring, D. W., Allison, J. D., Brown, W. S., Paul, L. K., et al. (2004). Neural substrates of emotion as revealed by functional magnetic resonance imaging. *Cognitive Behavioral Neurology, 17*, 9–17.

MacLean, P. D. (1985). Evolutionary psychiatry and the triune brain. *Psychological Medicine, 15*, 219–221.

MacLean, P. D. (1977). The triune brain in conflict. *Psychotherapy and Psychosomatics, 28*, 207–220.

McGaugh, J. L. (2004). The amygdala modulates the consolidation of memories of emotionally arousing experiences. *Annual Review of Neuroscience, 27*, 1–28.

Mather, M., Canli, T., English, T., Whitfield, S., Wais, P., Ochsner, K., et al. (2004). Amygdala responses to emotionally valenced stimuli in older and younger adults. *Psychological Science, 15*, 259–263.

Miller, N. E. (1961). Some recent studies on conflict behavior and drugs. *American Psychologist, 16*, 12–24.

Miller, N. E. (1959). Liberalization of basic S-R concepts: Extensions to conflict behavior, motivation and social learning. In S. Koch (Ed.), *Psychology: A study of a science. Study 1* (pp. 198–292). New York: McGraw-Hill.

Miller, N. E. (1951). Comments on theoretical models illustrated by the development of a theory of conflict behavior. *Journal of Personality, 20*, 82–100.

Murphy, F. C., Nimmo-Smith, I., & Lawrence, A. D. (2003). Functional neuroanatomy of emotions: A meta-analysis. *Cognitive Affective and Behavioral Neuroscience, 3*, 207–233.

Nitschke, J. B., Sarinopoulos, I., Mackiewicz, K. L., Schaefer, H. S., & Davidson, R. J. (2006). Functional neuroanatomy of aversion and its anticipation. *Neuroimage, 29*, 106–116.

Norris, C. J., Chen, E. E., Zhu, D. C., Small, S. L., & Cacioppo, J. T. (2004). The interaction of social and emotional processes in the brain. *Journal of Cognitive Neuroscience, 16*, 1818–1829.

Öhman, A., Lundqvist, D., & Esteves, F. (2001). The face in the crowd revisited: A threat advantage with schematic stimuli. *Journal of Personality and Social Psychology, 80*, 381–396.

Oppenheimer, S. (1993). The anatomy and physiology of cortical mechanisms of cardiac control. *Stroke, 24*, 13–15.

Oppenheimer, S. (2006). Cerebrogenic cardiac arrhythmias: cortical lateralization and clinical significance. *Clinical Autonomic Research, 16*, 6–11.

Oppenheimer, S. M., Gelb, A., Girvin, J. P., & Hachinski, V. C. (1992). Cardiovascular effects of human insular cortex stimulation. *Neurology, 42*, 1727–1732.

Osgood, C. E., Suci, G. J., & Tannenbaum, P. H. (1957). *The measurement of meaning.* Urbana, IL: University of Illinois Press.

Pecina, S., Smith, K. S., & Berridge, K. C. (2006). Hedonic hot spots in the brain. *Neuroscientist, 12*, 500–511.

Phelps, E. A. (2006). Emotion and cognition: Insights from studies of the human amygdala. *Annual Review of Psychology, 57*, 27–53.

Phelps, E. A., & Ledoux, J. E. (2005). Contributions of the amygdala to emotion processing: From animal models to human behavior. *Neuron, 48*, 175–187.

Pizzagalli, D. A., Sherwood, R. J., Henriques, J. B., & Davidson, R. J. (2005). Frontal brain asymmetry and reward responsiveness: A source-localization study. *Psychological Science, 16*, 805–813.

Porter, R. (1987). Corticomotoneuronal projections: synaptic events related to skilled movement. *Proceedings of the Royal Society London B, Biological Sciences, 231*, 147–168.

Pratto, F., & John, O. P. (1991). Automatic vigilance: The attention grabbing power of negative social information. *Journal of Personality and Social Psychology, 61*, 380–391.

Reynolds, S. M., & Berridge, K. C. (2003). Glutamate motivational ensembles in nucleus accumbens: Rostrocaudal shell gradients of fear and feeding. *European Journal of Neuroscience, 17*, 2187–2200.

Reynolds, S. M., & Berridge, K. C. (2002). Positive and negative motivation in nucleus accumbens shell: Bivalent rostrocaudal gradients for GABA-elicited eating, taste "liking"/"disliking" reactions, place preference/avoidance, and fear. *Journal of Neuroscience, 22*, 7308–7320.

Robinson, T. E., & Berridge, K. C. (2003). Addiction. *Annual Review of Psychology, 54*, 25–53.

Robinson, B. M., & Elias, L. J. (2005). Novel stimuli are negative stimuli: Evidence that negative affect is reduced in the mere exposure effect. *Perceptual and Motor Skills, 100*, 365–372.

Root, J. C., Wong, P. S., & Kinsbourne, M. (2006). Left hemisphere specialization for response to positive emotional expressions: A divided output methodology. *Emotion, 6*, 473–483.

Russell, J. A., & Carroll, J. M. (1999). On the bipolarity of positive and negative affect. *Psychological Bulletin, 125*, 3–30.

Sabatinelli, D., Bradley, M. M., Fitzsimmons, J. R., & Lang, P. J. (2005). Parallel amygdala and inferotemporal activation reflect emotional intensity and fear relevance. *Neuroimage, 24*, 1265–1270.

Sherrington, C. S. (1906). *The integrative action of the nervous system*. New Haven: Yale University Press.

Shiffrin, R. M., & Schneider, W. (1984). Automatic and controlled processing revisited. *Psychological Review, 91*, 269–276.

Smith, N. K., Larsen, J. T., Chartrand, T. L., Cacioppo, J. T., Katafiasz, H. A., & Moran, K. E. (2006). Being bad isn't always good: Evaluative context moderates the attention bias toward negative information. *Journal of Personality and Social Psychology, 90*, 210–220. PDF

Steiner, J. E., Glaser, D., Hawilo, M. E., & Berridge, K. C. (2001). Comparative expression of hedonic impact: Affective reactions to taste by human infants and other primates. *Neuroscience and Biobehavioral Reviews, 25*, 53–74.

Thurstone, L. L. (1931). The measurement of attitudes. *Journal of Abnormal Psychology, 26*, 249–269.

Tranel, D., Gullickson, G., Koch, M., & Adolphs, R. (2006). Altered experience of emotion following bilateral amygdala damage. *Cognitive Neuropsychiatry, 11*, 219–232.

Winston, J. S., Gottfried, J. A., Kilner, J. M., & Dolan, R. J. (2005). Integrated neural representations of odor intensity and affective valence in human amygdala. *Journal of Neuroscience, 25*, 8903–8907.

Wise, R. A. (2006). Role of brain dopamine in food reward and reinforcement. *Philosophical Transactions of theRoyal Society of London. Series B Biological Sciences, 361*, 1149–1158.

Zahm, D. S. (1999). Functional–anatomical implications of the nucleus accumbens core and shell subterritories. *Annals of the New York Academy Sciences, 877*, 113–128.

Zajonc, R. B. (1968). Attitudinal effects of mere exposure. *Journal of Personality and Social Psychology: Monograph Supplement, 9*, 1–27.

Zald, D. H., & Pardo, J. V. (1997). Emotion, olfaction, and the human amygdala: Amygdala activation during aversive olfactory stimulation. *Proceedings of the National Academy of Sciences, U.S.A., 94*, 4119–4124.

Evaluation Asymmetry

19 How Approach and Avoidance Decisions Influence Attitude Formation and Change

J. Richard Eiser and Russell H. Fazio

CONTENTS

As Benjamin Franklin once remarked, in this world nothing can be said to be certain, except death and taxes—and, we might add, uncertainty. Uncertainty is not merely a fact of life, it is a challenge to the survival of all living creatures. With uncertainty comes *risk*—of damage, death, or deprivation, of failure to feed or reproduce. For us humans, not all decisions are so obviously a matter of life and death, but most if not all have consequences that may be construed as benefits or costs, as good or bad, as states of affairs to be attained or avoided. It is therefore vital to our happiness and well-being, if not our actual survival, that we learn to distinguish objects or activities that will provide us with benefits from those that will lead us to incur costs. This process

of learning constitutes *attitude formation*, since it results in us acquiring favorable attitudes toward objects associated with benefits and unfavorable attitudes toward objects associated with costs.

In this chapter, we shall be concerned with how individuals acquire attitudes toward novel objects in contexts where such learning depends on their own behavior and specifically on their willingness to expose themselves to risk within an uncertain environment. We start by describing some of the factors that affect decision making under uncertainty, stressing in particular how different decision–outcome combinations vary in their diagnosticity, i.e., in their potential to confirm or disconfirm prior hypotheses and evaluative beliefs.

We then apply these ideas to the issue of how individuals acquire attitudes toward novel objects through experience. We describe a phenomenon we term learning asymmetry, whereby individuals show fewer errors in their learning of bad objects than good objects. In other words, individuals rarely evaluate bad objects positively, but tend to evaluate a proportion of good objects negatively. The reason for this is that false-positive beliefs will lead to approach, and hence discovery that the objects approached are actually bad, whereas false-negative beliefs may persist uncorrected since individuals fail to discover that some of the objects they have avoided are actually good. A series of experiments and simulations explore these processes in greater detail, and also consider the impact on attitude acquisition of socially communicated information about the attitude objects. We then consider the implications of these findings for positivity biases in self-conceptions and risk-averse decision making.

In terms of how our chapter relates to others in this book, we regard attitudes as evaluative judgments. By virtue of their marking the valence of some object, issue or person, attitudes necessarily have action implications. Favorable attitudes provide a motivation to approach and unfavorable attitudes a motivation to avoid. Wherever favorable and unfavorable attitudes (or approach and avoidance motivations) coexist (Cacioppo & Berntson, 1994), this gives rise to uncertainty about what actions to perform. Furthermore, whereas approach and avoidance motivations can coexist to varying degrees, decisions to approach or avoid are mutually exclusive. We cannot both approach and avoid the same object at the same time. So the translation of attitudes and motivations into behavior involves a form of decision making, whether conscious or unconscious, under conditions of uncertainty with regard to costs and benefits. This in turn gives rise to two questions: first, how are decisions to approach or avoid guided by perceived costs and benefits? And second, how does the experience of costly and beneficial outcomes shape the formation of attitudes toward objects in our social environment?

COSTS AND BENEFITS

Attempts to specify how costs and benefits relate to decision making have been traditionally dominated by economic rather than psychological theories. Furthermore, the purpose of much classical economic theory has been prescriptive (defining how a rational actor should decide) rather than descriptive (investigating how decisions are actually made). Yet it is precisely the introduction of costs

and benefits that turns the problem of decision making under uncertainty into one of the motivations, and hence a more broadly psychological topic of study than one concerned simply with people's cognitive ability to process ambiguous information. It goes without saying, or should, that we are motivated to make correct decisions and avoid errors. But, when decisions have consequences, not all errors are equally costly and not all correct decisions are equally beneficial. Furthermore, the steps required to avoid certain kinds of errors can themselves be costly or risky.

This is a problem faced in a number of safety-critical industries: if there is no such thing as zero risk, how much effort and expenditure should be devoted to making an improbable risk even more remote? As Fischoff, Slovic, Lichtenstein, Read, and Combs (1978) once asked, "how safe is safe enough?" Evidently, there is no absolute right or wrong answer to this question. Nonetheless, there are ways to address it relatively systematically, provided we (or society) can agree on a common metric for balancing, say, the cost of extra safety procedures against that of the accident that may thereby be prevented. The difficulty is that this last calculation is often controversial (take the issue of nuclear accidents, or terrorist attacks, for example). Estimates of the precise likelihood of such events may be hotly disputed and many people would strongly resent the notion that consequences of disasters (e.g., numbers of lives lost) can be translated into some kind of crude monetary equivalent.

Such calculations increasingly pervade public policy, for example where health economists are called upon to advise on the cost-effectiveness of different medical treatments so that scarce resources are used to maximum effect. The trouble is that, whereas it is relatively easy to measure (monetary) cost, measuring effectiveness is far more controversial and contains a large subjective element. The current approach is to rely on a derived measure termed Quality Adjusted Life Years (QALYs), essentially – how many more years of life will the treatment provide and what will be the gain in the patient's quality-of-life during these years (Gold, Siegel, Russell, Weinstein, 1996)? Apart from methodological questions of how best to measure quality-of-life for different patient groups (Eiser, 2004), there are a host of essentially ethical questions hidden behind superficially technical calculations: Are all groups—for example, young and old, parents and childless—equally deserving (Nord, Pinto, Richardson, Menzel, & Ubel, 1999)? Is it better to concentrate resources on large benefits for a few, or small benefits for many (Dolan, 1998; Olsen, 2000)?

Such difficulties arise most acutely when we are required to express preferences between things that are qualitatively very different, but undeniably many real-life choices are like this—balancing the enjoyment from a holiday or night out against the embarrassment of failing to complete a work assignment on time, the attractions of a new job in a different city against the distress of lost friendships. Since we cannot be in two places at once, or spend the same money twice, every choice has an opportunity cost—what we have to give up for what we choose to do. But even when we are comparing like with like, real-life decisions can still be difficult. The reason for this is simple but profound: *we cannot always be sure what the consequences of our decisions will be*.

DECISION MAKING, UNCERTAINTY, AND RISK

Apart from death and taxes, another fact of life is that decisions cannot always be avoided or postponed, even if we are uncertain of the consequences. If we could predict consequences correctly and with certainty, there would be no risk, but in real life such conditions are rare. We need to make decisions on the basis of incomplete and imperfect data. How can we do this? One starting point for thinking about this question is the classic theory of perceptual discrimination, Signal Detection Theory (SDT) (Swets, 1973). The basic problem this theory addresses is that of describing the "discrimination performance" of a perceiver faced with the task of identifying whether or not a piece of stimulus information is evidence of a "signal" or merely "noise." For instance, how does a radar operator tell the difference between a blip on a screen due to an approaching aircraft and one due to atmospheric disturbance? How reliably can a safety inspector (or even an automatic device such as a smoke detector) distinguish danger from safety? How well can a doctor diagnose a particular medical condition from a set of clinical symptoms?

In all these dilemmas the decision maker is faced typically with a mass of different pieces of information, some relevant and others irrelevant. So a first question is how well the decision maker can process this accumulated information to derive some estimate of the likelihood that a signal is actually present. Within SDT, the extent to which such estimates are well-calibrated with actual probabilities is referred to as sensitivity or discrimination ability. Behaviorally, better discrimination ability will tend to be reflected in more accurate decisions and fewer errors. However, even well-calibrated decision makers, well-trained air-traffic controllers or physicians, can sometimes make mistakes, so a second question is how many such mistakes, or rather *particular kinds* of mistakes, matter.

Although we can assume that correct responses will be more beneficial than incorrect ones, the extent to which this is so can vary considerably. Correct decisions can take the form of saying a signal is present when it is (hit) or saying that noise is mere noise (all clear). Incorrect decisions involve treating a signal as noise (miss) or noise as a signal (false alarm). Suppose, for example, the fire alarm sounds in the building where you work. It quite often sounds, since it is tested at least once a week, but this is not at its regular time. What do you do? Of course, you should leave the building. But then, a few minutes after you get outside, the alarm stops and you are told it had been set off accidentally by electricians doing some maintenance work, so you return to your desk. It was a false alarm, as a result of which you have wasted half-an-hour: a cost, to be sure, but a quite trivial one compared with staying in the building and perhaps losing one's life if there really had been a fire. But the trouble is the more often alarms turn out to be false, the less ready you may be to react to them as real—the well known "cry wolf" problem. In other circumstances, however, false alarms can be more costly than misses. Gigerenzer (2002) recounts several examples where patients may be recommended to undergo aggressive and distressing medical treatments following unreliable diagnostic tests, or for conditions that are so slow to develop as to have no significant implications for (older) patients' life-expectancy or quality-of-life if left untreated.

An enduring contribution of SDT, and its major relevance to approach and avoidance motivation, is that it characterizes decision-making performance not merely in terms of overall accuracy, but also in terms of "criterion" or response bias. This refers to the tendency to give responses in one direction, for example, to say the signal is present, or that the patient has a specific condition. Depending where the criterion is set, some ambiguous pieces of information may be over interpreted as a signal (false alarm), and others wrongly discounted as noise (miss). Now, although the use of a particular criterion will increase the chance of particular kinds of errors, there is no absolute answer to the question of what the best criterion should be. If you change the criterion, you will decrease the chance of some kinds of errors but you will simultaneously increase the chance of others. So the choice of what criterion to adopt depends on the relative perceived costs and benefits of different outcomes resulting from correct and incorrect decisions.

A minor difficulty in extending the SDT framework to more general issues of approach and avoidance motivation is that the terminology of signal versus noise implies a kind of "figure-ground" distinction between the detection of danger and safety. This is fair enough for contexts such as medical screening where the aim is correct detection of an abnormal condition. Conventionally, screening test results that indicate the presence of an abnormality are termed "positive" and those indicating an absence of disease are termed "negative." Even within the medical context, this terminology is potentially confusing at least for some patients since, evidently, a positive test result is bad and a negative result good. When considering more general approach–avoidance situations, however, we may be equally concerned with the detection of good (safe, desirable, rewarding) objects as with detecting those that are bad (dangerous, undesirable, costly). Put differently, we may be just as concerned with identifying good objects to approach, as with identifying bad objects to avoid.

Figure 19.1 illustrates the different decision–outcome combinations according to their conventional definitions, as well as how these might be applied to more general approach–avoidance decisions. A hit refers to correct detection of danger, a miss a failure to detect danger, and so on. Hits are conventionally termed "true-positives," but for clarity we refer to these as instances of true-positive diagnosis to remind the reader of their medical usage. In an approach–avoidance context, treating a dangerous signal as dangerous (a hit) constitutes a case of "correct avoidance" whereas treating a dangerous signal as safe (a miss) constitutes a case of "incorrect approach." As will soon become clear, we shall spend much time considering the processes that might lead to false alarms or instances of incorrect avoidance. Conventionally such responses would be termed false-positives, but we regard this as somewhat confusing from the perspective of approach–avoidance motivation and attitude theory (since positive normally suggests a favorable attitude and a willingness to approach). In the following, therefore, we shall sometimes refer to false alarms as *false-negative avoidance* decisions (rather than false-positive diagnoses of danger), in that it is more intuitive to think of negative as reflecting an unfavorable evaluation.

ANTECEDENTS OF RISK ACCEPTANCE AND AVERSION

A considerable literature has looked at the antecedents of people's readiness, or reluctance, to engage in various forms of risk-taking. In many case, researchers have considered characteristics predictive of a predisposition to risk or caution as relatively stable personality traits that generalize across situations. Examples include Zuckerman's (1994) research on sensation-seeking and Higgins's (1998) notion of promotion and prevention regulatory focus. Such behavioral tendencies may possibly reflect underlying differences in temperament (Elliot & Thrash, 2002) or behavioral activation and inhibition systems (Gray, 1990). Social anthropologists have also attempted to identify subcultural types characterized by supposedly general orientations of acceptance or concern toward a range of societal and technological risks (Boholm, 1996; Douglas, 1986). In such cases, the antecedents of such predispositions and orientations are assumed to lie, at least partly, in the individual's upbringing and experience of parental encouragement or discipline, and in experiences of autonomy or powerlessness

Action / Object valence	Avoid Treat as bad, dangerous	Approach Treat as good, safe
Bad, dangerous	True-positive diagnosis Correct avoidance Hit	False-negative diagnosis Incorrect approach Miss
Good, safe	False-positive diagnosis Incorrect avoidance False alarm	True-negative diagnosis Correct approach All clear

FIGURE 19.1   Decision–outcome combinations.

within the political and economic system. Our own focus is narrower, but arguably more easily amenable to empirical investigation. We are concerned with how response biases toward greater risk acceptance (approach) or risk aversion (avoidance) may be shaped and reinforced by an individual's experiences within a specific learning environment.

Experiences can affect attitudes and motivations in several ways. A fair amount of work has looked at how individuals come to regard objects more positively or negatively, either as a function of mere familiarity (Zajonc, 1968, 1980) or through a process of associative learning based on the co-occurrence of novel objects with others of established valence (De Houwer, Thomas, & Baeyens. 2001; Olson & Fazio, 2001, 2002, 2006). Such learning can be characterized as "passive" in the sense that the relevant learning experiences to which individuals are exposed are independent of their own behavior. Put differently, information gain within this paradigm comes essentially risk-free. (Note that our concern here is with whether there are risks associated with information search per se, rather than with any risks associated with consequential changes in behavior, which of course could be either adaptive or maladaptive.)

Our own focus is not on such passive learning, although it undoubtedly occurs, but instead on learning that is contingent on individuals' *active* exploration of their environment. This links with a large literature on *reinforcement learning* (Sutton & Barto, 1998). The essential feature of reinforcement learning is that learners receive *feedback* as a consequence of their actions. For example, a rat that explores a given arm of a maze may receive a food pellet or an electric shock. Learners who perform different actions receive different feedback, but if no action is performed, no feedback is provided. Positive feedback (e.g., food) increases the likelihood of an action being repeated (hence, approach), whereas negative feedback (e.g., shock), decreases its likelihood (hence, avoidance)—the familiar "law of effect." The slightly more subtle point is that the reinforcement learning paradigm is one in which the relation between action and learning experience is *dynamic*. Feedback is not only contingent on, but also shapes, the learner's actions.

A FUNDAMENTAL ASYMMETRY

Because of this dynamic relation, there is a fundamental asymmetry between approach and avoidance behaviors. At its simplest, approach behavior exposes the learner to potential feedback and learning experience whereas avoidance behavior generally does not. However, since such feedback could be either positive or negative, approach involves risk. Conversely, avoidance involves not merely escape from known danger, but a way of reducing uncertainty and hence, risk. Let us consider how this applies to the 2 × 2 matrix of decision–outcome combinations shown in Figure 19.1. If feedback is contingent on approach, learners should be unable to distinguish between false-negatives and true-negatives. In other words, learners should have no way of confirming or disconfirming the negative expectancies that led them to avoid a given object or action. More than 50 years ago, Solomon and Wynne (1954) established that avoidance behavior by animals is highly resistant to extinction. For instance, rats will continue to avoid an area of their cage where they have previously received an electric shock long after the reinforcement schedule has been changed so that the area can be safely visited. This again can be seen as a direct consequence of the dynamics of action and feedback: if the chosen action (avoidance) means that the rat never gets feedback that is inconsistent with prior negative expectancies, these expectancies will remain in force and lead to continued avoidance. Among humans, phobias, but also negative prejudices against out-groups, may reflect much the same process (as we shall discuss in more detail shortly). In such instances, adoption of a risk-averse response bias is likely to be self-sustaining.

How might feedback affect learners' ability to distinguish true- and false-positives? In a simple situation where feedback is immediate and unambiguous, discrimination should improve quickly. True positives should be rewarded and false-positives punished. (Shortly we shall describe an experimental paradigm that demonstrates this effect.) However, not all situations in real life are so clear cut. Physicians may often prescribe treatments on the basis of unreliable positive test results (as noted previously, positive means here that the disease is present, not that it is good news). If the patient's condition then improves, then that can be taken to prove that both the diagnosis and prescription were correct, when actually the patient might have improved anyway, and possibly faster without the treatment. Similarly, if the patient's condition worsens, that again just proves the correctness of the diagnosis and the seriousness of the medical condition that is resisting treatment. Likewise, many situations and systems can be relatively "forgiving" of unsafe behaviors (i.e., false-positive "approaches"). Many unhealthy habits lead to illness, but often only after many years. Not all instances of unsafe sexual intercourse result in pregnancy or infection. Not all cases of unsafe driving lead to accidents. But every time someone appears to get away with doing something dangerous, their perception of the risk is likely to be lowered and, assuming the behavior is otherwise pleasurable or rewarding, the chance of them behaving the same way again will be increased. Once again, incomplete feedback (in this case, delayed or inconsistent punishment of false-positive risk-taking) can lead to selective interpretations of contingencies between decisions and outcomes that are biased in the direct of confirming prior beliefs.

RISK AVERSION IN THE STANDARD GAMBLE

Before concluding this section, we need briefly to consider work involving a slightly different definition of "risk-aversion." This involves a procedure known to economists as the "standard gamble" where participants indicate their preferences between two options of the same expected value. An example would be:

Option A: Winning $10 for sure.
Option B: A 10% chance of winning $100, but a 90% chance of winning nothing.

In terms of this paradigm, Option B is seen as "riskier" since the consequences are less certain. Preference for Option A is therefore defined as "risk averse." The same problems can be rephrased in terms of chances of losing rather than winning, and this makes a big difference. According to Kahneman and Tversky's (1979) prospect theory, when the problem is defined in terms of gains, participants tend to be risk averse, i.e., prefer Option A, but when it is defined in terms of losses, they tend to be risk-seeking, i.e., prefer Option B rather than accept a sure loss.

What may underlie risk-averse and risk-seeking preferences within this paradigm? Interestingly, these too may reflect the learner's history of feedback. March (1996) used computer simulation to argue that risk aversion for gains could be a direct product of learning experience, rather than any kind of personality trait or higher-order conscious process. In his simulations, the learning system was presented with two classes of objects, one of which (the "sure thing" option) always produced a moderate reward, and the other of which (the "risky" option) sometimes produced a much larger reward, but more often produced nothing (the reward magnitudes and probabilities being arranged so that the expected value associated with the two classes of objects was the same, as in the choice between Options A and B above). The learning system had to choose whether to approach or avoid these objects on the basis of its expectations developed over time. The

learning algorithms used meant that these expectations were modified by experience of the value of individual objects, if and only if they were approached.

March's findings showed strong evidence for risk aversion for gains. The argument goes something like this. Whenever an object of the sure thing class is presented, it is consistently associated with a good outcome, and so approach is strongly reinforced. Before long, all sure thing objects will be approached. By contrast, most risky objects will produce no good outcome or reward at all, and so the tendency to approach these will be weakened. As a consequence, sure thing objects will be more likely to be approached and risky objects avoided.

"Ah, but what about the fact that the two classes of objects have the same expected value?" (an economist might ask). "Should not the extra value of the occasional large rewards in the risky class compensate for their infrequency?" True, but this only applies if both classes are fully sampled. Once (as a function of the reinforcement process) the system starts differentially to approach the sure thing class and avoid the risky class, the chances are that it will never sample enough of the risky class to discover it contains a few high rewards. Unlike human participants in standard gamble experiments (or lottery players, perhaps), the learning system does not know that there is a jackpot out there, unless and until it finds it.

ATTITUDE LEARNING THROUGH EXPLORATION

All of the above lines of research suggest that the outcomes experienced by individuals as a consequence of their decisions should be a major influence on attitude formation. At its simplest, we should come to hold favorable attitudes toward objects associated with positive outcomes and unfavorable attitudes toward objects associated with negative outcomes. Such attitudes are a source of approach and avoidance motivations, in that we should tend to approach positively valued objects toward which we hold favorable attitudes, and avoid negatively valued objects toward which we hold unfavorable attitudes. Approach and avoidance then, as explained, will in their turn influence the outcomes we experience.

Although these ideas are relatively simple at a theoretical level, there has been little attempt to investigate them empirically in the context of human attitude formation. Part of the reason may simply be the practical difficulty of achieving experimental control over the outcomes individuals experience while also controlling for, or eliminating variation in, their prior attitudes. This appears to exclude the typical style of much attitude research, where individuals are asked to state their opinion on some real-life social issue, or express (implicitly or explicitly) their liking or disliking for an actual social group. For this reason, we sought to develop a new experimental paradigm within which individuals would be presented with novel objects about which they could have no prior preconceptions of their value, but where they could learn to identify some objects as "good" and others as "bad."

To this end, we devised a computer game (BeanFest) involving a virtual world filled with different kinds of "beans" (Fazio, Eiser, & Shook, 2004). These beans are presented visually on the computer screen, and their appearance varies along two dimensions: shape (round to oblong) and number of speckles. Participants are told that some of the beans they see will be good, and will provide them with energy if eaten, whereas others will be bad, and will lead to a loss of energy if eaten. For each bean presented, participants therefore have to decide if they want to "eat" or "not eat" it (i.e., approach or avoid). They are instructed that their survival or success in the game depends on them learning to identify which beans are good and should be eaten and which are bad and should be avoided. The critical feature of our (standard) procedure is that, if a bean is eaten, the participant receives consistent and immediate feedback about its true valence (in the form of a gain or loss of "energy" points), but if a bean is avoided, the participant receives no feedback whatsoever.

We took particular care over the relationship between the valence of the beans and their visual attributes, so that the discrimination learning task could not be performed by focusing simply on one dimension and ignoring the other. There were 10 levels of each attribute, producing 100 possible attribute combinations, or stimulus patterns. However, participants only had to learn to discriminate between 36 of these. Of these 18 were good and 18 bad, and arranged in six separate clusters distributed across the 10×10 matrix shown in Figure 19.2. (In half the conditions, the valences were reversed from those shown, but this made no difference to the results to be described.) As can be seen, all beans within a single cluster or region had the same valence, thus enabling a form of generalization learning. (Participants were not shown the matrix, nor informed about the proportion of good and bad beans.)

The basic procedure consisted first of a set of six practice trials involving one bean from each region. To ensure that they gained some preliminary idea of the beans and to familiarize themselves with the feedback procedure, participants were instructed to answer "Yes" to each of these when asked if they wanted to eat them. This was followed by a learning, or game, phase, consisting of three blocks of 36 trials, with each bean being presented once within each block. During this phase, participants

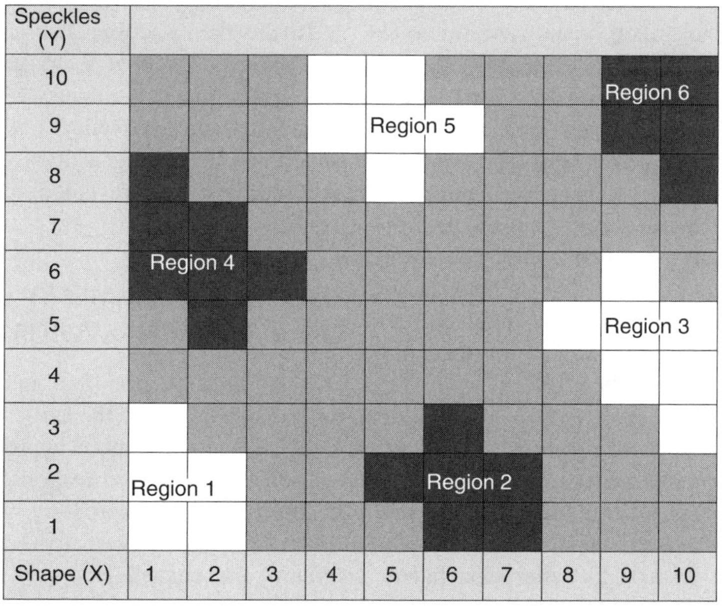

FIGURE 19.2 The BeanFest matrix. Regions 1, 3, and 5 comprise good beans; 2, 4, and 6, bad beans.

could monitor the effects of their behavior on their total energy level via an "energy meter" on the screen. If they ate a good bean, a +10 appeared after "Effect of Bean." If they ate a bad bean, −10 appeared in the same place. An additional feature included in the original version of the game was that, whatever they did, participants lost 1 energy unit or point on each trial, to simulate the idea that, if they never ate, they would eventually starve. Hence, another caption read "Energy Loss via Time" and took the value −1 on all trials. A third caption "Net Gain or Loss" was therefore followed by +9 whenever a good bean was eaten and −11 whenever a bad bean was eaten. If, however, the participant responded "No" when asked if they wanted to eat a bean, "Effect of Bean" remained blank, and a −1 was shown against the next two captions. In addition, participants could see their current energy level in numerical and visual analog form. In the original version of the game, their starting level was 100 units and they were told that, if the level dropped to 0, this symbolized "death." (Variations in procedure across different versions of the game included removing the energy loss via time, and setting different starting levels.)

When the game (the learning phase) reached its obvious conclusion, a final "test phase" began. At this point, the game was over. Hence, no energy meter was displayed. On each trial, a bean was presented and participants indicated whether they thought the bean was good or bad, i.e., whether it increased or decreased energy levels when eaten. The stimuli presented included both some from the original training set and others, not previously presented, from elsewhere in the 10 × 10 matrix. Responses to the former (original) beans were taken to provide a measure of participants' discrimination learning. Given that the game itself had concluded, these responses are unaffected by participants' current energy needs or consideration of the risk of a false-positive decision to "eat." The latter (novel) beans were included to see if such learning generalized to other beans with similar visual features. In our first two experiments, we included only a selection of original and novel beans, but in subsequent experiments, the test phase involved presentation of all 100 possible patterns, i.e., all 36 of the original training set plus 64 novel beans.

Our very first experiment (Experiment 1 of Fazio et al., 2004) yielded a number of clear and interesting effects. On average, participants were successful in learning. The mean phi coefficient relating the actual valence of the game beans to the participant's classifications during the test phase was substantially better than chance. Indeed, over 50% of the participants were characterized by statistically significant phi coefficients. Moreover,

these attitudes generalized to the novel beans. On the basis of Euclidean distances within the matrix, each novel bean could be classified as closer to a positive game bean, closer to a negative game bean, or equidistant. Responses to these novel beans were strongly affected by this proximity variable. Novel beans closer to a negative (i.e., more strongly resembling a negative game bean) were more likely to be classified as bad than were equidistant beans, and novel beans closer to a positive were the most likely to be classified as good.

However, two intriguing valence asymmetries also emerged. The first we refer to as a *learning asymmetry* effect. Although classification of positive and negative game beans were both well above chance levels, identification of bad beans was more accurate than identification of good beans. Good beans were more likely to be wrongly categorized as bad than the reverse. Consideration of the novel beans revealed a *generalization asymmetry* effect as well: participants' estimates of the valence of novel beans were biased toward the negative. Novel beans that were equidistant between a positive and a negative game bean were likely to be regarded as negative. Thus, resemblance to a known negative was weighted more heavily than resemblance to a known positive. Additional analyses showed this generalization asymmetry to be a phenomenon in and of itself, independent of the learning asymmetry. Although the generalization and learning asymmetries are strongly correlated across participants, the generalization asymmetry is apparent over and above the effects that the learning asymmetry itself has on generalization.

In the next sections, we consider the mechanisms that underlie each of these valence asymmetries. We first discuss the learning asymmetry and various experiments that have proven pivotal to our understanding of the forces that bring it about. We then consider what our research has revealed about the generalization asymmetry.

LEARNING ASYMMETRY DEPENDS ON APPROACH–AVOIDANCE

Our explanation for the learning asymmetry effect follows directly from the earlier theoretical discussion. If feedback is contingent on approach (here, "eating"), then true-positive approach responses will be reinforced and false-positives corrected by gain and loss feedback, respectively. However, false-negative avoidance will remain uncorrected since no feedback is provided to such responses and hence participants will fail to distinguish reliably between true-negatives (bad beans) and false-negatives (good beans assumed to be bad). The consequence is that participants' estimates of the valence of the stimuli will be predominantly negative. This argument rests on the assumption that learning asymmetry as assessed during the test phase reflects levels of avoidance versus approach during the learning phase, since these levels determine the feedback received. Direct evidence to support this assumption comes from the fact that the learning asymmetry was significantly negatively correlated with the overall amount of approach behavior during the learning (game) phase: the more participants chose to sample the beans, the more feedback they received and the better they became at identifying good as well as bad beans.

Another way of establishing that the learning asymmetry effect arises from the dependence of feedback on approach is to remove the fundamental constraint of the game and provide feedback on every trial, irrespective of whether participants chose to eat a bean or not. This change was introduced in the "full feedback" condition of Fazio et al.'s (2004) Experiment 2, where, if participants chose to eat a bean, they were informed of the "Effect of Bean," as before. However, if they chose not to eat, their energy level was unchanged, but they still received feedback alongside a caption reading "Effect Bean Would Have Had." The consequence was an elimination of the learning asymmetry effect, the only condition in which this has been observed.

This last finding is consistent with the conclusions of a series of computer simulations (Eiser, Fazio, Stafford, & Prescott, 2003) in which we trained a neural network to differentiate between "good" and "bad" input patterns corresponding to the beans in the BeanFest stimulus array. In the *full feedback* conditions, we employed the familiar backpropagation of error ("backprop") learning algorithm (McClelland & Rumelhart, 1988). The way this algorithm operates is broadly as follows. When the network is presented with a given input (bean), it produces an output, corresponding to an estimate of the bean's valence (how good or bad it is). This estimate is then compared with a target value, representing the correct output or true valence of the bean, and the "error," i.e., discrepancy between the output and target value, is calculated. The connection weights (that govern how activation is fed forward from the input through a layer of "hidden" units to the output) are then modified to reduce this error so that the next time the same input is presented, the output should be closer to the target value. The consequence is that "learning" takes place both when the network selects an action equivalent to approach or eating a bean and when it selects an action equivalent to

avoidance. In other words, regardless of whether the network approaches (eats) or avoids a given bean, it will be told whether the bean is good or bad, and so will be more likely to approach it next time it is presented if it is good, and less likely to approach it if it is bad. The simulations using the standard version of this algorithm produced perfect or near perfect learning of both good and bad beans, in other words, no learning asymmetry. In the *contingent feedback* conditions, however, we adapted the algorithm so that the connection weights were updated only if the network selected an action equivalent to approach (eating). In other words, learning only took place on trials where the network approached a bean to discover its valence, thus transforming the paradigm from one of supervised to reinforcement learning. The differences between the conditions were striking. Whereas the network continued to display perfect or near perfect learning of bad beans, it consistently failed to identify a proportion of the good beans, instead responding to them as though they were bad. In other words, we reproduced the learning asymmetry effect within an artificial learning system where, as in the human experiments, feedback depended on active exploration.

EFFECTS OF VALUE EXTREMITY

Feedback in the BeanFest game not only provides information to participants, it also results in gains and losses. In the standard version of the game these gains and losses were symmetrical (+10 versus −10 points on each trial). But what would we expect if gains were stronger than losses, or vice versa? In terms of a reinforcement learning perspective, stronger positive reinforcements from eating a good bean should lead to more approach, whereas stronger punishments from eating a bad bean should lead to more avoidance. In terms of a more cognitive (SDT) decision perspective, greater gains from a good bean increase the benefits of a true-positive, and hence encourage adoption of a more risk-accepting (approach) response criterion, whereas greater losses from a bad bean increase the costs of a false-positive and hence should lead to more risk aversion. Either way, the predictions are the same.

One of the experiments reported by Fazio et al. (2004) tested this specifically. In the extreme positive condition, the gains from each good bean remained at +10, but the costs of eating a bad bean were reduced to −2. Conversely, in the extreme negative condition, the costs of a bad bean remained at −10, but the gains from a good bean were only +2. As predicted, the extreme negative condition produced a dramatic decrease in approach behavior during the game, relative to the extreme positive condition.

The test phase data showed the learning asymmetry effect, although statistically evident in both conditions, to be significantly greater in extreme negative condition. Moreover, a mediational analysis indicated that this effect of condition on the learning asymmetry was mediated by the differences in approach behavior produced by the extremity manipulation.

PROMOTION VERSUS PREVENTION FOCUS AND GAIN–LOSS FRAMING IN BeanFest

So far we have been describing structural factors within the BeanFest game that influence the learning asymmetry. But what of other cues or motivational factors that might trigger differential levels of approach and avoidance? According to Higgins (1998), individuals vary in the extent to which they generally interpret uncertain situations as offering the achievement of potential success and gain ("promotion focus") and as requiring precautions against the occurrence of failure and loss ("prevention focus"). Although Higgins et al. (2001) suggest that such individual differences may have their roots in contrasting parenting practices, more experimental approaches have explored techniques for priming promotion- and prevention-focused interpretations of specific problems and situations that (as is the case with BeanFest) involve potential success and failure and gain and loss. There are close affinities here to the concept of "gain–loss framing" (Kahneman & Tversky, 1984), where preferences for different options can be affected by whether the same outcome is presented as a gain over a less desirable reference point (e.g., lives saved as a result of treatment) or a loss compared with a more desirable reference point (e.g., lives lost despite treatment).

To this end we adopted a technique devised by Friedman and Foerster (2001) for priming approach and avoidance behavior through promotion and prevention cues. This involved participants tracing routes on visually presented mazes. In the promotion focus condition, these mazes were presented as involving an animal seeking food at the end point of the maze. In the prevention condition, these involved an animal escaping from a larger predator, with the end point of the maze being a safe refuge. Each participant completed three mazes (under the same focus), once before the BeanFest game and twice at intervals between blocks of the game. In addition, participants in the promotion focus condition started the game with 0 points and were told to try and get 100, whereas those in the prevention focus condition started with 100 points and were told to try to avoid dropping to 0, with no "energy loss via time." (This

manipulation of points targets had not been found to influence game behavior or learning by itself in a previous version of the experiment.) As predicted, promotion focus led to a significant reduction in the learning asymmetry, with more good beans and fewer bad beans being correctly identified, compared with the prevention focus condition. Mediational analysis indicated that this effect of focus on learning asymmetry was mediated by differences in approach behavior during the game, with promotion focus leading to more approach than prevention focus. These findings suggest that motivations triggered by promotion and prevention cues external to the BeanFest game itself may lead to greater risk acceptance or aversion, with consequent effects on attitude formation.

SOCIALLY TRANSMITTED ATTITUDES AND INDIRECT EXPERIENCE

Our focus so far has been on how individuals acquire attitudes from their own experience, without any guidance for other people about what actions or objects should be approached or avoided. However, in many real-life contexts, our social interactions will be partly guided by socially transmitted attitudes, expectancies, encouragements, warnings, prejudices, and other kinds of information. Reliance on socially transmitted knowledge and experience is clearly functional in that it means that we do not have to discover everything for ourselves. The literature on social learning processes in personality and social development (Bandura, 1977; Mischel, 1973) is one of the many traditions of work that emphasize this theme. However, the implications of this for attitude formation have been relatively under-researched in comparison to topics such as the acquisition of behavioral and cultural norms. Even when the importance of socially transmitted expectancies for attitude–behavior relations has been more explicitly recognized, as with the inclusion of the subjective norm component in the theory of planned behavior (Ajzen, 1991), specific consideration of how such subjective norms have been acquired—and how this might combine with attitude formation processes more generally—has been largely lacking.

What then might be the combined effect on attitude learning of participants' own direct experience and evaluative information received indirectly from other people? Previous research has compared the effects of direct and indirect experience (indicating among other things that attitudes based on direct experience are more predictive of behavior, Fazio & Zanna, 1981, and more resistant to counter-persuasion, Wu & Shaffer, 1987). Here, though, we are not concerned with the relative effectiveness of direct and indirect experience for behavioral prediction so much as with how they might interact dynamically. Specifically, might socially transmitted information (indirect experience) guide individuals' exploratory behavior and hence shape the direct experience on the basis of which individuals' attitudes are formed? What happens when such direct experience confirms or disconfirms such expectations?

A first attempt to address this question was made in Experiment 5 in Fazio et al. (2004). Before playing the BeanFest game, participants were told that the main focus of the experiment was on "how well people can learn across generations." They would therefore be shown comments supposedly written by previous participants. These comments were presented to participants individually in folders, each containing two hand-written notes. One note was supposedly from a "first generation" player, the second from a "second generation" player who had been shown the first generation player's note. The first player reported having been very successful and passed on the advice either to eat or avoid a specific class of beans (circular ones with few speckles, i.e., region 1 in Figure 19.2), whereas the second player reported having followed this advice and found it "very helpful." Participants then played the game as in other conditions, either with the valences of the beans as in the original matrix shown in Figure 19.2, or with the valences reversed. This meant that the particular beans participants were advised to either eat or avoid were actually good (original matrix) or bad (reverse matrix).

Our main interest was in the effect of misleading information, in conditions where participants were advised either to eat beans that turned out to be bad, or avoid beans that were actually good. The main finding was that participants were able to discount the former kind of advice, since by sampling the bad beans they discovered their true value. In the latter condition, however, they tended to follow the advice to avoid the beans in question and therefore failed to discover that they were in fact good. In other words, the impact of advice was mediated by participants' own direct experience of the beans.

In a sequel to this study (Eiser, Shook, & Fazio, 2007), we looked at the effects of advice that the set of beans taken as a whole (rather than just those in a single region) were predominantly good, and to be eaten, or bad and to be avoided. The same cover story of learning across generations was used, but this time participants only read the note from a first generation player, without corroboration from a second generation player. We anticipated that the former (good) advice would lead to a reduction in the learning asymmetry effect compared with the condition

where participants were told most beans were bad. This was in fact the case, provided that participants did indeed start the game by following the advice they had been given; in other words, the effect of advice on learning was mediated by participants' actual approach or avoidance behavior.

THE GENERALIZATION ASYMMETRY

As noted earlier, participants in the BeanFest experiments show evidence of generalizing the attitudes that they develop toward the game beans to novel beans. The more closely a novel bean resembles a known positive (or negative), the more likely it is to be classified as positive (or negative). Despite this effect of resemblance, a strong asymmetry is also evident. It takes less resemblance to a negative to be declared negative than it takes resemblance to a positive to be declared positive. This generalization asymmetry has proven remarkably robust. It has been evident consistently across the various experiments that we have conducted. It has not been moderated to any significant degree by the manipulations that influenced the learning asymmetry. So, the generalization asymmetry was apparent regardless of whether feedback during the game was or was not contingent on approach behavior, regardless of whether positive or negative beans assumed more extreme values, and regardless of whether participants were induced to adopt a promotion or a prevention focus.

Recent research by Shook, Fazio and Eiser (2007) provides the most extensive analysis of the generalization asymmetry to date. This investigation examined attitude generalization as a function of visual similarity to objects that varied from extremely positive to mildly positive to mildly negative to extremely negative. Instead of employing the standard matrix in which three regions are associated with a value of +10 and three with a value of −10, Shook et al. reduced the value of good beans in one of the three regions to +2 (while leaving the remainder at +10) and at the same time changing that of bad beans in one region only to −2 (while leaving the remainder at −10). Each bean, i.e., each cell of the matrix, was treated as the unit of analysis, with the average response to the bean across participants representing the presumed value of the bean. (Actually, four matrices, varying the location of the +2 and −2 regions, were included so as to unconfound value with specific visual characteristics.)

Other things being equal, the more similar a novel bean was visually to a previously experienced game bean (i.e., the closer in the matrix), the more it was judged to share the same valence. As predicted, this tendency was even stronger for novel beans that more closely resembled previously experienced extreme negative beans than for those resembling (i.e., near in the matrix to) either extreme positive or mild negative beans. The extra potency of losses over gains was further evidenced by the fact that the tendency to rate novel beans similar to a mild negative (–2) bean as bad was of comparable strength to the tendency to rate novel beans similar to an extreme positive (+10) bean as good.

Shook et al. conducted additional analyses to predict participants' judgments of the novel beans from their individual responses to the original game beans (as distinct from the actual values of these game beans). The question addressed was whether any given novel bean would be judged as more similar in value to how those in the nearest region of original game beans were judged, or to those in the second nearest region of game beans (that would in fact be of opposite valence to the first). As expected, novel beans tended to be judged as more similar in value to the game beans in the nearer region than to those in the region slightly further away, but this effect of proximity was less marked when the nearer region was judged positive and the second region negative.

This last finding is important in confirming that the generalization asymmetry is more than just a by-product of the learning asymmetry. In other words, one might expect some tendency for novel beans to be seen as predominantly negative just because participants typically succeed in identifying more negative than positive beans during the learning phase. In fact, this is what happens in the simulations reported by Eiser et al. (2003). The network's "judgments" of the value of novel beans showed clear evidence of generalization on the basis of similarity, or proximity within the matrix, to the learnt values of the beans presented during the learning phase. In other words, if the network classified a training bean as bad (or good), it classified novel beans adjacent to it in the matrix similarly. There was a tendency for some novel beans adjacent to good training beans to be judged as bad, but only if the good training beans themselves were misclassified as bad. In other words, any tendency to predict novel beans to be bad rather than good in these simulations depends entirely on the learning asymmetry. This is not the case in the human experiments. The generalization asymmetry still is apparent after controlling for the learning asymmetry.

Unlike the learning asymmetry, the generalization asymmetry does not depend on a structural mechanism involving the contingent relation between information gain and approach behavior (since it is found also under conditions of full feedback), nor is it purely a function of how well participants learn to differentiate the original stimuli. Instead, it appears to be an illustration of the frequently discussed proposition that negativity is more powerful than positivity (Baumeister, Bratslavsky, Finkenauer, & Vohs, 2001; Cacioppo, Gardner, & Bernston, 1997; Rozin & Royzman, 2001; Taylor, 1991). When judging a novel stimulus, perceivers weigh its negative features more heavily than its positive features.

Another dramatic illustration of this negativity bias—this tendency to weigh the negative more heavily than the positive—was apparent in a recent study conducted by Eiser et al. (2007). The study focused on participants' self-assessments after playing the BeanFest game. Participants provided evaluative ratings regarding the efficacy of the strategy with which they approached playing the game. A straightforward hypothesis would have been that participants would evaluate their own game strategy more positively both if it led to more positive reinforcements (true-positive approaches to good beans leading to a gain in points), and also to fewer negative reinforcements (false-positive approaches to bad beans leading to a loss in points). Interestingly, participants' evaluations of their own strategy were strongly inversely related to the number of bad beans they approached, but not at all related to the number of good beans they approached. This is further evidence of how negative information looms larger than positive in its influence on evaluative judgment—in this case, with respect to self-assessments.

IMPLICATIONS FOR PREJUDICE

We have described the findings from our BeanFest experiments in some detail, not because, obviously, we have any special interest in beans—real or virtual—but rather because we believe the processes underlying participants' choices in this simple game may have wider relevance to people's cognitions, feelings, and behavior in their real social environment. The starting point for any such extrapolation is a set of related ideas centering around the notion of uncertainty. We inevitably have incomplete knowledge of our physical and social environment, and because of this, every action we perform involves some element of risk. One way of reducing uncertainty and hence risk is by gaining more knowledge, but extra knowledge rarely if ever comes risk-free. To find out more about unfamiliar places, people, activities, etc., we have to be prepared to approach and engage with them and to allow our own happiness or unhappiness, gains or losses, to be affected by them in ways we can predict only imperfectly, if at all. So a trade-off has to be struck between the gains of new knowledge and experience on the one hand, and the effort, cost, and even danger of seeking such knowledge.

This could be viewed as directly analogous to the issue of "energy budgets" in animal foraging (Bateson, 2002): will the energy expended in hunting or foraging be adequately compensated for by the energy gained from a new source of food? If animals fail to manage their energy budget efficiently, they will not survive, and for this simple reason we can assume that selection processes lead animals to be reasonably efficient in this respect, at least so long as the environment remains fairly stable. As humans, we still need to make trade-offs but the equations are far less well defined or deterministic, and the personal penalties for dysfunctional choices are often far less obvious or at least immediate.

From a societal perspective, some of the most dysfunctional choices are those involving prejudice against an out-group. In particular, we can ask why negative attitudes and stereotypes persist in ways that are unsupported by evidence. This is clearly only one of the very many questions that could be asked, along with why certain out-groups historically have been the target of prejudice to a greater extent than others, why prejudiced beliefs involve particular kinds of stereotypic content and how these may be linked to broader ideologies, why prejudice may lead to discrimination, dehumanization, and extermination. The last thing we wish to appear to do is to trivialize these issues, or suggest that they can all be reduced to the structure of a simple computer game. Yet even so, we believe that there may be some continuity between the processes underlying the persistence of false-negative avoidant tendencies and beliefs in our experiments and such real-world phenomena. The common link is that positive attitudes constitute a basis for motivation to approach, and negative attitudes a basis for motivation to avoid (Zajonc, 1998). To the extent that individuals can act out such motivations, they will interact with people they like and avoid interaction with people they dislike. The consequence of avoiding interaction is a lack of direct experience that might well disconfirm previous negative beliefs. Hence, false-negative avoidant tendencies and beliefs (prejudices) may well persist relatively unchallenged by experience.

One might well ask where such positive and negative attitudes come from in the first place. If we take "the first place" to mean an individual's earliest encounters with members of particular groups, these could well differ in the extent to which they are experienced as pleasant or unpleasant, reassuring or threatening. The relationship between attitudes and approach–avoidance behavior is essentially dynamic. As with all dynamic systems, we may witness an extreme sensitivity to differences in initial conditions (Eiser, 1994), so that small events can steer the social development of different individuals in directions of increasing divergence. Furthermore, as our experiments also show, socially transmitted beliefs, based supposedly on others' experience, can have a similar effect in terms of steering approach or avoidance. Nor is such reliance on others' opinions and advice irrational or unreasonable in the broader scheme of things. Reading consumer reports, travel guides, theater reviews, etc., can save us time, money, and disappointment, even if we also learn that we need to take some of these with a pinch of salt. When parents advise their children against accepting lifts from strange men, this is clearly sensible precautionary advice, even if not all strange men are molesters.

The difficulty is being able to distinguish the types of advice that are reasonable and well-founded from those that are not. This difficulty is even greater when the advice or attitudes we receive from others leads to avoidance, and where the costs of avoidance (including false-negative avoidance decisions) are affordable. Someone might take it into their head to avoid certain kinds of unfamiliar foods or ethnic cuisines—maybe they have been treated to horror stories of unhygienic practices or suspicious ingredients—but they are unlikely to starve as a consequence. Likewise, in many social contexts, individuals may neither have much opportunity nor feel any special need to form close friendships across ethnic, linguistic, or religious divides. Even without any perception of danger, it may simply be thought to involve more effort for no obvious gain. Similarity remains an important default cue for attraction (Berscheid & Walster, 1978). All this implies that many socially transmitted prejudices and negative attitudes may be assimilated in a relatively "mindless" (Langer, Blank, & Chanowitz, 1978) or uncritical way, and this may be especially the case where the target groups are ones with which the individual has only limited, if any, opportunity for direct interaction.

When such interaction opportunities do arise, invalid negative prejudices diminish the likelihood that they will be pursued. Precisely such avoidance as a function of negative racial attitudes has been demonstrated in recent research. Towles-Schwen and Fazio (2003) observed a relation between automatically activated racial attitudes and participants' expressed willingness to enter various situations involving interracial interaction. Plant and Devine (2003) likewise found that engagement in interracial interaction was inhibited by anticipated anxiety. The BeanFest findings illustrate what can happen when the relevant attitudes are unwarrantedly negative. The resulting avoidance behavior markedly reduces the chances of discovering the invalidity of the negative attitudes.

Another set of questions relate to how prejudices might be overcome, especially through direct experience. If risk-averse avoidance of interaction with out-group members underlies the persistence of prejudice, then perhaps part of the answer is to increase the opportunities for such interaction. Such reasoning is the basis for the "contact hypothesis" that increased opportunity for intergroup contact can lead to an attenuation of prejudice (Deutsch & Collins, 1951; Pettigrew, 1997). However, most of the research evidence suggests that it is the quality of contact, in particular formation of interethnic friendships, rather than contact per se, that is important. This is consistent with our argument that increased approach does not automatically lead to a blanket increase in positive attitudes, but rather to more complete feedback. This then allows more accurate identification of positive attitude objects (i.e., more true-positive approaches), along with a more evidence-based avoidance of negative attitude objects (i.e., fewer false-positive approaches, or more true-negative avoidances). In less technical terms, this can lead to a more differentiated view of out-group members as individuals, with some of whom friendships are easier, and with others, less so.

IMPLICATIONS FOR SELF-EVALUATIONS AND HAPPINESS

The reinforcements we receive from our social interactions not only lead us to hold positive and negative attitudes about other people, they critically affect the way we think about ourselves. If other people are nice to us, and show that they like us, then this surely "proves" that we are likable, and worth being nice to. Conversely, if people are nasty to us, and show they dislike us, then this just goes to show that we are nasty too, and do not deserve to be liked. A wide variety of studies suggest that our self-evaluations are related to how we believe others evaluate us (Bem, 1972; Fazio, 1987). Similarly, success can boost our self-esteem while failure or other negative life-events can damage it. If such failure persists, it can lead to depression. Naturally, there are individual differences in resilience to setbacks, and one moderating factor may be the extent to which success or failure is attributed internally to one's own character, skill, or effort (or the lack of these), or externally to chance or the actions of others (Mullen & Riordan, 1988). However, such interactions need to be interpreted in context. Overall we are dealing with some powerful main effects: good events make us

feel good and tend to raise our self-esteem, whereas bad events make us feel bad and tend to lower our self-esteem (Crocker & Wolfe, 2001).

But here we confront an interesting paradox. Despite the fact that we are risk averse in many of our personal life-choices (implying that we see much of the world as beset with danger), and despite the fact that negative events typically appear to have a greater impact on social judgments than do positive events (Baumeister et al. 2001; Rozin & Royzman, 2001; Skowronski & Carlston, 1989), most of us describe ourselves as relatively happy, much of the time. Furthermore, if asked to compare ourselves with "average" others, we generally tend to rate ourselves, within the constraints of modesty, as more likely to experience success and less like to experience failure or mishaps such as illness or injury and as better on a wide variety of attributes (Alicke, Klotz, Breitenbecher, Yurak, & Vredenburg, 1995; Weinstein, 1980, 1982). Although the strength of such reported effects depends to some extent on the format in which such questions are asked (Eiser, Pahl, & Prins, 2001), the overall message still seems relatively clear: most of us, for much of the time, are relatively pleased with ourselves and with our lot in life.

This tendency is all the more remarkable in the light of the fact that people can adapt surprisingly readily to changing life circumstances. In broad terms, we may overestimate the extent of any lasting changes to our happiness from positive and negative life-events (Wilson & Gilbert, 2003). Brickman, Coates, and Janoff-Bulman (1978) found that lottery winners reported little lasting gain in happiness. Likewise, the loss in well-being as a consequence of misfortune, injury, serious illness, or bereavement may be less severe in actual experience than in imagination (Lehman, Wortman, & Williams, 1987). But such homeostatic adaptive processes do not reduce everyone's sense of happiness and well-being to "average." On the contrary, on average most of us tend to see ourselves as somewhat happier than average (Diener & Diener, 1996).

Although it is almost a truism that all social judgments (including judgments of our own happiness and well-being) are relative rather than absolute (Eiser & Stroebe, 1972), there is nothing fixed about the standards of comparison we use, and to which our judgments are relative. Most of the work of comparative or unrealistic optimism appears paradoxical in that it asks participants to compare themselves with an interpersonal standard or average. The finding that respondents, on average, rate themselves as somewhat above average suggests the operation of some kind of positivity bias, but this just pushes the question one step on. If we show a positivity bias in our self-appraisals, how has this come about? How does it reflect our personal history and experience of reinforcements?

A possible answer is that, when we experience events as relatively positive or negative, we are not generally performing any interpersonal comparison (even if asked to do so), but rather comparing our experience with an intrapersonal or subjective standard. Still we are left with the question of why we mostly rate experiences as better than average, when our subjective standard may adapt to our personal distribution of good and bad events. But this is not such a difficult question to answer if we take account of how such subjective standards adapt to reflect the full distribution of our experiences. The classic theory of adaptation processes in social judgment is Helson's (1947, 1964) adaptation-level theory, according to which all experiences are judged against a weighted average of all previous experiences along the relevant sensory continuum. Later research (see Eiser & Stroebe, 1972, for an early review) showed Helson's formulation to be too simplistic. Among many other considerations, account needs to be taken of the shape (i.e., skewness) of the distribution of the stimulus events presented or experienced. According to Parducci (1963), a better prediction of an individual's subjective average or adaptation-level can be derived from a combination of the midpoint between the extremes of the stimulus distribution and the median (a so-called range-frequency compromise). If the stimulus distribution is normal (or rectangular), the midpoint and median will coincide, and equal the arithmetic mean. However, if there is any skew, they will diverge.

What has any of this to do with happiness? Well, Parducci (1984) offers an interesting and plausible speculation. Suppose most people's distributions of life-events are positively skewed, i.e., characterized by relatively frequent events that are moderately positive, and rather fewer, but somewhat more extreme, negative events. If this is the case, then the midpoint of their distribution would be lower than their median and, since their adaptation-level (subjective average) lies between the midpoint and the median, the majority of events would be experienced as better than average. The result: happiness.

This is a neat argument, but it raises an obvious question: why should most people's experiences of life-events be distributed as Parducci suggests? We can offer an answer in two parts. First, the possibility that negative events are experienced as more extreme fits well with the broader evidence on the salience of negative information. Second, a predominance of moderately positive outcomes

follows directly from the general tendency for risk-averse decision making, where individuals approach familiar objects they are confident are good, thus obtaining a satisfactory return of true-positives, while avoiding objects about whose valence they are less certain, thus minimizing the number of false-positive approaches, or nasty surprises, even at the price of missing out on available rewards of which they are unaware (false-negative avoidances).

Any general statements of this kind need obviously to be hedged around with a number of caveats. One of the most obvious is that the argument rests on the assumption that we can mostly avoid bad things happening to us, in other words, that conditions allow our approach and avoidance motivations to carry forward into approach and avoidance behaviors. Risk aversion is only functional if risks can indeed be avoided. If they cannot, the consequence is not happiness but a kind of learnt helplessness (Alloy, Abramson, & Francis, 1999; Seligman, 1975). For individuals deprived of free choice in oppressive life-circumstances or abusive relationships, positive outcomes may be the exception, and negative outcomes the norm. Another is that there is huge variation in the kinds of experiences that different individuals find pleasant and unpleasant. One person's fear may be another's excitement, one person's boredom another's mellow relaxation. The origins of such differences lie far beyond the scope of the present chapter, but do not affect our basic argument insofar as we assume that it will be individuals' personal evaluations of different outcomes that guide their approach–avoidance behavior.

A more general limitation is that there are many other aspects of feedback other than mere valence that may affect the processes described. Although our experimental situation fits within a general reinforcement learning paradigm, the more general literature on reinforcement learning emphasizes the importance of several parameters of reinforcement schedules beyond those we have manipulated. Note that, in BeanFest, every good bean is good, and every bad bean is bad, on every occasion they are presented and sampled. We have not explored the subtleties of partial reinforcement, variable interval or ratio schedules, or other such variations that were studied intensively in the animal learning literature for most of the last century. Our narrower focus reflects the limitations of our own efforts rather than any dismissal of the lessons that might be drawn from this wider literature. Nonetheless, we are struck by how few of these lessons have been drawn by social psychologists in general, and attitude theorists in particular.

CONCLUDING REMARKS

Like all contributors to this volume, we regard the distinction between approach and avoidance motivations as fundamental to psychological theory across many different areas. Our own focus has been on how such motivations interface with attitude processes as studied by social psychologists. Relating attitudes and motivations to each other immediately draws attention to the behavioral implications of attitudes. For the best part of 70 years or more, researchers have been concerned about such implications, but mainly from the perspective of how well attitude predicts behavior. We have argued for a more dynamic view of this relationship. Attitudes may motivate approach and avoidance, but approach and avoidance in their turn shape the experiences on which our attitudes are based. One of the simplest to state, but at the same time most startling and profound, challenges for attitude theory is the fact that different individuals can disagree in their evaluations of the same attitude object or issue, and sometimes violently. It is almost a truism that such differences in attitude reflect different selective perceptions of the issue, but what gives rise to such selectivity? We hope we have demonstrated that part of the answer can lie in the divergent experiences, and hence learning histories, that arise from different levels of risk acceptance, exploration, and hence discovery associated with approach and avoidance under conditions of uncertainty.

REFERENCES

Ajzen, I. (1991). The theory of planned behavior. *Organization Behavior and Human Decision Processes, 50*, 179–211.

Alicke, M. D., Klotz, M. L., Breitenbecher, D. L., Yurak, T. J., & Vredenburg, D. S. (1995). Personal contact, individuation, and the better-than-average effect. *Journal of Personality and Social Psychology, 68*, 804–825.

Alloy, L. B., Abramson, L. Y., & Francis, E. L. (1999). Do negative cognitive styles confer vulnerability to depression? *Current Directions in Psychological Science, 8*, 128–132.

Bandura, A. (1977). Self-efficacy: Toward a unifying theory of behavioral change. *Psychological Review, 84*, 191–215.

Bateson, M. (2002). Recent advances in our understanding of risk-sensitive foraging preferences. *Proceedings of the Nutrition Society, 61*, 1–8.

Baumeister, R. F., Bratslavsky, E., Finkenauer, C., & Vohs, K. D. (2001). Bad is stronger than good. *Review of General Psychology, 5*, 323–370.

Bem, D. J. (1972). Self-perception theory. In L. Berkowitz (Ed.), *Advances in experimental social psychology* (Vol. 6, pp. 1–62). New York: Academic Press.

Berscheid, E., & Walster, G. W. (1978). *Interpersonal attraction* (2nd ed.). Reading, MA: Addison-Wesley.

Boholm, A. (1996). Risk perception and social anthropology: Critique of cultural theory. *Ethnos, 61*(1–2), 64–84.

Brickman, P., Coates, D., & Janoff-Bulman, R. (1978). Lottery winners and accident victims: Is happiness relative? *Journal of Personality and Social Psychology, 36*, 917–927.

Cacioppo, J., & Berntson, G. (1994). Relationship between attitudes and evaluative space: A critical review with emphasis on the separability of positive and negative substrates. *Psychological Bulletin, 115*, 401–423.

Cacioppo, J. T., Gardner, W. L., & Berntson, G. G. (1997). Beyond bipolar conceptualizations and measures: The case of attitudes and evaluative space. *Personality and Social Psychology Review, 1*, 3–25.

Crocker, J., & Wolfe, C. T. (2001). Contingencies of self-worth. *Psychological Review, 52*, 177–193.

De Houwer, J., Thomas, S., & Baeyens, F. (2001). Associative learning of likes and dislikes: A review of 25 years of research on human evaluative conditioning. *Psychological Bulletin, 127*, 853–869.

Deutsch, M., & Collins, M. E. (1951). *Interracial housing: A psychological investigation of a social experiment.* Minneapolis, MN: University of Minnesota Press.

Diener, E., & Diener, C. (1996). Most people are happy. *Psychological Science, 7*, 181–185.

Dolan, P. (1998). The measurement of individual utility and social welfare. *Journal of Health Economics, 17*, 39–52.

Douglas, M. (1986). *Risk acceptability according to the social sciences.* London: Routledge & Kegan Paul.

Eiser, C. (2004). *Children with cancer: The quality of life.* Mahwah, NJ: Erlbaum.

Eiser, J. R. (1994). *Attitudes, chaos and the connectionist mind.* Oxford: Blackwell.

Eiser, J. R., Fazio, R. H., Stafford, T., & Prescott, T. J. (2003). Connectionist simulation of attitude learning: Asymmetries in the acquisition of positive and negative evaluations. *Personality and Social Psychology Bulletin, 29*, 1221–1235.

Eiser, J. R., Pahl, S., & Prins, Y. R. A. (2001). Optimism, pessimism and the direction of self-other comparisons. *Journal of Experimental Social Psychology, 37*, 77–84.

Eiser, J. R., Shook, N. J., & Fazio, R. H. (2007). Attitude learning through exploration: Advice and strategy appraisals. *European Journal of Social Psychology, 37*, 1046–1056.

Eiser, J. R., & Stroebe, W. (1972). *Categorization and social judgement.* London: Academic Press.

Elliot, A. J., & Thrash, T. M. (2002). Approach–avoidance motivation in personality: Approach and avoidance temperaments and goals. *Journal of Personality and Social Psychology, 82*, 804–818.

Fazio, R. H. (1987). Self-perception theory: A current perspective. In M. P. Zanna, J. M. Olson, & C. P. Herman (Eds.), *Social influence: The Ontario symposium* (Vol. 5, pp. 129–150). Hillsdale, NJ: Erlbaum.

Fazio, R. H., Eiser, J. R., & Shook, N. J. (2004). Attitude formation through exploration: Valence asymmetries. *Journal of Personality and Social Psychology, 87*, 293–311.

Fazio, R. H., & Zanna, M. P. (1981). Direct experience and attitude–behavior consistency. In L. Berkowitz (Ed.), *Advances in experimental social psychology* (Vol. 14, pp. 161–202). San Diego, CA: Academic Press.

Fischoff, B., Slovic, P., Lichtenstein, S., Read, S., & Combs, B. (1978). How safe is safe enough? A psychometric study of attitudes towards technological risks and benefits. *Policy Sciences, 9*, 127–152.

Friedman, R. S., & Foerster, J. (2001). The effects of promotion and prevention cues on creativity. *Journal of Personality and Social Psychology, 81*, 1001–1013.

Gigerenzer, G. (2002). *Reckoning with risk: Learning to live with uncertainty*. London: Penguin.

Gold, M. R., Siegel, J. E., Russell, L. B., & Weinstein, M. C. (1996). *Cost-effectiveness in health and medicine*. Oxford: Oxford University Press.

Gray, J. (1990). Brain systems that mediate both emotion and cognition. In J. Gray (Ed.), *Psychobiological aspects of relationships between emotion and cognition* (pp. 239–288). Hillsdale, NJ: Erlbaum.

Higgins, E. T. (1998). Promotion and prevention: Regulatory focus as a motivational principle. In M. P. Zanna (Ed.), *Advances in experimental social psychology* (Vol. 30, pp. 1–46). New York: Academic Press.

Higgins, E. T., Friedman, R., Harlow, R., Idson, L. C., Ayduk, O., et al. (2001). Achievement orientations from subjective histories of success: Promotion pride versus prevention pride. *European Journal of Social Psychology, 31*, 3–23.

Helson, H. (1947). Adaptation-level as frame of reference for prediction of psychophysical data. *American Journal of Psychology, 60*, 1–29.

Helson, H. (1964). *Adaptation-level theory*. New York: Harper & Row.

Kahneman, D., & Tversky, A. (1979). Prospect theory: An analysis of decision under risk. *Econometrics, 47*, 263–291.

Kahneman, D., & Tversky, A. (1984). Choices, values, and frames. *American Psychologist, 39*, 341–350.

Langer, E. J., Blank, A., & Chanowitz, B. (1978). The mindlessness of ostensibly thoughtful action: The role of 'placebic' information in interpersonal interaction. *Journal of Personality and Social Psychology, 36*, 635–642.

Lehman, D., Wortman, C., & Williams, A. (1987). Long-term effects of losing a spouse or a child in a motor vehicle crash. *Journal of Personality and Social Psychology, 52*, 281–231.

March, J. G. (1996). Learning to be risk averse. *Psychological Review, 103*, 309–319.

McClelland, J., & Rumelhart, D. (1988). *Explorations in parallel distributed processing*. Cambridge, MA: MIT Press.

Mischel, W. (1973). Towards a cognitive social learning reconceptualization of personality. *Psychological Review, 80*, 252–283.

Mullen, B., & Riordan, C. A. (1988). Self-serving attributions for performance in naturalistic settings: A meta-analytic review. *Journal of Applied Social Psychology, 18*, 3–22.

Nord, E., Pinto, J. L., Richardson, J., Menzel, P., & Ubel, P. (1999). Incorporating societal concerns for fairness in numerical valuations of health programmes. *Health Economics, 8*, 25–39.

Olsen, J. A. (2000). A note on eliciting distributive preferences for health. *Journal of Health Economics, 19*, 541–550.

Olson, M. A., & Fazio, R. H. (2001). Implicit attitude formation through classical conditioning. *Psychological Science, 12*, 413–417.

Olson, M. A., & Fazio, R. H. (2002). Implicit acquisition and manifestation of classically conditioned attitudes. *Social Cognition, 20*, 89–103.

Olson, M. A., & Fazio, R. H. (2006). Reducing automatically activated racial prejudice through implicit evaluative conditioning. *Personality and Social Psychology Bulletin, 32*, 421–433.

Parducci, A. (1963). Range-frequency compromise in judgment. *Psychological Monographs, 77* (2, Whole No. 565).

Parducci, A. (1984). Value judgments: Towards a relational theory of happiness. In J. R. Eiser (Ed.), *Attitudinal judgment* (pp. 3–21). New York: Springer-Verlag.

Pettigrew, T. F. (1997). Generalized intergroup contact effects on prejudice. *Personality and Social Psychology Bulletin, 23*, 173–185.

Plant, E. A., & Devine, P. G. (2003). The antecedents and implications of interracial anxiety. *Personality and Social Psychology Bulletin, 29*, 790–801.

Rozin, P., & Royzman, E. B. (2001). Negativity bias, negativity dominance, and contagion. *Personality and Social Psychology Review, 5*, 296–320.

Seligman, M. E. P. (1975). *Helplessness*. San Francisco, CA: Freeman.

Shook, N. J., Fazio, R. H., & Eiser, J. R. (2007). Attitude generalization: Similarity, valence and extremity. *Journal of Experimental Social Psychology, 43*, 641–647.

Skowronski, J. J., & Carlston, D. E. (1989). Negativity and extremity biases in impression formation: A review of explanations. *Psychological Bulletin, 105*, 131–142.

Solomon, R. L., & Wynne, L. C. (1954). Traumatic avoidance learning: The principles of anxiety conservation and partial irreversibility. *Psychological Review, 61*, 353–385.

Sutton, R. S., & Barto, A. G. (1998). *Reinforcement learning: An introduction*. Cambridge, MA: The MIT Press.

Swets, J. A. (1973). The receiver operating characteristic in psychology. *Science, 182*, 990–1000.

Taylor, S. E. (1991). Asymmetrical effects of positive and negative events. The mobilization-minimization hypothesis. *Psychological Bulletin, 110*, 67–85.

Towles-Schwen, T., & Fazio, R. H. (2003). Choosing social situations: The relation between automatically-activated racial attitudes and anticipated comfort interacting with African Americans. *Personality and Social Psychology Bulletin, 29*, 170–182.

Weinstein, N. D. (1980). Unrealistic optimism about future life events. *Journal of Personality and Social Psychology, 39*, 806–820.

Weinstein, N. D. (1982). Unrealistic optimism about suscep-
    tibility to health problems. *Journal of Behavioral Medi-
    cine*, *5*, 441–460.
Wilson, T. D., & Gilbert, D. T. (2003). Affective forecasting. In
    M. P. Zanna (Ed.), *Advances in experimental social psy-
    chology* (Vol. 35, pp. 345–411). New York: Elsevier.
Wu, C., & Shaffer, D. R. (1987). Susceptibility to persuasive
    appeals as a function of source credibility and prior expe-
    rience with the attitude object. *Journal of Personality and
    Social Psychology*, *52*, 677–688.

Zajonc, R. B. (1968). Attitudinal effects of mere exposure. *Journal
    of Personality and Social Psychology Monograph*, *9*, 1–27.
Zajonc, R. B. (1980). Feeling and thinking: Preferences need no
    inference. *American Psychologist*, *35*, 151–175.
Zajonc, R. B. (1998). Emotion. In D. Gilbert, S. Fiske, &
    G. Lindzey (Eds.), *The handbook social psychology* (4th
    ed., pp. 591–632). New York: McGraw-Hill.
Zuckerman, M. (1994). *Behavioral expressions and bioso-
    cial bases of sensation seeking*. Cambridge: Cambridge
    University Press.

Part V

Emotion and Well-Being

Structure of Emotions

20 | # Motivations and Emotivations: Approach, Avoidance, and Other Tendencies in Motivated and Emotional Behavior

Ira J. Roseman

CONTENTS

The concepts of motivation and emotion have been used across cultures and historical time periods to help explain human behavior. But motivation and emotion often are assigned to do similar theoretical work: accounting for the energy of behavior, that is, determining whether or not any action will occur and/or the magnitude or intensity of action (e.g., Hull, 1943; Lindsley, 1951). Motivation and emotion are usually also held to influence the direction of behavior: determining which particular behaviors will occur. But determining direction is not as unique a function of these variables, given that situational, learning history, and cognitive factors are also held to influence behavior specificity.

Perhaps in part because both variable types can account for the energization of action, during some periods in the history of psychology either motivation or emotion—but not both—has played relatively dominant roles in the mainstream of psychological theorizing. For example, from the 1920s through the 1950s, motivational or motive-like constructs such as instinct, drive, and reinforcement were much discussed and emotion got relatively short shrift; from the 1960s through the present, emotion became more dominant and there has been correspondingly less theoretical and research interest in motivation (though interest in motivational constructs seems to have been rising since the 1980s; see, e.g., Sorrentino & Higgins, 1986).

But while motivation and emotion may perform similar functions in psychological theories, and a number of theories do not distinguish between them (e.g., Murray, 1938; Plutchik, 1962), it is also true that different properties have been ascribed to motivational and emotional constructs, and some theoretical systems include both types of variables (e.g., as described below). In this chapter I will examine the general similarities, differences, and relationships between motivations and emotions, and also consider whether there are different types of motivations and emotions which have different types of effects upon behavior.

MOTIVATIONS AND EMOTIONS: WHY DO WE NEED THEM (BOTH)?

What is a motive? What is an emotion? How are the two alike, and how do they differ? These are simple, straightforward questions, but they do not currently have simple, straightforward answers. Theorists disagree, at least to some extent, about how motivation should be defined, and disagree profoundly about the nature of emotion.

WHAT IS MOTIVATION?

Kleinginna and Kleinginna (1981a,b) reviewed many definitions of both motivation and emotion, and proposed what they hoped might be integrative conceptualizations. They suggested (1981b, p. 272) that the term *motivation* refers to internal mechanisms that proximally energize behavior and give it direction (facilitating some actions while inhibiting others). In the introductory chapter to this volume, Elliot also identifies motivational processes as energizing and directing behavior, either toward positive stimuli or away from negative stimuli. A broader definition was adopted in Madsen's (1968, 1974) review of more than 40 motivation theories: motivation was defined as encompassing "all variables which arouse, sustain, and direct behavior" (1968, p. 46; see also Reeve, 2005).

However, Cofer and Appley (1964), in their classic volume *Motivation: Theory and Research*, argued that a definition of motivation which encompasses all internal and external causes of behavior is too broad. Nonmotivational causes of behavior, in their view, include externally applied force (such as a shove), the simple physical structure of an organism, and existing habits. They suggest that motivation might be postulated based on any or all of the following properties: "that behavior occurs at all, that a variety of responses is facilitated by some operation (like deprivation of food), that responses vary in vigor, that behavior has direction, that certain kinds of subsequent event may strengthen (and other kinds may weaken) a behavioral sequence" (p. 13).

If we combine

1. Kleinginna and Kleinginna's (1981b) conception of motivation as an internal state that serves to energize and direct behavior,
2. Cofer and Appley's distinction between merely caused versus motivated behavior, and their motivational properties of

a. Facilitation of varied responses and

b. Strengthening or weakening of behavioral sequences by subsequent events, and

3. Elliot's emphasis on approach and avoidance,

we may arrive at a conception of motivated action as behavior that can be described as at least partly determined by its consequences (e.g., increasing positive stimuli or decreasing negative stimuli)—that is, behavior which seems goal directed (for other conceptualizations of motivation in terms of goal-directed action, see Gollwitzer & Bargh, 1996).

I use the phrase "described as" (rather than actually) determined by its consequences, because future states cannot cause present behavior. Instead, some current state or process that is consequence-related (such as an expectation of future goal attainment or a process which repeatedly compares current states to fixed or variable set points or ranges) is causing motivated behavior, so that behavior is facilitated until the current representation or state corresponds more closely to a target set point or range, or less closely to an unsatisfactory set point or range (referred to by Carver & Scheier, 1998, as goals and antigoals respectively). For example, eating is motivated behavior which can be described (in part) as directed toward keeping levels of glucose, lipids, and the hormone ghrelin within target ranges (see Carlson, 2007, for a digestible summary). A motivation, then, is an internal state that produces behavior which can be described as moving toward desirable reference values or away from undesirable reference values.

WHAT IS AN EMOTION?

Kleinginna and Kleinginna (1981a) suggested emotion be defined as "a complex set of interactions among subjective and objective factors, mediated by neural/hormonal systems, which can: (a) give rise to affective experiences such as feelings of arousal, pleasure/displeasure; (b) generate cognitive processes such as emotionally relevant perceptual effects, appraisals, labeling processes; (c) activate widespread physiological adjustments to the arousing conditions; and (d) lead to behavior that is often, but not always, expressive, goal-directed, and adaptive" (p. 355). Similarly, in their introduction to the recent *Handbook of Affective Sciences*, Davidson, Scherer, and Goldsmith (2003) define emotion as "a relatively brief episode of coordinated brain, autonomic, and behavioral changes that facilitate a response to an external or internal event of significance to the organism" (p. xiii).

Building on Averill's (1980) conception of emotion as a *syndrome* of responses (none of which must occur in every instance of the emotion), I have defined emotions as syndromes of "(a) *phenomenology* (thoughts and feeling qualities); (b) *physiology* (neural, chemical, and other physical responses in the brain and body); (c) *expressions* (signals of emotion state, such as facial, vocal, and postural responses); (d) *behaviors* (action tendencies or readinesses); and (e) *emotivations* (emotional motivations, conceptualized as characteristic goals that people want to attain when the emotion is experienced)" (Roseman, 2001, p. 75).

SIMILARITIES BETWEEN MOTIVATIONS AND EMOTIONS

According to these definitions, motivations and emotions have a number of similarities. Both are internal states or processes (and thus may be able to account for individual differences in response to the same event or situation). Both are used to explain the energy and direction of behavior. Both may lead to goal-directed action.

DIFFERENCES BETWEEN MOTIVATIONS AND EMOTIONS

Although motivations and emotions may have a number of similar properties, there are some internal states that tend to be conceptualized chiefly as motivations and others that are more typically identified as emotions. For example, hunger, thirst, sexual desire, and need for achievement have typically been seen as motivations; whereas joy, sadness, fear, and anger are typically regarded as emotions. These and a number of other prototypical motivations and emotions are shown in Table 20.1. The fair amount of consensus, at least on these exemplars, suggests that some differentiation of the two classes may be possible.

A number of authors have written about differences between motivations (instincts, drives, needs, motives,

TABLE 20.1

Some States Typically Regarded either as Motivations or as Emotions

Motivations	Emotions
Hunger	Joy (or happiness)
Thirst	Sadness
Sexual drive	Fear
Competence motivation	Anger
Need for achievement	Love
Need for approval	Disgust
Need for power	Shame
Cognitive dissonance	Pride
Need for cognition	Distress

desires, goals, etc., depending on the terminology of the day) and emotions. I will discuss especially the formulations of affect theory pioneer Silvan Tomkins.

Motivations as Specific Purpose Mechanisms; Emotions as General Purpose Mechanisms

Tomkins (1970) proposed that compared to motives ("drives"), emotions ("affects") are more general with regard to "object" (p. 105). By this he meant that motives are activated by specific conditions, and direct behavior toward specific ends. For example, hunger is characteristically activated by food deprivation (and its biochemical and visceral consequences), thirst by water deprivation, and need for affiliation by the absence of desired social interaction; and these motives direct behavior specifically toward food, water, and social contact (one cannot generally satisfy one motive with the object of another).

In contrast, emotions can be produced by contingencies applicable to *any* motive. For example, attaining food or water or companionship or any current goal can elicit happiness; a threat to having food or water or companionship or any desired state can elicit fear; and another person's interference with attainment of any motive can elicit anger (see Scherer, 1988, for examples of the range of events that can elicit joy, sadness, fear, and anger).

Motivations as Relatively Deliberative; Emotions as Relatively Impulsive

If motivated behavior can be described as influenced by its consequences, then it may be regarded as instrumental or goal-directed. Goal-directed action has been said to have the property of equifinality (Heider, 1958; Tesser, Martin, & Cornell, 1996)—a variety of means may be employed to approach a desired end or avoid one that is undesired. Insofar as cognitive processing influences enactment of particular motivated behaviors, goal-directed action may be described as *relatively* deliberative. For example, according to Expectancy-Value models of motivation (see Feather, 1982), a person may assess whether or not to take a particular action, or which of several possible actions to take, based on expected consequences (Ajzen, 1991; Atkinson, 1964; Gollwitzer, 1996). Note that such "deliberation" may occur without awareness, as when people unconsciously choose particular words to convey an intended meaning, or decide how to turn the steering wheel to stay on the road while driving (Bargh & Barndollar, 1996); or it may have occurred previously and merely be recalled or activated in a current situation, and as when people have previously decided what foods they will eat if hungry at breakfast time (cf. Ajzen, 2002); or it

may be based on nonconscious beliefs or expectations, as when an implicit belief that ability is malleable leads to persistence in the face of failure (Dweck, 1999) or when a new person's resemblance to someone known triggers an unconscious expectation of acceptance or rejection and influences social approach or avoidance (Andersen, Reznik, & Glassman, 2005; Lewicki, 1985).

In contrast, much emotional behavior seems relatively impulsive (though I will also argue below for the existence of some deliberative emotional behavior). It seems we often do not plan how to enact our joy, sadness, fear, or anger to the same extent that we plan how to satisfy our hunger, social, or achievement needs (e.g., choosing which foods to eat, which people to approach, or which career goals to pursue). Particular emotions are linked to readinesses or tendencies to engage in particular actions, such as freezing in fear, yelling in anger, and doing nothing in sadness (Frijda, 1986; Lazarus, 1991; Roseman, Wiest, & Swartz, 1994). Many emotion researchers have commented on the feeling of relative compulsion that accompanies much emotional behavior. For example, Frijda (1986) described emotions as having "the character of urges or impulses" that "clamor for attention and for execution" (p. 78). For a recent similar perspective, see Strack and Deutsch (2005) who distinguish between reflective and impulsive motivational systems, with the latter often triggered by positive or negative affect.

Emotions Preempt Motivations

The main distinction between motivations and emotions mentioned by Tomkins (1970) is that emotions typically take precedence over motivations. Tomkins argued that sexual drive, for example, which was accorded such importance in Freudian theory, is easily disrupted by emotions such as anxiety or shame. Many other examples could be cited. Research indicates that when afraid: infants reduce exploratory behavior (see Kobak, 1999), adults reduce achievement striving (Birney, Burdick, & Teevan, 1969), and rats reduce eating (e.g., when a predator may be present; Fanselow & Lester, 1988). Although mild sadness may facilitate eating and socializing, intense sadness (as in grief or a major depressive episode) more often results in loss of appetite, loss of libido, a reduction in socializing, and loss of interest in activities formerly pursued (American Psychiatric Association, 2000; World Health Organization, 2007). Frustration caused by preventing children from playing with attractive toys was observed to lead to aggressive play which destroyed the very toys that had been sought (Klein, 1982, discussing the findings of Barker, Dembo, & Lewin, 1941). Even positive emotions such as joy, which can increase eating, sexual behavior, and social motivation, may reduce *sustained* pursuit of any of these or other specific motives, replacing it with "free activation" (Frijda, 1986), which involves increased distractibility (as in manic episodes, which are typically characterized by elevated mood; see American Psychiatric Association, 2000) and responsiveness to whatever features of a stimulus situation seem likely to sustain good mood or reward (Isen, 2000; Roseman, Swartz, Newman, & Nichols, 2007).

Note that the primary contention here is that emotions preempt *pursuit* of nonemotional motivations, rather than eliminating those motivations. But I am not suggesting that emotions result in an absence of goal pursuit. Instead I will argue below that each emotion engenders its own (emotion-specific) motivation, which tends to take precedence over nonemotional motivations, such as those listed in Table 20.1. Nor do emotions of *any* strength preempt all nonemotional motivation, as shown by instances in which emotions are regulated in order to achieve social, sexual, or achievement goals (see Gross, 1999). Rather, it may be proposed that emotions tend to preempt nonemotional motivations of comparable (or lesser) strength.

RELATIONSHIPS BETWEEN MOTIVATIONS AND EMOTIONS

At the influential Loyola Symposium on Feelings and Emotions, Leeper (1970) proposed that motives are related to emotions in two ways. First, emotions are perceptions of what a person "regards as the most significant realities in his life" (p. 164). This suggests that emotions *result* in part from motives.

Many contemporary emotion theorists make similar claims. For example, I have proposed (Roseman, 1984, 2001) that positive and negative emotions are produced by perceptions about the consistency versus inconsistency of situations with a person's current motives. Scherer (1984, 2001) views positive versus negative emotions as produced by goal-conducive versus goal-obstructive evaluations, as well as by intrinsically pleasant and unpleasant events. Frijda (1986, 2007) regards emotions as responses to match and mismatch of events with an individual's "concerns." Lazarus (1991, 2001) viewed emotions as arising in part from appraisals of goal-congruence versus incongruence; the dimension is "motivational congruence" in Smith and Kirby's (2001) theory.

Research supporting this claim indicates that emotions indeed result in part from motives: an emotion is caused by having some motive (goal, preference, etc.), and perceiving that a stimulus or event has implications for attainment of that motive (e.g., Roseman, 1991; Roseman & Evdokas, 2004; van Reekum et al., 2004).

Second, according to Leeper, emotions *are* motives. That is, emotions motivate behavior, giving it energy and direction. This perspective is explicitly or implicitly endorsed by a number of motivation theorists (e.g., Brown, 1961; Murray, 1938; Weiner, 1985) and most emotion theorists (e.g., Frijda, 1986; Izard, 1991; Lazarus, 1991; Plutchik, 1980). But many of the latter see emotions as causes of behavior, rather than as motivators which establish goals to guide action. This fits with the view, discussed above, that emotions prompt impulsive behavior rather than planful instrumental action.

However, there is reason to believe that emotional processes can also engender goals that guide behavior, just as do hunger, thirst, need for achievement, and other motivations. For example, fear may motivate a person to engage in a variety of behaviors (e.g., freezing, hiding, fleeing, calling for help, and defensive aggression) that move the person away from some danger and toward safety (cf. Plutchik, 1980). Anger may motivate a person to engage in a variety of aggressive actions (behaviors intended to hurt someone), such as hitting, criticizing, taunting, thwarting, giving the silent treatment, and so forth (Berkowitz, 1999; Underwood, 2003). Love may motivate a person to engage in a variety of behaviors that increase interpersonal closeness, such as physical proximity maintenance, caregiving, and initiating sexual contact (Shaver, Morgan, & Wu, 1996). In accord with this view, research participants recalling experiences of: fear, say that they wanted to get to safety; anger, say that they wanted to hurt someone; and love, say that they wanted to be close to someone—more than do participants recalling experiences of other emotions (Roseman et al., 1994, 2007). Indeed, unless we recognize that emotions involve action toward a goal, it is difficult to adequately understand (a) what the different behaviors that may be enacted when feeling a particular emotion have in common (e.g., in anger, yelling at someone and giving the silent treatment may have extremely different surface properties but serve the same goal—hurting the target in some way, for example, making the target feel bad) and (b) sequences of emotional behaviors, in which one behavior (e.g., the silent treatment) fails to attain an emotion's goal (making the target feel bad) and is then replaced by another behavior (e.g., criticizing or thwarting).

Thus I am proposing (cf. Roseman et al., 1994) that emotional behavior is organized at two levels: the level of action readiness patterns, in which particular emotions are linked to particular actions (given particular stimulus conditions); and the level of emotivational goals, in which particular emotions are linked to emotion-specific goals (which can organize a wider variety of behaviors aiming to achieve those goals).

FUNCTIONS OF MOTIVATIONS AND EMOTIONS

Why might an organism have two systems—motivational and emotional—for energizing and directing behavior? I suggested above that motivational processes are often more deliberative than emotions, selecting among alternative actions those that are relatively likely to increase motive attainment in light of situational conditions and outcome expectancies; whereas emotional processes are often more impulsive, involving greater reliance on relatively prespecified, evolution-tested patterns of action readiness. Behavior organized by emotivational goals occupies a middle ground: an emotion urges the adoption of its more general emotion-related goal (e.g., hurting another person, when feeling anger) instead of a more specific motivational goal (e.g., gaining approval; maintaining a friendship), but there is flexibility in selecting the particular actions that aim to achieve that goal (e.g., criticizing; thwarting; refusing to interact with the person).

Together with behavior that is neither motivated nor emotional, this set of processes provides organisms with multiple behavior control systems suitable for situations that differ in the need for rapid action. That is, affectively neutral states would seem to exert the least constraint on action, permitting an infinite range of behaviors that might be initiated or sorted through in a temporally unlimited manner. Motivations allow for relatively flexible action, with behaviors that can be generated or selected at least partly based on their potential to advance current goals and block antigoals. Comparatively, emotivational goals reduce flexibility in *goal* selection—decreasing response time by increasing focus on a particular general purpose goal (such as getting to safety) in place of more time-consuming processing of multiple specific purpose goals. Emotional action tendencies and readinesses further constrain the set of behaviors that are likely to be initiated, with the smaller number of action options permitting even faster response. Thus the motivation system allows for relatively flexible behavior when conditions permit, and the emotion system allows for more preprogrammed behavior when faster action is needed.

This formulation fits conceptions of emotions as "emergency" responses (Cannon, 1932) or "coping mechanisms" (Lazarus & Folkman, 1984). As such, it may seem most suited to negative emotions (Fredrickson, 1998) such as fear and anger. Faced with an immediate threat, it may be vital to have in the behavioral repertoire preorganized readinesses for responses such as flight and fight to cope quickly with the crisis (see, e.g., LeDoux, 1996; Tooby & Cosmides, 1990).

But the framework can be extended to encompass positive emotions as well, if we recognize the existence of time-limited opportunities that should be seized before they slip away (Roseman et al., 2007). One example is the appearance of another person who is appraised as having the potential to greatly enhance motive fulfillment (e.g., as a potential mate, caregiver, close friend, or other important relationship partner). The positive emotion of love (what Shaver et al., 1996, call "surge love") may be the emotional response to such a stimulus, involving readiness for behaviors that form, maintain, and strengthen relationships.

Similarly if the emotion of pride is a response to positive outcomes caused by the self (Roseman, 1991; Stipek, 1995) and engenders readiness for culturally syntonic self-display and self-assertion, it may serve to seize an opportunity (for acquiring social standing, dominance, resources, etc.) at a moment in time when those behaviors are most likely to meet with success, insofar as other people can see or be shown evidence of the self-caused positive outcomes (Roseman et al., 2007).

Overall, then, positive and negative emotions provide ways for organisms to seize opportunities and cope with crises, by engendering time-tested patterns of action readiness when there may not be time to more deliberatively consider the relative advantages, disadvantages, and potential consequences of particular behaviors or behavior alternatives.

Determinants of Motivated and Emotional Behavior

What factors influence whether action is governed primarily by nonaffective processes, by motivations, by emotivational goals, or by emotional action tendencies? As shown in Table 20.2, two possible determinants are *motive-relevance* and *actual or potential change in motive-relevance* perceived in a situation.

According to Table 20.2, if a situation lacks relevance to all active motives—for example, because no motives are active at a given time, or the person perceives that action would have no impact on progress toward active goals or preferences (cf. Bandura, 1997)—behavior would be neither motivated nor emotional. Behavior may nonetheless occur (organisms may be active even when not motivated or emotional), but it would lack goal-directedness, persistence, and felt compulsion to act. In contrast, in situations perceived as relevant to active motives, behavior may be under motivational control—flexibly directed toward wanted states or activities and away from unwanted ones. However, insofar as situations are not just motive-relevant, but involve actual or potential *changes* in motive-relevant events, emotion(s) may be generated (and the larger the changes, the more intense the emotions). If the changes are relatively large, emotions (joy, fear, anger, etc.) are likely to be relatively intense (as compared to

TABLE 20.2

Some Determinants of Behavior Control by Nonaffective and Affective Processes

Eliciting Condition	Processes Governing Behavior
Lack of relevance to active motives (e.g., no active motives or no possible effect on active motives)	Nonaffective (e.g., situational or cognitive) determinants
Motive-relevance (not unmodifiable match or mismatch with actively wanted or unwanted states or activities)	Motivational goals and preferences
Relatively large actual or potential change in motive-relevant events	Emotivational goals
Very large actual or potential change in motive-relevant events	Emotional readinesses and action tendencies

Note: As discussed by Izard (2000), the term *affect* is used by some psychologists to refer only to emotions, and by other psychologists to encompass both motivations and emotions. It is used here in the latter sense. This table does not attempt to list all determinants of motivational and emotional processes, but focuses instead on hypothesized differential determinants (e.g., it omits the importance and the imminence of desired and undesired states, which appear to influence the intensity of both motivation and emotion).

motives such as hunger, sex, need for achievement, etc.), and emotivational goals (e.g., sustaining a situation in joy, getting to safety in fear, getting revenge in anger) would increasingly come to govern action in place of the original motivational goals and preferences (which may remain active, but become increasingly subordinate as emotions get more and more intense). If changes in motive-relevant events are very large, emotion intensity would increase still further and the flexible pursuit of emotivational goals increasingly give way to behavior dominated by emotion-specific action readinesses and tendencies.

As an example, consider a student taking a college course. If the course lacks relevance to the student's current motives, she would be neither motivated nor emotional about her course performance (but may still take the course, e.g., because instructed to do so, or in accord with familial models or scripts). If the course is perceived as motive-relevant (e.g., to a desire to progress, or do well, or not do poorly) but relatively little actual or potential change in a motive-relevant outcome is envisioned, the student's behavior would be motivated (show persistent, goal-directed effort, e.g., in reading course material) but not particularly emotional. If a relatively large change from prior or expected outcome is imagined or perceived (e.g., a final exam is announced, and the student thinks about the prospect of doing significantly better or significantly worse than she otherwise might do), she would have an emotional response (e.g., hope or fear), and her behavior would be correspondingly guided by the emotivational goal of her emotion (e.g., making the envisioned outcome happen, or getting to safety) to the relative exclusion of other goals (either emotivational goal could be pursued by focused studying or by other means, such as seeking assistance or engaging in self-handicapping). If a

great change is envisioned, our student may feel intense emotion (e.g., hope or fear) and her behavior may be dominated by the action readinesses or tendencies of her emotion (e.g., in hope, eager anticipation, such as fantasies of success and its sequelae, and excited, preoccupied waiting or approach behavior; in fear, tense vigilance, such as watching out for and thinking about the potential for failure, and aroused passive or active avoidance behavior, e.g., periods of paralysis, thoughts of bailing out, and frantic studying or dropping the course).

The theory just outlined posits an adaptive matching between the conditions requiring organismic response (the degree of actual or potential change in motive-relevant events) and the functional characteristics of the behavior control system mobilized to govern action (in particular, the latencies of response that are characteristic of the different systems). As the immediate implications for active motives increase in magnitude, one moves from nonaffective to motivational to emotivational to emotional behavior, and action becomes more and more focused and constrained. The fewer the behavioral options generated, the smaller the need for cognitive involvement in selecting among options, and thus the more rapid a response can be.

A number of other theorists have suggested that change or rate of change is a key determinant of emotion activation or intensity. For example, Frijda (1988, 2007) posits a Law of Change: "Emotions are elicited not so much by the presence of favorable or unfavorable conditions but by actual or expected changes in favorable or unfavorable conditions" (Frijda, 2007, p. 10), and contends that the greater the change, the stronger the subsequent emotion. Carver and Scheier (e.g., 1998) have proposed that emotion is generated by the rate of progress toward goals or away from antigoals, in comparison to a desired rate; larger differences from this "reference rate" are held to produce more intense emotions.

In comparison, motivational processes may not require change, or any particular degree or threshold amount of change. For example, hunger may be generated when glucose or fatty acids in the blood are below target levels, or when ghrelin levels are high; and thirst when blood flow to the heart or kidneys is too low (Carlson, 2007). These hunger- and thirst-generating mechanisms appear to be at least partly dependent on levels rather than changes in the monitored substances, as it is possible to be chronically hungry or thirsty. For example, patients with Prader–Willi Syndrome have chronically high levels of ghrelin and continual hunger (DelParigi et al., 2002). Similarly, achievement striving and persistence may be engendered by dispositionally high competence perceptions and mastery or "performance-approach" goals (Elliot, 1997).

However, motivational processes may also be affected by change, as when hunger is triggered by the smell of food (Carlson, 2007), thirst by changes in osmotic pressure (Liedtke et al., 2000), and achievement motivation by perceived progress toward goals (Schunk, 2003). Yet consistent with the hypothesized influence of change on emotion, it is possible that significant or large changes in degree of fulfillment of these motives simultaneously generate emotions such as excitement (Tomkins, 1979), distress (Brunner, 1993), or joy (Summerfield & Green, 1986).

Alternative Determinants

It is also possible that, contrary to Table 20.2, change is not required for emotion initiation, and that the key determinant of emotional dominance over motivation is *degree of match or mismatch* with current goals or antigoals, which is then reflected in emotion intensity. As Frijda (1988, 2007) observes, many instances in which an absence of change reduces emotional intensity may be cases of habituation or "adaptation," (Helson, 1964) in which desires or expectations shift as a function of current state (e.g., we get used to an increased salary and set our sights higher; thus we cease to be happy not because change is required for happiness, but because a new level of aspiration makes our current state no longer match what we desire). Frijda also notes some cases—all of negative emotions, which leads him to posit a Law of Hedonic Asymmetry—in which it seems that people do *not* adapt but rather feel continued or increasing negative affect in response to unchanging aversive states. Among the examples given are irritations, such as noise (Frederick & Loewenstein, 1999), and chronic intractable pain.

One could come up with explanations for these apparent exceptions to the Law of Change: the cited studies examined intermittent rather than constant noise, perhaps preventing adaptation; over time one might increasingly want either noise or chronic pain to cease, thus accounting for intensification; and, as Frederick and Loewenstein (1999) point out, in degenerative diseases, chronic pain worsens over time, reducing adaptation. But it may also be possible to explain apparent change or rate of change effects as special cases of match or mismatch with a positive or negative reference state. For example, in Carver and Scheier's (1998) theory, people are said to have a desired rate of change. Perhaps that rate should be taken as their goal—the frame of reference from which degree of goal match and mismatch should be calculated.

Suppose that as the size of match or mismatch with reference states increases, emotions increase faster in intensity than do motivations. If so, as the size of match or mismatch grows, behavior might come first under increasing control of motivations, then emotivational goals, and then emotional action readinesses and tendencies. If this were the case, greater match or mismatch with reference states might be what produces increasingly constrained behavior, and the functional rationale would be that greater match or mismatch makes faster action advantageous (in order to more quickly respond to states that are more undesired or desired).

WHY INCORPORATE BOTH MOTIVATIONS AND EMOTIONS INTO THEORIES OF BEHAVIOR?

If motivations and emotions have significant similarities, and both provide energy and direction to behavior, why should both constructs be included in our theories? In accord with the above discussion, one answer to this question is that motivations and emotions also seem to have different empirically observable characteristic properties (narrow vs. broad initiating conditions, relatively deliberative vs. impulsive influence on behavior, and subordinate vs. preemptive tendencies).

There may be other distinguishing characteristics as well. For example, a number of emotions seem to have expressive properties that most motivations lack, such as distinctive pan-cultural facial displays (Darwin, 1872/1965; Ekman, 1999; Izard, 1971), vocal patterns (Scherer, Johnstone, & Klasmeyer, 2003), and postures (Darwin, 1872/1965; Tracy & Robins, 2004). By signaling an organism's emotional state, and readiness for emotional behaviors such as attack (e.g., in anger), flight (e.g., in fear), submission (e.g., in shame), and assertion (e.g., in pride), emotional expressions may serve as preprogrammed *social coping* mechanisms which rapidly and relatively effortlessly help individual organisms (Levenson, 1999), and groups or species of organisms (Keltner & Haidt, 1999), deal with opportunities and crises by exerting influence on other organisms. For example, expressions of anger may serve as threat displays that deter conspecifics—and sometimes other species—from a course of action (see, e.g., Fessler, 2006). Postural expressions of fear may elicit fear in conspecifics, facilitating flight (de Gelder, Snyder, Greve, Gerard, & Hadjikhani, 2004). Such rapid, effortless signaling may be more important under the conditions of significant change held to generate emotions, than under the less potentially urgent circumstances that generate motivational processes.

The primary brain circuitry of motivations and emotions may also differ. For example, Berridge and his colleagues (e.g., Berridge, 2004) distinguish motivational "wanting" sites in the nucleus accumbens (which are dopaminergic and influence working for food) from emotional "liking" sites in particular areas of the accumbens shell and ventral pallidum (which respond to opioids and influence facial responses to pleasant tastes).

In short, both motivations and emotions are needed to adequately describe and explain behavior. Motivation constructs (along with either expectancies, or comparisons of existing and potential states to reference states) are needed to describe and account for much behavior that occurs under normal circumstances: behavior that is goal-directed, persistent, and tailored to specific situations. Emotion constructs are needed to describe and account for the relatively impulsive deployment of a limited number of general purpose strategies and responses that have evolved (along with quick appraisals of basic cross-situational dimensions that nondeliberatively predict which emotion strategies are likely to be most successful in which types of situations) to deal with crises and potentially time-limited opportunities.

To return to our earlier example, motivational constructs (such as need for achievement or competence motivation) are needed to adequately explain why some college students devote persistent daily effort to attending lectures and reading and studying course material (despite fatigue, obstacles to comprehension, the easy availability of sensory and social pleasures, etc.). Emotional constructs (such as hope, fear, and guilt) are needed to adequately explain why various equally motivated students respond to an impending final exam with not only studying but also eagerness, anticipatory fantasies, and excited effort; or tense watching out for signs of approaching failure and periods of paralysis; or ruminative self-reproach.

In arguing for inclusion of both motivation and emotion in models of behavior, I am not alone. For example, all theories claiming that emotions result from appraisals of events in terms of motives, goals, or concerns (e.g., Carver & Scheier, 1998; Frijda, 1986; Lazarus, 1991; Roseman, 2001; Scherer, 2001; Smith & Kirby, 2001) implicitly if not explicitly encompass both types of variables. So do all theories which regard emotions as a distinct subtype or manifestation of motivations, or attempt to distinguish their properties (e.g., Buck, 1985; Tomkins, 1970). But fewer theories attempt to encompass both motivations and emotions as distinct yet roughly coequal determinants of action, and that is what is being advocated here.

TWO TYPES OF MOTIVATION AND EMOTIONS

TWO TYPES OF MOTIVATION

In the introductory chapter of this volume, Elliot traces the history of a distinction between approach and avoidance motivations for over two thousand years (see also Elliot, 1999). As Elliot shows, some version of the distinction can be found in descriptive and prescriptive philosophical accounts of human action, and is present in very many theories proposed by psychologists. The contributions to this volume reflect the continuing relevance of the distinction across many subfields of psychology.

Elliot's introductory chapter also discusses alternative conceptualizations of the approach versus avoidance distinction, including the terms appetitive versus motivation relevant to aversive, which he regards as covering roughly the same conceptual ground. In my model of emotion-eliciting appraisals (Roseman, 1984), I have used the latter distinction to refer to motivation relevant to states-to-be-attained versus states-to-be-prevented. The term "appetitive" was meant to incorporate the seeking aspect of appetitive behavior (to approach or maximize some states), without necessarily limiting what is sought to objects, such as food, which would subsequently be consumed or engaged with in a consummatory manner (Craig, 1918; cf. Lang, 1995). "Aversive" refers to motivations that avoid or minimize other states. In our empirical research, the meaning has best been captured by distinguishing between wanting to "get or keep" versus "get rid of or avoid" something (Roseman, Antoniou, & Jose, 1996). This phrasing indicates that the positive and negative reference states which guide motivated behavior may or may not be currently present in a situation.

Two Types of Emotions (When Emotions Are Motivations)

In emotion theory and research, positive versus negative emotion is a perpetual and central theme (Tolman, 1923; Tomkins, 1962, 1963; Watson & Tellegen, 1985). Although some theorists have challenged the classification of emotions into positive and negative groups or question the basis for the classification (Kristjánsson, 2003; Solomon & Stone, 2002), most analyses recognize positive versus negative emotion as a fundamental and important distinction.

While emotions may be categorized as positive versus negative according to their putative adaptive value (e.g., healthful vs. harmful, as discussed by Solomon & Stone, 2002), or people's attitude toward emotions (approving vs. disapproving of their experience or expression; see, e.g., Tsai, Knutson, & Fung, 2006), the most widely recognized version of the distinction is in terms of subjective feeling quality (e.g., Barrett, Mesquita, Ochsner, & Gross, 2007; Wundt, 1904). Emotions such as joy, love, and pride feel pleasant, and emotions such as sadness, fear, and shame feel unpleasant.

This division is immediately apparent when research participants are asked to sort emotions into groups (Shaver, Schwartz, Kirson, & O'Connor, 1987), or make similarity judgments among emotion words (Russell, 1980) or faces (Abelson & Sermat, 1962). It is also apparent when participants rate the emotions of others (Roseman, 1991) or their own ongoing experience of emotions (Barrett, 2006b). Positive emotions tend to covary, at least to some extent; so do negative emotions.

The hedonic quality of positive versus negative emotions enables them to also serve as motives—people may behave to experience more of positive emotions generally (Tomkins, 1987), or particular positive emotions such as joy, love, or pride (e.g., Atkinson, 1964; Tennov, 1979), or less of negative emotions generally (Taylor, 1991; Tomkins, 1987), or particular negative emotions such as panic, disappointment, or regret (Barlow, 1988; van Dijk, Zeelenberg, & van der Pligt, 2003; Zeelenberg, Beattie, van der Pligt, & de Vries, 1996).

What Is Approached or Avoided in Motivated and Emotional Behavior?

How should we characterize that which people want to get or keep in appetitive (approach) motivation and get rid of or avoid in aversive (avoidance) motivation? Although some theories have focused primarily on the maximization of positive emotions and minimization of negative emotions (e.g., Tomkins, 1970, claimed that nonemotional motives

require emotional "amplification" to affect behavior), it does not seem that emotions are in fact the only motivators. Nor must pleasure and pain be involved in motivating action. At least at low to moderate levels of motive intensity, people seem to regulate many different processes or parameters (e.g., perceptual constancies, speech production, self-verification), at least somewhat independently of the happiness or sadness, or pleasure or pain, it makes them feel. To give another example: people seek accurate understanding not just because it makes them feel joy, or pleasure, or even competence, but seemingly for its own sake (Chaiken, Liberman, & Eagly, 1989; Heider, 1958). We also seek to categorize stimuli, to evaluate stimuli, and to correct for bias, often without conscious awareness (Glaser & Kihlstrom, 2005; Petty & Wegener, 1993).

To encompass a very wide variety of approached versus avoided states and activities, it would seem that a very general formulation of the regulated entities must be offered. One candidate is rewards versus punishments (Gray, 1987; Gray & McNaughton, 2000). A possible advantage of this conceptualization is its potential linkage to distinct brain systems, such as those that mediate appetitive versus aversive information processing, (e.g., nucleus accumbens, ventral pallidum, and paraventricular nucleus of the hypothalamus vs. central amygdala and bed nucleus of the stria terminalis, as described by Cacioppo, Larsen, Smith, & Berntson, 2004).

Why Have Two Types of Motivation and Emotions?

The existence of appetitive versus aversive motivational systems and positive versus negative emotions may provide an important mechanism for prioritizing action. At comparable levels of affective strength, higher priority may be given to aversive (avoidance) motives and negative emotions as compared with appetitive (approach) motives and positive emotions (cf. Carver, 2003; Maslow, 1955). Indeed there is considerable evidence of such prioritization (Baumeister, Bratslavsky, Finkenauer, & Vohs, 2001; Taylor, 1991). For example, as discussed by Baumeister et al. (2001), most people (83%, according to a study of wagering by Atthowe, 1960) try harder to avoid losses than to obtain comparable gains (see also Kahneman & Tversky, 1984); the effects of punishment and negative reinforcers on behavior are generally stronger than the effects of reward and comparable positive reinforcers (Constantini & Hoving, 1973); and people report more often trying to get out of bad moods than to get into or prolong good moods (Baumeister, Heatherton, & Tice, 1994).

Moreover, differentiation of importance or urgency may provide a functional explanation for the evolution of two motivational systems, and the assignment of particular regulated parameters to one system or the other in the process of natural selection. For example, sexual motivation seems predominantly to involve appetitive motivation and pleasure seeking (e.g., van Furth, Wolterink, & van Ree, 1995); and though people may seek to eat particular foods in order to get pleasant tastes, eating as a response to prolonged food deprivation involves aversive motivation (reduction of unpleasant feelings of hunger; see Ashton, 2002). Perhaps this is because reproduction, while ultimately essential for the continuation of the species, is less time urgent than satisfying basic nutritional needs. Similarly, the need to cope with crises that is signaled by negative emotion seems more urgent than the need to seize opportunities that is signaled by positive emotions. As Elliot (2006) put it, avoidance goals are concerned with survival, and approach goals with thriving. Or to state it another way, if one doesn't reproduce or seize an opportunity today, one can try again tomorrow; but if one doesn't survive today, there will be no further opportunities (cf. Baumeister et al., 2001, p. 358).

Note that the "bad is stronger than good" principle (Baumeister et al., 2001) does not itself require two different systems of motivation or emotion. Organisms could have only approach (appetitive) goals, and respond with higher priority to departures from the goals than to progress toward them. More attention and effort could be mobilized toward avoiding losses than achieving gains, and to minimizing losses that occurred (Taylor, 1991), even if the gains and losses were only of desired objects or states. Instead, the existence of two motivational systems (with favorable and unfavorable outcomes possible in each) suggests some nonredundant functions, such as a more differentiated prioritization or action control system. I will consider further the utility of having four possible outcomes (improvement or worsening with respect to approach or avoidance motivation) in discussing motivation-linked emotions, below.

DISCRETE EMOTIONS: BEYOND TWO TYPES

There Is More to Emotions Than Positive and Negative

Most theories of emotion, from ancient (Aristotle, 1966/350 BC; Galen [see Irwin, 1947]) to classical (Descartes, 1649/1968, Spinoza, 1677/2000) to modern (Izard, 1991; Oatley & Johnson-Laird, 1987; Plutchik,

1980; Tomkins, 1962, 1963), including theories and taxonomies generated in other cultures (Hejmadi, Davidson, & Rozin, 2000; Romney, Moore, & Rusch, 1997), maintain that there are more varieties of emotion than just positive and negative. For example, Ekman (1992) argued that there are at least seven different emotions, based on evidence of pan-cultural facial displays for happiness, sadness, fear, anger, disgust, surprise, and contempt (according to Keltner, Ekman, Gonzaga, & Beer, 2003, there is now some evidence of expressions for embarrassment, shame, amusement, sympathy, and love as well). Panksepp (1998, p. 88), citing neuroanatomical and neurochemical evidence, also identified seven emotional systems: play (joy), panic, fear, rage, seeking, care, and lust. Frijda (1986, p. 88) distinguished 17 different patterns of "action readiness" and on this basis listed 17 emotions. de Rivera (1977), citing distinctive patterns of phenomenology, posited 48 emotions. Citing evidence of distinctive profiles of phenomenology, physiology, expression, action tendencies, and goals, as well as antecedent appraisals, I have proposed a system encompassing 17 emotions: 16 positive- or negative-valenced emotions, and the neutral-valenced emotion of surprise (Roseman, 2001).

There is also clearly disagreement about which states should be regarded as emotions (Ortony & Turner, 1990), although some of these can be understood as differences in terminology (e.g., what Panksepp, 1998, refers to as the "seeking" emotion system may correspond to hope in other emotion theories, e.g., Lazarus, 1991; Roseman, 2001). The more important disagreements would seem to be based in part on different definitions of emotions and thus different criteria for identifying and distinguishing between putative emotion states (e.g., phenomenological conceptualizations suggest more emotions than do universal expressive displays).

Only Degrees of Positive Versus Negative Affect and Arousal?

In recent years, James A. Russell and Lisa Feldman Barrett (Barrett, 2006a; Russell, 2003; Russell & Barrett, 1999) have led a challenge to the discrete emotion perspective, citing the variability of responses observable across instances of the same emotion, such as anger; and low correlations among the different responses proposed to constitute an emotion (e.g., subjective, physiological, facial, and behavioral responses). Russell and Barrett contend that what appear to lay persons and many emotion theorists as different emotions are really cultural or linguistic categories arbitrarily imposed on a simpler, dimensional affective reality (cf. Russell, 1980; Russell & Mehrabian, 1977). They claim that joy, sadness, fear, anger, and so forth correspond principally to particular combinations of valence and arousal.

In my view, some variability in responses across instances of an emotion and relatively low correlations among different emotion components are empirical realities (see, e.g., Cacioppo, Berntson, Larsen, Poehlmann, & Ito, 2000). But there are good reasons to expect such variability, and ways to explain it systematically. (a) As discussed above, at least when emotion intensity is not extremely high, emotivational goals may tailor emotional behavior toward responses seen as effective in specific situations (e.g., in fear, seeking safety by concealment or by calling for help). (b) Emotion regulation may alter or control emotions or their individual component responses (as when people suppress anger or mask facial displays of disgust to conform to social norms; see, e.g., Ekman, 1972; Gross, Richards, & John, 2006). (c) Other nonemotional processes may compete with emotions to influence physiology, expression, behavior, and phenomenology. For example, depending on the situation one was in, talking could alter facial expression; task demands (e.g., filling out a questionnaire vs. running on a treadmill) would affect heart rate and blood pressure; and nonemotional motives (such as keeping a job, or caring for an interaction partner) could constrain or shape behavior (e.g., the likelihood and form of angry attack).

The critique of discrete emotions is also empirically inadequate because it fails to account for relationships between particular emotions and particular responses that do exist. For example, Russell (2003) and Barrett (2006a) simply do not explain why the same facial and vocal expressions (e.g., smiling and laughter with happiness, downturned lips and weeping with sadness) would be associated with the same emotion concepts and similar eliciting conditions (e.g., reunions vs. separation from loved others) across all human cultures (Boucher & Brandt, 1981; Ekman, 1972; Izard, 1971; Keltner et al., 2003); or why such expressions are found in children born blind or even blind, deaf, and retarded (e.g., Charlesworth, 1970; Dumas, 1932; Eibl-Eibesfeldt, 1970, 1972; Mistschenka, 1933; as reviewed in Collier, 1985).

Existing relationships between subjectively experienced emotions and behaviors are also not adequately explained. For example, although people do not necessarily attack when feeling angry, and can attack when feeling fear or other emotions, aggression is more likely when feeling anger than when feeling no emotion, and more likely when feeling anger than when feeling other emotions, such as happiness, sadness, fear, surprise, or love (Berkowitz, 1999; Consedine, Strongman, & Magai, 2003; Roseman et al., 1994; Scherer & Wallbott, 1994).

Similarly, freezing is more likely when feeling fear than when feeling anger, sadness, joy, disgust, or other emotions (Bracha, 2004; Gray & McNaughton, 2000).

Nor can the various emotions differentiated by discrete emotions theorists and researchers be adequately accounted for simply by combinations of valence and arousal. Fear and anger, both high arousal negative emotions in dimensional accounts, differ significantly in characteristic facial expression (e.g., brows raised, lips stretched vs. brows lowered and squarish lips), physiology (e.g., pallor vs. flushing), behavior (as just described), and subsequent effects (see, e.g., Demaree, Everhart, Youngstrom, & Harrison, 2005; Ekman & Friesen, 1975; Lerner & Keltner, 2000; Mackie, Devos, & Smith, 2000).

As discussed above, the valence of emotions is an important dimension of variation. This hedonic characteristic divides emotions into positive versus negative groups which then have in common that they are sought versus avoided. But though there may be few cases of invariance, there are many documented significant relationships between particular emotions and particular emotional responses. Neither a two-group analysis of emotions (positive vs. negative) nor a two-dimensional model is sufficient to account for them.

SPECIFYING EMOTION RESPONSE SYNDROMES AND STRATEGIES

Based in part on prior emotion theories and empirical studies (e.g., Davitz, 1969; Izard, 1977), my students, colleagues, and I have developed many specific hypotheses about relationships between particular emotions and particular phenomenology, behaviors, and emotivational goals; and have conducted four studies to test these a priori hypotheses (Fischer & Roseman, 2007; Roseman, 2002; Roseman et al., 1994; Roseman et al., 2007). The studies ask participants to recall intense experiences of particular emotions, and answer questions about what they thought, felt, felt like doing, actually did, and wanted in the experiences that they described. Some results are shown in Table 20.3.

In these studies we found some responses that differentiated each of the 17 emotions in the model of the emotion system that I have proposed (Roseman, 2001). A number of these relationships have also been found in studies by other investigators (e.g., Consedine et al., 2003; Scherer & Wallbott, 1994; Shaver et al., 1987; see Roseman et al., 1994, 2007, for examples).

Perhaps most relevant to the present chapter was the support found for specific emotivational goals for many emotions (e.g., in joy, wanting to make an experience last

TABLE 20.3

Some Responses Found to Differentiate Particular Emotions as Predicted

Emotion	Responses
Surprise	Feel yourself breathe in suddenly
	Think that what was happening was unexpected
	Remain motionless
	Want to figure out what was going on
Hope	Think that you could be optimistic about the future
	Feel like planning for the future[a]
	Want to approach something
	Want what you were thinking of to happen
Joy	Feel a sense of lightness in your movements
	Feel like jumping up and down
	Celebrate
	Want to make the experience last longer
Relief	Feel tension leaving your body
	Think that the worst was over
	Rest
	Want to get on to something else
Affection	Feel warm all over
	Think that you belonged with someone
	Feel like holding someone
	Want to be close to someone
Pride	Feel more powerful
	Think that you had accomplished something
	Assert yourself
	Want to seek recognition
Fear	Feel your heart pounding
	Think of how bad things could get
	Feel like running away
	Want to get to a safe place
Sadness	Feel a lump in your throat
	Think about what you were missing
	Feel like doing nothing
	Want to be comforted
Distress	Think that you did not know what to do to make things less upsetting
	Feel like moving away from something
Frustration	Feel impatient
	Think about an obstacle that was in your way
	Want to overcome some obstacle
Disgust	Think that something was offensive
	Wrinkle your nose
(Interpersonal) Dislike	Think of something in another person that you didn't want to be around
	Feel like avoiding interactions with someone

(Continued)

TABLE 20.3   (continued)
Some Responses Found to Differentiate Particular Emotions as Predicted

Emotion	Responses
	Minimize your contact with someone
	Want to be far away from someone
Anger	Feel ready to explode
	Criticize the other person
	Want to hurt someone
Contempt	Feel revolted by another person
	Think that someone was unworthy of respect
	Feel like saying something unflattering about another person
	Want another person to be rejected by your group
Regret	Think of what a mistake you made
	Feel like correcting your mistake
Guilt	Think that you were in the wrong
	Feel like offering an apology
	Scold yourself for something
	Want to make up for what you did wrong
Shame	Feel small
	Feel like hiding your face
	Blush

Note: Based on data from Fischer and Roseman (2007); Roseman (2002), Roseman et al. (2007); Roseman et al. (1994).

[a] Response was only marginally different from other emotions tested.

longer; in fear, wanting to get to safety; in anger, wanting to hurt someone; in love, wanting to be close to someone). These findings indicate that there is more to emotions than approach and avoidance (or appetitive and aversive) goals. Rather, it seems that a component of each emotion is a distinctive goal (or goals) that people feeling the emotion want to pursue. Indeed people may seek to pursue emotivational goals even if they are not aware of their emotion (e.g., wanting to hurt someone even though one is not aware of being angry) or not aware of the goal itself (see Carver, Ganellen, Froming, & Chambers, 1983).

Hypothesized phenomenological, expressive, behavioral, and emotivational responses for each emotion in the proposed model are shown in the boxes in Figure 20.1. Proceeding outward, from an emotion box to its borders around the chart, shows the combinations of appraisals proposed to elicit each of the emotions (see Roseman, 2001, for a full discussion).

Examination of the emotion syndromes shown in Figure 20.1 suggests they are not made up of unrelated responses that just happen to be part of one emotion rather than another. Instead, the various responses characteristic of a particular emotion seem related to and supportive of each other, forming a "package" of responses (Keltner et al., 2003) that constitutes a "strategy" for coping with a particular type of situation (cf. Lazarus, 1991).

Like "reproductive strategies," emotion strategies are not consciously formulated and pursued by individuals, but are organizing principles of emotional response likely to have been shaped by evolution. For example, as shown in Figure 20.1, in response to unexpectedness (Reisenzein, 2000), the emotion of surprise implements a response strategy of suspending action and processing information in order to adjust to the disconfirmed expectancy. Proposed strategies for other emotions are shown in angle brackets at the bottom of each box in the chart.

EMOTION FAMILIES

Below surprise, the strategies of the other emotions shown in Figure 20.1 form four main groups or "emotion *families*." Each family contains distinct but related

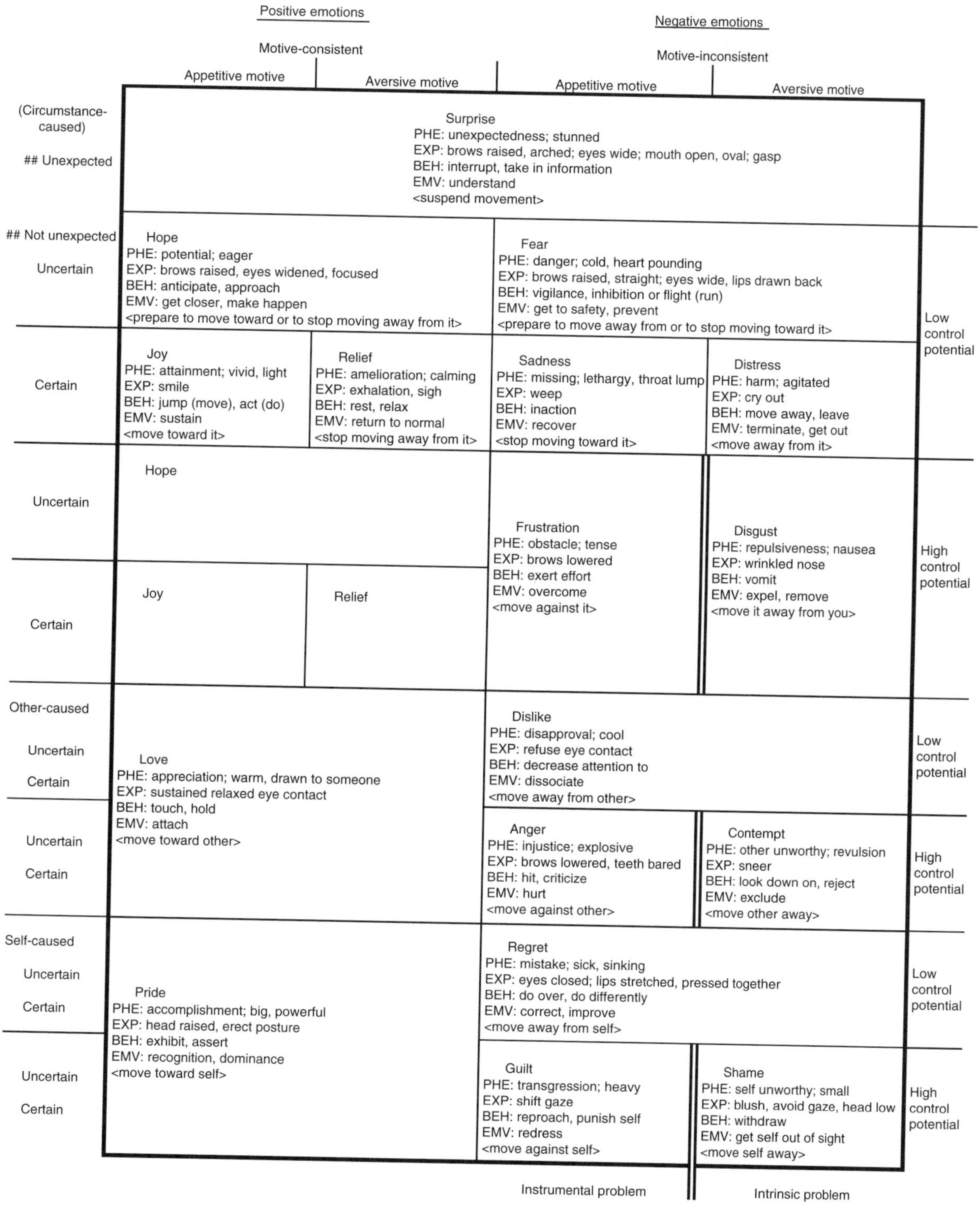

FIGURE 20.1 Structural model of the emotion system. Emotion components: PHE = phenomenological; EXP = expressive; BEH = behavioral; EMV = emotivational goal. Strategies integrating the response components for each emotion are given in angle brackets. Appraisal combinations eliciting each emotion are shown in unshaded areas around the borders of the chart. Adapted from "A model of appraisal in the emotion system: Integrating theory, research, and applications" by I. J. Roseman, in *Appraisal Processes in Emotion* (pp. 70–71) by K. R. Scherer, A. Schorr, & T. Johnstone (Eds.), 2001, New York: Oxford University Press. By permission of Oxford University Press.

strategies whose members cope either with motive-relevant events in general, or with events caused by other people, or with events caused by the self.

The five positive emotions in Figure 20.1 form a family of "contacting" emotions, which increase proximity to and/or interaction with impersonal, interpersonal, or intrapersonal stimuli. The response strategy of joy involves increased contact with rewarding stimuli via "movement toward" them, increasing interaction with them. Relief reduces "movement away" from stimuli—increasing contact via relaxation and decreased defensive responding. Hope increases contact by preparing to move toward or to stop moving away from stimuli. The preparation involves a focusing of attention, anticipation, and if possible, action to produce desired outcomes. Love moves one person toward another (or others), increasing interpersonal closeness, and forming, maintaining, or strengthening interpersonal bonds. Pride moves one toward oneself, in the sense of bringing one's behavior closer to one's own identity and self-conceptions, and promoting self-expression and self-assertion.

Distress, sadness, fear, interpersonal dislike, and regret form a family of "distancing" emotions, which increase distance from impersonal, interpersonal, or intrapersonal stimuli, thus reducing contact and/or interaction with them. Distress actively moves one away from stimuli. Sadness reduces movement toward them. Fear, like hope, is conceptualized as a 'remote coping' response, which prepares a person to move away from or to stop moving toward a stimulus. The vigilance that is characteristic of fear is the counterpart to hope's anticipation—watching out for danger and prompting freezing and/or preparation for flight. The responses of interpersonal dislike move one away from other persons, increasing social distance, for example, by minimizing interaction and connection with them. Regret involves moving away from oneself, in the sense of distancing one's future behavior from what one has done previously (e.g., a regretted course of action).

Disgust, contempt, and shame form a family of "rejection" emotions. Unlike the distancing emotions, which move the self away from something, rejection emotions move something away from the self. The coping strategy of disgust is to get less of something offensive by moving it out of or away from the self. In contempt, another person is moved away from the self, in a type of rejection that is specialized for interpersonal relationships. This social rejection involves looking down on someone and seeking to have the contemptible person rejected by one's in-group and excluded from social interactions. In shame the self is moved away, hidden, withdrawn, and excluded from social interactions.

Finally, frustration, anger, and guilt constitute a family of attack emotions, which move against objects and events in general, against other persons, or against the self. The coping strategy of frustration (which in this conceptualization corresponds to what Smith & Lazarus, 1990, called the emotion of "challenge/determination") moves against something to try to force a change in its state or behavior. It often involves an increased exertion of effort (Amsel, 1992), for example, to overcome an obstacle. In anger, effortful movement against is organized into an interpersonal attack, in which there is an attempt to get revenge, hurt the other person in some way, make the target feel bad. This type of attack is specialized to deal with other sentient beings, who can be hurt (e.g., by feeling pain, or censure, or thwarting of their goals). In guilt, one moves against the self, for example, by self-reproach or by offering an apology or reparation (incurring a social or material cost to redress a negative outcome one has caused).

More to Emotions Than Approach and Avoidance

The existence of contacting, distancing, rejection, and attack emotion families reveals that even when emotions are grouped according to the kind of coping strategies they represent, distinguishing between approach and avoidance classes still provides an insufficient or incomplete description of emotional behavior.

Positive and negative emotions, as valenced states, are indeed themselves approached and avoided, or maximized and minimized. However in the emotion system there are at least three distinct minimization processes: distancing, rejection, and attack. Distancing emotions cope with motive-inconsistent events by accommodating to them, moving away from them. But rejection and attack emotions cope with motive-inconsistent events by contending with them (Arnold, 1960), attempting to change the environment by actively moving stimuli away from the self or by attacking them.

Why Do Emotions Prompt More Than Approach and Avoidance?

The model offered in the first part of this chapter proposed that whereas motivated behavior may be generated by any degree of match or mismatch between a current situation and an actively wanted or unwanted state, emotional behavior is elicited by significant *changes* in such match or mismatch (or alternatively, by relatively *large* match or mismatch with reference states). Thus motivations guide behavior under relatively normal circumstances when an organism can utilize specific purpose behaviors, including behaviors acquired through instrumental learning, to approach desired states or avoid undesired states in ways tailored to the requirements of specific situations. For human beings, in the absence of great change in motive-relevant events, there is more likely to be time to consider particular actions and alternatives, assess their expected consequences in the particular situation at hand, and select an action partly informed by such assessments. In contrast, greater changes are likely to necessitate more rapid response, and I have described emotional behavior as often less planful and deliberative, and more preprogrammed and impulsive than motivated behavior. Moreover, I have argued that emotions typically take precedence over nonemotional motives, which is functionally adaptive because of the greater urgency of their eliciting conditions.

These contrasts between motivation and emotion may provide an explanation for why there are more varieties of emotion (contacting, distancing, rejection, and attack) than varieties of motives (approach and avoidance). Specifying only that something should be done to approach or avoid particular conditions (i.e., establishing goals or antigoals to guide behavior) may be sufficient if action is not needed urgently. But in the face of the larger changes that can create crises and time-limited opportunities, the more constrained action control that is characteristic of emotion, which permits faster response, may be advantageous.

More constrained guidance of behavior would seem especially important when dealing with the motive-inconsistent events that cause negative emotions. As shown in Figure 20.1, the *distancing emotions* (fear, sadness, distress, interpersonal dislike, regret) accommodate to stimuli (moving away, increasing distance from them) in situations appraised as low in control potential. Being constrained to move away is relatively likely to be helpful in such situations, reducing negative outcomes while conserving resources. If instead, an organism attempted to contend with stimuli (tried to change or get rid of them) when control potential is low, the effort is likely to be futile.

In contrast, when control potential is high, accommodating to stimuli may well result in a less than optimal adaptation. Contending with stimuli (e.g., getting rid of something rather than getting used to it; changing a person's behavior rather than avoiding the person on a continuing basis) may lead to better outcomes, especially in the medium and long term. According to Figure 20.1, the *attack emotions* (frustration, anger, and guilt) contend with motive-inconsistent stimuli by moving against them, when it is perceived that control potential is relatively high, and the problem is instrumental (a goal blockage). These are situations in which an urge to attack (a problem, another person, or the self) is most likely to be useful: the

person feeling the emotion is relatively powerful, and if the target is not intrinsically negative but merely blocking a goal, an attack may succeed in forcing some change.

However if a problem is intrinsic to an object, event, or person, attacking it cannot succeed in forcing it to change, even if the person reacting to the problem is relatively powerful. According to Figure 20.1, in such situations a *rejection emotion* (disgust, contempt, or shame) is elicited, which urges a person to move the emotion-producing stimulus away from the self. Such active rejection of a stimulus (moving it away or getting rid of it) may minimize its impact on one's outcomes and be the best one can do in this type of situation (Fischer & Roseman, 2007).

APPROACH VERSUS AVOIDANCE MOTIVATION AS A DETERMINANT OF SPECIFIC EMOTIONS

Most of the motivation-plus-cognition theories of emotion, and many other theories, implicitly or explicitly maintain that events related to *any* motive can give rise to an emotion. For example, as discussed above, many theories claim that happiness can be produced by fulfillment of any motive (hunger, thirst, sexual drive, need for achievement, etc.), fear by a threat to any motive, and anger by another person's interference with any motive.

A few theories claim that there are linkages between particular motives or types of motives and particular emotions. For example, Lazarus (1991) proposed that anger results in part from events incongruent with the goal of preserving or enhancing self- or social-esteem (a view similar to that of Aristotle, 1966/350 B.C., who claimed that anger results specifically from unjustified "slights"), guilt from incongruence with moral goals, and shame from incongruence with goals involving living up to an "ego ideal." However, other authors disagree with the motive-emotion linkages proposed by Lazarus, citing cases of anger in response to any physically or psychologically aversive event, such as pain, heat, frustration, and so forth (Berkowitz, 1998) especially if other people caused or were responsible for it (Roseman, 1991; Scherer, 1993; Smith & Kirby, 2004); and guilt in response to self-caused outcomes that may be unrelated to morality, such as going off a diet or not preparing sufficiently for an exam (Roseman, 2001; cf. Frijda, 1993).

REWARD-MAXIMIZING VERSUS PUNISHMENT-MINIMIZING MOTIVATION AS A DETERMINANT OF JOY-AND-SADNESS VERSUS RELIEF-AND-DISTRESS

I have proposed (Roseman, 2001; see Figure 20.1) that consistency and inconsistency of certain events with reward-related versus punishment-related motives are likely to produce different emotions. The precise claims are that consistency with a reward-maximizing motive ("getting something that you want") gives rise to joy; inconsistency with a reward-maximizing motive (not getting something that you want) gives rise to sadness; consistency with a punishment-minimizing motive (not getting something you don't want) gives rise to relief; and inconsistency with a punishment-minimizing motive (getting something you don't want) gives rise to distress. These hypotheses have been supported, for example, when measuring appraisals in recalled emotion experiences (Roseman et al. 1996; Roseman, Spindel, & Jose, 1990), and (for joy and relief) in research manipulating appraisals and measuring emotions (Roseman & Evdokas, 2004).

Similar proposals have been made by other theorists. In the model proposed by Higgins (e.g., 1987, 1997), having a "promotion focus" (a concern with aspirations and accomplishments) makes a person likely to experience "cheerfulness" emotions (e.g., happiness, satisfaction) if a positive outcome is present, and "dejection emotions" (e.g., disappointment, dissatisfaction, sadness) if a positive outcome is absent. In contrast, a "prevention focus" (a concern with responsibilities and safety) makes one likely to experience "quiescence" emotions (e.g., relaxed, secure) if a negative outcome is absent, and "agitation" emotions (e.g., uneasy, threatened, afraid) if a negative outcome is present.

Support for Higgins' formulation has been obtained in a number of studies. For example, Higgins, Shah, and Friedman (1997) found that in individuals with more of a promotion orientation, congruence between the person's actual and ideal self was associated with more cheerfulness emotions, and discrepancy between actual and ideal self was associated with more dejection emotions. In individuals with more of a prevention orientation, congruence between actual and ideal self was associated with more quiescence emotions, and discrepancy between actual and ideal self was associated with greater agitation emotions. Higgins et al. (1997) also found that inducing promotion focus led to greater change on a continuum from dejection to cheerfulness, whereas inducing prevention focus led to greater change on a continuum from agitation to quiescence.

Carver and Scheier (1998, p. 165) proposed that "discrepancy-reducing meta systems" (analogous to approach motivation) produce "elation/joy" if discrepancy reduction is occurring faster than a person's (minimum) desired rate, and "depression" if discrepancy reduction is slower than desired. For "discrepancy-enlarging systems" (analogous to avoidance motivation), progress (away from

undesired states) that is above an individual's standard is hypothesized to produce relief, and progress that is below standard is hypothesized to produce anxiety. Among the support cited for these relationships is a connection between the failure to attain incentives and depression, and between threat and anxiety (Ahrens & Haaga, 1993; Wickless & Kirsch, 1988; cited in Carver, 2003).

While there are differences among these three theories in formulation of the motivational distinction (reward-maximizing vs. punishment-minimizing; promotion-focus vs. prevention-focus; discrepancy-reducing vs. discrepancy-enlarging), and in the specific associated emotions (joy vs. cheerfulness vs. elation/joy; relief vs. quiescence; sadness vs. dejection vs. depression; distress vs. agitation vs. anxiety), all three posit similar relationships between approach- versus avoidance-like motivational orientations and specific emotions.

Why might such relationships exist? According to Figure 20.1, the negative emotion of distress increases distance between a person and a stimulus by moving the person away from the stimulus (i.e., via attempts to escape from the unwanted state). This active movement away in distress seems appropriate when dealing with high priority crises (those arising from punishment-minimizing motives). The positive emotion of relief allows increased contact with a stimulus by stopping the distancing.

According to Figure 20.1, the positive emotion of joy increases contact with a stimulus by actively moving a person toward it, and increasing interaction with it; the negative emotion of sadness allows increased distance by reducing this movement toward something. The active movement toward stimuli in joy seems appropriate when dealing with rewards (lower in priority than aversive states); and the passive failure to pursue incentives in sadness seems appropriate for lower priority situations (stimuli that need not be urgently pursued).

If punishment-minimizing motives are those with greater urgency, then the responses of related emotions might well have priority: the movement away in distress would have priority over movement toward in joy. Distress would also have greater power to influence behavior than sadness.

Some data cited by Baumeister et al. (2001) are consistent with this formulation. For example, as discussed above, Baumeister et al. (1994) found that attempts to get out of bad moods were more frequently reported than attempts to get into or maintain good moods. Also, Major, Zubek, Cooper, Cozzarelli, and Richards (1997) found that negative affectivity but not positive affectivity influenced distress. Leith and Baumeister (1996) reported that, unlike low-arousal negative moods such as sadness, high-arousal negative moods led research participants to "curtail information processing and make snap decisions" (Baumeister et al., 2001, p. 334). These findings are consistent with the depiction of distress as a more powerful, higher priority emotion than sadness. That is, it may be adaptive to have a lower priority emotion (sadness) which prompts us to cease pursuit of rewards; and a higher priority emotion (distress) which demands, more loudly, persistently, and actively, that we maintain efforts to escape from punishing events.

Thus two types and four degrees of prioritization are provided by this system, with priority-appropriate responses specified for each one: negative over positive emotions, and within these classes, avoidance-linked (distancing-related) over approach-linked (contacting-related) emotions.

SUMMARY

In this chapter I have argued that an adequate account of behavior must include both motivations and emotions, which energize and direct behavior under different conditions and in different ways. I proposed that relatively small changes of adaptive significance can give rise to motivational processes, which are relatively planful, deliberative, and specific-purpose responses, tailored to the specific situations in which they occur. Larger changes of adaptive significance give rise to emotional processes, which take precedence over comparable strength or weaker motives. If changes are only moderately large, emotion-specific emotivational goals tend to replace motivational goals in guiding behavior. Very large changes produce less deliberative, more impulsive, more preprogrammed general purpose emotional behaviors, governed more by stimulus-contingent patterns of action readiness.

In agreement with the theoretical framework of this volume, the model I proposed recognizes the two basic varieties of motivational processes that have been labeled approach and avoidance motivation. As positive and negative emotions have hedonic valence, they also serve as motives, states to be maximized and minimized respectively.

I next discussed the nature of emotions as syndromes of response that form coping strategies. Different positive emotions constitute distinct ways of coping with different types of opportunities, while different negative emotions are distinct ways of coping with different types of crises. I described a model consisting of 16 positive and negative emotions plus surprise (which is a neutral-valenced emotional reaction to unexpectedness). The positive and negative emotions can be grouped into four families—contacting, distancing, rejection, and attack emotions,

which move toward a stimulus, move away from a stimulus, move a stimulus away from the self, or move against a stimulus. Specific emotions apply each family's strategy either to objects and events in general (including distinct reactive and preparatory coping strategies), to other people, or to the self. Thus the emotion system cannot be adequately described just in terms of appetitive and aversive or approach and avoidance processes. Behavior guidance mechanisms beyond approach and avoidance, such as attack and rejection, must be recognized; and the specific varieties of contacting, distancing, rejection, and attack strategies that are specialized to deal with impersonal, interpersonal, and intrapersonal opportunities and crises (i.e., the individual discrete emotions shown in Figure 20.1) also appear to have distinctive properties that are worthy of attention.

Finally, I discussed causation of the specific emotions of joy and sadness (by success and failure, respectively, in maximizing reward) and relief and distress (by success and failure in minimizing punishment), as proposed in my model of appraisal and emotion; discussed two other theories that make similar claims, and some evidence supporting these theories; and considered why, from a functional perspective, having different emotions related to appetitive (approach) and aversive (avoidance) motives might make adaptive sense.

REFERENCES

Abelson, R. P., & Sermat, V. (1962). Multidimensional scaling of facial expressions. *Journal of Experimental Psychology*, *63*, 546–554.

Ahrens, A. H., & Haaga, D. A. F. (1993). The specificity of attributional style and expectations to positive and negative affectivity, depression, and anxiety. *Cognitive Therapy and Research*, *17*, 83–98.

Ajzen, I. (1991). The theory of planned behavior. *Organizational Behavior and Human Decision Processes*, *50*, 179–211.

Ajzen, I. (2002). Residual effects of past on later behavior: Habituation and reasoned action perspectives. *Personality and Social Psychology Review*, *6*, 107–122.

American Psychiatric Association. (2000). *Diagnostic and statistical manual of mental disorders* (4th ed., Text Revision). Washington, DC: Author.

Amsel, A. (1992). *Frustration theory: An analysis of dispositional learning and memory*. Cambridge: Cambridge University Press.

Andersen, S. M., Reznik, I., & Glassman, N. S. (2005). The unconscious relational self. In R. Hassin, J. S. Uleman, & J. A. Bargh (Eds.), *The new unconscious* (pp. 421–481). New York: Oxford University Press.

Aristotle (1966). Rhetoric. In *Aristotle's rhetoric and poetics* (W. R. Roberts, Trans.). New York: Modern Library. (Original work published 350 B.C.)

Arnold, M. B. (1960). *Emotion and personality*. New York: Columbia University Press.

Ashton, H. (2002). Motivation: Reward and punishment systems. In E. Perry, H. Ashton, & A. Young (Eds.), *Neurochemistry of consciousness* (pp. 83–104). Amsterdam: John Benjamins.

Atkinson, J. W. (1964). *An introduction to motivation*. New York: Van Nostrand.

Atthowe, J. M. (1960). Types of conflict and their resolution: A reinterpretation. *Journal of Experimental Psychology*, *59*, 1–9.

Averill, J. R. (1980). A constructivist view of emotion. In R. Plutchik & H. Kellerman (Eds.), *Emotion: Theory, research and experience* (Vol. 1, pp. 305–339). New York: Academic Press.

Bandura, A. (1997). *Self-efficacy: The exercise of control*. New York: W.H. Freeman.

Bargh, J. A., & Barndollar, K. (1996). Automaticity in action: The unconscious as repository of chronic goals and motives. In P. M. Gollwitzer & J. A. Bargh (Eds.), *The psychology of action* (pp. 457–471). New York: Guilford Press.

Barker, R., Dembo, T., & Lewin, K. (1941). *Frustration and reggression: An experiment with young children*. Iowa City: University of Iowa Press.

Barlow, D. H. (1988). *Anxiety and its disorders: The nature and treatment of anxiety and panic*. New York: Guilford Press.

Barrett, L. F. (2006a). Are emotions natural kinds? *Perspectives on Psychological Science*, *1*, 28–58.

Barrett, L. F. (2006b). Valence as a basic building block of emotional life. *Journal of Research in Personality*, *40*, 35–55.

Barrett, L. F., Mesquita, B., Ochsner, K. N., & Gross, J. J. (2007). The experience of emotion. *Annual Review of Psychology*, *58*, 387–403.

Baumeister, R. F., Bratslavsky, E., Finkenauer, C., & Vohs, K. D. (2001). Bad is stronger than good. *Review of General Psychology*, *5*, 323–370.

Baumeister, R. F., Heatherton, T. F., & Tice, D. M. (1994). *Losing control: How and why people fail at self-regulation*. San Diego, CA: Academic Press.

Berkowitz, L. (1998). Affective aggression: The role of stress, pain, and negative affect. In R. G. Geen & E. Donnerstein (Eds.), *Human aggression: Theories, research, and implications for social policy* (pp. 49–72). San Diego, CA: Academic Press.

Berkowitz, L. (1999). Anger. In T. Dalgleish & M. J. Power (Eds.), *Handbook of cognition and emotion* (pp. 411–428). New York: Wiley.

Berridge, K. C. (2004). Pleasure, unconscious affect and irrational desire. In A. S. R. Manstead, N. H. Frijda, & A. H. Fischer (Eds.), *Feelings and emotions: The Amsterdam symposium* (pp. 43–62). New York: Cambridge University Press.

Birney, R. C., Burdick, H., & Teevan, R. C. (1969). *Fear of failure*. New York: Van Nostrand.

Boucher, J. D., & Brandt, M. E. (1981). Judgment of emotion from American and Malay antecedents. *Journal of Cross-Cultural Psychology*, *12*, 272–283.

Bracha, H. S. (2004). Freeze, flight, fight, fright, faint: Adaptationist perspectives on the acute stress response spectrum. *CNS Spectrum*, *9*, 679–685.

Brown, J. S. (1961). *The motivation of behavior*. New York: McGraw-Hill.

Brunner, F. P. (1993). Pathophysiologie der Dehydratation [Pathophysiology of dehydration]. *Schweizerische Rundschau fur Medizin Praxis*, *82*, 784–787.

Buck, R. (1985). PRIME Theory: An integrated approach to motivation and emotion. *Psychological Review*, *92*, 389–413.

Cacioppo, J. T., Berntson, G. G., Larsen, J. T., Poehlmann, K. M., & Ito, T. A. (2000). The psychophysiology of emotion. In M. Lewis & J. M. Haviland-Jones (Eds.), *Handbook of emotion* (2nd ed., pp. 173–191). New York: Guilford Press.

Cacioppo, J. T., Larsen, J. T., Smith, N. K., & Berntson, G. G. (2004). The affect system: What lurks below the surface of feelings? In A. S. R. Manstead, N. H. Frijda, & A. H. Fischer (Eds.), *Feelings and emotions: The Amsterdam conference* (pp. 223–242). New York: Cambridge University Press.

Cannon, W. B. (1932). *The wisdom of the body*. New York: Norton.

Carlson, N. R. (2007). *Physiology of behavior*. Boston: Allyn & Bacon.

Carver, C. S. (2003). Pleasure as a sign you can attend to something else: Placing positive feelings within a general model of affect. *Cognition and Emotion*, *17*, 241–261.

Carver, C. S., Ganellen, R. J., Froming, W. J., & Chambers, W. (1983). Modeling: An analysis in terms of category accessibility. *Journal of Experimental Social Psychology*, *19*, 403–421.

Carver, C. S., & Scheier, M. F. (1998). *On the self-regulation of behavior*. New York: Cambridge University Press.

Chaiken, S., Liberman, A., & Eagly, A. H. (1989). Heuristic and systematic information processing within and beyond the persuasion context. In J. S. Uleman & J. A. Bargh (Eds.), *Unintended thought* (pp. 212–252). New York: Guilford.

Charlesworth, W. R. (1970). *Surprise reactions in congenitally blind and sighted children*. Bethesda, MD: National Institute of Mental Health Progress Report.

Cofer, C. N., & Appley, M. H. (1964). *Motivation: Theory and Research*. New York: Wiley.

Collier, G. (1985). *Emotional expression*. Hillsdale, NJ: Lawrence Erlbaum Associates.

Consedine, N. S., Strongman, K. T., & Magai, C. (2003). Emotions and behaviour: Data from a cross-cultural recognition study. *Cognition and Emotion*, *17*, 881–902.

Constantini, A. F., & Hoving, K. L. (1973). The effectiveness of reward and punishment contingencies on response inhibition. *Journal of Experimental Child Psychology*, *16*, 484–494.

Craig, W. (1918). Appetites and aversions as constituents of instincts. *Biological Bulletin*, *34*, 91–107.

Darwin, C. R. (1965). *The expression of the emotions in man and animals*. Chicago: University of Chicago Press. (Original work published 1872).

Davidson, R. J., Scherer, K. R., & Goldsmith, H. H. (Eds.) (2003). Introduction. *Handbook of the affective sciences* (pp. xiii–xvii). New York: Oxford University Press.

Davitz, J. R. (1969). *The language of emotion.* New York: Academic Press.

de Gelder, B., Snyder, J., Greve, D., Gerard, G., & Hadjikhani, N. (2004). Fear fosters flight: A mechanism for fear contagion when perceiving emotion expressed by a whole body. *Proceedings of the National Academy of Sciences, 101,* 16701–16706.

DelParigi, A., Tschop, M., Heiman, M. L., Salbe, A. D., Vozarova, B., Sell, S. M., Bunt, J. C., & Tataranni, P. A. (2002). High circulating ghrelin: A potential cause for hyperphagia and obesity in Prader–Willi Syndrome. *Journal of Clinical Endocrinology and Metabolism, 87,* 5461–5464.

Demaree, H. A., Everhart, D. E., Youngstrom, E. A., & Harrison, D. W. (2005). Brain lateralization of emotional processing: Historical roots and a future incorporating "dominance." *Behavioral and Cognitive Neuroscience Reviews, 4,* 3–20.

de Rivera, J. (1977). A structural theory of the emotions. *Psychological Issues, 10,* No. 4, Monograph No. 40.

Descartes, R. (1968). The passions of the soul. In *The Philosophical works of Rene Descartes* (Vol. 1). London: Cambridge University Press. (original work published 1649)

Dumas, F. (1932). La mimique des aveugles. *Bulletin de l'Academie de Medicin, 107,* 607–610.

Dweck, C. S. (1999). *Self-theories: Their role in motivation, personality and development.* Philadelphia: Psychology Press.

Eibl-Eibesfeldt, I. (1970). *Ethology: The biology of behavior.* New York: Holt, Rinehart, and Winston.

Eibl-Eibesfeldt, I. (1972). *Love and hate: The natural history of behavior patterns.* (G. Strachan, Trans.). New York: Holt, Rinehart, and Winston.

Ekman, P. (1972). Universals and cultural differences in facial expressions of emotion. In J. K. Cole (Ed.), *Nebraska symposium on motivation, 1971* (Vol. 19, pp. 207–283). Lincoln: University of Nebraska Press.

Ekman, P. (1992). An argument for basic emotions. *Cognition and Emotion, 6,* 169–200.

Ekman, P. (1999). Basic emotions. In T. Dalgleish & M. J. Power (Eds.), *Handbook of cognition and emotion* (pp. 45–60). New York: Wiley.

Ekman, P., & Friesen, W. V. (1975). *Unmasking the face.* Englewood Cliffs, NJ: Prentice-Hall.

Elliot, A. J. (1997). Integrating "classic" and "contemporary" approaches to achievement motivation: A hierarchical model of approach and avoidance achievement motivation. In P. Pintrich & M. Maehr (Eds.), *Advances in motivation and achievement* (Vol. 10, pp. 143–179). Greenwich, CT: JAI Press.

Elliot, A. J. (1999). Approach and avoidance motivation and achievement goals. *Educational Psychologist, 34,* 149–169.

Elliot, A. J. (2006). Approach and avoidance motivation. *Motivation and Emotion, 30,* 111–116.

Fanselow, M. S., & Lester, L. S. (1988). A functional behavioristic approach to aversively motivated behavior: Predatory imminence as a determinant of the topography of defensive behavior. In R. C. Bolles & M. D. Beecher (Eds.), *Evolution and learning* (pp. 185–212). Hillsdale, NJ: Erlbaum.

Feather, N. T. (Ed.) (1982). *Expectations and actions: Expectancy-value models in psychology.* Hillsdale, NJ: Erlbaum.

Fessler, D. M. T. (2006). The male flash of anger. In J. Barkow (Ed.), *Missing the revolution: Darwinism for social scientists* (pp. 101–117). New York: Oxford University Press.

Fischer, A. H., & Roseman, I. J. (2007). Beat them or ban them: The characteristics and social functions of anger and contempt. *Journal of Personality and Social Psychology, 93,* 103–115.

Frederick, S., & Loewenstein, G. (1999). Hedonic adaptation. In D. Kahneman, E. Diener, & N. Schwarz (Eds.), *Well-being: The foundations of hedonic psychology* (pp. 302–329). New York: Russell Sage Foundation.

Fredrickson, B. L. (1998). What good are positive emotions? *Review of General Psychology, 2,* 300–319.

Frijda, N. H. (1986). *The emotions.* New York: Cambridge University Press.

Frijda, N. H. (1988). The laws of emotion. *American Psychologist, 43,* 349–358.

Frijda, N. H. (1993). The place of appraisal in emotion. *Cognition and Emotion, 7,* 357–387.

Frijda, N. H. (2007). *The laws of emotion.* Mahwah, NJ: Lawrence Erlbaum Associates.

Glaser, J., & Kihlstrom, J. F. (2005). Compensatory automaticity: Unconscious volition is not an oxymoron. In R. Hassin, J. S. Uleman, & J. A. Bargh (Eds.), *The new unconscious* (pp. 171–195). New York: Oxford University Press.

Gollwitzer, P. M. (1996). The volitional benefits of planning. In P. M. Gollwitzer & J. A. Bargh (Eds.), *The psychology of action: Linking cognition and motivation to behavior* (pp. 287–312). New York: Guilford Press.

Gollwitzer, P. M., & Bargh, J. A. (Eds.). (1996). *The psychology of action: Linking motivation and cognition to behavior.* New York: Guilford Press.

Gray, J. A. (1987). *The psychology of fear and stress* (2nd ed.). Cambridge, UK: Cambridge University Press.

Gray, J. A., & McNaughton, N. (2000). *The neuropsychology of anxiety* (2nd ed.). New York: Oxford University Press.

Gross, J. J. (1999). Emotion and emotion regulation. In L. A. Pervin & O. P. John (Eds.), *Handbook of personality: Theory and research* (2nd ed.) (pp. 525–552). New York: Guilford Press.

Gross, J. J., Richards, J. M., & John, O. P. (2006). Emotion regulation in everyday life. In D. K. Snyder, J. A. Simpson, & J. N. Hughes (Eds.), *Emotion regulation in couples and families: Pathways to dysfunction and health* (pp. 13–35). Washington, DC: American Psychological Association.

Heider, F. (1958). *The psychology of interpersonal relations.* New York: Wiley.

Hejmadi, A., Davidson, R., & Rozin, P. (2000). Exploring Hindu Indian emotion expressions: Evidence for accurate recognition by Americans and Indians. *Psychological Science, 11*, 183–187.

Helson, H. (1964). *Adaptation-level theory: An experimental and systematic approach to behavior.* New York: Harper & Row.

Higgins, E. T. (1987). Self-discrepancy: A theory relating self and affect. *Psychological Review, 94*, 319–340.

Higgins, E. T. (1997). Beyond pleasure and pain. *American Psychologist, 52*, 1280–1300.

Higgins, E. T., Shah, J., & Friedman, R. (1997). Emotional responses to goal attainment: Strength of regulatory focus as moderator. *Journal of Personality and Social Psychology, 72*, 515–525.

Hull, C. L. (1943). *Principles of behavior.* New York: Appleton-Century-Crofts.

Irwin, J. R. (1947). Galen on the temperaments. *Journal of General Psychology, 36*, 45–64.

Isen, A. M. (2000). Positive affect and decision making. In M. Lewis & J. Haviland-Jones (Eds.), *Handbook of emotions* (2nd ed., pp. 417–435). New York: Guilford.

Izard, C. E. (1971). *The face of emotion.* New York: Appleton-Century-Crofts.

Izard, C. E. (1977). *Human emotions.* New York: Plenum Press.

Izard, C. E. (1991). *The psychology of emotions.* New York: Plenum Press.

Izard, C. E. (2000). Affect. In A. E. Kazdin (Ed.), *Encyclopedia of psychology* (Vol. 1, p. 88). New York: Oxford University Press.

Kahneman, D., & Tversky, A. (1984). Choices, values and frames. *American Psychologist, 39*, 341–350.

Keltner, D., Ekman, P., Gonzaga, G. C., & Beer, J. S. (2003). Facial expression of emotion. In R. Davidson, K. Scherer, & H. H. Goldsmith (Eds.), *Handbook of affective sciences* (pp. 415–432). New York: Oxford University Press.

Keltner, D., & Haidt, J. (1999). Social functions of emotions at four levels of analysis. *Cognition and Emotion, 13*, 505–522.

Klein, S. B. (1982). *Motivation: Biosocial approaches.* New York: McGraw-Hill.

Kobak, R. (1999). The emotional dynamics of disruptions in attachment relationships: Implications for theory, research, and clinical intervention. In J. Cassidy & P. R. Shaver (Eds.), *Handbook of attachment: Theory, research, and clinical applications* (pp. 21–43). New York: Guilford.

Kleinginna, P., Jr., & Kleinginna, A. (1981a). A categorized list of emotion definitions, with suggestions for a consensual definition. *Motivation and Emotion, 5*, 345–379.

Kleinginna, P., Jr., & Kleinginna, A. (1981b). A categorized list of motivation definitions, with suggestions for a consensual definition. *Motivation and Emotion, 5*, 263–291.

Kristjánsson, K. (2003). On the very idea of negative emotions. *Journal for the Theory of Social Behaviour, 33*, 351–364.

Lang, P. (1995). Studies of motivation and attention. *American Psychologist, 50*, 372–385.

Lazarus, R. S. (1991). *Emotion and adaptation.* New York: Oxford University Press.

Lazarus, R. S. (2001). Relational meaning and discrete emotions. In K. R. Scherer, A. Schorr, & T. Johnstone (Eds.), *Appraisal processes in emotion: Theory, methods, research* (pp. 37–67). New York: Oxford University Press.

Lazarus, R. S., & Folkman, S. (1984). *Stress, appraisal, and coping.* New York: Springer.

LeDoux, J. E. (1996). *The emotional brain: The mysterious underpinnings of emotional life.* New York: Simon & Schuster.

Leeper, R. W. (1970). The motivational and perceptual properties of emotions as indicating their fundamental character and role. In M. B. Arnold (Ed.), *Feelings and emotions: The Loyola symposium* (pp. 151–168). New York: Academic Press.

Leith, K. P., & Baumeister, R. F. (1996). Why do bad moods increase self-defeating behavior? Emotion, risk taking, and self-regulation. *Journal of Personality and Social Psychology, 71*, 1250–1267.

Lerner, J. S., & Keltner, D. (2000). Beyond valence: Toward a model of emotion-specific influences on judgment and choice. *Cognition and Emotion, 14*, 473–493.

Levenson, R. W. (1999). The intrapersonal functions of emotion. *Cognition and Emotion, 13*, 481–504.

Lewicki, P. (1985). Nonconscious biasing effects of single instances on subsequent judgments. *Journal of Personality and Social Psychology, 48*, 563–574.

Liedtke, W., Choe, Y., Marti-Renom, M. A., Bell, A. M., Denis, C. S., Sali, A., et al. (2000). Vanilloid receptor-related osmotically activated channel (VR-OAC), a candidate vertebrate osmoreceptor. *Cell, 103*, 525–535.

Lindsley, D. (1951). Emotion. In S. S. Stevens (Ed.), *Handbook of experimental psychology.* New York: Wiley.

Mackie, D. M., Devos, T., & Smith, E. R. (2000). Intergroup emotions: Explaining offensive action tendencies in an intergroup context. *Journal of Personality and Social Psychology, 79*, 606–616.

Madsen, K. B. (1968). *Theories of motivation* (4th ed.). Copenhagen, Denmark: Munksgaard.

Madsen, K. B. (1974). *Modern theories of motivation.* New York: Halstead Press.

Major, B., Zubek, J. M., Cooper, M. L., Cozzarelli, C., & Richards, C. (1997). Mixed messages: The implications of social conflict and social support for adjustment to abortion. *Journal of Personality and Social Psychology, 72*, 1349–1363.

Maslow, A. (1955). Deficiency motivation and growth motivation. In M. R. Jones (Ed.), *Nebraska symposium on motivation, 1955* (Vol. 3, pp. 1–30). Lincoln, NE: University of Nebraska Press.

Mistschenka, M. N. (1933). Ueber die mimische Gesichtsomotorik der Blinden. *Folia Neuropathologica, 13*, 24–43.

Murray, H. (1938). *Explorations in personality.* New York: Oxford University Press.

Oatley, K., & Johnson-Laird, P. N. (1987). Towards a cognitive theory of emotions. *Cognition and Emotion, 1*, 29–50.

Ortony, A., & Turner, T. J. (1990). What's basic about basic emotions? *Psychological Review, 97,* 315–331.

Panksepp, J. (1998). *Affective neuroscience: The foundations of human and animal emotions.* New York: Oxford.

Petty, R. E., & Wegener, D. T. (1993). Flexible correction processes in social judgment: Correcting for context-induced contrast. *Journal of Experimental Social Psychology, 29,* 137–165.

Plutchik, R. (1962). *Emotion: A psychoevolutionary synthesis.* New York: Harper & Row.

Plutchik, R. (1980). A general psychoevolutionary theory of emotion. In R. Plutchik & H. Kellerman (Eds.), *Emotion: Theory, research, and experience: Vol. 1. Theories of emotion* (pp. 3–33). New York: Academic Press.

Reeve, J. (2005). *Understanding motivation and emotion* (4th ed.). Hoboken, NJ: Wiley.

Reisenzein, R. (2000). The subjective experience of surprise. In H. Bless & J. P. Forgas (Eds.), *The message within: The role of subjective experience in social cognition and behavior* (pp. 262–279). Philadelphia: Psychology Press.

Romney, A. K., Moore, C. C., & Rusch, C. D. (1997). Cultural universals: measuring the semantic structure of emotion terms in English and Japanese. *Proceedings of the National Academy of Sciences, 94,* 5489–5494.

Roseman, I. J. (1984). Cognitive determinants of emotions: A structural theory. *Review of Personality and Social Psychology, 5,* 11–36.

Roseman, I. J. (1991). Appraisal determinants of discrete emotions. *Cognition and Emotion, 5,* 161–200.

Roseman, I. J. (2001). A model of appraisal in the emotion system: Integrating theory, research, and applications. In K. R. Scherer, A. Schorr, & T. Johnstone (Eds.), *Appraisal processes in emotion: Theory, methods, research* (pp. 68–91). New York: Oxford University Press.

Roseman, I. J. (2002). Distancing, attack, and exclusion emotions: A summary of progress in differentiating negative emotions. In A. Kappas (Ed.), *Proceedings of the 12th International Conference of the International Society for Research on Emotions* (pp. 199–204). Cuenca, Spain: International Society for Research on Emotions.

Roseman, I. J., Antoniou, A. A., & Jose, P. E. (1996). Appraisal determinants of emotions: Constructing a more accurate and comprehensive theory. *Cognition and Emotion, 10,* 241–277.

Roseman, I. J., & Evdokas, A. (2004). Appraisals cause experienced emotions: Experimental evidence. *Cognition and Emotion, 18,* 1–28.

Roseman, I. J., Spindel, M. S., & Jose, P. E. (1990). Appraisals of emotion-eliciting events: Testing a theory of discrete emotions. *Journal of Personality and Social Psychology, 59,* 899–915.

Roseman, I. J., Swartz, T. S., Newman, L., & Nichols, N. (2007). *Phenomenology, behaviors, and goals also differentiate positive emotions.* Manuscript submitted for publication.

Roseman, I. J., Wiest, C., & Swartz, T. S. (1994). Phenomenology, behaviors, and goals differentiate discrete emotions. *Journal of Personality and Social Psychology, 67,* 206–221.

Russell, J. A. (1980). A circumplex model of affect. *Journal of Personality and Social Psychology, 39,* 1161–1178.

Russell, J. A. (2003). Core affect and the psychological construction of emotion. *Psychological Review, 110,* 145–172.

Russell, J. A., & Barrett, L. F. (1999). Core affect, prototypical emotional episodes, and other things called emotion: Dissecting the elephant. *Journal of Personality and Social Psychology, 76,* 805–819.

Russell, J. A., & Mehrabian, A. (1977). Evidence for a three-factor theory of emotions. *Journal of Research in Personality, 11,* 273–294.

Scherer, K. R. (1984). Emotion as a multicomponent process: A model and some cross-cultural data. *Review of Personality and Social Psychology, 5,* 37–63.

Scherer, K. R. (1988). *Facets of emotion: Recent research.* Hillsdale, NJ: Erlbaum.

Scherer, K. R. (1993). Studying the emotion-antecedent appraisal process: An expert system approach. *Cognition and Emotion, 7,* 325–355.

Scherer, K. R. (2001). Appraisal considered as a process of multi-level sequential checking. In K. R. Scherer, A. Schorr, & T. Johnstone (Eds.), *Appraisal processes in emotion: Theory, methods, research* (pp. 92–120). New York: Oxford University Press.

Scherer, K. R., Johnstone, T., & Klasmeyer, G. (2003). Vocal expression of emotion. In R. J. Davidson, H. H. Goldsmith, & K. R. Scherer (Eds.), *Handbook of affective sciences* (pp. 433–456). New York: Oxford University Press.

Scherer, K. R., & Wallbott, H. G. (1994). Evidence for universality and cultural variation of differential emotion response patterning. *Journal of Personality and Social Psychology, 66,* 310–328.

Schunk, D. H. (2003). Self-efficacy for reading and writing: Influence of modeling, goal setting and self-evaluation. *Reading and Writing Quarterly, 19,* 159–172.

Shaver, P. R., Morgan, H. J., Wu, S. (1996). Is love a basic emotion? *Personal Relationships, 3,* 81–96.

Shaver, P., Schwartz, J., Kirson, D., & O'Connor, C. (1987). Emotion knowledge: Further exploration of a prototype approach. *Journal of Personality and Social Psychology, 52,* 1061–1086.

Smith, C. A., & Kirby, L. D. (2001). Toward delivering on the promise of appraisal theory. In K. R. Scherer, A. Schorr, & T. Johnstone (Eds.), *Appraisal processes in emotion: Theory, methods, research* (pp. 121–138). New York: Oxford University Press.

Smith, C. A., & Kirby, L. D. (2004). Appraisal as a pervasive determinant of anger. *Emotion, 4,* 133–138.

Smith, C. A., & Lazarus, R. S. (1990). Emotion and adaptation. In L. A. Pervin (Ed.), *Handbook of personality theory and research* (pp. 609–637). New York: Guilford Press.

Solomon, R. C., & Stone, L. D. (2002). On "positive" and "negative" emotions. *Journal for the Theory of Social Behaviour, 32,* 417–435.

Sorrentino, R. M., & Higgins, E. T. (1986). Motivation and cognition: Warming up to synergism. In R. M. Sorrentino & E. T. Higgins (Eds.), *Handbook of motivation and cognition: Foundations of social behavior* (pp. 3–19). New York: Guilford Press.

Spinoza, B. (2000). Ethics (G. H. R. Parkinson Trans.). New York: Oxford University Press. (Original work published 1677)

Stipek, D. (1995). The development of pride and shame in toddlers. In K. W. Fischer & J. P. Tangney (Eds.), *Self-conscious emotions: The psychology of shame, guilt, embarrassment, and pride* (pp. 237–252). New York: Guilford Press.

Strack, F., & Deutsch, R. (2005). Reflection and impulse as determinants of conscious and unconscious motivation. In J. P. Forgas, K. D. Williams, & S. M. Laham (Eds.), *Social motivation: Conscious and unconscious processes* (pp. 91–112). Cambridge, UK: Cambridge University Press.

Summerfield, A. B., & Green, E. J. (1986). Categories of emotion-eliciting events: A qualitative overview. In K. R. Scherer, H. G. Walbott, & A. B. Summerfield (Eds.), *Experiencing emotion: A cross-cultural study* (pp. 50–65). New York: Cambridge.

Taylor, S. E. (1991). Asymmetrical effects of positive and negative events: The mobilization-minimization hypothesis. *Psychological Bulletin, 110,* 67–85.

Tennov, D. (1979). *Love and limerence: The experience of being in love.* New York: Stein & Day.

Tesser, A., Martin, L. L., & Cornell, D. P. (1996). On the substitutability of self-protective mechanisms. In P. M. Gollwitzer & J. A. Bargh (Eds.), *The psychology of action: Linking cognition and motivation to behavior* (pp. 48–68). New York: Guilford Press.

Tolman, E. C. (1923). A behavioristic account of the emotions. *Psychological Review, 30,* 217–227.

Tomkins, S. S. (1962). *Affect, imagery, consciousness. Vol. I. The positive affects.* New York: Springer.

Tomkins, S. S. (1963). *Affect, imagery, consciousness. Vol. II. The negative affects.* New York: Springer.

Tomkins, S. S. (1970). Affect as the primary motivational system. In M. B. Arnold (Ed.), *Feelings and emotions: The Loyola symposium* (pp. 101–110). New York: Academic Press.

Tomkins, S. S. (1979). Script theory: Differential magnification of affects. In H. E. Howe Jr. & R. A. Dienstbier (Eds.), *Nebraska symposium on motivation, 1978* (Vol. 26, pp. 201–236). Lincoln, NE: University of Nebraska Press.

Tomkins, S. S. (1987). Script theory. In J. Aronoff, A. I. Rubin, & R. A. Tucker (Eds.), *The emergence of personality* (pp. 147–216). New York: Springer.

Tooby, J., & Cosmides, L. (1990). The past explains the present: Emotional adaptations and the structure of ancestral environments. *Ethology and Sociobiology, 11,* 375–424.

Tracy, J. L., & Robins, R. W. (2004). Show your pride: Evidence for a discrete emotion expression. *Psychological Science, 15,* 194–197.

Tsai, J. L., Knutson, B., & Fung, H. H. (2006). Cultural variation in affect valuation. *Journal of Personality and Social Psychology, 90,* 288–307.

Underwood, M. K. (2003). *Social aggression among girls.* New York: Guilford Press.

van Dijk, W. W., Zeelenberg, M., & van der Pligt, J. (2003). Blessed are they who expect nothing: Lowering expectations as a way of avoiding disappointment. *Journal of Economic Psychology, 24,* 505–516.

van Furth, W. R., Wolterink, G., & van Ree, J. M. (1995). Regulation of masculine sexual behavior: Involvement of brain opioids and dopamine. *Brain Research Reviews, 21,* 162–184.

van Reekum, C., Banse, R., Johnstone, T., Etter, A., Wehrle, T., & Scherer, K. R. (2004). Psychophysiological responses to appraisal responses in a computer game. *Cognition and Emotion, 18,* 663–688.

Watson, D., & Tellegen, A. (1985). Toward a consensual structure of mood. *Psychological Bulletin, 98,* 219–235.

Weiner, B. (1985). An attributional theory of achievement motivation and emotion. *Psychological Review, 92,* 548–573.

Wickless, C., & Kirsch, I. (1988). Cognitive correlates of anger, anxiety, and sadness. *Cognitive Therapy and Research, 12,* 367–377.

World Health Organization (2007). *ICD Version 2007.* http://www.who.int/classifications/apps/icd/icd10online

Wundt, W. (1904). *Principles of physiological psychology.* (E. B. Titchener, Trans., from the 5th German ed., published 1902). New York: Macmillan.

Zeelenberg, M., Beattie, J., van der Pligt, J., & de Vries, N. K. (1996). Consequences of regret aversion: Effects of expected feedback on risky decision making. *Organizational Behavior and Human Decision Processes, 65,* 148–158.

21 Functions of Emotions and Emotion-Related Dysfunction

Eric Youngstrom and Carroll E. Izard

CONTENTS

The goal of this chapter is to review the function and dysfunction of emotions within an overarching framework of approach and avoidance. The discussion of emotions will adopt an explicitly functionalist perspective, as described in the first section. The function of emotions and emotion-related dysfunction are addressed in the second and third sections. Whereas most prior evolutionary treatments of the functionality of emotions have concentrated on the survival value of emotions, our discussion also adds the element of reproductive advantage. We will argue that much of the function and dysfunction of emotions in human culture has been affected by sexual selection as well as survival pressures. Finally, and perhaps most provocatively, we explore the idea of memetic replication with regard to emotion. We argue that emotions offer a powerful ally for the propagation of memes, and hopefully will offer some provocative ideas about the plasticity with which both culture and self are developing.

FUNCTIONALIST PERSPECTIVE ON EMOTIONS

The word "emotion" is used every day in conversation, with a naïve, folk-psychology definition that is readily intuited. However, it proves exceedingly difficult to define what an emotion is in precise technical terms (Solomon, 2000). Consistent with a large body of prior work, we define an emotion as a system that involves and organizes many different processes and levels of analysis (Izard, 1991; Lazarus, 1991). Emotions connect sensory perceptions with very rapid appraisals of the valence and importance of the percepts. The appraisals are connected to physiological responses and cognitive processes, and these in turn are often connected to behavioral outputs. One of the hallmarks of emotions as systems is that there is some looseness in the connections between the different levels or processes. It is possible to have emotions without explicit cognitive involvement or behavioral output, for example. However, the stronger the emotional experience, the greater the entrainment of these different processes and levels of analyses (Cacioppo & Berntson, 1999).

EMOTIONS AS EVOLVED CAPACITY: THREE LEVELS OF ANALYSIS

Why develop emotions? What problems of fitness do emotions help solve from the perspective of natural selection? Many functionalist models of emotion explicitly theorize that emotions are an evolved capacity of biological organisms (Cosmides & Tooby, 2000; Plutchik, 1980, 1993). On the basis of this conceptualization, emotions evolved because they increased the "fitness" of organisms. Most discussions of emotion have emphasized the role of emotions in enhancing fitness in terms of survival (Darwin, 1872/1965; Izard, 1972, 1991; Lazarus, 1991).

Less frequently discussed is the fact that emotions can also improve the fitness of an organism by contributing to success in sexual reproduction. Dawkins' (1989) discussion of the "selfish gene" as the appropriate level of analysis for biological evolution is informative in this regard. The ultimate determinant of genetic fitness is how many copies of a gene that pass on to subsequent generations, and not whether a particular organism survives. An organism acts as a vehicle carrying the genes until the organism is able to

reproduce. Both survival and reproductive success are gates through which the stream of genes must pass in order to flow into subsequent generations. Although less often studied, it seems likely that emotions can play a large role in terms of influencing reproductive success. This opens the possibility of emotions being subject to sexual selection pressures as well as survival selection pressures, with the consequence that emotional systems might evolve in ways that are not evident when viewed through the lens of survival fitness (Miller, 2000; Ridley, 1993).

A third level of selection might also be fruitful to consider in the context of the functionality of emotions. Dawkins (1989) pointed out that the process of natural selection could operate on "replicant" units besides biological genes, and he speculated that behaviors might offer another potential form of replicant. Specifically, he coined the term "meme" to refer to a unit of behavior (including cognition) that could be copied and reproduced by other agents. Memes could be words, concepts, objects (such as clothes, or clothing fashions), or processes (such as tool-making, or making a pun). Other authors have subsequently elaborated on the concept of meme as a unit of selection among ideas and behaviors (Aunger, 2002; Blackmore, 1999; Distin, 2004). It is possible for memes to propagate because they are "infectious" ideas, apart from their relationship to biological, survival, or reproductive fitness. We will explore the role of emotions in an approach and avoidance framework, moving through the three different forms of selection: survival selection, sexual selection, and memetic selection.

FUNCTIONS OF EMOTIONS

Emotions are not the only behavioral response system observed in nature. Operant conditioning appears to be possible without having sufficient neural circuitry to have even a rudimentary affective system. Protozoa can approach food and attempt to avoid dangerous environmental stimuli such as extreme heat or toxic chemicals—but it does not seem appropriate to interpret the avoidance as an indicator of fear. Organisms as neurologically simple as planaria (flatworms) can be conditioned by the application of aversive stimuli, suggesting that approach and avoidance represent some of the most fundamental motivational systems for organisms (Elliot, 2006; Zechmeister & Nyberg, 1982). This is not surprising given the value that approach and avoidance can have in navigating fundamental threats to survival. But why have selection processes further elaborated the basic dimensions of approach and avoidance into more complex emotion systems? And why have emotions not been selected against once cognition develops? The fictional Vulcans of Star Trek found it highly illogical that emotions would persist once cognition became sufficiently developed. To them it seemed evident that rational analysis would produce consistent survival and social advantages compared to emotional responses.

Specialization

Emotions represent an opportunity for more nuanced response than offered by the blunt tools of undifferentiated approach and avoidance. The difference between shyness, fright, and terror is not just a matter of degree of avoidance (Izard, 1992). Similarly, although episodes of anger and enthusiasm might represent comparable degrees of approach motivation, these emotions are triggered by highly different environmental cues, and they galvanize extremely discrepant behavioral responses (Carver, 2004; Davidson, Ekman, Saron, Senulis, & Friesen, 1990; Izard, 1992). Emotions also offer a more flexible system of interpreting environmental stimuli and organizing responses than is possible with instincts or other stereotypic behaviors that are triggered by innate releasing mechanisms (Cosmides & Tooby, 2000).

Rapid Appraisal

Emotions also provide a more rapid system for response and appraisal than offered by cognition (LeDoux, 1992). Contrary to the Vulcans' perception, emotions maintain a survival advantage even after cognitive capacity has emerged, because they afford more rapid appraisal and response. At a neuropsychological level, the "deep structures" of emotional circuitry (brainstem, amygdala, hypothalamus) receive sensory input before it reaches the cortex—the seat of cognition (Panksepp, 2000). Cognitive processes at the cortical level then further interpret the now emotionally charged and filtered perceptions, and they can direct a behavioral response (LeDoux & Phelps, 2000). Cognition can also influence or regulate emotion by means of reciprocal inputs into the prefrontal cortex, which functional imaging studies indicate is one of the main areas involved in emotion regulation (Phan, Wager, Taylor, & Liberzon, 2002).

However, there are also projections from the amygdala and proximal structures that can organize behavioral responses without cortical input. The subcortical pathway can function without any cortical input, to the point that it remains intact even if the cortex is physically removed (LeDoux, 1992; LeDoux & Phelps, 2000). The subcortical pathway also processes information more rapidly than the cortically mediated system, enabling more rapid responses.

As has been pointed out by other emotion theorists, emotions also have the advantage of avoiding a "paralysis of analysis" in everyday tasks (Cosmides & Tooby, 2000). Mild emotional responses guide us through mundane choices almost effortlessly. What do we want for breakfast? Which tie or blouse should we wear? Emotional appraisals gently guide us along. A purely cognitive analysis could bog down into careful investigation of the nutritional value of different breakfast alternatives, or the time involved in their preparation, or their economic costs. Emotions similarly navigate most social interactions in a precognitive fashion, analyzing nonverbal cues and only involving cognition after the fact or when unusually complex situations are encountered.

Emotions may be a form of "fast and frugal" heuristic, offering a rapid algorithm for processing information (Gigerenzer & Goldstein, 1996; Todd & Gigerenzer, 2000). In fact, a productive line of research and modeling has developed by trying to "reverse engineer" how people process information and make decisions (Arkes & Ayton, 1999; Todd & Gigerenzer, 2000). Although people (and animals) clearly are not fitting regression equations or Bayesian models in their heads to interpret data (Arkes, 1991), they are able to handle huge volumes of information and make decisions that often closely approximate complicated statistical procedures in terms of their accuracy (Todd & Gigerenzer, 2000). Emotions provide a constellation of services that facilitate decision making that is not only fast, but also frugal—enabling decisive choices on the basis of relatively few data points. Emotions accomplish this frugality by filtering data for cues that are salient to survival, reproductive, or social needs, and then concentrating attention preferentially on these cues. Emotions also augment the retrieval of relevant experience through mechanisms such as mood-congruent recall enhancement. Conversely, emotions also weight the encoding of memories. The experience of intense fear can provoke learning that is stamped by the amygdala to create an impression that lasts a lifetime (Orr, Pitman, Lasko, & Herz, 1993; Shin et al., 1997).

Rapid Response

An additional benefit of emotions, as opposed to the fast and frugal heuristics generated by cognitive scientists or Vulcans, is that they also organize and motivate rapid behavioral responses. Subcortical systems make us jump away at the sight of a snake, while the Vulcan's cortical response systems are still trying to decide whether the reptile is a poisonous or harmless. The rapidity of response is not just a matter of more rapid appraisal. The emotional circuitry also can innervate simple automatic avoidance behaviors and energize fairly complicated behaviors without waiting for the frontal cortex to assess different strategies and decide on a best course. Once fear circuitry captures control, perceptual frames shift so that other environmental stimuli are reappraised in a search for hiding places, viable escape routes, or sources of aid (Cosmides & Tooby, 2000). Although the Vulcan is still cataloging the evidence for different risks and options, any emotional being will have decided whether the threat appears to be a false alarm (and begin de-escalating the emotional cascade), a minor nuisance (triggering relief or annoyance responses), a manageable challenge (perhaps triggering an angry approach response), an avoidable danger (leading to a hiding or flight response), or an unavoidable threat (unleashing a volley of defensive aggression). Once the Vulcan decides on an appropriate course of action, he or she then must act without the benefit of the cascade of physiological changes that emotions have set in motion. For humans, adrenaline, changes in heart rate, changes in blood flow (leaving the digestive system and viscera, and flooding to the peripheral musculature; Tomaka, Blascovich, Kibler, & Ernst, 1997), and other physiological changes all prepare the organism for vigorous action to increase or preserve its fitness. Although emotions probably developed as "natural kinds" in evolution (Panksepp, 2000), there evidently is a great deal of flexibility in the physiological responses (Cacioppo & Berntson, 1999) and behavioral acts associated with an emotion, allowing complexity that enhances fitness at the same time as it frustrates researchers.

SURVIVAL FITNESS

Approach and avoidance represent the most fundamental impulses relevant to an organism's survival (Elliot, 2006; Schneirla, 1959). Approach orients and motivates effort towards acquiring food and shelter. Avoidance monitors for threats and then actively impels organisms away from them. More subtly, avoidance-related emotions might promote survival by averting conflict with other animals within the same social group. Displays of submission, and inhibition of aggression displays, play an important role in preventing or terminating violent behavior that might otherwise injure animals. Darwin observed this in the behavior of wolves as well as primates, and other ethologists have subsequently confirmed and extended documentation of these displays across species as well as across human cultures. Similarly, approach-oriented emotions play a crucial role in survival fitness by providing motivation for organisms to seek food, to challenge competitors for food, or to organize other effortful behaviors in the pursuit of survival goals (Elliot, 2006).

Emotions evolved increasingly complex elaborations on the two basic themes of approach and avoidance. Panksepp has described three broad categories of emotions, with the lowest being "reflexive affects" including approach-related systems such as gustatory pleasure or lust; and avoidance-related circuitry such as gustatory

disgust or pain (Panksepp, 2000). The second category is what Panksepp terms the "Blue-Ribbon, Grade-A Emotions," relying on circuitry situated in the mid-level of the brain with sensory, motor, and cortical connections that enable functioning as "sensory-motor emotional command" systems. On the approach side, these emotions include joy, affection, and interest, as well as (less intuitively) anger. On the avoidance side, emotions would include fear, sadness, shyness, and the like. Panksepp, like Darwin and others, believes that both the category 1 and category 2 emotions are present in fairly homologous fashion, and involve similar brain circuitry, in mammals. These loosely correspond with what others have described as "discrete emotions," with some specificity in neural circuitry (Phan et al., 2002) as well as behaviors such as facial displays (Ekman, 1994; Ekman & Friesen, 1971; Izard, 1971, 1994). The third and most elaborated category is the "higher sentiments," which have markedly greater involvement of the forebrain. In Panksepp's view, these emotions involve creating blends of lower category emotions with more cognitive inputs. Some of these may follow channelization suggested by neural architecture, resulting in an emotion that is archetypal or universally experienced in a way that could be conceptualized as being a "discrete emotion" (Izard, 1972, 1992). Other such "higher sentiments" might be highly determined by cultural specifics or individual learning history, and might lead to behaviors such as artistic expression that clearly have an affective component, but without necessarily being reducible to a single emotion (Izard, 1992).

At its most fundamental level, approach is the function of the "seeking system," or the ascending medial forebrain bundle dopamine system (Panksepp, 2000). Activation of this system accompanies the urge for animals to explore their environment, learning about the rewards in their surroundings through trial and error. Panksepp argues that the seeking system does not directly encode pleasure or reward status. It is possible that the discrete emotion of interest or excitement is related to this seeking system, to the extent that interest or excitement is activating but only secondarily showing a positive hedonic valence.

Enjoyment and joy also reflect positive, approach-oriented emotions. These emotions more strongly involve positive valenced encoding, and in mammals may be more tied to social cues. Panksepp has described the importance of play in mammals, and posited an evolved "play system" in the brain. Observers of humans and animals note that play appears important in developing skills (such as hunting or courtship), promoting self-efficacy, and determining social dominance (Boulton & Smith, 1995; Wilson, 1980).

On the avoidance side, emotions play a powerful role in organizing perceptions of threats and responding rapidly. The fear system is the prototype for avoidance. There are some evolutionarily prepared fears that are innate or at least more easily learned, including fears of snakes, of heights, and of open spaces (Mineka, Davidson, Cook, & Keir, 1984). There are also fears of social rejection or defeat that can be expressed in humans as avoidant behavior in the form of shyness (Kagan, 1997b) or social phobia (Kagan, 1997a). It is also possible for fear to be learned readily via classical conditioning, creating a wide range of generalized fear associations that can be as unique as an individual's learning experience (Zechmeister & Nyberg, 1982).

REPRODUCTIVE FITNESS AND SEXUAL SELECTION

A second major way that emotions contribute to genetic fitness is by means of sexual selection. For genes to propagate, the organism carrying the genes must not only survive, but also reproduce. Reproduction is an affectively laden enterprise, with the emotions becoming more complex and flexible with the evolution of social groups and cognitive abilities.

Affiliation

At the most basic level, there appears to be an evolved circuitry for "lust," motivating mate selection, courtship, and copulatory behaviors. Interestingly, the lust systems appear to involve different architecture and neurotransmitters for male versus female animals (Becker, Breedlove, & Crews, 1992; Crenshaw & Goldberg, 1996). The female lust system is more dependent on oxytocin (versus vasopressin in males); and oxytocin plays a major role in the neurocircuitry of caregiving, including behaviors such as grooming and nursing, and affects related to attachment (Petersen, Caldwell, Jirikowski, & Insel, 1992). In more social mammals, these emotions of caring, bonding, and love motivate the parent to protect the offspring, and the offspring to remain close to the parent. This proximity promotes survival, particularly during the much-prolonged infancy and childhood linked to the sudden evolutionary increase in human cranial size (Konner, 1981); but then attachment-related behaviors are recruited and used as part of the repertoire for courtship and assortative mating (Stevens, 1982).

Competition

Humans as a species have relatively few offspring, which require a substantial investment of time and energy to survive to reproductive maturity. From a genetic perspective, genes favoring nurturing behavior and some degree of parental investment in the offspring would promote both survival and later reproductive success for persons carrying those genes. At the same time, there is a genetic pressure for "choosiness." The costs of pregnancy and parenthood to a female are high (Buss, 1994). Women genetically predisposed to be selective about partners are more likely to be able to choose partners with desirable genes (for physical health, cognitive capacity, or attractive personality). They also are more likely to be able to marshal resources in support of themselves and their children, by demanding greater displays of fidelity and paternal investment, and also by mating with more powerful members of the social group (Ellis, 1995).

Males also want to mate with the most desirable partners that they can, but the much lower costs invested in contributing sperm versus the minimal maternal contribution from ovum to weaning (let alone the more extended maternal investments typically made in humans) create an evolutionary pressure suggesting that at least some males would explore Casanova-like strategies of pursuing as many partners as possible, and others would be tempted to wander (Buss, 1995b). Interestingly, there is evidence for "social Machiavellianism" in female primates, too, where they may seek to partner with a good provider, but then have opportunistic liaisons with other partners with different desirable genetic attributes (Ellis, 1995; Ridley, 1993).

The details of sexual selection are fascinating, and any attempt at detailed treatment would derail the course of the present chapter. The central point for our purposes is that sexual selection is not simply a matter of pursuing or attracting a partner. There is a crucial component of selecting the "right" partner, which introduces a huge element of competition into the process. The competition includes intra-sex contests to capture the attention of the most attractive suitor, or to win access to the most desired partner. Sexual selection can focus on attributes and preferentially select for them, independently of their survival advantage. In fact, if the advantage in terms of sexual preference outweighs the risks in terms of survival, then it is possible for sexual selection to result in heritable changes that actually handicap the survival of the carrier (Zahavi, 1991). The classic example is the male peacock's tail; but the argument has been made that any attribute that shows rapid evolutionary change in the absence of clear survival advantages might be a good candidate for sexual selection (Miller, 2000). Sexual selection is also unusual compared to survival selection in that it has greater freedom in terms of what attributes it can seize upon, and also how rapidly it can drive changes. The rapid inflation of the size of the human brain might be attributable to sexual selection (Miller, 2000; Ridley, 1993). Sexual selection also would provide a mechanism for selecting persons more capable of emotion regulation, and more nuanced displays of emotion expression.

Runaway

Competition also can lead to an "arms race" between the sexes, where sexual selection drives change at a pace that is much more rapid than survival selection would produce (Ridley, 1993). The sexual selection argument for brain development hinges on the idea that humans would preferentially choose mates who were more intelligent, articulate, charming, and clever. People possessing these attributes would be more likely to mate at all, more likely to have multiple partners, and more likely to have their offspring survive to reproductive maturity (by virtue of the indirect effect of other desirable genes, as well as via the environmental benefits that come with having higher-status parents) and achieve their own reproductive successes. A consequence of this would be that genes for larger brains and more skillful emotion expression and regulation would become more common in the gene pool.

This sort of sexual selection could lead to a "runaway" escalation in the attributes targeted for selection. Take for example the ability to use behaviors from the caregiving emotional repertoire. The first human ancestors able to invoke these behaviors as part of courtship instead of only during caregiving would have held an enormous advantage. Females able to express these emotions and behaviors during courtship would be demonstrating their capacity to be a good mother. Males showing similar behaviors would be displaying a capacity for exceptional paternal involvement. As these individuals achieved greater reproductive success, their genes would become more common. However, the very success of the genes would in time mean that most of the population would eventually possess the beneficial genes, and what had been the jewel in the crown of fitness indicators now has become commonplace. This creates circumstances favoring the selection of individuals who happen to possess even more extreme degrees of the attribute, creating a positive feedback loop that leads to extremely rapid, "runaway" change in the sexually selected attributes (Miller, 2000; Ridley, 1993).

In the realm of emotions, sexual selection in humans appears to have produced a runaway process where the point of departure was the mammalian emotional toolbox. Sexual selection took these basic emotion processes and then favored those who could employ these emotions more flexibly in the service of courtship and reproduction. The pressure to demonstrate greater facility with emotions and social relationships may have contributed to the development of verbal expression, language, and cognitive development (Miller, 2000). In turn, these created a more complex social environment for more sophisticated displays of emotion. This feedback loop has literally exploded into the staggering array of behaviors ranging from gossip to dance to romantic poetry and the many forms of music. What chance would a Vulcan have against a human competitor in the dating game? A human could use emotions to size up the competition quickly, almost intuitively, and concentrate her efforts on the best matches while the Vulcan was still cataloging the features of the first person encountered. And once the Vulcans had identified a promising candidate some hours later, their dry catalog of the logical advantages of partnership would not be heard over the pulses of a samba that the emotional competitors were dancing.

Approach, Avoidance, and Sex

From the perspective of sexual competition, emotions would be extremely valuable in multiple ways. Approach emotions are crucial in identifying potential partners, as well as motivating courtship behaviors. In many cultures, the experience of romantic love is an emotional state that verges on religious ecstasy or hypomania (Johnson, 1983). There is a narrowing of attention onto the desired person, a sense of extreme well-being when connected with that person, a feeling of grandiosity about the relationship, and often marked increases in energy and decreased need for sleep. Feelings of lust can motivate extreme effort in animals; humans in love can display the same intensity with greater nuance. Approach emotions such as anger are also invaluable in navigating intra-sex competition. Without anger, it would be difficult for suitors to motivate their best performances, and few would be as willing to risk the losses—of social standing or physical injury— potentially accompanying the pursuit of a desired partner (Buss, 1995a). Anger also energizes assertive behaviors to ward off perceived competitors. People have a tendency to overestimate the attractiveness of competitors, which motivates greater effort to present oneself in the best light possible (Hill, 2006).

Avoidance emotions would also be crucial in rapidly evaluating complex social situations and deciding which potential partners to reject. It makes evolutionary sense to avoid pursuing partners who are too far above or below oneself in terms of desirability, given the investment involved in actually raising a child, and the limited number of children that humans have (relative to other animals). Avoiding pursuit of partners who are "out of reach" also makes sense if the courtship is going to consume resources without much likely return on the investment, or if there are competitors who are likely to impose costs (either physical injury or social derogation) if the person enters the fray (Buss, 1994). Avoidance emotions like shyness would help to shield people from exposure to the risks of direct competition. Shyness also supports a strategy of waiting to see which potential partners are motivated enough to continue to pursue even without immediate displays of receptivity. In other words, shyness might be an evolutionary tactic for helping separate serious partners from more casual suitors (Miller, 2000). If this hypothesis is correct, then it would make evolutionary sense for shyness to be more commonly expressed in women than men, because biological factors would favor women concentrating on the quality instead of quantity of partners (Buss, 1994). Consistent with this hypothesis, shyness appears more common in females (Kessler, 1998; Youngstrom & Green, 2003), and it also appears more socially handicapping in males when present (Snyder, Smith, Augelli, & Ingram, 1985).

Other avoidance emotions would be valuable in rejecting unwanted partners. The sense of disgust one feels on a bad blind date is not due to a biologically toxic effect, but instead reflects an emotion that initially developed for the purpose of avoiding poisons being recruited to guide avoidance behaviors in a complex social situation. Displays of social disgust or contempt will terminate flirtation far more quickly and thoroughly than any factual enumeration about the reasons for incompatibility. Sadness acting as an avoidance emotion is crucial for motivating withdrawal from situations where the relationship is damaged or lost, preventing further losses and providing space for recovery. Conversely, strategies for regulating sadness can lead to social exchanges that elicit empathic responding and social support (Izard, 1991; Izard & Ackerman, 2000).

The importance of emotions to our ancestors' sexual success is written across our bodies as well as our brains. The eyes and the muscles immediately around them are central to the facial expression of most emotions (Ekman, 1993; Izard, 1971; Izard, 1990). Humans, unlike other primates, have evolved very white scleras that make the eyes more visible. The greater contrast between the eye and the rest of the face makes it easier to discern emotion expressions, and also to divine where the other person is directing their attention. Both of these become increasingly valuable in complex social groups (The Economist, 2006). Humans have also become attuned to nonverbal cues about emotional and physical traits. Women are able

to look at facial photographs of unfamiliar males and make judgments that correlate highly with the men's assayed testosterone levels, or their attitudes towards children (indexed by the men's performance on a picture sorting task)—both with correlations around .6 (Roney, Hanson, Durante, & Maestripieri, 2006). Women also appear to have an advantage in terms of recognizing facial expressions of emotion, consistent with both attachment promotion and threat sensitivity fitness models of emotion (Hampson, van Anders, & Mullin, 2006).

SOCIAL AND INTERPERSONAL FUNCTIONS: BUILDING, MAINTAINING, AND CHANGING NETWORKS

Implicit in the discussion above are some of the ways that emotions influence social and interpersonal functions. Recent neuroimaging data indicate that social situations trigger emotions differently and engage distinct brain regions as compared with nonsocial stimuli (Britton et al., 2006). Approach and avoidance emotions are constantly alert to social cues. At the survival level, these include cues about whether a person is a friend or foe (Hampson et al., 2006). Far more attacks and deaths have resulted from intraspecies violence than from encounters with poisonous animals or other predators for most of humanity's recent evolutionary history. Humans appear to have gotten particularly good at recognizing expressions of anger in others, especially in dominant males, for just this reason (Allan & Gilbert, 2002).

Approach and avoidance may also work in an opponent process to help people quickly gauge the perceived controllability of social situations and their dominance or social status within the group. Dominance has important consequences in terms of social interactions, access to resources, and assortative mating. Approach emotions would help drive efforts to climb the social ladder, often through play (Panksepp, 2000), but sometimes in more serious confrontations. Avoidance emotions become vital to de-escalate conflicts and have the loser retreat before sustaining serious injury (Wilson, 1980). Avoidance emotions such as sadness and submissiveness displays also may help people to remain in the social group by advertising that they are no longer challenging the victor's status (Allan & Gilbert, 1997; Gilbert & Allan, 1998).

Studies of conflict in families suggest that an additional layer of meaning may have developed for emotional interactions beyond the surface content of the exchange. Emotional conflicts often involve deeper issues pertaining to intimacy or power within a relationship. If the conflict is about power, then winning or losing the argument matters a great deal to the participants, precisely because social dominance is at stake. However, if the conflict is about intimacy, then the content does not appear to be important; nor does "winning" matter as much. Instead, the intensity of the conflict communicates important information about the perceived importance of the relationship (Emery, 1992). It is our closest friends and lovers who can provoke the greatest extremes of emotional response. When we are able to discuss the strengths and weaknesses of a relationship with Vulcan-like dispassion, then the flame has gone out. On the basis of this model, even avoidance emotions can communicate important information about intimacy. Paradoxically, the profoundness of the sadness or pain at the rupture of a relationship reveals the importance of the intimacy.

Finally, much recent work emphasizes the value of positive, approach-oriented emotions for "broadening" awareness and "building" social networks (Fredrickson, 1998). Research with couples indicates that stable relationships tend to have partners expressing five times as many positive, approach emotions towards each other as negative emotions, including both anger and avoidant emotions (Gottman, 1994). "Stonewalling," an extreme form of withdrawal, also appears to be a particularly toxic pattern of interaction found in relationships that are close to dissolution (Gottman, 1994).

INTRAPERSONAL FUNCTIONS: SCULPTING THE SELF

Approach and avoidance emotions also play a fundamental role in shaping the development of personality, individual differences, and a person's self-identity (Elliot, 2006; Elliot, Gable, & Mapes, 2006). General tendencies towards behavioral activation and inhibition have a genetic component (Loehlin, 1992). These dispositional tendencies begin influencing temperament in infancy (Kagan, 1997b). People with lower activation thresholds for approach emotions are more likely to have higher activity levels. People with lower thresholds for avoidance emotions will have greater sensitivity to cues of threat, and are more likely to be shy and withdrawn as toddlers. These emotions continue to filter perceptions of experiences, fundamentally altering the perceived developmental environment. These emotion tendencies also change the transactions that the person has with peers and adults. Even in the same classroom, the experiences of a shy, anxious child versus a curious and energetic one are radically different.

In addition to changing the perceptions, emotional responses, and behaviors elicited by significant others in the environment, approach and avoidance emotions also shift the valence and weight of recalled memories (Mogg &

Mathews, 1990). Mood congruent biases in perception and memory continue to color learning history (Mogg, Bradley, Williams, & Mathews, 1993). Even as cognitive abilities develop, our thoughts work on percepts tinted by emotion, and we compare our experiences with memories selected for relevance based on our emotional state. Finally, besides providing scaffolding for organizing our interpretations and reactions to experiences, approach and avoidance also represent foundational dimensions for individual differences in motivation for behavior. Out of this cycle of experience, memory, and reinforcement grow temperamental styles (Kagan, 1997a). With continued cognitive development and experience, temperamental tendencies become personality traits. Genetic differences contribute to propensities for personality to grow in certain directions, but learning history can shift the course, although many environments will contribute to the self-reinforcing tendency of emotion systems. This process of development has been described as the formation of "affective-cognitive structures," or "emotion schemas," (Izard, 2007), a terminology that nicely captures the composite and interactive nature of emotion and cognition as components of personality (Izard, Libero, Putnam, & Haynes, 1993).

RUNAWAY SOFTWARE: EMOTIONS, MEMES, AND CULTURE

Many researchers are beginning to think about ideas or behaviors as being something that can replicate and either become more common or extinguish, in a manner analogous to genetic replication (Blackmore, 1999). Just as the Earth provided a primordial soup that allowed amino acids to develop, and from which emerged DNA with self-replicating capabilities; so genetic evolution created increasingly complicated nervous systems until the capacity for imitative learning emerged and became sufficiently developed to create a new environment where memes could replicate and compete (Jablonka & Lamb, 2005).

The concept is appealing on multiple levels. Viewed in this way, culture cannot be fully explained by a biological reductionism. Instead, culture and perhaps consciousness are emergent properties that only become possible when the underlying architecture is sufficiently rich and complex, but then begin to interact in a way that is at least partially independent of the architecture (Dennett, 1991). Another analogy could be made to computers. Initially they were calculators, hardwired for specific computations and purposes—analogous to the biologically reflexive responses, or instinctive innate releasing mechanisms and stereotypical responses. As computers become more powerful, it became possible to shift more functions into "software" instead of hardwired circuits. Software allowed the same computer to be used for different purposes, and much more flexibly. As memory capacity increased even further, software became more complicated (and less stable). The current world of Internet browsers, shared applications, cookies, spyware, and viruses represents a state of development where software often propagates across computers without conscious knowledge of the user, and it also can result in unpredictable behavior (Aunger, 2002).

One of the points of this analogy is that because both culture and software operate at an emergent level, it is not possible to make deterministic predictions about them based on the underlying architecture. Scientists cannot look at a functional image of a person's brain and know what languages they speak, nor what they will choose for lunch, any more than we could look at the motherboard of a computer and tell whether it is currently running a word processor or an Internet browser, or both at the same time.

A converse implication is that there are still constraints on the operation of the system based on the underlying architecture. Software no longer runs if there is physical damage to the memory or hard drive, just as culture or consciousness may cease to function if there is damage to the underlying brain. More subtly, the underlying architecture imposes some limits and creates probabilistic influences on the emergent systems. In terms of culture and consciousness, we cannot react to colors outside the spectrum that is visible to our optic system, or to tastes (even of toxins) not discernible by our gustatory system. Our brain must impose order on a jumble of sensory information, analogous to processing millions of web search "hits" every minute. The algorithms our brains use to rank the sensory "hits" were developed and optimized by our evolutionary history and its legacy in our nervous system.

Put another way, our search and ranking algorithms for navigating our environment are more emotional than rational. Our emotional nature shapes the playing field on which memes compete. Not all memes have emotional content, but the memes that do are at a considerable advantage in terms of grabbing attention, getting "chosen" for long-term memory, and getting shared with others. In terms of practical benefits, the contributions of theoretical physics objectively far outweigh pop culture, but apparently that is not the over-riding factor in the popularity of memes among emotional beings. Consider the number of people who could recite the three laws of thermodynamics versus humming a few bars of Michael Jackson's song "Thriller," which sold more than 59 million copies worldwide.

The environment occupied by memes has also changed with extreme rapidity. Some animals show evidence of vicarious learning of simple behaviors—arguably the protean form of memes. The development of language not only created a larger number of potential memes, but also increased their complexity and the number of people who could be exposed to the meme. The printed word further changed the memetic environment: (1) memes preserved in writing could last much longer, like spores or cryogenic freezing for biological replicants; (2) written memes could be exposed to much larger audiences; and (3) writing itself became another evolutionary niche that memes could occupy. The rise of mass media further increased the bandwidth through which memes could be broadcast, and also added the possibility of sound and color being attached to the memes—some of the secret weapons that "Thriller" used to out-propagate the Laws of Thermodynamics.

The Internet and computer games represent another quantum advance in the changes to the memetic environment. The Internet makes possible communication with literally hundreds of millions of people, and it now combines the durability of the printed word with the sensory appeal of sound, color, and animated motion. The result is a much larger audience exposed to memes, as well as accelerated competition. At present, virtual reality is available to a much smaller audience, but goes a step further than the typical Internet download in terms of sensory stimulation. The latest generation of videogames (e.g., X-Box, Playstation 3, Wii) are arguably the most widely distributed virtual reality systems. Even a cursory examination of the content shows that our choice of topics on the Internet and in games is driven by evolved emotional preferences. It does not flatter our species that more people will play "First Person Shooter" games such as Doom than will visit the Louvre, but these preferences make evolutionary "sense" given the greater importance that survival or sexual competition had as compared to aesthetic appreciation for the bulk of our evolutionary history. Aesthetics became a growth stock in the human market only once sexual selection focused on it, and artistic sensibility became a way of advertising fitness to potential mates (Miller, 2000).

What is fascinating about the Internet and virtual reality from an emotional perspective is that these media allow for activities that are based on evolved preferences for rewards, without the same potential costs that were present for most of our evolutionary history. An interesting parallel can be made to diet. For 2 million years, sugar, fat, and salt were present only in trace quantities in most available foodstuffs. Our taste preferences and drives evolved to provide motivation sufficient to incur the necessary costs to spend a day gathering nuts, or to brave hunting down a large mammal. Suddenly, in the evolutionary eye-blink of the last 10,000 years, the agricultural and industrial revolutions have changed our environment so that there is a profligacy of nutrients compared to the strength of our urges to consume them (Konner, 1985). We have sufficient motivation to spend a day foraging, impelling us impulsively to grab a Snickers bar at the checkout line; sufficient drive to hunt a mastodon guiding our choices at a drive-through fast food restaurant. A McDonald's Big Mac caters to our evolved preferences for fat and salt. Our choices of violent, sexual, or thrill-seeking content paint a similarly unflattering portrait of the legacy of our evolutionary environment on our choices of memes. Horror films, sad songs, elegiac poetry—all of these serve no obvious biological function in terms of survival or sexual selection. Instead, these are "junk food of the mind"—things that achieve their popularity by pandering to evolved preferences for approach and avoidance.

The bottom line is that, in the emergent world of consciousness and culture, not all memes are emotional. But the memes that carry an emotional charge are at a tremendous advantage, with the billows of approach and avoidance adding wind to the meme's sails at the moments of perception, attention, interpretation, and action. It is a substantial competitive edge, and the consequences of these probabilistic preferences are writ large across our popular culture. Supermarket tabloids provide a clearer window onto our evolutionary memetic legacy than do college textbooks or doctoral dissertations, even though the latter represent higher accomplishments by highly evolved minds.

EMOTION-RELATED DYSFUNCTION

Psychopathology presents one of the fundamental challenges to a functionalist approach to emotions. If emotions served an evolutionary purpose, why do emotions feature so prominently in pathological conditions? How could a good thing turn so bad? And how could an adaptive system that improves survival and sexual fitness go so wrong so often? Mental disturbances that involve severe emotional dysregulation are not a freakish oddity. Instead, emotional imbalance is the mainstay of psychopathology, to the point that scholars can argue that emotional dysfunction is the core construct of almost all mental illness (Bradley, 2000).

MODELS OF EMOTION AND PSYCHOPATHOLOGY

There are a variety of models that offer different explanations of the role of emotions in psychopathology.

Conflict as Normative Development

To some degree, conflict is an unavoidable part of maturation. Children and adolescents change roles and test the boundaries of relationships with authority figures and peers as they grow and master new skills (Emery, 1992). Approach emotions will motivate limit-testing behavior. Avoidance emotions will de-escalate conflict and promote periods of stability where the status quo of relationships and authority are maintained. Although parents, teachers, and sometimes youths will seek mental health services for these sorts of developmental conflicts, typically these do not represent psychopathology or emotion dysfunction so much as the inevitable bumps and scrapes of growing up.

Too Much of a Good Thing (Statistical Models of Extremity)

A related model of psychopathology would be the statistical extremity definition. Anger might serve an adaptive function on average, and there are individual differences in the tendency to activate or express anger. At the extremes of the distribution, there will be those who are extremely likely (or unlikely) to express anger. Persons in the top 5% of tendency to show hostility are likely to experience more adverse interpersonal interactions, as are people who are similarly reticent or incapable of showing anger. At either extreme, individual differences in anger could increase the likelihood of the person experiencing the "harmful dysfunction" that is considered a hallmark of psychopathology (Wakefield, 1997). Extremes in the tendency to experience other emotions are also likely to be associated with, and might even be a causal mechanism for, psychopathology. Extreme shyness appears linked with social phobia and perhaps other forms of anxiety (Heiser, Turner, & Beidel, 2003). Extremely low levels of positive affect (anhedonia) are implicated in depression (Clark & Watson, 1991). An important caveat is that statistical extremity need not signify an underlying genotypic extremity. Environmental factors play a large role in dulling or honing the edges of emotional expression. Traumatic events can have profound consequences on later emotional development (Porter, 1998), and cultural factors also do much to potentiate or mitigate emotional extremes.

Dysfunction as Transaction: Right Feelings, But at the Wrong Place and Time

Developmental models of psychopathology often focus on the transaction between the person and the environment (Chess & Thomas, 1989; Kazdin & Kagan, 1994). The same behavior might be adaptive on the playground, but inappropriate in the classroom; or behavior that is frighteningly disinhibited in the view of one parent might be within tolerable limits for another. Changes in the environment, precipitated by shifts in culture or technology, might alter perceptions of what is adaptive versus counterproductive, much as changes in food production have shifted our dietary environment away from the Paleolithic larder of our origins. The human emotional repertoire evolved primarily under circumstances where social groups might include up to a few dozen individuals, all of whom knew each other, and with a strong pressure for xenophobia towards strangers (Konner, 1981). Our emotional systems are likely to be stressed by the density and complexity of social relationships in postagricultural or postindustrial societies. At the same time, technology has magnified the consequences of emotional expression. Evolved anger responses to perceived social challenges among primates in the modern phenomenon of "road rage," and evolved jealousy responses to perceived infidelity turn lethal when a gun is added to the equation.

Within mental health, the transactional argument has received its fullest expression in the realm of attention-deficit/hyperactivity disorder, which psychiatry argues is a medical illness (American Psychiatric Association, 2001), but which others interpret as pathologizing individual differences in temperament that are within normal limits (Carey, 1998). A similar debate is now occurring with pediatric bipolar disorder, which some believe is a biological entity, and opponents argue is another example of "disease mongering" (Healy, 2006), or attempts to pathologize normal emotional experiences so as to increase the demand for medical services to treat the "problem" (Heath, 2006; Scott, 2006).

An advantage of transactional models is that they can account for psychopathology even when adaptively evolved emotion systems appear to be intact. It is not that the emotion system is damaged or categorically dysfunctional. Instead, adaptive emotions can become linked to maladaptive learning histories, cognitions, or social environments in "emotion schemas" (Izard, in press). A drawback of transactional models is that they do not draw sharp boundaries around a condition to delineate pathology. Instead of yielding a clear definition, transactional models imply that pathology is "negotiable," and can be changed by modifying the behavior, the setting, or both. This fuzziness appeared anathema to common sense, "medical model" definitions of pathology. However, current understanding of gene–environment interactions is demonstrating that genetic polymorphisms transact with the environment in complicated ways, such that a particular nutrient or caregiving environment might be essential to one subgroup, and toxic or irrelevant to another. Transactional models also provide a convenient solution for the puzzle of how emotions could be adaptive yet bound so tightly to psychopathology. The riddle is resolved if the environment where the emotion is problematic differs substantially from the context where the emotion system originally evolved to be adaptive.

Mutation—Fractures in an Otherwise Good System

A fourth model of emotion and psychopathology would concentrate on harmful mutations as an explanation of dysfunction in the emotional system. Examples can be found of single gene mutations or chromosomal deletions that result in severe emotional dysregulation, such as Williams syndrome—with its associated hyper-sociality and lack of fear of strangers, or Huntington's chorea—a single-gene trinucleotide repeat expansion that is associated with anxiety, depression, or extreme aggression. However, these mutations tend to be rare (affecting only 1 in 7,500 births for Williams syndrome, and up to 8 per 100,000 births for Huntington's chorea). Given the extreme social and reproductive consequences of such dysregulation of the emotion systems, it is unlikely that these mutations would persist long in a population unless their deleterious effects appeared well after reproductive maturity (as is typically the case with Huntington's chorea), or perhaps if lower doses of the mutation were associated with positive effects. The beneficial effect of low doses has been demonstrated with Sickle cell disease, where carriers with one copy of the recessive allele show enhanced resistance to malaria. More speculatively, there is evidence that low doses of bipolar disorder, in the form of mild illness or in the presumed loading of unaffected family members, are associated with increased creativity and productivity (Jamison, 1993; Simeonova, Chang, Strong, & Ketter, 2005). On the basis of this argument, mutations that increased approach-oriented emotions might provide advantages in moderate doses, though sometimes becoming deleterious in extreme concentrations.

Sneaky Value Added (Subtle or Counterintuitive Adaptive Value)

A final model for emotions and psychopathology hypothesizes subtle or indirect benefits sufficient to outweigh the costs to the replicating unit. There are multiple variations on this theme that have been proposed. Depression, which clearly involves short-term costs for the individual, may yield important social benefits by allowing the person to remain a member of the community in spite of setbacks or losses (Gilbert & Allan, 1998; Plutchik, 1993), or it might benefit the individual by preventing the wasteful expenditure of energy and resources in pursuit of a failed cause (Izard, 1992).

By shifting the focus from the organism to the gene, kinship selection models become plausible, whereby emotions might have evolutionary advantage even though the person expressing them may not have offspring of their own. Another provocative model is that sexual selection pressure drove the elaboration of the human brain as a marker of reproductive fitness, making it consume a disproportionate amount of energy and involve the expression of a disproportionate number of genes precisely because mental health status would then provide a quick and accurate method of sampling the genetic and developmental history of the organism (Miller, 2000). In this view, paying attention to emotional functioning becomes an excellent way of gauging not just mental health, but also reproductive and survival fitness more generally, precisely because so many things could go wrong with the emotion systems due to harmful mutations, poor environment, or acute trauma. Healthy displays of emotion are like the "miner's canary" whose sensitivity provides warning of accumulated toxins.

A third, and perhaps more disturbing, possibility arises if memes are considered as the unit of replication. From a memetic view, psychopathology could be an extremely effective way of propagating memes, even though the organism suffers harmful dysfunction, or the genes fail to propagate. Van Gogh was severely unhappy, dying childless of suicide; but his artwork has retained iconic status, with pieces auctioning for millions of dollars, and literally millions of reproductions of paintings such as "Starry Night" continuing to sell around the world. The cliché of the tortured artists suffering for their work might hold some truth viewed from a memetic level. Doses of approach and avoidance emotion that would be toxic at the interpersonal level and counterproductive from a genetic point of view may actually contribute to memetic success. Phenomena such as suicide contagion in schools, or suicide bombing, propagate memes widely and often indelibly on the minds exposed to them. A less violent example, albeit equally challenging at the genetic level of explanation, would be the popularity of celibacy within many organized religions. If it is possible for memetic selection to occur independently of the biological adaptiveness of the idea or behavior (and self-immolation presents the most extreme philosophical example of this scenario), then psychopathology becomes much easier to explain within an adaptive framework. The behavior becomes adaptive from the perspective of the meme, regardless of the consequences to the carrier, much as

inducing a terminal cough is adaptive from the perspective of the pathogen for influenza or pneumonic plague.

If the memetic model is correct, then there are important implications in terms of mental health. Recent policies of minimizing the publicity around suicides or terrorist attacks may help curb the spread of the memes of risk for these behaviors. Avoiding glamorization of violence or suicide also helps decrease replication by avoiding associations with "popular" memes that could accelerate the spread of linked memes. In other words, avoiding associations with sex, social status, or other emotionally provocative cues would decrease the spread of the meme. The more that a meme can co-opt evolved emotion systems, the easier it is for the meme to be perceived, remembered, and replicated in "copy-cat" behaviors (Aunger, 2002).

APPROACH AND AVOIDANCE EMOTIONAL MODELS OF PSYCHOPATHOLOGY: BEHAVIORAL INHIBITION SYSTEM AND BEHAVIORAL ACTIVATION SYSTEM

A dimensional framework has already been elaborated for understanding psychopathology in terms of approach and avoidance. Gray focused on neuroanatomical models and described three major motivational systems: The Behavioral Activation System (BAS), the Behavioral Inhibition System (BIS), and the Fight/Flight System (FFS) (Gray, 1985; Gray & McNaughton, 1996). Gray's model specifies neural circuitry and behavioral outputs for each of these systems. Others have developed questionnaires and behavior checklists to assess human behaviors, emotions, and personality traits that correlated with BAS and BIS (Carver & White, 1994; Depue & Iacono, 1989). BAS is the "gas pedal" that orients attention and impels the organism towards cues of reward, galvanizing approach behavior. BIS is the "brake pedal" that is attuned to cues of threat, inhibits approach, and potentially motivates avoidance. Data from multiple levels of analysis from imaging, psychophysiology, and factor analyses of questionnaires all indicate that BAS and BIS are separate systems, not opposite ends of a bipolar continuum (Beauchaine, 2001; Corr, 2001; Matthews & Gilliland, 1999). The interesting implication of this is that it is possible for an individual to experience any combination of activation of these two systems, including intense activation of both at the same time.

Multiple investigators have applied the BIS and BAS constructs to psychopathology, including extensive work by Quay with children and adolescents (Quay, 1985, 1993), and Fowles' review with adult psychopathology (Fowles, 1994). As the BIS and BAS constructs have also extended into personality research and social psychology, points of

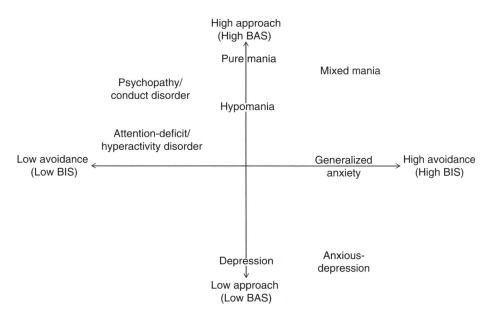

FIGURE 21.1   Relationship of clinical disorders to dysregulation of approach and avoidance systems.

overlap have become evident (Elliot & Thrash, 2002). Approach is roughly isomorphic with BAS, which also has a strong overlap with "positive affect" in the Tellegen-Watson model of affect (Watson & Tellegen, 1985), or with positive-valence plus high activation in other dimensional models of affect, or the high energy pole of Thayer's energy-tension model (Thayer, 2001). Avoidance corresponds well with BIS, which overlaps with "negative affect" in the Tellegen-Watson model. Figure 21.1 illustrates where many common forms of psychopathology fall in terms of dysregulated approach and avoidance.

Overactivity of the BIS (potentially due to low activation threshold, or due to exaggerated responsiveness of the BIS to threat, or due to longer latency to recovery once triggered) is associated with more negative affect, especially fear and worry. Chronic activation is correlated with trait neuroticism at the personality level, and with anxiety disorders at the acute pathology level (Matthews & Gilliland, 1999). Interestingly, high BIS activation (or high negative affect in the "Tripartite Model" of depression and anxiety) is most strongly linked to generalized anxiety disorder (and possibly separation anxiety in youths) (Chorpita, Albano, & Barlow, 1998), but not so tightly to phobias, which may often involve a strong disgust reaction instead (Watson, 2000).

BIS deficits are thought to be associated with conditions such as attention-deficit/hyperactivity disorder (ADHD), where low BIS results in impulsivity due to failure to inhibit behavior (Quay, 1997). Low BIS is also expected to contribute to the development of antisocial behavior (clinically diagnosed as conduct disorder or antisocial personality disorder in *DSM* parlance, and sometimes conceptualized as "psychopathy" in research) due to the lack of inhibition and also perhaps due to a failure to learn rapidly in response to punishment (Quay, 1993). Inadequate levels of avoidance motivation clearly are a risk factor for disinhibited, externalizing psychopathology.

Dysregulation of the approach system (i.e., BAS) also conveys marked risk for emotional and behavioral problems. High levels of BAS may contribute to "reward dominance," where the urge to obtain a goal overrides any cues for inhibition (Fowles & Dindo, 2006; Quay, 1993). The combination of high BAS and low BIS predisposes an individual to antisocial behavior, as they focus only on rewards and not potential negative consequences for actions.

Low BAS is an important component of major depression. Although depression also tends to involve high levels of negative affect (the nonspecific or shared component of both anxiety and depression), the more distinctive feature of depression is the lack of positive affect, energy, and motivation (Clark & Watson, 1991). Clinically, this manifests in symptoms of sadness (the opposite of happiness in dimensional models of state affect), loss of interest in activities, anergia or fatigue, and anhedonia. Less obviously, low trait BAS due to a high activation threshold might be a risk factor for substance use and other sensation-seeking behaviors (the hypo-arousal hypothesis; Zuckerman, 1999).

The combination of approach and avoidance, or BAS and BIS, can also be fruitfully applied to the construct of bipolar disorder. Previously known as "manic depression," bipolar disorder is an illness that can present any of a variety of mood states, including major or minor depression, euthymia (or mood within normal limits), hypomania, mania, or mixed states that combine manic and depressed symptoms in the same episode (American Psychiatric Association, 2001; Kraepelin, 1921). This dizzying range of clinical states can be challenging to recognize and categorize correctly. It is much more simple and elegant to conceptualize the illness as involving fluctuations in the BIS and BAS symptoms. High BAS activation and BIS suppression would characterize a pure, uncomplicated manic state with elevated mood, increased energy, and goal directed activity. Hypomania would involve more moderate amounts of BAS hyperactivation. Depressed states would entail very low BAS (resulting in the anergia and anhedonia of depression), with high levels of BIS adding the anxious, tense negative affectivity also often seen in depression. High BAS and BIS activation during the same episode would create a "mixed state," involving the high energy of mania with the negativity, tension, and anxiety of depression (Depue & Lenzenweger, 2001). Recent work in bipolar disorder has found good evidence for the BAS dysregulation component in particular, with the interesting findings that successes and positive life events can be destabilizing for people prone to mania (Johnson, 2005), and that mania may be associated with distinct cognitive and perceptual biases from depression (Reilly-Harrington, Alloy, Fresco, & Whitehouse, 1999).

It is important to note that although an approach and avoidance framework provides a parsimonious unifying framework that fits a broad variety of disorders, it does not provide a complete fit for all pathology. For example, approach and avoidance are not likely to be the primary dimensions contributing to eating disorders, obsessive-compulsive disorder, pervasive developmental disorders, or tic disorders—even though all of these typically include some degree of anxiety (Bradley, 2000). Approach and avoidance will also not be the salient dimensions for mental retardation or learning disabilities.

Even acknowledging these limitations, the explanatory power of approach and avoidance in the realm of psychopathology is impressive. Not only do these dimensions figure prominently in multiple disorders, but they also facilitate integration of personality, emotional, behavioral, psychophysiological, and neural aspects of functioning. The involvement of these two dimensions in multiple disorders also provides a plausible explanation for the high rates of psychiatric comorbidity observed in both epidemiological and clinical samples. Purportedly distinct disorders may be sharing a common underlying mechanism, such as BIS or BAS dysregulation (Caron & Rutter, 1991).

CONCLUSION

Organisms with appropriately calibrated emotional responses are more likely to survive and to reproduce. Discrete emotions can be organized to a large degree within a two-dimensional framework of approach and avoidance. However, discrete emotions evolved because they offered more differentiated ways of optimally addressing adaptational events. Emotions rapidly process a wealth of information, carefully attuned to cues of goals to approach or threats to avoid. Much of the information processing is happening precognitively, appraising nonverbal behavior and details that would be difficult to articulate consciously.

Human intelligence and culture introduced new levels of flexibility and complexity. Behavior is no longer driven by instinct and the stereotypic responses to innate releasing mechanisms, nor is it always led by emotion. Individuals developed the capacity to regulate emotions, and as social environments became more complex, it became possible and often beneficial to mask emotions or to feign emotional states different than what was actually felt. With the development of meta-emotional capacities, it became possible to recruit and blend emotions for other purposes, rather than primarily experiencing them as a response to the environment. Positive, approach-oriented emotions serve a crucial role in "broadening and building" social networks and cementing significant relationships. Negative, approach-oriented emotions such as anger and contempt serve to motivate action, to assert oneself or attempt to climb in social rank, and to defend that rank. Negative, avoidance-oriented emotions serve to not only avoid threats to survival, but also to help define social outgroups (promoting affiliation within a group), and also facilitate assortative mating.

Dawkins' concept of memes as replicable units of behavior offers a speculative but intriguing way of thinking about culture and ideas, and explaining behavior. The behavior or idea itself becomes the new unit of replication (not the selfish biological gene), and this change in type of replicant creates a new arena for adaptive events to select among myriad memes. Memes that have an attached "charge" in terms of approach or avoidance have a tremendous advantage for increasing their chances of propagation. Such charged memes are more likely to be appraised as important by evolved emotion systems, and thus are more likely to capture cognitive attention and to motivate behaviors (including the re-expression of the meme). Other memes, lacking a direct association with approach and avoidance, may be able to replicate by virtue of other features, but they operate at a distinct disadvantage.

Future functionalist views of emotions may want to consider how emotions contribute to survival, sexual, and memetic adaptation, and to consider how other domains (such as attachment or culture) are influenced by these processes. The emergent properties to our neurocognitive and our social systems add fascinating complexity. Although approach and avoidance systems initially evolved to facilitate survival, these dimensions were both conserved and elaborated in the service of sexual selection, and may now be reciprocally influencing memetic selection. Approach and avoidance are tools that now are often being turned to new purposes loosely linked, if at all, to their biological origins.

REFERENCES

Allan, S., & Gilbert, P. (1997). Submissive behaviour and psychopathology. *British Journal of Clinical Psychology*, *36*, 467–488.

Allan, S., & Gilbert, P. (2002). Anger and anger expression in relation to perceptions of social rank, entrapment and depressive symptoms. *Personality and Individual Differences*, *32*, 551–565.

American Psychiatric Association. (2001). *Diagnostic and statistical manual of mental disorders* (4th—Text Revision ed.). Washington, DC: Author.

Arkes, H. R. (1991). Costs and benefits of judgment errors: Implications for debiasing. *Psychological Bulletin*, *110*, 486–498.

Arkes, H. R., & Ayton, P. (1999). The sunk cost and Concorde effects: Are humans less rational than lower animals? *Psychological Bulletin*, *125*, 591–600.

Aunger, R. (2002). *The electric meme: A new theory of how we think*. New York: Free Press.

Beauchaine, T. P. (2001). Vagal tone, development, and Gray's motivational theory: Toward an integrated model of autonomic nervous system functioning in psychopathology. *Development and Psychopathology*, *13*, 183–214.

Becker, J. B., Breedlove, S. M., & Crews, D. (1992). *Behavioral endocrinology*. Cambridge, MA: MIT Press.

Blackmore, S. (1999). *The meme machine*. New York: Oxford University Press.

Boulton, M. J., & Smith, P. K. (1995). The social nature of play fighting and play chasing: Mechanism and strategies underlying cooperation and compromise. In J. H. Barkow, L. Cosmides, & J. Tooby (Eds.), *The adapted mind: Evolutionary psychology and the generation of culture* (pp. 429–449). New York: Oxford.

Bradley, S. J. (2000). *Affect regulation and the development of psychopathology*. New York: Guilford Press.

Britton, J. C., Phan, K. L., Taylor, S. F., Welsh, R. C., Berridge, K. C., & Liberzon, I. (2006). Neural correlates of social and nonsocial emotions: An fmri study. *Neuroimage*, *31*, 397–409.

Buss, D. M. (1994). *The evolution of desire: Strategies of human mating*. New York: Basic Books.

Buss, D. M. (1995a). Mate preference mechanisms: Consequences for partner choice and intrasexual competition. In J. H. Barkow, L. Cosmides, & J. Tooby (Eds.), *The adapted mind: Evolutionary psychology and the generation of culture* (pp. 249–266). New York: Oxford.

Buss, D. M. (1995b). Psychological sex differences: Origins through sexual selection. *American Psychologist*, *50*, 164–168.

Caccioppo, J. T., & Berntson, G. G. (1999). The affect system: Architecture and operating characteristics. *Current Directions in Psychological Science*, *8*, 133–137.

Carey, W. B. (1998). Temperament and behavior problems in the classroom. *School Psychology Review*, *27*, 522–533.

Caron, C., & Rutter, M. (1991). Comorbidity in child psychopathology: Concepts, issues and research strategies. *Journal of Child Psychology and Psychiatry*, *32*, 1063–1080.

Carver, C. S. (2004). Negative affects deriving from the behavioral approach system. *Emotion*, *4*, 3–22.

Carver, C. S., & White, T. L. (1994). Behavioral inhibition, behavioral activation, and affective responses to impending reward and punishment: The BIS/BAS Scales. *Journal of Personality and Social Psychology*, *67*, 319–333.

Chess, S., & Thomas, A. (1989). The practical applications of temperament to Psychiatry. In W. B. Carey & S. C. McDevitt (Eds.), *Clinical and educational applications of temperament research* (pp. 23–35). Amsterdam: Swets and Zeitlinger.

Chorpita, B. F., Albano, A. M., & Barlow, D. H. (1998). The structure of negative emotions in a clinical sample of children and adolescents. *Journal of Abnormal Psychology*, *107*, 74–85.

Clark, L. A., & Watson, D. (1991). Tripartite model of anxiety and depression: Psychometric evidence and taxonomic implications. *Journal of Abnormal Psychology*, *100*, 316–336.

Corr, P. J. (2001). Testing problems in J. A. Gray's personality theory: A commentary on Matthews and Gilliland (1999). *Personality and Individual Differences*, *30*, 333–352.

Cosmides, L., & Tooby, J. (2000). Evolutionary psychology and the emotions. In M. Lewis & J. M. Haviland-Jones (Eds.), *Handbook of emotions* (2nd ed., pp. 91–115). New York: Guilford Press.

Crenshaw, T., & Goldberg, J. P. (1996). *Sexual pharmacology: Drugs that affect sexual functioning*. New York: Norton.

Darwin, C. (1872/1965). *The expression of the emotions in man and animals*. Chicago: University of Chicago.

Davidson, R. J., Ekman, P., Saron, C. D., Senulis, J. A., & Friesen, W. V. (1990). Approach-withdrawal and cerebral asymmetry: Emotional expression and brain physiology: I. *Journal of Personality and Social Psychology, 58,* 330–341.

Dawkins, R. (1989). *The selfish gene.* (2nd ed.). New York: Oxford.

Dennett, D. (1991). *Consciousness explained.* Boston: Little Brown.

Depue, R. A., & Iacono, W. G. (1989). Neurobehavioral aspects of affective disorders. *Annual Review of Psychology, 40,* 457–492.

Depue, R. A., & Lenzenweger, M. F. (2001). A neurobehavioral dimensional model. In W. J. Livesley (Ed.), *Handbook of personality disorders: Theory, research, and treatment* (pp. 136–176). New York: Guilford.

Distin, K. (2004). *The selfish meme: A critical reassessment.* New York: Cambridge University Press.

Ekman, P. (1993). Facial expression and emotion. *American Psychologist, 48,* 384–392.

Ekman, P. (1994). Strong evidence for universals in facial expressions: A reply to Russell's mistaken critique. *Psychological Bulletin, 115,* 268–287.

Ekman, P., & Friesen, W. V. (1971). Constants across cultures in the face and emotion. *Journal of Personality and Social Psychology, 17,* 124–129.

Elliot, A. J. (2006). The hierarchical model of approach–avoidance motivation. *Motivation and Emotion, 30,* 111–116.

Elliot, A. J., Gable, S. L., & Mapes, R. R. (2006). Approach and avoidance motivation in the social domain. *Personality and Social Psychology Bulletin, 32,* 378–391.

Elliot, A. J., & Thrash, T. M. (2002). Approach–avoidance motivation in personality: approach and avoidance temperaments and goals. *Journal of Personality and Social Psychology, 82,* 804–818.

Ellis, B. J. (1995). The evolution of sexual attraction: Evaluative mechanisms in women. In J. H. Barkow, L. Cosmides, & J. Tooby (Eds.), *The adapted mind: Evolutionary psychology and the generation of culture* (pp. 267–288). New York: Oxford.

Emery, R. (1992). Family conflicts and their developmental implications: A conceptual analysis of meanings for the structure of relationships. In W. Hartup & C. Shantz (Eds.), *Family conflicts* (pp. 270–298). New York: Cambridge University Press.

Eyeing up the collaboration. (2006, Nov 2). *The Economist,* 2.

Fowles, D. C. (1994). A motivational theory of psychopathology. In W. D. Spaulding (Ed.), *Integrative views of motivation, cognition, and emotion* (Vol. 41, pp. 181–238). Lincoln, NE: University of Nebraska Press.

Fowles, D. C., & Dindo, L. (2006). A dual-deficit model of psychopathy. In C. J. Patrick (Ed.), *Handbook of psychopathy* (pp. 14–34). New York: Guilford Press.

Fredrickson, B. L. (1998). What good are positive emotions? *Review of General Psychology, 2,* 300–319.

Gigerenzer, G., & Goldstein, D. G. (1996). Reasoning the fast and frugal way: Models of bounded rationality. *Psychological Review, 103,* 650–669.

Gilbert, P., & Allan, S. (1998). The role of defeat and entrapment (arrested flight) in depression: An exploration of an evolutionary view. *Psychological Medicine, 28,* 585–598.

Gottman, J. M. (1994). *What predicts divorce? The relationship between marital processes and marital outcomes.* Hillsdale, NJ: Erlbaum.

Gray, J. A. (1985). Issues in the neuropsychology of anxiety. In A. H. Tuma & J. Maser (Eds.), *Anxiety and the anxiety disorders* (pp. 5–25). Hillsdale, NJ: Erlbaum.

Gray, J. A., & McNaughton, N. (1996). The neuropsychology of anxiety: Reprise. In D. A. Hope (Ed.), *Perspectives in anxiety, panic and fear* (Vol. 43, pp. 61–134). Lincoln, NE: University of Nebraska Press.

Hampson, E., van Anders, S. M., & Mullin, L. I. (2006). A female advantage in the recognition of emotional facial expressions: Test of an evolutionary hypothesis. *Evolution and Human Behavior, 27,* 401–416.

Healy, D. (2006). The latest mania: Selling bipolar disorder. *PLoS Medicine, 3,* e185.

Heath, I. (2006). Combating disease mongering: Daunting but nonetheless essential. *PLoS medicine, 3,* e146.

Heiser, N. A., Turner, S. M., & Beidel, D. C. (2003). Shyness: Relationship to social phobia and other psychiatric disorders. *Behaviour Research and Therapy, 41,* 209–221.

Hill, S. E. (2006). Overestimation bias in mate competition. *Evolution and Human Behavior, 4,* 1–9.

Izard, C. E. (1971). *The face of emotion.* New York: Appleton-Century-Crofts.

Izard, C. E. (1972). *Patterns of emotions.* San Diego: Academic Press.

Izard, C. E. (1990). Facial expressions and the regulation of emotions. *Journal of Personality and Social Psychology, 58,* 487–498.

Izard, C. E. (1991). *The psychology of emotions.* New York: Plenum Press.

Izard, C. E. (1992). Basic emotions, relations among emotions, and emotion-cognition relations. *Psychological Review, 99,* 561–565.

Izard, C. E. (1994). Innate and universal facial expressions: Evidence from developmental and cross-cultural research. *Psychological Bulletin, 115,* 288–299.

Izard, C. E. (2007). Basic emotions, natural kinds, emotion schemas, and a new paradigm. *Perspectives on Psychological Science, 2,* 260–280.

Izard, C. E., & Ackerman, B. P. (2000). Motivational, organizational, and regulatory functions of discrete emotions. In M. Lewis & J. M. Haviland-Jones (Eds.), *Handbook of emotions* (2nd ed., pp. 253–264). New York: Guilford Press.

Izard, C. E., Libero, D. Z., Putnam, P., & Haynes, O. M. (1993). Stability of emotion experiences and their relations to traits of personality. *Journal of Personality and Social Psychology, 64,* 847–860.

Jablonka, E., & Lamb, M. J. (2005). *Evolution in four dimensions: Genetic, epigenetic, behavioral, and symbolic variation in the history of life.* Cambridge, MA: MIT Press.

Jamison, K. R. (1993). *Touched with fire: Manic-depressive illness and the artistic temperament.* New York: Free Press.

Johnson, R. A. (1983). *We*. San Francisco: Harper and Row.

Johnson, S. L. (2005). Life events in bipolar disorder: Towards more specific models. *Clinical Psychology Review*, *25*, 1008–1027.

Kagan, J. (1997a). Conceptualizing psychopathology: The importance of development profiles. *Development and Psychopathology*, *9*, 321–334.

Kagan, J. (1997b). Temperament and the reactions to unfamiliarity. *Child Development*, *68*, 139–143.

Kazdin, A. E., & Kagan, J. (1994). Models of dysfunction in developmental psychopathology. *Clinical Psychology: Science and Practice*, *1*, 35–52.

Kessler, R. C. (1998). Sex differences in DSM-III-R psychiatric disorders in the United States: Results from the National Comorbidity Survey. *Journal of American Medical Women's Association*, *53*, 148–158.

Konner, M. (1981). *The tangled wing: Biological constraints on the human spirit*. New York: Holt, Rinehart, and Winston.

Konner, M. (1985). Cuisine sauvage. *The Sciences*, *25*, 5.

Kraepelin, E. (1921). *Manic-depressive insanity and paranoia*. Edinburgh: Livingstone.

Lazarus, R. S. (1991). *Emotion and adaptation*. New York: Oxford University Press.

LeDoux, J. (1992). Emotion and the amygdala. In J. P. Aggleton (Ed.), *The amygdala: Neurobiological aspects of emotion, memory, and mental dysfunction* (pp. 339–351). New York: Wiley.

LeDoux, J. E., & Phelps, E. A. (2000). Emotional networks in the brain. In M. Lewis & J. M. Haviland-Jones (Eds.), *Handbook of emotions* (2nd ed., pp. 157–172). New York: Guilford Press.

Loehlin, J. C. (1992). *Genes and environment in personality development* (Vol. 2). Thousand Oaks, CA: Sage.

Matthews, G., & Gilliland, K. (1999). The personality theories of H. J. Eysenck and J. A. Gray: A comparative review. *Personality and Individual Differences*, *26*, 583–626.

Miller, G. (2000). *The mating mind*. New York: Random House.

Mineka, S., Davidson, M., Cook, M., & Keir, R. (1984). Observational conditioning of snake fear in rhesus monkeys. *Journal of Abnormal Psychology*, *93*, 355–372.

Mogg, K., Bradley, B. P., Williams, R., & Mathews, A. (1993). Subliminal processing of emotional information in anxiety and depression. *Journal of Abnormal Psychology*, *102*, 304–311.

Mogg, K., & Mathews, A. (1990). Is there a self-referent mood-congruent recall bias in anxiety? *Behaviour Research and Therapy*, *28*, 91–92.

Orr, S. P., Pitman, R. K., Lasko, N. B., & Herz, L. R. (1993). Psychophysiological assessment of posttraumatic stress disorder imagery in World War II and Korean combat veterans. *Journal of Abnormal Psychology*, *102*, 152–159.

Panksepp, J. (2000). Emotions as natural kinds within the mammalian brain. In M. Lewis & J. M. Haviland-Jones (Eds.), *Handbook of emotions* (2nd ed., pp. 137–156). New York: Guilford Press.

Petersen, C. A., Caldwell, J. D., Jirikowski, G. F., & Insel, T. R. (1992). *Oxytocin in maternal, sexual, and social behaviors*

(Vol. 652). New York: Annals of the New York Academy of Sciences.

Phan, K. L., Wager, T., Taylor, S. F., & Liberzon, I. (2002). Functional neuroanatomy of emotion: A meta-analysis of emotion activation studies in PET and fmri. *Neuroimage*, *16*, 331–348.

Plutchik, R. (1980). *Emotion: A psychoevolutionary synthesis*. New York: Harper and Row.

Plutchik, R. (1993). Emotions and their vicissitudes: Emotions and psychopathology. In M. Lewis & J. M. Haviland (Eds.), *Handbook of emotions* (pp. 53–66). New York: Guilford Press.

Porter, S. (1998). Without conscience or without active conscience? The etiology of psychopathy revisited. *Aggression and Violent Behavior*, *1*, 179–189.

Quay, H. C. (1985). Attention deficit disorder and the behavioral inhibition system: The relevance of the neuropsychological theory of Jeffrey A. Gray. In L. M. Bloomingdale & J. A. Sergeant (Eds.), *Attention deficit disorder: Criteria, cognition, intervention* (pp. 117–125). Oxford: Pergamon Press.

Quay, H. C. (1993). The psychobiology of undersocialized aggressive conduct disorder: A theoretical perspective. Special Issue: Toward a developmental perspective on conduct disorder. *Development and Psychopathology*, *5*, 165–180.

Quay, H. C. (1997). Inhibition and attention deficit hyperactivity disorder. *Journal of Abnormal Child Psychology*, *25*, 7–13.

Reilly-Harrington, N. A., Alloy, L. B., Fresco, D. M., & Whitehouse, W. G. (1999). Cognitive styles and life events interact to predict bipolar and unipolar symptomatology. *Journal of Abnormal Psychology*, *108*, 567–578.

Ridley, M. (1993). *The Red Queen: Sex and the evolution of human nature*. New York: Harper Collins.

Roney, J. R., Hanson, K. N., Durante, K. M., & Maestripieri, D. (2006). Reading men's faces: women's mate attractiveness judgments track men's testosterone and interest in infants. *Proceedings of Biological Science*, *273*, 2169–2175.

Schneirla, T. (1959). An evolutionary and developmental theory of biphasic processes underlying approach and withdrawal. In *Nebraska symposium on motivation* (pp. 1–42). Lincoln, NE: University of Nebraska Press.

Scott, S. (2006). The medicalisation of shyness: From social misfits to social fitness. *Sociology of Health and Illness*, *28*, 133–153.

Shin, L. M., McNally, R. J., Kosslyn, S. M., Thompson, W. L., Rauch, S. L., Alpert, N. M., et al. (1997). A positron emission tomographic study of symptom provocation in PTSD. *Annals of the New York Academy of Sciences*, *821*, 521–523.

Simeonova, D. I., Chang, K. D., Strong, C., & Ketter, T. A. (2005). Creativity in familial bipolar disorder. *Journal of Psychiatric Research*, *39*, 623–631.

Snyder, C. R., Smith, T. W., Augelli, R. W., & Ingram, R. E. (1985). On the self-serving function of social anxiety: Shyness as a self-handicapping strategy. *Journal of Personality and Social Psychology*, *48*, 970–980.

Solomon, R. C. (2000). The philosophy of emotions. In M. Lewis & J. M. Haviland-Jones (Eds.), *Handbook of emotions* (2nd ed., pp. 3–15). New York: Guilford Press.

Stevens, A. (1982). *Archetypes: A natural history of the self.* New York: Quill.

Thayer, R. E. (2001). *Calm energy: How people regulate mood with food and exercise.* New York: Oxford University Press.

Todd, P. M., & Gigerenzer, G. (2000). Precis of simple heuristics that make us smart. *The Behavioral and Brain Sciences, 23,* 727–741; discussion 742–780.

Tomaka, J., Blascovich, J., Kibler, J., & Ernst, J. M. (1997). Cognitive and physiological antecedents of threat and challenge appraisal. *Journal of Personality and Social Psychology, 73,* 63–72.

Wakefield, J. C. (1997). When is development disordered? Developmental psychopathology and the harmful dysfunction analysis of mental disorder. *Development and Psychopathology, 9,* 269–290.

Watson, D. (2000). *Mood and temperament.* New York: Guilford Press.

Watson, D., & Tellegen, A. (1985). Toward a consensual structure of mood. *Psychological Bulletin, 98,* 219–235.

Wilson, E. O. (1980). *Sociobiology: The abridged edition.* Cambridge, MA: Harvard University Press.

Youngstrom, E. A., & Green, K. W. (2003). Reliability generalization of the self-report of emotions across gender, ethnicity, age, and socioeconomic status when using the Differential Emotions Scale. *Educational and Psychological Measurement, 63,* (Special Issue: Reliability Generalization), 279–295.

Zahavi, A. (1991). On the definition of sexual selection, Fisher's model, and the evolution of waste and of signals in general. *Animal Behaviour, 42,* 501–503.

Zechmeister, E. B., & Nyberg, S. E. (1982). *Human Memory: An Introduction to Research and Theory.* Monterey, CA: Brooks/Cole Publishing Co.

Zuckerman, M. (1999). *Vulnerability to psychopathology: A biosocial model.* Washington, DC: American Psychological Association.

22 Approach, Avoidance, and Emotional Experiences

Charles S. Carver, Yael E. Avivi, and Jean-Philippe Laurenceau

CONTENTS

Over the past two and a half decades, a broad principle has reemerged with renewed vigor in mainstream psychology. The principle is that two distinct classes of action tendencies serve as the building blocks from which complex behavior arises. Sometimes these are discussed simply as action tendencies: approach and avoidance (or withdrawal). Sometimes they are discussed in terms of the corresponding motivational tendencies: appetitive and aversive. In either case, the argument is that these two sets of tendencies are components, from which grows the complexity of human behavior (Davidson 1998). The reemergence of this principle as a central theme is reflected throughout this volume.

The idea that complex behavior reduces to approach and avoidance tendencies is not new, of course. It is implicit, for example, in the two facets of the Freudian superego. The ego ideal represents desired behaviors, to which the person aspires. The conscience represents behaviors that are forbidden and to be avoided. The idea of approach and avoidance as the building blocks of behavior is not generally attributed to Freud, however. It is more often linked to the writings of Miller and Dollard (1941; Miller, 1944), who viewed approach and avoidance tendencies in terms of gradients. The premise that these two tendencies are building blocks also led, during that period, to the idea that the two tendencies are managed by different structures in the nervous system (Konorski, 1948; Miller, 1944; Schneirla, 1959).

In the past 25 years or so, similar themes have gradually reemerged, in a family of theories with roots in neuropsychology, psychopathology, animal conditioning, and psychopharmacology. The theories that make up this family generally hold that appetitive motivation and approach behaviors are managed by what is variously termed a behavioral activation system (Fowles, 1980; Cloninger, 1987), behavioral approach system (Gray, 1981, 1987, 1990, 1994a,b), behavioral engagement system (Depue, Krauss, & Spoont, 1987), or behavioral facilitation system (Depue & Collins, 1999). Aversive motivation and withdrawal or avoidance behavior are said to be managed by a system that has been called a behavioral inhibition system (Cloninger, 1987; Gray, 1981, 1987, 1990, 1994b) or a withdrawal system (Davidson, 1984, 1988, 1995, 1998). These two broad systems are believed to have partially distinct neural substrates and to exert distinct influences on action. This family of theories is very influential today.

FEEDBACK, ACTION, AND AFFECT

The authors of this chapter became interested in approach and avoidance processes by somewhat circuitous paths. The first author has long been broadly interested in the structure of "behavior-in-general." The second and third authors have been interested primarily in close relationships and some of the factors that contribute to their ongoing dynamics and their success or lack of success. For somewhat separate reasons, we have all come to find ourselves thinking about motivational tendencies to approach and to avoid.

For many years the first author has explored a view of the person as a complex organization of self-regulating feedback loops (Carver & Scheier, 1990, 1998, 1999), which is yet another set of ideas with a considerable history (MacKay, 1966; Powers, 1973). Most people who are only vaguely familiar with the concept of a feedback loop probably associate it with descriptions of electromechanical or electronic devices. Those who have passing familiarity with the application of the concept to living systems (but not much more than that) probably think of its application to physiological systems such as those that maintain homeostatic control over blood pressure, body temperature, and so on. The viewpoint that Carver and Scheier have explored over a considerable period is that the structural elements that underlie homeostasis also underlie attempts to attain desired goals.

ACTION

In this view, goal pursuit entails having a goal, assessing where one presently stands with respect to that goal, and taking steps to reduce any discrepancy sensed between the present state and the desired state (the goal). These are the functional elements of a discrepancy reducing feedback loop. The operation of the loop is continuous and iterative; the process repeats as needed, until there is a match between what is and what was intended.

This model can be applied to motor-control goals such as reaching and grasping; it can also be applied to goals that are more abstract (e.g., being honest, being productive, forming a strong relationship). It can be applied to goals that are static; it can also be applied to goals that are moving and evolving targets (e.g., developing a research career, having a sound marriage, raising children to hold the right kind of personal values).

Discrepancy reducing feedback processes are essentially approach processes. They represent one kind of meta-theoretical framework for understanding the regulation of actions that involve approach.

Although discrepancy reducing loops are the most commonly discussed feedback process, there is also a second kind: discrepancy *enlarging* loops. These loops act to increase distance from comparison values. The comparison values in this case might be thought of as "antigoals," values that the system tries not to embody. An intuitive example is a feared or disliked possible self (Markus & Nurius, 1986; Ogilvie, 1987). A discrepancy enlarging loop compares present conditions to the undesired state (the antigoal) and tries to increase the discrepancy between the two. These processes thus create avoidance, escape, or withdrawal.

These two kinds of feedback processes differ both in the direction of the resultant effect on behavior (i.e., approach versus avoid) and also in how "directive" they are. That is, discrepancy reducing systems have a particular value as a target. They continue to home in on the target, even if the target is moving. In contrast, discrepancy enlarging systems have no specific aim. Their function is to create distance from the antigoal. Getting away is getting away, no matter what direction the escape happens to take.

In living systems, however, the functioning of a discrepancy enlarging process is generally constrained in some way by a discrepancy reducing process. What may begin as purely avoidance often leads a bit later to approach. Thus, an avoidance loop acts to increase distance from the antigoal; at some point an incentive becomes identified and an approach loop begins to engage. Once this happens, the person is simultaneously trying to avoid the antigoal and approach the goal (assuming that both loops remain active). Thus, many cases of active avoidance of a threat also involve approach of an incentive.

An example of active avoidance plus approach is the "ought self" (Higgins, 1996). The ought self is a goal to approach, but the person approaches it in order to escape from a source of disapproval. Thus, for example, Higgins and Tykocinski (1992) found that people whose sense of self was dominated by discrepancies between actual self and ought self were focused on the avoidance of negative occurrences. In contrast, people whose sense of self was dominated by discrepancies between actual self and their *ideals* were more likely to be striving for affirmative goals. Other research suggests that persons approach the ought self in order to avoid the feared (Carver, Lawrence, & Scheier, 1999).

Avoidance blended with approach is also represented in Ryan and Deci's (1999) concept of introjected values. Introjected values are goals that people try to attain and conform to. However, they try to attain these positive goals in order to avoid feelings of blame or guilt. Thus, although approach is involved, the first and most basic motive in these cases is an avoidance motive: the desire to avoid punishment or self-punishment.

Approach and avoidance motives sometimes overlap in achievement-related behavior, as well. This is reflected, for example, in Elliot and Church's (1997) hierarchical model of achievement motivation (for review see Elliot, 2006). People with a strong motive to avoid failure are energized at the core by an avoidance process. Yet sometimes this leads to the engagement in approach processes. Thus, these individuals prevent themselves from failing by actively pursuing success.

Affect

Feedback functions can exist in many different forms. Carver and Scheier (1990, 1998) have also used the feedback principle to make an argument about processes that underlie affect. Affect refers to the subjective experience of valence, the experience of positivity or negativity arising from a particular experience (Russell & Carroll, 1999). In many ways affect is the heart of emotion, though the term emotion often incorporates connotations of physiological changes that frequently accompany hedonic experiences.

The Carver and Scheier argument was that the subjective experience of affect reflects the error signal (the detection of a discrepancy) in a layer of feedback systems that exists in parallel to the systems that manage action. The function of the second layer is to monitor, and ultimately influence, how well the first layer (the organization of behavioral loops) is doing at moving the person toward desired goals and away from threats. The affect-related loop has the same structural elements as the behavioral loop, but it has a different kind of reference value. Carver and Scheier suggested that the affect loop has as its criterion a rate of progress occurring in the behavioral loop. The criterion rate is compared to the sensed rate of progress of the behavior system, and the result (the "error" between the two) is experienced as affect.

Behavioral discrepancies can exist in numerous ways. For example, when reaching for an object, one may reach

too high, too low, too far to the right, too far to the left, not far enough from one's body, etc. A loop that monitors rate, however, can in principle detect only two sorts of discrepancies. The sensed rate can be above the criterion or below the criterion. If the rate of goal-related progress is below the criterion, the second system's error signal is experienced as negative affect. If the rate is exactly at the criterion, the person is affect-free, because the error signal is zero. If the rate exceeds the criterion, the error signal is experienced as positive affect.

In essence, this theory holds that positive feelings mean that you are doing better at something than you need to (or expect to), and negative feelings mean that you are doing worse than you need to (or expect to; for broader discussion see Carver, 2003; Carver & Scheier, 1998, chapters 8 and 9). This view on affect rejects the idea that affect arises purely from attainment of a goal per se. Instead, it emphasizes the idea that progress toward goals across time is computed continuously while the person is engaged in goal-directed behavior. This position allows for the existence of affect to exist while the person is on the way to goals. Indeed, it allows for continually varying hedonic experiences (negative to positive and back and forth again), while the goal-directed behavior plays out over time.

Research Support

There is now at least a modest accumulation of evidence to support the idea that affect follows this rate or velocity function. For example, Hsee and Abelson (1991), who came to this hypothesis independently of Carver and Scheier (1990), presented laboratory participants with hypothetical scenarios depicting a desirable outcome, in this case improvement in class standing. They held constant the amount of change (a shift from 30th to 70th percentile), and varied the amount of time in which it occurs. The outcome of interest was levels of satisfaction or dissatisfaction with the outcome displayed. Participants expressed more satisfaction when improving to a high outcome than when having a constant high outcome; they expressed more satisfaction after reaching a given outcome at a fast velocity than after reaching the same outcome at a slow velocity; and they expressed more satisfaction after a change involving a high velocity over a short distance than after a change involving a lower velocity over a greater distance. All of these effects appear to indicate the involvement of a velocity function in affect.

Negative changes in this research showed a similar link between velocity and affective potency. That is, participants were more satisfied with a constant low salary than with a salary that dropped from higher to the same low level; they were less dissatisfied after slow drops than after fast drops; and they were less dissatisfied after an extended, gradual drop than after a small, fast drop. The velocity effect was also replicated in a study in which participants watched a graphic simulation of changes in the price of a hypothetical stock. Participants preferred a fast velocity when the outcome was improving and a slow one when the outcome was declining.

Lawrence, Carver, and Scheier (2002) tested the velocity effect in personal experience, rather than hypothetical situations. They manipulated participants' perceptions of progress toward an actual goal. Participants engaged in a task that was disguised as measure of social intuition. In reality, the task was simply an opportunity to provide false feedback of doing well or doing poorly. Participants received performance feedback after each of six 10-trial blocks. All received the same final total score: 50% accuracy. However, for some people, scores increased over blocks; for other people, scores decreased over blocks; and for other people, scores were stable across blocks. Increases in rate of perceived success over time predicted positive changes in mood; decreases in perceived success over time predicted negative changes in mood. Thus, mood change related to changes in how well things were going. Indeed, it is noteworthy that the total number of successes experienced by people with downward trajectories by the time of the mood rating was greater than the total number of successes experienced by people with upward trajectories. Yet the mood of the former was worse than the mood of the latter. Presumably this was due to the difference in trajectories.

Another study bearing on the velocity hypothesis was conducted by Brunstein (1993). In it, undergraduates reported subjective well-being over the several months of an academic term, as a function of various goal-related perceptions, including goal progress. At the beginning of the semester, participants listed six long-term goals. At subsequent assessments (4, 10, and 14 weeks later), participants rated progress toward these goals and their subjective well-being. Perceived progress at each assessment was positively and strongly correlated with concurrent well-being. Greater progress was additionally related to greater subsequent well-being.

A later study refined this picture, by taking into account individual differences in participants' motive dispositions and how those dispositions related to participants' goals (Brunstein, Schultheiss, & Grässmann, 1998). In this study, participants' goals were separated into those that were congruent with their dominant motives and those that were incongruent with those motives. Greater progress toward motive-congruent goals related to better emotional well-being, as one might expect. However, having greater progress toward goals that did not fit with the person's core motives did not relate to better emotional well-being.

Results that are conceptually similar to all of these emerged from a study of female fibromyalgia patients (Affleck et al., 1998). Patients made reports of their progress on social-interpersonal goals from one day to another. These daily ratings of progress toward social goals were positively associated with increases in positive mood and decreases in negative mood, controlling for that day's levels of pain and fatigue.

Action Consequences of Affect

Let us return to the idea that affect reflects the error signal in a feedback loop. If this were so, then affect would be a signal to *adjust* one's rate of progress. That is, if the input function of the affect loop is a sensed rate of progress in action, the output function must be a *change* in rate of that action. Thus, the affect loop has a direct influence on what occurs in the action loop. This view thus implies a natural link between affect and action, a theme that is very congruent with contemporary views of emotion (Frijda, 1986, 1988).

Negative feelings imply a rate that is too low. Consistent with theory, the first response to negative feelings usually is to try harder. If trying harder (or trying "smarter") does increase progress, the result is that the negative feeling goes away.

Some increases in rate output are straightforward. If you are lagging behind at something, you may be able to speed up. Sometimes the changes are less straightforward. The rates of many "behaviors" are defined not by a pace of physical action but in terms of choices among potential actions, or entire programs of action. For example, increasing your rate of progress on a project at work may mean choosing to spend a weekend working rather than going to the beach. Increasing your rate of being kind means choosing to do an action that reflects that value when an opportunity arises. Thus, adjustment in rate must often be translated into other terms, such as concentration, or allocation of time and effort.

For negative feelings, this principle seems completely intuitive. What this view predicts for positive feelings, however, is counterintuitive to many people. In this view, positive feelings arise when things are going better than they need to. This view argues that people who exceed the criterion rate of progress (who have positive feelings) will ease back on subsequent effort in this domain. They are likely to "coast" a little (cf. Frijda, 1994, p. 113)—not necessarily stop, but ease back such that subsequent rate of progress returns to the criterion. Although this hypothesis is interesting, it has not been much studied, and it is not addressed further here (see Carver, 2003, for further discussion).

The existence of two feedback systems functioning in concert with one another turns out to be quite common in an application of feedback concepts that is quite different from the one now under discussion. This other application is the literature of control engineering (Clark, 1996). Engineers have long since found that having two feedback systems working together—one controlling position, one controlling velocity—permits the device in which they are embedded to respond in a way that is both quick and stable (i.e., prevents overshoots and oscillations).

The combination of quickness and stability in responding is valuable in the kinds of devices that engineers deal with, but its value is not limited to such devices. A person with very reactive emotions is prone to overreact, and oscillate behaviorally. A person who is emotionally unreactive is slow to respond even to events where there is great urgency. A person whose reactions are between the two extremes responds quickly but without undue overreaction and oscillation. For biological entities, being able to respond quickly yet accurately confers an adaptive advantage. This combination of quick and stable responding may be a consequence of having both behavior-managing and affect-managing control systems. Affect causes responses to be quicker (because this control system is time sensitive) and as long as the affective system is not over-responsive, the responses are also stable.

It is also of interest that the behavioral responses that are presumed to be linked to the affects would also lead ultimately to reduction of the affects. Thus, the affect system seems to be, in a very basic sense, a self-regulating system (cf. Campos, Frankel, & Camras, 2004).

AFFECTS LINKED TO APPROACH AND TO AVOIDANCE

Recall our starting point: the idea that there exist both approach and avoidance behavioral systems. Presumably both approach and avoidance can give rise to the experience of affects. The Carver and Scheier (1990, 1998) view holds that positive affect results from doing well and negative affect from doing poorly. Certainly it is possible to do either well or poorly at either approach or avoidance. But doing well at moving *toward* a desired goal is not precisely the same experience as is doing well at moving *away* from a threat (see also Elliot & Sheldon, 1997). Doing poorly at attaining a desired end is not the same experience as is doing poorly at escaping a punishment.

Relying in part on insights from Higgins and his collaborators (reviewed, for example, in Higgins, 1996, 1997), Carver and Scheier (1998) argued that affective experiences can be organized along two bipolar dimensions. One dimension is generated by affect loops that concern approach behavior. It includes elation at one end (when things are going very well) and despair and despondency (when things are going very poorly) at the other end. The second dimension is generated by affect loops that concern avoidance. This dimension includes fear at one end (when things are going poorly) and relief and serenity at the other end (when things are going very well; Roseman, 1984, has expressed a similar view; see also Frijda, 1986, 1988; Ortony, Clore, & Collins, 1988).

This is not the same argument as underlies other depictions involving two dimensions of affect. The best known dual-dimensional model is known by the terms positive and negative affect, or positive and negative activation (Cacioppo, Gardner, & Berntson, 1999; Watson, Wiese, Vaidya, & Tellegen, 1999). That theoretical view argues for two unipolar dimensions, one of which is grounded in approach, the other in avoidance. The Carver and Scheier view, in contrast, argues for two bipolar dimensions. This difference, which may at first seem subtle and minor, is in fact quite important. This issue is addressed in greater detail a bit later on.

APPROACH AND AVOIDANCE SENSITIVITIES

Having noticed the general resemblance between two kinds of feedback loops (discrepancy reducing and discrepancy enlarging) and two classes of motives (appetitive and aversive), Carver and Scheier and some of their colleagues became interested in how deeply intertwined these two sets of ideas might be. Gray (1981, 1987, 1990, 1994a,b), Fowles (1980), and a number of others (Depue & Iacono, 1989), had pointed to the potential importance of individual differences in the functioning of appetitive and aversive motivational systems. One obvious path for study, then, was individual differences.

It seems reasonable to suggest that people vary in the sensitivity or the strength of these broad motivational systems. Some people by nature are readily engaged in active pursuit of whatever incentives arise (e.g., an upcoming social event, an unexpected opportunity for professional gain); others are less drawn to them. Some people by nature are vigilant to the possibility of threats or dangers in the environment (e.g., criticism or punishment for mistakes, dimly lit parking lots); others are less responsive to this sort of cue. If the neurobiological systems that manage approach and avoidance are independent in their sensitivities, then individual differences in responsiveness to incentive and threat will also be independent, yielding all combinations of highs and lows.

Drawing on the literature pertaining to this family of biobehavioral theories, Carver and White (1994) devised a set of self-report measures that they called the BIS/BAS scales. These scales reflect the self-rated sensitivity of the behavioral approach system and behavioral inhibition (or withdrawal) system. In their initial validation research, Carver and White found that people higher in BAS sensitivity (but not BIS sensitivity) reported larger increases in happiness in response to a rewarding outcome. They also found that people higher in BIS sensitivity (but not BAS sensitivity) reported larger increases in anxiety in response to a threat.

These findings were exactly as would be expected from the biological models of appetitive and aversive motives from which the scales were designed. That is, a person with a highly sensitive approach system should experience more positive affect than a person with a less sensitive approach system, given cues of reward, but this variable should not influence responses to cues of threat. In the same way, a person with a highly sensitive avoidance system should experience more anxiety than a person with a less sensitive avoidance system, given cues of threat, but this variable should not influence responses to cues of reward.

The BIS/BAS scales have proven useful for a wide variety of potential research applications. They have, for example, been used to examine views of personality in which approach and avoidance are considered to be the driving forces behind the trait dimensions of extraversion and neuroticism (Carver, Sutton, & Scheier, 2000; Carver & White, 1994; Elliot & Thrash, 2002; Zelenski & Larsen, 1999). They have also been linked to several aspects of psychopathology (Johnson & Carver, 2006; Johnson, Turner, & Iwata, 2003; Meyer, Johnson, & Carver, 1999; Meyer, Johnson, & Winters, 2001).

ISSUES IN CONCEPTUALIZING AFFECT

A particularly interesting application of the BIS/BAS scales is the use of them to investigate whether a given phenomenon pertains to approach or to avoidance. A measure of BAS and BIS sensitivities would seem to represent a very useful methodological tool for such investigations. BAS and BIS sensitivities can be assessed and then related (separately) to any behavioral or experiential phenomenon that might be of interest. If the phenomenon actually derives from functioning of the avoidance system, it should relate to individual differences in BIS

sensitivity. If the phenomenon actually derives from functioning of the approach system, it should relate to individual differences in BAS sensitivity. Thus, individual differences can be used to shed light on broad principles about general phenomena (cf. Underwood, 1975).

Approach-Related Negative Affect

This strategy has been used to examine the roots of two negative affects about which there has been disagreement: sadness and anger (Carver, 2004). As noted earlier, disagreements exist about the dimensionality of affect. One widely held view is that there is a dimension of positive affect and a separate dimension of negative affect. Each of these dimensions is unipolar, ranging from absence of that affect to intense experience of that affect.

This view has a number of theoretical sources. For example, Gray (1981, 1990, 1994b) held that the BIS is engaged by cues of punishment and by cues of frustrative nonreward. He thus saw BIS as responsible for negative feelings in response to either of these sorts of cue. Similarly, he held that BAS is engaged by cues of reward or of escape from (or avoidance of) punishment. He thus saw BAS as responsible for positive feelings in response to such cues. Gray's view thus was one in which each system is responsible for affect of one hedonic tone (positive for BAS, negative for BIS).

A similar position has long been taken by Watson, Tellegen, and their colleagues, first with respect to moods (Watson & Tellegen, 1985) and more recently with respect to affects with more focused origins (Watson et al., 1999). In recent years this viewpoint has increasingly pointed to neurobiological theories of motivation and action (Davidson, 1998; Fowles, 1993; Gray, 1994a) that appear to provide a conceptual basis for why these dimensions are fundamental (Watson et al.). That is, each dimension is now linked explicitly to a category of motives: appetitive and aversive. Other theorists in personality and social psychology and related areas have also taken similar positions (Cacioppo et al., 1999; Lang, Bradley, & Cuthbert, 1998).

In contrast to this position, the Carver and Scheier (1998) analysis, described earlier, assumes two bipolar dimensions. More specifically, Carver and Scheier argued that certain negative affects arise when an approach process is doing poorly at attaining its goals. The affects in question are sadness, frustration, and anger. If this were so, it should follow that the intensity of those negative affects under conditions that normatively evoke them would relate to individual differences in BAS sensitivity. Specifically, greater BAS sensitivity should lead to greater intensity of these affects. If, however, all negative affects have their roots in the BIS, that should not happen. Instead, stronger experiences of those negative affects should all relate instead to greater BIS sensitivities.

It is of particular importance here that all items of the BAS scales focus on affective and behavioral responses to the presence of incentive cues. More specifically, BAS-related items describe positive emotional and behavioral reactions to three aspects of the possibility of obtaining incentives (being motivated to seek them, being persistent in pursuit of them, and having positive feelings when obtaining them). No BAS item refers in any way to an adverse event, nor is there any hint of negative affect in the content of any BAS item. The opposite is true of BIS items. Each references a threatening event, and assesses emotional responsiveness to the threat. On the basis of the semantic content of the items, then, there should be a bias toward linking of BIS items to reports of adverse affective experiences.

These competing theories were tested in three studies (Carver, 2004). In Study 1, participants were led to believe that by performing well at a laboratory task they could obtain bonus credits toward a course requirement. However, they were all caused to perform at a level that failed to yield the bonus credits. Under these conditions of frustrative nonreward, reports of being sad and frustrated related significantly and positively to Fun seeking, a BAS scale. They did not relate significantly to the BIS scale.

In Study 2, participants imagined themselves in three hypothetical scenarios. All were written to be anger-eliciting and also potentially anxiety-eliciting at the same time. Reports of the feeling that would be experienced in those situations were aggregated into those pertaining to anger and those pertaining to nervousness. Nervousness related positively to BIS sensitivity, as would be expected

on the basis of all of the theories under study. In contrast, anger related positively to Reward responsiveness, a BAS scale, but only weakly to BIS.

In Study 3, conducted within two weeks of the terrorist attacks of September 2001, participants were asked to report their feelings about the events of that day. Levels of fear related positively to BIS sensitivity, as expected. Greater anger related to greater Reward responsiveness and Drive, both BAS scales. It appears from these results, and others reviewed in that article, that certain negative affects do indeed relate to inadequacy of approach. These findings are not consistent with a view in which all negative affects relate to a dimension of avoidance motivation.

Clearly anger and sadness are different from each other, and a theoretical model that places both of them on the same dimension should also be clear about their relationship to each other and to the approach function more generally. It has been argued that a key issue here is a variable that has not been considered thus far in this chapter: the extent of the person's confidence of being able to bring the desired rate back to the criterion (Figure 22.1; see Carver, 2004, for detail). Anger appears to be aimed at regaining lost ground. Implicit in that affect is a degree of confidence of being able to regain that ground. Sadness appears to imply that the effort seems pointless, the opportunity lost, the reward gone. Yet, despite these very real differences, it seems possible to relate both of these qualities to the function of approaching (or failing to approach) desired ends.

AVOIDANCE-RELATED POSITIVE AFFECT

Most work that compares these two dimensional positions to each other has examined negative affects that

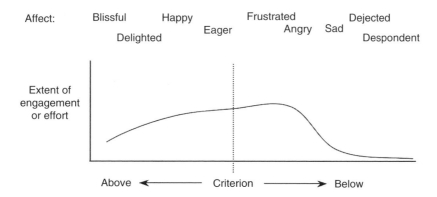

FIGURE 22.1 Hypothesized approach-related affects as a function of doing well versus doing poorly compared to criterion velocity. A second (vertical) dimension indicates the degree of behavioral engagement posited to be associated with affects at different degrees of departure from neutral. Adapted from "Negative affects deriving from the behavioral approach system," by C. S. Carver, 2004, *Emotion, 4*, p. 3.

Carver and Scheier argued should relate to approach. However, there is at least a little information concerning the other prediction that differs between the theories: that some positive affects should relate to an avoidance motivational tendency. One such affect is relief. Relief is a positive affect that occurs when a threat is removed. The removal of a threat would seem to be an indication that avoidance of the threat is going very well.

Recall that Gray (1990, 1994b) held that BAS is engaged both by cues of reward and by cues of escape from (or avoidance of) punishment. The latter is the circumstance that should induce relief. In contrast, the Carver and Scheier (1998) model holds that relief should occur when avoidance is going well—as when a threat disappears. These contrasting predictions have now been tested in two studies (Carver, in press).

Participants in both studies were asked to imagine themselves in hypothetical scenarios, some of which were written to be relief-eliciting. Participants then rated how they would feel in those situations, along several dimensions, including relief. These ratings then were related to participants' BIS/BAS scores obtained previously. In both studies, greater relief was related most strongly to greater BIS sensitivity. Relations with BAS scales were mixed. Greater relief related to greater Reward responsiveness but also to lower Fun seeking. These results appear to offer at least some support for the existence of a bipolar affective dimension relating to avoidance.

RELATIONSHIP-SPECIFIC APPROACH AND AVOIDANCE

Given these arguments—separate approach and avoidance functions, separate affective consequences of doing well and doing poorly at approach and avoidance—how far can they be extended? One emerging frontier for extending all of these themes is the domain of social and intimate relationships (Gable, 2006). The experience of emotion is certainly a core element in the functioning of such relationships (Berscheid, 1983). Given the arguments outlined earlier in this chapter, we would expect approach and avoidance processes to play separate roles in how such relationships are experienced. We would also expect the roles to differ from one another in important ways.

Let us consider close relationships, in particular, from this view. What goals do people have in close relationships? One relationship goal that has been noted repeatedly in the literature is intimacy (Peplau & Gordon, 1985; Reis, 1990; Reis, Senchak, & Solomon, 1985), the feeling of connectedness with another person (Laurenceau, Rivera, Schaffer, & Pietromonaco, 2004). Many regard

this connection as a universal human need (Baumeister & Leary, 1995; Ryan & Deci, 2000). People in romantic relationships try to maintain desired levels of intimacy, by self-disclosing to their partner and by conveying a sense understanding and responsiveness toward their partner (Laurenceau, Barrett, & Pietromonaco, 1998; Laurenceau, Barrett, & Rovine, 2005; Reis & Shaver, 1988). The goal of intimacy is sufficiently important that it presumably is always active at some level in the minds of people who are in romantic relationships, thereby influencing their experiences (Fitzsimons & Bargh, 2003).

Not all reference values that pertain to close relationships are desired conditions, however. Some are conditions to avoid—threats rather than incentives. An obvious threat in relationships is conflict, or interpersonal pain (Simpson, Oriña, & Ickes, 2003). Guerrero and Andersen (2000) suggested that each person has a level of relationship conflict that is intolerable, and that this represents a feared state to avoid. Indeed, conflict is so salient a factor in relationships that it is often taken as the main indicator of relationship functioning (Fincham & Beach, 1999). Although conflict and (loss of) intimacy are related, they are not simply opposite ends of a single dimension. Intimacy is an incentive; conflict is a threat.

In the same way, people have social motives that are broader than those that pertain to intimate relationships per se (Elliot, Gable, & Mapes, 2006; Gable, 2006). People have the desire to affiliate with other people and the desire to avoid rejection from others. The former is an approach motive, the latter is an avoidance motive. These motives pertain to social relations with friends and acquaintances, as well as with intimate others.

As we shift our attention here from the more general conceptual statement on approach and avoidance to the context of relationships, at least three issues arise. One of them is whether the velocity principle pertains to the relationship domain. A second issue is whether approach and avoidance motives relate to distinct affective experiences in the relationship domain, as they do in other domains. A third issue is whether approach and avoidance tendencies in relationships differ in any important way from more general tendencies toward approach and avoidance. At least some information is presently available pertaining to each of these issues.

Velocity and Distinct Contributions of Approach and Avoidance

Let us consider first the velocity principle. The velocity idea has been applied to the relationship context in several places. For example, Baumeister and Bratslavsky

(1999) reviewed indirect evidence suggesting that rapid increases in intimacy relate to positive emotions such as passion. They suggested that passion is a function of the rate of change in intimacy over time. Thus, passion should not derive only from the current level of intimacy, but from the rate with which intimacy changes. The notion of rapid change in intimacy has been similarly discussed in terms of self-expansion (Aron & Aron, 1986; Aron, Norman, & Aron, 2001), with rapid expansion yielding the feelings associated with falling in love.

Several studies have produced evidence that bears fairly directly on this issue. For example, Karney and Frye (2002) found that married couples evaluate their happiness, or their satisfaction with the relationship, more on the basis of perceptions of recent improvements than from perceptions of the quality of the relationship at that particular time. Karney and Bradbury (1997) also found that decreasing satisfaction over time (compared to low initial satisfaction) predicted dissolution of relationships over a period of 4 years.

Another recent study investigated romantic partners using a daily diary methodology (Laurenceau, Troy, & Carver, 2005). Participants used electronic devices to record perceived levels of, and perceived changes in, both intimacy and conflict twice daily over 10 consecutive days. Perceived increases in intimacy related to positive affect (passion and excitement) above and beyond perceptions of current intimacy (which also related to positive affect), among both male and female partners. Perceived increases in conflict related to anxious affect above and beyond perceptions of current conflict (which also related to anxiety), but only among males. These findings pertaining to perceptions of change are consistent with the velocity principle.

The findings from this study also indicated that the approach and avoidance tendencies made distinct contributions to participants' affective experiences in the relationship. That is, it was only perceptions of increased intimacy (i.e., approach of a desired state) that related to positive, intimacy-related emotions. Perceptions of conflict played no role in those emotions. The complementary pattern occurred for feelings of anxiety. It was only perceptions of increased conflict (i.e., avoidance going poorly) that related to anxiety. Perceptions concerning intimacy played no role in that emotion.

Another project that bears on the velocity principle (though not the separation of approach and avoidance) was reported by Avivi, Laurenceau, and Carver (2007). This research examined one sample of dating couples in a cross-sectional design and followed a second sample of committed romantic couples in a longitudinal design. As

in the Laurenceau, Troy, and Carver (2005) project, participants rated their perceptions of progress toward goals. In this case, however, it was the perception of progress toward goals that were perceived as being shared by both members of the couple. These perceptions of goal progress again related to a relationship-related outcome: in this case, perceptions of the relationship's quality.

RELATIONSHIP-SPECIFIC FUNCTIONS?

Another issue that arises when shifting the focus to the domain of close relationships is whether there is something special about this class of goals. When Carver and White (1994) developed their measure of the sensitivity of people's approach and avoidance systems, they intentionally created a very general measure. It was intended to apply to all sorts of incentive and threat situations. At that point, it had not occurred to them that there might be reasons for distinguishing among behavioral domains.

However, neurobiological evidence suggests that there may be *social* incentive and threat systems, which are partially overlapping but also partially separate from the more general appetitive and aversive systems (Depue & Morrone-Strupinksy, 2005; Panksepp, 1998). Thus, there may be individual differences in specialized sensitivities to incentives and threats *within the domain of intimate relationships*. The global BIS/BAS scales do not focus on close relationships as specific sources of incentives and threats. As a result, they may lack sensitivity in predicting behaviors and outcomes that are relationship-specific. If these theoretical ideas have any substance, what would be needed is a more focused measure of incentive and threat sensitivities, aimed specifically at close relationships.

At least two groups of researchers have begun to address this issue. Elliot et al. (2006) developed a measure intended to assess social approach and avoidance goals in friendships. They found that higher levels of the desire for affiliation predicts greater adoption of friendship-related approach goals, and that higher levels of fear of rejection predicts greater adoption of friendship-related avoidance goals. The holding of those goals, in turn, predicted subjective well-being and physical symptoms. Adoption of approach goals led to greater subjective well-being, and adoption of avoidance goals led to greater levels of physical symptoms.

In another project, Kleinman, Kaczynski, Laurenceau, and Carver (2007) developed a set of self-report scales intended to measure relationship-specific incentive and threat sensitivities. They called this measure the RAp/RAv scales (standing for relationship approach and relationship avoidance). The focus of this measure is somewhat different from that of Elliot et al. in two respects. First, the Kleinman et al. (2007) scales target intimate relations in particular, whereas the Elliot et al. scales target friendships. Second, the RAp/RAv scales are aimed at assessing sensitivities of postulated focused incentive and threat systems, whereas the Elliot et al. measure assesses the holding of goals (though they also supplemented that measure with measures of motives for affiliation and fear of rejection in some research). It remains to be seen whether the two new measures will prove to differ from each other in their focus of convenience, or will instead overlap in their prediction of relevant outcomes.

The RAp/RAv items were modeled on the items of the BIS/BAS scales, but each new item refers explicitly to the respondent's close relationship. The new scales have a reasonably sound factor structure, and there is also evidence of convergent and discriminant validity (Kleinman et al., 2007). Kleinman et al. (2007, Study 4) have also used these scales to predict the affective reactions of newlyweds after they engaged in two relationship-focused tasks. The first task was a pair of 12-min conversations about each of two topics identified by the couple as being sources of marital conflict. The second task was a conversation about the couple's positive feelings for each other. The outcomes of interest were the levels of anxiety reported after the conflict task and positive affect reported after the positive task (both adjusted for the respective baseline affect).

Among wives, RAp scores related to greater positive affect after the positive conversation task and did not relate to anxiety after the conflict conversation task. RAv scores related to greater anxiety after the conflict task and did not relate to positive affect after the positive task. Of particular interest, this pattern of associations remained, even after controlling for BIS and BAS scales. Among husbands, the results were somewhat less clearcut. Husbands' RAp scores predicted positive affect after the positive conversation. Contrary to prediction, however, husbands' RAv scores did not significantly predict anxiety after the conflict conversation, after controlling for baseline affect. Again, these relationships remained unchanged after controlling for the BIS and BAS scales.

Initial investigations thus suggest the potential usefulness of the RAp/RAv scales in predicting relationship-related outcomes. Moreover, these scales predicted the outcomes even when taking into account global incentive and threat sensitivity, in the form of the BIS/BAS scales. Thus, this research suggests that there may be considerable merit in distinguishing global approach and avoidance

sensitivities from more focused approach and avoidance sensitivities.

Many questions about this latter issue remain to be examined. For example, this pattern of results may simply represent a specific case of a more general principle concerning the breadth versus narrowness of psychological constructs. That is, attitudes and expectancies typically predict other outcomes better if they are at the same level of abstraction as the other outcome than if they are not. In the same way, a measure of sensitivities to relationship incentives and threats may be better predictors of relationship outcomes than a measure of broader sensitivities purely because it is at the right level of specificity. Alternatively, it may be the case that there is something unique about relationship functioning, which gives it a kind of privileged status in the neurobiology of behavior and emotion (cf. Carter, 1998; Young & Wang, 2004). These are issues that will take time to sort out.

CLOSING COMMENT

It seems clear that approach and avoidance functions are deeply embedded in the nature of human personality (Zuckerman, 2005). It also seems clear that these functions—each of which in itself is fairly simple—can lead to great complexity. In this chapter we have described multiple ways in which these functions have emerged in our own thinking and research efforts. As noted earlier, our interest in these functions as building blocks of behavior arose as a function of our interest in other constructs. Yet pursuit of those other constructs led us to undertake a closer consideration of approach and avoidance. We believe that these conceptual principles are extremely useful as organizing themes for theory development, and that they thus will continue to be central figures in psychology for a good long time.

REFERENCES

Affleck, G., Tennen, H., Urrows, S., Higgins, P., Abeles, M., Hall, C., et al. (1998). Fibromyalgia and women's pursuit of personal goals: A daily process analysis. *Health Psychology, 17,* 40–47.

Aron, A., & Aron, E. N. (1986). *Love and the expansion of self: Understanding attraction and satisfaction.* New York: Hemisphere Publishing.

Aron, A., Norman, C. C., & Aron, E. N. (2001). Shared self-expanding activities as a means of maintaining and enhancing close romantic relationships. In J. H. Harvey & A. E. Wenzel (Eds.), *Close romantic relationships: Maintenance and enhancement* (pp. 47–66). Mahwah, NJ: Lawrence Erlbaum Associates.

Avivi, Y. E., Laurenceau, J- P., & Carver, C. S. (2007). Linking romantic relationship quality to perceptions of relationship goal sharing and goal progress. Manuscript under review.

Baumeister, R. F., & Bratslavsky, E. (1999). Passion, intimacy, and time: Passionate love as a function of change in intimacy. *Personality and Social Psychology Review, 3,* 46–67.

Baumeister, R. F., & Leary, M. R. (1995). The need to belong: Desire for interpersonal attachments as a fundamental human motivation. *Psychological Bulletin, 117,* 497–529.

Berscheid, E. (1983). Emotion. In H. H. Kelley, E. Berscheid, A. Christensen, J. H. Harvey, T. L. Huston, G. Levinger E. McClintock, L. A. Peplau & D. R. Peterson (Eds.), *Close relationships* (pp. 110–168). New York: Freeman.

Brunstein, J. C. (1993). Personal goals and subjective well-being: A longitudinal study. *Journal of Personality and Social Psychology, 65,* 1061–1070.

Brunstein, J. C., Schultheiss, O. C., & Grässmann, R. (1998). Personal goals and emotional well-being: The moderating role of motive dispositions. *Journal of Personality and Social Psychology, 75,* 494–508.

Cacioppo, J. T., Gardner, W. L., & Berntson, G. G. (1999). The affect system has parallel and integrative processing components: Form follows function. *Journal of Personality and Social Psychology, 76,* 839–855.

Campos, J. J., Frankel, C. B., & Camras, L. (2004). On the nature of emotion regulation. *Child Development, 75,* 377–394.

Carter, C. S. (1998). Neuroendocrine perspectives on social attachment and love. *Psychoneuroendocrinology, 23,* 779–818.

Carver, C. S. (2003). Pleasure as a sign you can attend to something else: Placing positive feelings within a general model of affect. *Cognition and Emotion, 17,* 241–261.

Carver, C. S. (2004). Negative affects deriving from the behavioral approach system. *Emotion, 4,* 3–22.

Carver, C. S. (in press). Threat sensitivity, incentive sensitivity, and the experience of relief. *Journal of Personality.*

Carver, C. S., Lawrence, J. W., & Scheier, M. F. (1999). Self-discrepancies and affect: Incorporating the role of feared selves. *Personality and Social Psychology Bulletin, 25,* 783–792.

Carver, C. S., & Scheier, M. F. (1990). Origins and functions of positive and negative affect: A control-process view. *Psychological Review, 97,* 19–35.

Carver, C. S., & Scheier, M. F. (1998). *On the self-regulation of behavior.* New York: Cambridge University Press.

Carver, C. S., & Scheier, M. F. (1999). Themes and issues in the self-egulation of behavior. In R. S. Wyer, Jr. (Ed), *Advances in social cognition* (Vol. 12). Mahwah, NJ: Erlbaum.

Carver, C. S., Sutton, S. K., & Scheier, M. F. (2000). Action, emotion, and personality: Emerging conceptual integration. *Personality and Social Psychology Bulletin, 26,* 741–751.

Carver, C. S., & White, T. L. (1994). Behavioral inhibition, behavioral activation, and affective responses to impending reward and punishment: The BIS/BAS scales. *Journal of Personality and Social Psychology, 67,* 319–333.

Clark, R. N. (1996). *Control system dynamics.* New York: Cambridge University Press.

Cloninger, C. R. (1987). A systematic method of clinical description and classification of personality variants: A proposal. *Archives of General Psychiatry, 44,* 573–588.

Davidson, R. J. (1984). Affect, cognition, and hemispheric specialization. In C. E. Izard, J. Kagan, & R. Zajonc (Eds.), *Emotion, cognition, and behavior* (pp. 320–365). New York: Cambridge University Press.

Davidson, R. J. (1988). EEG measures of cerebral asymmetry: Conceptual and methodological issues. *International Journal of Neuroscience, 39,* 71–89.

Davidson, R. J. (1995). Cerebral asymmetry, emotion, and affective style. In R. J. Davidson & K. Hugdahl (Eds.), *Brain asymmetry* (pp. 361–387). Cambridge, MA: MIT Press.

Davidson, R. J. (1998). Affective style and affective disorders: Perspectives from affective neuroscience. *Cognition and Emotion, 12,* 307–330.

Depue, R. A., & Collins, P. F. (1999). Neurobiology of the structure of personality: Dopamine, facilitation of incentive motivation, and extraversion. *Behavioral and Brain Sciences, 22,* 491–517.

Depue, R. A., & Iacono, W. G. (1989). Neurobehavioral aspects of affective disorders. *Annual Review of Psychology, 40,* 457–492.

Depue, R. A., Krauss, S. P., & Spoont, M. R. (1987). A two-dimensional threshold model of seasonal bipolar affective disorder. In D. Magnusson & A. Öhman (Eds.), *Psychopathology: An interactional perspective* (pp. 95–123). Orlando, FL: Academic Press.

Depue, R. A., & Morrone-Strupinksy, J. V. (2005). A neurobehavioral model of affiliative bonding: Implications for conceptualizing a human trait of affiliation. *Behavioral and Brain Sciences, 28,* 313–395.

Elliot, A. J. (2006). The hierarchical model of approach–avoidance motivation. *Motivation and Emotion, 30,* 111–116.

Elliot, A. J., & Church, M. A. (1997). A hierarchical model of approach and avoidance achievement motivation. *Journal of Personality and Social Psychology, 72,* 218–232.

Elliot, A. J., & Sheldon, K. M. (1997). Avoidance achievement motivation: A personal goals analysis. *Journal of Personality and Social Psychology, 73,* 171–185.

Elliot, A. J., Gable, S. L., & Mapes, R. R. (2006). Approach and avoidance motivation in the social domain. *Personality and Social Psychology Bulletin, 32,* 378–391.

Elliot, A. J., & Thrash, T. M. (2002). Approach–avoidance motivation in personality: Approach and avoidance temperaments and goals. *Journal of Personality and Social Psychology, 82,* 804–818.

Fincham, F. D., & Beach, S. R. H. (1999). Conflict in marriage: Implications for working with couples. *Annual Review of Psychology, 50,* 47–77.

Fitzsimons, G. M., & Bargh, J. A. (2003). Thinking of you: Nonconscious pursuit of interpersonal goals associated with relationship partners. *Journal of Personality and Social Psychology, 84,* 148–163.

Fowles, D. C. (1980). The three arousal model: Implications of Gray's two-factor learning theory for heart rate, electrodermal activity, and psychopathy. *Psychophysiology, 17,* 87–104.

Fowles, D. C. (1993). Biological variables in psychopathology: A psychobiological perspective. In P. A. Sutker & H. E. Adams (Eds.), *Comprehensive handbook of psychopathology* (2nd ed., pp. 57–82). New York: Plenum Press.

Frijda, N. H. (1986). *The emotions.* Cambridge, UK: Cambridge University Press.

Frijda, N. H. (1988). The laws of emotion. *American Psychologist, 43,* 349–358.

Frijda, N. H. (1994). Emotions are functional, most of the time. In P. Ekman & R. J. Davidson (Eds.), *The nature of emotion: Fundamental questions* (pp. 112–126). New York: Oxford University Press.

Gable, S. L. (2006). Approach and avoidance social motives and goals. *Journal of Personality, 74,* 175–222.

Gray, J. A. (1981). A critique of Eysenck's theory of personality. In H. J. Eysenck (Ed.), *A model for personality* (pp. 246–276). Berlin: Springer-Verlag.

Gray, J. A. (1987). Perspectives on anxiety and impulsivity: A commentary. *Journal of Research in Personality, 21,* 493–509.

Gray, J. A. (1990). Brain systems that mediate both emotion and cognition. *Cognition and Emotion, 4,* 269–288.

Gray, J. A. (1994a). Personality dimensions and emotion systems. In P. Ekman & R. J. Davidson (Eds.), *The nature of emotion: Fundamental questions* (pp. 329–331). New York: Oxford University Press.

Gray, J. A. (1994b). Three fundamental emotion systems. In P. Ekman & R. J. Davidson (Eds.), *The nature of emotion: Fundamental questions* (pp. 243–247). New York: Oxford University Press.

Guerrero, L. K., & Andersen, P. A. (2000). Emotion in close relationships. In C. Hendrick & S. Hendrick (Eds.), *Close relationships: A source book* (pp. 171–183). Thousand Oaks, CA: Sage Publications.

Higgins, E. T. (1996). Ideals, oughts, and regulatory focus: Affect and motivation from distinct pains and pleasures. In P. M. Gollwitzer & J. A. Bargh (Eds.), *The psychology of action: Linking cognition and motivation to behavior* (pp. 91–114). New York: Guilford Press.

Higgins, E. T. (1997). Beyond pleasure and pain. *American Psychologist, 52,* 1280–1300.

Higgins, E. T., & Tykocinski, O. (1992). Self-discrepancies and biographical memory: Personality and cognition at the level of psychological situation. *Personality and Social Psychology Bulletin, 18,* 527–535.

Hsee, C. K., & Abelson, R. P. (1991). The relative weighting of position and velocity in satisfaction. *Psychological Science, 2,* 263–266.

Johnson, S. L., & Carver, C. S. (2006). Extreme goal setting and vulnerability to mania among undiagnosed young adults. *Cognitive Therapy and Research, 30,* 377–395.

Johnson, S. L., Turner, R. J., & Iwata, N. (2003). BIS/BAS levels and psychiatric disorder: An epidemiological study. *Journal of Psychopathology and Behavioral Assessment, 25,* 25–36.

Karney, B. R., & Bradbury, T. N. (1997). Neuroticism, marital interaction, and the trajectory of marital satisfaction. *Journal of Personality and Social Psychology, 72,* 1075–1092.

Karney, B. R. & Frye, N. E. (2002). "But we've been getting better lately": Comparing prospective and retrospective views of relationship development. *Journal of Personality and Social Psychology, 82,* 222–238.

Kleinman, B. M., Kaczynski, K. J., Laurenceau, J- P., & Carver, C. S. (2007). Assessment of relationship-specific approach and avoidance sensitivities: The RAp/RAv scales. Manuscript under review.

Konorski, J. (1948). *Conditioned reflexes and neuron organization.* Cambridge, UK: Cambridge University Press.

Lang, P. J., Bradley, M. M., & Cuthbert, B. N. (1998). Emotion, motivation, and anxiety: Brain mechanisms and psychophysiology. *Biological Psychiatry, 44,* 1248–1263.

Laurenceau, J- P., Barrett, L. F., & Pietromonaco, P. R. (1998). Intimacy as an interpersonal process: The importance of self-disclosure, and perceived partner responsiveness in interpersonal exchanges. *Journal of Personality and Social Psychology, 74,* 1238–1251.

Laurenceau, J- P., Barrett, L. F., & Rovine, M. J. (2005). The interpersonal process model of intimacy in marriage: A daily-diary and multilevel modeling approach. *Journal of Family Psychology, 19,* 314–323.

Laurenceau, J- P., Rivera, L. M., Schaffer, A. R., & Pietromonaco, P. R. (2004). Intimacy as an interpersonal process: Current status and future directions. In D. J. Mashek & A. Aron (Eds.), *Handbook of closeness and intimacy* (pp. 61–78). Mahwah, NJ: Lawrence Erlbaum Associates.

Laurenceau, J- P., Troy, A. B., & Carver, C. S. (2005). Two distinct emotional experiences in romantic relationships: Effects of perceptions regarding approach of intimacy and avoidance of conflict. *Personality and Social Psychology Bulletin, 31,* 1123–1133.

Lawrence, J. W., Carver, C. S., & Scheier, M. F. (2002). Velocity toward goal attainment in immediate experience as a determinant of affect. *Journal of Applied Social Psychology, 32,* 788–802.

MacKay, D. M. (1966). Cerebral organization and the conscious control of action. In J. C. Eccles (Ed.), *Brain and conscious experience.* Berlin: Springer-Verlag.

Markus, H., & Nurius, P. (1986). Possible selves. *American Psychologist, 41,* 954–969.

Meyer, B., Johnson, S. L., & Carver, C. S. (1999). Exploring behavioral activation and inhibition sensitivities among college students at risk for bipolar spectrum symptomatology. *Journal of Psychopathology and Behavioral Assessment, 21,* 275–292.

Meyer, B., Johnson, S. L., & Winters, R. (2001). Responsiveness to threat and incentive in bipolar disorder: Relations of the BIS/BAS scales with symptoms. *Journal of Psychopathology and Behavioral Assessment, 23,* 133–143.

Miller, N. E. (1944). Experimental studies of conflict. In J. McV. Hunt (Ed.), *Personality and the behavior disorders* (Vol. 1, pp. 431–465). New York: Ronald Press.

Miller, N. E., & Dollard, J. (1941). *Social learning and imitation*. New Haven, CT: Yale University Press.

Ogilvie, D. M. (1987). The undesired self: A neglected variable in personality research. *Journal of Personality and Social Psychology, 52,* 379–385.

Ortony, A., Clore, G. L., & Collins, A. (1988). *The cognitive structure of emotions*. New York: Cambridge University Press.

Panksepp, J. (1998). *Affective neuroscience: The foundations of human and animal emotions*. New York: Oxford University Press.

Peplau, L., & Gordon, S. (1985). Women and men in love: Gender differences in close heterosexual relationships. In V. O'Leary, R. Unger, & B. Wallston (Eds.), *Women, gender, and social psychology* (pp. 257–292). Hillsdale, NJ: Lawrence Erlbaum Associates.

Powers, W. T. (1973). *Behavior: The control of perception*. Chicago: Aldine.

Reis, H. T. (1990). The role of intimacy in interpersonal relations. *Journal of Social and Clinical Psychology, 9,* 15–30.

Reis, H., Senchak, M., & Solomon, B. (1985). Sex differences in the intimacy of social interaction: Further examination of potential explanations. *Journal of Personality and Social Psychology, 48,* 1204–1217.

Reis, H., & Shaver, P. (1988). Intimacy as an interpersonal process. In S. W. Duck (Ed.), *Handbook of personal relationships: Theory, research, and intervention* (pp. 367–389). Chichester, UK: John Wiley & Sons, Ltd.

Roseman, I. J. (1984). Cognitive determinants of emotions: A structural theory. In P. Shaver (Ed.), *Review of personality and social psychology* (Vol. 5, pp. 11–36). Beverly Hills, CA: Sage Publications.

Russell, J. A., & Carroll, J. M. (1999). On the bipolarity of positive and negative affect. *Psychological Bulletin, 125,* 3–30.

Ryan, R. M., & Deci, E. L. (1999). Approaching and avoiding self-determination: Comparing cybernetic and organismic paradigms of motivation. In R. S. Wyer, Jr. (Ed.), *Advances in social cognition* (Vol. 12, pp. 193–215). Mahwah, NJ: Erlbaum.

Ryan, R. M., & Deci, E. L. (2000). Self-determination theory and the facilitation of intrinsic motivation, social development, and well-being. *American Psychologist, 55,* 68–78.

Schneirla, T. C. (1959). An evolutionary and developmental theory of biphasic processes underlying approach and withdrawal. In M. R. Jones (Ed.), *Nebraska symposium on motivation* (Vol.7, pp. 1–42). Lincoln: University of Nebraska Press.

Simpson, J. A., Oriña, M. M., & Ickes, W. (2003). When accuracy hurts, and when it helps: A test of the empathic accuracy model in marital interactions. *Journal of Personality and Social Psychology, 85,* 881–893.

Underwood, B. J. (1975). Individual differences as a crucible in theory construction. *American Psychologist, 30,* 128–134.

Watson, D., & Tellegen, A. (1985). Toward a consensual structure of mood. *Psychological Bulletin, 98,* 219–235.

Watson, D., Wiese, D., Vaidya, J., & Tellegen, A. (1999). The two general activation systems of affect: Structural findings, evolutionary considerations, and psychobiological evidence. *Journal of Personality and Social Psychology, 76,* 820–838.

Young, L. J., & Wang, Z. (2004). The neurobiology of pair bonding. *Nature Neuroscience, 7,* 1048–1054.

Zelenski, J. M., & Larsen, R. J. (1999). Susceptibility to affect: A comparison of three personality taxonomies. *Journal of Personality, 67,* 761–791.

Zuckerman, M. (2005). *Psychobiology of personality* (2nd ed.). New York: Cambridge University Press.

Anger

23 Anger and Approach–Avoidance Motivation

Eddie Harmon-Jones, Carly Peterson, Philip A. Gable,
and Cindy Harmon-Jones

CONTENTS

"Anger is a great force. If you control it, it can be transmuted into a power which can move the whole world."—William Shenstone (Scottish Writer, 1714–1763)

"Anger and jealousy can no more bear to lose sight of their objects than love."—George Eliot (English Writer, 1819–1880)

Contemporary theories of motivation and emotion assume that positive emotions are associated with approach motivation and that negative emotions are associated with withdrawal motivation. For instance, Watson and colleagues wrote, "…accumulating evidence suggests that the self-report NA [*negative affect*] dimension represents the subjective component of the withdrawal-oriented BIS… In contrast, variations in self-rated PA [*positive affect*] reflect the operation of the BFS [*behavioral facilitation system*]" (italicized information added; Watson, Wiese, Vaidya, & Tellegen, 1999, p. 830). These and similar theories (Lang, 1995) have been very influential in contemporary psychology and have led to important advances in understanding basic processes involved in emotion and motivation, the physiological and neural underpinnings of emotion and motivation, and disorders of emotion and motivation. At the same time, the assumption that positive emotions are always associated with approach motivation and that negative emotions are always associated with withdrawal motivation can be misleading.

For the emotions of fear and disgust, the assumption that these negative affects are exclusively associated with avoidance motivation is tenable. Both fear and disgust impel the organism to flee from the source of the threat. In contrast, anger violates the association of negative affect and avoidance motivation. Instead of motivating avoidance, anger often motivates approach, causing the organism to go toward the threat. Less research has been conducted on anger than on other negative affects by scientists who study emotion. However, past research by scientists who study aggression and other behavioral phenomena has suggested that anger may be associated with approach rather than avoidance motivation. In this chapter, we will review the evidence on the motivational functions of anger.

ANGER AS AN EMOTION

Emotions can be considered processes that involve involuntary action readiness (Frijda, 1986). Basic emotions, such as anger, provide organisms with relatively complex and biologically prepared behavioral potentials that assist in coping with major challenges to their welfare (Panksepp, 1998). However, for organisms with larger, more complex brains, these inherited behavioral potentials only suggest ways of behaving. Emotions can be regulated and thus may not directly affect behavior. Thus, while humans may possess the same emotional instincts as lower animals, we are not as controlled by the dictates of emotions and thus we have more choices (Panksepp, 1994).

An emotion is not a "thing" but is best considered a complex process that is made up of basic processes such as feelings of pleasure or displeasure, facial expression components, particular appraisals, and particular action plans and activation states (Frijda, 1993). Anger is a relatively unpleasant feeling, and is described using words like annoyed, angry, and enraged, which in our view, express differences in intensity (cf., Lewis [1993]; however, suggested that rage and anger are qualitatively different). When left uncontrolled or uninhibited, its facial expression involves the muscles of the brow moving inward and downward, thus "creating a frown and a foreboding appearance around the eyes, which seem to be fixed in a hard stare toward the object of anger. The nostrils dilate and the wings of the nose flare out. The lips are opened and drawn back in a rectangle-like shape, revealing clenched teeth. Often the face flushes red" (Izard, 1977, p. 330). Because humans are taught to control anger and its expression, the expressions of anger vary considerably from one person to another.

In this chapter, we will review recent research and theoretical advances in the study of basic processes involved in anger. We will focus our review on the causes of anger, its subjective feeling and motivational components, and some of its neural components. In doing so, we will consider all of the component processes typically involved in anger—its feelings, appraisals (under causes), action plans and activation states (under motivation), and physiology. However, we will not review the literature on angry facial expressions, as it is beyond the scope of this chapter (for a review, see Russell & Fernández-Dols, 1997).

CAUSES OF ANGER

Anger is often thought to result from physical or psychological restraint or from interference with goal-directed activity (Darwin, 1872; Izard, 1977; Lewis, 1993). This action-oriented approach to understanding the cause of anger is consistent with postulations advanced by other major theoretical perspectives.

REINFORCEMENT APPROACHES

Neo-behaviorists suggested that the actual or signaled arrival or termination of pleasant or unpleasant events (positive or negative reinforcers) was the primary cause of emotions (Mowrer, 1960). Gray (1987) extended these ideas by including stimulus omissions and interactions with individuals' resources, such as ability to deal with events (see also, Rolls, 1999). According to these models, angry emotions (like frustration, anger, and rage) occur as a result of the omission of a positive reinforcer or the termination of a positive reinforcer. Along these lines, Lewis (1993) proposed that the thwarting of a goal-directed action is an unlearned cause of anger. In one experiment, after 2- to 8-month-old infants were conditioned to move one of their arms in order to see a picture of another baby's smiling face, the infants were exposed to an extinction phase in which the arm movement no longer revealed the happy picture. This "frustrating" event caused the majority of the infants to exhibit anger-like facial expressions (Lewis, Alessandri, Sullivan, 1990).

Similarly, in considering the causes of anger, Berkowitz (1989) extended the original frustration-aggression model (Dollard, Doob, Miller, Mowrer, & Sears, 1939) with a cognitive neo-associative model of anger and aggression. According to this model, any unpleasant situation, including pain, discomfort, frustration, or social stress, provokes negative affect. This negative affect is associated with fight and flight motivation. The individual's prior experiences have formed associations that provide cues relating to the present situation. If these cues lead him or her to desire primarily to escape, then the flight system is activated and the person experiences mostly fear. If the cues lead him or her to desire to attack, then the fight system is activated and he or she experiences mostly anger.

COGNITIVE APPRAISAL APPROACHES

The other main theoretical approach aimed at understanding the causes of anger is the cognitive approach taken by appraisal theorists. These theorists propose that emotions are caused by an individual's appraisal of a situation. All appraisal theorists agree that anger is evoked in negatively appraised situations. However, negatively appraised situations are associated with all of the emotions considered to be negative, including fear, sadness, and anger. Therefore, appraisal theorists have sought the necessary conditions required in order to cause anger, rather than a different negative emotion, to be evoked.

Anger-evoking situations are often described as situations where the individual's goals are blocked. To clarify what is meant by "goals," some theorists state that the instigating circumstance must be evaluated as personally significant in some way, so that it has goal relevance, if there is to be an angry reaction (Lazarus, 1991). Goals are defined very broadly by some researchers, including not only consciously sought goals, but also basic needs.

One condition that has been proposed as necessary for anger to occur is an appraisal of "*other-blame*," that is, an assessment by the individual that someone or something has wrongly caused the negative situation to occur (Lazarus, 1991; Ortony, Clore, & Collins, 1988). Another condition proposed to cause anger is an appraisal that the negative event was wrong, unfair, or improper (Shaver, Schwartz, Kirson, & O'Connor, 1987; Frijda, Kuipers, & ter Schure, 1989; Roseman, 1991). Lazarus proposed that, in order for anger to occur, the individual must perceive a threat against self-esteem (Lazarus, 1991). Another characteristic that appraisal theorists have proposed as necessary for anger is an appraisal of *high coping potential* in the negative situation. By this, they mean that individuals become angry when they believe that they have a high likelihood of being able to rectify the negative situation and to prevent the undesired consequences (Lazarus, 1991; Stein & Levine, 1989). In negative situations where the individual appraises low coping potential, by contrast, these theorists propose that sadness, fear, or anxiety are experienced instead of anger.

The idea that anger results from an appraisal that the situation is (a) negative, (b) threatens self-esteem, (c) is caused by others, and (d) is one that we expect to be able to rectify has intuitive appeal. That is, many of us can easily recall instances where we experienced anger and it seemed that the anger resulted from such appraisals. However, our intuitions may be wrong. Indeed, the appraisal literature has been criticized for failing to provide evidence as to whether appraisals cause emotion or whether emotion motivates the individual to make appraisals. Frijda (1993; Frijda & Zeelenberg, 2001) and Parkinson and Manstead (1992) have noted that, because of the verbal-report methods employed in most investigations in this area, it is unclear whether the identified appraisal characteristics preceded or followed the arousal of the emotional experience. "Nothing in the data resists the interpretation that the relevant appraisals were consequences rather than precedents of the emotional reactions" (Parkinson & Manstead, 1992, p. 129).

Other scientists have questioned the necessity of specific appraisals for anger (Berkowitz & Harmon-Jones, 2004). For example, Berkowitz and Harmon-Jones have argued that once the fight system and anger are activated, the person begins to make appraisals and to do other cognitive processing of the situation, in order to determine who or what to attack, and how or whether to follow through behaviorally with these impulses. This conception differs from the appraisal models in that it proposes that an appraisal of the provoking situation is not necessary in order to produce emotion. According to Berkowitz and Harmon-Jones, appraisals are involved in the experience of anger, but come later in the process, and occur with anger, or are provoked by anger, rather than causing anger. (However, as appraisals occur, they may enhance or alter the emotion process.) Berkowitz's cognitive neo-associative model better accounts for all of the data, including atypical anger occurrences that do not fit well into models that assume the necessity of self-relevance, goals, and blameworthy behavior by another person. Moreover, appraisal theorists' definitions of "goals," "cognitions," and "appraisals" are sometimes so overly broad that they are untestable (for example, the "goal" of not experiencing discomfort).

Regarding the necessity of the appraisal of "other-blame," it has been suggested that, while other-blame does often occur along with anger, that it is the emotion of anger that motivates the individual to seek someone or something to blame for the negative situation. Fridja (1993) reports a number of instances where angry persons blamed, and even aggressed against, inanimate objects in a way that many would characterize as irrational, lending support to the idea that blaming is motivated by anger rather than the other way around.

Lazarus' claim that self-esteem threats are necessary for anger elicitation has also been questioned. While self-esteem threats may be common in anger-evoking situations, studies have shown that persons sometimes report experiencing anger in response to the frustration of transient goals that do not have high personal relevance. Moreover, it is not likely that the 2-month-old infants in Lewis and colleagues' experiments (1990) were concerned about self-esteem.

Finally, the claim that high coping potential is necessary for the experience of anger has recently been challenged by an experiment in which coping potential was manipulated and found to affect cortical activation (see below) but not the subjective experience of anger (Harmon-Jones, Sigelman, Bohlig, & Harmon-Jones, 2003).

MOTIVATIONAL COMPONENTS OF ANGER: SUBJECTIVE AND BEHAVIORAL EVIDENCE

Theorists have suggested that anger is an emotion that evokes behavioral tendencies of approach (Darwin, 1872; Ekman & Friesen, 1975; Plutchik, 1980; Young, 1943). Of course, emotions are complex phenomena and both approach and withdrawal tendencies can be elicited in a given situation. However, we believe that the dominant behavioral tendency associated with anger is approach.

In the animal behavior literature, a distinction has been made between offensive or irritable aggression and defensive aggression (Moyer, 1976). It has been posited that irritable aggression results from anger and that pure irritable aggression "involves attack without attempts to escape from the object being attacked" (Moyer, 1976, p. 187). A number of aggression researchers have suggested that offensive aggression is associated with anger, attack, and no attempts to escape, whereas defensive aggression is associated with fear, attempts to escape, and attack only if escape is impossible (Blanchard & Blanchard, 1984; Lagerspetz, 1969; Moyer, 1976). In demonstrating that organisms evidence offensive aggression and that this is an approach behavior, Lagerspetz (1969) found that under certain conditions mice would cross an electrified grid to attack another mouse.

Other research has demonstrat that damage to the amygdala, a brain region involved in defensive behavior, has no effect on offensive aggression but reduces reactivity to nonpainful threat stimuli (Blanchard & Takahashi, 1988; Busch & Barfield, 1974). Further evidence supporting the conceptualization of anger as involved in offensive aggression comes from research on testosterone, which has been found to be associated with anger and aggression in humans (Olweus, 1986). In this research, testosterone treatments have been found to decrease defensive (fear) responses in a number of species (Boissy & Bouissou, 1994; Vandenheede & Bouissou, 1993). Taken together, these diverse lines of research suggest that

offensive aggression is associated with different neural systems, hormones, and behaviors than defensive aggression. Moreover, these offensive aggressive behaviors are likely associated with anger (Blanchard & Blanchard, 1984; Moyer, 1976).

In research with humans, anger has been found to be associated with attack (Berkowitz, 1993). Moreover, Depue and Iacono (1989) have suggested that irritable aggression is part of the behavioral facilitation system, a biobehavioral system similar to the behavioral approach system (BAS) (Gray, 1987). Whether anger results in a general tendency to approach as compared to a specific tendency to aggress is currently a topic of debate with some suggesting the former (Lewis, 1993) and some the latter (Berkowitz, 1999; Berkowitz, 2000).

In support of the idea of anger evoking approach motivation, (Lewis et al. 1990; Lewis, Sullivan, Ramsey, & Alessandri, 1992) conditioned infants to pull a string to receive a reward. They found that infants who displayed anger when the reward was withdrawn demonstrated the highest levels of joy, interest, and required arm pull when the learning portion of the task was reinstated. Thus, subsequent to frustrating events, anger may maintain and increase task engagement and approach motivation.

In other research, Baron (1977) demonstrated that angry individuals are reinforced positively by signs of their tormentor's pain. Participants who had been deliberately provoked by another individual had an opportunity to assault him in return. Indications that their first attacks were hurting their target led to increased aggression for previously provoked participants, but to reduced aggression for unprovoked participants. The initial signs of their victim's suffering showed the angry persons they were approaching their aggressive goal and thus evoked even stronger assaults from them.

Additional support for the idea that anger is associated with approach motivation comes from research testing the conceptual model that integrated reactance theory with learned helplessness theory (Wortman & Brehm, 1975). According to this model, how individuals respond to uncontrollable outcomes depends on their expectation of being able to control the outcome and the importance of the outcome. When an individual expects to be able to control outcomes that are important, and those outcomes are found to be uncontrollable, psychological reactance should be aroused. Thus, for individuals who initially expect control, the first few bouts of uncontrollable outcomes should arouse reactance, a motivational state aimed at restoring control. After several exposures to uncontrollable outcomes, these individuals should become convinced that they cannot control the outcomes and should show decreased motivation (i.e., learned helplessness). In other words, reactance will precede helplessness for individuals who initially expect control. In one study testing this model, individuals who exhibited angry feelings in response to one unsolvable problem had better performance and were presumably more approach motivated on a subsequent cognitive task than did participants who exhibited less anger (Mikulincer, 1988).

Other research has revealed that state anger relates to high levels of self-assurance, physical strength, and bravery (Izard, 1991), inclinations associated with approach motivation. In addition, trait anger has been found to relate to high levels of assertiveness and competitiveness (Buss & Perry, 1992). Lerner and Keltner (2001) found that anger (both trait and state) is associated with optimistic expectations, whereas fear is associated with pessimistic expectations. Moreover, happiness was associated with optimism, making anger and happiness appear more similar to each other in their relationship with optimism than fear and anger. Although Lerner and Keltner (2001) interpreted their findings as being due to the appraisals associated with anger, it seems equally plausible that it was the approach motivational character of anger that caused the relationship of anger and optimism. That is, anger creates optimism because anger engages the approach motivational system and produces greater optimistic expectations.

Other evidence supporting the idea that anger is associated with an approach-orientation comes from research on bipolar disorder. The emotions of euphoria and anger often occur during manic phases of bipolar disorder (Cassidy, Forest, Murry, & Carroll, 1998; Depue & Iacono, 1989; Tyrer & Shopsin, 1982). Both euphoria and anger may be approach-oriented processes, and a dysregulated or hyperactive approach system may underlie mania (Depue & Iacono, 1989; Fowles, 1993). Furthermore, lithium carbonate, a treatment for bipolar disorder, reduces aggression (Malone, Delaney, Luebbert, Cater, & Campbell, 2000), suggesting that anger and aggression correlate with the other symptoms of bipolar disorder.

Other individual different studies support the hypothesis that trait anger is related to trait approach motivation, or more specifically, trait BAS. BAS is a concept from Gray's motivation theory, which posits that a BAS and behavioral inhibition system (BIS) motivate and guide behavior. In theory, the BAS is a motivational system that is sensitive to signals of conditioned reward, nonpunishment, and escape from punishment. Its activation causes movement toward goals. The BIS is hypothesized to be sensitive to signals of conditioned punishment, nonreward, novelty, and innate fear stimuli. The BIS inhibits behavior, increases arousal, prepares for vigorous action, and increases attention toward aversive stimuli. Carver and White's (1994) BIS/BAS questionnaire assesses individual differences in BIS and BAS sensitivity. Sample items from the BIS scale include: "I worry about making mistakes" and "I have very few fears compared to my friends (reverse scored)." Sample items from the BAS include: "It would excite me to win a contest," "I go out of my way to get things I want," and "I crave excitement and new sensations." In two studies, Harmon-Jones (2003) showed that trait BAS was positively related to trait anger, as assessed by the Buss and Perry (1992) aggression questionnaire, at the simple correlation level. Smits and Kuppens (2005) have replicated the relationship between BAS and trait anger. They also found that measures of the anger-coping styles of anger-out versus anger-in relate to BAS and BIS. That is, anger-out, or the tendency to express one's anger outwardly, related directly with BAS and inversely with BIS. In contrast, anger-in, or the tendency to turn one's anger inward, related directly with BIS and inversely with BAS.

Other research has extended this work by showing that trait levels of BAS sensitivity relate to self-reported anger responses to laboratory manipulations of anger. For instance, Carver (2004) found that trait BAS predicts state anger in response to situational anger manipulations. Putman, Hermans, and van Honk (2004) found that trait BAS predicts attentional vigilance to angry faces presented below conscious thresholds, suggesting that individuals with stronger approach motivational sensitivities selectively attend to angry faces as in a dominance confrontation.

Additional support for anger's association with approach motivation comes from two experiments that examined the speed with which movement of angry and fearful faces toward or away from the direction of gaze is accurately detected (Adams, Ambady, Macrae, & Kleck, 2006). In one experiment, faces displaying anger or fear were presented in the center of a computer monitor. The gaze of the forward facing target was manipulated so that it appeared that the individual was looking to the left or the right. After 1000 ms, the faces shifted to the right or the left, and the participants were instructed to make a right or left mouse click in the same direction the face appeared to move. In other words, it appeared as if the faces were either approaching (moving toward their gaze fixation) or withdrawing (moving away from their gaze fixation). Reaction time results revealed that participants were quicker to detect angry faces moving in the direction of their gaze than any other facial display/movement direction combinations.

These results suggest that that an approach behavioral intent is conveyed by facial expressions of anger.

MOTIVATIONAL COMPONENTS OF ANGER: ASYMMETRICAL FRONTAL CORTICAL ACTIVITY

The above evidence using self-report and behavioral measures suggests that anger is often associated with approach rather than avoidance or withdrawal motivation. Guided by this past work, we have examined anger as a way to better understand the psychological and behavioral functions of asymmetrical frontal cortical activity. Over three decades of research has suggested that the left and right frontal cortical regions are asymmetrically involved in emotional and motivational processes. During this period, some scientists suggested that the left frontal cortical region is involved in the expression and experience of positive affect, whereas the right frontal cortical region is involved in the expression and experience of negative affect.

Some of the earliest research suggestive of the idea that the left and right frontal cortices were involved in different emotional or motivational processes was provided by work with individuals who had suffered damage to the left or right frontal cortical region. In this research, it was found that individuals who suffered damage to the right frontal cortex were more likely to evidence mania, whereas individuals who suffered damage to the left frontal cortex were more likely to evidence depression (see review by Robinson & Downhill, 1995). This research is consistent with the view that mania may be associated with increased left frontal activity and increased approach tendencies, because the approach motivation functions of the left frontal cortex are released and not restrained by the withdrawal system in the right frontal cortex.

BASELINE EEG AND INDIVIDUAL DIFFERENCES

A number of additional studies have examined the relationship between asymmetrical frontal cortical activity recorded during resting baseline with other measures of trait affect and motivation. This research is based on the idea that baseline asymmetrical frontal cortical activity reflects a trait (Tomarken, Davidson, Wheeler, & Kinney, 1992). Depression has been found to relate to resting frontal asymmetrical activity, with depressed individuals showing relatively less left than right frontal brain activity (Henriques & Davidson, 1990; Jacobs & Snyder,

1996). Other research has revealed that trait positive affect is associated with greater left than right frontal brain activity, whereas trait negative affect is associated with greater right than left frontal brain activity (Tomarken, Davidson, Wheeler, & Doss, 1992). In this past research, trait positive and negative affect were assessed using the Positive and Negative Affect Schedule (Watson, Clark, & Tellegen, 1988). Watson et al. have recently stated that they consider this scale a measure of activated positive affect and activated negative affect (Watson et al., 1999), because the items on the scales assess activated or aroused positive and negative affects (e.g., active, interested, afraid, distressed) not ones lower in arousal (e.g., happy, sad).

Other research has found that trait BAS relates to greater left than right frontal brain activity (Coan & Allen, 2003; Harmon-Jones & Allen, 1997; Sutton & Davidson, 1997). In this research, BAS was measured by Carver and White's (1994) BIS/BAS questionnaire.

Studies have produced inconsistent results regarding the relationship of behavioral inhibition sensitivity (BIS; "I worry about making mistakes.") and frontal brain asymmetry. One study found a significant relationship between BIS and greater right than left frontal activity (Sutton & Davidson, 1997), while two others found a nonsignificant relationship (Coan & Allen, 2003; Harmon-Jones & Allen, 1997). While researchers have hypothesized that right frontal brain activity increases during withdrawal, BIS may not be equivalent to withdrawal motivation (Harmon-Jones & Allen, 1997). It is also possible that BIS taps withdrawal oriented attentional processes rather than withdrawal oriented action processes (Peterson, Gable, & Harmon-Jones, in press). This possibility is consistent with Gray's (1987) original conception of BIS as a "stop, look, and listen" system.

BASELINE EEG AND RESPONSES TO EMOTION-ELICITING STIMULI

Resting baseline frontal asymmetrical activity also predicts emotional responses to emotion-eliciting stimuli. Individuals with relatively greater right than left frontal activity exhibit larger negative affective responses to negative emotion-inducing films (fear and disgust) and smaller positive affective responses to positive emotion-inducing films (happiness) (Tomarken, Davidson, & Henriques, 1990; Wheeler, Davidson, & Tomarken, 1993). In a related vein, research has found that resting baseline frontal asymmetrical activity predicts evaluative responses to novel stimuli that have been repeatedly exposed to participants (Harmon-Jones & Allen, 2001). According to theory, exposing individuals to novel stimuli without reward or punishment (mere exposure) signals safety. Individuals with greater relative right frontal activity reported more favorable attitudes toward familiarized stimuli than did individuals with relative left frontal activity. Other research has found that relative right frontal activity at baseline predicts crying in response to maternal separation in 10-month-old infants (Davidson & Fox, 1989).

Although these effects are based on correlational evidence and hence subject to alternative explanations, one experiment has more strongly suggested that frontal asymmetry is causally involved in the production of these emotional responses. In this experiment, neurofeedback training was used to manipulate asymmetrical frontal cortical activity (Allen, Harmon-Jones, & Cavender, 2001). Participants were randomly assigned to receive neurofeedback training designed to increase right frontal relative to left frontal activity or to receive training in the opposite direction. Systematic alterations of frontal asymmetry were observed as a function of neurofeedback training. Moreover, subsequent self-reported affect in response to emotionally evocative film clips was significantly influenced by the direction of neurofeedback training. Individuals trained to increase left frontal activity reported more positive affect in response to the happy film clip than individuals trained to increase right frontal activity.

EEG Activity During Emotional Situations

Research has also demonstrated that asymmetrical frontal brain activity is associated with state emotional responses. For instance, 10-month-old infants exhibited increased left frontal activation in response to a film clip of an actress generating a happy facial expression as compared to an actress generating a sad facial expression (Davidson & Fox, 1982). Newborn infants (2–3 days old) evidenced greater relative left-sided activation in frontal regions in response to sucrose as compared with water (Fox & Davidson, 1986). Frontal brain activity has been found to relate to facial expressions of positive and negative emotions, as well. For example, Coan, Allen, and Harmon-Jones (2001) found that voluntary contractions of the facial musculature to form a happy facial expression produced relatively greater left frontal activity, while voluntary contractions of the facial musculature to form a fearful facial expression produced relatively less left frontal activity.

EXPLANATIONS OF THE ASYMMETRICAL FRONTAL BRAIN ACTIVITY AND EMOTION RELATIONSHIP

The functions of the left and right frontal cortices of the brain continue to spark ongoing debate in the study of emotion. Various researchers have provided evidence that activity in the left frontal cortex relates to positive emotions, approach motivation, or both, while activity in the right frontal cortex relates to negative emotions, withdrawal motivation, or both (Davidson, 1998, Tomarken & Keener, 1998). Because positivity versus negativity was confounded with approach versus withdrawal in the past work cited above, it was impossible to determine whether the activity in the frontal hemispheres related to the valence of emotion (positive versus negative) or the direction of motivation (approach versus withdrawal).

Because anger is a negatively valenced, approach-motivated emotion, it presents an opportunity to examine the true relationship of asymmetrical frontal activity and emotional valence or motivational direction. In one of the first studies examining this, Harmon-Jones and Allen (1998) found that trait anger related to increased left frontal activity and decreased right frontal activity.

More recently, Harmon-Jones (2004) addressed an alternative explanation for these results. The alternative explanation suggested that persons with high levels of trait anger might experience anger as a positive emotion, and this positive feeling or attitude toward anger could be responsible for anger being associated with relative left frontal activity. After developing a valid and reliable assessment of attitude toward anger, a study was conducted to assess whether resting baseline asymmetrical activity related to trait anger and attitude toward anger. Results indicated that relative left frontal activity related to anger and not attitude toward anger. Moreover, further analyses revealed that the relationship between trait anger and left frontal activity was not due to anger being associated with a positive attitude toward anger.

To address the limitations of the above correlational studies, experiments have been conducted in which anger is manipulated and its effects on regional brain activity are examined. In Harmon-Jones and Sigelman (2001), participants were randomly assigned to a condition in which another person insulted them or to a condition in which another person treated them in a neutral manner. Immediately following the treatment, EEG activity was assessed. As predicted, individuals who were insulted evidenced greater relative left frontal activity than individuals who were not insulted. Additional analyses revealed that within the insult condition, reported anger and aggression were positively correlated with relative left frontal activity. Neither of these correlations was significant in the no-insult condition. These results suggest that relative left-frontal activation was associated with more anger and aggression in the condition in which anger was evoked.

Recent experimental evidence has replicated these results and also revealed that state anger evokes both increased left and decreased right frontal activity. Moreover, a manipulation of sympathy for the person who would later insult the participant revealed that sympathy reduced the effects of insult on left and right frontal activity (Harmon-Jones, Vaughn-Scott, Mohr, Sigelman, & Harmon-Jones, 2004). This research suggests that experiencing sympathy for another individual may reduce aggression toward that individual (see review by Miller & Eisenberg, 1988) by reducing the relative left frontal activity associated with anger.

In the two experiments just described, the designs were tailored in such a way as to evoke anger that was approach oriented. Although most instances of anger involve approach inclinations, not all instances of anger are associated with approach motivation. To manipulate approach motivation independently of anger, Harmon-Jones et al. (2003) performed an experiment in which the ability to cope with the anger-producing event was manipulated. On the basis of the past research that has revealed that coping potential affects motivational intensity (Brehm & Self, 1989), it was predicted that the expectation of being able to take action to resolve the anger-producing event would increase approach motivational intensity relative to expecting to be unable to take action.

Participants were exposed to an anger-eliciting situation. To manipulate coping potential, in one condition participants were led to believe that they could act to change the angering situation, while in the other condition participants were led to believe that there was nothing they could do to change the situation. Both conditions evoked significant increases in anger (over baseline) and the degree of anger did not differ between conditions. Consistent with predictions, participants who expected to engage in the approach-related action evidenced greater left frontal activity than participants who expected to be unable to engage in approach-related action. Moreover, within the action-possible condition, participants who evidenced greater left frontal activity in response to the angering event also evidenced greater self-reported anger, providing support for the idea that anger is often an approach-related emotional response. In the condition where action was not possible, greater left frontal activity did not relate to greater anger. In our view, this is because, although anger usually

leads to approach motivation, when action is not possible, approach motivation remains low, even if angry feelings are high. Finally, within the action-possible condition, participants who evidenced greater left frontal activity in response to the event were more likely to engage in behavior that could change the situation.

This research suggests that the left frontal region is most accurately described as a region sensitive to approach motivational intensity. It was only when anger was associated with an opportunity to resolve the anger-producing event that participants evidenced the increased relative left frontal activation. The increase in left frontal cortical activation during instances of anger where approach-related action is possible has been replicated (Harmon-Jones, Lueck, Fearn, Harmon-Jones, 2006). However, the results of these two experiments should not be taken to indicate that such explicit manipulations of action possibility are always necessary. Manipulations of action possibility may only potentiate the effects of emotion manipulations on asymmetrical frontal cortical activity. Indeed, in a recent study, participants were exposed to anger-inducing pictures (and other pictures) and given no explicit manipulations of action expectancy. Across all participants, a null effect of relative left frontal asymmetry occurred. However, individual differences in trait anger related to relative left frontal activity to the anger-inducing pictures, such that individuals high in trait anger showed greater left frontal activity to anger-producing pictures (controlling for activity to neutral pictures; Harmon-Jones, 2007).

The reviewed research has revealed that the left frontal cortical region is involved in approach-motivated anger. A few studies using brain imaging technologies other than EEG have been conducted. In one, positron emission tomography (PET) was measured while men were exposed to personally created angry or neutral mental imagery scripts (Dougherty et al., 1999). Results revealed that as compared to neutral imagery, anger imagery caused an increase in the left orbital frontal cortex, the right anterior cingulate cortex, the bilateral anterior temporal poles, left precentral gyrus, bilateral medial frontal cortex, and bilateral cerebellum. Thus, the increase in activity in the left orbital frontal cortex is consistent with the anger research results obtained using EEG.

However, Dougherty et al. (1999) interpreted the increase in left orbital frontal cortical activity very differently. They ascribed the increase "to inhibition of aggressive behavior in the face of anger" (p. 471). While this interpretation is consistent with some speculations of the role of the left orbital frontal cortex in response inhibition (Mega, Cummings, Salloway, & Malloy, 1997), it is inconsistent with the EEG results showing that increased left frontal activity is associated with increased aggression and approach behavior (Harmon-Jones & Sigelman, 2001; Harmon-Jones et al., 2003). The interpretation that the left frontal cortical region is involved in the inhibition of anger and aggression is also inconsistent with lesion data suggesting that mania results from damage to the right frontal region (Robinson & Downhill, 1995) and results obtained when the left relative to right frontal cortex is activated and angry attentional processes are measured (d'Alfonso, van Honk, Hermans, Postma, & de Haan, 2000). However, EEG is likely assessing dorsolateral frontal cortical activity and not orbital frontal activity, and left orbital frontal activity may be involved in the inhibition of anger, whereas left dorsolateral frontal activity may be involved in approach motivations like anger. An increase in dorsolateral frontal cortical activity may not have been found in the PET study because no approach opportunity was presented to the participants. In fact, it is possible that approach motivation may be more difficult to evoke under the conditions of immobility required during PET.

Of course, it may be difficult to compare anger induced by imagery to anger induced by insulting feedback or goal blocking, as in the EEG experiments. In the imagery experiments, there was no report of a significant association between reported anger and regional brain activity. In the EEG experiments, self-reported anger has been found to correlate significantly with relative left frontal activity. Such correlations assist in determining whether the brain activation is related to emotional experience or some other nonemotional variable.

In the previously discussed studies, the psychological variables of approach motivation and anger were manipulated and the physiological variable of relative left frontal activation was measured. Experimental approaches that manipulate brain activity provide complementary rather than redundant information about the relationship between brain activity and psychological/behavioral functions. As noted by Sarter, Berntson, and Cacioppo (1996), studies that manipulate brain activity and observe its effects on psychological/behavioral outcomes provide different information than studies that manipulate psychological processes and observe their effects on brain activity. The two experimental approaches differ in their heuristic power, with the brain manipulation studies providing stronger inferences. The change of psychological and behavioral function by change of neuronal processes in certain regions can establish a particular brain region as necessary for a particular psychological function. Although both assessment of and manipulation of brain

activity can be studied experimentally, studies that examine the effects of a psychological process on brain activity are limited in the causal inferences that can be advanced, because the experimental alteration of a particular psychological process often alters brain activity in multiple regions, including those that presumably underlie the psychological process of interest. It remains possible that an alternate and perhaps undetected brain event could be causally mediating the relationship between the psychological process and the brain activity of interest. Although the reviewed research suggests that approach-oriented anger evokes left frontal activity, the causal inferences that can be drawn from this literature are limited because the evidence is based on studies examining the effects of a manipulated psychological process on brain activity.

Fortunately, other research has addressed these limitations by manipulating regional brain activity and observing its effects on anger processes. For example, d'Alfonso et al. (2000) used slow repetitive transcranial magnetic stimulation (rTMS) to inhibit the left or right prefrontal cortex. Slow rTMS reduces cortical excitability, so that rTMS applied to the right prefrontal cortex decreases its activation and causes the left prefrontal cortex to become more active, while rTMS applied to the left prefrontal cortex causes activation of the right prefrontal cortex. They found that rTMS applied to the right prefrontal cortex caused selective attention toward angry faces whereas rTMS applied to the left prefrontal cortex caused selective attention away from angry faces. Thus, an increase in left prefrontal activity led participants to attentionally approach angry faces, as in an aggressive confrontation. In contrast, an increase in right prefrontal activity led participants to attentionally avoid angry faces, as in a fear-based avoidance. These results have been conceptually replicated by van Honk and Schutter (2006). The interpretation of these results is supported by research demonstrating that attention toward angry faces is associated with high levels of anger, BAS, and testosterone, and that attention away from angry faces is associated with high levels of social anxiety and cortisol (van Honk, Tuiten, de Haan, van den Hout, & Stam, 2001; van Honk et al., 1998, 1999).

We recently extended the work of van Honk and colleagues by examining whether a manipulation of asymmetrical frontal cortical activity would affect behavioral aggression. On the basis of the past research showing that contraction of the left hand increases right frontal cortical activity and that contraction of the right hand increases left frontal cortical activity (Harmon-Jones, 2006), we manipulated asymmetrical frontal cortical activity by having participants contract their right or left hand.

That is, participants squeezed a small ball in one hand or the other hand. Participants then received insulting feedback ostensibly from another participant. They then played a reaction time game on the computer against the other ostensible participant. Participants were told they could give the other participant a blast of 60, 70, 80, 90, or 100 dB white noise for up to 10 s if they were fastest to press the shift key when an image appeared on the screen. Results indicated that participants who squeezed with their right hand gave significantly louder and longer noise blasts to the other ostensible participant than those who squeezed with their left hand (Peterson, Shackman, & Harmon-Jones, 2008).

In summary, the idea that anger is associated with approach motivational tendencies is supported by behavioral and neuroimaging evidence. However, it is possible that some instances of anger, such as anger mixed with fear, may be associated with withdrawal motivational tendencies (Zinner, Brodish, Devine, & Harmon-Jones, in press). In addition, some individuals may have learned to control their angry approach tendencies and may have instead converted these angry tendencies into withdrawal-oriented behaviors (Hewig, Hagemann, Seifert, Naumann, & Bartussek, 2004). More research is needed to understand whether and how this type of angry expression may emerge.

SUBJECTIVE FEELINGS ASSOCIATED WITH ANGER

The conception of anger advanced in this chapter is much broader than some others, which suggest that there are different kinds of anger. For example, Ellsworth and Scherer (2002, p. 575) wrote, "Rather than a single emotion of anger, there can be many varieties of 'almost anger' and many nuances of the anger experience." We do not reject such a possibility, but instead suggest a broader view that proposes that there is an important commonality overriding the "nuances" of anger experience. Spielberger et al. (1983, 1995) reflected this notion in regarding anger as encompassing low intensity feelings such as irritation or annoyance as well as high intensity feelings such as fury and rage. A factor analysis of the items in his State Anger scale (such as "I am furious" and "I feel irritated") obtained only a single factor, suggesting that the feelings tapped by these items reflected a unitary affective state varying in intensity. Spielberger's (Spielberger et al., 1983, 1995) distinction between "anger-in" and "anger-out," it should be noted, refers to differences in the *predisposition* (i.e., *trait*) *to openly express* the motoric concomitants of anger rather than

qualitative differences in the nature of the angry feelings (Spielberger et al., 1995). Our conception of anger experience is in accord with the prototype view of emotion concepts advanced by Shaver et al. (1987). Shaver et al. found that the anger prototype indicates that a variety of feelings labeled *irritation, annoyance, exasperation, disgust,* and *hate* are often included within the general notion of anger. In sum, there is some justification to not regarding the various "nuances" of anger experience as distinctly different emotional or affective states.

It is often held that emotions, unlike moods, are about something in particular; they have a more definite cause and a more specific target. However, this clarity or focus is a matter of degree, as Frijda (1986, pp. 59–60) recognized, and people can vary in the extent to which they believe they know what produced the mood they are experiencing. As Frijda put it, the distinction between mood and emotion is "unsharp" (1986, p. 60). If people can vary in the extent to which they have a clear conception of the cause of their affective arousal, where do we place the cutting point on this continuum, putting mood on one side and emotion on the other?

Anger is often regarded as a negative emotion by laypersons as well as psychological scientists. However, what is meant by negative is not always clearly defined in the literature. Emotions can be regarded as positive or negative (1) because of the conditions that evoked the emotion, (2) because of the emotion's adaptive consequences, (3) or because of the emotion's subjective feel.

Thus, the emotion of anger can be viewed as negative when considering the conditions that evoked the emotion, because anger is evoked by aversive events. Anger could be viewed as either positive or negative when considering its adaptive consequences, depending upon the outcome of the behaviors evoked by anger. However, one would also need to define for whom the consequences are adaptive—the individual experiencing the anger or the individual or group toward whom the individual directs his or her behavior, and whether the consequences are adaptive in the short- or long term. Finally, anger could be viewed as either positive or negative when considering the subjective feel or evaluation of the emotion, depending on whether an individual likes or dislikes the subjective experience of anger.

In considering the valence of an emotion, the definition of emotion must also be considered. Although there is no completely accepted definition of emotion, some scientists focus on the stimulus conditions when defining an emotion (e.g., a negative situation blamed on another causes anger), whereas other scientists focus on the responses evoked when defining an emotion (e.g., anger involves certain physiological changes, behavioral expressions, and subjective feelings). The stimulus-based definitions indicate that the individual's evaluation of the stimulus causing the emotion determines the valence of the emotion (Lazarus, 1991). Thus, most appraisal theorists regard whether the emotion-evoking situation is appraised as positive or negative as the most important and frequent way of distinguishing positive from negative emotions. By this definition, then, anger is a negative emotion.

Response-based definitions of emotion indicate that the individual's subjective evaluation of the feeling determines the valence of the emotion. When anger is examined as a subjective experience, however, it is not necessarily negative; it can be subjectively accepted or rejected. Anger can be evaluated positively by the person experiencing the emotion, as when an individual says, "I like how it feels when I am furious." Although most persons find the experience of anger unpleasant, some individuals find it relatively less unpleasant (Harmon-Jones, 2004).

In general, both state and trait studies examining the valence of anger indicate that most individuals regard anger as a negative experience. However, there are some individuals who routinely find the experience of anger less negative than others (Harmon-Jones, 2004). Moreover, these individual differences in attitudes toward anger relate positively to Buss and Perry (1992) trait anger and trait hostility (as measured by the Positive and Negative Affect Schedule-Expanded (PANAS-X) of Watson & Clark, 1991), although the correlations are not so high as to suggest redundancy. These individual differences in attitude toward anger also relate negatively to trait fear (as measured by PANAS-X). Attitudes toward anger do not relate to self-reported affect intensity or social desirability. Thus, while the valence of anger is predominantly negative, some individuals find it less negative than others, and these attitudes toward anger may have important consequences. It is important to note that these individual differences in attitudes toward anger do not explain why trait anger relates to relative left frontal cortical activity (Harmon-Jones, 2004).

RELATIONSHIP TO OTHER EMOTIONAL EXPERIENCES

In a given situation, anger may be the primary or even sole emotional experience. However, often times, anger occurs amid other negative emotions, as many conceptual perspectives recognize (Berkowitz, 1989). The idea that anger could co-occur with measures of positive affect is less often recognized. In a recent experiment, anger was manipulated using an interpersonal insult and self-reported affect was measured following the insult (Harmon-Jones et al., 2004). In addition to reporting feeling more anger, insult condition participants reported feeling more active, alert, determined, proud, and strong than the no-insult control condition participants. These latter items are from the PANAS measure of activated positive affect (Watson et al., 1988). On the surface, these results suggest that the insult manipulation caused more activated positive affect. Such an interpretation would be consistent with the idea that the activated positive affect scale is measuring approach motivation (Watson, 2000). However, another interpretation is that the words did not reflect feelings of positivity in this situation in which anger was present.

These results for activated positive affect have since been replicated using a different anger manipulation. In addition, in this more recent study, trait BAS was positively related to both reported anger and reported activated positive affect, providing convergent evidence. Moreover, anger and activated positive affect were positively correlated, happiness and activated positive affect were positively correlated, and happiness and anger were negatively correlated (Harmon-Jones, Harmon-Jones, Abramson, & Peterson, 2008). Taken together, these results suggest that the PANAS measure called activated "positive activation" or PA may be a better measure of approach motivation or "pounce affect" than of positivity. In other words, the PA subscale may actually describe an action-tendency of approach—a motivation to "pounce." The "pouncing" measured by these items may be an enthusiastic approach to a delicious dessert, a lustful embrace of an attractive mate, or an angry attack on an enemy.

CONCLUSION

Empirical and theoretical developments on anger and its relationship with motivational direction were reviewed. Many models of anger suggest that anger occurs as a result of goal blocking, consistent with the idea that anger may often occur in approach motivated situations. Other theoretical and empirical developments have revealed that, unlike other negative emotions, anger responses are associated with approach motivation instead of withdrawal or avoidance motivation. Recent research and theoretical developments on anger have shed new light on our understanding of the relationship between motivational direction and emotional valence. Whereas most previous dimensional models of emotion and motivation suggested that approach motivation was only associated with positive affect, the evidence now suggests that at least one negative affect, anger, is often associated with approach motivation. These results suggest that dimensional models of emotion are in need of revision and that the motivational direction of emotion needs to be considered as independent of the valence of emotion. Practically, the reviewed evidence may assist in understanding why anger presents problems for the individual and society, but it also suggests that anger may provide some beneficial functions.

ACKNOWLEDGMENT

Portions of the research described within this chapter were supported by a grant from the National Science Foundation (BCS 0350435) and by a grant from the National Institute of Mental Health (R03 MH60747–01).

REFERENCES

Adams, R. B. J., Ambady, N., Macrae, C. N., & Kleck, R. E. (2006). Emotional expressions forecast approach-avoidance behavior. *Motivation and Emotion, 30*, 179–188.

Allen, J. J. B., Harmon-Jones, E., & Cavender, J. (2001). Manipulation of frontal EEG asymmetry through biofeedback alters self-reported emotional responses and facial EMG. *Psychophysiology, 38*, 685–693.

Baron, R. A. (1977). Effects of victim's pain cues, victim's race, and level of prior instigation upon physical aggression. *Journal of Applied Social Psychology, 9*, 103–114.

Berkowitz, L. (1989). Frustration-aggression hypothesis: Examination and reformulation. *Psychological Bulletin, 106*, 59–73.

Berkowitz, L. (1993). *Aggression: Its causes, consequences, and control.* New York: McGraw-Hill.

Berkowitz, L. (1999). Anger. In T. Dalgleish & M. Power (Eds.), *Handbook of cognition and emotion* (pp. 411–428). Chichester, UK/New York: John Wiley and Sons.

Berkowitz, L. (2000). *Causes and consequences of feelings.* Cambridge: Cambridge University Press.

Berkowitz, L., & Harmon-Jones, E. (2004). Toward an understanding of the determinants of anger. *Emotion, 4*, 107–130.

Blanchard, D. C., & Blanchard, R. J. (1984). Affect and aggression: An animal model applied to human behavior. *Advances in the Study of Aggression, 1*, 1–62.

Blanchard, D. C., & Takahashi, S. N. (1988). No change in intermale aggression after amygdala lesions which reduce freezing. *Physiology & Behavior, 42*, 613–616.

Boissy, A., & Bouissou, M. F. (1994). Effects of androgen treatment on behavioral and physiological responses of heifers to fear-eliciting situations. *Hormones and Behavior, 28*, 66–83.

Brehm, J. W., & Self, E. (1989). The intensity of motivation. In M. R. Rosenzweig & L. W. Porter (Eds.), *Annual Review of Psychology* (Vol. 40, pp. 109–131). Palo Alto, CA: Annual Reviews, Inc.

Busch, D. E., & Barfield, R. J. (1974). A failure of amygdaloid lesions to alter agonistic behavior in the laboratory rat. *Physiology & Behavior, 12*, 887–892.

Buss, A. H., & Perry, M. (1992). The aggression questionnaire. *Journal of Personality and Social Psychology, 63*, 452–459.

Carver, C. S. (2004). Negative affects deriving from the behavioral approach system. *Emotion, 4*, 3–22.

Carver, C. S., & White, T. L. (1994). Behavioral inhibition, behavioral activation, and affective responses to impending reward and punishment: The BIS/BAS scales. *Journal of Personality and Social Psychology, 67*, 319–333.

Cassidy, F., Forest, K., Murry, E., & Carroll, B. J. (1998). A factor analysis of the signs and symptoms of mania. *Archives of General Psychiatry, 55*, 27–32.

Coan, J. A., & Allen, J. J. B. (2003). Frontal EEG asymmetry and the behavioral activation and inhibition systems. *Psychophysiology, 40*, 106–114.

Coan, J. A., Allen, J. J. B., & Harmon-Jones, E. (2001). Voluntary facial expression and hemispheric asymmetry over the frontal cortex. *Psychophysiology, 38*, 912–925.

d'Alfonso, A. A. L., van Honk, J., Hermans, E., Postma, A., & de Haan, E. H. F. (2000). Laterality effects in selective attention to threat after repetitive transcranial magnetic stimulation at the prefrontal cortex in female subjects. *Neuroscience Letters, 280*, 195–198.

Darwin, C. (1872/1965). *The expression of the emotions in man and animals.* Chicago, IL: The University of Chicago Press.

Davidson, R. J. (1998). Anterior electrophysiological asymmetries, emotion, and depression: Conceptual and methodological conundrums. *Psychophysiology, 35*, 607–614.

Davidson, R. J., & Fox, N. A. (1982). Asymmetrical brain activity discriminates between positive and negative affective stimuli in human infants. *Science, 218*, 1235–1237.

Davidson, R. J., & Fox, N. A. (1989). Frontal brain asymmetry predicts infants' response to maternal separation. *Journal of Abnormal Psychology, 98*, 127–131.

Depue, R. A., & Iacono, W. G. (1989). Neurobehavioral aspects of affective disorders. *Annual Review of Psychology, 40*, 457–492.

Dollard, J., Doob, L., Miller, N., Mowrer, O., & Sears, R. (1939). *Frustration and aggression.* New Haven, CT: Yale University Press.

Dougherty, D. D., Shin, L. M., Alpert, N. M., Pitman, R. K., Orr, S. P., Lasko, M., et al. (1999). Anger in health men: A PET study using script-driven imagery. *Biological Psychiatry, 46*, 466–472.

Ekman, P., & Friesen, W. V. (1975). *Unmasking the face: A guide to recognizing emotions from facial clues.* Englewood Cliffs, NJ: Prentice-Hall.

Ellsworth, P. C. & Scherer, K. R. (2002). Appraisal processes in emotion. In R. J. Davidson, H. Goldsmith, & K. R. Scherer (Eds.), *Handbook of the affective sciences.* New York/Oxford, UK: Oxford University Press.

Fowles, D. C. (1993). Behavioral variables in psychopathology: A psychobiological perspective. In P. B. Sutker & H. E. Adams (Eds.), *Comprehensive handbook of psychopathology* (2nd ed., pp. 57–82). New York: Plenum Press.

Fox, N. A., & Davidson, R. J. (1986). Taste-elicited changes in facial signs of emotion and the asymmetry of brain electrical activity in human newborns. *Neuropsychologia*, *24*, 417–422.

Frijda, N. H. (1986). *The emotions*. Cambridge, UK/New York: Cambridge University Press.

Frijda, N. H. (1993). The place of appraisal in emotion. *Cognition and Emotion*, *7*, 357–387.

Frijda, N. H., Kuipers, P., & ter Schure, E. (1989). Relations among emotion, appraisal, and emotional action readiness. *Journal of Personality and Social Psychology*, *57*, 212–228.

Frijda, N. H., & Zeelenberg, M. (2001). Appraisal: What is the dependent? In K. R. Scherer, A. Schorr, & T. Johnstone (Eds.), *Appraisal processes in emotion*. Oxford, UK/New York: Oxford University Press.

Gray, J. A. (1987). *The psychology of fear and stress*. London: Cambridge University Press.

Harmon-Jones, E. (2003). Anger and the behavioural approach system. *Personality and Individual Differences*, *35*, 995–1005.

Harmon-Jones, E. (2004). On the relationship of anterior brain activity and anger: Examining the role of attitude toward anger. *Cognition and Emotion*, *18*, 337–361.

Harmon-Jones, E. (2006). Unilateral right-hand contractions cause contralateral alpha power suppression and approach motivational affective experience. *Psychophysiology*, *43*, 598–603.

Harmon-Jones, E. (2007). Trait anger predicts relative left frontal cortical activation to anger-inducing stimuli. *International Journal of Psychophysiology*, *66*, 154–160.

Harmon-Jones, E., & Allen, J. J. B. (1997). Behavioral activation sensitivity and resting frontal EEG asymmetry: Covariation of putative indicators related to risk for mood disorders. *Journal of Abnormal Psychology*, *106*, 159–163.

Harmon-Jones, E., & Allen, J. J. B. (1998). Anger and prefrontal brain activity: EEG asymmetry consistent with approach motivation despite negative affective valence. *Journal of Personality and Social Psychology*, *74*, 1310–1316.

Harmon-Jones, E., & Allen, J. J. B. (2001). The role of affect in the mere exposure effect: Evidence from psychophysiological and individual differences approaches. *Personality and Social Psychology Bulletin*, *27*, 889–898.

Harmon-Jones, E., Harmon-Jones, C., & Abramson, L. Y. (2007). *On the association of anger and PANAS positive affect*. Manuscript in preparation.

Harmon-Jones, E., Lueck, L., Fearn, M., & Harmon-Jones, C. (2006). The effect of personal relevance and approach-related action expectation on relative left frontal cortical activity. *Psychological Science*, *17*, 434–440.

Harmon-Jones, E., & Sigelman, J. (2001). State anger and prefrontal brain activity: Evidence that insult-related relative left prefrontal activation is associated with experienced anger and aggression. *Journal of Personality and Social Psychology*, *80*, 797–803.

Harmon-Jones, E., Sigelman, J. D., Bohlig, A., & Harmon-Jones, C. (2003). Anger, coping, and frontal cortical activity: The effect of coping potential on anger-induced left frontal activity. *Cognition and Emotion*, *17*, 1–24.

Harmon-Jones, E., Vaughn-Scott, K., Mohr, S., Sigelman, J., & Harmon-Jones, C. (2004). The effect of manipulated sympathy and anger on left and right frontal cortical activity. *Emotion*, *4*, 95–101.

Henriques, J. B., & Davidson, R. J. (1990). Regional brain electrical asymmetries discriminate between previously depressed and healthy control subjects. *Journal of Abnormal Psychology*, *99*, 22–31.

Hewig, J., Hagemann, D., Seifert, J., Naumann, E., & Bartussek, D. (2004). On the selective relation of frontal cortical asymmetry and anger-out versus anger-control. *Journal of Personality and Social Psychology*, *87*, 926–939.

Izard, C. E. (1977). *Human emotions*. New York: Plenum Press.

Izard, C. E. (1991). *The psychology of emotions*. New York: Plenum Press.

Jacobs, G. D., & Snyder, D. (1996). Frontal brain asymmetry predicts affective style in men. *Behavioral Neuroscience*, *110*, 3–6.

Lagerspetz, K. M. J. (1969). Aggression and aggressiveness in laboratory mice. In S. Garattini & E. B. Sigg (Eds.), *Aggressive behavior* (pp. 77–85). New York: Wiley.

Lang, P. J. (1995). The emotion probe. *American Psychologist*, *50*, 372–385.

Lazarus, R. S. (1991). *Emotion and adaptation*. New York: Oxford University Press.

Lerner, J. S., & Keltner, D. (2001). Fear, anger, and risk. *Journal of Personality and Social Psychology*, *81*, 146–159.

Lewis, M. (1993). The development of anger and rage. In R. A. Glick & S. P. Roose (Eds.), *Rage, power, and aggression* (pp. 148–168). New Haven, CT: Yale University Press.

Lewis, M., Alessandri, S. M., & Sullivan, M. W. (1990). Violation of expectancy, loss of control, and anger expressions in young infants. *Developmental Psychology*, *26*, 745–751.

Lewis, M., Sullivan, M. W., Ramsey, D. S., & Alessandri, S. M. (1992). Individual differences in anger and sad expressions during extinction: Antecedents and consequences. *Infant Behavior & Development*, *15*, 443–452.

Malone, R. P., Delaney, M. A., Luebbert, J. F., Cater, J., & Campbell, M. (2000). A double-blind placebo-controlled study of lithium in hospitalized aggressive children and adolescents with conduct disorder. *Archives of General Psychiatry*, *57*, 649–654.

Mega, M. S., Cummings, J. L., Salloway, S., & Malloy, P. (1997). The limbic system: An anatomic, phylogenetic, and clinical perspective. *Journal of Neuropsychiatry and Clinical Neuroscience*, *9*, 315–330.

Mikulincer, M. (1988). Reactance and helplessness following exposure to unsolvable problems: The effects of attributional style. *Journal of Personality and Social Psychology*, *54*, 679–686.

Miller, P. A., & Eisenberg, N. (1988). The relation of empathy to aggressive and externalizing/antisocial behavior. *Psychological Bulletin*, *103*, 324–344.

Mowrer, O. H. (1960). *Learning theory and behavior*. New York: John Wiley and Sons.

Moyer, K. E. (1976). *The psychobiology of aggression.* New York: Harper and Row.

Olweus, D. (1986). Aggression and hormones: Behavioral relationship with testosterone and adrenaline. In D. Olweus, J. Block, & M. Radke-Yarrow (Eds.), *Development of antisocial and prosocial behavior: Research, theories, and issues* (pp. 51–72). Orlando, FL: Academic Press.

Ortony, A., Clore, G. L., & Collins, A. (1988). *The cognitive structure of emotions.* New York: Cambridge University Press.

Panksepp, J. (1994). The basics of basic emotions. In P. Ekman & R. J. Davidson (Eds.), *The nature of emotion: Fundamental questions* (pp. 20–24). New York: Oxford University Press.

Panksepp, J. (1998). *Affective neuroscience: The foundations of human and animal emotions.* New York: Oxford University Press.

Parkinson, B., & Manstead, A. S. R. (1992). Appraisal as a cause of emotion. In M. S. Clark (Ed.), *Review of personality and social psychology Vol. 13* (pp. 122–149). Newbury Park, CA: Sage.

Putman, P., Hermans, E., & van Honk, J. (2004). Emotional stroop performance for masked angry faces: It's BAS, not BIS. *Emotion, 4,* 305–311.

Peterson, C. K., Gable, P., & Harmon-Jones, E. (in press). Asymmetrical frontal ERPs, emotion, and behavioral approach/inhibition sensitivity. *Social Neuroscience.*

Peterson, C. K., Shackman, A. J., & Harmon-Jones, E. (2008). The role of asymmetrical frontal cortical activity in aggression. *Psychophysiology, 45,* 86–92.

Plutchik, R. (1980). *Emotion: A psychoevolutionary synthesis.* New York: Harper and Row.

Robinson, R. G., & Downhill, J. E. (1995). Lateralization of psychopathology in response to focal brain injury. In R. J. Davidson & K. Hugdahl (Eds.), *Brain asymmetry* (pp. 693–711). Cambridge, MA: Massachusetts Institute of Technology.

Rolls, E. T. (1999). *The brain and emotion.* Oxford: Oxford University Press.

Roseman, I. J. (1991). Appraisal determinants of discrete emotions. *Cognition and Emotion, 5,* 161–200.

Russell, J. A., & Fernández-Dols, J. M. (1997). *The psychology of facial expression.* Paris: Cambridge University Press.

Sarter, M., Berntson, G. G., & Cacioppo, J. T. (1996). Brain imaging and cognitive neuroscience: Toward strong inference in attributing function to structure. *American Psychologist, 51,* 13–21.

Shaver, P., Schwartz, J., Kirson, D., & O'Connor, C. (1987). Emotion knowledge: Further exploration of a prototype approach. *Journal of Personality and Social Psychology, 52,* 1061–1086.

Smits, D. J. M., & Kuppens, P. (2005). The relations between anger, coping with anger, and aggression, and the BIS/BAS system. *Personality and Individual Differences, 39,* 783–793.

Spielberger, C. D., Jacobs, G. A., Russell, S. F., & Crane, R. S. (1983). Assessment of anger: The state-trait anger scale. In J. N. Butcher & C. D. Spielberger (Eds.), *Advances in personality assessment* (Vol. 2, pp. 159–187). Hillsdale, NJ: Erlbaum.

Spielberger, C. D., Reheiser, E. C., & Sydeman, S. J. (1995). Measuring the experience, expression, and control of anger. In H. Kassinove (Ed.), *Anger disorders: Definition, diagnosis, and treatment* (pp. 49–67). Washington, DC: Taylor & Francis.

Stein, N. L., & Levine, L. J. (1989). The causal organization of emotional knowledge: A developmental study. *Cognition and Emotion, 3,* 343–378.

Sutton, S. K., & Davidson, R. J. (1997). Prefrontal brain asymmetry: A biological substrate of the behavioral approach and inhibition systems. *Psychological Science, 8,* 204–210.

Tomarken, A. J., Davidson, R. J., & Henriques, J. B. (1990). Resting frontal brain asymmetry predicts affective responses to films. *Journal of Personality and Social Psychology, 59,* 791–801.

Tomarken, A. J., Davidson, R. J., Wheeler, R. E., & Doss, R. (1992). Individual differences in anterior brain asymmetry and fundamental dimensions of emotion. *Journal of Personality and Social Psychology, 62,* 676–687.

Tomarken, A. J., Davidson, R. J., Wheeler, R. E., & Kinney, L. (1992). Psychometric properties of resting anterior EEG asymmetry: Temporal stability and internal consistency. *Psychophysiology, 29,* 576–592.

Tomarken, A. J., & Keener, A. D. (1998). Frontal brain asymmetry and depression: A self-regulatory perspective. *Cognition and Emotion, 12,* 387–420.

Tyrer, S., & Shopsin, B. (1982). Symptoms and assessment of mania. In E. S. Paykel (Ed.), *Handbook of affective disorders* (pp. 12–23). New York: Guilford Press.

van Honk, J., & Schutter, D. J. L. G. (2006). From affective valence to motivational direction: The frontal asymmetry of emotion revised. *Psychological Science, 17,* 963–965.

van Honk, J., Tuiten, A., de Haan, E., van den Hout, M., & Stam, H. (2001). Attentional biases for angry faces: Relationships to trait anger and anxiety. *Cognition and Emotion, 15,* 279–297.

van Honk, J., Tuiten, A., van den Hout, M., Koppeschaar, H., Thijssen, J., de Haan, E., et al. (1998). Baseline salivary cortisol levels and preconscious selective attention for threat: A pilot study. *Psychoneuroendocrinology, 23,* 741–747.

van Honk, J., Tuiten, A., Verbaten, R., van den Hout, M., Koppeschaar, H., Thijssen, J., et al. (1999). Correlations among salivary testosterone, mood, and selective attention to threat in humans. *Hormones and Behavior, 36,* 17–24.

Vandenheede, M., & Bouissou, M. F. (1993). Effect of androgen treatment on fear reactions in ewes. *Hormones and Behavior, 27,* 435–448.

Watson, D. (2000). *Mood and temperament.* New York: Guilford Press.

Watson, D., & Clark, L. A. (1991). *The PANAS-X: Preliminary manual for the positive and negative affect schedule—expanded form.* Unpublished manuscript.

Watson, D., Clark, L. A., & Tellegen, A. (1988). Development and validation of brief measures of positive and negative affect: The PANAS scales. *Journal of Personality and Social Psychology, 54,* 1063–1070.

Watson, D., Wiese, D., Vaidya, J., & Tellegen, A. (1999). The two general activation systems of affect: Structural findings, evolutionary considerations, and psychobiological evidence. *Journal of personality and social psychology*, *76*, 820–838.

Wheeler, R. E., Davidson, R. J., & Tomarken, A. J. (1993). Frontal brain asymmetry and emotional reactivity: A biological substrate of affective style. *Psychophysiology*, *30*, 82–89.

Wortman, C. B., & Brehm, J. W. (1975). Responses to uncontrollable outcomes: An integration of reactance theory and the learned helplessness model. In L. Berkowitz (Ed.), *Advances in experimental social psychology* (Vol. 8., pp. 278–336). New York: Academic Press.

Young, P. T. (1943). *Emotion in man and animal: Its nature and relation to attitude and motive*. New York: John Wiley and Sons.

Zinner, L., Brodish, A., Devine, P. G., & Harmon-Jones, E. (in press). Anger and asymmetrical frontal cortical activity: Evidence for an anger-withdrawal relationship. *Cognition and Emotion*.

Well-Being

24 Approach–Avoidance Goals and Well-Being: One Size Does Not Fit All

Maya Tamir and Ed Diener

CONTENTS

April and Avalon are equally committed to their goals and work equally hard to achieve them. Their goals, however, are quite distinct. April wants to become a regional manager and works hard to climb up the promotion ladder. Avalon wants to keep her job and works hard not to lose her position as a regional manager. Whereas April is driven by an approach goal (i.e., get promoted), Avalon is driven by an avoidance goal (i.e., not get demoted). Do these distinct goals carry any implications for well-being? Are certain goals more conducive to well-being than others? Are some goals more conducive to the well-being

of one person than another? These and related questions are explored in the present chapter.

Since the early philosophical discussions of well-being, it has been conceptualized from two distinct perspectives—one emphasizing hedonic pleasure and one emphasizing meaning in life. Aristippus, for instance, argued that the purpose of life is to maximize pleasure. Indeed, the hedonic perspective assumes that well-being is enhanced by experiences of pleasure and impaired by experiences of pain. Current hedonic approaches emphasize pleasures of the mind and the body, as indicated primarily by momentary experiences of pleasant (vs. unpleasant) affect (Kahneman, 1999).

Aristotle, on the other hand, argued that true happiness is a function of virtue. Thus, an alternative perspective to well-being assumes that it is dependent upon the experience of meaning and value in life (Ryan & Deci, 2000; Ryff, 1989). That is, meaning involves a unified purpose in life that is consistent with one's values. According to this approach, well-being is enhanced by the experience of meaning in life and impaired when life experiences are not personally meaningful or valuable to the individual.

These two approaches to well-being highlight pleasure and meaning in life as two, conceptually distinct, sources of well-being. Pleasure and meaning, however, are often related to one another. Experiences of pleasure and pain can make events meaningful. For instance, a student may feel more drawn and personally committed to a topic taught in class, if she enjoys the lectures. In addition, the extent to which an event is personally meaningful can determine the hedonic consequences of the event. For instance, doing well on an exam is likely more pleasant and rewarding, if the exam covers a topic the student views as personally meaningful (Emmons, 1996).

Pleasure and meaning in life are, nevertheless, conceptually distinct sources of well-being that can have different underpinnings and different implications. In exploring well-being, therefore, it is important to acknowledge both pleasure and meaning in life as critical determinants. Accordingly, in the present context, we define well-being as involving frequent experiences of pleasant affect, infrequent experiences of unpleasant affect, and a sense of meaning in life. This approach to well-being is reflected, to some extent, in research on subjective well-being, where meaning in life is an important contributor to life satisfaction (Diener, Oishi, & Lucas, 2003).

The present chapter reviews the potential implications of approach and avoidance goals for well-being. In the first part of the chapter, we review the general implications of approach and avoidance goals for well-being. We begin by explaining why motivation features so prominently in accounts of well-being. We then review the implications of approach and avoidance goals for affective experiences and meaning in life, focusing on the potential contributions of the process and the outcome of goal pursuit. In the second part of the chapter, we argue that the link between approach–avoidance goals and well-being can be fully understood only when examined from an individual difference perspective. In particular, we propose that the extent to which approach

and avoidance goals are beneficial for well-being may depend on the desirability and feasibility of such goals for the individual.

MOTIVATION IS CENTRAL TO WELL-BEING

Motivation is arguably one of the most important building blocks of well-being (Diener, 1984). In part, this is because motivation is linked to pleasure and pain as well as to meaning in life. As noted earlier, affect-based approaches view momentary pleasant and unpleasant affective experiences as critical determinants of well-being (Kahneman, 1999; Kubovy, 1999). Momentary affective experiences, in turn, arise in response to events that are motivationally relevant (Frijda, 1988).

Pleasant feelings signal an event that promotes the individual's goals. For instance, when an individual aspires to be a good student, doing well on an exam is likely to result in pleasant affect. Unpleasant feelings signal an event that hinders the individual's goals. For instance, if an individual is motivated to be a good student, doing poorly on an exam is likely to lead to unpleasant affect. If, however, the individual is not motivated to be a good student, doing poorly on an exam is less likely to lead to unpleasant affect.

Whereas pleasure-based theories of well-being highlight the role of motivation in determining affective experiences, meaning-based theories highlight the role of motivation in creating meaning in life. A personally meaningful life, according to such approaches, is one that is characterized by the pursuit of self-defining goals that are consistent with the person's core beliefs and values (Ryan & Deci, 2000; Waterman, 1993). For example, graduating from medical school would contribute to the well-being of an individual who has always dreamt of becoming a doctor, but it would not necessarily contribute to the well-being of an individual who has always dreamt of becoming a movie star.

IMPACT OF MOTIVATION: ACTIVITY AND TELIC THEORIES OF WELL-BEING

Motivation can influence well-being by underlying both affective experiences and meaning in life. According to Diener (1984), such effects may depend on either the process or the outcome of motivational pursuits. The roles of the process and the outcome of goal pursuits are highlighted in activity and telic theories of well-being, respectively.

Activity theories of well-being focus on the process of goal pursuit. According to such theories, it is the active pursuit of goals, rather than their fulfillment, that contributes to well-being (Cantor, 1990; Palys & Little, 1983). The impact of goal pursuits on well-being, primarily goals that involve conscious objectives that are pursued in daily life, has been demonstrated in research on current concerns (Klinger, 1975), personal projects (Palys & Little, 1983), and personal strivings (Emmons, 1986). Such research demonstrates that the active pursuit of goals is an important determinant of well-being.

Unlike activity theories, telic theories of well-being focus on the outcome of goal pursuits. Telic theories maintain that well-being is enhanced when a person successfully attains a goal, and impaired when a person fails to attain a goal (Diener, 1984). Successful pursuits may be defined in terms of adequate progress toward the target end-state (Carver & Scheier, 1990) or in terms of final goal implementation (Gollwitzer, 1999). In other words, the successful pursuit of goals is an important determinant of well-being (Ryan & Deci, 2000).

In summary, both the pursuit and the fulfillment of goals can promote well-being. Consistent with affect-based theories, motivational pursuits underlie the experience of positive and negative affect. Consistent with meaning-based theories, motivational pursuits give meaning to life. But are some motivational pursuits more conducive to well-being than others? In other words, do specific goals differ in their affective or meaning-related consequences? The answer lies in the distinction between approach and avoidance goals.

APPROACH AND AVOIDANCE GOALS ARE CENTRAL TO WELL-BEING

In the beginning of the chapter, we introduced two coworkers, April and Avalon. Although both work equally hard to attain their goals, April pursues an approach goal (i.e., is motivated to attain desirable outcomes) whereas Avalon pursues an avoidance goal (i.e., is motivated to avoid undesirable outcomes). This distinction between approach and avoidance is one of the most critical and influential distinctions in the study of motivation (see Elliot, 2008).

From a functional point of view, both approach and avoidance goals are necessary for successful adaptation. Whereas approach motivation facilitates growth and flourishing, avoidance motivation facilitates protection and survival. Avoidance goals, for example, help individuals avoid taking unnecessary risks (Lauriola & Levin, 2001) or consuming harmful substances (Worth, Sullivan, Hertel, Rothman, & Jeffery, 2005). Approach and avoidance motivation promote distinct types of affective,

cognitive, and behavioral processes, both of which are relevant to adaptive functioning.

Although it is beneficial to pursue at least some degree of both approach and avoidance goals, pursuing such goals may carry different implications for well-being. What balance, therefore, of approach to avoidance goals should an individual pursue to optimize well-being? The answer, of course, depends on the differential implications of approach and avoidance goals for affective and meaningful experiences in life. In the sections that follow, we review such implications focusing on the process and the outcome of goal pursuits.

APPROACH–AVOIDANCE GOALS AND WELL-BEING: AN ACTIVITY THEORY PERSPECTIVE

What are the affective consequences of approach and avoidance goals and how do these consequences impact well-being? We begin to address these questions by focusing on the process of goal pursuit (i.e., adopting an activity perspective). In the following sections, we first explore conceptual differences in the process of approach and avoidance goal pursuits and then review some empirical evidence.

CONCEPTUAL DISTINCTIONS

According to activity theories, well-being is determined by the process of goal pursuit. From this perspective, approach and avoidance goals are likely to carry different implications for well-being, only to the extent that there are substantive differences in the process of pursuing these goals. As we describe below, there are reasons to believe that the process of pursuing approach goals is qualitatively distinct from that of pursuing avoidance goals.

The pursuit of approach goals should be more manageable than that of avoidance goals. According to cybernetic control models (Carver & Scheier, 1998), the pursuit of approach goals involves diminishing the discrepancy between a current state and a desired state. On the other hand, the pursuit of avoidance goals involves enlarging the discrepancy between a current state and an undesired state. From this conceptual viewpoint, the pursuit of approach goals should be more manageable than the pursuit of avoidance goals, because progress is more tangible and easier to monitor (Elliot, Sheldon, & Church, 1997; Higgins, 1997).

To demonstrate this point, let us return to our two coworkers. April can monitor progress in her goal pursuit as she climbs up the promotion ladder. If she fails to get promoted to assistant regional manager, she knows that she is not making sufficient progress toward her desired position. If, however, she gets the promotion, she knows that she is getting closer to obtaining her goal. April, therefore, can easily monitor success and failure in her goal pursuit and experience pleasant or unpleasant affect as a result.

Avalon, on the other hand, may have a harder time monitoring her progress. If she is demoted to assistant regional manager, she knows that she is failing in obtaining her goal of keeping her position. But what would indicate to her that she is succeeding in her goal pursuit? Finding indications of success in pursuing avoidance goals can often be challenging. Thus, Avalon may be more likely to detect failures than successes in her goal pursuit, making it more likely for her to experience unpleasant affect.

In addition, the pursuits of approach and avoidance goals likely differ in the cognitions they give rise to. If goal pursuits involve constant comparisons of a current state to an end-state (Carver & Scheier, 1998), the pursuit of approach goals involves constantly monitoring positive outcomes, making them more accessible during goal pursuit. On the other hand, the pursuit of avoidance goals involves constantly monitoring negative outcomes, making them more accessible during goal pursuit. Thus, the pursuit of approach goals can maintain positive cognitions, whereas the pursuit of avoidance goals can maintain negative cognitions (Elliot & Sheldon, 1998; Higgins, Roney, Crowe, & Hymes, 1994).

April and Avalon, therefore, may have different thoughts accessible to them in their daily lives. April may think of what it would be like to be the regional manager in her company and such thoughts might engender pleasant affect. Avalon, on the other hand, may think of what it would be like to lose her job and such thoughts may engender unpleasant affect.

Overall, the process of pursuing approach goals is different from the process of pursuing avoidance goals. Approach goals appear to be easier to monitor and more manageable than avoidance goals. In addition, whereas approach goals elicit positive cognitions, avoidance goals elicit negative cognitions. According to activity theories, therefore, the pursuit of approach goals should be more likely than the pursuit of avoidance goals to promote well-being.

Empirical Evidence

According to activity theories of well-being, the process of pursuing approach goals should be more conducive to

well-being than that of avoidance goals. Indeed, there are now several lines of research supporting this prediction. For example, Elliot and his collaborators (for a recent review, see Elliot & Friedman, 2007) asked participants to list goals that best describe what they are trying to achieve in life. After categorizing these goals as either approach- or avoidance-oriented, they created an avoidance (relative to approach) index for each participant.

Using this procedure, the authors found that pursuing more approach than avoidance goals was associated with higher levels of well-being. In particular, pursuing more approach than avoidance goals was associated with higher levels of well-being in retrospective ratings (Elliot et al., 1997) and with less physical symptoms, such as headaches, sore throat, and dizziness (Elliot & Sheldon, 1998).

The beneficial role of approach (vs. avoidance) goals has been demonstrated with respect to general goals and with respect to goals in specific life domains. In the achievement domain, pursuing approach achievement goals was associated with higher levels of subjective well-being (Elliot & Sheldon, 1997). Similarly, in the social domain, pursuing approach friendship goals was associated with higher levels of subjective well-being (Elliot, Gable, & Mapes, 2006).

Consistent with core assumptions of activity theories, the relationships between approach–avoidance goals and well-being were fully mediated by perceptions of progress and competence in goal pursuit. Approach goals predicted higher perceptions of personal progress and competence in goal pursuit, which in turn, predicted higher levels of subjective well-being (Elliot & Sheldon, 1997; Elliot et al., 1997).

There is also reason to believe that the pursuit of approach versus avoidance goals exerts a causal influence on well-being. For instance, Coats, Janoff-Bulman, and Alpert (1996) presented participants with tasks, framed in terms of either approach or avoidance goals. Pursuing approach (vs. avoidance) goals was associated with higher perceptions of success in the task and with higher levels of task satisfaction. Consistent with the predictions of activity theories, such research suggests that pursuing approach (vs. avoidance) goals leads to greater perceived progress, which in turn, promotes satisfaction with the experience as a whole.

Taken together, according to activity theories of well-being, the pursuit of approach goals is more conducive to well-being than the pursuit of avoidance goals. This is primarily because it is easier to monitor and assess progress when pursuing approach compared to avoidance goals. Approach goals are more manageable than avoidance goals and they elicit positive (vs. negative) cognitions. The available evidence is consistent with these predictions, suggesting that pursuing more approach than avoidance goals leads to greater perceived progress and efficacy, which in turn, promote well-being.

APPROACH–AVOIDANCE GOALS AND WELL-BEING: A TELIC THEORY PERSPECTIVE

In the previous section, we examined the differential implications of approach and avoidance goals, focusing on the process of goal pursuit. However, as mentioned earlier, both the process and the outcome of goal pursuit can influence well-being. In this section, therefore, we review the implications of success or failure in approach and avoidance goal pursuits and their anticipated impact on well-being.

According to telic theories, well-being is determined by the outcome of goal pursuit. Contrary to the account of activity theories, from the telic perspective, approach and avoidance goals are likely to carry different implications for well-being, only to the extent that success or failure in pursuing approach goals has different consequences than success or failure in pursuing avoidance goals. As we describe below, the outcome of approach and avoidance goal pursuits indeed results in distinct affective experiences.

Affective experiences are assumed to be driven by the appetitive and defensive motivational systems (i.e., approach and avoidance, respectively) (Davidson, 1993; Gray, 1990; Lang, 1995). An active approach system is linked to feelings such as excitement and elation whereas an active avoidance system is linked to feelings such as anxiety and fear (see Carver, 2008; Harmon-Jones, 2008). Such affective experiences are most likely to arise as a function of success or failure in goal pursuit.

According to cybernetic control models (Carver & Scheier, 1998), affective reactions reflect the speed of progress in goal pursuit. Pleasant feelings arise when the rate of progress toward a goal is faster than anticipated, whereas unpleasant feelings arise when the rate of progress toward a goal is slower than anticipated (Carver, 2004). Thus, both approach and avoidance goals should have the potential of inducing pleasant as well as unpleasant feelings as a function of progress in goal pursuit. When pursuing approach goals, desirable outcomes elicit excitement whereas undesirable outcomes elicit sadness. When pursuing avoidance goals, desirable outcomes elicit calmness whereas undesirable outcomes elicit anxiety.

For example, April may feel pleasant affect (i.e., excitement) when she is promoted and she may feel unpleasant affect (i.e., sadness) when she fails to get that promotion. Similarly, Avalon may feel pleasant affect (i.e., relief or calmness) when she discovers that the board decided to keep her on the job and she may feel unpleasant affect (i.e., anxiety) when she hears that the board decided to give her job to another employee.

According to telic theories, therefore, the outcomes of approach and avoidance goal pursuits lead to distinct affective experiences, yet both have the potential of eliciting pleasant (e.g., excitement and relief) as well as unpleasant (e.g., sadness and anxiety) affective experiences. Well-being, in turn, likely reflects the frequency rather than the intensity of affective experiences (Diener & Lucas, 2000).

According to telic theories, the extent to which approach or avoidance goals promote well-being depends on the frequency of success or failure when pursuing such goals. This, of course, is assuming that all pleasant emotions contribute to well-being and all unpleasant emotions impair well-being. In other words, according to telic theories, if success is always more likely when pursuing approach (vs. avoidance) goals, approach goals should be more likely to contribute to well-being compared to avoidance goals. However, if there are cases in which success is more likely when pursuing avoidance (vs. approach) goals, in such cases, avoidance goals should theoretically be more likely to contribute to well-being than approach goals.

APPROACH–AVOIDANCE GOALS AND MEANING IN LIFE

In the previous sections, we suggested that the process and the outcome of pursuing approach and avoidance goals can have different implications for well-being. In daily life, however, individuals likely pursue multiple goals, some of which are more important or meaningful than others. The impact of approach and avoidance goals on well-being, therefore, may vary as a function of how important or meaningful the goal is for the individual (Brunstein, Schultheiss, & Maier, 1999; Emmons, 1986).

According to both activity and telic theories, goals that are personally meaningful are likely to have a greater impact on well-being (Carver & Scheier, 1990; Palys & Little, 1983). Indeed, there is evidence to suggest that only progress toward personally meaningful goals predict increases in well-being (Brunstein, Schultheiss, & Grassman, 1998). The perceived importance of goals also determines the time spent on goal-relevant activities in daily life (Cantor et al. 1991; Emmons, 1991).

Personal meaning determines the extent to which well-being is influenced by the outcome of goal pursuits. In a daily diary study, Oishi, Diener, Suh, and Lucas (1999) found that within-person changes in life satisfaction were strongly linked to success in domains that individuals valued. Similarly, Sheldon and Elliot (1999) found that goal fulfillment was associated with greater well-being, but only if the goals were consistent with the individual's core values.

April and Avalon can help demonstrate the importance of personally meaningful goals. Both of them want to get in shape and learn how to play the piano. For April, however, getting in shape is far more meaningful than playing the piano whereas the opposite is true for Avalon. Exercising, therefore, is more likely to promote the well-being of April compared to Avalon, whereas playing the piano is more likely to promote the well-being of Avalon compared to April.

Are approach goals more meaningful to individuals than avoidance goals? There is currently no evidence to suggest that approach and avoidance goals differ in how meaningful or important they are to individuals, nor is there a reason to expect them to differ (Elliot & Church, 2002). To the extent that any goal can be personally meaningful, individuals may be able to experience meaning in life as they pursue approach or avoidance goals, as long as the goals they pursue are meaningful to them.

It is theoretically possible, therefore, that some individuals view approach goals as more meaningful than avoidance goals. As an example, for April, winning the $100 prize in the pumpkin pie festival may be more meaningful than selling enough pies to cover her $100 investment. It is also theoretically possible, however, that some individuals view avoidance goals as more meaningful than approach goals. For Avalon, for example, selling enough pies to cover her investment is more important than winning the monetary prize. To the extent that both April and Avalon can fill their life with meaning by pursuing goals that are important to them, April is more likely to find meaning in life by pursuing approach goals, whereas Avalon is more likely to find meaning in life by pursuing avoidance goals.

In summary, both approach and avoidance goals have the potential of promoting well-being by filling life with meaning. What is it, however, that leads individuals to view some goals as more meaningful than others? Clearly, individuals vary dramatically in the goals that they find personally meaningful. In the remainder of the chapter, we explore the role of individual differences in moderating the link between approach–avoidance goals and well-being.

INDIVIDUAL DIFFERENCES MODERATE THE LINK BETWEEN APPROACH–AVOIDANCE GOALS AND WELL-BEING

The importance of individual differences has been highlighted in research on motivation as well as in research on well-being. Individual differences are critical in determining the propensity to pursue approach or avoidance goals (see Larsen, 2008). Individual differences are also critical in predicting overall levels of well-being (for a review, see Diener & Lucas, 1999). In fact, individuals who typically pursue approach goals tend to have higher levels of well-being, whereas those who typically pursue avoidance goals tend to have lower levels of well-being (Carver, Sutton, & Scheier, 2000; Urry et al., 2004).

Prior research on individual differences assumed that the link between approach–avoidance goals and well-being is relatively fixed. In other words, there is a fixed balance between approach and avoidance goals that is optimal for well-being. From this perspective, individual differences cannot change the link between approach–avoidance goals and well-being, but they can determine which goals are more likely to be pursued and what level of well-being the individual is predisposed to experience.

In this chapter, however, we propose a novel approach. We argue that the link between approach–avoidance goals and well-being is relatively dynamic. In other words, the balance between approach and avoidance goals that is optimal for well-being varies as a function of individual differences. For some individuals, increasing the pursuits of approach (vs. avoidance) goals may be beneficial for well-being, whereas for others this may carry little benefit. In other words, individual differences can change the nature of the link between approach–avoidance goals and well-being.

What kind of individual differences might moderate the link between approach–avoidance goals and well-being? Building on activity and telic theories, two types of individual differences may be critical. Activity theories emphasize the importance of goal desirability. From this perspective, individual differences in the desirability of goals should moderate the link between goals and well-being. Second, telic theories emphasize the importance of goal feasibility (i.e., the likelihood of successful goal pursuits). From this perspective, individual differences in the feasibility of goals should moderate the link between goals and well-being.

The desirability and feasibility of goals also feature prominently in theories of self-regulation as determinants of the personal value of goals (Ajzen, 1985; Gollwitzer, 1990; Heckhausen & Leppmann, 1991). In the following sections, therefore, we discuss the importance of individual differences in the desirability and feasibility of approach–avoidance goals and the potential implications of such differences for well-being. We begin by reviewing individual differences in the desirability of goals and proceed to review individual differences in the feasibility of goals. In each case, we review the role of individual differences from a theoretical perspective and then discuss one empirical example.

DESIRABILITY OF APPROACH AND AVOIDANCE GOALS: AN ACTIVITY THEORY PERSPECTIVE

Individuals prefer to pursue goals that are desirable to them. The desirability of goals, in turn, is determined by the perceived attractiveness of goal attainment. Focusing on pleasure as the determinant of well-being, goal desirability should be determined by the degree of pleasant affect that is expected to result from goal attainment. The pursuit of goals that are expected to yield pleasant affect when attained (i.e., desirable goals) should promote well-being.

Focusing on meaning as the determinant of well-being, goal desirability should be determined by the extent to which the goal is consistent with a person's daimon, or true self (Ryan & Deci, 2000; Waterman, 1993). The pursuit of authentic (i.e., desirable) goals should promote well-being (Harter, 2002). For example, the self-concordance model (Sheldon & Elliot, 1999) maintains that the pursuit of self-concordant goals (i.e., goals that are consistent with the core values of the individual) moderates the link between goal attainment and well-being. Such moderation was found to be independent of self-efficacy, indicating that the desirability of goals can be separable from their feasibility.

Individual differences in the desirability of approach–avoidance goals, therefore, may moderate their impact on well-being. For instance, if April perceives approach goals as more desirable than Avalon, she may find working for a promotion more rewarding and meaningful. The process of pursuing approach goals, therefore, may be more conducive to the well-being of April than Avalon.

Indeed, we argue that individuals who view approach goals as more desirable than avoidance goals should be more likely to benefit from pursuing approach goals.

However, individuals who view avoidance goals as more desirable than approach goals may not benefit as much from pursuing approach goals. To support this argument, in the next section we review cultural differences as reflecting individual differences in the desirability of approach and avoidance goals.

DESIRABILITY OF APPROACH–AVOIDANCE GOALS: CULTURAL DIFFERENCES AS AN EXAMPLE

In this section, we focus on the role of culture in determining the desirability of approach and avoidance goals and the implications of such differences for well-being (for reviews on cultural differences in well-being, see Diener et al., 2003; Diener & Suh, 2000; Tov & Diener, 2007). We have emphasized the role of goal desirability as moderating the impact of goals on well-being. Indeed, many agree that the implications of a goal for well-being depend on the extent to which it is considered desirable in a given culture (Cantor & Sanderson, 1999).

The role of culture in determining the desirability of goals has been explored primarily in the context of individualistic versus collectivistic cultures, focusing on the comparison between European Americans and Asians, respectively (e.g., Oishi, Schimmack, Diener, & Suh, 1998). In this context, there is evidence that culture determines the desirability of goals. For instance, individualistic goals are perceived as more desirable in individualistic cultures whereas collectivistic goals are perceived as more desirable in collectivistic cultures (Triandis, 1995). Furthermore, the pursuits of goals that are desirable according to cultural norms are more likely to promote well-being. For instance, pursuing goals that are consistent with individualistic values promoted well-being among European Americans but not Asian Americans. On the other hand, pursuing goals that are consistent with collectivistic values promoted well-being among Asian Americans, but not European Americans (Oishi & Diener, 2001).

Individualistic and collectivistic cultures also differ in the extent to which approach and avoidance goals are considered desirable. In particular, compared to collectivistic cultures, individualistic cultures view approach goals as more desirable (Elliot, Chirkov, Kim, & Sheldon, 2001; Lee, Aaker, & Gardner, 2000). If well-being is enhanced by the pursuit of desirable goals, pursuing more approach than avoidance goals should promote the well-being of members of individualistic cultures (e.g., European Americans) but not the well-being of members of collectivistic cultures (e.g., Asians). This indeed seems to be the case. Although pursuing more approach than avoidance goals was conducive to the well-being of

European Americans, this was not the case for Asian Americans, Koreans, and Russians (Elliot et al., 2001).

It appears, therefore, that pursuing more approach than avoidance goals is conducive to well-being particularly in cultures that view approach goals as more desirable than avoidance goals. The pursuit of more approach than avoidance goals, however, does not promote well-being in cultures that consider approach and avoidance goals as equally desirable. This may be because the desirability of approach–avoidance goals influences how meaningful they are to the individual. More meaningful pursuits are more likely to promote well-being.

Can the desirability of approach–avoidance goals also carry affective implications? In general, approach goals are associated with excitement or sadness whereas avoidance goals are associated with calmness or anxiety. Although the affective implications of approach and avoidance goals are likely consistent across individuals, their impact on well-being may differ across cultures. For instance, if approach and avoidance goals differ in their desirability across cultures, the affective experiences that are linked to approach and avoidance may also differ in their desirability across cultures.

On the basis of an instrumental approach to emotion (Tamir, 2005; Tamir, Chiu, & Gross, 2007), individuals seek out either emotions that are pleasant or emotions that are instrumental for important goal pursuits. For instance, although it is unpleasant to experience, an individual may view anger as desirable when her goal is to confront a wrong-doer. Applying these assumptions to the present context, one could argue that cultures value affective experiences that are associated with the pursuit of culturally desirable goals.

The idea that some cultures may value excitement, for example, more highly than other cultures may sound surprising to some. However, consistent with the predictions of the instrumental approach to emotion, there is now evidence that cultures differ in the affective experiences that they value. In a large cross-cultural study, Eid and Diener (2001) found that pride, which reflects approach goals, was viewed as more desirable by members of individualistic cultures.

More recently, Tsai and her colleagues (Tsai, Knutson, & Fung, 2006) found that even after controlling for actual affect, European Americans valued feelings such as excitement that reflect approach goals. On the other hand, Asian Americans and Chinese valued feelings such as calmness and relief that reflect avoidance goals. In other words, members of individualistic (vs. collectivistic) cultures view approach-related affect as more desirable, whereas members of collectivistic (vs. individualistic) cultures view avoidance-related affect as more desirable.

What are the implications of cross-cultural differences in affect valuation for well-being? One compelling question for future research is whether approach-related emotions are stronger predictors of well-being among individualistic cultures, whereas avoidance-related emotions are stronger predictors of well-being among collectivistic cultures. Although this hypothesis has not been tested directly, it is consistent with the idea that the impact of emotional experiences on well-being depends upon the desirability of such experiences in a given culture (Markus & Kitayama, 1994; Schimmack, Radhakrishnan, Oishi, Dzokoto, & Ahadi, 2002). Another important question involves the specific cultural beliefs that underlie such differences. Given that the studies reviewed above involved mainly Asian samples, it may be useful to explore whether the obtained cultural differences are associated with collectivism, broadly construed, or with the Confucian system, more specifically.

In summary, the research reviewed in this section demonstrates that cultures differ in the desirability of approach and avoidance goals. Whereas individualistic (vs. collectivistic) cultures view approach goals as more desirable, collectivistic (vs. individualistic) cultures view avoidance goals as more desirable. As a result, the pursuit of approach goals is more meaningful to members of individualistic cultures and the emotions they give rise to are considered more desirable.

It is, therefore, not surprising that the pursuit of approach (vs. avoidance) goals promotes well-being in individualistic, but not collectivistic, cultures. What about the pursuit of avoidance goals? Such pursuits do not necessarily impair well-being in members of collectivistic cultures. Whether or not the pursuit of avoidance (vs. approach) goals can promote well-being in collectivistic cultures remains to be seen.

FEASIBILITY OF APPROACH AND AVOIDANCE GOALS: A TELIC THEORY PERSPECTIVE

As outlined earlier, both the process and the outcome of goal pursuit has implications for well-being. Indeed, individuals differ not only in how desirable a goal is for them but also in how feasible it is. Feasibility is determined by individuals' judgments of their capabilities to perform relevant goal-directed behaviors (i.e., self-efficacy, Bandura, 1977) and the beliefs that these behaviors will be successful (Oettingen & Gollwitzer, 2004). Individuals prefer to pursue goals that are feasible to them (Brunstein, 1993) and the pursuit of feasible goals, in turn, promotes well-being (Brunstein et al., 1999).

Feasibility or self-efficacy might be based on inherent skills and prior experience in pursuing the goal (Bandura, 1977).

Individual differences in the feasibility of approach–avoidance goals, therefore, may moderate their impact on well-being. For instance, if successfully pursuing approach goals is more feasible for April than for Avalon, winning the first prize in the country fair may be more conducive to the well-being of April than Avalon.

Indeed, we argue that individuals for whom approach goals are more feasible than avoidance goals should be more likely to benefit from pursuing approach goals. What about individuals for whom avoidance goals are more feasible than approach goals. Might it be possible that for these individuals, the pursuit of avoidance goals may be beneficial in some respect? To explore these questions in the next section, we review evidence for regulatory fit as reflecting individual differences in the feasibility of approach and avoidance goals.

FEASIBILITY OF APPROACH–AVOIDANCE GOALS: REGULATORY FIT AS AN EXAMPLE

Might the pursuit of approach or avoidance goals be more feasible to some individuals compared to others? Research on regulatory fit suggests that the answer is yes. Regulatory fit is the sense of value that arises when people act in a way that sustains their motivational orientation (Higgins, 2000). For example, if an individual is primarily motivated to approach, framing a goal in terms of a desired end-state increases the value of pursing the goal. Similarly, if an individual is primarily motivated to avoid, framing a goal in terms of avoiding an undesired end-state increases the value of pursing that goal.

When individuals pursue goals in a way that fits their motivational orientation, they are more engaged in goal pursuit, view the pursuit as more valuable, and are more likely to be successful (Förster, Higgins, & Idson, 1998; Higgins, Idson, Freitas, Spiegel, & Molden, 2003; Higgins et al., 1994; Shah, Higgins, & Friedman, 1998). Individuals also experience greater enjoyment during goal pursuit when they pursue the goal in a manner that fits their dispositional orientation (Freitas & Higgins, 2002).

Such effects may be driven by the greater feasibility of motivationally consistent goals. Mann, Sherman, and Updegraff (2004) found that individuals were more effective in promoting health behaviors when health messages were framed in ways that matched their underlying motivational dispositions. Individuals who were approach motivated were more successful when health messages were framed as approach goals, whereas individuals who were avoidance motivated were more successful when

health messages were framed as avoidance goals. Consistent with the emphasis of a telic approach on feasibility, the effects were fully mediated by perceptions of self-efficacy in goal pursuit (Sherman, Mann, & Updegraff, in press).

Thus, if April is an approach-oriented person, she might find working toward winning the first prize in the pumpkin pie festival more feasible than selling enough pies. Such pursuits would be more enjoyable to her and she might eventually be more successful at them. On the other hand, if Avalon is an avoidance-oriented person, she might find selling enough pies to cover her expenses more feasible than winning the first prize. She might be more motivated to do so, and ultimately she might be more successful in doing so.

The feasibility of approach–avoidance goals influences how meaningful they are to the individual. But what are the implications of greater goal feasibility for affective experiences? Recent evidence suggests that the feasibility of goals may determine the intensity of goal-related emotional reactions. Idson, Liberman, and Higgins (2000) found that compared to approach-oriented individuals, avoidance-oriented individuals were less happy following the successful pursuit of approach goals and less sad following the unsuccessful pursuit of approach goals. On the other hand, they were calmer and more relieved following the successful pursuit of avoidance goals and more anxious following the unsuccessful pursuit of avoidance goals.

These findings are astounding because they suggest that the affective consequences of goal pursuits might vary across individuals. April, for instance, may feel better (i.e., more excited) if she wins the first prize at a competition, whereas Avalon may feel better (i.e., more relieved) if she manages to sell enough pies to cover her expenses. The intensity of affective reactions to success and failure in goal pursuit may depend on how feasible the goal is for the individual.

Furthermore, the implications of affective experience for well-being may also differ as a function of goal feasibility. In fact, individual differences in approach and avoidance motivation influence the extent to which well-being depends on pleasant and unpleasant affective experiences. Empirical evidence for this hypothesis was recently provided by Updegraff, Gable, and Taylor (2004). These authors demonstrated that the more approach-oriented individuals were, the more they tended to base their judgments of well-being on the frequency of their pleasant affect. This finding suggests that the weight of pleasant and unpleasant affect in judgments of well-being may itself vary as a function of motivational dispositions.

In summary, research on regulatory fit demonstrates that the feasibility of approach and avoidance goals varies as a function of basic motivational orientations. Pursuing approach goals may be more feasible for approach-oriented individuals, whereas pursuing avoidance goals may be more feasible for avoidance-oriented individuals. The pursuit of feasible goals, in turn, is likely to promote well-being because it is more meaningful, the chances of success are higher, and success leads to more intense pleasant experiences.

On the basis of this analysis, approach-oriented individuals may be expected to experience greater well-being when pursuing more approach than avoidance goals. What about avoidance-oriented individuals? On the one hand, as discussed earlier, avoidance goals are harder to monitor and engender negative cognitions. Avoidance goals, therefore, should theoretically impair the well-being of avoidance-oriented individuals in some ways. On the other hand, as discussed in this section, avoidance goals may be more meaningful and feasible for avoidance-oriented individuals. Avoidance goals, therefore, could theoretically also contribute to the well-being of avoidance-oriented individuals in some ways. What are the implications of pursuing avoidance goals for avoidance-oriented individuals? We conclude this chapter by discussing this conflicting goal pursuit.

CONFLICTING GOAL PURSUITS OF AVOIDANCE-ORIENTED INDIVIDUALS

In the previous sections, we argued that individual differences in the desirability and feasibility of goals can moderate the impact of such goals on well-being. In particular, we proposed that approach goals may be more desirable and feasible for individuals who are high (vs. low) in approach motivation. On the other hand, avoidance goals may be more desirable and feasible for individuals who are high (vs. low) in avoidance motivation. As we have demonstrated above, the pursuit of desirable and feasible goals is likely to promote well-being.

Approach-oriented individuals, therefore, benefit from approach goals because of the general attributes of these goals and because of their desirability and feasibility. What about avoidance-oriented individuals? On the one hand, these individuals are likely to suffer some negative consequences when pursuing avoidance goals because of the attributes of such goals. On the other hand, avoidance-oriented individuals may attain some benefits from pursuing avoidance goals because such goals are more feasible and perhaps more desirable to them. Avoidance-oriented individuals, therefore, are likely to experience some degree of conflict in their goal pursuits.

Avalon, for example, may find avoidance goals difficult to monitor and pursuing such goals make her focus on unpleasant future outcomes. Nevertheless, she might find such goals to be personally meaningful, she might be more successful at obtaining them, and she may experience more intense pleasant affect as a result. It is therefore possible that the pursuit of avoidance goals is not as harmful for Avalon as it is for April. However, does the pursuit of avoidance goals benefit Avalon in any way?

We have begun to explore this interesting possibility in the context of trait neuroticism, a trait that is closely related to the avoidance motivational system (Carver et al., 2000; Elliot & Thrash, 2002). We began by examining whether individuals who are high (vs. low) in neuroticism can benefit from the ability to successfully pursue avoidance goals (Tamir, Robinson, & Solberg, 2006).

Specifically, we examined neurotic individuals who varied in the extent to which they were skilled at identifying threats. Individuals who can quickly identify threats are more likely to successfully avoid them (Öhman, 2001; Robinson, 1998). Therefore, we expected individuals high in neuroticism to benefit from being skilled at threat identification. Our results supported this hypothesis. Neurotic individuals who were relatively skilled at threat identification experienced lower levels of negative affect in their daily lives over a week long period as well as higher levels of satisfaction in various life domains (Tamir et al., 2007). These findings suggest that individuals high (vs. low) in neuroticism may benefit in some respects from the successful pursuit of avoidance goals.

Emotions can also promote successful goal pursuits. For instance, emotions direct attention toward potentially threatening or rewarding information (Mogg & Bradley, 1998; Oatley & Johnson-Laird, 1987; Tamir & Robinson, 2007), instigate physiological responses that support approach or avoidance behaviors (Frijda, 1988; Panksepp, 1982), and signal the effectiveness with which people are pursuing their goals (Carver, 2001). In particular, avoidance-related emotions, such as worry or anxiety, may promote the successful pursuit of avoidance goals (Parrott, 2002).

If avoidance emotions (e.g., worry) promote the pursuit of avoidance goals, would the experience of such emotions promote the successful goal pursuits of neurotic individuals? Furthermore, assuming that successful goal pursuits promote well-being, would neurotic individuals be motivated to experience such emotions when engaged in goal pursuit? We recently tested these counterintuitive hypotheses by having neurotic individuals perform an anagram task following either a happy or a worried mood induction (Tamir, 2005). Individuals who were high in neuroticism solved more anagrams correctly following a worried (vs. happy) mood induction. Furthermore, individuals high (vs. low) in neuroticism were more motivated to increase their level of worry when they expected to perform a motivationally significant task.

Taken together, these findings demonstrate that neurotic individuals may benefit, at least in some respect, from the ability to effectively pursue avoidance goals. These findings, however, do not necessarily show that pursuing avoidance goals is beneficial for the well-being of avoidance-oriented individuals. Instead, we propose that pursuing avoidance goals may have mixed implications (i.e., harmful in some respects and beneficial in others) for avoidance-oriented individuals.

In summary, we argue that approach and avoidance goals can have both main effects as well as interactive effects on well-being. Some implications of goal pursuits are likely identical across individuals. Other implications of goal pursuits, however, likely differ among individuals. For instance, individuals differ in the extent to which approach and avoidance goals are desirable or feasible to them, leading such goals to have potentially different implications for affective experiences and meaning in life. For some individuals (e.g., approach-oriented), pursuing avoidance goals carries little benefit. For other individuals (e.g., avoidance-oriented), pursuing avoidance goals may carry at least some temporary benefits. The overall impact of avoidance goals on well-being may be influenced by the relative weight of their different implications (e.g., the cognitive content they evoke vs. how personally meaningful they are) and by the degree of conflict they evoke. Exploring the overall impact of avoidance goals on the well-being of avoidance-oriented individuals is an important endeavor for future research.

Approach goals also elicit positive cognitions, by leading individuals to focus on desirable outcomes. Avoidance goals, on the other hand, are more difficult to monitor and they elicit negative cognitions, by leading individuals to focus on undesirable outcomes. These characteristics make the pursuit of approach goals generally beneficial for well-being.

In this chapter, however, we argued that the implications of approach and avoidance goals for well-being can also vary dramatically across individuals. Well-being, for instance, is enhanced by the pursuit of personally meaningful experiences. In particular, the pursuit of goals that are desirable and feasible is conducive to well-being. The desirability and feasibility of approach and avoidance goals vary as a function of motivationally relevant individual differences.

Which goals are most likely to promote well-being? A combination of both approach and avoidance goals is important for adaptive functioning. We have argued that the extent to which individuals should pursue more approach than avoidance goals is influenced by the desirability and feasibility of these goals for a given individual. Individuals for whom approach goals are desirable or feasible may experience greater well-being if their goal pursuits are heavily skewed toward approach goals. This, however, is not the case for individuals for whom avoidance goals are desirable or feasible. Such individuals may not necessarily benefit from pursuing approach goals and may even benefit in certain ways from pursuing avoidance goals. As we have learned from April and Avalon, no single mix of approach and avoidance goals is optimal for the well-being of all individuals. Instead, to maximize well-being, individuals may need to find the mix that fits them best.

SUMMARY

What is the source of happiness? What gives meaning to life? What makes life worth living? Greater well-being results from experiencing more frequent pleasant and less frequent unpleasant affect and from having personally meaningful experiences in life. In this chapter, we argued that the pursuits of approach and avoidance goals are inextricably linked to well-being because both the process and the outcome of their pursuits can shape affective experiences as well as provide meaning to life.

What are the differential implications of approach and avoidance goals for well-being? Some of these implications are consistent across individuals. In particular, approach goals are likely easier to monitor so that perceived progress is likely greater during their pursuit.

REFERENCES

Ajzen, I. (1985). From intentions to actions: A theory of planned behavior. In J. Kuhl & J. Beckman (Eds.), *Action control: From cognition to behavior* (pp. 11–39). Berlin: Springer-Verlag.

Bandura, A. (1977). Self-efficacy: Toward a unifying theory of behavioral change. *Psychological Review, 84,* 191–215.

Brunstein, J. C. (1993). Personal goals and subjective well-being: A longitudinal study. *Journal of Personality and Social Psychology, 65,* 1061–1070.

Brunstein, J. C., Schultheiss, O. C., & Grassman, R. (1998). Personal goals and emotional well-being: The moderating role of motive dispositions. *Journal of Personality and SocialPsychology, 75,* 494–508.

Brunstein, J. C., Schultheiss, O. C., & Maier, G. W. (1999). The pursuit of personal goals: A motivational approach to well-being and life adjustment. In J. Brandtstadter &

R. M. Lerner (Eds.), *Action and self-development: Theory and research through the life span* (pp. 169–196). Thousand Oaks, CA: Sage Publications.

Cantor, N. (1990). From thought to behavior: "having" and "doing" in the study of personality and cognition. *American Psychologist*, *45*, 735–750.

Cantor, N., & Sanderson, C. A. (1999). Life task participation and well-being: The importance of taking part in daily life. In D. Kahneman, E. Diener, & N. Schwarz (Eds.), *Well-being: The foundations of hedonic psychology* (pp. 230–243). New York: Russell Sage Foundation.

Cantor, N., Norem, J., Langston, C., Zirkel, S., Fleeson, W., & Cook-Flannagan, C. (1991). Life tasks and daily life experience. *Journal of Personality*, *59*, 425–451.

Carver, C. S. (2001). Affect and the functional bases of behavior: On the dimensional structure of affective experience. *Personality and Social Psychology Review*, *5*, 345–356.

Carver, C. S. (2004). Negative affects deriving from the behavioral approach system. *Emotion*, *4*, 3–22.

Carver, C. S., Avivi, Y. E., & Laurenceau, J.-P. Approach, avoidance, and emotional experiences. In A. J. Elliot (Ed.), *Handbook of approach and avoidance motivation*. (pp. 385–398). Boca Raton, Florida: Taylor & Francis.

Carver, C. S., & Scheier, M. (1990). *Principles of self-regulation: Action and emotion*. New York: Guilford Press.

Carver, C. S., & Scheier, M. F. (1998). *On the self-regulation of behavior*. New York: Cambridge University Press.

Carver, C. S., Sutton, S. K., & Scheier, M. F. (2000). Action, emotion, and personality: Emerging conceptual integration. *Personality and Social Psychology Bulletin*, *26*, 741–751.

Coats, E. J., Janoff-Bulman, R., & Alpert, N. (1996). Approach versus avoidance goals: Differences in self-evaluation and well-being. *Personality and Social Psychology Bulletin*, *22*, 1057–1067.

Davidson, R. J. (1993). The neuropsychology of emotion and affective style. In M. Lewis & J. M. Haviland (Eds.), *Handbook of emotions* (pp. 143–154). New York: Guilford Press.

Diener, E. (1984). Subjective well-being. *Psychological Bulletin*, *95*, 542–575.

Diener, E., & Lucas, R. E. (1999). Personality and subjective well-being. In D. Kahneman, E. Diener, & N. Schwarz (Eds.), *Well-being: The foundations of hedonic psychology* (pp. 213–229). New York: Russell Sage Foundation.

Diener, E., & Lucas, R. E. (2000). Subjective emotional well-being. In M. Lewis & J. M. Haviland-Jones (Eds.), *Handbook of emotions* (2nd ed., pp. 325–337). New York: Guilford Press.

Diener, E., Oishi, S., & Lucas, R. E. (2003). Personality, culture, and subjective well-being: Emotional and cognitive evaluations of life. *Annual Review of Psychology*, *54*, 403–425.

Diener, E., & Suh, E. M. (2000). *Culture and subjective well-being*. Cambridge, MA: MIT press.

Eid, M., & Diener, E. (2001). Norms for experiencing emotions in different cultures: Inter- and intranational differences. *Journal of Personality and Social Psychology*, *81*, 869–885.

Elliot, A. J. (2008). Approach and avoidance motivation. In A. J. Elliot (Ed.), *Handbook of approach and avoidance motivation* (pp. 3–14). Boca Raton, Florida: Taylor & Francis.

Elliot, A. J., & Church, M. A. (2002). Client-articulated avoidance goals in the therapy context. *Journal of Counseling Psychology*, *49*, 243–254.

Elliot, A. J., & Friedman, R. (2007). Approach-avoidance: A central characteristic of personal goals. In B. R. Little, K. Salmela-Aro, & S. D. Phillips (Eds.), *Personal project pursuit: Goals, action, and human flourishing* (pp. 97–118). Mahwah, NJ: Lawrence Erlbaum.

Elliot, A. J., & Sheldon, K. M. (1997). Avoidance achievement motivation: A personal goals analysis. *Journal of Personality and Social Psychology*, *73*, 171–185.

Elliot, A. J., & Sheldon, K. M. (1998). Avoidance personal goals and the personality–illness relationship. *Journal of Personality and Social Psychology*, *75*, 1282–1299

Elliot, A. J., & Thrash, T. M. (2002). Approach–avoidance motivation in personality: Approach and avoidance temperaments and goals. *Journal of Personality and Social Psychology*, *82*, 804–818.

Elliot, A. J., Gable, S. L., & Mapes, R. R. (2006). Approach and avoidance motivation in the social domain. *Personality and Social Psychology Bulletin*, *32*, 378–391.

Elliot, A. J., Sheldon, K. M., & Church, M. A. (1997). Avoidance personal goals and subjective well-being. *Personality and Social Psychology Bulletin*, *23*, 915–927.

Elliot, A. J., Chirkov, V. C., Kim, Y., & Sheldon, K. M. (2001). A cross-cultural analysis of avoidance (relative to approach) personal goals. *Psychological Science*, *12*, 505–510.

Emmons, R. A. (1986). Personal strivings: An approach to personality and subjective well-being. *Journal of Personality and Social Psychology*, *51*, 1058–1068.

Emmons, R. A. (1991). Personal strivings, daily life events, and psychological and physical well-being. *Journal of Personality*, *59*, 453–472.

Emmons, R. A. (1996). Striving and feeling: Personal goals and subjective well-being. In P. M. Gollwitzer & J. A. Bargh (Eds.), *The psychology of action: Linking cognition and motivation to behavior* (pp. 313–337). New York: Guilford Press.

Förster, J., Higgins, E. T., & Idson, L. C. (1998). Approach and avoidance strength during goal attainment: Regulatory focus and the "goal looms larger" effect. *Journal of Personality and Social Psychology*, *75*, 1115–1131.

Freitas, A. L., & Higgins, E. T. (2002). Enjoying goal-directed action: The role of regulatory fit. *Psychological Science*, *13*, 1–6.

Frijda, N. H. (1988). The laws of emotion. *American Psychologist*, *43*, 349–358.

Gollwitzer, P. M. (1990). *Action phases and mind-sets*. New York: Guilford Press.

Gollwitzer, P. M. (1999). Implementation intentions: Strong effects of simple plans. *American Psychologist*, *54*, 493–503.

Gray, J. A. (1990). Brain systems that mediate both emotion and cognition. *Cognition and Emotion*, *4*, 269–288.

Harmon-Jones, E., Peterson, C., Gable, P. A., & Harmon-Jones, C. Anger and approach–avoidance motivation. In A. J. Elliot (Ed.), *Handbook of approach and avoidance motivation.* (pp. 399–414). Boca Raton, Florida: Taylor & Francis.

Harter, S. (2002). Authenticity. In C. R. Snyder & S. J. Lopez (Eds.), *Handbook of positive psychology* (pp. 382–394). New York: Oxford University Press.

Heckhausen, H., & Leppmann, P. K. (1991). *Motivation and action.* New York: Springer-Verlag.

Higgins, E. T. (1997). Beyond pleasure and pain. *American Psychologist, 52,* 1280–1300.

Higgins, E. T. (2000). Making a good decision: Value from fit. *American Psychologist, 55,* 1217–1230.

Higgins, T. E., Idson, L. C., Freitas, A. L., Spiegel, S., & Molden, D. C. (2003). Transfer of value from fit. *Journal of Personality and Social Psychology, 45,* 20–31.

Higgins, E. T., Roney, C. J. R., Crowe, E., & Hymes, C. (1994). Ideal versus ought predilections for approach and avoidance distinct self-regulatory systems. *Journal of Personality and Social Psychology, 66,* 276–286.

Idson, L. C., Liberman, N., & Higgins, E. T. (2000). Distinguishing gains from nonlosses and losses from nongains: A regulatory focus perspective on hedonic intensity. *Journal of Experimental Social Psychology, 36,* 252–274.

Kahneman, D. (1999). Objective happiness. In D. Kahneman, E. Diener, & N. Schwarz (Eds.), *Well-being: The foundations of hedonic psychology* (pp. 3–25). New York: Russell Sage Foundation.

Klinger, E. (1975). Consequences of commitment to and disengagement from incentives. *Psychological Review, 82,* 1–25.

Kubovy, M. (1999). On the pleasures of the mind. In D. Kahneman, E. Diener, & N. Schwarz (Eds.), *Well-being: The foundations of hedonic psychology* (pp. 134–154). New York: Russell Sage Foundation.

Lang, P. J. (1995). The emotion probe: Studies of motivation and attention. *American Psychologist, 50,* 372–385.

Larsen, R. J. & Augustine, A. A. (2008). Basic personality dispositions related to approach and avoidance: Extraversion/neuroticism, BAS/BIS, and positive/negative affectivity. In A. J. Elliot (Ed.), *Handbook of approach and avoidance motivation* (pp. 151–164). Boca Raton, Florida: Taylor & Francis.

Lauriola, M., & Levin, I. P. (2001). Personality traits and risky decision-making in a controlled experimental task: An exploratory study. *Personality and Individual Differences, 31,* 215–226.

Lee, A. Y., Aaker, J. L., & Gardner, W. L. (2000). The pleasures and pains of distinct self-construals: The role of interdependence in regulatory focus. *Journal of Personality and Social Psychology, 78,* 1122–1134.

Mann, T.L., Sherman, D. S., & Updegraff, J. A. (2004). Dispositional motivations and message framing: A test of the congruency hypothesis. *Health Psychology, 23,* 330–334.

Markus, H. R., & Kitayama, S. (1994). The cultural shaping of emotion: A conceptual framework. In S. Kitayama & H. R. Markus (Ed.), *Emotion and culture: Empirical studies of mutual influence* (pp. 339–351). Washington, DC: American Psychological Association.

Mogg, K., & Bradley, B. P. (1998). A cognitive-motivational analysis of anxiety. *Behavioral Research and Therapy, 36,* 809–848.

Oatley, K., & Johnson-Laird, P. N. (1987). Towards a cognitive theory of emotions. *Cognition and Emotion, 1,* 29–50.

Oettingen, G., & Gollwitzer, P. M. (2004). Goal setting and goal striving. In M. B. Brewer & M. Hewstone (Eds.), *Emotion and motivation* (pp. 165–183). Malden, MA: Blackwell Publishing.

Öhman, A. (2001). Emotion drives attention: Detecting the snake in the grass. *Journal of Experimental Psychology: General, 130,* 466–478.

Oishi, S., & Diener, E. (2001). Goals, culture, and subjective well-being. *Personality and Social Psychology Bulletin, 27,* 1674–1682.

Oishi, S., Diener, E., Suh, E., & Lucas, R. E. (1999). Value as a moderator in subjective well-being. *Journal of Personality, 67,* 157–184.

Oishi, S., Schimmack, U., Diener, E., & Suh, E. M. (1998). The measurement of values and individualism-collectivism. *Personality and Social Psychology Bulletin, 24,* 1177–1189.

Palys, T. S., & Little, B. R. (1983). Perceived life satisfaction and the organization of personal project systems. *Journal of Personality and Social Psychology, 44,* 1221–1230.

Panksepp, J. (1982). Toward a general psychobiological theory of emotions. *Behavioral and Brain Sciences, 5,* 407–467.

Parrott, W. G. (2002). The functional utility of negative emotions. In L. F. Barrett & P. Salovey (Eds.), *The wisdom in feeling: Psychological processes in emotional intelligence* (pp. 341–359). New York: Guilford Press.

Robinson, M. D. (1998). Running from William James' bear: A review of preattentive mechanisms and their contributions to emotional experience. *Cognition and Emotion, 12,* 667–696.

Ryan, R. M., & Deci, E. L. (2000). On happiness and human potentials: A review of research on hedonic and eudaimonic well-being. *Annual Review of Psychology, 52,* 141–166.

Ryff, C. D. (1989). Happiness is everything, or is it? Explorations on the meaning of psychological well-being. *Journal of Personality and Social Psychology, 57,* 1069–1081.

Schimmack, U., Radhakrishnan, P., Oishi, S., Dzokoto, V., & Ahadi, S. (2002). Culture, personality, and subjective well-being: Integrating process models of life satisfaction. *Journal of Personality and Social Psychology, 82,* 582–593.

Shah, J., Higgins, E. T., & Friedman, R. S. (1998). Performance incentives and means: How regulatory focus influences goal attainment. *Journal of Personality and Social Psychology, 74,* 285–293.

Sheldon, K. M., & Elliot, A. J. (1999). Goal striving, need satisfaction, and longitudinal well-being: The self-concordance model. *Journal of Personality and Social Psychology, 76,* 482–497.

Sherman, D. K., Mann, T. L., & Updegraff, J. A. (2006). Approach/avoidance orientation, message framing, and health behavior: Understanding the congruency effect. *Motivation and Emotion, 30,* 165–169.

Tamir, M. (2005). Don't worry, be happy? Neuroticism, trait-consistent affect regulation, and performance. *Journal of Personality and Social Psychology, 89,* 449–461.

Tamir, M., Chiu, C. Y., & Gross, J. J. (2007). Business or pleasure? Utilitarian versus hedonic considerations in emotion regulation. *Emotion, 7,* 546–554.

Tamir, M., & Robinson, M. D. (2007). The happy spotlight: Positive mood and selective attention to rewarding information. To appear in *Personality and Social Psychology Bulletin, 33,* 1124–1136.

Tamir, M., Robinson, M. D., & Solberg, E. C. (2006). You may worry, but can you recognize threats when you see them?: Neuroticism, threat identifications, and negative affect. *Journal of Personality, 74,* 1481–1506.

Triandis, H. C. (1995). *Individualism and collectivism.* Boulder, CO: Westview.

Tov, W., & Diener, E. (2007). Culture and subjective well-being. In S. Kitayama & D. Cohen (Eds.), *Handbook of cultural psychology* (pp. 691–713). New York: Guilford Press.

Tsai, J. L., Knutson, B., & Fung, H. H. (2006). Cultural variation in affect valuation. *Journal of Personality and Social Psychology, 90,* 288–307.

Updegraff, J. A., Gable, S. L., & Taylor, S. E. (2004). What makes experiences satisfying? The interaction of approach-avoidance motivations and emotions in well-being. *Journal of Personality and Social Psychology, 86,* 496–504.

Urry, H. L., Nitschke, J. B., Dolski, I., Jackson, D. C., Dalton, K. M., Mueller, C. J., et al. (2004). Making a life worth living: Neural correlates of well-being. *Psychological Science, 15,* 367–372.

Waterman, A. S. (1993). Two conceptions of happiness: Contrasts of personal expressiveness (eudaimonia) and hedonic enjoyment. *Journal of Personality and Social Psychology, 64,* 678–691.

Worth, K. A., Sullivan, H. W., Hertel, A. W., Rothman, A. J., & Jeffery, R. W. (2005). Avoidance goals can be beneficial: A look at smoking cessation. *Basic and Applied Social Psychology, 27,* 107–116.

Part VI

Cognition

Challenge and Threat Appraisal

25 Challenge and Threat

Jim Blascovich

CONTENTS

The biopsychosocial model (BPSM) of challenge and threat has evolved over the last decade or so, becoming increasingly more complex as more evidence has accumulated (Blascovich, 2007; Blascovich & Mendes, 2000; Blascovich & Tomaka, 1996). This chapter begins with a discussion of the relationships of the model's banner motivational constructs and the more general concepts of approach and avoidance motivation as elucidated in the introductory chapter to this volume and elsewhere, a comparison that has not been explored in any detail in the past. Such a comparison not only informs our challenge-threat model but also may help expand understanding of approach–avoidance motivation more generally. The current version of the BPSM of challenge and threat motivation is presented subsequently with attention to selected approach–avoidance energization models.

CHALLENGE–THREAT AS APPROACH–AVOIDANCE

Based on his broad and informed knowledge of the history of approach and avoidance motivational theory as well as his own contributions, Elliot (this volume; Elliot & Trash, 2002) defines *approach* motivation as *the energization of behavior directed toward positive or desirable stimuli* and *avoidance* motivation as *the energization of behavior directed away from negative or undesirable stimuli*. Elliot (this volume) argues convincingly that both energization and direction are necessary elements of approach–avoidance motivation. However, he points out that the direction of movement may in some cases (i.e., those associated with automatic evaluation) be predispositional and covert rather than overt, but still result in underlying physiological and somatic responses preparatory for approach and withdrawal.

There are, of course, at least two other logical possibilities regarding the relationship of energization and direction; specifically, energization toward negative stimuli, and energization away from positive stimuli. What may energize and "move" people in these directions has to do with relationships among goals. Specifically, energization toward a positive superordinate but distal goal (e.g., entering a profession) may require energization or movement toward a negative subordinate proximal goal (e.g., taking very difficult exams). Furthermore, energization away from a negative superordinate distal goal (e.g., going bankrupt, going to jail) may require energization and movement away from a positive subordinate proximal goal (e.g., creating an overly optimistic business plan, selling recreational drugs). Hence, as Elliot (2006) and others have pointed out, one must take motivational hierarchies into account to understand

approach and avoidance especially as they relate to approach–avoidance conflicts.

According to the BPSM, challenge results when an individual's evaluated resources outweigh situational demands and threat results when evaluated situational demands outweigh an individual's resources. If individuals were merely motivated by purely hedonistic goals of experiencing positive affect and avoiding negative affect on a moment by moment basis (as might be the case for infants, young children at times, and addicts), then challenge would map onto approach (and energization and task engagement) and threat onto avoidance (and energization and task disengagement) and that would be the end of it.

However, in order to achieve a desirable superordinate goal (e.g., entering a profession), an individual may be required to approach a series of subordinate goals (e.g., doing well on exams in school) that may prove threatening (i.e., ones in which an individual may not evaluate himself or herself as having personal resources that outweigh situational demands) to reach. Yet the superordinate goal is perceived as desirable enough (or the alternative to reaching the superordinate goal is so undesirable; e.g., flipping burgers for a living) that individuals will be energized to approach a necessary but negative subordinate goal and perform in what they themselves evaluate as threatening situations, even to the point of jeopardizing their physical well-being (Anderson et al., 1993; Blascovich, 2007).

In order to provide an understanding of the ways in which challenge and threat constructs relate to approach and avoidance, one must take into account the context within which the BPS model of challenge and threat is generally applied, the hierarchical nature of goals, and Elliot's important caveat regarding a possible disjunction between predispositions and actual (and we would add "gross") movements, If one does so, the concepts of challenge and threat relate to Elliot's approach–avoidance definitions albeit in a perhaps unexpected but important way.

The BPS focuses on contexts that are labeled *motivated performance situations*, ones that we assume are goal relevant and, hence, task engaging for individuals, and ones that require instrumental cognitive responses (e.g., answering questions on exams, presenting material in lectures, the "gives" and "takes" of bargaining and negotiation, arguing and debating, making chess moves, chiseling stone to create sculpture, etc.). Within this type of context, challenge clearly fits within Elliot's notions of energization and movement or approach toward positive or desirable stimuli.

Arguably, however, the BPSM construct of threat can also be categorized as an approach construct but one involving movement toward negative or undesirable stimuli. Furthermore, because of the disjunction between hedonic qualities of movement (i.e., toward) and affect (i.e., negative stimuli) for threat, the nature of threat approach undoubtedly differs from that of challenge as there is likely a tension between the need to approach and the desire to avoid. Hence, it fits long-lived notions of approach–avoidance conflict.

Although both challenge and threat involve psychological, physiological, and sometimes overt physical movement toward a goal, threat includes at least predispositional (in Elliot's terms) elements (e.g., neurophysiological and somatic ones) of movement away from a goal. Because of this tension, threat is likely the more variable, fragile, disruptible, and stressful of the two. Because both challenge and threat as so defined involve approach, they can be regarded as anchors of a bipolar motivational continuum separating them by degree of avoidance (see more discussion of this continuum below).

INTEGRATION OF PHYSIOLOGICAL ENERGIZATION AND EVALUATION THEORY

OVERVIEW

The BPSM of challenge and threat is so named because it attempts an integration of biological, psychological, and social psychological levels of analysis to explain motivational processes within human performance contexts, which in our view are necessarily social because nearly every aspect of human performance is influenced by the actual, imagined, and implied presence of others. The model also integrates processes within each of these levels of analysis. Within the biological level, the BPSM focuses on the interplay between autonomic and endocrine influences on the cardiovascular system. Within the psychological level, it incorporates cognitive and affective influences on evaluative processes. Within the social psychological level, it integrates intraindividual, interindividual, and environmental influences. Challenge/threat motivation is rooted in all three levels of analysis and the interplay within and among them. Hence, in our view, challenge and threat represent person/situation-evoked motivational states with affective, cognitive, and physiological antecedents and consequences.

THEORETICAL ROOTS

Biological Component

The BPSM is rooted in physiological energization theory, specifically Richard Dienstbier's (1989) theory of physiological toughness. Based nearly exclusively on animal work, Dienstbier theorized that differing patterns of cardiovascular responses during potentially threatening performance situations (e.g., foraging for food in the vicinity of predators) represent differences in the near term for task performance and in the far term for survival. His work identified central nervous system controlled neural and endocrine processes that give rise to two different patterns of cardiovascular responses in potentially threatening performance situations, such as those necessary for survival among members of the same mammalian species (e.g., squirrels): one for those animals who appear to thrive during and following performance and one for animals who do not.

Dienstbier labeled the performance and survival enhancing pattern as "physiological toughness," leaving the performance and survival reducing pattern to be labeled "physiological weakness." In terms of neurophysiological processes, both the physiological toughness and physiological weakness patterns involve sympathetic neural and adrenal medullary (SAM) axis activation. Such activation produces increased sympathetic neural stimulation increasing myocardial (i.e., heart muscle) contractility, more specifically left ventricle contractility (VC) and heart rate (HR). The left ventricle is the final pumping chamber of the heart forcing blood to the body through the aortic value and via the aorta. The adrenal medullary aspect of SAM axis activation eventuates in the release of epinephrine into the bloodstream further increasing HR and dilating the arteries, thereby decreasing total systemic peripheral vascular resistance (TPR). The result is relatively large increases in blood flow as measured by cardiac output (CO). However, in addition to SAM activation, physiologically weak animals experience activation of the hypothalamic pituitary adrenal (HPA) axis, more specifically the pituitary adrenal cortical (PAC) axis, along with the SAM activation. This HPA activation results in sustained adrenal cortical release of cortisol that dampens the SAM effects on TPR, thereby eliminating SAM-driven decreases in TPR (and often actually increasing TPR), thereby decreasing SAM-driven CO.

By providing a neurophysiological rationale based on the SAM and HPA axes, specifying a set of measurable cardiovascular responses (VC, HR, CO, and TPR) sensitive to SAM and HPA activation, and specifying distinctive patterns among critical cardiovascular responses within that set, Dienstbier presented a clear distinction of functional and dysfunctional cardiovascular response patterns during goal-relevant performance situations in animals. Subsequently, we (see below) experimentally tested his notions regarding these responses in humans in order to verify whether or not they presented as clear a distinction of functionality during goal-relevant performance situations as in animals.

Psychological Component

The BPSM is rooted in cognitive appraisal theories, particularly that of Lazarus (1991) and his colleagues (Lazarus & Folkman, 1984). Indeed, in the past we freely borrowed and used the term appraisal as in "appraisal of personal resources and situational demands" (cf. Blascovich & Tomaka, 1996). However, over time and in concert with increasing evidence of the important operational role of nonconscious or automatic processes, particularly those related to affect in everyday behavior (cf. Blascovich & Mendes, 2000), we realized that the determining processes were often much less conscious than the label "cognitive appraisal" implies. Subsequently, we came to label the central psychological process as one of "evaluation," which we believe not only has less conscious and cognitivistic connotations but also allows for the incorporation of more purely affective influences.

Integration

Lazarus and Folkman's appraisal model (1984) on coping and stress suggested that the human antecedents of what Dienstbier (1989) had described in animals as physiological toughness and weakness involved cognitive appraisals or evaluations of goal relevance, performance demands, and coping resources. If such evaluations in humans were predictably associated with Dienstbier's specified cardiovascular patterns of toughness and weakness responses, the biological and psychological aspects of performance motivation within a unified theory could be integrated. Furthermore, if Dienstbier's work generalizes to humans, the cardiovascular patterns he identified could be utilized to identify motivational states in humans as a function of personality, social psychological, and context factors.

Hence, we hypothesized that if an individual evaluated his or her personal resources as meeting or exceeding the demands of a goal-relevant performance situation, a positive hedonically toned motivational state, which we labeled challenge, would result. We also hypothesized that if an individual evaluated his or her personal resources as not meeting the demands, a negative hedonically toned motivational state would result, which we labeled threat.

VALIDATIONAL STUDIES

Our empirical validational studies involved laboratory-based motivated performance situations as described above (ones that are goal relevant and task engaging and that require instrumental cognitive responses; i.e., active coping tasks; Obrist, 1981). These performance situations involved laboratory tasks such as vocal serial subtraction (i.e., "mental arithmetic") and giving speeches, tasks often used by scientists in the cardiovascular psychophysiology community. The validational studies fall into three categories: correlational, experimental, and predictive.

Measurement and recording equipment, including electrocardiographic, impedance cardiographic, and hemodynamic (i.e., blood pressure) measurement technologies described elsewhere (Blascovich, 2000; Blascovich & Seery, in press), allowed the assessment and or derivation of the cardiovascular response patterns (see Figure 25.1) of VC, HR, CO, and TPR specified by Dienstbier noninvasively in humans. In all of these studies, resting baseline measurements were recorded followed by measures during task performance. As is the common practice in cardiovascular psychophysiology research, reactivity scores were calculated by subtracting the last minute of asymptoted baseline values from corresponding values assessed during the tasks.

Correlational

We ran a series of correlational experiments to ascertain the association between self-reported evaluations of personal resources and situational demands made prior to task performance and patterns of cardiovascular responses during subsequent motivated task performance. In accord with the general hypotheses derived from our integration of Lazarus and Folkman's (1984) appraisal theory and Dienstbier's theory of physiological toughness, we hypothesized that evaluations of personal resources exceeding situational demands would result in a challenge motivational state that would be associated with increases in HR, VC, and CO, and a decrease in TPR, and that an evaluation of demands exceeding resources would be associated with increases in HR and VC, but little change in CO and little change or even increases in TPR (see Figure 25.1). As Figure 25.2 illustrates, our hypotheses were confirmed in these experiments (Tomaka, Blascovich, Kelsey, & Leitten, 1993) thereby extending the generalizability of Dienstbier's work to humans.

Experimental

In order to determine whether the relationship between the evaluation of perceived demands and resources causes the cardiovascular patterns specified by Dienstbier, we experimentally manipulated overall challenge and threat evaluations prior to task performance and assessed subsequent CVR patterns during task performance. In this experiment (Study 1 in Tomaka, Blascovich, Kibler, & Ernst, 1997), manipulations of instructional content via

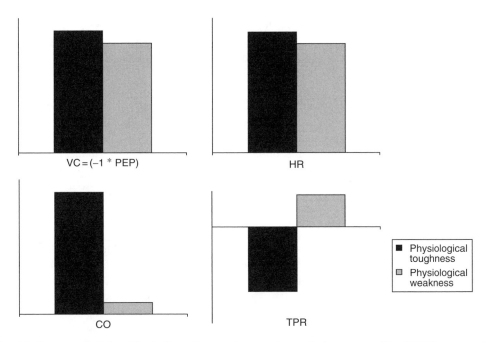

FIGURE 25.1 Dienstbier's patterns of physiological toughness—increased ventricular contractility (VC), heart rate (HR), cardiac output (CO), and decreased total peripheral resistance (TPR)—and weakness—increased VC, HR, little or no increase in CO and little change in or increased TPR.

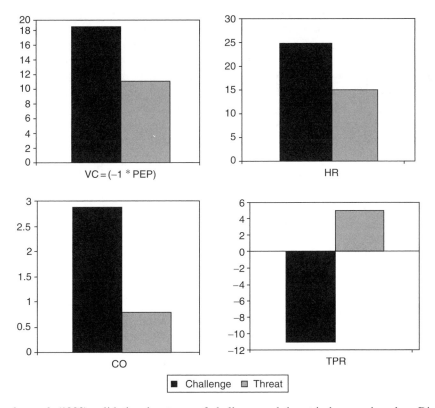

FIGURE 25.2 Tomaka et al. (1993) validational patterns of challenge and threat in humans based on Dientbier's patterns of physiological toughness and weakness, respectively (see Figure 25.1).

cognitive manipulation (practice vs. criterion) together with affective manipulation via instructional tone (friendly vs. hostile vocal tone) of task instructions led to the hypothesized challenge and threat patterns of CVR as we predicted.

In another (Hunter, 2001), we manipulated whether participants received instructions informing them that they would either be read or sing the U.S. national anthem while we recorded their cardiovascular responses. In order to give them an experience of what this would be like, participants were instructed to read or sing the first couple of stanzas. Significantly more of the participants who anticipated and practiced singing exhibited the cardiovascular pattern associated with threat than individuals who anticipated and practiced reading. Significantly more of the participants who anticipated and practiced reading evidenced the challenge pattern than individuals who anticipated and practiced singing.

We also examined the possibility of a reversal of causality, a version of the neo-Jamesian hypothesis, to determine whether the physiological toughness and weakness cardiovascular patterns could somehow cause challenge and threat evaluations, respectively. To do so, we performed two experiments (Studies 2 and 3 in Tomaka et al., 1997) in which we experimentally manipulated physiology via physical means so that participants would experience a pattern of cardiovascular responses that mimic the challenge and threat patterns. In one study, participants either pedaled a bicycle ergometer (i.e., "exercise bike") at a moderate workload (i.e., 50 watts) or sat stationary on it. Aerobic exercise is accompanied by a pattern of cardiovascular responses that mimics physiological toughness or challenge, whereas sitting stationery does not. In the other study, participants either immersed their hands in a warm or ice bath (i.e., pressors). The warm pressor typically is accompanied by a pattern of cardiovascular responses that mimics physiological toughness or challenge; the cold pressor typically is accompanied by a pattern that mimics physiological weakness or threat. In each study, we asked participants to self-report evaluations of demands and resources for an upcoming serial subtraction task during the manipulation (i.e., while on the ergometer or with hand immersed in the bath). Demand/resource evaluations did not differ as a function of the physical manipulations in either study, suggesting that interoception from the experience of the different cardiovascular patterns was not causally linked to demand/resource evaluations. Taken together, these experimental validational experiments indicate that the demand/resource evaluations are causally linked to Dienstbier's patterns in humans. That is, these

experimental studies provided strong evidence that Dienstbier's patterns mapped on to our challenge and threat constructs.

Predictive

More recently, we (Blascovich, Seery, Mugridge, Weisbuch, & Norris, 2004) conducted a study to determine if the challenge–threat patterns of CVR are predictive of future performance. Members (position players other than pitchers; i.e., hitters) of our university's varsity baseball and softball teams participated. Each athlete was required to give two three-minute speeches during which we recorded relevant cardiovascular data. One of the speeches was irrelevant to baseball/softball and served as a control for determining the level of cardiovascular responses related to challenge–threat caused by giving a speech in the laboratory experiment ("Why I am a good friend"). The second speech served as the experimental speech and was baseball-relevant ("How I would approach a critical hitting situation"). We derived a unitary physiological index of challenge–threat derived from our multiple cardiovascular measures for each speech. We collected offensive baseball statistics such as the runs generated index, batting averages, etc. during the varsity baseball season which began approximately 6 months after the experiment. Controlling for the unitary cardiovascular index of challenge–threat during the control speech, the unitary cardiovascular index of challenge-threat reliably predicted the major measures of offensive baseball performance during the baseball-relevant speech (the runs generated index, batting averages, etc.) such that the greater the challenge the better the performance. Additionally, because there were no effects of sport (exclusively male-played baseball vs. exclusively female played softball) on these predictive relationships; gender was not a factor.

SUMMARY

The validational studies confirm strongly that challenge and threat motivational states as defined and delineated in the BPSM involve the neuroendocrine processes described in Dienstbier's theory of physiological toughness. Furthermore, given the assertion that both challenge and threat involve approach-like motivational states, the commonality of SAM access activity to both challenge and threat is likely associated with a physiological predisposition of movement toward a goal, and HPA activity is likely associated with a rudimentary predisposition to withdraw from a goal if necessary during threat. Most importantly, these validational studies demonstrate that psychological and biological substrates of motivational states are integrated and operate interactively.

Additionally, these studies have validated distinctive patterns of cardiovascular responses as indexes of challenge and threat motivation. These indexes provide several methodological advantages—as they can be continuously and covertly recorded online—making them relatively impervious to sources of measurement error associated with more subjective self-report measures (e.g., impression management). Most importantly, these indexes can and have been used to test the motivational aspects of a wide range of personality and social psychological theories, not only informing these theories, but also providing further convergent validation of the indexes themselves.

BIOPSYCHOSOCIAL MODEL OF CHALLENGE AND THREAT

Overview

Figure 25.3 depicts the general components of the BPSM as described above. The model describes the theoretical processes underlying the generation of challenge–threat states *within* a motivated performance situation. The challenge–threat process is initiated when an individual becomes task engaged in a personally goal-relevant motivated performance situation requiring the performer to make resource and demand evaluations that result in energizing the individual for performance in ways consistent with challenge and threat. Interim performance

feedback informs reevaluation of demands and resources. Hence, the processes specified by the BPS *follow* a positive determination of goal relevance by the individual.

Nature and Limitations of Motivated Performance Situations

Goal Relevance and Task Engagement

Because, by definition, motivated performance situations assume goal relevance, it follows that an individual's performance must reach some standard in order to reach the self-relevant goal. Motivated performance situations differ from other more passive goal-relevant situations (e.g., watching a desirable movie) because they require *instrumental* actions that can be evaluated by others or the performers themselves. These actions are instrumental in the sense that they are necessary for the performance to continue to completion. If for example, a student was taking a standardized exam (e.g., SAT or GRE), the instrumental responses would take the form of answering each question in turn. If the student stopped answering questions before completing the exam, the situation would change dramatically from one of motivated performance to something more passive such as enduring emotional responses that do not require the same sort of instrumental cognitive responses. Within a motivated performance situation, instrumental actions may be primarily mental (e.g., silently rehearsing a speech) or more overt (e.g., giving a practice speech) in terms of affective, cognitive, and behavioral actions.

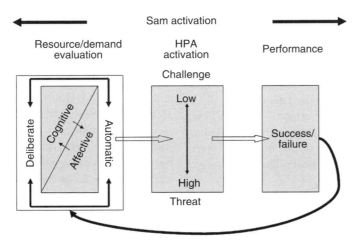

FIGURE 25.3 General components of the biopsychosocial model (BPS) of challenge and threat.

Limits of Generalizability

Note that the proponents of the BPS model have not extended its external validity nor the use of its indexes beyond motivated performance, or what some label active coping (cf. Obrist, 1981), situations. Furthermore, even within the limited motivated performance situation context, the cardiovascular indexes have not been validated in metabolically demanding ones (e.g., running a marathon), though research has shown that metabolic demands do not necessarily mask motivated performance situation driven changes in the relevant cardiovascular measures (Rousselle, Blascovich, & Kelsey, 1995).

Nevertheless, these limitations do not minimize the external validity of the BPS model severely because motivated performance situations are ubiquitous in human societies. Most economies appear to be based on production and marketing of goods, services, or information that require a plethora of supportive activities, perhaps all of which are goal relevant for workers and require instrumental responses; that is, they are, motivated performance situations. Of course, motivated performance situations extend beyond work. They are also ubiquitous in terms of many interpersonal interactions, education and learning, recreation, volunteering, etc.

TASK ENGAGEMENT AND ENERGIZATION

The goal relevance of a motivated performance situation drives task engagement; that is, the importance of the task to the individual determines the initial preparedness for action via the sympathetic neural component of the SAM axis. Hence, in terms of the cardiovascular markers, ventricular contractility (VC), which is largely sympathetically determined, and HR, which is both sympathetically and parasympathetically determined should increase relatively quickly, with neuroendocrine modulation of TPR and CO following a short time later (due to the relative speed of neural rather than endocrine activation). Continued modulation of all four cardiovascular responses depends on factors related to ongoing challenge–threat evaluations and activation of the HPA axis. Hence, neither HR nor VC increases can be regarded as distinctive to either challenge or threat, but rather mark task engagement proximally and goal relevance distally.

RESOURCE/DEMAND EVALUATIONS

Once an individual is engaged in a motivated performance situation, a cybernetic evaluation–feedback process ensues. This process modulates challenge–threat motivation. Given increased VC and HR, the modulation can be marked by fluctuations in HPA axis influences on CO and TPR with increased CO and decreased TPR pointing toward the challenge end of the continuum and decreased or static CO and static or increased TPR pointing toward the threat end of the continuum (see Figure 25.1). Individuals iteratively reevaluate personal resources and situational demands as they gain additional experience in the motivated performance task situation including interim successes and failures. Such experience influences fluctuations within and between relevant evaluation factors (see below). Furthermore, we have experimentally demonstrated that these resource/demand evaluations can occur deliberately (i.e., consciously), automatically (i.e., unconsciously), or both. Furthermore, these dual processes can influence each other (cf. LeDoux, 1996). Finally, the evaluations can be primarily cognitive (e.g., semantic), affective (e.g., hedonic), or both.

If the evaluative calculus results in unreasonable "ratios" of resources to demands; that is, ones which are extremely high (i.e., little or no probability of failure) or extremely low (little or no probability of success), the net effect will be disengagement because the task loses goal relevance (i.e., pragmatic meaning) for the performer, an argument based on Yerkes-Dodson's Law. For example, if a rank amateur chess player were about to face a grand master, there would be little goal relevance and neither the amateur nor the master would likely be task engaged. However, if such calculus results in a midrange probability of success or failure (e.g., a chess match between two grand masters), goal relevance will be maintained and task engagement sustained. Furthermore, inherent or external interim feedback during performance via iterative reevaluation can skew the ratio in ways that decrease or increase goal relevance and task engagement.

The most complex aspect of resource/demand evaluations involves specification of the factors or dimensions (i.e., antecedents) that may enter into the evaluation calculus. This complexity stems from the number of possible factors to be evaluated, their myriad interrelationships, and their subjectivity. Initially (Blascovich & Tomaka, 1996; Blascovich & Mendes, 2000), the BPS specified factors hierarchically within separate resource and demand categories. However, over time the model has been revised in this regard in recognition of the likelihood that almost any factor has implications for both resources and demands. Hence, factors are now specified (cf. Blascovich, 2007) as bipolar ones with regard to effects on resource and demand evaluations.

Specified factors entering into this affective–cognitive evaluative calculus (see Figure 25.4) are ones within a Lewinian (1936) framework of person by situation factors

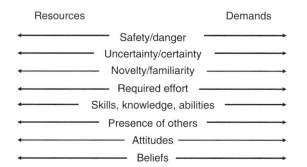

Resources   Demands

Safety/danger

Uncertainty/certainty

Novelty/familiarity

Required effort

Skills, knowledge, abilities

Presence of others

Attitudes

Beliefs

FIGURE 25.4   Factors in resource/demand evaluations.

that can interact among one another. They include: psychological and physical danger/safety, uncertainty/certainty, novelty/familiarity, required effort, skills and knowledge, the presence of others, affective cues, attitudes and beliefs, etc. In other words, far more dimensions than those directly related to the performance requirements of the task itself (e.g., task difficulty) can influence the evaluation. For example, on the face of it, quickly serially subtracting "3's" (or even on occasion "1's") from a four digit number would seemingly be challenging for almost anyone with an eighth grade education. However, in a situation in which such subtraction is carried out vocally, known to be monitored by highly evaluative others such as psychologists during a "psychology experiment," and for which sensors have been placed on the individual to record their physiology, the performer's evaluation of resources and demands is not so straightforward. Furthermore, these factors are not completely independent of each other. Rather, they tend to overlap (e.g., uncertainty/certainty and novelty/familiarity) and can be interactive or synergistic. For example, uncertainty can increase evaluated danger or required effort. Finally, although these factors are illustrative of ones that enter into resource/demand evaluations, undoubtedly, they do not represent the full set.

Generally, perceptions of the levels of contributions of any of these factors to resource/demand evaluations are filtered via intraindividual processes including individual differences related to temperament, dispositional traits and states, and quality of self-knowledge. In addition, various interindividual social psychological processes can moderate the factors. Hence, the antecedents of demand/resource evaluations and reevaluations are complex indeed.

Physiological Modulation of Energization

As depicted in Figure 25.3, once an individual becomes task engaged in a goal-relevant motivated performance situation, SAM activation energizes him or her to perform. Once so engaged, however, continual iterative resource/demand evaluations modulate SAM activation via HPA activation depending on the resource/demand ratio. If resources are sufficient to meet demands, little or no HPA activation occurs and challenge (i.e., Dienstbier's physiological toughness pattern) predominates. If resources are insufficient HPA activation occurs and threat (i.e., physiological weakness pattern) predominates.

Performance and Feedback

According to the BPSM, individuals' performance generally parallels the resource/demand ratio such that a challenge ratio leads to better performance than a threat ratio. However, both challenge and threat states are motivating and performance under threat may suffice for an individual to reach a goal. In certain cases, performance during threat may exceed performance during challenge. For example, threat appears to be related to better performance on vigilance tasks than challenge (Hunter, 2001).

Of course, initial subjective judgments of the levels and interactions of antecedent resource/demand factors may prove inaccurate during an individual's task performance itself, thereby causing those subjective judgments to vary during the task. Indeed, such judgments can cause fluctuations in the performer's motivational state and concomitant variations in HPA axis activity (Quigley, Barrett, & Weinstein, 2002). For example, when a student is beginning a graduate record exam, he or she may evaluate personal resources as exceeding situational demands perhaps by believing he or she is well-prepared and knowledgeable. Upon experiencing uncertainty regarding the correct answer to a question or two, reevaluation may occur causing the performer to believe that he or she is not so well-prepared and knowledgeable. Answering more questions may further move the performer via reevaluation toward threat or may move the performer in the direction of challenge; for example, if the test taker starts experiencing certainty regarding his or her answers to questions. At the extremes, individuals may evaluate the motivated performance situation as one in which their resources so outweigh the demands, or vice-versa, that it loses goal relevance and, hence, they become disengaged.

RESEARCH

Overview

Research supporting the BPS of challenge and threat has appeared in the literature over the last 15 years. This work has not only taken the form of validational work as described above, but also includes a substantial body of work using the cardiovascular indexes of challenge and threat to test many personality and social psychological theories including ones focused on intraindividual processes and ones focused on interindividual processes. This kind of research is based on the rationale that if a personality or social psychological theory can be examined within a motivated performance situation and hypotheses deduced regarding resource/demand evaluations, then that theory can be tested via the BPSM using the cardiovascular indexes of challenge and threat. Furthermore, such work can come full circle to support the BPSM of challenge and threat in two ways, via identification of intraindividual and interindividual processes affecting resource/demand evaluations and via convergent validation of the cardiovascular indexes. Here, a sampling of such substantive research is reviewed.

INTRAINDIVIDUAL PROCESSES

As indicated above, the antecedent factors that enter into the evaluative calculus underlying challenge and threat are filtered or moderated by intraindividual processes such as temperament, dispositions, attitudes, and beliefs. Although we have not studied temperament, we believe that our model is consistent with that of Elliot and Thrash (2002). However, we have studied how other intraindividual processes influence on the challenge and threat evaluation processes. A few are described here.

Dispositions: Belief in a Just World

Individuals vary dispositionally in their justice beliefs, with some adhering to the belief that individuals get what they deserve while others do not. Dispositional belief in a just world has been thought to protect individuals existentially by giving meaning to their lives and enabling them to adapt to life demands (Lerner, 1980). Hence, we hypothesized that dispositional belief in a just world should moderate challenge–threat evaluations and, thus, challenge–threat motivational states.

Tomaka and Blascovich (1994) tested this hypothesis by having participants who had completed Rubin and Peplau's (1975). Belief in a Just World (BJW) scale performs a serial subtraction task, a task not particularly related to justice beliefs, in a laboratory-based motivated performance situation. Cardiovascular responses assessed during a sequence of two performance periods demonstrated that those participants high in dispositional belief in a just world not only self-reported a higher ratio of resources to demands but also exhibited the

cardiovascular pattern associated with challenge motivation. Those participants low in dispositional belief in a just world not only self-reported a higher ratio of demands to resources but also exhibited a cardiovascular pattern consistent with threat motivation.

Dispositions: Stability of Self-Esteem

More recently, we (Seery, Blascovich, Weisbuch, & Vick, 2004) examined the relationships among level of self-esteem, self-esteem stability, and cardiovascular reactions to performance feedback. Prior research on level of self-esteem and performance feedback (McFarlin & Blascovich, 1981) has indicated that individuals with high self-esteem following failure feedback expect to perform even better on the same motivated performance task (i.e., a version of the Remote Association Task; McFarlin & Blascovich, 1984) in the future than those receiving success feedback. Furthermore, this research also indicates that individuals with low self-esteem expect to perform worse in the future whether they receive either success or failure feedback. Similarly, Swann, Pelham, and Krull (1989) demonstrated self-verification processes such that high and low self-esteem individuals seek confirmation via high and low performance feedback, respectively.

In the interim, personality psychologists (Kernis, Cornell, Sun, Berry, & Harlow, 1993) have convincingly demonstrated that self-esteem must not only be examined in terms of level (i.e., high to low) but also in terms of within person variability over time. Hence, in terms of self-esteem, individuals may be assessed not only from high to low globally, but also in terms of stability–instability. Hence, individuals with stable high self-esteem differ in important respects from those with unstable high self-esteem. Similarly, individuals with stable low self-esteem differ in important respects from those with unstable low self-esteem.

In the Seery et al. (2004) experiments, individuals preassessed for self-esteem level and stability, participated in a challenge–threat experiment in which they performed in a motivated performance situation involving the remote associates task (RAT) in two sessions. The RAT in the first session was manipulated via selection of items (i.e., easy or difficult version) to produce relative success or failure. Participants are well aware of whether or not they perform well or poorly on easy and difficult versions of the RAT because the nature of the task makes it inherently clear whether they have correctly answered an item (McFarlin & Blascovich, 1984). The two experiments reported in Seery et al. differed only slightly in the wording of confirming verbal performance feedback following the first task. After receiving this verbal performance feedback, participants were told that the first task was a practice task and that the criterion task would follow. Subsequently, they completed a moderately difficult version of the RAT. Prior to, and during performance on the second task, the cardiovascular measures necessary to distinguish challenge from threat were recorded.

Seery et al. (2004) hypothesized that the effects of self-esteem level, stability of self-esteem, and performance feedback would interact such that individuals high in stability and high in self-esteem would experience challenge during the second task despite failure performance feedback on the first task, but those unstable high self-esteem individuals would experience threat following failure feedback on the first task. In addition, Seery et al. expected that those low in stability and low in self-esteem would experience challenge following success feedback, but those high in stability and low in self-esteem would not. In both studies, participants with unstable high self-esteem experienced greater threat following failure feedback during criterion task performance than those with stable high self-esteem, and participants with unstable low self-esteem experienced greater challenge than those with stable low self-esteem.

Attitudes: Functionality

In the long history of the study of attitudes in social psychology, many theorists (Allport, 1935; Fazio, 1989) have maintained that attitudes (e.g., attitudes toward food items) function to ease decision-making in motivated performance situations that individuals face constantly in daily life. Accordingly, in terms of the BPS of challenge and threat, one would hypothesize that individuals with preexisting attitudes toward decision alternatives would be relatively challenged and that individuals without such attitudes would be threatened during a motivated performance situation involving a decision-making task for which such attitudes are relevant.

Based on earlier work establishing an experimental attitude testing paradigm (Fazio, Blascovich, & Driscoll, 1992), Blascovich et al. (1993) essentially hypothesized that preexisting attitudes would serve as a resource to individuals finding themselves in a motivated performance situation in which the attitudes were relevant. In other words, preexisting attitudes would predispose individuals toward challenge in such a situation; whereas, without such attitudes individuals would be predisposed to threat.

In two experiments (Studies 2 and 3 in Blascovich et al., 1993), participants rehearsed attitudes to a random set of 15 novel abstract paintings out of a larger group of 30 such paintings. This procedure had been previously demonstrated (Fazio et al., 1992) to increase attitude accessibility toward targeted attitude objects, enabling individuals to make pairwise preference judgments more quickly between pairs of the paintings toward which participants had rehearsed attitudes than pairs of paintings that were novel.

In the relevant experiments, Blascovich et al. (1993) confirmed the challenge–threat hypotheses. Specifically, participants exposed to paintings from the familiar rehearsed set exhibited the challenge pattern of cardiovascular reactivity while making rapid pairwise judgments of them. Participants exposed to paintings from the novel unrehearsed set exhibited the threat pattern.

Beliefs

In a recent study, Weisbuch-Remington, Mendes, Seery, & Blascovich (2005) examined how religious beliefs might influence resource/demand evaluations. Based on anthropological, sociological, and psychological theories, they reasoned that learned religious beliefs should serve as a resource for believers during relevant goal-relevant motivated performance situations. Furthermore, they created an experimental paradigm in which they primed religious beliefs outside of participants' awareness, and conducted two experiments to test their hypotheses.

In both experiments, participants were exposed subliminally to positive and negative graphic Christian religious icons or symbols. Each experiment involved two tasks. The first involved an estimation task in which participants were instructed to indicate the number of tiles in an abstract mosaic that actually served as the mask for the subliminal cues.

The first experiment included only participants who during a previous apparently unrelated mass prescreening activity had indicated they were religious and Christian. Following, this task, participants were instructed to give a speech. Half were randomly assigned to give a speech about their own death and the other half gave a speech about going to the dentist. The results indicated that participants exposed to positive Christian subliminal cues prior to the speech exhibited the challenge pattern of cardiovascular reactivity during the speech, while participants exposed to negative Christian cues exhibited the threat pattern. Furthermore, these effects were stronger during the death speech than the dentist speech.

The second experiment included both Christian and non-Christian participants, and all participants gave the death speech. Again, Christian participants exposed to positive Christian subliminal cues exhibited the challenge pattern and Christian participants exposed to negative Christian subliminal cues exhibited the threat pattern. However, non-Christian participants were not affected by the subliminal cues. These experiments confirmed the role of learned beliefs in resource/demand evaluations. Importantly, they also indicate that such evaluations can take place nonconsciously.

Interindividual Processes

In addition to antecedent intraindividual factors, interindividual processes can also affect the evaluative resource/ demand calculus underlying challenge and threat. Among the interindividual processes that we have examined are: social facilitation, social comparison, stigma, and stereotype threat. These are reviewed briefly here.

Social Facilitation

The presence of observers and coactors should heighten the evaluative nature of motivated performance situations by increasing the psychological danger associated with failing to perform at a level that others present would perceive as good or acceptable. Hence, drawing on the BPSM, one would hypothesize that if a well-learned task is performed in the presence of such an audience, challenge is more likely to occur because failing to perform is unlikely. However, if a novel task is performed in the presence of an audience threat is more likely to occur because failing to perform well is more likely.

Blascovich, Mendes, Hunter, and Salomon (1999) tested these hypotheses in a classic social facilitation experiment. The experiment consisted of two phases. In the first, participants learned one of two equally difficult tasks (number categorization or pattern recognition) and mastered it by performing to criterion. In the subsequent phase, participants were randomly assigned to perform either the well-learned task or the novel task (i.e., the one they did not perform or learn in the first phase). Within each performance task condition, participants were randomly assigned to perform alone or in the presence of two confederates.

The results supported the hypotheses drawn from the BPS in two regards. First, task engagement, as indicated by the cardiovascular measures occurred only in the audience conditions during the second, criterion phase. Second, in the audience condition paired with the well-learned task, participants exhibited the challenge pattern of cardiovascular responses. In the audience condition paired with the novel task, participants exhibited the threat pattern. These results not only supported the BPS, but also delineated differences in patterns of physiological

"arousal" associated with social facilitation and inhibition for the first time since Zajonc (1965) included physiological arousal in his social facilitation theory.

Social Comparison

Another classic social influence process that should affect resource/demand evaluations in motivated performance situations involving other performers is social comparison (Festinger, 1954). Although several social comparison researchers have incorporated the role of general arousal in theories of social comparison (Major, Testa, & Bylsma, 1991; Wills, 1991) and a few social comparison studies incorporated simple HR or skin conductance measures to assess such arousal, the motivational arousal construct underlying social comparison theory has been poorly delineated.

Drawing on the BPSM and social comparison theory, Mendes, Blascovich, Major, and Seery (2001) hypothesized that participants performing in a motivated performance situation with partners who performed better than they did (i.e., upward social comparison) would experience threat and that participants paired with partners who performed worse (i.e., downward social comparison) would experience challenge. These experiments began with a brief participant–partner (i.e., a confederate) face-to-face interaction, followed by solo performance of a word finding task (similar to the game of Boggle) by the participant with veridical performance feedback. Subsequently, participants received information regarding their partner's solo performance, which was the manipulation of upward or downward comparison. Finally, the participant and partner performed as a team during a final word finding task.

As predicted, participants were task engaged (i.e., significant increases in VC during the final criterion task) whether they were in the upward or downward comparisons conditions. Also, as predicted, participants in the upward comparison condition exhibited a pattern of cardiovascular responses associated with threat, and participants in the downward comparison condition exhibited a pattern of cardiovascular responses associated with challenge.

Stigma

Social interactions between members of stigmatized (e.g., African-Americans, disfigured individuals, people low in socio-economic status, persons with mental illness) and nonstigmatized (e.g., Anglo-Americans, attractive individuals, people high in socio-economic status, and mentally healthy persons) groups have received much attention from social psychologists over the past half-century, particularly over the last two decades or so.

Theorists have maintained that interacting with stigmatized individuals cause nonstigmatized individuals uncertainty, discomfort, anxiety, and danger during social interactions (Crocker, Major, & Steele, 1998). Similarly, by virtue of membership in socially devalued groups, stigmatized individuals may feel particularly susceptible to negative performance stereotypes increasing their sense of psychological danger (e.g., stereotype threat; Steele, 1992). Hence, it is not surprising that, since Goffman's (1963) seminal work on stigma, social psychological theorists have considered social interactions between stigmatized and nonstigmatized individuals as threatening to the interactants.

However, it is only in the new millennium that researchers have been able to demonstrate physiological evidence of threat, based in both nonstigmatized and stigmatized interactants during social interactions. This work began with the application of the BPSM of challenge and threat to such investigation. Blascovich, Mendes, Hunter, Lickel, and Kowai-Bell (2001) hypothesized that, during interactions with stigmatized others, members of nonstigmatized groups would experience resource/demand evaluations in which demands outweighed resources resulting in threat motivation.

Their work involved pairing nonstigmatized and stigmatized individuals as partners in cooperative motivated performance situations involving speech and word finding tasks. In their initial studies, the investigators experimentally manipulated stigma by placing opaque or transparent facial birthmarks on confederates (cf. Kleck & Strenta, 1980) who subsequently interacted with nonstigmatized others in the cooperative situations. Their results demonstrated that the nonstigmatized partners exhibited cardiovascular response patterns associated with threat when interacting with a birthmarked partner and challenge when interacting with a nonbirthmarked partner (Experiments 1 & 2; 2001).

Blascovich and colleagues demonstrated similar effects when nonstigmatized individuals were partnered with African-Americans of the same gender compared to nonstigmatized individuals partnered with other nonstigmatized individuals (Experiment 3; 2001; Mendes, Blascovich, Lickel, & Hunter, 2002). Furthermore, using the birthmark manipulation on genuine participants, this research group has demonstrated that stigmatized individuals are also threatened when interacting with nonstigmatized individuals (reference forthcoming).

Stereotype Threat

According to Steele and Aronson's (1995) stereotype threat theory, performing in a domain in which one is negatively stereotyped is associated with feelings of anxiety, uncertainty, etc. This "stereotype threat" stems from the possibility that one's performance might confirm a negative stereotype and can result in poorer performance, thereby confirming the stereotype. Blascovich, Spencer, Quinn, and Steele (2001) published a paper demonstrating heightened cardiovascular responses among stereotype-threatened African-Americans taking a supposed verbal abilities test, however, they did not report cardiovascular measures that could confirm threat vis-à-vis the BPS.

Recently, Vick, Seery, Blascovich and Weisbuch (in press) hypothesized that situations raising the salience of negative self-relevant stereotypes negatively affect resource/demand evaluations in a motivated performance situation. Specifically, stereotype-threatened individuals should experience increased demand evaluations (e.g., greater uncertainty, more psychological danger) thereby increasing the likelihood of threat. Some nonphysiological research supports these notions, confirming that stereotype-threatened individuals have lower expectations for performance and increased self-doubt (Steele & Aronson, 1995). They tested these hypotheses in a situation involving gender-math stereotypes involving male and female participants.

In the Vick et al. experiment, participants completed a difficult math test, one that they had been led to believe was either gender-biased in favor of males or gender-fair, while appropriate cardiovascular data were assessed. During the test, stereotype-threatened women exhibited a cardiovascular pattern associated with threat, while nonstereotyped-threatened women exhibited challenge. Interestingly, the cardiovascular patterns were reversed for men. Specifically, men exhibited challenge when a male gender bias was implied, but threat when it was not.

SUMMARY

The BPSM of challenge and threat has evolved over the last 15 years, becoming richer in detail and amassing validational evidence for its putative cardiovascular indexes of challenge and threat. The BPSM is at its essence a motivational model, one integrating biological, psychological (cognitive and affective), and social psychological (intrapersonal and interpersonal) levels of analysis. The BPSM is a domain specific (i.e., motivated performance situations) model, though this is arguably a quite broad and ubiquitous domain. The model fits within the family of approach–avoidance theories of motivation, although we argue that both challenge and threat involve approach, with the latter modulated by avoidance like neurophysiological processes.

Research has demonstrated the applicability of the model in many domains pertinent to personality and social psychology. The research reviewed above as well as other research (Allen, Blascovich, & Mendes, 2002; Blascovich, Mendes, & Seery, 2002; Mendes, Blascovich, Hunter, Lickel, & Jost, in press; Mendes, Reis, Seery, & Blascovich, 2003) provides support for many of the processes specified by the BPSM. Furthermore, it demonstrates the utility of the model for testing theories focused on intraindividual and interindividual processes pertinent to person and situational influences in daily life by testing them within the context or empirical model of motivated performance situations.

REFERENCES

Allen, K., Blascovich, J., & Mendes, W. B. (2002). Cardiovascular reactivity and the presence of pets, friends, and spouses: the truth about cats and dogs. *Psychosomatic Medicine, 64*(5), 727–739.

Allport, G. W. (1935). Attitudes. In C. Murchison (Ed.), *Handbook of social psychology*. Worchester, MA: Clark University Press.

Anderson, N., McNeilly, M., & Myers, H. (1993). A biopsychosocial model of race differences in vascular reactivity. In J. Blascovich & E. S. Katkin (Eds.), *Cardiovascular reactivity to psychological stress and disease* (pp. 83–110). Washington, DC: American Psychological Association.

Blascovich, J. (2007). Challenge, threat, and health. In J. Shah & W. Gardner (Eds.), *Handbook of motivation science* (pp. 481–493). New York: Guilford.

Blascovich, J., Ernst, J. M., Tomaka, J., Kelsey, R. M., Salomon, K. A., & Fazio, R. H. (1993). Attitude as a moderator of autonomic reactivity. *Journal of Personality and Social Psychology, 64*, 165–176.

Blascovich, J., & Mendes, W. B. (2000). Challenge and threat appraisals: The role of affective cues. In J. Forgas (Ed.), *Feeling and thinking: The role of affect in social cognition* (pp. 59–82). Cambridge, UK: Cambridge University Press.

Blascovich, J., Mendes, W. B., Hunter, S. B., Lickel, B., & Kowai-Bell, N. (2001). Perceiver threat in social interactions with stigmatized others. *Journal of Personality and Social Psychology, 80*, 253–267.

Blascovich, J., Mendes, W., Hunter, S., & Salomon, K. (1999). Social facilitation, challenge, and threat. *Journal of Personality and Social Psychology, 77*, 68–77.

Blascovich, J., Mendes, W. B., & Seery, M. (2002). Intergroup encounters and threat: A multi-method approach. In D. Mackie & E. Smith (Eds.), *From prejudice to intergroup emotions: Differentiated reactions to social groups* (pp. 89–110). New York: Psychology Press.

Blascovich, J., Seery, M., Mugridge, C., Weisbuch, M., & Norris, K. (2004). Predicting athletic performance from cardiovascular indicators of challenge and threat. *Journal of Experimental Social Psychology, 40*, 683–688.

Blascovich, J., Spencer, S., Quinn, D., & Steele, C. (2001). African-Americans and high blood pressure: The role of stereotype threat. *Psychological Science, 12*, 225–229.

Blascovich, J., & Tomaka, J. (1996). The biopsychosocial model of arousal regulation. In M. Zanna (Ed.), *Advances in Experimental Social Psychology Vol. 28* (pp. 1–51). New York: Academic Press.

Crocker, J., Major, B., & Steele, C. (1998). Social stigma. In D. T. Gilbert, S. T. Fiske et al. (Eds.), *The handbook of social psychology* (4th ed., Vol. 2). Boston: McGraw-Hill.

Dienstbier, R. A. (1989). Arousal and physiological toughness: Implications for mental and physical health. *Psychological Review, 96*, 84–100.

Elliot, A. J. (2006). The hierarchical model of approach–avoidance motivation. *Motivation and Emotion, 30*, 111–116.

Elliot, A. J., & Trash, T. M. (2002). Approach–avoidance motivation in personality: Approach and avoidance temperaments and goals. *Journal of Personality and Social Psychology, 82*(5), 804–818.

Fazio, R. H. (1989). On the power and functionality of attitudes: The role of attitude accessibility. In A. R. Pratkanis, S. J. Breckler, & A. G. Greenwald (Eds.), *Attitude structure and function* (pp. 153–179). Hillsdale, NJ: Lawrence Erlbaum.

Fazio, R. H., Blascovich, J., & Driscoll, D. M. (1992). On the functional value of attitudes: The influence of accessible attitudes upon the ease and quality of decision-making. *Personality and Social Psychology Bulletin, 18*, 388–401.

Festinger, L. (1954). A theory of social comparison processes. *Human Relations, 7*, 117–140.

Goffman, E. (1963). *Stigma*. Englewood Cliffs, NJ: Prentice-Hall.

Hunter, S. B. (2001). Performance under pressure: The impact of challenge and threat states on information processing. Unpublished doctoral dissertation, University of California, Santa Barbara.

Kernis, M. H., Cornell, D. P., Sun, C., Berry, A., & Harlow, A. (1993). There's more to self-esteem than whether it is high or low: The importance of stability of self-esteem. *Journal of Personality and Social Psychology, 65*(6), 1190–1204.

Kleck, R. E., & Strenta, A. (1980). Perceptions of the impact of negatively valued physical characteristics on social interaction. *Journal of Personality and Social Psychology, 39*, 861–873.

Lazarus, R. S. (1991). Progress on a cognitive-motivational-relational theory of emotion. *The American Psychologist, 46*(8), 819–834.

Lazarus, R. S., & Folkman, S. (1984). *Stress, appraisal, and coping*. New York: Springer.

Lerner, M. J. (1980). *The belief in a just world*. New York: Plenum.

Lewin, K. (1936). *Principles of topological psychology*. New York: McGraw-Hill.

LeDoux, J. E. (1996). The emotional brain: The mysterious underpinnings of emotional life. New York: Simon & Schuster.

Major, B. N., Testa, M., & Bylsma, W. H. (1991). Responses to upward and downward social comparisons: The impact of esteem-relevance and perceived control. In J. M. Suls & T. A. Wills (Eds.), *Social comparison* (pp. 230–260). Hillsdale NJ: Erlbaum.

McFarlin, D. B., & Blascovich, J. (1981). The effects of self-esteem and performance feedback on affective preferences and cognitive expectations. *Journal of Personality and Social Psychology*, *4*, 521–531.

McFarlin, D. B., & Blascovich, J. (1984). On the remote associates test (RAT) as an alternative to illusory performance feedback: A methodological note. *Basic and Applied Social Psychology*, *5*, 223–228.

Mendes, W. B., Blascovich, J., Hunter, S. B., Lickel, B., & Jost, J. T. (2007). Threatened by the unexpected: Physiological responses during social interactions with expectancy-violating partners. *Journal of Personality and Social Psychology*, *93*, 698–716.

Mendes, W. B., Blascovich, J., Lickel, B., & Hunter, S. (2002). Challenge and threat during interactions with White and Black men. *Personality and Social Psychology Bulletin*, *28*, 939–952.

Mendes, W. B., Blascovich, J., Major, B., & Seery, M. (2001). Effects of social comparisons on challenge and threat reactivity. *European Journal of Social Psychology*, *31*, 477–479.

Mendes, W. B., Reis, H. T., Seery, M., & Blascovich, J. (2003). Cardiovascular correlates of emotional disclosure and suppression: Do content and gender context matter. *Journal of Personality and Social Psychology*, *84*, 771–792.

Obrist, P. (1981). *Cardiovascular psychophysiology: A perspective*. New York: Plenum.

Quigley, K. S., Barrett, L. F., & Weinstein, S. (2002). Cardiovascular patterns associated with threat and challenge appraisals: A within-subjects analysis. *Psychophysiology*, *39*(3), 292–302.

Rousselle, J. G., Blascovich, J., & Kelsey, R. M. (1995). Cardiorespiratory response under combined psychological and exercise stress. *International Journal of Psychophysiology*, *20*, 49–58.

Rubin, Z., & Peplau, L. A. (1975). Who believes in a just world? *The Journal of Social Issues*, *31*(3), 65–89.

Seery, M., Blascovich, J., Weisbuch, M., & Vick, S. B. (2004). The relationship between self-esteem, self-esteem stability, and cardiovascular reactions to performance feedback. *Journal of Personality and Social Psychology*, *87*, 133–145.

Steele, C. M. (1992). Race and the schooling of Black Americans. *The Atlantic Monthly*, *269*(4), 68–78

Steele, C. M., & Aronson, J. (1995). Stereotype threat and the intellectual test performance of African Americans. *Journal of Personality and Social Psychology*, *69*(5), 797–811.

Swann, W. B., Pelham, B. W., & Krull, D. S. (1989). Agreeable fancy or disagreeable truth? Reconciling self-enhancement and self-verification. *Journal of Personality and Social Psychology*, *57*(5), 782–791.

Tomaka, J., & Blascovich, J. (1994). Effects of justice beliefs on cognitive appraisal of and subjective, physiological, and behavioral responses to potential stress. *Journal of Personality and Social Psychology*, *67*, 732–740.

Tomaka, J., Blascovich, J., Kelsey, R. M., & Leitten, C. L. (1993). Subjective, physiological, and behavioral effects of threat and challenge appraisal. *Journal of Personality and Social Psychology*, *65*, 248–260.

Tomaka, J., Blascovich, J., Kibler, J., & Ernst, J. M. (1997). Cognitive and physiological antecedents of threat and challenge appraisal. *Journal of Personality and Social Psychology*, *73*, 63–72.

Vick, S. B., Seery, M. D., Blascovich, J., & Weisbuch, M. (in press). The effect of gender stereotype activation on challenge and threat motivational states. *Journal of Experimental Social Psychology*

Weisbuch-Remington, M., Mendes, W. B., Seery, M. D., & Blascovich, J. (2005). The non-conscious influence of religious symbols in motivated performance situations. *Personality and Social Psychology Bulletin*, *31*, 1203–1216.

Wills, T. A. (1991). Similarity and self-esteem in downward social comparison. In J. M. Suls & T. A. Wills (Eds.), *Social comparison* (pp. 51–78). Hillsdale NJ: Erlbaum.

Zajonc, R. B. (1965). Social facilitation. *Science*, *149*, 269–274.

Mental Control

26 Thought Suppression and Psychopathology

Sadia Najmi and Daniel M. Wegner

CONTENTS

There are very few theories of psychopathology that trace all disorders of the mind to a single common cause. The demon-possession theory gave it a good try for a while, at least in the medieval popular mind. And later, as psychology developed, theorists with big ideas made their own suggestions for unifying themes: Freud and repression, Adler and inferiority, Rogers and low self-regard, Skinner and contingencies of reinforcement. Students of introductory psychology can name these and more, and can also note that in every case there are major exceptions to these one-factor theories. Something as miraculously complex as the human mind is susceptible to potential pathological influences with similar complexity, so theories suggesting a common theme will always fall prey to the criticism of oversimplification. Still, we plan in this chapter to make the same darn mistake—by examining the potential role of thought suppression as a causal factor in, if not all, then a wide range of psychological disorders.

Why would we stumble off to perform a fool's errand? Our attraction to this idea comes from a basic realization about mental disorder. The inner life of disorder is often painful, unpleasant, a focus of suffering—and thus will commonly motivate thought suppression as a *reaction*. People typically do not want to think about their sorrows, their symptoms, their fears, their abnormalities, the voices in their heads—they hope to avoid their psychopathological mental states. This reaction, then, could be very broad, a standard and stereotypical response to mental turmoil in every form of psychopathology in which a person remains conscious and experiences distress. And while the suppression of thoughts may seem to be an effective solution, this strategy can have profound and unexpected consequences in the unwanted magnification of the psychological influences of the suppressed thought. The unifying feature of this approach to psychopathology, then, is not that thought suppression might somehow *initiate* a significant range of the psychological disorders, but rather that it may expand their psychological damage, prolong their course, and make them more resistant to treatment. The unifying theme of thought suppression is not that it is a general cause of disorder, but that it is a general human response to distress that may seriously complicate any disorder that arises.

This chapter begins by describing the phenomena of suppression and considering how suppression might complicate disorders. Next, we review the evidence to date for a role of suppression in various forms of mood, anxiety, and impulsive disorders. We then consider recent theoretical proposals regarding a potential role of thought suppression in psychosis. Throughout, we illustrate how suppression is differentially implicated in distinct forms of psychopathology, in some instances potentially as an etiological mechanism, but more often as a disorder-complicating moderator of psychopathology. More broadly, suppression is characterized in this chapter as a product of avoidance motivation that has detrimental consequences for psychological functioning and well-being.

SUPPRESSION OF UNWANTED THOUGHTS

The idea that trying to keep things out of mind can be a factor in psychopathology has always been a central tenet in Freudian psychoanalysis and in psychodynamic psychology. Although there remains significant debate on this issue (Erdelyi, 2006), the predominant sentiment underlying this approach has been that attempts to stop thinking can be successful—that people can indeed control their minds (Wegner, Eich, & Bjork, 1994). In contrast to this presumption, the initial experimental studies of thought suppression revealed that suppression simply does not work (Wegner, Schneider, Carter, & White, 1987). People cannot keep the thought of a white bear out of mind for 5 minutes, let alone suppress something for a lifetime. The fact is, though, that people often try not to think about things despite the futility of the enterprise.

Thought suppression is one of various strategies that people may use to manage or control thoughts that trigger unpleasant emotions. Conceptualized this way, it is a prime cognitive exemplar of avoidance motivation. What is most critical to pathology of intrusive thoughts is that this strategy is often unsustainable, especially in the face of competing cognitive demands. Moreover, when the strategy fails, the unwanted thoughts often do not return to their initial baseline level and instead escalate to a much higher level of frequency. According to the ironic process theory of mental control (Wegner, 1994), this occurs because mental control involves processes that usually work together to effect thought suppression, but that can fail and yield intrusions under conditions of high mental load. The theory posits an effortful and conscious operating process that diverts attention away from unwanted thoughts, and an effortless and unconscious ironic monitoring process that both maintains vigilance for occurrences in awareness of the unwanted thought, and triggers further action of the operating process if the unwanted thought appears in awareness. These two processes work hand in hand to ensure that unwanted thoughts remain outside of awareness. Ironically, however, by maintaining vigilance for the unwanted thought, the monitoring system helps assure that the unwanted thought never becomes dormant.

Research has demonstrated two characteristics of suppressed thoughts—the ease of return to suppressed thoughts, and the difficulty of escape from suppressed thoughts. In the original thought suppression experiment, Wegner et al. (1987) found evidence for ease of return—after a period of thought suppression, people instructed to discontinue suppression of the thought and instead to begin thinking about it reported more returns of the thought than occurred without prior suppression. Subsequent studies revealed that this effect is particularly likely to occur under conditions of mental load. The ease of return illustrated by this "rebound effect" has since been observed repeatedly (see reviews by Abramowitz, Tolin, & Street, 2001; Rassin, 2005; Wenzlaff & Wegner, 2000). Common to these studies with clinical and nonclinical populations is the finding that the unwanted thought is faster to return to consciousness while it is being actively suppressed.

Studies examining the phenomenon of hyperaccessibility in interference effects have shown evidence for the difficulty of escape from suppressed thoughts. Wegner and Erber (1992) found that people suppressing a thought under cognitive load showed interference with the task of color-naming in a modified Stroop (1935) paradigm. Remarkably, this interference was even greater than the interference found when people were concentrating on the thought under load. These results imply that people could not disengage attention to escape from the unwanted thought, and this difficulty became more pronounced with the imposition of cognitive load. This effect, too, has been observed repeatedly (Arndt, Greenberg, Solomon, Pyszczynski, & Simon, 1997; Klein, 2007; Newman, Duff, & Baumeister, 1997; Page, Locke, & Trio, 2005).

The ease of return and difficulty of escape from unwanted thoughts may underlie a certain asymmetry in the way unwanted thoughts are linked to other thoughts—the remarkable phenomenon that we find ourselves being reminded of a particular unwanted thought by most everything that comes to mind, but the idea itself seems to remind us of nothing more than our desire to eliminate it from consciousness. This unusual asymmetry in the way unwanted thoughts are linked to other thoughts was examined in a recent study (Najmi & Wegner, in press). Participants who were asked to suppress a thought or to concentrate on it completed a task assessing the influence of priming on reaction time to word/nonword judgments (associative priming lexical decision task). Results indicated that suppression under cognitive load produced a sort of asymmetric priming. Priming with the associate of a suppressed word speeded reaction time to the suppressed word, but priming with a suppressed word did not speed reaction time to associated words. This suggests that suppression induces an unusual form of cognitive accessibility in which movement of activation toward the suppressed thought from associates is facilitated but movement of activation away from the suppressed thought to associates is undermined. Thus, suppression of an unwanted thought ironically increases its return while precluding other related thoughts from entering into awareness.

SUPPRESSION AND PSYCHOPATHOLOGY

Early theories of psychopathology portrayed a state of mind much like the one produced by simple instructions to suppress. These theories described psychopathological states in terms of the *idée fixe*—a thought that intrudes repeatedly upon consciousness and becomes difficult to control—and pointed to such fixed ideas as the very basis of mental disorder (Janet, 1894; Ribot, 1881). In presenting William James' views on psychopathology, Taylor (1984) provides a list of "exceptional mental states" characterized by an *idée fixe*, highlighting the notion that characteristic of many emotional disorders is perseverative thinking of aversive thoughts and attempted control of these thoughts in the service of emotion regulation.

Ironically, it may be avoidance of the thoughts that fuels their persistence. James suggests that this "power of the buried idea" may underlie symptoms of hysteria, while intolerance and avoidance of uncertainty (*folie du doute* or doubting mania) may mark the beginnings of obsessive thinking (Taylor, 1984). Although theories of psychopathology have grown more sophisticated than this, there remains evidence that unwanted intrusive thoughts characterize a range of emotional disorders (Clark, 2005). Intrusive thoughts are typically experienced as ego-dystonic and unacceptable, they cause distress, and interrupt current mental activity (Rachman, 1978, 1981). The drive to eliminate thoughts from consciousness may create the precise formula for turning the ordinary experience of unwanted thoughts into the painful experience of persistent intrusions that characterize many forms of psychopathology, from obsessive-compulsive disorder (OCD) and posttraumatic stress disorder (PTSD) to depression and beyond (Clark, 2005).

It is often the case that overwhelming intrusions have no obvious beginnings. For example, in the case of patients with OCD, it is nearly impossible to identify when the unwanted thought of contamination or blasphemy first gained acute emotional import. One approach to this problem is to suggest that suppression itself is the cause of subsequent obsession. This idea was developed in a theory of *synthetic obsessions* (Wegner, 1989) that oriented much of the early empirical investigation of thought suppression in psychopathology toward testing the idea that suppression failure was a primary etiological process in certain forms of psychopathology. This possibility remains open, as little research assessing the causal role of thought suppression in OCD and other forms of psychopathology has been reported as yet (but see Wegner & Zanakos, 1994; Wenzlaff, 2005).

In focusing our approach in this chapter on the potential for thought suppression to play a role across a wide range of psychopathologies, we will set aside for now the specific analysis of a potential etiological role for suppression in any one disorder. Rather, we will examine the associations that have been observed between psychological disorders and various indicators of thought suppression tendencies and effectiveness. A review by Wenzlaff and Wegner (2000) presented empirical findings related to the suppression of intrusive thoughts in PTSD, OCD, and depression. In the sections that follow, we expand this earlier review to incorporate more recent findings in these areas and in a wider array of disorders.

SUPPRESSION AND POSTTRAUMATIC STRESS DISORDER

Two of the primary characteristics of PTSD—unwanted intrusions of traumatic recollections and avoidance of all things associated with the trauma—suggest that individuals with PTSD are motivated to suppress trauma-related thoughts. Most empirical investigations of the effects of thought suppression in PTSD indicate that the disorder is characterized by a bias in the ability to suppress trauma-related thoughts. Shipherd and Beck (1999) examined the effects of instructed suppression of rape-related thoughts in female sexual assault survivors with PTSD and those without PTSD following the sexual assault. They found that trauma survivors with PTSD experienced a postsuppression rebound in the frequency of rape-related thoughts, whereas trauma survivors without PTSD did not experience a rebound.

A more recent study (Shipherd & Beck, 2005) replicated these findings in a follow-up investigation of the deliberate suppression of trauma-related thoughts in survivors of motor vehicle accidents with and without PTSD. These researchers found that both groups successfully suppressed trauma-related thoughts *temporarily*, but that the PTSD group experienced a postsuppression rebound, whereas the no-PTSD group did not. In this study, participants were given an additional task of suppressing a personally relevant thought that was not related to the trauma. In this task, the PTSD group did not experience a rebound effect, suggesting that this effect was specific to the suppression of their trauma-related thoughts. However, in a further follow up study (Beck, Gudmundsdottir, Palyo, Miller, & Grant, 2006), both PTSD and no-PTSD groups showed a postsuppression rebound of trauma-related thoughts, suggesting that difficulties in suppressing trauma-related thoughts may be ubiquitous, and not specific to PTSD.

Results to date suggest, then, that attempted suppression of trauma-related thoughts and their subsequent rebound may exacerbate trauma-related intrusions. Whether ineffective suppression is a precursor of PTSD or a consequence of the disorder cannot be determined by these studies. Furthermore, while the jury is still out on whether or not PTSD is associated with a bias in ability to suppress trauma-related thoughts, it is clear that suppression complicates the disorder by escalating the intrusions. Finally, it is interesting to note that Harvey and Bryant (1998) observed a postsuppression rebound effect for accident-related thoughts in survivors of motor vehicle accidents with acute stress disorder (ASD), but a follow-up study (Guthrie & Bryant, 2000) found that these effects were temporary. It may be that the effects of attempted suppression of trauma-related thoughts is fleeting but that repeated, failed, attempts at suppressing trauma-related thoughts contribute to the escalation of intrusions from acute stress disorder to PTSD.

SUPPRESSION AND OBSESSIVE-COMPULSIVE DISORDER

OCD is characterized by the avoidance of anxiety that is produced by persistent obsessions. Although the relentlessness of unwanted intrusive thoughts is a defining feature of OCD, several studies have established that the experience of unwanted intrusive thoughts with obsessional content is a normative phenomenon (Purdon & Clark, 1993; Rachman & de Silva, 1978; Salkovskis & Harrison, 1984). This idea was foreshadowed in James's *degeneracy theory of mental illness* (Taylor, 1984) in which he suggested that cognitive and behavioral avoidance and the intensity of unwanted thoughts lie on a dimension from normalcy to pathology.

Indeed, empirical studies have established that the difference between "normal" and "clinical" obsessions is a matter of degree rather than kind. Nonclinical individuals indicate that their most common negative intrusive thoughts occur a few times a year (Purdon & Clark, 1994a,b). Normal individuals who report significant recurrence of distressing unwanted thoughts also return high scores on the *White Bear Suppression Inventory*, a scale developed to assess motivation to suppress thoughts (Wegner & Zanakos, 1994). Compared to nonclinical individuals, however, OCD patients experience more frequent, distressing intrusive thoughts, perceive them to be less controllable, and more strongly try to resist them using maladaptive mental control strategies such as thought suppression (Janeck & Calamari, 1999; Rachman & de Silva, 1978). According to the cognitive-behavioral perspective on OCD (Rachman, 1997; Salkovskis, 1985), the intrusive thoughts that characterize many psychological disorders may persist because of three types of processes "(a) preexisting ideas, beliefs or schemas, (b) faulty interpretation and appraisal of the intrusion, and (c) futile efforts to intentionally control or suppress unwanted cognitions" (Clark, 2001, p. 125). According to Salkovskis's model of OCD, dysfunctional appraisals of responsibility and unsuccessful attempts to neutralize and control the intrusive thoughts cause normal intrusive thoughts to escalate into clinical obsessions. Thus, according to the model, thought suppression alone is not the cause of obsessions, but rather it is the suppression of unwanted, intrusive thoughts motivated by the need to eliminate them from consciousness in order to avert harm.

With a few exceptions (Kelly & Kahn, 1994; Purdon & Clark, 2001), the paradoxical effects of suppressing obsessional thoughts in nonclinical samples have been observed fairly consistently. In a series of studies, Salkovskis and colleagues (Salkovskis & Campbell, 1994; Salkovskis & Reynolds, 1994; Trinder & Salkovskis, 1994) observed a suppression-related increase in intrusive thoughts both in the lab and over a 4-day naturalistic follow-up. McNally and Ricciardi (1996) presented nonclinical participants with a list of thoughts reflecting various themes of obsessions and asked them to identify one that they had previously experienced. They observed a marginally significant tendency for the obsessional thought to occur more often after suppression whereas neutral thoughts tended to occur less frequently after suppression.

To date, there has not been much investigation of the effects of instructed suppression of obsessional thoughts in OCD. One problem in conducting the thought suppression experiment with OCD patients is the difficulty of finding an appropriate control condition. Tolin et al. (2002b) note that instructing individuals with OCD to suppress an obsessional thought is essentially a "nonintervention" since individuals in the nonsuppression control group are being asked to act against what they would naturally do. Purdon, Rowa, and Antony (2005) found that individuals with OCD exerted effort to suppress their obsessional thought despite explicit instructions not to suppress, and that this suppression effort was correlated with their perceived urgency to control the thought. This may explain the absence of suppression rebound or enhancement effects in the studies of instructed suppression of obsessional thoughts conducted with clinical samples of OCD patients (Janeck & Calamari, 1999; Purdon et al., 2005). Tolin et al. (2002b) argue that if individuals with OCD have general deficits in their ability to control thoughts, this will be manifested in their ability to control neutral thoughts. Moreover, this design overcomes the problem of spontaneous suppression of obsessional thoughts in the OCD control group. Consistent with their hypothesis, they found that individuals with OCD had higher occurrences of a neutral target thought after suppressing compared to baseline.

The initial observations of thought suppression suggested that it is not very successful (Wegner et al., 1987). What does this mean for the role of suppression in OCD if we conclude that the rebound or enhancement effect is not experienced by the majority of OCD subjects instructed to suppress their obsessions? One possibility is that suppression works temporarily. If so, it serves as a neutralization strategy; that is, it terminates exposure to the obsession thereby curtailing habituation of the anxiety associated with the obsession (Roemer & Borkovec, 1994) and preventing disconfirmation of the perceived negative consequences of the obsession. Another possibility is that suppression fails. Failed suppression can serve to increase the salience of the unwanted thought and the need to control it in order to avoid the perceived negative consequences. Failure of suppression is associated with worse mood, and faulty appraisals of suppression failure may lead to greater effort to suppress (Purdon et al., 2005). Conceptualized this way, it may well be the case that repeated attempts at suppression serve to exacerbate an already existent obsessional state.

Faulty appraisals of the failure of suppression and faulty beliefs about the need to control thoughts and about the controllability of thoughts may be both causal precursors of the obsessional state as well as complicating factors that further aggravate it. Purdon and Clark (2000) have argued that certain individuals hold preexisting metacognitive beliefs that result in thought suppression, namely, that unwanted thoughts can and should be controlled and that intrusive thoughts are the product of an unhealthy mind. For example, Tolin et al. (2002a) observed that OCD patients were more likely than anxious and nonanxious controls to attribute a failure of thought suppression to internal, negative attributions (e.g., "I am mentally weak"). These beliefs may predispose the individual to exert greater control over thoughts, and consequently, to suffer the counterproductive effects of mental control. Indeed, results from studies using correlational designs such as path analysis (Smári & Hólmsteinsson, 2001) and structural equation modeling (Rassin, Muris, Schmidt, & Merckelbach, 2000) suggest that negative thought appraisal predicts suppression, which in turn predicts OCD symptoms.

SUPPRESSION AND DEPRESSION

Research investigating the role of thought suppression in depression has yielded two primary inferences: One is the fairly robust observation that the motivated avoidance of depressotypic intrusions results in a rebound of these cognitions (Wenzlaff, Wegner, & Roper, 1988), and the other is the suggestion that the suppression of depressive thoughts may mask a cognitive vulnerability to depression (Wenzlaff & Bates, 1998).

According to Wenzlaff (2005) there are a number of reasons why depressed individuals are prone to experiencing the suppression-induced rebound of depressotypic intrusions. Consistent with the idea of a depressive schema underlying the disorder that makes depressotypic information more accessible (Beck, 1967), depressed individuals are likely to undertake suppression by choosing distracters that are mood congruent and hence closely linked to their suppression target (Wenzlaff et al., 1988). This finding has been replicated reliably in studies of suppression in dysphoric individuals (Conway, Howell, & Giannopoulos, 1991; Howell & Conway, 1992; Renaud & McConnell, 2002; Wenzlaff, Wegner, & Klein, 1991). A recent study extended these findings to the domain of autobiographical memory (Dalgleish & Yiend, 2006). Results showed that in dysphoric individuals, the suppression of a negative memory resulted in increased activation of other negative information (presumably distracters used in order to achieve suppression), thereby rendering negative information more accessible on a subsequent autobiographical-memory retrieval task.

Moreover, depressed mood may deplete cognitive resources needed for an effortful cognitive process such as suppression. Hartlage, Alloy, Vázquez, and Dykman (1993) have observed that depression interferes mostly with effortful processing and only minimally with automatic processing. Thus, ironic process theory (Wegner,

1994) predicts that suppression undertaken during a depressed mood would impair functioning of the effortful operating process (which diverts attention away from the target thought) and leave unhindered the functioning of the automatic monitoring process (which maintains vigilance for the target thought), thereby increasing accessibility of the target thought.

The hypothesis that suppression conceals a cognitive vulnerability to depression was proposed by Wenzlaff and Bates (1998) and tested in a series of studies with individuals at high risk for depression (e.g., individuals remitted from depression). Theories of cognitive vulnerability to depression assert that depressive schemata may be latent but can be activated by conditions similar to those experiences that were initially responsible for creation of the schemata (Beck, Rush, Shaw, & Emery, 1979). Other models based on Bower's (1987) associative network model (Miranda & Gross, 1997) predict that because depressive schemata are likely to develop in a negative emotional context, they should be associated with a negative mood in memory. When the individual is no longer experiencing the negative mood, the associated depressotypic cognitions should be less accessible, thereby allowing them to become dormant or latent. It appears, however, that studies aimed at revealing negative schemata in remitted depressed individuals using methods of mood induction are, at best, equivocal (Ingram, Miranda, & Segal, 1998). According to Wenzlaff and Bates (1998), one possible reason why such attempts at revealing depressive schemata fail may be that remitted depressed individuals are trying to suppress the very thoughts investigators are attempting to detect. In this sense, the depressive cognitions of remitted-depressed individuals are latent not in that they are inactive but because their influence is concealed by active suppression.

Research in this area supports the idea that thought suppression masks a cognitive vulnerability to depression, that this vulnerability becomes apparent when mental control is disabled (e.g., when rehearsing a 9 digit number during the task), and that this effect is particularly pronounced among those who engage in chronic thought suppression (Wenzlaff & Bates, 1998; Wenzlaff & Eisenberg, 2001; Wegner & Zanakos, 1994; Wenzlaff, Meir, & Salas, 2002; Wenzlaff, Rude, Taylor, Stultz, & Sweatt, 2001). One such study, for example, revealed that the imposition of a cognitive load caused remitted-depressed individuals to interpret recorded homophones in a more negative fashion (performing more similar to depressed than to control subjects), and that this was not the case without the cognitive load. Similar studies have been done using scrambled sentences which could be unscrambled to form depression-relevant (i.e., depressotypic) themes. In all of these studies, the increase in negative thinking induced by the cognitive load was significantly correlated with Wegner and Zanakos's (1994) measure of propensity to suppress unwanted thoughts. The rationale behind these studies is that if remitted depressed individuals are actively suppressing depressotypic thinking, it should be possible to detect the suppressed negative bias by imposing a cognitive load. Taken together, results of these studies are consistent with the hypothesis that the active suppression of depressotypic thoughts may serve to mask an underlying depressive schema in individuals at risk for depression.

SUPPRESSION OF WORRY IN GENERALIZED ANXIETY DISORDER AND INSOMNIA

Worry is conceptualized as thoughts that are motivated by the avoidance of emotionally negative imagery and of concomitant aversive somatic sensations (Borkovec & Inz, 1990). Although worry is initiated in order to avoid imagery of future catastrophe and of current anxiety sensations, it quickly becomes undesirable in itself and is experienced as increasingly uncontrollable (Borkovec & Roemer, 1995). Thus, an important difference between worries and other unwanted intrusive thoughts (e.g., those in OCD) is that they are ego-syntonic and hence the motivation to suppress them is not obvious. However, once the worries themselves become unwelcome, they may initiate a cycle of self-perpetuating counterproductive attempts at controlling them. Nevertheless, a study conducted by Behar, Vescio, and Borkovec (2005) to distinguish between the effects of thought- versus image-suppression about a worrisome target did not reveal a rebound effect for either group.

A cardinal feature of generalized anxiety disorder (GAD) is the persistence of uncontrollable worries. Becker, Rinck, Roth, and Margraf (1998) tested the hypothesis that patients with GAD show a bias in ability to suppress their worries. Consistent with their hypothesis, they observed that GAD patients found it more difficult to suppress thoughts of their worries than thoughts of a neutral target. However, Mathews and Milroy (1994) did not observe a suppression-specific rebound effect for worries in a nonclinical sample of excessive worriers. They found that worriers had more frequent worry thoughts than nonworrying individuals regardless of mental control instruction. Taken together, these findings suggest that thought suppression may play a limited role in exacerbating worries in GAD.

Harvey (2003) further illuminated the role of thought suppression in the maintenance of worry by investigating its effects in clinical insomnia. Worries surface as a persistent cognitive activity in clinical insomnia (Borkovec, 1982). Harvey (2003) found that compared to control participants, insomniacs reported a greater use of suppression to control their presleep worries. Furthermore, insomniacs instructed to suppress their self-identified worry reported worse sleep quality and longer sleep-onset latency than did insomniacs in the no-suppression condition. The intriguing finding is that this was the case in the absence of a rebound of the worrying thought for the suppression group, suggesting that the act of suppression—possibly due to the effort devoted to the endeavor—appears to exacerbate the disorder.

SUPPRESSION AND ALCOHOL USE AND ABUSE

Alcohol abuse is conceptualized as a disorder of overactivation of approach motivation toward the positive effects of alcohol (Palfai & Ostafin, 2003) coupled with underactivation of avoidance motivation away from its negative consequences (Ostafin, Palfai, & Wechsler, 2003). It follows that cognitive avoidance strategies at odds with this pattern of motivation—such as the suppression of positive alcohol-related thought—meet with little success.

The research on thought suppression in alcohol use was motivated by a finding that individuals in the process of quitting smoking experienced an enhancement of smoking-related intrusions under suppression (Salkovskis & Reynolds, 1994). Palfai, Colby, Monti, and Rohsenow (1997) tested the hypothesis that in a sample of heavy social drinkers, suppression of urges to drink would lead to increased accessibility of alcohol-related information, particularly information regarding expectancies about the effects of alcohol. In their study, heavy social drinkers were exposed to their usual alcoholic drink during which one group was instructed to suppress the urge to drink alcohol and the other group received no instructions. Following this, both groups made timed judgments about the applicability of a number of alcohol outcome expectancies. As hypothesized, those in the suppression condition were faster to endorse alcohol outcome expectancies than those in the control condition. This suppression-induced hyperaccessibility of alcohol-related information in heavy social drinkers is consistent with results of a study conducted with a sample of alcohol abusers. In this study, Klein (2007) found that alcoholic subjects who had tried to suppress thoughts of alcohol prior to performing a modified Stroop task showed increased interference for the word "alcohol" as compared to those alcoholic subjects who had expressed thoughts about alcohol freely prior to the task. These results are consistent with the idea that suppression leads to hyperaccessibility (Wegner & Erber, 1992) of suppressed information and that this bias in information-processing may play a role in maintaining the disorder.

The effects of suppression in alcohol abuse have also been assessed, though less directly, on biological indicators of psychological well-being, such as heart-rate variability (HRV). HRV has been shown to be positively correlated with measures of cognitive flexibility and with the ability to regulate emotion (Johnsen et al., 2003). Consistent with this idea, Ingjaldsson, Laberg, and Thayer (2003) found a negative association between HRV and the propensity to suppress unwanted thoughts in chronic alcohol abuse. These results support earlier findings that suggest that low HRV is associated with impaired cognitive control and rigid thinking (Thayer & Lane, 2002), and that thought suppression is particularly counterproductive for mitigating alcohol-related urges and cravings (Palfai, Colby et al., 1997; Palfai, Monti, Colby, & Rohsenow, 1997).

It is interesting to note that the suppression of alcohol-related urges may have cross-substance effects. For instance, Palfai, Colby et al. (1997) have discovered that those who had previously suppressed their urge to drink alcohol showed an increase in smoking behavior. It remains to be seen whether these cross-substance effects are specific to the relationship between alcohol and smoking or if they can be extended to the suppression of other unwanted urges. Confirmation of the latter would expand considerably the scope of suppression-related negative consequences for addictions.

SUPPRESSION AND SELF-INJURIOUS THOUGHTS AND BEHAVIORS

Self-injurious thoughts and behaviors (SITB) include suicidal ideation, suicide attempts, and nonsuicidal self-injury (NSSI) or direct, deliberate destruction of body tissue in which there is no intent to die (e.g., cutting or burning one's skin). Recent conceptualizations of SITB suggest that it is a disorder of avoidance motivation in that it functions to avoid aversive cognitive and emotional experiences (Baumeister, 1990; Boergers, Spirito, & Donaldson, 1998; Chapman, Gratz, & Brown, 2005; Nock & Prinstein, 2004, 2005). Take the example of a 13-year-old patient who has an argument with her boyfriend. She has a predisposition for high emotional reactivity and is immediately overwhelmed by anger, sadness, fear of her boyfriend forsaking her, and thoughts of her own worthlessness, among a host of other negative cognitions and emotions. She cannot bear the emotional arousal, tries to not think about it, fails, only thinks about it more, and then finds some, though minimal, relief in focusing on thoughts of cutting herself. Ultimately, it is the behavior of cutting that helps reduce her emotional arousal.

Research has suggested that when people try to suppress thoughts, they tend to undertake an *unfocused distraction* strategy—the iterative use of many different distracters rather than just one focus—and experience a rebound of the suppressed thought (Wegner, Schneider, Knutson, & McMahon, 1991). However, this rebound effect is less likely to occur if suppression is undertaken using a *focused distracter* thought (Wegner et al., 1987). This successful focused distraction from certain thoughts is often an adaptive strategy for reducing the frequency of the thoughts or the distress associated with them (Johnstone & Page, 2004; Salkovskis & Campbell, 1994). However, it may be maladaptive in cases when the distracter itself is harmful, such as in the example above, when SITB becomes the focused distracter from thoughts that create aversive emotions.

A study by Najmi, Wegner, and Nock (2007) tested a model suggesting that the propensity to suppress unwanted thoughts is a cognitive mediator of the relationship between emotional reactivity and SITB. Results of this cross-sectional study revealed that the self-reported propensity to suppress unwanted thoughts partially mediates the relationship between emotional reactivity and the frequency of NSSI and suicidal ideation. Moreover, those with a higher tendency to suppress unwanted thoughts reported engaging in NSSI primarily in order to reduce aversive emotions. Thus, the general tendency to suppress unwanted thoughts was demonstrated in the need to suppress the specific aversive thoughts and emotions that trigger NSSI.

SUPPRESSION AND PSYCHOSIS

The study of thought suppression in psychosis has not attracted many researchers, probably because they recognize that other factors are likely to cause such disorders, and that the study of suppression is thus unlikely to get to the heart of the problem. However, this approach may obscure how suppression could be involved in the amplification of symptoms. As discussed above, ironic process theory predicts that when mental capacity is compromised by cognitive load, the control falls below a baseline level and produces the opposite of the intended effect. However, this is not unique to thoughts, but in fact is the

same process at work when people are burdened by competing cognitive demands as they try to relax (Wegner, Broome, & Blumberg, 1997), concentrate (Wegner, Erber, & Zanakos, 1993), sleep (Ansfield, Wegner, & Bowser, 1996), avoid being prejudiced (Macrae, Bodenhausen, Milne, & Jetten, 1994), or ignore pain (Cioffi & Holloway, 1993; Masedo & Esteve, 2007). Could suppression of psychotic symptoms also serve to intensify them? The ironic process theory suggests an exploration of the intriguing possibility that suppression may play a role in the persistence of hallucinations in psychotic disorders (Morris & Wegner, 2000).

The hypothesis that hallucinations are maintained by avoidance motivation follows from the idea that auditory hallucinations share certain features with the intrusion of unwanted thoughts (Morrison, Haddock, & Tarrier, 1995). Much like auditory hallucinations, intrusive thoughts often take the form of repetitive, ego-dystonic, unacceptable images, or impulses, which, if appraised negatively, can generate feelings of "mental pollution" (Rachman, 1994). Morrison and Baker (2000) found that patients who experienced auditory hallucinations had more intrusive thoughts than did the no-hallucinations schizophrenia control group and the nonpsychiatric control group. Furthermore, patients who experienced auditory hallucinations found their intrusive thoughts more distressing, uncontrollable, and unacceptable than did the control groups, and the degree of distress caused by the voices was associated with their negative appraisal of the voices.

According to Morrison et al.'s (1995) heuristic model, auditory hallucinations are experienced when intrusive thoughts are attributed to an external source in order to reduce cognitive dissonance. They propose that this dissonance is caused by the lack of concordance between the intrusive thoughts and preexisting metacognitive beliefs such as those concerning the controllability of these thoughts. This is consistent with Bentall's (1990a,b) hypothesis that implicates faulty metacognitive beliefs as a critical factor that influences attempted suppression and persistence of auditory hallucinations, an idea that has been suggested earlier regarding maintenance of intrusive thoughts in OCD.

Analogous to the research on intrusive thoughts, Barrett and Etheridge (1992) have found that hallucinations are a normative experience. Thus it is possible that what makes a normal hallucination clinically significant might in part be failed cognitive avoidance strategies, such as suppression. Morrison (1998) suggests that the process underlying disturbing intrusive thoughts in anxiety disorders and disturbing intrusive auditory hallucinations in psychotic disorders may in fact be similar. The cognitive model of panic (Clark, 1986) suggests that panic attacks result from a predisposition to misinterpret certain bodily sensations, especially common somatic responses to anxiety, in a catastrophic manner, appraising them as being indicative of immediate danger. This predisposition is maintained in part by cognitive and behavioral avoidance that prevents disconfirmation of threat (Salkovskis, 1996). Morrison (1998) suggests that appraisals of hallucinations in psychosis may be analogous to this catastrophic misinterpretation in panic.

Although there are as yet no empirical studies addressing this hypothesis directly, there exists some preliminary evidence consistent with the proposed framework. For example, it has been shown that individuals who experience auditory hallucinations exhibit stronger metacognitive beliefs regarding the uncontrollability of mental events, in comparison with psychiatric and non-psychiatric controls (Baker & Morrison, 1998). To the extent that beliefs about controllability influence attempts at mental control, as has been suggested in the case of intrusive thoughts in OCD, these findings are consistent with the possibility that attempts to avoid or suppress might play a role in the maintenance of hallucinations. Morrison and Wells (2000) assessed various strategies used to control unwanted thoughts—distraction, social control, punishment, worry, and reappraisal—and showed that individuals with schizophrenia used significantly more punishment and worry strategies and significantly less distraction strategies than did control subjects. Romme, Honig, Noorthorn, and Escher (1992) found that use of distraction as a coping strategy was inversely correlated with ability to cope with hallucinations, whereas Nayani and David (1996) found that the use of distraction coping strategies was correlated with reports of worsening the hallucinations. Although these results do not assess thought suppression per se, they are consistent with the idea that the use of certain cognitive techniques can exacerbate or maintain auditory hallucinations in a manner similar to that which occurs with unwanted, intrusive thoughts.

According to Bentall (1990a,b), auditory hallucinations may reflect a bias, rather than a deficit, in the monitoring of internal events, and this bias may be influenced in part by beliefs and in part by negative reinforcement in the form of anxiety reduction. For instance, the misattribution of certain kinds of internally generated events, such as negative, ego-dystonic, thoughts about the self, as being externally generated may be reinforced by a temporary reduction in anxiety. Bentall's ideas are consistent with those of Morrison et al. (1995), namely that beliefs inconsistent with intrusive thoughts lead to cognitive

dissonance which is then reduced when the intrusive thoughts are attributed to an external source, as in auditory hallucinations. The individual, instead of remaining indifferent to the appraisal of the hallucination, will then engage in counterproductive avoidance strategies, such as suppression (Morrison, 1998, 2001; Morrison et al., 1995).

The idea that hallucinations are maintained by suppression of self-discrepant, ego-dystonic, thoughts (Morrison & Baker, 2000; Morrison et al., 1995) was examined empirically by García-Montes, Perez-Alvarez, and Fidalgo (2003) using a nonclinical sample. They investigated the effects of the repeated suppression of self-discrepant thoughts on the vividness of auditory illusions. They found that when discrepancy of thoughts was high, suppression indeed increased the quality of the illusions reported by participants; on the other hand, when discrepancy of thoughts was low, their suppression had no effect on the quality of auditory illusions. This study of illusions in a nonclinical sample provides a basis for examining the phenomenon of hallucinations in a clinical sample.

Treatment using the normalizing approach of Kingdon and Turkington (1993), in which they propose the use of psychoeducation regarding the commonness of hallucinations, may help to prevent catastrophic misinterpretation of hallucinations and the subsequent use of misguided mental control to get rid of them. A model for this exists in the treatment of OCD in which the original thought suppression experiment (Wegner et al., 1987) has been used for several years now as a behavioral experiment in therapy. Patients have been invited to suppress thoughts of a neutral target, e.g., giraffe, and the subsequent occurrence of the giraffe images is then used as the basis for educational discussion about the need to control thoughts (Baer, 2001; Salkovskis & Campbell, 1994).

SUPPRESSION AND DREAMS

As a final note on mental disorder and suppression, it is worth noting that one of the more insidious symptoms of disorder—recurrent distressing nightmares (Hartmann, Russ, van der Kolk, Falke, & Oldfield, 1981)—might also be open to a suppression analysis. Wegner, Wenzlaff, and Kozak (2004) asked participants in a nonclinical sample to spend some time before bed attempting to suppress the thought of a person; those in comparison conditions either thought about the person for this time or thought about anything (after having their attention directed to the person). Dream diaries collected the next morning revealed that thinking about the person increased the likelihood of dreaming about the person, but that suppression of thoughts about the person increased such dreaming even more. This was true regardless of the emotional valence of the person (attractive or not), suggesting that the tendency to suppress thoughts in waking may make them return in dreams. If people suffering from severely distressing thoughts in the daytime put them aside through suppression, it makes sense that they might end up paying for this strategy with horrific nightmares. The role of such processes in psychopathology has yet to be discerned, but these results suggest that thought suppression may play a part in magnifying mental distress.

CONCLUSION

Taken together, studies on thought suppression in psychopathology present a more nuanced picture now than was emerging in the early years of its investigation. Some evidence is consistent with the idea that the counterproductive effects of suppression are causally implicated in the disorder, but for the most part a more parsimonious conclusion is that thought suppression acts as a complication of the disorder. The detrimental effects of suppression are often different across a wide range of emotional disorders. Suppression is rarely successful in the long run, but in some cases it can be successful in the short-term and prevent exposure to and habituation of undesirable emotional states; in other cases, suppression is often counterproductive, exacerbating aversive thoughts, and concomitant aversive emotions; finally, faulty beliefs about the possibility of successful suppression and subsequent attributions of the inevitable failure of suppression can exacerbate the negative emotional state and trigger further futile suppression attempts. In one way or another, suppression, like most experiential avoidance strategies, is detrimental to psychological well-being. Future research should focus on evaluating the relative merits of alternatives.

Recently reported successes of mindful-acceptance based techniques in the treatment of emotional disorders (Bach & Hayes, 2002; Foa & Wilson, 2001; Hayes, Strosahl, & Wilson, 1999; Roemer & Orsillo, 2002; Segal, Williams, & Teasdale, 2002) suggest a possible mechanism that encourages exposure to unwanted thoughts and feelings, at the very least by explicitly discouraging suppression. Wenzlaff (2005) suggested that one way of understanding mindfulness-based therapies is that they work against avoidance motivation, specifically the individual's tendency to try to suppress unwanted thoughts. "The instruction to be mindful instead promotes an abandonment of mental control intentions.... This kind of therapy may have salutary effects because it replaces the

use of a self-defeating mental control technique with a simple relaxation of the control motive" (p. 74).

ACKNOWLEDGMENT

The research reported here was supported in part by NIMH Grant MH49127.

REFERENCES

Abramowitz, J. S., Tolin, D. F., & Street, G. P. (2001). Paradoxical effects of thought suppression: A meta-analysis of controlled studies. *Clinical Psychology Review*, *21*, 683–703.

Ansfield, M., Wegner, D. M., & Bowser, R. (1996). Ironic effects of sleep urgency. *Behaviour Research and Therapy*, *34*, 523–531.

Arndt, J., Greenberg, J., Solomon, S., Pyszczynski, T., & Simon, L. (1997). Suppression, accessibility of death-related thoughts, and cultural worldview defense: Exploring the psycho-dynamics of terror management. *Journal of Personality and Social Psychology*, *73*, 5–18.

Bach, P., & Hayes, S. C. (2002). The use of acceptance and commitment therapy to prevent the rehospitalization of psychotic patients: A randomized controlled trial. *Journal of Consulting and Clinical Psychology*, *70*, 1129–1139.

Baer, L. (2001). *The imp of the mind: Exploring the silent epidemic of obsessive bad thoughts*. New York: Dutton/Penguin Books.

Baker, C., & Morrison, A. P. (1998). Metacognition, intrusive thoughts and auditory hallucinations. *Psychological Medicine*, *28*, 1199–1208.

Barrett, T. R., & Etheridge, J. B. (1992). Verbal hallucinations in normals: I: People who hear voices. *Applied Cognitive Psychology*, *6*, 379–387.

Baumeister, R. F. (1990). Suicide as escape from self. *Psychological Review*, *97*, 90–113.

Beck, A. T. (1967). *Depression: Causes and treatment*. Philadelphia: University of Pennsylvania Press.

Beck, A. T., Rush, A. J., Shaw, B. F., & Emery, G. (1979). *Cognitive therapy of depression*. New York: Guilford Press.

Beck, J. G., Gudmundsdottir, B., Palyo, S. A., Miller, L. M., & Grant, D. M. (2006). Rebound effects following deliberate thought suppression: Does PTSD make a difference? *Behavior Therapy*, *37*, 170–180.

Becker, E. S., Rinck, M., Roth, W. T., & Margraf, J. (1998). Don't worry and beware of white bears: Thought suppression in anxiety patients. *Journal of Anxiety Disorders*, *12*, 39–55.

Behar, E., Vescio, T. K., & Borkovec, T. D. (2005). The effects of suppressing thoughts and images about worrisome stimuli. *Behavior Therapy*, *36*, 289–298.

Bentall, R. P. (1990a). The illusion of reality: A review and integration of psychological research on hallucinations. *Psychological Bulletin*, *107*, 82–95.

Bentall, R. P. (1990b). The syndromes and symptoms of psychosis: Or why you can't play twenty questions with the concept of schizophrenia and hope to win. In R. P. Bentall (Ed.), *Reconstructing schizophrenia* London: Routledge.

Boergers, J., Spirito, A., & Donaldson, D. (1998). Reasons for adolescent suicide attempts: associations with psychological functioning. *Journal of the American Academy of Child and Adolescent Psychiatry, 37*(12), 1287–1293.

Borkovec, T. D. (1982). Insomnia. *Journal of Consulting and Clinical Psychology, 50*, 880–895.

Borkovec, T. D., & Inz, J. (1990). The nature of worry in generalized anxiety disorder: A predominance of thought activity. *Behaviour Research and Therapy, 28*, 153–158.

Borkovec, T. D., & Roemer, L. (1995). Perceived functions of worry among generalized anxiety disorder subjects: Distraction from more emotionally distressing topics? *Journal of Behavior Therapy and Experimental Psychiatry, 26*, 25–30.

Bower, G. H. (1987). Commentary on mood and memory. *Behaviour Research and Therapy, 25*, 443–455.

Chapman, A. L., Gratz, K. L., & Brown, M. Z. (2005). Solving the puzzle of deliberate self-harm: The experiential avoidance model. *Behaviour Research and Therapy, 44*, 371–394.

Cioffi, D., & Holloway, J. (1993). Delayed costs of suppressed pain. *Journal of Personality and Social Psychology, 64*, 274–282.

Clark, D. A. (2001). Unwanted mental intrusions in clinical disorders: An introduction. *Journal of Cognitive Psychotherapy: An International Quarterly, 16*, 161–178.

Clark, D. A. (2005). *Intrusive thoughts in clinical disorders: Theory, research, and treatment.* New York: Guilford Press.

Clark, D. M. (1986). A cognitive approach to panic. *Behaviour Research and Therapy, 24*, 461–470.

Conway, M., Howell, A., & Giannopoulos, C. (1991). Dysphoria and thought suppression. *Cognitive Therapy and Research, 15*, 153–166.

Dalgleish, T., & Yiend, J. (2006). The effects of suppressing a negative autobiographical memory on concurrent intrusions and subsequent autobiographical recall in dysphoria. *Journal of Abnormal Psychology, 115*(3), 467–473.

Erdelyi, M. H. (2006). The unified theory of repression. *Behavioral and Brain Sciences, 29*, 499–551.

Foa, E. B., & Wilson, E. (2001). *Stop Obsessing! How to overcome your obsessions and compulsions.* New York: Bantam.

García-Montes, J. M., Pérez-Álvarez, M., & Fidalgo, A. M. (2003). Influence of the suppression of self-discrepant thoughts on the vividness of perception of auditory illusions. *Behavioural and Cognitive Psychotherapy, 31*, 33–34.

Guthrie, R., & Bryant, R. A. (2000). Attempting suppression of traumatic memories over extended periods in acute stress disorder. *Behaviour Research and Therapy, 38*(9), 899–907.

Hartlage, S., Alloy, L. B., Vázquez, C., & Dykman, B. (1993). Automatic and effortful processing in depression. *Psychological Bulletin, 113*, 247–278.

Hartmann, E., Russ, D., van der Kolk, B., Falke, R., & Oldfield, M. (1981). A preliminary study of the personality of the nightmare sufferer: Relationship to schizophrenia and creativity. *American Journal of Psychiatry, 138*, 794–797.

Harvey, A. G. (2003). The attempted suppression of presleep cognitive activity in insomnia. *Cognitive Therapy and Research, 27*, 593–602.

Harvey, A. G., & Bryant, R. A. (1998). The effect of attempted thought suppression in acute stress disorder. *Behaviour Research and Therapy, 36*, 583–590.

Hayes, S. C., Strosahl, K., & Wilson, K. G. (1999). *Acceptance and commitment therapy: An experiential approach to behavior change.* New York: Guilford Press.

Howell, A., & Conway, M. (1992). Mood and the suppression of positive and negative self-referent thoughts. *Cognitive Therapy and Research, 16*, 535–555.

Ingjaldsson, J. T., Laberg, J. C., & Thayer, J. F. (2003). Reduced heart rate variability in chronic alcohol abuse: Relationship with negative mood, chronic thought suppression, and compulsive drinking. *Biological Psychiatry, 54*, 1427–1436.

Ingram, R. E., Miranda, J., & Segal, Z. V. (1998). *Cognitive vulnerability to depression.* New York: Guilford Press.

Janeck, A. S., & Calamari, J. E. (1999). Thought suppression in obsessive-compulsive disorder. *Cognitive Therapy and Research, 23*, 497–509.

Janet, P. (1894). Histoire d'une idee fixe. *Revue Philosophique, 37*, 121–163.

Johnsen, B. H., Thayer, J. F., Laberg, J. C., Wormnes, B., Raadal, M., Skaret, E., et al. (2003). Attentional and physiological characteristics of patients with dental anxiety. *Journal of Anxiety Disorders, 17*, 75–87.

Johnstone, K. A., & Page, A. C. (2004). Attention to phobic stimuli during exposure: The effect of distraction on anxiety reduction, self-efficacy and perceived control. *Behaviour Research and Therapy, 42*, 249–275.

Kelly, A. E., & Kahn, J. H. (1994). Effects of suppression of personal intrusive thoughts. *Journal of Personality and Social Psychology, 66*, 998–1006.

Kingdon, D. G., & Turkington, D. (1993). *Cognitive behavioural therapy of schizophrenia.* New York: Guilford Press.

Klein, A. A. (2007). Suppression-induced hyperaccessibility of thoughts in abstinent alcoholics: A preliminary investigation. *Behaviour Research and Therapy, 45*, 169–177.

Macrae, C. N., Bodenhausen, G. V., Milne, A. B., & Jetten, J. (1994). Out of mind but back in sight: stereotypes on the rebound. *Journal of Personality and Social Psychology, 67*, 808–817.

Masedo, A. I., & Esteve, M. R. (2007). Effects of suppression, acceptance and spontaneous coping on pain tolerance, pain intensity and distress. *Behaviour Research and Therapy, 45*, 199–209.

Mathews, A., & Milroy, R. (1994). Effects of priming and suppression of worry. *Behaviour Research and Therapy, 32*, 843–850.

McNally, R. J., & Ricciardi, J. N. (1996). Suppression of negative and neutral thoughts. *Behavioural and Cognitive Psychotherapy, 24*, 17–25.

Miranda, J., & Gross, J. J. (1997). Cognitive vulnerability, depression, and the mood-state hypothesis: Is out of sight out of mind? *Cognition and Emotion, 11*, 585–605.

Morris, W. L., & Wegner, D. M. (2000). *Disowning our unwanted thoughts: Thought suppression and introspective alienation.* Paper presented at the Poster presented at the American Psychological Society, Miami Beach, FL.

Morrison, A. P. (1998). A cognitive analysis of auditory hallucinations: are voices to schizophrenia what bodily sensations are to panic? *Behavioural and Cognitive Psychotherapy, 26,* 289–302.

Morrison, A. P. (2001). The interpretation of intrusions in psychosis: An integrative cognitive approach to hallucinations and delusions. *Behavioural and Cognitive Psychotherapy, 29,* 257–276.

Morrison, A. P., & Baker, C. A. (2000). Intrusive thoughts and auditory hallucinations: a comparative study of intrusions in psychosis. *Behaviour Research and Therapy, 38,* 1097–1106.

Morrison, A. P., Haddock, G., & Tarrier, N. (1995). Intrusive thoughts and auditory hallucinations: A cognitive approach. *Behavioural and Cognitive Psychotherapy, 23,* 265–280.

Morrison, A. P., & Wells, A. (2000). Thought control strategies in schizophrenia: A comparison with non-patients. *Behaviour Research and Therapy, 38,* 1205–1209.

Najmi, S., & Wegner, D. M. (in press). The gravity of unwanted thoughts: Asymmetric priming effects in thought suppression. *Consciousness and Cognition.*

Najmi, S., Wegner, D. M., & Nock, M. K. (2007). Thought suppression and self-injurious thoughts and behaviors. *Behaviour Research and Therapy, 45,* 1957–1965.

Nayani, T. H., & David, A. S. (1996). The auditory hallucination: A phenomenological survey. *Psychological Medicine, 26,* 177–189.

Newman, L. S., Duff, K. J., & Baumeister, R. F. (1997). A new look at defensive projection: Thought suppression, accessibility, and biased person perception. *Journal of Personality and Social Psychology, 5,* 980–1001.

Nock, M. K., & Prinstein, M. J. (2004). A functional approach to the assessment of self-mutilative behavior. *Journal of Consulting and Clinical Psychology, 72,* 885–890.

Nock, M. K., & Prinstein, M. J. (2005). Contextual features and behavioral functions of self-mutilation among adolescents. *Journal of Abnormal Psychology, 114,* 140–146.

Ostafin, B. D., Palfai, T. P., & Wechsler, C. E. (2003). The accessibility of motivational tendencies toward alcohol: Approach, avoidance, and disinhibited drinking. *Experimental and Clinical Psychopharmacology, 11,* 294–301.

Page, A. C., Locke, V., & Trio, M. (2005). An online measure of thought suppression. *Journal of Personality and Social Psychology, 88*(3), 421–431.

Palfai, T. P., Colby, S. M., Monti, P. M., & Rohsenow, D. J. (1997). Effects of suppressing the urge to drink on smoking topography: A preliminary study. *Psychology of Addictive Behaviors, 11,* 115–123.

Palfai, T. P., Monti, P. M., Colby, S. M., & Rohsenow, D. J. (1997). Effects of suppressing the urge to drink on the accessibility of alcohol outcome expectancies. *Behaviour Research and Therapy, 35,* 59–65.

Palfai, T. P., & Ostafin, B. D. (2003). Alcohol-related motivational tendencies in hazardous drinkers: Assessing implicit response tendencies using the modified-IAT. *Behaviour Research and Therapy, 41,* 1149–1162.

Purdon, C. L., & Clark, D. A. (1993). Obsessive intrusive thoughts in nonclinical subjects. Part I. Content and relation with depressive, anxious and obsessional symptoms. *Behaviour Research and Therapy, 31,* 713–720.

Purdon, C. L., & Clark, D. A. (1994a). Obsessive intrusive thoughts in nonclinical subjects. Part II. *Behaviour Research and Therapy, 32,* 403–410.

Purdon, C. L., & Clark, D. A. (1994b). Perceived control and appraisal of obsessional intrusive thoughts: A replication and extension. *Behavioural and Cognitive Psychotherapy, 22,* 269–285.

Purdon, C. L., & Clark, D. A. (2000). White bears and other elusive intrusions: Assessing the relevance of thought suppression for obsessional phenomena. *Behavior Modification, 24,* 425–453.

Purdon, C. L., & Clark, D. A. (2001). Suppression of obsession-like thoughts in nonclinical individuals: Impact on thought frequency, appraisal and mood state. *Behaviour Research and Therapy, 39,* 1163–1181.

Purdon, C. L., Rowa, K., & Antony, M. M. (2005). Thought suppression and its effects on thought frequency, appraisal and mood state in individuals with obsessive-compulsive disorder. *Behaviour Research and Therapy, 43,* 93–108.

Rachman, S. J. (1978). An anatomy of obsessions. *Behaviour Analysis and Modification, 2,* 235–278.

Rachman, S. J. (1981). Unwanted intrusive cognitions. *Advances in Behaviour Research and Therapy, 3,* 89–99.

Rachman, S. J. (1994). Pollution of the mind. *Behaviour Research and Therapy, 32,* 311–314.

Rachman, S. J. (1997). A cognitive theory of obsessions. *Behaviour Research and Therapy, 35,* 793–802.

Rachman, S. J., & de Silva, P. (1978). Abnormal and normal obsessions. *Research and Therapy, 16,* 233–248.

Rassin, E. (2005). *Thought suppression.* New York: Elsevier.

Rassin, E., Muris, P., Schmidt, H., & Merckelbach, H. (2000). Relationship between thought-action fusion, thought suppression and obsessive-compulsive symptoms: A structural equation modeling approach. *Behaviour Research and Therapy, 38,* 889–897.

Renaud, J. M., & McConnell, A. R. (2002). Organization of the self-concept and the suppression of self-relevant thoughts. *Journal of Experimental Social Psychology, 38,* 79–86.

Ribot, T. (1881). *Les maladies de la mémoire.* Paris: Baillière.

Roemer, L., & Borkovec, T. D. (1994). Effects of suppressing thoughts about emotional material. *Journal of Abnormal Psychology, 103,* 467–474.

Roemer, L., & Orsillo, S. M. (2002). Expanding our conceptualization of and treatment for generalized anxiety disorder: Integrating mindfulness/acceptance-based approaches with existing cognitive-behavioral models. *Clinical Psychology: Science and Practice, 9,* 54–68.

Romme, M. A. J., Honig, A., Noorthorn, E. O., & Escher, A. D. M. A. C. (1992). Coping with hearing voices: An emancipatory approach. *British Journal of Psychiatry, 161,* 99–103.

Salkovskis, P. M. (1985). Obsessional-compulsive problems: A cognitive-behavioral analysis. *Behaviour Research and Therapy, 23,* 571–583.

Salkovskis, P. M. (1996). Cognitive-behavioural approaches to the understanding of obsessive-compulsive problems. In R. M. Rapee (Ed.), *Current controversies in the anxiety disorders* (pp. 103–133). New York: Guilford Press.

Salkovskis, P. M., & Campbell, P. (1994). Thought suppression induces intrusion in naturally occurring negative intrusive thoughts. *Behaviour Research and Therapy, 32*, 1–8.

Salkovskis, P. M., & Harrison, J. (1984). Abnormal and normal obsessions—A replication. *Behaviour Research and Therapy, 23*, 571–584.

Salkovskis, P. M., & Reynolds, M. (1994). Thought suppression and smoking cessation. *Behaviour Research and Therapy, 32*, 193–201.

Segal, Z. V., Williams, J. M. G., & Teasdale, J. D. (2002). *Mindfulness and the prevention of depression: A guide to the theory and practice of mindfulness-based cognitive therapy.* New York: Guilford Press.

Shipherd, J. C., & Beck, J. G. (1999). The effects of suppressing trauma-related thoughts on women with rape-related posttraumatic stress disorder. *Behaviour Research and Therapy, 37*, 99–112.

Shipherd, J. C., & Beck, J. G. (2005). The role of thought suppression in posttraumatic stress disorder. *Behavior Therapy, 36*, 277–287.

Smári, J., & Hólmsteinsson, H. E. (2001). Intrusive thoughts, responsibility attitudes, thought action fusion and chronic thought suppression in relation to obsessive-compulsive symptoms. *Behavioural and Cognitive Psychotherapy, 29*, 13–20.

Stroop, J. R. (1935). Studies of interference in serial verbal reactions. *Journal of Experimental Psychology, 18*, 643–662.

Taylor, E. (1984). *William James on exceptional mental states.* Amherst: University of Massachusetts Press.

Thayer, J. F., & Lane, R. D. (2002). Perseverative thinking and health: Neurovisceral concomitants. *Psychology and Health, 17*, 695–695.

Tolin, D. F., Abramowitz, J. S., Hamlin, C., Foa, E. B., & Synodi, D. S. (2002a). Attributions for thought suppression failure in obsessive-compulsive disorder. *Cognitive Therapy and Research, 26*, 505–517.

Tolin, D. F., Abramowitz, J. S., Przeworski, A., & Foa, E. B. (2002b). Thought suppression in obsessive-compulsive disorder. *Behaviour Research and Therapy, 40*, 1255–1274.

Trinder, H., & Salkovskis, P. M. (1994). Personally relevant intrusions outside the laboratory: Long-term suppression increases intrusion. *Behaviour Research and Therapy, 32*, 833–842.t

Wegner, D. M. (1989). *White bears and other unwanted thoughts: Suppression, obsession, and the psychology of mental control.* New York: Viking/Penguin.

Wegner, D. M. (1994). Ironic processes of mental control. *Psychological Review, 101*, 34–52.

Wegner, D. M., Broome, A., & Blumberg, S. J. (1997). Ironic effects of trying to relax under stress. *Behaviour Research and Therapy, 35*, 11–21.

Wegner, D. M., Eich, E., & Bjork, R. A. (1994). Thought suppression. In D. Druckman & R. A. Bjork (Eds.), *Learning, remembering, believing: Enhancing human performance* (pp. 277–293). Washington, DC: National Academy Press.

Wegner, D. M., & Erber, R. E. (1992). The hyperaccessibility of suppressed thoughts. *Journal of Personality and Social Psychology, 63*, 903–912.

Wegner, D. M., Erber, R. E., & Zanakos, S. (1993). Ironic processes in the mental control of mood and mood-related thought. *Journal of Personality and Social Psychology, 65*, 1093–1104.

Wegner, D. M., Schneider, D. J., Carter, S., III., & White, L. (1987). Paradoxical effects of thought suppression. *Journal of Personality and Social Psychology, 53*, 5–13.

Wegner, D. M., Schneider, D. J., Knutson, B., & McMahon, S. R. (1991). Polluting the stream of consciousness: The effect of thought suppression on the mind's environment. *Cognitive Therapy and Research, 15*, 141–152.

Wegner, D. M., Wenzlaff, R., & Kozak, M. (2004). Dream rebound: The return of suppressed thoughts in dreams. *Psychological Science, 15*, 232–236.

Wegner, D. M., & Zanakos, S. (1994). Chronic thought suppression. *Journal of Personality, 62*, 615–640.

Wegner, D. M., & Zanakos, S. (1994). Chronic thought suppression. *Journal of Personality, 62*, 610–640.

Wenzlaff, R. M. (2005). Seeking solace but finding despair: The persistence of intrusive thoughts in depression. In D. A. Clark (Ed.), *Intrusive thoughts in clinical disorders: Theory, research, and treatment* (pp. 54–85). New York: Guilford Press.

Wenzlaff, R. M., & Bates, D. E. (1998). Unmasking a cognitive vulnerability to depression: How lapses in mental control reveal depressive thinking. *Journal of Personality and Social Psychology, 75*, 1559–1571.

Wenzlaff, R. M., & Eisenberg, A. R. (2001). Mental control after dysphoria: evidence of a suppressed, depressive bias. *Behavior Therapy, 32*, 27–45.

Wenzlaff, R. M., Meir, J., & Salas, D. M. (2002). Thought suppression and memory biases during and after depressive moods. *Cognition and Emotion, 16*, 403–422.

Wenzlaff, R. M., Rude, S. S., Taylor, C. J., Stultz, C. H., & Sweatt, R. A. (2001). Beneath the veil of thought suppression: Attentional bias and depression risk. *Cognition and Emotion, 15*(4), 435–452.

Wenzlaff, R. M., & Wegner, D. M. (2000). Thought suppression. In S. T. Fiske (Ed.), *Annual review of psychology* (Vol. 51, pp. 59–91). Palo Alto: Annual Reviews.

Wenzlaff, R. M., Wegner, D. M., & Klein, S. B. (1991). The role of thought suppression in the bonding of thought and mood. *Journal of Personality and Social Psychology, 60*, 500–508.

Wenzlaff, R. M., Wegner, D. M., & Roper, D. (1988). Depression and mental control: The resurgence of unwanted negative thoughts. *Journal of Personality and Social Psychology, 55*, 882–892.

Orienting and Attentional Processes

27 Motivational and Attentional Components of Personality

Douglas Derryberry and Marjorie Reed

CONTENTS

Although approach and avoidance motivation are most often discussed in terms of behaviors, it is now clear that such motivation also regulates attention. From a motivational perspective, states related to appetitive and defensive needs appear to bias attention in favor of stimuli capable of satisfying or blocking that need. Given defensive needs, for example, attention to signals predicting danger and safety is enhanced. Such enhancement helps link sensory and response pathways, making it easier for the individual to avoid the danger and approach safety (Derryberry & Reed, 2002; Posner & Rothbart, 1998).

Motivational influences on attention are also important because they provide a mechanism through which motivational states can influence a wide range of cognitive processes. In these cases, attention is directed away from sensory channels toward more internal pathways involved in conceptual, affective, and response processing. For example, achievement-related needs may bias attention toward stored information related to success and failure, and social needs may allocate attention toward information related to acceptance and rejection. Such information can be used in thinking about the past, in anticipating the future, and in formulating coping strategies that help the person approach positive outcomes and avoid negative outcomes (Matthews, 1997).

In addition, motivated attention is important in that attention is one of the processes that stabilize information in memory (Grossberg, 1999). Enhanced attention helps store motivationally significant information in memory, building representations that are more developed regarding sources of success and failure. These representations can then be called upon to help guide behavior in future situations. When viewed in terms of learning and development, it is not hard to see that motivational influences on attention may play a central role in personality development. As the child grows older, underlying approach and avoidance processes bias attention in relation to the individual's unique needs and environment, gradually shaping representations of the self, others, and the future. Combined with the underlying motivational systems, such representations are often viewed as central to personality (Derryberry & Reed, 1996; Elliot & Thrash, 2002).

This chapter consists of three sections. We begin with a theoretical overview, briefly laying out physiological and psychological models of motivation, attention, and personality. The second section describes three sets of reaction time studies that we have used to explore motivational and personality influences on attention. These studies demonstrate that in situations involving approach or avoidance, attention is modulated by the previous outcome of success or failure and by personality traits of Extraversion, Anxiety, and Attentional Control. Finally, the last section returns to a developmental perspective to consider interactions among motivational, attentional, and representational processes in the development of personality.

TEMPERAMENT FRAMEWORK FOR MOTIVATION, ATTENTION, AND PERSONALITY

In laying out our temperament framework, we briefly describe circuitry relevant to approach and avoidance behavior, followed by a description of attentional systems and their connections with the motivational systems. We then consider how individual differences in these systems are related to personality and clinical problems.

MOTIVATIONAL SYSTEMS

Since physiological mechanisms are covered in other chapters, we provide a brief outline of our theoretical model. The model is based on multiple, parallel motivational systems such as those involved in appetitive, defensive, and nurturant needs. These motivational systems share control over other circuits involved in orchestrating approach and avoidance behavior. In addition to controlling behavior, the motivational systems regulate attention to environmental stimuli relevant to the current need.

The motivational systems are distributed throughout the brain, providing a variety of approach and avoidance behaviors. If we look at the defensive system, for example, individual motor and autonomic components arise from circuits in the medulla. These components are coordinated by descending projections from the midbrain's periaqueductal gray (PAG) area. The PAG contains columns of cells that elicit distinct avoidance behaviors depending upon the nature of the immediate threat. An explosive form of escape behavior is elicited when an organism is under immediate threat but has an escape route. If the organism is cornered with no escape route, then defensive aggression is triggered in an attempt to fight off the predator. If the organism is injured and defensive aggression is not possible, then a form of tonic immobility (playing dead) can be activated (Bandler & Shipley, 1994; Keay & Bandler, 2001).

The PAG columns are reciprocally connected with higher circuits within the limbic system and cortex. These circuits allow more complex avoidance behavior in relation to stimuli that are spatially and temporally more distant. Descending connections from the hypothalamus are thought to be involved in more directed forms of escape (active avoidance) given a more distant threat. Connections from the amygdala appear to orchestrate avoidance (e.g., active or passive avoidance) in relation to conditioned stimuli that signal threat, whereas hippocampal projections help co-ordinate a form of "risk assessment" when an organism cautiously enters an area previously occupied by a threat (Gray & McNaughton, 1996). Descending connections from the orbital and medial frontal cortex provide further fine tuning of avoidance behaviors, presumably in relation to more abstract dangers such as failure, rejection, and so on. As can be seen, the defensive circuitry appears to have evolved in such a way as to take increasing advantage of distant stimuli, dangers that are spatially and temporally more distant from the individual.

The circuitry underlying appetitive motivation is less well understood, but appears to be similarly distributed across the brain. Within the PAG, for example, columns have been located related to sexual and feeding behavior. These behaviors are strongly regulated from the hypothalamus, as well as via descending projections from the amygdala and frontal cortex. Again, it is likely that the higher projections regulate approach in relation to more abstract types of rewards. Additional research has found that approach is regulated via critical circuits converging on the nucleus accumbens, a ventral extension of the striatum. Most of this forebrain circuitry is under the facilitatory influence of dopaminergic projections arising from the midbrain. The approach-related circuitry has been discussed in terms of a "behavioral activation system" (Gray, 1987), a "behavioral facilitation system" (Depue & Collins, 1999), and an "expectancy-foraging system" (Panksepp, 1998).

ATTENTIONAL SYSTEMS

Appetitive and defensive systems possess extensive connections to the brain's attentional systems. The resulting attentional control increases the efficacy of approach and avoidance by facilitating relevant stimuli (e.g., rewards to be approached, dangers to be avoided). The attentional effects can be exerted in several ways, perhaps best described in terms of Posner's three interacting attentional systems (Posner & Raichle, 1994).

Posner has discussed a "vigilance" system involving norepinephrine projections from the brainstem's locus coeruleus to the cortex. This system is thought to lack the specificity required for highly selective attention, but nevertheless to be involved in tonic maintenance and phasic adjustments in general alertness. Phasic alerting may enhance signal-to-noise ratios across multiple sets of synapses, biasing relatively large forebrain circuits in relation to motivationally significant stimuli. Also, the noradrenergic system plays an important role in neuronal plasticity, helping to store important information in memory (Berridge & Waterhouse, 2003; Gu, 2002).

In addition to the noradrenergic systems, a number of other projection systems are likely to be involved in general attentional functions. These include the serotonergic projections from the raphe nuclei, dopaminergic projections from the ventral tegmental area, histaminergic projections from the hypothalamus, and cholinergic projections from the nucleus basalis (Gu, 2002). Together with the noradrenergic projections, these systems form an intricate network that exerts highly complex neuromodulatory effects on distinct cortical layers and regions. All of these projection systems appear closely linked to motivation, with the source nuclei receiving inputs from the PAG, hypothalamus, amygdala, and frontal cortex.

A second set of attentional circuits is involved in orienting attention from one specific location to another. This "posterior attentional system" is distributed across the midbrain's superior colliculus, the pulvinar nucleus of the thalamus, and the parietal lobe within the cortex. Its functioning can be best understood in terms of component operations that allow attention to "disengage" (parietal lobe) from one location, "move" (superior colliculus) to a new location, and "engage" (thalamus) or enhance that location (Posner & Raichle, 1994). So far, fewer motivational inputs to the orienting system have been identified compared to the vigilance system. The frontal cortex has direct projections to most of the orienting circuitry, as does the vigilance-related systems, but other motivation-related regions, such as the amygdala and hypothalamus, have less direct or weaker connections.

A third attentional system is located within the frontal cortex and the anterior cingulate region. This "anterior attentional system" is viewed as a voluntary, executive system responsible for regulating the posterior attentional system and controlling attention to semantic and response information (Posner & Raichle, 1994; Rothbart, Derryberry, & Posner, 1994). A similar formulation can be found in Shallice's "supervisory attentional system" (Stuss, Shallice, Alexander, & Picton, 1995). Posner and Rothbart (1998) suggest that the anterior system underlies the conscious, "effortful control" of behavior through which the individual can regulate more reactive motivational functions. In addition, we have suggested that individual motivational systems can recruit the anterior system during voluntary motivational states (Derryberry, Reed, & Pilkenton-Taylor, 2003). Connections through which motivational states may access voluntary attention are plentiful, including ascending frontal connections from the PAG, hypothalamus, amygdala, and hippocampus (Ongur & Price, 2000).

To provide a more functional example, consider someone entering a grocery store and scanning for a tasty food item. Individual food items are processed in detail within the cortex and then delivered to the motivational systems (though more direct inputs from the thalamus are also available; LeDoux, 2000). If a rewarding item is detected, attention will be directed toward the item to facilitate processing and evaluation. In more detail, brainstem vigilance mechanisms (e.g., the noradrenergic projections) will exert a relatively general alerting effect on the cortex; attention will orient (disengage, move, and engage) to the new location, facilitating the further processing of the food information in that location; and within the anterior system, additional conceptual information may be brought into play, prepotent response and conceptual pathways may be inhibited, and the orienting will be brought under voluntary control. This regulated information will then converge on the approach and avoidance systems, and if approach is more strongly activated, then the reaching response will be guided (via the enhanced sensory information) toward the food item. In addition, attention will help stabilize the relevant pathways in memory in order to update the individual's "food map" for future use. This memory effect is likely to involve several attentional components, such as the ascending noradrenergic effect on the cortex (Berridge & Waterhouse, 2003; Grossberg, 1999).

PERSONALITY

Most temperament models assume that the motivational systems vary in reactivity or strength across individuals and that these differences underlie major personality dimensions. As the approach system increases in strength, individuals are thought to move from the introverted to the extraverted end of the Extraversion dimension. Thus, extraverts should be more sensitive to rewarding stimuli, more likely to attend to and to approach these stimuli, and more likely to experience feelings such as hope, desire, and positive anticipation (Depue & Collins, 1999; Eysenck & Eysenck, 1985; Gray, 1987; Watson & Clark, 1992). Given the idea that attention facilitates learning, extraverts would be expected to develop representations that feature positive as opposed to negative elements. Because they feed back into the motivational systems, the extravert's "optimistic" representations should preferentially engage the appetitive circuitry, leading to increased probability of future approach behavior (Derryberry & Reed, 1996).

In contrast, the defensive or avoidance system is usually related to neuroticism. As one moves from the "stable" to the "neurotic" end of this dimension, the individual becomes more sensitive to negative information, more likely to attend to it, to avoid it, and to suffer from negative emotions such as anxiety, depression, and anger. In addition, attention to negative information may lead to relatively negative and pessimistic representations, thereby increasing the probability of future avoidance (Eysenck & Eysenck, 1985; Watson & Clark, 1992).

It is worth noting that some models propose that the underlying motivational process does not map directly onto Extraversion and Neuroticism, but rather aligns with two other dimensions running diagonally within the two-dimensional space (Gray, 1987; Wallace, Newman, & Bachorowski, 1991). Thus, approach reactivity is viewed as increasing along an "Impulsivity" dimension running from stable introversion to neurotic extraversion, and avoidance reactivity (behavioral inhibition) is viewed as increasing along an "Anxiety" dimension that runs from the stable extravert to the neurotic introvert.

In contrast to motivational tendencies, traditional personality models have not addressed attentional capabilities. In early studies, however, we found that differences in self-reported "attentional focusing" and "attentional shifting" were evident and related to other personality measures (Derryberry & Rothbart, 1988). For example, the attentional measures were negatively related to measures of negative emotions, suggesting that individuals with better control can use their attention to reduce negative affect. Rothbart and Posner went on to build a developmental model in which individual differences in frontal circuits related to executive attention are proposed to underlie a dimension of "Effortful Control" (Posner & Raichle, 1994; Rothbart & Bates, 1998). Effortful control is thought to

provide a voluntary means of controlling more reactive approach and avoidance tendencies. For example, good effortful control may allow an individual to inhibit a prepotent approach (or avoidance) response, and thus execute a more situationally appropriate avoidance (or approach) response. As described later in the section on reaction time studies, we have combined our earlier shifting and focusing scales into a single measure of "Attentional Control" (Derryberry & Reed, 2002). Unpublished work has found Attentional Control to correlate most strongly with the dimension of conscientiousness ($r = .5$ to $.6$), but to also correlate with Neuroticism ($r = -.3$ to $-.4$) and Extraversion ($r = .2$ to $.3$).

REACTION TIME STUDIES OF APPROACH AND AVOIDANCE

We will return to personality in the last section of the chapter where we adopt a developmental perspective. But first, it is necessary to provide specific evidence for the types of motivational, attentional, and personality processes that have driven our theorizing. The studies we will describe seem particularly relevant to the theme of this handbook because we have always framed our paradigms around approach and avoidance orientations. We first describe the general paradigm, followed by three sets of experimental findings.

BASIC EXPERIMENTAL PARADIGM

Our primary goal has always been to examine the theoretical ideas expressed above by investigating attentional biases related to approach and avoidance states. It is possible to elicit these states fairly easily by using a game framework within which participants can gain or lose points on each trial. Positive (approach-related) trials led to a gain of 10 points if the response was accurate and faster than the participant's median reaction time from the last game (success), but no loss of points if the response was too slow (failure). In contrast, negative (avoidance-related) targets led to a loss of 10 points if the response was slower than the median RT (failure), and no loss of points if the response was faster (success).

Because the criterion for success and failure was based on each person's average speed, cumulative scores (across a block of trials or a set of blocks) tended to stay close to zero. This made the games more challenging and prevented confounding by states related to particularly low or high scores. Participants were simply told that the game is programmed to be challenging, and that the average score, at the end of the set of blocks, tended to be close to zero. They were told that sometimes their score would be above zero, at other times below zero, but that their overall goal should be to break zero at the end of the set. In motivational terms, we assumed that participants were motivated to "approach" winning points and to "avoid" losing points, and that this underlying motivation could be manipulated, with some precision, by the signals presented on each trial.

Each trial consisted of three signals. First, a cue appeared, signaling whether the trial would be positive or negative in nature. For example, some studies used a cue on the right side to signal the opportunity to gain points and a cue on the left side to signal the chance of losing points. Other studies used the letter M to signal a positive trial and the letter W a negative trial. These signals were assumed to elicit a brief, phasic motivational state related to approach or avoidance. Second, the effect of this state is assayed by presenting a simple target within 500 ms following the cue. Targets could involve a simple dot to be detected, a word to be categorized, or a letter to be categorized. They could match or mismatch the cue in location or meaning. Third, a feedback signal was presented roughly 1 s after the response. These signals took several different forms across different studies, including smiling and frowning faces, green and red squares, and so on. The feedback signal was assumed to elicit an outcome-related motivational state (success or failure) that might extend across time to influence cue and target processing on the next trial.

Here is an example using our simplest spatial orienting task (Posner, 1978). The trial begins with a cue in the form of an arrow pointing up on the right side of the screen, signaling that if the subsequent target appears on the right 10 points can be gained, but if the target appears on the left no points can be gained. The cue is assumed to activate a positive, approach-related state that motivates an attentional shift to the more important right side of the screen. A simple detection target appears on the right or left side of the screen. If the target appears in the attended (e.g., right) location, the RT will be fast because attention has already moved and facilitated detection on the right (a "valid" trial). But if the target appears in the unattended location (e.g., left), then the RT will be slow because attention must be shifted from the attended to the unattended targeted location (an "invalid" trial). The relative strength of this attentional bias can be estimated by subtracting the fast RTs on the attended (right) side from the slower RTs to targets on the unattended (left) side (i.e., invalid–valid RTs). Thus, it is possible to compute the size of this basic attentional effect on both approach and avoidance trials. The bias can also be

assessed in relation to the outcome of the previous trial, to determine whether previous success and failure influence subsequent attention.

We designed this paradigm because it allows improved control of the targeted motivational processes and attentional processes. Other success and failure manipulations have been shown to elicit the intended positive and negative emotions (Nummenmaa & Niemi, 2004). Our game format allows honest success and failure feedback in a relatively balanced mix, with no danger of participants not believing the feedback. Importantly, it allows assessment of approach and avoidance motivation within the same person. Both types of contexts involved the same number of points and thus the same distance toward or away from the goal. In most studies, positive and negative signals were also made as identical as possible in terms of their physical properties, varying only in location (left or right) or orientation (M or W, 2 or 5).

The design also provides better control over attention. For one thing, we were able to partially disentangle attentional from response effects by using the same exact response (a key press with the right index finger) for both types of targets. In addition, we were able to track attentional movement across time by presenting the targets at varying intervals (SOAs: stimulus onset asynchronies) following a cue. Furthermore, these paradigms can be modified to provide a more precise view of attention itself. They can be used to break attention down into components such as Posner's disengage, move, and engage operations, and to examine more voluntary as opposed to involuntary processes.

A main disadvantage, at least in the context of approach and avoidance motivation, is that our paradigm focuses on a specific type of avoidance motivation in which one performs an arbitrary response (neither approaching or avoiding in structural terms) in order to avoid a negative outcome. Although this may not fit well within the more classic notions of avoidance (physically avoiding an object or location), it is nevertheless a common form of motivation that may be found in contexts of performance, achievement, and social acceptance where success and failure are primary outcomes. We have performed a few studies in which subjects physically avoided a certain target location, but the results can be difficult to interpret given the more complex programming required for avoidance than approach responses.

We will summarize the results from three sets of studies completed across the last 15 years. The first focuses on approach motivation and the conditions under which it is enhanced. The second set of studies focuses on avoidance motivation, underlying attentional mechanisms, and individual differences. The last set describes studies investigating attentional effects of relative value, where a conflict is set up by presenting two simultaneous targets differing in incentive value (e.g., worth 5 points or 2 points).

APPROACH-RELATED PROCESSING

One of our initial questions was whether the cue-elicited attentional effect would be stronger for positive trials (where points could be gained) or negative trials (where points could be lost). Some have argued that the human processing system is basically biased toward positive information, a tendency sometimes referred to as the "Pollyanna Effect" (Matlin & Stang, 1978). However, others, such as Kahneman and Tversky (1979) and Baumeister, Bratslavsky, Finkenauer, and Vohs (2001) have argued that humans show a general "loss aversion," viewing losses as more important than equivalent gains.

We approached this question by comparing the strength of attentional effects elicited by positive and negative cues. As described above, such effects can be estimated by computing the difference between valid trials (where cue and target match) and invalid trials (where cue and target mismatch requiring a reorienting of attention). Our earliest studies presented positive (an arrow pointed up) and negative (an arrow pointed down) cues to indicate whether points could be gained or lost. This was followed by a state-descriptive adjective that was to be categorized as positive (e.g., happy) or negative (e.g., sad). Although both kinds of cues elicited strong attentional effects, we could find no general differences between the positive and negative cues (Derryberry, 1988). Other studies using a spatial orienting task presented cues in a positive or negative location, followed by a detection target in the cued or uncued location. Again, orienting was found to both positive and negative locations, but with no general biases favoring one location or the other (Derryberry & Reed, 1994). Thus, we have been unable to find any general differences in the overall attentional effects related to approach and avoidance motivation. We suspect that such general effects will be difficult to find because motivational states are not always equally active, and thus, will only lead to attentional biases under certain circumstances.

Although a positive attentional bias is not generally active, such an effect does arise following failure. In other words, the outcome states of success and failure alter motivational activity and appear to change the impact of positive and negative incentives. In our early studies with state adjectives, we found what we termed an "incongruent effect," i.e., following positive feedback,

attentional effects were equal for positive (61 ms) and negative (57 ms) cues, but following negative feedback, attentional effects were stronger for positive (56 ms) than negative (32 ms) cues (Derryberry, 1988). Using the spatial orienting paradigm, attentional effects following positive feedback were equal for positive (17 ms) and negative (16 ms) cues, but following negative feedback, attentional effects were stronger for positive (17 ms) than negative (10 ms) cues (Derryberry & Reed, 1994). Similar examples of incongruent effects can be found in Derryberry (1993) and more recently in Rothermund (2003).

Such effects suggest that approach and avoidance motivation are modulated by the previous outcome, with failure enhancing the attentional impact of positive relative to negative cues. This type of effect would be adaptive in helping the person to continue approaching a task following a failure. The incongruent effect is generally compatible with the notion that motivational states have "inertial tendencies," such that approach-related motivation may build in strength following failure (Atkinson & Birch, 1978). The effect is also consistent with neural models featuring positive and negative motivational systems that are connected by reciprocal inhibitory neurons (Grossberg & Schmajuk, 1987). When one system (e.g., avoidance) is weakened by repeated activation, the other system (e.g., approach) is disinhibited, resulting in a rebound enhancement.

In addition to regulation by the previous outcome, the attentional effects are also influenced by the more enduring motivational processes related to personality. Our spatial orienting studies have employed measures of extraversion, neuroticism, anxiety, and impulsivity to investigate models such as Gray's (1987). Predictions are fairly clear from these models that extraverts (or neurotic extraverts) should show relatively strong attentional effects under approach conditions (potential gain), whereas neurotics (or neurotic introverts) should show stronger effects in avoidance situations (potential loss).

Two sets of studies have found such differences (Derryberry, 1987; Derryberry & Reed, 1994). Averaged across the two 1994 studies, positive cues elicited greater attention in extraverts (35 ms) than introverts (25 ms) and negative cues elicit greater attention in introverts (26 ms) than extraverts (18 ms). Thus, we find evidence for the Pollyanna effect and the loss aversion effect, but importantly, in different individuals. As suggested by models such as Gray's (1987), the approach or behavioral activation system should be engaged more strongly in extraverts than introverts and should facilitate approach behavior given positive cues. The behavioral inhibition system should be engaged more strongly in introverts and should inhibit approach and direct attention to threats requiring potential avoidance.

A closer look at this data suggests that the Extraversion effect is strongest in neurotic extraverts and neurotic introverts, and that it interacts with the failure-related enhancement of the positive bias. Averaged across the two studies, failure-related increase in the positive bias is greatest in neurotic extraverts. Following failure, neurotic extraverts show an attentional effect of 39 ms for positive cues and 16 ms for negative cues, whereas stable extraverts show an effect of 30 ms for positive and 23 ms for negative cues Thus, extraverts and especially neurotic extraverts respond to failure with enhanced attention to positive cues affording the opportunity to gain points, while introverts show no changes in response to positive cues.

This effect may reflect a basic motivational difference between extraverts and introverts. Extraverts may show enhanced approach motivation following failure that allows them to remain optimistic and to persist in the face of difficulties (which may or may not prove adaptive). Such a process is supported by the work of Newman and his colleagues with extraverts and psychopaths (Newman, 1987; Wallace et al., 1991). These researchers proposed that negative feedback engages a nonspecific arousal system related to neuroticism, which in turn facilitates the positive and negative motivational processes related to extraversion (Wallace et al.). As a result, negative feedback should enhance attention to positive cues in neurotic extraverts and to negative cues in neurotic introverts.

In summary, our studies suggest that the positive bias is rather elusive, appearing in only some people under some conditions. In general, approach and avoidance motivation appear roughly equal in terms of their effects on attention. However, approach motivation gets stronger after unsuccessful compared to successful outcomes, with this enhancement effect appearing primarily in extraverts.

Avoidance-Related Processing

We turn now to a set of studies examining negative attentional effects. Again, we found that an individual difference approach was essential to studying such effects. As predicted by models such as Gray's, anxious individuals (e.g., neurotic introverts) showed a relative general bias favoring negative cues that signaled a potential loss of points. In the 1994 studies, for example, the attentional effect of a negative cue is stronger in neurotic introverts (25 ms) than neurotic extraverts (15 ms). Unlike the positive bias, the negative bias did not depend on the previous outcome (Derryberry & Reed, 1994). In general, the negative bias is consistent with many other findings that anxious

individuals (who tend to be neurotic introverts) show an attentional bias favoring threatening information (MacLeod & Mathews, 1988; Fox, Russo, Bowles, & Dutton, 2001).

Several of our studies have attempted to examine the specific operations underlying this negative attentional bias. Although so far we have spoken in terms of an overall "attentional effect" computed by subtracting RTs following valid cues from those following invalid cues, it is possible to begin to consider underlying operations by examining the valid and invalid trials separately. Given a valid cue, attention must disengage from a neutral location (a fixation point), move to the cued location, and engage the cued location. But given an invalid cue, attention must also disengage from the cued location, move to the uncued location, and then engage the target. Such an analysis suggests that valid trials primarily reflect the time required by the move and engage operations, whereas invalid trials reflect in large part the extra time required to disengage attention.

Almost all of our studies have found motivational and personality effects to appear on invalid rather than valid trials. Typically RTs will be similar given valid cues but different given the invalid cues that require attention to be disengaged from the cued location. In our 1994 studies, introverts (especially neurotic introverts) showed greater delays given invalid negative cues than did extraverts (Derryberry & Reed, 1994). This pattern suggests that high anxious people are not faster than low anxious people in moving to and engaging a cued negative location, but rather, are slow to disengage from that location once it has been attended. The delayed disengagement has been replicated by Derryberry and Reed (2002) and also by Fox et al. (2001).

Although more research is needed, the delayed disengagement provides an interesting approach to understanding anxious cognition. It may be misleading to say that an introvert or anxious person is more likely to attend to or notice perceptual or conceptual threats. In contrast, the impaired disengagement may make it difficult to respond to other relevant information, such as the safety signals that are beneficial in coping with the threat. While less anxious people may shift away, more anxious people may become "stuck" in worrisome and ruminative lines of thought. As more anxiety is elicited, a positive feedback loop can be established leading to increasingly pessimistic thought, stronger anxiety, and stronger tendencies to employ avoidant coping strategies. It thus becomes important to consider mechanisms through which this loop can be attenuated and hopefully broken.

Our most recent studies have focused on the relationship between negative biases and individual differences in attentional control. Earlier we described models suggesting that

that individuals differ not only in underlying motivational systems, but also in their capacity to use executive, effortful attentional mechanisms. In early questionnaire work, we developed scales to measure individual differences in "Attentional Focusing" and "Attentional Shifting" (Derryberry & Rothbart, 1988). More recently, we have combined the focusing and shifting measures into a single, 20-item measure of "Attentional Control" which we have used in conjunction with our other personality measures.

One set of RT studies (Derryberry & Reed, 2002) examined the anxiety-related attentional bias reported above (Derryberry & Reed, 1994), which we suspected would be decreased in people with good attentional control. The design was a modified spatial orienting task where the approach and avoidance trials, rather than being randomly interspersed, were separated into positive games (where points could be gained) and negative games (where points could be lost). Pretarget cues appeared in the left or right visual field. Rather than indicating the incentive value of the upcoming target, they signaled whether a target in that location would be "difficult" or "easy." The criteria for "fast" and "slow" responses were adjusted such that the difficult cues (an arrow pointing down) signaled that targets in that location would result in slow responses on 75% of the trials. The easy cues (an arrow pointing up) indicated that targets in that location would be responded to fast 75% of the time such that the cue predicted positive feedback. Thus, the difficult cues tagged a dangerous location by predicting negative feedback, whereas the easy cues labeled a safe location by predicting positive feedback. In addition, in order to examine shifts in attention between the dangerous and safe locations across time, we presented the detection targets at two intervals, either 250 ms or 500 ms following the cue.

When the target appeared 250 ms after the cue, the anxiety-related bias was evident. All high anxious subjects were slow to disengage from invalid negative cues. Individual differences in attentional control were not influential at this short delay. When the target appeared after 500 ms, however, attentional control attenuated the effects of anxiety. Anxious subjects with poor attentional control were still slow to shift from threatening cues, as if they were stuck at the negative location. In contrast, anxious persons with good attentional control were better able to disengage and shift from the dangerous to the safe location (as were all low anxious participants).

This is an important finding for it suggests that a general mechanism (attentional control) helps some people attenuate their anxiety. In social situations, for example,

they may be better able to shift from cues related to potential rejection by one person to signals of acceptance from others. In thinking about the self, good attention may facilitate attention to positive as well as negative traits, and to the possibility of succeeding as well as failing in an achievement task. In adopting coping strategies, attentional skill may allow the person to make use of more difficult but effective coping strategies (e.g., positive reappraisal) as opposed to simpler but less effective strategies (e.g., disengagement). In general, attentional control should allow the person to take advantage of more relevant information, and thus to employ more informed and effective coping strategies (Derryberry, Reed, & Pilkenton-Taylor, 2003).

In summary, our studies provide additional evidence, besides that arising from Stroop and Dot-probe tasks, of an attentional bias favoring threatening cues in high trait anxious individuals. They also provide additional evidence that the bias involves delays in the disengage attentional operation. Most intriguing, our studies indicate that individuals vary in their ability to control attention, and that while some anxious individuals may have difficulty disengaging from threat, others are better able to do so.

Processing Relative Value

A third set of studies has examined attention to stimuli carrying different point values. Selecting between stimuli possessing different incentive values within the same valence is a common occurrence in everyday life. We must often choose which of several attractive activities (e.g., two movies) or between several less attractive activities (e.g., two chores) to approach. Although such decisions can be complex, we wanted to begin with a model task that would be as simple as possible. Thus, we examined attentional preferences for targets that differed in terms of the number of points that could be gained or lost. Such biases can be estimated in terms of a "value effect," computed by subtracting the faster RTs to high value targets from those to slower low value targets.

An initial study presented a composite target on each trial that consisted of two symbols: a letter M or W signaled whether points could be gained or lost, respectively, and a number 2 or 5 signaled how many points were at stake (Derryberry, 1993). Subjects were instructed to categorize the target as valuable (M2, M5, W2, W5) by pressing one key or as worthless (M3, W4, A5, V2) by pressing another key. As expected, RTs were consistently faster given high value (M5, W5) than low value targets (M2, W2), with a mean value effect (low value RTs–high value RTs) of roughly 25 ms. When a pretarget cue was presented before the target (e.g., M followed by M5), an incongruent feedback effect was found. Positive feedback led to slow shifts from negative cues whereas negative feedback was followed by slow shifts from positive cues. This is consistent with our previously discussed findings (Derryberry, 1988).

However, when the target was presented with no preceding cue, so that attentional shifts from cue to target were not involved, the incongruent effect was replaced with a congruent effect. Failure was followed by roughly equal value effects for positive and negative targets (30 ms), but success led to larger value effects for positive (50 ms) than negative (0 ms) targets. This effect is consistent with other findings of congruency, such as those showing that positive affect leads to an increased optimism regarding potential gains (Nygren & Isen, 1985) and to decreased estimates of risk (Johnson & Tversky, 1983). More generally, these findings suggest that feedback elicits multiple parallel effects. A congruent effect favoring high value targets that may function to stabilize and prolong the motivational state, and an incongruent effect that may help attenuate or shift the motivational state.

More recent studies have moved from feedback effects to concentrate on individual differences. The studies used a modified spatial orienting task in which different point values were assigned to the two sides of the screen. Positive and negative valences were presented in alternating games where points could be gained but not lost and games where points could be lost but not gained. Several studies began each trial by presenting two numbers on the screen, such as a 2 on the left and a 5 on the right. These numbers indicated how many points were at stake given a detection target at either location. Before the target appeared, one of the numbers turned red, signaling which number was more likely to be targeted. Thus, we were interested in the general bias favoring the high value location, and how this effect might interact with the attentional validity effect generated by the red cue. As expected, subjects showed faster RTs to the cued location (attentional effect) and also to the higher valued location (value effect).

Interactions between these two effects depended on individual differences. Both studies found a stronger interaction in participants with good attentional control. Participants with poor attention showed similar attentional effects (i.e., invalid–valid RTs) for low value (5 ms) and high value (10 ms) locations, whereas those with good attention showed greater attention to high value (20 ms) than low value locations (−5 ms). Not only did they shift strongly to a cued high value location, good attenders tended to shift away from cued low value location. These findings are interesting in that this type of relative value

or preference coding is carried out within the orbital frontal cortex (Schultz, Tremblay, & Hollerman, 1998), an area with important connections to the anterior cingulate region (i.e., Posner's executive attentional system).

A nearly identical, noninteracting, effect was found for Extraversion. Introverts showed similar attentional effects to low (5 ms) and high value (10 ms) cues, but extraverts showed stronger orienting to high value (15 ms) than low value (−5 ms) locations. Thus, both extraverts and good attenders show enhanced performance at high value locations, patterns suggesting a more flexible and effective strategy that can result in a higher score. Although more research is required, several aspects of the data suggest separate mechanisms may be involved in extraverts and good attenders. The Attentional Control effect is consistent with our other studies in focusing on the invalid trials, suggesting delays in shifting attention from the high value cues. In contrast, the Extraversion effect is limited to valid trials and involves higher error rates (i.e., pressing the key following a high value cue on trials when no target was presented). Such differences suggest that the Attentional Control effect may reflect attention whereas the Extraversion effect may reflect response potentiation elicited by the high value cue.

Our studies of incentive value are consistent with our studies of approach- and avoidance-related processing. On the one hand, attentional processes appear to be modulated as a function of the previous outcome, though incentive value is subject to a congruent as well as an incongruent influence. In addition, people differ in their orienting to high value targets; both good attenders and extraverts show facilitated processing when expecting a high value target.

More generally, our findings suggest that approach and avoidance motivation are quite flexible. They vary in relation to ongoing states resulting from success and failure, with feedback exerting two complementary effects on subsequent processing. A congruent effect functions in the absence of pretarget cues and facilitates high value positive targets following positive feedback. Such an effect may serve to lock in and enhance approach motivation, something that would be adaptive when responses are achieving success. When a pretarget cue is presented, an incongruent potential is revealed that increases the attentional impact of cues differing in valence from the previous outcome. Such an effect is important in countering the congruent effect, and thus making it easier for the person to break loose and shift to an alternative state of approach or avoidance.

Regarding the attentional effects, our findings indicate that feedback and temperament influence attention by regulating the time to disengage from certain types of stimuli. Although this may suggest that motivational pathways function by directly adjusting the disengage circuitry, we cannot say for sure that this is the real locus of the effect. The problem is that slow disengagement may also arise as an indirect consequence of facilitating the engage mechanism. Thus, anxious people may tend to strongly engage threatening stimuli, making it more difficult for them to disengage. An effect of enhancing engagement would make sense in that it affords a more direct influence in facilitating the processing and storage of the important information.

Finally, our findings support approaches to personality based on the notion that personality is framed around basic forms of motivation related to approach and avoidance (Elliot & Thrash, 2002). Extraversion does appear related to approach motivation, though the effect is relatively subtle and appears primarily after negative feedback. Anxiety is consistently related to avoidance situations involving threat. However, evidence suggests that individuals vary in terms of other systems related to voluntary attention, and that these differences in Attentional Control are crucial to understanding the effects of Extraversion and Anxiety. Therefore, we will focus on personality in the final section, describing some of the potential interactions arising between extraversion, anxiety, and attentional control.

MOTIVATED ATTENTION AND PERSONALITY DEVELOPMENT

A developmental perspective is especially useful for viewing the motivational and attentional components of personality. We adopt such a perspective in this final section, and explore both the benefits and the costs related to certain personality profiles. As will be seen, approach and avoidance motives, along with attention and the child's developing representations, are at the heart of the self-organizing processes which shape the child's personality.

Approachful Children

Beginning with approach motivation, children who are more extraverted or impulsive will be more sensitive to environmental rewards and thus more likely to approach a variety of objects and people. Such approach can be beneficial in providing the child with more opportunities to learn about the various rewards available in the world. Because they show biases toward positive cues following failure, extraverted children may find it easier to remain optimistic without becoming discouraged. In addition, their friendly approach of other people tends to elicit positive affect in return, allowing the child to benefit from pleasant and stimulating social interactions. As the child becomes older and forms more complex representations, the attentional bias should function to stabilize the more positive components of the representations. In thinking about the self, for example, the child's failures may be associated with positive as well as negative information, providing for a sense of confidence and efficacy. Along similar lines, noticing positive aspects of an unsuccessful outcome provides additional options for coping. Such children are likely to adopt the more adaptive approach-based rather than avoidant strategies.

On the other hand, children with strong approach motivation can also run into trouble. A major goal of socialization is to bring approach tendencies into line with cultural standards. The more impulsive children may find themselves making inappropriate approaches, leading to punishment from their friends, family, or teachers. Newman has suggested that such failures may further enhance approach motivation, such that the child fails to learn from the failure because the approach orientation interferes with attention to the faulty behaviors and relevant rules. The extraverted child may utilize approach-oriented strategies, but they may be less optimal strategies such as those involving confrontation and lacking planning. In addition, the child's persistence following failure may make it difficult to shift to a new coping strategy. Finally, the child with strong approach motivation may be vulnerable to frustration and anger when approach is unsuccessful (Carver, 2004; Derryberry & Rothbart, 1997). In the most serious cases, children with strong approach motivation will be vulnerable to externalizing or impulsive disorders, such as conduct disorder and hyperactivity (Derryberry et al., 2003; Fowles, 1994).

Avoidant Children

In contrast, more fearful children prone to avoidance may tend to inhibit approach of new people and situations. This may make it easier for them to avoid impulsive problems, resulting in praise from parents and teachers for their good behavior. Although they may be less likely to elicit high-stimulating social interactions, fearful or shy children may still evoke rewarding social interactions, though these may be fewer in number and calmer in nature. High anxious children show more empathy (Rothbart, Ahadi, & Hershey, 1994) and an enhanced development of conscience (Kochanska, 1997;

Kochanska, Coy, & Murray, 2001; Kochanska, Gross, Lin, & Nichols, 2002) compared to low anxious children. One explanation is that they pay greater attention to punishment, to their behavior and feelings of guilt, to negative cues indicating feelings of others, and to the principle involved in moral behavior. Attention results in a binding of these feelings and behaviors to the moral principle.

Unfortunately, anxious children can run into problems in several ways. In behavioral terms, their tendency to avoid certain situations can make it difficult to learn the skills required to cope with stressful situations. In addition, their performance in social situations may be impaired due to their general inhibition and difficulty in disengaging from negative cues (e.g., perceived frowns, potential embarrassment). In performance or achievement contexts, anxious children may respond to failure with discouragement and less effort, especially if they are introverted and lack the facilitation of approach found in extraverts. Their difficulty in disengaging from negative information may lead to memory representations that emphasize negative aspects of the self (e.g., as incompetent), others (as rejecting), and of the world in general (as dangerous). In more extreme cases, such children will be vulnerable to internalizing disorders such as childhood anxiety (e.g., overanxious disorder; school phobia) and depression (Derryberry et al., 2003; Fowles, 1994).

Our examples above describe adaptive and maladaptive outcomes in terms of a single motivational system. It is important to note, however, that these systems interact and thus all systems need to be taken into consideration. From such a perspective, it can be seen that the most vulnerable children will be those with strong approach and weak avoidance systems and those with strong avoidance and weak approach systems. For example, children with strong approach and weak avoidance are most likely to be overly impulsive and disinhibited, and limited in their capacity to learn from mistakes and to develop strong moral principles (Quay, 1993). Conversely, children with strong avoidance and weak approach are most likely to be overly inhibited, withdrawn, and to give up in the face of even minor failure. If anxious children had a strong approach system, then they could temper their withdrawal and gain more environmental rewards (Derryberry & Rothbart, 1997).

ATTENTIONAL CONTROL

Especially important interactions involve attentional control. In general, good attention should help the child avoid problems related to the extremes of approach and avoidance motivation. Children with strong approach tendencies and poor attentional control will be most vulnerable to impulsive, externalizing problems (especially if they are also low in anxiety). In contrast, children with good attentional control will be better able to delay the gratifications and resist the temptations accompanying strong approach motivation. Mischel has found that the ability to delay gratification (e.g., to wait 10 min before approaching an attractive object) depends on various attentional strategies that serve to amplify the "cool" relative to the "hot" aspects of the situation. For example, children are better able to delay eating a marshmallow when they look away from it or think of it as a puffy white cloud (Mischel, 1983; Metcalfe & Mischel, 1999). It is worth noting that this attention-related ability shows remarkable stability, with preschool ability to delay gratification predicting competent coping during adolescence (Shoda, Mischel, & Peake, 1990) and coping with rejection sensitivity in the early thirties (Mischel & Ayduk, 2002).

As mentioned above, another potential problem related to strong approach motivation involves frustration and anger when the goal is blocked. Good attentional control can protect against such problems by allowing more effective use of coping strategies. In a study of 4–6 year-old children, boys with good attentional control were found to deal with anger by using nonhostile, verbal methods rather than more overt aggressive methods (Eisenberg, Fabes, Nyman, Bernzweig, & Pinulas, 1994). A more recent study examined the effectiveness of different anger-regulating strategies in three and a half year-olds while they waited to eat a cookie (Gilliom, Shaw, Beck, Schonberg, & Lukon, 2002). Children who used strategies of voluntarily directing attention away from the cookie (e.g., distraction, passive waiting) were most effective in controlling their anger, whereas those who focused on the cookie showed increased anger. When assessed at the age of six, children who had used passive waiting and distraction strategies showed fewer externalizing symptoms, whereas those who focused on the cookie showed more externalizing.

Finally, attentional control may constrain problematic approach behavior by facilitating empathy and conscience development. Although empathy and morality can arise from strong fear motivation, they are also related to strong "effortful control" (Kochanska, 1997; Rothbart et al., 1994). An attentional explanation suggests that morality involves complex representations linking behaviors, feelings, and principles. Children with good attentional control may have the flexibility required to shift between and thereby progressively link the relevant sources of information. Once internalized, the child's moral principles can provide powerful constraints on approach behavior.

In cases of anxiety, it is again children with poor attentional control who will most likely suffer from their fears. Such children may have difficulty shifting attention from anxious content in social or achievement situations, resulting in an increase in their anxiety and consequent decrease in their performance. After the punishing event, anxious children may continue to think about their failures, giving rise to cognitive representations that are biased in favor of negative aspects of the self and the world.

In contrast, anxious children with good attention can benefit in many ways. In anticipating a novel social situation, for example, such children should be better able to disengage from the possible threats that they might encounter in the situation (e.g., strangers), and shift their attention to possible sources of reward (e.g., fun games). The more balanced anticipation should make it more likely that these children will approach rather than avoid the situation, and thus gain from the experience. Upon entering the social situation, anxious children with good attention should be better able to disengage from the threatening aspects and to shift attention to a source of safety or reassurance (e.g., their friends). Again, this should attenuate their anxiety, improve performance, and make them more likely to enjoy the situation. Afterwards, as these children think about the experience, their attentional flexibility should allow them to develop representations that are more balanced, featuring positive as well as negative memories. They may also be able to utilize cognitive coping strategies such as positive reappraisal ("It wasn't as bad as I had feared") or compensation ("I was scared but I was still friendly").

Although more research is needed, these ideas are supported by findings of negative relations between attentional control and anxiety in adults (Derryberry & Rothbart, 1988) and children (Rothbart et al., 1994). Attentional control has also been found to moderate the effects of negative emotionality on social competence and shyness (Eisenberg, et al., 2001), and as described above, good attentional control allows anxious adults to shift from a threatening to a safe location (Derryberry & Reed, 2002). Related ideas can be found in Lonigan, Vasey, Phillips, and Haze (2004), Mathews, Yiend, and Lawrence (2004), and Muris and Dietvorst (2006).

CONCLUSION

This chapter has developed the idea that we can gain a better understanding of approach and avoidance motivation by going beyond behavior to study effects on attention and related cognitive processes. When this is done, we can see that attention arises from a highly complex set of

systems that work together to control alertness, orienting, and executive functions. This attentional complexity affords motivational processes a range of mechanisms through which to influence information processing. Although most current research has focused on a few motivational processes (e.g., anxiety) and mechanisms (e.g., orienting), we are only beginning to appreciate the many potential ways in which motivation might influence attention and cognition.

Similarly, the complexity of motivational states may go beyond our usual formulations. We have described our rather obvious findings that approach-related states are regulated depending on the previous outcome or feedback. This regulation is not simple, however, and appears to involve at least two complementary effects. A congruent effect serves to strengthen and prolong the motivational state, while an incongruent effect prepares a shift to a new state. In addition, feedback signals appear to interact with attentional systems at the highest executive levels within the anterior cingulate (Luu, Tucker, Derryberry, Reed, & Poulsen, 2003). This is consistent with the notion that feedback-related states are among the brain's most important forms of self-regulation.

Finally, our research suggests that we can gain a better understanding of personality by adopting a developmental perspective that focuses on the systems related to approach and avoidance. Depending on their temperament and environment, each child will possess diverse tendencies to approach and avoid. The related motivational systems will recruit attentional systems to regulate forebrain processing in an adaptive way. Because attention is fundamental to learning, this regulation can be viewed as a progressive binding and sculpting of the child's representations, an extension of the motivational systems into the cortex. But at the same time, the representations feed back upon the motivational circuitry, providing the motivational systems with the enhanced evaluative and strategic potential arising from the cortex's architecture. Thus, motivational and cognitive processes become progressively intertwined, and we can better appreciate the extent to which personality is a self-organizing process.

REFERENCES

Atkinson, J. W., & Birch, D. (1978). *An introduction to motivation.* New York: Van Nostrand-Reinhold.

Bandler, R., & Shipley, M. T. (1994). Columnar organization in the midbrain periaqueductal gray: modules for emotional expression? *Trends in Neurosciences, 17,* 379–389.

Baumeister, R. F., Bratslavsky, E., Finkenauer, C., & Vohs, K. D. (2001). Bad is stronger than good. *Review of General Psychology, 5*(4), 323–370.

Berridge, C. W., & Waterhouse, B. D. (2003). The locus coeruleus–noradrenergic system: Modulation of behavioral state and state-dependent cognitive processes. *Brain Research Reviews, 42,* 33–84.

Carver, C. S. (2004). Negative affects deriving from the behavioral approach system. *Emotion, 4,* 3–22.

Depue, R. A., & Collins, P. F. (1999). Neurobiology of the structure of personality: Dopamine, facilitation of incentive motivation, and extraversion. *Behavioral and Brain Sciences, 22,* 521–555.

Derryberry, D. (1987). Incentive and feedback effects on target detection: A chronometric analysis of Gray's model of temperament. *Personality and Individual Differences, 8,* 855–865.

Derryberry, D. (1988). Emotional influence on evaluative judgments: Roles of arousal, attention, and spreading activation. *Motivation and Emotion, 12,* 23–55.

Derryberry, D. (1993). Attentional consequences of feedback: Congruent, incongruent, and focusing effects. *Motivation and Emotion, 17,* 65–89.

Derryberry, D., & Reed, M. A. (1994). Temperament and attention: Orienting toward and away from positive and negative signals. *Journal of Personality and Social Psychology, 66,* 1128–1139.

Derryberry, D., & Reed, M. A. (1996). Regulatory processes and the development of cognitive representations. *Development and Psychopathology, 8,* 215–234.

Derryberry, D., & Reed, M. A. (2002). Anxiety-related attentional biases and their regulation by attentional control. *Journal of Abnormal Psychology, 111,* 225–236.

Derryberry, D., Reed, M. A., & Pilkenton-Taylor, C. (2003). Temperament and coping: Advantages of an individual differences approach. *Development and Psychopathology, 15,* 1049–1066.

Derryberry, D., & Rothbart, M. K. (1988). Affect, arousal, and attention as components of temperament. *Journal of Personality and Social Psychology, 55,* 958–966.

Derryberry, D., & Rothbart, M. K. (1997). Reactive and effortful processes in the organization of temperament. *Development and Psychopathology, 9,* 633–652.

Eisenberg, N., Cumberland, A., Spinrad, T., Fabes, R., Shepard, S., Reiser, M., et al. (2001). The relations of regulation and emotionality to children's externalizing and internalizing problem behavior. *Child Development, 74,* 1112–1134.

Eisenberg, N., Fabes, R. A., Nyman, M., Bernzweig, J., & Pinulas, A. (1994). The relations of emotionality and regulation to children's anger-related reactions. *Child Development, 65,* 109–128.

Elliot, A. J., & Thrash, T. M. (2002). Approach–avoidance motivation in personality: Approach and avoidance temperaments and goals. *Journal of Personality and Social Psychology, 82*(5), 804–818.

Eysenck, H. J., & Eysenck, M. W. (1985). *Personality and individual differences: A natural science approach.* New York: Plenum.

Fowles, D. C. (1994). A motivational theory of psychopathology. In W. G. Spaulding (Ed.), *Nebraska symposium on motivation, Vol. 41: Integrative views of motivation, cognition, and emotion* (pp. 181–238). Lincoln, NE: University of Nebraska Press.

Fox, E., Russo, R., Bowles, R., & Dutton, K. (2001). Do threatening stimuli draw or hold visual attention in subclinical anxiety? *Journal of Experimental Psychology: General, 130,* 681–700.

Gilliom, M., Shaw, D. S., Beck, J. E., Schonberg, M. A., & Lukon, J. L. (2002). Anger regulation in disadvantaged preschool boys: Strategies, antecedents, and the development of self-control. *Developmental Psychology, 38,* 222–235.

Gray, J. A. (1987). *The psychology of fear and stress.* (2nd ed.). New York: McGraw-Hill.

Gray, J. A., & McNaughton, N. (1996). The neuropsychology of anxiety: Reprise. In D. A. Hope (Ed.), *Nebraska symposium on motivation: Perspectives on anxiety, panic, and fear.* (Vol. 43, pp. 61–134). Lincoln, NE: University of Nebraska Press.

Grossberg, S. (1999). The link between brain learning, attention, and consciousness. *Consciousness and Cognition, 8,* 1–44.

Grossberg, S., & Schmajuk, H. A. (1987). Neural dynamics of attentionally modulated Pavlovian conditioning: Conditioned reinforcement, inhibition, and opponent processing. *Psychobiology, 15,* 215–240.

Gu, Q. (2002). Neuromodulatory transmitter systems in the cortex and their role in cortical plasticity. *Neuroscience, 111,* 815–835.

Johnson, E., & Tversky, A. (1983). Affect, generalization, and the perception of risk. *Journal of Personality and Social Psychology, 45,* 20–31.

Kahneman, D., & Tversky, A. (1979). Prospect theory: An analysis of decisions under risk. *Econometrika, 47,* 263–291.

Keay, K. A., & Bandler, R. (2001). Parallel circuits mediating distinct emotional coping responses to different kinds of stress. *Neuroscience and Biobehavioral Reviews, 25,* 669–678.

Kochanska, G. (1997). Multiple pathways to conscience for children with different temperaments: From toddlerhood to age 5. *Developmental Psychology, 33,* 228–240.

Kochanska, G., Coy, K. C., & Murray, K. T. (2001). The development of self-regulation in the first four years of life. *Child Development, 72,* 1091–1111.

Kochanska, G., Gross, J. N., Lin, M., & Nichols, K. E. (2002). Guilt in young children: Development, determinants, and relations with a broader system of standards. *Child Development, 73,* 461–482.

LeDoux, J. E. (2000). Emotion circuits in the brain. *Annual Review of Neuroscience, 23,* 155–184.

Lonigan, C. J., Vasey, M. W., Phillips, B. M., & Haze, R. A. (2004). Temperament, anxiety, and the processing of threat-relevant stimuli. *Journal of Clinical Child and Adolescent Psychology, 33,* 8–20.

Luu, P., Tucker, D. M., Derryberry, D., Reed, M., & Poulsen, C. (2003). Electrophysiological responses to errors and feedback in the process of action regulation. *Psychological Science, 14,* 47–53.

MacLeod, C., & Mathews, A. (1988). Anxiety and the allocation of attention to threat. *Quarterly Journal of Experimental Psychology*, *40*, 653–670.

Mathews, A., Yiend, J., & Lawrence, A. D. (2004). Individual differences in the modulation of fear-related brain activation by attentional control. *Journal of Cognitive Neuroscience*, *16*, 1683–1694.

Matlin, M. W., & Stang, D. J. (1978). *The Pollyanna principle: Selectivity in language, memory, and thought*. Cambridge, MA: Schenkman.

Matthews, G. (1997). *Cognitive science perspectives on personality and emotion*. (Ed.). Amsterdam: Elsevier.

Metcalfe, J., & Mischel, W. (1999). A hot/cool-system analysis of delay of gratification: Dynamics of willpower. *Psychological Review*, *106*, 3–19.

Mischel, W. (1983). Delay of gratification as process and as person variable in development. In D. Magnusson & V. P. Allen (Eds.), *Human development: An interactional perspective* (pp. 149–165). New York: Academic Press.

Mischel, W., & Ayduk, O. (2002). Self-regulation in a cognitive—affective personality system: Attentional control in the service of the self. *Self and Identity*, *1*, 113–120.

Muris, P., & Dietvorst, R. (2006). Underlying personality characteristics of behavioral inhibition in children. *Child Psychiatry and Human Development*, *36*, 437–445.

Newman, J. P. (1987). Reaction to punishment in extraverts and psychopaths: Implications for the impulsive behavior of disinhibited individuals. *Journal of Research in Personality*, *21*, 464–480.

Nummenmaa, L., & Niemi, P. (2004). Inducing affective states with success-failure manipulations: A meta-analysis. *Emotion*, *4*, 207–214.

Nygren, T. E., & Isen, A. M. (1985). Examining probability estimation: Evidence for dual subjective probability functions. *Paper presented at the Meeting of the Psychonomic Society*. MA: Boston.

Ongur, D., & Price, J. L. (2000). The organization of networks within the orbital and medial prefrontal cortex of rats, monkeys and humans. *Cerebral Cortex*, *10*, 206–219.

Panksepp, J. (1998). *Affective neuroscience*. New York: Oxford.

Posner, M. I. (1978). *Chronometric explorations of mind*. Hillsdale, NJ: Erlbaum.

Posner, M. I., & Raichle, M. E. (1994). *Images of mind*. New York: Scientific American Library.

Posner, M. I., & Rothbart, M. K. (1998). Attention, self-regulation and consciousness. *Philosophical Transactions of the Royal Society of London B*, *353*, 1915–1927.

Quay, H. C. (1993). The psychobiology of undersocialized aggressive conduct disorder: A theoretical perspective. *Development and Psychopathology*, *5*, 165–180.

Rothbart, M. K., Ahadi, S. A., & Hershey, K. L. (1994). Temperament and social behavior in childhood. *Merrill-Palmer Quarterly*, *40*, 21–39.

Rothbart, M. K., & Bates, J. E. (1998). Temperament. In W. S. E. Damon & N. V. E. Eisenberg (Eds.), *Handbook of child psychology*: (Vol. 3, pp. 105–176). *Social, emotional and personality development*. (5th ed.). New York: Wiley.

Rothbart, M. K., Derryberry, D., & Posner, M. I. (1994). A psychobiological approach to the development of temperament. In J. E. Bates & T. D. Wachs (Eds.), *Temperament: Individual differences at the interface of biology and behavior* (pp. 83–116). Washington, DC: American Psychological Association.

Rothermund, K. (2003). Motivation and attention: Incongruent effects of feedback on the processing of valence. *Emotion*, *3*, 223–238.

Schultz, W., Tremblay, L., & Hollerman, J. R. (1998). Reward prediction in primate basal ganglia and frontal cortex. *Neuropharmacology*, *37*, 421–429.

Shoda, Y., Mischel, W., & Peake, P. K. (1990). Predicting adolescent cognitive and self-regulatory competencies from preschool delay of gratification: Identifying diagnostic conditions. *Developmental Psychology*, *26*, 978–986.

Stuss, D. T., Shallice, T., Alexander, M. P., & Picton, T. W. (1995). A multidisciplinary approach to anterior attentional functions. In J. Grafman, K. J. Holyoak, & F. Boller (Eds.), *Annals of the New York Academy of Sciences, Volume 769*. Structure and functions of the human prefrontal cortex, New York: The New York Academy of Sciences.

Wallace, J. F., Newman, J. P., & Bachorowski, J. (1991). Failures of response modulation: Impulsive behavior in anxious and impulsive individuals. *Journal of Research in Personality*, *25*, 23–44.

Watson, D., & Clark, L. A. (1992). On traits and temperament: General and specific factors of emotional experience and their relation to the five-factor model. *Journal of Personality*, *60*, 441–476.

Framing

28 How Persons and Situations Regulate Message Framing Effects: The Study of Health Behavior

Alexander J. Rothman, Jhon T. Wlaschin, Roger D. Bartels, Amy Latimer, and Peter Salovey

CONTENTS

Joan flips through her mail and notices a postcard from her health plan urging her to get a mammogram. Across the top it reads, "The costs of not having a mammogram." Across town, Carla notices a similar postcard. However, the slogan on her card reads, "The benefits of having a mammogram." Six months later, the health plan finds that women who received a card with a loss-framed appeal (such as Joan received) were more likely to have obtained a mammogram than were women who received a card with a gain-framed appeal (such as Carla received). The observation that the manner in which a message is framed can affect people's behavioral decisions is fascinating and has intrigued both basic and applied behavioral scientists.

Over the past 15 years, investigators have worked to specify the factors that guide the impact of gain- and loss-framed appeals and have strived to provide practitioners with a set of guidelines that could be used to maximize the impact of health communication programs

(Rothman, Bartels, Wlaschin, & Salovey, 2006; Rothman, Kelly, Hertel, & Salovey, 2003; Rothman & Salovey, 1997; Rothman, Stark, & Salovey, 2006). To date, two perspectives have guided our understanding of when loss- and gain-framed messages are maximally persuasive. One view has emphasized the manner in which the function of the health behavior—in particular, whether it is designed to detect or to prevent a health problem—moderates the impact of framed appeals (Rothman & Salovey, 1997), whereas the other view has emphasized how people's dispositional sensitivity to favorable or unfavorable outcomes moderates the impact of framed appeals (Mann, Sherman, & Updegraff, 2004). In this chapter, we examine the conceptual frameworks that underlie each of these perspectives and review the available empirical evidence. We then provide a new conceptualization of framing effects that integrates the two dominant perspectives. Specifically, we propose that people's responses to framed appeals are contingent on their self-regulatory tendencies and the accessibility of these tendencies is a function of people's dispositional preferences and features of the behavioral decision. We believe this new perspective has the potential not only to advance our understanding of when and how gain- and loss-framed messages are effective, but also to generate new, innovative predictions regarding other aspects of health cognition and health behavior.

MESSAGE FRAMING AND HEALTH BEHAVIOR: THE FUNCTION OF THE BEHAVIOR

Health communications can be framed in terms of the benefits afforded by adopting a health behavior (a gain-framed appeal) or in terms of the costs associated with failing to adopt a health behavior (a loss-framed appeal). As illustrated in the earlier example, a brochure promoting mammography could emphasize the benefits of screening—"By getting a mammogram you give yourself the best chance of detecting breast cancer early"—or the costs of not screening—"By failing to get a mammogram, you will miss the best chance of detecting breast cancer early." The premise that altering how information is framed can affect people's behavioral decisions was motivated by the framing postulate of Prospect Theory (Tversky & Kahneman, 1981). According to Prospect Theory, people's preferences are sensitive to how information is framed: people act to avoid risks when considering the potential gains afforded by a decision (they are risk-averse in their preferences), but are willing to take risks when considering the potential losses afforded by their decision (they are risk-seeking in their preferences).

Rothman and Salovey (1997) proposed that predictions regarding the relative influence of gain- and loss-framed messages on health behavior can be derived from the conceptual framework outlined in Prospect Theory. Given the premise that people are more willing to take risks when faced with loss-framed information but are more risk-averse when faced with gain-framed information, the influence of a given frame on behavior should depend on whether the behavior under consideration is perceived to reflect a risk-averse or risk-seeking course of action. To the extent a decision to engage in a health behavior involves some degree of uncertainty or risk, people will be more responsive to a loss-framed message. Conversely, to the extent a health behavioral decision affords a relatively certain or safe outcome, people will be more responsive to a gain-framed message.

Consistent with this perspective, a taxonomy of health-relevant situations—classifying them as risk-averse or risk-seeking—was developed that affords predictions as to when gain- or loss-framed health appeals are maximally persuasive (Rothman & Salovey, 1997; Rothman et al., 2003). When people are considering a behavior that they perceive involves some risk of an unpleasant outcome (e.g., it may detect a health problem), loss-framed appeals should be more persuasive. When people are considering a behavior that they perceive involves a relatively low risk of an unpleasant outcome (e.g., it prevents the onset of a health problem), gain-framed appeals should be more persuasive. At the heart of this taxonomy is the observation that the function served by a health behavior can serve as a reliable heuristic for whether people construe a behavior as a relatively risky or safe course of action.

The primary function of detection or screening behaviors such as colonoscopy or mammography is to detect the presence of a health problem. Because of this emphasis on the behavior's ability to inform people that they are symptomatic or ill, choosing to initiate the behavior may be considered a risky decision. In contrast, the primary function of prevention behaviors, such as the regular use of sunscreen or condoms, is to prevent the onset of an illness and maintain a person's current health status. Thus, choosing to adopt a prevention behavior affords people a relatively safe option as there are few potential costs associated with performing them. The primary risk associated with these behaviors concerns the decision not to take action (e.g., failing to apply sunscreen when one's skin is exposed to the sun places one at risk for skin cancer). Taken together, this framework suggests that loss-framed appeals would be more effective in promoting the use of detection behaviors but gain-framed appeals would be more effective in promoting the use of prevention behaviors.

DETECTION AND PREVENTION BEHAVIORS: A FIRST LOOK

The distinction between prevention and detection behaviors has proven to be a relatively useful heuristic for understanding the impact of message framing on health behavior. Research on detection behaviors has tended to reveal an advantage for loss-framed appeals, with the majority of these studies having focused on promoting cancer screening practices (e.g., screening mammography and breast self-examination [BSE]; Banks et al., 1995; Cox & Cox, 2001; Finney & Iannoti, 2002; Meyerowitz & Chaiken, 1987; Schneider et al., 2001; colorectal cancer screening; Myers et al., 1991). Although no study has shown gain-framed appeals to be more effective than loss-framed appeals in promoting cancer screening behaviors, several studies have either failed to find an advantage for either frame (Lalor & Hailey, 1990; Lauver & Rubin, 1990; Lerman et al., 1992) or have found the effect to be limited to a specific subset of individuals (Apanovitch, McCarthy, & Salovey, 2003; Finney & Iannoti, 2002; Schneider et al., 2001).

Fewer empirical studies have examined prevention behaviors than have examined detection behaviors. However, research has generally supported the prediction that gain-framed messages should effectively promote behaviors that prevent the onset of health problems (Detweiler, Bedell, Salovey, Pronin, & Rothman, 1999; Jones, Sinclair, & Courneya, 2003; Linville, Fischer, & Fischhoff, 1993; Millar & Millar, 2000; Rothman, Salovey, Antone, Keough, & Martin, 1993; but see McCaul, Johnson, & Rothman, 2002).

Although the pattern of findings across studies is generally consistent with the guiding framework, the most persuasive evidence that framing effects are contingent on the function of the advocated behavior comes from a study in which a single health behavior served either a detection or a prevention function. Rothman, Martino, Bedell, Detweiler, and Salovey (1999) presented participants with framed messages advocating the use of a mouthrinse that was designed either to detect the presence of plaque (i.e., a detection behavior) or to prevent the accumulation of plaque (i.e., a prevention behavior). The results of the study revealed the predicted interaction between frame and behavior: participants were more likely to request a free sample of the plaque-detecting mouthrinse after having read a loss-framed message, but were more likely to request a free sample of the plaque-preventing mouthrinse after having read a gain-framed message. Rivers, Pizarro, Schneider, Pizarro, and Salovey (2005) conceptually replicated these findings in a randomized field study examining Pap test utilization.

SPECIFYING THE DISTINCTION BETWEEN DETECTION AND PREVENTION BEHAVIORS

The empirical evidence indicates that the function of the behavior regulates the impact of gain- and loss-framed messages. But this premise is grounded on an underlying assumption regarding how people construe the behavior. For example, it is because detection behaviors are perceived to afford a degree of uncertainty and risk that loss-framed appeals are thought to be more persuasive. To the extent there is variability in how a given behavior is construed, the relative influence of loss- and gain-framed messages will vary. Early evidence of this premise was reported by Meyerowitz, Wilson, and Chaiken (1991) who found that loss-framed messages were most effective

in promoting BSE, but only for those women who perceived the behavior to be relatively risky.

To experimentally test the assumption that the risk posed by adopting a behavior is responsible for the relative impact of framed messages, Bartels, Kelly, and Rothman (2006) manipulated the risk implications posed by both a prevention behavior (a vaccine) and a detection behavior (a screening test). In one study, participants read about a new vaccine for West Nile virus (i.e., a prevention behavior). Some participants learned that the vaccine was effective for 9 out of 10 people who are vaccinated and thus there was no risk to being vaccinated, whereas other participants learned that the vaccine was effective for only 6 out of 10 people who are vaccinated and thus relying on the vaccine to protect their health posed some degree of risk. Consistent with predictions, participants who considered a vaccine whose effectiveness was uncertain were more persuaded by a loss-framed article, whereas participants who considered a vaccine whose effectiveness was assured were more persuaded by a gain-framed article.

A second study examined what happens when one varies the risk implications associated with a detection behavior. In this case, participants learned about a fictitious enzyme, Thioamine Acelytase (TAA) that was said to either confer a health benefit (i.e., the enzyme made them more resistant to a complex set of pancreatic disorders) or indicate a health problem (i.e., the enzyme made them more susceptible to a complex set of pancreatic disorders; for a full description, see Croyle & Ditto, 1990). We predicted that participants would perceive testing for the potentially harmful enzyme to be a relatively risky decision, and therefore, a loss-framed message would render them more willing to schedule a test at the university health center. On the other hand, participants would ascribe little risk to testing for the beneficial enzyme, and therefore, a gain-framed message would render them more willing to schedule a test. The relative rates with which participants were willing to schedule a TAA screening test at the university health center were consistent with predictions, but this was true only for those individuals who had previously utilized the university health services.

Recent research on framing effects and attitudes toward condoms has provided a conceptually similar pattern of results. Kiene and colleagues (Kiene, Barta, Zelenski, & Cothran, 2005) explored the thesis that using condoms is seen to pose little risk when construed in terms of the health benefits they afford, but is seen as risky when construed in terms of the interpersonal negotiations associated with deciding whether to use them. Consistent with prior studies, Kiene et al. (2005) found that gain-framed messages were more effective when health concerns were salient, but loss-framed messages were more effective when interpersonal concerns were salient. The proposed framework may also help explain why O'Connor, Ferguson, and O'Connor (2005) found that loss-framed appeals were more effective in promoting interest in using a new hormonal contraceptive pill for men. One might imagine that because the contraceptive pill eliminates the need for unpleasant partner negotiations the pill would be construed as a health promoting behavior. However, a systematic assessment of how men construe taking a hormonal drug for contraception revealed that using a new biomedical treatment evoked a broad range of concerns regarding the risk of side effects and the uncertainty of using a new treatment. Given this focus on the risks posed by the behavior, a loss-framed advantage is not unexpected. However, one might hypothesize that as the procedure becomes more familiar and there is limited evidence of troubling side effects people might begin to construe the pill as a health promoting behavior, affording an advantage for gain-framed appeals.

Taken together, these studies provide further evidence that how people construe a health behavior regulates the impact of gain- and loss-framed appeals. At the heart of this view is the thesis that health behaviors systematically elicit from people a set of thoughts and feelings and that it is the fit between this psychological state and the message frame that regulates its impact on decision-making and behavior. We will return to this thesis after examining evidence for how dispositional factors can moderate the impact of framed appeals.

MESSAGE FRAMING AND HEALTH BEHAVIOR: THE ROLE OF DISPOSITIONAL FACTORS

If the way in which people construe a health behavior moderates the impact of framed appeals, one might hypothesize that people's dispositional inclination to think about the decisions they face in terms of gains or losses might similarly affect their reaction to gain- and loss-framed messages. Several independent teams of investigators have demonstrated that people systematically differ in the degree to which they monitor for and respond to favorable and unfavorable outcomes. Some investigators have focused on the tendency with which people are motivated to approach or seek out favorable outcomes or to avoid unfavorable outcomes (Carver & White, 1994; see also Elliot & Thrash, 2002), whereas others have emphasized the notion that people differ in

their sensitivity to the presence or absence of positive and negative events (Higgins, 1999). In either case, researchers have pursued the thesis that people who are sensitive to positive outcomes (as indexed by higher scores on promotion focus [Higgins, 1999]) or are motivated to approach favorable goals (as indexed by higher scores on behavioral activation [Carver & White, 1994]) respond more favorably to gain-framed appeals, whereas people who are sensitive to negative outcomes (as indexed by higher scores on prevention focus [Higgins, 1999]) or are motivated to avoid unfavorable goals (as indexed by higher scores on behavioral inhibition [Carver & White, 1994]) respond more favorably to loss-framed appeals.

Several studies have provided empirical support for the thesis that these dispositional factors moderate the impact of framed health appeals (Latimer et al., 2007; Mann et al., 2004; Sherman, Mann, & Updegraff, in press; for similar findings outside the health domain, see Cesario, Grant, & Higgins, 2004; Lee & Aaker, 2004). For example, in a study designed to encourage dental flossing, undergraduate students who had a relatively stronger avoidance orientation (as indexed by a difference between their behavioral activation and their behavioral inhibition scores; Carver & White, 1994) reported flossing more after having read a loss-framed message, whereas those who had a relatively stronger approach orientation reported flossing more after having read a gain-framed message (Mann et al., 2004). A similar pattern of results emerged in an experiment encouraging inactive adults to increase their participation in physical activity (Latimer et al., 2007). In this study, individuals were categorized in terms of whether they were more promotion- or prevention-oriented. When given gain-framed messages, promotion-oriented people reported engaging in more physical activity at the follow-up interview than did prevention-oriented people. When given loss-framed messages, prevention-oriented participants tended to report more physical activity at the follow-up interview than did the promotion-oriented individuals, but this difference was not statistically significant.

What might account for the finding that dispositional tendencies can moderate the impact of framed appeals? The observed benefit of matching message frame to a person's disposition is consistent with the broader finding that tailoring a message to fit an individual's needs and characteristics enhances persuasion (Kreuter & Skinner, 2000; Kreuter & Wray, 2003). Messages can be tailored to a variety of characteristics such as demographics (Kreuter, Strecher, & Glassman, 1999), stage of change (Marshall et al., 2003), and dispositional factors (Latimer, Katulak, Mowad, & Salovey, 2005). Tailored messages are thought to be effective because they enhance the perceived relevance or importance of the message, which in turn increases the likelihood that the message will be processed systematically (Cacioppo & Petty, 1984; Eagly & Chaiken, 1993). All else being equal, greater elaboration of a strong health message is desirable as well-reasoned attitudes are more stable over time and better predictors of behavior (Petty & Wegener, 1998). Consistent with this perspective, studies have demonstrated that tailored messages are more likely to be read and remembered than are nontailored messages (Skinner, Strecher, & Hospers, 1994), are more likely to be discussed with others (Brug, Steenhuis, van Assema, & de Vries, 1996), and are perceived as more interesting and engaging (Brug et al., 1996; Kreuter, Bull, Clark, & Oswald, 1999).

Regulatory focus theory (Higgins, 1998) similarly suggests that messages that are tailored to a person's dispositional outlook may have increased persuasive impact. According to the theory, individuals experience *regulatory fit* when they think about or utilize behavioral strategies that match their promotion/prevention orientation. Regulatory fit makes people "feel right" about what they are doing and strengthens their engagement with and valuation of goal-directed behaviors (Higgins, 2000; Higgins et al., 2003; Spiegel, Grant-Pillow, & Higgins, 2004). This suggests that the match between message content and disposition might not only enhance the degree to which people process a message but also affect the psychological experience elicited by engaging with and responding to the message.

MESSAGE FRAMING AND HEALTH BEHAVIORS: INTEGRATING SITUATIONAL AND DISPOSITIONAL FACTORS

To date, there is evidence that framing effects differ based on people's dispositional tendencies as well as on features of the behavioral decision. In both cases, the *fit* between how the message is framed and the person or situation is thought to maximize the effectiveness of the framed appeal. Yet, these two lines of work have been examined independently and efforts considering how these two approaches might be related to each other have only begun to appear (Rothman et al., 2006). We believe that these two, heretofore, independent sets of moderating factors may in fact rest on the operation of a single set of underlying cognitive and affective processes. Specifically, the self-regulatory foci described in regulatory focus theory may provide an effective way to conceptualize the psychological processes that regulate the impact of gain- and loss-framed messages.

Research on regulatory focus theory (Higgins, 1998, 1999) has demonstrated that people will adopt a prevention or promotion focus because it reflects either a chronic dispositional tendency or a mindset that is induced temporarily by features of the situation. We believe that when people contemplate or engage in a specific class of health behavior, they experience a predictable set of thoughts and feelings that represent a mindset that is conceptually analogous to the two self-regulatory orientations proposed by Higgins—prevention focus and promotion focus. The extent to which a health behavior is perceived to afford the opportunity to either achieve a desired state (i.e., promote health) or monitor for an unwanted outcome (i.e., detect an illness) may serve as a strong situation that evokes a unique set of thoughts and feelings, which in turn regulate how people respond to gain- and loss-framed messages.

In some sense health behaviors can be said to engender a "personality" in that they evoke a pattern of thoughts and feelings that are consistently present whenever a person contemplates or engages in the behavior. Behaviors that promote health such as exercise or sunscreen are designed to afford favorable outcomes when performed consistently. Thus, when people think about engaging in these behaviors, they are more likely to attend to the presence or absence of favorable outcomes. For example, regular exercise affords the opportunity to be in shape (i.e., the presence of a favorable outcome), whereas failing to exercise can result in being out of shape (i.e., the absence of favorable outcome). Thus, intentions to perform these behaviors are typically grounded in the goal of maintaining or maximizing health, fitness, and well-being. Moreover, the motivation to engage in this type of behavior is thought to represent a personal choice that is expressed as an eagerness to advance toward a desired outcome. Finally, achieving the goals associated with these behaviors should elicit feelings of satisfaction, whereas failing to achieve these goals should elicit feelings of disappointment. Taken together, these psychological experiences are consistent with Higgins' characterization of a promotion-focused self-regulatory process (Higgins, 1999).

Screening behaviors such as mammography or blood cholesterol testing may engender a different set of thoughts and feelings. Because these behaviors are designed to determine the presence or absence of a health problem, we propose that when people think about engaging in these behaviors they focus on the presence or absence of unfavorable outcomes. For example, a mammogram is perceived to indicate whether you do or do not have breast cancer. Screening represents a process through which people monitor vigilantly for unwanted outcomes. Therefore, the decision to perform a screening behavior may feel more like a duty or an obligation (i.e., something one ought to do) than a desirable choice (i.e., something one wants to do). Finally, having attained goals associated with these behaviors (i.e., the absence of a problem) should elicit feelings of relief, whereas failing to achieve these goals (i.e., the presence of a problem) should elicit feelings of anxiety. Taken together, this set of psychological experiences is consistent with Higgins' characterization of a prevention-focused self-regulatory process.

What evidence is there that different classes of health behaviors systematically evoke distinct patterns of thoughts, motivations, and feelings? In an initial study, participants were asked to write about the thoughts and feelings they have when contemplating either exercising or having a cholesterol test (Wlaschin, Rothman, Bartels, & Bachnick, 2006). We predicted that when people think about engaging in a behavior designed to promote health (e.g., exercise), they will report thoughts and feelings consistent with a promotion-focus mindset, whereas when people think about a behavior designed to detect the presence of a health problem (e.g., cholesterol test), they will report thoughts and feelings consistent with a prevention-focus mindset.

Participants' responses were coded in terms of their fit with either a prevention or promotion mindset. Statements that described a desire to achieve a positive outcome, feelings along a satisfaction/disappointment continuum, and internal or ideal motivations were coded as promotion-oriented. Statements that described the desire to avoid negative outcomes, feelings along an anxious/calm continuum, and external or ought motivations were coded as prevention-oriented. As predicted, people who wrote about exercise provided more promotion-oriented statements than prevention-oriented statements, whereas people who wrote about a cholesterol test provided more prevention-oriented than promotion-oriented statements (see Figure 28.1). Those participants who indicated they would be willing to engage in the behavior were also asked to indicate which statement best characterized their willingness to perform the behavior—they would do the behavior because they liked to do it or they would do the behavior because they ought to do it. The decision to exercise was more likely to be characterized as a desirable choice (66% vs. 29%), whereas the decision to get a cholesterol test was more likely to be characterized as an obligation (71% vs. 34%). Finally, the different behaviors elicited two distinct patterns of emotional experience. When people thought about an exercise program, they were much more likely to describe any associated emotions with terms related to satisfaction and dejection. On

the other hand, when people thought about the cholesterol test, their affective reactions were typically grounded in feelings of worry and relief.

The clear motivational and emotional distinction between these two behaviors suggests that each experience evokes a particular regulatory mindset. However, one must be cautious in interpreting these initial findings. In particular, it is important to recognize that there are likely to be behaviors for which people differ systematically in the mindset that is elicited. For example, Apanovitch et al. (2003) assessed women's beliefs about HIV screening. Women who believed they had some risk of HIV infection construed the behavior as a means for detecting HIV. Other women who felt they were at low risk of HIV infection construed the behavior more as a means for confirming they were HIV free. How people think about a screening test for HIV may depend on the certainty of the outcome. An uncertain outcome may create feelings of anxiety and people may be more motivated to have an HIV test out of a sense of obligation or responsibility rather than a personal choice. People who are confident that the HIV test would assure them that they are not HIV positive would naturally be less worried about being screened and view the test more as a means for confirming health. Certainty in this outcome should afford a sense of satisfaction and people may be more willing to take the test as a personal choice rather than as an obligation. In fact, Apanovitch et al. found that women who construed an HIV test as health affirming were more likely to get tested after viewing the gain-framed video,

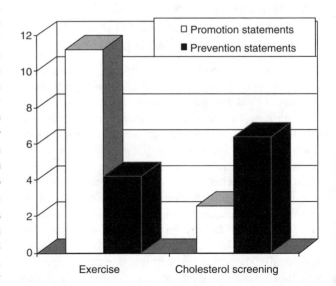

FIGURE 28.1 Mean number of total prevention and promotion statements for exercise and cholesterol screening.

whereas those who construed the behavior in terms of disease detection were somewhat more likely to get tested after viewing the loss-framed video.

Although Wlaschin et al. (2006) found considerable consistency in how participants construed exercise or a cholesterol test, one could imagine situations in which people might differ in how they conceptualize engaging in exercise or having a cholesterol test. For example, people with a history of low cholesterol—either due to family history or to having had a series of normal test results—would come to construe the procedure as a means for affirming their vascular health. In a similar manner, people who have to follow an exercise plan in response to a health problem might be less likely to construe the decision to exercise as a personal choice and be more likely to construe it as a duty and obligation (see Rothman et al., 2003 for a discussion of a related series of issues).

There may also be behaviors that more readily afford the adoption of different construals. For example, a regular dental visit can be perceived as an opportunity to enhance the health of one's teeth or to learn whether one has dental problems. To the extent that the prospect of a dental visit elicits thoughts about detecting cavities, it should induce a prevention-oriented mindset, whereas if it elicits thoughts about keeping one's teeth healthy and clean, it should induce a promotion-oriented mindset. In a recent survey of college undergraduates, we found that slightly more than two-thirds of the sample construed a regular dental visit as an opportunity to have their teeth cleaned and to promote the health of their teeth and gums, with the remaining third adopting a cavity-detection construal (Wlaschin, Bartels, & Rothman, 2007). Consistent with findings reported for cholesterol and exercise, students who focused on the detection of cavities were more likely to report affective and motivational concerns that were consistent with a prevention-oriented mindset (e.g., feelings of relief and anxiety), whereas those who focused on having their teeth cleaned were more likely to report affective and motivational concerns that were consistent with a promotion-focused mindset (e.g., feelings of satisfaction and disappointment). For example, people with a teeth-cleaning mindset were more likely to characterize attending a dental visit as reflecting a personal choice, whereas those who adopted a cavity-detection mindset characterized attending a dental visit as a duty or obligation.

Given the thesis that behaviors may differ in the types of construal they evoke and that, moreover, for certain behaviors there is variability among people in the specific construal that is evoked, what determines the type of construal that is adopted? Why is a mammogram typically construed as an illness-detection behavior? Why are students more likely to think about a dental visit in terms of healthy teeth and gums than about cavities? Although these questions have received limited empirical attention, we believe there are, at least, three critical determinants. First, how people construe a given behavior is likely to reflect the manner in which they are socialized to think about that behavior. For example, to the extent that information presented in the media or communicated by health professionals regarding mammography emphasizes its ability to detect cancer, people are likely to adopt an illness-detection construal. We are in the process of examining one facet of this hypothesis by conducting an archival analysis of newspaper and magazine articles about cholesterol screening and about physical exercise to determine whether the media consistently uses a given construal when communicating about each of these behavioral domains. For example, we anticipate that the media will portray deciding whether to exercise as a personal choice but deciding whether to have a cholesterol test as an obligation or duty. In addition, building on a recent finding by Semin and colleagues (Semin, Higgins, de Montes, Estourget, & Valencia, 2005) that promotion-focused statements utilize more abstract words (e.g., adjectives, state verbs), whereas prevention-focused statements utilize more concrete words (e.g., descriptive action verbs) we also plan to examine whether articles about exercise and cholesterol employ more abstract and concrete words, respectively.

Second, personal experience with the behavior as well as the experience of close others may shape how people perceive the behavior. In the dental health area, the extent to which visits to the dentist during childhood were characterized by cavities likely affords the development of an illness-detecting construal. If this construal makes people less eager to visit the dentist (e.g., because they are worried the dentist will find a problem), it may elicit a pattern of behavior that undermines dental health which, in turn, increases the likelihood that when the dental visit does occur their experience is less pleasant, which reinforces the initial construal. At the same time, a repeated series of favorable experiences (e.g., visits to the dentist at which no cavities are found) may over time induce a more favorable construal of a dental visit. The experiences of friends and family may also shape how one thinks about a behavior. Because events that involve the presence of disease are more memorable than those that involve the absence of disease, the adverse experiences of others may prove to have a particularly influential effect on how people think about a screening test.

A person's chronic tendency to adopt a promotion- or prevention-oriented mindset might also affect the extent to which a particular behavioral construal develops. Messages and experiences that match a person's dispositional tendencies are likely to resonate and be easier to recall. The moderating impact of disposition might be particularly important in domains where the media or health professionals provide an inconsistent or weak construal or in new or novel behavioral domains where a dominant construal has yet to emerge. Finally, there may be some behaviors that fail to evoke a particularly strong promotion- or prevention-oriented mindset. In these situations, a person's chronic tendency to adopt a prevention-oriented or a promotion-oriented mindset may have a direct effect on decision-making independent of the existence of any particular behavioral construal.

The thesis that a prevention- or promotion-oriented mindset can be evoked either by features of the behavioral domain or the person offers a unifying framework for thinking about the persuasive impact of gain- and loss-framed messages. Prior demonstrations that framing effects depend on whether a behavior is perceived in terms of the possibility of an unwanted outcome (Bartels et al., 2006; Rothman et al., 1999) can now be understood within this broader conceptual framework. When a behavior leads people to focus on the presence or absence of a negative outcome—which is what a screening behavior typically does, it can be understood to have induced a prevention-focused mindset that, in turn, elicits a unique set of affective and motivational concerns that guide decision-making and behavior. At the same time, when a behavior leads people to focus on the presence or absence of a positive outcome—which is what a health promotion or prevention behavior typically does, it can be understood to have induced a promotion-focused mindset that, in turn, affords its own unique set of affective and motivational concerns.

One potentially important advantage of thinking about a behavior in terms of its ability to evoke a prevention- or a promotion-oriented mindset is that it provides investigators with a broader set of dimensions to specify how a particular behavior is construed and, thus, generate predictions regarding the differential impact of gain- and loss-framed appeals. For example, it might be difficult to specify the risk implications people ascribe to a treatment regimen, but it could be possible to determine whether the regimen evokes feelings of anxiety or calm or feelings of disappointment or satisfaction. Alternatively, one could examine the extent to which the behavior is perceived to represent an obligation or duty. These affective and motivational markers could then be used to predict whether the treatment should be categorized as a prevention- or a promotion-oriented behavior and to guide the dissemination of gain- or loss-framed appeals.

However, some behaviors may fail to elicit a systematic or strong mindset. It is under these conditions (i.e., when the situation is weak) that we expect dispositional differences in people's sensitivity to favorable and unfavorable outcomes to regulate the impact of framed messages. Flossing, the behavior examined in the studies by Mann and colleagues (Mann et al., 2004; Sherman et al., in press) may prove to be a good example of a behavior that does not elicit strong affective or motivational concerns. Alternatively, it may be the case that framing effects are maximized when there is consistency between the mindset evoked by the behavior and a person's personality. Recall that Latimer et al. (2007) found that when encouraging exercise there was a gain-frame advantage for promotion-focused people but not a loss-framed advantage for prevention-focused people. This may provide some suggestive support for the thesis that tailoring messages that harmonize with a person's chronic regulatory disposition *and* the general construal of the behavior will afford the most persuasive effect. However, additional research is needed that examines the impact of behavior and disposition on framing simultaneously before any firm conclusions can be drawn.

PREVENTION- AND PROMOTION-ORIENTED HEALTH BEHAVIORS: IMPLICATIONS BEYOND MESSAGE FRAMING

The premise that health behaviors systematically induce a promotion- or a prevention-oriented mindset affords predictions not only regarding how and when people will respond to gain- and loss-framed messages, but also about other aspects of health judgment and behavioral decision-making. For example, Higgins and colleagues have observed that promotion- and prevention-focused people differ in how they judge the utility of a particular course of action. Classical models of utility suggest that people weight the likelihood (i.e., expectancy) and value of potential outcomes in a multiplicative manner that allows them to maximize utility. Across a series of studies, promotion-focused people were shown to weight expectancy and value in this manner when making behavioral decisions (Shah, Higgins, & Friedman, 1998). However, the behavioral decisions made by prevention-focused people did not reflect the normative relation between expectancy and value. Instead, prevention-focused people were more responsive to the value of a potential outcome and, in particular, as perceived value increased were less sensitive to information about the likelihood of the outcome. This pattern of judgment is thought to reflect the tendency for prevention-focused individuals to construe actions in terms of obligations and duties.

The differential weighting of expectancy and value may have interesting implications for the application of several models of health behavior that rely on the assumption that people weight expectancy and value in a multiplicative manner. For example, several models assume that people assess the threat posed by an event (e.g., contracting the flu) based on a weighting of its perceived personal risk (i.e., likelihood) and perceived severity (i.e., value) and that perceptions of threat predict people's willingness to take precautionary action (Weinstein, 1993). For behaviors that induce a promotion-oriented mindset, this predicted pattern of relations among constructs should hold. On the other hand, when people contemplate performing a behavior that induces a prevention-oriented mindset, people may not act in a manner that reflects the expected weighting of risk and severity. Instead, they may prove to be more responsive to the perceived severity of the outcome when considering a precautionary behavior. This is not to suggest that people in a prevention-oriented mindset are not responsive to perceptions of personal risk, but rather that perceptions of risk do not moderate the impact of perceived severity on behavioral decisions.

A similar analysis could be applied to facets of other models that rely on the normative weighting of expectancy and value. The extended parallel process model (Witte, 1992) offers an interesting example. In this model, people's behavioral decisions are thought to rest on an interaction between judgments of threat and self-efficacy such that action is most likely when people are provided information that induces perceptions of both high threat and high efficacy. In light of the present framework, we would predict that this relation would be particularly robust when applied in behavioral domains that induce a promotion-oriented mindset (e.g., behaviors that prevent HIV infection), but be less effective when applied in behavioral domains that induce a prevention-oriented mindset (e.g., screening behaviors). Of course, the viability of these predictions, as well as those outlined in the preceding paragraph, awaits empirical scrutiny.

Recently, researchers have demonstrated that the adoption of a promotion- as compared to a prevention-oriented mindset evokes greater attention to long-term outcomes (Pennington & Roese, 2003) and more global (i.e., abstract) attributes (Förster & Higgins, 2005). This would suggest that health promoting behaviors may elicit greater attention to, and perhaps weighting of, long-term outcomes. For

example, people may be willing to initiate exercise or to start eating more fruits and vegetables based on the prospect of delayed outcomes. On the other hand, decision-regarding behaviors that induce a prevention-oriented mindset may be particularly sensitive to short-term outcomes. This might possibly help to explain why perceptions of screening behaviors rest primarily on their ability to detect the presence of disease and not on the longer-term health benefits that are afforded by the treatment options that come from early detection. In fact, to the extent that people can focus on the longer-term benefits associated with a screening behavior, their construal of that behavior should change dramatically (see Orbell, Perugini, & Rakow, 2004) for an interesting demonstration regarding attitudes toward colorectal cancer screening.

The observation that people who adopt a prevention-oriented mindset are focused on more concrete factors might suggest that prevention-oriented behaviors will lead people to be more interested in information about how a behavior is performed. People may find that they are more reassured by instructions about how to engage in the behavior than by more general information about why a person should do it (Vallacher & Wegner, 1987). Because a prevention focus has been shown to induce a more conservative and cautious approach to decision-making (Higgins, 2000), behaviors that induce a prevention-oriented mindset should evoke a similar pattern of behavior. To the extent that prevention-oriented behaviors are perceived to be more prescriptive, one would predict that they would elicit limited debate about the wisdom of the behavior, and thus lead people to be more likely to follow instructions and comply with prevention-oriented than with promotion-oriented behaviors. For example, one would predict that people perceive behavioral guidelines for a screening behavior (which should induce a prevention-oriented mindset) as rules that must be followed, whereas behavioral guidelines for exercise (which should induce a promotion-oriented mindset) are perceived as a general framework that can be modified according to personal preference. An additional consequence of this approach is that people may also find it easier to maintain prevention-oriented behaviors over time (Fugelstad, Rothman, & Jeffery, in press).

Finally, specifying the degree to which a behavior induces a prevention- or a promotion-oriented mindset may have implications for the impact an implementation intention intervention has on behavior. Implementation intention interventions ask people to specify how, when, and where they will implement their intention to act and have been shown to dramatically increase the likelihood that stated intentions are translated into action (Armitage,

2004; Sheeran & Orbell, 1999, 2000; for a review, see Gollwitzer & Sheeran, 2006). Because implementation plans render salient the specific structural and situational factors that underlie people's ability to take action, one might predict that this intervention strategy would be particularly effective for behaviors that induce a prevention-focused mindset as this type of information would likely resonate with its emphasis on procedural details. On the other hand, one might expect that precisely because these behaviors already prompt people to focus on the specific, concrete details associated with performing the behavior, any additional benefit afforded by the implementation plan would be attenuated. From this perspective, one would expect implementation intention interventions to be more effective for behaviors that induce a promotion-focused mindset as they would compensate for the fact that people might focus more on general, abstract concerns and less on procedural details. Although investigators have begun to elucidate the processes that underlie the impact of implementation intentions, the degree to which features of the behavior regulate its effectiveness remains to be specified. The conceptual framework outlined above offers a potentially promising line of inquiry.

FINAL THOUGHTS

Research on message framing has proven quite successful in producing both clinically and statistically significant behavioral outcomes, but has proven less successful at specifying the mechanisms that underlie these effects. To a certain extent, this state of affairs reflects the fact that the guiding theoretical frameworks have focused on the role of moderating factors—behavioral and dispositional factors that regulate the persuasiveness of gain- and loss-framed appeals. The new, integrative framework described in this chapter may afford an opportunity to address this discrepancy and to revitalize theorizing about message framing. By providing a psychologically richer account of the moderating factors identified in prior research it offers investigators a range of variables that could serve to clarify how framed appeals are perceived and processed and how they subsequently affect behavioral decision-making.

The new framework also provides an opportunity to extend research on message framing in two important directions. First, it can inform how to apply message framing in new behavioral domains. Message framing research has focused primarily on screening behaviors and prevention behaviors—reflecting the classes of behaviors highlighted by Rothman and Salovey (1997)—and it has been unclear how to apply message framing to other behavioral domains

such as treatments or efforts at cessation. The broader set of psychological states that are predicted to characterize a prevention- or promotion-oriented mindset may provide investigators with a more productive and functional set of dimensions upon which to classify a behavior, which in turn can guide predictions regarding the impact of gain- or loss-framed appeals.

Second, there is an opportunity to better situate how our understanding of message framing effects fits within the broader study of health cognition and health behavior (Rothman & Salovey, in press). Message framing effects may be but one of a series of effects that can be derived from the mindset that people adopt when thinking about their health. Moreover, the focus within message framing research on features of health behaviors may provide an opportunity to think about how other phenomena may or may not generalize across behavioral domains. To date, psychological theories of health decision-making offer a rich description of people's thoughts and feelings, but little guidance as to the applicability of these states across behavioral domains. Thus, questions regarding the generalizability of predictions and findings across health domains are difficult to answer. The thesis that behaviors systematically elicit a set of self-regulatory tendencies may provide a framework with which to begin to answer those questions.

REFERENCES

Apanovitch, A. M., McCarthy, D., & Salovey, P. (2003). Using message framing to motivate HIV testing among low-income, ethnic minority women. *Health Psychology, 22,* 60–67.

Armitage, C. J. (2004). Evidence that implementation intentions reduce dietary fat intake: A randomized trial. *Health Psychology, 23,* 319–323.

Banks, S. M., Salovey, P., Greener, S., Rothman, A. J., Moyer, A., Beauvais, J., et al. (1995). The effects of message framing on mammography utilization. *Health Psychology, 14,* 178–184.

Bartels, R., Kelly, K. M., & Rothman, A. J. (2006). *Specifying the impact of behavior: An analysis of how and when message frames impact behavioral decision-making.* Unpublished manuscript, University of Minnesota, Minneapolis.

Brug, J., Steenhuis, I., van Assema, P., & de Vries, H. (1996). The impact of a computer-tailored nutrition intervention. *Preventative Medicine, 25,* 236–242.

Caccioppo, J. T., & Petty, R. E. (1984). The Elaboration Likelihood Model of persuasion. *Advances in Consumer Research, 11,* 673–675.

Carver, C. S., & White, T. L. (1994). Behavioral inhibition, behavioral activation, and affective responses to impending reward and punishment. *Journal of Personality and Social Psychology, 67,* 319–333.

Cesario, J., Grant, H., & Higgins, E. T. (2004). Regulatory fit and persuasion: Transfer from "feeling right." *Journal of Personality and Social Psychology*, 86, 388–404.

Cox, D., & Cox, A. D. (2001). Communicating the consequences of early detection: The role of evidence and framing. *Journal of Marketing*, 65, 91–103.

Croyle, R. T., & Ditto, P. H. (1990). Illness cognition and behavior: An experimental approach. *Journal of Behavioral Medicine*, 13, 31–52.

Detweiler, J. B., Bedell, B. T., Salovey, P., Pronin, E., & Rothman, A. J. (1999). Message framing and sun screen use: Gain-framed messages motivate beach-goers. *Health Psychology*, 18, 189–196.

Eagly, A. H., & Chaiken, S. (1993). *The psychology of attitudes*. Orlando, FL: Harcourt, Brace, Jovanovich.

Elliot, A. J., & Thrash, T. M. (2002). Approach–avoidance motivation in personality: Approach and avoidance temperaments and goals. *Journal of Personality and Social Psychology*, 82, 804–818.

Finney, L., & Iannoti, R. (2002). Message framing and mammography screening: A theory-driven intervention. *Behavioral Medicine*, 28, 5–14.

Förster, J., & Higgins, E. T. (2005). How global versus local perception fits regulatory focus. *Psychological Science*, 16, 631–636.

Fugelstad, P., Rothman, A. J., & Jeffery, R. W. (in press). Getting there and hanging on: The effect of regulatory focus on performance in smoking and weight loss interventions. *Health Psychology*.

Gollwitzer, P. M., & Sheeran, P. (2006). Implementation intentions and goal achievement: A meta-analysis of effects and process. *Advances in Experimental Social Psychology*, 38, 69–119.

Higgins, E. T. (1998). Promotion and prevention: Regulatory focus as a motivational principle. In M. P. Zanna (Ed.), *Advances in experimental social psychology* (Vol. 30, pp. 1–46). New York: Academic Press.

Higgins, E. T. (1999). Promotion and prevention as a motivational duality: Implications for evaluative processes. In S. Chaiken & Y. Trope (Eds.), *Dual process theories in social psychology*. New York: Guilford Press.

Higgins, E. T. (2000). Making a good decision: Value from fit. *American Psychologist*, 55, 1217–1230.

Higgins, E. T., Idson, L. C., Freitas, A. L., Spiegel, S., & Molden, D. C. (2003). Transfer of value from fit. *Journal of Personality and Social Psychology*, 84, 1140–1153.

Jones, L., Sinclair, R., & Courneya, K. (2003). The effects of source credibility and message framing on exercise intentions, behaviors, and attitudes: An integration of the elaboration likelihood model and prospect theory. *Journal of Applied Social Psychology*, 33, 179–196.

Kiene, S. M., Barta, W. D., Zelenski, J. M., & Cothran, D. L. (2005). Why are you bringing up condoms now? The effect of message content on framing effects of condom use messages, *Health Psychology*, 24, 321–326.

Kreuter, M. K., Bull, F. C., Clark, E. M., & Oswald, D. L. (1999). Understanding how people process health information: A comparison of tailored and non-tailored weight-loss materials. *Health Psychology*, 18, 487–494.

Kreuter, M. W., & Skinner, C. S. (2000). Tailoring: What's in a name? *Health Education Research*, 15, 1–4.

Kreuter, M. W., Strecher, V. J., & Glassman, B. (1999). One size does not fit all: The case for tailoring print materials. *Annals of Behavioral Medicine*, 21, 276–283.

Kreuter, M. W., & Wray, R. J. (2003). Tailored and targeted health communication: Strategies for enhancing information relevance. *American Journal of Health Behavior*, 27, S227–S232.

Latimer, A. E., Rivers, S. E., Rench, T. A., Katulak, N. A., Mowad, L. Z., Higgins, E. T., et al. (2007). *A field experiment testing the utility of regulatory fit messages for encouraging participation in physical activity*. Unpublished manuscript, Yale University, New Haven, CT.

Latimer, A. E., Katulak, N., Mowad, L., & Salovey, P. (2005). Motivating cancer prevention and early detection behaviors using psychologically tailored messages. *Journal of Health Communication*, s137–s156.

Lalor, K. M., & Hailey, B. J. (1990). The effects of message framing and feelings of susceptibility to breast cancer on reported frequency of breast self-examination. *International Quarterly of Community Health Education*, 10, 183–192.

Lauver, D., & Rubin, M. (1990). Message framing, dispositional optimism, and follow-up for abnormal Papanicolaou tests. *Research in Nursing and Health*, 13, 199–207.

Lee, A. Y., & Aaker, J. L. (2004). Bringing the frame into focus: The influence of regulatory fit on processing fluency and persuasion. *Journal of Personality and Social Psychology*, 86, 205–218.

Lerman, C., Ross, E., Boyce, A., Gorchov, P. M., McLaughlin, R., Rimer, B., et al. (1992). The impact of mailing psychoeducational materials to women with abnormal mammograms. *American Journal of Public Health*, 82, 729–730.

Linville, P. W., Fischer, G. W., & Fischhoff, B. (1993). AIDS risk perceptions and decision biases. In J. B. Pryor & G. D. Reeder (Eds.), *The social psychology of HIV infection* (pp. 5–38). Hillsdale, NJ: Lawrence Erlbaum.

Mann, T., Sherman, D., & Updegraff, J. (2004). Dispositional motivations and message framing: A test of the congruency hypothesis in college students. *Health Psychology*, 23, 330–334.

Marshall, A. L., Bauman, A. E., Owen, N., Booth, M. L., Crawford, D., & Marcus, B. H. (2003). Population-based randomized controlled trial of a stage-targeted physical activity intervention. *Annals of Behavioral Medicine*, 25, 194–202.

McCaul, K. D., Johnson, R. J., & Rothman, A. J. (2002). The effects of framing and action instructions on whether older adults obtain flu shots. *Health Psychology*, 21, 624–628.

Meyerowitz, B. E., & Chaiken, S. (1987). The effect of message framing on breast self-examination attitudes, intentions, and behavior. *Journal of Personality and Social Psychology*, 52, 500–510.

Meyerowitz, B. E., Wilson, D. K., & Chaiken, S. (1991, June). *Loss-framed messages increase breast self-examination for women who perceive risk*. Paper presented at the annual convention of the American Psychological Society, Washington, DC.

Millar, M., & Millar, K. (2000). Promoting safe driving behaviors: The influence of message framing and issue involvement. *Journal of Applied Social Psychology, 30,* 853–856.

Myers, R. E., Ross, E. A., Wolf, T. A., Balshem, A., Jepson, C., & Millner, L. (1991). Behavioral interventions to increase adherence to colorectal cancer screening. *Medical Care, 29,* 1039–1050.

O'Connor, D. B., Ferguson, E., & O'Connor, R. C. (2005). Intentions to use hormonal male contraception: The role of message framing, attitudes and stress appeals. *British Journal of Psychology, 96,* 351–369.

Orbell, S., Perugini, M., & Rakow, T. (2004). Individual differences in sensitivity to health communications: Consideration of future consequences. *Health Psychology, 23,* 388–396.

Pennington, G. I., & Roese, N. J. (2003). Regulatory focus and temporal distance. *Journal of Experimental Social Psychology, 39,* 563–576.

Petty, R. E., & Wegener, D. T. (1998). Attitude change: Multiple roles for persuasion variables. In D. Gilbert, S. Fiske, & G. Lindsay (Eds.), *Handbook of social psychology* (pp. 323–390). New York: McGraw Hill.

Rivers, S. E., Pizarro, D. A., Schneider, T. R., Pizarro, J., & Salovey, P. (2005). Message framing and Pap test utilization among women attending a community health clinic. *Journal of Health Psychology, 10,* 67–79.

Rothman, A. J., Bartels, R. D., Wlaschin, J., & Salovey, P. (2006). The strategic use of gain- and loss-framed messages to promote healthy behavior: How theory can inform practice. *Journal of Communication, 56,* S202–S221.

Rothman, A. J., Kelly, K. M., Hertel, A., & Salovey, P. (2003). Message frames and illness representations: Implications for interventions to promote and sustain healthy behavior. In L. D. Cameron & H. Leventhal (Eds.), *The self-regulation of health and illness behavior* (pp. 278–296). London, UK: Routledge.

Rothman, A. J., Martino, S. C., Bedell, B. T., Detweiler, J. B., & Salovey, P. (1999). The systematic influence of gain- and loss-framed messages on interest in and use of different types of health behavior. *Personality and Social Psychology Bulletin, 25,* 1355–1369.

Rothman, A. J., & Salovey, P. (1997). Shaping perceptions to motivate healthy behavior: The role of message framing. *Psychological Bulletin, 121,* 3–19.

Rothman, A. J., & Salovey P. (2007). The reciprocal relation between principles and practice: Social psychology and health behavior. In A. Kruglanski & E. T. Higgins (Eds.), *Social psychology: Handbook of basic principles* (2nd edn.) (pp. 826–849). New York: Guilford Press.

Rothman, A. J., Salovey, P., Antone, C., Keough, K., & Martin, C. D. (1993). The influence of message framing on intentions to perform health behaviors. *Journal of Experimental Social Psychology, 29,* 408–433.

Rothman, A. J., Stark, E., & Salovey, P. (2006). Using message framing to promote healthy behavior: A guide to best practices. In J. Trafton (Ed.), *Best practices in the behavioral management of chronic diseases,* (Vol. 3, pp. 31–48). Institute for Disease Management: Los Altos, CA.

Schneider, T. R., Salovey, P., Apanovitch, A. M., Pizarro, J., McCarthy, D., Zullo, J., et al. (2001). The effects of message framing and ethnic targeting on mammography use among low-income women. *Health Psychology, 20,* 256–266.

Semin, G. R., Higgins, E. T., de Montes, L. G., Estourget, Y., & Valencia, J. F. (2005). Linguistic signatures of regulatory focus: How abstraction fits promotion more than prevention. *Journal of Personality and Social Psychology, 89,* 36–45.

Shah, J., Higgins, E. T., & Friedman, R. S. (1998). Performance incentives and means: How regulatory focus influences goal attainment. *Journal of Personality and Social Psychology, 74,* 285–293.

Sheeran, P., & Orbell, S. (1999). Implementation intentions and repeated behavior: Augmenting the predictive validity of the theory of planned behavior. *European Journal of Social Psychology, 29,* 349–369.

Sheeran, P., & Orbell, S. (2000). Using implementation intentions to increase attendance for cervical cancer screening. *Health Psychology, 19,* 283–289.

Sherman, D. K., Mann, T. L., & Updegraff, J. A. (in press). Approach/avoidance orientation, message framing, and health behavior: Understanding the congruency effect. *Motivation and Emotion.*

Skinner, C. S., Strecher, V. J., & Hospers, H. (1994). Physicians' recommendations for mammography: Do tailored messages make a difference? *American Journal of Public Health, 84,* 43–49.

Spiegel, S., Grant-Pillow, H., & Higgins, E. T. (2004). How regulatory fit enhances motivational strength during goal pursuit. *European Journal of Social Psychology, 34,* 39–54.

Tversky, A., & Kahneman, D. (1981). The framing of decisions and the rationality of choice. *Science, 221,* 453–458.

Vallacher, R. R., & Wegner, D. M. (1987). What do people think they're doing? Action identification and human behavior. *Psychological Review, 94,* 3–15.

Weinstein, N. D. (1993). Testing four competing theories of health-protective behavior. *Health Psychology, 12,* 324–333.

Witte, K. (1992). Putting the fear back into fear appeals: The extended parallel process model. *Communication Monographs, 59,* 329–349.

Wlaschin, J. T., Bartels, R. D., & Rothman, A. J. (2007, January). *Regulatory focus and health behavior: Testing how behaviors can evoke a prevention or promotion mindset.* Presented at the annual meeting of the Society for Personality and Social Psychology, Memphis, TN.

Wlaschin, J. T., Rothman, A. J., Bartels, R. D., & Bachnick, L. (2006, May). *Behaviors with personality: Testing the mindset evoked by prevention and detection behaviors.* Presented at the annual meeting of the American Psychological Society, New York.

Part VII

The Self

Self-Regulation

29 Distinguishing Levels of Approach and Avoidance: An Analysis Using Regulatory Focus Theory

Abigail A. Scholer and E. Tory Higgins

CONTENTS

Jack and Jill walk down the aisle, now officially a married couple. Both beam at their friends and family on this special day. Both know that marriage will not always be this blissful, but both have the goal of having a good marriage. While Jack is thinking, "I am going to do all that I can to build a good marriage," Jill reflects, "I am going to be careful not to mess up this good marriage." Jack recalls the advice his mother gave him that morning, "The secret of a good marriage is never to go to bed angry," while Jill remembers the words of her mother, "Show him you love him every day. You can't express it too often."

What does it mean to approach and avoid? Both Jack and Jill are approaching the same desired end-state (a good marriage), yet there are clear differences in the strategies and tactics each plans to use to achieve that goal. The strategic preference of Jack to "do all that he can" to have a good marriage reflects strategic approach (eagerly approaching matches to "good marriage"), whereas the strategic preference of Jill to be "careful not

to mess up" reflects strategic avoidance (vigilantly avoiding mismatches to "good marriage"). And while Jack embraces approach at the strategic level, tactically he advocates avoidance ("don't go to bed angry"). In contrast, Jill endorses strategic avoidance while tactically embracing approach (telling spouse "I love you" every day).

In this chapter, we argue that one cannot fully answer the question of what it means to approach and avoid without considering the different levels at which approach and avoidance occur. As Andrew Elliot reviews in the introductory chapter, though the interest in approach and avoidance motivations has a long and rich history, there has been considerable variability in the ways that researchers have approached this issue. In particular, approach and avoidance motivations have been studied and conceptualized at various levels of abstraction. Distinguishing between these levels, we argue, is critical for understanding both the antecedents and consequences of self-regulation with regard to approach and avoidance.

LEVELS OF APPROACH AND AVOIDANCE: AN OVERVIEW

There are a number of theories that have discussed the importance of distinguishing between levels of self-regulation. Different approaches have emphasized the importance of different kinds of distinctions—between goals and subgoals (Miller, Galanter, & Pribram, 1960), between principles, programs, and sequences of movement (Carver & Scheier, 1998), between low and high levels of action identification (Vallacher & Wegner, 1985, 1987), between life-task goals, strategies, and plans or tactics (Cantor & Kihlstrom, 1987), between self-regulatory systems and strategies (Higgins, 1997; Higgins, Roney, Crowe, & Hymes, 1994), and between temperaments, motive dispositions, goals, and behaviors (Elliot, 2006; Elliot & Church, 1997; Gable, 2006; Pervin, 1989, 2001). Although these approaches differ somewhat in the preferred terminology and number of these levels, a common thread runs throughout: at any lower level in the hierarchy, there are multiple means (e.g., goals, subgoals, programs, strategies, tactics, or behaviors) that can serve a higher level.

In this chapter, we address the distinction between levels of self-regulation specifically with respect to levels of approach and avoidance in the service of self-regulation (Elliot, 2006; Elliot & Church, 1997; Gable, 2006; Higgins, 1997; Higgins et al., 1994). We propose that within a hierarchy of approach and avoidance motivations, the levels of approach and avoidance are independent. Thus, approach or avoidance at one level is independent of approach or avoidance at another level (cf. Elliot & Church, 1997; Elliot & Thrash, 2002; Gable, in press; Higgins, 1997; Higgins et al., 1994). In the present discussion of levels of approach and avoidance, we distinguish between three levels: the system, strategic, and tactical levels (Higgins, 1997; Scholer, Stroessner, & Higgins, in press). Our approach shares many similarities with other hierarchical models of approach and avoidance motivation, but we differ in the distinctions among the levels that we emphasize. For example, the hierarchical model of approach and avoidance motivation proposed by Elliot and colleagues (Elliot, 2006; Elliot & Church, 1997) emphasizes how underlying motives and temperaments can be served by different goals, whereas we emphasize how underlying approach and avoidance goals can be served by different strategies and tactics. In the concluding section of the chapter, we return to a discussion of the similarities and differences between these approaches.

At the *system* level, approach and avoidance motivations have been defined in relation to whether behavior is energized by positive stimuli (desirable end-states or reference points) or negative stimuli (undesirable end-states or reference points) (Carver & Scheier, 1981, 1990, 1998; Elliot & Thrash, 2002; Freud, 1920/1952; Gray, 1982; Lang, 1995; Lewin, 1935; Miller, 1944; Mowrer, 1960). The system level is characterized by the end-states that regulate behavior as goals, standards, or reference points. This is perhaps the most ubiquitous way in which approach and avoidance motivations have been conceptualized and correspond to the idea of *regulatory reference* (Higgins, 1997). While the system level tells us about whether an individual is regulating in regards to a desired end-state (e.g., a goal to get an A in a course) or undesired end-state (e.g., a goal to avoid an F), it does not tell us about the strategic or tactical ways in which the approach or avoidance system's directional motivation may be playing out.

At the *strategic* level, approach and avoidance motivations are about the *means or process* of moving towards desired end-states or moving away from undesired end-states. Strategies reflect the general plans or means for goal pursuit. Critically, there are different ways both of approaching desired end-states and of avoiding undesired end-states. Regarding the most common case of approaching desired end-states, strategic means are about whether one is approaching eagerly (moving towards the desired end-state by approaching matches to it) or approaching vigilantly (moving towards the desired end-state by avoiding mismatches to it). Though less commonly discussed, there are also different ways of avoiding undesired end-states. To move away from an undesired end-state at the system level, one can either strategically approach mismatches or strategically avoid matches to it (Higgins et al., 1994). Thus, approach and avoidance at the strategic level differs from approach and avoidance at the system level because the strategic level is about the means or process, rather than about the endpoints. Approach and avoidance at the strategic level differ from the tactical level (which we discuss next) because the strategic level is about broad-level descriptions of the means rather than the more specific instantiations of those means.

At the tactical level, approach and avoidance are reflected in the specific ways in which one might, for example, eagerly approach matches to a desired end-state in a *particular context*. Tactics are thus the instantiation of a strategy in a given context and are about the means or process at a more concrete, in-context level (Cantor & Kihlstrom, 1987; Higgins, 1997). Just as approach and avoidance are reflected in the strategic level, so too are approach and avoidance reflected in the tactical level. For example, in the signal detection sense, approach and avoidance tactics are reflected in the bias for the acceptance threshold that one adopts. A bias towards a lenient or liberal criterion for acceptance represents approach; this is a tactic that maximizes hits (even at the cost of false alarms)—a so-called risky bias. In contrast, a bias towards a strict criterion for acceptance represents avoidance; this is a tactic that maximizes correct rejections (even at the cost of misses)—a so-called conservative bias. In the opening example, tactics encompassed the different kinds of behaviors that Jack and Jill embraced for pursuit of a good marriage ("not going to bed angry" versus "expressing 'I love you' every day"). Our distinction between strategy and tactics also parallels the military distinction between strategy (long range planning and development for victory) and tactics (how troops are actually deployed in a particular combat situation).

Our notion of the tactical level that implements a strategy in a particular situation is broader than approach and avoidance at the behavioral level, especially as it has been described in the literature. It is common to associate approach and avoidance at the behavioral level with action and inaction, respectively (cf. Gray, 1982). These associations do not always characterize the full range of behavioral possibilities, however. For example, taking action at the behavioral level in the service of the same tactic may reflect either approach or avoidance depending on the circumstances. To illustrate, imagine that Donald is walking down a city street and thinks he sees an old college buddy walking towards him. Donald tries to decide if he should approach this man and say hello. If Donald adopts a lenient criterion of acceptance (an approach tactic), he is likely to decide, "Yes, that's him" and approach the man to say hello (behavioral approach). However, if instead Donald wonders if the man approaching him is the escaped (and dangerous) convict that he saw on the morning news, the adoption of the same lenient criterion for acceptance is likely to lead to a different behavioral response. Here, adopting an approach tactic (a lenient criterion for acceptance) is again likely to lead Donald to decide, "Yes, that's him." But this time such a decision will lead to an avoidance action at the behavioral level, not an approach action. Donald is unlikely to approach the convict to have a little chat; rather, he is likely to walk away and perhaps even notify the authorities. In this example, then, we see that either an approach behavioral action or an avoidance behavioral action can reflect the same approach tactic (a lenient criterion for acceptance).

It is also possible that the same tactic could be instantiated by either action or inaction at the behavioral level. To illustrate, if Jack's avoidance tactic is "to not go to bed angry," he might either stop thinking about what Jill did that angered him that day (inaction at the behavioral level) or try to remind himself of why he loves being with her (action at the behavioral level). In other words, "not going to bed angry" could be instantiated by thinking about the nice things your partner did for you that day (action) or by not thinking about the mean things (inaction).

Thus, the tactical level as we are defining it here is broader than the behavioral level defined simply as activation or inhibition, action or inaction. It involves the constellation of responses or behaviors (motor movements, attention, etc.) that embody a strategy played out in a specific context. While a discussion of hierarchical levels of approach and avoidance could include these lower behavioral levels, they are not the focus of our discussion here. We raise the point, however, because the behavioral level has been the focus of other theories of approach and avoidance (notably Gray, 1982, 1990; Miller, 1944; Mowrer, 1960), and we want to be clear that our conceptualization of tactics is at a broader level than simply activation or inhibition of behavior or approach versus avoidance at the behavioral output level.

Our perspective may be illuminated further by considering how one influential theory of approach and avoidance relates to our distinction between the system, strategic, and tactical levels. Gray (1982, 1990) proposed two motivational–behavioral systems that regulate behavior: a behavioral approach system (also referred to as a behavioral activation system) (Fowles, 1980, 1987) and a behavioral inhibition system (BIS). In Gray's conception, the behavioral approach system (BAS) responds to inputs related to signals of conditioned reward—either the presence of reward (e.g., food) or the absence of punishment (e.g., safety). It is important to note that these inputs (reward, nonpunishment relief) are functionally equivalent in the model (Fowles, 1987; Gray, 1982). These inputs result in *behavioral* approach or action. Thus, BAS is a theory of approach at the highest level of our hierarchy (its inputs are desired end-states such as food and safety), but it is also a theory of approach at a lower level than we discuss here, in that its outputs are behavioral action and approach (e.g., approach learning, active avoidance, skilled escape, predatory aggression). Similarly, BIS responds to inputs related to conditioned punishment— either to the presence of punishment or the absence of reward (frustrative nonreward). As in BAS, these inputs are functionally equivalent: punishment and frustrative nonreward are believed to activate the same underlying neural substrate (Fowles, 1987; Gray, 1982). Activation of BIS results in behavioral inhibition (e.g., passive avoidance and extinction). Thus, BIS is a theory of avoidance at the highest level of our hierarchy (its inputs are undesired end-states) but its outputs are behavioral, reflecting inhibition of some ongoing behavior.

While this dual emphasis on different levels of the approach and avoidance hierarchy has been reflected in the various ways that the BAS/BIS conceptions have been applied to the study of emotions and personality, the fact that the model involves two different levels of approach–avoidance analysis—one very high (system) and one very low (behavioral)—has received little attention. Indeed, many have concluded that these dimensions simply represent fundamental approach versus avoidance motivations (Carver, Sutton, & Scheier, 2000; Elliot & Thrash, 2002; Gable, Reis, & Elliot, 2003). The fact that the BAS/BIS distinction involves two levels of approach–avoidance analysis raises the issue of whether it is reasonable to assume, as the BAS/BIS distinction does, at least implicitly, that approach behaviors necessarily go with approaching desired end-states and avoidance behaviors necessarily go with avoiding undesired end-states. As suggested by our earlier discussion, we do not believe that this assumption is necessary (cf. Higgins, 1997).

While not denying the ubiquitous or fundamental nature of approach and avoidance motivations, we argue that consideration of an approach and avoidance hierarchy such as we propose here will elucidate some issues within self-regulation while raising some important new questions. Does some underlying general "approach" disposition increase the likelihood that a person will approach at all levels of analysis? When is avoidance at the strategic level likely to reflect approach at the system level? Are the costs of avoidance at the system level the same as the costs of avoidance at the strategic level? What are the implications of concordance or divergence between approach (or avoidance) at different levels in the hierarchy?

In sum, we suggest that it is important to distinguish how individuals approach and avoid at multiple levels of analysis. In the following sections, we use regulatory focus theory (Higgins, 1997) and empirical evidence from studies testing regulatory focus theory to illustrate the importance of distinguishing among the system, strategic, and tactical levels. We then explore the implications of these distinctions for understanding approach and avoidance motivations in self-regulation. In the remainder of the chapter we will not describe evidence for the distinction between the tactical versus behavioral levels of approach–avoidance as this has not been formally addressed yet by regulatory focus theory (or by any other theory of which we are aware). We do believe the distinction is important, however, and deserves future research attention. For example, as discussed earlier, at these levels as well there could be implications of concordance or divergence between approach–avoidance at the tactical level and approach–avoidance at the behavioral output level.

APPROACH AND AVOIDANCE LEVELS IN REGULATORY FOCUS

One of the original contributions of regulatory focus theory was to distinguish between the system and strategic levels of self-regulation. Until recently, the tactical level of self-regulation was not emphasized. We begin with an overview of regulatory focus theory, including a discussion of the relation of the theory to approach and avoidance more generally, and then go on to discuss experimental evidence that makes it clear why the system/strategic/tactical distinction is both necessary and useful.

Building on earlier distinctions (Bowlby, 1969, 1973; Higgins, 1987; Mowrer, 1960), regulatory focus theory distinguishes between two coexisting regulatory systems or general orientations that serve critically important but different survival needs (Higgins, 1997). The promotion orientation regulates nurturance needs and is concerned with growth, advancement, and accomplishment. Individuals in a promotion focus are striving towards ideals, wishes, and aspirations and are particularly sensitive to the presence and absence of positive outcomes (gains and nongains). In contrast, the prevention orientation regulates security needs. Individuals in a prevention focus are concerned with safety and responsibility and with meeting one's oughts, duties, and responsibilities. Prevention-focused individuals are particularly sensitive to the absence and presence of negative outcomes (nonlosses and losses). At the system level, regulatory focus theory is orthogonal to the system-level distinction between approaching desired end-states and avoiding undesired end-states because promotion and prevention orientations each involve *both* approaching desired end-states (e.g., approaching accomplishment or safety, respectively) and avoiding undesired end-states (e.g., avoiding nonfulfillment or danger, respectively).

Regulatory focus theory also distinguishes between the different strategic ways that individuals pursue different desired end-states (Higgins, 1997; Higgins et al., 1994). Although the same desired end-state (e.g., having a good marriage) can be pursued by both promotion-focused and prevention-focused individuals, they have different preferred strategies for doing so. Thus, promotion-focused individuals prefer to use eager approach strategies (approaching matches to desired end-states, approaching mismatches to undesired end-states) whereas prevention-focused individuals prefer to use vigilant avoidance strategies (avoiding mismatches to desired end-states, avoiding matches to undesired end-states). The eager strategic means preferred by individuals in a promotion-focus reflect their concerns with advancement and accomplishment and their pursuit of ideals and growth. The vigilant strategic means preferred by individuals in a prevention focus reflect their concerns with safety and responsibility and the need to guard against mistakes. Thus, at the strategic level of approach and avoidance, differences between promotion and prevention foci relate to differences in preference for using eager approach and vigilant avoidance strategies, respectively.

EMPIRICAL EVIDENCE FOR THE SYSTEM–STRATEGY DISTINCTION IN THE CASE OF REGULATORY FOCUS

How do we know that the system level and the strategic level are truly independent? For example, how do we know that when a prevention-focused individual pursues the goal of "good marriage" they are approaching at the system level while avoiding at the strategic level? We review empirical evidence in this section that supports the claim that these are independent levels of self-regulation.

A study that capitalized on the classic "goal looms larger" effect provides especially clear evidence for the independence of the system and strategic levels (Förster, Higgins, & Idson, 1998). The finding that motivational strength increases as the distance from a goal decreases has been labeled the "goal looms larger" effect (Lewin, 1935; Miller, 1944, 1959). The initial work was done with rats (Brown, 1948), but the effect has been replicated across many contexts (Losco & Epstein, 1977; Smith, 1965, 1969). Why is it that a goal looms larger as we approach it? As we approach the desired end-state, each step takes us closer to the goal, thus reducing the goal discrepancy. The contribution of any one of those steps to the value of success depends on the magnitude of the discrepancy that it reduces; thus, each subsequent step reduces a greater proportion of the discrepancy, assuming the steps are of equal size (Förster et al., 1998). The motivational properties subsequently "loom larger" as one gets closer to a goal, increasing the strength of strategic motivations likely to produce success (see Brendl & Higgins, 1995, for a review).

While the goal looms larger effect posits that motivation should increase as one approaches ever nearer to the desired end-state, it does not specify what type of motivation may be increasing. Thus, it could be that either strategic approach motivation or strategic avoidance motivation increases. Imagine two individuals preparing for a date. Both promotion- and prevention-focused individuals may be motivated to have their evening date end in a pleasant kiss; at the system level, both individuals are approaching a desired end-state (a pleasant kiss as the successful ending to the date). However, as the eve of the date approaches, a promotion-focused individual may eagerly purchase a box of mints (approaching a match to the pleasant kiss) whereas a prevention-focused individual may be careful to avoid the garlic bread at lunch (avoiding a mismatch to the pleasant kiss). Thus, as a goal looms larger for prevention- and promotion-focused individuals, promotion-focused individuals should show an increase in strategic approach motivation (getting more and more enthusiastic) whereas prevention-focused individuals should show an increase in strategic avoidance motivation (getting more and more careful). Förster et al. (1998) tested these ideas in a series of studies.

In one study (Förster et al., 1998, Study 3), the goal for all participants was to perform well on an anagram task (as payment depended on good performance). The effects of regulatory focus were evaluated both as a chronic variable (measured in an earlier session) and as a manipulated variable. Participants were assigned to one of the two framing conditions: promotion or prevention (the regulatory focus manipulation). To assess the differential strength of approach or avoidance strategic motivations, two different types of anagrams were presented. Participants were told that for each green anagram for which they found all possible solutions, they would gain a point (*strategic approach* problems). They were told that for each red anagram for which they found all possible solutions, they would avoid losing a point (*strategic avoidance* problems). Motivational strength in this study was measured by persistence (duration of time participants spent working on the anagrams). According to the goal looms larger effect, persistence should increase for anagrams late in the set relative to those early in the set. Indeed, to be confident that both promotion- and prevention-focused participants are, indeed, approaching a desired end-state at the system level, a goal looms larger effect is needed for *all* participants.

However, the way in which motivational strength increases for promotion- versus prevention-focused participants should differ. According to regulatory focus theory and the argument that the system versus strategic levels are independent, promotion-focused individuals should show greater approach strength at the strategic level as the goal looms larger whereas prevention-focused individuals should show greater avoidance strength at the strategic level as the goal looms larger. The design allowed differences in the motivational strength of these two strategies to be assessed via persistence on the two different types of anagram problems (red or green). The specific prediction was that promotion-focused participants would persist longer on green (strategic approach) anagrams late versus early in the task, whereas prevention-focused participants would persist longer on red (strategic avoidance) anagrams late versus early in the task. For both the situational manipulation of regulatory focus and for chronic regulatory focus, these predicted effects were obtained, independent of both outcome valence and outcome expectancy. In other words, while all participants showed evidence of the "goal looms larger" effect from steadily approaching a desired end-state, this resulted in increasing strategic approach motivation for promotion-focused participants but increasing strategic avoidance motivation for prevention-focused participants (for further evidence of these effects, see also Förster, Grant, Idson, & Higgins, 2001).

The basic assumptions underlying studies testing regulatory fit theory (Higgins, 2000) also support the independence of the system and strategic levels of approach and avoidance. Regulatory fit theory posits that individuals derive value from using strategic means that fit their underlying regulatory orientations. As we have discussed, one way to differentiate between types of strategic means is to recognize that people may use either approach strategic means or avoidance strategic means. Within the context of regulatory focus theory, approach strategic means (eager means) fit a promotion focus whereas avoidance strategic means (vigilant means) fit a prevention focus. When individuals experience regulatory fit by using strategic means that sustain their underlying orientation, they "feel right" about what they are doing (Higgins, 2000) and also experience increased engagement (Higgins, 2006). Regulatory fit theory is not restricted to fit between regulatory focus orientations and means (Avnet & Higgins, 2003; Bianco, Higgins, and Klem, 2003), but it is the evidence within regulatory focus theory that is germane to our present discussion of approach and avoidance motivations within self-regulation. Of most relevance to the current discussion, such regulatory fit effects could *not* occur if the strategic level of approach and avoidance was not dissociable from the system level of approach and avoidance. Across the studies that we will review, everyone is approaching a desired end-state at the system level, but the value of what people are doing is intensified when they pursue goals with eager approach or vigilant avoidance strategies that fit their regulatory system orientation.

A series of studies found support for the idea that the value created when people use strategic means that fit their regulatory orientation not only affects the value of the goal pursuit activity but also affects the value of subsequent object appraisals (Higgins, Idson, Freitas, Spiegel, & Molden, 2003). Higgins et al. gave participants an unexpected gift—a choice between a university logo coffee mug and a cheap disposable pen. These gifts had been preselected so that the mug was seen as more desirable by almost everyone. All participants were asked to focus on the positive attributes of the objects (desired end-states), but the strategic ways in which they were asked to do so differed. Half of the participants were told to think about what they would gain by choosing the mug and what they would gain by choosing the pen (eager approach strategy). The other half of the participants were told to think about what they would lose by not choosing the mug and what they would lose by not choosing the pen (vigilant avoidance strategy).

In both conditions, participants were focusing on desired end-states; in both conditions making the choice itself resulted in a desired end-state (owning the positive attributes of the mug they selected). Thus, across conditions, the system level of approach was held constant. Of interest was how the fit or nonfit between participants' chronic regulatory focus orientations (assessed by the Self-Guide Strength Measure) (Higgins, Shah, & Friedman, 1997) and the assigned strategy would affect the value of the mug. Value of the mug was measured by the amount of their own money that participants were willing to spend to purchase the mug. The price offered to buy the mug was almost 70% higher under regulatory fit than under nonfit (Higgins et al., Study 2). Thus, although all participants were approaching a desired end-state, the strategic means they used had a dramatic impact on their experience of the decision activity, which in turn intensified the attractiveness of the mug, as reflected in the price they were willing to pay to buy it.

It is notable that there was no main effect of the strategic means in these studies; in other words, it was not better overall to use approach strategic means or avoidance strategic means. This highlights an important distinction between the benefits and costs of approach and avoidance at the system level versus the benefits and costs of approach and avoidance at the strategic level. While a number of studies have found support for the idea that approach goals result in better outcomes than avoidance goals (Elliot & Harackiewicz, 1996; Elliot & Sheldon, 1997, 1998; Elliot, Sheldon, & Church, 1997), this may be primarily in regards to approach and avoidance at the system level. Approaching desired end-states as reference points may indeed have benefits that avoiding undesired end-states do not. However, at the strategic level value may be derived more from a fit between the strategic means and one's regulatory orientation, rather than from a main effect of approach versus avoidance per se.

What processes other than assigning monetary value are impacted by regulatory fit? In one study (Higgins et al., 2003, Study 5), all of the participants had to think about things that would improve the transition from elementary school to middle school (i.e., all participants were approaching a desired end-state at the system level). However, half of the participants had to do this by using an approach strategy (thinking of improvements that could be *added* to middle school to maximize the positive aspects of middle school) while half of the participants had to do this using an avoidance strategy (thinking of things that should be *eliminated* from middle school to ensure that students avoid negative experiences). Regulatory focus was again measured using the Self-Guide Strength Measure (Higgins et al., 1997). Not only did participants rate middle school experiences as more important under fit, but they also performed better by generating more options for improving middle school.

Shah, Higgins, and Friedman (1998) also found that participants performed better on an anagram task under fit. For participants with a chronic promotion focus, strategic approach framing led to better performance. In contrast, for participants with a chronic prevention focus, strategic avoidance framing led to better performance. Freitas and Higgins (2002) further found that under fit individuals reported greater task enjoyment and greater subjective perceptions of success. This is additional evidence that at the strategic level neither approach nor avoidance strategies per se produce better outcomes overall (in terms of performance or subjective well-being). Instead, these strategies have differential effects dependent on their relation to one's underlying regulatory focus orientation (fit versus nonfit).

Spiegel, Grant-Pillow, and Higgins (2004) extended these findings to real-life health behaviors. In one study, for example, participants were told that they were participating in a two-session study to track the nutritional habits of college students (Study 2). In the initial session, all participants were given health messages to read that advocated pursuit of the same desired end-state—eating more fruits and vegetables. The key manipulations took place as part of the messages that participants received. Although all participants were given the same message ("eat more fruits and vegetables"), a promotion versus prevention focus was manipulated through the concerns (accomplishments versus safety, respectively) that were highlighted within the messages. Additionally, within each regulatory focus condition, participants were asked either to imagine the benefits they would get if they complied with the health message (strategic approach) or the costs they would incur if they did not comply with the health message (strategic avoidance). Participants were asked to keep a nutritional log for the following week;

the critical dependent variable was whether participants in conditions of fit would consume more fruits and vegetables than participants in conditions of nonfit. Indeed, participants in conditions of fit ate more fruits and vegetables in the week following the first session than participants in conditions of nonfit.

All of the work that we have reviewed so far makes clear that approach at the system level may be served by either approach or avoidance strategies. Indeed, the literature in general has paid much more attention to exploring how individuals approach desired end-states than avoid undesired end-states (Higgins, 1997). However, a few studies have examined how avoidance at the system level can also be served by approach or avoidance strategies (Grant, Higgins, Baer, & Bolger, 2006; Higgins et al., 1994). These studies provide further evidence for the independence of the system and strategic levels.

Higgins et al. (1994, Study 2) found support for the notion of the independence of the system and strategic levels in an investigation that included both desired and undesired end-states. Regulatory focus was manipulated by either having participants write a brief essay about how their current hopes and goals changed as they were growing up (promotion manipulation) or how their current duties and obligations changed as they were growing up (prevention manipulation). Participants were then presented with a story about the life of an individual over several days. In the story, the target faced a number of different episodes that differed at the system level (e.g., involved desired versus undesired end-states). The target either used approach or avoidance strategies in dealing with these situations. An example of an episode involving an undesired end-state would be a target who "disliked eating in crowded places." In one version, the target might deal with this undesired end-state by approaching a mismatch: "At noon I picked up a sandwich from a local deli and ate outside." In contrast, the target might deal with this undesired end-state by avoiding a match: "At noon I avoided eating at the school cafeteria." The primary dependent variable was recall for these episodes. The underlying assumption was that activation of the prevention or promotion system should increase accessibility and sensitivity to regulatory forms associated with the activated system, thus impacting recall for episodes that are associated with those forms (Higgins & Tykocinski, 1992). Of particular interest was whether regulatory focus orientation would impact recall at the system or the strategic level.

Participants in a promotion focus had better memory for episodes in which the target used approach strategies (e.g., approaching matches to desired end-states or approaching mismatches to undesired end-states). Recall was better for approach strategies, irrespective of whether the episode involved a desired or undesired end-state. In contrast, participants in a prevention focus had better memory for episodes in which the target used avoidance strategies (e.g., avoiding mismatches to desired end-states, avoiding matches to undesired end-states). Again, recall was better for avoidance strategies, regardless of whether the episode involved a desired or undesired end-state. In other words, regulatory focus orientation involved sensitivity to the strategic ways in which individuals were pursuing desired end-states and avoiding undesired end-states, rather than to sensitivity at the system level.

Grant et al. (2006) further investigated the impact of regulatory fit on coping with undesired end-states (daily life problems). In a daily diary study, participants reported the "most upsetting or bothersome incident" that happened to them each day. Participants also completed a daily measure of distress as well as a coping measure that assessed the use of eager (approach) strategies and vigilant (avoidance) strategies for coping. Prior to beginning the diary portion of the study, all participants completed the regulatory focus questionnaire (Higgins et al., 2001), a chronic measure of regulatory focus that assesses the extent to which participants believe that they have achieved success within the promotion and prevention systems.

Using the principles of regulatory fit theory, Grant et al. (2006) predicted that regulatory fit would increase a strategy's effectiveness by influencing the extent to which individuals would "feel right" about whatever coping strategies they used, thereby directly reducing the experience of distress. Specifically, they predicted that on days when participants used more coping strategies that fit their underlying orientations, they would experience *less* distress. Grant et al. also predicted that there would be a significant impact of nonfit: on days when participants used more coping strategies that did not fit their underlying orientations, they would experience *more* distress. At the system level, all participants were avoiding an undesired end-state (daily stressors). Support for the regulatory fit predictions would provide evidence that there are different strategic ways that individuals can avoid undesired end-states. Both predictions were supported. Promotion-focused individuals who used eager (approach) coping strategies to deal with undesired end-states experienced less distress than promotion-focused individuals who used vigilant (avoidant) coping strategies. Similarly, prevention-focused individuals who used vigilant strategies reported less distress than prevention-focused individuals who used eager coping strategies. It is important to note that there was no main effect of promotion or

prevention pride on distress; chronic regulatory orientation did not affect reactivity to stress. What were critical were the strategic ways in which individuals coped with daily stressors. While there was some evidence in this study that approach strategies generally led to less distress than avoidance strategies, the fit or nonfit between participants' underlying orientations and the strategy employed was especially important for well-being.

STRATEGIES VERSUS TACTICS

In the previous section, we reviewed evidence for the independence of the system and strategic levels of approach and avoidance. We extend our discussion here to explore what it means for the strategic and tactical levels of approach and avoidance to be independent. Tactics reflect the specific ways in which one might approach matches to desired end-states or avoid mismatches to undesired end-states *in a particular context*. Given our supposition that these levels are independent, the tactics that serve a particular strategy may shift depending on the context. While it may be that much of the time, approach tactics are more likely to follow from approach strategies and that avoidance tactics are more likely to follow from avoidance strategies, this will not always be the case. If the strategic and tactical levels of approach and avoidance are independent, then the same approach tactic could serve either strategic approach (eagerness) or strategic avoidance (vigilance), and the same avoidance tactic could serve either strategic approach or strategic avoidance. In addition, the same strategy (eager approach or vigilant avoidance) could be better served by either an approach tactic in one case or an avoidance tactic in another case.

EMPIRICAL EVIDENCE FOR THE STRATEGY–TACTIC DISTINCTION

As reviewed earlier, the original conception of regulatory focus theory made a critical distinction between the system and the strategic levels of approach and avoidance (Higgins, 1997). However, regulatory focus theory has historically tended to conflate the strategic and tactical levels, especially for those predictions made within a signal detection framework (Crowe & Higgins, 1997). As we will see, this was in part because the research emphasis was on those cases where the initial state of the participants was in the neutral to slightly positive region. In the current section, we discuss how recent work within regulatory focus theory—where the initial state is no longer only in the neutral to slightly positive region—makes clear that the strategic and tactical levels of approach and avoidance also need to be treated as independent.

Given that individuals in a promotion focus prefer approach strategies (e.g., eagerly approaching matches to desired end-states), have general concerns with advancement, growth, and accomplishment, and exhibit greater sensitivity to the presence and absence of positive outcomes, the original prediction was that those in a promotion focus would also adopt approach tactics in a signal detection paradigm. In a signal detection paradigm, an individual is differentiating between "signal" and "noise" under uncertainty. Responses are influenced in part by a bias for where one sets the criterion for acceptance. A lenient threshold for acceptance maximizes the chances of hits, while also increasing the chances of false alarms. Within the signal detection framework, a bias to set a lenient threshold has been described as "liberal" or "risky" (Crowe & Higgins, 1997; Swets, 1973; Tanner & Swets, 1954). Thus, given the promotion focus concerns with advancement and the desire to achieve hits or positive outcomes, the prediction was that promotion-focused individuals should exhibit a risky bias in the signal detection framework; they should be willing to incur false alarms to insure hits.

In contrast, individuals in a prevention focus were predicted to exhibit a conservative bias, an avoidance tactic, within the signal detection framework. A conservative bias reflects the adoption of a strict criterion for acceptance. Such a tactic minimizes the chances of false alarms—ensuring correct rejections at the cost of potentially increased misses. Given the prevention focus concerns with security and safety, and the greater sensitivity to the presence and absence of negative outcomes, the prediction was that the avoidance strategies of prevention-focused individuals would also result in avoidance tactics.

Indeed, in two studies that examined regulatory focus tactical differences in a signal detection framework (Crowe & Higgins, 1997; Friedman & Förster, 2001), promotion-focused individuals were shown to have a risky bias (approach tactic) and prevention-focused individuals were shown to have a conservative bias (avoidance tactic). However, both of these studies examined these tactical differences with regards to neutral stimuli—nonwords (Crowe & Higgins, 1997) or neutral words (Friedman & Förster, 2001). It is possible that in the neutral case concordance between approach (avoidance) strategies and approach (avoidance) tactics is more likely. As long as a concordant tactic serves the underlying strategy, it may more easily and naturally be adopted.

When, then, might strategies and tactics diverge? If a concordant tactic no longer serves the strategy, we hypothesized that a tactic that is instrumentally effective should be preferred, even if it is not concordant. Within regulatory focus theory, we thought that a shift in the valence of the signals themselves—from neutral to negative—might demonstrate the independence of strategies and tactics. Given prevention focus concerns with the absence or presence of negative outcomes, an individual in a prevention focus should be especially concerned with negativity in the environment. Prevention-focused individuals should be especially motivated not to "miss" negative objects and events because this negativity poses a direct threat to the primary concern of individuals in a prevention focus—safety and security. Consequently, we predicted that when negative conditions were involved, individuals in a prevention focus would show a willingness to incur false alarms to insure that no negative information is missed—an approach tactic serving their strategic vigilance. If individuals in a prevention focus do adopt risky tactics in order to vigilantly deal with negative conditions, this would be evidence for the independence of the strategic and tactical levels of self-regulation.

We conducted a series of six studies to examine this prediction that prevention-focused individuals would adopt an approach tactic (i.e., a risky bias) when confronting negative signals (Scholer, et al., in press). All of these studies employed the same basic recognition memory signal detection paradigm. Regulatory focus was experimentally manipulated in every study. Across the studies, we tested a number of potential moderators: the nature of the regulatory focus manipulation; the timing of the regulatory focus manipulation; whether valence was manipulated between or within-participants; and the presentation speed of the stimuli. None of these moderators impacted the strength of the basic finding. In *every* study, individuals in a prevention focus exhibited a *risky* bias in the recognition memory signal detection. This bias was risky relative to the conservative bias that prevention-focused participants showed towards positive words *and* relative to the risky bias promotion-focused participants showed towards negative words. A significant meta-analysis confirmed the consistency of this pattern across the six studies. This is clear evidence of the independence of the strategic and tactical levels of approach and avoidance. When conditions are positive, one tactic (a conservative bias, or avoidance tactic) is adopted by participants in a prevention focus to serve their vigilant avoidance strategy; when conditions are negative, a different tactic (a risky bias, or approach tactic) is adopted by participants to serve the same vigilant avoidance strategy.

In other contexts, what kinds of tactics represent approach versus avoidance tendencies? Within the decision-making domain, much attention has been paid to contexts in which individuals are risk-seeking versus risk-averse (Kahneman & Tversky, 1979, 2000). Risk-seeking in the traditional decision-making sense (i.e., choosing gambles over certainty) can be seen as an approach tactic, whereas risk aversion (i.e., preferring certainty over gambles) can be seen as an avoidance tactic. In the signal detection studies we described, we found evidence that tactical approach (a risky bias) could serve a vigilant avoidant strategy. Would we find evidence of this dissociation in other decision-making domains with a different operationalization of a "risky" approach tactic?

We used a stock-investment paradigm to investigate this question (Scholer, Zou, Fujita, Stroessner, & Higgins, 2008). Participants arrived at the lab and completed a battery of questionnaires, including the Self-Guide Strength measure, a measure of chronic promotion-focus strength (the chronic accessibility of ideals) and chronic prevention-focus strength (the chronic accessibility of oughts; see Higgins et al., 1997). After completing these questionnaires, participants were paid for their participation. They were then given a choice to leave the study or to invest their payment in a second, stock-investment study. Participants were told that, in general, participants walked away with additional money in the stock-investment study but that there was a chance that they could lose real money. Most participants decided to invest in the stock-investment study.

After making their initial investment decision, participants tracked the performance of their stock over time. At the end of the first round, all participants learned that they had lost not only their original investment but also additional money (manipulation checks confirmed that participants did indeed experience their situation as a real loss). At this point, participants were given a choice between investing in two stocks for the second round of the study, a risky stock and a conservative stock. The expected value of these stocks was equivalent, but the risky stock was riskier both in the objective sense that its variance was greater (Markowitz, 1952) and in the subjective sense (participants rated the risky stock as riskier). In a state of loss, would prevention-focused participants prefer the riskier stock? Indeed, as chronic prevention-focus strength increased, the probability of selecting the risky option also increased substantially.

In this first stock-investment study, only the risky option had the potential of returning participants to their break-even point. Given that the underlying motivation of prevention-focused individuals concerns doing what is necessary to remain secure, to restore safety, this choice necessitated a risky option: it was the only tactic that

could return participants to "safety." Interested in exploring more deeply what might be motivating the risky choice of prevention-focused participants in this study, we considered what might happen if prevention-focused participants had the option of a conservative tactic that *could* return them to their break-even point. If a conservative tactic could return them to the status quo, to safety, the necessity of choosing a risky tactic would no longer exist. We predicted that in this case they would evince a stronger preference for the conservative avoidance tactic because it more naturally suits the vigilant avoidance strategy preferred by individuals in a prevention focus. While the instrumental effectiveness of the tactics will normally triumph, when tactics are equivalent in instrumentality, we propose that there may be a preference for tactic–strategy concordance. Specifically, the notion was that if both a risky approach tactic and a conservative avoidance tactic served the vigilant avoidance strategy of restoring the status quo (restoring safety), participants with a strong prevention focus would prefer the conservative avoidance tactic.

To examine this question, we ran a second study replicating the first stock-investment study with the addition of a new condition. In the new condition, participants had a choice between the same risky stock and a new conservative stock that did have the potential to get participants back to their break-even point. As in the other condition, the expected value of these stocks was equivalent but the risky stock was riskier both in the objective and subjective sense. We replicated the findings of Study 1 in the original condition where the conservative option would *not* bring participants back to safety (the status quo); as prevention-focus strength increased, participants were more likely to choose the risky option. However, when prevention-focused participants had a conservative option that *could* return them to safety, their tactical preference shifted dramatically back to a clear preference for the conservative tactic. Within the same study, then, we have clear evidence of the independence of the strategic and tactical levels of approach and avoidance in self-regulation. In one condition (where the conservation choice would not restore the status quo), an approach tactic (the risky stock) served a vigilant avoidance strategy, whereas in the other condition (where the conservation choice *would* restore the status quo), an avoidance tactic (the conservative stock) served the vigilant avoidance strategy.

Thus, there is evidence both within the classic "signal versus noise" signal detection framework and within the traditional "choosing between options" decision-making framework that approach and avoidance strategies (eagerness versus vigilance) are independent of approach and avoidance tactics. The empirical evidence we presented in this section highlighted how a vigilant avoidance strategy can be served by both approach and avoidance tactics. We are currently exploring the flip side of this issue: when and how eager approach strategies might be served by avoidance, as well as approach, tactics.

APPROACH AND AVOIDANCE HIERARCHIES: MULTIPLE PERSPECTIVES

In this chapter, we have illustrated one way of conceptualizing a hierarchy of approach and avoidance motivations. Our model is inspired by regulatory focus theory, which historically emphasized the different *strategic* ways that individuals can approach desirable end-states or avoid undesirable end-states as reference points at the system level, and that recently recognizes the different *tactical* ways that individuals can serve their strategic preferences. Our model shares similarities with Elliot and colleagues' (Elliot, 2006; Elliot & Church, 1997; Elliot, Gable, & Mapes, 2006; Gable, 2006) hierarchical model of approach and avoidance motivation but differs in both significant and subtle ways in how we parse and define the levels within the hierarchy.

Both models emphasize that the highest level does not specify *how* individuals go about approaching or avoiding. In our characterization, the system level is akin to a goal: "I want to approach a good marriage" versus "I want to avoid a bad marriage." In Elliot's model, goals per se do not enter at the highest level; rather, this level reflects underlying approach and avoidance motives and temperaments. Goals enter as mid-level constructs that specify how individuals strategically go about addressing the underlying approach and avoidance motives and temperaments. Thus, goals for Elliot provide direction for the underlying motives and temperaments and in some ways incorporate aspects of both the system and strategic levels of our model (e.g., achievement goals such as "My goal in this class is to get a better grade than most of the students" or "I just want to avoid doing poorly in this class") (Elliot & Church, 1997).

Much of the work exploring the implications of Elliot's hierarchical model of approach and avoidance motivation has been done in the achievement domain, exploring differences between two types of approach goals (performance-approach goals, mastery-approach goals) and two types of avoidance goals (performance-avoidance goals, mastery-avoidance goals) (Elliot & Church, 1997; Elliot & McGregor, 2001). Recently, the hierarchical model of approach and avoidance motivation has been extended to the social domain, examining differences in goals reflecting positive social outcomes (approaching affiliation and intimacy) versus goals involving negative social outcomes (avoiding rejection and conflict) (Elliot, Gable, & Mapes, 2006; Gable, 2006). These goals represent the channels through which approach and avoidance motives and temperaments are "concretized"; the independence in the approach and avoidance hierarchy posited by Elliot and colleagues is that an avoidance motive disposition (e.g., need to avoid failure) can be served by an approach goal (e.g., performance-approach goal, such as "I am motivated by the thought of outperforming my peers in this class") (Elliot & Church, 1997). Our model takes this a step further by positing that approach (avoidance) *goals* can be served by *either* approach or avoidance strategies. Furthermore, in our conception, both an approach strategy and an avoidance strategy *can* serve either approaching desirable or avoiding undesirable end-states (or reference points). Our model also goes further by distinguishing approach and avoidance tactics from approach and avoidance strategies.

While these approaches differ in emphasis, there are many ways in which they complement each other's strengths and share a common perspective. While the approach–avoidance hierarchy of Elliot and colleagues emphasizes the interactions between dispositional motives and temperaments and goals, we focus primarily on the relations among goals, strategies, and tactics. It will be interesting in future work to consider how these two approaches might together suggest new ways in which to study approach and avoidance motivations in self-regulation. For instance, Elliot (2006) has suggested that "avoidance motivation is posited to be problematic at all levels of the hierarchy" (p. 115; see also Elliot & Sheldon, 1997, 1998; Emmons, 1996). However, this perspective emerges primarily in reference to the dispositional and goal levels of the hierarchy. We do not disagree that avoidance at those levels (or at the system level in our model) often leads to poorer outcomes. However, we argue that avoidance at the *strategic* level, or at the *tactical* level, is *not* inherently problematic. Indeed, regulatory fit theory provides evidence of times when avoidance strategies lead to better performance (Förster et al., 2001), enjoyment (Freitas & Higgins, 2002), and subjective well-being (Grant et al., 2006).

We have also emphasized in this chapter that despite promotion sometimes being characterized as synonymous with systemic approach and prevention with systemic avoidance (cf. Gable, 2006), promotion and prevention orientations are *not* the same as approach and avoidance at the system level. In part, we suspect that this confusion has arisen because at the strategic level of the approach and avoidance hierarchy, rather than the system level, such parallels *can* be drawn. Further, some measures of approach and avoidance orientations, such as the well-known Carver and White (1994) BAS/BIS questionnaire, have tended to emphasize promotion system concerns and eager-related tactics in the approach scales, perhaps causing scientists to perceive too strong an association between BAS, *as measured in this questionnaire,* and promotion focus (cf. Eddington, Dolcos, Cabeza, Krishnan, & Strauman, in press). It is also possible that this confusion reflects an actuarial reality that promotion goals tend to be reflected more often in approach at the system level and prevention goals may tend to be reflected more often in avoidance at the system level. Indeed, a preference for eager strategies and the concerns of the promotion system do result in greater sensitivity to the presence and absence of positive outcomes, just as a preference for vigilant strategies and the concerns of the prevention system result in greater sensitivity to the absence and presence of negative outcomes. However, although individuals in a promotion- or prevention-focused state have differential sensitivity to positive and negative outcomes, this does not mean that promotion-focused individuals only pursue desired end-states and that prevention-focused individuals only avoid undesired end-states. At the system level, both promotion- and prevention-focused individuals avoid undesired end-states and approach desired end-states. Thus, when measuring or manipulating approach and avoidance at the system level, it is important to differentiate between whether an individual is pursuing a desired end-state and whether that individual is in a promotion- or prevention-focused state.

Consideration of the dimension of regulatory focus at the system level further suggests that beyond the benefits of pursuing approach versus avoidance, there are additional benefits that result when there is a fit between an individual's regulatory focus orientation and the approach or avoidance *strategy* that is employed. For all individuals, approaching a desired end-state (e.g., good marriage) is posited to typically result in better outcomes than avoiding an undesired end-state (e.g., bad marriage). However, imagine two individuals both pursuing a good marriage. A promotion-focused individual is likely to represent that end-state as an ideal whereas a prevention-focused individual is likely to represent that end-state as an ought. Given the different ways in which these individuals represent the desired end-state at the system level, eager approach strategies will result in better outcomes for the promotion-focused individual and vigilant avoidance strategies will result in better outcomes for the prevention-focused individual; in other words, regulatory fit produces better outcomes. Thus, the idea that "approach

is better" at all levels of the hierarchy does not hold up when one considers the orthogonal but related dimension of regulatory focus at the system level. This also suggests that the fit between one's underlying regulatory focus orientation and the employed strategy may have a greater impact on well-being than the compatibility or concordance between approach (avoidance) at the system level and approach (avoidance) at the strategic level.

TARGETING THE HIERARCHY: IMPLICATIONS FOR INTERVENTIONS

In this closing section, we would like to explore briefly some potential implications of how thinking about approach and avoidance in this way might be of interest not only for understanding self-regulation in theory, but also in practice. The interest that many of us have in self-regulation is motivated, at least in part, by an understanding of how to make real differences for the ways that individuals struggle to self-regulate effectively (Vohs & Baumeister, 2004). How might thinking about distinctions between the system, strategic, and tactical levels of approach and avoidance help us design and target interventions that are more effective?

Individuals sometimes have maladaptive strategies for getting along in the world; these strategies are also served by more (or less) adaptive tactics, depending on the context. If one accepts the premise that the strategic and tactical levels of self-regulation are independent, it follows that interventions could be targeted at either the strategic or the tactical level. Although speculative, it seems plausible that in some cases, it may be easier to help an individual to first adopt new, more adaptive tactics (framed as serving an existing strategy) and then work to modify or challenge the underlying strategy if needed. Imagine an individual who has the goal of avoiding rejection (system-level avoidance). She may adopt an avoidance strategy (avoid matches to rejection); this strategy can be served by multiple tactics. For example, she could preemptively reject after conflict (Downey, Freitas, Michaelis, & Khouri, 1998), self-silence her own needs in the face of potential rejection (Ayduk, May, Downey, & Higgins, 2003), or increase ingratiation efforts (Romero-Canyas & Downey, 2005). While all of these tactics serve the underlying strategy, some may be preferred because they are less maladaptive in certain situations (though admittedly all are maladaptive to some extent). Additionally, there may well be other, even more adaptive tactics that could be implemented. Thus, if the underlying systemic and strategic preferences are harder to initially alter, the adoption of more adaptive tactics might be an easier first step.

Such an approach reflects a potential therapeutic advantage of considering hierarchies of self-regulation.

The Grant et al. (2006) diary study suggests a further implication of the present model of approach and avoidance motivations. In the daily diary study, promotion-focused individuals who used eager coping strategies to cope with a stressor did better than promotion-focused individuals who used vigilant coping strategies, whereas the reverse was true for prevention-focused individuals. Thus, interventions that identify the best way to frame a coping strategy in terms of approach versus avoidance for a given client may be particularly effective. For instance, people suffering from clinical depression tend to have a dominant promotion focus, and those suffering from clinical anxiety tend to have a dominant prevention focus (Strauman, 1992). If new (and generally positive) tactics for coping with the client's everyday problems are being proposed (e.g., by the therapist), then it would make sense to frame a new intervention tactic as serving an eager (approach) strategy for the depressed client and as serving a vigilant (avoidance) strategy for the anxious client— thereby intensifying the attractiveness of the tactical activity to the client and increasing the likelihood that he or she will engage in it. For example, the tactics of choosing to exercise more or to improve one's eating habits, which benefit clients with either type of clinical problem, could be framed differentially. In other words, the tactical direction of the therapist to these two clients could be the same (e.g., "begin an exercise regimen") but the framing of the tactic could be tailored to reflect the eager approach or vigilant avoidance strategy that would be most motivating given the client's underlying system-level symptoms and diagnosis (promotion-related depression or prevention-related anxiety).

In closing, we have found that thinking about approach and avoidance motivations at the system, strategic, and tactical levels has been generative for us in exploring both theoretical and applied issues. Although we have begun to answer some questions, our exploration raises as many (or more) new questions as it answers. But that is as it should be. We ourselves have struggled with the difficulties in clearly defining these levels and certainly recognize that our way of parsing these motivations is not the only alternative. We believe that the field is entering a new conceptual growth period for the study of approach and avoidance motivations in self-regulation, and thus it is timely for this volume to appear. We also believe that identifying the levels at which individuals are approaching or avoiding is critical in order to fully understand and predict effective and ineffective self-regulation.

ACKNOWLEDGMENT

The research reported in this paper was supported by Grant 39429 from the National Institute of Mental Health to E. Tory Higgins. Correspondence concerning this chapter may be sent to E. Tory Higgins, Department of Psychology, Columbia University, Schermerhorn Hall 406, 1190 Amsterdam Avenue, New York, 10027.

REFERENCES

Avnet, T., & Higgins, E. T. (2003). Locomotion, assessment, and regulatory fit: Value transfer from "how" to "what." *Journal of Experimental Social Psychology, 39,* 525–530.

Ayduk, O., May, D., Downey, G., & Higgins, E. T. (2003). Tactical differences in coping with rejection sensitivity: The role of prevention pride. *Personality and Social Psychology Bulletin, 29,* 435–448.

Bianco, A. T., Higgins, E. T., & Klem, A. (2003). How "fun/importance" fit affects performance: Relating implicit theories to instructions. *Personality and Social Psychology Bulletin, 29,* 1091–1103.

Bowlby, J. (1969). *Attachment (attachment and loss, Vol.1).* New York: Basic Books.

Bowlby, J. (1973). *Separation: Anxiety and anger (attachment and loss, Vol.2).* New York: Basic Books.

Brendl, C. M., & Higgins, E. T. (1995). Principles of judging valence: What makes events positive or negative? *Advances in Experimental Social Psychology, 28,* 95–160.

Brown, J. S. (1948). Gradients of approach and avoidance responses and their relation to motivation. *Journal of Comparative and Physiological Psychology, 41,* 450–465.

Cantor, N., & Kihlstrom, J. F. (1987). *Personality and social intelligence.* Englewood Cliffs, NJ: Prentice Hall.

Carver, C. S., & Scheier, M. F. (1981). *Attention and self-regulation: A control theory approach to human behavior.* New York: Springer-Verlag.

Carver, C. S., & Scheier, M. F. (1990). Origins and functions of positive and negative effect: A control-process view. *Psychological Review, 97,* 19–35.

Carver, C. S., & Scheier, M. F. (1998). *On the self-regulation of behavior.* Cambridge: Cambridge University Press.

Carver, C. S., Sutton, S. K., & Scheier, M. F. (2000). Action, emotion, and personality: Emerging conceptual integration. *Personality and Social Psychology Bulletin, 26,* 741–751.

Carver, C. S., & White, T. L. (1994). Behavioral inhibition, behavioral activation, and affective responses to impending reward and punishment: The BIS/BAS scales. *Journal of Personality and Social Psychology, 67,* 319–333.

Crowe, E., & Higgins, E. T. (1997). Regulatory focus and strategic inclinations: Promotion and prevention in decision-making. *Organizational Behavior & Human Decision Processes, 69,* 117–132.

Downey, G., Freitas, A. L., Michaelis, B., & Khouri, H. (1998). The self-fulfilling prophecy in close relationships: Rejection sensitivity and rejection by romantic partners. *Journal of Personality and Social Psychology*, 75, 545–560.

Eddington, K. M., Dolcos, F., Cabeza, R., Krishnan, K. R. R., & Strauman, T. J. (2007). Neural correlates of promotion and prevention goal activation: An fMRI study using an idiographic approach. *Journal of Cognitive Neuroscience*, 19, 1152–1162.

Elliot, A. J. (2006). The hierarchical model of approach–avoidance motivation. *Motivation and Emotion*, 30, 111–116.

Elliot, A. J., & Church, M. A. (1997). A hierarchical model of approach and avoidance achievement motivation. *Journal of Personality and Social Psychology*, 72, 218–232.

Elliot, A. J., Gable, S. L., & Mapes, R. R. (2006). Approach and avoidance motivation in the social domain. *Personality and Social Psychology Bulletin*, 32, 378–391.

Elliot, A. J., & Harackiewicz, J. M. (1996). Approach and avoidance achievement goals and intrinsic motivation: A mediational analysis. *Journal of Personality and Social Psychology*, 70, 461–475.

Elliot, A. J., & McGregor, H. A. (2001). A 2×2 achievement goal framework. *Journal of Personality and Social Psychology*, 80, 501–519.

Elliot, A. J., & Sheldon, K. M. (1997). Avoidance achievement motivation: A personal goals analysis. *Journal of Personality and Social Psychology*, 73, 171–175.

Elliot, A. J., & Sheldon, K. M. (1998). Avoidance personal goals and the personality–illness relationship. *Journal of Personality and Social Psychology*, 75, 1282–1299.

Elliot, A. J., Sheldon, K. M., & Church, M. A. (1997). Avoidance personal goals and subjective well-being. *Personality and Social Psychology Bulletin*, 23, 915–927.

Elliot, A. J., & Thrash, T. M. (2001). Achievement goals and the hierarchical model of achievement motivation. *Educational Psychology Review*, 13, 139–156.

Elliot, A. J., & Thrash, T. M. (2002). Approach–avoidance motivation in personality: Approach and avoidance temperaments and goals. *Journal of Personality and Social Psychology*, 82, 804–818.

Emmons, R. A. (1996). Striving and feeling: Personal goals and subjective well-being. In P. M. Gollwitzer & J. A. Bargh (Eds.), *The psychology of action: Linking cognition to motivation to behavior* (pp. 313–337). New York: The Guilford Press.

Förster, J., Grant, H., Idson, L. C., & Higgins, E. T. (2001). Success/failure feedback, expectancies, and approach/avoidance motivation: How regulatory focus moderates classic relations. *Journal of Experimental Social Psychology*, 37, 253–260.

Förster, J., Higgins, E. T., & Idson, L. C. (1998). Approach and avoidance strength during goal attainment: Regulatory focus and the "goal looms larger" effect. *Journal of Personality and Social Psychology*, 75, 1115–1131.

Fowles, D. C. (1980). The three arousal model: Implications of Gray's two-factor learning theory for heart rate, electrodermal activity, and psychopathy. *Psychophysiology*, 17, 87–104.

Fowles, D. C. (1987). Application of a behavioral theory of motivation to the concepts of anxiety and impulsivity. *Journal of Research in Personality*, 21, 417–435.

Freitas, A. L., & Higgins, E. T. (2002). Enjoying goal-directed action: The role of regulatory fit. *Psychological Science*, 13, 1–6.

Freud, S. (1952). *A general introduction to psychoanalysis*. New York: Washington Square Press. (Original work published 1920).

Friedman, R. S., & Förster, J. (2001). The effects of promotion and prevention cues on creativity. *Journal of Personality and Social Psychology*, 81, 1001–1013.

Gable, S. L. (2006). Approach and avoidance social motives and goals. *Journal of Personality*, 74, 175–222.

Gable, S. L., Reis, H. T., & Elliot, A. J. (2003). Evidence for bivariate systems: An empirical test of appetition and aversion across domains. *Journal of Research in Personality*, 37, 349–372.

Gray, J. A. (1982). *The neuropsychology of anxiety: An enquiry into the functions of the septo-hippocampal system*. New York: Oxford University Press.

Gray, J. A. (1990). Brain systems that mediate both emotion and cognition. *Cognition and Emotion*, 4, 269–288.

Grant, H., Higgins, E. T., Baer, A., & Bolger, N. (2006). *Coping style and regulatory fit: Emotional ups and downs in life.* Unpublished Manuscript.

Higgins, E. T. (1987). Self-discrepancy: A theory relating self and affect. *Psychological Review*, 94, 319–340.

Higgins, E. T. (1997). Beyond pleasure and pain. *American Psychologist*, 52, 1280–1300.

Higgins, E. T. (2000). Making a good decision: Value from fit. *American Psychologist*, 55, 1217–1230.

Higgins, E. T. (2006). Value from hedonic experience and engagement. *Psychological Review*, 113, 439–460.

Higgins, E. T., Friedman, R. S., Harlow, R. E., Idson, L. C., Ayduk, O. N., & Taylor, A. (2001). Achievement orientations from subjective histories of success: Promotion pride versus prevention pride. *European Journal of Social Psychology*, 31, 3–23.

Higgins, E. T., Idson, L. C., Freitas, A. L., Spiegel, S., & Molden, D. C. (2003). Transfer of value from fit. *Journal of Personality and Social Psychology*, 84, 1140–1153.

Higgins, E. T., Roney, C. J. R., Crowe, E., & Hymes, C. (1994). Ideal versus ought predilections for approach and avoidance: Distinct self-regulatory systems. *Journal of Personality and Social Psychology*, 66, 276–286.

Higgins, E. T., Shah, J., & Friedman, R. (1997). Emotional responses to goal attainment: Strength of regulatory focus as moderator. *Journal of Personality and Social Psychology*, 72, 515–525.

Higgins, E. T., & Tykocinski, O. (1992). Self-discrepancies and biographical memory: Personality and cognition at the level of psychological situation. *Personality and Social Psychology Bulletin*, 18, 527–535.

Kahneman, D., & Tversky, A. (1979). Prospect theory: An analysis of decision under risk. *Econometrica*, 47, 263–291.

Kahneman, D., & Tversky, A. (2000). *Choices, values, and frames*. New York: Cambridge University Press.

Lang, P. J. (1995). The emotion probe: Studies of motivation and attention. *American Psychologist, 50*, 372–385.

Lewin, K. (1935). *A dynamic theory of personality.* New York: McGraw-Hill.

Losco, J., & Epstein, S. (1977). Relative steepness of approach and avoidance gradients as a function of magnitude and valence of incentive. *Journal of Abnormal Psychology, 86*, 360–368.

Markowitz, H. (1952). Portfolio selection. *Journal of Finance, 7*, 77–91.

Miller, G. A., Galanter, E., & Pribram, K. H. (1960). *Plans and the structure of behavior.* New York: Henry Holt and Co.

Miller, N. E. (1944). Experimental studies of conflict. In J. McV. Hunt (Ed.), *Personality and the behavior disorders* (Vol. 1, pp. 431–465). New York: Ronald Press.

Miller, N. E. (1959). Liberalization of basic S-R concepts: Extensions to conflict behavior, motivation, and social learning. In S. Koch (Ed.), *Psychology: A study of a science—General systematic formulations, learning and special processes* (Vol. 2, pp. 196–292). New York: McGraw-Hill.

Mowrer, O. H. (1960). *Learning theory and behavior.* New York: Wiley.

Pervin, L. A. (1989). Goal concepts in personality and social psychology: A historical introduction. In L. A. Pervin (Ed.), *Goal concepts in personality and social psychology* (pp. 1–17). Hillsdale, NJ: Lawrence Erlbaum Associates.

Pervin, L. A. (2001). A dynamic systems approach to personality. *European Psychologist, 6*, 172–176.

Romero-Canyas, R., & Downey, G. (2005). Rejection sensitivity as a predictor of affective and behavioral responses to interpersonal stress: A defensive motivational system. In K. D. Williams, J. P. Forgas, & W. von Hippel (Eds.), *The social outcast: Ostracism, social exclusion, rejection, and bullying* (pp. 131–154). New York: Psychology Press.

Scholer, A. A., Zou, X., Fujita, K., Stroessner, S. J., & Higgins, E. T. (2008). When risk-seeking becomes a motivational necessity. *Manuscript under review.*

Scholer, A. A., Stroessner, S. J., & Higgins, E. T. (in press). Responding to negativity: How a risky tactic can serve a vigilant strategy. *Journal of Experimental Social Psychology.*

Shah, J., Higgins, E. T., & Friedman, R. S. (1998). Performance incentives and means: How regulatory focus influences goal attainment. *Journal of Personality and Social Psychology, 74*, 285–293.

Smith, N. W. (1965). GSR measures of cigarette smokers' temporal approach and avoidance gradients. *Psychological Record, 15*, 261–268.

Smith, N. W. (1969). Spatial conflict gradients of cigarette smokers: A methodology. *Journal of General Psychology, 80*, 287–290.

Spiegel, S., Grant-Pillow, H., & Higgins, E. T. (2004). How regulatory fit enhances motivational strength during goal pursuit. *European Journal of Social Psychology, 34*, 39–54.

Strauman, T. J. (1992). Self-guides, autobiographical memory, and anxiety and dysphoria: Toward a cognitive model of vulnerability to emotional distress. *Journal of Abnormal Psychology, 101*, 87–95.

Swets, J. A. (1973). The relative operating characteristic in psychology. *Science, 182*, 990–1000.

Tanner, W. P., Jr., & Swets, J. A. (1954). A decision-making theory of visual detection. *Psychological Review, 61*, 401–409.

Vallacher, R. R., & Wegner, D. M. (1985). *A theory of action identification.* Hillsdale, NJ: Lawrence Erlbaum Associates.

Vallacher, R. R., & Wegner, D. M. (1987). What do people think they're doing? Action identification and human behavior. *Psychological Review, 94*, 3–15.

Vohs, K., & Baumeister, R. F. (2004). Understanding self-regulation: An introduction. In R. F. Baumeister & K. D. Vohs (Eds.), *Handbook of self-regulation: Research, theory, and applications* (pp. 1–9). New York: The Guilford Press.

Self-Esteem and Self-Concept

30 Approach and Avoidance Motivations in the Self-Concept and Self-Esteem

Dianne M. Tice and E. J. Masicampo

CONTENTS

How do we come to know ourselves and what impact does our self-knowledge have on the way we behave? Over time, each of us gathers information that instructs us of who we are and what we are like. We learn about ourselves through our experiences, and we form positive or negative evaluations for the various characteristics we perceive ourselves to have. Social psychologists refer to these aspects of self-knowledge collectively as the self-concept. Our self-concepts provide us with information about ourselves, and this information in turn influences the actions we take and the goals we decide to pursue. If we know that we like something, then we seek it out. If we think we can accomplish a task, then we will happily engage it. The purpose of this chapter is to examine these relationships—namely, how knowledge about one's self is tied to motivated behavior.

This chapter will review the relationship between motivation and the self-concept, particularly with regard to self-esteem and approach and avoidance motivations. Many of our motivations are driven not merely by the content of our self-concepts, but by the way we evaluate our self-concepts, or our levels of self-esteem. Each of us expends a great deal of energy toward maintaining certain (usually positive) evaluations of ourselves and this self-esteem maintenance can manifest itself in a wide range of behaviors, including self-handicapping (Tice, 1991), world view defense (Greenberg, Pyszczynski, & Solomon, 1986), and aggressive behavior toward others (Tesser, 1988). Furthermore, by utilizing the approach–avoidance distinction, we can gain a better understanding of when, why, and by whom these various behaviors are likely to be performed.

We will review the social psychological literature with a special focus on findings related to the function of self-esteem, how self-esteem has been defined and measured, and the behaviors individuals engage in that relate to self-esteem maintenance. As we review this literature, we will make reference to two primary modes by which the self-concept and self-esteem relate to approach and avoidance motivations. First, we review evidence that individual differences in self-esteem level relate to dispositional tendencies toward approach- and avoidance-related behaviors. We will also expound on these findings by suggesting ways that the more distinct self-esteem components may relate to motivated behavior. Second, we suggest that the content of individuals' self-concepts can help predict the contexts under which approach and avoidance behaviors will be engaged.

Before starting, it is vital to acknowledge that self-esteem is discussed and conceptualized in two very different ways by social and personality psychologists, and that these different ways have quite different implications for approach and avoidance motivation. One widespread conceptualization emphasizes individual differences in level of self-esteem (and related traits). As we shall propose, these different levels of self-esteem are associated with different kinds of social strategies. In particular, high self-esteem appears to foster an approach strategy, whereas low self-esteem is associated with more avoidance strategies. The other conceptualization treats self-esteem as itself a motivation rather than a trait, in the sense that people are widely seen as striving to think well of themselves. The self-esteem motive can be deconstructed into self-enhancement, which is primarily an approach motive in the sense that one seeks to approach positive outcomes, and self-protection, which is mainly concerned with the avoidance of failure and loss. We shall suggest, furthermore, that the trait and the motivation are intertwined.

PURSUIT OF SELF-ESTEEM

The notion that people strive to think well of themselves, and that they also strive to be well thought of by others, is hardly new in modern social psychology. On the contrary, it is a relatively ancient observation and underlies many conceptions of human vanity and hypocrisy. Pride—especially puffing up an inflated, unwarranted sense of superiority over others—was regarded by medieval theologians as one of the Seven Deadly Sins. Before them, hubris was presented as one of humankind's most dangerous failings in ancient mythology, and humans who fancied themselves to be on the level with the gods were often punished with severe comeuppances.

Functions of Self-Esteem

The benefits of having high self-esteem are manifold and some researchers have argued that the motive to see one's self in a positive regard is universal (Sedikides, Gaertner, & Toguchi, 2003). However, researchers have

largely taken for granted the fact that each of us has a desire to see ourselves in a positive light (however, see Swann, 1997 for an important opposing view). Few have bothered to ask why this is so. What is the function of self-esteem? Why is high self-esteem beneficial at all and why should we seek it?

There are two major social psychological models as they relate to this issue: terror management theory (TMT; Greenberg et al., 1986) and sociometer theory (Leary, Tambor, Terdal, & Downs, 1995; Leary & Baumeister, 2000). Each theory provides a framework for understanding both why we have self-esteem and what we do to maintain it.

Greenberg and colleagues (1986) put forth the idea that self-esteem serves as a buffer against the potentially paralyzing anxiety brought about by the awareness of one's own mortality. Based on the work of cultural anthropologist Ernest Becker, TMT suggests that one uniquely human characteristic is that we are each aware of our own impending death. This awareness of mortality coupled with the inborn urge to defy death causes a potentially paralyzing anxiety within each individual. Accordingly, we use culture and religion to achieve symbolic immortality, thereby defeating on some level the looming threat of death. Furthermore, self-esteem informs us of whether or not we are adhering to the culture to which we feel we belong.

According to Sociometer Theory (Leary et al., 1995), self-esteem serves as a gauge that informs us of our level of inclusion with others. This theory is based on the idea that humans rely on others to survive, thus belonging to social groups is an innate human need (Baumeister & Leary, 1995). As such, social exclusion is seen as detrimental to human functioning and survival, and self-esteem is suggested as the primary tool by which we avoid any instances of social rejection. Inclusion from others makes us feel good, and so we seek acceptance as a form of self-esteem fulfillment. Exclusion decreases self-esteem, and so when we try to boost our self-esteem we work to once again gain acceptance from others.

Why is the purpose of self-esteem important for the approach–avoidance distinction? Each theory of self-esteem has unique consequences for self-esteem maintenance and how approach and avoidance motivations should be understood as they relate to self-esteem. The authors of Sociometer Theory, for instance, suggest that "human beings possess a fundamental motive to seek inclusion and to avoid exclusion from important social groups" (Leary et al., 1995, p. 519). Thus, self-esteem related approach behaviors should be manifested in one's behavior toward maintaining interpersonal relationships, whereas self-esteem related avoidant behaviors should come in the form of avoiding social exclusion and rejection. On the other hand, TMT focuses on self-esteem as an anxiety buffer. From this perspective, self-esteem maintenance should be particularly important when threats to mortality-related anxiety are high. Moreover, one might expect that (risky) acts of self-enhancement will be relatively higher and acts of self-protection lower when mortality concerns are absent and thus pose no threat to the individual.

Where the two theories overlap is also informative for our understanding of approach and avoidance motivations. To the extent that self-esteem is conceptualized as a buffer against mortality-related anxiety, or as a monitor that warns a person of harmful social-exclusion situations, both theories seem to frame self-esteem maintenance as a largely avoidant behavior. This may have larger consequences for motivation as a whole, beyond behaviors directly related to self-esteem or the self-concept. Self-esteem maintenance then may relate to avoidant behaviors in general, such that individuals will behave in avoidant, self-protective ways when a self-esteem threat is present. Conversely then, perhaps approach behaviors are only possible when self-esteem is high and threats to self-esteem are absent. This idea is consistent with the suggestion by Baumeister, Campbell, Krueger, and Vohs (2003) that high self-esteem seems beneficial only to the extent that it impels behavior. Baumeister et al. (2003) suggested that high self-esteem appears linked to greater initiative. People with high self-esteem are, for example, said to initiate behaviors more and persist longer in the face of failure. Thus, when self-esteem maintenance is unnecessary and esteem needs are met, individuals are free to seek other behaviors and to adopt a general approach orientation toward goals.

Do people seek self-esteem beyond its functional level? In other words, do people seek high levels of self-esteem for its own sake or only in the face of ego-threats such as mortality salience or social exclusion? If self-esteem is seen largely as a defense mechanism, then it may best be understood through the scope of avoidant behavior.

The following section reviews some documented cases of self-esteem maintenance. While previous research has not focused on the approach and avoidance distinction in relation to self-esteem maintenance, we review the previous research with this distinction in mind, and we suggest likely instances of this fundamental separation. Patterns in this research are consistent with the proposed idea that individual differences in self-esteem level produce differences in approach and avoidance behaviors.

SELF-DECEPTION: APPROACHING GOOD, AVOIDING BAD

Modern psychology owes a debt to Calvinist Protestantism, because the Calvinists developed a much more thorough understanding of self-deception than had prevailed earlier. Calvin held that because God knows everything, God knows whether each person is going to end up in heaven or in hell, in which case everyone's fate is already "predestined." Calvin added that it was usually possible to figure which of those fates awaited any particular person, especially because God tended to favor the Elect with worldly success to complement their virtuous piety and good works. Generations of Calvinists therefore became fascinated with trying to persuade themselves that they were headed for heaven. Along the way, they noticed that their neighbors were likewise trying to fancy themselves members of the Elect, and they became aware of how people try to twist the facts to furnish a flattering picture of self.

Self-deception, as documented in today's research laboratories, is perhaps less focused than in the Puritan era on persuading oneself about one's eternal fate. (How much this reflects a change in the self-deceptive goals of individuals, and how much it reflects the relatively secular emphases of modern research methods, could be debated to some extent.) But the basic truth continues to be widely assumed and often confirmed. People twist and spin the facts so as to enable them to think well of themselves. We now summarize some of the patterns of self-deception that psychologists have documented.

By self-deception we mean the broad range of cognitive strategies people employ in order to enable them to think well of themselves. This broad definition is more in keeping with everyday, colloquial usages of the term and with modern research findings, as opposed to stricter and narrower definitions that required proof that the same person can both know something and not know it simultaneously (Sackeim & Gur, 1979). It does assume that people have a basic self-esteem motivation, which is to say they are driven to create and hold generally favorable views of themselves. This assumption—that pretty much everyone desires a measure of self-respect and self-esteem—appears uncontroversial in modern social psychology as practiced in Western civilizations, although there remain some questions about cultural relativity. In particular, Heine, Lehman, Markus, and Kitayama (1999) proposed that Japanese persons do not have the same "self-enhancement" motive and instead strive for humility and self-improvement. But perhaps there are commonalities even there, insofar as Japanese too seek the respect of others and like to regard them-selves as good members of valued groups (Sedikides et al., 2003). Perhaps the Japanese have the same goal of being a good person and are simply more disciplined than others at rejecting self-deception as a way to get there, so that substantive goodness rather than cognitive distortion is the most effective means of satisfying this goal. This may be reflected in the Japanese orientation toward self-improvement, as well as their cultural tradi-tion of committing suicide in response to personal disgrace.

It is certainly clear that, at least from the perspective of what is best for society, becoming a better person is the preferred way to earn self-esteem. But that requires hard work, discipline, and the sacrifices of virtue. Thus, it is probably not surprising that many persons, at least in the West, occasionally indulge in self-deception. Self-deception offers a shortcut to self-esteem. Instead of actually becoming a better person, one can simply con-vince oneself that one already is a better person. The path of self-congratulation is ever gentler and less steep than the path of virtue.

Self-deception, as practiced by modern Westerners and observed by social psychologists, is often a liberal mix of approach and avoidance. Self-deception is essen-tially a manipulation of information. One approaches information (and/or its implications) that offers positive views of self, and one avoids information (and implica-tions) that threaten negative views of self. Let us review some of the relevant findings.

The self-serving bias is a well-documented pattern by which people interpret events in ways that benefit their self-esteem. A review by Zuckerman (1979) concluded already at that early date that the evidence was consistent and robust. The essence of the self-serving bias is that people attribute outcomes in a biased manner. Success is attributed to internal causes, whereas failure is attributed to external causes. This well-documented pattern can be decomposed into two biases. Success is approached, in the sense that it is pulled closer to the self by means of embracing it and seizing responsibility. Failure is avoided, in that the self distances itself from it and from responsi-bility for it.

Information processing strategies also use selective approach and avoidance in the service of self-deception. One of these is simply to devote more time to thinking about and elaborating on good information than bad information (Crary, 1966; Kuiper & Derry, 1982; Mischel, Ebbesen, & Zeiss, 1976). People replay flattering events in their memory but prefer not to dwell on or relive humiliating moments; and to the extent they can direct

their minds to follow that pattern, memory will become slanted toward emphasis on positive events that make the self look good. The relative approach and avoidance of evaluative information about the self was specifically studied by Baumeister and Cairns (1992) who allowed participants to self-select the amount of time they spent reading computer-presented feedback about their person-alities. Participants spent significantly longer reading their feedback when it was good than when it was bad. Moreover, this pattern was especially pronounced among repressors, who tend to exhibit the strongest and clearest patterns of self-deception.

The selective avoidance of disturbing information was the key to Greenwald's (1988) so-called junk mail theory of self-deception. Greenwald sought to address one of the classic philosophical dilemmas of self-deception and indeed selective attention generally, which is the appar-ent impossibility or paradox of using one's mind to keep things out of one's mind. That is, how do you know not to look at something until you see it—whereupon it is already too late to avoid looking? The analogy to junk mail offered a solution. People cannot prevent themselves entirely from receiving and recognizing junk mail, but often they can recognize it from the envelope and then discard it without opening and reading it. Applied to self-deception, the idea is that people do not entirely avoid threatening information but they can minimize it by turn-ing attention away as soon as they recognize its unwel-come aspect. Partial avoidance is thus an important strategy for self-deception.

Mentally approaching and avoiding other people is another strategy that can be used in self-deception. As Festinger (1954) pointed out early in the rise of social psychology, many traits are objectively meaningless and can only be evaluated in comparison with other people. Hence the selection of comparison targets becomes a potentially decisive factor in how one evalu-ates oneself. There is ample evidence that people are often quite strategic about choosing to compare them-selves with people who are doing less well than they themselves are doing, so that they can maintain a favor-able verdict about their own qualities (Crocker & Major, 1989; Taylor & Brown, 1988; Wills, 1981). This strategy too has both approach and avoidance aspects: people avoid comparing themselves with others who are doing better and would make them feel bad, while they seek out comparison targets who will give them the favor-able contrast they seek.

Moreover, the approach and avoidance of others in the service of self-deception is more than an idle cogni-tive exercise. Tesser's (1988) Self-Evaluation Maintenance

(SEM) theory holds that people are most threatened to be outperformed on personally important things by people who are close to them. Hence if a relationship partner or other close friend begins to perform too well in a sphere that is central to one's own self-definition, one may begin to distance oneself from the friend at potentially significant cost to the relationship. In this case, the wish to avoid any bad implications about the self can take the form of avoiding a significant other person.

COMPETING MOTIVES IN SELF-KNOWLEDGE

Social psychologists have not been alone in recognizing that people have an extensive thirst to learn about themselves. Astrologers, fortune tellers, writers of magazine self-quizzes, the self-help book industry, and a great many others have catered to this thirst, and in fact the Delphic oracle in ancient Greece advertised with the slogan "know thyself," although it is possible that the phrase had a somewhat different connotation back then. Nonetheless, it is apparent that people are well motivated to approach information about the self.

Not all information is equally approachable, however. Indeed, the precise nature of the motivation to seek self-knowledge was the basis of lively controversy for many years. Three main theories came to dominate the battle, and rather than one of them being the winner, the consensus gradually emerged that all are genuine and distinct motives. In a sense, the battle moved from a dispute between researchers to an everyday conflict within people's minds and behaviors. The three motives operate, sometimes together, sometimes at cross-purposes.

One motive is the desire to hold a favorable view of self. This motive, termed positivity or self-enhancement, is understood largely as the preference for favorable and flattering feedback. It is associated with the desire to raise one's self-esteem from wherever it is, although in some versions the desire simply to cling to an established (though possibly inaccurate and unjustified) favorable view of self is enough.

The second motive is based on consistency. Its most ardent advocate was Swann (1987), who has favored the term self-verification. That term emphasizes that the person is not really seeking to learn new information about the self so much as to verify already established beliefs (including ones that may be inaccurate or unjustified). Self-verification and self-enhancement motives can be regarded as concurring in the preference for information that confirms favorable views of self, but of course they differ sharply when it comes to predicting what sort of information will be approached and preferred by people with unfavorable views of self.

The third motive is the simple desire for accurate, correct information about oneself. This so-called diagnosticity motive (see Trope, 1983, 1986) is marked by the quest to find out the truth, regardless of whether it is favorable or unfavorable, and regardless of whether it confirms or shatters the existing views of self.

As social psychologists compiled studies and findings demonstrating these various motives, a landmark attempt to pit them against each other so as to test their relative power was conducted by Sedikides (1993). He concluded that the self-enhancement motive tended to dominate the others and in a sense was the strongest of the three. The consistency motive came second, as a genuine and powerful motive. And diagnosticity or accuracy was also genuine, but weaker than the other two. Thus, to different degrees, and in different circumstances, people seek all three types of information.

The rank ordering of these three motives has implications for understanding approach and avoidance processes in self-esteem. The one thing that all three motives agree on is the strong dislike of being insulted—insofar as we define insults to consist of negative evaluations of the self that are inaccurate or unfair and contrary to existing self-knowledge. Furthermore, the two stronger motives (positivity and consistency) also concur in predicting that people will have a strong dislike for any evaluations that are more negative than what they already think about themselves. Put another way, any broad desire to learn more about oneself will be tempered by a strong wish to avoid criticism.

Thus, despite the general information-seeking (approach) pattern, avoidance will tend to take precedence. People are more strongly motivated to avoid bad information about the self than to approach good information. This may be part of the broader pattern by which bad is stronger than good (Baumeister, Bratslavsky, Finkenauer, & Vohs, 2001). Yet the very breadth of that pattern indicates why the fear of criticism does not turn people into information-avoiders as a general orientation. Whatever the (greater) power of individual bad events, life remains largely good because of the preponderance of good events. In the same way, people mostly hear favorable things about themselves, partly just because of other people's politeness and reluctance to transmit bad news (Tesser & Rosen, 1972). They also probably remain generally optimistic (Taylor & Brown, 1988), and so they may approach unknown information and diagnostic situations in the possibly mistaken expectation that what they learn about themselves will be gratifying.

ORIGINS AND COSTS OF PURSUING SELF-ESTEEM

Although some researchers have attempted in recent years to explain the need for self-esteem (Leary et al., 1995; Greenberg et al., 1986), psychologists have largely taken for granted that self-esteem is both necessary and good for the individual. The simple and obvious explanation for self-esteem has been that it has so many adaptive consequences that people seek it out for the sake of these benefits.

With self-esteem, however, the case for adaptive benefits has become clouded. To be sure, it has had its advocates. Indeed, spurred by a mass of early research findings showing many positive correlations between (high) self-esteem and various positive outcomes that included academic and occupational success, popularity, and avoidance of a broad range of personal and psychological problems, many American groups and institutions began to put efforts and resources into trying to increase self-esteem across various broad segments of the population. The most famous of these was the California Task Force to promote self-esteem and personal and social responsibility (see California Task Force, 1990), which hoped that increasing the self-esteem of all California citizens would lead to a host of benefits, including reductions in crime, drug dependency, and teen pregnancy, and various improvements ranging from academic performance to more tax revenues for the state. Although that group disbanded in the 1990s, the self-esteem movement remains influential across the United States, particularly in schools, where it is hoped that raising the youngers' self-esteem will lead to better performance in school as well as various other moral and socially desirable outcomes.

The hope that raising self-esteem will produce a host of positive outcomes has, however, been battered by the accumulation of research findings. An extensive review by Baumeister and colleagues (2003) and a less extensive but still authoritative one by Emler (2002) concluded that the benefits of high self-esteem are far less than previously thought. The exciting findings that initially fostered so many fond hopes have been found to be subject to the familiar problem of drawing causal conclusions from correlational findings. For example, although it is true that higher self-esteem is moderately correlated with getting better grades in school, the correlation appears to arise because academic success leads to higher self-esteem, not because self-esteem somehow results in doing better on tests (Bachman & O'Malley, 1976). Third variable explanations are also relevant: coming from a well-off family appears to contribute to both higher self-esteem and better academic performance (Bachman & O'Malley, 1976).

Indeed, artificial attempts to boost self-esteem, such as by the sort of self-flattering exercises happily practiced in many schools, may if anything be counterproductive. One of the few rigorous experimental tests of such interventions was recently carried out by Forsyth, Kerr, Burnette, and Baumeister (2007). Struggling students were randomly assigned to receive either just a weekly review question, or that same question accompanied by either a self-esteem boost or an exhortation to take personal responsibility for one's schoolwork. Final examination scores revealed that the group whose self-esteem was boosted scored significantly worse than the other groups and significantly worse than their own midterm examination performance.

A possible implication of these disturbing findings is that when people begin to focus on self-esteem as an end in itself, they often abandon rather than renew their efforts to change their behaviors and performances for the better. To understand why that might happen, it is necessary to reconsider why people want self-esteem so much in the first place. As we said, if high self-esteem led directly to a great many positive outcomes, the pursuit of self-esteem would be unsurprising and even rational and adaptive. In the apparent absence of so many benefits, however, one must ask why that motivation seems so pervasive. Why have evolution and culture shaped people to want self-esteem, if self-esteem confers so few benefits?

Terror management theory (Greenberg, et al., 1986) and sociometer theory (Leary et al., 1995) which we reviewed earlier in this chapter shed some light on this issue. Greenberg and colleagues (1986) suggest that self-esteem serves as a buffer against the anxiety brought about by the awareness of one's own mortality. Sociometer Theory (Leary et al.), on the other hand, proposes that self-esteem serves as a gauge that informs us of our level of social inclusion.

The Terror Management view depicts the quest for self-esteem as part of the generally self-deceptive project. The idea is that self-esteem helps shield the person from awareness of impending death. This has, however, the important value that it will enable the person to function from day to day, whereas a full awareness of mortality would supposedly paralyze the person with terror. To be sure, self-esteem does not really do any good in preventing death, but it helps the person downplay the thought of it.

The function of self-esteem in Sociometer Theory is much clearer. People need acceptance from others, and self-esteem tells them whether they are likely to get it. Low self-esteem signifies a high likelihood of social exclusion and rejection, and so people in that state should be motivated to change so as to improve their prospects of acceptance. Leary and Schreindorfer (1997) showed that low self-esteem was uncorrelated with death anxiety (contrary to the Terror Management view) but substantially correlated with social anxiety.

These views thus suggest why people might desire self-esteem even though its objective benefits are small. They also suggest, however, that the pursuit of self-esteem as an end in itself might have problematic, even undesirable consequences.

One problem with pursuing self-esteem was explicated by Leary and Baumeister (2000). According to the sociometer view, the purpose of self-esteem is to tell you whether you are the sort of person whom others will want to accept and include, such as by befriending, hiring, or marrying you. Low self-esteem should signify that one's eligibility is low, and so one should change the self so as to make it more appealing to others. That process would possibly lead eventually and, most important, indirectly, to a rise in self-esteem, by way of becoming a better person. But some individuals may be tempted to skip the hard work of improving the self and instead simply revise their opinion of themselves based on dubious or phony reassurances. Rather than become a better person, it is easier and pleasanter to merely claim and think that one is a better person. The more people focus on self-esteem as the goal rather than as a signal of goal attainment, the more they will be tempted to "fool the meter" by self-deceptive processes.

The findings cited above by Forsyth et al. (2007) capture this problem. According to sociometer theory, the link between getting good grades and self-esteem should be there because people know (correctly) that good grades will improve their chances of future social acceptance. Doing poorly in school should threaten self-esteem, which ideally would lead to redoubled efforts to perform better such as by studying harder. However, apparently the students who were encouraged to focus on maintaining their self-esteem reduced their effort, either because they decided that their own high self-worth did not need any objective validation in terms of good grades, or simply because they found it easier to think well of themselves when they avoided spending time and effort on a class that had already provided esteem-threatening feedback in terms of a low midterm grade. Making self-esteem the goal and focus of their motivation thus led them to do worse rather than better.

A broad and masterful indictment of the dangers of pursuing self-esteem for its own sake was furnished by Crocker and Park (2004). Crocker and Park argued that the importance of self-esteem lies in the way people define, pursue, and maintain their levels of self-esteem,

rather than people's self-esteem levels per se. A major thrust of their argument is that in domains in which individuals' self-esteem is contingent, self-esteem goals tend to override other, often beneficial goals related to that domain. For instance, Crocker (2003) found that individuals who based their self-esteem on academics were more concerned with obtaining good grades than they were with actual learning. In important domains, positive performance becomes a means to validate the self rather than an opportunity to learn, improve, or master ones goals, and negative performance becomes a major self-threat rather than an opportunity to learn from one's mistakes.

Crocker and Park (2004) reviewed a wide range of self-defeating behaviors and strategies that people engage in when operating in domains important to their self-esteem. Individuals will often avoid thinking about or selectively forget negative feedback (Crary, 1966; Mischel et al., 1976), and focus on receiving positive feedback without trying to understand what led to their success (Carver, 2003). Such self-serving behavior often undermines a person's ability to improve on the given domain. People also tend to become focused on themselves in self-relevant domains to the point that their inattention to others compromises interpersonal relationships (Park & Crocker, 2003). Furthermore, feeling that one has to do something in order to feel worthy threatens their sense of autonomy in that domain, and leads to high levels of stress and anxiety that can diminish one's self-regulatory capacity and even compromise both mental and physical health (Dykman, 1998).

Many of these potential costs of self-esteem pursuit are not inherent to either an approach or an avoidance orientation to motivation. Crocker and Park (2004) acknowledge that while high and low self-esteem individuals may approach or avoid self-relevant domains in different ways, both types of behavior can have costs for the individual. Thus, the consequences of self-esteem related behavior will hinge not only on one's motivational orientation, but how people define self-worth for themselves and in what domains they decide to pursue it.

TRAIT DIFFERENCES IN SELF-ESTEEM

We turn now from the pursuit of self-esteem to trait differences in self-esteem. This section will review the relationship between self-esteem level and motivation. Findings in the self-esteem literature are consistent with research on approach–avoidance motivations such that a subset of self-esteem related behaviors can be defined as approaching desired, positive outcomes, while others are aimed at avoiding undesired, negative outcomes.

In addition, trait self-esteem levels have been found to be closely related to individual differences in the chronic preference for one motivational orientation (approach or avoidance) over the other. We will review the literature on self-esteem and how it relates to motivation for the purpose of illuminating this relationship between the self-concept and approach–avoidance behaviors.

Self-esteem is perhaps the most studied construct in social psychological research on the self (Baumeister et al., 2003), and self-esteem's development and maintenance have been found to be a large factor in determining one's goals and motivations. The most common conceptualization of self-esteem is as a person's positive or negative evaluation of him- or herself (James, 1890). Thus, individuals are said to have either a positive (or high) self-esteem or a negative (or low) self-esteem. Although reliable self-esteem differences have been measured, a number of positive benefits have been conferred to the positive (as opposed to negative) evaluation of the self (Baumeister et al.), and furthermore, the inborn desire to evaluate one's self in a positive regard has become axiomatic in the psychological literature (Crocker & Wolfe, 2001; Pyszczynski, Greenberg, Solomon, Arndt, & Schimel, 2004; Tesser, 1988). The tendency to seek out favorable self-knowledge has been observed as taking precedence over other motivations related to the evaluation of the self-concept, including the motivations to obtain accurate self-relevant feedback (self-assessment) and to confirm one's existing views about one's self (self-verification; Sedikides, 1993). This desire to view one's self in a positive regard has been seen as both powerful and universal (Sedikides et al., 2003), and thus serves as a common focal point in the literature on self-esteem and the self-concept.

A wide range of behaviors aimed at producing a positive view of the self have now been documented, and the relationships between them dovetail quite nicely with the literature on the distinction between approach and avoidance motivations. The approach–avoidance distinction refers to the idea that human behavior relies on two primary motivational systems (Carver & Scheier, 1998; Gray, 1981; Elliot, 1997; Higgins, 1997). Gray (1981) differentiated between a behavioral approach system (BAS) which deals with appetitive motivations and approach behaviors, and a behavioral inhibition system (BIS) which deals with aversive motivations and withdrawal behaviors. Carver and Scheier (1981) developed a similar motivational model based on two self-regulating feedback systems. One system, a discrepancy-reducing feedback system, maps quite well onto Gray's BAS idea. Similarly, a second discrepancy-enlarging feedback

system which focuses on avoidant behavior is reminiscent of the BIS. A third line of research that is consistent with this theme is work by Higgins (1996) on the distinction between promotion and prevention as self-regulatory foci. In theory, each focus (promotion and prevention) is applicable to both approach and avoidance goals, but some researchers suggest (Carver, Sutton, & Scheier, 2000) that the promotion focus tends to deal with appetitive goals while the prevention focus tends to deal with aversion goals. All three lines of research support the idea of two fundamental human motivations: roughly, approach and avoidance. Furthermore, each of the previous theories also supports the idea of measurable individual differences in the chronic preferences for one motivation system over the other.

Do individual differences in motivation relate to chronic self-esteem levels? One sweeping formulation of motivational differences that depend on level of self-esteem was proposed by Baumeister, Tice, and Hutton (1989). In some respects anticipating the sociometer theory, particularly with regard to putting an emphasis on interpersonal goals and motives, they began by examining the actual responses to trait scales that resulted in being classified as high or low in self-esteem. Somewhat surprisingly, they did not find that low self-esteem scores came from describing oneself in unflattering terms, which the literal definition of low self-esteem would imply. Rather, they found that low scores on self-esteem were only relatively low, and in absolute terms they were medium, noncommittal responses. They went on to propose that neutral, noncommittal descriptions of self (unlike negative, self-derogating ones) could well serve effective functions, specifically with regard to protecting the self from the dangers of extravagant claims. They followed earlier work by McFarlin and Blascovich (1981), which resolved the earlier and intense debates about the motivational orientation of people with low self-esteem. Contrary to views that low self-esteem was characterized by a positive desire for failure (e.g., to confirm negative views of self), McFarlin and Blascovich showed that people with low self-esteem had the same values and aspirations as people with high self-esteem, namely to succeed and be liked—the people with low self-esteem simply had less confidence that they would actually achieve those goals.

Thus, people of different levels of self-esteem agree in their desire to succeed but differ in their perceived likelihood of reaching it. The differential confidence leads to a different orientation toward risky undertakings. People with high self-esteem expect frequent success and are therefore willing to take some risks. Their optimistic, confident outlook predisposes them to look for new ways to achieve success and thereby to glorify the self. In contrast, people with low self-esteem anticipate that many undertakings will turn out badly. For them, avoiding embarrassment, humiliation, and other failures becomes a central focus. To be sure, they would like just fine to achieve a great new success or to discover something new and wonderful about themselves, but they do not expect many such fine outcomes. Moreover, having less self-esteem to start, they are less willing than others to gamble with it. Baumeister, Cooper, and Skib (1979) compared self-esteem to money. Those with plenty of it are more willing to gamble and speculate in the hope of achieving a sizable return. Those with only a little of it must avoid taking chances and only invest it in the safest opportunities.

Hence the balance between approaching and avoiding may be different as a function of trait level of self-esteem. Risky endeavors that contain the chances of both dramatic success and embarrassing failure will appeal far more to approach-oriented people having high self-esteem than to avoidance-oriented people with low self-esteem. It is true (contrary to some early theories) that both high and low self-esteem go with preferring success over failure, and when one is immersed in working toward a goal, people of all levels of self-esteem will try to do well. But in terms of who will seek out such a high-risk, high-payoff undertaking, different levels of trait self-esteem will push people in different ways. For those with low self-esteem, avoidance of failure will be paramount, whereas for those with high self-esteem, the chance to approach success will outweigh most risks of possible failure.

A direct test of this motivational theory of self-esteem was provided by Tice (1991). She used the strategic behavior of self-handicapping which was first identified by Jones and Berglas (1978; see also Berglas & Jones, 1978; Frankel & Snyder, 1978). Self-handicapping refers to a seemingly self-destructive pattern by which people act in ways that reduce their own chances of success. For example, in preparation for an upcoming examination, a prudent strategy would be to study hard and then get a good night's sleep, whereas a self-handicapper might avoid studying and spend the night on a drunken outing. The appeal of such strategies is that they alter the attributional calculus so as to bias it in the self-handicapper's favor. In the preceding example, the unprepared and hungover test-taker is protected against being shown to be stupid or incompetent, because failure on the test will be attributed to the obstacles (lack of preparation and alcoholic hangover) rather than to lack of ability. Meanwhile, to perform well despite not having studied nor properly slept would be taken as a sign of unusually high ability.

Thus, self-handicapping has two attributional benefits. It avoids negative implications of failure while enhancing the credit one would get for success. Tice (1991) undertook to separate these two attributional benefits, by means such as describing an upcoming test as only suited for identifying exceptionally low or exceptionally high levels of talent. Her findings supported the view that high self-esteem is oriented toward self-enhancement whereas low self-esteem aims for self-protection. People who scored high in self-esteem were more likely to engage in self-handicapping when it was a strategy for self-enhancement and when self-protection was irrelevant (such as if the test was described as suited only for identifying exceptionally gifted individuals, so that any scores but extremely high ones were meaningless). People with low self-esteem, in contrast, engaged in self-handicapping mainly to protect themselves against failure.

To be sure, Tice (1991) found that the self-protection motive was more common. Both high and low self-esteem were associated with some degree of self-protective self-handicapping (although the pattern was stronger among people with low than high self-esteem). This fits our earlier assertion of the primacy of avoidance: everyone wants to avoid losing self-esteem.

More recent findings have demonstrated that the tendency for low (and high) self-esteem individuals to engage in avoidance (and approach) related behaviors applies to personal goals in general (Heimpel, Elliot, & Wood, 2006), and not just self-evaluation or self-presentation. Thus, self-esteem level seems intimately tied to dispositional approach and avoidance behaviors, and a more detailed understanding of this relationship hinges on a more accurate definition of what it means to have high or low self-esteem. In the following section, we continue our assessment of motivation and self-esteem with a review of the research that has focused on defining exactly what self-esteem is, what the construct comprises of, and how it should be measured.

DEFINITION AND MEASUREMENT

The definition and measurement of self-esteem has not been without controversy. The most common conceptualization of self-esteem is as a person's positive or negative evaluation of him- or herself (James, 1890). However, this unidimensional view of self-esteem has been somewhat inconsistent in its predictions for high and low self-esteem individuals' behavioral and psychological outcomes (Baumeister et al., 2003; Kernis, 2003). For instance, although there is an abundance of research suggesting that high self-esteem is unequivocally beneficial to the individual, some theorists have begun to question this assumption based on such findings as those indicating that high self-esteem individuals may have fragile self-concepts that make them susceptible to overly defensive behaviors. Unidimensional self-esteem has also proven somewhat inconsistent in its predictions for interpersonal behaviors; some theorists have suggested that low self-esteem causes aggression toward others, while research findings suggest that high self-esteem (or some kinds of high self-esteem) can facilitate the same antisocial behavior. Together, these data suggest that self-esteem is perhaps a more complicated construct than a unidimensional scale would suggest.

Rosenberg (1965) developed a scale based on a unidimensional definition of self-esteem several decades ago and it still serves as the major tool for assessing self-esteem today (Blascovich & Tomaka, 1991). However, a close inspection of the Rosenberg Self-Esteem Scale (RSES) has yielded results that indicate more than one dimension of self-esteem, with positive feelings loading onto one factor and negative feelings loading onto another (Marsh, 1996). Others have suggested that the RSES does indeed follow a single common factor (Gray-Little, Williams, & Hancock, 1997) and others have argued that the two-factor findings are an artifact of language (Corwyn, 2000; Dunbar, Ford, Hunt, & Der, 2000).

Elliot and Mapes (2005) recently suggested that a two-factor model of global self-esteem may not be a meaningless artifact of the RSES. They propose utilizing the apparent separation between negative and positive self-evaluations in future research, and they cite the approach–avoidance distinction as a rationale for this approach. Consistent with this suggestion, the coexistence of dual attitudes has been well documented in the literature, and this ambivalence has furthermore been seen as predictive of approach versus avoidance motivations. Thus, the approach–avoidance distinction provides one direction toward resolving the controversy of self-esteem measurement, and future research on this distinction may shed light on some of the individual differences in self-esteem motivation.

Work by Showers (1992) suggests that the manner in which we store our self-knowledge has important consequences for self-evaluation. Her research showed that the compartmentalization of positive and negative information about the self explained variance in self-esteem beyond the mere amount of positive and negative content in the self-concept. Similarly, Pelham (1991) revealed that individuals seem to harbor pockets of positive and negative self-evaluation such that even depressed individuals were found to have specific self-views that were just as positive as those held by nondepressed persons. The evidence provided by Showers (1992) and Pelham (1991) suggests that measures of global self-esteem are incomplete measures of self-evaluation (see also Harter, Waters, & Whitesell, 1998), and so it should not be surprising that global measures have yielded variable success in predicting behavioral outcomes. More research needs to be done on the relationship between motivated behavior and self-evaluation in specific domains. Although individuals with low self-esteem have been shown to avoid negative self-evaluations, in which domains does this trend apply? If low self-esteem individuals harbor pockets of positive self-evaluation, how do they maintain these pockets? One possibility is that they behave similarly to high self-esteem individuals in domains in which they hold strong, positive self-evaluations. Such confidence in one's domain-specific abilities may allow those with low global self-esteem to take more risks and approach positive evaluations in these particular contexts. On the other hand, they may be especially self-protective in such domains, for the reason that these domains serve as their only avenues toward self-worth.

Taken together, the findings on self-esteem measurement suggest that future research must take into account a much more detailed measure of self-evaluation than the traditional unidimensional approach. To what extent do people feel good about themselves? To what extent do people evaluate themselves negatively? Furthermore, in which domains do these evaluations occur and in which domains does the individual feel most personally invested? A complete understanding of one's motivations must take these questions into account. We begin to touch on the interaction between these various issues in the next section as we review some of the interpersonal strategies people use to maintain their self-esteem.

Motivation in the Self-Concept: Self-Esteem Maintenance in Action.

Regardless of the exact function of self-esteem, researchers are in agreement that most individuals are motivated to achieve and maintain high levels of self-esteem. The ways in which people do this are manifold and we review many of these strategies below. These lines of research have rarely, if ever, acknowledged the approach and avoidance distinction. We speculate about how such factors would play into these phenomena.

There are many social cognitive strategies by which individuals work to maintain positive self-evaluations. One way individuals can increase their feelings of self-worth is by associating themselves with other individuals or groups that have performed well on some domain.

This idea of basking in the reflected glory (BIRGing; Cialdini et al., 1976; Cialdini & Richardson, 1980) of others was famously illustrated by the observation by Cialdini and colleagues (1976) that college students are more likely to adorn their university's clothing immediately following a win rather than a loss by the school's football team. By associating themselves with winners, individuals are able both to feel good about themselves and to present themselves in a positive light. On the other hand, people avoid negative self-evaluations by distancing themselves from those who are performing poorly. By cutting of reflected failure (CORFing; Snyder, Lassegard, & Ford, 1986), individuals are able to protect themselves from potential negative evaluations. In either case, self-esteem maintenance has a strong influence on the affiliations one will make.

The trend of relating self-enhancement to approach motivations and self-protection to avoidance motivations may not be as straightforwardly applied in the case of BIRGing and CORFing as it can be in other situations. For instance, although BIRGing may resemble an approach-oriented behavior to the extent that it involves seeking out positive evaluations, this tendency to reflect in the positive performance of others appears to be a rather risk-free instance of self-evaluation. In the cases of BIRGing and CORFing, one need not perform in order to meet expectations, one must simply choose to share in another's success or choose not to share in another's failure. Thus, it seems reasonable that in this case, those with low self-esteem need not fear the act of approaching positive evaluations since there are no negative consequences for doing so. In fact, evidence suggests that individuals with low self-esteem are not only undeterred by this form of "safe" self-enhancement but are actually more likely to engage in it than individuals who are high in self-esteem. Brown, Collins, and Schmidt (1988) found that low self-esteem individuals were more likely to self-enhance by displaying favoritism toward well-performing others than those with high self-esteem. More specifically, the findings by Brown and colleagues (1988) suggest that low self-esteem people are more likely to enhance their self-worth in situations where they are not directly implicated in the domain being evaluated. Somewhat consistent with this are findings suggesting that individuals are more likely to BIRG when their self-concepts are vulnerable—that is, individuals have been found to BIRG more often after incidents of self-threat (Cialdini et al., 1976).

While the reflection processes in BIRGing and CORFing involve identifying with the performances of others, social comparison strategies, as the name suggests,

involve comparing one's own performance with the performance of others. Social comparison theory was originally predicated on the inborn motivation to obtain accurate self-knowledge. Individuals were said to compare themselves with others in order to gain a more clear understanding of themselves and their place in the world (Festinger, 1954). More recent research has focused on how individuals use social comparison as a tool for self-enhancement (Suls, Martin, & Wheeler, 2002; Wood, 1989). There are two main mechanisms by which people are able to do this. First, individuals can make downward social comparisons—they can choose to compare themselves with worse-off others in order to make themselves appear better off and to boost their self-esteem. Wood, Taylor, and Lichtman (1985), for instance, found that many women with breast cancer spontaneously compare themselves with other patients who are in worse condition. Secondly, there is some evidence that upward social comparisons can also increase self-regard. The option to compare oneself with those who are better off can be a fairly dangerous strategy in that one risks appearing inferior, however, to the extent that individuals are able to use this type of comparison to motivate themselves toward self-improvement (Berger, 1977; Blanton, Buunk, Gibbons, & Kuyper, 1999; Vrugt & Koenis, 2002), or convince themselves that they are similar to the better-off others (Wheeler, 1966), upward comparisons can be beneficial for one's self-regard.

Findings suggest that low self-esteem individuals are more likely to seek self-enhancement through social comparisons when such comparisons are perceived to be safe. For instance, those low in self-esteem are more likely to seek social comparisons when they have received success (rather than failure) feedback, and in addition are more likely to do so than those with high self-esteem. These findings are consistent with the BIRGing literature in the suggestion that low self-esteem individuals are perfectly willing to seek positive self-regard so long as the situation is deemed to be of little risk. It is likely that low self-esteem individuals are more likely to take advantage of downward social comparisons while high self-esteem individuals are more likely to make upward social comparisons. If upward social comparisons are only beneficial to the extent that they impel individuals toward active self-improvement, then one intuitive conclusion is that those who are high in self-esteem and of an approach-oriented motivation will be most likely to engage in it. On the other hand, Elliot and Mapes (2005) propose that self-improvement motives may parallel an aversion to the deterioration of one's abilities. However, the factors that dictate whether self-improvement will be driven by a desire for self-enhancement or an aversion to deterioration remains to be seen.

Tesser and colleagues (Tesser, 1988; Tesser, Campbell, & Smith, 1984; Tesser & Smith, 1980) provide a comprehensive account of the interaction between the reflection and comparison processes outlined above, and they review a variety of behaviors by which individuals may work to maintain positive self-regard with relation to these variables. Though BIRGing and social comparison can both be used as strategies to enhance one's self-esteem, the two processes present near opposite responses to the performance of others—reflection requires one to identify with another's performance while comparison requires one to contrast one's own performance with the performance of others. Furthermore, the two processes appear to have the opposite result in any given situation. One consequence of BIRGing is that the closer the other person is whose performance one is reflecting in, and the better that person's performance, the greater the benefit for the BIRGing individual's self-worth. In contrast, when comparing one's performance to the performance of another, the closer the other person is to the individual and the better the other person's performance, the greater the negative impact will be for the individual's self-worth. What dictates whether one will engage in reflection or comparison when confronted with the performance of another? An understanding of the interaction between the reflection and comparison processes requires relating them to an important third variable: relevance. A task is considered relevant to an individual to the extent that the task is central to the individual's self-concept, the individual strives to perform well at the task, and the individual freely chooses to engage in the task. According to Tesser's Self-Evaluation Maintenance (SEM; 1988) model, the comparison process will take precedence for tasks that are relevant, while the reflection process will take precedence for tasks that are not.

The SEM model describes a variety of strategies by which individuals maintain positive self-regard. A few of these strategies include affecting the performance of others (Tesser & Smith, 1980), changing one's own performance (Tesser et al., 1984), modifying relationship closeness (Pleban & Tesser, 1981), and adjusting task relevance (i.e., adjusting one's self-concept; Tesser & Paulhus, 1983). To provide an example of these strategies, imagine that a self-described cellist finds out a close friend and fellow orchestra member is eligible for the spot as the first-chair cellist in the orchestra. Because cello performance in this case is relevant to the individual, comparison becomes the more important process. One strategy the individual can engage in would be to sabotage her friend's performance in order to avoid looking inferior by comparison. Alternatively, the individual can start working harder in order to boost her relative performance and perhaps herself become eligible for the principal cellist position. She can also distance herself from her friend thereby reducing the strength of the comparison. Finally, she may decide to abandon music altogether in order to reduce the relevance of the domain and allow herself to focus on other tasks. This strategy would also allow her to reflect in the glory of her friend's no longer threatening abilities.

The particular strategy that an individual will choose to pursue in situations like that in the previous example will likely depend in large part on the context (e.g., some strategies may not be plausible in a given situation); however, it is reasonable to assume that there are many individual differences in strategy preference as well. Approach-oriented people may be more likely to try to improve their own performance when threatened by such a comparison. Those who are more avoidant in nature, particularly those who are less confident in themselves or their abilities, may be more likely to flee a given situation—possibly by abandoning the domain altogether or by stepping away from the relationship in order to avoid hurtful comparisons.

Given the wide range of positive and negative consequences that can result from each of these strategies, a firm understanding of both the contextual variables and the individual differences that predict strategy preferences should prove very valuable. This is certainly true with regard to the strategy of hurting another's performance in cases of social comparison, or alternatively helping another's performance when presented with the possibility of reflecting in their subsequent glory. These behaviors present an interesting subset of anti- and prosocial behaviors. Are certain people more likely to hurt or help the performance of another? When self-worth is implicated in prosocial behavior as they are in these situations, how does self-esteem level interact with behavior? How do approach and avoidance dispositions relate to such behaviors? Again, the relationships here are speculative. High self-esteem may help serve as a buffer against the threatening aspects of such situations, and may additionally impel self-enhancing (rather than self-protective) behaviors. Of course, self-enhancement may come in the form of self-improvement or just as plausibly the disruption of another's performance, which would be consistent with findings suggesting that high self-esteem individuals may be particularly capable of aggressive behaviors.

A likely moderating factor in any act of self-esteem maintenance will be the content of people's self-concept and the contingencies of their self-worth. Although people may be threatened by the performance of another, if they are particularly invested in that domain they will not be likely to walk away from it. Additionally, if that person is particularly invested in his or her relationship with the comparison target, or if that person is personally invested in interpersonal relationships in general, then he or she may not be likely to hinder the other's performance or create distance in the relationship.

CONCLUSION

We have examined the relationship between the self-concept and motivation with a special emphasis on self-evaluation and the seemingly universal pursuit of high self-esteem. We reviewed research on the self that has suggested that high self-esteem is directly related to approach-oriented aspects of self-esteem maintenance, while low self-esteem is connected with the avoidance-oriented aspects of self-esteem maintenance. In other words, research indicates that those with high and low self-esteem are particularly oriented toward self-enhancement and self-protection, respectively. While research does suggest that low self-esteem individuals will engage in self-enhancement in situations that are deemed "safe" from a self-evaluative standpoint, the relationship between self-esteem level and approach–avoidance orientation seems to hold up in a variety of processes, including self-handicapping (Tice, 1991) and the pursuit of personal goals in general (Heimpel et al., 2006).

We have also reviewed recent research on the functions of self-esteem. Self-esteem theories such as sociometer theory (Leary et al., 1995) and TMT (Greenberg et al., 1986) suggest that self-esteem maintenance may be a largely avoidant process to the extent that individuals are oriented toward avoiding social exclusion or mortality-related anxiety. This is consistent with the observed relationship between self-esteem level and motivation orientation. Those with low self-esteem should be particularly attuned to self-evaluative motives, while those with high self-esteem levels should feel free to approach a much wider range of goals and behaviors, an idea that is consistent with a number of findings.

Research on the strategies by which people maintain their feelings of self-worth, such as self-deception, BIRGing (Cialdini et al., 1976) and CORFing (Snyder et al., 1986), social comparison (Wood, 1989), and SEM (Tesser, 1988), also promise to be an insightful resource for understanding motivation. Though few have addressed how these strategies relate to the approach and avoidance distinction, research suggests that the answer will come by combing these strategies with more detailed accounts and measurements of the self-concept—such as domain specific self-evaluation and contingencies of self-worth. A firm grasp on these aspects of the self-concept may help psychologists understand a wide range of motivated behavior.

REFERENCES

Bachman, J. G., & O'Malley, P. M. (1976). Self-esteem in young men: A longitudinal analysis of the impact of educational and occupational attainment. *Journal of Personality and Social Psychology, 35,* 365–380.

Baumeister, R. F., & Cairns, K. J. (1992). Repression and self-presentation: When audiences interfere with self-deceptive strategies. *Journal of Personality and Social Psychology, 11,* 131–148.

Baumeister, R. F., & Leary, M. R. (1995). The need to belong: Desire for interpersonal attachments as a fundamental human motivation. *Psychological Bulletin, 117,* 497–529.

Baumeister, R., Bratslavsky, E., Finkenauer, C., Vohs, K. (2001), Bad is stronger than good, *Review of General Psychology, 5,* 323–370.

Baumeister, R. F., Campbell, J. D., Krueger, J. I., & Vohs, K. D. (2003). Does high self-esteem cause better performance, interpersonal success, happiness, or healthier lifestyles? *Psychological Science in the Public Interest, 4,* 1–44.

Baumeister, R. F., Cooper, J., & Skib, B. A. (1979). Inferior performance as a selective response to expectancy: Taking a dive to make a point. *Journal of Personality and Social Psychology, 37,* 424–432.

Baumeister, R. F., Tice, D. M., & Hutton, D. G. (1989). Self-presentational motivations and personality differences in self-esteem. *Journal of Personality, 57,* 547–579.

Berger, S. M. (1977). Social comparison, modeling, and perseverance. In J. M. Suls & R. L. Miller (Eds.), *Social comparison processes: Theoretical and empirical perspectives* (pp. 209–234). Washington, DC: Hemisphere.

Berglas, S., & Jones, E. E. (1978). Drug choice as a self-handicapping strategy in response to noncontingent success. *Journal of Personality and Social Psychology, 36,* 405–417.

Blanton, H., Buunk, B. P., Gibbons, F. X., & Kuyper, H. (1999). When better-than-others compare upward: Choice of comparison and comparative evaluation as independent predictors of academic performance. *Journal of Personality and Social Psychology, 76,* 420–430.

Blascovich, J., & Tomaka, J. (1991). Measures of self-esteem. In J. P. Robinson, P. R. Shaver, & L. S. Wrightsman (Eds.), *Measures of personality and social psychological attitudes* (Vol. 1, pp. 115–160). New York: Academic Press.

Brown, J. D., Collins, R. L., & Schmidt, G. W. (1988). Self-esteem and direct versus indirect forms of self-enhancement, *Journal of Personality and Social Psychology, 55,* 445–453.

California Task Force to Promote Self-esteem and Personal and Social Responsibility (1990). Toward a state of self-esteem. Sacramento: California State Department of Education.

Carver, C. S. (2003). Pleasure as a sign you can attend to something else: Placing positive feelings within a general model of affect. *Cognition & Emotion, 17,* 241–261.

Carver, C. S., & Scheier, M. F. (1981). The self-attention-induced feedback loop and social facilitation. *Journal of Experimental Social Psychology, 17,* 545–568.

Carver, C. S., & Scheier, M. F. (1998). *On the self-regulation of behavior.* New York: Cambridge University Press.

Carver, C. S., Sutton, S. K., & Scheier, M. F. (2000). Action, emotion, and personality: Emerging conceptual integration. *Personality and Social Psychology Bulletin, 26,* 741–751.

Cialdini, R. B., Borden, R. J., Thorne, A., Walker, M. R., Freeman, S., & Sloan, L. R. (1976). Basking in reflected glory: Three (football) field studies. *Journal of Personality and Social Psychology, 34,* 366–375.

Cialdini, R. B., & Richardson, K. D. (1980). Two indirect tactics of image management: Basking and blasting. *Journal of Personality and Social Psychology, 39,* 406–415.

Corwyn, R. F. (2000). The factor structure of global self-esteem among adolescents and adults. *Journal of Research in Personality, 34,* 357–379.

Crary, W. G. (1966). Reactions to incongruent self-experiences. *Journal of Consulting Psychology, 30,* 246–252.

Crocker, J. (2003). [Contingencies of self-worth and self-validation goals in achievement domains]. Unpublished raw data.

Crocker, J. & Major, B. (1989). Social stigma and self-esteem: The self-protective properties of stigma. *Psychological Review, 96*(4), 608–630.

Crocker, J., & Park, L. E. (2004). The costly pursuit of self-esteem. *Psychological Bulletin, 130,* 392–414.

Crocker, J., & Wolfe, C. T. (2001). Contingencies of self-worth. *Psychological Review, 108,* 593–623.

Dunbar, M., Ford, G., Hunt, K., & Der, G. (2000). Question wording effects in the assessment of global self-esteem. *European Journal of Psychological Assessment, 16,* 13–19.

Dykman, B. M. (1998). Integrating cognitive and motivational factors in depression: Initial tests of a goal-orientation approach. *Journal of Personality and Social Psychology, 74,* 139–158.

Elliot, A. J. (1997). Integrating "classic" and "contemporary" approaches to achievement motivation: A hierarchical model of approach and avoidance achievement motivation. In P. Pintrich & M. Maehr (Eds.), *Advances in motivation and achievement* (Vol. 10, pp. 143–179). Greenwich, CT: JAI.

Elliot, A. J., & Mapes, R. R. (2005). Approach–avoidance motivation and self-concept evaluation. In A. Tessesr, J. Wood, & D. Stapel (Eds.), *On building, defending, and regulating the self: A psychological perspective* (pp. 171–196). Washington, DC: Psychological Press.

Emler, N. (2002). The costs and causes of low self-esteem. *Youth Studies Austraia, 21,* 45–48.

Festinger, L. (1954). A theory of social comparison processes. *Human Relations, 7,* 11–16.

Forsyth, D. R., Kerr, N. A., Burnette, J. L., & Baumeister, R. F. (2007). Attempting to improve the academic performance of struggling college students by bolstering their self-esteem: An intervention that backfired. *Journal of Social and Clinical Psychology, 26,* 447–459.

Frankel, A., & Snyder, M. L. (1978). Poor performance following unsolvable problems: Learned helplessness or egotism? *Journal of Personality and Social Psychology, 36,* 1415–1423.

Gray, J. A. (1981). A critique of Eysenck's theory of personality. In H. J. Eysenck (Ed.), *A model for personality* (pp. 246–276). Berling: Springer-Verlag.

Gray-Little, B., Williams, V. S. L., & Hancock, T. D. (1997). An item response theory analysis of the Rosenberg Self-Esteem Scale. *Personality and Social Psychology Bulletin, 23,* 443–451.

Greenberg, J., Pyszczynski, T., & Solomon, S. (1986). The causes and consequences of a need for self-esteem: a terror management theory. In R. F. Baumeister (Ed.), *Public self and private self* (pp. 189–212). New York: Springer-Verlag.

Greenwald, A. G. (1988). Self-knowledge and self-deception. In J. Lockard & D. Paulhus (Eds.), *Self-deception: An adaptive mechanism?* (pp. 113–131). Englewood Cliffs, NJ: Prentice Hall.

Harter, S., Waters, P., & Whitesell, N. R. (1998). Relational self-worth: Differences in perceived worth as a person across interpersonal contexts among adolescents. *Child Development, 69,* 756–766.

Heimpel, S. A., Elliot, A. J., & Wood, J. V. (2006). Basic personality dispositions, self-esteem, and personal goals: an approach-avoidance analysis. *Journal of Personality, 74,* 1293–1319.

Heine, S. J., Lehman, D. R., Markus, H. R., & Kitayama, S. (1999). Is there a universal need for positive self-regard? *Psychological Review, 106,* 766–794.

Higgins, E. T. (1996). Emotional experiences: The pains and pleasures of distinct regulatory systems. In R. D. Kavanaugh, B. Zimmerberg, & S. Fein (Eds.), *Emotion: Interdisciplinary perspectives* (pp. 203–241). Hillsdale, NJ: Lawrence Erlbaum Associates.

Higgins, E. T. (1997). Beyond pleasure and pain. *American Psychologist, 52,* 1280–1300.

James, W. (1890). *The principles of psychology.* New York: Holt.

Jones, E. E., & Berglas, S. (1978). Control of attributions about the self through self-handicapping strategies: The appeal of alcohol and the role of underachievement. *Personality and Social Psychology Bulletin, 4,* 200–206.

Kuiper, N. A., & Derry, P. A. (1982). Depressed and nondepressed content self-reference in mild depressives. *Journal of Personality, 50,* 67–80.

Kernis, M. H. (2003). Toward a conceptualization of optimal self-esteem. *Psychological Inquiry, 14,* 83–89.

Leary, M. R., & Baumeister, R. F. (2000). *The nature and function of self-esteem: Sociometer theory.* In M. P. Zanna (Ed.), *Advances in experimental social psychology* (Vol. 32, pp. 1–62). San Diego, CA: Academic Press.

Leary, M. R., & Schreindorfer, L. S. (1997). Unresolved issues with terror management theory. *Psychological Inquiry, 8,* 26–29.

Leary, M. R., Tambor, E. S., Terdal, S. K., & Downs, D. L. (1995). Self-esteem as an interpersonal monitor: The sociometer hypothesis. *Journal of Personality and Social Psychology, 68*, 518–530.

Marsh, H. W. (1996). Positive and negative global self-esteem: a substantively meaningful distinction or artifactors? *Journal of Personality and Social Psychology, 70*, 810–819.

McFarlin, D. B., & Blascovich, J. (1981). Effects of self-esteem and performance feedback on future affective preferences and cognitive expectations. *Journal of Personality and Social Psychology, 40*, 521–531.

Mischel, W., Ebbesen, E. B., & Zeiss, A. M. (1976). Determinants of selective memory about the self. *Journal of Consulting and Clinical Psychology, 44*, 92–103.

Park, L. E., & Crocker, J. (2003). *The interpersonal costs of seeking self-esteem.* Unpublished manuscript.

Pelham, B. W. (1991). On the benefits of misery: Self-serving biases in the depressive self-concept. *Journal of Personality and Social Psychology, 61*, 670–681.

Pleban, R., & Tesser, A. (1981). The effects of relevance and quality of another's performance on interpersonal closeness. *Social Psychology Quarterly, 44*, 278–285.

Pyszczynski, T., Greenberg, J., Solomon, S., Arndt, J., & Schimel, J. (2004). Why do people need self-esteem? A theoretical and empirical review. *Psychological Bulletin, 130*, 435–468.

Rosenberg, M. (1965). *Society and the adolescent child.* Princeton, NJ: Princeton University Press.

Sackeim, H. A., & Gur, R. C. (1979). Self-deception, other-deception, and self-reported psychopathology. *Journal of Consulting and Clinical Psychology, 47*, 213–215.

Sedikides, C. (1993). Assessment, enhancement, and verification determinants of the self-evaluation process. *Journal of Personality and Social Psychology, 65*, 317–338.

Sedikides, C., Gaertner, L., & Toguchi, Y. (2003). Pancultural self-enhancement. *Journal of Personality and Social Psychology, 84*, 60–79.

Showers, C. (1992). Compartmentalization of positive and negative self-knowledge: Keeping bad apples out of the bunch. *Journal of Personality and Social Psychology, 62*, 1036–1049.

Snyder, C. R., Lassegard, M., & Ford, C. E. (1986). Distancing after group success and failure: Basking in reflected glory and cutting off reflected failure. *Journal of Personality and Social Psychology, 51*, 382–388.

Suls, J., Martin, R., & Wheeler, L. (2002). Social comparison: Why, with whom, and with what effect? *Current Directions in Psychological Science, 11*, 159–163.

Swann, W. (1987). Identity negotiation: Where two roads meet. *Journal of Personality and Social Psychology, 53*, 1038–1051.

Swann, W. B., Jr. (1997). The trouble with change: Self-verification and the self. *Psychological Science, 8*, 177–180.

Taylor, S. E., & Brown, J. D. (1988). Illusion and well-being—a social psychological perspective on mental-health. *Psychological Bulletin, 103*(2), 193–210.

Tesser, A. (1988). Toward a self-evaluation maintenance model of social behavior. In L. Berkowitz (Ed.), *Advances in experimental social psychology* (Vol. 21, 181–227). San Diego, CA: Academic Press.

Tesser, A., Campbell, J., & Smith, M. (1984). Friendship choice and performance: Self-evaluation maintenance in children. *Journal of Personality and Social Psychology, 46*, 561–574.

Tesser, A., & Paulhus, D. (1983). The definition fo self: Private and public self-evaluation management strategies. *Journal of Personality and Social Psychology, 44*, 672–682.

Tesser, A., & Rosen, S. (1972). Similarity of objective fate as a determinant of the reluctance to transmit unpleasant information: The MUM effect. *Journal of Personality and Social Psychology, 23*, 46–53.

Tesser, A., & Smith, J. (1980). Some effects of friendship and task relevance on helping: You don't always help the one you like. *Journal of Experimental Social Psychology, 16*, 582–590.

Tice, D. M. (1991). Esteem protection or enhancement? Self-handicapping motives and attributions differ by trait self-esteem. *Journal of Personality and Social Psychology, 60*, 711–725.

Trope, Y. (1983). Self-assessment in achievement behavior. In J. Suls & A. G. Greenwald (Eds.), *Psychological perspectives on the self* (Vol. 2). Hillsdale, NJ: Erlbaum.

Trope, Y. (1986). Self-enhancement and self-assessment in achievement behavior. In R. Sorrentino & E. T. Higgins (Eds.), *Handbook of motivation and cognition* (Vol. 2, pp. 350–378). New York: Guilford.

Vrugt, A., & Koenis, S. (2002). Perceived self-efficacy, personal goals, social comparison, and scientific productivity. *Applied Psychology: An International Review, 51*, 593–607.

Wheeler, L. (1966). Motivation as a determinant of upward comparison. *Journal of Experimental Social Psychology, Supplement 1, 20*, 263–271.

Wills, T. A. (1981). Downward comparison principles in social psychology. *Psychological Bulletin, 90*, 245–271.

Wood, J. V. (1989). Theory and research concerning social comparisons of personal attributes. *Psychological Bulletin, 106*, 231–248.

Wood, J. V., Taylor, S. E., & Lichtman, R. R. (1985). Social comparison in adjustment to breast cancer. *Journal of Personality and Social Psychology, 67*, 713–731.

Zuckerman, M. (1979). Attribution of success and failure revisited: or The motivational bias is alive and well in attribution theory. *Journal of Personality, 47*, 245–287.

Self-Knowledge

31 Secrets of Resilience: Approaching Negative Self-Aspects Without Aversion

Carolin J. Showers and Kristy L. Boyce

CONTENTS

Motives to approach and to avoid traditionally have not been conceptualized as self-relevant motives. Yet, from a physiological perspective, the activation of the BAS and BIS system depends heavily on appraisals mediated by self-perceptions of control and efficacy, as articulated in Carver and Scheier's (1998) control theory model. From a traditional personality perspective, approach motivation is characteristic of individuals with high achievement orientation, who are generally confident with high self-esteem; whereas avoidance motivation is characteristic of trait-anxious individuals, whose self-concept is likely to be insecure (Atkinson & Birch, 1970). More recently, hypothesized correspondences between self-discrepancies and promotion versus prevention goals make a concrete link between the structure of the self-concept and fundamental motivational orientations, highlighting the inherent role of the self in motivation (Higgins, 1997).

Yet, all of these perspectives to date imply that a positive and secure self-concept fosters confidence and the motive to approach positive stimuli and outcomes; whereas a negative, insecure self-concept fosters anxiety and the motive to avoid negative stimuli and outcomes. In the present chapter, we consider the prevailing concern of what we call a resilient self, that is, a self that is well-prepared to cope with negative experience or stress. This concern is how to approach negative stimuli (i.e., negative attributes or experiences) without an aversive response. We argue that the approach–avoidance framework offers unique insights regarding this concern. In fact, this circumstance has been addressed indirectly by the hierarchical model of approach–avoidance motivation (Elliot & Thrash, 2001).

On the face of it, approach toward negative stimuli without aversion is anathema to approach–avoidance models. The avoidance system allows for vigilance to negative stimuli, but is accompanied by aroused physiological states and impulses to avoid or withdraw (Lang, Bradley, & Cuthbert, 1998). What Elliot and Thrash (2001) proposed is that, at times, the approach system can work in service of long-term avoidance goals—that is, an individual can work toward a positive outcome in the short-term in order to avoid the feared outcome in the long-term. So, for example, a college student who fears failing a multiple-choice test can mobilize her efforts by preparing elaborate outlines of every chapter in the textbook, thereby ensuring adequate (and possibly exceptional) performance on the exam (cf. Norem & Illingworth, 1993; Showers, 1992c).

The premise of the present chapter is even more general and far-reaching, namely that at least some individuals may be motivated to approach negative attributes or feelings about the self, without aversion, in order to address or make sense of the concerns they pose. For instance, consider the individual who, when faced with the prospect of a social interaction that will make him feel shy, says to himself "I'm shy, but I'm a loyal friend." Although the initial thought of his shyness may conjure the motivation to avoid focusing on this negative attribute, such an individual quickly converts that motivation to an approach state by linking shyness to a positive attribute (loyalty), thereby making attention to the social self more rewarding. Individuals who respond in this way should, over time, be increasingly willing to approach their negative attributes or experiences, because they do not experience the same aversive conditioning as someone in whom the initial avoidance motivation proceeds unchecked.

Thus, we contend that the possibility that individuals sometimes approach negative stimuli with minimal aversion represents an important lacuna in approach–avoidance models. Although previous work on the hierarchy of motivational states does address this issue, negative approach systems are understudied. We suggest that the ability to approach negative stimuli without aversion is an important feature of resilience and good coping, and that,

therefore, a full exploration of these processes within the framework of approach–avoidance models will be a fruitful contribution to the literature.

ROLE OF SELF-STRUCTURE

Recent research on the evaluative structure of the self may offer insight into how individuals are able to approach negative stimuli with minimal aversion. Showers' (1992a) model of evaluative self-organization focuses on how individuals represent positive and negative self-beliefs, and the associative links and category structures which represent them. This is largely a cognitive information processing model, but since the cognitive elements are valenced self-beliefs, affective, and motivational processes are inherently involved. Evaluative self-structures are presumably influenced by underlying self-relevant motivations (e.g., self-enhancement or self-accuracy) (Cantor & Kihlstrom, 1987). In turn, evaluative self-structures likely facilitate certain self-motives (in a bidirectional fashion) (Showers, 1995). Similarly, evaluative self-structures may be both influenced by emotionality and affective processes (such as reactivity or intensity) (cf. Niedenthal, Halberstadt, & Innes-Ker, 1999), and have important emotional consequences. In the present chapter, we extend previous theorizing about affective and motivational processes associated with evaluative self-organization by considering them through the framework of approach–avoidance models and systems.

Previous formulations (Showers & Zeigler-Hill, 2007) suggested distinct motivational characterizations for individuals with relatively positive or relatively negative self-concepts and relatively integrative or relatively compartmentalized self-structures (as described below). As an overview, for individuals with largely positive self-concepts, those with compartmentalized self-structures seem to experience a need for self-enhancement, whereas integrative self-structures were associated with a need for realism. For individuals with largely negative self-concepts, the motivation of individuals with integrative self-structures might be characterized as struggling to cope, whereas those who were compartmentalized showed strategies of resignation or withdrawal (giving up). Here, we will extend these motivational considerations by applying an approach–avoidance framework and, more concretely, their possible manifestations in preference for certain types of achievement goals (e.g., mastery versus performance). In addition, we will examine what that framework suggests with regard to more traditional self-goals and coping strategies, such as self-enhancement versus realism; or active coping versus withdrawal.

BASIC MODEL OF EVALUATIVE ORGANIZATION

This model of self-structure was developed to understand how individuals process and organize positive and negative beliefs about the self (Showers, 1992a, 1995). The so-called basic model of evaluative organization considers the association between self-structure and mood or self-esteem. In particular, the model identifies two alternative approaches to organizing self-knowledge, referred to as "compartmentalized" or "integrative." Numerous empirical studies have documented the association between an integrative or compartmentalized style of self-organization and the individual's mood or self-esteem (Showers, 1992b; Showers & Kevlyn, 1999; Showers & Ryff, 1996). Extensions of the model consider the dynamics of self-structure (i.e., how and when an individual's self-structure might change) and the implications for the stability of self-esteem (Showers, 2000; Zeigler-Hill & Showers, 2007). In addition, this model has been tested in a variety of special populations (college students with eating disorders (McMahon, Showers, Reider, Abramson, & Hogan, 2003); college students who had experienced childhood maltreatment (Showers, Zeigler-Hill, & Limke, 2006); and counseling clients (Showers, Limke, & Zeigler-Hill, 2004) to help understand their unique self processes. The general compartmentalization model has also been extended beyond the case of self-structure to the case of how people organize knowledge about someone else (e.g., a parent or a romantic partner), linking the individual's parent or partner structure to their global attitudes toward that person and the quality of their relationship (Showers & Kevlyn, 1999; Showers & Zeigler-Hill, 2004).

ASSUMPTIONS

A fundamental assumption of the compartmentalization model of evaluative self-organization is the belief that the self is multifaceted and consists of multiple selves or personae (Cantor & Kihlstrom, 1987; Markus & Wurf, 1987). The self-concept is viewed as an enormous repertoire of self-relevant information, including both episodic and semantic knowledge. This knowledge is organized into categories (or some kind of network structure), which represent a person's multiple selves. In any behavioral context, one or more of these selves is activated, creating a working self-concept. This working self-concept consists of subsets of self-knowledge associated with the activated selves. The model of evaluative self-organization is an information processing model that suggests how the organization of positive and negative self-beliefs across multiple self-aspects may influence global feelings about the self and represent self-relevant motivations (cf. Showers, 1995).

COMPARTMENTALIZATION AND INTEGRATION

The terms compartmentalization and integration refer to the evaluative structure of a person's multiple selves (or self-aspect categories). In individuals with compartmentalized self-structures, the specific attributes of their multiple selves tend to be either purely positive or purely negative—that is, they likely have both positive and negative attributes in their self-concept, but they are associated with distinct self-aspects (e.g., "me as an honors student": intelligent, hardworking, curious; "me before exams": weary, disorganized, tense). In individuals with evaluatively integrative self-structures, a similar set of positive and negative attributes may be endorsed, but the attributes within each self-aspect category tend to be mixed (e.g., "me in drama class": creative, involved, disorganized, lazy). According to the model, these evaluative structures may affect individuals' global feelings about the self. For example, if a compartmentalized individual most often experiences the Honors student self (which is purely positive), then that individual should feel quite good. However, when the exam self is activated, the individual will feel quite bad. In contrast, the integrative individual who typically experiences a mixture of positive and negative attributes regardless of which multiple self is activated should have less extreme and perhaps more stable feelings about the self.

Note that in the case of the compartmentalized self, overall feelings depend on whether the positive self-aspects or the negative self-aspects are most important or salient. These individuals can be identified as positively compartmentalized or negatively compartmentalized to distinguish them. Similarly, integrative individuals may have a self that is predominantly positive or negative, and so they too may be identified as positive integrative or negative integrative. However, the two integrative types should be more similar in their overall self-evaluations than the two compartmentalized types, because integrative self-aspect categories contain a mixture of positive and negative attributes. Note also that although we have labeled compartmentalized and integrative structures in a discrete fashion, in fact this feature of self-structure is measured on a continuum from perfectly compartmentalized (no self-aspect categories with attributes of mixed valence) to perfectly integrative (equal proportions of positive and negative attributes across all self-aspect categories) (cf. Showers, 1992a).

Thus, the model of evaluative self-organization predicts an association between the self-structure and a person's mood or self-esteem that can be summarized as follows. For individuals with largely positive self-concepts (i.e., when positive attributes or self-aspects are important or salient), positive compartmentalization should be associated with more positive mood and higher self-esteem than positive integration. This is because the compartmentalized structure helps to isolate negative self-beliefs, minimizing their likelihood of activation. However, for individuals with relatively negative self-concepts (i.e., when negative attributes or self-aspects are important or salient), negative integration should be associated with less negative mood and higher self-esteem than negative compartmentalization. This is because integrative organization minimizes the impact of negative self-beliefs that likely could not be avoided.

These associations between type of self-structure and current mood or self-esteem have been documented in multiple correlational studies (Showers, 1992a,b; Showers, Abramson, & Hogan, 1998; Showers & Kling, 1996; Showers & Ryff, 1996).

METHODOLOGY

Most empirical studies based on the model of evaluative organization have employed a card-sorting task to assess self-concept structure (Showers, 1992a). In this task, participants are given 40 cards that each contains a potentially self-descriptive attribute (20 positive and 20 negative attributes). This task is similar to one used by Linville (1987) to assess self-complexity, although Linville's version uses 33 cards, the majority of which contain positive attributes.

Participants are asked to think of the different aspects of the self and sort the cards into groups such that each group describes a different part of the self. Participants are allowed flexibility to choose the number of self-aspect groups as well as the number and valence of adjectives they include in each group. Once participants have completed this section of the task, they are asked to rate the positivity, negativity, and importance of each group.

This task provides three measures that are used to examine self-structure. The first of these measures is the phi coefficient, which is based on a chi-square statistic (Cramer's v; Cramer, 1945/1974). Phi provides an index of compartmentalization by contrasting the proportion of positive and negative attributes in each of the groups with that which would be expected based on chance (i.e., equal proportions of negative attributes across all groups). The phi coefficient is a continuous measure of

compartmentalization, ranging from 0 (perfect integration) to 1 (perfect compartmentalization). A score of 0 means that equal proportions of negative attributes appear in all groups, whereas a score of 1 means that the positive and negative adjectives are completely segregated into different self-aspect groups. Table 31.1 presents sample integrative and compartmentalized self-descriptive card sorts generated by actual research participants, and their calculated phi values.

The second measure is an index of differential importance (DI) (Pelham & Swann, 1989). Although based on theory by Pelham and Swann, the card sort measure of DI does not employ their Self Attributes Questionnaire. Instead, this index is computed by correlating importance ratings and the positivity–negativity ratings across an individual's self-aspect groups (cf. Showers, 1992a). A positive value of DI indicates that a participant perceives her relatively positive groups to be more important than her relatively negative groups, whereas negative values indicate that negative groups are perceived to be more important than positive groups. A third measure is negativity (neg), the proportion of negative attributes used in an individual's card sort that are negative. The measures of DI and neg are used together to distinguish positively compartmentalized from negatively compartmentalized card sorts, and positively integrative from negatively integrative card sorts (Showers & Kevlyn, 1999).

In addition to the card-sorting task, several other tasks have been used to assess evaluative organization. One alternative measure of compartmentalization is a *listing task* (Showers, 1992b). In this task, participants generate a list of attributes to describe themselves in a specific domain (e.g., academic situations; social situations), with instructions to list the attributes in the order in which they come to mind. The order of positive and negative attributes listed is then analyzed by calculating the extent of clustering of similarly valenced attributes (i.e., the tendency for positive attributes to be listed together and for negative attributes to be listed together). An evaluatively clustered list in which positive adjectives are followed by other positive traits and negative adjectives are followed by other negatives is considered to be compartmentalized. A list in which positive and negative adjectives are intermixed together is considered integrative. Therefore, this task should reflect the tendency to compartmentalize or integrate positive and negative attributes on recall or, possibly, the evaluative structure of self-knowledge stored in memory.

The *paragraph task* (McMahon et al., 2003; Showers, 1992b) can be conceptualized as a measure of integrative ability or potential. In this task, participants identify an

TABLE 31.1
Examples of Actual Card Sorts Illustrating Compartmentalization and Integration

Panel A: Compartmentalized Organization

Me at Home	Me at Work	Me in Class	Me in Norman, OK	Me and My Sorority	Me with People I do not Know	Me When I am Stressed
Giving	Successful	Successful	Successful	Successful	–Weary	–Hopeless
Confident	Capable	Capable	Confident	Giving	–Inferior	–Not the "real me"
Comfortable	Confident	Independent	Comfortable	Confident	–Tense	–Uncomfortable
Lovable	Comfortable	Organized	Independent	Comfortable		–Sad and blue
Outgoing	Needed	Interested	Fun and Entertaining	Lovable		–Irritable
		Hardworking				
Happy	Communicative		Interested	Fun and Entertaining		–Disorganized
Friendly	Organized		Outgoing			–Tense
Optimistic	Interested		Hardworking	Interested		
	Outgoing		Happy	Outgoing		
	Hardworking		Friendly	Energetic		
	Happy		Optimistic	Happy		
	Friendly			Friendly		

Panel B: Integrative Organization

Family	Religion	Student	African American	Intimate Relationship	Friendship	Dreams (as in Goals)	Perfectionist
Organized	Needed	Successful	–Hopeless	Comfortable	Giving	Independent	Successful
–Irritable	Organized	–Lazy	Organized	–Irritable	–Uncomfortable	Organized	–Disagreeing
–Disagreeing	Giving	Mature	Confident	–Immature	–Insecure	–Weary	–Irritable
–Self-centered	Happy	–Irritable	–Irritable	–Insecure	–Irritable		Capable
Communicative	–Irritable	Organized		–Inferior	–Isolated		Confident
Lovable	Optimistic	Intelligent		Organized	Organized		Organized
Fun and Entertaining		Interested		–Tense	Friendly		Intelligent
	Hardworking						
Energetic	–Tense	Hardworking			–Not the "real me"		Outgoing
		–Tense					Hardworking
							–Tense

Source: From "Self-structure and self-esteem stability: The hidden vulnerability of compartmentalization," by V. Zeigler-Hill and C.J. Showers, 2007, *Personality and Social Psychology Bulletin, 33*, p. 143.

Note: Negative attributes are identified by a minus sign. Panel A: compartmentalization = 1.00; differential importance = .80; and proportion of negative attributes = .17. Panel B: compartmentalization = .32; differential importance = .65; and proportion of negative attributes = .40.

extremely negative attribute that describes them and write about how that attribute relates to other aspects of the self, as well as the consequences it has for them. The paragraph or individual sentences are then coded for the presence of integrative thinking (e.g., I am shy, but I am a loyal friend). Individuals that tend to integrate negative information are linking their negative attributes to other more positive features of the self, which should help to minimize the impact of negative self-beliefs.

Finally, a variation on an affective priming task is currently being tested as a measure of underlying integrative processes or potential (Boyce & Showers, 2007). In this reaction time task, participants are shown a potentially self-relevant prime followed by a target word and asked to decide if the target is "good" or "bad." Primes and targets are positive and negative self-descriptive adjectives. On the basis of the work of Fazio, Sanbonmatsu, Powell, and Kardes (1986), one would expect participants to have the quickest reaction times on trials for which prime and target share the same valence, due to the spreading activation of valence through memory. However, individuals who are able to integrate negative traits with positive traits may have relatively quicker reaction times on trials with incongruent valence—that is, trials on which the valence of the prime (e.g., negative) is different from the target valence (e.g., positive). However, this research is still exploratory (cf. Graham & Clark, 2006).

LONG-TERM OUTCOMES

Data on current mood and self-esteem, however, do not present a complete picture of the associations between evaluative organization and psychological well-being. Although concurrent well-being data suggest advantages to positive compartmentalization and negative integration, some potential drawbacks of these organizational styles and strategies are revealed in longitudinal and diary studies, and also in studies of special populations.

First, consider positively compartmentalized college students, whose concurrent mood and self-esteem are high (Showers, 1992a). Daily diary data reveal their vulnerability to changes in self-esteem, corresponding to everyday life events (Zeigler-Hill & Showers, 2007). Although compartmentalized individuals' baseline level of self-esteem is high, their self-esteem is actually relatively unstable, fluctuating in response to positive and negative events reported each day. Presumably, negative events activate negative compartments of self, causing a substantial (but temporary) impact on self-esteem. In

contrast, individuals with positively integrative structures show greater self-esteem stability, both in daily diary data and in response to social rejection in the laboratory.

Second, negatively integrative individuals may experience a concurrent lift in their feelings, given the proportion of negative attributes they endorse, but longitudinal results suggest that over time, attempts to integrate important negative beliefs may wear themselves out. This is most apparent in a study of college students' perceptions of their romantic partners (Showers & Zeigler-Hill, 2004). Although individuals with negatively integrative perceptions reported relatively positive feelings about their partner at the outset of the study (given the proportion of negative attributes they perceived), 1 year later they were especially likely to have ended the relationship. Hence, negative integration may help an individual make the best of a bad situation, but over time, that integrative perspective may be difficult to maintain and the relationship may ultimately fail. Perhaps positive integration (i.e., integration in the context of largely positive beliefs) is more likely to be associated with realism and resilience over the long-term.

Consistent with the romantic partners study, a study of college students who reported childhood maltreatment suggested that integration of important negative attributes may reflect an ongoing struggle with important negative beliefs rather than successful resolution of those concerns (Showers, Zeigler-Hill, & Limke, 2006). In this study, college students indicated whether specific events associated with sexual or emotional maltreatment had occurred to them before age 15. Those who had experienced the most severe maltreatment (i.e., both sexual and emotional events) had relatively integrative self-structures, presumably to help them cope with important negative self-beliefs. Those who had one type of maltreatment (especially sexual maltreatment, but not both) were relatively compartmentalized, presumably to help isolate any negative self-beliefs. Interestingly, the integrative structures of those with severe maltreatment were not associated with enhanced psychological well-being; well-being in the severely maltreated was consistently poor. However, for individuals with only one type of maltreatment (especially sexual maltreatment, but not both), integration was associated with more negative adjustment (i.e., borderline features, depression, and maladaptive defenses). We interpret this as showing that integration in this population reflects the ongoing struggle with negative self-beliefs. When a maltreated person can compartmentalize negative self-beliefs, then coping may be either more straightforward or more complete, and psychological well-being is good.

LINKS BETWEEN SELF-ORGANIZATION AND SELF-MOTIVES

Each type of self-organization (i.e., positive compartmentalization, positive integration, negative integration, and negative compartmentalization) can be understood in terms of underlying motives that may contribute to that self-structure or that may emerge when an individual with that structure experiences stressful life events. Characteristic ways of organizing self-knowledge may affect individuals' responses to stress and their goals for effective coping. It may also affect their goals in settings in which performance will be evaluated. Here, we will consider each type of self-structure and outline the likely motivations and preferred types of goals consistent with that self-structure, emphasizing approach–avoidance motives and achievement goals, in conjunction with characteristic styles of coping for individuals with that self-structure, as inferred from previous research.

POSITIVE COMPARTMENTALIZATION

Because individuals with positively compartmentalized self-structures primarily access their positive compartments, negative attributes are characteristically avoided or ignored. One might infer that these individuals value self-enhancement over self-accuracy or realism. Consistent with this, individuals with positively compartmentalized selves report the most positive mood and highest self-esteem. However, these positive feelings may sometimes be unrealistic. Our study of romantic partners found that individuals with positively compartmentalized perceptions of their partners had more positive attitudes toward them at the outset of the study than individuals with positively integrative perceptions, but were more likely to break up over the course of 1 year (Showers & Zeigler-Hill, 2004). In addition, Zeigler-Hill and Showers (2007) found that individuals with positively compartmentalized selves had relatively unstable self-esteem and were especially sensitive to negative interpersonal events and social rejection.

If individuals with positively compartmentalized self-structures wish to avoid their negative attributes, it is likely that their motivations could be characterized as high in approach motivation and low in avoidance. Moreover, their characteristic achievement orientation could be characterized as performance-approach (cf. Elliot & Church, 1997). However, the gist of the literature on evaluative organization suggests that individuals for whom approach is the sole motivation may have hidden vulnerabilities if they cannot adopt a different motivational perspective in appropriate circumstances. In motivational terms, if the prospect of failure suddenly looms large, a person who is unfamiliar with the avoidance state may have difficulty harnessing their anxiety to direct effort toward avoiding feared outcomes.

INTEGRATION

In contrast to individuals with positively compartmentalized selves who avoid or ignore negative attributes and experiences, integrative individuals preserve access to negative attributes, but cushion their impact on the self. This approach may be more realistic, since negative attributes are acknowledged rather than ignored. It also may require high effort or resources, because the individual may be preserving detailed self-thoughts (rather than assimilating concrete beliefs into a broader impression) and continually has to confront distressing negative self-beliefs. One advantage of this approach, however, may be that chronic access to at least some negative beliefs inoculates the individual against stress when it occurs. If people are accustomed to processing salient negative beliefs and linking them to other more positive attributes, they may be well-prepared to cope with salient negative beliefs when additional stressors arise. In other words, individuals with integrative self-structures may be more modest in their typical self-perceptions, but may show good resilience when extreme stressors occur (Showers & Zeigler-Hill, 2007).

Individuals with positively integrative self-structures (i.e., integration within a basically positive self-concept) are likely to be the most realistic in their self-representations. (Most people have predominantly positive self-beliefs.) Moreover, the more positive self-beliefs one has, the easier it should be to make integrative associations between salient negative beliefs and positive attributes. Thus, these individuals are likely to be most resilient.

Consistent with this, we expect that positively integrative individuals would show moderate levels of both approach and avoidance motivations. This should be an ideal motivational frame, since it affords the greatest flexibility (cf. Elliot, 2006). In terms of specific achievement goals, these individuals with their realistic perspective should prefer mastery goals. Their access to a mix of positive and negative self-beliefs gives them a realistic perspective on their current level of skill, while their approach motivation should help them set appropriate goals for self-improvement.

Individuals with negatively integrative structures might best be characterized as good copers. They will have a relatively negative self-concept, which they are chronically trying to resolve. The risk for them is that the integration of many important negative attributes is so effortful that they wear themselves out. In many cases, negative integration may be temporary until the negative concerns are resolved or recompartmentalized. In other cases, the individual may become an expert at integration, able to think in this complex fashion with relative ease and minimal drain on cognitive resources. In some cases, the prevalence and importance of negative attributes may reflect subjective perceptions. Anxious individuals who are struggling to cope might be the prototype of negative integration.

An individual who is anxious yet coping would seem to have high avoidance motivation with moderate levels of approach motivation (to spur the effort to cope). The dominant achievement goal would seem to be performance-avoidance, perhaps with performance-approach goals adopted in the service of avoidance. Thus, their goals may have a hierarchical structure, as proposed by Elliot and Thrash (2001).

In their hierarchical model, Elliot and Thrash (2001) separate the different components that interact to produce an individual's achievement motivation (cf. Elliot & Church, 1997). Specifically, their model includes a higher order construct (i.e., motive dispositions) and a midlevel construct (i.e., achievement goals). Motive dispositions describe relatively abstract motives that individuals have, including the need for achievement and the need to avoid failure, among others. These higher order motives are theorized to lead individuals to adopt more concrete achievement goals. The achievement goals then directly influence a person's goal-related behavior. Elliot and Thrash (2001) argue that motive dispositions and achievement goals are independent constructs, a position that allows for a more flexible understanding of how general motives and specific goals can affect each other to lead to behavior. Thus, this model allows a person to have a dominant motive to avoid failure, but also to use concrete performance-approach goals to alleviate this fear of failure.

Negative Compartmentalization

Negative compartmentalization is the alternative to negative integration. These individuals have relatively negative self-concepts, but may do little in the way of coping. They may seem overwhelmed by their negative attributes, and may be characterized by low-arousal anxiety or depression. One possibility is that negative compartmentalization represents a failed attempt to isolate or avoid one's negative attributions via positive compartmentalization. Alternatively, negatively compartmentalized

structures may afford stability even if they do not imply happiness. For example, in our study of romantic partners, individuals who had negatively compartmentalized perceptions of their partner showed low relationship satisfaction, but were relatively unlikely to break up (Showers & Zeigler-Hill, 2004). In other words, they appeared to have unhappy, but stable, relationships.

These depressed, negatively compartmentalized individuals would likely reveal low approach and low avoidance motivation. Unlike anxious individuals who are vigilant to negative stimuli in order to avoid feared outcomes, depressed individuals are more likely simply to withdraw. In performance contexts, they should endorse neither mastery, performance-approach, nor performance-avoid goals.

DYNAMIC MODEL: CHANGE IN SELF-STRUCTURE

To the extent that these four types of self-structure represent alternative strategies for managing positive and negative self-beliefs, it is reasonable to expect flexibility, that is the potential shift from one structure or strategy to another as circumstances and salient beliefs change. For example, we have suggested that healthy individuals may shift from a positively compartmentalized self-structure to the more effortful integrative style of thinking when negative attributes are salient. In a study of self-structure associated with body dissatisfaction and disordered eating in college-aged women, McMahon et al. (2003) found that participants who were relatively compartmentalized in their overall self-concept structure, but who switched to an integrative style of thinking about specific negative characteristics, also reported the least negative mood. Thus, the most adaptive form of evaluative self-organization may be one that is flexible, shifting from relative compartmentalization to relative integration depending on the salience of positive and negative attributes and one's goals for accuracy, optimism, or resilience.

Another study that examined stability and change in self-structure over the course of almost 2 years (Showers et al., 1998) obtained results that contradicted the hypothesis that individuals would shift toward a more integrative style of self-organization in times of stress. Instead, individuals who seemed to be coping well (low vulnerability to depression, but experiencing major stressful life events) were more compartmentalized when stress was high than when stress was low. We interpret this to mean that compartmentalization is more effective as a coping strategy than was previously imagined. Because of its ease and efficiency, self-organization by valence may be an effective strategy as long as compartmentalization is successfully maintained (i.e., as long as compartmentalization effectively isolates important negative attributes). Compartmentalization may be an especially useful strategy for college students, given the complexity of their lives. For instance, if college students tend to have multiple selves that are relatively independent and nonoverlapping, compartmentalization may be especially effective for them.

Interestingly, some of the clearest evidence of shifts toward integration emerged from our study of romantic relationships (Showers & Zeigler-Hill, 2004), in which integration of partner-structure increased over the course of a year for individuals who were experiencing high relationship conflict or who described their partner in relatively negative terms (but not both). Moreover, increases in integration were associated with better relationship outcomes (i.e., ongoing status) only if the couple experienced low conflict. Thus, as suggested earlier, increased integration may reflect the effort of an ongoing struggle with negative beliefs that is not always successful in the long run. Finally, preliminary results of a psychological treatment study suggest that individuals who seek psychological treatment experience shifts toward increased evaluative integration of the self over a 2- to 3-month period. A more detailed discussion of a dynamic model of evaluative self-organization appears in Showers (2002).

The present approach–avoidance systems perspective suggests the intriguing possibility that a physiological shift from approach (BAS) to avoidance (BIS) systems may accompany or even underlie or precede change in evaluative self-structure, as described above. The approach–avoidance framework inherently allows for flexibility without implying that evaluative structures need to be stable and unchanging. Moreover, the approach–avoidance goals framework emphasizes the contribution of the individual's perspective and goal choice in accomplishing these structural shifts.

ADDITIONAL FEATURES OF SELF-STRUCTURE AND LINKS TO SELF-MOTIVES

As should be clear from the previous sections, one advantage of the model of evaluative organization is its ability to make very explicit predictions about motivations. In particular, the compartmentalization model is an information processing model that specifies the cognitive processes that take place when individuals are confronted with positive or negative information or experience, as well as the long-term outcomes that these processes would predict. As outlined above, evaluative organization specifies four

specific groups of individuals whose achievement goals, approach–avoidance motives, and likelihood of resilience can be differentiated and explained.

However, evaluative self-organization is not the only feature of self-structure that can be linked to resilience and the ability to cope with stress. Whereas the content of the self-concept may represent a reasonably accurate reflection of both positive and negative attributes and experiences in individuals' lives, structural features of the self may reflect an individual's goals and motives; the self-structure, rather than the self-concept content, may be the source of the individual's ability to cope (Showers et al., 1998). A variety of features of self-structure influence the attention, salience, or importance an individual gives positive or negative aspects of the self. In their most adaptive forms, these features of self-structure may enable individuals to approach negativity without aversion.

MULTIPLE SELVES PERSPECTIVES

Self-complexity is one dimension of self-structure that may allow individuals to approach negative information or experience without aversion. Self-complexity has two components (1) the number of aspects a person uses to describe the self, and (2) the distinctiveness of the aspects (Linville, 1987; Rafaeli-Mor & Steinberg, 2002). (One distinction between evaluative organization and self-complexity is that self-complexity does not take the valence of traits into account, whereas evaluative organization does assess the valence of the self-concept). Specifically, an individual's multiple self-aspects are said to be distinctive if the attributes contained in one aspect of the self are different from, or independent of, those in other aspects of the self-concept. Therefore, a person's level of self-complexity increases as the number and distinctiveness of her self-aspects increase.

The many distinct self-aspects of individuals with high self-complexity should buffer them from negative outcomes under conditions of stress (Koch & Shepperd, 2004; Linville, 1987; see also Showers & Zeigler-Hill, 2003). Particularly, those with higher self-complexity are less affected by negative events because this negative information is restricted to a small amount of self-knowledge, while other independent self-aspects are left unaffected. For example, a person with high complexity may have multiple self-aspects that describe her as a mother, wife, teacher, researcher, and writer, while a person with low complexity might only have two self-aspects describing her family life and work life. If the first individual receives negative teaching evaluations, this should only affect her "teaching" aspect, while her other self-aspects are unaffected. However, if the second person receives the same information this would relate to everything that falls within her "work" aspect, and thus affect her more broadly.

Due to the buffering effect of complexity, individuals with higher self-complexity should react less strongly to stressors than those with low self-complexity. Importantly, these individuals may show lower avoidance motivation because they are able to approach negativity without an extreme aversive reaction. Individuals with high self-complexity may also exhibit moderate approach motives because their resilience should provide them with a greater opportunity to focus attention on and approach positive information instead of exerting their energy toward circumventing negative information.

A second structural feature of the self-concept that cushions the effect of negative attributes and experience is differential importance. The model of differential importance (DI) and differential certainty attempts to explain differences in self-esteem by taking into account both the certainty and importance of positive and negative self-views (Pelham & Swann, 1989). As described above, individuals have high DI if they perceive their relatively positive aspects of the self to be more important than their relatively negative self-aspects.

Pelham and Swann (1989) found that, for individuals who had many negative self-views, self-esteem was greater when they placed greater importance on their positive self-views, as compared to their negative self-views (i.e., when they showed high differential importance). Thus, even though their self-concepts contained a great deal of negative information, these individuals still exhibited relatively high levels of self-esteem because they were able to put more emphasis on their positive attributes.

This ability to minimize negative information should help those with high DI to be resilient to incoming negative information. When forced to deal with this information, these individuals have the ability to minimize its importance and shift attention and importance to the positive aspects that they have. Because of this ability, we predict that individuals with high DI should have lower avoidance motivation than those with low DI (those placing more importance on negative aspects than positive aspects). Individuals with high DI should be able to confront negative information without extreme emotional reactions or unpleasantness. Furthermore, the emphasis that they place on positive attributes should allow them to develop moderate levels of approach motivations by shifting their attention and effort to seeking additional positive information.

SELF-CONCEPT CLARITY, SELF-STABILITY, AND CONTINGENCIES OF SELF-WORTH

In addition to focusing on the multiple selves that an individual can have, researchers have begun to examine the fragility, or insecurity, of the self-concept as it relates to self-structure (Crocker & Wolfe, 2001; Kernis, Paradise, Whitaker, Wheatman, & Goldman, 2000). According to these perspectives, a self-concept is fragile if the perception of self-worth is uncertain and easily changed by external information or events. Some features of the self-concept associated with self-fragility include self-concept clarity, self-esteem instability, and contingencies of self-worth.

These models share the common characteristic of measuring variability in self-descriptions and self-worth. However, each model also has its own distinct formulation and predictions. Self-concept clarity refers to having a self-concept that is clearly and confidently defined, temporally stable, and internally consistent (Campbell, 1990; Campbell et al., 1996). Thus, an individual is said to have high self-concept clarity if he knows which traits describe him, if these descriptions stay constant through time, and if these descriptions relate to specific behaviors. In contrast, those with low self-concept clarity are unsure about how to describe themselves and tend to change their self-views more easily. Empirical studies have found low self-clarity to be correlated with low self-esteem, negative affect, high neuroticism, and high levels of depression (Campbell et al.). Additionally, low self-concept clarity has been correlated with unstable self-esteem (Kernis et al., 2000). Self-esteem instability describes a tendency for individuals to display short-term fluctuations in global self-esteem (Kernis & Goldman, 2003). These fluctuations can reflect responses to daily positive and negative events and can lead to more depressive symptoms and lower levels of self-determination.

Individuals with low self-concept clarity and self-esteem instability lack definite beliefs about the traits that describe them. This lack of certain self-knowledge allows their moods and self-esteem to be greatly influenced by outside events. Although the focus on fragility has framed this self-uncertainty as a negative outcome, it is also possible to view uncertainty or instability as a source of flexibility or resilience. If we imagine a person with low self-esteem and either low self-clarity or unstable self-esteem, we can consider whether self-uncertainty might actually offer relief from an otherwise negative self-concept. These individuals may prefer self-knowledge that is uncertain but sometimes (even if only rarely) positive, over confirmed, stable negative self-beliefs. Although there may often be costs to uncertainty, the glimmers of hope it provides may sometimes motivate resilience in the face of threat (cf. Pelham, 1991).

A study by Hannover (2002) makes a relevant argument for the usefulness of low self-concept clarity for individuals with an interdependent self-construal. For those with interdependent construals, it is particularly important to achieve group harmony and have positive relationships within different social groups. Hannover theorizes that having low self-concept clarity would be more adaptive for individuals with interdependent construals because it would give them flexibility to adjust to various social contexts. In other words, because individuals with low self-concept clarity lack a strong sense of who they are, they may actually interact more effectively with others by changing to fit the social environment. Thus, in some circumstances, having a flexible sense of self can lead to better outcomes and make a person more resilient to negativity.

On the basis of the fact that low self-concept clarity and self-esteem instability have been associated with relatively negative self-concepts, we do not expect these individuals to be high in approach motivation. However, if these characteristics afford resilience, either in terms of flexibility to adjust to different social contexts or by providing glimmers of hope in the face of an otherwise negative self-concept, avoidance motivation may be lower than for individuals with clear and stable negative self-concepts. The fact that uncertain individuals have negative self-beliefs combined with glimmers of hope may allow them to approach negative self-knowledge or experience without aversion. Thus, we would predict that these fragile individuals may show moderate levels of approach motivation and relatively low levels of avoidance motivation. This motivational structure affords them the flexibility to change their behavior as needed in response to an environment that is often adverse.

Our discussion of self-concept clarity and self-esteem instability has characterized these features of self-structure as representing strategies that a person can use when dealing with negative feedback (i.e., using one's uncertainty of self-knowledge to defend against potentially damaging negative information). To the extent that contingencies of self-worth (CSW) also create low self-clarity or unstable self-esteem, similar outcomes may be expected. Specifically, a person is said to have contingent self-worth if he places particular importance on a certain domain of the self and stakes his self-worth on success in this area (Crocker & Wolfe, 2001). Crocker and Wolfe (2001) describe seven domains of the self for which people may construct contingencies: approval, appearance, God's love, family support, academic competency,

competition, and virtue. Accordingly, if college students place importance on the area of academic competency (i.e., if their self-worth is contingent on academic success) then their self-esteem may increase when they succeed and decrease when they fail in this domain.

Literature on CSW has focused on the harsh implications of failure in a contingent domain. Crocker, Brook, Niiya, and Villacorta (2006) explain that, because declines in self-esteem following failure can be highly painful, contingent self-esteem can create a prevailing motivation to protect and maintain the self. This goal of protecting the self should produce vigilance toward negativity and, hence, an avoidance perspective. More specifically, in an achievement domain, this contingency might translate into a tendency to adopt performance-avoidance goals in an attempt to ensure that failure does not occur.

However, it seems plausible that CSW in a domain can sometimes be accompanied by high self-efficacy, such that contingent individuals generally believe that they can succeed in that domain. More specifically, if individuals are able to attain success in their contingent domains this should allow them to exhibit high stable self-esteem (Crocker & Wolfe, 2001). In these cases, we would predict that individuals could reveal an approach motivation due to the fact that they strongly believe that they can succeed in a domain and increase their self-esteem. In a related vein, Niiya, Crocker, and Bartmess (2004) showed that the negative effects of failure for those with academic CSW can be attenuated by priming them with an incremental theory of intelligence. In this work, individuals primed to believe that they could increase their intelligence in the future showed a less severe drop in self-esteem after an academic failure. In other words, activation of incremental self-theories may mimic the hypothesized effects of high self-efficacy, and link CSW to approach rather than avoidance motives.

Thus, although CSW in its prototypical form is likely associated with strong avoidance motives and performance-avoid goals, it may sometimes be associated with using self-uncertainty to one's advantage. Moreover, if contingencies are likely to be satisfied, CSW may even be associated with approach goals, despite the inherent fragility of this self-structure.

SELF-STRATEGIES: SELF-ENHANCEMENT VERSUS SELF-VERIFICATION

Most researchers would agree that people are motivated to understand themselves and the ways in which others see them (Fiske, 2004; Taylor, 1998). There are a number of different self-strategies that people can use to do this, depending on the type of information that is the most appealing to them (Tesser, Crepaz, Beach, Cornell, & Collins, 2000). For instance, one of the most well-researched strategies is the self-enhancement motive (Sedikides, 1993; Kwan, John, Kenny, Bond, & Robins, 2004). Individuals use this strategy because they are interested in obtaining positive or favorable information about themselves. This could also be called an enhancement bias because individuals only receive a limited amount of information about themselves and are motivated to avoid learning about any information that could reflect negatively on them. Sedikides's data suggest that self-enhancement is one of the most dominant strategies used to evaluate one's self.

Nonetheless, there are alternative strategies that can actually lead individuals to approach negative information. Self-verification is a strategy for understanding the self in which people are motivated to have their own self-beliefs validated by others (Swann & Read, 1981). They seek consistency between the attributes that they believe describe them and the attributes that other people use to describe them. Importantly, these individuals may be motivated to verify *negative* beliefs that they hold about themselves, as well as positive beliefs. Thus, if a person believes that he is an incompetent tennis player, he will seek out others to verify this belief. Individuals guided by this motive may seek verification of negative self-beliefs from others because they would rather have others see them truthfully than have them set high expectations that they cannot meet. Knowing that others understand and accept their weaknesses alleviates the stress of wondering whether others will feel disappointed with them in the future (Swann & Read, 1981; Swann, Stein-Seroussi, & Giesler, 1992).

Presumably, a self-verification motive could lead individuals to approach self-consistent information (both positive and negative) without aversion, if this information offers the benefit of validating their own beliefs about the self. To the extent that most individuals have a substantial number of both positive and negative beliefs in their repertoire of self-knowledge (cf. Schwartz & Garamoni, 1986), we would expect them to show moderate to high levels of approach motivation when positive attributes are salient and (because of the benefits of self-verification) only moderate levels of avoidance motivation with regard to salient negative attributes. Moreover, like the negatively integrative individuals, self-verifying individuals with important negative self-beliefs may adopt a mixture of approach–avoid tactics in the service of higher-level avoidance goals (e.g., I want my romantic partner to verify my current negative self-views in order to prevent future disaster in my relationship).

Other features of self-knowledge, self-structure, and self-strategies are not addressed in detail here because they have their own chapters in the present volume. For example, self-presentation phenomena comprise strategies of portraying the self so that one relates well to others in a social group (Baumeister, 1982). Self-presentation could reflect higher levels of avoidance motivation if individuals who self-present are unduly anxious about being accepted by others, but other forms of self-presentation may be associated with resilience. Research on self-discrepancies has already been related to promotion or prevention focus and achievement goals (Higgins, 1997). Self-discrepancies emphasize the contrast between a person's perception of the actual self-concept and both the self they wish they had (ideal) and the self they should have (ought). These different discrepancies can lead individuals to exhibit different achievement goals and adopt a focus on promotion versus prevention goals. Finally, Friedman and Förster (2000) have developed approach–avoidance goal manipulations using specific behaviors. These perspectives on self-knowledge and self-strategies offer additional understanding of potential resilience to negativity within an approach–avoidance framework.

CONCLUSION

To summarize, this chapter has reviewed literature on evaluative organization of the self, as well as other features of self-structure, linking each feature to approach and avoidance motivation and (where appropriate) performance versus mastery goals. Specifically, we propose that the resilience of individuals who construct positively integrative structures for their self-beliefs may correspond to moderate levels of both approach and avoid motives (i.e., motivational flexibility) and a preference for mastery goals. The predominance of avoidance motives in individuals with negatively integrative self-structures may serve them well in the short-term, but may often carry long-term costs, consistent with the view that this perspective functions best as a short-term strategy. In contrast, individuals who tend toward positively compartmentalized self-structures may prefer a performance-approach framework that is optimal in benign circumstances, but which may be unrealistically positive in times of stress, especially if the self-structure and concomitant motives are rigid and inflexible. Finally, individuals with negatively compartmentalized self-structures should simply be low in both approach and avoidance motivations, given a perspective that allows the illusion of some positive potential with low motivation for any substantive change.

Additionally, we discussed other features of self-structure that may characterize resilient individuals who can approach negative self-knowledge or experience without aversion. In addition to the positively integrative self-structure that characterizes resilient individuals according to the model of evaluative self-organization, other features of self-structure associated with resilience may include high self-complexity; high differential importance (especially for individuals with a relatively negative self-concept); some instances of low self-concept clarity, self-esteem instability, or even contingent self-worth; and a preference for self-verification strategies. We propose that these structural features and strategies associated with good coping may stem from moderate levels of approach motives and low to moderate avoidance motives, affording an optimal level of flexibility. This flexibility allows resilient individuals to adjust their motives and mastery/performance goals to fit the current environment. Although much of the literature tends to treat approach and avoidance motives as mutually exclusive (although see Elliot, 2006 for an exception), an interest in resilience highlights the need to examine the flexibility of individuals who display moderate levels of both approach and avoidance goals, the ability of these individuals to adapt to a range of motivational contexts, and the ways in which motivational flexibility can affect behavioral outcomes.

REFERENCES

Atkinson, J. W., & Birch, D. (1970). *The dynamics of action*. New York: Wiley.

Baumeister, R. F. (1982). A self-presentational view of social phenomena. *Psychological Bulletin, 91*, 3–26.

Boyce, K. L., & Showers, C. J. (2007). *Reverse priming as a result of self-focus and stimulus extremity*. Poster presentation at annual meeting of the Society for Personality and Social Psychology, Memphis, TN. January 25–27.

Campbell, J. D. (1990). Self-esteem and clarity of the self-concept. *Journal of Personality and Social Psychology, 59*, 538–549.

Campbell, J. D., Trapnell, P. D., Hein, S. J., Katz, I. M., Lavallee, L. F., & Lehman, D. R. (1996). Self-concept clarity: Measurement, personality correlates, and cultural boundaries. *Journal of Personality and Social Psychology, 70*, 141–156.

Cantor, N., & Kihlstrom, J. F. (1987). *Personality and social intelligence*. Englewood Cliffs, NJ: Prentice-Hall.

Carver, C., & Scheier, M. (1998). *On the self-regulation of behavior*. New York: Cambridge University Press.

Cramer, H. (1974). *Mathematical methods of statistics*. Princeton, NJ: Princeton University Press. (Original work published 1945).

Crocker, J., Brook, A. T., Niiya, Y., & Villacorta, M. (2006). The pursuit of self-esteem: Contingencies of self-worth and self-regulation. *Journal of Personality, 74*, 1749–1771.

Crocker, J., & Wolfe, C. T. (2001). Contingencies of self-worth. *Psychological Review, 108*, 593–623.

Elliot, A. J. (2006). The hierarchical model of approach–avoidance motivation. *Motivation and Emotion, 30*, 111–116.

Elliot, A. J., & Church, M. A. (1997). A hierarchical model of approach and avoidance achievement motivation. *Journal of Personality and Social Psychology, 72*, 218–232.

Elliot, A. J., & Thrash, T. M. (2001). Achievement goals and the hierarchical model of achievement motivation. *Educational Psychology Review, 12*, 139–156.

Fazio, R. H., Sanbonmatsu, D. M., Powell, M. C., & Kardes, F. R. (1986). On the automatic activation of attitudes. *Journal of Personality and Social Psychology, 50*, 229–238.

Fiske, S. T. (2004). *Social beings: A core motives approach to social psychology* (1st ed.). New York: Wiley.

Friedman, R. S., & Förster, J. (2000). The effects of approach and avoidance motor actions on the elements of creative insight. *Journal of Personality and Social Psychology, 79*, 477–492.

Graham, S. M., & Clark, M. S. (2006). Self-esteem and organization of valenced information about others: The 'Jekyll and Hyde'-ing of relationship partners. *Journal of Personality and Social Psychology, 90*, 652–665.

Hannover, B. (2002). One man's poison ivy is another man's spinach: What self-clarity is in independent self-construal, a lack of context-dependency is in interdependent self-construal. *Revue Internationale de Psychologie Sociale, 15*, 65–88.

Higgins, T. E. (1997). Beyond pleasure and pain. *American Psychologist, 52*, 1280–1300.

Kernis, M. H., & Goldman, B. M. (2003). Stability and variability in self-concept and self-esteem. In M. R. Leary & J. P. Tangney (Eds.), *Handbook of self and identity* (pp. 106–127). New York: Guilford Press.

Kernis, M. H., Paradise, A. W., Whitaker, D. J., Wheatman, S. R., & Goldman, B. N. (2000). Master of one's psychological domain? Not likely if one's self-esteem is unstable. *Personality and Social Psychology Bulletin, 26*, 1297–1305.

Koch, E. J., & Shepperd, J. A. (2004). Is self-complexity linked to better coping? A review of the literature. *Journal of Personality, 72*, 727–760.

Kwan, V. S. Y., John, O. P., Kenny, D. A., Bond, M. H., & Robins, R. W. (2004). Reconceptualizing individual differences in self-enhancement bias: An interpersonal approach. *Psychological Review, 111*, 94–110.

Lang, P., Bradley, M., & Cuthbert, B. (1998). Emotion, motivation, and anxiety: Brain mechanisms and psychophysiology. *Biological Psychiatry, 44*, 1248–1263.

Linville, P. W. (1987). Self-complexity as a cognitive buffer against stress-related illness and depression. *Journal of Personality and Social Psychology, 52*, 663–676.

Markus, H., & Wurf, E. (1987). The dynamic self-concept: A social psychological perspective. *Annual Review of Psychology, 38*, 299–337.

McMahon, P. D., Showers, C. J., Reider, S. L., Abramson, L. Y., & Hogan, M. E. (2003). Integrative thinking and flexibility in the organization of self-knowledge. *Cognitive Therapy and Research, 27,* 167–184.

Niedenthal, P. M., Halberstadt, J. B., & Innes-Ker, A. H. (1999). Emotional response categorization. *Psychological Review, 106,* 337–361.

Niiya, Y., Crocker, J., & Bartmess, E. N. (2004). From vulnerability to resilience: Learning orientations buffer contingent self-esteem from failure. *Psychological Science, 15,* 801–805.

Norem, J. K., & Illingworth, K. S. (1993). Strategy-dependent effects of reflecting on self and tasks: Some implications of optimism and defensive pessimism. *Journal of Personality and Social Psychology, 65,* 822–835.

Pelham, B. W. (1991). On the benefits of misery: Self-serving biases in the depressive self-concept. *Journal of Personality and Social Psychology, 61,* 670–681.

Pelham, B. W., & Swann, Jr., W. B. (1989). From self-conceptions to self-worth: On the sources and structure of global self-esteem. *Journal of Personality and Social Psychology, 57,* 672–680.

Rafaeli-Mor, E., & Steinberg, J. (2002). Self-complexity and well-being: A research synthesis. *Personality and Social Psychology Review, 6,* 31–58.

Schwartz, R. M., & Garamoni, G. L. (1986). A structural model of positive and negative states of mind Asymmetry in the internal dialogue. In P. C. Kendall (Ed.), *Advances in cognitive-behavioral research and therapy* (Vol. 5, pp. 1–62). New York: Academic Press.

Sedikides, C. (1993). Assessment, enhancement, and verification determinants of the self-evaluation process. *Journal of Personality and Social Psychology, 65,* 317–338.

Showers, C. J. (1992a). Compartmentalization of positive and negative self-knowledge: Keeping bad apples out of the bunch. *Journal of Personality and Social Psychology, 62,* 1036–1049.

Showers, C. J. (1992b). Evaluatively integrative thinking about characteristics of the self. *Personality and Social Psychology Bulletin, 18,* 719–729.

Showers, C. J. (1992c). The motivational and emotional consequences of considering positive or negative possibilities for an upcoming event. *Journal of Personality and Social Psychology, 63,* 474–484.

Showers, C. J. (1995). The evaluative organization of self-knowledge: Origins, processes, and implications for self-esteem. In M. H. Kernis (Ed.), *Efficacy, agency, and self-esteem* (pp. 101–120). New York: Plenum.

Showers, C. J. (2000). Self-organization in emotional contexts. In J. P. Forgas (Ed.), *Feeling and thinking: The role of affect in social cognition* (pp. 283–307). Paris: Cambridge University Press.

Showers, C. J. (2002). Integration and compartmentalization: A model of self-structure and self-change. In D. Cervone & W. Mischel (Eds.), *Advances in personality science* (pp. 271–291). New York: The Guilford Press.

Showers, C. J., Abramson, L. Y., & Hogan, M. E. (1998). The dynamic self: How the content and structure of the self-concept change with mood. *Journal of Personality and Social Psychology, 75,* 478–493.

Showers, C. J., & Kevlyn, S. B. (1999). Organization of knowledge about a relationship partner: Implications for liking and loving. *Journal of Personality and Social Psychology, 76,* 958–971.

Showers, C. J., & Kling, K. C. (1996). Organization of self-knowledge: Implications for recovery from sad mood. *Journal of Personality and Social Psychology, 70,* 578–590.

Showers, C. J., Limke, A., & Zeigler-Hill, V. (2004). Self-structure and self-change: Applications to psychological treatment. *Behavior Therapy, 35,* 167–184.

Showers, C. J., & Ryff, C. D. (1996). Self-differentiation and well-being in a life transition. *Personality and Social Psychology Bulletin, 22,* 448–460.

Showers, C. J., & Zeigler-Hill, V. (2007). Compartmentalization and integration: The evaluative organization of contextualized selves. *Journal of Personality, 75,* 1181–1204.

Showers, C. J., & Zeigler-Hill, V. (2003). Organization of Self-knowledge: Features, functions, and flexibility. In M. R. Leary & J. Tangeny (Eds.), *Handbook of self and identity* (pp. 47–67). New York: Guilford.

Showers, C. J., & Zeigler-Hill, V. (2004). Organization of partner knowledge: Relationship outcomes and longitudinal change. *Personality and Social Psychology Bulletin, 30,* 1198–1210.

Showers, C. J., Zeigler-Hill, V., & Limke, A. (2006). Self-structure and childhood maltreatment: Successful compartmentalization and the struggle of integration. *Journal of Social and Clinical Psychology, 25,* 473–506.

Swann, W. B., & Read, S. J. (1981). Self-verification processes: How we sustain our self-conceptions. *Journal of Experiment Social Psychology, 17,* 351–372.

Swann, W. B., Stein-Seroussi, A., & Giesler, R. B. (1992). Why people self-verify. *Journal of Personality and Social Psychology, 62,* 392–401.

Taylor, S. E. (1998). The social being in social psychology. In D. T. Gilbert, S. T. Fiske, & G. Lindzey (Eds.), *The handbook of social psychology* (pp. 58–95). New York: McGraw-Hill.

Tesser, A., Crepaz, N., Beach, S. R. H., Cornell, D., & Collins, J. C. (2000). Confluence of self-esteem regulation mechanisms: On integrating the self-zoo. *Personality and Social Psychology Bulletin, 26,* 1476–1489.

Zeigler-Hill, V., & Showers, C. J. (2007). Self-structure and self-esteem stability: The hidden vulnerability of compartmentalization. *Personality and Social Psychology Bulletin, 33,* 143–159.

Self-Access

32 The Functional Architecture of Approach and Avoidance Motivation

Julius Kuhl and Sander L. Koole

CONTENTS

When a young man marries a woman just because he cannot bear his loneliness any longer, we would not be surprised when this marriage does not bring him much happiness. Simply marrying somebody to avoid being alone does not guarantee marital happiness, common interests, personal well-being, or mutual understanding and growth, to name just a few approach goals neglected by the young man in our example. Avoidance goals, even when they are perfectly accomplished, terminate or prevent aversive states, but they do not necessarily promote the satisfaction of needs (Elliot, chapter 1, this volume; Higgins, 1998). Instead, avoidance motivation is associated with reduced subjective well-being and impaired subjective competence (Elliot & Sheldon, 1997) and increased physical symptoms (Elliot & Sheldon, 1998).

The negative consequences of avoidance motivation are intuitively compelling. But what might be the psychological mechanisms that underlie the relationship between avoidance motivation and its negative consequences? An intuitive understanding of its negative consequences does not really tell us why avoidance motivation should have those detrimental effects. In the present chapter, we therefore aim to develop a more scientifically grounded understanding of the psychology of approach and avoidance motivation. In particular, we examine the functional architecture that underlies approach and avoidance motivation. Because we assume that approach versus avoidance is a fundamental distinction to personality functioning, we highlight the connections between approach and avoidance motivation and basic personality systems. Our functional approach focuses on the psychological processes that underlie the two most fundamental achievements of personality functioning (Kuhl, 2000a, 2000b, 2001; Kuhl & Koole, 2004): The enactment of difficult intentions (volitional efficiency) and the repeated integration of new (self-alien) experiences into an ever-growing network of personal wisdom (self-development).

The plan of this chapter is threefold. First, we discuss a hierarchical model of personality functioning. Second, we give a brief summary of PSI theory. In the third part, we describe in more detail how the distinction between approach and avoidance motivation is integrated by the theory of personality system interactions across different levels of personality functioning. We devote special attention to self-regulation as the highest level of personality functioning. We conclude that approach and avoidance are not, as they may appear at first glance, confined to simple forms of motivation (e.g., related to fight or flight). As we will show, approach and avoidance systems may regulate even highly complex motivational phenomena such as self-determination and free will.

A HIERARCHICAL MODEL OF PERSONALITY FUNCTIONING

Over the past century or so, psychologists have developed quite a few different approaches to personality (for an overview, see Carver & Scheier, 2004). For example, whereas Skinner and Hull (and, with some elaborations, social learning theories) describe personality in terms of acquired habits, that is, response dispositions that are automatically triggered by stimuli associated with them, other theories place more emphasis on individual differences in arousal (Eysenck) or affect (Freud, Gray), and still others describe personality with higher-level constructs such as motives (Murray, Atkinson, McClelland), cognitive schemas or "constructs" (Kelly), or the need to develop an authentic self and bring behavior in accordance

with it (Rogers). Given this wide array of different personality constructs, it is a formidable challenge to arrive at an integrative theory of personality functioning.

PSI theory (Kuhl, 2000a, 2001) takes a first step toward an integrative theory of personality, by proposing that leading theories of personality each focus on a different level of personality functioning. More specifically, PSI theory proposes seven levels of personality functioning, which are displayed in Table 32.1. The lowest, most basic level of personality functioning is formed by the smallest unit of motor and perceptual systems that can still be controlled by motivational or volitional processes. The highest level of personality functioning is formed by systems that support intentional action and self-determination.

The lower levels of personality functioning are assumed to be both phylo- and ontogenetically older than the higher levels. Moreover, a steep gradient of increasing degrees of freedom in behavior control can be discerned across the seven levels of personality functioning, which highlights the compatibility of our taxonomy with hierarchical models of approach and avoidance motivation (Cacioppo & Berntson, 1999; Carver & Scheier, 1998; Elliot, 1997). The "gradient of freedom" starts with very few degrees of freedom at the lowest level, where behavior is determined by S-R associations that permit only one dominant response to a given stimulus. With each higher level, the degrees of freedom (or the number of possible responses to a given stimulus) increase. The highest degrees of freedom are associated with the participation of the integrated self in the guidance of decision making and action control. On this level, even goals are exchangeable as long as they are somehow compatible with a person's needs, values, integrated social norms, and other self-aspects.

LEVEL 1: ELEMENTARY COGNITION

At the most basic level, PSI theory distinguishes between a system that supports the automatic control of behavior, *intuitive behavior control* (IBC), and a system that supports the perception of isolated objects, *object recognition*. The behavior that is governed by intuitive behavior control is strongly dependent on the presence of triggering stimuli. Prototypical examples of intuitive behavior control are S-R learning (Skinner, 1953), behavioral priming (Bargh, Chen, & Burrows, 1996), and the largely automatic control of behavior through specifying the exact time and place for performing an intended action (Gollwitzer, 1999). Examples of intuitive behavior control are small talk based on automatized routines of exchanging polite and culturally scripted words, the

TABLE 32.1

Approach and Avoidance Components within Seven Levels of Personality Functioning, Related Theories of Personality (1), and Operationalizations (2)

Level of Personality		Theories (1) and Operationalizations (2)
Approach-Related	**Avoidance-Related**	
Level 1 (Low-level cognition)		(1) Hull, Skinner, Witkin
Habits	*Objects*	(2) Valence-independent enactment; behavioral priming (Bargh
Intuitive Behavior Control: IBC	Object Recognition: OR	et al., 1996)
Level 2 (Temperament)		(1) Pavlov, Eysenck
Motor activation	*Sensory arousal*	(2) Determinants of activation/arousal (EDA): motor activity,
Opportunistic energization of motor or sensory networks		white noise (Lang,1995; Thayer,1978)
Level 3 (Affect)		(1) Freud, Gray
Positive and facilitating	*Negative and inhibiting*	(2) Reward versus punishment (Gupta & Nagpal, 1978)
Object conditioning of positive and negative valence		
Level 4 (Progression versus regression)		(1) Freud
Top–down	*Bottom–up*	(2) Elementary versus configurational conditioning (Schmajuk
Degree of modulation of Levels 1–3 through Levels 5–7		& Buhusi, 1997)
Level 5 (Instrumental versus experiential motives):		(1) Murray, Atkinson, McClelland
Instrumental needs	*Experiential needs*	(2) Motives (Atkinson, 1958); Motive-goal congruence
(achievement, power)	(affiliation, self-growth)	(Brunstein, 2001; Baumann et al., 2005)
Motives as "intelligent needs" (networks of context-specific possible actions from autobiographical memory)		
Level 6 (Knowing and feeling: high-level cognition)		(1) Kelly, Jung
Analytical thinking (either–or)	*Holistic feeling (both–and)*	(2) Summation priming (Beeman et al., 1994); Coherence
Independence of experience, affect, and need states	Dependence of experience, affect, and need states	judgments (Bowers et al., 1990)
Level 7 (Agency)		(1) Rogers (Freud versus Jung)
Self-control	*Self-maintenance*	(2) Volition (Kuhl & Kazén, 1999); self-complexity (Linville,
Intention memory (IM)	Extension memory (EM/Self)	1987; Showers & Kling, 1996); self-determination (Deci & Ryan, 2000)

intuitive exchange between mother and baby during face-to-face interaction, and a driver taking the well-known route to his office.

Object recognition is assigned to the same fundamental level of personality functioning. The primary function of object recognition is to recognize single objects independently of the context in which they appear. An "object" is defined here as a perceptual or semantic entity that can be labeled and recognized as separate from the context. For example, Witkin's (1950) concept of field-independence can be related to the object recognition function. Examples of object recognition are recognizing a new car model on the freeway despite the fact that one has only seen this new model at an exhibition rather than on the road, or

recognizing a single angry face among a crowd of faces with a different emotional expression (Öhman, Lundqvist, & Esteves, 2001). An example of a maladaptive use of object recognition would be a psychotherapist perceiving a patient as an exemplar of a particular clinical category rather than as a complex human being with an elaborate past and a rich life context that entails many propensities and resources beyond her particular symptoms.

LEVEL 2: TEMPERAMENT

The second level of personality functioning is referred to as temperament, and controls the intensity or energization of behavior. Temperament is further divided into a *sensory arousal* and a *motor activation* component. For example, motor activation increases whenever a person has engaged in rigorous physical exercise, such as walking up and down a flight of stairs several times. Analogously, sensory arousal increases whenever a person has perceived a strong stimulus, such as a loud noise. Either type of temperament component intensifies processes across levels of personality. At a subjective level, it is often difficult to distinguish between arousal and affect (see Level 3), given that increases in affect often involve elevated levels of arousal. Nevertheless, psychophysiological (Lang, 1995) and even self-report (Thayer, 1978) methods for disentangling arousal and affect have been developed.

LEVEL 3: AFFECT

The third level of personality functioning is affect. At this level, specific objects become linked to a specific affective valence. In agreement with other modern emotion theories (Cacioppo & Gardner, 1999), PSI theory distinguishes between *positive* and *negative affect*. The distinction between positive and negative affect is conceptually and empirically supported by various lines of research (Cacioppo & Berntson, 1999; Diener & Emmons, 1985; Higgins, 1987; Taylor, 1991; Watson, Wiese, Vaidya, & Tellegen, 1999). Positive affect is typically experienced as elated emotion, ranging from satisfaction to joy, whereas inhibited positive affect is typically experienced as dejected emotion, ranging from a "neutral" or aloof mood to listlessness, dejection, or even depression. Negative affect is typically experienced as agitated emotion, ranging from sadness to anxiety, whereas inhibited negative affect is typically experienced as peaceful emotion, ranging from calmness to deep relaxation. The third level corresponds to reward and punishment systems, and is therefore most directly linked to approach and avoidance motives. We return to this issue in the next section.

LEVEL 4: PROGRESSION VERSUS REGRESSION

On the fourth level of personality functioning, a decision is made as to whether the three elementary levels (Levels 1–3), or the three higher levels of control (Levels 4–7) govern experience and behavior. When the lower levels acquire the predominant control over the person's behavior, we speak of *regression*. When the higher levels acquire the predominant control over the person's behavior, we speak of *progression*. The Freudian concept of regression (Freud, 1938/1989) can be related to this level

because it describes impaired high-level control of affective responses and habitual behavior (i.e., Levels 1–3).

Today, regression of experience and behavior to lower-level functioning (i.e., to uncontrollable habits, arousal, impulsivity, and affect-driven behavior) can be related to the stress-dependent inhibition of the hippocampus that normally mediates top–down control of emotional experience and motor behavior at lower levels through higher-order systems (Jacobs & Nadel, 1985; Sapolsky, 1992; Schmajuk & Buhusi, 1997). When the hippocampus is inhibited by excessive amounts of the stress hormone cortisol, task-oriented goals or any volitional effort cannot inhibit impulsive behavior elicited by some stimulus in the environment (e.g., when in front of a lion's cage in the zoo, fear of wild animals cannot be inhibited by the high-level knowledge that the lion cannot leave its cage) nor can unwanted affective responses be suppressed (e.g., fear of failure although it interferes with one's effort to concentrate on an exam): Experience and behavior regresses to and is governed by elementary response dispositions that do not obey task-motivation, higher insights, or volitional control intentions.

This functional account of regression and progression can be related to the concept of threat and challenge, respectively (Blascovich & Tomaka, 1996). Whereas challenge is marked by activation of the sympathetic-adrenal-medullary (SAM) axis which enhances left ventricular contractility and cardiac output, but decreases peripheral vascular resistance, threat is marked by not only activation of the SAM axis, but also by activation of the pituitary-adrenal-cortical (PAC) axis which is associated with inhibition of hippocampal activity and its dampening effects on the PAC-axis (including an inhibition of the challenge-related increase of both cardiac output and peripheral resistance).

LEVEL 5: MOTIVES

At the fifth level of personality functioning, behavior is governed by motives. PSI theory's conception of motives draws on the classic work on implicit motives by McClelland, Heckhausen, and associates (Heckhausen, 1991; McClelland, Koestner, & Weinberger, 1989). Motives are conceived as "intelligent needs." This means that motives are assumed to be grounded in the person's basic needs, which specify the essential nutriments that the person needs for his or her well-being. Motives connect these needs with networks of context-specific possible actions that are represented in autobiographical memory. As such, motives allow individuals to pursue their basic needs in an intelligent, context-sensitive manner. PSI theory distinguishes between two basic classes of motives. *Instrumental motives* involve a means-end perspective, that is, the enactment of these motives is based on clear-cut intentions and instrumental activities that are considered means toward accomplishing intended goals. Achievement and power motives are among the most important instrumental motives. *Experiential motives* are characterized by more holistic enactment that is based on integrative competence rather than dichotomies between means and ends or exclusive alternatives (such as winners or losers, success or failure, own or others' needs). The most important examples of experiential motives are affiliation and self-growth motives.

LEVEL 6: COMPLEX COGNITION

At the sixth level of personality functioning, behavior is guided by complex cognition. What makes cognition at this level complex is that it consists of configurations of elements rather than separate elements. Moreover, complex cognition is abstract and removed from the person's immediate perceptual experience. PSI theory distinguishes two forms of complex cognition. *Analytic thinking* consists of logical-symbolic thought that operates in a sequential, step-by-step mode and typically takes the form of "if … then" statements. *Holistic feeling* consists of associative thought that considers many different elements simultaneously in computing an integrative representation. Holistic feeling is closely connected with emotion and somatic systems. It can be distinguished from intuitive behavior control (elementary intuition) because the operation of holistic feeling can be partly expressed in explicit language, whereas intuitive behavior control is completely implicit.

LEVEL 7: AGENCY

The seventh and highest level of personality functioning is the level of agency. At this level, the other levels of personality functioning are co-ordinated in a manner that enables the person to control his or her thoughts, feelings, and behavior in a top–down manner. PSI theory distinguishes between two agent systems, intention memory and extension memory. Intention memory is a system that maintains symbolic representations of intentions activated in working memory, while at the same time inhibiting intuitive behavior control (to prevent premature enactment of the intention). Intention memory is thus a vital system in the regulation of intentional action (Goschke & Kuhl, 1993; Kazén & Kuhl, 2005). Extension

memory is conceived as a huge network integrating a vast amount of personally relevant experiences abstracted from autobiographical memory. Extension memory plays an important role in detecting coherence between complex configurations of stimuli (Baumann & Kuhl, 2002) and in establishing congruence between explicit goals and more implicit needs (Baumann, Kaschel, & Kuhl, 2005; Baumann & Kuhl, 2003).

INTERACTIONS BETWEEN PERSONALITY SYSTEMS

PSI theory's hierarchical model (Kuhl, 2001) thus posits seven separate levels of personality functioning with two opposing subsystems on each level. An important implication of the model is that human behavior is determined by a complex array of personality systems. For some pathological individuals, one system or level may be sufficient to understand their behavior. For instance, highly impulsive individuals may rely predominantly on intuitive behavior control, whereas highly neurotic individuals may have a chronic activation of the negative affect system. Among fully functioning individuals, however, all seven levels with their different subsystems will be more or less relevant in understanding their personality functioning. Of course, this is especially true as circumstances vary over time. Under specific circumstances, one personality system may be sufficient in understanding human behavior. For instance, in solving a logical syllogism, most individuals will call on their analytic thinking system. With time and varying circumstances, personality functioning becomes more dynamic and needs to operate on multiple levels, switching back and forth between different systems.

An important question thus becomes which principles determine the dynamic interaction between personality systems. PSI theory integrates experimental and neurobiological research that helps to illuminate the basic principles of personality system interactions (Kuhl, 2000a, 2000b, 2001). In general terms, PSI theory assumes that affective changes are critical to the interaction between low-level systems (intuitive behavior control and object recognition) and high-level systems (intention memory and extension memory). Affect is thus central to the dynamics of personality system interactions.

Positive and negative affect are assumed to play distinct roles in regulating the dynamics of personality system interactions. It is important to note that this modulation function of positive and negative affect is postulated over and above the direct impact that positive and negative affect have on approach and avoidance behavior

(Neumann, Förster, & Strack, 2003). Positive and negative affect are thus assumed to serve a dual function, which consists of (1) facilitating approach and avoidance behavior toward specific objects and (2) regulation of personality system interactions. The regulatory function of affect may have evolved because affect systems lie at an intermediate level in the hierarchy of personality systems. Due to this central position within the overall personality architecture, affect systems are well positioned to co-ordinate the interplay between lower- and higher-level systems. According to PSI theory, positive affect plays a key role in the dynamics between intuitive behavior control (Level 1) and intention memory (Level 7). Specifically, positive affect facilitates enactment of *difficult* intentions (i.e., *volitional efficiency*) once they are loaded into intention memory, that is, after an explicit intention has been formed (Figure 32.1). Positive affect thus helps the intuitive behavior control system to get to know what the current intention is (which enables intuitive behavior control to find some routine in its repertoire that may help enact the current intention). In more technical parlance, positive affect modulates the interaction between intuitive behavior control and intention memory.

The presumed modulation function of positive affect has received ample empirical support (Fuhrmann & Kuhl, 1998; Goschke & Kuhl, 1993; Kazén & Kuhl, 2005; Kuhl & Kazén, 1999).

The modulation function of positive affect can also be stated in reverse form, when it is applied to inhibited positive affect. On the basis of the modulation function of positive affect, inhibited positive affect should be associated with hesitation and "passive goal awareness" (Kuhl & Beckmann, 1994), that is, a discrepancy between actual behavior and plans, goals, or ideals activated in intention memory. Research has indeed confirmed that individuals high on hesitation display an impaired ability to upregulate positive affect (Baumann, Kaschel, & Kuhl, 2005; Jostmann, Koole, Van der Wulp, & Fockenberg, 2005; Koole & Jostmann, 2004). Research on the relationship between ideal-actual self-discrepancies (or promotion focus) and dejected emotion is thus consistent with this modulation function of positive affect (Higgins, 1987; Higgins, Shah, & Friedman, 1997).

According to PSI theory, negative affect plays a key role in the dynamics between object recognition (Level 1) and extension memory (Level 7). Specifically, persistent negative affect impairs access to extension memory. Persistent negative affect presumably energizes the object recognition system, which isolates single instances of new experience (objects) and inhibits their integration into coherent network of personal wisdom (i.e., the integrated self). As a result, individuals who have an impaired ability to downregulate negative affect (i.e., "ruminators" or *state-oriented* individuals) should show deficits on various functions that rely on self-access and other coherence-depending functions (such as the coherence-detection task mentioned earlier). For example, successful integration of all personally relevant autobiographical experience in extension memory is an ideal basis for integration of actual goals and behavior with a mature form of moral judgment that derives decisions as to what is good or bad behavior in a given situation from the expected consequences for both

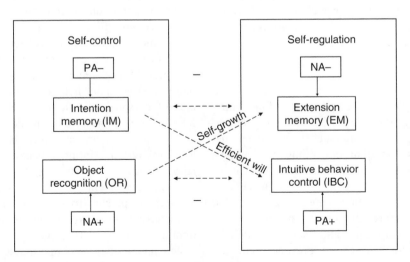

FIGURE 32.1 PSI theory: Illustration of a change from low (PA−) to high (PA+) positive affect facilitating enactment of intentions (efficient will) and change from high (NA+) to low (NA−) negative affect facilitating integration of some isolated (unexpected or painful) experience into the coherent network (EM) of personal experience (self-growth).

others and oneself (rather than from self-alien norms) integrated across a host of personal and cultural experiences. According to PSI theory, integration of personal goals into a coherent self-system is impaired when excessive negative affect inhibits self-access. The empirical relationship between negative affect (i.e., agitated emotions such as anxiety and nervousness) and the discrepancy between conscience (ought goals, duties and responsibilities) and actual goals (Higgins et al., 1997) are consistent with this implication of PSI theory.

Empirical findings show such integration deficits in participants having an impaired capacity to downregulate negative affect (i.e., state-oriented participants). For example, when observed in negative mood states (either induced or reported) state-oriented participants show impaired perception of coherence among personality traits or other concepts (Baumann & Kuhl, 2002; Bolte, Goschke, & Kuhl, 2003), impaired discrimination between externally assigned and self-chosen goals (Baumann & Kuhl, 2003; Kazén, Baumann, & Kuhl, 2003; Kuhl & Kazén, 1994), and impaired disengagement from unwanted (task-irrelevant) thoughts and emotions (Baumann & Kuhl, 2003; Brunstein & Olbrich, 1985; Koole, 2004; Koole & Van den Berg, 2005; Kuhl, 1981; Kuhl & Baumann, 2000; Kuhl & Weiss, 1994).

Taken together, PSI theory introduces a different type of explanation to existing theories of human motivation. Classical motivation theories heavily rely on the contents of thought, emotions, and intentions when explaining motivated behavior. By contrast, PSI theory focuses on functional effects of psychological systems and their interactions. For example, when a student repeatedly fails to sit down at home and prepare himself for the next exam, content-related explanations would refer to control beliefs ("I cannot understand this topic anyway") or the content of his intentions ("I will go out to play baseball"). According to PSI theory, there may be an additional explanation that operates over and above possible effects of mental contents: The student may even have positive control beliefs and the intention to work, but his intention memory might not be able to make contact with intuitive behavior control (e.g., because he is stuck in dejected affect which impairs transfer of information from intention memory to intuitive behavior control).

Another example illustrates the modulation function of negative affect: Learned helplessness as indicated by generalized performance deficits observed after exposure to uncontrollable failure (Hiroto & Seligman, 1975) is typically attributed to contents of beliefs or intentions ("I failed on the first task, so I will fail on any other task

as well" and "I will not even try"). Alternatively, it may result from a functional rather than a motivational or cognitive deficit: To the extent that negative affect elicited by the failure experience cannot be downregulated when confronting a task that differs markedly from the task one failed to solve, access to extension memory and the integrated self may be impaired which would cause deteriorated performance, especially at complex tasks that draw upon this system. In accordance with this alternative account, helplessness effects are observed even when participants do not generalize their performance deficits experienced at the training task to the subsequent task and even when they do not show any motivational deficits (Kuhl, 1981; Kuhl & Weiss, 1994).

APPROACH AND AVOIDANCE ACROSS SEVEN LEVELS OF PERSONALITY FUNCTIONING

From the perspective of PSI theory, approach and avoidance motivation play a very basic role in the functional architecture of personality. The fundamental importance of approach and avoidance motivation is presumably derived from its adaptive significance during the evolution of the human species. Mostly likely, the ability to efficiently approach opportunities and avoid dangers facilitated the survival of our prehuman ancestors. Accordingly, basic approach and avoidance mechanisms were built into the architecture of personality at a very early stage, probably around the time that our ancestors acquired affect systems at Level 3.

However, the significance of approach and avoidance motivation extends beyond the affective level of personality functioning. A basic principle in personality architecture is that more elementary levels are encompassed by more complex levels of personality functioning (Kuhl, 2001). This principle is likely predicated on nature's inclination to build more complex neurological structures on top of more primitive structures (Panksepp, 1998). The organization of more elementary levels of personality thus forms a groundplan for the organization of more complex levels of personality. Because of this structural organization, certain systems within the personality architecture are more likely to form connections between each other than other systems.

PSI theory's hierarchical model of personality architecture thus allows us to make predictions about the connections of approach and avoidance systems across all seven levels of personality functioning. On the basis of structural considerations, PSI theory suggests that certain personality systems may be more compatible with approach motivation whereas other personality systems may be more compatible with avoidance motivation. A schematic overview of the approach and avoidance components at each level is provided in Table 32.1. Notably, these hypotheses about the approach–avoidance components at each of the seven levels of personality should be taken as possible guides for future research more than as clear-cut conclusions from available research.

Just because certain systems are less compatible with one type of motivation, does not mean that these systems are in reality never recruited in the service of that motivation. One reason for this difficulty derives from the operation of approach versus avoidance at multiple levels of personality functioning (Cacioppo & Berntson, 1999). To the extent that approach versus avoidance effects can dissociate across levels of personality, approach effects on one level can be counteracted by avoidance effects on another level.

Another reason for the notion that we cannot expect that approach and avoidance processes are always translated into approach or avoidance behavior, respectively, may be seen in the fact that mechanisms that have evolved over millennia of evolution are often used for purposes other than the original one. An example of such an "*exaptation effect*" (Gould & Vrba, 1982) is the functional significance of bird feathers that originally served for thermoregulation and were later used for flying. To use a more psychological example, when people experience fear during a horror movie, they usually give a positive evaluation of this movie and might even decide to see it again on a later occasion (for empirical evidence, see Martin, Abend, Sedikides, & Green, 1997). Thus, it is possible that people sometimes learn to use negative affect for approach behavior, even though the original function of negative affect was presumably to facilitate avoidance behavior. In the present context, we refer to such exaptation effects as *functional crossover*. Although functional crossover adds a layer of complexity to our analysis, it is theoretically meaningful as it testifies to the inherent plasticity in personality functioning.

APPROACH AND AVOIDANCE IN ELEMENTARY PERSONALITY FUNCTIONING

APPROACH AND AVOIDANCE IN ELEMENTARY COGNITION (LEVEL 1)

What might be the relationship of simple habits and object perception to the approach–avoidance distinction on the first level of personality functioning? According to

PSI theory, automatic (or intuitive) control of approach behavior does not require the conscious perception of objects to the same extent that avoidance behavior does. This claim is illustrated by neuropsychological evidence associated with *object agnosia* (Goodale & Milner, 1992). A patient suffering from this disease could not see an object in front of her (e.g., a glass) or describe its size, but she could spread her thumb and index finger according to the size of that object when asked to grasp it. Intuitive control of approach behavior which is organized by a brain system different from systems underlying object perception (e.g., dorsal versus ventral visual systems) contains an intuitive perceptual component that continues to work even when conscious object perception is not available, *provided the relevant action is ongoing* (that is, the implicit perceptual component of IBC is available only during performance).

It should be noted that in PSI theory, the terms "automatic" and "intuitive" can be distinguished on the basis of the extensiveness and flexibility of habitual behavior (based on S-R learning). In line with common terminology, automatic is used to denote rather rigid habitual behavior that does not require positive valence to be elicited (e.g., daily tooth-brushing which is performed irrespective of how much fun it is). On the other hand, intuitive behavior includes a wider range of the behavioral repertoire that is typically associated with positive affect: An example of intuitive behavior is social interaction that is neither planned nor controlled, but much less rigid and confined than the S-R type of behavior performed independently of its valence.

In contrast to the postulated association between approach motivation and intuitive behavior control, object perception might have a deeply rooted affinity with avoidance motivation. A plausible theoretical reason for this assumption can be seen in the generalization and decontextualization function of object perception postulated by PSI theory: When encountering a dangerous situation it seems adaptive to make sure that one will *recognize* the source of that danger in the future, even if it occurs in quite different contexts (Öhman et al., 2001). High certainty of context-independent recognition may be more important (even life-saving) for dangerous objects than for positive incentives. Context-independent recognition requires decontextualization, a crucial feature of object perception (cf. the construct of field-independence; Witkin, 1950) whereas approach behavior requires a great sensitivity for contextual information.

Indeed, locomotion involves parallel processing of information for online control of one's movements according to the weight, size, and position of objects (relative to one's own position) in space (Berthental & Pinto, 1993; Paillard, 1991) and it places considerable demands on the integration of contextual information across modalities (Clifton, Rochat, Robin, & Berthier, 1994). Empirical evidence consistent with a special association between context sensitivity and intuitive behavior control stems from behavioral priming studies that typically involve casual or implicit primes (e.g., classifying nouns and adjectives that "happen" to be related to old age) affecting automatic behavior (Bargh et al., 1996). Nonetheless, according to the evolutionary principle of functional crossover, intuitive behavior control can also be utilized by avoidance motivation and object perception can be useful for approach purposes.

APPROACH AND AVOIDANCE IN TEMPERAMENT (LEVEL 2)

Activation and arousal have been used interchangeably to denote a global energization function presumably associated with "temperament" (Duffy, 1962; Eysenck, 1967). However, research on animal and human behavior has demonstrated the separability of (motor) activation and (sensory) arousal (Pribram & McGuiness, 1975; Thayer, 1978). Conceding the possibility that both activation and arousal can affect either intuitive behavior control or object recognition, PSI theory (Kuhl, 2001) proposes an original link between activation and approach, on the one hand, and arousal and avoidance, on the other hand.

Avoidance-related stimuli (e.g., unpleasant levels of noise) typically increase sensory arousal (more than motor activation) as operationalized by object recognition measures or sensory thresholds (Broadbent & Gregory, 1965; Eysenck, 1982). In contrast, approach-related stimuli (e.g., some desired food) activate motor behavior more than sensory arousal as expressed in theories of incentive motivation and related research (Bolles, 1975; Lewin, 1935). Again, despite the possibility that approach and avoidance components may dissociate across levels of personality, we expect that links among approach and among avoidance components across levels of personality should be more likely to occur than dissociations across levels.

Consistent with this reasoning, experimental induction of motor activation (e.g., stepping up and down a chair several times) facilitates perception of blurred (only implicitly perceived) objects that are hard to identify on a conscious level (recall that *implicit* rather than explicit perception is associated with intuitive behavior control as illustrated by Goodale and Milner's case of object agnosia), whereas it does not affect conscious perception of clear-cut objects (Matthews, Davies, & Lees, 1990). The link between object recognition and arousal (expected on the basis of a common link to avoidance motivation) is difficult to investigate. This is because measures of object recognition are typically confounded with intuitive behavior control because participants typically need some form of motor behavior (e.g., pushing a key) to indicate what they have seen. However, in an experiment in which object recognition and motor behavior were unconfounded by assessing perceptual performance through a subsequent memory test, arousal (induced by white noise) facilitated object recognition (Broadbent & Gregory, 1965).

APPROACH AND AVOIDANCE IN AFFECT (LEVEL 3)

Whereas the first and the second levels of personality functioning can work irrespective of the valence of objects (e.g., strong habits are performed independent of their positive or negative valence), the third level brings positive and negative valence into play. This is the level where the most clear-cut links to approach and avoidance motivation have been found (see the other chapters in this volume).

According to PSI theory, valence brings incentive motivation into play which results in consistent approach or avoidance reactions to the same objects. Objects associated with positive valence elicit consistent approach and negatively valenced objects elicit consistent avoidance behavior whereas individuals who are mainly motivated from Level 2 (activation or arousal) may respond to the same object in different (even opposing) ways at different times in an opportunistic fashion. An increased level of activation may facilitate approach to an object the organism happens to be confronted with without implying consistent approach behavior toward that object on future occasions.

This opportunistic feature of activation-based approach behavior is illustrated in Jung's description of extraverts who would change their behavior according to their current mood or opportunities encountered in the here and now, without showing introverts' high degree of "object loyalty" in terms of consistent behavior toward the same object or person on future occasions. In contrast, the association of valence with an object (e.g., positive attachment to a person or the positive incentive value of a steak) presumably leads to more consistent behavior toward that object (Bolles, 1975; Freud, 1938). This increase in consistency can be explained: Affect is more easily conditioned to a stimulus than a certain level of activation or arousal.

A particular form of anger can directly increase approach motivation (Harmon-Jones & Allen, 1998) through establishing the interaction between IM (intention memory) and IBC, which we consider the functional basis of the "invigoration of the will" through temperament (Ach, 1910). Presumably, this type of anger improves the enactment of intentions more through motor activation (Level 2: temperament) than through positive affect (Level 3).

APPROACH AND AVOIDANCE IN HIGHER PERSONALITY FUNCTIONING

For the moment, we postpone the intermediate level of personality, which deals with movement between elementary and higher levels of personality functioning. Our discussion thus turns to the three higher-order levels listed in Table 32.1, that is, motives, analytic versus holistic cognition, and intentional control versus holistic self-regulation.

APPROACH AND AVOIDANCE IN MOTIVES (LEVEL 5)

In PSI theory, motives are conceived of as "intelligent needs." Their close connection with holistic feeling (Level 6), extension memory, and the integrated self (Level 7) is what enables them to find intelligent ways for need satisfaction, that is, the ways that take into account the current context (e.g., using fork and knife rather than one's hands at a formal dinner party) and compatibility with the integrated self (which provides emotional support for motive enactment).

According to PSI theory, achievement and power motives have their original roots in instrumental approach motivation (Elliot, 2005; Winter, 1996). Specifically, achievement motivation is primarily characterized by affective change along the approach dimension (McClelland, Atkinson, Clark, & Lowell, 1953; see also Kazén & Kuhl, 2005). A typical achievement-motivated episode starts with some difficult task (which initially dampens positive affect because goal attainment must be postponed) and ends with succeeding at that task (which re-establishes positive affect). Means-end analysis associated with instrumental activity is associated with left rather than right-hemispheric processing (Levy & Trevarthen, 1976). The latter evidence triangulates with studies linking left-hemispheric processing to approach (Harmon-Jones & Allen, 1998). Despite the hypothesized compatibility between achievement motivation and approach, the role of fear of failure and avoidance concerns is so obvious in the achievement domain that the postulated primacy of approach in achievement motivation may appear as a rather academic issue (Elliot, 2005).

In fact, the elaboration of the old dichotomous (approach–avoidance) taxonomy of achievement motivation into a 2 × 2 model differentiates high- and low-level forms of motivation within both approach and avoidance orientations (Elliot & McGregor, 2001): High-level achievement motivation combines the creativity and emotional support of the self with approach or avoidance orientations, respectively (*mastery* motivation), whereas low-level achievement motivation is characterized by an (object-related) outcome rather than a self-referential focus. We recently developed a nonreactive method for fourfold assessment of achievement (as well as affiliation and power) motives resulting from this taxonomy (plus a fifth *passive-avoidance* category). This nonreactive measure capitalizes on the advantages of the traditional TAT by using spontaneous fantasies rather than explicit responses to questionnaire items, while being less time-consuming to score and yielding much better psychometric properties than the traditional TAT (Kazén & Kuhl, 2005; Kuhl, 2002; Scheffer, 2003).

Empirical evidence for the postulated affinity between left-hemispheric processing and power motivation was recently obtained in a study confirming left-hemispheric dominance for power motivation (independent of positive or negative valence) (Kuhl & Kazén, 2007). The latter association is consistent with the notion that affiliation and intimacy in dyadic relationships involve exchange on a personal level which is tantamount to the integrated self. Findings showing empathy to be associated with right-hemispheric dominance (Adolphs, Damasio, Tranel, Cooper, & Damasio, 2000) are also consistent with our relating the affiliation motive to the operation of the right hemisphere.

Less obvious seems the postulated basic association between affiliation and avoidance (Table 32.1). Indirect evidence for this link is that right-hemispheric dominance is associated with both affiliation (Kuhl & Kazén, 2006) and negative affect (Davidson, 1993). More directly to the point, there is empirical evidence for evolutionary and ontogenetic primacy of the link between avoidance motivation and affiliation (MacDonald, 1992). Both in animals as well as in human infants the primary function of the need for affiliation, attachment, and proximity seems to be protection and safety, two concerns that have a deeply rooted avoidance focus (MacDonald, 1992). Nonetheless, functional crossover opens affiliation to positive affect and approach motivation. People from independent cultures might tend to overestimate this link because there is a greater value attached to positive affect in many independent cultures compared to the majority of interdependent cultures (MacDonald, 1992).

APPROACH AND AVOIDANCE IN HIGH-LEVEL COGNITION AND AGENCY (LEVELS 6 AND 7)

Levels 6 and 7 are closely interconnected with Level 5. Achievement and power motives are more dependent on analytical thinking, explicit intentionality, and ego-control, whereas affiliation and self-growth motives are naturally more closely interacting with the vast integrative potential of extension memory and the self that develops from innumerable autobiographical episodes and receives continuous input from emotions and needs (whose level of satisfaction is indicated by emotions).

The parallel processing power of extension memory is the functional basis for its ability to integrate a virtually unlimited amount of inputs and constraints: The ability of extension memory to simultaneously take in a virtually unlimited number of information units is a computational feature that results in an enormous integrative competence, that is, in the ability to find cognitive and behavioral solutions that simultaneously satisfy innumerable needs and values (own and others'), and take account of situational constraints, personal competences, and cultural norms and expectations. In contrast, the step-by-step (sequential) nature of analytical thinking cannot take account of as many different constraints which renders complex decision making very difficult when it solely relies on sequential processing (i.e., left-hemispheric processing).

The self integrates the personally relevant part of extension memory. Because of its intimate interrelatedness with emotions, the self is the most potent functional basis for the recruitment of positive (intrinsic) motivation (Deci & Ryan, 2000) and for profound and permanent coping with painful experience (Linville, 1987; Rothermund & Meiniger, 2004; Showers & Kling, 1996). Up to 40 self-regulatory functions can be distinguished and assessed which range from goal formation in intention memory, generation of initiative and self-motivation, disengagement from intrusive or ruminating thoughts, and other aspects of self-relaxation, self-compatibility checking (e.g., for discovering self-alien introjects), and many more (Kuhl & Fuhrmann, 1998).

VERTICAL INTERACTIONS WITHIN APPROACH AND AVOIDANCE SYSTEMS: AFFECT MODULATIONS AND PROGRESSION VERSUS REGRESSION

In addition to the "horizontal" distinction between approach and avoidance components at each level of personality, "vertical" interactions within approach and within avoidance orientations can be investigated across levels of personality (Table 32.1). The two modulation assumptions of PSI theory mentioned earlier focus on the vertical link between valence-related approach or avoidance components (Level 3 in Table 32.1) and corresponding high-level systems. In fact, the assumed basic association between valence-based approach (Level 3) and intentional control (Level 7), on the one hand, and valence-based avoidance (Level 3) and holistic self-representations (Level 7), on the other hand, is the basis for the two affect modulation assumptions described earlier.

In light of the close connection between self-access and the avoidance axis (especially: high versus low negative affect) one might wonder how the NA-self relationship can be reconciled with findings demonstrating *self-positivity* (Koole, Dijksterhuis, & Van Knippenberg, 2001). One answer might be that self-positivity has a profound basis in finding positive sides of and meaning in negative experience, a process that presumably involves the self-system providing an extended network of personal experience (Frankl, 1986; Kuhl, 2000a; Linville, 1987; Rothermund & Meiniger, 2004; Showers & Kling, 1996). This would be an example of functional crossover: Despite its deeply rooted link with the avoidance axis, self-access can be utilized for direct recruitment of positive affect (self-motivation) in order to strengthen approach motivation (Koole & Jostmann, 2004).

It goes without saying that the postulated functional priority of avoidance over approach in self-maintenance requires further empirical testing. Some preliminary support comes from neuropsychological research. Holistic and polysemantic processing as well as self-access are associated with the right hemisphere and analytic-instrumental processing with the left hemisphere (Craik et al., 1999; Keenan et al., 2001; Levy & Trevarthen, 1976; Rotenberg, 2004; Springer & Deutsch, 1997). In addition, right-hemispheric activation is associated with negative affect and left-hemispheric activation with positive affect (Davidson, 1993; Harmon-Jones, 2006). Taken together, these findings are consistent with PSI theory's assumption concerning natural links between negative affect and holistic processing versus positive affect and intentional (analytical) action control. Evidence from neuropsychological studies confirms the assumption that the right prefrontal cortex is involved in both holistic processing in general and self-referential processing in particular (Beeman et al., 1994; Craik et al.; Keenan et al., 2001), and that the self-referential part supported by the right prefrontal cortex involves implicit rather than explicit self-representations (Kircher et al., 2002).

Our approach–avoidance look at the architecture of personality is almost complete at this point. However, the role of Level 4 still requires some elaboration. In fact, the functional significance of progression and regression may help acquire an understanding of the intricate relationship between cognitive systems, affect, and approach–avoidance: At first glance, the notion that nonanalytic, holistic processing is "associated" with negative affect seems to be inconsistent with empirical evidence suggesting excessive negative affect *interferes* with holistic processing as assessed by coherence judgments and self-access (Baumann & Kuhl, 2002, 2003). For instance, state-oriented individuals who report having problems terminating negative affect and related ruminations do not seem to be successful in their attempts to cope with negative affect by accessing coherence-producing functions (self-related or not). An extreme case of a similar phenomenon has been observed in depressed and suicidal patients who seem to be unable to find (polysemantic or "holistic") meaning in their lives despite their enduring attempts to activate the hemisphere that should provide all-encompassing meaning due to its holistic and polysemantic nature (as indicated by physiological arousal of right prefrontal networks; Davidson, 1993; Rotenberg, 2004; Weinberg, 2000). Empirical evidence shows that state orientation may, in fact, be regarded as a nonpathological analogue of depression (Kuhl, 1981; Kuhl & Helle, 1986).

What happens to depressed or state-oriented people who undermine their attempts to seek meaning and self-congruence to failure when exposed to excessive life stress or experimentally induced negative affect? How can we reconcile the assumed association between holistic self-maintenance functions and negative affect with the finding that for some people (i.e., state-orientated ones) negative affect seems to be associated with *impaired* functioning of self-related (presumably holistic) functions? Consistent with PSI theory is the argument that the inability to cope with negative affect (typical of state-oriented or depressed individuals) causes a dissociation between physiological arousal of the holistic self-system (presumably supported by the right prefrontal cortex) and its efficiency (Rotenberg, 2004). According to this view, both action- and state-oriented or depressed and nondepressed individuals activate the holistic, self-referential system when negative affect is aroused (even more so than action-oriented individuals: Biebrich & Kuhl, 2004). However, for some reason, the failure to downregulate negative affect impairs efficient functioning of that system.

This is where the fourth level of our architecture of personality deserves special attention. One of the mechanisms that explains the dissociation between physiological arousal of the right hemisphere (Davidson, 1993) and

its malfunctioning in state-oriented or depressed people when exposed to life stress or aversive stimuli, respectively, operates on Level 4, which may be related to the Freudian concept of regression. Recall that regression may be accounted for by a stress-sensitive structure of the brain that is inhibited when the level of stress (as assessed, for example, by the concentration of the stress hormone cortisol) exceeds a critical intensity (Jacobs & Nadel, 1985; Sapolsky, 1992). The hippocampus mediates, among other things, the top–down modulation of low-level processing (cf. Level 1, 2, and 3 in Table 32.1) through high-level systems in humans (Jacobs & Nadel, 1985) and in animals (Schmajuk & Buhusi, 1997). Consequently, we can explain the failure of high-level systems to regulate affect by meaning-providing structures or useful personal experience (provided by self-access): Whenever stress exceeds a critical level and cannot be downregulated within a critical time window (which seems to happen to state-oriented more often than to action-oriented individuals), high-level systems lose their impact on low-level structures. This can result in the perseverance of unwanted habits (such as compulsive cleaning: Level 1 in Table 32.1) or unpleasant affect (such as the elicitation of strong anxiety when crossing a high bridge, despite the firm knowledge that it will not break down: Level 3 in Table 32.1).

Presumably, regression is more deeply associated with avoidance because its prime function is to prepare the organism for simple forms of avoidance (e.g., fight or flight) by shutting off high-level control of behavior. This renunciation of high-level control seems especially adaptive in an environment that provides many unpredictable risks: Whenever dangerous events cannot be reliably predicted it makes sense to inhibit cognitive systems that try to make sense out of the environment by relying on prognostic attempts of the cognitive apparatus.

Aligning the two modes of control (i.e., top–down versus bottom–up control) with the approach–avoidance distinction, we therefore propose that regression (i.e., the bottom–up flow of control) is associated with avoidance and the release of regression corresponds to self-confrontational coping. On the other hand, progression typically facilitates intelligent top–down approach because it puts low-level systems under the control of the current task or goal, whereas the inhibition of progression amounts to bottom–up control of behavior guided by impulses (generated on the temperament or affective level) or habits including external control. Despite this aligning of approach–avoidance with progression and regression, respectively, the crossover hypothesis permits that progression can be associated with avoidance (e.g., loading intention memory with an avoidance goal) and regression can serve approach purposes (e.g., when behavioral impulses toward wanted objects cannot be controlled by high-level systems).

The negative affect modulation assumption of PSI theory (and its reversal) describes the intricate relationship between negative affect and high-level functioning: Excessive and persevering negative affect (presumably associated with state orientation) impairs the efficiency of high-level coping that depends on holistic processing and self-access. In other words, when negative affect exceeds a critical intensity, it becomes difficult to bring painful or anxiety-inducing events in contact with the experiential knowledge of the self which normally helps see aversive events in perspective ("despite this failure I know that I have been successful in so many other situations") or provides meaning to them ("this loss has brought a new task to my life").

The integrated self is the ideal system for this deep and sustained coping effect because it encompasses extended networks of autobiographical experience, needs, values, options for future action, and creative solutions. Access to these extended networks (extension memory) facilitates detection of some experience, need, or behavioral option that may help cope with the aversive event (Frankl, 1986). This effect is further facilitated by another functional characteristic of the integrated self. The close connection between this (right-hemispheric) system and the autonomic (emotional) nervous system (Cacioppo, Gardner, & Berntson, 1999; Dawson & Schell, 1982; Wittling, 1990) provides a functional basis for changing affective responses associated with aversive experience. To the extent that excessive negative affect inhibits self-access, this form of deep and sustained coping is impaired, which gives way for the well-known self-avoiding defense mechanisms (e.g., denial, embellishment, suppression, intellectualization).

SELF-CONFRONTATIONAL COPING

As a final question we may ask: Why should the self be especially suited for dealing with negative affect and avoidance (Linville, 1987; Rothermund & Meiniger, 2004; Showers & Kling, 1996), a feature that fits with neurobiological evidence for the close association between negative affect, withdrawal, and right-hemispheric activation (Davidson, 1993)?

We can see one reason for this relationship in the *multidirectionality* of negative affect and avoidance: Avoidance motivation defines a direction of locomotion to be avoided rather than defining which way to go. In Lewin's topological representation of psychological forces, negative valence was illustrated by arrows pointing away from the locus of negative valence in all directions (Lewin, 1938). We propose that this model nicely illustrates the enormous demands on parallel processing for intelligent coping with avoidance: The highest level of parallel processing (i.e., the level of the integrated self) is the best functional basis for fast processing of an extended number of possible ways (directions) of avoiding an aversive event. Finding the personally best way among this host of possible directions that promise to overcome or avoid a negative experience may be tantamount to the search for meaning that Frankl (1986) described as the most powerful and uniquely human way of coping (Kuhl, 2006). This view is largely consistent with a neurobehavioral animal model that associates anxiety (as opposed to fear) with high-level, integrative functions (hippocampal and prefrontal) that mediate inhibition of dominant responses and support cognitive search for conflict resolution (McNaughton & Corr, 2004). However, arguing more from a motivational rather than from a neurobehavioral perspective, we confine the term approach to clearcut approach motivation rather than to situations that start with avoidance motivation and lead to search activity (Rotenberg, 2004) which may eventually result in approach behavior. Nonetheless, the two terminologies are compatible with our terminology focusing on motivation whereas McNaughton and Corr's use a behavioral criterion for defining approach and avoidance.

In contrast, in the case of approach motivation, that is, when a clear-cut approach goal is available, cognitive reduction on the direct path toward that goal as performed by analytical thinking and intention memory may be more adaptive than parallel processing of many possible ways to approach it. As a result, cognitive reduction to one goal and task-related information only, which is typically provided by explicit, verbal cognition and the left hemisphere (Kircher et al., 2002; Marcel, 1983; Schore, 2003; Springer & Deutsch, 1997), should be more adaptive for approach than for avoidance motivation. As mentioned, this is consistent with neurobiological findings that demonstrate an association between left-hemispheric activation and approach motivation (Davidson, 1993; Harmon-Jones & Allen, 1998). Nonetheless, there is the possibility of functional crossover among this association of approach and avoidance with sequential and parallel processing systems, respectively (i.e., approach with analytical thinking and intention memory versus avoidance with extension memory and the integrated self).

For example, even if the primary (original) purpose of the integrated self has evolved for dealing with the cognitive complexity of avoidance, the enormous computational power of its parallel processing capacity can be utilized for exploring creative ways for realizing approach goals, especially when important existential decisions (involving the whole person with his or her needs, values, propensities, and experience) are to be made. The parallel processing capacity of the right hemisphere (especially its prefrontal parts involved in self-representation and self-regulation) is better equipped for integration of both positive and negative emotions than the analytic and discriminative processing characteristic of the left hemisphere: According to Cacioppo et al. (1999), emotion-generating circuits share with cognitive parallel processing systems the collapsing of multiple input dimensions (e.g., the temperature, sweetness, or texture of a gustatory stimulus). The loss of information associated with this multidimensional integration can be considered a functional prerequisite for computing instantaneous overall utility of a given situation necessary for a fast approach or avoidance response.

The self-inhibiting impact of negative affect is offset by the beneficial effects of self-access on the downregulation of negative affect (reversal of the second modulation assumption): Successful activation of holistic processing and self-access helps downregulate negative affect in a more reliable way than accomplished by any other coping or defense mechanism. Empirical findings are consistent with this notion. In addition to the cited evidence for the relationship between negative affect and impaired self-access and deteriorated detection of coherence in state-oriented individuals (Baumann & Kuhl, 2002, 2003), empirical findings demonstrate that state orientation predicts the intensity and development of psychosomatic symptoms (Baumann et al., 2005; Baumann, Kaschel, & Kuhl, 2007). This particular study revealed that motives mediate the relationship between state orientation and psychosomatic illness (i.e., Levels 3 and 4 affecting Levels 6 and 7): The significant prediction of psychosomatic symptoms by the interaction of state orientation (Level 4) and negative affect (Level 3) was significantly reduced when the discrepancy between implicit motives and explicit goals was statistically controlled.

Discrepancy between goals and motives is a form of self-incongruence which may be regarded as a hidden stressor. Negative affect associated with this stressor should impair self-access which in turn reduces the ability of the self-system to regulate emotions and other somatic processes that only this system has privileged access to, according to PSI theory. Loss of privileged access to emotions, needs, motives, and other somatically anchored organismic processes also explains why so-called extrinsic goals (such as status or money) do not easily bring happiness and satisfaction with life (Kasser & Ryan, 1993): Goal attainment does not really

reach organismic needs and emotions unless goal motivation emanates from the self. According to PSI theory, the functional basis of this basic tenet of self-determination theory (Deci & Ryan, 2000) can be seen in the close connectivity between the implicit self of the right hemisphere and the autonomic nervous system of the brain (Cacioppo et al., 1999; Dawson & Schell, 1982; Schore, 2003; Wittling, 1990).

SUMMARY, CONCLUSION, AND FUTURE DIRECTIONS

In the present chapter, we have situated approach and avoidance motivation within the functional architecture of personality. We first discussed the personality architecture as postulated by PSI theory (Kuhl, 2000a, 2001). PSI theory distinguishes seven levels of personality functioning, which include elementary cognition, temperament, affect, progression and regression, motives, high-level cognition, and agency. At each of these levels, our analysis distinguished two personality systems, which include intuitive behavior control versus object recognition, motoric activation versus perceptual arousal, positive versus negative affect, progression versus regression, instrumental versus experiential motives, knowing versus feeling, and self-control versus self-maintenance.

To become a fully functioning person, high- and low-level systems need to interact with each other. According to PSI theory, these personality system interactions are regulated by affect: Changes between low and high positive affect regulate the interaction between intention memory and intuitive behavior control, which is necessary for volitional action. Changes along the negative affect dimension regulate the interaction between extension memory and object recognition, which is necessary for personal growth.

We then related approach and avoidance motivation to the framework of PSI theory. At first glance, approach and avoidance motivation relate primarily to positive and negative affect systems. This straightforward relation, however, probably underestimates the broad and fundamental significance of approach and avoidance motivation. Indeed, we proposed that the functional significance of approach and avoidance motivation cuts across the entire spectrum of personality functioning, thereby implicating all seven levels of the functional architecture of personality. Because the organization of higher personality systems tends to subsume that of lower personality systems, it is possible to delineate which personality systems are particularly compatible with approach and avoidance motivation. Approach motivation is particularly compatible with the axis of personality systems that support intuitive behavior control, motor activation, positive affect, progression, instrumental motives, analytic thinking, and self-control. Avoidance motivation is particularly compatible with the axis of personality systems that support object recognition, perceptual arousal, negative affect, regression, experiential motives, holistic feeling, and self-maintenance (Table 32.1).

Our review of the literature found some initial empirical support that related approach versus avoidance motivation to the hypothesized profile of compatible functional systems. At the same time, it is apparent that approach versus avoidance motivation do not conform rigidly to the hypothesized profiles. Indeed, our review yielded several examples of functional crossover, in which approach versus avoidance motivation were linked to systems that should be theoretically less compatible with the respective motivation. These examples of functional crossover highlight the inherent flexibility and plasticity in personality functioning. As we suggested, this flexibility may arise either because of the complex hierarchical nature of approach versus avoidance motivation (Elliot, 2005) or because people find ways to recruit personality systems for motivations for which these personality systems were not originally "designed" during the course of evolution.

Whenever functional crossover occurs, it may give rise to forms of behavior regulation that are inherently somewhat unstable. This is because functional crossover involves the collaboration of personality systems that were not originally designed by nature to collaborate with each other. For instance, functional crossover may break down more easily under high demands or stress or require special kinds of executive control to ensure the smooth collaboration between the inherently less compatible systems. It is thus likely that behavior that results from functional crossover still differs in subtle ways from behavior that results from inherently compatible personality systems.

For future research, the approach–avoidance distinction is especially intriguing within the highest level of personality functioning. Theoretical and empirical research is especially needed to spell out the far-reaching implications of the functional connection between avoidance and self-determination. Suffice it to say, in concluding, that according to our hypothesis concerning a special link between negative affect and the integrated self, avoidance motivation should be even more deeply involved in free self-determination than approach motivation. This notion is in accordance with existential philosophy, according to which there is a deep link between freedom of choice and anxiety (Heidegger, 1927/1996). Moreover, this notion is also consistent with empirical evidence that the self plays a major role in coping with existential

threats such as mortality salience (for an overview, see Greenberg, Koole, & Pyszczynski, 2004). Our argument concerning the multidirectionality of avoidance motivation can be regarded as a functional account of Heidegger's claim of existential anxiety emanating from the virtually unlimited range of existential possibilities associated with "Da-Sein," his philosophical term for the totality of subjective representations relevant for one's existence.

At the outset of this chapter, we introduced our readers to a young man who chose to get married because he could not bear his loneliness. At the end of this chapter, we are in a position to shed some more light on the intuition that getting married to avoid being alone is unlikely to bring someone happiness. To the extent that negative affect associated with avoidance motivation is strong enough to inhibit extension memory, experiential motives (especially the affiliation motive), and the integrated self, our young man might have difficulties developing a satisfying relationship on a personal level, which would require functions associated with the right hemisphere such as affiliation motivation and empathy, holistic processing, and self-access. Unlike local affect associated with an isolated event (e.g., positive affect associated with a single success), happiness requires an overall positive evaluation of a variety of life events on the basis of their relevance for personal (i.e., self-related) needs (Deci & Ryan, 2000). Without access to the integrative function of the self-system, it will be difficult to even *experience* overall happiness (irrespective of the objective amount of happy events occurring).

Our functional-design analysis of approach and avoidance motivation is admittedly more abstract than traditional motivational theories. Nevertheless, unraveling the functional architecture of approach and avoidance motivation can be extremely useful in understanding the basic psychological mechanisms that underlie the effects of approach and avoidance motivation. A deeper understanding of these basic mechanisms, in turn, can be of great practical use in providing motivational support to people in everyday life situations (Kuhl, Kazén, & Koole, 2006). For instance, the present analysis may suggest some grounds for hope for our lonely young man: Once his self-growth would permit him at some point of his development to downregulate the negative affect associated with his avoidance motivation through self-confrontation, his weakness may be turned into a source of strength. Successful self-confrontation may help to turn the inhibiting aspects of excessive avoidance motivation into facilitating resources for a mutually satisfying relationship, further personal growth and overall well-being.

REFERENCES

Ach, N. (1910). *Über den Willensakt und das Temperament* [On temperament and the act of will]. Leipzig: Quelle & Meyer.

Adolphs, R., Damasio, H., Tranel, D., Cooper, G., & Damasio, A. R. (2000). A role for somatosensory cortices in the visual recognition of emotion as revealed by three-dimensional lesion mapping. *Journal of Neuroscience, 20*, 2683–2690.

Atkinson, J. W. (1958). *Motives in fantasy, action, and society.* Princeton, NJ: Van Nostrand.

Bargh, J. A., Chen, M., & Burrows, L. (1996). Automaticity of social behavior: Direct effects of trait construct and stereotype activation on action. *Journal of Personality and Social Psychology, 71*, 230–244.

Baumann, N., Kaschel, R., & Kuhl, J. (2005). Striving for unwanted goals: Stress-dependent discrepancies between explicit and implicit achievement motives reduce subjective well-being and increase psychosomatic symptoms. *Journal of Personality and Social Psychology, 89*, 781–799.

Baumann, N., Kaschel, R., & Kuhl, J. (2007). Affect sensitivity and affect regulation in dealing with positive and negative affect. *Journal of Research in Personality, 41*, 239–248.

Baumann, N., & Kuhl, J. (2002). Intuition, affect, and personality: Unconscious coherence judgments and self-regulation of negative affect. *Journal of Personality and Social Psychology, 83*, 1213–1223.

Baumann, N., & Kuhl, J. (2003). Self-infiltration: Confusing assigned tasks as self-selected in memory. *Personality and Social Psychology Bulletin, 29*, 487–497.

Beeman, M., Friedman, R. B., Grafman, J., Perez, E., Diamond, S., & Lindsay, M. B. (1994). Summation priming and coarse coding in the right hemisphere. *Journal of Cognitive Neuroscience, 6*, 26–45.

Berthental, B. I., & Pinto, J. (1993). Dynamical constraints in the perception and production of human movements. In E. Thelen & L. Smith (Eds.), *Dynamical systems in development* (Vol. 2, pp. 209–239). Cambridge, MA: Bradford Books.

Biebrich, R., & Kuhl, J. (2004). Handlungsfähigkeit und das Selbst [Action competence and the self: Individual differences in coping with "inner capitulation"]. *Zeitschrift für Differentielle und Diagnostische Psychologie, 25*, 57–77.

Blascovich, J., & Tomaka, J. (1996). The biopsychosocial model of arousal regulation. In M. Zanna (Ed.), *Advances in experimental social psychology* (Vol. 28, pp. 1–51). New York: Academic Press.

Bolles, R. C. (1975). *Learning theory.* New York: Holt, Rinehart & Winston.

Bolte, A., Goschke, T., & Kuhl, J. (2003). Emotion and intuition. *Psychological Science, 14*, 416–422.

Bowers, K. S., Regehr, G., Balthazard, C., & Parker, K. (1990). Intuition in the context of discovery. *Cognitive Psychology, 22*, 72–110.

Broadbent, D. E., & Gregory, M. (1965). Effects of noise and of signal rate upon vigilance analysed by means of decision theory. *Human Factors, 7*, 155–162.

Brunstein, J. C. (2001). Persönliche Ziele und Handlungs-versus Lageorientierung: Wer bindet sich an realistische und bedürfniskongruente Ziele? [Personal goals and action versus state orientation: Who commits himself to realistic and motive-congruent goals?] *Zeitschrift für Differentielle und Diagnostische Psychologie, 22*, 1–12.

Brunstein, J. C., & Olbrich, E. (1985). Personal helplessness and action control: An analysis of achievement-related cognitions, self-assessments, and performance. *Journal of Personality and Social Psychology, 48*, 1540–1551.

Cacioppo, J. T., & Berntson, G. G. (1999). The affect system: Architecture and operating characteristics. *Current Directions in Psychological Science, 8*, 133–137.

Cacioppo, J. T., & Gardner, W. L. (1999). Emotions. *Annual Review of Psychology, 50*, 191–214.

Cacioppo, J. T., Gardner, W. L., & Berntson, G. G. (1999). The affect system has parallel and integrative processing components: Form follows function. *Journal of Personality and Social Psychology, 76*, 839–855.

Carver, C. S., & Scheier, M. F. (1998). *On the self-regulation of behavior.* New York: Cambridge University Press.

Carver, C. S., & Scheier, M. F. (2004). *Perspectives on personality.* Boston, MA: Allyn & Bacon.

Clifton, R., Rochat, P., Robin, D., & Berthier, N. (1994). Multimodal perception in the control of infant reaching in the dark. *Journal of Experimental Psychology: Human Perception and Performance, 20*, 876–886.

Craik, F. I. M., Moroz, T. M., Moscovitch, M., Stuss, D. T., Winocur, G., Tulving, E., et al. (1999). In search of the self: A positron emission tomography study. *Psychological Science, 10*, 26–34.

Davidson, R. J. (1993). Cerebral asymmetry and emotion: Conceptual and methodological conundrums. *Cognition and Emotion, 7*, 115–138.

Dawson, M. E., & Schell, A. M. (1982). Electrodermal responses to attended and nonattended significant stimuli during dichotic listening. *Journal of Experimental Psychology: Human Perception and Performance, 8*, 315–324.

Deci, E. L., & Ryan, R. M. (2000). The "what" and "why" of goal pursuits: Human needs and the self-determination perspective. *Psychological Inquiry, 11*, 227–268.

Diener, E., & Emmons, R. A. (1985). The independence of positive and negative affect. *Journal of Personality and Social Psychology, 47*, 1105–1117.

Duffy, E. (1962). *Activation and behavior.* New York: Wiley.

Elliot, A. J. (1997). Integrating the "classic" and "contemporary" approaches to achievement motivation: A hierarchical model of approach and avoidance achievement motivation. In M. L. Maehr & P. R. Pintrich (Eds.), *Advances in motivation and achievement* (Vol. 10, pp. 143–179). Greenwich, CT: JAI Press.

Elliot, A. J. (2005). A conceptual history of the achievement goal construct. In A. Elliot & C. Dweck (Eds.), *Handbook of competence and motivation* (pp. 52–72). New York: Guilford.

Elliot, A. J., & McGregor, H. A. (2001). A 2 × 2 achievement goal framework. *Journal of Personality and Social Psychology, 80*, 501–519.

Elliot, A. J., & Sheldon, K. M. (1997). Avoidance achievement motivation: A personal goals analysis. *Journal of Personality and Social Psychology*, *73*, 171–185.

Elliot, A. J., & Sheldon, K. M. (1998). Avoidance personal goals and the personality–illness relationship. *Journal of Personality and Social Psychology*, *75*, 1282–1299.

Eysenck, H. J. (1967). *The biological basis of personality*. Springfield, IL: Charles C. Thomas.

Eysenck, M. W. (1982). *Attention and arousal: Cognition and performance*. New York: Springer.

Frankl, V. E. (1986). Logotherapy and the challenge of suffering. *Review of Existential Psychology and Psychiatry*, *20*, 63–67.

Freud, S. (1938/1989). *Abriß der Psychoanalyse*. Frankfurt, Germany: Fischer.

Fuhrmann, A., & Kuhl, J. (1998). Maintaining a healthy diet: Effects of personality and self-reward versus self-punishment on commitment to and enactment of self-chosen and assigned goals. *Psychology and Health*, *13*, 651–686.

Gollwitzer, P. M. (1999). Implementation intentions: Strong effects of simple plans. *American Psychologist*, *54*, 493–503.

Goodale, M. A., & Milner, A. D. (1992). Separate visual pathways for perception and action. *Trends in Neuroscience*, *15*, 20–25.

Goschke, T., & Kuhl, J. (1993). The representation of intentions: Persisting activation in memory. *Journal of Experimental Psychology: Learning, Memory, and Cognition*, *19*, 1211–1226.

Gould, S. J., & Vrba, E. (1982). Exaptation—a missing term in the science of form. *Paleobiology*, *8*, 4–15.

Greenberg, J., Koole, S. L., & Pyszczynski, T. (2004). *Handbook of experimental existential psychology*. New York: Guilford.

Gupta, B. S., & Nagpal, M. (1978). Impulsivity/sociability and reinforcement in verbal operant conditioning. *British Journal of Psychology*, *69*, 203–206.

Harmon-Jones, E. (2006). Unilateral right-hand contractions cause contralateral alpha power suppression and approach motivational affective experience. *Psychophysiology*, *43*, 598–603.

Harmon-Jones, E., & Allen, J. J. B. (1998). Anger and frontal brain activity: EEG asymmetry consistent with approach motivation despite negative valence. *Journal of Personality and Social Psychology*, *74*, 1310–1316.

Heckhausen, H. (1991). *Motivation and action*. Berlin: Springer-Verlag.

Heidegger, M. (1927/1996). *Sein und Zeit* [Being and Time; transl. By J. Stambaugh]. Albany, New York: State university of New York press.

Higgins, E. T. (1987). Self-discrepancy: A theory relating self and affect. *Psychological Review*, *94*, 319–340.

Higgins, E. T. (1998). Promotion and prevention focus as a motivational principle. In M. P. Zanna (Ed.), *Advances in experimental social psychology* (Vol. 30, pp. 1–46). San Diego: Academic Press.

Higgins, E. T., Shah, J., & Friedman, R. (1997). Emotional responses to goal attainment: Strength of regulatory focus as moderator. *Journal of Personality and Social Psychology*, *72*, 515–525.

Hiroto, D. W., & Seligman, M. E. P. (1975). Generality of learned helplessness in man. *Journal of Personality and Social Psychology*, *31*, 311–327.

Jacobs, W. J., & Nadel, L. (1985). Stress-induced recovery of fears and phobias. *Psychological Review*, *92*, 512–531.

Jostmann, N., Koole, S. L., Van der Wulp, N., & Fockenberg, D. (2005). Subliminal affect regulation: The moderating role of action versus state orientation. *European Psychologist*, *10*, 209–217.

Kasser, T., & Ryan, R. M. (1993). A dark side of the American dream: Correlates of financial success as a central life aspiration. *Journal of Personality and Social Psychology*, *65*, 410–422.

Kazén, M., Baumann, N., & Kuhl, J. (2003). Self-infiltration and self-compatibility checking in dealing with unattractive tasks and unpleasant items: The moderating influence of state vs. action-orientation. *Motivation and Emotion*, *27*, 157–197.

Kazén, M., & Kuhl, J. (2005). Intention memory and achievement motivation: Volitional facilitation and inhibition as a function of affective contents of need-related stimuli. *Journal of Personality and Social Psychology*, *89*, 426–448.

Keenan, J. P., Nelson, A., O'Connor, M., & Pascual-Leone, A. (2001). Self-recognition and the right hemisphere. *Nature*, *409*, 305.

Kircher, T. T. J., Brammer, M., Bullmore, E., Simmons, A., Bartels, M., & David, A. S. (2002). The neural correlates of intentional and incidental self processing. *Neuropsychologia*, *40*, 683–692.

Koole, S. L. (2004). Volitional shielding of the self: Effects of action orientation and external demands on implicit self-evaluation. *Social Cognition*, *22*, 117–146.

Koole, S. L., Dijksterhuis, A., & van Knippenberg, A. (2001). What's in a name: Implicit self-esteem and the automatic self. *Journal of Personality and Social Psychology*, *80*, 669–685.

Koole, S. L., & Jostmann, N. B. (2004). Getting a grip on your feelings: Effects of action orientation and external demands on intuitive affect regulation. *Journal of Personality and Social Psychology*, *87*, 974–990.

Koole, S. L., & Van den Berg, A. E. (2005). Lost in the wilderness: Terror management, action orientation, and evaluations of nature. *Journal of Personality and Social Psychology*, *88*, 1014–1028.

Kuhl, J. (1981). Motivational and functional helplessness: The moderating effect of action vs. state orientation. *Journal of Personality and Social Psychology*, *40*, 155–170.

Kuhl, J. (2000a). A Functional-design approach to motivation and self-regulation: The dynamics of personality systems interactions. In M. Boekaerts, P. R. Pintrich, & M. Zeidner (Eds.), *Handbook of self-regulation* (pp. 111–169). San Diego: Academic Press.

Kuhl, J. (2000b). The volitional basis of personality systems interaction theory: Applications in learning and treatment contexts. *International Journal of Educational Research*, *33*, 665–703.

Kuhl, J. (2001). *Motivation und Persönlichkeit: Interaktionen psychischer Systeme [Motivation and personality: Architectures of mood and mind].* Göttingen, Germany: Hogrefe.

Kuhl, J. (2002). *Manual of the Operant Motive Test (OMT).* Germany: University of Osnabrück.

Kuhl, J. (2006). Sinn und Selbstregulation: Wann helfen und wann stören Gefühle [Meaning and self-regulation: When are emotions helpful and when are they harmful]? In O. Wiesmeyr & A. Battyani (Eds.), *Der Wille zum Sinn* Weinheim: Beltz.

Kuhl, J., & Baumann, N. (2000). Self-regulation and rumination: Negative affect and impaired self-accessibility. In W. Perrig & A. Grob (Eds.), *Control of human behavior, mental processes and consciousness* (pp. 283–305). Mahwah: Erlbaum.

Kuhl, J., & Beckmann, J. (1994). *Volition and personality: Action versus state orientation.* Göttingen/Seattle: Hogrefe.

Kuhl, J., & Fuhrmann, A. (1998). Decomposing self-regulation and self-control: The volitional components checklist. In J. Heckhausen & C. Dweck (Hrsg.), *Life span perspectives on motivation and control* (S. 15–49). Mahwah, NJ: Erlbaum.

Kuhl, J., Kazén, M., & Koole, S. L. (2006). Putting self-regulation theory into practice: A user's manual. *Applied Psychology: An International Review, 55,* 408–418.

Kuhl, J., & Helle, P. (1986). Motivational and volitional determinants of depression: The degenerated-intention hypothesis. *Journal of Abnormal Psychology, 95,* 247–251.

Kuhl, J., & Kazén, M. (1994). Self-discrimination and memory: State orientation and false self-ascription of assigned activities. *Journal of Personality and Social Psychology, 66,* 1103–1115.

Kuhl, J., & Kazén, M. (1999). Volitional facilitation of difficult intentions: Joint activation of intention memory and positive affect removes Stroop interference. *Journal of Experimental Psychology: General, 128,* 382–399.

Kuhl, J., & Kazén, M. (2007). Motivation, affect, and hemispheric asymmetry: Power versus intimacy. Submitted manuscript, University of Osnabrück, Germany.

Kuhl, J., & Koole, S. L. (2004). Workings of the will: A functional approach. In J. Greenberg, S. L. Koole, & T. Pyszczynski (Eds.), *Handbook of experimental existential psychology* (pp. 411–430). New York: Guilford.

Kuhl, J., & Weiss, M. (1994). Performance deficits following uncontrollable failure: Impaired action control or generalized expectancy deficits? In J. Kuhl & J. Beckmann (Eds.), *Volition and personality: Action versus state orientation* (pp. 317–328). Göttingen: Hogrefe.

Lang, P. J. (1995). The emotion probe: Studies of motivation and attention. *American Psychologist, 50,* 372–385.

Levy, J., & Trevarthen, C. (1976). Metacontrol of hemispheric function human split-brain patients. *Journal of Experimental Psychology, 3,* 299–312.

Lewin, K. (1935). *A dynamic theory of personality: Selected papers.* New York: McGraw-Hill.

Lewin, K. (1938). *The conceptual representation and the measurement of psychological forces.* Durham, NC: Duke University Press.

Linville, P. W. (1987). Self-complexity as a cognitive buffer against stress-related illness and depression. *Journal of Personality and Social Psychology, 52,* 663–676.

MacDonald, K. (1992). Warmth as a developmental construct: An evolutionary analysis. *Child Development, 63,* 753–773.

Marcel, A. J. (1983). Conscious and unconscious perception: Experiments on visual masking and word recognition. *Cognitive Psychology, 15,* 197–237.

Martin, L. L., Abend, T., Sedikides, C., & Green, J. D. (1997). How would I feel if…? Mood as input to a role fulfillment evaluation process. *Journal of Personality and Social Psychology, 73,* 242–253.

Matthews, G., Davies, D. R., & Lees, J. L. (1990). Arousal, extraversion, and individual differences in resource availability. *Journal of Personality and Social Psychology, 59,* 150–168.

McClelland, D. C., Atkinson, J. W., Clark, R. A., & Lowell, E. L. (1953). *The achievement motive.* New York: Appleton-Century-Crofts.

McClelland, D. C., Koestner, R., & Weinberger, J. (1989). How do self-attributed and implicit motives differ? *Psychological Review, 96,* 690–702.

McNaughton, N., & Corr, P. J. (2004). A two-dimensional neuropsychology of defense: Fear/anxiety and defensive distance. *Neuroscience and Biobehavioral Reviews, 28,* 285–305.

Neumann, R., Förster, J., & Strack, F. (2003). Motor compatibility: The bidirectional link between behavior and evaluation. In J. Musch & K. C. Klauer (Eds.), *The psychology of evaluation: Affective processes in cognition and emotion* (pp. 371–391). Mahwah, NJ: Lawrence Erlbaum.

Öhman, A., Lundqvist, D., & Esteves, F. (2001). The face in the crowd revisited: A threat advantage with schematic stimuli. *Journal of Personality and Social Psychology, 80,* 381–396.

Paillard, J. (1991). Motor and representational framing of space. In J. Paillard (Ed.), *Brain and space* (pp. 163–182). New York: Oxford University Press.

Panksepp, J. (1998). *Affective neuroscience: The foundations of human and animal emotions.* New York: Oxford University Press.

Pribram, K. H., & McGuiness, D. (1975). Arousal, activation, and effort in the control of attention. *Psychological Review, 82,* 116–149.

Rotenberg, V. S. (2004). The peculiarity of the right-hemisphere function in depression: Solving the paradoxes. *Progress in Neuro-Psychopharmacology and Biological Psychiatry, 28,* 1–13.

Rothermund, K., & Meiniger, C. (2004). Stress-buffering effects of self-complexity: Reduced affective spillover or self-regulatory processes? *Self and Identity, 3,* 263–282.

Sapolsky, R. M. (1992). *Stress, the aging brain, and the mechanism of neuron death.* Cambridge, MA: MIT Press.

Scheffer, D. (2003). *Die Messung impliziter Motive* [The assessment of implicit motives]. Göttingen, Germany: Hogrefe.

Schmajuk, N. A., & Buhusi, C. V. (1997). Stimulus configuration, occasion setting, and the hippocampus. *Behavioral Neuroscience, 111*, 235–257.

Schore, A. N. (2003). *Affect regulation and the repair of self.* New York: Norton.

Showers, C. J., & Kling, K. C. (1996). Organization of self-knowledge: Implications for recovery from sad mood. *Journal of Personality and Social Psychology, 70*, 578–590.

Skinner, B. F. (1953). *Science and human behavior.* New York: Macmillan.

Springer, S. P., & Deutsch, G. (1997). *Left brain, right brain.* San Francisco: Freeman.

Taylor, S. E. (1991). Asymmetrical effects of positive and negative events: The mobilization-minimization hypothesis. *Psychological Bulletin, 110*, 67–85.

Thayer, R. E. (1978). Toward a psychological theory of multidimensional activation (arousal). *Motivation and Emotion, 2*, 1–34.

Watson, D., Wiese, D., Vaidya, J., & Tellegen, A. (1999). The two general activation systems of affect: Structural findings, evolutionary considerations, and psychobiological evidence: The structure of emotion. *Journal of Personality and Social Psychology, 76, 5*, 820–838.

Weinberg, I. (2000). The prisoners of dispair: Right hemisphere deficiency and suicide. *Neuroscience and Biobehavioral Reviews, 24*, 799–815.

Winter, D. G. (1996). *Personality: Analysis and interpretation of lives.* New York: McGraw-Hill.

Witkin, H. A. (1950). Individual differences in ease of perception of embedded figures. *Journal of Personality, 19*, 1–15.

Wittling, W. (1990). Psychophysiological correlates of human brain asymmetry: Blood pressure changes during lateralized presentation of an emotionally laden film. *Neuropsychologia, 28*, 457–470.

Part VIII

Social Context

Culture

33 Approach and Avoidance Motivation Across Cultures

Takeshi Hamamura and Steven J. Heine

CONTENTS

The distinction between approach and avoidance motivation has been of enormous value for understanding the functioning of the mind. It has also been of much use in aiding cultural psychologists to better understand the interplay between culture and mind. Cultural psychology has primarily been concerned with how culture and mind influence each other (Shweder, 1991). In particular, much research has been conducted exploring how individuals from different cultures vary in terms of how they evaluate themselves (Cousins, 1989; Markus & Kitayama, 1991). Various findings about cultural differences in the self-concept have led to a number of different accounts for why people view themselves in the ways that they do (Cohen, Hoshino-Browne, & Leung, in press; Heine, Lehman, Markus, & Kitayama, 1999; Kitayama, Markus,

Matsumoto, & Norasakkunkit, 1997). It is the thesis of this chapter that the framework of approach and avoidance motivation can integrate many of the findings from the cross-cultural exploration of the self-concept.

This chapter first introduces how the approach and avoidance distinction fits with cross-cultural research on self-evaluation. Then, we discuss how the approach and avoidance framework can be utilized in developing a number of novel hypotheses in cross-cultural research. Last, we review how cross-cultural research can, in turn, be utilized to inform the mechanisms underlying approach and avoidance motivation. As the majority of this research has contrasted East Asians and Westerners, our focus for the review is also on research with these cultures.

CULTURAL VARIATION IN SELF-ENHANCEMENT MOTIVATION

How do individuals from different cultures vary in their self-evaluations? At one level, it would seem that there should be much universality with respect to how people evaluate themselves. For example, people everywhere should be motivated to view themselves as living up to the cultural norms with respect to what it is to be a good person (Norenzayan & Heine, 2005). At the same time, however, to the extent that the nature of social relations varies across cultures, what constitutes a culturally valued person should also vary across cultures (Heine et al., 1999). In individualistic cultures such as much of the West, people learn (via their socialization, participating in cultural institutions, interaction with others) that it is valued to think of themselves as a unique and self-sufficient entity. Towards this objective, individuals come to focus on their positive self-characteristics in order to positively distinguish themselves from others, that is, they come to have high self-esteem. According to this view, strategies which help enable individuals to have high self-esteem should be favored in individualistic cultures. Self-enhancement, defined as the motivation to elaborate on positive self-characteristics relative to negative ones, is a motivation that should thus serve to bring one closer to the culturally shared ideals of a good person in such cultural contexts.

In contrast, in hierarchical collectivistic cultural environments such as East Asia, where the self is embedded in a social network, being a culturally valued person importantly entails maintaining one's "face." Face has been defined as "the respectability and/or deference which a person can claim for himself from others by virtue of the relative position he occupies in his social network and the degree to which he is judged to have functioned adequately in that position" (Ho, 1976, p. 883). Being a good person in East Asian contexts is associated with being a person with a successfully maintained face. We submit that concepts such as face and self-esteem are universally accessible (they can be seen as existential universals) (Norenzayan & Heine, 2005), however, we argue that self-esteem is prioritized more in the West whereas face is prioritized more in East Asia (Hamamura & Heine, in press; Heine, 2005). In the following sections, we explore some of the psychological implications of the notion that the conception of a "good person" held commonly among East Asians differs from that typically held among Westerners.

If the motivation to view the self in a positive light is prioritized to a greater extent among Westerners than it is

for East Asians, it follows that there should be cultural variation in the extent to which Westerners and East Asians self-enhance (Heine et al., 1999). This rationale is supported by many studies. A recent meta-analysis of all published cross-cultural self-enhancement studies ($k = 46$) showed a striking absence of self-enhancement among East Asians ($d = -.01$) compared to strong evidence for self-enhancement among Westerners ($d = .87$) (Heine & Hamamura, 2007). The conclusion we draw from these findings is that self-enhancing motivations are more prevalent among Westerners than among East Asians.

There are three objections that are commonly made regarding this conclusion: (1) cross-cultural self-enhancement research does not take account the fact that different cultures value different characteristics. People everywhere self-enhance on those characteristics that are important to them, and the cultural differences would be greatly reduced if East Asians were asked to evaluate themselves in domains that are of much concern to them (Kobayashi & Brown, 2003; Sedikides, Gaertner, & Toguchi, 2003); (2) collectivistic East Asians self-enhance by enhancing their group selves (Brown & Kobayashi, 2002; Muramoto & Yamaguchi, 1997); and (3) the cultural differences reflect different self-presentation norms across cultures, not differences in people's motivations (Kobayashi & Greenwald, 2003; Kurman, 2003). We discuss each of these alternative accounts below.

The first account predicts universal self-enhancement on those characteristics that an individual views to be important, and it suggests that this pattern should hold across cultures. A few studies have indeed found this pattern (Brown & Kobayashi, 2002; Sedikides et al., 2003) although the opposite pattern (i.e., East Asians show less self-enhancement for more important traits) has been found in other studies (Heine & Lehman, 1995; Heine & Renshaw, 2002; Kitayama et al., 1997). A meta-analysis of all cross-cultural studies on this topic reveals that cultures differ significantly on the correlation between traits importance and self-enhancement in that East Asians do not exhibit the pattern of greater self-enhancement for traits that are especially important to them ($r = -.01$) whereas Westerners do ($r = .18$) (Heine, Kitayama, & Hamamura, in press; note that a meta-analysis with different inclusion criteria conducted by Sedikides, Gaertner, & Vevea, 2005, concluded that East Asians do self-enhance more for important traits; also see Sedikides, Gaertner, & Vevea, in press. We invite readers to compare the different meta-analyses and draw their own conclusions). Furthermore, the few studies that do identify tendencies among East Asians to self-enhance more on especially important domains do so almost exclusively with measures of the "better-than-average effect," a measure that is compromised by a person positivity bias (Klar & Giladi, 1997; Sears, 1983). When this bias is circumvented, the better-than-average effect no longer reveals self-enhancement among East Asians for especially important traits (Hamamura & Heine, 2007; Heine et al., in press). Hence, although this alternative account benefits from a certain intuitive appeal, overall, the data do not support it.

The second account, that East Asians direct their self-enhancing motivations to their groups, has also been explored in a number of different studies. Two cross-cultural studies have found no difference between Westerners and East Asians in their group-enhancing tendencies (Brown & Kobayashi, 2002; Endo, Heine, & Lehman, 2000). These two studies are in support of this alternative account. On the other hand, eight studies have found that Westerners enhance their groups more than East Asians. This cultural difference has emerged for people's evaluations of their romantic relationships (Endo et al., 2000), their family members, universities, and social groups (Heine & Lehman, 1997), their evaluations of their countries (Rose, 1985), their cities (Kitayama, Palm, Masuda, Karasawa, & Carroll, 1996), their children (Stevenson & Stigler, 1992), their sports teams (Snibbe, Kitayama, Markus, & Suzuki, 2003), their gender (Bond, Hewstone, Wan, & Chiu, 1985), and in their collective self-esteem (Crocker, Luhtanen, Blaine, & Broadnax, 1994). In contrast, we are not aware of any published studies that have found greater group-enhancing tendencies among East Asians compared with Westerners which would be expected if this alternative account was correct. In sum, a consideration of the cross-cultural research on this topic finds that, overall, group-enhancing tendencies are stronger among North Americans than among East Asians. Hence, the observed cultural variation in self-enhancement cannot be explained in terms of any purported East Asian group-enhancing motivations.

The third alternative account for cultural variation in self-enhancement is that the differences arise from self-presentational norms and not from genuine cultural differences in motivations. That is, either East Asians are feigning modesty or Westerners are feigning bravado, and this is preventing us from having an accurate view of each culture's self-enhancing motivations. This is a very difficult question to assess with confidence as our ability to assess the private thoughts of individuals is limited by our methods. Nonetheless, two studies that sought private behavioral measures of self-enhancement found that whereas Westerners showed a self-enhancing pattern of responses, East Asians showed an overall self-critical pattern of responses (Heine, Kitayama, Lehman, Takata,

Ide, & Leung, et al., 2001; Heine, Takata, & Lehman, 2000). That the East Asian responses were, if anything, more self-critical in these studies than in questionnaire studies would argue against the account that East Asians are feigning modesty. Furthermore, a number of other studies have also found clear evidence for a lack of East Asian self-enhancement using measures that would seem protected from self-presentational concerns (Oishi & Diener, 2003; Ross, Heine, Wilson, & Sugimori, 2005; White & Lehman, 2005).

However, research conducted with implicit measures of self-esteem, such as the Implicit Associates Test and the birthday-number effect, reveal that East Asians have as positive views of themselves as do Westerners (Kitayama & Karasawa, 1997; Kitayama & Uchida, 2003; Kobayashi & Greenwald, 2003). We submit that these latter findings might indicate that cultures do not differ in the extent to which people come to have warm feelings about themselves. Rather, the cultural differences primarily lie with respect to how positively people assess their own competence (cf., Tafarodi & Swann, 1996). The question of what cross-cultural comparisons of implicit measures of self-esteem are telling us will be further illuminated once we have a better understanding of what these measures are assessing (Bosson, Swann, & Pennebaker, 2000; Hofmann, Gawronski, Gschwendner, Le, & Schmitt, 2005).

SUMMARY OF SECTION

The available evidence converges to indicate a pronounced cultural discrepancy in tendencies to self-enhance. Whereas Westerners consistently show evidence for strong self-enhancing motivations, East Asians do not (Heine & Hamamura, 2007). The relative absence of evidence for self-enhancing motivations among East Asians calls into question the ways that East Asians evaluate themselves. As the next section discusses, the distinction of approach and avoidance motivation is of much utility for illuminating how East Asians and Westerners work towards becoming a good person in their respective cultures.

CULTURES AND SELF-REGULATION: APPROACH AND AVOIDANCE MOTIVATION

Self-regulation coordinates cognitions, emotions, and behaviors and is essential for the attainment of goals and the adherence to social norms (Baumesiter & Heatherton, 1996). To the extent that social norms and goals which govern psychological processes are importantly influenced by culture, patterns of self-regulation should also differ across cultures.

Self-esteem and face are two ways to instantiate the motivation to be a culturally valued person, and their relative prioritization varies across cultures. These two conceptions of being a good person can be distinguished from each other in a number of ways. One important distinction is with respect to their ease of management. On the one hand, self-esteem is something that is relatively easy to manage as individuals have at least some control over it. People have a variety of self-deceptive tactics at their disposal by which they can interpret self-relevant information in a way that is flattering to themselves. For example, they can attend to and elaborate more on positive informative, they can exaggerate the positivity of their self-assessments, or they can make attributions for their performance in a self-serving way (see Taylor & Brown, 1988, for a review). In Western contexts these can be viewed as adaptive strategies, as they bring the self closer to the culturally valued goal of having a positive view of one's self. These various self-deceptive tactics can be seen as examples of an approach motivation, as they are all consistent with the goal of securing positive information about the self. People who are self-enhancing work towards securing a positive self-view and largely ignore, or discount, information that would threaten this conception. According to this view, approach motivation is integral in Westerners' attempts to build upon the self-resource that they tend to prioritize: namely, self-esteem.

In contrast, compared to self-esteem, face is considerably more difficult to manage. On the one hand, there are few opportunities for people to increase their face because the amount of face that people can claim is determined by their position in the social hierarchy. Such opportunities are limited to occasions in which one moves up the social hierarchy (e.g., a graduate student becomes a professor). On the other hand, face is chronically vulnerable for loss because it is successfully managed only to the extent that the individual is able to live up to the expectations of others—expectations that are often unknown to the individual and that vary depending on the audience. In other words, unlike self-esteem, the fate of one's face is largely determined by relevant others' evaluations. For example, if a teacher is perceived as incompetent by students, his or her face as a teacher may be in jeopardy. Hence, face is something that is difficult to gain but easy to lose. To the extent that East Asians are concerned about this inherently vulnerable resource, their self-regulation should be oriented more towards avoiding the loss of face. In other words, an avoidance orientation should be more adaptive for East Asians in their quest to become a culturally valued person (Hamamura & Heine, in press; Heine, 2005).

In sum, we propose that different conceptions of what it entails to be a good person and an inherent asymmetry

between the ease of acquiring self-esteem and of not losing face, give rise to cultural variation in self-regulation. An approach focus is more adaptive and should be more common among North Americans, whereas an avoidance focus is more adaptive and should predominate more among East Asians.

This rationale is confirmed by a growing corpus of cross-cultural research. First, there is evidence that people are socialized to develop particular motivational styles in culturally distinct ways from a very young age. For example, in their investigation of Japanese and American mothers' behaviors, Caudill and Weinstein (1969) identified a strong positive correlation between the frequency of American mothers' chatting with their babies and their infants' "happy vocals." In contrast, there was no correlation between the mothers' chatting and the babies' "unhappy vocals." The American mother thus appears to elicit and reinforce her baby's happy vocalizations, reflecting an approach orientation in her mothering style. In contrast, the chatting of Japanese mothers was significantly correlated with their babies' unhappy vocals and not with their happy vocals. Caudill and Weinstein argued that the Japanese mothers' chatting served to soothe their babies—an effort to eliminate their problems, rather than to approach happy states. Similar findings have been documented from a set of studies in which parents in Taiwan and the United States were interviewed regarding their attitudes towards child rearing (Miller, Wang, Sandel, & Cho, 2002; Miller, Wiley, Fung, & Liang, 1997). The researchers explored the stories that parents often used about the child's past behaviors to socialize them. European-American parents more frequently described telling stories that focused on a past success of the child. In contrast, the Taiwanese parents were more likely to tell stories about past transgressions of the child (Miller et al., 1997; also see similar findings by Wang, 2004). East Asians thus appear to be socialized to adopt a predominantly avoidance outlook, whereas Westerners are socialized more towards an approach orientation.

These cultural differences in socialization are paralleled by many findings for cultural differences in approach–avoidance motivation later in life. For example, Elliot, Chirkov, Kim, and Sheldon (2001) found that Asian-Americans and Koreans were more likely to embrace avoidance personal goals relative to European-Americans. Quite often, for many participants of Asian background, important concerns are to avoid not living up to others' expectations. Likewise, Lee, Aaker, and Gardner (2000) found that Americans rated a tennis game that was framed as an opportunity to win as more important than one that was framed as an opportunity to avoid a loss, whereas the reverse pattern was observed among Chinese participants.

Winning is thus not necessarily the name of the game, in some cultures it may be better labeled "not losing." Similarly, Lockwood, Marshall, and Sadler (2005) found that negative role models—someone that people want to ensure they do not become like—are more motivating for Asian-Canadians, whereas positive role models are more motivating for European-Canadians. The findings of these studies converge across methods to demonstrate that a concern with not failing is of greater motivational significance among East Asians than Westerners.

Cultural variation in approach and avoidance motivation is also evident in studies that have explored people's reactions to successes and failures. On the one hand, successes are diagnostic of one's strengths and they thus should be particularly motivating for individuals with an approach focus (Idson & Higgins, 2000). Moreover, in Western cultural contexts where motivations to positively distinguish the self from others are prioritized, individuals would fare better by adopting an approach focus to reveal their strengths. According to this reasoning, Westerners who succeed on a task should be more motivated to continue working on the task relative to East Asians. In contrast, failures are diagnostic of one's shortcomings and these should be especially motivating for those with an avoidance focus (Idson & Higgins, 2000). The identification of shortcomings is particularly informative for the purpose of self-improvement and face management as shortcomings indicate where one's face might be vulnerable to loss. It follows, then, that East Asians who have failed on a task and have identified a shortcoming should be more motivated to continue working on that task, in an effort to correct the shortcoming, compared to Westerners.

This rationale has been confirmed in a number of studies. In one series of studies, Canadians and Japanese participants received either success or failure feedback on a task (Heine et al., 2001). When they were subsequently given an opportunity to work again on that task in private, Canadians who received success feedback persisted longer compared to those receiving failure feedback (replicating a pattern that has been identified in a number of Western studies) (Feather, 1966; Shrauger & Rosenberg, 1970), indicating an approach orientation. In stark contrast, Japanese who received failure feedback persisted longer than those receiving success feedback, indicating an avoidance orientation. Similarly, Oishi and Diener (2003) found that whereas European-American participants who performed well on a task tended to choose the same task over a different task 2 weeks later, such a pattern was not observed among Asian-Americans; that is their successful performance did not affect Asian-Americans' subsequent choice of which task to choose.

Again, this is evidence for cultural variation in approach–avoidance motivation.

Similarly, much research finds that East Asians tend to view negative feedback as more useful to them, whereas Westerners are more likely to show the opposite pattern (Heine et al., 2000; White & Lehman, 2005). To the extent that cultural differences in approach and avoidance motivation underlie this observed difference, an experimental procedure that manipulates one's motivation should reverse this pattern. Indeed, when an approach motivation is experimentally induced to Japanese participants (by reading a scenario of someone receiving a bonus for good performance), positive feedback was evaluated as equally useful as negative feedback eliminating the pattern observed in a control as well as in an avoidance condition (a scenario of a salary reduction for poor performance) in which participants evaluated negative feedback to be more useful than positive (Ozaki, 2005). In other words, Japanese evaluations of positive and negative feedback became more similar to Western norms when they explicitly adopted an approach orientation. This suggests that a key reason for cultural differences in the perceived utility of positive feedback relates to chronic cultural differences in approach motivation.

Furthermore, manipulations that prime East Asian identity have also been shown to affect approach–avoidance motivation in ways that are parallel to the findings from cross-cultural studies. For example, in one study, Briley and Wyer (2002) gave Hong Kong Chinese a questionnaire that was written either in English or Cantonese. The rationale was that the language should prime bilingual participants' respective networks of cultural information (Ross, Xun, & Wilson, 2002). They found that those participants who answered the questionnaires in English were more approach focused as indicated by their greater endorsement of approach-oriented proverbs (e.g., "try any doctor when critically ill"), compared to those who answered the questionnaire in Cantonese, who showed greater endorsement of avoidance proverbs (e.g., "ponder your faults and you will avert misfortune"; also see conceptually similar findings from Briley, Morris, & Simonson, 2005). That is, bilingual participants would switch between motivational states depending on the language that they spoke, indicating that their two languages were each associated with motivational states that paralleled the cultural differences.

The above studies provide convergent evidence that East Asians are more likely to adopt an avoidance outlook compared with Westerners. However, there is one area of research that consistently reveals the opposite pattern of results. When it comes to taking risks in financial ventures, a number of studies indicate that, relative to Westerners,

East Asians are more likely to prefer pursuing more risky, although potentially lucrative, strategies. For example, Hsee and Weber (1999) compared the financial decision making of Chinese and Americans in response to a number of hypothetical scenarios. In these studies, when participants were asked to choose between an uncertain loss of a large amount of money (e.g., 50% chance of losing $2000) and a certain loss of a smaller amount of money (e.g., losing $1000 for sure), the Chinese were less risk averse (i.e., they were more willing to take a risk and choose the uncertain option) in comparison with Americans. This pattern of cultural differences was replicated by Mandel (2003) with a prime of independence–interdependence, which suggests that financial risk seeking is associated with feelings of interdependence. Hsee and Weber (1999) explained these findings in terms of a "social cushion" that protects interdependent individuals from financial misfortune. If times go bad, the reasoning goes, people with a stronger social network have a greater social cushion (e.g., friends, extended family) that can help absorb the blow of their misfortune. However, this kind of cushion should only be able to mitigate the impact of financial misfortunes. A social network is of less utility for absorbing the negative consequences of risky behavior that makes one's health or social reputation vulnerable (Mandel, 2003). Hence, there appears to be an important boundary condition regarding cultural variation in terms of an avoidance focus. In domains, such as making investment choices, where one's interdependent network can potentially cushion the harmful effects of a loss, East Asians do not show more of an avoidance orientation compared to Westerners.

SUMMARY OF SECTION

A growing body of cross-cultural research on approach–avoidance motivation yields a converging set of findings. East Asians tend to adopt more of an avoidance outlook compared with Westerners. These cultural differences have been identified with a number of different East Asian and Western samples, with a wide variety of different experimental methods, and for a number of domains, with the important exception of investment choices.

CROSS-CULTURAL RESEARCH OF PHENOMENA IMPLICATED IN AN APPROACH–AVOIDANCE FRAMEWORK

The distinction of approach–avoidance motivation is an integral aspect of many psychological theories (Cacioppo, Gardner, & Berntson, 1999; Elliot & Church, 1997;

Higgins, 1997). As such, the observed cultural variation in approach and avoidance motivation allows for the generation of a number of novel hypotheses regarding cultural differences in a variety of psychological phenomena. We discuss some of these below.

REGULATORY FIT

Much recent research has suggested that regulatory fit, or the concordance between one's chronic regulatory focus (approach or avoidance focus) and the regulatory strategy that is demanded by a particular task at hand (e.g., trying to win or trying to prevent a loss) serves to boost one's motivation (Aaker & Lee, 2006; Higgins & Spiegel, 2004). To the extent that there are cultural differences in chronic regulatory focus, it follows that the framing of tasks will affect East Asians and Westerners differently. For example, when Canadian and Japanese participants were instructed that performance on a puzzle was to either be monetarily rewarded for each correct response (approach condition) or punished for each incorrect response (avoidance condition), Canadians were able to perform better on the puzzle in the approach condition relative to the avoidance condition. In contrast, Japanese tended to perform better in the avoidance condition compared to the approach condition (Hamamura & Heine, 2006). This demonstrates that regulatory fit is associated with positive motivational consequences across cultures although Canadians and Japanese differ in terms of what kinds of strategies tend to fit better with their chronic orientations.

In contrast, situations where one's chronic regulatory focus is mismatched with the demands of a task may give rise to negative consequences. One such potential negative consequence is in terms of health outcomes. Much prior research conducted in North America reports a link between having an avoidance focus and poor physical and mental health (Elliot & Sheldon, 1997; Elliot & Sheldon, 1998). One possible conclusion is that this relation reflects some universal disadvantages associated with an avoidance focus. However, another possibility is that this relation reflects the consequences of having a mismatch between culturally encouraged approach orientations among Westerners and an individual-level avoidance focus. Perhaps having goals that are at odds with dominant cultural values leads to negative outcomes because of a lack of regulatory fit. This latter alternative suggests that the negative health consequences that have been observed among Western individuals with an avoidance focus should not be as prevalent among East Asians. A few studies find evidence that is consistent with this reasoning. For example, Elliot et al. (2001) found that an avoidance orientation was not a negative predictor of subjective well-being for Asian-Americans or Koreans, although it was for Americans. Likewise, Takagi (2005) found that whereas avoidance personal goals were predictive of greater loneliness and worse health outcomes among Canadians, they actually predicted lower levels of loneliness and better health among Japanese. Furthermore, Heine and Lehman (1999) found that a correlation between an actual-ideal self-discrepancy (which indicates the extent to which one is failing at an approach goal) and depression was significantly weaker among Japanese compared to Canadians, suggesting that unsatisfied approach motivation was less of a problem for Japanese individuals. In sum, these studies indicate that negative mental and physical health outcomes of particular kinds of regulatory focus that are found among North Americans are largely absent among East Asians. These findings suggest that such negative outcomes might arise from a lack of regulatory fit rather than being due to an avoidance orientation per se.

TEMPORAL CONSTRUAL

Approach and avoidance motivations have also been linked to temporal construals. Temporal construal theory states that future events are construed differently depending on their temporal distance, that is, distant future events tend to be represented in an abstract, general, and decontextualized manner, whereas, in contrast, near-future events tend to be represented in a concrete and contextualized manner (Trope & Liberman, 2003). A recent study has demonstrated that an approach focus is more common when a distant future perspective is taken, whereas an avoidance focus comes to predominate when a near future perspective is adopted (Pennington & Roese, 2003; see also Forster & Higgins, 2005). The rationale is that the concern with security that characterizes an avoidance focus is better achieved when people direct their attention to concrete aspects of events where potential threats might lie. On the other hand, the concern with growth which characterizes an approach focus is better achieved; people concentrate on abstract aspects of events where opportunities for growth can be more commonly found.

This line of research suggests that there may be potential cultural differences in temporal construals. It follows that East Asians, with their relatively more dominant avoidance orientation, should tend to be more near-future oriented in their construal of future events. In contrast, Westerners, with a more pronounced approach orientation,

should be relatively more distant-future oriented. A few preliminary studies have found evidence for such a pattern. For example, Hamamura and Heine (2006) found that the personal goals of Japanese tend to be of a shorter time frame relative to the personal goals of Canadians (i.e., goals that can be achieved in days and weeks as opposed to months and years). Likewise, Lee (2006) reported that when Asian-Americans and Koreans were asked to imagine an event that they would be responsible for organizing, they tended to assume that it would occur nearer in the future (e.g., the event will take place in 2 weeks) compared to European-Americans who tended to have more distant future orientations (e.g., 2 years from now). Hence, preliminary findings suggest that temporal construal is another phenomenon that is implicated by cross-cultural research on approach–avoidance motivation.

ANTICIPATING FUTURE EVENTS

Cultural differences in approach–avoidance motivation also have implications for how people from different cultures anticipate future events. Whereas anticipating positive events should enhance the motivation of those with an approach focus, anticipating negative events should be more motivating and lead to more productive outcomes among those with an avoidance focus (Grant & Higgins, 2003). Consistent with this rationale, cross-cultural research has found greater optimism for Westerners relative to East Asians (Lee & Seligman, 1997). For example, Heine and Lehman (1995) found that, compared to Canadians, Japanese were less optimistic in that they were much less likely to believe that positive events (e.g., living past the age of 80, owning a home sometime in the future) would happen to them. Furthermore, Japanese were more pessimistic than Canadians in that they were more likely to believe that negative events (e.g., have a heart attack before the age of 50, drop out of university) would happen to them. Other studies have found further support for this cultural difference (Chang & Asakawa, 2003; Hamamura, Heine, & Takemoto, 2007). In sum, North Americans and East Asians differ in terms of the kinds of future events they anticipate as cultural variation in approach–avoidance motivation would predict.

MOTIVATED INFORMATION PROCESSING

Another area where the application of the approach–avoidance motivation distinction has been fruitful is the field of information processing. Prior research has identified that a chronic motivational orientation sensitizes one to stimuli that are consistent with their orientation (i.e., approach focused individuals should become more sensitive to stimuli that are framed in terms of the presence or absence of positive outcomes). Moreover, research shows that this pattern extends even to stimuli that are not relevant to the self. For example, Higgins and Tykocinski (1992) found that when chronically approach and avoidant oriented participants read a list of events that a stranger had experienced, approach-oriented individuals recalled more events pertaining to the presence or absence of positive outcomes (e.g., finding a $20 bill on street, or finding that a movie one wanted to see was no longer showing) whereas avoidance oriented individuals recalled more events pertaining to the presence or absence of negative outcomes (e.g., getting stuck in the subway, or having an unpleasant class canceled).

Attending to the approach–avoidance distinction provides a foundation for predicting cultural variation in information processing. Specifically, Westerners with a more chronic approach focus should be more sensitive to information pertaining to positive rather than negative outcomes whereas East Asians, with a more chronic avoidance orientation should show the opposite preference. A few studies support this rationale. For example, in a study of autobiographical memory, Endo and Meijer (2004) found that, among Americans, memories of successes were more accessible relative to memories of failures. In contrast, among Japanese, memories of successes and failures were equally accessible. In addition, Endo and Meijer (2004) found that Americans perceived the positive impact of their success memories to be greater than the negative impact of their failure memories, whereas Japanese showed the opposite pattern. This difference in information processing may even affect people's evaluations of their subjective well-being. Oishi (2002) found that European-Americans' overall satisfaction ratings across a week were better predicted by the level of satisfaction that was reached in their happiest day of the week. In contrast, for Asian-Americans, their overall satisfaction was better predicted by the level that was reached in their unhappiest day of the week. In a cross-cultural replication of Higgins and Tykocinski (1992), Meijer, Heine, and Yamagami (1999) found that after studying a list of events that happened in a stranger's life, Japanese participants better recalled information pertaining to negative outcomes, whereas Americans had better recall for information regarding positive outcomes. Likewise, Hamamura and Heine (2006) extended this research by investigating people's recall of movie reviews. They found that Japanese participants recalled movie reviews that were framed in terms of the presence or absence of negative information relatively better. In contrast, Canadians tended to have better recall of reviews framed in terms of the presence or absence of positive information. Similarly, Aaker and Lee (2001) found that Hong Kong Chinese had better recall for the details from a tennis match when the game was framed as preventing a loss whereas European-Americans exhibited better recall when the game was framed as an opportunity to win. In sum, these studies provide converging evidence that cultural variation in approach–avoidance motivation orientation affects memory in predictable ways.

EMOTIONAL CONSEQUENCES

Much research has revealed that approach and avoidance motivations are associated with different emotional states. Specifically, emotional experiences associated with approach motivation tend to be located along a dimension that ranges from cheerfulness to dejection (e.g., happy, disappointed). In contrast, the emotional experiences that are associated with an avoidance focus tend to fall along a dimension that runs from relaxation to agitation (e.g., calm, uneasy) (Carver and Scheier, 1998; Higgins, Shah, & Friedman, 1997; Mowrer, 1960). The different emotional consequences of approach and avoidance motivation predict that there should be cultural variation in the kinds of emotions that people experience and seek. For example, Lee et al. (2000) found that when Americans reacted to a scenario of a tennis match, they more strongly experienced emotions that were associated with an approach motivation (i.e., happiness, dejection) compared with those associated with an avoidance focus (i.e., relaxation, agitation). In contrast, Chinese participants showed the precise opposite pattern, and experienced avoidance related emotions more strongly than they did approach related emotions.

This proposed cultural difference in emotional experience has also been observed in recent research by Tsai and her colleagues (Tsai, Knutson, & Fung, 2006a; Tsai, Louie, Chen, & Uchida, 2006b; Tsai, Miao, & Seppala, 2007). They propose that cultures vary in the kinds of emotional states that people are motivated to pursue something which they term "ideal affect." Westerners, they argue, are more likely to seek out high arousal positive (HAP) emotional states, such as feeling enthusiastic, or excited. These states would seem to parallel those achieved through the successful completion of approach goals. In contrast, East Asians, they argue, strive to attain low arousal positive (LAP) emotional states, such as feeling calm and relaxed. These parallel those states achieved by successfully completing avoidance goals.

Evidence for these cultural differences has been found in several studies. For example, Chinese were found to value LAP emotions more and HAP emotions less compared with Americans (Tsai et al., 2006a). Furthermore, these preferred emotional states appear to be learned through socialization. An investigation of best selling children's storybooks in Taiwan and the United States revealed that Taiwanese storybooks contained more characters with calm expressions, and who were engaged in less arousing activities, compared to American storybooks, and children preferred those characters who demonstrated the culturally appropriate emotions (Tsai et al., 2006b). Further evidence for this cultural difference has been identified in the dominant religious teachings and practices of the respective cultures. A content analysis of classic Christian and Buddhist texts (e.g., the Gospels of the Bible and the Lotus Sutra), as well as contemporary Christian and Buddhist self-help books, revealed that high arousal states were encouraged more in the Christian texts whereas the low arousal states were more encouraged in the Buddhist texts. Moreover, Tsai and colleagues noted that some Christian sects include enthusiastic religious practices such as jumping, shouting, and applause, whereas Buddhist religious practices more often emphasize meditation and the calming of one's mind (Tsai et al., 2007). In sum, these studies indicate that different emotional states are preferred across cultures, and these are consistent with predictions that are derived from cultural variation in approach–avoidance motivation.

SUMMARY OF SECTION

Approach–avoidance motivation has been found to implicate a number of psychological phenomena. Given the cultural variability that has been documented with respect to approach and avoidance orientations, it follows that East Asians and Westerners should also differ in terms of the various phenomena that are influenced by different motivational outlooks. Convergent cross-cultural differences have been documented for studies of regulatory fit, temporal construal, optimism and pessimism, motivated informational processing, and emotional consequences.

MECHANISMS UNDERLYING CROSS-CULTURAL VARIATION IN APPROACH–AVOIDANCE MOTIVATION

As reviewed above, many studies have found evidence for cross-cultural variation in approach–avoidance motivation and in psychological phenomena that are implicated by the respective motivations. However, it is important to

underscore that these cultural differences do not suggest that either type of motivation is absent across cultures. Indeed, the distinction between approach and avoidance motivation is evident across species, even for the most basic organisms (e.g., amoebas), underscoring the fundamental role both modes of motivation play for many, if not all, living organisms (Elliot, 1999). It seems reasonable to assume that the two modes of motivation are functional universals, or mental process that universally serve the same function, although their accessibility may differ importantly across cultures (Norenzayan & Heine, 2005). To the extent that approach–avoidance motivation is universally available, it suggests that observed cultural differences could be reduced or even reversed with appropriate experimental manipulations. Cross-cultural studies that investigate how the correlates of approach and avoidance motivation are influenced by various manipulations are critical for identifying the mechanisms that underlie these motivations. This is one way that cultural variation can be used to inform the nature of universal theories: it serves to spotlight where one should more effectively target the search for mechanisms. Whatever variables underlie observed cultural differences in motivations likely play a key role in the manifestation of the motivations in other contexts as well.

For example, one way to consider why East Asian and Western cultures differ in their reliance on approach and avoidance motivation is to explore another variable for which East Asians and Westerners have been shown to reliably differ: lay theories of achievement (Dweck & Leggett, 1988). Many studies have found evidence for heightened entity theories of achievement among Westerners compared with East Asians (Norenzayan, Choi, & Nisbett, 2002; Stevenson & Stigler, 1992). How might entity theories of achievement be associated with an approach motivation? To the extent that people view abilities as largely fixed and entity-like, it follows that they should not devote much effort towards tasks in which they perform poorly. Entity theorists would fare better by avoiding tasks in which they fail, as future efforts would be unlikely to lead to successes. In contrast, entity theorists should focus their effort on tasks in which they perform well, as they will likely continue to succeed on those tasks in the future. Hence, entity theorists are able to approach positive outcomes by devoting effort to tasks at which they are especially talented. On the other hand, incremental theorists would seem to fare better by devoting their effort to those tasks for which there is the most room for improvement. Future failures can be avoided if one is able to improve one's abilities on the tasks by making sufficient efforts. If this reasoning is correct, entity theorists should be more likely to demonstrate an approach motivation and incremental theorists should evince more of an avoidance motivation.

One study tested this hypothesis by manipulating American and Japanese participants' theories of achievement (Heine et al., 2001, Study 3). Participants in one condition were led to believe that a task had an incremental basis (i.e., trying harder would improve one's performance), whereas those in another condition were led to believe the task had an entity basis (i.e., performance was largely unrelated to efforts). A third condition, a control group, received no manipulation. Participants' persistence on a task following failure was then assessed. For Americans, the entity manipulation had no effect on their performance: they persisted as long on the task if they had received entity instructions as they did in the control group. Apparently, the entity instructions were redundant with most American participants' lay theory of achievement regarding this task. In contrast, Americans who received incremental instructions persisted significantly longer on the task, suggesting that the incremental instructions heightened American participants' avoidance focus. On the other hand, Japanese who received incremental instructions persisted as long as those who were in the control group; these instructions did not appear to contain novel information to them. In contrast, Japanese who received the entity instructions persisted less than those in the other conditions, suggesting that the instruction heightened their approach focus. In sum, manipulations of lay theories yield parallel findings as those from previous cross-cultural studies, and suggest that entity theorists should be more likely to demonstrate approach motivations, whereas incremental theorists should be more likely to demonstrate avoidance motivations.

Cultural differences in approach and avoidance orientations have also been explained in another way. The most commonly discussed psychological difference between East Asians and Westerners is that East Asians tend to view the self as part of an interdependent network, whereas Westerners more commonly view the self as an independent agent (Markus & Kitayama, 1991). Could these cultural differences in self-concept help make sense of the observed cultural differences in approach–avoidance motivation? In one study, Lee et al. (2000, Study 3) contrasted how Americans viewed a tennis game depending on whether it was described as a team event (which should prime thoughts of interdependence) or as a solo event (which should prime thoughts of independence). When Americans received the interdependence prime, they viewed tennis games framed as an opportunity to avoid a loss as more important than those games framed as opportunities for victories—the precise pattern that Lee et al. had demonstrated among Chinese.

Another source of evidence that cultural differences in the self-concept underlie differences in approach–avoidance motivation comes from research on regulatory fit. Regulatory fit theory, as discussed earlier, suggests that a fit between regulatory focus that a particular task at hand demands (i.e., approaching a success or avoiding a failure) and people's chronic motivation focus (i.e., approach or avoidance) serves to intensify emotional and motivational reactions (Aaker & Lee, 2006; Higgins & Spiegel, 2004). To the extent that independence and interdependence are associated with approach and avoidance motivations, respectively, it follows that when independence is primed people should experience regulatory fit with approach stimuli, whereas when interdependence is primed people should experience regulatory fit with avoidance stimuli. This rationale was tested in a study by Aaker and Lee (2001). They had participants evaluate a product that was presented to them either in approach or avoidance terms (i.e., participants were asked to focus on the presence or absence of positive or negative qualities) after they were primed with independence or interdependence. The participants had a more favorable evaluation of the product presented in approach terms under the independence priming whereas the product presented in avoidance term was evaluated more favorably in the interdependence condition. These studies suggest that self-concept is importantly related to approach–avoidance orientation.

SUMMARY OF SECTION

Cultural variation in psychological processes can serve to spotlight the underlying mechanisms of those processes. Knowing that East Asians are more likely to adopt an avoidance orientation compared with Westerners has led to research that demonstrates that avoidance orientations are facilitated by other variables which are more characteristic of those from East Asian cultures: namely, incremental theories of abilities and interdependent self-concepts.

CONCLUSION

The distinction of approach and avoidance orientations provides new insight into cross-cultural research on motivations. We suggest that cultural differences exist in approach–avoidance motivation because cultures shape the kinds of self-resources that people come to prioritize.

In Western contexts, people come to prioritize a self-view that includes the sense that one is an autonomous and self-sufficient entity; a view that is fostered by having high self-esteem. Furthermore, self-esteem is a resource that is accumulated relatively easily given people's abilities to selectively attend to information that bolsters it. For this reason, a chronic approach focus is favored. In contrast, in East Asian contexts, people come to favor a self-view that includes the sense that one maintains a valuable position within a social network; a view that is fostered by successfully maintaining one's face. Because face, in comparison with self-esteem, is a resource that is always vulnerable as it is subject to the whims of others in one's social network, a habitual avoidant outlook is more functional. These different ways of evaluating the self importantly shape the relative predominance of approach and avoidance motivation across cultures.

Approach and avoidance motivations are fundamental and universal psychological processes. It is precisely these kinds of core psychological processes which should provide some of the most interesting vistas from which to observe how the mind is shaped by culture. As the research reviewed in this chapter reveals, many of the identified differences in the ways of thinking between East Asians and Westerners can be better understood by considering them from the perspective of approach–avoidance motivation. Although approach and avoidance motivations are universally available, that they are prioritized differently across cultures leads to an array of different psychological consequences that cut across a number of topics of research that are typically viewed as largely unrelated. East Asians are more likely to chronically take on an avoidance perspective than are Westerners, and this increasingly well-documented fact can help to explain why a wide variety of other psychological differences emerge between the two cultures.

REFERENCES

Aaker, J. L., & Lee, A. Y. (2001). "I" seek pleasures and "We" avoid pains: The role of self-regulatory goals in information processing and persuasion. *Journal of Consumer Research, 28,* 33–49.

Aaker, J. L., & Lee, A. Y. (2006). Understanding regulatory fit. *Journal of Marketing Research, 43,* 15–19.

Baumesiter, R. F., & Heatherton, T. F. (1996). Self-regulation failure: An overview. *Psychological Inquiry, 7,* 1–15.

Bond, M. H., Hewstone, M., Wan, K. -C., & Chiu, C. -K. (1985). Group-serving attributions across intergroup contexts: Cultural differences in the explanation of sex-typed behaviors. *European Journal of Social Psychology, 15,* 435–451.

Bosson, J. K., Swann, W. B., & Pennebaker, J. W. (2000). Stalking the perfect measure of implicit self-esteem: The blind men and the elephant revisited? *Journal of Personality and Social Psychology, 79,* 631–643.

Briley, D. A., Morris, M. W., & Simonson, I. (2005). Cultural chameleons: Biculturals, conformity motives, and decision making. *Journal of Consumer Psychology, 15,* 351.

Briley, D. A., & Wyer, R. S., Jr. (2002). The effect of group membership salience on the avoidance of negative outcomes: Implications for social and consumer decisions. *Journal of Consumer Research, 29,* 400–415.

Brown, J. D., & Kobayashi, C. (2002). Self-enhancement in Japan and America. *Asian Journal of Social Psychology, 5,* 145–168.

Cacioppo, J. T., Gardner, W. L., & Berntson, G. G. (1999). The affect system has parallel and integrative processing components: Form follows function. *Journal of Personality and Social Psychology, 76,* 839–855.

Carver, C. S., & Scheier, M. F. (1998). *On the self-regulation of behavior.* New York: Cambridge University Press.

Caudill, W., & Weinstein, H. (1969). Maternal care and infant behavior in Japan and America. *Psychiatry, 32,* 12–43.

Chang, E. C., & Asakawa, K. (2003). Cultural variations on optimistic and pessimistic bias for self versus a sibling: Is there evidence for self-enhancement in the West and for self-criticism in the East when the referent group is specified? *Journal of Personality and Social Psychology, 84,* 569–581.

Cohen, D., Hoshino-Browne, E., & Leung, A. K. -y. (2007). Culture and the structure of personal experience: Insider and outsider phenomenologies of the self and social world. In M. Zanna (Ed.), *Advances in experimental social psychology* (Vol. 39, pp. 1–67). San Diego: Academic Press.

Cousins, S. D. (1989). Culture and selfhood in Japan and the U.S. *Journal of Personality and Social Psychology, 56,* 124–131.

Crocker, J., Luhtanen, R., Blaine, B., & Broadnax, S. (1994). Collective self-esteem and psychological well-being among White, Black, and Asian college students. *Personality and Social Psychology Bulletin, 20,* 503–513.

Dweck, C. S., & Leggett, E. L. (1988). A social-cognitive approach to motivation and personality. *Psychological Review, 95,* 256–273.

Elliot, A. J. (1999). Approach and avoidance motivation and achievement goals. *Educational Psychologist, 34,* 149–169.

Elliot, A. J., Chirkov, V. I., Kim, Y., Sheldon, K. M. (2001). A cross-cultural analysis of avoidance (relative to approach) personal goals. *Psychological Science, 12,* 505–510.

Elliot, A. J., & Church, M. A. (1997). A hierarchical model of approach and avoidance achievement motivation. *Journal of Personality and Social Psychology, 72,* 218–232.

Elliot, A. J., & Sheldon, K. M. (1997). Avoidance achievement motivation: A personal goals analysis. *Journal of Personality and Social Psychology, 73,* 171–185.

Elliot, A. J., & Sheldon, K. M. (1998). Avoidance personal goals and the personality–illness relationship. *Journal of Personality and Social Psychology, 75,* 1282–1299.

Endo, Y., Heine, S. J., & Lehman, D. R. (2000). Culture and positive illusions in close relationships: How my relationships are better than yours. *Personality and Social Psychology Bulletin*, *26*, 1571–1586

Endo, Y., & Meijer, Z. (2004). Autobiographical memory of success and failure experiences. In Y. Kashima, Y. Endo, E. S. Kashima, C. Leung, & J. McClure (Eds.), *Progress in Asian social psychology* (Vol. 4, pp. 67–84). Seoul, Korea: Kyoyook-Kwahak-Sa Publishing Company.

Feather, N. (1966). Effects of prior success and failure on expectations of success and subsequent performance. *Journal of Personality and Social Psychology*, *3*, 287–298.

Forster, J., & Higgins, E. T. (2005). How global versus local perception fits regulatory focus. *Psychological Science*, *16*, 631–636.

Grant, H., & Higgins, E. T. (2003). Optimism, promotion pride, and prevention pride as predictors of quality of life. *Personality and Social Psychology Bulletin*, *29*, 1521–1532.

Hamamura, T., & Heine, S. J. (2006). *Self-regulation across cultures: new perspectives on culture and cognition research.* Paper presented at the International Conference of the Cognitive Science, Vancouver, BC.

Hamamura, T., & Heine, S. J. (2007). Self-enhancement, self-improvement, and face among Japanese. In E. C. Chang (Ed.), *Self-criticism and self-enhancement: Theory, research, and clinical implications* (pp. 105–122). Washington, DC: American Psychological Association.

Hamamura, T., Heine, S. J., & Takemoto, T. (2007). *Why the better than average effect is a worse than average measure of self-enhancement.* Unpublished manuscript. University of British Columbia.

Heine, S. J. (2005). Constructing good selves in Japan and North America. In R. M. Sorrentino, D. Cohen, J. M. Olson, and M. P. Zanna (Eds.), *Culture and social behavior: The tenth Ontario symposium* (pp. 115–143). Hillsdale, NJ: Lawrence Erlbaum.

Heine, S. J., & Hamamura, T. (2007). In search of East Asian self-enhancement. *Personality and Social Psychology Review*, *11*, 4–27.

Heine, S. J., Kitayama, S., & Hamamura, T. (2007). Inclusion of additional studies yields different conclusions: Comment on Sedikides, Gaertner, & Vevea (2005), Journal of Personality and Social Psychology. *Asian Journal of Social Psychology*, *10*, 49–58.

Heine, S. J., Kitayama, S., Lehman, D. R., Takata, T., Ide, E., Lueng, C., et al. (2001). Divergent consequences of success and failure in Japan and North America: An investigation of self-improving motivations and malleable selves. *Journal of Personality and Social Psychology*, *81*, 599–615.

Heine, S. J., & Lehman, D. R. (1995). Cultural variation in unrealistic optimism: Does the west feel more vulnerable than the east. *Journal of Personality and Social Psychology*, *68*, 595–607.

Heine, S. J., & Lehman, D. R. (1997). The cultural construction of self-enhancement: An examination of group-serving biases. *Journal of Personality and Social Psychology*, *72*, 1268–1283.

Heine, S. J., & Lehman, D. R. (1999). Culture, self-discrepancies, and self-satisfaction. *Personality and Social Psychology Bulletin*, *25*, 915–925.

Heine, S. J., Lehman, D. R., Markus, H. R., & Kitayama, S. (1999). Is there a universal need for positive self-regard? *Psychological Review*, *106*, 766–794.

Heine, S. J., & Renshaw, K. (2002). Interjudge agreement, self-enhancement, and liking: Cross-cultural divergences. *Personality and Social Psychology Bulletin*, *28*, 578–587.

Heine, S. J., Takata, T., & Lehman, D. R. (2000). Beyond self-presentation: Evidence for self-criticism among Japanese. *Personality and Social Psychology Bulletin*, *25*, 71–78.

Higgins, E. T. (1997). Beyond pleasure and pain. *American Psychologist*, *52*, 1280–1300.

Higgins, E. T., & Spiegel, S. (2004). Promotion and prevention strategies for self-regulation: A motivated cognition perspective. In R. F. Baumeister & K. D. Vohs (Eds.), *Handbook of self-regulation: Research, theory and applications* (pp. 171–187). New York: Guilford Press.

Higgins, E. T., & Tykocinski, O. (1992). Self-discrepancies and biographical memory: Personality and cognition at the level of the psychological situation. *Personality and Social Psychology Bulletin*, *18*, 527–535.

Higgins, E. T., Shah, J., & Friedman, R. (1997). Emotional responses to goal attainment: Strength of regulatory focus as moderator. *Journal of Personality and Social Psychology*, *72*, 515–525.

Ho, D. Y. (1976). On the concept of face. *The American Journal of Sociology*, *81*, 867–884.

Hofmann, W., Gawronski, B., Gschwendner, T., Le, H., & Schmitt, M. (2005). A meta-analysis on the correlation between the impolict association test and explicit self-report measures. *Personality and Social Psychology Bulletin*, *31*, 1369–1385.

Hsee, C. K., & Weber, E. U. (1999). Cross-national differences in risk preferences and lay predictions for the differences. *Journal of Behavioral Decision Making*, *12*, 165–179.

Idson, L. C., & Higgins, E. T. (2000). How current feedback and chronic effectiveness influence motivation: Everything to gain versus everything to lose. *European Journal of Social Psychology*, *30*, 583–592.

Kitayama, S., & Karasawa, M. (1997). Implicit self-esteem in Japan: Name letters and birthday numbers. *Personality and Social Psychology Bulletin*, *23*, 736–742.

Kitayama, S., Markus, H. R., Matsumoto, H., & Norasakkunkit, V. (1997). Individual and collective processes in the construction of the self: Self-enhancement in the United States and self-criticism in Japan. *Journal of Personality and Social Psychology*, *72*, 1245–1267.

Kitayama, S., Palm, R. I., Masuda, T., Karasawa, M., & Carroll, J. (1996). Optimism in the U.S. and pessimism in Japan: perceptions of earthquake risk. Unpublished manuscript, Kyoto University.

Kitayama, S., & Uchida, Y. (2003). Explicit self-criticism and implicit self-regard: Evaluating self and friend in two cultures. *Journal of Experimental Social Psychology*, *39*, 476–482.

Klar, Y., & Giladi, E. E. (1997). No one in my group can be below the group's average: A robust positivity bias in favor of anonymous peers. *Journal of Personality and Social Psychology*, *73*, 885–901.

Kobayashi, C., & Brown, J. D. (2003). Self-esteem and self-enhancement in Japan and America. *Journal of Cross-Cultural Psychology, 34*, 567–580.

Kobayashi, C., & Greenwald, A. G. (2003). Implicit-explicit differences in self-enhancement for Americans and Japanese. *Journal of Cross-Cultural Psychology, 34*, 522–541.

Kurman, J. (2003). Why is self-enhancement low in certain collectivist cultures? An investigation of two competing explanations. *Journal of Cross-Cultural Psychology, 34*, 496–510.

Lee, A. Y. (2006). *Temporal perspectives of the independence and interdependent self.* Paper presented at the Hong Kong International Conference on Cultural Influences on Behavior.

Lee, A. Y., Aaker, J. L., & Gardner, W. L. (2000). The pleasures and pains of distinct self-construals: The role of interdependence in regulatory focus. *Journal of Personality and Social Psychology, 78*, 1122–1134.

Lee, Y. T., & Seligman, M. E. P. (1997). Are Americans more optimistic than the Chinese? *Personality and Social Psychology Bulletin, 23*, 32–40.

Lockwood, P., Marshall, T. C., & Sadler, P. (2005). Promoting success or preventing failure: Cultural differences in motivation by positive and negative role models. *Personality and Social Psychology Bulletin, 31*, 379–392.

Mandel, N. (2003). Shifting selves and decision making: The effects of self-construal priming on consumer risk-taking. *Journal of Consumer Research, 30*, 30–40.

Markus, H. R., & Kitayama, S. (1991). Culture and the self: Implications for cognition, emotion, and motivation. *Psychological Review, 98*, 224–253.

Meijer, Z., Heine, S. J., & Yamagami, M. (1999). *Remember those good ol' days? Culture, self-discrepancies and biographical memory.* Symposium presentation at the 3rd conference of the Asian Association of Social Psychology, August 4–7, 1999, Taipei, Taiwan.

Miller, P. J., Wang, S., Sandel, T., & Cho, G. E. (2002). Self-esteem as folk theory: A comparison of European American and Taiwanese mothers' beliefs. *Parenting: Science and Practice, 2*, 209–239.

Miller, P. J., Wiley, A. R., Fung, H., & Liang, C. (1997). Personal storytelling as a medium of socialization in Chinese and American families. *Child Development, 68*, 557–568.

Mowrer, O. (1960). *Learning theory and behavior.* New York: Wiley.

Muramoto, Y., & Yamaguchi, S. (1997). Another type of self-serving bias: Coexistence of self-effacing and group-serving tendencies in attribution in the Japanese culture. *Japanese Journal of Experimental Social Psychology, 37*, 65–75.

Norenzayan, A., Choi, I., & Nisbett, R. E. (2002). Cultural similarities and differences in social inference: Evidence from behavioral predictions and lay theories of behavior. *Personality and Social Psychology Bulletin, 28*, 109–120.

Norenzayan, A., & Heine, S. J. (2005). Psychological universals: What are they and how can we know? *Psychological Bulletin, 131*, 763–784.

Oishi, S. (2002). The experiencing and remembering of well-being: A cross-cultural analysis. *Personality and Social Psychology Bulletin, 28*, 1398–1406.

Oishi, S., & Diener, E. (2003). Culture and well-being: The cycle of action, evaluation, and decision. *Personality and Social Psychology Bulletin, 29*, 939–949.

Ozaki, Y. (2005). *Effect of regulatory focus on success/failure feedback.* Paper presented at the Annual Meeting of the Japanese Society of Social Psychology.

Pennington, G. L., & Roese, N. J. (2003). Regulatory focus and temporal distance. *Journal of Experimental Social Psychology, 39*, 563–576.

Rose, R. (1985). National pride in cross-national perspective. *International Social Science Journal, 103*, 85–96.

Ross, M., Heine, S. J., Wilson, A. E., & Sugimori, S. (2005). Cross-cultural discrepancies in self-appraisals. *Personality and Social Psychology Bulletin, 31*, 1175–1188.

Ross, M., Xun, W. Q. E., & Wilson, A. E. (2002). Language and the bicultural self. *Personality and Social Psychology Bulletin, 28*, 1040–1050.

Sears, D. O. (1983). The person-positivity bias. *Journal of Personality and Social Psychology, 44*, 233–250.

Sedikides, C., Gaertner, L., & Toguchi, Y. (2003). Pancultural self-enhancement. *Journal of Personality and Social Psychology, 84*, 60–79.

Sedikides, C., Gaertner, L., & Vevea, J. L. (2005). Pancultural self-enhancement reloaded: A meta-analytic reply to Heine (2005). *Journal of Personality and Social Psychology, 89*, 539–551.

Sedikides, C., Gaertner, L., & Vevea, J. L. (2007). Inclusion of theory-relevant moderators yield the same conclusions as Sedikides, Gaertner, and Vevea (2005): A meta-analytical reply to Heine, Kitayama, and Hamamura (2007). *Asian Journal of Social Psychology, 10*, 59–67.

Shrauger, J. S., & Rosenberg, S. E. (1970). Self-esteem and the effects of success and failure feedback on performance. *Journal of Personality, 38*, 404–417.

Shweder, R. A. (1991). *Thinking through cultures: Expeditions in cultural psychology.* Cambridge, MA: Harvard University Press.

Snibbe, A. C., Kitayama, S., Markus, H. R., & Suzuki, T. (2003). They saw a game: A Japanese and American (football) field study. *Journal of Cross-Cultural Psychology, 34*, 581–595.

Stevenson, H. W., & Stigler, J. W. (1992). *The learning gap: Why our schools are failing and what we can learn from Japanese and Chinese education.* New York: Summit Books.

Tafarodi, R. W., & Swann, W. B., Jr. (1996). Individualism-collectivism and global self-esteem: Evidence for a cultural trade-off. *Journal of Cross-Cultural Psychology, 27*, 651–672.

Takagi, K. (2005). *Approach-avoidance goals and psychological well-being, health, and interpersonal relationship outcomes across Euro-Canadian, Japanese, and Mexican cultures.* Unpublished Master's thesis. University of British Columbia.

Taylor, S. E., & Brown, J. D. (1988). Illusion and well-being: A social psychological perspective on mental health. *Psychological Bulletin, 103*, 193–210.

Trope, Y., & Liberman, N. (2003). Temporal construal. *Psychological Review, 110*, 401–421.

Tsai, J. L., Knutson, B., & Fung, H. H. (2006a). Cultural variation in affect valuation. *Journal of Personality and Social Psychology, 90,* 288–307.

Tsai, J. L., Louie, J. Y., Chen, E. E., & Uchida, Y. (2006b). Learning what feelings to desire: Socialization of ideal affect through children's storybooks. *Personality and Social Psychology Bulletin, 32,* 1–14.

Tsai, J. L., Miao, F., & Seppala, E. (2007). Good feelings in Christianity and Buddhism: Religious differences in ideal affect. *Personality and Social Psychology Bulletin, 33,* 409–421.

Wang, Q. (2004). The emergence of cultural self-constructs: Autobiographical memory and self-description in European American and Chinese children. *Developmental Psychology, 40,* 3–15.

White, K., & Lehman, D. R. (2005). Culture and social comparison seeking: The role of self-motives. *Personality and Social Psychology Bulletin, 31,* 232–242.

Stereotyping

34 Interracial Interactions: Approach and Avoidance

E. Ashby Plant and Patricia G. Devine

CONTENTS

In today's increasingly diverse society, people have the opportunity to interact with individuals from many different racial and ethnic groups. Historically in the United States, society was segregated, which effectively limited interracial contact. When interracial contact occurred, it was often not by choice (e.g., African Americans forced to serve Whites) and almost always involved clear roles and scripts for how to behave in the interaction. In contemporary society, however, not only are interracial interactions likely more frequent, people typically have at least some choice as to whether or not they interact with outgroup members. That is, people may choose to approach interracial interactions or avoid them. Of course, there are also times that, regardless of whether one would choose to interact, interracial interactions are unavoidable. Furthermore, interracial interactions are less often scripted in contemporary society, though at the same time, strong norms discouraging expressions of prejudice exist. With no clear scripts to guide interactions and no way to divine

others' intentions or attitudes, interracial interactions in contemporary society create new challenges to interactants, often making the road to intergroup interactions rocky and difficult to traverse (Devine & Vasquez, 1998).

Recent years, however, have witnessed an ever-burgeoning literature addressing the nature of these challenges from the perspective of majority as well as minority group members. In reviewing and synthesizing this literature, we have found the distinction between approach and avoidance motivation to provide a useful framework for identifying the nature and consequences of these new challenges. Hence, in the current chapter, we consider how approach and avoidance motivations play out in interracial contexts in determining (1) whether people chose to interact and (2) how they regulate their behavior in interracial contexts. In exploring these issues, we consider the experiences of White people interacting with racial and ethnic minority group members as well as the experiences of people from ethnic and racial minority groups interacting with White people. Although we believe that many of the same factors influence the experiences for both groups (e.g., expectations concerning the quality of the interaction, anxiety about the interaction), we believe there are also some important differences in the self-regulatory challenges members of these groups face in interracial interactions (e.g., being the historic target vs. perpetrator of racial bias).

In what follows, we first consider general issues of approach and avoidance motivation in the context of self-regulation. We then review relevant research on interracial interactions using the framework of approach and avoidance motivation. We first consider interracial interactions from the majority group perspective and then consider the minority group perspective. Although we review these literatures separately, ultimately the implications of approach and avoidance motivations play out in the context of intergroup settings in which people have to interact with each other. Therefore, we conclude by considering the implications of approach and avoidance for dynamic interactions.

APPROACH AND AVOIDANCE MOTIVATION

As reviewed in the introductory chapter of this volume (Elliot, 2008), an important distinction is made in classic and contemporary motivation and self-regulation theories between motivational systems that focus on approaching desired end-states and those that focus on avoiding undesired end-states (Atkinson, 1964; Carver & Scheier, 1998). The motivation to approach a desired end-state produces interest in and the active pursuit of the end-state and the adjustment of behavior to reduce the discrepancy between current behavior and the desired end-state. As such, people motivated to achieve a desired end-state tend to pursue success-related behaviors, such as persistence in the face of failure and setting realistic, approach-related goals (Atkinson & Litwin, 1960; Elliot & Church, 1997; Elliot & Harackiewicz, 1996; Feather, 1967; Hembree, 1988; Mahone, 1960). The motivation to avoid an undesired end-state, in contrast, produces the tendency to avoid performing actions that are expected to produce the undesired end-state and the adjustment of behavior to amplify the discrepancy between current behavior and the undesired end-state. People who are motivated to avoid an undesired end-state tend to set avoidance-related goals and to pursue behaviors that are likely to provide an excuse for failure, presumably in an attempt to avoid negative implications for the self-concept (Atkinson & Litwin, 1960; Elliot & Church, 1997; Feather, 1967; Hembree, 1988; Mahone, 1960).

We believe that conceptualizing interracial interactions in terms of approach and avoidance motivations

provides a useful approach for understanding challenges faced by majority and minority group members in such interactions. These motivational concerns are reflected, we posit, in people's decisions about whether to enter into intergroup interactions and, if they engage in interracial interactions, their goals and primary concerns for these interactions. People's decision to engage in or avoid interracial interactions can be framed as the decision to approach a positive end-state or avoid a negative end-state. Further, in considering whether people possess approach or avoidance motivation when they engage in interracial interactions, it is important to reflect upon what people are likely trying to accomplish in interracial interactions. For example, in regulating their responses in intergroup interactions, some people may be primarily focused on having a positive interaction. To this end, they pursue the goal of treating their interaction partner in a fair, friendly manner (i.e., approach a desired end-state). Others, however, may be primarily concerned with preventing a negative interaction and therefore, may be focused on the potential for a negative interaction. In interracial interactions, the concern with bias or prejudice (either being the perpetrator or target of bias) may be a salient undesired end-state. As a result, people focused on the potential for a negative outcome may pursue the goal of avoiding negative outcomes during the interaction (i.e., avoid an undesired end-state). Such concerns could have implications for a variety of issues beyond whether people enter interracial interactions, including for example, their perceived quality of the interaction, the interaction partner's perceived quality of the interaction, the dynamics of ongoing interactions, and whether people wish to pursue subsequent interracial interactions.

With these considerations as a backdrop, we now review some of the literature on interracial interactions using this approach and avoidance motivation framework. For both the majority and minority group perspective, we first reflect upon the decision of whether or not to enter interracial interactions and then the implications of approach and avoidance motivations for responses within the context of an interaction.

MAJORITY GROUP PERSPECTIVE

CHOOSING TO APPROACH OR AVOID INTERRACIAL INTERACTIONS

As noted above, in contemporary society people often have the choice whether or not they want to participate in interracial interactions. For White people, there seem to be two key factors that are likely to contribute to a desire to avoid interracial interactions, racial antipathy and a concern that the interaction will not go well. Not surprisingly, there is some evidence that White people who possess more negative attitudes toward Black people (either implicitly or explicitly) tend to report having less contact with Black people (Brigham, 1993; Levin, van Laar, & Sidanius, 2003; Towles-Schwen & Fazio, 2001, 2006). Similarly, White, non-Hispanic people who report negative attitudes toward Hispanic people also report a greater desire to avoid interacting with Hispanic people than those with less negative attitudes (Plant, Butz, & Tartakovsky, in press). As for the impact of implicit prejudice, Towles-Schwen and Fazio (2006) found that automatically activated negative attitudes among Whites were associated with a shorter duration of roommate relationships with Black roommates. Thus, negative attitudes toward outgroup members are likely to be one factor that contributes to the avoidance of interracial contact.

However, negative attitudes toward the outgroup are not the only source of outgroup avoidance. A major factor in determining whether White people report that they want to avoid interracial interactions is their expectations about the likely outcome of such interactions. If White people anticipate that interracial interactions will go poorly and be unpleasant, these negative outcomes can be a salient negative end-state that White people may desire to avoid. Consistent with this idea, White people who are concerned that interracial interactions will not go well tend to report a heightened desire to avoid interracial interactions (Britt, Boniecki, Vescio, Biernat, & Brown, 1996; Gudykunst, 1993; Plant, 2004; Plant & Butz, 2006; Plant & Devine, 2003; Plant & Devine, 2007; Shelton & Richeson, 2005; Vorauer, 2006; Vorauer, Main, & O'Connell, 1998) and given the chance, will actually avoid such interactions (Plant & Devine, 2003). Further, there is some evidence that this influence of expectancies on avoidance is due to the impact of negative expectancies on interracial anxiety (Plant & Devine, 2003). White people who anticipate that interracial interactions will go poorly tend to report heightened anxiety about these interactions which, in turn, predicts the tendency to avoid them. Anxiety is related to avoidance of intergroup interactions even when controlling for intergroup attitudes, indicating that attitudes and expectancies/anxiety have independent contributions to the decision to approach or avoid intergroup contact (Plant et al., in press). It is also worth noting, however, that not all who are anxious will avoid interracial contact. There is some evidence that White people who are personally, internally motivated to respond without prejudice will not avoid interracial interactions even if they are anxious about them (Plant, 2004).

In identifying the nature of the negative expectations that White people have regarding interracial interactions, recent work has begun to clarify the types of negative end-states that White people may be trying to escape when avoiding interracial interactions. In general, these negative expectancies revolve around concerns about the likelihood that the interaction will end poorly and that the outgroup member will view the person in a negative manner. Vorauer and colleagues have identified the importance of concerns among White people that outgroup members will stereotype them based on the negative stereotype of Whites as prejudiced (i.e., the meta-stereotype; Vorauer, 2006; Vorauer et al., 1998). Such evaluative concerns have a range of negative implications for intergroup interactions including avoidance. Shelton and Richeson (2005) found that White people explained their avoidance of interactions with Black people as being due to fear of rejection, indicating that interracial avoidance may serve the purpose of averting the highly negative experience of being socially rejected. Plant and Butz (2006; also see Butz & Plant, 2006) demonstrated that low levels of self-efficacy regarding one's ability to respond in a nonbiased manner during interracial interactions predicted avoidance. Specifically, being concerned that they would come across as racially biased during interracial interactions caused White people to both desire to avoid an upcoming interaction with a Black person and, after having participated in the interaction, wish to avoid future interactions with that outgroup member. For these people, the potential of being viewed in a racially biased manner likely represented a highly negative end-state that they were driven to avoid even if it meant cutting off contact with the outgroup member.

There is somewhat less evidence regarding what increases White people's tendency to approach interracial interactions. Presumably, low levels of those factors that contribute to avoidance would likely lead to a higher likelihood of approach (e.g., positive attitudes toward outgroup members would increase approach), but the absence of avoidance does not necessarily lead to active approach of interracial contact. There is some evidence, however, that White people with more positive expectations about the outcome of interactions reported having more positive interracial contact during the subsequent 2 weeks than those with more negative expectations (Plant, 2004). Thus, expecting positive outcomes from interracial interactions can lead people to approach them. Plant (2004) also found that people who reported that it is personally important for them to respond without prejudice (i.e., the internally motivated) were more likely to have positive interactions with Black people over the following 2 weeks and were less interested in avoiding interactions with Black people. Moreover, for those who are internally motivated, interracial interactions may represent a chance to respond consistently with their personal standards and approach their nonprejudiced identity (Brodish & Devine, 2007).

WITHIN INTERRACIAL INTERACTIONS: APPROACH AND AVOIDANCE GOALS

The complexities of interracial interactions do not end with the decision to engage in an interaction or avoid it altogether. After choosing to engage in an interaction with an outgroup member or being required to interact if the situation does not permit avoiding it, White people must decide how to manage the interracial interaction. That is, they must determine their goal for the interaction (e.g., make a new friend, avoid angering the new boss) and how best to respond during the course of the interaction to meet the interaction goal. If White people are motivated to have a positive interaction or simply to avoid a negative interaction, they must decide how best to bring the outcome to fruition. The research on approach and avoidance motivation suggests that whether people chose to focus on approaching a positive interaction or avoiding a negative interaction is likely to have a range of implications for their self-regulatory choices within the interracial interaction as well as the likelihood of meeting their goal.

In considering whether White people possess an approach or avoidance motivation when regulating behavior in interracial interactions, it is important to reflect upon what they are likely trying to accomplish in interracial interactions. To the extent that White people are primarily focused on having a positive interaction, they may pursue the goal of treating their interaction partner in a pleasant, egalitarian manner (i.e., approach a desired end-state). In contrast, to the extent that White people are primarily concerned with preventing a negative interaction and, therefore, may be focused on the potential for a negative interaction, responding with racial bias is likely to be a highly salient undesired end-state. As a result, they may pursue the goal of avoiding negative outcomes and prejudiced behavior during the interaction (i.e., avoid an undesired end-state).

We suggest that in interracial interactions, whether White people are primarily concerned with approaching a desired end-state of a pleasant interaction or avoiding an undesired end-state of overt bias in the interaction depends the reasons underlying their motivation to respond without prejudice. Plant and Devine (1998)

argued that in examining the regulation of prejudice, it is important to consider not only *whether* people are motivated, but also the reasons *why* they are motivated to respond without prejudice. For example, some people are strongly motivated to respond without prejudice in interracial interactions because they possess personally important nonprejudiced beliefs (Devine, 1989; Devine & Monteith, 1993, 1999; Devine, Monteith, Zuwerink, & Elliot, 1991; Plant & Devine, 1998). It is also possible to be strongly influenced by social norms discouraging the expression of bias in interracial interactions and to be motivated to control the expression of prejudice to avoid negative reactions from others (Crandall, Eshleman, & O'Brien, 2002; Dunton & Fazio, 1997; Plant & Devine, 1998). We posit that these distinct reasons for responding without prejudice will have important implications for regulatory behavior in interracial settings. More specifically, our emerging program of research leads us to suggest that these different reasons for responding without prejudice lead to regulatory efforts that reflect approach and avoidance orientations. It should be noted that because we are arguing that individual differences in the reasons underlying people's motivation to respond without prejudice has implications for their motivational tendencies (approach or avoidance) in the context of interracial interactions, the language can become awkward (motivation resulting in motivation). As a result, throughout this chapter, we frequently refer to approach and avoidance motivational tendencies as orientations. In what follows, we first review some of the previous work on internal and external motivation to respond without prejudice and then outline how they may map onto approach and avoidance orientations for the regulation of racial bias.

INTERNAL AND EXTERNAL MOTIVATION TO RESPOND WITHOUT PREJUDICE

In order to capture these distinct reasons for responding without prejudice, Plant and Devine (1998) developed and validated two scales, the internal (personal) motivation to respond without prejudice scale (IMS) and the external (normative) motivation to respond without prejudice scale (EMS) (Plant & Devine, 1998). Plant and Devine demonstrated that the IMS was highly correlated with traditional measures of prejudice, such that higher levels of internal motivation were associated with lower prejudice scores. The EMS, in contrast, was only modestly correlated with traditional prejudice measures such that high levels of external motivation were associated with high prejudice scores. In addition, only a small correlation was found between the EMS and measures of social evaluation (e.g., Leary, 1983, Interaction Anxiety Scale), suggesting that the EMS assesses a specific concern with how prejudiced responses will be evaluated rather than a general concern with social evaluation. Also providing evidence of the discriminant validity of the scales, neither the IMS nor the EMS was related to measures of social desirability (Crowne & Marlowe, 1960) or self-monitoring (Snyder & Gangestad, 1986). Moreover, the IMS and EMS were found to be largely independent (average $r = -.14$). Thus, people can be motivated to respond without prejudice primarily for internal reasons, primarily for external reasons, for both internal and external reasons, or they may not be particularly motivated for either type of reason.

We propose that internal motivation to respond without prejudice results in an approach orientation in interracial interactions whereas external motivation to respond without prejudice results in an avoidance orientation. Consider that highly internally motivated people want to respond without prejudice in order to respond consistently with personally important nonprejudiced values. That is, they want to approach a desired end-state of pleasant, egalitarian responding. People externally motivated, in contrast, want to respond without prejudice in order to avoid negative reactions from others. Their primary concern is with avoiding an undesired end-state of biased responding that would result in social disapproval. These distinct approach and avoidance motivational tendencies should have implications for White people's goals in interracial interactions (Carver & Scheier, 1998; Elliot, Gable, & Mapes, 2006; Higgins, 1997). In addition, people should be particularly drawn to strategies for interracial interactions that address their motivational concerns (Elliot, 2006; Shah, Higgins, & Friedman, 1998).

Consistent with this argument, Plant and Devine (2008) explored people's efforts to regulate their racial bias for an upcoming interracial interaction and the intentions underlying their self-regulatory efforts. White participants were presented with an opportunity to work on a computer program that they were led to believe would help them to respond without prejudice during the interaction. When participants were led to believe that the program would reduce detectable, overt racial bias that would be apparent to their Black partner in an upcoming interracial interaction, White participants who were highly externally motivated to respond without prejudice spent more time on the program than those less externally motivated. Such efforts are consistent with a desire to avoid an undesired end-state of racial bias and the

resulting social sanction for the upcoming interaction. In contrast, when the program was framed as eliminating bias that would be unlikely to be detected by others but could still result in a subtle bias, only highly internally motivated participants who anticipated that bias was a possibility in the interaction spent extensive time working on the program. This type of response is consistent with the intention of being free of all bias and thereby, approaching true egalitarian responding.

Brodish and Devine (2006) further demonstrated that among individuals who are externally motivated, those who were also internally motivated were more likely to endorse, activate, and pursue the goal to reveal their non-prejudiced identity in interracial interactions. Thus, they seemed to be focused on approaching an impression in the interaction consistent with their egalitarian self-concept. In contrast, participants who were primarily externally motivated to respond without prejudice were more focused on pursuing the goal of concealing their prejudice; that is, avoiding a prejudiced impression.

These previous findings are consistent with our suggestion that internal motivation to respond without prejudice results in an approach orientation for interracial interactions and external motivation to respond without prejudice results in an avoidance orientation for interracial interactions. However, the previous work does not provide a direct link between our individual difference measures and approach and avoidance motivations. Moreover, the previous work does not demonstrate how these motivational approaches to interracial interactions play out in people's goals and strategies for the interactions. Below, we provide some initial evidence linking internal motivation to an approach focus and external motivation to an avoidance focus for interracial interactions (Plant & Devine, 2007). The first study examines whether White people's source of motivation to respond without prejudice is related to their self-reported goals and strategies in interracial interactions with Black people. The second study examines the extent to which approach and avoidance goals are automatically activated upon exposure to Black and White faces as a function of White people's source of motivation to respond without prejudice.

SELF-REPORTED GOALS AND STRATEGIES FOR INTERRACIAL INTERACTIONS

As a first step in exploring these issues, Plant and Devine (2008) explored White people's self-reported goals and strategies for an anticipated interaction with a Black person. Of particular interest was whether these goals and strategies reflected an approach or avoidance focus and whether the tendency to report goals and strategies reflecting an approach or avoidance focus varied as a function of their source of motivation to respond without prejudice. Participants who were highly internally motivated were expected to be more likely to generate goals and strategies for the interaction that focused on approaching egalitarianism (positive end-state) compared to those less internally motivated to respond without prejudice. In addition, participants who were highly externally motivated were expected to be more likely to generate goals and strategies for the interaction that focused on avoiding racial bias (negative end-state) than those less externally motivated to respond without prejudice.

White introductory psychology students who had completed the IMS and EMS as a part of a mass testing session early in the semester were invited to participate if their scores fell in the top or bottom 30% of the IMS and EMS distributions. Participants completed open-ended questions assessing their anticipated goals and strategies when interacting with a Black person. For the assessment of participants' goals, they were asked the following open-ended question: "Think about having an interaction with a Black person you have never met before in a social setting. What would your goal be in the interaction?" For the assessment of the participants' strategies, they were asked to list the strategies they would use in interactions with Black people to be nonprejudiced.

Two independent judges, who were blind to the participants' IMS and EMS scores, coded participants' responses to the goal and strategy questions in order to determine whether participants generated approach themes (i.e., focused on approaching a positive, egalitarian interaction) and avoidance themes (i.e., focused on avoiding overt bias) in their goals and strategies. If participants generated a goal that reflected the desire to treat the hypothetical Black interaction partner without bias and, thereby, approach the desired end-state of egalitarian responding (e.g., "treat the person as I would anyone else"; "get to know them and become friends"), they were coded as having an approach goal. If participants generated a goal that reflected the desire to avoid overtly biased responses and, thereby, avoid the undesired end-state of overt bias (e.g., "avoid having a bad interaction"; "wouldn't want to look uncomfortable"), they were coded as having an avoidance goal. If participants generated a strategy that reflected behaviors likely to result in a positive interaction (e.g., "smile"; "be friendly"), they were coded as having an approach strategy. If participants generated a strategy that reflected the avoidance of overtly biased behaviors likely to result in a negative interaction (e.g., "avoid

making racist jokes"; "not make offensive statements"), they were coded as having an avoidance strategy.

Analysis of the presence or absence of approach themes in participants' goals revealed the anticipated effect of IMS, such that high IMS participants were more likely to generate goals with an approach theme than low IMS participants. Table 34.1 presents percentages and frequencies for the approach and avoidance goals and strategies as a function of IMS and EMS separately. Although participants rarely generated goals with avoidance themes, the analyses of the presence or absence of avoidance themes revealed an effect of EMS, such that, as expected, high EMS participants were more likely to generate goals with an avoidance theme than low EMS participants. For the analysis of the strategies, consistent with expectations, the analyses of the presence or absence of approach themes revealed an effect of IMS, such that high IMS participants were more likely to generate approach strategies than low IMS participants. The analyses of the presence of absence of avoidance strategies revealed an effect of EMS, such that, as expected, high EMS participants were more likely to generate avoidance strategies than low EMS participants.

TABLE 34.1

Percentage of Goals and Strategies That Reflected Approach and Avoidance

Themes	Low IMS (N = 50)	High IMS (N = 61)
Approach goals	34%[a]	56%[b]
	(17)	(34)
Avoidance goals	10%	5%
	(4)	(4)
Approach strategies	40%[a]	59%[b]
	(20)	(36)
Avoidance strategies	36%	34%
	(18)	(21)
	Low EMS (N = 52)	High EMS (N = 59)
Approach goals	50%	42%
	(26)	(25)
Avoidance goals	2%[a]	12%[b]
	(2)	(6)
Approach strategies	44%	56%
	(23)	(33)
Avoidance strategies	21%[a]	48%[b]
	(11)	(28)

Note: Percentages with different superscripts on the same row differ with $p < .05$. The frequencies for each group are presented in parentheses below the percentages.

Plant and Devine's (2008) findings were highly consistent with the idea that internal motivation to respond without prejudice results in an approach orientation for interracial interactions. Specifically, those who were motivated to respond without prejudice because it is personally important (i.e., high IMS) were more likely than those low in internal motivation to generate goals and strategies for the interaction that focused on approaching a pleasant, egalitarian interaction. In addition, the findings supported the proposition that external motivation was related to an avoidance orientation for interracial interactions. High EMS people were more likely than those low in external motivation to generate goals and strategies for the interaction that focused on avoiding overt bias.

ACTIVATION OF APPROACH AND AVOIDANCE UPON EXPOSURE TO BLACK FACES

The findings from Plant and Devine's (2008) first study suggest that whether White people's self-reported goals and strategies for interactions with Black people focus on approaching egalitarianism or avoiding overt bias is influenced by their motivation to respond without prejudice. To the extent that participants' reports of their goals for interracial interactions reflect chronic regulatory tendencies, then these concerns are likely to become automatically activated upon exposure to relevant cues (Bargh, 1990; Bargh & Barndollar, 1996). To the extent that people who are highly internally motivated to respond without prejudice are chronically concerned with approaching egalitarianism in interracial interactions, then we would expect that general approach-related concepts would be highly accessible when exposed to Black people. Further, to the extent that people who are highly externally motivated are chronically concerned with avoiding overt bias for interracial interactions, then we would expect that general avoidance-related concepts would be highly accessible when they are exposed to Black people. To explore this possibility, Plant and Devine (2008) examined whether concepts conceptually related to approach and avoidance goals are automatically activated upon exposure to Black people as a function of the source of participants' motivation to respond without prejudice. Specifically, the accessibility of approach- and avoidance-related goals was examined by assessing the speed of response to these concepts following exposure to Black versus White faces.

Previously, researchers have shown that when environmental cues relevant to a chronic goal are primed (i.e.,

activated), people respond more quickly to words related to that goal (Bargh & Barndollar, 1996; Bargh, Raymond, Pryor, & Strack, 1995). To the extent that exposure to a Black person activates approach- or avoidance-related goals for White people, then responses to approach and avoidance concepts reflecting these goals should be facilitated (i.e., made more quickly) following exposure to a Black face as compared to a White face. To examine these possibilities, Plant and Devine (2008) had White participants complete a lexical decision task, in which they indicated as quickly as possible whether a string of letters was a word or nonword. Prior to each decision, participants were presented with either a White or Black face prime. Of particular interest was the speed of response to approach- and avoidance-related words following exposure to Black faces, controlling for the speed of response to these words following White faces.

White introductory psychology students who completed the IMS and EMS as a part of a mass testing session early in the semester were considered eligible for the study if their responses fell into the top or bottom 30% of the IMS and EMS distributions. The design of the study was a 2 (IMS: high vs. low) × 2 (EMS: high vs. low) × 2 (Face Prime: Black vs. White) × 2 (Letter String: approach vs. avoid) mixed-model factorial, with face prime and letter string as repeated measures. Of interest was participants' speed of response to the approach and avoidance words following a Black face prime controlling for the speed of response to similar words following a White face prime (Table 34.2). Specifically, participants completed a computer task where they were primed with Black and White faces prior to being presented with approach- and avoidance-related words and nonwords (SOA 450 ms). The average speed of response in seconds was then computed for the approach- and avoidance-related words following the Black and White faces separately (e.g., approach words following Black faces; avoidance words following White faces).

Analyses were conducted on participants' speed of response to the approach and avoidance words following Black face primes with the average speed of response to the corresponding words following White face primes as the covariate in each analysis with IMS and EMS as factors. The analysis of the speed of response to approach-related words following Black face primes revealed the predicted main effect of IMS, such that high IMS participants responded more quickly to the approach-related words following Black faces than low IMS participants. The analysis of the speed of response to avoidance-related words following Black face primes, consistent with expectations, revealed a main effect of EMS, such that

TABLE 34.2

Latency to Respond to Words Following Black Face Primes Controlling for Speed Following White Face Primes

	Low IMS (N = 46)	High IMS (N = 52)
Approach words	992.94[a]	853.87[b]
	(36.86)	(34.46)
Avoidance words	1121.10	1089.00
	(37.82)	(35.47)
	Low EMS (N = 48)	High EMS (N = 50)
Approach words	910.39	936.43
	(35.99)	(35.04)
Avoidance words	1165.61[a]	1044.49[b]
	(37.18)	(36.16)

Note: Means with different superscripts on the same row differ with $p < .05$. The standard errors are presented in parentheses below the means.

high EMS participants responded more quickly to the avoidance-related words following Black faces than low EMS participants.

These findings indicate that internally motivated people have approach goals automatically activated upon exposure to Black faces and externally motivated people have avoidance goals automatically activated upon exposure to Black faces. Drawing upon Bargh's (Bargh, 1990; Bargh & Barndollar, 1996) automotive theory, these findings suggest that for internally and externally motivated people, approach and avoidance regulatory concerns are likely to be chronically activated in relevant situations (e.g., exposure to a Black person).

These findings lend further support to the utility of conceptualizing people's source of motivation to respond without prejudice in terms of its implications for their orientation (approach or avoidance) for interracial interactions. Taken together, the findings from Plant and Devine's (2008) work demonstrate that highly, internally motivated White people are more likely to anticipate pursuing goals and strategies that focus on approaching egalitarianism during an interaction with a Black person and to have their approach-related goals automatically activated upon exposure to a Black person than are less internally motivated White people. In addition, highly externally motivated White people are more likely to anticipate pursing goals and strategies that focus on avoiding overt bias during such

interactions and to have their avoidance-related goals automatically activated upon exposure to a Black person than are less externally motivated White people. We now turn to the implications of approach and avoidance concerns for the quality of interracial interactions.

IMPLICATIONS OF APPROACH AND AVOIDANCE ORIENTATION FOR INTERRACIAL INTERACTIONS

Plant and Devine's (2008) findings provided insight into who among White people is likely to possess approach or avoidance motivation for interracial interactions and the implications of these motivational concerns for people's goals and strategies for such interactions. This foundation is an essential step to understanding interracial interactions and it leaves us better prepared to take on the challenges of exploring ongoing, dynamic interactions. However, thus far, the work does not speak to the likely implications of possessing approach or avoidance motivation for the perceived quality of interracial interactions.

There is reason to suspect that having avoidance motivation may be less beneficial for the course of interracial interactions than possessing an approach orientation. We anticipate that in an interracial interaction, a White person who pursues strategies such as smiling and being friendly is likely to have a far more pleasant interaction than someone who pursues strategies such as avoiding the use of stereotypes (Reis & Shaver, 1988). Further, actively trying to avoid or suppress the use of a stereotype causes the stereotype to become highly accessible in the person's mind and influence the treatment of outgroup members (Macrae, Bodenhausen, Milne, & Jetten, 1994). Thus, some avoidance strategies may actually backfire and result in a more biased response.

In addition, focusing on the undesired end-state of bias in interracial interactions may result in heightened anxiety in these interactions, which may lead to avoidance behaviors and more negative attitudes about the outgroup (Devine, Evett, & Vasquez-Suson, 1996; Islam & Hewstone, 1993; Plant & Devine, 2003; Stephan & Stephan, 1985). Focusing on a positive outcome, in contrast, may lead to the pursuit of success-related behaviors, such as persistence in the face of failure and setting realistic goals (Atkinson & Litwin, 1960; Elliot & Church, 1997; Elliot & Harackiewicz, 1996; Feather, 1967; Hembree, 1988; Mahone, 1960). In addition, there is some evidence that taking on an approach-focus for an interracial interaction (i.e., seeing it as an opportunity for intercultural dialogue) results in less depletion of self-regulatory strength following the interaction than pursuing an avoidance focus (i.e., avoiding the appearance of preju-dice; Trawalter & Richeson, 2006). Further, Shelton (2003) found that when White people tried not to be pre-judiced (i.e., took on an avoidance orientation), they experienced more anxiety and enjoyed an interaction with a Black person less than if they were not trying to avoid prejudice. Interestingly, though they enjoyed the interac-tion less, participants trying to avoid prejudice were liked more by their Black partner than control group partici-pants who were not told to avoid prejudice, which may indicate that some motivation to respond without preju-dice is better than none. In the Shelton (2003) work, how-ever, there was not a group that worked to approach a good interaction, so it is difficult to know how that would have influenced the partner's experience. In addition, although Vorauer and Turpie (2004) also found that heightened evaluative concerns had positive implications for how White participants responded to outgroup mem-bers, it was only for participants higher in prejudice. Such concerns were actually disruptive for those low in preju-dice who may typically respond positively in interracial interactions.

It is also worth considering that in Study 2, as summa-rized previously, externally motivated participants responded with the automatic activation of avoidance-related concepts, such as "withdraw" and "escape" when exposed to Black faces. The activation of such concepts in interracial interactions may lead to avoidance behav-iors (e.g., standing further away, making less eye contact). In addition, it may mean that externally motivated people are more likely to choose to avoid interracial interactions all together. One highly effective way to avoid coming across as biased in an interracial interaction is to avoid that interaction altogether (though, of course, avoiding interactions could be perceived as bias de facto). In con-trast, the automatic activation of approach-related con-cepts, such as "embrace" and "unite," among internally motivated people may result in intimate and warm inter-actions and possibly the active pursuit of interracial interactions. It will be important to examine such impli-cations of possessing approach or avoidance concerns in interracial interactions for behavior in actual ongoing interactions.

As a final note, although the focus for this section was on motivation to respond without prejudice, there are likely other factors that also predict approach and avoid-ance responses within intergroup interactions for majority group members. For example, Dovidio et al. (2002) found that White participants' implicit prejudice was associated with less nonverbal friendliness (less approach) in their interactions with a Black compared to White partner.

These processes could complicate matters in that one's intentions (e.g., to approach) could be inconsistent with implicit biases that are known to be difficult to control (Devine et al., 1996; Devine, Plant, Amodio, Harmon-Jones, & Vance, 2002).

MINORITY PERSPECTIVE

We now consider the experiences of minority group members with a focus on both their decisions to approach or avoid interracial interactions and their approach and avoidance orientation within interracial interactions. Historically, far less research has been conducted exam-ining minority group members' responses and behaviors in intergroup settings (Shelton, 2000), assuming, at least implicitly, that minority group members are passive tar-gets of prejudice. This perspective has been challenged in recent years (Devine et al., 1996; Shelton, 2003) and, indeed, one of the exciting developments in intergroup relations research is a focus on minority group members' experiences (i.e., their attitudes, expectancies, goals) and the role they play in intergroup interactions (Brigham, 1993; Butz & Plant, 2006; Livingston, 2002; Mendoza-Denton, Downey, Purdie, Davis, & Pietrzak, 2002; Monteith & Spicer, 2000; Plant, 2004; Shelton & Richeson, 2006). The vast majority of the existing work tends to focus on minority group members' (and particu-larly Black people's) experiences in interactions with majority group members, specifically White people. As a result, the focus of this review will be on minority group members' experiences in interactions with White people. As with the review of the majority group perspective, we first summarize the work examining the decision to approach or avoid interactions with White people and then consider the implications of being approach or avoidance oriented for responses in interactions with White people.

CHOOSING TO APPROACH OR AVOID INTERRACIAL INTERACTIONS

For minority group members, the decision of whether to enter interracial interactions with White people or avoid them may be more restricted than for majority group members. By virtue of being in the numerical minority, minority group members may often have little choice whether to interact with White people (e.g., in work, retail, educational settings). Further, because historically, White people have held positions of power more often than minority group members and in some cases this has not changed, minority group members may be compelled to interact with and get along with majority group members or be put at a disadvantage (e.g., professionally). Indeed, even among college students, there is some evidence that Black students have far more contact with White people than White students have with Black people, which may in part reflect having little choice whether to interact with Whites in some situations (Brigham, 1993).

When minority group members do have a choice whether or not to interact with White people, the factors that predict whether minority group members want to approach or avoid interactions with White people are in some cases similar to those factors that influence majority group members' decisions to interact with minority group members. However, there are also some important differences. Similar to the situation for White people, minority group members' negative attitudes toward White people are associated with the avoidance of interracial contact (Brigham, 1993; Johnson & Lecci, 2003; Levin et al., 2003; Livingston, 2002; Plant, 2004; Shelton & Richeson, 2006). For example, Hispanic participants who reported more negative attitudes toward White people both reported less previous contact with White people and a greater desire to avoid an upcoming interaction with a White person (Plant et al., in press). Brigham (1993) also found that for Black people, negative attitudes toward White people were associated with low levels of contact with White people. Further, longitudinal work by Levin et al. indicates that ethnic minority group members' negative attitudes may lead to decreased outgroup contact. Thus, negative attitudes may be an important factor in contributing to the avoidance of contact with White people for minority group members.

Also, consistent with the experience of majority group members, minority group members are likely to approach interracial interactions if they possess positive expectations regarding the outcomes of these interactions and avoid them if they anticipate negative outcomes. However, the types of outcomes that are most salient to minority group members in deciding whether to engage in interracial interactions differ somewhat compared to those for White people. One salient negative outcome that minority group members experience in the context of interracial interactions with White people is that they will be the target of bias and stereotyping from White people, which can contribute to the avoidance of intergroup contact (Livingston, 2002; Mendoza-Denton et al., 2002; Monteith & Spicer, 2000; Pinel, 1999; Plant, 2004; Steele, 1997; Tropp, 2003). For example, Plant (2004) demonstrated that Black participants who were concerned about being the target of bias in interactions with White people

had fewer interracial interactions during the subsequent 2 weeks and were more interested in avoiding interactions with White people. Interestingly, Black participants who expected less bias from White people had more previous experience with White people, suggesting that contact may decrease negative expectations regarding interracial interactions. Unfortunately, since negative expectations breed avoidance, it may be difficult to alleviate negative expectations of bias once formed.

Consistent with the experiences of White people in interracial interactions, Black participants report that they would avoid interracial interactions out of fear of rejection from White people (Shelton & Richeson, 2005). However, it is possible that the reasons Black and White people anticipate being rejected differ somewhat. For example, Black people may fear being rejected because of White people's prejudice toward them. White people may fear being rejected because of Black people's frustration at being the targets of racial bias. Unlike for White people, self-efficacy concerns and fears of coming across as biased generally may be less prominent for minority group members because of more chances for interracial contact over the course of their lives (cf. Plant et al., in press).

WITHIN INTERRACIAL INTERACTIONS: APPROACH AND AVOIDANCE GOALS

Once in an interaction with a majority group member, minority group members must decide what outcome they desire for the interaction. Within the context of the interaction, minority group members may choose to approach a positive interaction or avoid a negative interaction. As discussed in the previous section, for minority group members, the concern that they may be the target of prejudice is likely to loom large in interactions with White people (Feagin, 1991; Crocker et al., 1991; Mendoza-Denton et al., 2002; Pinel, 1999). This concern may take the form of constantly being "on guard" for signs of bias on the part of majority groups members and culminate in low feelings of trust in being treated fairly by the other. In many ways, this could complicate the unfolding dynamics of interracial interactions such that they may see signs of bias when none are intended or present (Devine et al., 1996). Moreover, to prevent the possibility for the other to view them in light of their group membership, minority group members may adopt an avoidance motivation, whereby they specifically focus on avoiding behavior that might be seen as confirming stereotypes about their group and behaviors that may elicit prejudice.

However, when minority group members anticipate the possibility of prejudice, the cause of the negative outcome is external to the self (i.e., the prejudice of the majority group member). As a result, minority group members may feel that their best tactic for interracial interactions is to focus on approaching a good interaction as opposed to focusing on avoiding a negative outcome that they may not be able to control (i.e., the outgroup member's bias). Consistent with this idea, Shelton, Richeson, and Salvatore (2005) found that stigma consciousness can lead Black people to pursue compensatory behaviors that encourage a positive interaction, such as increased engagement and self-disclosure. These behaviors would seem to reflect more of an approach than avoidance motivation, as they would move the actor toward a positive interracial interaction. Indeed, these compensatory strategies were found to improve the experience of White people in the interracial interaction (Shelton et al., 2005). Interestingly, these behaviors did not lead to a better experience for the Black people, which may have been due to the behaviors making the Black people feel inauthentic in the interaction. These findings are an interesting parallel to Shelton's (2003) work showing that White people who tried to appear nonprejudiced made a better impression on their Black interaction partner but enjoyed the interaction less. Clearly efforts to improve the experience of outgroup interaction partners can come at a cost.

Similar to concerns about being the target of bias, minority group members experience concerns about confirming stereotypes about their group (Steele, 1997; Steele & Aronson, 1995). Previous work on stereotype threat supports the idea that, in some contexts, minority group members may focus on avoiding the confirmation of a stereotype about their group, which can have negative implications for performance in those arenas (Steele, 1997; Steele & Aronson, 1995). For example, concerns about confirming the stereotype that minority group members are less intelligent and academically inclined than White people may lead minority group members to focus on avoiding stereotype confirmation. The negative implications of focusing on avoiding the stereotype confirmation as opposed to focusing on approaching success may account for the negative performance implications of stereotype threat (Smith, 2006). Similar to the implications of stereotype threat in performance settings, it is possible that concerns about confirming stereotypes in interpersonal interactions may also result in an avoidance focus in intergroup interactions. That is, one could speculate that concerns about being perceived as behaving consistently with the stereotype of one's group may lead minority group members to focus on *not* behaving in ways that are consistent with the stereotype of their group

(e.g., not seeming unintelligent or lazy, not being too into athletics or music). As a result, they may be less likely to focus on behaviors that may result in a positive interaction (e.g., finding common interests, actively gathering information about the interaction partner). Such a focus on avoiding a stereotypic impression in interracial interactions could result in less pleasant interactions for all involved.

BRINGING IT TOGETHER: DYNAMIC INTERACTIONS

Thus far, we have focused primarily on the majority and minority group members' responses to interracial interactions in isolation. However, interactions are by definition dynamic interchanges. It seems inescapable that the behaviors and responses of one interactant will influence the experiences of the other interactant (Devine et al., 1996). To date, the research exploring ongoing interactions where neither interactant is a confederate are extremely limited (but see Shelton et al., 2005; Shelton, 2003). Whether an individual decides to approach or avoid interracial interactions will certainly have an impact on the outgroup member. For example, deciding to avoid an interracial interaction can lead to the outgroup member feeling rejected (Shelton & Richeson, 2005). Such feelings of rejection could certainly contribute to negative expectations and attitudes about future intergroup interactions. Further, if people want to avoid interactions but cannot escape them, they are likely to respond in an awkward, avoidant manner in the interaction (Plant & Butz, 2006). These responses come across as avoidant may be interpreted as intergroup bias (Plant & Butz, 2006), and could contribute to negative expectations and attitudes for the interaction partner.

Of course, it is also possible that interracial interactions can go well, particularly if the interaction partners have an approach motivation for the interaction. Such positive interactions can have a range of implications including improving intergroup attitudes and expectations for future interactions (Allport, 1954; Pettigrew & Tropp, 2006). It will be important in future work to identify those factors that create an approach motivation for both majority and minority group members. For those who avoid intergroup interactions out of concerns that they will go poorly, breaking the cycle of avoidance will be a critical first step to moving forward. Simply getting people to engage in intergroup interactions may help to improve negative expectancies at least in most situations. Further, once people engage in interactions, perhaps if one interactant has an approach orientation for the interaction, it can help the other person to overcome any negative expectancies and shift to an approach orientation as well. In general, getting people to shift their focus from what can go wrong in intergroup interactions to what can go right may be an important advance in encouraging approach motivation. Our hope is that the framework of approach and avoidance motivations for intergroup interactions that we have introduced here can help identify promising avenues to encourage positive intergroup contact.

REFERENCES

Allport, G. W. (1954). *The nature of prejudice*. Reading, MA: Addison-Wesley.

Atkinson, J. W. (1964). *An introduction to achievement motivation*. Princeton, NJ: Van Nostrad.

Atkinson, J. W., & Litwin, G. H. (1960). Achievement motive and test anxiety conceived as motive to approach success and motive to avoid failure. *Journal of Abnormal and Social Psychology, 60*, 52–63.

Bargh, J. A. (1990). Auto-motives: Pre-conscious determinants of social interaction. In E. T. Higgins & R. M. Sorrento (Eds.), *Handbook of motivation and cognition: Foundations of social behavior* (Vol. 2, pp. 93–130). New York: Guilford Press.

Bargh, J. A., & Barndollar, K. (1996). Automaticity in action: The unconscious as repository of chronic goals and motivates. In P. M. Gollwitzer & J. A. Bargh (Eds.), *The psychology of action* (pp. 457–481). New York: Guilford Press.

Bargh, J. A., Raymond, P., Pryor, J. B., & Strack, F. (1995). Attractiveness of the underling: An automatic power → sex association and its consequences for sexual harassment and aggression. *Journal of Personality and Social Psychology, 68*, 768–781.

Brigham, J. C. (1993). College students' racial attitudes. *Journal of Applied and Social Psychology, 23*, 1933–1967.

Britt, T. W., Boniecki, K. A., Vescio, T. K., Biernat, M., & Brown, L. M. (1996). Intergroup anxiety: A person X situation approach. *Personality and Social Psychology Bulletin, 22*, 1177–1188.

Brodish, A. B., & Devine, P. G. (2007). *To conceal or reveal? Distinct interpersonal goals for interracial interactions*. Unpublished manuscript.

Butz, D. A., & Plant, E. A. (2006). Perceiving outgroup members as unresponsive: Implications for approach-related emotions, intentions, and behavior. *Journal of Personality and Social Psychology, 91*, 1066–1079.

Carver, C. S., & Scheier, M. F. (1998). *On the self-regulation of behavior*. Cambridge: University Press.

Crandall, C. S., Eshleman, A., & O'Brien, L. (2002). Social norms and the expression and suppression of prejudice: The struggle for internalization. *Journal of Personality and Social Psychology, 82*, 359–378.

Crocker, J., Voelk, K., Testa, M., & Major, B. (1991). Social stigma: The affective consequences of attributional ambiguity. *Journal of Personality and Social Psychology, 60*, 218–228.

Crowne, D. P., & Marlowe, D. (1960). A new scale of social desirability independent of psychopathology. *Journal of Consulting Psychology, 24*, 349–354.

Devine, P. G. (1989). Stereotypes and prejudice: Their automatic and controlled components. *Journal of Personality and Social Psychology, 56*, 5–18.

Devine, P. G., Evett, S. R., & Vasquez-Suson, K. A. (1996). Exploring the interpersonal dynamics of interracial context. In R. M. Sorrentino & E. T. Higgins (Eds.), *Handbook of motivation and cognition: The interpersonal context* (Vol. 3, pp. 423–464). New York: Guilford Press.

Devine, P. G., & Monteith, M. J. (1993). The role of discrepancy-associated affect in prejudice reduction. In D. M. Mackie & D. L. Hamilton (Eds.), *Affect, cognition, and stereotyping: Interactive processes in group perception* (pp. 317–344). San Diego: Academic.

Devine, P. G., & Monteith, M. J. (1999). Automaticity and control in stereotyping. In S. Chaiken & Y. Trope (Eds.), *Dual process theories in social psychology* (pp. 339–360). New York: Guilford Press.

Devine, P. G., Monteith, M. J., Zuwerink, J. R., & Elliot, A. J. (1991). Prejudice with and without compunction. *Journal of Personality and Social Psychology, 60*, 817–830.

Devine, P. G., Plant, E. A., Amodio, D. M., Harmon-Jones, E., & Vance, S. L. (2002). Exploring the relationship between implicit and explicit prejudice: The role of motivations to respond without prejudice. *Journal of Personality and Social Psychology, 82*, 835–848.

Devine, P. G., & Vasquez, K. A. (1998). The rocky road to positive intergroup relations. In J. L. Ebberhardt & S. T. Fiske (Eds.), *Confronting racism: The problem and the response* (pp. 234–262). Thousand Oaks, CA: Sage Publications.

Dovidio, J. F., Kawakami, K., & Gaertner, S. L. (2002). Implicit and explicit prejudice and interracial interaction. *Journal of Personality and Social Psychology, 82*, 62–68.

Dunton, B. C., & Fazio, R. H. (1997). An individual difference measure of motivation to control prejudiced reactions. *Personality and Social Psychology Bulletin, 23*, 316–326.

Elliot, A. J. (2006). The hierarchical model of approach-avoidance motivation. *Motivation and Emotion, 30*, 111–116.

Elliot, A. J. (2008). Approach and avoidance motivation. In A. Elliot (Ed.), *Handbook of approach and avoidance motivation* Mahwah, NJ: Lawrence Erlbaum Associates.

Elliot, A. J., & Church, M. A. (1997). A hierarchical model of approach and avoidance achievement motivation. *Journal of Personality and Social Psychology, 72*, 218–232.

Elliot, A. J., Gable, S. L., & Mapes, R. (2006). Approach and avoidance motivation in the social domain. *Personality and Social Psychology Bulletin, 32*, 378–391.

Elliot, A. J., & Harackiewicz, J. M. (1996). Approach and avoidance achievement goals and intrinsic motivation: A mediational analysis. *Journal of Personality and Social Psychology, 70*, 461–475.

Feagin, J. R. (1991). The continuing significance of race: Anti-black discrimination in public places. *American Sociological Review*, *56*, 101–116.

Feather, N. T. (1967). Level of aspiration and performance variability. *Journal of Personality and Social Psychology*, *6*, 37–46.

Gudykunst, W. B. (1993). Toward a theory of effective interpersonal and intergroup communication: An anxiety/uncertainty management perspective. In R. L. Wiseman & J. Koester (Eds.), *Intercultural communication theory* (pp. 8–58). Thousand Oaks, CA: Sage.

Hembree, R. (1988). Correlates, causes, effects, and treatment of test anxiety. *Review of Educational Research*, *58*, 47–77.

Higgins, E. T. (1997). Beyond pleasure and pain. *American Psychologist*, *52*, 1280–1300.

Islam, M. R., & Hewstone, M. (1993). Dimensions of contact as predictors of intergroup anxiety, perceived out-group variability, and out-group attitude: An integrative model. *Personality and Social Psychology Bulletin*, *19*, 700–710.

Johnson, J. D., & Lecci, L. (2003). Assessing anti-white attitudes and predicting perceived racism: The Johnson-Lecci scale. *Personality and Social Psychology Bulletin*, *29*, 299–312.

Leary, M. R. (1983). Social anxiousness: The construct and its measurement. *Journal of Personality Assessment*, *47*, 66–75.

Levin, S., van Laar, C., & Sidanius, J. (2003). The effects of ingroup and outgroup friendship on ethnic attitudes in college: A longitudinal study. *Group Processes and Intergroup Relations*, *6*, 76–92.

Livingston, R. W. (2002). The role of perceived negativity in the moderation of African Americans' implicit and explicit racial attitudes. *Journal of Experimental Social Psychology*, *38*, 405–413.

Macrae, C. N., Bodenhausen, G. V., Milne, A. B., & Jetten, J. (1994). Out of mind but back in sight: Stereotypes on the rebound. *Journal of Personality and Social Psychology*, *67*, 808–817.

Mahone, C. H. (1960). Fear of failure and unrealistic vocational aspiration. *Journal of Abnormal and Social Psychology*, *60*, 253–261.

Mendoza-Denton, R., Downey, G., Purdie, V., Davis, A., & Pietrzak, J. (2002). Sensitivity to status-based rejection: Implications for African American students' college experience. *Journal of Personality and Social Psychology*, *83*, 896–918.

Monteith, M. J., Ashburn-Nardo, L., Voils, C. I., & Czopp, A. M. (2002). Putting the breaks on prejudice: On the development and operation of cues for control. *Journal of Personality and Social Psychology*, *83*, 1029–1050.

Monteith, M. J., & Spicer, C. V. (2000). Contents and correlates of Whites' and Blacks' racial attitudes. *Journal of Experimental Social Psychology*, *36*, 125–154.

Monteith, M. J., Voils, C. I., & Ashburn-Nardo, L. (2001). Taking a look underground: Detecting, interpreting, and reacting to implicit racial biases. *Social Cognition*, *19*, 395–417.

Pettigrew, T., & Tropp, L. (2006). A meta-analytic test of intergroup contact theory. *Journal of Personality and Social Psychology*, *90*, 751–783.

Pinel, E. C. (1999). Stigma consciousness: The psychological legacy of social stereotypes. *Journal of Personality and Social Psychology*, *76*, 114–128.

Plant, E. A. (2004). Responses to interracial interactions over time. *Personality and Social Psychology Bulletin*, *30*, 1458–1471.

Plant, E. A., & Butz, D. A. (2006). The causes and consequences of an avoidance-focus for interracial interactions. *Personality and Social Psychology Bulletin*, *32*, 833–846.

Plant, E. A., Butz, D. A., & Tartakovsky, M. (in press). Interethnic interactions: Expectancies, emotions, and behavioral intentions. *Group Process and Intergroup Relations*.

Plant, E. A., & Devine, P. G. (1998). Internal and external motivation to respond without prejudice. *Journal of Personality and Social Psychology*, *75*, 811–832.

Plant, E. A., & Devine, P. G. (2003). The antecedents and implications of interracial anxiety. *Personality and Social Psychology Bulletin*, *29*, 790–801.

Plant, E. A., & Devine, P. G. (2007). [Motivation to respond without prejudice and Approach and Avoidance Orientations]. Unpublished raw data.

Plant, E. A., & Devine, P. G. (2008). *The intention underlying the control of prejudice: To hide or to be free of bias.* Manuscript in revision.

Reis, H. T., & Shaver, P. (1988). Intimacy as an interpersonal process. In S. W. Duck (Ed.), *Handbook of personal relationships* (pp. 367–389). Oxford, England: Wiley.

Shah, J., Higgins, T. E., & Friedman, R. S. (1998). Performance incentives and means: How regulatory focus influences goal attainment. *Journal of Personality and Social Psychology*, *74*, 285–293.

Shelton, J. N. (2000). A reconceptualization of how we study issues of racial prejudice. *Personality and Social Psychology Review*, *4*, 374–390.

Shelton, J. N., (2003). Interpersonal concerns in social encounters between majority and minority group members. *Group Processes and Intergroup Relations*, *6*, 171–186.

Shelton, N. J., & Richeson, J. A. (2005). Intergroup contact and pluralistic ignorance. *Journal of Personality and Social Psychology*, *88*, 91–107.

Shelton, J. N., & Richeson, J. (2006). Ethnic minorities' racial attitudes and contact experiences with White people. *Cultural Diversity and Ethnic Minority Psychology*, *12*, 149–164.

Shelton, J. N., Richeson, J., & Salvatore, J. (2005). Expecting to be the target of prejudice: Implications for interethnic interactions. *Personality and Social Psychology Bulletin*, *31*, 1189–1202.

Smith, J. L. (2006). The interplay among stereotypes, performance–avoidance goals, and women's math performance expectations. *Sex Roles*, *54*, 287–296.

Snyder, M., & Gangestad, S. (1986). On the nature of self-monitoring: Matters of assessment, matters of validity. *Journal of Personality and Social Psychology*, *51*, 125–139.

Steele, C. M. (1997). A threat in the air: How stereotype shape intellectual identify and performance. *American Psychologist*, *52*, 613–629.

Steele, C. M., & Aronson, J. (1995). Stereotype threat and the intellectual test performance of African Americans. *Journal of Personality and Social Psychology, 69*, 797–811.

Stephan, W. G., & Stephan, C. W. (1985). Intergroup anxiety. *Journal of Social Issues, 41*, 157–175.

Towles-Schwen, T., & Fazio, R. H. (2001). On the origins of racial attitudes: Correlates of childhood experiences. *Personality and Social Psychology Bulletin, 27*, 162–175.

Towles-Schwen, T., & Fazio, R. H. (2006). Automatically activated racial attitudes as predictors of the success of interracial roommate relationships. *Journal of Experimental Social Psychology, 42*, 698–705.

Trawalter, S., & Richeson, J. A. (2006). Regulatory focus and executive function after interracial interactions. *Journal of Experimental Social Psychology, 42*, 406–412.

Tropp, L. R. (2003). The psychological impact of prejudice: Implications for intergroup contact. *Group Processes and Intergroup Relations, 6*, 131–149.

Vorauer, J. D. (2006). An information search model of evaluative concerns in intergroup interaction. *Psychological Review, 113*, 862–886.

Vorauer, J. D., Main, K. J., & O'Connell, G. B. (1998). How do individuals expect to be viewed by members of lower status groups? Content and implications of meta-stereotypes. *Journal of Personality and Social Psychology, 75*, 917–937.

Vorauer, J. D., & Turpie, C. A. (2004). Disruptive effects of vigilance on dominant group members' treatment of outgroup members: Choking versus shining under pressure. *Journal of Personality and Social Psychology, 87*, 384–399.

Social Comparison

35 A Reunion for Approach–Avoidance Motivation and Social Comparison

Jerry Suls and Ladd Wheeler

CONTENTS

Leon Festinger was a student or colleague of Kurt Lewin from 1939 until Lewin's death in 1947, and Lewin's theorizing about positive and negative valences led to the distinction between approach and avoidance motivation (Elliot, 1997; see Elliot, chapter 1, this volume; Higgins, 2000). However, there is no mention of approach–avoidance or positive–negative valence in social comparison theory (Festinger, 1954a,b). Festinger had used these concepts in the classic paper on level of aspiration (LOA)

(Lewin, Dembo, Festinger, & Sears, 1944) and had in fact previously published on the "resultant valence theory" (Festinger, 1942b). We would guess that these notions of positive and negative valence would be deeply embedded in Festinger's mind. Their apparent absence in his subsequent work is surprising.

However, we show that Festinger (1954a,b) borrowed important elements of the LOA paper for his formulation of comparison theory. Also, by formally reintroducing social comparison to approach–avoidance motivation, we hope to provide more clarity about the current state of knowledge concerning comparison processes for ability and trait evaluation.

In this chapter, we first briefly describe the LOA and classic social comparison theories, noting their connections and what Festinger borrowed from earlier research by himself and colleagues. Appreciation of these connections leads us to a reconceptualization of social comparison and its positive and negative consequences for self-evaluation. Specifically, we describe responses to social comparison and selection of comparison information in a new approach–avoidance framework. For our purposes, approach will refer to those situations in which the person wants to excel on the comparison dimension. Conversely, avoidance will refer to the desire to avoid failure on the comparison dimension. The other dimension in this framework is the actual status of the comparison target relative to the person, whether the target is inferior or superior to the person and by how much.

HISTORICAL BACKGROUND

LEVEL OF ASPIRATION

In the 1930s, Lewin and his students, Dembo (1931) and Hoppe (1930), turned their attention to the question of how people set goal levels. LOA was defined as the degree of difficulty of the goal toward which a person is striving and was seen as relevant when there is a range of perceived difficulty to attain goals. It also was recognized that there is variation in valence among goals differing in difficulty. Succeeding at a task known to be difficult should be particularly satisfying; failing at a simple task should be particularly unsatisfying.

In a representative LOA experiment, a subject performs a task to obtain a score. Following the first trial, the subjects learn about their performance and then are asked what score they will try to make the next time. The task is attempted again and the subject receives another score. Prior to each trial, the subject is asked to report what score he/she is aiming for next (i.e., level of aspiration). This sequence continues over a series of trials. In this paradigm, a common observation is that doing better versus doing worse across trials influences the LOA set by the subjects.

By the mid-1940s, an appreciable amount of research had been conducted by Lewin and his colleagues and by others to understand factors that affect LOA. The purpose of Lewin et al.'s (1944) review paper was to evaluate the state of evidence and propose a general theory of LOA. Three factors were identified as important contributors to LOA: (a) the valence of seeking success; (b) the valence of avoiding failure; (c) the probability of success/failure. "The strength of these forces and values corresponding to the subjective probability depend on many aspects of the individual…particularly on the way he sees his past experience and on the scales of reference which are characteristics of his culture and his personality" (Lewin et al., p. 376).

These factors were implicated by several sources of empirical evidence. For example, researchers noted that the vast majority of research subjects reported LOA's which were above their previous performance score (Gould, 1939). This was seen as a manifestation of the cultural emphasis on improvement. In the theory of LOA, past experience was seen as acting on the perceived probability of future success or failure.

The valence of success or failure was seen to follow a general rule–as the difficulty of the task increases so does the valence of success (while the valence of failure decreases). This general tendency was modifiable, however, by other factors, including the performance standards of relevant social groups. The valence of failure should be high and valence of success low at a performance level below the group's standard (or average). Conversely, the valence of success should be high and valence of failure low at a performance level at or above the group standard. There can be, however, group standards that prohibit either low or high levels of performance. True Gentlemen should not receive an academic grade either higher or lower than a "C." Departure in either direction would entail a high negative valence and a low positive valence.

Direct evidence of the role of social reference standards was provided by Festinger (1942a). Using the LOA experimental protocol, Festinger manipulated the source and nature of performance norms that subjects received about other groups. He found that undergraduates would lower their aspirations if they found themselves performing above the group average and raise their aspirations if they scored below the group average. Thus, subjects changed their aspirations to be in agreement with their peers. The status of the group also made a difference. The undergraduates raised their aspirations the most when they were told they scored below high school students and lowered their aspirations the most when told they scored above graduate students.

The most direct legacy of LOA was for theories of achievement motivation where valence and probability figured importantly, as well as personality (Atkinson, 1959, 1964). But LOA also informed Festinger's (1954a,b) Social Comparison Theory.

Social Comparison Theory

In the mid-to-late 1940s, Festinger, Lewin, and their associates turned their attention to the study of group dynamics. In his Informal Social Communication theory, Festinger (1950) emphasized the action of social pressures, such as communication between group members and the rejection of deviates, to attain agreement or uniformity in the group. Uniformity of opinion was desirable, Festinger thought, because it provides confidence in one's opinion or facilitates group goals. A short time later, when Festinger was asked to review and integrate empirical findings about social influence in groups (which resulted in two papers describing social comparison theory; 1954a,b), his thinking had shifted from an emphasis on the power of the group over the individual to how individuals use groups to evaluate themselves. In the new theory, Festinger carried over the idea about people wanting to know whether their opinions were correct, but also extended it to the evaluation of abilities. That is, people also want to know what their abilities allow them to do. He proposed that comparisons with others could provide this information when objective standards were unavailable or nonexistent. His idea about pressures toward uniformity from informal social communication was extended to the comparison process. Finding agreement with others should make us feel more confident. In the case of abilities, observing those with similar abilities allows us to know what our own possibilities for action are; "if they were successful at 'X,' probably I can be too."

In social comparison theory, the emphasis was on accurate self-evaluation—for opinions, "Am I correct?" and for abilities, "Can I do X?" For both questions, the "similarity hypothesis" was a key element. As Festinger (1954b) noted, "There is a tendency to stop comparing oneself with others who are very divergent. This tendency increases if others are perceived as different from oneself in relevant dimensions" (p. 217). In other words, people who are similar are especially useful in generating accurate evaluations. Festinger, however, did not clearly specify the basis of similarity. Subsequent researchers clarified that the similarity was on characteristics correlated or predictive of an ability or opinion (Goethals & Darley, 1977; Martin, Suls, & Wheeler, 2002; Suls, Martin, & Wheeler, 2000; Wheeler, Martin, & Suls, 1997). These characteristics are referred to as *related attributes* by social comparison researchers.

In his 1954 statements, Festinger almost completely ignored the valence of comparison information; whether the comparison would make the recipient feel worthwhile or worthless was irrelevant. In fact, the theory allowed for the possibility that someone may purposely not perform their best so they can be similar and "fit in" with other group members (Radloff, 1966). However, valence crept into the theory via the unidirectional drive upward, a legacy of the LOA work. For abilities, Festinger observed there is a value set on doing better and better ("a unidirectional drive upward"), which does not normally apply to opinions. This means there is an inherent conflict between pressures to uniformity for purposes of accurate self-evaluation and the need to be superior (see discussion of Hypothesis V; Festinger, 1954a). We would add, however, that this also applies to other personal attributes and many kinds of opinions because some opinions and personal attributes are seen as better than others to possess (Jones & Gerard, 1965). For Festinger (1954a), "The implication is that, with respect to the evaluation of abilities, a state of social quiescence is never reached." In other words, in a social group there will be a continuous attempt to be better, or at least think one is better, than everyone else.

Connections Between Social Comparison and LOA

Festinger borrowed at least two important themes from LOA. The first was the idea that similar others serve as a critical reference standard. He had shown this in his earlier LOA research. After learning they had performed above or below other undergraduates, subjects moved their aspiration level closer to their peer group's performance.

The second idea he adapted was the unidirectional drive upward, which he observed might apply only in Western culture which stresses individual achievement and competition. This was suggested by empirical evidence with the LOA paradigm demonstrating that subjects typically set higher goals on each succeeding trial. People want to improve.

LOA also may have been influential in another way. Festinger's idea that ability self-evaluation works the same way as opinion, evaluation probably seemed surprising to initial readers of his theory. In the 1950s, group processes, opinions, and persuasion were the popular social psychology topics. But Festinger's introduction of ability is understandable in the context of his earlier LOA research, which presumed that aspirations are based partly on ability self-assessment.

Still, the absence of discussion of the affective consequences of social comparisons (only touched on in the unidirectional drive upward) seems like an oversight for a researcher who had been previously studied how people select goals to maximize feelings of success and minimize feelings of failure. Our speculation is that the oversight might be the result of Festinger's well-known disdain for *bubba* (commonsense) psychology and his predilection for empirical demonstrations of counter-intuitive behavior. The affective effects of social comparison might have seemed too obvious–people should feel better about themselves when they are superior and worse when they are inferior to others. As subsequent research has demonstrated (Buunk, Collins, Taylor, VanYperen, & Dakof, 1990), however, the outcomes of comparison are not so simple, but Festinger did not wait to find out. He dropped social comparison theory and moved to his theory of cognitive dissonance, the last research he did in social psychology.

For nearly a decade and a half, researchers studying social comparison focused mainly on the striving for accurate self-evaluation and tests of the similarity hypothesis (see Latane, 1966). The emphasis shifted after publication of Wills' (1981) downward comparison theory, which posited that people who feel threatened should compare with others who are worse-off, thereby boosting feelings of subjective well-being. Subsequent research, consistent with Wills' theory, showed that medical patients seemed to benefit from strategic downward comparisons (Wood, Taylor, & Lichtman, 1985). The idea that social comparisons could be self-enhancing or self-protective rather than self-evaluative became a major research topic, which continues to the present day. Also, empirical support for another motive—directing comparison in the interest of improving the self—also appeared (see Wood, 1989). With the recognition of these additional motivations for social comparison, the relevance of valence was clearly appreciated. But the accumulated research from the 1980s to the present day has presented a wide range of findings across different kinds of outcomes (Collins, 1996; Wheeler & Suls, in press). A number of theories have been presented (see Suls & Wheeler, 2000; Stapel & Suls, 2007), but none seem to subsume all of the data and none have formally incorporated approach and avoidance. With regard to the latter, this seems important because the desire to attain success (i.e., self-enhancement) may operate differently in social comparison than the desire to avoid failure (i.e., self-protection). Later in this chapter, we describe our approach–avoidance model and assess how well it handles the empirical evidence.

BRINGING APPROACH AND AVOIDANCE BACK HOME

The legacy of LOA theory, particularly its emphasis on achieving success and avoiding failure, has considerable relevance when we are uncertain about choosing a goal or a course of action (as in the LOA paradigm). Similarly, distinguishing between approach toward success and avoidance of failure has utility for understanding the affective reactions to unbidden forced or spontaneous comparisons. We begin with the general premise that we want to find out we are worthwhile people. To accomplish this, people want to excel on the comparison dimension—this can be conceptualized as approach. Conversely, people want not to fail on the comparison dimension—avoidance. One can feel worthwhile as a person either by excelling or by not failing. In the social world, these general tendencies are played out among an array of superior, similar, and inferior comparison targets.

The distinction between approach and avoidance motivation has not been fully appreciated in social comparison (but see Lockwood, 2002). We described earlier how downward comparison was believed to serve self-enhancement. However, the empirical literature tends to lump self-protection with self-enhancement and assume they work similarly. This may be in error because self-enhancement represents the desire to excel; self-protection is quite different because it represents a desire to avoid failure (see Elliot & Mapes, 2005).

In the next section, we describe how approach and avoidance influence the selection of appropriate comparisons to evaluate ability. After describing the role of these motives for comparison selection, we will describe the affective responses that result from being exposed to superior or inferior comparison targets.

"CAN I DO X?": COMPARISON SELECTION AND MOTIVES

To understand the role of approach and avoidance in comparison selection, we first must describe how the process by which people make comparisons to evaluate their abilities is understood currently. The proxy comparison model (Martin, 2000; Martin et al., 2002; Wheeler et al., 1997) builds on Festinger's theory and the attributional reformulation (Goethals & Darley, 1977) that clarified his similarity hypothesis. The model focuses on the selection of comparison information in situations where someone must decide whether to undertake a novel and consequential task where failure would have costs. Should a college graduate accept admission at a prestigious medical school where the receipt of a degree confers future benefits but the flunk-out rate is high? Does someone have the ability to swim to a lovely island across a wide bay? Serious consequences may occur if people miscalculate about their capabilities in attempting a novel task. If the person has not tried this before, there is no objective standard available, but certain kinds of social comparisons can help to make the decision.

According to the proxy model, one can find out whether he/she can do "X," if there is a person who already has undertaken the unfamiliar task—that is, a proxy. Not every person who has tried "X" is an informative choice, however. The proxy model describes the configuration of variables—similarity to self, effort expended, and related attributes—that make a proxy appropriate.

These variables are defined by three premises. If one finds someone else who has succeeded at "X" (e.g., medical school or swimming the bay successfully), this proxy is a good indicator of one's own likely future performance *if* both self and proxy performed similarly on a prior related task *and* the proxy is known to have exerted maximal effort on that prior occasion. If it is unclear that proxy exerted maximum effort then he/she may not be an appropriate index (e.g., if proxy was fatigued when performing comparably to self), his/her prior performance might be an underestimate of proxy's actual ability, making his/her success at "X" a poor prognosticator for the self.

In the absence of information about proxy's maximum effort, proxy can still be informative if self and proxy share characteristics that are predictive of performance (i.e., related attributes). If, however, it is known that proxy performed at maximum effort, then standing on related attributes is irrelevant. Unpacking this argument with an example: if Stan knows that he and Gus ran 25 laps in 10 min and he was confident that this represented Gus' best or maximal effort, then Stan can infer he should be able to match Gus' subsequent performance in a marathon. Whether Gus runs several times a week (i.e., a related attribute) should not change Stan's expectation of matching proxy-Gus' performance on the new task. In sum, the proxy model predicts that related attribute information should be disregarded when there is information that proxy performed at maximal effort on the prior related task. Lacking that, related attributes similarity can serve as a substitute and establish that proxy's performance indicates whether self can do X.

The proxy model predictions have received support in several experiments. In an important study that inspired the formulation of the proxy model, Jones and Regan (1974) found that subjects preferred to affiliate with someone who performed similarly to them on an initial test of ability and who had already attempted the task at issue. Smith and Sachs (1997) reported that confidence in performance predictions was highest when the proxy's score was similar.

Martin et al. (2002) reported the results of several lab experiments using a physical strength paradigm to test the three main predictions. Consistent with the model, subjects used a proxy's success on a novel task (Task 2) to predict their own performance if both had performed similarly on a prior related task and proxy was known to have exerted maximal effort on that occasion. In another study, whether proxy had performed at maximum effort was ambiguous, but information about a related attribute (hand size) was manipulated. Subjects used related attribute information about hand width to make their performance predictions about task 2.

The third premise was tested by manipulating information about proxy's prior performance (maximum, ambiguous) and related attribute information. When subjects did not know whether proxy's performance was their maximum, subjects used the related attribute information as a basis for their predictions. When proxy's performance represented maximum effort, subjects predicted that they would perform at the same level as proxy did on task 2, regardless of related attributes. Comparable support was found for these predictions in a paradigm involving a novel intellectual task.

Where do approach and avoidance motivations play a role? They were not discussed in the proxy model or experiments, but they are implicitly part of the basic premises. As stated earlier, the theory is assumed to apply in cases where the task is novel (hence, there is uncertainty about the outcome) and successful performance would lead to personal rewards, but failure would be costly. People want to know whether they "can do X?" so that they maximize the possibility of success (approach) and minimize the possibility of failure (avoidance). If there were no rewards for succeeding, then there is no reason to consider trying "X." The question is asked precisely because there is something important to be gained. But because failure is costly, there also is strong motivation not to fail. Lacking other information about a novel challenge, finding an appropriate proxy—someone who has attempted it previously—is critical. By comparing with a proxy (defined by similar prior performance under best effort *or* related attributes), the person maximizes the informational potential and balances the desire for success versus fear of failure.

The proxy model has a clear connection to approach and avoidance motivation because it applies to novel situations where there are both incentives for succeeding and serious costs for failing. Festinger (1954a) also recognized that inaccurate evaluation was costly: "The holding of … inaccurate appraisals of one's abilities can be punishing or even fatal in many situations," (p. 117).

There is a need for research that manipulates rewards of success and costs of failure to assess how selection of the proxy may change. Earlier work indicated that offering appreciable monetary incentives did not affect performance prediction accuracy (Martin et al., 2002), but this is different from effects of the gains or costs associated with performance quality. In social comparison research, the rewards of success and costs of failure have not been manipulated. Also, individual differences in approach or avoidance motivation have not been directly measured so we do not know much about the interplay of the motives and comparison selection. We speculate that inordinate focus on success may cause people to focus on proxy superstars who are wholly inappropriate and lead them to attempt tasks that exceed their capabilities. Conversely, too much focus on fears of failure may cause people to rely on proxies who lead them to be overly cautious in choosing their goals.

MOTIVES AND REACTIONS TO SOCIAL COMPARISON

Contemporary researchers find that comparison with a target can produce self-evaluations that are displaced toward the comparison target (i.e., assimilation) or evaluations that are displaced away from the target (i.e., contrast). Recognition that assimilation might be a consequence of comparison represented a change in thinking because the assumption in the 1980s and 1990s was that contrast was the main outcome of social comparison (Suls, Martin, & Wheeler, 2002). An illustrative study is Morse and Gergen's (1970) "Mr. Clean–Mr. Dirty experiment" where the self-esteem of subjects increased after being exposed to a disheveled, disorganized student but decreased after being exposed to a well-dressed, very competent college student.

More recent evidence, however, demonstrates that comparison also can lead to assimilation. For example, Brown, Novick, Lord, and Richards (1992) found that low self-esteem females who had the same birthday as an attractive comparison target female assimilated their own attractiveness ratings toward that target. However, if they did not have the same birthday, they contrasted their attractiveness ratings away from her.

Since the recognition that social comparisons can lead to contrast or to assimilation, social psychologists have been actively studying what conditions lead to one or the other outcome and have developed a number of conceptual models. By now, several variables have been identified. Some contemporary theories of assimilation-contrast emphasize how different kinds of information are made accessible by the comparison target or by surrounding conditions (Markman & McMullen, 2003; Mussweiler, 2003; Stapel & Koomen, 2001b). We find these cognitive

explanations to be interesting but incomplete. When motives, such as self-enhancement or self-improvement, are discussed, they seem tacked-on rather than fully incorporated into the theory. (In fairness, the Markman and McMullen model considers affect more explicitly than the other models, but mainly as an outcome of comparison; Markman, McMullen, & Elizaga, 2007.) But we think that an appreciation of the interplay of approach and avoidance motivation has the potential for a satisfying integration that acknowledges both cognitive and affective influences (see also Lockwood, 2002; Higgins, 2000). To advance our arguments, first we must describe a contemporary cognitive assimilation-contrast theory that we find attractive. We chose the selective accessibility model (SAM; Mussweiler, 2003) as the vehicle from which we launch our approach–avoidance comparison model because of its parsimony and preference for absolute rather than subjective rating outcomes. However, Stapel's (2007; Stapel & Koomen, 2000; Stapel & Suls, 2004) interpretation-comparison model probably might just as readily have been used. In the interests of space and complexity, we have focused on SAM. After reviewing SAM, we describe our approach–avoidance perspective.

THE SELECTIVE ACCESSIBILITY MODEL

Mussweiler (2003; see also Mussweiler & Strack, 2000a,b) proposes that whether assimilation versus contrast occurs depends on the information that is accessible and used during the comparison. The process is guided by an initial, holistic assessment of the similarity between the target and the self. This rapid initial screening results in a general judgment of "similar" or "dissimilar." Cognitive psychologists who have studied object recognition note that people rapidly consider a small number of salient features to determine whether an object and a target are generally similar or dissimilar. For social comparison, this might comprise salient characteristics or category membership, such as gender or age. Once the initial assessment is made, retrieval tends to focus on hypothesis-consistent evidence (Klayman & Ha, 1987). In the context of comparison, a general impression of similarity with the target sets in motion a process of "similarity testing" (e.g., "We both like history"). Because there are many facets of the self, people can recall or construe self-knowledge in such a way that accessible knowledge is consistent with the initial holistic impression. The consequence is that the self-evaluations are drawn closer to the target after selective search for similarity—leading to assimilation.

An initial, general impression of dissimilarity, however, should prompt selective retrieval of target-inconsistent knowledge about the self (e.g., "He likes barbershop quartets, but I like bebop"). There, too, information can be recalled or construed consistently with the impression of difference. After dissimilarity search, self-evaluations are displaced from the comparison target—leading to contrast.

Empirical support for the SAM has taken several forms. In a representative experiment, Mussweiler (2001) used a procedural priming task (Smith, 1994) with a picture comparison task to induce subjects to focus on either similarities or differences. Specifically, subjects were assigned either to find the similarities or the differences between two scenes. This manipulation was used to prime the subjects to engage in similarity versus dissimilarity testing. Then, in a supposedly unrelated experiment, subjects read about another college student who was described either adjusting well or poorly to college. After making their impressions of the other student, subjects evaluated their own adjustment to college by answering such questions as, "How often have you typically gone out per month?" and "How many friends do you have at the university?" Consistent with predictions from SAM, subjects who had been primed earlier to focus on similarities named more social activities and friends after comparison with a well-adjusted target than a poorly adjusted target. Conversely, subjects primed to focus on differences, contrasted self-evaluations away from the high standard; that is, reported their adjustment to college was worse after comparison with a well-adjusted target than a poorly adjusted target. Thus, assimilation versus contrast with a comparison target occurred depending on whether subjects had been primed to focus on similarities or differences. Other research has found evidence, consistent with SAM, that priming social standards makes certain kinds of standard-consistent or standard-inconsistent information more cognitively accessible and hence faster to access in a lexical priming task (Mussweiler & Strack, 2000b).

One of the strengths of SAM is that selective accessibility provides a parsimonious cognitive explanation for the moderating factors reported to influence whether assimilation or contrast with a comparison target occurs. Lockwood and Kunda (1997) found that subjects would assimilate to a superior target if they believed the likelihood of reaching the same success was possible for them. Thus, the likelihood of attaining better standing is important. This is also related to Stapel and Koomen's (2000) idea that assimilation to the target is facilitated when the person thinks that the relevant attribute is mutable, that is, can be changed. Major, Testa, and Blysma (2001) also proposed that perceived control was important in determining responses to comparisons. If the target was superior, subjects should assimilate if they thought they had control over the attribute. In these empirical examples, the likelihood of improvement to the comparison target was high; assimilation with the target was the outcome.

Another moderator that strengthens assimilation is psychological closeness to the comparison target, such as sharing related attributes with another person. In the study by Brown et al. (1992), described earlier, assimilation presumably occurred for the subjects who shared a birthday with the target because psychological closeness was salient. Sharing a social category, increasing the feeling of "we-ness," should also increase psychological closeness and is associated with assimilative outcomes (Stapel & Koomen, 2001a), as should comparison with ingroup rather than outgroup members (Mussweiler & Bodenhausen, 2002).

Mussweiler (2003) notes that each of these factors should lead to a holistic impression of similarity leading to further testing for similarity. If information about the self is retrieved that is consistent with the target then assimilation should result.

Conversely, contrast should occur in the absence of psychological closeness, when people think they do not share the same likelihood for future success, or do not have the same related attributes. Researchers also find that a highly distinct or extreme comparison target (e.g., Albert Einstein for intelligence, Mother Teresa for charity) produces contrast (Stapel & Koomen, 2000). Such extreme exemplars, according to SAM, should create an initial impression of dissimilarity with the target and prompt testing for dissimilarity, thereby resulting in contrastive self-evaluations.

In SAM, similarity testing frequently operates as the default. Research indicates that people initially tend to focus on similarities rather than differences in comparisons. Festinger's (1954a) theory and its extensions (Goethals & Darley, 1977; Wheeler et al., 1997) also are consistent with this idea. Whether similarity is a default because it is well practiced (Smith, 1994) or follows attributional logic (see description of proxy model) are not mutually exclusive possibilities. But the search for similarity should be short-circuited when a target initially perceived as extreme or distinct does not share related attributes or has some salient attribute suggesting the self and target are probably quite different. Then the holistic impression of dissimilarity should set in motion a search for differences that leads to contrast.

There are other models, with origins in psychophysics, that do not account for contrast with selective accessibility (Biernat, Manis, & Nelson, 1991; Manis & Paskewitz,

1984; Ostrom & Upshaw, 1968; Manis, Biernat, & Nelson, 1991).* In these alternative accounts, a comparison target serves as a judgmental anchor that changes the meaning of the scale of evaluation. For example, in the company of Yao Ming (7'6″), the authors might rate themselves as "very short" though objectively we both are of average height. In this case, Ming serves as a reference point that influences the interpretation of the points on the rating scale. As a consequence, "average" and "short" take on a different meaning for us as raters than if Earl Boykins (5'5″) was the reference point.

The SAM acknowledges that both selective accessibility (via difference seeking) and the change of meaning induced by reference points can produce contrast. But SAM views the latter as only affecting the language or ratings that people use to describe their judgments and not the underlying cognitive or perceptual process. Selective accessibility is thought to directly affect the mental representation of the self-evaluation. Moreover, if the similarity default is operating, then there is always a battle between assimilation (via selective accessibility) and use of the target as a contrastive standard when a subjective rating is the measure of self-evaluation (because of the change in scale interpretation). This means, with a few exceptions, that both reference points and selective accessibility (via difference search) may account for contrast outcomes. On the other hand, an assimilative outcome on a subjective rating scale is strong evidence that the influence of selective accessibility (via similarity testing) was greater than any effect of reference point. For these reasons, Mussweiler (2003) prefers to demonstrate comparison effects on absolute judgments rather than on subjective rating scales. But, to date, there is more research available that reports rating scale outcomes. This will be a relevant consideration when we review the relevant evidence.

THE ROLE OF MOTIVES

Neither the selective accessibility or reference point theories have formal mechanisms addressing the role of motives on responses to comparisons with superior or inferior others. The cognitive mechanisms grind away

seemingly disinterested in whether the comparison outcome reflects positively or negatively on the self. Mussweiler, Epstrude, and Ruter (2005) note, however, that people motivated to preserve a positive self-image when confronted with a low standard may focus more on dissimilarity testing. Stapel and Schwinghammer (2004) have shown that defensiveness may prompt construal of comparison targets in ways that protect self-esteem (also see Stapel & Van der Zee, 2006). But a systematic approach to personal motivations is missing in SAM, which does not differentiate between the motivation to succeed versus that to avoid failure. When self-enhancement is considered, approach and avoidance motivations are lumped together.

We propose that people should be interested in the outcome of social comparisons because they want to find out and confirm that they are worthwhile. This means that people are always oriented upward whether they want to approach success or avoid failure. The central question is "How close am I to those people up there?" When the approach motive is high, the person wants to know this so he can get there. When avoidance is high, they hope the gap is not so great that it makes them feel and look bad. Translated into approach–avoidance terms, people should want to excel on the comparison dimension and avoid failure on the comparison dimension. We assume, however, that situational factors and individual differences determine whether approach or avoidance is salient. (Much of this volume is devoted to these topics.) The approach–avoidance distinction is represented by the two levels of the first factor in the 2×4 scheme that we propose (see Table 35.1). The second factor refers to the status of the comparison target, which considers both direction—upward/downward—and extremity: from extremely superior, slightly superior, and slightly inferior to extremely inferior.

THE APPROACH–AVOIDANCE MODEL OF COMPARISON

In our scheme, the comparison effects of features identified in research, such as closeness, related attributes, attainability, mutability, and extremity, are considered in light of the approach or avoidance tendencies. This is best explained by describing how approach–avoidance should work in assimilation-contrast terms in each cell of the 2×4 matrix.

In Scenario A, the desire to excel (approach) is difficult to satisfy with someone who is highly superior, such as Einstein, Gandhi, or a fashion model. In the case of a superstar, the likelihood of psychological closeness, attainability, or related attributes also is probably low and immediately apparent; thus, selective search for differences

---

* Changes in reference point interpretation do not account for assimilation phenomena as easily (Wedell, Hicklin, & Smarandescu, 2007). Some related models posit an inclusion process leading to assimilation when the comparison other has attributes that are potentially relevant to the self-representation. Under such circumstances, the person and the comparison target are assigned to the same category—assimilation (Schwarz & Bless, 1992; Stapel & Koomen, 2001b).

TABLE 35.1

Comparison Responses as a Function of Approach–Avoidance Motivation and Target Direction and Extremity

Motivation	Target Direction and Extremity			
	Highly Superior	Slightly Superior	Slightly Inferior	Highly Inferior
Approach	A Contrast	B Assimilation	C Contrast	D Ignore or maybe contrast
Avoidance	E He/she is a noncomparable genius.	F Derogate (lower) the target to your level.	G Emphasize your differences from that person to avoid possibility of assimilation.	H Contrast

should commence. Of course, in the interest of self-enhancement, it would be optimal to cease comparison with such targets or find someone not quite so brilliant. But the target's extremity probably engages dissimilarity search, leading to contrast. We doubt, however, that the self-evaluation is repelled so far that it shifts to the negative side of the continuum.

For Scenario B, exposure to a slightly superior other, combined with a personal desire to excel (approach), should yield assimilation. This possibility was first explicitly recognized by Collins (1996), but was implied by earlier evidence (Wheeler, 1966). According to SAM, the similarity search default contributes here, the distance from the target also is not too large, and any other relevant feature (e.g., closeness, related attributes, attainability) will further engage retrieval or construal of similarity with the target. Self-evaluations, therefore, should move closer to the superior other. Any initially detected feature that seems to negate the possibility of attainment or similarity, however, should terminate similarity seeking and discourage assimilation.

If the person is motivated to excel (approach) and exposed to a slightly inferior target then contrast should be the result (Scenario C). Although the distance from the target is not great, the person should be motivated to reject similarity testing. Also, if there are any features that might suggest similarity with the target, it is in the person's interest to ignore them. If the target is highly inferior, however, then either it is ignored or contrast occurs because of the initial impression of dissimilarity (Scenario D). We assume the target's extreme (inferior) status will frequently imply that there is a difference in related attributes between them. Selective retrieval of other differences should only reinforce that impression.

When avoidance is high and the target is highly superior, the simplest strategy to "save face" is to consider them a noncomparable genius (Scenario E). If the person is only slightly better, derogation of the target to your level is the best option (Scenario F). This is probably the scenario where pressure for selective construal of the comparison target or sabotage is the greatest (Scenario F).

To avoid failure when confronted with a slightly inferior target (Scenario G), it is best for the person to emphasize differences (i.e., dissimilarity search leading to contrast) because the person is not far from them. This tendency to find dissimilarity should be most intense, however, if the target is highly inferior, producing contrast (Scenario H).

It is noteworthy that contrast is considered more likely whenever the person compares with an inferior target (regardless of how different the target is; scenarios C, D, G, & H). Whether a person wants to excel (approach) or avoid failure (avoidance), downward assimilation is an unlikely outcome. This prediction is consistent with the empirical literature where instances of downward assimilation have rarely been documented (Wheeler & Suls, in press).

Another point concerns the unavoidable looseness of some predictions. Things work like this in general, but there are probably circumstances where a single salient attribute could create the opposite outcome. For example, a person might be extremely avoidant about academic situations and tend to derogate those who are more academically successful (Scenario F). But if the target happens to be a sibling then psychological closeness might become very salient and induce selective retrieval that results in (upward) assimilation. Or, for an aspiring student, assimilation toward a slightly better classmate might be short-circuited in the absence of an expectation about improving. There are, however, a wide variety of factors (extremity, related attributes, attainability, mutability, psychological closeness) that may effect the initial holistic impression of the comparison target. Because these features may not be highly correlated, the exact outcome may be difficult to predict; this looseness in the model seems necessary to remain true to the complexities and subtleties of comparison in social life. (Researchers, however, should manipulate all of these factors independently or keep some constant while manipulating others.)

RELEVANT EMPIRICAL EVIDENCE

Our approach–avoidance comparison model requires systematic empirical testing, but some tentative support for the predictions can be found in previous experiments that will be briefly described below. Before describing this evidence, a few issues should be noted. With a few exceptions, approach and avoidance have not been measured or manipulated in past comparison research (but see Lockwood, 2002). But our reading of the empirical literature suggested that certain situational or individual difference variables in some experiments can plausibly be considered as approach or avoidance. Also, we made some judgments about the extremity of the comparison target. A successful peer seemed to us to be slightly superior; figures like Einstein, Mother Teresa, or professional fashion models to be extremely superior.

Second, inclusion of no-comparison control groups or pre and post comparison self-evaluative ratings is atypical in the literature (Wheeler, 2000; Wheeler & Suls, in press). This is unfortunate because, in the absence of such information, it is not possible to unambiguously determine whether the upward target or downward target is attracting or repelling, or both are acting on self-ratings. For example, there may have been contrast with an upward target leading to lower self-ratings that nonetheless still are in the positive range. Alternatively, the self-ratings may have been repelled to the negative side of the continuum.

Finally, the outcomes of most relevant research are in the form of subjective rating scales, so these were the focus of our review. But for some scenarios, relevant data using self-evaluation were unavailable. In those cases, we had to rely on studies with different kinds of outcomes, such as mood, self-esteem, and motivation. This is not our preference because we have previously shown that self-evaluations, affect, and behavior do not necessarily respond in the same way to upward/downward comparisons (Suls & Wheeler, 2007; Wheeler & Suls, in press). In fact, we have strongly advocated for defining

assimilation and contrast in social comparison as displacements in *self-evaluations* toward or away from targets. For the present, however, we had to deviate from our preference.

Approach and a Highly Superior Target (Scenario A)

Cash, Cash, and Butters (1983) exposed women to photographs of very physically attractive women (taken from magazines), but described as other college students. Subjects' self-ratings of attractiveness decreased—producing a contrast effect. Brown et al. (1992) also found contrast effects, except when the target shared a similarity with the subject (such as a birthday or similar attitudes). In the latter condition, we assume that the shared attribute increased the similarity search and produced assimilation, as predicted for Scenario B. In Cash et al. (1983), there was also a condition that attached a label (Calvin Klein or Cover Girl) to the photo to emphasize the stimulus person's status as a professional model. Subjects' self-attractiveness ratings were unaffected (i.e., no contrast) in the "model condition." This suggests that subjects ceased comparing with the photos because the models were perceived to be irrelevant to them (see Scenario E).

Thornton and Moore (1993) also examined effects of exposure to very physically attractive targets on self-evaluations. Two experiments collected self-ratings after exposure to attractive targets versus a no-comparison control group. Both men and women rated themselves lower in attractiveness after exposure to same-sex attractive photographs—a negative contrast effect.

In an experiment mentioned earlier, Morse and Gergen's (1970) subjects were recruited with the cover story of applying for a summer part-time job; therefore we assume they were oriented toward success. Although the comparison target was a college student, the experiment was conducted in the 1960s in a midwestern university town. "Mr. Clean" was a job applicant who was well groomed, dressed in a suit and with an attaché case. Thus, we think Mr. Clean probably created a very high (i.e., extreme) standard. When subjects were exposed to Mr. Clean, self-esteem ratings decreased from baseline, suggestive of a (negative) contrast effect. In a supplementary analysis (based on the experimenter's ratings of the subject's appearance and demeanor), those who resembled Mr. Dirty showed the largest contrast effect after being exposed to Mr. Clean.

Approach and a Slightly Superior Target (Scenario B)

This case should produce assimilation, an outcome reported by Lockwood and Kunda (1997) who had first-year and senior college student subjects read a description of a very successful senior of matching major and gender. We assume that college students in general are motivated to succeed and read the materials about another student with that set. First-year students were inspired and made higher self-ratings on traits relevant to career success (i.e., assimilation) than subjects not exposed to any target. However, subjects who also were seniors (like the target), and therefore no longer had time to attain the same success (i.e., low attainability), did not show any more positive reaction than those subjects in the no-comparison control condition.

In an experiment that shares many features with Lockwood and Kunda (1997), Stapel and Schwinghammer (2004; Study 1) had college students who were psychology majors read a (fictitious) newspaper article about another student who was described in either very positive or very negative terms. Subsequently, the subjects completed ratings about themselves. A reliable contrast effect was found; inclusion of a no-comparison control showed that the upward comparison lowered and downward comparison increased self-evaluations. Of course, this conflicts with our prediction and Lockwood and Kunda's finding of assimilation. However, Stapel and Schwinghammer's target was simply described as a *psychology student*, whether the target was a senior should not have been clear to the subjects. Also, the attributes on which the target excelled or was deficient were relatively enduring (intelligent, well liked, and friendly vs. unintelligent, not liked, and unfriendly). We speculate that the absence of salient clues for similarity and low likelihood of attainability prompted difference search. But this does suggest that the occurrence of assimilation versus contrast in Scenario B is temperamental.

Nosanchuk and Erickson (1985) conducted a study of social comparison among experienced bridge players, who should have been motivated to win given their commitment to team playing. Although respondents claimed to compare with players of similar ability, often those named were objectively superior according to lifetime playing records. The results suggest that average players assimilated their ability to the higher level. This is not surprising as the subjects still had the possibility of getting better.

Testa and Major (1990) led subjects to believe their performance on a test could improve or not and then they learned about an upward comparison target who performed slightly better. When subjects believed they could improve, they felt more positively and were more persistent than those who believed improvement was impossible. The downward comparison had no differential effects in this study.

Approach and a Slightly or Extremely Inferior Target (Scenarios C & D)

In these cases, the comparison target is worse-off than the subject. Morse and Gergen's (1970) results are relevant to C & D, but it is difficult for us to decide whether Mr. Dirty represents an instance of slight or extreme inferiority. In the 1960s, Mr. Dirty was probably a more common sight on college campuses (one of us was encouraged to "Get clean for Gene [McCarthy]!" in the 1960s'; we declined!) and probably did not stand out as much as Mr. Clean. Fortunately, contrast is predicted for both Cells C and D; however, when the target is very extreme, the subject might also ignore the target as irrelevant.

With these considerations in mind, it is noteworthy that after being exposed to Mr. Dirty, subjects' self-esteem increased from baseline—a (positive) contrast effect. The smallest change was seen in "neat" subjects suggesting they found Mr. Dirty to be highly inferior (more like Scenario D) or irrelevant to them. But those subjects who resembled Mr. Dirty (and therefore were closer in reality to him) actually showed the largest increase in self-esteem—a (positive) contrast effect (Scenario C).

Lockwood (2002) examined the role of perceived vulnerability in response to downward comparisons. First-year college students read about another first-year student who was doing poorly in the transition to college. Lockwood posited subjects would not feel vulnerable to another's predicament because they were doing OK in their first year of college. We also assume that low vulnerability should have oriented the student subjects toward success rather than avoidance of failure. Lockwood predicted and found that subject's self-ratings became more positive (vs. no-comparison target)—a contrastive self-evaluation, which is consistent with our analysis of scenario C. (To obtain the contrast effect, it was also necessary for Lockwood to instruct subjects to think about how they might become like the other student.)

Avoidance and a Highly Superior Target (Scenario E)

When avoiding failure is salient (whether because of situational or chronic needs), people should try to find a way to make their distance from the top irrelevant. Hoffman, Festinger, and Lawrence (1954) had subjects work in three-person competitive bargaining tasks. When subjects were falsely told that one of the players (an accomplice) was clearly superior, they competed considerably less with him and more against each other. Since the task was difficult (probably raising concerns about losing points) and competition is one way to acquire comparison information, this result is consistent with our prediction that comparison ceases with a very superior other when avoidance motivation is strong.

More definitive evidence comes in the form of the so-called "genius effect," demonstrated by Alicke, LoSchiavo, Zerbst, and Zhang (1997). They found that when subjects did not perform well on difficult problems compared to an accomplice—which should have made avoidance salient—they tended to aggrandize the superior performer's abilities. That is, subjects rated him/her as much more intelligent. Alicke et al. (1997) proposed that seeing the superior performer as a genius allowed the subject to reduce self-esteem threat. Observer-subjects who learned about the relative performance of the subject and the accomplice did not make differential ratings of ability. These results are quite consistent with the idea that a salient desire to avoid failure after being exposed to a highly superior other prompts perception of the other as a "noncomparable genius."

Cash et al.'s (1983) finding no contrast when female subjects were exposed to photographs labeled as professional models may also be relevant to Scenario E. Although we think most young people are motivated to be seen as attractive (approach in cells A and B), learning that they are comparing to a model might make avoidance salient. Putting the models in the "noncomparable beauty category" makes them irrelevant to self—hence, there was no contrast in that condition.

Avoidance and a Slightly Superior Target (Scenario F)

Our analysis suggests that exposure to a slightly superior target, combined with a motive to avoid failure, should lead to derogation of the target to one's own level. After all, the target is not so superior that this is impossible at least in one's own mind. Unfortunately, subjective construal of comparison targets or sabotage is not frequently measured, but a study by Tesser and Smith (1980) has relevance. They found that when subjects were outperformed by a friend on a self-relevant task, the subjects subsequently provided fewer clues to help the friend, presumably to lower his/her performance and make him more comparable to the self.

Avoidance and a Slightly Inferior Target (Scenario G)

Some studies have shown that depressed students (Gibbons, 1986; Study 2) and students in a negative mood (Aspinwall & Taylor, 1993) report more positive affect after exposure to a worse-off peer. This has also been found among persons low in self-esteem (Aspinwall & Taylor, 1993). If we assume that these subjects were very concerned about avoiding failure then the changes in affect suggest they saw differences with the target. Admittedly, this must be considered speculative.

More direct evidence can be found in an experiment conducted by Lockwood (2002). First-year college students read a description of a graduate who was having great difficulty obtaining employment and making the transition from college. In this case, Lockwood thought the subjects could perceive that they were vulnerable to the same predicament, thus their wanting not to fail should have been strong. Relative to a no-comparison control group, subjects rated themselves less positively. This might be indicative of assimilation—contrary to our prediction. In this scenario, our model predicts people should try to distance themselves to avoid possibility of assimilation. It should be noted, however, that subject's mean ratings were above the midpoint so subjects still saw themselves in relatively positive terms. A different dependent variable showed results more consistent with our prediction. Lockwood also measured the degree to which subjects planned to act in ways to prevent failure. Consistent with the idea that people would try to emphasize their differences with a slightly inferior target to avoid assimilation, subjects exposed to the unsuccessful graduate reported thinking of more specific strategies they would use in the future to avoid failure.

Avoidance and a Highly Inferior Target (Scenario H)

The effects of extreme comparison targets have been studied. For example, Stapel and Blanton (2004) found that subjects primed with "Clown" made more positive self-evaluations than those primed with Einstein. But to our knowledge, no experimental studies have looked at comparisons with highly inferior targets in situations that manipulated or measured approach–avoidance motivation.

According to our model, this scenario should produce contrast. Some indirect support for this prediction comes from Wood et al.'s (1985) study of cancer survivors who we assume wanted to avoid thoughts about negative outcomes (i.e., disease recurrence, coping difficulties). The fact that the vast majority of them reported that they were doing much better than most cancer patients is consistent.

We think that the appeal of gossip about celebrities might also fall into this category (Brickman & Bulman, 1977; Suls, 1977). Famous actors, musicians, and politicians can serve as foils for the rest of us when we learn about the terrible predicaments to which they fall victim. The most "trashtastic" current celebrity can serve as an extreme negative standard for contrast, which may account for the high level of interest in gossip.

Coda

For some scenarios, the evidence we reviewed is somewhat thin. Perhaps the biggest limitation of the review, however, concerns whether the upward or downward target is attracting or repelling, or both are acting. As noted above, we cannot always ascertain whether contrast with an upward target repels the subject below a psychological midpoint or whether the subject hovers at or somewhat above the midpoint. Conversely, the evidence does not indicate whether contrast with a downward comparison leads to a self-evaluation above the midpoint or only slightly distanced from the inferior target. Our view, however, is that because people want to feel worthwhile, their self-evaluations should be somewhat positive even if their self-ratings are displaced (i.e., contrasted) from someone who is superior. Exposed to a downward comparison, people also probably try their best to see themselves on the positive side of the dimension, not just as less inferior.

The Case of the Similar Comparison Target

The 2 × 4 table does not address responses to similar targets. It might be imagined that comparison with others of similar standing would not produce any shifts in self-evaluation because the person should be satisfied to find a fellow to share the same rung on the social ladder. Often, in the case of opinions, finding such agreement is satisfying (Festinger, 1954a,b; Suls et al., 2000). The present approach, however, concerns comparison of personal attributes that are relevant to success and failure. Earlier, we described the unidirectional drive upward and how it prevents a state of "social quiescence" (Festinger, 1954a). If we are to learn about someone who has performed at the same level, there will be an upward drive to outdo him/her. There may be cultural constraints on this tendency. Festinger (1954a) observed that non-Western cultures that de-emphasize competitive and achievement may not exhibit the unidirectional drive. But in the societies most extensively studied to date by comparison researchers, the striving to be better and do better seems prevalent. Thus, people are oriented toward targets who are somewhat better than themselves. Evidence for preferred upward comparison choices (Blanton, Buunk, Gibbons, & Kuyper, 1999; Huguet, Dumas, Monteil, & Genestoux, 2001; Suls & Tesch, 1978; Thornton & Arrowood, 1966; Wheeler, 1966; Wheeler et al., 1969) consistently documents this tendency.

CONCLUSIONS AND IMPLICATIONS

To show how they are relevant to contemporary issues, we wanted to reacquaint the reader with elements of LOA research that Festinger used in his classic social comparison theory. The integration of these motivational concepts with contemporary theory and research provides a better understanding of how people select comparison information to evaluate their capabilities. Furthermore, distinguishing between approach and avoidance motives provides a more comprehensive way to predict when upward or downward comparisons lead to assimilation versus contrast. Previous writers and researchers have emphasized how self-enhancement can affect both the search for comparison information and comparison responses (Wills, 1981; Wood, 1989). However, self-enhancement lumps together two very different motives—the need to excel and the need to avoid failure. Our approach–avoidance model shows how these motives can produce different outcomes depending on the direction and extremity of the comparison target.

Contemporary social cognitive theories of assimilation contrast (Mussweiler, 2003; Stapel & Koomen, 2001a,b) informed our analysis, but motives previously have not been systematically or formally included as an integral component of these cognitive models. The relevant evidence that we found provides support for our approach–avoidance model although the available evidence is admittedly limited and rests in some instances on plausible but unverified assumptions. Nonetheless, we think the 2 × 4 model has sufficient support to serve as a generative framework to pose more refined questions, to conduct studies with more informative results, and to provide a common ground for self-evaluation researchers and motivation researchers. Finally, we hope this chapter can serve as a trustworthy map to encourage the next explorers to approach, rather than avoid, this challenging territory.

ACKNOWLEDGMENTS

Preparation of this chapter was partially supported by grants from National Science Foundation BCS-9910592 and National Science Foundation BCS-SGER 0634901 to JS and by the Australian Research Council DP0449717 to LW. Also, we are grateful to Majorie Seaton for her splendid comments and suggestions and to Bryan Koestner for his excellent questions.

REFERENCES

Alicke, M., LoSchiavo, F. M., Zerbst, J., & Zhang, S. (1997). The person who outperforms me is a genius: Maintaining perceived competence in upward social comparison. *Journal of Personality and Social Psychology, 73*, 781–789.

Aspinwall, L., & Taylor, S. E. (1993). Effects of social comparison direction, threat and self-esteem on affect, and self-evaluation and expected success. *Journal of Personality and Social Psychology, 64*, 708–722.

Atkinson, J. W. (1959). Motivational determinants of risk-taking behavior. *Psychological Review*, *64*, 359–372.

Atkinson, J. W. (1964). *An introduction to motivation*. New York: Van Nostrand.

Biernat, M., Manis, M., & Nelson, T. E. (1991). Stereotypes and standards of judgment. *Journal of Personality and Social Psychology*, *60*, 485–499.

Blanton, H., Buunk, B. P., Gibbons, F. X., & Kuyper, H. (1999). When better-than-others compare upward: Choice of comparison and comparative evaluation as independent predictors of academic performance. *Journal of Personality and Social Psychology*, *76*, 420–430.

Brickman, P., & Bulman, R. J. (1977). Pleasure and pain in social comparison. In J. Suls & R. L. Miller (Eds.), *Social comparison processes: Theoretical and empirical perspectives* (pp. 149–186). Washington, DC: Hemisphere.

Brown, J. D., Novick, N. J., Lord, K. A., & Richards, J. M. (1992). When Gulliver travels: Social context, psychological closeness, and self-appraisals. *Journal of Personality and Social Psychology*, *62*, 717–727.

Buunk, B. P., Collins, R. L., Taylor, S. E., VanYperen, N. W., & Dakof, G. A. (1990). The affective consequences of social comparison: Either direction has its ups and downs. *Journal of Personality and Social Psychology*, *59*(6), 1238–1249.

Cash, T., Cash, D., & Butters, J. (1983). Mirror, mirror, on the wall…: Contrast effects and self-evaluations of physical attractiveness. *Personality and Social Psychology Bulletin*, *9*, 351–358.

Collins, R. L. (1996). For better or for worse: The impact of upward social comparisons on self-evaluations. *Psychological Bulletin*, *119*, 51–69.

Dembo, T. (1931). Der Aerger also dynamisches Problem. *Psychologische Forschung*, *15*, 1–144.

Elliot, A. J. (1997). Integrating "classic" and "contemporary" approaches to achievement motivation: A hierarchical model of approach and avoidance achievement motivation. In P. Pintrich & M. Maehr (Eds.), *Advances in motivation and achievement* (Vol. 10, pp. 143–179). Greenwich, CT: JAI Press.

Elliot, A. J., & Mapes, R. (2005). Approach–avoidance motivation and self-concept evaluation. In A. Tesser, J. Wood, & D. A. Stapel (Eds.), *On building, defending and regulating the self: A psychological perspective* (pp. 171–196). New York: Psychology Press.

Festinger, L. (1942a). Wish, expectation and group standards in level of aspiration. *Journal of Abnormal and Social Psychology*, *37*, 184–200.

Festinger, L. (1942b). A theoretical interpretation of shifts in level of aspiration. *Psychological Review*, *49*, 235–250.

Festinger, L. (1950). Informal social communication theory. *Psychological Review*, *57*, 271–282.

Festinger, L. (1954a). A theory of social comparison processes. *Human Relations*, *7*, 117–140.

Festinger, L. (1954b). Motivation leading to social behavior. In M. R. Jones (Ed.), *Nebraska symposium on motivation* (pp. 191–218). Lincoln, NE: University of Nebraska Press.

Gibbons, F. X. (1986). Social comparison and depression: Company's effect on misery. *Journal of Personality and Social Psychology*, *51*, 140–148.

Goethals, G., & Darley, J. (1977). Social comparison theory: An attributional approach. In J. Suls & R. Miller (Eds.), *Social comparison processes: Theoretical and empirical perspectives* (pp. 259–278). Washington, DC: Hemisphere.

Gould, R. (1939). An experimental analysis of "level of aspiration." *Genetic Psychology Monographs*, *21*, 1–116.

Higgins, E. T. (2000). Regulatory focus. *American Psychologist*, *55*, 1217–1230.

Hoffman, P. J., Festinger, L., & Lawrence, D. H. (1954). Tendencies toward group comparability in competitive bargaining. *Human Relations*, *7*, 141–159.

Hoppe, F. (1930). Erfolg und misserfolg. *Psychologisches Forchung*, *14*, 1–62.

Huguet, P., Dumas, F., Monteil, J. M., & Genestoux, N. (2001). Social comparison choices in the classroom: Further evidence for students' upward comparison tendency and its beneficial impact on performance. *European Journal of Social Psychology*, *31*, 557–578.

Jones, E. E., & Gerard, H. B. (1965). *Foundations of social psychology*. New York: Wiley.

Jones, S., & Regan, D. (1974). Ability evaluation through social comparison. *Journal of Experimental Social Psychology*, *10*, 133–146.

Klayman, J., & Ha, Y. -W. (1987). Confirmation, disconfirmation, and information in hypothesis-testing. *Psychological Review*, *94*, 211–228.

Latane, B. (Ed.) (1966). Studies in social comparison. *Journal of Experimental Social Psychology*, Suppl. 1.

Lewin, K., Dembo, T., Festinger, L., & Sears, P. (1944). Level of aspiration. In J. McV. Hunt (Ed.), *Personality and the behavior disorders* (pp. 338–378). New York: Ronald Press.

Lockwood, P. (2002). Could it happen to you? The impact of downward social comparisons on the self. *Journal of Personality and Social Psychology*, *82*, 343–358.

Lockwood, P., & Kunda, Z. (1997). Superstars and me: Predicting the impact of role models on the self. *Journal of Personality and Social Psychology*, *73*, 91–103.

Major, B., Testa, M., & Blysma, W. (2001). Responses to upward and downward social comparisons: The impact of esteem-relevance and perceived control. In J. Suls & T. A. Wills (Eds.), *Social comparison: Contemporary theory and research* (pp. 237–260). Hillsdale, NJ: Lawrence Erlbaum Associates.

Manis, M., Biernat, M., & Nelson, T. F. (1991). Comparison and expectancy processes in human judgment. *Journal of Personality and Social Psychology*, *61*, 203–211.

Manis, M., & Paskewitz, J. (1984). Judging psychopathology: Expectation and contrast. *Journal of Personality and Social Psychology*, *20*, 217–230.

Markman, K., & McMullen, M. (2003). A reflection and evaluation model of comparative thinking. *Personality and Social Psychology Review*, *7*, 244–267.

Markman, K., McMullen, N. M., & Elizaga, R. (2007). Counterfactual thinking, persistence and performance: A test of the reflection and evaluation model. *Journal of Experimental Social Psychology* (in press).

Martin, R. (2000). "Can I do X?": Using the proxy comparison model to predict performance. In J. Suls & L. Wheeler (Eds.), *Handbook of social comparison: Theory and research* (pp. 67–80). New York: Kluwer Academic/Plenum.

Martin, R., Suls, J., & Wheeler, L. (2002). Ability evaluation by proxy: The role of maximum performance and related attributes in social comparison. *Journal of Personality and Social Psychology, 82,* 781–791.

Morse, S., & Gergen, K. J. (1970). Social comparison, self-consistency, and the concept of the self. *Journal of Personality and Social Psychology, 16,* 148–156.

Mussweiler, T. (2001). 'Seek and ye shall find': Antecedents of assimilation and contrast in social comparison. *European Journal of Social Psychology, 31,* 499–509.

Mussweiler, T. (2003). Comparison processes in social judgment: Mechanisms and consequences. *Psychological Review, 110,* 472–489.

Mussweiler, T., & Bodenhausen, G. (2002). I know you are, but what am I? Self-evaluative consequences of judging in-group and out-group members. *Journal of Personality and Social Psychology, 82,* 19–32.

Mussweiler, T., Epstrude, K., & Ruter, K. (2005). The knife that cuts both ways: Comparison processes in social perception. In M. Alicke, D. Dunning, & J. Krueger (Eds.), *The self in social judgment* (pp. 109–130). New York & Hove: Psychology Press.

Mussweiler, T. and Strack, F. (2000a). Consequences of social comparison: Selective accessibility, assimilation, and contrast. In J. Suls & L. Wheeler (Eds.), *Handbook of social comparison: Theory and research* (pp. 253–270). New York: Kluwer Academic/Plenum.

Mussweiler, T., & Strack, F. (2000b). The "Relative Self": Informational and judgmental consequences of comparative self-evaluation. *Journal of Personality and Social Psychology, 79,* 23–38.

Nosanchuk, T. A., & Erickson, B. H. (1985). How high is up? Calibrating social comparison in the real world. *Journal of Personality and Social Psychology, 48,* 624–634.

Ostrom, T., & Upshaw, H. (1968). Psychological perspective and attitude change. In A. G. Greenwald, T. Brock, & T. M. Ostrom (Eds.), *Psychological foundations of attitudes* (pp. 217–242). New York: Academic Press.

Radloff, R. (1966). Social comparison and ability evaluation. *Journal of Experimental Social Psychology,* Suppl. 1, 6–26.

Schwarz, N., & Bless, H. (1992). Constructing reality and its alternatives: An inclusion/exclusion model of assimilation and contrast effects in social judgments. In L. Martin & A. Tesser (Eds.), *The construction of social judgments* (pp. 217–245). Hillsdale, NJ: Lawrence Erlbaum Associates.

Smith, E. R. (1994). Procedural knowledge and processing strategies in social cognition. In R. S. Wyer & T. K. Srull (Eds.), *Handbook of social cognition* (2nd ed., Vol. 1, pp. 99–152). Hillsdale, NJ: Lawrence Erlbaum Associates.

Smith, W., & Sachs, P. (1997). Social comparison and task prediction: Ability similarity and the use of a proxy. *British Journal of Social Psychology, 36,* 587–602.

Stapel, D. A. (2007). In the mind of the beholder: The Interpretation Comparison Model of accessibility effects. In D. A. Stapel & J. Suls (Eds.), *Assimilation and contrast in social psychology* (pp. 143–164). New York & Hove: Psychology Press.

Stapel, D. A., & Blanton, H. (2004). From seeing to being: Subliminal social comparisons affect implicit and explicit self-evaluations. *Journal of Personality and Social Psychology, 27,* 468–481.

Stapel, D. A., & Koomen, W. (2000). Distinctiveness of others, mutability of selves: Their impact on self-evaluations. *Journal of Personality and Social Psychology, 79*(6), 1068–1087.

Stapel, D. A., & Koomen, W. (2001a). I, we, and the effects of others on me: How self-construal level moderates social comparison effects. *Journal of Personality and Social Psychology, 80,* 766–781.

Stapel, D. A., & Koomen, W. (2001b). The impact of interpretation versus comparison goals on knowledge accessibility effects. *Journal of Experimental Social Psychology, 37,* 134–149.

Stapel, D. A., & Schwinghammer, S. A. (2004). Defensive social comparison and the constraints of reality. *Social Cognition, 22,* 147–167.

Stapel, D. A., & Suls, J. (2004). Method matters: Effects of explicit versus implicit social comparisons on activation, behavior, and self-views. *Journal of Personality and Social Psychology, 87,* 860–875.

Stapel, D. A., & Suls, J. (Eds.). (2007). *Assimilation and contrast in social psychology.* New York & Hove: Psychology Press.

Stapel, D. A., & Van der Zee, K. (2006). The self salience model of other-to-self effects: Integrative principles of self-enhancement, complementarity and imitation. *Journal of Personality and Social Psychology, 90,* 258–271.

Suls, J. (1977). Gossip as social comparison. *Journal of Communication, 27,* 164–168.

Suls, J., & Tesch, F. (1978). Students' preferences for information about their test performance: A social comparison study. *Journal of Applied Social Psychology, 8,* 189–197.

Suls, J., Martin, R., & Wheeler, L. (2000). Three types of opinion comparison: The Triadic Model. *Personality and Social Psychology Review, 4,* 219–237.

Suls, J., Martin, R., & Wheeler, L. (2002). Social comparison: Why, with whom, and with what effect?. *Current Directions in Psychological Science, 23,* 159–163.

Suls, J., & Wheeler, L. (Eds.). (2000). *Handbook of social comparison.* New York: Kluwer/Plenum.

Suls, J., & Wheeler, L. (2007). Psychological magnetism: A brief history of assimilation and contrast in psychology. In D. A. Stapel & J. Suls (Eds.), *Assimilation and contrast in social psychology* (pp. 9–44). New York: Psychology Press.

Tesser, A., & Smith, J. (1980). Some effects of task relevance on friendship and helping: You don't always help the one you like. *Journal of Experimental Social Psychology, 16,* 582–590.

Testa, M., & Major, B. (1990). The impact of social comparisons after failure: The moderating effects of perceived control. *Basic and Applied Social Psychology*, *11*, 205–218.

Thornton, D., & Arrowood, A. J. (1966). Self-evaluation, self-enhancement, and the locus of social comparison. *Journal of Experimental Social Psychology*, Suppl. 1, 40–48.

Thornton, D., & Moore, S. (1993). Physical attractiveness contrast effect: Implications for self-esteem and evaluations of the social self. *Personality and Social Psychology Bulletin*, *19*, 474–480.

Wedell, D. H., Hicklin, S. K., & Smarandescu, L. O. (2007). Contrasting models of assimilation and contrast. In D. Stapel & J. Suls (Eds.), *Assimilation and contrast in social psychology* (pp. 45–74). New York: Psychology Press.

Wheeler, L. (1966). Motivation as a determinant of upward comparison. *Journal of Experimental Social Psychology*, Suppl. 1, 27–31.

Wheeler, L. (2000). Individual differences in social comparison. In J. Suls & L. Wheeler (Eds.), *Handbook of social comparison* (pp. 141–158). New York: Kluwer Academic/Plenum.

Wheeler, L., Shaver, K., Jones, R., Goethals, G. R., Cooper, J., Robinson, J. E., et al. (1969). Factors determining choice of a comparison other. *Journal of Experimental Social Psychology*, *5*, 219–232.

Wheeler, L., Martin, R., & Suls, J. (1997). The proxy social comparison model for self-assessment of ability. *Personality and Social Psychology Review*, *1*, 54–61.

Wheeler, L., & Suls, J. (2007). Assimilation in social comparison: Can we agree on what it is? *La Revuew Internationale de Psychologie Sociale*, *20*, 31–51.

Wills, T. A. (1981). Downward comparison principles in social psychology. *Psychological Bulletin*, *90*, 245–271.

Wood, J. V. (1989). Theory and research concerning social comparison of personal attributes. *Psychological Bulletin*, *106*, 231–248.

Wood, J. V., Taylor, S., & Lichtman, R. (1985). Social comparison in adjustment to breast cancer. *Journal of Personality and Social Psychology*, *49*, 1169–1183.

Social Exclusion

36 I Am Approaching the Decision to Avoid You: An Approach and Avoidance Perspective on Research on Social Exclusion and Rejection

Roy F. Baumeister and Seth Gitter

CONTENTS

As cultural animals, humans live by rules set up by the community. Government, religions and, on a more micro level, local community and social groups have developed rules and laws that guide and direct behavior. Those who abide by society's rules are rewarded for their behavior. Those who disobey face severe punishments. Quite possibly the most used and oldest form of punishment is social rejection/ostracism. Although the practices of banishment and exile, so readily used by early humankind, have fallen out of favor in recent years, people still rely on rejection in some form or another to encourage appropriate behavior in social contexts.

Rejection looms large and one simple slip can lead an individual to lose relationships that are so important to him or her. With rejection being such a looming threat in the social world across evolutionary history, one would expect strong motivational responses to the threat and occurrence of social exclusion. For early humans, rejection was likely to lead to death. As a result, people should

have developed a strong predisposition to avoid the occurrence of rejection and to react quickly after rejection.

Recently, there has been an increased interest in studying appetitive/approach and aversive/avoidance motives with regard to the social domain (Elliot, Gable, & Mapes, 2006; Gable, 2006). Although research is currently being devoted to the motivational factors that draw people together, little, if any, research has been directed to identifying similar motivational factors that pull people apart. To address this disparity in the literature, our aim in this chapter is to present supportable evidence to suggest how motivational systems allow individuals to navigate the tortuous waters between acceptance and exclusion.

THE NEED TO BELONG

Baumeister and Leary (1995) suggest that humans have a fundamental motivation to form groups and relationships and to sustain these connections (see also Bowlby, 1969,

1973; Maslow, 1968). It is even suggested that many of the other motivations that people have (e.g., need for achievement) are driven by or derived from a need to belong to a social group (Baumeister & Leary, 1995)—as the attainment of these goals would facilitate being perceived as a good relationship partner. Belonging to groups could therefore be considered to be one of the most important positive outcomes that motivate and guide human behavior. Yet belongingness seems to serve the purpose of attaining other outcomes as well. In this next section we look to the relevant literature presented by Baumeister and Leary (1995) on the need to belong. We focus on the distinction between specific approach and avoidance motivation factors associated with this need.

The need to belong likely developed over human evolutionary history, as individuals who had a strong motivation to form social bonds with others would have survived and reproduced better than individuals who lacked this need. Many positive outcomes can be acquired through striving to affiliate with others, suggesting that the need to belong is driven by a strong approach motivation. Group members would be more successful than individuals at procuring food—through hunting and food-sharing. Individuals might also find it much more difficult than group members to acquire a mate (a necessary condition for reproduction). Individuals who are motivated to affiliate would also be much more successful at raising children to reproductive age than individuals who would be less motivated to stay with the child. Additionally, groups can benefit by sharing vigilance duties, thereby improving avoidance of predators and other enemies. This might be suspect as a twinge of avoidant motivation present in the need to belong as the individual is attempting to avoid some negative outcome. Yet research by Rofe (1984) suggests that people are driven to be with others under the threat of possible danger elicited by such cues as illness, danger, nightfall, and disaster. Essentially, individuals seek out others for protection rather than simply trying to avoid the threat of danger. Therefore, the threats to survival drive individuals to affiliate with others, suggesting avoiding threat leads to approaching allies. Belonging to groups therefore appears to function to a great degree to ensure the attainment of outcomes necessary to survive in a harsh environment. This drive is likely elicited by approach motivation.

Modern life has obviated some of the pragmatic need for belongingness. If nothing else, the meteoric rise in single-person households demonstrates this. We no longer need to have somebody watching out for marauding tigers. Individuals still depend on others to provide resources for them (e.g., food, protection), but there is a reduced need to interact with others to acquire these resources. For example rather than relying on group members to engage in cooperative hunting, today an individual can simply pick up a filling and tasty and slightly nutritious meal by passing through a drive-through. But evolution has done its work, and people still crave social connection regardless of whether they absolutely need it for survival.

The relationship between an individual and those he or she relies upon for certain resources is decidedly reduced compared to the relationships our ancestors forged to ensure survival, and indeed the global economy allows people to have mutually beneficial interactions with far-off strangers they will never meet. Evolution likely did not select for people who sought out relationship partners merely to obtain resources. Rather it is more likely that those individuals who had a strong motivation to seek out relationship partners, and consequently suffered when alone, were more likely to survive due to the benefits of engaging in relationships. One of the most widely supported findings in the behavioral sciences is that individuals who lack relationships suffer from decrements in health, adjustment, and well-being (see Berscheid & Reis, 1998 for review). Although the modern day environment may seem to reduce the need to associate with others for the direct procurement of resources, affiliating with others remains an important need that can produce substantial benefits over being alone.

Indeed individuals today retain similar needs to develop relationships as those suggested to be prevalent in our ancestors. The ease with which individuals form relationships with others implies a strong approach motivation. This is evident in research showing proximity (or the mere experience of interacting with another) to be one of the biggest factors in predicting whether a relationship will occur between two people (Festinger, Schachter, & Back, 1950)—even overcoming the role that similarity plays in forming social bonds (Nahemov & Lawton, 1975). Research on minimal group paradigms has also shown the ease with which cohesive groups form (Brewer, 1979). Relationships can even develop in the presence of adverse circumstances (Latane, Eckman, & Joy, 1966) and with individuals who were once disliked (Sherif, Harvey, White, Hood, & Sherif, 1961/1988; Wilder & Thompson, 1980). It appears that people are willing to start a relationship with just about anyone that they encounter, suggesting a strong approach orientation to the development of relationships.

Even individuals who appear, at least on the surface, to lack this persistent need to form relationships still desire them. Individuals who suffer from social anxiety disorder (SAD) and those who are shy are very resistant to engaging others in social interaction. Yet this seems to be more a result of fears concerning evaluation than a lack of a need to form relationships. When shy individuals interact with others, they engage in a large degree of "innocuously sociable" behavior (Leary, 1983) such as smiling and nodding, as well as verbally reinforcing those they are interacting with. Schlenker and Leary (1982) suggest that the reactions of individuals suffering from SAD seem to stem from the discrepancy between the strong desire to make a positive impression and the worry or expectation that they will be unable to do so. For shy and SAD individuals the concern with belonging seems to remain pervasive. Rather, their dissociation from interaction seems to stem from a low self-efficacy to form the desired impression rather than a lack of desire to form relationships.

Forming relationships does not seem to be enough to satiate the need to belong as people seem to benefit little by simply having relationships. Rather these relationships need to consist of strong bonds of mutual caring (Baumeister & Leary, 1995). Individuals should therefore also be motivated to further the development of their relationships with others. Seemingly, those individuals who engage in approach-oriented behavior toward developing their current relationships benefit greatly. Elliot et al. (2006) found that individuals who espoused strong approach goals with their current friendships benefited more than individuals who espoused avoidance social goals. Individuals with strong approach social goals (e.g., "I am trying to deepen my relationships with my friends") reported greater relationship satisfaction, lowered perceptions of loneliness, and a greater number and impact of positive relationship experiences compared with individuals who espoused a more avoidant stance to their friendships (e.g., "I am trying to avoid disagreements and conflicts with my friends") who experienced more loneliness and a greater number and impact of negative relationship events. In the long-term, individuals who scored higher in friendship approach goals showed an increase in subjective well-being, whereas individuals who scored higher in friendship avoidance goals showed an increase in physical symptomology. Seemingly, individuals benefit by continually devoting time and resources to their current relationship partners.

The need to belong is such a strong motivation that it would likely make individuals reluctant to reject others. Indeed, individuals seem disinclined to sever ties that they have formed with others, including relationships that are based on loosely established ties, and even abusive relationships (see Baumeister & Leary, 1995 for review).

Anecdotally, many of our research assistants express great difficulty at having to tell research participants that they have been rejected by someone else. They feel pained at the possibility of a distraught or surprised look on the face of the participant upon hearing this. The saving grace of this experience is to see the look of relief on the participant's face upon learning of the deception of the experiment during the debriefing.

Experimental evidence confirms that people are at least reluctant to reject others outright. Folkes (1982) compared women's real reasons for rejecting a potential date to the reasons they told the luckless men. Although most women explained the rejection as based on some factor external to the requestor (e.g., she was busy on the evening he picked), the true reason tended to involve something internal to him, such as that he was unattractive, unintelligent, or poor. Converging evidence comes from research on unrequited love. People who have to reject would-be-lovers often experience extreme guilt over having to reject someone they once considered a close friend (Baumeister, Wotman, & Stillwell, 1993; Baumeister & Dhavale, 2001). Even though the experience is almost always negative for them, rejectors are reluctant to exclude the would-be-lovers entirely. Unfortunately this often results in the would-be-lover doubling his or her efforts, likely resulting in an even more stressful situation for the rejector. Seemingly rejection is something that is not taken lightly, experienced as very aversive, and often avoided until all other options have been exhausted.

In the modern environment, it is likely impossible for an individual to accept all others. As humans are incredibly social animals, individuals may occasionally confront others who are vying for their affection—affection that may already be tied up with other relationship partners. Devoting time and resources to new relationship partners limits the amount of time and resources an individual can devote to already established ties. Humans therefore should have developed specific parameters with which to discriminate between the possible relationship partners within the environment—seeking out the most advantageous relationships to devote time and resources to. Although rejecting people may be an aversive experience, some individuals will need to be rejected in favor of others.

REJECTING STRANGERS

Although it may seem paradoxical, satiation of the need to belong may actually be one factor that results in the exclusion of some individuals. Individuals have a limited amount of time and resources to devote to their relationships (Audy, 1980; Leary, 2001; Tooby & Cosmides, 1996). In order to devote the requisite time and resources to relationships of high importance, individuals need to exclude others.

Research has shown that individuals do prefer a small group of intimate relationships to a large number of loosely established ties (Caldwell & Peplau, 1982; Reis, 1990). Even when an individual is immersed in a highly social environment and has access to a large number of possible relationship partners, he or she will tend to devote the majority of his or her time to the same five or six individuals (Wheeler & Nezlek, 1977). Parker and Asher (1993) found that the quality of one's relationships is more important for producing positive psychological outcomes than the sheer quantity of relationships. The findings of Elliot et al. (2006) also attest to the benefits acquired by being motivated to approach those relationships that one has already established. Individuals with strong approach goals have much more satisfactory relationships with others and show greater increases in subjective well-being over time compared to individuals with low approach goals and those with a strong avoidance goals—who seemed to suffer as a result of their relationships. Seemingly, a strong approach motivation to continually engage in current relationships appears to result in the by-default rejection of others.

Other more direct forms of stranger rejection have also been identified and seem to result from stigmatization—the process of ascribing negative global evaluations to a person based on a single defining negative characteristic (Goffman, 1963). Several different theories have been presented to explain processes of stigmatization each with its own interpretation of what is likely to be stigmatized as well as the process through which stigmatization occurs (Crocker, Major, & Steele, 1998; Elliot, Ziegler, Altman, & Scott, 1982; Goffman, 1963; Jones et al., 1984; Kurzban & Leary, 2001). Regardless of the process, however, the major function of stigma is to identify individuals to be avoided or excluded from social interaction (Kurzban & Leary, 2001).

The basic premise of functional stigma avoidance (Kurzban & Leary, 2001) is that humans, over the course of evolutionary history, would likely develop specific adaptations to identify and avoid other individuals who could pose threats to survival, reproduction, and resource acquisition. If an individual is assessed to be a threat to any one of these factors, he or she would be more likely than individuals who do not exhibit these characteristics to be rejected from group interaction. Insofar as these stigmas identify an individual as unfit for social interaction, it is likely that stigma serves largely as an avoidance

cue. For example, parasite avoidance is indeed a factor that should result in the avoidance of an individual to facilitate survival and reproduction. Due to the possibility of contagion when interacting with someone who is ill, those of our ancestors who were sensitive to and readily avoided anyone with a marker of parasitic infection would have been more likely to survive than those who didn't.

In some instances clear markers (such as infested sores and a higher incidence of coughing) are present that would suggest an individual is infected. Other identifying features are much more subtle however. The ability to withstand environmental and genetic stressors in both humans and animals is reflected in facial/bodily symmetry, as the presence of parasites usually leads to asymmetrical features (see Grammer & Thornhill, 1994; Kurzban & Leary, 2001 for review). Humans and other animals have been shown to have a preference for facial and bodily symmetry (Bruce & Morgan, 1975; Gangestad & Thornhill, 1997). These systems become especially sensitive at key times. Specifically, women become more sensitive to facial symmetry, even detecting it through scent, when they are able to become pregnant (Thornhill & Gangestad, 1999). Parasitic avoidance therefore seems to have partly risen from a motivation to avoid reproduction with unhealthy partners.

There may be some question as to whether sensitivity to symmetry is an approach or avoidance motivation. Researchers often frame their findings to suggest a *preference* for symmetrical faces over asymmetrical faces. Preferences motivate an individual to attain things that provide resources and benefits needed for reproduction (Orians & Heerwagen, 1992). Therefore, the preference for symmetrical faces may be an approach motivation to attain healthy partners. Nevertheless, this preference is only in a relative sense in that individuals rate symmetrical others as more attractive than asymmetrical others. Rather, parasitic avoidance mechanisms are likely similar to other evolutionary avoidance systems that are overly sensitive to the possibility of a negative outcome (e.g., fear; Haselton & Buss, 2000). The costs of mating with someone who appears to be healthy, but is not (miss), is much greater than the cost of not mating with someone who appears unhealthy, but is actually healthy (false positive)—oversensitizing the system to false positives. Therefore, it seems more likely that our preference for symmetrical faces arose from avoidance of parasites rather than to approach individuals free from parasites.

Another function of stigmatization is to avoid relationships that could lead to unfair reciprocal exchange (Kurzban & Leary, 2001). One of the suggested reasons for the development of the need to belong is that individuals who belonged to groups would benefit by engaging in exchange with one another (Baumeister & Leary, 1995). There are certain restrictions that limit an individual's ability to benefit from dyadic cooperation however. For a person to benefit from exchange, he or she should (1) readily cooperate with others—but only when reciprocation is likely, (2) be especially sensitive to individuals who violate social contracts, and (3) quickly reject any person who is unwilling to engage in fair exchange (Cosmides & Tooby, 1992). If reciprocal exchange were guided only by approach motivation and an individual were indiscriminately prosocial with others, he or she would be more likely than an individual that followed these rules to give resources to others and not receive anything in exchange. Avoidance motivation should therefore guide decisions to exclude others who appear unable or unwilling to reciprocate.

Indeed, humans have developed specific adaptations to identify cheaters—those individuals who take more than they give. Cosmides (1985) reviewed the literature examining performance on the Wason selection task. The Wason selection task is widely used to assess an individual's ability to detect conditional rules (Wason, 1966). Normally individuals perform quite poorly on these tasks. Most of the errors on this task are errors of omission in which participants fail to identify disconfirming information (Chapman & Johnson, 2002). When these tasks are framed as social contract violations, however, such as taking benefits without paying costs, individuals solve them much more easily and accurately, with approximately 75% of participants correctly solving the problem (Cosmides, 1985). Crucially, performance increased because participants' sensitivity to disconfirming information increased on these social contract problems compared to standard conditional logic problems. In social contract problems the disconfirming instance is one in which an individual might be cheating by receiving some benefit without meeting the criteria necessary to receive that benefit. Individual increases in performance on social contract problems appear to result from a strong sensitization to the possibility of being cheated on and the desire to avoid this outcome.

Cheater detection is only one avoidance motivated function in dyadic cooperation. Kurzban and Leary (2001) also proposed that the predictability of a potential relationship partner will influence whether he or she is selected as an exchange partner. Individuals who associate with those who are unpredictable cannot be sure that they will receive resources in exchange. Basically, successful exchange requires coordination between individuals (Cosmides & Tooby, 1992). In order to coordinate exchange, an individual needs to be able to infer the intentions of his or her exchange partners. People generate expectations about

individuals based on societal norms. When individuals violate these norms, they break from expectations. This break from expectations leads observers to evaluate them as unpredictable and results in the norm-violating individual being evaluated more negatively than individuals who follow social norms (Kiesler, 1973). Humans appear to have developed systems sensitized to identify individuals who appear unwilling and unable to engage in fruitful, mutually beneficial exchange.

REJECTING CURRENT RELATIONSHIP PARTNERS

Undoubtedly it is harder to reject a partner from an ongoing relationship than to reject a stranger before any relationship starts. Indeed the research attests to the resistance of committed relationships to dissolution (see Baumeister & Leary, 1995 for review). Although it would be expected that extreme negative experiences, such as abuse, would result in relationship dissolution, a great number of people are reluctant to end abusive relationships (Roy, 1977; Strube, 1988). Similarly, the experience of infidelity might be expected to be a deal-breaker in romantic relationships, yet a goodly proportion of individuals who experienced infidelity in a former relationship suggest that the infidelity was not the cause of the break-up (approximately 25%; Hall & Fincham, 2006). People even seem reluctant to end relationships with people that they have little interest in. Studies of unrequited love have shown that although the experience is more negative for the would-be-loved individual, these people are very reluctant to completely reject their would-be-lovers (Baumeister et al., 1993; Baumeister & Dhavale, 2001).

Interdependence theory (Kelley & Thibault, 1978) and investment model theory (Rusbult, 1980a) suggest that individuals consider more than just the negative experiences associated with their relationships. Rather, an individual's satisfaction with his or her relationship is a result of a comparison of the rewards (e.g., perceived similarity, attractiveness of partner) and costs (e.g., time and monetary costs) present in the relationship compared to the expectations that one has for his or her partner. If a relationship partner continues to produce more rewards and fewer costs than his or her comparison level, satisfaction will be high and the relationship will continue. If costs rise or rewards decline to the point that an individual is not meeting his or her comparison level however, satisfaction will be low and the relationship is at threat of termination. Indeed the relative weight of rewards and costs compared to a relationship partner's comparison level influences an individual's level of satisfaction and commitment for both friendships (Rusbult, 1980b) and romantic relationship partners (Rusbult, 1980a).

A direct corollary can be drawn between relationship satisfaction and approach and avoidance motivation. Approach-oriented systems are attuned to seeking out situations in which rewards exceed costs, whereas avoidance-oriented systems are attuned to avoiding situations high in costs (Gable, Reis, & Elliot, 2003). Therefore, individuals who are currently satisfied with their relationship should engage in approach-oriented behavior toward sustaining the relationship due to the relatively high proportion of rewards compared to costs. Individuals in unsatisfactory relationships on the contrary should be motivated by avoidance forces due to the relatively high proportion of costs compared to rewards.

Besides satisfaction level, other competitive forces appear to push and pull at relationships. People today live in a socially rich world with many alternative partners available. Interdependence theory (Kelley & Thibault, 1978) and Rusbult's investment model (1980a) posit that the comparison level of alternative partners will also influence decisions to stay or leave current relationship partners. This is very similar to the comparison level of one's current relationship partner, except that it refers to the attractiveness of alternative partners. Even if a person is moderately satisfied with his or her current relationship partner, if there are more attractive alternatives available in the environment, relationship dissolution may still occur. Kenrick, Neuberg, Zierk, and Krones (1994) showed men and women pictures of either attractive or dominant opposite sex individuals. Women shown dominant male faces and men shown attractive female faces rated lower satisfaction with their current partner. Approach forces toward external sources (in this case attractive alternative partners) therefore also function in decisions to maintain or dissolve a relationship.

Earlier, however, we suggested that a strong approach motive serves to encourage continued engagement in current relationships. This presents a difficult barrier to new potential partners vying for someone's affection. The strong motive to maintain current relationships should make it difficult for a new potential partner to be considered as a replacement—even if this new potential partner is perceived to have a slightly higher comparison level. This is because individual members of a long-term relationship have a large number of resources (such as time, effort, and mutual possessions) tied to their relationship (Rusbult, 1980a). These could be considered as "sunk costs" of the relationship that cannot be retrieved if the relationship is ended. This should make individual members averse to relationship dissolution, insofar as these

lost resources cannot be fully reclaimed. The avoidance of losing resources therefore plays a key role in sustaining long-term relationships.

Rusbult (1983) tested the influence of these factors (rewards/costs, comparison level, comparison level for alternative partners, and investment) on one another as well as their role in influencing stay/leave decisions in romantic relationships in a longitudinal study. Most important for this chapter are those factors that influenced stay/leave decisions. Of those relationships that ended, rewards increased less and costs grew more than those who stayed in the relationship. It is likely that approach forces were considerably less and avoidance forces to leave the relationship greater because of the shift in rewards and costs, respectively, for those who left compared to those who stayed. Additionally for those who left the relationship, alternative quality of attractive partners increased over time, and individuals invested less in their partners. In this case the approach motivation to leave the partner may have increased, whereas the avoidance motivation to maintain resources was reduced by investing less in the relationship.

As the decision to end a relationship is influenced by both approach and avoidance motivation, it could be expected that the course of relationship dissolution might also wax and wane as a result of approach and avoidance forces. Using a script generation procedure, Battaglia, Richard, Daterri, and Lord (1998) developed a script of relationship dissolution processes. The script reflected a long lasting process of indecisiveness that fluctuated between decisions aimed at ending the relationship and decisions aimed at trying to repair the relationship. These fluctuations appeared to shift between approach and avoidance tendencies during which "Characteristic approach behaviors, for instance 'try to work things out', 'communicate feelings' and 'get back together', alternate with typical avoidance behaviors, such as 'act distant', 'physical distance/avoidance' and date other people' throughout the 16 step script" (Battaglia et al., 1998, p. 841).

RESPONSES TO EXCLUSION THREATS

Inclusion is such an important and pervasive need (Baumeister & Leary, 1995) that threats to this need result in negatively affective states such as guilt, anxiety, jealousy, depression, and loneliness (Baumeister, Stillwell, & Heatherton, 1994; Baumeister & Tice, 1990; Leary, 1990). The general association between exclusion threats and negatively affective states suggests that threats to inclusion will result in motivated cognition and behavior to avoid exclusion from current relationship partners.

This places a potentially powerful tool in the hand of relationship partners. Insofar as it can be expected that individuals will engage in behavior to avoid exclusion, relationship partners may be able to use exclusion threats to encourage motivated behavior to avoid relationship dissolution. Indeed, individuals appear to induce guilt (Baumeister, Stillwell, & Heatherton, 1995) and jealousy (Vangelesti, Daly, & Rudnick, 1991) to elicit more appropriate relationship-regulation behaviors on the part of their partners.

For example, Baumeister et al. (1995) found that guilt induction appears to be a frequently used and moderately successful tactic to redistribute power and resources within a relationship. Guilt is an important weapon of the weak in the sense that it enables people with little or no objective power to exert influence over others who have more power. Additionally, Baumeister et al. found that individuals who felt guilty, whether induced or not, for a past transgression against their partner were more likely to change their behavior, apologize for the transgression, and/or say that they learned a lesson than individuals who did not feel guilty. Individuals who induce guilt in their partners therefore seem motivated by both approach forces to attain positive outcomes in relationships, and avoidance forces to reduce the likelihood of future transgressions by their partner. Individuals induced to feel guilty on the other hand are motivated by forces to avoid relationship dissolution.

Similarly, jealousy is quite effective at encouraging motivated cognition and behavior to avoid relationship dissolution. Jealousy has been shown to elicit compensatory behaviors in which the jealous individual expends more attention and resources to the relationship partner (Fleischman, Spitzberg, Andersen, & Scott, 2005) as well as specific attentional biases directed at detecting possible threats from worthy competitors in an effort to avoid losing the relationship (Maner, Gailliot, Rouby, & Miller, 2007). Because of the specific threat of jealousy that one's relationship partner will reallocate his or her attention to another potential partner, jealousy motivates individuals to engage in behavior directed at the partner and to potential rivals to reduce the threat of rejection.

Other forms of negative affect seem important in reducing the threat of rejection. Anxiety and depression are negative affective states that co-occur with real or imagined threats to social exclusion (Schlenker & Leary, 1982; Baumeister & Tice, 1990; Allen & Badcock, 2003). The relationship between these negatively affective states and threats to exclusion has led many to suggest that they function to ward off exclusion threats. Specifically, anxiety functions to encourage regulated behavior to fulfill self-presentational concerns (Schlenker & Leary, 1982), whereas depression functions to elicit socially cautious behavior (Allen & Badcock, 2003).

Feelings of anxiety can aid individuals in appropriate self-regulatory and self-presentational behaviors. When an individual engages in social interaction it is important for him or her to act in a socially desirable manner and to be perceived positively by others (Schlenker, 1980). Individuals who do not follow normative standards fail to contribute to the group, or are perceived as unattractive by the group are at threat of exclusion (Baumeister & Tice, 1990). In response to such threats, anxiety causes people to focus attention on potentially threatening social evaluations and to reassess their current behavior as appropriate or inappropriate (Smith, Ingram, & Brehm, 1983). If the behavior may lead to a negative evaluation, the individual can then cease that behavior in favor of more socially desirable responses (Schlenker & Leary, 1982). Anxiety therefore appears to function as a warning system to weed out behavior that would result in negative evaluations from others.

Similar to anxiety, feelings of sadness or depression can occur in response to exclusion threats (Leary, 1990). According to the social risk hypothesis (Allen & Badcock, 2003), depression evolved to elicit a risk-averse response predisposition for those individuals who may be currently at risk for social exclusion. In that perspective, due to the threat of exclusion faced by individuals experiencing depression, depressed individuals should favor cautious, low-risk social behavior. High-risk social behaviors may benefit the depressed individual greatly, as success could quickly restore his or her relationships. These big risks carry with them a high cost however, because failure could result in complete exclusion from social relationships. Taking smaller social risks should therefore be the optimal strategy for individuals suffering from depression. Success may only slightly raise an individual's social standing, yet these smaller risks carry with them a lower likelihood of failure resulting in exclusion. Indeed individuals experiencing moderate levels of depression seem especially attentive to socially relevant information (Badcock & Allen, 2003; Matthews, Ridgeway, & Williamson, 1996), are more likely to over-perceive the risks in social endeavors (Allen & Badcock, 2003), and are less likely to engage in socially risky behavior (Forgas, 2002).

Although interpersonal regulation may be guided by anxious and depressed states, it can also lead to self-defeating social behaviors (Allen & Badcock, 2003; Baumeister & Tice, 1990; Schlenker & Leary, 1982). The chronic experience of rejection can lead to strong feelings of anxiety that preclude individuals from engaging in social interactions in the first place (Baumeister & Tice, 1990; Downey & Feldman, 1996; Schlenker & Leary, 1982). Shy individuals and those who suffer from SAD are constantly concerned with the evaluations of others. The result is often a complete avoidance of social interaction. Similarly, although moderately depressed individuals benefit from being averse to social risks, clinical levels of depression can hamper an individual's social relationships. Risk-averse behavior can become so pervasive that it results in individuals becoming dysregulated and avoiding social contact (Gilbert, 2001). Additionally, although individuals at moderate levels of depression can elicit care from close-relationship partners through signaling behaviors (Clark, Ouellette, Powell, & Milberg, 1987; Biglan et al., 1985), these behaviors can become so pervasive that the relationship partners of severely depressed individuals will begin to distance themselves from the relationship (Coyne, 1976).

Emotion is not the only function that can reduce relationship threats. Several have suggested that an individual's perception of his or her social standing is monitored by cognitive systems that fluctuate with varying levels of inclusion and exclusion (Leary, Tambor, Terdal, & Downs, 1995; Allen & Badcock, 2003). According to sociometer theory (Leary et al., 1995), self-esteem serves this function. Through a series of experiments the authors showed that high self-esteem individuals have higher perceptions of inclusion compared to individuals with low self-esteem. State ratings of self-esteem also seem to decrease with increasing levels of rejection (Buckley, Winkel, & Leary, 2004). Self-esteem may therefore function like a gas gauge of social acceptance, lighting up to warn people when their level of social inclusion is reaching critically low levels (Leary et al.).

The major functional difference between self-esteem and emotional response systems to rejection is that self-esteem systems can result in both avoidant and approach social motives. At high levels of self-esteem, individuals feel secure in their relationships and as a result engage in self-enhancement strategies, whereas at low levels of self-esteem, individuals are less secure in their relationships and tend to engage in more self-protective strategies (see Baumeister, Tice, & Hutton, 1989; Sommer, 2001 for reviews). Individuals high in self-esteem seem to buffer themselves against rejection threats by affirming other relationships (Murray, Holmes, MacDonald, & Ellsworth, 1998), terminating the threatened relationship (Rusbult, Morrow, & Johnson, 1987), and seeking out new relationship partners (Sommer, Williams, Ciarocco, & Baumeister, 2001). Individuals low in self-esteem who perceive

threats of exclusion on the other hand tend to devalue the source of the possible exclusion (Murray et al., 1998), to neglect and ignore threatened relationships (Rusbult et al., 1987), and to engage in "defensive ostracism" (Sommer et al., 2001). In response to exclusion threats, high self-esteem individuals appear to be motivated by approach forces aimed at developing other relationships, whereas low self-esteem individuals are motivated to avoid information that threatens their relationships, often resulting in relationships falling apart.

RESPONSES TO ACTUAL REJECTION

Much human behavior appears to be motivated at defusing rejection threats before they occur. Yet even these attempts can fail and ironically can sometimes increase the person's likelihood of being rejected. If an individual is unsuccessful at avoiding threats to exclusion, one expected reaction might be behavior motivated to establish new relationships. After rejection, however, many individuals appear to engage in a host of self-defeating behaviors such as increased levels of aggression, decreased prosocial behavior, and a reduction in the motivation to engage in self-regulatory behaviors important for engaging in social interactions (see Blackhart, Baumeister, & Twenge, 2006 for review). On the surface these behaviors appear maladaptive and would likely result in a continued lonely existence. But new work has begun to elucidate the reasons why rejected individuals fail to engage in the self-regulation necessary for social success (DeWall & Baumeister, 2006) as well as to show that, under the right conditions, rejection can cause people to approach new relationships (Maner, DeWall, Baumeister, & Schaller, 2007).

Self-regulation is crucial for functioning in a social world, so one might expect that individuals faced with a lonely future would be more than willing to engage in motivated behavior aimed at repairing those relationships. Much evidence points to the contrary however. When rejection is experienced, individuals appear to fail to monitor and correct their behavior (Baumeister, DeWall, Ciarocco, & Twenge, 2005).

Self-awareness is an important component of self-regulation (Carver & Scheier, 1981). For an individual to regulate his or her behavior, attention must be directed at the self to identify whether the current behavior being enacted is meeting evaluative standards. Individuals appear motivated to avoid self-awareness when they are faced with negative evaluative feedback however. If an individual has received negative information about his or her character, having to direct attention at the self would result in the individual having to confront this apparent shortcoming. Self-awareness after rejection would likely be an aversive experience of analyzing one's character flaws to identify the reason one was rejected. Indeed, research shows that when rejected, individuals avoid self-awareness (Twenge, Catanese, & Baumeister, 2003).

Why? Introspection following rejection might be profitable for the future and long-term success, but it would be fairly unpleasant. After the experience of social exclusion, rejected individuals may perceive that future attempts at affiliation are unlikely to result in the desired outcome. Avoiding a negative self-perception may have much more drastic consequences in the here and now. Therefore, the monitoring system necessary for engaging in effective self-regulation is avoided momentarily to defuse the effect of negative feedback on an excluded individual's self-perception.

Recent research on the emotions experienced (or not experienced) after exclusion suggests one other reason why rejected individuals fail to engage in motivated behavior. It might be expected that rejection, considered by most to be a distressing experience, would decrease positive affect and increase negative affect. Nevertheless, when examined in the laboratory, rejection experiences seem to have little effect on mood (Baumeister, Twenge, & Nuss, 2002; Gardner, Pickett, & Brewer, 2000; Twenge, Baumeister, Tice, & Stucke, 2001). Even when rejection is found to decrease mood, the change in mood does not seem to mediate the behavioral responses to social exclusion (Buckley et al., 2004; DeWall & Baumeister, 2006; Williams, Cheung, & Choi, 2000). Rather it seems that rejection results in a numbing to both emotional and physical pain, both in the ability to experience one's own pain as well as the emotional and physical pain of others (DeWall & Baumeister, 2006; Twenge, Baumeister, DeWall, Ciarocco, & Bartels, 2007). Emotional and physical insensitivity may be an adaptive response to social exclusion, insofar as it would effectively reduce the distress that is assumed to occur after social exclusion. It may however have drastic consequences for social interaction. Positive and negative affective systems have been shown to be inherently linked to both approach and avoidance motivation, respectively (Cacioppo & Gardner, 1999; Depue & Iacono, 1989). People generally want to avoid experiences that would lead to negative affect and approach experiences that result in positive affect. The apparent lack of emotional sensitivity may however leave the rejected individual unable or unwilling to engage in motivated behavior to avoid these states.

Recently, DeWall (in preparation) and Twenge et al. (2007) have produced studies identifying the lack of empathy as a mediating factor in the disinhibition of aggressive responses and inhibition of prosocial responses by excluded individuals. The results of these studies suggest that the maladaptive behavior of excluded individuals arises due to a lack of empathic emotion that normally results in more socially appropriate behavior. In these situations, normal or included individuals would respond with emotional distress and a corresponding motivation to avoid this distress through prosocial behavior and inhibiting the urge to engage in aggressive behavior. Those who have been excluded however lack the emotional systems that would distress the individual in the first place (DeWall & Baumeister, 2006). Lacking these feelings of associated distress disengages the normal motivational propensity to avoid empathic distress through engagement of prosocial behavior and inhibition in aggression. The emotional numbness of excluded individuals therefore appears to reduce avoidance motivation by wiping away the crucial signal to engage in effective self-regulation.

It is entirely possible that the emotional numbness experienced after social exclusion may stifle approach behavior as well. DeWall and Baumeister's (2006) findings showed excluded individuals lack the ability to experience both negative *and* positive affect. As positive affect is inherently linked to approach motivation, it could be assumed that the inability for excluded individuals to experience positively affective states may reduce this motivational propensity as well. Although a rejected individual may be unable to experience positive affect, it is entirely plausible that he or she will still seek it out. Indeed, when enticed by a tangible reward (such as cash), excluded individuals appear to retain the ability to engage in self-regulation (Baumeister et al., 2005). Approach motivation may therefore be sustained in the behavior of rejected people. A likely place to identify approach motivation is in the domain where it is currently thwarted—specifically redeveloping social relationships. Recent findings by Maner et al. (2007) suggest that excluded individuals will continue to engage in self-regulated behavior toward attaining positive social experiences, but only when the outcome is highly likely.

Early research on rejection suggested rejected individuals were unwilling to engage in behavior that would increase the likelihood of reconnecting with others. If the need to belong is a fundamental human motive (Baumeister & Leary, 1995) it would be expected that rejected individuals would engage in behaviors to reduce their thwarted belongingness. Nevertheless, rejected individuals engage in a host of behaviors that would not be beneficial to building new social relationships (Blackhart et al., 2006). Several studies have shown that rejection and ostracism lead to aggressive responses, not only to the source of the rejection, but also to individuals completely unrelated to the rejection experience (Buckley et al., 2004; Twenge et al., 2001; Twenge & Campbell, 2003; Warburton, Williams, & Cairns, 2006). Additionally, Twenge et al. (2007) have shown that individuals who have been rejected engage in less prosocial behavior compared to those who have been included or did not receive acceptance/exclusion feedback. Being highly aggressive and refusing to engage in prosocial behavior would likely not result in an individual being a highly valued candidate for social interaction.

This evidence of antisocial tendencies among rejected persons seems inconsistent with other findings showing that exclusion can sometimes lead to behavior that could be seen as aimed at fostering reconnection. Williams and Sommer (1997) found that ostracized women (but not men) put forth increased effort toward a group task, which could be considered a promising strategy to make oneself attractive to the group. Williams et al. (2000) found that ostracized individuals were more likely than accepted individuals to conform to others' opinions, which could be seen as an ingratiation strategy (though it could also reflect mere passivity). Rejected individuals have also been shown to have better memory for information regarding other people's affiliation and rejection experiences, which may function to encourage more appropriate social behavior in future interactions, although it may simply reflect greater sensitivity due to being primed by one's own rejection (Gardner et al., 2000).

In an attempt to resolve the contradiction between these findings and the findings of others showing that rejected individuals engage in antisocial behaviors, Maner et al. (2007) proposed that rejected individuals will engage in affiliative behaviors only when the perceived possibility of forming a relationship is high. Through several studies, Maner and colleagues showed that individuals who experienced or imagined social exclusion were more interested in joining a group to form new friends (Study 1), were more likely to choose to work with others (Study 2), perceive others as more friendly and less hostile (Studies 3 & 4), and were more rewarding of a new interaction partner who was not an initial source of the exclusion experience (Studies 5 & 6). These studies seem to confirm the social reconnection hypothesis in that excluded individuals appear to be optimistic about future social interactions and take the opportunity to engage in social reconnection opportunities.

What then could result in the findings of previous studies showing that individuals who had been rejected were less than willing to engage in affiliative behavior? Maner and colleagues suggest that the degree to which an individual perceives social interaction to lead to actual social connection will alter affiliative responses to rejection. Specifically, three boundary conditions were tested and supported. The first factor is simply whether the individuals are engaging in interactions with the individual who had previously rejected them, or a novel potential relationship partner. Although rejected individuals, compared to control, rated novel relationship partners as friendlier and less hostile (Studies 4 & 5) and assigned greater rewards to these novel relationship partners—even though giving less rewards to their partner would result in a greater sum of money they could win in a raffle (Study 5)—they rated the individual who had rejected them as less friendly and more hostile (Studies 4 & 5) and were less benevolent toward this individual (Study 5). Another boundary condition was tested and identified in Study 6. Specifically participants were led to believe that they would either later meet their novel interaction partner or not. Those who were rejected and expected to meet their new interaction partner later were much more rewarding to this novel partner than those who did not expect to meet their partner and those who were not rejected in the first place. Apparently then excluded individuals seem to retain the motivation to seek out new relationship partners, but only if doing so is likely to result in future interaction.

Besides suggesting that individuals who have been excluded appear to continue to engage in approach-motivated behavior, the research of Maner et al. (2007) seems to suggest that at least a modicum of avoidance motivation remains intact after social exclusion. Specifically, many of the findings in these studies were moderated by a crucial individual difference, evaluation anxiety. Those individuals who had been excluded and scored high on a measure of anxiety showed no evidence of a desire to reconnect with others. Even when highly anxious excluded individuals interacted with a new partner (unrelated to the initial rejection experience) and had been led to expect that they would meet this person later, they seemed reluctant to engage in prosocial behavior. This suggests that for some individuals, the experience of rejection may lead to fears about future rejection. High anxious individuals who had faced a previous rejection may have expected a similar result of interacting with a new partner. The pervasive fear of negative evaluation and future rejection from others may therefore stifle even the strongest of motivations.

CONCLUSION

The purpose of this chapter has been to examine the effects of social rejection and exclusion in terms of approach and avoidance. Rejection is itself generally the result of a sort of avoidance, in the sense that rejection means that others have elected to avoid the person. But the rejected person's responses include a rich mixture of approach and avoidance tactics.

The decision to reject someone seems inherently to be a matter of avoidance, but this appearance can be misleading. For example, in modern societies, people are legally allowed to have only one spouse at a time, and most premarital romantic relationships follow the same dyadic rule, and so a person might reject one potential partner simply because of a stronger (approach) desire to affiliate with someone else. Even during the processes of rejecting someone and breaking off a romantic attachment, people may be ambivalent and thus torn between their lingering attraction to the partner and their various reasons for wanting to separate — thus, a classic approach/ avoidance conflict.

The rejected person tends to avoid the people who rejected him or her. There is some wish to form new relationships to replace the lost one, and that wish is essentially an approach motivation (i.e., to approach new partners and relationships), but this is tempered by the painful sensitivity that makes the rejected person eager to avoid being rejected again. The reluctance to risk another rejection entails an avoidance of some possible interactions and partners. Rejected people avoid self-awareness, presumably because it is highly aversive to dwell on what faults or flaws in themselves may have contributed to the rejection, and this lack of self-awareness curtails learning and introspection and may interfere with self-regulation.

The threat of rejection seems to evoke powerful and deeply rooted motivations, most likely because the need to belong is very basic to the human psychological makeup insofar as belongingness was essential to human biological strategies for survival and reproduction. The threat of rejection generally evokes a variety of negative affective and emotional responses, and people wish to avoid these. Many behaviors are thus indirectly shaped by the wish to avoid anxiety and other negative emotions that are associated with the possibility of rejection. For example, shy people may avoid social settings because they fear rejection, but this very avoidance conflicts with their often quite strong desire to approach others so as to form relationships and thereby escape from loneliness. Self-esteem may also be threatened by possible rejection,

and people may therefore engage in a variety of behaviors to protect or enhance their self-esteem.

Within relationships, too, approach and avoidance dynamics may be affected by the fear of rejection. One destructive pattern occurs when a partner who fears rejection seeks to preempt the devastating blow by distancing himself or herself from the relationship (e.g., devaluing the partner or the relationship), thereby contributing to its demise.

The novelist E.M. Forster once wrote, "Only connect!" but such advice is impractical, especially in a world where time is limited and monogamy is enforced. Human beings have a deeply rooted set of impulses to approach others to form relationships, but the complications of human social life lead to a great many avoidance impulses as well. Analyzing the phenomena of belongingness and rejection in those terms offers a fresh set of insights into how humans relate to each other.

REFERENCES

Allen, N. B., & Badcock, P. B. T. (2003). The social risk hypothesis of depressed mood: Evolutionary, psychosocial, and neurobiological perspectives. *Psychological Bulletin, 129,* 887–913.

Audy, J. R. (1980). Man the lonely animal: Biological roots of loneliness. In J. Hartog, J. R. Audy, & Y. A. Cohen (Eds.), *The anatomy of loneliness* (pp. 111–128). New York: International Universities Press

Badcock, P. B. T., & Allen, N. B. (2003). Adaptive Social Reasoning in depressed moods and depressive vulnerability. *Cognition and Emotion, 17,* 647–670.

Battaglia, D. M., Richard, F. D., Daterri, D. L., & Lord, C. G. (1998). Breaking up is (relatively) easy to do: A script for the dissolution of close relationships. *Journal of Social and Personal Relationships, 15,* 829–845.

Baumeister, R. F., DeWall, C. N., Ciarocco, N. J., & Twenge, J. M. (2005). Social exclusion impairs self-regulation. *Journal of Personality and Social Psychology, 88,* 589–604.

Baumeister, R. F., & Dhavale, D. (2001). Two sides of romantic rejection. In M. R. Leary (Ed.), *Interpersonal rejection* (pp. 55–72). New York: Oxford University Press.

Baumeister, R. F., & Leary, M. R. (1995). The need to belong: Desire for interpersonal attachments as a fundamental motivation. *Psychological Bulletin, 117,* 497–529.

Baumeister, R. F., Stillwell, A. M., & Heatherton, T. F. (1994). Guilt: An interpersonal approach. *Psychological Bulletin, 115,* 243–367.

Baumeister, R. F., Stillwell, A. M., & Heatherton, T. F. (1995). Personal narratives about guilt: Role in action control and interpersonal relationships. *Basic and Applied Social Psychology, 17,* 173–198.

Baumeister, R. F., & Tice, D. M. (1990). Anxiety and social exclusion. *Journal of Social and Clinical Psychology, 9,* 165–195.

Baumeister, R. F., Tice, D. M., & Hutton, D. G. (1989). Self-presentational motives and personality differences in self-esteem. *Journal of Personality*, *57*, 547–579.

Baumeister, R. F., Twenge, J. M., & Nuss, C. K. (2002). Effects of social exclusion on cognitive processes: Anticipated loneliness reduces intelligent thought. *Journal of Personality and Social Psychology*, *83*, 817–827.

Baumeister, R. F., Wotman, S. R., & Stillwell, A. M. (1993). Unrequited love: On heartbreak, anger, guilt, scriptlessness, and humiliation. *Journal of Personality and Social Psychology*, *64*, 377–394.

Berscheid, E., & Reis, H. T. (1998). Attraction and close relationships. In T. Gilbert, S. T. Fiske & G. Lindzey (Eds.), *The handbook of social psychology*. (Vol. 2, 4th ed. pp. 193–281). New York: McGraw-Hill.

Biglan, A., Hops, H., Sherman, L., Friedman, L. S., Arthur, J., & Osteen, V. (1985). Problem solving interactions of depressed women and their husbands. *Behavior Therapy*, *16*, 431–451.

Blackhart, G. C., Baumeister, R. F., & Twenge, J. M. (2006). Rejection's impact on self-defeating, prosocial, antisocial, and self-regulatory behaviors. In K. D. Vohs & E. J. Finkel (Eds.), *Self and relationships: Connecting intrapersonal and interpersonal processes* (pp. 237–253). New York: Guilford Press.

Bowlby, J. (1969). *Attachment and loss: Vol. 1. Attachment.* New York: Basic Books.

Bowlby, J. (1973). *Attachment and loss: Vol. 2. Separation anxiety and anger.* New York: Basic Books.

Brewer, M. B. (1979). Ingroup bias in the minimal intergroup situation: A cognitive-motivational analysis. *Psychological Bulletin*, *86*, 307–324.

Bruce, V. G., & Morgan, M. J. (1975). Violations of symmetry and repetition visual patterns. *Perception*, *4*, 239–249.

Buckley, K. E., Winkel, R. E., & Leary, M. R. (2004). Reactions to acceptance and rejection: Effects of level and sequence of relational evaluation. *Journal of Experimental Social Psychology*, *40*, 14–28.

Cacioppo, J. T., & Gardner, W. L. (1999). Emotions. *Annual Review of Psychology*, *50*, 191–214.

Caldwell, M. A., & Peplau, L. A. (1982). Sex differences in same-sex friendship. *Sex Roles*, *8*, 721–732.

Carver, C. S., & Scheier, M. F. (1981). *Attention and self-regulation: A control theory approach to human behavior.* New York: Springer-Verlag.

Chapman, G. B., & Johnson, E. J. (2002). Incorporating the irrelevant: Anchors in judgments of belief and value. In T. Gilovich, D. Griffin, & D. Kahneman (Eds.), *Heuristics and biases: The psychology of intuitive judgment* (pp. 120–138). New York: Cambridge University Press.

Clark, M. S., Ouellette, R., Powell, M. C., & Milberg, S. (1987). Recipient's mood, relationship type, and helping. *Journal of Personality and Social Psychology*, *53*, 94–103.

Cosmides, L. (1985). Deduction or Darwinian algorithms? An explanation of the "elusive" content effect on the Wason selection task. Doctoral dissertation, Department of Psychology, Harvard University: University Microfilms, #86–02206.

Cosmides, L., & Tooby, J. (1992). Cognitive adaptations for social exchange. In J. Barkow, L. Cosmides, & J. Tooby (Eds.), *The adapted mind* (pp. 163–228). New York: Oxford University Press.

Coyne, J. C. (1976). Depression and response to others. *Journal of Abnormal Psychology*, *85*, 186–193.

Crocker, J., Major, B., & Steele, C. (1998). Social stigma. In D. T. Gilbert, S. T. Fiske, & G. Lindzey (Eds.), *The handbook of social psychology* (Vol. 2, 4th ed. pp. 504–533). Boston, MA: McGraw-Hill.

Depue, R. A., & Iacono, W. (1989). Neurobehavioral aspects of affective disorders. In M. R. Rosenweigh & L. W. Porter (Eds.), *Annual review of psychology* (pp. 457–492). Palo Alto, CA: Annual Reviews.

DeWall, C. N. I can't feel your pain, so I inflict pain on you: Emotional insensitivity as a mechanism underlying aggressive responses to rejection. Manuscript in preparation.

DeWall, C. N., & Baumeister, R. F. (2006). Alone but feeling no pain: Effects of social exclusion on physical pain tolerance and pain threshold, affective forecasting, and interpersonal empathy. *Journal of Personality and Social Psychology*, *91*, 1–15.

Downey, G., & Feldman, S. I. (1996). Implications of rejection sensitivity for intimate relationships. *Journal of Personality and Social Psychology*, *70*, 1327–1343.

Elliot, A. J., Gable, S. L., & Mapes, R. R. (2006). Approach and avoidance motivation in the social domain. *Personality and Social Psychology Bulletin*, *32*, 378–391.

Elliot, G. C., Ziegler, H. L., Altman, B. M., & Scott, D. R. (1982). Understanding stigma: Dimensions of deviance and coping. *Deviant Behavior*, *3*, 275–300.

Festinger, L., Schachter, S., & Back, K. (1950). *Social pressures in informal groups: A study of a housing community.* Palo Alto, CA: Stanford University Press.

Fleischman, A. A., Spitzberg, B. H., Andersen, P. A., & Scott, C. R. (2005). Tickling the monster: Jealousy induction in relationships. *Journal of Social and Personal Relationships*, *22*, 49–73.

Folkes, V. S. (1982). Communicating the reasons for social rejection. *Journal of Experimental Social Psychology*, *18*, 235–252.

Forgas, J. P. (2002). Feeling and doing: Affective influences on interpersonal behavior. *Psychological Inquiry*, *13*, 1–28.

Gable, S. L. (2006). Approach and avoidance social motives and goals. *Journal of Personality*, *74*, 175–222.

Gable, S. L., Reis, H. T., & Elliot, A. J. (2003). Evidence for bivariate systems: An empirical test of appetition and aversion across domains. *Journal of Research in Personality*, *37*, 349–372.

Gangestad, S. W., & Thornhill, R. (1997). The evolutionary psychology of extra-pair sex: The role of fluctuating asymmetry. *Evolution and Human Behavior*, *18*, 69–88.

Gardner, W. L., Pickett, C. L., & Brewer, M. B. (2000). Social exclusion and selective memory: How the need to belong influences memory for social events. *Personality and Social Psychology Bulletin*, *26*, 486–496.

Gilbert, P. (2001). Depression and stress: A biopsychosocial exploration of evolved functions and mechanisms. *Stress: The International Journal of the Biology of Stress, 4,* 121–135.

Grammer, K., & Thornhill, R. (1994). Human (Homo sapiens) facial attractiveness and sexual selection: The role of symmetry and averageness. *Journal of Comparative Psychology, 108,* 233–242.

Goffman, I. (1963). *Stigma: Notes on the management of spoiled identity.* Englewood Cliffs, NJ: Prentice Hall

Hall, J. H., & Fincham, F. D. (2006). Relationship dissolution following infidelity: The role of attributions and forgiveness. *Journal of Social and Clinical Psychology, 25,* 508–522.

Haselton, M. G., & Buss, D. M. (2000). Error management theory: A new perspective on biases in cross-sex mind reading. *Journal of Personality and Social Psychology, 78,* 81–91.

Jones, E. E., Farina, A., Hastorf, A. H., Markus, H., Miller, D. T., & Scott, R. A. (1984). *Social stigma: The psychology of marked relationships.* New York: Freeman.

Kelley, H. H., & Thibault, J. W. (1978). *Interpersonal relations: A theory of interdependence.* New York: Wiley.

Kenrick, D. T., Neuberg, S. L., Zierk, K. L., & Krones, J. M. (1994). Evolution and social cognition: Contrast effects as a function of sex, dominance, and physical attractiveness. *Personality and Social Psychology Bulletin, 20,* 210–217.

Kiesler, S. B. (1973). Preference for predictability or unpredictability as a mediator of reactions to norm violations. *Journal of Personality and Social Psychology, 27,* 354–359.

Kurzban, R., & Leary, M. R. (2001). Evolutionary origins of stigmatization: The functions of social exclusion. *Psychological Bulletin, 127,* 187–208.

Latane, B., Eckman, J., & Joy, V. (1966). Shared stress and interpersonal attraction. *Journal of Experimental Social Psychology, 1,* 80–94.

Leary, M. R. (1983). *Understanding social anxiety: Social, personality, and clinical perspectives.* Beverly Hills, CA: Sage.

Leary, M. R. (1990). Responses to social exclusion: Social anxiety, jealousy, loneliness, depression, and low self-esteem. *Journal of Social and Clinical Psychology, 9,* 221–229.

Leary, M. R. (2001). Toward a conceptualization of interpersonal rejection. In M. R. Leary (Ed.), *Interpersonal rejection* (pp. 3–20). New York: Oxford University Press.

Leary, M. R., Tambor, E. S., Terdal, S. K., & Downs, D. L. (1995). Self-esteem as an interpersonal monitor: The sociometer hypothesis. *Journal of Personality and Social Psychology, 68,* 518–530.

Maner, J. K., DeWall, C. N., Baumeister, R. F., & Schaller, M. (2007). Does social exclusion motivate interpersonal reconnection? Resolving the porcupine problem. *Journal of Personality and Social Psychology, 92,* 42–55.

Maner, J. K., Gailliot, M. T., Rouby, A., & Miller, S. (2007). Can't take my eyes off of you: Mating-goals and biases in attentional adhesion. *Journal of Personality and Social Psychology, 93,* 389–401.

Maslow, A. H. (1968). *Toward a psychology of being.* New York: Van Nostrand.

Matthews, A., Ridgeway, V., & Williamson, D. A. (1996). Evidence for attention to threatening stimuli in depression. *Behaviour Research and Therapy, 34,* 695–706.

Murray, S. L., Holmes, J. G., MacDonald, G., & Ellsworth, P. C. (1998). Through the looking glass darkly? When self-doubts turn into relationship insecurities. *Journal of Personality and Social Psychology, 75,* 1459–1480.

Nahemov, L., & Lawton, M. P. (1975). Similarity and propinquity in friendship formation. *Journal of Personality and Social Psychology, 54,* 811–819.

Orians, G. H., & Heerwagen, J. H. (1992). Evolved responses to landscapes. In J. H. Barkow, L. Cosmides, & J. Tooby (Eds.), *The adapted mind.* New York: Oxford University Press.

Parker, J. G., & Asher, S. R. (1993). Friendship and friendship quality in middle childhood: Links with peer group acceptance and feelings of loneliness and social dissatisfaction. *Developmental Psychology, 29,* 611–621.

Reis, H. T. (1990). The role of intimacy in interpersonal relations. *Journal of Social and Clinical Psychology, 9,* 15–30.

Rofe, Y. (1984). Stress and affiliation: A utility theory. *Psychological Review, 91,* 235–250.

Roy, M. (1977). *Battered women.* New York: Van Nostrand.

Rusbult, C. E. (1980a). Commitment and satisfaction in romantic associations: A test of the investment model. *Journal of Experimental Social Psychology, 16,* 172–186.

Rusbult, C. E. (1980b). Satisfaction and commitment in friendships. *Representative Research in Social Psychology, 11,* 86–105.

Rusbult, C. E. (1983). A longitudinal test of the investment model: The development (and deterioration) of satisfaction and commitment in heterosexual involvements. *Journal of Personality and Social Psychology, 45,* 101–117.

Rusbult, C. E., Morrow, G. D., & Johnson, D. J. (1987). Self-esteem and problem-solving behavior in close relationships. *British Journal of Social Psychology, 26,* 293–303.

Schlenker, B. R. (1980). *Impression Management: The Self-Concept, Social Identity, and Interpersonal Relations.* Monterey, CA: Brooks/Cole Publishing.

Schlenker, B. R., & Leary, M. R. (1982). Social anxiety and self-presentation: A conceptualization and model. *Psychological Bulletin, 92,* 641–669.

Sherif, M., Harvey, O. H., White, B. J., Hood, W. R., & Sherif, C. W. (1988). *The Robbers Cave experiment: Intergroup conflict and cooperation.* Middletown, CT: Wesleyan University Press. (Original work published 1961).

Smith, T. W., Ingram, R. E., & Brehm, S. S. (1983). Social anxiety, anxious self-preoccupation, and recall of self-relevant information. *Journal of Personality and Social Psychology, 44,* 1276–1283.

Sommer, K. L. (2001). Coping with rejection: Ego defensive strategies, self-esteem, and interpersonal relationships. In M. R. Leary (Ed.), *Interpersonal rejection* (pp. 167–188). New York: Oxford University Press.

Sommer, K. L., Williams, K. D., Ciarocco, N. J., & Baumeister, R. F. (2001). When silence speaks louder than words: Explorations into the intrapsychic and interpersonal consequences of social ostracism. *Basic and Applied Social Psychology, 23,* 225–243.

Strube, M. J. (1988). The decision to leave an abusive relationship: Empirical evidence and theoretical issues. *Psychological Bulletin, 104,* 236–250.

Thornhill, R., & Gangestad, S. W. (1999). The scent of symmetry: A human scent pheromone that signals fitness? *Evolution and Human Behavior, 20,* 175–201.

Tooby, J., & Cosmides, L. (1996). Friendship and the banker's paradox: Other pathways to the evolution of adaptations for altruism. *Proceedings of the British Academy, 88,* 119–143.

Twenge, J. M., Baumeister, R. F., Tice, D. M., & Stucke, T. S. (2001). If you can't join them, beat them: Effects of social exclusion on aggressive behavior. *Journal of Personality and Social Psychology, 81,* 1058–1069.

Twenge, J. M., & Campbell, W. K. (2003). Isn't it fun to get the respect that we're going to deserve? Narcissism, social rejection, and aggression. *Personality and Social Psychology Bulletin, 29,* 261–272.

Twenge, J. M., Catanese, K. R., & Baumeister, R. F. (2003). Social exclusion and the deconstructed state: Time perception, meaninglessness, lethargy, lack of emotion, and self-awareness. *Journal of Personality and Social Psychology, 85,* 409–423.

Twenge, J. M., Baumeister, R. F., DeWall, C. N., Ciarocco, N. J., & Bartels, J. M. (2007). Social exclusion decreases prosocial behavior. *Journal of Personality and Social Psychology, 92,* 56–66.

Vangelesti, A. L., Daly, J. A., & Rudnick, J. R. (1991). Making people feel guilty in conversations: Techniques and correlates. *Human Communication Research, 18,* 3–39.

Warburton, W. A., Williams, K. D., & Cairns, D. R. (2006). When ostracism leads to aggression: The moderating effects of control deprivation. *Journal of Experimental Social Psychology, 42,* 213–220.

Wason, P. (1966). Reasoning. In B. M. Foss (Ed.), *New horizons in psychology.* Harmondsworth: Penguin.

Wheeler, L., & Nezlek, J. (1977). Sex differences in social participation. *Journal of Personality and Social Psychology, 35,* 742–754.

Wilder, D. A., & Thompson, J. E. (1980). Intergroup contact with independent manipulations of in-group and out-group interactions. *Journal of Personality and Social Psychology, 38,* 589–603.

Williams, K. D., Cheung, C. K. T., & Choi, W. (2000). Cyberostracism: Effects of being ignored over the internet. *Journal of Personality and Social Psychology, 79,* 748–762.

Williams, K. D., & Sommer, K. L. (1997). Social ostracism by coworkers: Does rejection lead to loafing or compensation? *Personality and Social Psychology Bulletin, 23,* 693–706.

Sexual Behavior

37 A Dyadic Perspective on Approach and Avoidance Motives for Sexual Behavior

M. Lynne Cooper, Amelia E. Talley, Meli S. Sheldon, Ash Levitt, and Lindsay L. Barber

CONTENTS

The notion that people use sex strategically to achieve different goals, and that these differences shape the experience and expression of their sexuality, is central to a motivational perspective. According to this view, the key to understanding behavior lies in the needs and purposes served by the behavior. Regardless of outward similarities, behaviors undertaken in service of different needs are thought to be psychologically distinct, and should therefore exhibit unique patterns of antecedents, correlates, and consequences. This perspective suggests that sexual behaviors motivated by different needs (e.g., to strengthen a bond vs. avoid rejection) should be triggered by unique antecedents, characterized by qualitatively different styles of behavior and emotions, and ultimately result in distinct consequences. Thus, according to this view, human sexual behavior cannot be adequately understood without taking into account the nature of the underlying needs that motivate it.

Although needs or motives* vary along many dimensions, a fundamental distinction can be drawn between approach and avoidance motives. Past research indicates that sexual behavior motivated by approach versus avoidance concerns is associated with distinctive styles of behaving and distinctive outcomes in both cross-sectional and longitudinal studies. In general, this body of research suggests that having sex for avoidant reasons (e.g., to escape or avoid negative moods, to avoid disapproval from one's partner or peers, to allay insecure feelings) is linked to negative feelings about sex and lower satisfaction, along with higher rates of casual sex, sexually transmitted infections (STIs), and unplanned pregnancies. In contrast, having sex for approach reasons (intimacy, enhancement) is associated with positive feelings about sex, higher satisfaction, and more adaptive behaviors overall, though certain approach motives also appear to foster sexual risk taking.

Although this body of research attests to the importance of approach–avoidance motives for understanding patterns and consequences of sexual behavior, it has been limited by an almost exclusive focus on the individual and his or her motives in isolation. The fact that sexual behavior is shaped by the needs and motives of two people has received little systematic attention. In this chapter, we use this observation as a jumping-off point for exploring how the approach–avoidance motives of intimate partners individually and jointly shape the nature and quality of sexual experiences within their relationship.

We begin this chapter with a review of existing research on approach–avoidance motives for sexual behavior, conducted exclusively on individuals rather than couples. We then review several lines of evidence from prior studies based on individuals that, nevertheless, suggest that individual-level analyses of highly interdependent behaviors, such as sexual behavior, are limited in important ways. Using data from a community sample of 299 young adult couples, we then summarize evidence showing (a) that the effects of approach–avoidance motives on sexual behavior are highly sensitive to a relationship context; (b) that both one's own motives and one's partner's motives shape individual sexual experience (particularly among men); and (c) that partner motives combine in synergistic ways (i.e., interact) to shape the sexual outcomes of both male and female relationship partners. We conclude by highlighting several new insights gained by moving to a dyadic level of analysis to examine the nature of approach–avoidance motives in the sexual arena.

WHAT MOTIVES UNDERLIE SEXUAL BEHAVIOR?

In our earlier work, we (Cooper, Shapiro, & Powers, 1998) hypothesized that two primary motivational dimensions underlie human sexual behavior. The first dimension distinguishes behaviors that involve the pursuit of positive or pleasurable experiences (appetitive or approach behaviors) from those that involve the avoidance of, or escape from, negative or painful ones (so-called aversive or avoidance behaviors). According to Gray (1970, 1987), approach and avoidance behaviors are regulated by neurologically distinct motivational systems. The behavioral inhibition system (BIS) regulates avoidance motivation and controls the experience of negative emotions, whereas the behavioral activation system (BAS) regulates approach motivation and controls the experience of positive emotions. Gray further hypothesized that individuals differ in a stable, trait-like manner in the relative sensitivity of the two systems. Consistent with this hypothesis, people who are high in BIS are especially responsive to threat and punishment cues, which predispose them to experience negative affect and respond in an avoidant or fearful manner. Conversely, individuals who are high in BAS are especially responsive to reward cues, which predispose them to experience positive affect and engage in reward-seeking behaviors (see Carver & White, 1994; Larsen & Ketelaar, 1991, for supporting evidence). Indeed, the stable personality traits of neuroticism and extroversion are thought to derive from the BIS and BAS systems, respectively (Gray, 1970; Larsen & Ketelaar, 1991). When applied to sexual behaviors, this distinction suggests that people can have sex to pursue or maintain

---

* Throughout this document, we use the term motive to refer to the underlying dynamics that drive or "energize" sexual behavior. The sex motives measure used in our research (developed and described in Cooper, Shapiro, & Powers, 1998) assesses the motivated use of sexual behavior to achieve, maintain, avoid, or escape different desired or undesired states. As such, this measure assesses a mid-range, hybrid construct that is part motive, part goal. Indeed, it is similar to what Elliot (2006) has called a "goal complex," because it specifies both the source or energization of behavior (what motivates or gives rise to the behavior; e.g., the desire to strengthen a relationship), as well as how the individual "directs" his or her efforts to satisfy the need or motive (in this case, via sexual behavior). However, because our measure refers to a relatively stable tendency to use sex to achieve certain ends (see Cooper et al., 1998, Study 4, for information on the temporal stability of this measure), whereas goals most often refer to more time-bound, situation specific behaviors, we believe that the term, motive or motive disposition, best captures the nature of the construct under review in the present chapter.

positive outcomes, such as physical pleasure or excitement, or to avoid or escape negative ones, such as rejection by socially significant others.

The second motivational dimension hypothesized to underlie human sexual behavior concerns the extent to which behavior is motivated by an intraindividual or self-focused concern versus an external, interpersonal, or social concern. This distinction is closely related to distinctions between agency versus communion (Bakan, 1966), autonomy/competence versus relatedness (Skinner & Wellborn, 1994), and exploration versus attachment (Bowlby, 1970). Thus, sexual behaviors motivated by self-focused concerns might serve agentic, identity, or autonomy/competence needs, such as having sex to affirm one's sense of identity or attractiveness, or to manage one's internal emotional experience. The latter can be thought of as an agentic striving to the extent that it involves mastery and control of one's emotional experience (McAdams, 1984). In contrast, sexual behavior motivated by social concerns might serve attachment or communal needs, such as having sex to achieve intimacy and communion in a relationship, or to gain another's approval. Thus, although intrapersonal motives can be pursued in an interpersonal context (as when one uses sex to self-affirm), and both intrapersonal and interpersonal motives can be seen as ultimately originating from a desire to manage one's emotions (either by direct manipulation of feeling states or indirectly by obtaining a valued outcome from a socially significant other), these motives nevertheless can be differentiated by the degree to which the outcomes sought are primarily self-focused or internal to the individual versus other-focused or external to the individual (i.e., social).

We hypothesized that these two dimensions combine to yield four broad classes of motivations for sexual behavior: (a) self-focused approach motives, such as having sex to enhance physical or emotional pleasure (i.e., enhancement motives); (b) self-focused avoidant motives, such as having sex to cope with threats to self-esteem or to minimize negative emotions (i.e., coping motives); (c) social approach motives, such as having sex to bond with socially significant others (i.e., intimacy motives); and (d) social avoidant motives, such as having sex to avoid social censure or rejection (i.e., peer- and partner-approval motives).

We validated this framework in a series of studies (Cooper et al., 1998, Studies 1–3). First, to determine how well people's spontaneously generated motives fit the hypothesized framework, we asked undergraduates to list the most important reasons why they had sex on a recent occasion of intercourse. Ninety-two percent of the resulting responses involved approach motives, both enhancement (49%) and intimacy (43%), whereas only 8% involved avoidant motives, including having sex to escape or cope with negative internal states (e.g., "So I could relieve stress") and to avoid rejection by one's peers or partner (e.g., "I felt that I had to because he was my boyfriend"). Thus, people spontaneously generated reasons within all hypothetical motive classes identified by our model, though their reasons were not equally distributed across these classes.

Factor analytic work carried out in three independent samples provided further support for the validity of this model, while at the same time suggesting a potentially important refinement. Using a set of Likert-type items intended to measure the four-motive constructs, we obtained six instead of four factors: two approach motive factors (intimacy, enhancement), as hypothesized, but four (instead of two) avoidant motive factors (coping, self-affirmation, partner approval, and peer approval). Despite this deviation from expectation, higher-order factor models showed that the correlations among the six factors could be explained by a four-factor structure in which intimacy and enhancement were treated as indicators of discrete factors (i.e., other- and self-focused approach factors, respectively); affirmation and coping motives were treated as indicators of a single, higher-order self-focused, avoidant factor; and peer- and partner-approval motives were treated as indicators of a single, higher-order social, avoidant factor (see Cooper et al., 1998, Study 3). These data suggest that although multiple, specific manifestations of avoidance motives exist, the four-motive typology is nevertheless a useful heuristic device for understanding the major distinctions among motive types.

Additional factor analytic work showed that nesting the four avoidant motives under a higher-order avoidance factor and the two approach motives under a higher-order approach factor provided a better fit to the data than nesting the three intrapersonal motives (enhancement, coping, self-affirmation) under a higher-order intrapersonal factor and the three social motives (intimacy, partner approval, peer approval) under a higher-order interpersonal factor (Cooper et al., 1998, Study 2). Although both two-factor models provided a significantly worse fit to the data than the four-factor model, these findings nevertheless indicate that the approach–avoidance distinction better accounts for the structure of sexual motivations than the self versus social distinction. In this sense then, the approach–avoidance distinction appears to be the more fundamental of the two to the psychological structure of sex motives.

Subsequent validation studies using the Cooper et al. (1998) measure of sexual motivations showed that rates of endorsement in both college (Cooper et al., Study 2) and community (Study 3) samples varied across motive type in a manner similar to that observed in the initial open-ended elicitation study: Enhancement and intimacy were by far the most commonly endorsed reasons for having sex followed by sex to affirm ones' self-worth, to cope with negative emotions, and for partner or peer approval. Moreover, this rank order was largely invariant across gender, race, and age groups (Study 3).

In sum, findings from this research indicate that people use sex to pursue a relatively small number of different goals, and that these goals can be parsimoniously characterized in terms of underlying differences in approach–avoidance motivation and self/internal versus social focus. At the same time, these dimensions and the specific motives that derive from them appear to differ in their importance; the approach–avoidance distinction better accounts for the underlying latent structure of sex motives and, within this dimension, approach motives are much more common, at least among young adults, than avoidance motives.

DOES HAVING SEX TO SATISFY DIFFERENT MOTIVES MATTER?

In the foregoing section, we characterized the nature and distribution of sexual motives among young adults. However, the larger question of whether these differences are consequential remains. Do the nature and quality of outcomes differ, for example, among individuals who use sex primarily to achieve intimacy with their partner compared with those who use sex primarily to cope with their insecurities? Consistent with a core assumption of the motivational perspective, existing research (reviewed below) suggests that they do.

APPROACH MOTIVES FOR SEX

People who have sex for approach reasons are, by definition, seeking a positive or rewarding outcome, be that a closer connection with their partner or a physically enjoyable and exciting experience. Accordingly, sexual behavior among such individuals should be seen as a way to obtain benefits and achieve important life goals—expectations that in turn should create positive emotional responses to sex (i.e., high erotophilia, low erotophobia; Fisher, Byrne, & White, 1983), and lead to more frequent and satisfying sexual experiences. At the same time, however, the contexts in which these experiences occur

should differ markedly for people who have sex to build intimacy versus enhance. Having sex within the context of a close emotional relationship should facilitate satisfaction among those who are primarily motivated to seek intimacy, whereas having sex with any attractive person may provide a suitable context for satisfaction of pleasure-seeking motivations. Indeed, to the extent that enhancement motives are partly driven by excitement and novelty seeking, as their hypothesized roots in the BAS suggest, a casual sex partner may even be preferred to a more intimate one among individuals who are primarily motivated by hedonic concerns.

Consistent with the above analysis, research indicates that both intimacy and enhancement motives are positively associated with need for sex and erotophilia, but negatively associated with erotophobia (Cooper et al., 1998, Study 3). Also as expected, individuals who have sex for intimacy and enhancement reasons report higher relationship satisfaction (which has been strongly linked to sexual satisfaction; Christopher & Sprecher, 2000; Rusbult & Van Lange, 2003) and more frequent intercourse (Cooper et al.; Impett, Peplau, & Gable, 2005). On the whole then, these data suggest that both intimacy and enhancement motives reflect a strong approach orientation to sex.

These similarities notwithstanding, the two motives are linked to distinct partner and risk profiles, as hypothesized. Whereas intimacy motives have been consistently associated with fewer and less risky, better-known sexual partners, enhancement motives have been associated with permissive attitudes toward casual, uncommitted sex, more sex partners (especially casual ones), and more risky sex practices (Browning, Hatfield, Kessler, & Levine, 2000; Cooper et al., 1998; Hill & Preston, 1996; Levinson, Jaccard, & Beamer, 1995). Intimacy motives have also been associated with more effective birth control use, fewer unplanned pregnancies, as well as lower rates of condom use (Cooper et al.; Gebhardt, Kuyper, & Dusseldorp, 2006; Hill & Preston, 1996). This pattern of findings appears to be directly attributable to the more committed relationship contexts in which people who use sex to achieve intimacy are likely to have sex (Cooper et al.; see also Schachner & Shaver, 2004). Finally, and in contrast, enhancement motives have been associated with both higher rates of STIs and unplanned pregnancies (Cooper et al.). Together these data suggest that although intimacy and enhancement motives are associated with positive feelings about sex, as their shared roots in the approach motivation system predict, sex motivated by these two concern, is nevertheless characterized by highly distinctive relational contexts, as well as distinctive patterns of behavior and associated consequences.

AVOIDANCE MOTIVES FOR SEX

People who have sex for avoidant reasons are, by definition, having sex to escape from, minimize, or avoid aversive states or anticipated negative outcomes, including generalized negative mood states, feelings of insecurity or inadequacy, or rejection by socially significant others. According to Elliot and colleagues (Elliot, Gable, & Mapes, 2006), the negative orientation characteristic of avoidance goals is thought to evoke a set of processes that undermine the quality of social interactions and the development of social bonds, including negatively valenced perceptions (e.g., interpreting partner behaviors in the worst possible light), attentional biases (e.g., heightened attention to negative partner qualities), memories (e.g., biased search for and recall of negative information), emotions (e.g., fear, mistrust), and behaviors (e.g., stonewalling one's partner). As a result, people who are primarily motivated by avoidance goals are more likely to associate sex with painful or unpleasant experiences and to experience negative emotional responses to sex (i.e., high erotophobia). As a result of these intervening processes, such individuals are also more likely to engender negative sexual situations. For all of these reasons, we expect less frequent, satisfying, and rewarding sex among individuals who are primarily motivated by avoidance goals.

Sexual behaviors motivated by avoidance concerns should also be riskier. This expectation rests on at least three different lines of reasoning. First, negatively valenced stimuli have been shown to garner more attention, to create stronger emotional reactions, and to more reliably elicit behavioral responses than comparable positively valenced stimuli (Baumeister, Bratslavsky, Finkenauer, & Vohs, 2001; Carver & Scheier, 1998). Because avoidant motives focus attention on negative rather than positive situations and possibilities, they may take precedence over other goals and considerations. Under such circumstances, if having sex is seen as an effective way to escape from or avoid an undesirable situation, then sex seems more likely to occur regardless of its advisability on that particular occasion or with that particular partner. A second and related point: risky behaviors are typically thought to involve a trade-off between short-term gains and long-term costs. According to Baumeister and Scher (1988), the propensity to choose immediate pleasure or relief is exacerbated under the influence of negative emotional states in part because being in a negative mood increases the attractiveness of immediate relief. Thus, individuals who use sex to escape negative emotional states may weigh the immediate

benefits of having sex more heavily than potential longer-term costs, thereby shifting the balance in favor of riskier sexual decisions. Finally, even though avoidance goals can assume a prepotent role in decision-making situations, they are nevertheless thought to provide a suboptimal structure for self-regulation (Carver & Scheier, 1998; Heimpel, Elliot, & Wood, 2006). As Carver and Scheier (1998) point out, avoidance goals provide something to move away from but nothing to move toward. In the absence of a concrete path for moving forward, individuals who are primarily focused on avoidance concerns may lack clear guidelines for evaluating behavioral alternatives and thus have greater difficulty regulating their behavior in line with their goals and values. Thus, through a variety of processes, we expect individuals who are primarily motivated by avoidant concerns to engage in less adaptive, riskier sexual behaviors.

A review of the existing literature reveals patterns of association that are largely consistent with these expectations. Consistent with the notion that avoidant motives are rooted in the BIS, all four avoidance motives have been linked to higher levels of neuroticism and erotophobia (Cooper et al., 1998). Interestingly, however, coping and affirmation motives have also been associated with higher levels of sexual desire and erotophilia (Cooper et al.; Hill & Preston, 1996), thus suggesting an approach-avoidant or ambivalent orientation toward sex among those who use sex to cope or affirm. However, because ambivalence is widely experienced as aversive (Priester & Petty, 1996), these findings can also be seen as consistent with the contention that both motives reflect BIS-driven, avoidant motivational processes. Unlike the pattern observed for coping and affirmation motives, individuals who are high (vs. low) in peer- and partner-approval motives do not differ in need for sex or in erotophilia (Cooper et al.), thus suggesting a predominantly negative (as opposed to ambivalent) orientation to sex among those who have sex for approval reasons. Finally, although specific associations between avoidant motives and sexual satisfaction have not been tested, avoidance motives have been linked to lower relationship satisfaction (Impett et al., 2005), which, as previously indicated, is strongly associated with sexual satisfaction.

Although these four motives appear to share a core set of negative emotional responses to sex, they have nevertheless been associated with distinctive behavioral patterns. For example, individuals who are high in sex to cope report more frequent masturbation (Hill & Preston, 1996), more casual sex partners (Cooper et al., 1998; Hill & Preston, 1996), but better birth control use and fewer unplanned pregnancies (Cooper et al.). This promiscuous but "safe" pattern suggests a certain calculated quality to the sexual behavior of individuals who use sex to cope (cf., Gold & Skinner, 1993). Individuals who are high in partner-approval motives also show greater involvement in risky sexual practices, but less birth control use and higher rates of unplanned pregnancies (Cooper et al.)—a pattern that is thought to reflect reluctance to assert oneself and risk partner disapproval in sexual situations (cf., Harlow, Quina, Morokoff, Rose, & Grimley, 1993; Jemmott & Jemmott, 1991). Having sex for peer approval, a phenomenon observed primarily among young adolescent males (Cooper et al., Studies 3 and 4) has been associated with a relative lack of sexual experience. Such individuals reported fewer lifetime intercourse experiences, fewer lifetime sex partners, less frequent sex in the past 6 months, and older age at first intercourse. These individuals also, however, showed steeper increases in sexual risk taking over time, thus suggesting that they eventually "catch-up" with or even exceed their peers, possibly as other motives supplant their initial reasons for having sex (Cooper et al., Study 4). Finally, having sex to affirm has been linked to an inconsistent pattern of sexual risk behaviors, perhaps owing at least in part to its statistical overlap with coping motives (Cooper et al.).

Summary

The foregoing review provides strong support for the idea that the reasons why people have sex are important for understanding sexual outcomes. Indeed, different motives for sex are characterized by distinct patterns of behaving and by distinct consequences. Moreover, although approach and avoidant sex motives have been related in a uniform and consistent manner to positive and negative emotional responses to sex, respectively, the distinctive pattern of behaviors associated with individual motives suggests that motives cannot be reduced to a simple approach–avoidance dichotomy. Instead, it appears that whether one is trying to use sex to address internal, self-focused needs, or social needs also matters, perhaps by selectively directing the individual to more impersonal versus intimate relational contexts.

LIMITATIONS OF STUDYING INDIVIDUALS AS OPPOSED TO COUPLES

As previously discussed, past research on sexual motivations has focused on one partner's goals and motives in isolation, essentially ignoring the fact that sexual behavior is intrinsically dyadic and thus involves the goals and motives of two people. As Kenny and Cook (1999) point

out, individualistic approaches such as this assume, without ever testing, that there are actor but not partner effects—in other words, that one's behavior is caused by his or her own standing on important predictors, but not by the partner's. In such studies, the partner is effectively deemed irrelevant.

Interestingly, however, even research using individuals (as opposed to couples) points to the fallacy of this position. Cooper, Agocha, and Sheldon (2000), for example, found that approach and avoidance motives for alcohol use accounted for 27% of the variance in alcohol outcomes on average, whereas approach and avoidance motives for sex accounted for only 6%, on average, of the variance in sexual behavior outcomes—a more than fourfold difference. Although it is possible that these differences stem from the differential validity of the two motive measures, there is no psychometric evidence to support this interpretation (cf., Cooper, 1994; Cooper et al., 1998). Rather we suspect that the observed differences reflect the fact that intrapersonal motives are less predictive of highly interdependent behaviors like sex than they are of largely individually determined behaviors like drinking.

Evidence from our earlier study on sex motives (Cooper et al., 1998) lends additional support to this interpretation. Specifically, we found a consistent pattern of relationship status × sex motive interactions in both cross-sectional (Study 3) and longitudinal (Study 4) analyses showing that individual motives (especially enhancement) more strongly predicted sexual behavior among uncoupled individuals than among those in steady or exclusive relationships. Indeed, in some cases motives only predicted behavior among uncoupled individuals, thus implying that sexual behavior enacted in some relationship contexts may be even more interdependent and hence jointly determined than in other contexts.

In our earlier sex motives study (Cooper et al., 1998, Studies 3 and 4), we also found a strong and consistent pattern of relationship status versus motive interactions predicting precautionary behaviors (i.e., birth control and condom use). Intimacy motives, for example, were significantly positively related to birth control and condom use in the context of an ongoing or exclusive relationship, but significantly negatively related in more casual relationship contexts (see Gebhardt, Kuyper, & Greunsven, 2003, for similar results). This pattern, though not specifically predicted, is consistent with evidence that condom and birth control use in casual relationship contexts are thought to convey advance planning for sex and, by extension, sexual permissiveness (Morrison, 1985)—an impression that people seeking intimacy in their sexual encounters would surely want to avoid conveying to their partner. In contrast, intimacy motives in a committed relationship context should encourage communication and cooperation between partners (Reis & Shaver, 1988), which in turn has been shown to facilitate precaution adoption (Sheeran, Abraham, & Orbell, 1999).

Interestingly, the reverse pattern of effects was found for enhancement motives—that is, enhancement was significantly positively related to condom use with casual sex partners, but significantly negatively related with committed sex partners (Cooper et al., 1998, Study 3). Moreover, in prospective analyses, enhancement motives were related to discontinuation of condom use among those who were stably partnered, but with maintenance of use among those who were not (Study 4). Thus, in a context where the need to protect oneself against STI/AIDS was likely perceived as low (i.e., in a stable relationship), those with high-enhancement needs were quick to abandon any protective measure that interfered with their pleasure. In contrast, taking pleasure in the physical aspects of one's sexuality appeared to facilitate (or at least, not undermine) protective measures in the context of more casual liaisons (cf., Gerrard, 1982).

Taken together, the cross-over interaction patterns observed for intimacy and enhancement motives suggest that precaution adoption is facilitated when the relationship context provides a good match to the individual's motives and needs, but may be impeded in the presence of a mismatch. More broadly and more important for the present chapter, they show that the effects of sex motives on sexual behaviors depend strongly on the relationship context and therefore cannot be understood in a decontextualized framework.

Evidence that motives are systematically linked to the probability of being in different relationship contexts provides yet more support for the importance of adopting an explicit dyadic perspective. In cross-sectional analyses, for example, we (Cooper et al., 1998, Study 3) found that mean levels of all motives, except enhancement, differed as a function of relationship status. Indeed, intimacy motives were higher among individuals who were either in an exclusive or nonexclusive sexual relationship, whereas all four avoidant motivations were higher among individuals who were not in any relationship. Although cross-sectional data such as these cannot address the issue of differential selection versus environmental influence, longitudinal data from our earlier study (Cooper et al., Study 4) suggest that at least some of the observed differences reflect the effects of selection into relationship environments that ostensibly foster need satisfaction. Indeed, we found that high-intimacy-motive individuals were, over a 1 1/2 year period, more likely to stay in

committed relationships if already in one at baseline or, if not, to move into a committed relationship. In contrast, people who were high in enhancement and coping motives were more likely to leave a committed relationship if they were in one at baseline or, if not, to stay unattached. Moreover, patterns of change and stability in relationship status were found to mediate, at least in part, the prospective effects of sex motives on sexual behavior.

Together these data suggest that failure to consider the relationship context in which sex occurs can lead to systematic underestimation of the predictability of sexual behavior from sex motives, particularly in committed relationships, as well as inaccuracies and distortions in the characterization of the motive–behavior relationship. Moreover, the fact that people appear to seek relationship environments partly on the basis of the environment's ability to satisfy their sexual needs and that these environments in turn mediate motive effects on behavior suggests that partner and relationship effects play a consequential role in shaping the nature and quality of sexual experience. Nevertheless, simply demonstrating that relationship context matters, as these data do, does little to inform us about how or why this context matters.

DYADIC ANALYSES OF APPROACH AND AVOIDANCE MOTIVES

In the remainder of this chapter, we begin to address these issues by reviewing findings from two studies (Cooper, 2008; Cooper et al., 2006) that illustrate important ways in which both partners' approach and avoidance motives shape sexual experiences within intimate relationships. The data for both studies were drawn from the same community sample of 299 Black and White young adult couples (average age = 24 years for men and 22 years for women). To participate, couple members had to be at least 18 years old and involved in a heterosexual, sexual relationship. Couples were interviewed face-to-face, separately and in private by a same-sex interviewer; more sensitive questions were self-administered to encourage honest responding. Relationships ranged in length from 1 month to 9 years, with a mean of nearly 3 years. Sixty-two percent of couples described their relationship as an "exclusive dating relationship," 47% were living together, and 43% were raising at least one child (see Collins, Cooper, Albino, & Allard, 2002, and Cooper et al., 2006, for details).

The primary outcomes examined in these studies included six different aspects of sexual experience, rated by both partners. These were the frequency of affectionate gestures (kissing, hugging, cuddling) initiated by both partners; frequency of sex (with one's primary partner) in the past 6 months; overall satisfaction with the sexual relationship; the use of verbal or physical coercion by the male partner; a dichotomous measure of cheating, defined as having one or more extrapair partners in the past 6 months when one's primary partner thought the relationship was monogamous; and a quantitative measure of the riskiness of these extrapair sex partners. Individuals with no extrapair partners (about 75% of the sample) were scored 0 on the latter two measures. On the basis of patterns of association with sexual satisfaction, affectionate gestures and frequency of sex were viewed as markers of positive sexual experience, whereas coercion and both measures of extrapair sex were viewed as markers of poor sexual functioning.* Finally, both partners completed the Cooper et al. (1998) sex motives measure. For all analyses, an internal avoidant motive composite was created by averaging the coping and affirmation subscales, which were correlated in the low .60s among both men and women. Thus, four male and four female motive measures (viz., intimacy, enhancement, internal avoidance, and partner approval) were used in all analyses, one reflecting each of the hypothesized quadrants in our original model.

TO WHAT EXTENT IS AN INDIVIDUAL'S SEXUAL EXPERIENCE INFLUENCED BY HIS OR HER PARTNER'S APPROACH AND AVOIDANCE MOTIVES FOR SEX?

Questions regarding the nature and extent of actor (influence of one's own motives on one's behavior) and partner (influence of partner motives on one's behavior) effects on sexual outcomes were examined in a series of regression models in which both self- and partner-motives were entered simultaneously. Results for the four measures of sexual experience within the relationship are displayed graphically in Figure 37.1. (Results for extrapair sex are discussed later.)

As shown in Figure 37.1, a number of interesting patterns emerged in the data. First, the quantity and quality of sexual experience among women was determined

almost exclusively by their own motivations. Indeed, only one significant partner effect was found among women—male intimacy motives, somewhat surprisingly, negatively predicted female reports of sex frequency. In contrast, the quantity and quality of male sexual experience was determined by both his own and his partner's motivations. In fact, for two of the four outcomes, male sexual experience was influenced solely by his partner's motives.

Second, the direct effects of avoidance motives on sexual experience were relatively few in number, but uniformly negative. Female avoidance motives were negatively related to both male and female partner reports of affectionate exchanges, and to female reports of sexual satisfaction. In addition, female partner-approval motives were positively related to both male and female reports of sexual coercion enacted by the male partner, as were male avoidance motives to his own reports of coercion. Thus, consistent with prior research using individuals (as opposed to couples), avoidant motivations appear to be detrimental to sexual functioning in romantic relationships.

In contrast, the pattern for approach motives was both more complex and less consistent with results of earlier studies using individuals. For example, although enhancement motives have been associated in past research with a pattern of high risk, promiscuous sex, female enhancement motives were associated with largely positive effects for both men and women, including increased frequency of sex and increased satisfaction. In contrast, male enhancement motives were unrelated to sexual functioning, as reported by both male and female partners.

Similarly, the effects of pursuing intimacy in the context of an intimate relationship also appeared more mixed than findings obtained in prior studies of individuals. For example, and as expected, female intimacy motives were related to higher perceived levels of affectionate exchange and higher sexual satisfaction among women, as were male intimacy motives to sexual satisfaction among men. At the same time, however, high-intimacy-motive women perceived their partners to use more coercive tactics, whereas women with high-intimacy-motive partners reported less frequent intercourse.

Motive effects on extrapair sex were examined in our earlier study (see Cooper et al., 2006, for details). These results showed that men whose sexual behavior was motivated by avoidance (including coping, self-affirmation, and partner-approval motives) had more risky extrapair partners, whereas women who used sex to affirm their attractiveness and self-worth (one of the measures in our

---

* Interestingly, however, the correlations between sexual satisfaction and coercion were modest in magnitude ($rs = -.15$, $p < .05$, for both genders), suggesting that the nature of the coercion used by men in the present sample was most likely mild. Consistent with this analysis, only 5% of males and 7% of females reported that the male partner had ever used any type of physical force to coerce his partner.

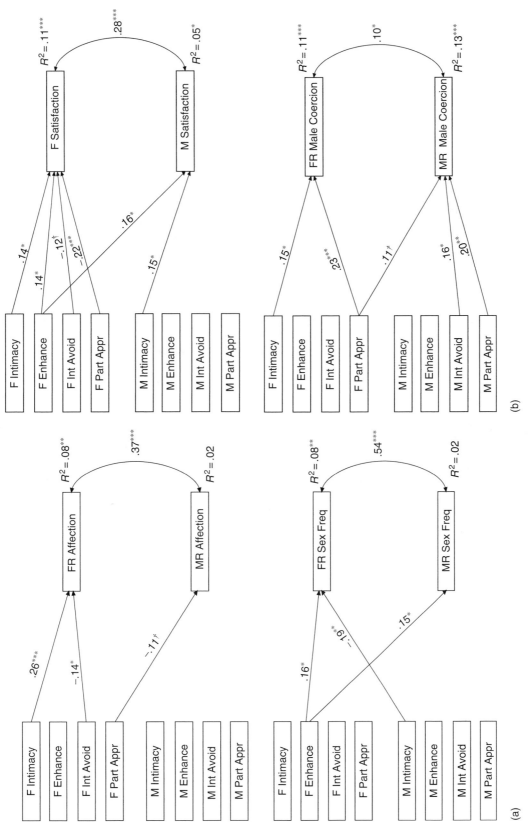

FIGURE 37.1 Actor-partner models predicting male and female sexual outcomes. *Note*: F = female; M = male; Int Avoid = internal avoidant; Part Appr = partner approval; FR = female report; MR = male report; Freq = frequency. † *p* < .10; * *p* < .05; ** *p* < .01; *** *p* < .001.

avoidant composite) had more risky extrapair partners. Perhaps most important for the present chapter, however, men with partners high in approval motives for sex were more likely to both cheat and have high-risk extrapair partners. In contrast, but consistent with the pattern described above, male partner motives did not predict extrapair sex among women.

Together these data indicate that the sexual experiences of men in relationships are profoundly shaped not only by their own motivations but also by their partner's. Men whose female partners were high in enhancement appeared to have more positive sexual experiences, whereas men whose female partners were high in partner-approval motives reported less adaptive sexual behaviors. Women's experiences, on the other hand, were almost entirely shaped by their own motivations, possibly reflecting women's role as the arbiter of sexual activity in relationships (Baumeister & Tice, 2001). Finally, comparing these results to results from earlier studies using individuals indicates that pursuing avoidance goals is associated with largely detrimental outcomes across relationship contexts, whereas the effects of pursuing approach goals depend more heavily on relationship context.

ARE THERE SYNERGISTIC (I.E., COUPLE LEVEL) EFFECTS OF APPROACH AND AVOIDANCE MOTIVES?

In the prior section, we showed that the sexual motivations of both partners, but particularly of the female partner, make unique contributions to sexual experience in intimate relationships. However, the presence of additive effects alone does not mean that the couple functions as a synergistic system in which the relationship "whole" is greater than the sum of its parts (i.e., the two partners' motivational strivings). To demonstrate synergy, the two partners' motives must interact to predict important outcomes. This possibility was recently examined using measures of sexual experience both within and outside the relationship (Cooper, 2008).

Because little is known about how partner motives combine to shape sexual outcomes, we wanted to allow for a wide range of plausible interaction patterns in our analyses. We therefore tested all possible male partner × female partner motive interactions and then examined both the pattern of significant effects (e.g., across motives, across dependent measures) and the shape of significant interactions to determine if they conformed to any of several plausible models of synergistic effects. Interactions were tested in blocks involving all possible

interactions for each of the four motives (e.g., all possible interactions involving male and female intimacy motives). Accordingly, a total of 48 blocks of interactions were tested (6 sexual outcomes × 4 motive classes × male and female reports).

Do Male and Female Partner Motives Interact? If So, Are These Synergistic Effects Equally Common Among Men and Women, Across Sexual Behaviors, and Across Specific Motives?

At the most general level, results of the interaction analyses showed that motives combine in a synergistic fashion to shape sexual experience among both men and women. Indeed, nearly half (21 of 48) of the interaction blocks tested were significant at $p < .10$, more than four times the number expected by chance alone. Examining results for male and female outcomes separately suggested that synergistic effects may be stronger among women than men: 54% of the blocks of interactions tested significantly predicted female outcomes, compared with only 33% of the blocks predicting male outcomes. Examining the pattern of effects *by dependent measure* raised the possibility that some sexual behaviors are more interdependent than others. Cheating was strongly determined by the interaction of partner motives among both men (3 of 4 blocks, $p < .05$) and women (3 of 4 blocks, $p < .05$), thus suggesting that straying from one's primary relationship reflects an interactive dynamic between properties of the person and of the relationship. In contrast, other patterns of effects differed across men and women. In particular, more consistent interaction effects were found for risky extrapair sex (4 of 4 blocks, $p < .05$) and for reports of male sexual coercion (3 of 4 blocks, $p < .10$) among women, and for sexual satisfaction (4 of 4 blocks, $p < .10$) among men. Examining the pattern of significant effects *by motive* suggested that the effects of enhancement motives on sexual outcomes were highly conditional among both men (3 of 6 blocks, $p < .10$) and women (4 of 6 blocks, $p < .10$). Among women only, the effects of intimacy motives (4 of 6 blocks, $p < .10$) and internal avoidant motives (3 of 6 blocks, $p < .10$) also appeared to depend heavily on the male partner's motivational pursuits.

What Is the Nature of These Synergistic Effects?

Although these data clearly indicate that male and female partner motives combine in a synergistic fashion to shape at least some sexual outcomes, the nature of these synergisms can be understood only by examining the form of the interactions. Accordingly, significant ($p < .10$) interactions ($n = 43$) were plotted and examined to determine the extent to which they conformed to several plausible patterns of synergistic effects.

We first considered a set of possibilities based loosely on exchange theory (Clark & Reis, 1988). This approach argues that sexual experiences should be most rewarding and functional in relationships where couple members contribute socially valued attributes—attributes that provide significant rewards but have minimal associated costs (Schmitt, 2002). In the context of a close romantic relationship, intimacy motives would be expected to serve as a positive or adaptive attribute and avoidance motives as negative or maladaptive attributes. However, it is less clear whether enhancement motives can be seen as unequivocally adaptive or maladaptive; thus, this perspective may not apply in any simple or straightforward way to enhancement motives.

The general notion that sexual functioning will be sensitive to the balance or combination of adaptive (intimacy) versus maladaptive (avoidance) motives could play out in a number of different ways. For example, couples in which both individuals are high in adaptive motives might experience unusually positive sexual outcomes, whereas couples in which both individuals are high in maladaptive motives might experience unusually negative outcomes. Similarly, couples in which both members are low in adaptive motives would be expected to experience poor sexual outcomes, whereas couples in which both members are low in maladaptive motives might experience less negative outcomes (though the mere absence of maladaptive motives might not be sufficient to foster high levels of adaptive functioning and positive outcomes). Alternatively, the presence of an adaptive motive in either partner might buffer the adverse effects of a maladaptive motive on sexual experience.

Examining the subset of significant interactions relevant to the exchange theory approach (i.e., intimacy × intimacy [$n = 2$], intimacy × avoidance [$n = 10$], and avoidance × avoidance [$n = 7$] interactions) revealed modest support for this perspective. Of the 19 relevant interactions examined, 6 interactions could be interpreted within this framework: three conformed to the buffering model, and 3 conformed to the notion that the cumulative effects of either low quantities of positive attributes or high quantities of negative attributes lead to particularly poor outcomes. Figure 37.2 provides an example of both patterns of synergistic effects.

As shown in the top panel of Figure 37.2, women who were high in internal avoidant motives coupled with a low intimacy partner were prone to have risky extrapair sex, perhaps in an effort to cope with negative emotions stemming from insecure feelings about their self-worth. In contrast, no such effect was observed among high-internal-avoidant-motive women coupled with high-intimacy men who may provide more effective support to their female partners. As shown in the bottom panel, low intimacy among men predicted elevations in the use of coercive strategies by the male partner only if the female partner was also low in intimacy.

We also considered the possibility that matching on motives might lead to superior outcomes, regardless of the adaptive nature of the motives involved. For example, couple members might be more satisfied because of the relative equality of their attributes (Hatfield, Walster, & Berscheid, 1978), or because similarity is self-validating (Swann, 1992). Alternatively, similarity in motives might lead to patterns of thoughts, feelings, and behaviors that are familiar and comfortable, even if maladaptive (cf., repetition compulsion; Freud, 1920). Or relatedly, similarity in motives might lead to less conflict or more easily managed conflict (cf., Gottman, 1994). However, little support was found for this perspective. Only a small number of interactions (6 of 48 tested) were obtained between like motives (e.g., male and female intimacy) and, of these, only one suggested that couples who shared similar motives (in this case, enhancement) experienced more adaptive outcomes (i.e., more affectionate gestures).

In addition, we examined the possibility that one partner's motives and preferences might disproportionately drive the couple's sexual outcomes to the extent that the other partner has sex for approval reasons (cf., the motivation to comply component of subjective norms in the theory of reasoned action; Ajzen & Fishbein, 1980). For example, we might expect male enhancement motives to more strongly determine intercourse frequency in relationships where the female partner is high versus low in partner-approval motives, or in other words, where the female partner has sex to please or appease her partner. We found strong support for this notion, with more than half of the significant partner-approval interactions (10 of 19) conforming to this pattern. Interestingly, however, this pattern held primarily for female partner-approval motives, with 8 of the 10 conforming interactions involving female approval motives. Figure 37.3 illustrates this pattern for female partner approval × male enhancement predicting female reports of sex frequency (top panel) and of sexual satisfaction (bottom panel). Consistent with

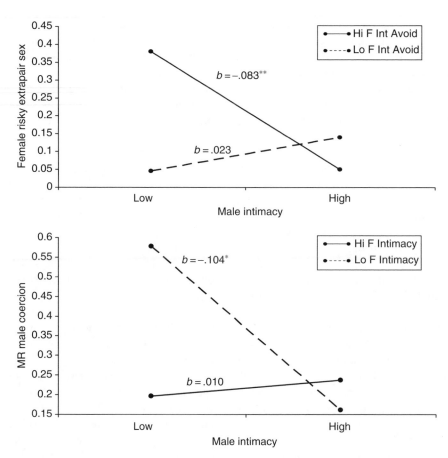

FIGURE 37.2   Illustrative interactions consistent with the exchange model. Top panel: Male intimacy × female internal avoidance predicting female risky extrapair sex. Bottom panel: Male intimacy × female intimacy predicting male reports of male coercion. *Note:* F = female; MR = male report; Int Avoid = internal avoidant. * $p < .05$; ** $p < .01$.

expectation, both plots indicate that male motives more strongly shaped sexual experience in couples where the woman was high as opposed to low in partner-approval motives.

Finally, given that more than half of all significant interaction coefficients (24 of 43) involved male enhancement, female enhancement, or both, we thought it important to examine these interactions to see what could be learned about the role of enhancement in intimate sexual relationships. Not surprisingly, a complex pattern of results was found in which enhancement motives were associated with harmful effects (especially increased infidelity and use of coercive tactics among men), but also with beneficial ones (increased frequency of physical and sexual contact), depending on the motivational context in which they were pursued. For example, high-enhancement men were more likely to use coercive tactics and to cheat when they were partnered with high-enhancement women (see Figure 37.4, top panel), and women with

high-enhancement partners were also more likely to cheat when they were low in either intimacy or partner-approval motives or high in internal avoidance (see Figure 37.4, bottom panel). In addition, both men and women were more likely to cheat in relationships where the woman was high in enhancement and the man was low in internal avoidance motives. On the more positive side, both men and women reported more frequent intercourse when the male partner was high (vs. low) in enhancement and the female partner was high in partner-approval motives (see Figure 37.3, top panel), and high-enhancement men reported more kissing, hugging, and cuddling when they were partnered with women high in enhancement or in intimacy motives. Finally, although female enhancement was primarily associated with positive effects on sexual satisfaction among both men and women (see Figure 37.1), the effects of male enhancement motives on satisfaction were for the most part negligible. Indeed, only two interactions were obtained predicting sexual satisfaction from

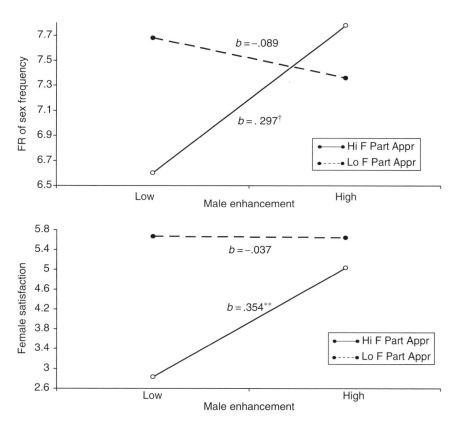

FIGURE 37.3 Illustrative interactions involving female partner-approval motives. Top panel: Male enhancement × female partner approval predicting female reports of intercourse frequency. Bottom panel: Male enhancement × female partner approval predicting female sexual satisfaction. *Note:* F = female; FR = female report; Part Appr = partner approval. $^{\dagger} p < .10$; ** $p < .01$.

male enhancement, and the effects were in one case negligible to positive (see Figure 37.3, bottom panel) and in the other, negligible to negative (not shown).

SUMMARY

At the most general level, these analyses indicate that male and female partner motives combine in a synergistic fashion to determine sexual experience within intimate relationships, that the expression or satisfaction of some motivations is particularly dependent on the nature of the partner's motivational pursuits, and that some behaviors are more synergistically determined than others. Examining the form of the interactions between male and female partner motives revealed a complex variety of forms, the overwhelming majority of which were readily interpretable. Nevertheless, the multitude of forms suggests that multiple distinct processes underlie and give rise to these interactions, and therefore that no single theoretical model will be adequate to understand the nature of these synergisms.

CONCLUDING THOUGHTS AND FUTURE DIRECTIONS

The present chapter highlights the utility of the approach–avoidance framework for understanding human sexual motivation. In this chapter, we showed that the structure of discrete sexual motivations can be usefully understood within the approach–avoidance framework, and indeed that this two-dimensional structure is superior to other plausible two-dimensional representations. Not surprisingly, this framework also provides important insights into the nature and meaning of different motivational strivings in the sexual domain, particularly their emotional valence. The approach–avoidance framework also provides broadly useful insights into the probable consequences of using sex to pursue approach and avoidance goals, although the straightforward expectation of positive effects accruing from approach pursuits and negative effects accruing from avoidant pursuits is clearly inadequate. This is particularly true for enhancement motives which may be considered a prototype of an approach

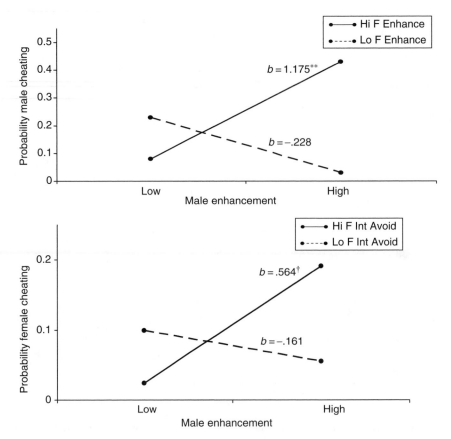

FIGURE 37.4 Illustrative interactions involving male enhancement motives. Top panel: Male enhancement × female enhancement predicting probability of male cheating. Bottom panel: Male enhancement × female internal avoidance predicting probability of female cheating. *Note:* F = female; Int Avoid = internal avoidance. [†] $p < .10$; ** $p < .01$.

motive, yet are associated with a complex pattern of both harmful and beneficial effects. Indeed, the evidence in this chapter strongly suggests that understanding how these motives play out in the lives of individuals and couples to shape sexual experience will require going beyond a simple approach–avoidance dichotomy to more carefully consider the relational context in which one's sexual goals are pursued, as well as the role of gender-specific dynamics that can transform the meaning of sexual behaviors for men and women. In the remainder of this chapter, we briefly explore several implications of these notions for understanding approach–avoidance sexual goals and their contributions to human sexual experience.

The Relational Context

At the most basic level, evidence presented in the present chapter indicates that whether sexual goals are pursued within or outside the context of a committed or exclusive relationship matters greatly and that failure to take relationship status into account risks underestimating the predictability of sexual behavior from sexual motives, as well as mischaracterizing or distorting these relationships. Thus, at a minimum, even studies of individuals need to take relationship status (e.g., committed vs. casual) into account.

Beyond this basic consideration, our dyadic analyses indicate that both partner's motives shape sexual experience in at least two important ways. First, all behaviors in the present analyses are, in part, determined by partner motive effects. Specifically, our findings reveal partner (but not actor) motive effects for two (male) outcomes, and both actor and partner motive effects (i.e., additive effects) for five (4 male, 1 female) additional outcomes. Thus, for the majority of outcomes, focusing solely on one partner's motives would substantially underestimate the predictability of sexual experience from approach and avoidance sex motives, particularly among men.

Second, we showed that all of the outcomes considered in the present chapter are jointly shaped by specific combinations of partner approach and avoidance motives among both men and women. From a psychological viewpoint, such findings indicate that the effects of one's own motivational pursuits on sexual experience within a close relationship cannot be understood in a vacuum, but rather depend importantly on the context provided by one's partner's goal pursuits.

Despite the meaningfulness of the individual interactions examined, the set of interactions as a whole do not lend themselves to parsimonious generalizations about the adaptive significance of specific motive combinations for individuals and couples. Although the form of various interactions can be seen as conforming to different models of how partner attributes combine to determine outcomes in a relationship (e.g., similarity, exchange), many do not conform to any of the common models. We suspect that this diversity of form reflects the inherent complexity of sexual behavior, and of the many functions it can serve and meanings it can assume in the context of an ongoing committed relationship. Alternatively or in addition, meaning and organization may reside at a higher, more complex level of analysis. For example, the entire configuration of motives of one partner may interact with the other partner's configuration. This, we believe, represents an important direction for future research.

GENDER SPECIFICITY OF MOTIVE EFFECTS

Human sexual behavior is strongly gender specific, both biologically and culturally. Thus, it is not surprising that we find pervasive gender differences in the effects of approach–avoidance motives on sexual behavior. These differences manifest in at least three important ways.

First, the pattern of actor and partner effects in Figure 37.1 illustrates what might be called a "female dominance effect" in which the woman's, but not the man's, motivations drive the sexual experience of both partners. This asymmetrical pattern of influence suggests that sexual outcomes are more interdependent among men than women, at least within the context of a committed relationship, possibly due to the disproportionate power women are thought to hold in the sexual arena (cf., Baumeister & Tice, 2001). There is, however, an important exception to this pattern: The sexual outcomes of both women and men in couples where the woman is high in partner-approval motives are more strongly determined by male partner motives. The converse is not true, however: In four of eight significant interactions involving male partner-approval motives, female motives more strongly determined outcomes when the male partner was low (not high) in approval motives. These data not

only provide additional evidence of the gender specificity of motive effects on sexual behavior, but also raise questions about what partner-approval motives assess among men if not the motivation to comply with or defer to their partner's sexual preferences.

Finally, the data in the present chapter also indicate that the effects of pursuing approach and avoidance goals depend importantly on whose motivational agenda—the man's or the woman's—we are talking about. In the actor-partner models (Figure 37.1), only three actor effects replicate across men and women (viz., intimacy motives → satisfaction, partner approval → coercion by the male partner, internal avoidant → risky extrapair sex), and no partner effect replicates. Although such findings may be partly attributable to methodological limitations of self-report measures, we suspect that these asymmetrical findings also reflect meaningful differences in how men and women pursue sexual goals, or in what specific sexual goals or specific sexual behaviors signify to men and women. Indeed, unless we are willing to write off all observed differences as methodological artifacts—an interpretation that we believe would be difficult to justify in the face of the many statistically reliable and psychologically meaningful results—we are faced with the conclusion that the effects of approach and avoidance sex motives on sexual behavior cannot be understood at a general or abstract level, but rather must take into account the highly gender specific nature of behaviors enacted in the sexual arena.

In this chapter, we presented evidence showing that individuals use sex to pursue a range of approach and avoidance goals in their relationships and that sexual outcomes are shaped to a nontrivial extent by the nature of these motivational pursuits. Specifying whether, or under what conditions, these pursuits lead to positive or negative sexual outcomes proved highly complex, however, owing to the gender specificity of sexual behaviors and to synergisms between partners' motivational pursuits. These findings point to the need to develop more complex models of approach and avoidance motives in the sexual domain, as well as a deeper understanding of the individual and dyadic processes by which people seek to meet these needs in various relational contexts.

REFERENCES

Ajzen, I., & Fishbein, M. (1980). *Understanding attitudes and predicting social behavior*. Englewood Cliffs, NJ: Prentice-Hall.

Bakan, D. (1966). *The duality of human existence: An essay on psychology and religion*. Oxford: Rand McNally.

Baumeister, R. F., Bratslavsky, E., Finkenauer, C., & Vohs, K. D. (2001). Bad is stronger than good. *Review of General Psychology, 5*, 323–370.

Baumeister, R. F., & Scher, S. J. (1988). Self-defeating behavior patterns among normal individuals: Review and analysis of common self-destructive tendencies. *Psychological Bulletin, 104*, 3–22.

Baumeister, R. F., & Tice, D. M. (2001). *The social dimension of sex*. Toronto: Allyn and Bacon.

Bowlby, J. (1970). Disruption of affectional bonds and its effects on behavior. *Journal of Contemporary Psychotherapy, 2*, 75–86.

Browning, J. R., Hatfield, E., Kessler, D., & Levine, T. (2000). Sexual motives, gender, and sexual behavior. *Archives of Sexual Behavior, 29*, 135–153.

Carver, C. S., & Scheier, M. F. (1998). *On the self-regulation of behavior*. New York: Cambridge University Press.

Carver, C. S., & White, T. L. (1994). Behavioral inhibition, behavioral activation, and affective responses to impending reward and punishment: The BIS/BAS Scales. *Journal of Personality and Social Psychology, 67*, 319–333.

Christopher, F. S., & Sprecher, S. (2000). Sexuality in marriage, dating, and other relationships: A decade review. *Journal of Marriage & the Family, 62*, 999–1017.

Clark, M. S., & Reis, H. T. (1988). Interpersonal processes in close relationships. *Annual Review of Psychology, 39*, 609–672.

Collins, N. L., Cooper, M. L., Albino, A., & Allard, L. (2002). Psychosocial vulnerability from adolescence to adulthood: A prospective study of attachment style differences in relationship functioning and partner choice. *Journal of Personality, 70*, 965–1008.

Cooper, M. L. (1994). Motivations for alcohol use among adolescents: Development and validation of a four-factor model. *Psychological Assessment, 6*, 117–128.

Cooper, M. L. (2008). Sexual experiences in intimate relationships: The product of both partners' needs and motives. Unpublished manuscript, University of Missouri, Columbia.

Cooper, M. L., Agocha, V. B., & Sheldon, M. S. (2000). A motivational perspective on risky behaviors: The role of personality and affect regulatory processes. *Journal of Personality, 68*, 1059–1088.

Cooper, M. L., Pioli, M., Levitt, A., Talley, A. E., Micheas, L., & Collins, N. L. (2006). Attachment styles, sex motives, and sexual behavior: Evidence for gender-specific expressions of attachment dynamics. In M. Mikulincer & G. S. Goodman (Eds.), *Dynamics of romantic love: Attachment, caregiving, and sex* (pp. 243–274). New York: Guilford Press.

Cooper, M. L., Shapiro, C. M., & Powers, A. M. (1998). Motivations for sex and risky sexual behavior among adolescents and young adults: A functional perspective. *Journal of Personality and Social Psychology, 75*, 1528–1558.

Elliot, A. J. (2006). The hierarchical model of approach–avoidance motivation. *Motivation Emotion, 30*, 111–116.

Elliot, A. J., Gable, S. L., & Mapes, R. R. (2006). Approach and avoidance motivation in the social domain. *Personality and Social Psychology Bulletin, 32*, 378–391.

Fisher, W. A., Byrne, D., & White, L. A. (1983). Emotional barriers to contraception. In D. Byrne & W. A. Fisher (Eds.), *Adolescents, sex, and contraception* (pp. 207–239). Hillsdale, NJ: Erlbaum.

Freud, S. (1920). *Beyond the pleasure principle. The standard edition of the complete psychology works of Sigmund Freud* (vol. 18). London: Hogarth Press.

Gebhardt, W. A., Kuyper, L., & Dusseldorp, E. (2006). Condom use at first intercourse with a new partner in female adolescents and young adults: The role of cognitive planning and motives for having sex. *Archives of Sexual Behavior, 35*, 217–223.

Gebhardt, W. A., Kuyper, L., & Greunsven, G. (2003). Need for intimacy in relationships and motives for sex as determinants of adolescent condom use. *Journal of Adolescent Health, 33*, 154–164.

Gerrard, M. (1982). Sex, sex guilt, and contraceptive use. *Journal of Personality and Social Psychology, 42*, 153–158.

Gold, R. S., & Skinner, M. J. (1993). Desire for unprotected intercourse preceding its occurence: The case of young gay men with an anonymous partner. *International Journal of STD and AIDS, 4*, 326–329.

Gottman, J. M. (1994). *What predicts divorce? The relationship between marital processes and marital outcomes*. Hillsdale, NJ: Lawrence Erlbaum Associates, Inc.

Gray, J. A. (1970). The psychophysiological basis of introversion–extraversion. *Behaviour Research and Therapy, 8*, 249–266.

Gray, J. A. (1987). Perspectives on anxiety and impulsivity: A commentary. *Journal of Research in Personality, 21*, 493–509.

Hatfield, E., Walster, G. W., & Berscheid, E. (1978). *Equity theory and research*. Boston, MA: Allyn and Bacon.

Harlow, L. L., Quina, K., Morokoff, P. J., Rose, J. S., & Grimley, D. M. (1993). HIV risk in women: A multifaceted model. *Journal of Applied Biobehavioral Research, 1*, 3–38.

Heimpel, S. A., Elliot, A. J., & Wood, J. V. (2006). Basic personality dispositions, self-esteem, and personal goals: An approach–avoidance analysis. *Journal of Personality, 74*, 1293–1319.

Hill, C. A., & Preston, L. K. (1996). Individual differences in the experience of sexual motivation: Theory and measurement of dispositional sexual motives. *Journal of Sex Research, 33*, 27–45.

Impett, E. A., Peplau, L. A., & Gable, S. L. (2005). Approach and avoidance sexual motives: Implications for personal and interpersonal well-being. *Personal Relationships, 12*, 465–482.

Jemmott, L. S., & Jemmott, J. B. (1991). Applying the theory of reasoned action to AIDS risk behavior: Condom use among Black women. *Nursing Research, 40*, 228–234.

Kenny, D. A., & Cook, W. (1999). Partner effects in relationship research: Conceptual issues, analytic difficulties, and illustrations. *Personal Relationships, 6*, 433–448.

Larsen, R. J., & Ketelaar, T. (1991). Personality and susceptibility to positive and negative emotional states. *Journal of Personality and Social Psychology, 61*, 132–140.

Levinson, R. A., Jaccard, J., & Beamer, L. (1995). Older adolescents' engagement in casual sex: Impact of risk perception and psychosocial motivations. *Journal of Youth and Adolescence, 24*, 349–364.

McAdams, D. P. (1984). Human motives and personal relationships. In V. Derlega (Ed.), *Communication, intimacy, and close relationships* (pp. 41–70). New York: Academic Press.

Morrison, D. M. (1985). Adolescent contraceptive behavior: A review. *Psychological Bulletin, 98*, 538–568.

Priester, J. R., & Petty, R. E. (1996). The gradual threshold model of ambivalence: Relating the positive and negative bases of attitudes to subjective ambivalence. *Journal of Personality and Social Psychology, 71*, 431–449.

Reis, H. T., & Shaver, P. (1988). Intimacy as an interpersonal process. In S. Duck, D. F. Hay, S. E. Hobfoll, W. Ickes, & B. M. Montgomery (Eds.), *Handbook of personal relationships: Theory, research and interventions* (pp. 367–389). Oxford: John Wiley & Sons.

Rusbult, C. E., & Van Lange, P. A. M. (2003). Interdependence, interaction and relationships. *Annual Review of Psychology, 54*, 351–375.

Schachner, D. A., & Shaver, P. R. (2004). Attachment dimensions and sexual motives. *Personal Relationships, 11*, 179–195.

Schmitt, D. P. (2002). Personality, attachment and sexuality related to dating relationship outcomes: Contrasting three perspectives on personal attribute interaction. *British Journal of Social Psychology, 41*, 589–610.

Sheeran, P., Abraham, C., & Orbell, S. (1999). Psychosocial correlates of heterosexual condom use: A meta-analysis. *Psychological Bulletin, 125*, 90–132.

Skinner, E. A., & Wellborn, J. G. (1994). Coping during childhood and adolescence: A motivational perspective. In D. L. Featherman, R. M. Lerner, & M. Perlmutter (Eds.), *Life-span development and behavior* (Vol. 12, pp. 91–133). Hillsdale, NJ: Erlbaum.

Swann, W. B. (1992). Seeking "truth," finding despair: Some unhappy consequences of a negative self-concept. *Current Directions in Psychological Science, 1*, 15–18.

Author Index

A

Aaker, J. L., 421, 478, 560, 562, 564, 566
Aarts, H., 296
Abelson, R. P., 352, 387
Abend, T., 542
Abercrombie, E. D., 94
Aberman, J. E., 29
Abi-Dargham, A., 121
Abraham, C., 621
Abramowitz, J. S., 448
Abramson, L. Y., 409
Abramson, L. Y., 337, 523–524
Achille, N. M., 155
Ach, N., 544
Ackerman, B. P., 373
Ackerman, J., 275, 279, 281–282
Adamec, R., 6
Adams, L. F., 110
Adams, M. S., 258
Adams, R. B. J., 403
Adolphs, R., 313–314, 544
Afarian, H., 42
Affleck, G., 388
Agnati, L. F., 91
Agocha, V. B., 620
Agrati, D., 137
Ahadi, S., 422
Ahadi, S. A., 190, 470
Ahern G. L., 35
Ahrens, A. H., 360
Aiken, K. J., 299
Aiken, L. S., 196
Ajzen, I., 223, 300, 332, 346, 421, 625
Akers, K. G., 44
Akil, H., 194
Aksan, N., 156, 188
Akwa, Y., 111
Albano, A. M., 379
Albarracín, D., 289–291
Alberts, S. C., 204
Albino, A., 621
Alburges, M. E., 100
Alcaro, A., 71, 77, 81
Alcock, J., 274
Aleman, D. O., 95
Alessandri, S. M., 400, 402
Alexander, G. E., 279
Alexander, M. P., 463
Algom, D., 157
Alicke, M., 596
Alicke, M. D., 336
Allan, S., 373, 377
Allard, L., 621
Allen-Arave, W., 257
Allen, J. J. B., 35–39, 237, 244, 404–405,
    543–544, 547
Allen, K., 444

Allen, N. B., 607–608
Alloy, L. B., 337, 380, 451
Allport, G., 307
Allport, G. W., 229, 289–290, 307,
    441, 581
Allsopp, J. F., 159
Alnwick, K. A., 110
Alpert, N., 418
Altman, B. M., 604
Altmann, J., 204
Alvarez-Pelaez, R., 55
Amaral, D. G., 61, 313
Amaral, E., 136
Amat, C., 129
Ambady, N., 403
Ames, C., 224–225, 227
Amodio, D. M., 579
Amo, L., 176
Amorapanth, P., 23, 25, 29
Amsel, A., 358
Anagnostaras, S. G., 129
Anderman, E. M., 227
Andersen, P. A., 392
Andersen, S. M., 346
Anderson, A. K., 314
Anderson, C., 277
Anderson, M. C., 236, 242
Anderson, N., 432
Anderson, R., 6
Anderson, R. C., 167, 174,
    178–179, 221
Andréen, K., 112
Andrew, R., 41
Andrews, M. W., 43
Anglada-Figueroa, D., 23
Angleitner, A., 195
Annas, P., 61–62
Anokhin, A. P., 39
Ansfield, M., 454
Antes, J. R., 237
Antone, C., 477
Anton, G., 96
Antoniou, A. A., 351
Antony, M. M., 451
Aono, T., 137–138
Apanovitch, A. M., 477, 480
Apiolaza, L. A., 174
Appley, M. H., 9, 344
Araneda, R. C., 129
Arbisi, P., 38
Archer, J., 137, 225, 227
Arcuri, L., 293
Aristotle, 353, 359
Arkes, H. R., 369
Armitage, C. J., 483–484
Armitage, K., 6
Armony, J. L., 20, 24
Arndt, J., 448, 512

Arneson, C. L., 190
Arnold, H. M., 131
Arnold, M., 7–8
Arnold, M. B., 293, 358
Aron, A., 62, 208, 393
Aronson, J., 443, 581
Arrowood, A. J., 597
Arseneault, L., 193
Arvanitogiannis, A., 83
Asakawa, K., 563
Ascher, J. A., 138
Asendorpf, J. B., 299
Asher, E. R., 211
Asher, S. R., 604
Ashton, H., 353
Ashton, M. C., 155
Aspinwall, L., 596
Aston-Jones, G., 91
Atkinson, J., 10
Atkinson, J. W., 8, 204–205, 217–218,
    220–221, 223, 346, 352,
    466, 521, 536–537, 544, 572,
    578, 586
Atthowe, J. M., 352
Audy, J. R., 604
Augelli, R. W., 373
Auger, A. P., 138
Augustine, A. A., 151–161, 174
Aunger, R., 368, 375, 378
Avena, N., 99
Avena, N. M., 89–102
Averill, J. R., 345
Avila, C., 211
Avivi, Y. E., 385–394
Avnet, T., 494
Axelrod, R., 257
Ayduk, O., 207, 471, 500
Ayers, G., 138
Ayton, P., 369
Aziz, N., 207

B

Babinsky, R., 314
Bachman, J. G., 510
Bachnick, L., 480
Bachorowski, J., 464
Bach, P., 456
Back, K., 602
Backstrom, T., 110, 112
Badcock, P. B. T., 607–608
Baer, A., 495
Baer, L., 455
Baeyens, F., 327
Bailey, J. M., 282
Bakan, D., 617
Baker, C., 455

Subject Index

A